Born in Shropshire in 1974, Dominic Sandbrook was educated at Balliol College, Oxford, the University of St Andrews and Jesus College, Cambridge. He taught history at the University of Sheffield and is currently a Senior Fellow at the Rothermere Institute, University of Oxford.

Praise for *Never Had It So Good*:

'The first volume of Dominic Sandbrook's spectacular history of the Sixties is a chronicle of how the realisation of irreversible national decline hit the British after the Suez crisis ... It is a tribute to Sandbrook's literary skill that his scholarship is never oppressive. Alternately delightful and enlightening, he has produced a book which must have been an enormous labour to write but is a treat to read'
Nick Cohen, *Observer*

'Sandbrook has a winning style – not too flashy, but always ready with a killer observation. His judgements are cool and self-assured, his wry wit ever-present but unobtrusive. Above all, he moves effortlessly from the particular to the general and back again, dazzling the reader with peculiar but telling facts, offering tart vignettes of politicians and cultural standard bearers, and demonstrating the extraordinary range of his reading. You should read this remarkable history of a much misunderstood era for both its immense sweep and the piquancy of its detail ... Without a doubt, this will rank as one of the outstanding historical books of 2005'
Christopher Silvester, *Sunday Express*

'There is much to be enjoyed and admired here. Sandbrook writes lucidly and with brio ... I find myself in awe of Sandbrook's apparent breadth and depth of reading, and his enthusiasm'
Sam Leith, *Spectator*

'Brilliant ... with a novelist's skill, [Sandbrook] picks his way through the unfolding drama ... As a popular, very readable history, this is a massive compendium of quiet, thoughtful information, occasionally punctuated with some very funny anecdotes'
Ray Connolly, *Daily Mail*

Also by Dominic Sandbrook

White Heat

NEVER HAD IT SO GOOD

A History of Britain from
Suez to the Beatles

DOMINIC SANDBROOK

ABACUS

First published in Great Britain in 2005 by Little, Brown
This paperback edition published in 2006 by Abacus
Reprinted 2006, 2008

A CIP catalogue record for this book is available
from the British Library.

ISBN 978-0-349-11530-6

Papers used by Abacus are natural, recyclable products made from
wood grown in sustainable forests and certified in accordance with
the rules of the Forest Stewardship Council.

Typeset in Spectrum by M Rules
Printed and bound in Great Britain by Clays Ltd, St Ives plc
Paper supplied by Hellefoss AS, Norway

Abacus
An imprint of
Little, Brown Book Group
100 Victoria Embankment
London EC4Y 0DY

An Hachette Livre UK Company

www.littlebrown.co.uk

For Ella

CONTENTS

Let's be frank about it; most of our people have never had it so good. Go around the country, go to the industrial towns, go to the farms, and you will see a state of prosperity such as we have never had in my lifetime – nor indeed ever in the history of this country. What is worrying some of us is 'Is it too good to be true?' or perhaps I should say 'Is it too good to last?'

Harold Macmillan, 20 July 1957

ACKNOWLEDGEMENTS

At the beginning of Kingsley Amis' novel *Lucky Jim*, the hero, a young history lecturer, is accosted by his head of department, Professor Welch. 'I was wondering about that article of yours,' Welch says. 'If I were you, Dixon, I should take all the steps I possibly could to get this article accepted in the next month or so.' Dixon can barely bring himself to meet Welch's eye; he contemplates the 'frenzied fact-grubbing and fanatical boredom' that have gone into his work on medieval shipbuilding, and concludes that 'the thing's worth could be expressed in one short hyphenated indecency'. In the end, he never does publish it; by the time that he leaves the university in deep disgrace, the article has been stolen by a rival historian, who passes it off in an Italian journal as his own work.

For most of the time when I was working on this book, I was also carrying out my duties as a lecturer in the history department of the University of Sheffield. At one point, in an unexpected echo of *Lucky Jim*, a senior colleague solemnly advised me to cancel the contract for what he liked to call my 'coffee-table book', and to devote myself instead to writing a serious scholarly article. Unfortunately, like Jim Dixon, I did not always show my elders the respect they deserved, and I ignored his advice. Unlike Dixon, however, I was fortunate in my colleagues, and I am pleased to thank everyone at Sheffield for their help and advice, especially Pertti Ahonen, Mike Braddick, Flurin Condrau, Simon Hall, Karen Harvey, Zoë Laidlaw, Simon Loseby, Patrick Renshaw, Barbara Schmucki, Joe Street and Ted Vallance. I am especially grateful to Robert Cook and Hugh Wilford, who were great sources of encouragement and guidance on everything from Gerry Anderson to Exeter City. And it is a particular pleasure to thank Jenny Atkins, Sarah Buchan, Alastair Eccles, Siân Findlay, Liza Gerrard, Catherine Karalis Isaac, Samantha Kenyon, Kim Lees, Danielle Leighton, Joe Merton, Charles Salt, David Senior, Elliot Shale, Lizzie Soutter, Mike Warbrick and Rachel Weallans for their dedication to Dick Nixon and their splendid camaraderie during the final days.

Andrew Clark, Joe Guinan, Simon Hall, Martin O'Neill and Andrew

Preston all read various drafts of the manuscript and offered characteristically incisive and uninhibited criticisms. Shona, Sulekha and Madhu Abhyankar were a great help with the chapter on immigration. Simon Hooper and Lauren Stewart were unstinting sources of hospitality during my research trips to London, and Kaele Stokes, James Davis, Vicky Scahill, Nathan Bavidge and Edward Meek were no less welcoming in Cambridge. I am deeply grateful to Andrew Wylie, Michal Shavit and the staff of the Wylie Agency, and I also want to thank Jessica Clark, Jenny Fry, Catherine Hill, Caroline Hogg, Iain Hunt, Ursula Mackenzie, Susan de Soissons, Duncan Spilling, David Young and everyone at Time Warner Books for their hard work and support. My parents and my brother Alex were, as ever, tremendous sources of encouragement, and, working from impenetrable instructions, they somehow managed to construct the desk on which this book was written: no mean achievement!

I owe a great deal to all those historians, commentators and critics who have already written about British politics, culture and society in the fifties and sixties. It seems only fair to single out for special mention those from whom I borrowed particularly enthusiastically, namely Anthony Aldgate, Asa Briggs, David Cannadine, Humphrey Carpenter, Alan Clayson, John Darwin, John Davis, Jonathon Green, Peter Hennessy, Robert Hewison, John Hill, Colin Holmes, Alistair Horne, Kevin Jefferys, Ian MacDonald, Ross McKibbin, Arthur Marwick, Philip Norman, Jeffrey Richards and Harry Ritchie. But this is only to scratch the surface, and I have tried to indicate in the endnotes and bibliography my numerous debts to my fellow historians. I also want to acknowledge the sterling work of the various unsung librarians and archivists in London, Cambridge, Oxford and Sheffield, without whom researching and writing this book would have been inestimably more difficult.

Finally, I want to acknowledge four outstanding debts. Simon Hooper apparently never tired of reading draft chapters, organising sixties-related diversions and exploring the culture of the period into the small hours. Lauren Stewart showed extraordinary patience to put up with endless conversations about Peter Sellers, Paul McCartney and Berni Inns. I am deeply grateful to Catherine Morley, whose faith, inspiration and support meant so much. And, above all, my thanks go to Tim Whiting, an outstanding editor and a very good friend.

PREFACE

HEADMASTER: Would it be impossibly naïve and old-fashioned of me to ask what it is you are trying to accomplish in this impudent charade?

FRANKLIN: You could say that we are trying to shed the burden of the past.

HEADMASTER: Shed it? Why must we shed it? Why not shoulder it? Memories are not shackles, Franklin, they are garlands.

FRANKLIN: We're too tied to the past. We want to be free to look to the future. The future comes before the past.

HEADMASTER: Nonsense. The future comes after the past. Otherwise it couldn't be the future . . . It's all very easy to be daring and outspoken, Franklin, but once you're at the helm the impetus will pass. Authority is a leaden cope. You will be left behind, however daring and outspoken you are. You will be left behind, just as I have been left behind. Though when you have fallen as far behind as I have, you become a character. The mists of time lend one a certain romance.

Alan Bennett, *Forty Years On* (1968)

Just as few adolescents can ever believe that their parents have been through the same stages of attitude and development before them, so one of the more frequently recurrent fallacies has been people's belief that their own age is without precedent, that some new order is coming to birth in which all the general assumptions previously made about human behaviour are becoming somehow outmoded. In few ages has this belief been more prevalent than our own.

Christopher Booker, *The Neophiliacs* (1969)

On 21 October 1960, at the Old Bailey in London, the prosecution opened their case in *Regina* v. *Penguin Books Limited*, charged under the terms of the Obscene Publications Act of 1959 for publishing D. H. Lawrence's novel *Lady Chatterley's Lover*. The trial lasted for six days and made headlines not only in London but in capitals across the world. It was, said one observer, 'a circus so hilarious, fascinating, tense and satisfying that none who sat through all its six days will ever forget them'.[1]

The *Lady Chatterley's Lover* trial was one of the great set-pieces of the sixties. On the one hand stood the old order, represented by the counsel for the prosecution, Mervyn Griffith Jones, described by one observer as 'high cheek-boned and poker-backed, a veteran of Eton, Trinity Hall (Cambridge), the Coldstream Guards and many previous obscenity cases; a voice passionate only in disdain, but barbed with a rabid belief in convention and discipline'.[2] It was Griffith Jones who opened the case by listing, with cold contempt, the obscenities used by Lawrence in his novel, and it was Griffith Jones who famously turned to ask the jury if this was 'a book that you would have lying around in your own house . . . a book you would even wish your wife or your servants to read?' On the other side, representing the new wave of frankness and freedom, stood Gerald Gardiner, counsel for Penguin Books and a founder member of the Campaign for Nuclear Disarmament (CND), supported by thirty-five expert witnesses ranging from the literary icons E. M. Forster and Rebecca West to the young Northern lecturer Richard Hoggart and the Bishop of Woolwich, John Robinson. And it was the Bishop who best captured the liberal spirit of the defence team. 'What I think is clear', he told the court, 'is that what Lawrence is trying to do is to portray the sex relationship as something essentially sacred . . . as in a real sense an act of holy communion.' Asked whether it was 'a book which in your view Christians ought to read', he replied, confidently: 'Yes, I think it is.'[3]

On 2 November, after retiring for three hours to consider their verdict, the jury returned to the courtroom and acquitted Penguin Books of all charges. The publishers' immediate reaction was to deliver some 200,000 copies of the novel, which had been lying in readiness in their warehouse, to booksellers up and down the country. Each paperback cost just 3s 6d, and it was hardly surprising, given the notoriety of the trial, that sales were sensational. In the next two years, Penguin claimed to sell no fewer than 3.3 million copies of *Lady Chatterley's Lover*; in one Yorkshire town copies of the book were said to be on display in the butcher's next to his lamb chops; and by the end of the decade, the story of Constance Chatterley and the gamekeeper Mellors had taken up its place as one of the bestselling books in modern British history.[4]

But there was more to the *Chatterley* affair than sales alone: as Bernard Levin put it a few years later, it offered a powerful 'collection of symbols for the decade that was just beginning'.[5] On the Sunday after the jury had handed down their verdict, Kenneth Tynan wrote in the *Observer* that the 'real battle' had been 'between all that Hoggart stood for, and all that Griffith Jones stood for; between Lawrence's England and Sir Clifford Chatterley's England; between contact and separation; between freedom and control; between love and death'.[6] Penguin themselves added a caption to new editions proclaiming that the trial 'was not just a legal tussle, but a conflict of generation and class'.[7] 'I feel that a window has been opened,' said Lawrence's stepdaughter, 'and fresh air has blown right through England.'[8]

For many observers, the *Chatterley* trial caught the mood of a society on the brink of a new era of hedonism, liberation and excitement, precisely those values that are most often associated with 'the sixties'. As early as 1969, in the first major work on the decade, the journalist Christopher Booker wrote that 'there was a feeling of modernity and adventure that would never be won so easily again'.[9] And almost twenty years later, two school-teachers wrote in a retrospective of the decade that the sixties had entailed 'youthful rebellion against war, racial prejudice and sexual repression . . . a mini-renaissance in which the right of individual expression was encouraged, applauded and nurtured by a generation whose naïve belief was that all we needed was love'.[10]

This is the most common interpretation of the sixties: a cultural renaissance that emphasised tolerance, freedom and, above all, love. In Jonathon Green's book *All Dressed Up*, one of the standard accounts of the period, he explains that 'the Sixties are as much a state of mind as a chronological concept', standing, 'rightly or not, as the dominant myth of the modern era':

> As the century draws to a close, it is hard not to see the Sixties as the pivotal decade. It was not the only momentous period and its perceived importance now may be ascribed to the current domination of media by those whose youth was played out against its gaudy wallpaper, but for all the importance of the Twenties and the Thirties, the years of the two World Wars, and the grim, destructive Eighties, the Sixties seem to stand in the centre of it all, sucking in the influences of the past, creating the touchstones of the future.[11]

Like so many other nostalgic veterans of the period, Green associates it with utopianism, non-conformity, sensuality and experimentation. It was all about 'dressing up', 'party-time': 'For some it was "party best", for others full-scale fancy dress, while for many, noses pressed to the window, it was merely the reflection, alluring or repellent, of those dead set on a good time.' Hence the title of his book, borrowed from John Lennon's comment that in the sixties 'we all dressed up'.[12]

This version of the sixties remains both popular and persuasive, and is the one most often echoed by Green's contemporaries in the arts and publishing worlds when they, too, look back on their youth. 'It was all an incredibly romantic era,' according to a journalist who worked on the underground press: 'girls were incredibly beautiful and luscious and they didn't have AIDS and didn't wear knickers. There was always enough money to be comfortable, there was good music, dope, sex, and above all there was not conforming.'[13] It is also a version largely confirmed by Arthur Marwick's monumental survey of the period, which covers not only Britain but also France, Italy and the United States. For Marwick, the story of the sixties is the story of an international 'cultural revolution' that transformed 'material conditions, family relationships, and personal freedoms for the vast majority of ordinary people'.[14] As Marwick explained in an interview publicising the book, 'it was a change in the relationships between children and parents; blacks and whites; men and women; social classes. The old conventions were thrown away.'[15] In his conclusion, he suggests that 'the sixties cultural revolution in effect established the enduring values and social behaviour for the rest of the century'.[16]

Both Green and Marwick, as should already be clear, are broadly in favour of the social and cultural changes they associate with the sixties. But there have also been plenty of commentators for whom the period was one of moral turpitude, artistic self-indulgence, social fragmentation and cultural decline. In 1977, for instance, the moral campaigner Mary Whitehouse wrote that Britain had sunk into an abyss of state-sponsored depravity, from 'pre-marital sex, abortion on demand [and] homosexuality' to 'abuse of the monarchy, moral values, law and order and religion'. An entire generation, she thought, had been taught to see 'sex as the great liberator, and self-control and self-denial as the only sins'.[17] This was an interpretation eagerly repeated during the following decade by Conservative politicians and journalists keen to contrast the achievements of Thatcherism with the alleged failures of the past. The Conservative party chairman, Norman Tebbit, notoriously attacked the BBC as 'the insufferable, smug, sanctimonious, naïve, guilt-ridden, wet, pink orthodoxy of that sunset home of the third-rate minds of that third-rate decade, the Sixties', and commented that the decade had been characterised by dirt, disorder, 'bad art . . . violence and soft pornography'.[18] Three years later, in 1988, Margaret Thatcher herself blamed 'Sixties culture' for 'the block mentality: tower blocks, trade union block votes, block schools' and the insidious cult of 'breaking the rules'.[19]

At the end of the 1990s the columnist Peter Hitchens argued that ever since the *Chatterley* trial British civilisation had been rapidly approaching 'the edge of extinction':

> We allowed our patriotism to be turned into a joke, wise sexual restraint to be mocked as prudery, our families to be defamed as nests of violence, loathing and abuse, our literature to be tossed aside like so much garbage, and our church to be turned into a department of the Social Security system . . . We lost our nerve and our pride. We thought there was something wrong with our own country, and so we scanned the world for novelties to import and adopt. We tore up every familiar thing in our landscape, adopted a means of transport wholly unfitted to our small, crowded island, demolished the hearts of hundreds of handsome towns and cities, and in the meantime we castrated our criminal law.

The changes underfoot since the sixties had, said Hitchens, 'brought about misery, decadence and ignorance . . . which threatens to abolish one of the happiest, fairest and kindest societies which has ever existed in this imperfect world'. And even his political adversaries appeared to agree. At first. Tony Blair had presented himself as a child of the sixties, posing with a guitar for press photographers and enthusiastically talking about his affection for the Beatles and their contemporaries. Eventually, however, he too decided to join the assault on the period. Unveiling a new criminal justice programme in the summer of 2004, Blair told his audience that the 1960s had been an era of 'freedom without responsibility', producing 'a group of young people who were brought up without parental discipline, without proper role models and without any sense of responsibility to or for others'. It was time for a return to 'rules, order and proper behaviour' and 'a community where the decent law-abiding majority are in charge'. It was time, he said, for 'the end of the 1960s liberal social consensus'.[20]

At first glance there seems to be little in common between writers like Jonathon Green and Arthur Marwick on the one hand, and the likes of Margaret Thatcher and Peter Hitchens on the other. While one group heaps praise upon an era of liberation and self-expression, the other condemns an age of moral decline and collapsing traditions. But the irony is that essentially they agree that what characterised the sixties in Britain was a process of breakneck, irreversible and unprecedented change, and their disagreement basically hinges on their attitude to the tremendous forces that the decade apparently unleashed. Indeed, this emphasis on change is echoed by dozens of other historians and commentators who have written about the period. For Christopher Booker it was a 'frenetic decade' in which 'conventions of dress, language and behaviour seemed to be dissolving like snow'.[21] For Bernard Levin, 'the Sixties saw an old world die and a new one come to birth'.[22] For Jeffrey Richards, Britain 'underwent a profound and far-reaching social and cultural revolution' in which 'rules, restrictions, conventions and traditions in both life and art were ditched'.[23] Even the sober Marxist historian Eric Hobsbawm, in his global history of the twentieth century, calls the sixties a 'golden age' of affluence and prosperity that 'generated a profound, and in many ways sudden, moral and cultural revolution, a dramatic transformation of the conventions of social and personal behaviour'.[24] As Marwick, the dean of sixties historians, puts it, the decade witnessed the birth of 'a unique civilization'. 'There has been nothing quite like it,' he wrote in his concluding words; 'nothing would ever be the same again.'[25]

This book presents a rather different version of British history in the sixties. As probably the first historian to write about the period whose earliest memories only just encompass the years before Thatcherism, I have very little interest either in celebrating an exaggerated golden age of hedonism and liberation, or in condemning an equally exaggerated era of moral degradation and national decline. What this book argues is that the British experience in the 1960s was much more complicated, diverse and contradictory than it has often been given credit for.

The example of the *Chatterley* trial, or perhaps what might better be called the myth of the *Chatterley* trial, is a case in point. Mervyn Griffith Jones' misjudged remark about 'wives and servants' and John Robinson's endorsement of Lawrence's 'Christian' book are very well known. What is less well known is that nine of the twelve jurors had already decided to acquit Penguin Books before the trial had even begun.[26] And far from the prosecution having the wholehearted support of a stuffy and monolithic Establishment, almost every newspaper in the country thought that the trial was a waste of time. The *Guardian* commented that 'there should be no great difficulty' in proving that Penguin Books were innocent, while even the *Daily Telegraph*, probably the most conservative paper of all, thought that 'the police would be better employed' in hunting down 'absolutely filthy' pornography than in attacking a novel that was clearly not in that class.[27] In fact, as Paul Ferris has argued, the Crown had little choice but to bring the case to court, because they needed to test the vague concept of 'literary merit' described in the new Obscene Publications Act of the previous year. As Griffith Jones himself told the Director of Public Prosecutions, prosecution was effectively inevitable: if no action was taken, it would 'make proceedings against any other novel very difficult' and effectively destroy the new legislation within months of its passage.[28]

To confuse matters further, there is plenty of evidence that millions of ordinary people were shocked rather than invigorated by the verdict. In Edinburgh, one woman bought a copy only to set it on fire on the pavement outside the bookshop. In South Wales, female library assistants were given permission to refuse to handle the book. The Home Office kept a file of examples of horrified letters from the public. 'England needs your help,' one man implored Harold Macmillan, the Prime Minister, begging him to step in to ban the book. A 'family man and grammar schoolmaster' reported that his Essex pupils found it 'impossible to buy "proper comics" in local shops, their place being taken by sex-filled trash'. And one anguished woman from Surrey wrote to the wife of the Home Secretary, R. A. Butler, explaining that she had a thirteen-year-old daughter at boarding school and was afraid that 'day girls there may introduce this filthy book at only three and sixpence . . . If a mistress protests, girls can reply that a clergyman has said "Every Christian should read it."'[29]

But, all in all, the truth was that the controversy was little more than a storm in a teacup. Although the book sold hundreds of thousands of copies, as might have been expected given its sensational content, it was never discovered how many readers had actually waded all the way through Lawrence's heavy, self-conscious prose. In the novelist's birthplace of Eastwood in Nottinghamshire, there was very little interest in the book at all; readers were reportedly much more interested in Alan Sillitoe's New Wave bestseller *Saturday Night and Sunday Morning*.[30] In November 1969, when the magazine *New Society* conducted a poll asking more than a thousand people of all ages and social backgrounds for their attitudes to the changes of the sixties, less than 1 per cent identified the *Chatterley* trial as the most important event of the decade, compared with the 39 per cent who selected man's conquest of space, the 14 per cent who chose the death of Winston Churchill, or even the 2 per cent who chose the marriage of Princess Margaret.[31]

The implication of all this is that the *Chatterley* trial's supposed 'conflict of generation and class' was rather more convoluted, and lends itself rather less well to a simplistic tale of liberation and repression, than is generally imagined. Indeed, for the man or woman in the street the *Chatterley* trial was simply not very important. One of the purposes of this book, therefore, is to argue for a messier and perhaps more complicated account of the sixties than already exists. Of course there were plenty of changes, as there are in most periods of modern history, but they were often painful, sluggish and controversial. Many of the most notable developments in British life, from the expansion of the suburbs to the changing role of women, built on the legacy of previous decades. There had been controversies about birth control, discussions of teenage affluence and arguments about American popular music in the 1920s and 1930s, and although these trends gathered pace after the interruption of the Second World War, they did not necessarily represent anything shockingly new. Even the so-called revolution in sexual attitudes of the later sixties reflected social and cultural trends that had been long under way. In other words, this book argues that, far from being a period of 'unprecedented intensity', as one account has it, or of staggering and unexpected change, the sixties revealed a fundamental continuity with older periods of British history.[32]

A second and related argument is that ordinary people often reacted to these developments in a much more contradictory, confused and apprehensive way than historians usually allow. The Victorian statesman Benjamin Disraeli once remarked that Britain was 'a very difficult country to move . . . a very difficult country indeed and one in which there is more disappointment to be looked for than success'.[33] This was no less true in the 1960s than it had been in previous decades. Even at the end of the decade, the battered pubs in the dilapidated Nottingham district of St Ann's still proudly displayed the Queen's portrait behind the bar.[34] British literature still largely clung to its traditional emphasis on the pragmatic and the idiosyncratic; music-hall traditions endured in songs and television shows; men devoted their weekends to gardening, bowling and fishing; and families decamped on holiday to Scarborough and Skegness. Indeed, there was no shortage of commentators struck not by the radical transformation of British life, but by its conservatism and conformity. 'Shouldn't one talk of the Cautious Sixties, rather than the Swinging Sixties?' asked *New Society* magazine in November 1969.[35] Even John Lennon, who fancied himself as the iconic rebel of the age, agreed. Jonathon Green borrowed Lennon's phrase 'we all dressed up' for his book on the sixties and the counter-culture, but Lennon was actually using it to describe the *absence* of a cultural revolution:

> The people who are in control and in power and the class system and the whole bullshit bourgeois scene is exactly the same except that there is a lot of middle-class kids with long hair walking around London in trendy clothes and Kenneth Tynan's making a fortune out of the word 'fuck'. But apart from that, *nothing happened except that we all dressed up*. The same bastards are in control, the same people are runnin' everything, it's exactly the same. They hyped the kids and the generation.
>
> We've grown up a little, all of us, and there has been a change and we are a bit freer and all that, but it's the same game, nothing's really changed . . . Nothing happening except that we grew up; we did our thing just like they were telling us. Most of the so-called 'Now Generation' are getting jobs and all of that. We're a minority, you know, people like us always were.[36]

This leads us to the third theme of this book. Almost all of those commentators who have written about the 1960s have memories either of the period itself or of the years that immediately followed it, and it is hard to resist the suspicion that they have found it difficult to separate their own private memories from their interpretation of the subject. Most books on the decade not only concentrate on change rather than continuity, but also pay extremely close attention to the affairs of a minority of well-educated, relatively affluent young people, precisely those people most likely to become writers, publishers, historians and so on. Indeed, Jonathon Green even goes so far as to dismiss with lofty contempt the tastes of 'the masses', which he says 'remained predictable and grimly banal'.[37] This may make for diverting, if slightly irritating, bar-room banter, but it hardly suggests a serious attempt to capture the wider experiences of the British population as a whole. For, as historians have found when writing about previous periods of British history, there was no such thing as a single national experience; and the phenomena that we often take as shorthand for the sixties were not universally popular. People rarely remember that the soundtracks of *The Sound of Music* and *South Pacific* comfortably outsold any of the Beatles albums of the decade; or that more people attended church than went to football matches; or that, far from turning against a supposedly repressive Establishment, most people were content to vote for socially conservative, Oxford-educated politicians like Harold Macmillan, Harold Wilson and Edward Heath. And so, to borrow the famous phrase of the historian E. P. Thompson, this book sets out to rescue 'from the enormous condescension of posterity' – as well as the enormous condescension of innumerable historians – the lives of the kind of people who spent the 1960s in Aberdeen or Welshpool or Wolverhampton, the kind of people for whom mention of the sixties might conjure up memories not of *Lady Chatterley*, the Pill and the Rolling Stones, but of bingo, Blackpool and Berni Inns.

Having set out the three major themes of this book, it makes sense to say a few words about its scope. Precisely when the sixties began and ended remains a matter of some debate. Robert Hewison, for example, defines the period as lasting from 1960 to 1975; David Mellor and Laurent Gervereau choose to begin in 1962 and end in 1973; and Eric Hobsbawm has a broader 'golden age' of affluence running from the late 1940s to the middle of the 1970s.[38] Perhaps most influentially, Arthur Marwick proposes a 'long sixties' from 1958 to 1974, which he divides into three periods: 'First Stirrings' from 1958 to 1963; the 'High Sixties' of 1964–9; and 'Catching Up' from 1969 to 1974.[39]

This chronology at first seems very persuasive, but it suffers from one important flaw. When Marwick refers to 'the sixties', he is talking about the phenomenon of a broad, international cultural revolution rather than the specifically British experience that is the subject of this book. From a British point of view, it would be odd to start in 1958 and not in 1956 – the year of the Suez crisis, the film *Rock Around the Clock*, the play *Look Back in Anger*, and so on. It was in the mid-fifties, after all, that rationing and austerity came to an end, consumer activity began rapidly escalating, the first commercial television channel was established, and the retreat from empire began in earnest. So the Suez crisis of 1956 seems to mark a reasonable starting point, although, to emphasise the central theme of continuity, there are occasional diversions into the early fifties or even further back. And as for the end of the sixties in Britain, 1974 seems much too late. The flavour of the early 1970s – inflation, strikes, the IRA bombings, football hooliganism, progressive rock and the ecology movement – seems very different from that of Swinging London and the bright, self-confident sixties. An alternative might be 1973, which historians often take to mark the end of the affluent sixties because it brought the shattering blow of the OPEC oil shock, but in Britain any sense of economic optimism was already long gone.

The most sensible solution, it seems to me, is to banish the early 1970s altogether and to end the story in the summer of 1970. By this point, the scientific optimism of the mid-sixties had evaporated, the fashion for 'flower power' was coming to an end, and the economy was already in something of a mess. A further attraction of 1970 is that it was the year of the Beatles' separation, the defeat of England, the football world champions, in Mexico, and the electoral defeat of Harold Wilson's Labour government, three events that for different groups around the country seemed to represent the end of a particular era.

Most readers will already have noticed that the period described is much longer than that promised by the subtitle of this book. In fact I originally set out to write one very long book charting the years from 1956 to 1970, and then discovered that it would take much longer than I had imagined to do justice to the complexities of the period. *Never Had It So Good* is therefore the first of two volumes, and examines the period between 1956 and the end of 1963: roughly, the years of Harold Macmillan and the affluent society. My justification for breaking the narrative at the end of 1963 is partly a question of national politics – the transition from Macmillan to Wilson, via Home – and partly a question of popular culture, with this point marking an approximate crossover between the world of skiffle, duffel coats and expresso bars on the one hand, and the world of the Rolling Stones, miniskirts and discotheques on the other. The latter world will be covered in the second volume, *White Heat*, which describes the rise and fall of Harold Wilson's optimistic 'New Britain' between 1964 and 1970.

As for the content of the book, I have not shied away from discussing familiar subjects like the Angry Young Men, the Profumo scandal and the rise of the Beatles. These were important phenomena that greatly intrigued many contemporary onlookers and also tell us much about British society in the middle of the last century. But I have also tried to pay attention to the less celebrated and glamorous corners of national life, from high-street shopping and children's toys to Little Chefs and the Gloucester music scene. At the same time, I have endeavoured to strike a balance between political and cultural narratives. Many writers, especially those who celebrate the alleged cultural revolution of the sixties, agree with Marwick that 'it is a mistake to concentrate on politics and changes of governments'.[40] I do not share this opinion. For one thing, the lives and livelihoods of millions of ordinary people often depended on the decisions taken by politicians. What was more, politics clearly mattered to people living in the sixties. Electoral turnout was very high, the two major parties were usually divided by the narrowest of margins, and the media devoted great attention to the activities of politicians and governments. Some features of the period, like CND and the satire boom, are barely comprehensible without some sense of the political context. So throughout the book there runs a clear political narrative, showing how politics and government both reflected and influenced broader developments in British society and culture.

As a legacy of my original plan to write a single enormous work covering the years between 1956 and 1970, I have held over discussion of some topics until the sequel to this book. In working out the structure of the two books, I have tried to address issues at the most appropriate point in the general narrative. So in *Never Had It So Good* there is quite a lot about consumerism, literature and the Cold War, but not very much about, say, fashion and design, architecture or sex, subjects that are addressed at greater length in *White Heat*. No doubt plenty of readers will wonder, on reading this book, why some vital topic close to their heart has been criminally ignored, and the only consolation I can offer is that it might feature in the sequel; although, of course, the truth is that it equally well might not.

Finally, a word on the title. Harold Macmillan's most famous phrase is often misquoted as 'You've never had it so good'; what he actually said was: 'Let's be frank about it, *most of our people* have never had it so good.' Macmillan was the dominant public figure of the era, and his words are often cited to evoke the optimism of the late fifties, the sense that Britain was enjoying a period of unprecedented affluence and progress. But, as Macmillan himself implicitly admitted, not all of his fellow citizens enjoyed the same prosperity. Some, like the Prime Minister himself, worried that it was too good to last, while others were troubled by the social changes that followed in its wake. What contemporaries called the affluent society was not universally popular, and confident dreams of a prosperous future were intermingled with gloomy fears of national decline. And in many ways, it is the tension between them that provides the story of this book.

PERMISSIONS

We are grateful for permission to reproduce extracts from the following material in this volume: *The Road to Wigan Pier* by George Orwell (Copyright © George Orwell, 1936), courtesy of Bill Hamilton as the Literary Executor of the Estate of the Late Sonia Brownell Orwell and Martin Secker & Warburg Ltd; *Years of Hope: Diaries, Papers and Letters, 1940–62* and *Out of the Wilderness: Diaries, 1963–67*, by Tony Benn, published by Hutchinson, courtesy The Random House Group Ltd; *The Fifties* by Peter Lewis, courtesy The Herbert Press, an imprint of A & C Black Publishers, 37 Soho Square, London W1D 3QZ; *The Entertainer* by John Osborne, courtesy Faber & Faber Ltd; *The Anatomy of Britain* by Anthony Sampson (Copyright © Estate of Anthony Sampson 1962), by permission of PFD on behalf of the Estate of Anthony Sampson; 'How to Get On in Society' by John Betjeman, reprinted by permission of John Murray Publishers; *The Art of the Possible: The Memoirs of Lord Butler* by R. A. Butler, courtesy Penguin Books and David Higham Associates; *Poor Me* by Adam Faith and *Trad Mad* by Brian Matthew, both by arrangement with Souvenir Press Ltd; *The Fifties and Sixties* by Miriam Akhtar and Steve Humphries, courtesy Macmillan Ltd; *Jill* by Philip Larkin, courtesy Faber & Faber Ltd; *The Letters of Kingsley Amis*, edited by Zachary Leader, reprinted by permission of HarperCollins Publishers Ltd. Copyright © Zachary Leader, 2000; *Lucky Jim* by Kingsley Amis, first published by Gollancz 1954, Penguin Books 1961. Copyright © Kingsley Amis, 1954; *In the Fifties* by Peter Vansittart, reprinted by permission of John Murray Publishers; *In Anger: Culture in the Cold War 1945–60* by Robert Hewison, courtesy Methuen Publishing Ltd; *Room at the Top* by John Braine, courtesy The Random House Group Ltd and David Higham Associates; *Look Back in Anger* by John Osborne, courtesy Faber & Faber Ltd; *Windrush: The Irresistible Rise of Multi-Racial Britain* by Mike Phillips and Trevor Phillips, reprinted by permission of HarperCollins Publishers Ltd. Copyright © Mike Phillips and Trevor Phillips, 1999; *The Third Floor Front: A View of Broadcasting in the 1960s* by Hugh Carleton Greene (Copyright © Hugh Carleton Greene 1969) by permission of PFD on behalf of the Estate of Hugh Carleton Greene; *Hurry On Down* by John Wain,

1

SUEZ

A squalid episode ends in a pitiable climb-down . . . Our moral authority in the world has been destroyed.

Daily Herald, 7 November 1956

The bastards! The *rotten bastards*! They've killed him! They've killed Mick! Those bloody wogs – they've murdered him! Oh, the rotten bastards!

John Osborne, *The Entertainer* (1957)

At five o'clock on a mild November morning, John Morrison looked out over the still and darkened waters. He had been in the air for an hour now. As light slowly broke across the southern Mediterranean, he grimly began to make the last preparations for the jump. 'As we stood up and hooked up', he recalled, 'I looked out of one of the windows and saw a Naval fighter diving across the bay with its guns going. Then the usual: RED on. Stand in the Door. GREEN on. GO! GO! GO! GO! . . . And out I went.' The crowded plane climbed away above him, and Morrison tumbled a thousand feet through a cloudless blue African dawn. A 'large piece of flak or something' ripped through his parachute canopy and 'tore a great big hole in it'. He struggled to get his weapons free as the earth came up at him, and then his body smashed into the ground 'with a hell of a bang'.[1]

This was the raffish town of Port Said, Egypt, on the morning of 5 November 1956, and Morrison was a corporal in the 3rd British Parachute Regiment. Around him his fellow paratroopers were already falling into formation, moving towards their objective: a walled cemetery to the east, where the Egyptian defenders had opened up with a vicious hail of machine-gun fire. It was grim and unrelenting stuff, a confused hell of heat and mosquitoes and blood and bullets. The fighting lasted for hours; by early afternoon, however, the exhausted Morrison and his comrades controlled the field.

That night, the paratroopers held their position in the cemetery overlooking the sparkling Mediterranean Sea. Nine miles to the north, just off the Egyptian coast, the British and French expeditionary fleet lay at anchor. As dawn broke on 6 November, the heavy crash of their guns broke into the silence of the port. 'We could see Port Said immediately in front of us,' one airman recalled, 'a great pall of black smoke rising into the sky above it.' By six o'clock the air was thick with the noise of helicopters lifting off from the decks, banking towards the Egyptian port, over the water and towards the central square where an enormous statue of Ferdinand de Lesseps, the architect of the Suez Canal, stood proudly amid the clamour of battle. As on the previous day, the struggle was intense but one-sided. By mid-afternoon, the British commandos had control of the major arteries and buildings of Port Said and were beginning to relax, yielding to the flush of exhilaration that follows close combat. The first phase of an immensely complicated and controversial operation had ended.[2]

When Egypt became the first Arab country to assert its independence from the decaying Ottoman Empire at the beginning of the nineteenth century, its potential wealth and superb strategic location made it the natural object of envious glances from the burgeoning imperial powers of Western Europe. British statesmen in particular had long been transfixed by the urge to stop any European rival from gaining control of the country and the eastern Mediterranean. They were initially suspicious of a scheme by the French engineer Ferdinand de Lesseps to build a canal through the Suez isthmus from Port Said to the Red Sea, even though it had obvious potential to improve trade and communications with their supreme imperial prize, India. But, shortly after the opening of the great waterway in 1869, the British Prime Minister Benjamin Disraeli began buying up shares in the Suez Canal Company, and before long British civil servants were poring through the Egyptian ruler's accounts, planning a new national infrastructure and sipping tea in the lavish rooms of Shepheard's Hotel in Cairo. In 1882, after nationalist riots in Alexandria, British troops were finally sent in to garrison the country and protect the Canal. For the next seventy years Egypt was a British possession, with thousands of British soldiers stationed in dusty garrison towns and hundreds of British officials working away in the grand offices of Cairo and Alexandria. The strategic priority of controlling the Canal coincided nicely with fashionable imperialist ideas about Britain's mission to spread the ideals of civilisation and justice throughout the developing world. The average Egyptian, needless to say, was less than content with this arrangement. The future President Anwar Sadat once recalled the loathsome spectacle of the 'typical British constable on his motorcycle tearing through the city streets day and night like a madman . . . I simply hated the sight of him.'[3]

Egypt remained a British possession in all but name until the end of the Second World War. Even in the early 1950s, contingency plans for a British nuclear exchange with the Soviet Union assumed that nuclear bombers would strike at southern Russia from Britain's airfields in the Suez Canal Zone. Meanwhile, the Middle East was now providing 70 per cent of the oil that powered the economies and armies of the industrialised West, and half of this oil reached European ports by tanker through the Canal. 'Suez remains of vast importance as the back door to Egypt and will no doubt be of great importance in the next war,' noted a Foreign Office paper in 1951, while Egypt was 'the essential central point from which to defend the Middle East and all that the Middle East entails'.[4] Along a narrow 120 mile strip from Port Said to Suez there stretched a long wilderness of airfields, barracks and warehouses inhabited by nearly forty thousand bored British soldiers.[5] They looked on their Egyptian neighbours with an unfriendly blend of racism, indifference and contempt. 'Nobody ever called the local people Egyptians,' explained one National Service conscript; 'it was always "the wogs".'[6] One Royal Engineer found on his desk a report of a traffic accident outside Cairo between a British army vehicle and a Rolls-Royce. 'Two Wogs were inside,' it read, 'and their names were King Farouk and Ali Ismael.' The officer recalled that he 'summoned the driver and took him to task, telling him he should not call King Farouk a wog, and he must rewrite the report. Back it came: "I asked them their names . . . they were King Farouk and another Wog called Ali Ismael."'[7]

From the Egyptian point of view, the continued presence of the British troops, with their alien ways and smug superiority, was becoming increasingly intolerable. In October 1951 the Egyptian Prime Minister Mustafa al-Nahhas announced the unilateral abrogation of the 1936 Anglo-Egyptian Treaty, proclaimed a state of emergency and demanded that British forces immediately evacuate the Canal Zone. But in Downing Street there was no intention of giving in to nationalist pressure; the Canal Zone bases were regarded as far too important. 'Tell them if we have any more of their cheek we will set the Jews on them,' Winston Churchill raged to his Foreign

Secretary Anthony Eden, 'and drive them into the gutter from which they should never have emerged.'[8] What followed was a long, bitter and bloody stalemate, with running clashes between Egyptian irregulars and nervous British servicemen around the depots and camps of the Canal Zone.[9] On 25 January 1952 a gun battle between British troops and Egyptian policemen at Ismailiya ended with fifty killed and a hundred more wounded. The following day Cairo exploded in riots, leaving thirty more dead and hundreds of shops burned and smashed. The symbols of British political and cultural occupation, from Shepheard's Hotel and Barclays Bank to car showrooms and cinemas, were despoiled in a frenzy of nationalist frustration. For the Egyptian government itself, this was little consolation. King Farouk sacked his ministers immediately after the conflagration and then, in July, was himself overthrown by nationalist officers and replaced by Mohammed Neguib, the most respected general in the Egyptian army. Two years later Neguib was deposed in his turn and a new leader emerged: Gamel Abdel Nasser.[10]

The son of a postal clerk from Alexandria, Nasser was an unusually dashing, self-confident and compelling figure. In 1936, at just eighteen, he had joined the army, and there he fell in with a group of ambitious young officers including his future successor Anwar Sadat. By the late 1940s he was the leading figure in the Free Officers Movement, which met regularly to talk over coffee and cigarettes about socialism, Islam and rebuilding Egypt as a force to be respected in the world. The Free Officers had played a vital role in the coup that kicked out King Farouk in 1952, and when Nasser himself took over two years later he was determined to make himself the dynamic expression of Egyptian pride and anti-imperial resentment.[11] For millions of people across the Arab world, Nasser was the very personification of Arab self-assertion against the great powers of the West. 'He had made us feel by all available means', wrote one Egyptian writer, 'that there existed in Egypt and the whole Arab world only one intelligence, one power, one personality.'[12]

Nasser's appeal to his countrymen owed something to his innate charm and much to his state-funded welfare and education programmes. But it also owed a great deal to his determination to tweak the tail of the British lion. The Free Officers' regime made it an explicit priority to dislodge the British from the Canal Zone, and negotiations began almost immediately after the coup.[13] Once he had toppled General Neguib and cemented his domestic position, Nasser grew more bullish. He used the army to crush dissidents at home, including the radical Muslim Brotherhood and the Communists, and insisted that Britain evacuate all personnel from the Canal bases. In October 1954 a deal was finally struck. British forces would be pulled out within twenty months, but would retain the option to return if an outside power attacked Turkey or a member of the Arab League. Nasser himself declared that Egypt and Britain could look forward to working together 'on a solid basis of mutual trust and confidence'.[14] But he evidently had little faith in the British word; and the events of the next two years were to destroy any confidence in London that Nasser was a reliable ally.

In February 1955 Nasser received a visit from the British Foreign Secretary and Churchill's heir apparent, Sir Anthony Eden. The purpose of Eden's visit was to explain to Nasser the significance of the Baghdad Pact, an anti-Communist alliance that he hoped would become 'a NATO for the Middle East'.[15] As far as Nasser was concerned, however, the Baghdad Pact was just another attempt by Britain to control the affairs of the Arab world, and he complained that it was designed to promote the interests of Iraq above those of Egypt. The two men met in the opulent surroundings of the British Embassy in Cairo, and although the encounter was far more cordial than some reports would have us believe, it was not an unqualified success. Eden greeted Nasser in Arabic and chatted with him relatively amiably about the recent developments in Anglo-Egyptian relations; at one point the two men even exchanged some of their favourite proverbs from the Koran. Eden's young wife Clarissa observed that Nasser gave a 'great impression of health and strength – terrifically broad and booming'. She thought that the meeting had been 'a good talk', despite the fact that Nasser was 'very bitter' about the Baghdad Pact.[16] Nasser, meanwhile, was impressed with Eden, but his admiration was tinged with resentment. 'What elegance!' he remarked to his confidant Mohammed Heikal. 'It was made to look as if we were beggars and they were princes!'[17]

Shortly after Eden's return to London, Britain signed the Baghdad Pact. Pakistan and Turkey joined later in the year, but Egypt declined and was left sitting on the sidelines. When Nasser heard the news, he was furious. Egyptian state radio denounced the alliance as a 'betrayal of Arabism', and warned that 'imperialism and its stooges' were undermining the Arab cause.[18] Relations with the British deteriorated still further when Eden refused to sell Nasser a consignment of armaments to build up the Egyptian army on the contentious northern border with Israel. Nasser therefore turned east and in September 1955 announced that he had arranged to buy hundreds of planes and tanks, not to mention guns, rocket launchers and other supplies, from Czechoslovakia. To British eyes, this was the final straw. Nasser's refusal to join the Baghdad Pact, the frequent denunciations of European imperialism on Radio Cairo and the Czech arms deal all added up to overwhelming proof that he had become little more than a tool of the Communist bloc. 'I suspect that his relations with the Soviet Union are a good deal closer than he admits to us,' Eden wrote to the American President Eisenhower in March 1956. 'We should accept, I think, that a policy of appeasement will bring us nothing in Egypt.'[19] And so on 19 and 20 July 1956 the American and British governments announced that they would be withdrawing their offer of over $200 million in funds for Nasser's pet project to build a High Dam at Aswan.[20]

Quite clearly this rebuff was meant as a personal insult to Nasser himself. But as a tactical move designed to preserve the standing of the Western powers in the Middle East, it was a total disaster. On 26 July, the anniversary of King Farouk's ejection from his throne, Nasser appeared before an enormous crowd in Alexandria and made a three-hour speech of thrilling, brazen defiance, broadcast live on Egyptian radio. Never again, he declared, would Egypt be considered part of the British sphere of influence. He harangued the British government for destroying the Aswan Dam deal, and then, unexpectedly, he embarked on a little lecture on the history of the Suez Canal. 'I went back in my memory to what I used to read about the year 1854,' he said. 'In this year Ferdinand de Lesseps arrived in Egypt.'[21] A hundred miles away, as soon as the words 'de Lesseps' had left Nasser's lips, the Egyptian army sprang into action, and armed personnel began moving into the offices and installations of the Canal Zone. Nasser repeated the words 'de Lesseps' fourteen more times, just in case his officers had missed the signal, but even before he had reached the end of his speech the operation was over. He was jubilant. 'In the past,' he told the cheering crowd, 'we were kept waiting in the offices of the British High Commissioner and the British Ambassador, but now they take us into account . . . Today we greet the fifth year of the revolution and in the same way as Farouk left us on 26 July 1952, the old Suez Canal Company also leaves us on the same day.'[22]

In London, it was night. Sir Anthony Eden, who had finally replaced Churchill a year earlier, was hosting a formal dinner in Downing Street for the visiting Prime Minister of Iraq. Shortly after ten o'clock, his duty

secretary interrupted the dinner and handed to the British Prime Minister
the message that Nasser had nationalised the Suez Canal. The great trial of
Eden's premiership was upon him.[23]

In July 1956, Sir Anthony Eden was the most experienced, the best-known
and probably the most popular politician in Britain. He had grown up in
the cosseted wealth of a country estate in County Durham, had been educated at Eton and Oxford, and had exhibited tremendous courage and
leadership in the trenches of the Somme. In 1923, at only twenty-six, he
had been elected as a Conservative MP, and at thirty-eight he was Foreign
Secretary. It was the age of the dictators, of Mussolini's brutal aggression
in Abyssinia and the bloody heartbreak of the Spanish Civil War. In 1938,
sick of the shabby farrago of appeasement, Eden resigned and the result
was a sensation. Cheering crowds gathered outside his house, and he
received over six thousand letters of congratulation, not least from the
Archbishop of Canterbury.[24] Eden's resignation was the making of him: it
won him enduring popular admiration and brought him into alliance
with Churchill, the most indomitable of appeasement's critics. 'Eden has
today paid a big cheque into the bank on which he can draw in future,'
remarked David Lloyd George.[25] When war finally broke out, he returned
to the Cabinet and eventually won back his old job at the Foreign Office.
Throughout the struggle, he stood at Churchill's side; he was closer to
him than any other member of the government, and even married his
attractive niece Clarissa. After the Labour landslide of 1945, George VI
offered to make Eden a Knight of the Garter; like Churchill, he refused.
He was now a political star, 'after Churchill, the most famous face in
Britain'.[26]

When the Conservatives regained power in 1951, Eden was made
Foreign Secretary once again. Four long years as heir apparent followed,
and then at last, on 6 April 1955, he made the short journey to
Buckingham Palace to be invested with the supreme responsibility of high
office. Later that day Eden was greeted in the Commons by genial tributes
from both sides of the House on what his sympathetic biographer calls 'a
happy and civilized occasion that emphasized the genuine affection and
regard felt for the new Prime Minister'.[27] According to the Gallup organisation, his public approval rating stood at a commanding 73 per cent.[28] 'It
is fortunate for Britain', enthused the *Yorkshire Post*, 'that there exists to succeed Sir Winston a leader who is a world statesman in his own right.'[29] A

French–English phrasebook published later that year suggested that the most appropriate translation for '*Il est très distingué*' was 'A regular Anthony Eden'.[30] He was that rare beast: a genuinely glamorous and cultivated politician, who read Arabic and Persian literature in the original and presented an image of effortless suavity bolstered by an unrivalled knowledge of international affairs and diplomatic history. At a point in British history when the country was feeling relatively self-satisfied, his moderate appeal to good manners and good sense was assured of a warm reception. Weeks after becoming Prime Minister, Eden fought and won an immediate general election, increasing the Conservative majority and enhancing his own reputation. When he greeted the cheering crowds on 26 May as the newly re-elected head of government, his high place in British political history seemed certain.[31]

Few people, therefore, realised that Eden's easy charm and unruffled competence was little more than a façade. The truth was that Eden, in the words of his authorised biographer, was 'an exceptionally tense, lonely and shy man'.[32] His Cabinet colleague R. A. Butler once remarked, shrewdly but unkindly, that he was 'part mad baronet, part beautiful woman'.[33] As a boy, Eden had always been highly strung and unhappy, and as a young man he had been lucky to emerge alive from the nightmarish bloodbath of Flanders, where two of his brothers had been killed. He had made an unhappy first marriage before finding happiness with Clarissa Churchill, and his beloved son Simon died in an air crash in Burma in 1945.[34] In the House of Commons Eden had few close friends: he was not naturally gregarious and shunned the masculine atmosphere of the gentleman's club. Like many shy and unhappy men, he sought solace in work. Although he loved art, literature and the countryside, he was obsessed by his job, pushing himself to the limits of physical and mental exhaustion. An unceasing string of ailments, from appendicitis and migraines to gallstones and jaundice, weighed heavily on an already sensitive and reserved man. In April 1953 disaster struck. Eden entered the London Clinic for a simple operation on his gall bladder, to be conducted by an experienced and respected surgeon. The surgeon's knife slipped; Eden's biliary duct was accidentally cut, and he lost large quantities of blood. A second operation to save his life was carried out: again Eden lost great amounts of blood, and on this occasion he came close to death. A third operation, which lasted for eight hours, repaired some of the damage, but Eden's health never entirely recovered.[35] He was, said his close friend and parliamentary private secretary Robert Carr, 'never the same man' again.[36]

Eden's fortunes as Prime Minister were not helped by the fact that his predecessor had lingered so long in Downing Street. By the time he finally succeeded to the top job, Eden was past his peak of vigour and imagination, and problems were mounting at home. He inherited a stuttering economy, with earnings and prices booming and Britain's balance of payments deficit yawning to over £450 million.[37] Churchill himself doubted Eden's capacity to govern; the night before his own resignation, he remarked: 'I don't believe Anthony can do it.'[38] His chief lieutenants, Rab Butler and Harold Macmillan, the Chancellor and Foreign Secretary respectively, were not close to him and had prime ministerial ambitions of their own. Butler's handling of the economy was less than competent; after cutting income tax in a pre-election budget spree, he was forced to reverse his generosity in the autumn and hitch taxes back up in order to fight off pressure on the pound.[39]

Less than a year after Eden had become Prime Minister there were whispers of discontent in the tea rooms of the Commons. A misjudged Cabinet reshuffle, which replaced Butler at the Treasury with the feline Macmillan, did not help matters.[40] Eden was perceived as weak, vacillating and insufficiently devoted to the economic concerns of the middle classes. To his critics on the back benches and in the Conservative press, the heroic statesman famous for opposing appeasement in the 1930s had become a feeble Prime Minister who appeased socialism at home and Arab nationalism abroad. There were whispers that an 'Eden-must-go' movement was gathering strength, and in January 1956 a notorious *Daily Telegraph* article, entitled 'The Firm Smack of Government', sneered that Eden was capable only of 'smoothing and fixing'. Eden's characteristic speaking gesture, the writer noted, was to clench his right fist, punch it into his left palm for emphasis – only to stop at the last minute: 'the smack is seldom heard'.[41]

By the late spring of 1956, a series of by-election defeats had weakened the Conservatives' confidence in Eden's political acumen, and his future in Downing Street was looking increasingly shaky.[42] The Egyptian imbroglio, therefore, gave Eden a sense of enormous frustration, and he began to see Nasser not as the leader of a rival state but as a private adversary with whom he was locked in mortal combat. He prided himself on his handling of foreign affairs, but Nasser's vituperative anti-imperialist broadcasts were undermining the British position elsewhere in the Arab world, not least in Iraq and Jordan. In March 1956, the young King Hussein abruptly dismissed the British commander of the Arab Legion in Jordan, General Sir John

Glubb, in a dramatic statement of anti-British intent and a serious blow to British prestige in the Middle East. Shortly after Glubb's dismissal, Eden received a memorandum from his friend Anthony Nutting, then Minister of State at the Foreign Office, urging him to exercise restraint and concilia-tion towards the Arab world. To Nutting's astonishment, he was then hauled out of a diplomatic dinner at the Savoy to hear Eden's thoughts on the telephone:

'What's all this poppycock you've sent me?' he shouted. 'I don't agree with a single word of it.'

I replied that it was an attempt to look ahead and to rationalise our position in the Middle East, so as to avoid in the future the kind of blow to our prestige that we had just suffered over Glubb.

'But what's all this nonsense about isolating Nasser or "neutralising" him, as you call it? I want him destroyed, can't you understand? I want him removed, and if you and the Foreign Office don't agree, then you'd better come to the Cabinet and explain why.'

I tried to calm him down by saying that, before deciding to destroy Nasser, it might be wise to look for some alternative, hostile or friendly. And the only result of removing Nasser would be anarchy in Egypt.

'But I don't want an alternative,' Eden shouted at me. 'And I don't give a damn if there's anarchy and chaos in Egypt.'

With that he hung up, leaving me to return to my dinner.[43]

Eden felt himself cursed. 'From now on, Eden completely lost his touch,' wrote Nutting. 'Gone was his old uncanny sense of timing, his deft feel for negotiation. Driven by the impulses of pride and prestige and nagged by mounting sickness, he began to behave like an enraged elephant charging senselessly at invisible and imaginary enemies in the international jungle.'[44]

When, on the night of 26 July, Eden heard that Nasser had nationalised the Canal, he recognised that this was the moment of decision. If he could act with swift and unwavering resolution, with the country behind him, then he could destroy Nasser once and for all, reverse the decline of his own government, and cast off the overbearing shadow of Churchill. As soon as he had heard the news, Eden summoned the Chiefs of Staff to discuss the possibility of military action. Although it was clear that such action could not be taken for several weeks, the Cabinet the following day agreed that though they would be 'on weak ground in basing our resistance on the narrow argument that Colonel Nasser had acted illegally', it was imperative that 'every effort must be made to restore effective international control over the Canal'. Co-operation with France and the United States was, of course, desirable, but not necessarily essential. The habits of empire died hard. Eden explained to his colleagues:

> The fundamental question before the Cabinet . . . was whether they were prepared in the last resort to pursue their objective by the threat or even the use of force, and whether they were ready, in default of assistance from the United States and France, to take military action alone.
>
> The Cabinet agreed that our essential interests in this area must, if necessary, be safeguarded by military action and that the necessary preparations to this end must be made. Failure to hold the Suez Canal would lead inevitably to the loss one by one of all our interests and assets in the Middle East and, even if we had to act alone, we could not stop short of using force to protect our position if all other means of protecting it proved unavailing.[45]

Eden's intense conviction that the nationalisation of the Canal was an intolerable affront was shared by much of the British population. The news was greeted with widespread outrage; a tin-pot Egyptian colonel could hardly be allowed to seize control of a vital international waterway through which passed a quarter of all British imports. Indeed, if Eden had not reacted at all to Nasser's actions, he would certainly have offended a large swathe of the electorate. *The Times* called Nasser's enterprise 'a clear affront and threat to Western interests'; it also refused the Egyptian leader the usual courtesy of the title 'President' or 'Colonel', referring to him merely as 'Nasser', while the *Mirror* called him 'Grabber Nasser'.[46] Although many Labour backbenchers were not convinced by the arguments for military action, their leader, Hugh Gaitskell, sounded even more belligerent than Eden. True, he suggested that the United Nations might be called in to resolve the dispute, but he also accused Nasser of plotting to destroy Israel and subvert the Arab world, and told MPs: 'It is all very familiar. It is exactly the same that we encountered from Mussolini and Hitler in those years before the war.'[47] Many other observers agreed. 'Remember Mussolini?' the *Mirror* asked its readers on 30 July. 'Mussolini ended up hanging upside down by his feet in a square in Milan. Remember Adolf Hitler? He ended up burning in a petrol-soaked blanket outside his bunker in the heart of devastated Berlin.'[48] 'No more Adolf Hitlers,' insisted the *Daily Herald*. 'There is no room for appeasement.'[49] Eden himself liked to repeat the parallel with Mussolini; indeed, he invested it with great personal significance. On 5 August he wrote to Eisenhower again and warned him that Nasser had 'embarked on a course which is depressingly familiar'. It was essential, Eden explained, to remove him and install 'a regime less hostile to the West'. He went on: 'I have never thought Nasser a Hitler, he has no warlike people behind him. But the parallel with Mussolini is close. Neither of us can forget the lives and treasures he cost us before he was finally dealt with.'[50]

Eisenhower, however, did not agree. The President was facing re-election in November, and like his Secretary of State, John Foster Dulles, he was extremely wary of being dragged into a conflict in the Middle East. Both warned Eden that the long-term consequences of an operation by Britain and France would be disastrous, and that American public opinion was firmly opposed to any such action.[51] There followed an elaborate and ultimately futile exercise in negotiation: even while the British military planners were refining the details of their proposed operations, two London conferences were organised to resolve the dispute and a short-lived Suez Canal Users' Association was formed, with negligible results.[52] Indeed, to most uninformed observers, August and September marked a strange hiatus in the inexorable build-up of tension. But the fact was that it would take over six weeks to assemble a task force to strike at Egypt, and Eden had not been put off by the Americans from his original plan of taking military action. On 2 August he called up selected military reserves. Five days later, the Chancellor of the Exchequer, Harold Macmillan, suggested that British war aims should be extended 'to bring about the fall of Nasser and create a government in Egypt which will work satisfactorily with ourselves and the other great powers'.[53] By now British planners took it for granted that the round of conferences scheduled for the next few weeks would come to nothing, and the invasion was scheduled for early September.

On 8 August, Eden broadcast to the nation, a clear sign of the seriousness of his intentions. 'Our quarrel is not with Egypt,' he explained, 'still less with the Arab world. It is with Colonel Nasser . . . The pattern is clear to many of us, my friends. We all know this is how fascist governments behave and we all remember only too well what the cost can be of giving in to fascism.' The cost of inaction, he argued, would be insupportable. 'If Colonel Nasser's action was to succeed, each one of us would be at the mercy of one man for the supplies on which we live; we could never accept that. With dictators you always have to pay a higher price later on, for the appetite grows with feeding.'[54]

Perhaps if he had struck now, Eden might have won broad public support. Instead he waited, hamstrung by the complicated timetable of military preparations. The empty charade of the London conferences dragged on with no resolution. Again and again Eisenhower and Dulles repeated their warnings against the use of force. 'It might cause a serious misunderstanding between our two countries because I must say frankly that there is as yet no public opinion in this country which is prepared to support such a move,' Eisenhower wrote on 8 September.[55] An opinion poll at the end of August found that only a third of the British public supported military action, dropping to 27 per cent if the Americans were not involved, with nearly a half firmly against it.[56] The proportion in favour of a military attack in Egypt was likely to fall still further as the weeks went by, as public opinion turned to other issues, and as the outrage at Nasser's nationalisation of the Canal faded from memory. At the beginning of September, however, the Chiefs of Staff told Eden that the plans had been changed. Their original scheme had been to land at Port Said; this had been altered to Alexandria; now they had decided to launch a massive air attack on Egypt, followed by a landing in Port Said after all. Eden reluctantly gave way, and as one of the planners remarked, 'it was back to the drawing board'.[57]

A month had now elapsed since Nasser's rhetorical triumph in Alexandria. The British task force lay at anchor off Malta and Cyprus. In Britain itself, khaki-painted trucks were still carrying stores and equipment to the southern ports. The press carried stories of men and machines moving south, forming a great Mediterranean armada that would regain the Canal from Nasser's control. But nothing happened. No orders came. Eden's domestic critics began to muster. The reservists, who had originally greeted the crisis with great enthusiasm, were muttering in frustration. One blimpish brigadier told an old soldiers' reunion: 'Politicians don't know Orientals like we do. They don't know that the only way to deal with them is to kick their backsides.'[58] When the Conservative party conference opened in Llandudno, there was little doubt that the majority of Eden's own activists were impatient for action. A mocking cartoon in *Punch* read: 'The grand old Anthony Eden / He had ten thousand men / He marched them up to the top of the hill / And marched them down again.'[59] Meanwhile, Eden's delicate health was buckling under the strain. In late September and early October he recorded in his diary that he was sleeping little and suffering severe abdominal pains – a legacy of his disastrous operation three years before. His wife was unwell, and while visiting her in University College Hospital Eden himself 'began to shake uncontrollably with a violent fever'. Drugs and stimulants kept him going, but there could be no doubt that he was desperately tired.[60]

At the beginning of October, a breakthrough came. From the outset Eden had planned the operation as a joint expedition with the French, who blamed Nasser for encouraging nationalism in Algeria. Talks on a peaceful settlement to the affair had now broken down in the United Nations and the French were sick of the rigmarole of negotiation and delay. They had begun secret discussions with Egypt's bitter enemy, Israel. On 30 September French and Israeli representatives met in Paris and agreed that a concerted operation offered benefits for all sides. Israel would attack from the east, sweeping across the Sinai desert towards the Canal; French forces would land at airfields just west of the Canal and seize the Canal itself. The French would see Nasser defeated and ousted; the Israelis would keep Sinai and control of the Gulf of Aqaba and the Straits of Tiran. On 14 October a French delegation arrived at Chequers and outlined the plan to Eden. Israel would launch its invasion across the Sinai. Britain and France would wait for them to defeat the Egyptians, then insist that both sides withdraw from the Canal. A joint Anglo-French occupation force would then move into the Canal Zone in the interests of protecting it for international traffic.[61] According to Anthony Nutting, who was a horrified observer at the meeting, Eden, 'doing his best to conceal his excitement . . . replied non-committally that he would give these suggestions very careful thought'.[62] In fact, the plan seemed perfect, and almost childishly simple. The focus now turned to Selwyn Lloyd, the Foreign Secretary, whom Eden sent in secret to France to discuss the plan with the Israelis. This, therefore, was the moment at which the conspiracy began.

Lloyd had been a curious and revealing choice for the Foreign Office: a loyal, clubbable deputy, but no visionary and certainly no great statesman. He was, as the historian Peter Clarke puts it, 'a successful, provincial, professional man', albeit one educated at Fettes and Cambridge.[63] He had done well out of the Second World War, acquiring both a safe Tory seat and the faithful, meticulous instincts of a decent officer. Cheerful, tactless, unimaginative, he had been a surprise choice to join the government in 1951. When Churchill first summoned him to 10 Downing Street, Lloyd admitted that 'he could not think why I had been sent for so soon'. Churchill asked him to go to the Foreign Office as Minister of State. Poor Lloyd was 'flabbergasted'. As he himself later recalled, with perhaps a little exaggeration, he replied: 'But Sir, there must be some mistake. I do not speak any foreign language. Except in war, I have never visited any foreign country. I do not like foreigners. I have never spoken in a Foreign Affairs debate in the House. I have never listened to one.' Churchill growled in return: 'Young man, these all seem to me to be positive advantages.'[64] Above all, he was dependable; by moving Lloyd to the Foreign Office just before Christmas 1955, Eden was confident that he would effectively be able to run his own private foreign policy.[65]

On 22 October Lloyd announced that he had a heavy cold and cancelled his existing appointments. Away from the cameras, he was bundled into a car and driven to an RAF airfield, from where he flew to the French military base at Villacoublay. He was then put in another car and driven to a villa in the Parisian suburb of Sèvres. On the way the car narrowly escaped a high-speed collision with a larger vehicle storming out of a side road. The rest of the journey, however, passed off without incident and a still shaken Lloyd was ushered in to meet the French Prime Minister, Guy Mollet, and his Foreign Minister Claude Pineau. The latter explained that the Israelis had made up their minds to attack Egypt. Lloyd then went in to see the Israeli representatives, 'a roomful of utterly exhausted people, mostly asleep'. 'I ought to have had a false moustache,' he announced to a stony silence. Their journey had been even worse than Lloyd's, having lasted seventeen hours. In the circumstances, the meeting was a tense and uneasy occasion. Lloyd found it hard to conceal his personal distaste for the arrangement, while the Israeli Prime Minister David Ben-Gurion and Chief of Staff Moshe Dayan were tired, aggressive and in no mood to be patronised.[66] Lloyd himself, according to his private secretary, was 'thoughtful': his problem was that since Eden was evidently in favour of the plan, he could hardly walk out of the meeting having rejected it.[67]

As subsequent accounts have made clear, the Sèvres meetings amounted to detailed planning of the Israeli invasion and its aftermath. The following day, Lloyd reported to the Cabinet that 'secret conversations' had been held with the Israelis in Paris.[68] British diplomats were then sent back to Sèvres and over the next few days the three sides came to an agreement. On the evening of 24 October, a protocol was finally typed up and signed. According to the deal, Israel would invade Egypt in five days' time, on the evening of 29 October, aiming to reach the Canal Zone by the following morning. Britain and France would then issue an appeal to both sides to stop fighting, to withdraw ten miles from the Canal, and to accept Anglo-French occupation of the Canal Zone in order 'to guarantee freedom of passage through the Canal by vessels of all nations until a final settlement'. If Nasser refused, then Britain and France would attack.[69] It seemed fool-proof, if not wholly honourable. Even the British signatories themselves found it hard to muster much pride in their handiwork. 'I think champagne was produced,' one diplomat recalled, 'but there was little sparkle in the atmosphere.' As he left the villa to return to London, he observed that 'the stars shone as brightly as I have ever seen them. It seemed wholly incongruous.'[70]

On 25 October, with just four days until the Israeli invasion, Eden put the plan to the Cabinet. He frankly admitted that Britain would be accused of 'collusion with Israel', but both he and Lloyd were strongly in favour. Indeed, the Prime Minister was evidently delighted that a solution had at last presented itself; as one colleague later recalled, he was 'bright-eyed and full of life', temporarily free of the weariness of the last few weeks.[71] The Chancellor, Harold Macmillan, was also impressed by the scheme, and confidently assured his colleagues that the Americans would not cause trouble. What he did not choose to tell them, however, was that American co-operation was vital to the operation, because the British economy was in one of its periodic bouts of crisis. The problem was the balance of payments deficit, which was encouraging speculation against sterling and weakening international confidence in the pound as a major currency. In August the Treasury warned Macmillan that because of the balance of payments issues, British gold and dollar reserves were going to be 'under considerable strain' over the coming months.[72] In September Macmillan's chief economic adviser told him that it was a 'vital necessity from the point of view of the currency and our economy of ensuring that we do not go it alone, and that we have the maximum US support'.[73] The pound was creaking under the strain: in August £129 million was lost from sterling accounts, and, after a pause in September, another £85 million disappeared in October.[74] But Macmillan chose to interpret the Treasury's advice in a quite different light. He argued that confidence in sterling would be restored with 'a quick and satisfactory settlement of this issue'.[75] In the crucial meeting, as in other Cabinet meetings before the final decision, Macmillan remained a keen supporter of a military strike. He was confident, too, of American support, even though Eisenhower and Dulles had been kept entirely in the dark. 'I know Ike,' the Chancellor told his colleagues. 'He will lie doggo!'[76] The alliance of Eden, Lloyd and Macmillan was decisive. Three other members dissented vigorously, but they did not resign, and collective responsibility bound them all to the Sèvres plan. With that, the die was cast.[77]

At dusk on 29 October, as agreed, the Israeli attack began with a parachute landing in the Mitla Pass. Soon afterwards came the rolling thunder of the long columns of tanks and infantry, rumbling implacably into the sands of the Sinai. Although Egyptian military intelligence had suspected that something was afoot, Nasser simply could not bring himself to believe the rumours of conspiracy. As one historian puts it, 'he had misplaced ideas of an Englishman's sense of honour'.[78] The Egyptian forces put up strong resistance, but were quickly cut off and surrounded; by the following morning, the Israelis were reported to be closing on the Canal Zone. The Cabinet met at ten that morning and agreed to issue the expected ultimatum. According to the minutes of the meeting, the Cabinet for the first time acknowledged the possible dangers of offending the United States, noting that 'we should do our utmost to reduce the offence to American public opinion which was liable to be caused by our notes to Egypt and Israel. Our reserves of gold and dollars were still falling at a dangerously rapid rate.'[79] But it was too late to worry about that now. In the afternoon the Egyptian and Israeli ambassadors were handed copies of the British and French ultimatum demanding that their armies retreat ten miles from the Canal. Eden also wrote to Eisenhower, who had been left dumbfounded by the sudden development of the operation. The British intervention, Eden explained, was 'not part of a harking back to the old colonial and occupational concepts', but instead would amount to 'strengthening the weakest point in the line against Communism'.[80] Eisenhower might appear a genial, bumbling old war hero, but in reality he was a shrewd and ruthless political operator. His anger at having been double-crossed by Eden, just one week before the presidential election, boded ill for the success of the plan.

Under the terms of the ultimatum, Egypt and Israel had twelve hours to pull their troops back from the Canal. Bewildered by the speed of events, but never quite losing his cool, Nasser rejected the Anglo-French demands. On the late afternoon of 31 October the first British attacks began, wave after wave of Canberra bombers sweeping down from Cyprus. Within a day control of the skies had been won, and 260 Egyptian aircraft had been destroyed for the loss of only three allied pilots, two British and one French. Unfortunately, the naval task force was still ploughing through the Mediterranean from Malta towards Port Said: although the Egyptian air defences had been smashed, there now followed a crucial delay before British troops could be landed to take control of the Canal. On 2 November the UN General Assembly met for the first time in emergency session and approved an American resolution calling for a ceasefire. Eden had entirely misjudged the international reaction to the British intervention: rather than approval, or even passivity, he faced a firestorm of protest. Only Australia, New Zealand and South Africa, the bastions of the old Commonwealth, backed Britain and France, and even their support was reluctant. In all other respects the Suez allies stood alone.[81]

British public opinion, meanwhile, was in tumult. Eden had partly been pushed into the Suez adventure by the belief that the Conservative press and electorate would never forgive him for 'appeasing' Nasser. *The Times* had run leaders with headlines like 'A Hinge of History' and 'Resisting the Aggressor', and one edition warned that the British people, 'in their silent way, know better than the critics. They still want Britain great.'[82] The *Daily Sketch* echoed this tone in September with its notorious headline: 'LET THE CRYBABIES HOWL! It's GREAT Britain Again'.[83] 'How good it is to hear the British Lion's roar!' wrote one reader in the *Daily Telegraph*.[84] In fact, public opinion was intensely divided. An opinion poll taken on 1 and 2 November found that 40 per cent supported Eden's general handling of the Middle Eastern situation, 46 per cent disagreed with it, and 14 per cent were unsure. As for military action against Egypt, 37 per cent supported it, 44 per cent opposed it, and 19 per cent had no opinion. But as the war intensified over the next few days, there was a heavy shift in favour of the government, and another poll found that on 10 and 11 November 53 per cent supported the war and 32 per cent opposed it. The majority of Conservative voters, of course, supported the government, along with a substantial minority of Labour and Liberal supporters.[85]

The Suez controversy did not follow conventional party lines; it splintered partisan allegiances, communities and even families. In John Osborne's play *The Entertainer*, first performed in 1957, the seventy-year-old Billy Rice is bewildered by 'all this business out in the Middle East', complaining: 'People seem to be able to do what they like to us.' His granddaughter Jean, on other hand, is 'steamed up about the way things were going' and attends an anti-war rally in Trafalgar Square. 'I should think you want your bloody head read,' is Billy's incredulous reaction.[86] Inside Buckingham Palace, too, opinions were divided. The Queen told one friend that she was 'having the most awful time', since 'my lady-in-waiting thinks one thing, one private secretary thinks another, another thinks something else'.[87] Lord Mountbatten, the First Sea Lord, defied the traditions of the Royal Navy by sending a letter to Eden expressing profound disagreement with the operation.[88] Many of Eden's parliamentary colleagues were openly furious. On 1 November, the day after the bombing began, the Speaker had to suspend the House of Commons for thirty minutes after 'the rage and passion' of MPs boiled over. 'I have never seen Members so angry,' wrote Anthony Wedgwood Benn in his daily diary.[89] Although Eden then spoke calmly and eloquently, it was barely possible to allay the outrage of many Labour members. His own party in the Commons was hardly united. Anthony Nutting and the Financial Secretary to the Treasury, Sir Edward Boyle, both resigned from the government, while six Conservative backbenchers also publicly opposed their own leader. Several more were thought to be ambivalent. The party in the country, on the other hand, was wholeheartedly behind Eden, who now seemed to have recaptured the firm smack of government. Downing Street was deluged with telegrams of support from the shires.[90] The Conservative press and the vast majority of provincial newspapers were similarly enthusiastic, although *The Times* remained undecided and both *The Economist* and the *Spectator* opposed military action.[91]

The Labour Party, meanwhile, was terribly caught between working-class patriotism and middle-class conscience. The young David Owen, who was spending his summer before university working on a construction project in Plymouth, recalled that his fellow builders overwhelmingly backed Eden's intervention on the principle that since 'the Gippos had hit us, we should hit them'.[92] Indeed, some Labour MPs, generally those from working-class backgrounds, hardly bothered to hide their sympathy for the government and support for the military operations. Others could not contain their revulsion that Eden had reverted to the tactics of nineteenth-century imperialism. Benn, for example, recorded his 'shame and disgust' at a debate at the Cambridge Union. Beside him sat a weeping Egyptian graduate student who was tormented by fears for his family; on the walls hung enormous posters reading 'Support Eden, not Nasser' and 'We are now committed and must support our troops'; the audience was 'a crowd of students laughing and screaming for war'.[93] On 4 November Benn went to Hugh Gaitskell's house to help him draft an address to the nation to be televised that evening.[94] Gaitskell had abandoned his warlike rhetoric of the summer, and told the television audience that Eden had 'violated the charter of the United Nations'. 'We are doing all this alone except for France: opposed by the world, in defiance of the world,' he insisted. 'It is not a police action; there is no law behind it.' Britain, he argued, must accept a ceasefire and allow the United Nations to settle the crisis, and Eden must resign.[95]

Although Gaitskell recognised that Suez was a tricky challenge for the Labour Party, he was enjoying the opportunity to savage the government. 'What's so wonderful, Dick,' he told Richard Crossman, 'is that we are morally in the right.'[96] Unfortunately for Gaitskell, the broadcast did not quite have the effect he intended. Many wavering Conservatives rallied to Eden's colours rather than throw in their lot with the heathen, and the broadcast inevitably suggested to international observers that the British governing class was fatally divided. Gaitskell himself came across as at best opportunistic and at worst unpatriotic, particularly after his ill-judged references to the dictators earlier in the year.[97] Eden's biographer Robert Rhodes James recalled that on his number 11 bus from Chelsea to Westminster the passengers, young and old, were fervent supporters of the government and 'contemptuous of the unpatriotic Socialist "intellectuals" who opposed it'.[98] One Air Corps colonel recalled listening to Gaitskell's address on board a naval carrier steaming towards the coast of Egypt. 'We were not impressed,' he remembered. In the past, he thought, the country had rallied to its troops; but 'now those troops were being vilified by one of the leaders of the country, in the defence of whose honour they were at that moment prepared to die'.[99]

The controversy at home only added to the enormous strain on Eden and his ministers, who now found themselves at the mercy of events. The Anglo-French fleet was still ploughing towards the Mediterranean; for the sake of appearances, it had waited for the British ultimatum before setting sail. Meanwhile, Egypt's air force had been destroyed, the Israelis were in control of the Sinai, and the world was in uproar. On 3 November, almost unbelievably under the circumstances, Eden's military chiefs suggested altering the invasion plans yet again and landing troops not at Port Said but at Haifa, a sign not only that the whole operation had been carelessly planned, but that nerves were cracking under the pressure. Eden insisted that the invasion go ahead as agreed, with all possible efforts to avoid civilian casualties and with military operations to be confined to the Canal Zone itself.[100] That evening he addressed the nation. The swagger of the Conservative tabloids was markedly absent from his tone:

> All my life I have been a man of peace, working for peace, striving for peace, negotiating for peace. I have been a League of Nations man and a United Nations man, and I am still the same man, with the same convictions, the same devotion to peace. I could not be other, even if I wished, but I am utterly convinced that the action we have taken is right . . .
>
> We have stepped in because the United Nations could not do so in time. If the United Nations will take over the police action we shall welcome it. Indeed, we proposed that course to them.[101]

Eden almost certainly did not believe that the United Nations would be able to act quickly to establish a peacekeeping force; his promise was made for political appearances, but it was a rash one. The following day, Sunday 4 November, while Soviet troops were fighting their way into Budapest to crush a Hungarian national uprising, an American-backed resolution to set up exactly such a UN peacekeeping force was passed in New York, leaving Eden in an awkward position. For the moment, though, he was determined that the next phase of the operation must go ahead. But he was a weary and resigned figure, weakened both by his persistent ill health and by sheer shock at the intensity of opposition to his plans. That morning's *Observer* had run an editorial unprecedented in its scorn for the 'folly and crookedness' of the government, and it was hard to disagree with its verdict that not since 1783 had Britain 'made herself so universally disliked'.[102] One Cabinet minister heard Eden pacing in the room above: 'Up and down, up and down, talking incessantly, that worried me.' Although he remained outwardly calm, Eden had seemed to age, 'looking tired and drawn'. The Suez Canal, admitted his wife, 'was flowing through the drawing room'.[103]

Late on the afternoon of the same Sunday, the Cabinet met to give their final approval. Selwyn Lloyd recalled that in the Cabinet Room they could hear the 'howling' and 'booing' of thirty thousand people at an anti-war demonstration in Trafalgar Square, which was being addressed by the Labour firebrand Aneurin Bevan.[104] Curiously enough, Eden's own wife Clarissa, an interested spectator at the rally, was recognised with friendly cheers, although she felt it wisest to return home.[105] After a long debate, the issue came to a vote. Twelve ministers wanted to continue; three to postpone; and three to abandon the mission entirely. Eden, Lloyd and Macmillan, of course, were all for going ahead. But for the first time there was a breach within the Cabinet itself. After a delay, with Eden considering his position, news came that Israel had refused to accept the UN conditions for a ceasefire. 'Everyone laughed & banged the table with relief – except Birch and Monckton [two dissenters] who looked glum,' wrote Clarissa Eden.[106] The Cabinet therefore agreed: the troops must go in.[107] That evening, Eden sent another heartfelt message to Eisenhower. 'I am sure that this is the moment to curb Nasser's ambitions,' he wrote. 'If you cannot approve, I would like you at least to understand the terrible decisions we have had to make. I remember nothing like them since the days when we were comrades together in the war. History alone can judge whether we have made the right decision.'[108]

On the shores of the Mediterranean, the military operations, despite all the problems of planning and organisation, were going extremely well. The British and French paratroopers landed in the early morning of 5 November and secured the airfields around Port Said and Port Fuad. At dawn on the following day ground troops landed in force and by nightfall Egyptian resistance had been crushed. The British and French commandos had lost only thirty-two men, the Egyptians over two thousand.[109] The way south, to complete control of the Canal, was now open. One British paratrooper, recalled from the reserves to the colours, remembered setting off with his platoon down the southern road late that night. They were in two tanks, swigging whisky to warm themselves against the frigid night air, buoyant that the mission was going so well. Then, suddenly, they were flagged down, twenty-three miles south of the coast. To their complete surprise and disappointment, their commander told them to halt. The Americans, he said, had 'stopped the advance'.[110]

It was American economic pressure, not military defeat, that stopped the operation in its tracks. Throughout the autumn there had been a steady haemorrhage of Britain's gold and dollar reserves as the position of sterling came under renewed pressure; in the first week of November alone, the Treasury lost almost $100 million from its currency reserves. With the Canal blocked and Britain's access to Middle Eastern oil cut off by the Syrians, the situation was now desperate.[111] On the morning of 6 November Macmillan telephoned Washington and asked for assistance: he was informed that only if the government agreed to a ceasefire before midnight would the Americans support a loan from the International Monetary Fund.[112] Before the Cabinet met that morning to consider the excellent military reports from Egypt, Macmillan muttered to Lloyd that 'in view of the financial and economic pressures we must stop'.[113] In the meeting itself, Lloyd admitted that the British were coming under tremendous pressure in the United Nations, and that the relationship with the United States was now in danger of collapsing completely. Macmillan, meanwhile, told his colleagues about the Americans' insistence on a ceasefire if the Treasury wanted its loan from the IMF. The alternative consequences, he implied, might be another devaluation of the pound and the end of sterling as a serious international currency. Other pressures came to bear. Some ministers were frightened that the Soviet Union might now intervene; others that the Conservative Party might be torn apart. Macmillan's gloom was decisive; Eden himself had been deserted by all but a handful of his colleagues.[114]

Early that afternoon, Eden telephoned Eisenhower to concede defeat and agree to a ceasefire in Egypt. He then went to announce the decision in the House of Commons, where he was greeted by the predictable cacophony of cheers and jeers. All the tension of the last few weeks had peaked and broken, leaving him 'aged and ill, defeated and broken'.[115] One observer described his appearance:

> The Prime Minister sprawled on the front bench, head back and mouth agape. His eyes, inflamed with sleeplessness, stared into the vacancies beyond the roof. His hands twitched at his horn-rimmed spectacles. The face was grey except where black-rimmed caverns surrounded the dying embers of his eyes. The whole personality seemed completely withdrawn.[6]

Nasser had won.

In the weeks after the ceasefire, the magnitude of Eden's defeat became painfully clear. The Americans even vetoed British attempts to stay in Egypt as part of the UN peacekeeping forces; there would be no loan to prop up the pound unless all British forces were withdrawn

unconditionally from Port Said. Macmillan, with all the zeal of the convert, became the champion of reconciliation with Washington and
withdrawal from Egypt. In Harold Wilson's trenchant phrase, the
Chancellor was 'first in, first out'.[7] While the British commandos waited
aimlessly in the dust of Port Said, Macmillan insisted that the position of
sterling was paramount. On 20 November he warned his colleagues that
the Treasury might have to choose between spending all its reserves to
maintain the value of the pound and allowing it 'to find its own level, with
the result that sterling might cease to be an international currency'.[118] A
week later, he repeated the warning: it was 'urgently necessary' to rebuild
relations with the United States, because the Treasury was about to
announce the extent of the drain on British finances, and it was imperative to have secured by then a loan from Washington. 'For this purpose,'
he explained, 'the good will of the United States was necessary; and it was
evident that this good will could not be obtained without an immediate
and unconditional undertaking to withdraw the Anglo-French force from
Port Said.'[119] After a few days' hesitation, the Cabinet gave way. Lloyd went
to the Commons on 3 December and announced that, since the operation
had been a complete success, the Anglo-French troops were being
withdrawn. It was a feeble attempt to conceal the extent of Eden's humiliation. Aneurin Bevan, with unsparing black wit, conveyed Labour
sympathy for Lloyd's 'having to sound the bugle of advance to cover his
retreat . . . I am bound to say, in conclusion, that having regard to the
obvious embarrassment of the Government, I feel I would be a bully if I
proceeded any further.' The Labour benches were exultant, the
Conservatives crushed.[120]

As for Eden, the pressure had taken its toll. Since his last illness in early
October his health had been precarious: although it now appears that the
stories about his dependence on Benzedrine were wildly exaggerated, he was
a lonely and haggard figure.[121] Whether he was seriously ill or simply
exhausted was unclear, but on 19 November his doctors advised him to take
a complete rest in a warmer climate. The solution was rather appropriate
after the cloak-and-dagger machinations of the preceding months: he
accepted an offer from Ian Fleming to retreat to his Jamaican house,
Goldeneye.[122] The announcement on 23 November that the Prime Minister
was off to Jamaica, with British troops still ensconced in Port Said, did not go
down well. Randolph Churchill, a frequent critic of Eden, wrote that
whereas Hitler had refused to withdraw his army from Stalingrad, 'even

Hitler did not winter in Jamaica'.[123] To make matters worse, Goldeneye was a long way from the Governor's mansion, where all official correspondence was sent, and Eden was effectively cut off from government deliberations until his return.

In London a triumvirate of Butler, Macmillan and the Lord President of the Council, the Marquess of Salisbury, controlled affairs. The Jamaican sojourn was relaxing enough, but Eden was chafing to return to Downing Street. He understandably found it infuriating to read by cable that Macmillan and Butler had agreed to pull British forces out of the Canal Zone, and that in his absence the Cabinet had effectively caved in to Eisenhower. On 14 December a tanned Eden arrived at London Airport and read a bland prepared statement: his original version denouncing the 'Moscow–Cairo axis', the Americans and the United Nations had been vetoed by his colleagues, a palpable signal of the shifting balance of power. Ever since his departure there had been intense speculation about his survival as Prime Minister; Clarissa Eden wrote that now 'everyone [was] looking at us with thoughtful eyes'.[124] 'Prime Minister Visits Britain' read one mocking headline.[125] In the Commons on 20 December, Eden was compelled to lie about the Sèvres conspiracy, telling the House: 'There were no plans to get together to attack Egypt . . . there was no fore-knowledge that Israel would attack Egypt.' He insisted: 'I would be compelled . . . if I had the same very disagreeable decisions to take again, to repeat them.'[126]

These were his last words in the House. After Christmas the doctors had another look at Eden and told him that his fevers and sleepless nights would almost certainly recur if he remained in 10 Downing Street. The news was a great disappointment to him, and although opinion polls suggested that Eden's popularity had actually improved as a result of the crisis, it was doubtful whether he still had the strength to fight for his political career.[127] 'In our opinion,' read his doctors' statement, 'his health will no longer enable him to sustain the heavy burdens inseparable from the office of Prime Minister.' Contrary to the historical myth, this was a genuine case of ill health, not a political pretext; as his wife put it, he simply 'wanted to stay alive'. On 9 January 1957, Eden told his Cabinet colleagues that he had decided to resign. The doctors, he said, had told him he 'would not last more than six weeks' as Prime Minister. At six o'clock he drove to Buckingham Palace to deliver his resignation to the Queen.[128] Ten days later, he left for a cruise to New Zealand, during which he struck up an unlikely rapport with his cabin steward, the future Deputy Prime Minister John Prescott.[129] On his return, Eden retired to his country farm, and died in 1977, at the age of seventy-nine.

The ghosts of Munich loomed heavily over Suez. Eden had been determined not to become another Chamberlain; he had been eager to step out from the shadow of Churchill; and he had been convinced that Nasser was Mussolini reborn. But instead of recapturing the spirit of the war, Eden had merely become a byword for prime ministerial folly.[130] For some observers, launching the operation had been bad enough, but abandoning it so swiftly was even worse. Churchill, who had initially been all for the operation, later remarked: 'I am not sure I should have dared to start, but I am sure I should not have dared to stop.'[131] Indeed, Eden's refusal to be *more* ruthless, to press home his military advantage with unflinching cynicism, is what strikes some historians.[132] Certainly the surrender left Eden's military chiefs bewildered and infuriated. 'We were shocked, very shocked,' recalled Sir Dermot Boyle, Chief of the Air Staff. 'And we felt terribly for the poor men on the ground who had done everything we wanted of them, done it extremely efficiently, and some of them had got killed, and yet they were being stopped when victory was, from their point of view, imminent.'[133] Not only had some British servicemen lost their lives; thousands of Egyptians had also died in a futile imperial adventure, only for the apparent victors to 'retreat like whipped dogs', as one account has it.[134]

But the expedition was plainly seriously flawed from the start. It was never clear whether the Anglo-French forces would be content with possession of the Canal Zone, or whether they would push on to Cairo. The French certainly had the aim of eliminating Nasser and installing a compliant replacement. Eden, however, never seemed sure whether Nasser would be 'destroyed' or allowed to remain. Even if the operation had been a success, it would have left thousands of British troops in uneasy possession of the Canal Zone, exactly the same unappealing scenario that had created the bitter quarrels of the early 1950s. If Eden meant this to be a permanent occupation, then he would need enormous quantities of men and resources for the complete suppression of Egyptian resistance. That these problems were never really resolved is testament to the tremendous pressure that Eden and his colleagues were under in the autumn of 1956; put kindly, they acted as they did simply because they felt they had to do *something*. Even if the

Americans had not forced the abandonment of the mission, it is still not easy to imagine a successful resolution of the crisis. As it was, the act of collusion with the Israelis represented a morally dubious gamble that ultimately left the Canal in Egyptian hands, Nasser entrenched in power, and British prestige and influence irreparably tarnished. There was no silver lining; the operation had been a complete disaster.[135]

The symbolic importance of the crisis was that it marked a confrontation between the old ambitions of British imperialism and the new realities of post-imperial retrenchment. Indeed, the Suez affair illustrated with striking clarity the decline of British imperial power. It was not, as some people tend to imagine, a cause of that decline; rather, it was a reflection of Britain's changed role in the world, partly as a result of two ruinously expensive global wars. Ever since 1945 British governments had been keenly conscious of the constraints that a battered economy would exercise on their imperial ambitions.[136] Selwyn Lloyd, for example, denied that 'one result of Suez was to make us realise that we could not act independently'. 'The fact was that we knew that all the time,' he explained. 'We were very conscious of our economic weakness and of the strain on our resources of expenditure overseas affecting our balance of payments.'[137] Eden expressed this well in a memorandum on 'the lessons of Suez' that he wrote shortly after returning from Jamaica, arguing: 'Surely we must review our world position and our domestic capacity more searchingly in the light of the Suez experience *which has not so much changed our fortunes as revealed realities.*'[138]

In fact, British imperial power had been ebbing for decades. Suez simply demonstrated it, powerfully and incontrovertibly, to the entire world. Even worse, any claims to moral superiority had been shattered by the suspicion that Eden had colluded with the Israelis in the attack on Egypt. Sir Pierson Dixon, the ambassador to the United Nations, noted that British influence had been 'greater than our actual strength' only so long as others thought that Britain would fight solely 'in defence of principle'. Now he felt that 'we had by our action reduced ourselves from a first-class to a third-class power. We revealed our weakness by stopping; and we threw away the moral position on which our world status largely depended.'[139] So, while the episode was not necessarily important in actually reducing British military and financial power, it was vitally important in changing the perception (both at home and abroad) of Britain's role in the world.[140] Certainly in Washington the feeling now was that British influence in the Middle East had been broken for good. The Secretary of State, the zealously dour John Foster Dulles, told the Senate Foreign Relations Committee that the British position had been 'severely weakened', adding, as regards Suez: 'Partly that created, partly it disclosed, the vulnerability of the British economic and financial position.'[141] 'I've just never seen a great power make such a complete *mess and botch* of things,' Eisenhower told his speech-writer. 'Of course, there's nobody, in a war, I'd rather have fighting alongside me than the British . . . But – *this* thing! My God!'[142]

A second consequence of the Suez crisis was the termination of the career of Sir Anthony Eden. He had been horrendously unlucky; a record of nine major internal operations tells its own story, and when he went under the knife again in 1970, it took two hours to make the first incision, so heavy was the scarring from the previous operations.[143] True, he might well have had to resign anyway because of his ill health; but he would not have had to take his leave in such humiliating circumstances. There was obviously great personal sadness for Eden in the Suez debacle, but there was also a sense that a glittering political career had been needlessly and tragically squandered. Writing nearly four decades later, Ben Pimlott remarked that if his illness had forced Eden to resign two years earlier, 'he would be remembered as one of the great politician–diplomats of the century, instead of by one traumatic word, which, more than any other, encapsulates British decline, senescence and delusions of grandeur'.[144] From the end of the Second World War until January 1957, Britain had been governed by men who had been prominent national figures in that conflict: Churchill, Attlee and Eden. When Eden resigned, it was as though a cord between the realities of the present and the glories of the past had been snapped. He was the last of the statesmen of the thirties to occupy 10 Downing Street and the last of the political heroes of the war to lead his party. His resignation was a powerful signal that the era of the world wars was over. The British people would have new leadership to carry them into the challenges of the 1960s.

There is little doubt that the humiliation of Suez and Eden's unhappy departure left a deep impression on the nation at large. Even in December 1956, weeks after the collapse of the operation, opinion polls found that a majority of the public supported the military intervention.[145] But the writer Peter Vansittart was not alone when he recalled that he did 'sense a change, in the streets, at bars, in homes and in "the media" after Suez: a lowering of expectations, a feeling that the good times had gone'.[146] As another observer put it, the age of 'going about as top people, deciding everything for the world', had vanished.[147] In Andrew Sinclair's satirical novel *The Breaking of Bumbo* (1959), the middle-class conscript hero harangues his fellow officers about the immorality of the invasion:

> Suppose we beat Egypt? We lose anyway, we've got to sell ourselves to live, and who'll buy John Bull, with a Boer War musket in his hand? . . . OK we think we're so damn wonderful still, and all we are is a lousy, punch-drunk ex-champ between a couple of really big men, jockeying around for the KO, not caring two damn hoots about us.[148]

For some this was hard to accept and bred a predictable sense of resentment, even despair. 'I think the defeat at Suez had a shattering effect on the morale at Whitehall,' said one Conservative minister later. 'The stench of defeat in the defence departments was really appalling.'[149] Over a hundred Conservative MPs endorsed a parliamentary motion accusing the Americans of 'gravely endangering the Atlantic Alliance', and many ordinary people shared their bitterness at the old ally. 'No Americans Served Here' read a sign outside one car showroom in Hertfordshire.[150] One young miner lamented: 'We should have gone right in there, but this country is not capable of it any more. Not even against the bloody wogs.'[151]

Few historians dispute that, if there is such a thing as a historical watershed, the Suez crisis was such a moment. In the aftermath of the crisis, no one could doubt that Britain's days as a great international power had passed, and Suez became a symbol of British retrenchment and reassessment, the end of the era of 'Britain Strong and Free' (as the 1951 Conservative manifesto had it).[152] But Eden's humiliation at Suez was not the only intimation in 1956 of the changes that were to sweep across Britain in the decade to come. Despite the gloom of international defeat, the heavy grey clouds that had hung over British life for almost twenty years were beginning to lift, and the austerity and sacrifices of the Second World War seemed a distant memory. Only two years previously, meat rationing had still been in force, but now high-street sales of cars, televisions, washing machines and records were reaching record levels. Old enemies were prospering: West Germany overtook Britain in car exports, and Japan became the world's foremost shipbuilder.[153] The first expresso bars were spreading across southern England; students were huddling around coffees and cigarettes in their distinctive duffel coats; the first skiffle musicians were finding a mass audience. In February Muffin the Mule made his television debut; in

May came the first performance of John Osborne's play *Look Back in Anger* at the Royal Court Theatre, and the first appearance of Elvis Presley in the British record charts with 'Heartbreak Hotel'; in September the film *Rock Around the Clock* was released in British cinemas. At the end of the year, the Atticus column in the *Sunday Times* summed up 1956 as the year of 'Rock 'n' Roll. Pizza. Cigarillos — cigarette-sized cheroots. Tortoiseshell-tinted hair. *The Outsider*. Records of *My Fair Lady*. Angry young men . . . Skiffle groups.'[154] To many people, Britain felt like a country on the verge of an exciting new era of opportunity and possibility; to many others, it felt like a country on the brink of a descent into materialism and madness. 'Outwardly it seemed that nothing had changed,' wrote the journalist Christopher Booker. 'Deep in the national psyche, however, was the knowledge that a very real watershed had been passed . . . The dam had burst.'[155]

2

BRITAIN IN 1956

'Come again, won't you?' Derek said to Gerald, once more shaking his hand. 'Perhaps you can tell me what happened in history after the Tudors. We never got any farther than Francis Drake and his bloody bowls at school. The glorious Armada, and back we went each year to the Ancient Britons in their woad. Not a word about why things were like they are now . . .'

Angus Wilson, *Anglo-Saxon Attitudes* (1956)

'Have you seen Jimmy's new suit? It's a conservative cut.'
'What's a conservative cut?'
'It's the same as a Socialist cut – only they're more polite about it.'

Take It from Here, early 1950s

In 1956 the United Kingdom of Great Britain and Northern Ireland was home to just over fifty million people. More than forty million lived in England, the southernmost of the four countries bound together under the British Crown, and also the largest, richest and most culturally influential. Of the rest, five million or so lived in Scotland, north of Hadrian's Wall; two-and-a-half million lived beyond the River Severn in Wales; and across the Irish Sea, one million more, both Catholics and Protestants, coexisted uneasily in the rump six counties of Northern Ireland, the other counties of Ireland having won independence under the partition of 1921. Smaller communities lived in the islands dotted around the British and Irish coasts: the Hebrides, the Orkneys, the Shetlands, the Isle of Wight, and the Crown dependencies of the Isle of Man and the Channel Islands.[1]

Britain in the fifties was one of the most conservative, stable and contented societies in the world. But perhaps the main impression that would have struck a foreign visitor in 1956 was that of sheer clamour and commotion. Not only was Britain extremely crowded by comparison with its neighbours, it was also easily the most urbanised country in Europe. Its population was more tightly packed into cities and towns than anywhere else on the Continent, and for seventy years it remained the case that eight out of ten Britons lived in urban communities.[2] Two great cities dominated the landscape of southern and central England: London, the capital, with its national institutions and massive, seething population of eight million, and Birmingham, the titan of Victorian industry, commerce and municipal politics, still gazing confidently out across the rolling hills of the Midlands.[3] Indeed, England was a country of cities and conurbations: Manchester, Liverpool, Leeds, Bradford, Sheffield, Newcastle, Hull and Middlesbrough, their mills and factories still alive with sweat and light and effort, linked to the capital and the south by a vast network of railways and roads. Around Cardiff, the largest city in Wales, there stretched miles of docks and steelworks, while in the coalfields of the South Wales valleys thousands of miners trudged to work every morning. On the banks of the Clyde, the yards rang with the cries of Scottish shipbuilders, and every Saturday afternoon thousands of urban workers poured into the football grounds of Rangers, Celtic, Hearts and Hibernian. Around each of these cities strands of suburbia rippled out into the countryside, bringing the noise and habits of the towns to country roads becoming increasingly crowded with cars and lorries. Just one in twenty people worked on the land in England and Wales, and only slightly more in Scotland; across the English Channel, in France, the figure was more like one in three.[4]

Indeed, the very landscape and people of Britain in 1956 bore witness to the immense social and economic changes the country had undergone since the early eighteenth century. There were now more than ten times as many people, most of whom lived longer and enjoyed better health. They worked in factories, mills, mines and shipyards; they lived in crowded urban terraces; they preferred to watch football matches and listen to the radio than pray and sing in church; and they enjoyed greater political power than their ancestors ever had, casting a vote every five years for their local parliamentary representative. Yet, despite all these changes, Britain struck many observers as a model of conservatism, order and stability. National life, wrote George Orwell in 1940, was 'somehow bound up with solid breakfasts and gloomy Sundays, smoky towns and winding roads, green fields and red pillar-boxes', a continuity stretching 'into the future and the past'. He also saw the British as a remarkably pragmatic, polite, law-abiding people, filled with a deep longing for the rural idyll that they had lost. Although their experience was overwhelmingly urban and collective, they jealously guarded their own privacy and individuality:

> We are a nation of flower-lovers, but also a nation of stamp-collectors, pigeon-fanciers, amateur carpenters, coupon-snippers, darts-players, crossword-puzzle fans. All the culture that is most truly native centres round things which even when they are communal are not official – the pub, the football match, the back garden, the fireside and the 'nice cup of tea'. The liberty of the individual is still believed in, almost as in the nineteenth century.[5]

Orwell was not alone in placing domesticity at the centre of the British character. As a writer in the *Birmingham Mail* proudly put it at the end of the Second World War, the British were 'not much given to mass gaiety', but were a nation of 'gardeners, family men, artificers and very individualistic at that'.[6] Many foreign observers agreed: the American philosopher George Santayana, for example, famously remarked that Britain was 'the paradise of individuality, eccentricity, heresy, anomalies, hobbies and humours'.[7]

While the British saw themselves as supremely individualistic, they also congratulated themselves on their moderation. Although their closest neighbours, the detestable French, might go in for wild gesticulations, extravagant oaths and public kissing, Britishness was supposed to be all about irony, inscrutability and self-restraint. Extremes of any kind were to be avoided. Some commentators even suggested that the British owed their equanimity to their temperate climate. They were not, they had to admit, a sunny people; perhaps the grey drizzle of the British weather was all for the best, since it encouraged such coolness and self-possession.[8] But even in the hottest climes the British kept their composure. As Noël Coward reminded his audience: 'In a jungle town where the sun beats down to the rage of man and beast / The English garb of the English sahib merely gets a bit more creased.'[9] Where else but in Britain could civil servants be nicknamed 'mandarins' after the supposed formality and inscrutability of the Chinese, and where else could the values of a game like cricket – patience, fortitude, stoicism – become emblematic of the national character?[10]

Cricketers in the fifties were still divided into two groups, Gentlemen and Players, and this was precisely the kind of thing that sustained the stereotype of the British as utterly obsessed with class. Like the weather, class was supposed to be a typically British obsession, despite the fact that, by comparison with its neighbours, Britain in 1956 was not particularly unequal or hierarchical.[11] Since the fissures of race, region and religion that divided other nations were comparatively weak in Britain, however, it is perhaps not surprising that people tended to classify themselves by social class. Sometimes they used the idea of class to mean 'us' as opposed to 'them': the rulers and the ruled, the rich and the poor or the Establishment and the masses.[12] Or they might talk about three groups: upper-class, middle-class and lower-class (or working class), supposed to reflect the old divisions of the nobility, bourgeoisie and commoners. Still, according to the historian David Cannadine, what best captured people's idea of class was the concept of social hierarchy, a carefully layered progression of time-honoured divisions from the grandest palace to the meanest slum.[13] As Evelyn Waugh put it, it was a question of 'precedence, a single wholly imaginary line . . . extending from Windsor to Wormwood Scrubs, of separate individuals, each justly and precisely graded'.[14] Class was not merely a matter of money; what determined one's position was a complicated network of factors: birth, breeding and education, occupation, income, expenditure, accent and deportment, friendships, political and cultural attitudes and values. Opinion polls found that well over 90 per cent of the population recognised the existence of social classes, and people rarely had much difficulty in defining their own place within the class structure.[15] In 1966, for example, a representative sample divided themselves, without prompting, into 'working class' (67 per cent), 'middle class' (29 per cent), 'upper class' (1 per cent), 'upper-working class' (1 per cent) and 'lower-middle class' (1 per cent). Only a further 1 per cent were unable to allocate themselves to any of the conventional classes. One 'twenty-five-stone eccentric' claimed that he belonged to the 'sporting class', but even if such a class existed, this was surely very unlikely.[16]

Surveys taken throughout the fifties and sixties consistently found that around two-thirds of the British public thought that they were working-class. In 1951, according to one estimate, the English working classes accounted for about thirty-two million people, some 72 per cent of the population. In Scotland and Wales, meanwhile, about three or four million more men and women also considered themselves working-class.[17] There is much more to say about working-class life in the 1950s and 1960s, but three points are particularly relevant here. One is that in many working-class areas, the old memories of dole queues, poverty and malnutrition had been wiped out by the Second World War and over a decade of full employment and high wages. Some communities, largely depending on their regional location and the success of their local industries, were still trapped in unemployment and poverty; but in many towns, especially in southern and central England, working-class families were animated by a spirit of optimism and ambition.[18] A second point is that the working classes were not especially politicised; like most other groups in British society, they generally regarded earnest political involvement as rather odd and not very respectable, and active members of any political party, even the Labour Party, were often the objects of some suspicion.[19] Finally, it would be entirely wrong to treat the working classes as one monolithic group. Although most of the population who thought of themselves as working-class were manual workers, there were considerable differences between, say, unskilled labourers, bin men, train drivers and small craftsmen. Similarly, other groups who considered themselves working-class, like pub landlords, the owners of little shops in industrial areas, foremen and junior technicians, did not think of themselves as equivalent to coal miners or manual factory workers. Occupational and economic differences might separate one street from another, or even one family from another, and there might also, in some cases, be unbridgeable gaps on religious, political or other lines. There was not one working class, rather a multitude of working classes.[20]

The middle classes defined themselves largely by their occupation, and in 1956 accounted for somewhere between fifteen and twenty million people. One very easy way to explain what characterised the middle classes is to say that they were simply those people who fell between being working-class and upper-class: they included secretarial and other office staff, local businessmen, lawyers, doctors, teachers and qualified professionals of all kinds, and a growing number of managers, scientists and researchers, technical staff, advertisers and salesmen.[21] Again, this was a matter of *classes* rather than one united class: a secretary or a clerk was likely to be considered 'lower-middle-class' and to live in more modest surroundings than a lawyer or a doctor, who might be very comfortably off and would be thought of as 'upper-middle-class'. Few occupations were as respectable as the traditional professions, especially the law, largely because Britain remained a conservative, legalistic, institutionalised society. Since the beginning of the century, however, there had been a proportionate increase in salaried employees, often working in offices, rather than professionals and the self-employed. There was also a noticeable increase in the proportion of women entering middle-class occupations, especially as nurses, teachers, secretarial workers, managers of restaurants and boarding houses, and other functions considered commensurate with a woman's 'natural' role.[22]

Most middle-class groups prided themselves on their 'respectability'; it was this, rather than their income, that they considered distinguished them from their social inferiors.[23] Sometimes they were quite open about their dislike of the lower orders, and in the north Oxford suburb of Summertown middle-class residents even erected two walls, topped with spikes and broken glass, to cut themselves off from the adjacent Cutteslowe council estate. Only in 1959, twenty-four years after they had been built, were the walls finally torn down by the local council.[24] But attitudes were harder to shift, and many middle-class voters evidently resented having to pay taxes towards universal benefits. 'The lower intellect people are mostly inclined towards Labour, aren't they?' remarked one woman in 1962. 'I think it's because they're the sort of people that won't do things for themselves. They want everything doing for them instead of working hard and saving a bit of money and buying a house. They'd rather live on a council estate.'[25] Indeed, there was usually a striking difference between the very look of working-class and middle-class homes. Two sociologists in the London suburb of Woodford in the late 1950s were particularly struck by the contrast:

> Our informants sometimes engulfed us in deep, velvet-covered settees, and handed us glasses of sherry which we had to hold gingerly in the left hand while unchivalrously scribbling notes with the right. In another street we were seated on hard upright chairs next to drying nappies and given a large cup of the sweet tea and sterilized milk which we had come to know in Bethnal Green.
>
> One house would have thick pile carpets, rooms fashionably decorated with oatmeal paper on three walls and a contrasting blue on the fourth, bookcases full of Charles Dickens, Agatha Christie and *Reader's Digest* condensed books, above the mantelpiece a water-colour of Winchelsea, Vat 69 bottles converted into table-lamps, French windows looking out onto a terra-cotta Pan in the middle of a goldfish bowl, the whole bathed in a permanent smell of Mansion polish.
>
> Five minutes away a smaller house had peeling paints showing

green beneath the cream, rexine-covered sofas polished in the sit-down places like a long-worn pair of trousers, brown linoleum cracked around the edges, and, in place of the polish, a faint but equally permanent smell of leaking gas and boiled greens.[26]

The middle-class ideal of respectability was often simply equated with 'moderation'. It was not respectable to be voluble, passionate or outspoken; it was certainly not respectable to 'make a scene'.[27] This reserve also applied to middle-class cultural tastes, which were self-consciously modest, unspectacular and inoffensive, for example, the Woodford 'bookcases full of Charles Dickens, Agatha Christie and *Reader's Digest* condensed books'.[28] The ideal middle-class life was quiet, contented and comfortable, the kind of unambitious, unassuming world celebrated by Richmal Crompton and Agatha Christie before the war.[29] In J. R. R. Tolkien's story *The Hobbit*, also published before the war but a phenomenal commercial success during the fifties and sixties, we discover that Mr Bilbo Baggins lives in 'a hobbit-hole, and that means comfort'. 'A very well-to-do hobbit', and part of a 'very respectable' family, his pleasures amount to taking tea, baking and eating cakes, and smoking his wooden pipe.[30] Invited by a visiting wizard to join him on a quest, he at first, like any good middle-class homeowner of the day, shows very little enthusiasm for such a dangerous enterprise:

'. . . I am looking for someone to share in an adventure that I am arranging, and it's very difficult to find anyone.'

'I should think so – in these parts! We are plain quiet folk and I have no use for adventures. Nasty disturbing uncomfortable things! Make you late for dinner! I can't think what anybody sees in them,' said our Mr Baggins, and stuck one thumb behind his braces, and blew out another even bigger smoke-ring.[31]

As the fifties progressed, it became harder to tell the difference between the wealthiest members of the Baggins classes and the old upper-class elite. In 1954 Professor Alan Ross of Birmingham University argued that the upper class was now distinguished 'solely by its language', although he did admit that certain odd habits, like playing real tennis and piquet, or disliking the telephone and the wireless, were also pretty good indicators. Language, he thought, could be divided into two categories: U, which was correct, upper-class usage; and non-U, reserved for the rest of the country.[32]

Pronunciation was one important part of this: an upper-class speaker pronounced the first syllable of *Catholic* with a long *a*, for instance; or *Ralph* and *golf* to sound like *Rafe* and *goff*.[33] But the most revealing element of someone's speech was his vocabulary, and Ross gave dozens of examples of the difference between U and non-U. It was non-U to say *corset, cycle, home, mirror* and, most notoriously, *serviette*; in each case, an upper-class speaker would say *stays, bike, house, looking-glass* and *napkin*. It was definitely non-U to say *Pardon*; an upper-class speaker said *What* or *Sorry*. It was non-U to say *Pleased to meet you*; the upper class said *How d'you do*. No upper-class speaker would call people *cultured* or *cultivated*; no upper-class speaker would have a *lounge*; and no upper-class speaker called people *wealthy* when they were really *rich*.[34] All in all, the only sure way of turning a boy into a U-speaker was 'to send him first to a good preparatory school, then to a good public-school'; 'similar arrangements' could be made for girls, if the parents were not going to employ a 'U-governess'.[35]

There could be no better illustration of the British fascination with social hierarchy than the eagerness with which the public greeted Professor Ross' thesis. His article had first been published in a Finnish philological journal, but it was then taken up by the upper-class novelist and socialite Nancy Mitford, who wrote an article about it for the magazine *Encounter* in September 1955. After a great storm of letters, Ross was persuaded to publish a simplified version of his piece in the November issue, and in 1956 Hamish Hamilton brought out a special book on the subject entitled *Noblesse Oblige*.[36] The debate was very well timed: class distinctions had taken a battering not only from the disruptions of wartime, but also from the impact of state education, rising affluence and social mobility. The Honourable Nancy Mitford, with her blue blood and cut-glass accent, was exactly the kind of person who might want to repel middle-class parvenus, and in her article for *Encounter* she enthusiastically threw herself into the U/non-U debate. She was also a very good example of the socially isolated upper-class woman who had been brought up by governesses in an extremely exclusive environment, and therefore preserved a way of speaking that astounded ordinary members of the public. In 1940 she had even been asked to leave her London firewatching unit because her fellow watchers could not stand her accent.[37]

Mitford thought that Professor Ross' only error had been to overlook some of the most hideous non-U howlers: the use of her Christian name by 'comparative strangers', for example, or being introduced 'without any prefix'. Whenever she received a letter that forgot her title, she added, she quickly tore it up. Other egregious non-U crimes included saying *Cheers* before drinking, saying *It was so nice seeing you* or similar, and eating *sweet* instead of *pudding*. Revealingly enough, Mitford thought that the very use of the word *Britain* was a non-U, middle-class alternative to the U *England*. To use the word *Scottish*, meanwhile, was certainly wrong; Mitford insisted on *Scotch*. And to say *Bye-bye* was 'dreadful'.[38] Her fellow contributors, meanwhile, were no less keen to point out their own favourite social blunders; the novelist Evelyn Waugh gravely reported hearing from no less a person than Nancy Mitford's own cousin that 'no gentleman ever wore a brown suit'.[39]

Food and drink, as Waugh pointed out, was another social minefield. When Lord Curzon was Chancellor of Oxford University, he was shown the proposed menu for a lunch in honour of the King at Balliol, only to dismiss it with the words: 'No gentleman has soup at luncheon.'[40] The upper class took their *lunch* or *luncheon* in the middle of the day, followed by *dinner* in the evening; lesser mortals, however, ate *dinner* at midday, no doubt in their shirtsleeves and potentially involving soup, and had *tea* at night.[41] In the cutlery world, fish knives were notoriously middle-class, since real gentlemen had silver that dated from long before their invention in the mid-nineteenth century.[42] Even the process of actually making and drinking tea was fraught with difficulty; nannies and governesses might think it respectable to put the milk in first, but their employers would never dream of it. 'Rather MIF [milk in first], darling,' one of Waugh's friends would say in condemnation of some social solecism.[43] In short, the non-U masses were confronted with such an obstacle course of vocabulary, manners and tastes that they were bound to stumble. As the playwright and broadcaster Alan Bennett recalled, when his working-class parents visited him at Oxford in the 1950s, shame and humiliation would inevitably descend. 'When we were at home,' he remembered, 'we inevitably had our dinner at lunchtime . . . But when I was at university and they came to see me, we'd go into the hotel dining room at night and the waiter would present the menu, and Mam would say the dread words, "Do you do a poached egg on toast?" and we'd slink from the dining room, the only family in England not to have its dinner at night.'[44]

The most memorable and enduring contribution to *Noblesse Oblige* was John Betjeman's prize-winning poem 'How to Get On in Society', in which almost every other word captures the helplessly non-U world of middle-class respectability:

Phone for the fish-knives, Norman,
    As Cook is a little unnerved;
You kiddies have crumpled the serviettes
    And I must have things daintily served.

Are the requisites all in the toilet?
    The frills round the cutlets can wait
Till the girl has replenished the cruets
    And switched on the logs in the grate.

In its final verse, the poem even makes fun of the middle-class, MIF way of pouring tea:

Milk and then just as it comes, dear?
    I'm afraid the preserve's full of stones;
Beg pardon, I'm soiling the doilies
    With afternoon tea-cakes and scones.

But, from the mid-fifties onwards, it was this affluent, middle-class world of modern gadgets, brown suits and serviettes that was in the ascendant.[45]

Only about forty thousand people could claim to be members of the upper class, a tiny social group but one with enormous political and economic power even in the post-war years. As Nancy Mitford was keen to point out, upper-class status was not defined by wealth alone: to join the upper class, a family had to spend their money in the right way, wear the right clothes at the right times, know the right people (Society), and attend the right events (the Season), such as Cowes, Ascot and Wimbledon. Upper-class boys were educated at public schools like Eton and Winchester and then went up to Oxford or Cambridge, or joined particular regiments, or merely strolled around the restaurants and clubs of the West End. Upper-class girls went to boarding schools like Roedean or Cheltenham Ladies' College and then gadded about town looking for suitable husbands. What made the upper class distinct from the wealthier members of the middle classes, therefore, was not so much their income as their expenditure. And even if the richest middle-class tycoons appeared at Cowes, the Boat Race and all the other events, splendidly attired in the appropriate regalia, still they would probably not pass the Mitford test.[46]

The wider changes in the British economy that had been under way since the previous century meant that, like any other social group, the upper class was itself evolving. Where the aristocracy and the landed families had once relied on income from their tenants, they now dabbled in finance, commerce and manufacturing. Conservative Party politics in particular was still dominated in the post-war years by the old public schools: in 1955, Eton alone accounted for one in five Conservative backbenchers and over half of Anthony Eden's Cabinet, while Winchester was particularly well represented on the Labour benches.[47] The institution of domestic service had not entirely died out, either: in 1960 there were still an estimated six hundred working butlers in Britain.[48] All in all, though, the role of the aristocracy was changing, as one historian puts it, 'from political activism to cultural stewardship'. In a political system based on the mass franchise, it was implausible to imagine that aristocrats could maintain their grip on power for long, and by the sixties even the Conservative Party had fallen beneath the advance of the grammar-school boys.[49] The gradual decline of British agriculture, the collapse of land prices and the increases in death duties and income tax meant that landed families found their massive country houses extremely burdensome to maintain. They were therefore forced to choose between opening them as tourist attractions, selling them to wealthy businessmen, and simply demolishing them. Over the course of the century, perhaps 1700 country houses were torn down, a sixth of those that had been standing in 1900.[50]

The reinvention of the country house as a tourist attraction was an immediate success, and by 1965 at least five hundred houses across the nation had been opened to the public.[51] At Ragley, the Marquess of Hereford even tried to lure in the great unwashed by giving them demonstrations of water-skiing; appropriately enough, he later took up a job in public relations. But the most famous impresario was the thirteenth Duke of Bedford, who succeeded to the title in 1953 when his father accidentally shot himself while hunting his missing flock of parakeets and homing budgerigars. The family home, the magnificent eighteenth-century pile of Woburn Abbey, was in a state of disrepair and the new Duke owed £4.5 million in death duties, so he decided to open it to the public for six months as a money-spinning venture. Despite the theft of the Duke's dog and the arrest of a visitor trying to steal a piece of the curtains as a souvenir, the venture proved a success, attracting 181,000 visitors. Within seven years Woburn Abbey was hosting over 430,000 visitors a year, almost double its nearest rivals Beaulieu and Chatsworth, and bringing in an annual haul of £53,875, not to mention the revenue from cream teas and souvenirs. It had a private zoo, a park with deer and bison, a playground and a working dairy, and the Duke even allowed it to be used as the set for the film *Nudist Paradise* in 1958, telling his critics: 'I wouldn't mind going nude myself.'[52]

The British family perhaps least likely to throw itself into commercial nudism was the House of Windsor. The monarchy stood at the top of the British social structure, but was nonetheless perceived as being somehow apart from it. Its appeal was based on a paradoxical combination of the sublime and the banal: the more popular monarchs like George III, Victoria and George V had all at various times managed to project both the splendour that befitted the anointed head of state and the carefully presented domesticity of an 'ordinary' family. To outside observers, the monarchy was a central part of Britain's national identity; daily life was drenched in the iconography of royalty, from coins and stamps to post boxes, prayers in church, the national anthem, the loyal toast, and history lessons for schoolchildren.[53] However, whether the actual sovereigns themselves quite lived up to the lofty expectations of majesty and magnificence was another matter, for Victoria's immediate successors had not been an especially inspiring lot. Edward VII ended up looking more like Falstaff than Prince Hal; George V was a gruff, slow, conservative sort of man; and Edward VIII was notoriously vain and unreliable.[54] After the Abdication crisis of 1936, the crown had passed to George's second son Bertie, who became George VI and was still on the throne at the beginning of the fifties. As the Duke of York, with few expectations of coming to the throne, Bertie had been devoted to his family and his beloved country recreations; he was horrified at the prospect of becoming king, and burst into tears when finally given the bad news. His wife, the former Elizabeth Bowes-Lyon, was made of sterner stuff, and took much more readily to a life of majesty; indeed, during the late thirties she was projected and perceived as the epitome of glamour and charm.[55] Bertie, however, was just like his father: devoted to his wife, possessed of an earthy and unsubtle sense of humour, delighted by shooting, uniforms and medals, unimaginative and slow, but somehow a rather decent sort of fellow.[56]

Since the royal family had all the attitudes and tastes of the landed gentry with whom they tended to associate, it was hardly surprising that the politics of the King and court were solidly Conservative. He was not impressed, for example, by arguments for the welfare state, nationalisation or trade unionism.[57] The Windsors also had cultural tastes that were more middlebrow than avant-garde, preferring a day's riding or shooting followed by a quiet family

evening, rather than the more taxing mental exertions of contemporary culture. On one occasion T. S. Eliot was invited to recite some of his poetry, with
less than successful results. The Queen Mother later told A. N. Wilson: 'We
had this rather lugubrious man in a suit, and he read a poem . . . I think it was
called "The Desert". And first the girls got the giggles, and then I did and then
even the King.' '"The Desert", Ma'am?' Wilson asked. 'Are you sure it wasn't
called *The Waste Land*?' 'That's it. I'm afraid we all giggled. Such a gloomy man,
looked as though he worked in a bank, and we didn't understand a word.'[58]
But, for all their limitations, George VI and his Queen made a far better job of
kingship than many of their predecessors, especially given the circumstances
of his accession and the fact that within three years the British were fighting
for their lives. Churchill, an ardent monarchist, wrote to the King in 1941:
'This war has drawn the Throne & the people more closely together than was
ever before recorded, & Yr Majesties are more beloved by all classes and conditions than any of the princes of the past.'[59] When George died in 1952 the
Windsors were far more popular than they had been at his accession, and his
daughter Elizabeth succeeded to the throne with probably as much public
goodwill as any that had gone before her.

Elizabeth was in Kenya on a royal tour when her father died in his sleep;
on the night of her return, Winston Churchill broadcast to the nation and
welcomed the dawn of a 'new Elizabethan age'.[60] In the House of
Commons, he declared:

> A fair and youthful figure, Princess, wife and mother, is the heir to all
> our traditions and glories . . . She comes to the Throne at a time when
> a tormented mankind stands uncertainly poised between world catas-
> trophe and a golden age. That it should be a golden age of art and
> letters we can only hope – science and machinery have their other tales
> to tell – but it is certain that if a true and lasting peace can be
> achieved . . . an immense and undreamed of prosperity, with culture
> and leisure ever more widely spread, can come . . . to the masses of the
> people.[61]

Elizabeth had been born in April 1926 and was brought up in the conservative atmosphere of the pre-war court. Like her younger sister Margaret, she
was not sent away to school, but was given a rather undemanding education
at home; her parents feared dreadful consequences if she became a 'blue-
stocking'. After her father's accession in 1936, a greater effort was made to

teach her imperial and constitutional history, but it was also announced that she was learning cookery and household skills, so that she would not look too much of an intellectual.[62] She enjoyed the typical childhood of an aristocratic girl in the thirties, a world of dogs and horses rather than blackboards and books. Her mother later explained that it was more important to 'spend as long as possible in the open air, to enjoy to the full the pleasures of the country, to be able to dance and draw and appreciate music, to acquire good manners and perfect deportment, and to cultivate all the distinctive feminine graces'.[63]

In 1947 Elizabeth married Prince Philip of Greece, a headstrong and assertively masculine figure with a blunt, abrupt, breezy style that shocked many of the more conservative courtiers.[64] But the future Queen was still very much her father's daughter: a reserved, self-disciplined and strong-willed young woman, without profound intellectual or imaginative interests, but with a sharp temper and occasional flashes of quick humour. In her early twenties, she was said to like knitting, reading the latest best-sellers, singing along to musical show tunes, riding, and gossiping over tea with her younger sister and their friends.[65] 'Moderation in all things' was her favourite quotation, and she was acutely conscious of her responsibilities as the future sovereign.[66] On her twenty-first birthday she made a memorable broadcast to the Commonwealth, pledging that her 'whole life, whether it be long or short, shall be devoted to your service and the service of our great Imperial family to which we all belong'.[67] When the news came of George VI's death, it was entirely typical of Churchill that, sitting up in bed with a cigar and surrounded by state papers, he burst into tears. It was equally typical of his new Queen that, although pale and solemn, she remained utterly composed.[68]

The new Queen's Coronation in June 1953 was the first major royal celebration to be shown live on television, and although only about three million people owned a set, the audience was estimated to have been between twenty and twenty-seven million people, over half of the adult population and easily a record. Since another twelve million people had listened to the coverage on the radio, there were therefore very few people who had not been swept up in the enthusiasm of the day.[69] The Coronation was also the cue for much talk in the press about a 'New Elizabethan Age', representing the happy union of tradition and progress, especially as the country was finally emerging from post-war rationing and austerity and the first glimmerings of an affluent middle-class revival were beginning to become apparent. That the new sovereign was a woman was an inspiration to many of her subjects. The young Margaret Thatcher, then an obscure law student, wrote an article called 'Wake Up, Women!' for the *Sunday Graphic*, insisting: 'Women can – AND MUST – play a leading part in the creation of a glorious Elizabethan era. Should a woman arise equal to the task, I say let her have an equal chance of competing for the leading Cabinet posts. Why not a woman Chancellor – or a woman Foreign Secretary?'[70]

The New Elizabethan spirit was given a boost by the fact that the Coronation coincided with the final ascent of Everest by a Commonwealth expedition. Later that summer the England cricket team regained the Ashes, and when, within a year, the Oxford medical student Roger Bannister became the first man in recorded history to run a mile in under four minutes, it seemed as though the old Corinthian character had been successfully revived.[71] *The Times* compared the conquest of Everest, news of which broke on the very morning of the Coronation, with Drake's voyage around the world; the *Daily Express*, meanwhile, ran the banner headline: 'BE PROUD OF BRITAIN ON THIS DAY', rejoicing that it had been 'a stroke in the true Elizabethan vein, a reminder that the old adventurous, defiant heart of the race remains unchanged'.[72] In her Coronation broadcast the Queen told her subjects that like her Tudor forebear she ruled a country that was 'great in spirit and well endowed with men who were ready to encompass the earth . . . rich in material resources [and] richer still in the enterprise and courage of its peoples'.[73] But one guest at the ceremony, the eminent Dutch historian J. H. Huizinga, could not bring himself to agree. He later wrote:

> I found myself jerked back to the reality of the times we lived in by the cold shower that, only too symbolically, poured down on the patiently waiting subjects of her with whose Coronation we had just inaugurated the second Elizabethan age . . . I grieved for the British because during those unforgettable hours in the Abbey, I had understood . . . their belief that history would not deal with them as it had dealt with all other nations that had strutted their brief moment of power and glory on the world's stage . . .
>
> But the more sympathetic comprehension one had for the high hopes with which they embarked on the second Elizabethan era, the more acutely one realised what a painful era it would be for them, how rich in disillusionment, frustration and humiliation.[74]

One of the reasons that contemporary observers discussed the new Queen and her family with such reverence was that they had already become part of a modern national myth, the glorious tale of Britain standing alone against the Nazi air armada during the Second World War. For millions of people in the fifties and sixties, the war against Hitler was not simply a distant memory, but one of the central experiences of their lives. In the summer of 1940 the nation had come close to defeat and occupation; during the Battle of Britain and the Blitz, the Luftwaffe had destroyed hundreds of thousands of homes, killed sixty thousand civilians and injured tens of thousands more; and over the course of the war, almost 300,000 British servicemen had been killed in action.[75] Even if the people of Britain had suffered much less than their European neighbours, they had still been changed by the experience, for good or ill. Many still looked back with pride on Britain's stand against the Nazis; while the feeble French and the countries of Continental Europe, east and west, had crumbled, the plucky British had kept on their feet. This was the attitude of David Low's famous wartime cartoon, showing 'Tommy' standing alone on the white cliffs of Dover, the sea raging about his feet, shaking his fist at the black waves of approaching German bombers, and shouting: 'Very well, Alone.' Perhaps only the British could have *welcomed* the fact that their allies had collapsed. George VI told his mother that he was pleased 'now that we have no allies to be polite to and pamper', while a Thames boatman shouted to a group of MPs: 'Now we know where we are! No more bloody allies!'[76]

This sense of British exceptionalism was slow to fade. Roy Denman, a civil servant who later helped to negotiate Britain's entry into the EEC, thought that memories of the war died hard:

> Britain had won the war. The continentals had not. Those who had fought Britain were wicked; those who had not were incompetent, for otherwise they would not have been defeated . . .
>
> For a great power to abandon its world role, the leadership of the Commonwealth, and its favoured position with the United States in order to throw in its lot with a bombed out, defeated rabble south of the Channel seemed to the British unthinkable.[77]

If anything, the old contempt for Continental Europe had been sharpened, not mellowed, by the experience of victory. It was hardly surprising, then, that British intellectuals and writers in the 1950s found that their interests and preoccupations were often very different from those of their neigh-bours.[78] The same kind of exceptionalism prevailed in sport, too. When Chelsea, the English league champions, were invited to participate in the inaugural European Cup in 1955, they were barred from doing so by the domestic football authorities. Even the Queen Mother, despite the German family connections of the House of Windsor, habitually referred to the Germans as 'the Huns', and when Prince Philip's relatives came to Balmoral, she told her staff: 'You certainly don't curtsey to Germans.'[79]

This romanticised, nostalgic patriotism remained a powerful force in British life for decades afterwards. Films and books about the Second World War made immense amounts of money; visitors queued to see museums and exhibitions about the experience of wartime; and television producers found that families were happy to spend their evenings curled up watching documentaries, drama serials, situation comedies and all manner of other programmes based on the war. The British had certainly been very fortu-nate to escape the trauma of invasion and occupation; but at the same time, this also meant that national myths were never challenged. They never felt that they needed to question their own innate superiority and virtue; and, for some historians, there existed a 'cenotaph culture', simplistic, traditional and self-satisfied. Peter Hennessy, for example, calls Britain in the 1950s 'the most settled, deferential, smug, un-dynamic society in the advanced world'.[80] This may seem a little extreme, but it contains more than a grain of truth. As Huizinga had remarked, the British remained strikingly com-placent about their place in the world, and indeed the talk of a second Elizabethan Age suggests that many were confident that they could recap-ture the heights of power and influence from which they had been displaced. That perhaps explains why the humiliation at Suez was such a shock.

The truth was that Britain in the fifties had still not recovered from the rigours of the war. It might have been a triumph for the national spirit, but it had been a catastrophe for the power of the Empire. Hundreds of thou-sands of British soldiers and citizens had been slaughtered; half a million houses had been destroyed; and the Treasury was utterly exhausted. Churchill and his ministers had borrowed $30 billion from the Americans under the Lend–Lease programme, owed the rest of the Empire almost £3 billion, and by the end of 1945 had run up a balance of payments deficit of £1 billion. Almost a third of the entire wealth of the country had been wiped out; and only by importing more food and raw materials from abroad was

Britain keeping itself afloat. Since the Americans abruptly cut off the Lend–Lease money at the end of the war, the Attlee government had been forced to send the economist John Maynard Keynes to Washington to beg for yet another loan, which eventually came to $3.75 billion. The terms were that sterling be made fully convertible with the dollar by July 1947; predictably and humiliatingly enough, when the time came, many investors rushed to change their pounds into dollars, wiping out most of the loan and forcing the government to backtrack and suspend convertibility.[81] Britain's finances were, in short, in a terrible mess.

The euphoria of the New Elizabethan Age was all the more striking when set against the backdrop of the deprivation and austerity of the immediate post-war years. For many people, things had actually got worse after the war. The shortages – of food, of fuel, of housing – were such that on the first anniversary of VE Day, as Susan Cooper later recalled, 'the mood of the British was one not of festivity but of bleak resignation, with a faint rebelliousness at the restrictions and looming crises that hung over them like a fog'.[82] 'We won the war,' one housewife was quoted as saying. 'Why is it so much worse?'[83] The winter of 1947 was the coldest of the century: there were shortages, and strikes, and everyone shivered; and in the spring the floods struck, closing down the London Underground, washing away the crops of thirty-one counties and pouring into thousands of homes.[84] By the following year, rationing had fallen well below the wartime level. The average adult in 1948 was entitled to a weekly allowance of thirteen ounces of meat, one-and-a-half ounces of cheese, six ounces of butter, one ounce of cooking fat, eight ounces of sugar, two pints of milk and one egg. Even dried egg, which had been a staple of meals in wartime, had disappeared from the shops.[85] Children at the beginning of the 1950s still wondered what their parents meant when they reminisced about eating oranges, pineapples and chocolate; they bathed in a few inches of water, and wore cheap, threadbare clothes with 'Utility' labels.[86] It was just as well that the British prided themselves on their ability to form an orderly queue; they had plenty of opportunities to prove it. Not until July 1954 did food rationing finally come to an end.

Austerity left its mark, and many people who had scrimped and saved through the post-war years found it hard to accept the attitudes of their juniors during the long boom that followed. As one housewife later commented: 'It makes you very careful and appreciate what you have got. You don't take things for granted.'[87] Caution, thrift and the virtues of 'making do' had become so ingrained during the long years of rationing that many people never forgot them and forever told each other, 'Waste not, want not,' or reminded themselves to put things aside 'for a rainy day', or complained that their children and grandchildren did not 'know the value of money'.[88] But by the mid-fifties, with a youthful Queen on the throne, rationing at an end and newspaper pundits talking of renewed achievement and ambition, there was a palpable sense of optimism in the air. Increasingly, the attention of the nation and its leaders would be fixed on domestic matters: on making and spending money, on families and jobs, on television and films, on pleasure and affluence.

The Palace of Westminster stands at the end of Whitehall overlooking the Thames as the physical manifestation of British tradition, a grandiloquent late-Gothic pastiche, designed not by medieval craftsmen but by Charles Barry and Augustus Pugin at the height of Victorian imperial ambition. It stands as a lavish monument to nineteenth-century conservatism, the expression in stone and wood of a nostalgic romanticism that takes in the arms of the English, Welsh, Scottish and Irish kingdoms, Tudor portraits, Arthurian frescos, the insignia of the great medieval orders of chivalry, images of Britain's patron saints and a glittering array of heraldic, royal and imperial decorations. At the State Opening of Parliament, when the monarch presides, robed and crowned, surrounded by peers in crimson robes, bishops and heralds and government ministers and ordinary Members, the link between Britain's imperial past and its present is rarely more striking.[89]

For an aspiring politician arriving on his or her first day as a Member of Parliament, the Palace of Westminster must be a proud, invigorating, awesome sight, its pinnacles soaring confidently above the bustle of the Embankment. For Mark Bonham Carter, who made his way to the House as a Liberal Member for the first time in 1958, it was an intimidating place:

> It's just like being back as a new boy at public school – with its ritual and rules, and also its background of convention, which breeds a sense of anxiety and inferiority in people who don't know the rules. Even the smell – the smell of damp stone stairways – is like a school. All you have of your own is a locker – just like a school locker. You don't know where you're allowed to go, and where not – you're always afraid you may be breaking some rule, or wandering into the Speaker's house by

mistake. In the smoking room, you're afraid to sit down in case you're in somebody's special chair. The only place where you can work is in the library: and even there you daren't ask the man for a book, because you don't know whether he's a librarian or an old member.[90]

In this heavy atmosphere of history and privilege, the House sat for thirty-six weeks a year, usually from the early afternoon until the late evening, with a long recess from August until October. As the clanging division bell sounded in the gloomy stone corridors, the Members might be found hurrying from the bars, the library or the dining, smoking and tea rooms towards the lobbies or the chamber.[91]

In the 1955 election, which had produced a handsome majority for Anthony Eden, the country had returned 345 Conservative members, 277 Labour, 6 Liberals and 2 others, giving the Conservatives an absolute majority of fifty-nine seats. The voters were remarkably loyal to the two major parties; this was a time when only a small number were likely to change their vote, and the fate of the country often turned on the decisions of a few hundred thousand people. Taking into account all the elections fought between 1950 and 1970, the average Conservative vote was 46 per cent and the average Labour vote 45.7 per cent.[92] Even in 1955, which had been a disappointing election for Labour, they had still won over twelve million votes, a figure little different from the elections of 1945, 1950 and 1951.[93] Quite simply, in the words of one commentator in the *Observer* in May 1955, the electorate was 'astonishingly evenly divided and strikingly immovable'.[94]

According to a detailed analysis of a marginal seat in Bristol, the typical Conservative voter was a retired middle-class teacher, a lay reader in the Church of England who had always voted for the Tories because they represented 'the general well-being of the people'.[95] Like most successful political parties, the Conservative Party encompassed a great range of ideological themes, from tradition, hierarchy and pageantry to imperialism, liberalism and free enterprise. Above all, it was a successful electoral machine, with a long history of attracting voters and producing competent governments.[96] Its parliamentarians, almost all men, were generally businessmen, barristers, soldiers and farmers.[97] Its support in the country at large has often been described as the political expression of provincial Anglicanism, and the bedrock of the Tory electorate was the shires of England, from Hampshire, Kent and Sussex up through Surrey and Berkshire towards East Anglia and the southern and western Midlands.[98]

Throughout the fifties, middle-class voters backed the Tories by a ratio of almost four to one, guaranteeing victory in a broad swathe of rural and sub-urban seats.[99]

But most people, of course, were not middle-class; how, then, could a middle-class party win elections? The answer was that the Conservatives con-sistently won between a third and a half of the working-class vote. Even during the darkest years of slump and unemployment before the war, one in every two manual workers had cast his ballot for a Conservative. It was an extraordinary achievement for a right-of-centre, middle-class party to have won such a following among the working classes, without a parallel anywhere in Europe.[100] It was a trick that had first been pulled off by the easy-going, paternalistic Worcestershire ironmaster Stanley Baldwin in the twenties and thirties; and his successors did not find it too difficult to repeat it. Working-class Conservatives, according to a survey at the end of the sixties, were not merely motivated by deference to their betters; instead, they genuinely thought that the Conservative Party was more likely to benefit them, since they shared its vision of a consensual, united, harmonious society free from class conflict.[101] Those workers who voted for Churchill, Eden and their suc-cessors were neither intimidated nor deluded; they weighed up their interests and in many cases believed that Conservative policies would best help them to realise their own economic and social ambitions. Had they not done so, a middle-class party would have had very little hope of ever winning power.[102]

Throughout the fifties and sixties, Conservative rhetoric tended to place great emphasis on the legacy of moderate Tory reformers like Disraeli and Baldwin, appealing to national unity rather than to class conflict. In October 1950, nine young Conservative MPs, including promising high-flyers like Edward Heath, Iain Macleod, Robert Carr and Enoch Powell, published a book, *One Nation*, reworking these themes for the post-war age. They pledged themselves to protect the Labour accomplishments of the NHS and the wel-fare state; they committed themselves to 'the maintenance of full employment', a 'vigorous housing drive' and 'maintaining the social services' and they insisted that a Conservative government must 'act as a balancing force, to ensure that liberty and order reinforce one another'.[103] The authors continued to hold regular meetings and dinners after publication, too, call-ing themselves the 'One Nation' group.[104] For Heath and Macleod, perhaps the two most promising young members in the party, this remained their creed for the rest of their careers. In 1962, for example, Macleod stunned the party conference with a frank restatement of his social goals:

The people of this country think that the society which we have
created is not sufficiently just . . . They are puzzled by the fact that still
in this twentieth century the child of a skilled manual labourer has
only one chance in a hundred of going to the university, while the child
of a professional man has 34 chances. They are puzzled that 42 per cent
of the people in this country still earn £10 a week or less . . .

The just society that we seek is a society which can confidently
invite the men and women who compose it to make their own way in
the world, because no reasonable opportunity is denied to them. You
cannot ask men to stand on their own two feet if you give them no
ground to stand on.[105]

Men like Macleod, Heath and Powell were destined to play critical roles in
the political history of the sixties, as we shall see.

The Labour Party had first been established in 1906 through an uneasy
alliance between the trade unions and a variety of socialist pressure groups,
and the Labour movement itself was a mixture of competing traditions and
impulses, sheltering syndicalists, Fabians, planners, corporatists, Christian
socialists, trade unionists, social democrats and so on.[106] It was common for
Conservatives to refer not to the Labour Party, but to 'the Socialists', and
indeed most Labour Members themselves talked a great deal about socialism
and identified themselves as socialists. Strictly speaking, however, socialism
was only one element among many in the making of the Labour Party.
Edmund Dell's verdict that 'over the years, socialism, repeatedly revised, was
drained of its original meaning and converted into little more than an
expression of good intentions' is a harsh one, but probably not far from the
truth.[107] It is also very doubtful whether most Labour voters, and even
many Members of Parliament, subscribed to or understood what was meant
by socialist ideas.[108] When the newly elected Labour MPs took their seats in
the Commons after the landslide victory of 1945 and began to sing the Red
Flag, it was soon obvious that many did not actually know the words.[109]
Indeed, Labour's post-war general secretary Morgan Phillips commented
that his party 'owed more to Methodism than to Marx'.[110] Middle-class
activists became more prominent in the sixties and seventies and, although
a minority, tended to exercise disproportionate influence within the party.
Most people, however, still saw the Labour Party principally as 'the political
wing of the trade union movement'.[111] Its typical voter, according to the
Bristol survey, was a working-class lorry driver and trade union member,

unstinting in his support because Labour stood for 'the average man' rather than 'the capitalist class'.[112] The unions put up most of the money for parliamentary campaigns, and until 1914 all the Labour MPs were themselves working-class.[113]

Unlike its European counterparts, the Labour Party was not primarily an instrument for the realisation of socialist ideology. Instead, it was above all 'a trade union party, created, financed and, in the last analysis, controlled by a highly decentralised trade union movement, which was already in existence before it came into being'.[114] The unions themselves were a heterogeneous and divided bunch, white collar and manual, skilled and unskilled, ideological socialists and cautious conservatives.[115] When Anthony Sampson came to publish his *Anatomy of Britain* in 1962, he found that the biggest union, the Transport and General Workers, had 1.3 million members, from London bus drivers to North Wales quarrymen; the Amalgamated Engineers had just under a million; the General and Municipal Workers had almost 800,000; and the National Union of Mineworkers, the most distinctive and close-knit of all, commanded the support of some 586,000 men.[116] By way of contrast, the smallest unions were the London Jewish Bakers (51 members), the Wool Shear Workers (56), the Spring Trap Makers (90) and the Coal Trimmers (127); equally incongruous groups included the actors (Equity), with over 9000 members, and the footballers (the PFA), with 2200.[117] Their members were often encouraged to pledge their loyalty not to the workers in general, but to those who worked in their particular trade; in some cases a union's greatest enemies were not the bosses but the other unions, who might make off with its members. Trade unionists were nominally committed to work together, but all too often sectionalism prevailed over solidarity.[118]

Many members were interested not in long-term ideological schemes, but in short-term, piecemeal gains, and evidently a considerable number actually voted for the Conservatives. By the fifties, the trade unions were sufficiently politically secure for a Conservative electoral victory to cause them relatively little concern. They had worked closely and successfully with the government during the war; the conventional mechanisms for collective bargaining were widely accepted by workers, employers and ministers; and membership had risen to over nine million.[119] While many historians like to emphasise the conflicts between the unions and government, the fact was that at the end of the war labour relations in Britain were the envy of many European countries, and certainly better than in the Continent's two strongest industrial powers, France and West Germany. There was nothing inevitable about the controversies of future decades.[120]

The parliamentary Labour Party in the fifties and sixties was divided between working-class trade unionists and a growing number of middle-class intellectuals; in 1959, there were thirty-six teachers, thirty-four miners, twenty-seven barristers and twenty-five journalists.[121] Most of the famous Labour names of the period were middle-class recruits, from Gaitskell, Crossman and Foot to Jenkins, Healey and Benn. They were professionals, public servants, technocrats, economists and educators rather than miners, railwaymen or dockers.[122] And for all the Tory warnings to the contrary, they were also, in general, social conservatives. Clement Attlee, the Prime Minister between 1945 and 1951 and one of the most revered figures in the history of the Labour Party, was a passionate supporter of the monarchy, the House of Lords, the Empire and, especially, his old school of Haileybury, cricket and the *Times* crossword. At the end of the 1951 election campaign, while Attlee was waiting for his own constituency result, he sat with his young Conservative opponent, Edward du Cann, chatting companionably and smoking his pipe. Du Cann noticed that among the piles:

> there were fifty or sixty spoiled papers, some mutilated, some with crosses in the wrong place, one or two with obscene messages and a dozen with the word 'socialism' written across them.
>
> 'What does that mean?' I asked Mr Attlee.
>
> 'They think I'm not socialist enough,' he replied. 'I know them of old.'[123]

For all Attlee's equanimity, Labour lost the 1951 election. To a great extent its leaders had run out of ideas, most of the commitments made in 1945 having already been enacted. It was not entirely clear what the party should do next.[124] The indefatigable Labour diarist Richard Crossman admitted that the Attlee government 'seemed to have exhausted the content of British socialism' and that new objectives had not yet been determined.[125] Four years later, in his seminal revisionist manifesto *The Future of Socialism*, Anthony Crosland declared that 'the much-thumbed guide-books of the past must now be thrown away'. 'Traditional socialism', he said, 'was largely concerned with the evils of traditional capitalism and with the need for its overthrow. But today traditional capitalism has been reformed and modified almost out of existence ... and the socialist finds himself pinioned by a new and unforeseen reality.'[126] For many on the left of the parliamentary party, this was anathema; but they were hardly buzzing with ideas for new socialist programmes.[127]

The dominant personality in the Labour Party in the fifties was undoubtedly the firebrand of the left, Aneurin ('Nye') Bevan. His supporters, the Bevanites, confidently predicted that the Conservative victory in 1951 would inevitably result in rising unemployment, which would sweep them back into office. Bevan himself told the 1952 party conference that it was 'a fact' that 'there is no means of preventing unemployment in a capitalist society'.[128] When this proved not to be the case, the keepers of the socialist flame were left rather flummoxed. They knew what they were against: as one account puts it, they were 'anti-upper class, anti-public school, anti-colonial, anti-capitalist and anti-American'. But what were they for? Their domestic programme boiled down to more nationalisation, which was unlikely to impress the electorate; so instead they concentrated on international issues like West German rearmament and, eventually, nuclear disarmament.[129] The fact was that, as another observer puts it, 'a dense mist was obscuring the path to the socialist summit and there was neither map nor compass'.[130]

Bevan was a hefty, brilliant Welsh orator from the coalmining community of Tredegar who had pulled himself up by his bootstraps from the pit to Parliament. When he was elected as Member for Ebbw Vale in 1929, he was a man of exceptional youth among the gerontocrats who usually represented South Wales' miners. Bevan was eloquent, passionate and fiercely independent; indeed, in the late thirties he was expelled from the party for flirting with the Communists. He was also the perfect example of what critics called 'champagne socialism'; his marriage proposal to Jennie Lee was made in the splendid surroundings of the Café Royal, and the Conservative MP Brendan Bracken ridiculed him for being 'a Bollinger Bolshevik'. After 1945, it was Bevan, as Minister of Health, who built the NHS, a formidable and enduring achievement; what was more, he also organised a house-construction programme that left a legacy of one million new homes. As a minister, therefore, he could point to a record that few British politicians could match, and he should have been a firm favourite to replace Attlee as party leader in 1954.[131]

Unfortunately for Bevan, many of his party colleagues detested him. Told that Bevan was his own worst enemy, the powerful trade unionist and

Foreign Secretary Ernest Bevin commented: 'Not while I'm alive he ain't.'[132] Herbert Morrison called him 'wicked', and Hugh Dalton wrote of his making 'a violent speech, of nauseating egoism and sweating with hatred'.[133] Even Richard Crossman, a great admirer of Bevan, called him 'unpredictable, irascible, brilliant and occasionally cowardly'.[134] And yet, for all his weaknesses, Bevan was a gifted and compelling political figure. When he was appointed to the Ministry of Health, his new permanent secretary privately described him as 'a terrible fellow' and told a friend that he was going to retire; several months later, he told the same friend that Bevan was 'the best Minister I've ever worked for' and that he would stay as long as Bevan did.[135]

Bevan's great rival in the Labour Party was Hugh Gaitskell, who later remarked that he won the leadership in 1954 principally 'because Bevan threw it at me by his behaviour'.[136] The son of a senior civil servant in the Raj, Gaitskell had been educated at Winchester and Oxford, and taught economics before working in the civil service during the war and then becoming an MP. At Oxford he had not been a bookworm like the young Harold Wilson, but an aesthete, moving on the edges of a bohemian, homosexual set; as a young lecturer in Nottingham with an eye for the ladies, he even admitted that he saw nothing wrong with having 'too much sex without the essential intellect'.[137] An emotional, reckless man, he later kept up an affair with Ann Fleming, the fashionable hostess and wife of James Bond's creator.[138] Not for nothing did the Tory grandee Lord Hailsham write that he was 'civilized but somewhat harem-bred'.[139] Gaitskell's commitment to socialism, unlike Bevan's, sprang from a streak of romantic moralism rather than the surroundings of his youth. As an adult education lecturer in the Nottinghamshire coalfield in the late 1920s, he had been shocked by the poverty and misery he saw, and from that point onwards he nursed an understated but nonetheless potent passion for social justice.[140] In the early fifties, having risen with astonishing speed to become Attlee's Chancellor of the Exchequer, he found himself adopted by the more conservative trade union leaders who were looking for a rival to match Bevan, and after Bevan had destroyed his own chances of the leadership by a series of resignations and tantrums, Gaitskell coasted home.[141]

When Gaitskell became Labour leader, he was the youngest party leader of the century. Many on the left of the party were suspicious of this privileged, well-heeled young man who had risen so quickly through the ranks, and rumours of his lifestyle did not impress many Labour stalwarts. He lived in comfort in suburban Hampstead, listening to jazz, playing croquet, enjoying good food and fine wines, and dancing into the small hours.[142] There were murmurs of discontent about the young middle-class intellectuals like Roy Jenkins and Anthony Crosland who gathered for dinner parties at his Hampstead home, chatting animatedly about art and music instead of politics and poverty.[143] There were also complaints about Gaitskell's rhetorical style, which although intellectually rigorous was also exceedingly dry, seldom revealing the passion of the man. In the public mind he was forever the civil servant; when people saw or heard him, they tended to think automatically of Whitehall and the BBC's highbrow Third Programme.[144] Harold Macmillan called Gaitskell 'a cold-blooded Wykehamist intellectual', and wrote after one debate that he 'might have been a lecturer in Economics'.[145] Unlike Macmillan and Bevan, Gaitskell often told his audiences what they did not want to hear, and unlike Bevan, he all too rarely had party members cheering in the aisles. The issues that he chose to discuss, like taxation, state education or colonial and racial questions, were associated more with a vague commitment to equality than with traditional socialist ambitions like public ownership and class solidarity. As his biographer puts it: 'His banner was Conscience and Reform, not class struggle.'[146]

The split between Bevan and Gaitskell offers an intriguing glimpse into the uncomfortable alliance between working-class inspiration and middle-class progressivism that lay at the heart of the Labour movement. On the one hand, there was the unpredictable, flashing, galvanising oratory of the South Wales miner; on the other, the logical, clear, rational analysis of the Oxford-educated civil servant. Since the late forties they had been the two clear rivals for pre-eminence in the Labour movement, and it was not surprising that Bevan was bitter. After an argument during the Attlee years, a friend reminded Bevan that Gaitskell was 'one of the really considerable men of the Government'. '*Considerable?*' he replied in disbelief. 'But he's nothing, nothing, nothing!'[147] The taunt that most people associated with Gaitskell, however, was Bevan's line about his being 'a desiccated calculating machine', even though it had originally been directed at Attlee.[148] Even so, in terms of policy there was less between them than was often imagined. It was not simply a question of left versus right, but largely a matter of what one writer calls 'colour': the brilliant red prophet of the pits versus the grey, suburban Whitehall mole.[149] Bevan probably never accepted that beneath his rival's surface coolness was a passionate commitment no less forceful and dynamic than his own. This 'faction for faction's sake' continued until 1957, when Gaitskell and Bevan ostensibly buried their differences and Bevan became Shadow Foreign Secretary.[150] He was never really at ease in the affluent society of the late fifties, and neither was he truly accepted by Gaitskell's advisers.[151] Even after his death in 1960, the bitterness lingered on.

The politicians of the fifties and sixties lived in a world that had been irrevocably altered by the Labour government elected in 1945. By the time Attlee left office in 1951, the foundations of what historians call the postwar settlement were in place: the welfare state; the commitment to maintaining full employment; the mixed, public–private economy; benevolent recognition of the trade unions; and British involvement in the Cold War.[152] The greatest of these accomplishments was the welfare state, based on the Liberal economist Sir William Beveridge's famous report of 1942. The report had called for a full-scale attack on the 'five giants', Want, Disease, Ignorance, Squalor and Idleness, that had blighted British life before the war, and Beveridge provided the blueprint for state-funded social security, a national health service, free education and government intervention to guarantee full employment and cheap housing.[153] Benefits were universal, from child benefit to schooling to medical treatment, and the funding came from a system of national insurance, whereby every employed person paid the same flat-rate contribution in return for the same benefits.[154] No other system in the world aimed so high or had such universal principles, and the welfare state became, in Peter Hennessy's words, 'the talisman of a better post-war Britain'.[155] It demanded a heavy financial commitment: between 1948 and 1958, for example, spending on state education doubled in real terms and, as a proportion of national income, grew by 75 per cent.[156] But the results were impressive. Thanks to the National Health Service, for example, the dramatic medical advances of the post-war years made an impact in every town and village in Britain. Between 1938 and 1956, cases of diphtheria declined from 65,000 to fifty-three, infant mortality fell by half, maternal mortality was reduced by five-sixths, and tuberculosis was virtually wiped out.[157] Although limited charges for prescriptions, dental treatment and glasses were introduced by Hugh Gaitskell in 1951, prompting a furious Bevan to resign from the Cabinet, the NHS by the late fifties was regarded as a national treasure and the subject of a genuine bipartisan consensus.[158]

Despite the achievement of building the welfare state, Attlee's government had not really been a very radical one. There were no serious efforts to reform the House of Lords, the civil service, local government, industrial relations, the banks or the legal system; even the public schools and old universities were, at the beginning of the fifties, stronger than they had been ten years before.[159] Indeed, the political commentator Anthony Howard even wrote in 1963 that Attlee had 'brought about the greatest restoration of traditional values since 1660'.[160] But this did make it much easier for the Conservatives to accept the welfare state and limited public ownership when they finally returned to power. The mood of the party was largely determined by younger Conservative members who saw themselves following in the footsteps of Disraeli and Baldwin. R. A. Butler, whose landmark legislation had already introduced free state education, later wrote that they had been working to develop 'an alternative policy to Socialism that was viable, efficient and humane, which would release and reward enterprise and initiative but without abandoning social justice or reverting to mass unemployment'.[161] Anthony Eden coined the phrase 'a nation-wide property-owning democracy' to describe the kind of society that the Conservatives wanted to build: one with more emphasis on private ownership and economic freedom than under Attlee, but with the same framework of social security and full employment.[162] And so, when Churchill returned to 10 Downing Street in 1951, he made little effort to roll back the welfare state or even to return the nationalised industries to private hands.[163] Unwilling to alienate working-class voters, his ministers appeared less interested in reversing the Labour legacy than in proving that they could manage it. 'I have come to know the nation and what must be done to retain power,' said Churchill: in other words, not much.[164]

For many contemporary observers, what characterised the fifties was not fierce political disagreement but an underlying mood of consensus and contentment. In 1953, Edward Hyams published his comic novel *Gentian Violet*, the tale of a working-class lad called James Blundell who advances in society thanks to his heroic war career and also contrives to maintain two identities. To his old mates he is still ordinary Jim Blundell, but to his new upper-class chums he is James Stewart-Blundell. The comic deception becomes even more complicated when he manages to win election to Parliament as both an industrial Labour Member and a rural Conservative. He has no difficulty in keeping up both roles; indeed, his fears of being found out once he arrives at the House of Commons prove to be without foundation:

Nobody noticed anybody else . . . A member might be on his feet talking away yet boring nobody, as nobody was obliged to listen . . . it
reduced the most ambitious and domineering public men to the status
of prefects, with certain privileges, like putting their feet on the
table . . . If democracy was to be found anywhere, Jim felt, it was here
in the House of Commons.

And Jim soon began to be very proud of being two members of it.[165]

This spirit of gentle good humour was an understandable reaction to the
rigours of wartime and austerity, but it was also reinforced by the political
values of the day. As the *Observer* put it in its Coronation supplement: 'The
country is today a more united and stabler society than it has been since the
"Industrial Revolution" began.'[166] This idea of consensus was more than just
a convenient and reassuring myth. In very general terms, both political parties were operating in the shadow of the Liberal economist John Maynard
Keynes. Put very simply, Keynes held that the market economy was not self-
regulating, but instead needed the supervising hand of government to
ensure that consumer demand was high. If demand were kept steady, then
unemployment would remain under control. Keynes was not a socialist: he
did not believe that the market economy should be overthrown, but instead
thought that governments should actively regulate demand by fiscal
means.[167]

By the end of the 1940s, the Keynesians were in full cry and classical, laissez-faire economists in retreat. 'The Government accept as one of their
primary aims and responsibilities the maintenance of a high and stable level
of employment after the war,' declared the wartime coalition's White Paper
on Employment Policy.[168] Seven years later, when Butler took over at the
Treasury, he congratulated himself on speaking 'in the accents of
Keynesianism', promising 'full employment and social security . . . [and]
strong central control over the operation of the economy'.[169] Both parties
accepted Keynes' argument that it was the duty of government to supervise
the operation of the economy in good times and bad, and both were pledged
to what was called Keynesian demand management. The story of British
government in the fifties and sixties, therefore, was in large part the story of
how successive Chancellors, Conservative and Labour, handled the problems of the economy.

Few prominent British politicians questioned the premises of Keynesian
management until the seventies, and if they did, they were usually

considered to be antediluvian crackpots. For the likes of Butler, Macmillan and Gaitskell, the Keynesian intellectual inheritance was close to being the holy grail of economic theory. All the same, the Keynesian model adopted during the post-war years had its limitations. As the social-ist economist Evan Durbin pointed out, Keynes' miracle 'cure' for unemployment might well 'simply lead to an accelerated inflation, and ultimately a rise in prices'.[170] Keynes himself was aware of the problem, but died without really addressing it. What refinements he might have devel-oped had he lived beyond 1946 could not be known, but since the simplified outlines of his ideas appealed to the understandable free-spending instincts of political leaders and civil servants, the 'ultimate manageability of the economy' was cheerfully taken for granted.[171] The men charged with the responsibility of managing the economy were politicians rather than pro-fessional economists, and it is doubtful whether many of Britain's post-war Chancellors really understood the extremely complicated ramifications of the theory they claimed to support.[172] Since the Attlee government had not taken the opportunity to build a more professional, streamlined unit in Whitehall to administer the welfare state, economic decisions were too often left to politicians who were under pressure to deliver vote-winning budgets just before a general election.[173] If the choice were between long-term economic responsibility and short-term political survival, very few people would have the courage to choose the former.

The economy over which Conservative and Labour Chancellors presided during the 1950s and 1960s was mixed, part public and part private. Attlee's Labour government had left most businesses in private hands, but had nationalised the cable and wireless companies, civil aviation, the coalmines, the gas and electricity utilities and the railways. Steel and road haulage had been nationalised only to be immediately sold off again by Churchill in the early fifties, and the Conservatives were not keen on taking any more busi-ness into public ownership. By 1960, therefore, the four major public corporations were the British Transport Commission, with 729,000 employees and an estimated turnover of £726 million; the National Coal Board, with 634,000 employees and a £937 million turnover; the various Electricity Boards, with 193,000 workers and a turnover of £340 million; and the Gas Boards, which had 124,000 workers and a turnover of £388 mil-lion.[174] These leviathans dwarfed any of the big private companies. British Railways, part of the British Transport Commission, employed six times as many workers as the chemical giant ICI; the Electricity Board, meanwhile, consumed enough capital to build a new ICI every three years.[175] But, although this represented a break from the thirties, the fact remains that the basic structures of the economy were not greatly altered. At the end of the 1950s, the two principal muscles of Britain's industrial strength were the coal and steel industries, just as they had been for decades previously. Indeed, some historians have suggested that the roots of Britain's post-war economic weakness lie in Attlee's failure to take more radical steps to modernise British industry.[176] On the other hand, no such steps were ever really likely. Britain had emerged from the war in a better state than its major European competitors, and neither Labour nor Conservative leaders saw any urgent need to tear down the old system and build another. Unemployment and inflation were both low, and the mixed economy that Attlee bequeathed to Churchill and Eden seemed to be working well.[177] 'The miracle has happened,' said *The Economist* in 1954: 'full employment without inflation.'[178]

According to the historian Correlli Barnett, the problems of the British economy in the late fifties and sixties can largely be blamed on the crippling burden of the welfare state.[179] This does not really stand up; countries like West Germany, France and Sweden, whose economies performed better during the same period, all spent more money on welfare, not less. Even though the NHS was unusual in its scope and ambition, British governments in the fifties actually spent less on health services, per head, than any other European countries except Ireland and Italy.[180] A more serious long-term problem was the tension between harmony at home and greatness abroad. Of all the Western allies, only the Americans spent more on defence than the British.[181] The maintenance of an army on the Rhine, the commitment to build an atomic bomb and the decision to hang on to British bases in the Far East have been seen by historians as burdensome, extravagant and even irresponsible, however understandable in the context of the Cold War.[182] Since both parties were pledged to maintain Britain's world role, defence spending as a proportion of total government expenditure remained very high: 23 per cent in 1950, 24 per cent in 1960 and 17 per cent in 1970.[183] In this context, it is hard to see the welfare state as a unique and crippling burden.[184] Ultimately the problem for successive governments in the 1950s and 1960s was that they wanted to avoid the hard choice between social security at home and strategic advantage abroad. No ambitious politician in the 1950s wanted to be the scapegoat who pulled out the rug from beneath the Empire or the Atlantic alliance, but equally no one wanted the reputation of an uncaring skinflint bent on slashing the welfare state to ribbons.

What was more, heavy spending on overseas defence commitments exacerbated the balance of payments problem, which, as one historian puts it, was 'poised like an axe over Britain's recovery'.[185] Put very simply, this had two dimensions. First, the pound was overvalued on the international exchange markets, standing at a fixed rate of $2.80.[186] At the same time, its attractiveness to international speculators was decreasing, because they doubted that the long-term health of the British economy justified its value. There were four severe sterling crises between 1947 and 1957, and through much of the sixties the pound was almost constantly under threat, so there was often talk of further devaluation. To devalue the pound, however, was a considerable political risk. British exporters would benefit, since their products would be cheaper overseas, but the price of imports would shoot up overnight, raising the spectre of domestic inflation. Devaluation would also be a serious blow to national prestige and the reputation of the government; it looked like giving in to foreign speculation.[187]

The second dimension concerned the balance of payments itself: in other words, the flow of money in and out of the United Kingdom. Britain's balance of trade was actually pretty healthy, since the total values of imports and exports were usually fairly similar.[188] What explained the persistent balance of payments problems were the persistent deficits on the capital account: in other words, the bill for maintaining Britain as a world power overseas, which had to be paid for in sterling. Governments continually urged British manufacturers to produce more goods for export, in order to try and make up for the deficit. But the danger was that rising production and economic growth would only encourage people to spend their money on imported goods, making the haemorrhage of sterling out of the country even worse. Successive Chancellors of the Exchequer were therefore faced with a delicate balancing act. They needed to promote economic growth to meet their political goals of prosperity and popularity; at the same time, they had to encourage businesses to produce goods for foreign as well as domestic markets; and, simultaneously, they had somehow to restrain consumers from spending too much on foreign imports. To compound their difficulties, international trade was becoming more competitive in the fifties and sixties, so the British share of export markets was bound to come under threat. Harold Macmillan, who served as Eden's last Chancellor, later admitted:

To maintain the British economy at the right level, between inflation and deflation, balancing correctly between too much and too little growth, was a delicate exercise. All the clever young economists and journalists and all the armchair experts could not resolve it. There were so many imponderables, and so many uncertainties. It was not a subject to be solved by mathematical formulae, or exact calculation. It was like bicycling along a tightrope.[189]

But in the early fifties these problems seemed little more than slight concerns. The mood was calm. The welfare state was up and running, rationing was coming to an end, the export industry was prospering, new houses were being built, and the new Conservative government seemed disinclined to challenge the substance of the Keynesian settlement. The personification of this mood of consensus was the mythical Mr Butskell, a conflation of the Conservative Chancellor Rab Butler and his Labour predecessor Hugh Gaitskell, invented by *The Economist* in 1954:

> Mr Butskell is already a well-known figure in dinner table conversations in both Westminster and Whitehall and the time has come to introduce him to a wider audience. He is a composite of the present Chancellor and the previous one . . . Whenever there is a tendency to excess Conservatism within the Conservative Party – such as a clamour for too much imperial preference, for a wild dash to convertibility, or even for a little more unemployment to teach the workers a lesson – Mr Butskell speaks up for the cause of moderation from the Government side of the House; when there is a clamour for even graver irresponsibilities from the Labour benches, Mr Butskell has hitherto spoken up from the other.[190]

The catchphrase caught on. Butler was, after all, on the One Nation wing of the Conservative Party; and Gaitskell was seen as suspiciously right-wing by his Labour critics.[191] Indeed, Butler recorded in his memoirs that he and Gaitskell had enjoyed a 'warm' relationship, and he thought that his Labour adversary was 'a man of great humanity and sticking power'. On the other hand: 'I shared none of his convictions, which were unquenchably Socialist, nor his temperament . . . Both of us, it is true, spoke the language of Keynesianism. But we spoke it with different accents and a differing emphasis.' According to Butler, whereas he favoured 'freedom and opportunity',

Gaitskell was keener on planning and controls.[192] Gaitskell, however, admitted that there was a lot of truth in the analogy. Soon after Butler had replaced him at the Treasury, and long before the publication of the 'Mr Butskell' article, Gaitskell privately observed that the Conservatives 'have really done exactly what we would have done, and have followed the same lines on controls, economic planning, etc. . . . Butler is on the extreme left of the Tory Party and is shrewd enough to understand that what they have got to do while in office is to live down the reputation inherited from their periods of office in the thirties.'[193]

Butler and Gaitskell had their differences, of course, but they also had a shared commitment to Keynesian management and moderate, professional administration.[194] The parallels between them were widely thought to reflect the wider affinities between the two parties and, beyond that, the mood of the country as a whole. There was no Conservative backlash against the welfare state, while on the Labour benches the verses of the Red Flag were sung more with nostalgic reverie than with socialist fervour.[195] 'Party differences', said Churchill in 1954, 'are now in practice mainly those of emphasis.'[196] Of course the two parties still had their genuine and bitter disagreements; they emphasised contrasting values and spoke to vastly different constituencies. Indeed, the loyalty of their voting blocs and the nail-biting closeness of elections in the early fifties suggest that the electorate still thought that they stood for very different things. Yet, however divergent their goals, they followed strikingly similar courses in office, especially by the standards of more fevered periods like the 1930s or the 1980s.[197] As the Conservative strategist Michael Fraser explained thirty years later, there was 'a good deal of common ground' between Labour and the Conservatives, even if there was no 'unity of aim'. 'The real position', he wrote, 'was like that of two trains, starting off from parallel platforms at some great London terminus and running for a time on broadly parallel lines but always heading for very different destinations.'[198]

Despite the excitement of the introduction of the welfare state and the tension of the Cold War, this was not an era of great political passion. Most partisan disagreements took place within the Butskellite framework; intellectual challenges to it, whether from left or right, tended to be ignored or derided. By the standards of other periods in the twentieth century, university common rooms were empty of political discussion or ideological ferment. Voters loyally turned out to support their favoured party, but displayed little active interest in public affairs. In 1953 a survey of political

activity in Derby found that only 11 per cent of those interviewed were members of a political party: of these, two-thirds still did not attend political
meetings.[199] Six years later, another survey discovered that barely 15 per cent
of respondents described themselves as 'very interested in politics', while a
further 20 per cent were unable to name a single major politician.[200] 'This is
an essentially satisfied country,' announced the *Daily Express* in 1955. 'The basic
problems of sharing wealth in an industrial community have been solved.'[202]

In intellectual circles, the epitome of the fifties consensus was the Anglo-
American monthly *Encounter*, an anti-Communist publication that appealed
to moderate readers of both left and right, celebrated the triumph of
Keynesianism and even proclaimed 'the end of ideology'. In April 1955 it ran
an article by the American sociologist Edward Shils, who taught at the
London School of Economics and Manchester, analysing the contentment
of British society in the age of Mr Butskell. British intellectuals, Shils said,
were united by their fondness for 'continental holidays, the connoisseurship
of wine and food, the knowledge of wild flowers and birds, acquaintance
with the writings of Jane Austen, a knowing indulgence for the worthies of
the English past, an appreciation of "more leisurely epochs", doing one's job
dutifully and reliably, the cultivation of personal relations'. These were
values that spoke more of conservatism and complacency than vigour and
originality. He explained:

> There are complaints here and there and on many specific issues, but
> – in the main – scarcely anyone here in Great Britain seems any longer
> to feel there is anything fundamentally wrong. On the contrary, Great
> Britain on the whole, and especially in comparison with other coun-
> tries, seems to the British intellectual of the mid-1950s to be all right
> and even much more than that. Never has an intellectual class found
> its society and its culture so much to its satisfaction.[202]

3

SUPERMAC

I've been thinking about this for a long time. Something for the benefit of the country as a whole. What should it be, I thought, become a blood donor or join the Young Conservatives? Anyway, as I'm not looking for a wife and I can't play table tennis, here I am.

'The Blood Donor', *Hancock's Half Hour* (1961)

Just after six on the evening of 9 January 1957, Sir Anthony Eden's car pulled into the forecourt of Buckingham Palace and the Prime Minister emerged for his final audience with the monarch. Within half an hour he was Prime Minister no longer, and the hunt was on for his replacement. The appointment was not in the hands of the national electorate, the Conservative Party membership or even the parliamentary party, because it was the Queen's royal prerogative to appoint a new first minister. Reports suggested that she would wait until the following day before summoning the chosen candidate to the Palace, as had been the case in 1955 when Eden had smoothly replaced Churchill. The following morning, therefore, British voters read over their breakfast tables the news that Eden was out and that, although no new Prime Minister had yet been appointed, there was only one likely replacement. The new leader, according to almost every major newspaper in the land, would be the man who had stood in for Eden during his recuperation in Jamaica, the current Home Secretary and former Chancellor, the moderate, lugubrious R. A. Butler.[1]

Eden and his wife certainly thought that Butler would succeed him.[2] So did Butler himself. That night he enjoyed a meal with his family in Smith Square and asked – rather tempting fate, so his sister thought – 'What shall I say in my broadcast to the nation tomorrow?'[3] Such reckless confidence was untypical of the man. He was the quintessential British public servant, his father being an Indian imperial administrator and later Master of Pembroke College, Cambridge. 'Rab' had been educated at Marlborough and Cambridge, where he emerged with a double first, and having been just too young to fight in the Great War, he moved smoothly into a Cambridge fellowship and then a safe Conservative seat. During the thirties he had been a consummate young man on the inside track, moving quickly up the political hierarchy, steadfastly loyal to his great hero Stanley Baldwin and the party leadership.[4] He became closely identified with appeasement, not merely because he was so faithful to Baldwin, Chamberlain and Halifax, but also because his own personal qualities – loyalty, reasonableness, decency, unambitious complacency and so on – were themselves associated with the failure to stand up to Hitler.[5] But, despite his links with the appeasers, Butler was one of the brightest stars of Churchill's wartime government. As Education Minister in 1944, he was responsible for the landmark legislation that introduced free schooling for all children under fourteen, and as Chancellor and Leader of the House in the fifties he was one of the keenest pioneers of the new consensual Conservatism. By 1957, few senior Tories were better known in the country, and certainly very few were as liberal. His characteristic appearance was a kind of stooping, slightly battered scruffiness, and he was a laconic, thoughtful man, capable of dryly withering asides and wicked indiscretions. And on 10 January 1957, he woke confident that within hours he would be asked to come to the Palace and accept the Queen's invitation to form a government.

Only one plausible rival stood between Butler and the leadership. This was a man whose career had been intertwined with his and had long been in Butler's shadow. Harold Macmillan was, at sixty-two, eight years older than Rab; he was an Old Etonian, a Balliol man, and the son-in-law of the Duke of Devonshire. But while Butler had been making himself indispensable to the Tory leadership in the thirties, Macmillan had been a rebel, speaking up for his poorer constituents in Stockton-on-Tees, temporarily resigning the party whip to write a book, *The Middle Way* (1938), on the need for centralised planning and economic nationalism, and even calling for a new party combining 'all that is best of Left and Right', to be led by Herbert Morrison.[6] While Butler was serving as one of Chamberlain's most trusted junior ministers, Macmillan dressed the guy on his family bonfire in a familiar frock-coat and black Homburg and equipped him with a rolled umbrella.[7] While Butler was content to support Baldwin's consensual Conservatism, Macmillan bitterly attacked 'casino capitalism', insisted that 'free competition' was dead, and called for the adoption of 'socialistic methods and principles'.[8] Butler was a solid, dependable Conservative; Macmillan himself admitted he was 'not a good Tory'.[9] Clement Attlee once called him 'by far the most radical man I've known in politics . . . He was a real left-wing radical in his social, human and economic thinking.' Macmillan had come very close to joining the Labour Party in the thirties; had he done so, Attlee said, he would have become its leader.[10] Instead, Macmillan stuck it out in the Conservative Party, was rewarded by Churchill with ministerial office, and proved an extremely effective housing minister in the early fifties. The Tories had made a rash promise to build 300,000 houses a year, more than even Bevan had managed, and Macmillan's qualities of drive and showmanship were ideally suited to the task. He scaled down the construction standards for council houses, lobbied hard for financial resources, and made so much fuss that when the target was reached in 1953 he reaped the benefit of the attendant publicity, triumphantly handing over the keys before the assembled press photographers.[11]

In December 1955 Macmillan was appointed Chancellor of the Exchequer, and within nine months he was caught up in the Suez controversy, where his record was less than impressive. During the Cabinet discussions of August 1956, he had, as one critic puts it, 'appointed himself, as it were, chief extremist', defying Treasury warnings and blithely assuring his colleagues that the Americans would go along with the invasion scheme.[12] And yet, when the crunch arrived, he was the first to crumble. Within the course of a couple of days he had gone, as Brendan Bracken remarked, from 'wanting to tear Nasser's scalp off with his own finger nails' to being 'leader of the bolters'.[13] By any standards this was a humiliating and yet curiously shameless exhibition. Macmillan had been consistently and spectacularly wrong and misleading, but now he had reversed himself completely. As one historian puts it: 'Considering the role he had played so far, all his talk of "all or nothing", of "selling Britain's last securities", of "dying in the last ditch", this was a sensational loss of nerve.'[14]

It was not Macmillan who had to clear up the Suez mess, but his main rival. Eden was away at Goldeneye, and Butler, as acting Prime Minister, was in charge of extricating the British forces in the least humiliating manner possible and trying to mend fences with the Eisenhower administration. The American terms were punitive, and the government was forced to agree to a total and unconditional withdrawal, with no chance of a bargain to save face. As the bearer of bad news to a mutinous Conservative Party, Butler was in a tricky position. After announcing the terms to the House of Commons on 22 September, he agreed to explain the situation to the 1922 Committee, the assembly of Tory backbenchers. That evening he made a vital and disastrous mistake. He took Macmillan, as Chancellor, with him, turning the occasion into a joint appearance. While Butler gave a quiet and low-key speech explaining the importance of the terms, Macmillan then followed with over thirty minutes of 'a veritable political organ voluntary . . . pulling out every stop and striking every majestic chord in his well-practised repertoire', dazzling his audience with his dramatic vigour.[15] Enoch Powell, then a young parliamentary secretary at the Ministry of Housing, later wrote that he never trusted Macmillan after that moment. It was 'one of the most horrible things that I remember in politics . . . seeing the way in which Harold Macmillan, with all the skill of the old actor manager, succeeded in false-footing Rab. The sheer devilry of it verged on the disgusting.'[16] Powell, however, was in a minority. Most backbenchers had fallen head over heels for Macmillan's rhetorical magic. Their patriotism and their pride had been wounded; they did not want to hear the blunt truths that Butler had to tell them, but they responded warmly to Macmillan's mixture of flattery, self-pity, anti-American resentment and shameless self-promotion. With his confident guardsman's bearing, he even *looked* more like a statesman than the scruffy, stooping, careworn Butler.[17]

The Queen had the right to invite any politician she chose to form a government, but in practice it was clear that she would allow herself be guided by the grandees of the Tory Establishment. Eden's last Cabinet had been held at five in the evening of his resignation, and after he had made his announcement to his colleagues, the meeting broke up. Excluding Eden, Macmillan and Butler, there remained fourteen members of the Cabinet, and, one by one, they were called by the Marquess of Salisbury, the Lord President of the Council, and Lord Kilmuir, the Lord Chancellor, to Salisbury's room in the Privy Council Offices. Kilmuir later recalled the scene:

> There were two light reliefs. Practically each one began by saying, 'This is like coming to the Headmaster's study.' To each Bobbety [Salisbury] said, 'Well, which is it, Wab or Hawold?' As well as seeing that remainder of the ex-Cabinet, we interviewed the Chief Whip and Oliver Poole, the Chairman of the Party. John Morrison, the Chairman of the 1922 Executive, rang me up from Islay the next day. An overwhelming majority of Cabinet Ministers was in favour of Macmillan as Eden's successor, and back-bench opinion, as reported to us, strongly endorsed this view.[18]

Although Butler was the favourite and by most accounts the more popular man in the country, he had won the support of only three of his Cabinet colleagues.[19] The following morning Lord Salisbury took the news to the Queen. Macmillan, meanwhile, was closeted in 11 Downing Street reading *Pride and Prejudice*, which he said was 'very soothing', and Butler was nervously strolling along the Embankment, telling a curious cameraman: 'I'm taking a walk – the best thing to do in the circumstances.' Just before noon Macmillan had the telephone call he was expecting, asking him to come to the Palace after lunch; shortly afterwards Butler received a visit from Edward Heath, the Chief Whip. Despite his nerves, Butler was still confident of victory. 'As I entered,' Heath later wrote, 'his face lit up with his familiar, charming smile . . . "I am sorry, Rab," I said, "it's Harold." He looked utterly dumbfounded.'[20]

Conspiracy theorists were quick to pick over the bones of the succession, alleging that it had all been a fix in favour of Macmillan. Salisbury was one of Macmillan's strongest backers, and it is just possible that he exerted influence over his more junior colleagues. On the other hand, both Salisbury and Kilmuir were respected party grandees and members of the House of Lords: under the undemocratic system of the early fifties, it is hard to see how else a name could have emerged.[21] Certainly Macmillan was the overwhelming choice of the Cabinet, although not of Anthony Eden, who was not formally consulted.[22] The truth is that Butler was never quite as popular among his Tory colleagues as was imagined. Many of the pro-Suez MPs thought that he had been a ditherer over the operation from the beginning and saw him as a convenient scapegoat for the failure of the enterprise. In private he had been wildly indiscreet, confiding his doubts to groups of Conservative Members in an almost self-destructive way. The fateful meeting of the 1922 Committee counted against him; he had been dishevelled, flat and mournfully honest at a time when MPs were desperate for comfort and charisma.[23] Butler was also unpopular with many Members who thought he was too clever by half, a fault often attributed to intelligent, witty Conservatives by their dimmer colleagues. Even after Macmillan had become Prime Minister, Butler treated him with a kind of dry, witty condescension. Macmillan loved to advertise his classical learning, and once greeted Butler, his deputy, while clutching a volume of Livy. Butler gently picked up the book and glanced at the cover. 'Ah, Livy,' he remarked; and then, slightly bemused: 'But I always thought of Livy as a fourth-form text.'[24]

The new Prime Minister, meanwhile, had a personal sparkle that Butler could never match. As his official biographer puts it, Macmillan was a man of paradoxes: 'by turns crofter and duke *manqué*, scholar and swordsman; he was compassionate and ruthless, pessimistic and optimist, fatalist and devout Christian'.[25] Identities came and went as the mood took him. His background, when examined closely, was much more complicated than Butler's. His father was a hard-working Scottish publisher, his mother a wealthy and domineering American Midwesterner. During the First World War he saw action with the Grenadier Guards, watched many of his friends die, was seriously wounded himself and returned to Britain something of an emotional wreck, transfixed by pessimism and guilt. As we have seen, he was in the thirties something of a radical, an early convert to Keynesianism who thought about joining Oswald Mosley's New Party before Mosley went over to fascism, and who might have joined the Labour Party had it been less economically cautious. He was a man fascinated by religion and spirituality, who toyed with conversion to Rome while a young man. Only Asquith and Churchill rivalled him as the best-read Prime Minister of the century; we have already encountered him reading Austen and Livy, and at many critical moments he would retire to immerse himself in the classics.[26]

Like Eden and Butler, Macmillan had also known deep sadness in his personal life. Eden made a disastrous first marriage; Butler's first wife died of cancer in December 1954.[27] Macmillan's marriage, meanwhile, was by any standards a harrowing business. His wife, Lady Dorothy Cavendish, was nineteen when they married in 1920, while he was twenty-six; she was sensual and selfish, while he was bookish and sensitive. She quite swiftly embarked on a lifelong affair with his fellow Tory MP Robert Boothby, who was later acknowledged as the father of the Macmillans' fourth child, Sarah. When Harold discovered the truth in 1929, an event that Boothby sardonically referred to as the 'Great Crash', he was shattered. For the rest of his life he remained faithful to his errant wife, whom he did not divorce: in other words, he was condemned to permanent abstinence. They kept up appearances for the sake of his career, but in private, as Dorothy put it, 'I am faithful to Bob.' Sarah Macmillan was told quite casually, and cruelly, that Boothby was her real father while she was an undergraduate at Oxford, and died at the age of forty after battling with severe alcoholism. She also had to cope with a broken marriage and the effects of an abortion forced on her by Dorothy for the sake of Harold's career, which left her sterile. All in all, it was not a happy story.[28] The evidence of Cabinet papers suggests that Macmillan worked extremely long hours. No doubt the unhappiness of his family life had a great deal to do with it.[29]

Macmillan needed to be a good actor to keep the pain of his marriage hidden from the public, and he was. Indeed, it was his talent as a performer, if a rather hammy one, that contemporary observers most associated with him. Bernard Levin, a very unsympathetic critic, thought that he came over as 'a down-at-heel actor resting between engagements at the decrepit theatres of minor provincial towns, his ability minimal for anything but hoodwinking fools by the thousands and million'.[30] And Macmillan was typically portrayed as an ageing relic of a bygone era, not least because he himself played up to this image. Although only sixty-two, he frequently put on the act of a man much older in order to win the sympathy of his audiences, to evoke a sense of pre-war nostalgia, or to affect a faded grandeur that he did not really possess.[31] It even seemed that, the further British power receded from its Edwardian heights, the more determined Macmillan became to conceal the decline by presenting himself as a breezy Edwardian grandee. *The Economist* quipped that Conservative Central Office were faced with the task of 'trying to project in 1958 a Prime Minister obstinately determined to reflect 1908'.[32]

Macmillan's appearance of doddering bonhomie masked the self-protecting ruthlessness essential for political success. Rab Butler told a friend that his new chief was conscientious and hard working, but also noted that he was 'ruthless' and had 'an infinite capacity for elasticity'.[33] Above all, Macmillan had the killer instinct. 'I like both Butler and Eden,' he wrote in 1952. 'They both have great charm. But it has been cruelly said that in politics there are no friends at the top. I fear it is so.'[34] Ever since Eden's departure for Jamaica, he had been planning ahead and busily working the Commons tea-room circuit. Like so many successful politicians, Macmillan saw his public role as a part to be played like any other, and he carefully used his antiquated manner to disguise the cool, cynical intelligence that had propelled him to the top. If intelligent observers recognised that there were elements of burlesque and self-parody in the performance, then no harm was done; indeed, the Edwardian self-confidence initially seemed a breath of fresh air after Eden's hollow earnestness. As L. A. Siedentrop noted seven years after Macmillan's retirement, he came close to resembling 'an American's Englishman – the slight exaggeration of a type':

the heavily hooded but wary eyes, the sagging jaw which suggested weariness, the toothiness, the shambling gait which contrasted so oddly with his controlled, precise and epigrammatic turn of phrase, the drawl in which wide-ranging historical observations and old-fashioned patriotic appeals were delivered, and, finally, the well-cut but rather ill-kempt clothes which went so well with the long but often dishevelled hair and moustache.

This exaggerated Englishness, full of 'languor, irony and careless elegance', was, as it turned out, the ideal remedy to soothe a nation wounded by the humiliation of Suez; not for nothing did Macmillan's shapeless cardigans acquire a minor following in the last years of the decade.[35]

Macmillan's ruthlessness was further disguised by yet another element of his style: his unflappability. When he arrived at No. 10, he brought with him an air of thoughtful calm to replace the anguish and anxiety of the Eden years. The klaxon on the prime ministerial car, which Eden had never been shy of using, was turned off permanently, and on the green-baize door of the private secretaries' office he pinned a handwritten quotation from Gilbert and Sullivan: 'Quiet calm deliberation disentangles every knot.'[36] At one early Cabinet meeting, when the discussion was expected to be long and fierce, each of the assembled ministers found in front of him on the Cabinet table a small packet of tranquillisers: a light-hearted point, perhaps, but a point well made. Unlike Eden, Macmillan was rarely on the telephone haranguing his ministers, even though he was never prepared to let them have free rein.[37] He divided life into things that were 'fun' and things that were 'a bore': being Prime Minister was fun, while serious crises and difficult ministers were bores.[38]

When with foreign observers, he played the laid-back English gentleman even more than usual. On one occasion he gave a lunch for the dour Soviet Minister of Culture and then walked her down the stairs of Admiralty House, where 'his hand waving laconically from side to side, [Macmillan] passed under review the portraits of prime ministers lining the stairs – Pitt, Gladstone, Campbell-Bannerman . . . as if to remind the Russian provincial that he was the latest in a long line of British brilliance and that after 300 years of it, he was exhausted by his own distinction'. He looked like 'a walrus descending a staircase in slow motion, flippers flapping nonchalantly from side to side as he indicated his illustrious forebears'.[39] He loved to play up his own languid manner: in an interview three decades later, he explained:

I found it much the most relaxed of the offices I held. You didn't work so hard. You didn't have to do all the work of the departments. Oh, you had the Cabinet to run and all that. I found I read a lot of books and so on. I rested a lot. It's a great mistake to get yourself into a state of nervous excitement all the time. Nobody should ever overdo it, you know. You can't make good judgements . . . You should read Jane Austen, and then you'll feel better, and then when they come in with some awful crisis, having read about *Pride and Prejudice* and so on, you'll feel better.[40]

Of course this was exaggerated. Macmillan worked exceptionally hard, not least because of his personal loneliness, and he was actually a very nervous man, so nervous that he was almost physically sick before major speeches or parliamentary appearances.[41] Still, appearance was all. As far as the voters knew, Macmillan was not the anxious, distrustful, driven man whose wife had cuckolded him with one of his own MPs, but the unflappable, elegant grandee whose idea of an entertaining evening was, as he so splendidly put it, 'going to bed with a Trollope'.[42]

Macmillan was formally invited by the Queen to form a government in the early afternoon of 10 January. He warned her, 'half in joke, half in earnest, that I could not answer for the new government lasting more than six weeks'.[43] On arriving in Downing Street, he remarked to one of his senior civil servants that he might not last thirty days: 'I don't think I shall be very good at this job. I'm afraid I'm no good as an actor.'[44] But this was, of course, just another of his acts. As he sat in the Cabinet Room planning his government, he was evidently determined to give no public impression of indecision or pessimism. That evening he called on Ted Heath, the Chief Whip, and together they headed off to the prestigious Turf Club for a celebration binge of oysters, steak and cognac, much to the entertainment of the press. As Heath recalled, when they went into the club there was only one other man at the bar, reading an *Evening Standard* with the banner headline 'MACMILLAN PRIME MINISTER':

The man looked up, saw the Prime Minister and then asked, rather casually, 'Have you had any good shooting recently?' 'No,' answered the Prime Minister. 'What a pity,' the man observed. We ordered our dinner, finished our drinks and then got up to make our way to the dining room. As the Prime Minister was going out, the fellow looked up and said, 'Oh, by the way, congratulations.'[45]

In the Butler home, Macmillan cattily remarked, 'there would have been plain living and high thinking'.[46] By contrast, this government would be all about public exhibitions of style and good cheer. Perhaps only Macmillan, with the problems of the country on his mind, could have brought it off. *The Times* commented the following day that he was 'a man of good will . . . of warm emotions and generous humanity' as well as 'a man of energy'.[47]

He would need those qualities, because his prospects appeared bleak. The Conservative Party was fractious and divided; when Macmillan appointed the ebullient Lord Hailsham as party chairman, Hailsham thought that the assignment was 'virtually impossible', since it was 'hard to exaggerate the disarray and loss of morale in the party, and unpopularity with the press and media of the Government in the months following Suez'.[48] The government clearly could not afford another crisis on the scale of that Egyptian debacle, or the party membership and the wider electorate would lose all confidence in the parliamentary leadership. Britain had not yet recovered from its humiliation in the United Nations; pessimistic talk of national decline was common, relations with the Americans and the French were very poor, and the perennial problem of dwindling currency reserves had been dramatically exposed. Any serious economic problems, from a downturn in trade figures to a major industrial strike, might damage international confidence in sterling and trigger another crisis, probably necessitating a humiliating devaluation of the pound. The new Prime Minister would, therefore, need to tread very carefully indeed.[49]

Seven days after taking office Macmillan made his first broadcast to the nation, an upbeat if somewhat hackneyed routine attacking the idea that Britain was in decline:

Every now and again since the war I have heard people say: 'Isn't Britain only a second- or third-class power now? Isn't she on the way out?' What nonsense! This is a great country, and do not let us be ashamed to say so . . . Twice in my lifetime I have heard the same old tale about our being a second-class power, and I have lived to see the answer . . . So do not let us have any more defeatist talk of second-class powers and of dreadful things to come. Britain has been great, is great, and will stay great, provided we close our ranks and get on with the job.

As for the rift with the United States, he assured his listeners that, while the damage was not irreparable, the British did not intend to be subservient:

The life of the free world depends on the partnership between us. Any partners are bound to have their differences now and then. I've always found it so . . . But true partnership is based on respect. We don't intend to part from the Americans, and we don't intend to be satellites.[50]

This sort of stuff evidently went down very well. The Labour MP Anthony Wedgwood Benn recorded in his diary that Macmillan 'had shown just the right quality of drama in his opening days at Number 10. His government is bold and his television performance was evidently a very dramatic one . . . If he succeeds in making an impact it will call for great skill by the Labour Party to make a successful challenge to him.'[51] In fact, Macmillan's cheerful affirmation of Britain's world role had been exactly the tonic that a miserable nation wanted. He survived longer than the six weeks that he had forecast to the Queen, not least by constantly telling his listeners that he was determined to preserve British influence in the super-power age. In one address to the 1922 Committee, he explained that British diplomacy would be governed not by imperial vanity but by national pride, a subtle but neat distinction, and added 'that the greatest moments in out history have not been those when we have conquered, but when we have led'. 'It was superb,' wrote the Tory MP Nigel Nicolson.[52] By the final debate on Suez in May 1957 Macmillan had, as his biographer says, 'got fully into his stride', telling the Commons: 'We are a great world power, and we intend to remain so.'[53]

Macmillan's first move had been to reshuffle his Cabinet. Butler, the disappointed rival, moved to the Home Office, and the sporting dignity with which he took his defeat won him more tributes than ever.[54] He was clearly the second man in the government and a prohibitive favourite to replace Macmillan in the event of disaster. Much more surprising was the retention of Selwyn Lloyd, the hapless Sèvres conspirator, as Foreign Secretary; this news was widely greeted, as one observer put it, with 'a long, cold arch of raised eyebrows'.[55] Macmillan later explained that to sack Lloyd would mean 'admitting that certain statements made about Suez were not absolutely correct': in other words, it would be a tacit confession that there had been both a conspiracy and a cover-up. 'You don't give in to the world and get rid of the man who was most responsible for the thing which you yourself have supported,' Macmillan remarked subsequently. 'It would have been the most miserable, cringing thing to do.' Macmillan also felt sorry for Lloyd, whose wife had abandoned him for a younger man, leaving him with their young child. Macmillan's own problems meant that he sympathised with Lloyd's plight and allowed him to spend weekends at Chequers, the prime ministerial mansion. Butler, on the other hand, thought very little of Lloyd. His wife had left him, he rather snobbishly remarked, 'because he got into bed with his sweater on! . . . You shouldn't be too sorry for him . . . he had a terrible chip – a feeling of being from the North Country – far from first class, and was lucky to get where he did.'[56] Macmillan knew that Lloyd was unimaginative; but he was also conscientious, loyal and pliable. Keeping him on meant that, just like Eden, the Prime Minister could hope to run the Foreign Office himself. As Aneurin Bevan put it, he was the monkey to Macmillan's organ grinder.[57]

Macmillan picked the rest of his team carefully. Salisbury and Kilmuir, the kingmakers behind his accession, kept their places. Butler's three alleged supporters, meanwhile, were moved to the House of Lords. The new Chancellor of the Exchequer, a position of vital importance, was Peter Thorneycroft, a self-confident character with a background in industry and finance who had put in a decent five-year stint at the Board of Trade. Elsewhere there was an injection of new blood. By 1957 a younger generation of Conservative politicians, many with strong One Nation sympathies, was breaking through, prominent examples being Iain Macleod (Minister of Labour), Enoch Powell (Financial Secretary to the Treasury), David Eccles (Trade), Lord Hailsham (Education), Edward Heath (Chief Whip) and Reginald Maudling (Paymaster General). This was largely overshadowed, however, by the fact that the Cabinet itself had a very narrow social base. Of the sixteen members in January 1957, six had been at Eton, only two had not attended a major public school, and, as usual, there were no women at all. Even more remarkably, the government as a whole was crammed to the seams with Macmillan's own relatives. By January 1958, the entire government comprised some eighty-five ministers, of whom thirty-five were related to Macmillan by marriage, including seven of the nineteen members of the Cabinet. While the government was popular, there was no cause for concern, but after the 1959 election satirists and commentators began to draw more and more attention to Macmillan's government of relatives. 'Mr Macmillan', commented one of his Tory critics in 1961, 'has more cousins and less opposition that any Prime Minister in our history.'[58]

Shortly after forming his first government, Macmillan made a list of his most pressing problems. They fell under six headings: national confidence; clearing up the Suez crisis; the Anglo-American relationship; the need to rethink defence priorities; the Commonwealth and Empire; and finally, the economy.[59] As far as the electorate was concerned, the priority was clearly the economy. Issues like the relationship with Eisenhower or the future of the Commonwealth were less than fascinating to the general public, and every British government during the fifties and sixties recognised that it lived or died by its economic management. While Macmillan was no longer the radical of the thirties, he still saw himself as being on the left of the Conservative Party, a firm believer in government intervention to ensure high consumer demand and economic expansion. On being confirmed by the 1922 Committee as party leader in January 1957, he reminded them of a line from Disraeli: 'We must be conservative to conserve all that is good and radical to uproot all that is bad.' His conception of the welfare state placed more emphasis on individual initiative, enterprise and the rights of business than was found on the Labour benches; he added that unless the Tories gave 'opportunity to the strong and able' they would 'never have the means to provide real protection for the weak and old'.[60] But he was not impressed by arguments for laissez-faire or passive government. 'The great thing', he once wrote in his diary, 'is to keep the Tory party on *modern* and *progressive* lines.'[61]

Macmillan was fortunate to be taking office in a period of very low unemployment, high wages and technological innovation. Rationing was fading into history, and all the talk was of supermarkets, washing machines, record players, televisions, advertisers and airline tickets – all the trappings of what *Queen* magazine would call 'the age of BOOM'.[62] The trick was to keep the economy expanding while ensuring that prices did not rise too quickly; at the same time, the government needed to restrain con-sumers from spending too much on imports, and to encourage manufacturers to produce goods for export overseas, in order to protect the country's vulnerable currency reserves. Macmillan himself, as we have seen, wrote that economic management was 'like bicycling along a tightrope', 'balancing correctly between too much and too little growth'.[63] He publicly admitted the difficulty in his famous remarks to a crowd at Bedford on 20 July 1957:

> Let's be frank about it; most of our people have never had it so good. Go around the country, go to the industrial towns, go to the farms, and you will see a state of prosperity such as we have never had in my lifetime – nor indeed ever in the history of this country. What is worrying some of us is 'Is it too good to be true?' or perhaps I should say 'Is it too good to last?' For amidst all this prosperity, there is one problem that has troubled us . . . ever since the war. It's the problem of rising prices. Our constant concern today is – can prices be steadied while at the same time we maintain full employment in an expanding economy? Can we control inflation? This is the problem of our time.[64]

Macmillan was often misquoted as having said, 'You've never had it so good,' an expression of Tory complacency.[65] In fact, he only used the phrase 'most of our people', therefore implicitly recognising that affluence was not universal, and the thrust of his speech was actually a warning against the dangers of inflation. If 'inflation prices us out of world markets', he went on, '. . . we will be back in the old nightmare of unemployment'.[66]

For all his apparent concern about rising prices, Macmillan was instinctively an expansionist who found it intensely disagreeable to curb his urge to spend more money. As the MP for Stockton in the thirties, he had seen the misery of joblessness at first hand and was obsessed by the prospect of falling demand and rising unemployment.[67] His favourite economic guru was Professor Roy Harrod, the loyal biographer and intellectual disciple of John Maynard Keynes. Harrod, like Macmillan, was an expansionist by instinct. Every few weeks he would send Macmillan a long letter of economic advice, which Macmillan would read, digest and often pass on to his Chancellor, much to the disgruntlement of the Treasury economists. So often was Harrod on the telephone to the Prime Minister that the Downing Street private secretaries often had trouble forcing him to get off the line.[68]

Macmillan, however, remained a great admirer of the Oxford economist, not least because Harrod told him what he was already hoping to hear. In 1959 he noted in his diary that the Treasury gave 'bad advice' to 'every Chancellor in turn . . . I have greater belief in Roy Harrod.'[69] Three years later, Macmillan wrote to his new Chancellor, Reginald Maudling: 'I regard him as a man of genius – considerable genius. He is often wrong, but then he is often right . . . Do not pass this on to your Department who have a great dislike of Roy.'[70] Like some of his Conservative successors, then, Macmillan was more interested in the advice of his academic favourite than the warnings of the Treasury civil servants. Another Chancellor, Derick Heathcoat Amory, later explained:

> He was terrified of one thing, a slump . . . he did ring me up occasionally. 'Don't you think there might be a slump in a month?' – that was the influence of Roy Harrod. He was always pleased by anything that was expansionary, almost a wild inflationist at that time . . . It was his instinct to be rebellious against the restrictive actions of the Treasury – he never liked the Treasury: 'What is wrong with inflation, Derry?'
>
> I'd reply 'You're thinking of your constituents in the 1930s?' – 'Yes, I am thinking of the under-use of resources – let's over-use them!'[71]

'Inflation is like sin,' commented *The Economist* in July 1957. 'Everybody is against it, but it goes on.'[72] Macmillan paid lip-service to the dangers of rising prices, but he never really took them seriously. Already in 1955, thanks to Butler's expansive pre-election budget, there had been a bout of economic 'stop–go', or more accurately, 'go–stop', a process by which a Chancellor would let the economy loose, there would be a short and dramatic boom as it began to overheat, and then severe remedial measures would have to be applied.[73] Part of the problem was that the economic information available to the Treasury was necessarily retrospective and limited. Macmillan himself, when Chancellor, had admitted that he was 'always, as it were, looking up a train in last year's Bradshaw'.[74] As Edmund Dell points out, a more appropriate parallel would be with the driver of an unfamiliar and unreliable motor vehicle:

> He is condemned to sitting in the driving seat, often without very much experience of this kind of driving, turning the wheel this way and that in accordance with his latest guess as to where he is at any particular moment, and in the hope that his actions are in some way positively linked to the direction of his vehicle. He can never be certain that he will not be confronted by a sudden crisis which will require a more than usually violent twist of the wheel to be sure that the vehicle actually reacts to his steering.[75]

Macmillan's first Chancellor was Peter Thorneycroft, an amiable, intelligent and able Tory social reformer and an effective parliamentary debater. He was both an obvious and a promising choice.[76] His two closest colleagues were also regarded as extremely able. The Economic Secretary, Nigel Birch, was another Old Etonian, a successful and wealthy City stockbroker with an acerbic manner and a reputation for intellectual honesty and independence. Curiously, he suffered from deteriorating eyesight and was forced to memorise his speeches because he could barely read his own notes. The Financial Secretary, meanwhile, was Enoch Powell, the bright young MP for Wolverhampton South-West.[77] Ominously, neither Birch nor Powell was a great admirer of the Prime Minister, and neither did they have much time for the new permanent secretary at the Treasury, Sir Roger Makins, whom they regarded as economically illiterate.[78]

The general outlook, meanwhile, was troubled, as Macmillan himself admitted at Bedford. Growth in 1956 had been only 1.1 per cent, while inflation had reached 4.9 per cent.[79] Even so, the government was unwilling to challenge the unions over pay, afraid that a series of strikes would alienate public opinion and destroy international confidence in the pound. The Minister of Labour, Iain Macleod, was therefore encouraged to seek settlements with the shipyard workers, engineers and railwaymen rather than face down their demands. Tory hardliners muttered about 'appeasement', but, as Macmillan himself noted, he was not yet strong enough to take 'a firm stand' against what he called 'industrial appeasement with continual inflation'.[80] Despite Macmillan's expansionist instincts, the Cabinet agreed to make a stab at deflation with a series of spending cuts, especially in defence, and in April Thorneycroft felt able to introduce a budget that was cautiously optimistic rather than violently deflationary. He cut taxes by £100 million and explained to his backbenchers that since exports were booming to record levels: 'I see some grounds for cheerfulness. As I see it, the temperature of the economy has been brought down to a more normal level . . . All this seems to be a basis not for standing still, but for going forward. Expansion must be the theme.'[81]

Within a month, however, Thorneycroft was sunk in gloom. Treasury experts were full of forebodings about the long-term future of sterling and doubts about the capacity of the government to resist the tide of inflation, especially since the government was granting the unions considerable pay increases.[82] The Chancellor's own solution was a statutory incomes policy that would keep pay increases under Treasury control. The Cabinet would have none of it.[83] In August, fears of British inflation and the news of the devaluation of the French franc unexpectedly launched a new run on the pound, and within a month £80 million of the reserves had disappeared.[84] Clearly Thorneycroft had to do something; but what? One option was to dust down the old idea of cutting the pound loose to float on the exchange markets; since the balance of payments was then favourable, this might well have proved a success. Most of the Cabinet, however, worried that this would further upset the Americans, and, if the pound fell in value, it would be yet another national humiliation. The idea was rejected.[85] In the end, Thorneycroft raised bank rate to 7 per cent, its highest level since 1921, and persuaded Macmillan to approve cuts in public investment and restrictions on credit. In other words, just a few months after his 'cheerful' budget, the Chancellor, in order to stave off the collapse of sterling, had introduced a tough, deflationary package that was bound to push a stuttering economy into recession. Within a few weeks the run on the reserves had stopped, but the September measures were not popular with industry, the voters or even much of the City. Opinion polls registered a 7 per cent decline in Conservative support after the deflationary package was announced and many observers evidently felt that, even if Thorneycroft had stemmed the haemorrhage, his 'kill or cure' remedy had been too severe.[86]

Unlike the man who had appointed him, Thorneycroft had been converted during the crisis to the belief that the fight against inflation was an absolute priority, even if this meant pushing up unemployment. In this he was not alone, since both his junior ministers were fascinated by the unfashionable idea of restricting the money supply to try and bring down inflation. Enoch Powell later recalled: 'Nigel Birch started to drop into my room to talk about the causes of inflation, I started to drop into his, and when we conferred with the Chancellor, we found we'd all come to the same conclusion.'[87] Even before joining the Treasury team, Powell had been in touch with various neo-liberal economic theorists; he was already a devotee of laissez-faire economic ideas, and had read and reviewed essays by the conservative thinker Friedrich Hayek. He was renowned among his colleagues even then for his 'ferocious anti-statism', an approach that was very different from the politically fashionable views of One Nation Tories like Butler, Macleod and Maudling.[88]

By any standards, Enoch Powell was one of the most controversial and influential politicians of the twentieth century, regarded by many historians as the founding father of Thatcherism. By the end of his career he was popularly associated with just one issue, the emotive subject of race, but he was a remarkable and divisive character even before he began to speak out against immigration. He was a strange individual even as a schoolboy in Birmingham during the 1920s. At weekends he would deliver formal lectures to his proud parents on the contents of the library books he had read that week, and was regarded by his schoolfellows as odd and austere, described to newcomers 'as a boy to stay clear of – "an unfriendly fellow, talks to no-one"'. He had a serious, pale face, cold blue eyes, and an exceptionally formal manner, as well as a brilliant mind; by the age of fourteen, he had already embarked on a private translation of Herodotus.[89]

At Trinity, Cambridge, where he was a grammar-school scholarship boy, Powell would work from just after five in the morning until after nine at night, and then retire. He quite literally had no social life at all. When invited by a Birmingham contemporary to come and have some tea, he replied: 'Thank you very much, but I came here to work.' He even refused the invitation of the Master and his wife to attend the traditional dinner for new arrivals at the college, explaining that 'pressure of work' prevented him from attending. No one had ever refused before. But he was, in truth, an outstanding scholar, and at just twenty-five he was appointed Professor of Greek at the University of Sydney, the youngest professor in the entire British Empire.[90] The experience of moving to Australia, as well as his service in the army during the Second World War, mellowed Powell a little, but by any other standards he was still an extraordinarily serious and severe figure. While he was driving with a fellow officer from Algiers to Cairo, Powell's intensity and lack of common sense were comically illustrated by a disastrous attempt to cook breakfast:

> The fire he had lit was being uncooperative, so he threw some petrol over it, causing the flames to flare up and singe his moustache. He cut his finger trying to cook the sausages and the water he was boiling fell over the flames and put the fire out. Strachan, who was more practical, offered to help. 'You keep away,' Powell snarled at him. 'If they want to be bloody-minded, I'll show them, by God I will.' The breakfast was not a success, nothing in Powell's life having prepared him for the culinary challenges he was now facing. Strachan tactfully drank his disgusting tea and ate his undercooked sausages, while Powell, unused to failure, stomped around muttering, 'Bloody inefficient! Bloody inefficient!', too angry to eat.[91]

After the war, Powell worked in the Conservative Research Department alongside other rising stars like Macleod and Maudling, and in 1950 was elected MP for Wolverhampton South-West. Even though he had fallen behind his old friend Macleod in the race for high office, it was still an achievement to be made Financial Secretary in 1957; in effect, he was the most important minister not in the Cabinet, responsible for examining every spending proposal made by every department. Powell as a minister, now married, was less intense than Powell the scholar, and he had made some firm friendships in the House, especially – curiously, some might think – with his fellow oddity Tony Benn.[92] He could still be tremendously stiff and self-disciplined and was ferociously well organised; he even kept a card index of all the constituents who had been to see him, with notes on each written in Greek so that only he could read them. Not only did he canvass in Wolverhampton almost every weekend, he made a point of visiting newcomers to the area, and later proudly recalled that he had campaigned in six languages that he spoke fluently: English, French, Italian, German, Greek and Urdu.[93] It is a great mistake to overlook, amid all the controversy about Powell's views on immigration, his exceptional intellectual intensity and the burning passion of his political convictions. Lord Annan, who had no sympathy for Powell's views, nevertheless thought that he was 'a true intellectual, more of an intellectual than any Labour politician: for he was also a scholar. No other politician had the ability to translate the law book of a medieval Welsh king, edit Greek texts with a dryness that made Housman look gushing, master the intricacies of the medieval House of Lords, and reinterpret the New Testament.'[94]

Powell was a man of almost obsessive passions, from Housman and Nietzsche to High Anglicanism and hunting.[95] He was, in short, a nineteenth-century romantic, zealous and uncompromising, a man of causes. His decision to join the Conservative Party, for example, was based less on social and economic principles than on sheer romantic traditionalism. It was the party of the Empire, the King and the flag, and that was good enough for him.[96] The affable Butler, who supervised the activities of the Conservative Research Department after 1945, later wrote:

> I remember that on one occasion he brought me a paper in which he argued that with ten divisions we could reconquer India. At his request I submitted the paper to Churchill, who seemed distressed and asked me if I thought Powell was 'all right'. I said I was sure he was, but explained that he was very determined in these matters.

Churchill summoned Powell to come and see him, 'shook his head sadly a great deal and said that it was too late for him to invade India and that, in any event, ten divisions would not be enough'. 'That particular hobby-horse', reported a relieved Butler, 'was heard of no more.'[97]

To Powell, the fight against inflation in 1957 was a crusade, and it seems likely that his ardour rubbed off on his two Treasury colleagues. Since the Cabinet were not prepared to try and curb inflation by picking a fight with the unions, Thorneycroft was adamant that they must restrict the supply of money themselves, even if that meant allowing unemployment to creep up to 3 per cent or higher. In August, the Chancellor convinced a reluctant Macmillan to agree that the public spending estimates for the next financial year should be frozen at the same level as those for the current year. Since prices had risen in the intervening period, this implied that there would have to be substantial spending cuts.[98] On 19 September, when announcing the deflationary package to protect the reserves, he declared his determination to fight 'the upward spiral of costs', adding: 'There can be no remedy for inflation and the steadily rising prices that go with it which does not include, and indeed is not founded upon, a control of the money supply.'[99] By this stage, Thorneycroft and his ministers had fallen out with most of their senior civil service advisers, most of whom disagreed that there was a direct link between the money supply and inflation.[100]

Roy Harrod, meanwhile, was busy telling Macmillan that 'the idea that you can reduce prices by limiting the quantity of money' was an 'antiquated doctrine'. Hardly any economist under the age of fifty, said Harrod, took it seriously, and if Macmillan went along with it he would provoke a rise in unemployment and would have Gaitskell and every economist in the country 'lambasting and ridiculing this policy'.[101] At the same time, Enoch Powell was touring the West Midlands praising Thorneycroft's deflationary measures to various Tory audiences. They would not succeed, he warned, 'without a limitation of public expenditure'. It was almost a moral issue: 'If inflation with its evil consequences at home and abroad is to be stopped, this increase in the money supply must be halted and halted without delay.'[102] Macmillan had of course already promised Thorneycroft that cuts would be made to ensure that the spending estimates were frozen for the next financial year. But since the Conservative Party had trailed at least five points behind Labour throughout the previous twelve months, it was highly unlikely that Macmillan would be able to restrain his own expansionist instincts and do as the Treasury ministers demanded.

By the end of November, spending bids from the various government departments were arriving daily at Powell's desk for consideration. He was horrified, and sent a memo to Thorneycroft complaining that they constituted 'the biggest increase ever recorded in peacetime' in public spending. The government, he thought, had to face down the farmers and the defence lobby as well as the demands for increased spending on the NHS and public buildings. In conclusion: 'We cannot go on blundering as we are at present.'[103] The Chancellor's chief economic adviser thought that Powell's ideas were madness. The economy was coasting along nicely; people were better off than ever before; why resort to such violent shock therapy to cure inflation when the potential costs in unemployment and unpopularity were so high? By this point, indeed, the Treasury advisers had largely abandoned their ministers.[104] And as the spending estimates made clear, the rest of the Cabinet had decided to go their own way as well. On 8 December, Thorneycroft complained to Macmillan that their colleagues had simply ignored the directive to hold their expenditure down to the levels of the current financial year. The following day, he told his own senior civil servant that there had to be 'an agonising reappraisal' in which nothing, not even the welfare state, could be 'immune'.[105] This was bound to offend not only his One Nation colleagues but also a Prime Minister who prided himself on his social conscience and dedication to economic growth. On 22 December, Macmillan recorded in his diary that he had just had 'a long talk' with a 'very worried Chancellor', who was demanding 'swingeing cuts in the Welfare State expenditure – more, I fear, than is feasible politically'. The following day he recorded that a small group of ministers had discussed the proposed cuts, including the abolition of Children's Allowance. All but Thorneycroft were 'bitterly opposed'; the embattled Chancellor, meanwhile, was 'in a very determined (also resigning) mood'.[106]

Two things were therefore clear. First, Macmillan himself had backed away from his earlier promise to cut spending; with Labour ahead in the polls and the country basking in a consumer boom, it was simply not 'feasible politically'. Second, the various Cabinet ministers were not prepared to acquiesce in the Treasury ministers' proposed cuts. Either Thorneycroft or Macmillan would have to give in, or one would have to go. It was unlikely to be the Prime Minister.

All the while, Powell was working hard behind the scenes to stiffen the Chancellor's resolve. On Christmas Eve he wrote to tell Nigel Birch that the Cabinet had refused to co-operate with the programme of cuts and that they ought therefore 'to fight this on resignation'. Thorneycroft must not be allowed to give in: 'It will be necessary to screw the Chancellor to the sticking point and, this done, to present the pistol at the right moment.' But Powell was confident that their ultimatum would work: 'I hardly see the cabinet, on the eve of the PM's departure [on a Commonwealth tour], facing the resignation of all three Treasury ministers because their colleagues refused the necessary co-operation in reducing expenditure.'[107] This was typical Powell. His own logic seemed irrefutable; it was barely conceivable to him that his fellow ministers could not see what he saw, and that they might put other priorities, such as full employment and social services, ahead of the need to fight inflation.

On New Year's Eve the Cabinet met to consider Thorneycroft's ultimatum. He wanted further savings of £153 million. Some £40 million, he said, could come from general trimmings; perhaps £50 million from health and welfare spending; and £65 million if the family allowance was withdrawn from second children. These would be unpopular, but he thought they were 'unavoidable'. At this his colleagues recorded their complete agreement him *in principle*, but one by one they objected to the 'drastic measures' he was proposing. The meeting broke up amid vague promises that more economies would be sought, and they agreed to reconvene in three days' time.[108]

On the morning of 3 January the Cabinet ministers reassembled in 10 Downing Street. The mood was tense. This time they were also joined by the Minister of Pensions and National Insurance, John Boyd-Carpenter, who was adamantly opposed to cuts in the family allowance and was himself determined to resign if Thorneycroft got his way. The discussion was again fruitless; only Reginald Maudling spoke in favour of the Chancellor's cuts. There was then an adjournment until 4.30, and when they reconvened in the Cabinet Room, Thorneycroft quietly announced that he was intending to resign. Macmillan then asked whether he would stay if they came up with cuts worth around £117 million, £36 million less than the original proposal. This evidently threw the Chancellor; while a man as zealous as Powell would have immediately refused, Thorneycroft asked for time to think. There now followed yet another adjournment, further increasing the tension. At 6.30 the ministers retook their seats with the exception of Lord Kilmuir and the Chancellor. Kilmuir, it was soon revealed, was reasoning with Thorneycroft in an adjoining room, but to little avail. Eventually Thorneycroft returned, looking, in Boyd-Carpenter's words, 'flushed and puffy'. He laid down his conditions for staying, and Boyd-Carpenter takes up the story:

> Chancellor said he wanted £30 million certain from 'Welfare' and to be free to seek economies on rest of civil side. Iain Macleod said this was like Hitler tactics. I said I didn't see why 'Welfare' should be specially singled out for a cut, as distinct from Civil Estimate generally.
>
> PM then said he would adjourn Cabinet and if on Monday agreement couldn't be reached, following discussions at weekend, he would have to consider question of placing resignation of Government in hands of Queen. He would very much regret this after all we had been through . . . It seemed a tragedy in the present state of the world to break up the Government over about half of one per cent of national expenditure, or perhaps over £10m.[109]

Macmillan, of course, had no such intention. He was merely presenting the Cabinet with a nightmare scenario: in effect, bluffing them into accepting Thorneycroft's resignation as a less painful solution.[110] As his diary reveals, he had by now lost all patience with his 'rude and *cassant*' Chancellor.[111]

The predictable denouement followed two days later, as the Cabinet met, unusually, on a Sunday evening. Macmillan came out against further cuts in either defence or welfare spending: cutting family allowance, for example, was 'neither politically nor socially desirable' and was 'contrary to the traditions of the Conservative Party'. On the other hand, he said, the Chancellor 'could feel assured of the wholehearted determination of his colleagues to support him in his disinflationary policy'.[112] Enoch Powell's biographer calls this 'a statement of pure flannel', which of course it was. Macmillan had never really shared Thorneycroft's commitment to anti-inflationary shock therapy, and by January 1958 had lost confidence in his entire Treasury team.[113] That morning he had held a private meeting with the Chancellor and appealed to him to 'accept the collective view'; Thorneycroft said he needed time to think, and Macmillan recorded that evening: 'I got the impression that he had made up his mind to resign, unless he got the full demand . . . He has obviously been pushed on by the Treasury Ministers.'[114] With the rest of the Cabinet backing Macmillan rather than Thorneycroft, the latter knew that he was beaten. The following morning, Powell went into Thorneycroft's office in the Treasury to be shown the figures. 'Will it do?' asked the Chancellor.

> Powell said to Thorneycroft: 'Shall we follow the former practice in the House of Lords, where the junior peer votes first?' And Powell put his hand on his breast and uttered, 'Not content'.
> 'I don't think it will do,' said Birch.
> 'I don't think it will do either,' said Thorneycroft. 'I'm going,' added the Chancellor, 'but that doesn't mean you have to.'
> However, there was no question of what they would do. At 10.30 the same morning Macmillan was handed the three resignation letters.[115]

Given that he had just lost his entire Treasury team, a setback that might have been expected to destroy his administration, Macmillan's reaction was masterful. The day after he was officially notified of the three ministers' resignations, he was off on his five-week Commonwealth tour. At the airport, surrounded by journalists, he casually remarked: 'I thought the best thing to do was to settle up with these little local difficulties and then turn to the wider vision of the Commonwealth.' It was a supposedly spontaneous put-down that he had been practising the night before, and it worked. Macmillan the imperturbable showman was still in command, despite the fact that his Chancellor and two other ministers had just walked out.[116] Inwardly he was furious, and more than a little frightened that Thorneycroft might have planned a rebellion in the parliamentary party. He confided to his diary that he thought the crisis had been 'carefully planned by the Chancellor of the Exchequer and the Treasury Ministers'.[117] He would refer to Thorneycroft later in life as 'that man who looked like an English butler, with the nice Italian wife – I forget his name . . .', while he described Birch as 'a natural intriguer' and Powell as a 'fanatic'. When Powell was recalled to the colours in 1960 as Minister of Health, Macmillan ordered that his seat at the Cabinet table be moved because, he said, 'I can't stand those mad eyes staring at me a moment longer.'[118] Meanwhile, any threat of a wider rebellion in 1958 had been averted. The press were carefully briefed on the rigidity and fanaticism of the three ministers, and thus the leading Tory newspaper, the *Telegraph*, concluded that they had resigned over 'a grain of dust'.[119] The point that Macmillan himself had gone back on his original promise to keep spending down – the root of all the trouble – was barely addressed. In playing down the affair, Macmillan was disingenuous, but he was also consummately skil-ful. A political disaster had been averted.[120]

There is little doubt that this was a critical moment in post-war political and economic history. In their belief that fighting inflation must take priority over keeping unemployment down, and in their eagerness to slash govern-ment spending to do so, the Treasury ministers were anticipating by twenty years the case that would be made by Margaret Thatcher and the neo-liberal right in the late seventies and early eighties. But as Alan Walters, a young aca-demic economist in the late fifties, admitted, at that time 'monetarists – and I was one – were looked on as being absurd'.[121] Thirty or forty years later, when controlling the money supply had become much more important to both Labour and Conservative politicians, many Thatcherite sympathisers saluted the three ministers as courageous, far-sighted pioneers.[122]

As it turned out, however, inflation did *not* dramatically increase after the Treasury resignations, and their doom and gloom, in the short term at least, looked rather exaggerated. The deflationary medicine that Thorneycroft had already administered had done the trick, and wage increases were abating. In the calendar year 1959, inflation actually reached its lowest level since the war, less than 1 per cent.[123] Equally, monetarist historians do not take into account the strong commitments of even Conservative ministers in 1958 to avoiding the unemployment and class antagonism of the twenties and thir-ties.[124] Most of the Cabinet simply believed that stagnation or job losses were worse prospects than a little inflation. Butler later remarked that the Treasury cuts would have undone welfare policies 'to which we have dedi-cated the service of our lives'.[125] Indeed, most of the more progressive ministers thought that the three departed monetarists were deranged and held Powell responsible. Iain Macleod concluded that Thorneycroft was 'obsessed and dominated' by Powell, and denounced free-market ideas as 'Enochery'.[126] 'Poor old Enoch,' he would say of his estranged friend. 'Driven mad by the remorselessness of his own logic.'[127] Two other potential stars of the future, Edward Heath and Viscount Hailsham, both found it difficult to trust Powell ever again, and regarded him as little short of insane.[128]

Macmillan, meanwhile, did not emerge from the affair with much credit, since he had personally abandoned Thorneycroft despite promising that he would support him. This was hardly a great victory for One Nation compassion, as some writers have suggested, since there were still going to be some cuts in services, and overall spending as a proportion of national income had fallen slightly since the Conservative victory in 1951.[129] Nor was there any sense that Macmillan had an alternative economic strategy, other than a vague idea of trimming expenditure to keep inflation down and then merrily returning to economic expansion. Perhaps the major difference between Macmillan and Thorneycroft was that the Prime Minister was preoccupied by the Tories' electoral prospects, and the Chancellor by the health of the economy as he understood it. Macmillan had even accepted Thorneycroft's argument, in principle, but then refused to implement it for fear of alienating working-class voters. This was, then, less a clash of two economic philosophies than a clash between electoral popularity and economic conviction.[130]

Thorneycroft had already put his finger on one of the basic flaws in the post-war settlement in a memorandum to Macmillan in December 1957. As he explained:

> With relatively few assets and large debts, we continue to live on the scale of a great power. We have the most expensive defence forces in Europe. We have joined the nuclear 'club'. We claim at the same time a very high standard of life. We seek to lead the world in the social services we provide.[131]

Like both his predecessors and his successors, Macmillan was unwilling to choose between the appurtenances of global power and comprehensive social provision, the assumption being that Britain could have both bombs and butter. He had already based his appeal to the Tory Party on a promise that Britain would 'stay great', but at the same time he was determined to prove that Conservatism stood for prosperity, jobs and compassion. Thorneycroft provided a forceful critique of this approach on 23 January in his resignation statement, accusing both major parties of trying to maintain Great Power status and a costly welfare state while owing enormous sums of money to overseas creditors and simultaneously struggling to prop up the pound. 'It has meant', he declared, 'that over twelve years we have slithered from one crisis to another. Sometimes it has been a balance of payments crisis and sometimes it has been an exchange crisis . . . It is a picture of a nation in full retreat from its responsibilities . . . It is the road to ruin.' The solution, he insisted, did not lie in applying endless remedies, but in acknowledging the root cause of the problem. 'The simple truth is that we have been spending more money than we should.'[132] It was a compelling speech and was acknowledged as such by backbenchers on both sides of the

House. But the Keynesian consensus was too strong to be swept aside by three dissident ministers. Macmillan, 'the great spender' as Thorneycroft affably dubbed him, still had a firm grip on power, and the philosophy of short-term growth still held sway.[133]

Macmillan's new Chancellor was Derick Heathcoat Amory, another amiable character and a paternalistic, conscientious war hero who ran a family textile company in his native Devon. As a former Liberal, Amory was more socially progressive than most of his Conservative colleagues. He was a bachelor of very simple habits, ate his meals in teashops, and was renowned for his honesty and lack of ambition. Amory had very few partisan instincts, which meant that he was popular on both sides of the House, and did not even regard himself as a professional politician. From Macmillan's point of view, he was an ideal choice, a well-liked and respected individual with few strong economic convictions of his own and therefore unlikely to rock the boat.[134] The economy was still recovering from Butler's ill-judged vote-winning spree and post-election retrenchment in 1955, and a fall in worldwide commodity prices late in 1957 provoked fears of a recession and rising unemployment. Controlling inflation, in short, was not a priority. One of Amory's first statements as Chancellor explained: 'We shall not keep the brakes on one day longer than we must. A steady expansion of the economy is wanted.'[135] Macmillan, meanwhile, was constantly badgering Amory for generous economic measures to stave off a potential slump. With a general election a year or so away, it was imperative for the Conservatives to cast themselves as the party of prosperity and to start clawing back Labour's advantage in the opinion polls. On 5 March 1958, for instance, Macmillan sent Amory an insistent memorandum:

The people need encouragement and I believe the view that high taxation is anti-inflationary has been pretty well exploded . . . Will the cinema tax have to be halved? Would this have to be offset by another pound on TV? The things I would think about are remission of stamp duty on house purchase. Best of all, abolish Schedule A [an unpopular tax on owner-occupied houses].[136]

Through the spring, however, the Conservatives' poll ratings were not improving but declining. Three by-elections were lost, and Conservative support fell by 6 per cent between January and May.[137] For all the internal wrangling of the Labour Party, it seemed likely that Hugh Gaitskell would be forming the next government. At the same time, the Liberal Party, the forgotten third force of British politics, was beginning to haul itself off the canvas. From the twenties onwards, the Liberals had been squeezed out of contention by the rise of Labour, by their own internal bickering and by the ability of the Conservatives to attract anti-socialist voters. In both 1951 and 1955 the Liberal vote had sunk to a pitiful level of less than 3 per cent, yielding just six seats in the Commons.[138] The Liberals were regarded as little more than a historical eccentricity, the province of middle-class eccentrics and a few West Country die-hards. From 1956, however, they benefited from the charismatic and determined leadership of Jo Grimond, who at forty-three was younger and potentially more appealing than either Macmillan or Gaitskell.

Grimond's first real breakthrough came in February 1958 with the Rochdale by-election, the first such event to be covered on television and therefore something of a media spectacle. In 1955 the victorious Conservative MP had won the seat with over twenty-six thousand votes. Now the Tory candidate finished third with fewer than ten thousand votes, while Labour won the seat with twenty-five thousand. The Liberal candidate, the popular ITN newsreader Ludovic Kennedy, sensationally took second place with over seventeen thousand, his party not even having bothered to contest the seat at the previous election.[139] Voting surveys found 'a general picture . . . of ill-defined frustration and disgruntlement' with the Conservatives, and Macmillan admitted that the result was 'a tremendous shock'.[140] In March, the Tories lost a straight fight to Labour in Kelvingrove, Glasgow. At the end of the month there followed an even more spectacular defeat at Torrington in Devon, when the Liberal candidate, Mark Bonham Carter, actually won the seat, by 219 votes. It was the first Liberal by-election victory in thirty years. As the grandson of Herbert Asquith, Bonham Carter could hardly have had stronger Liberal roots, but he had actually been planning to join the Conservatives until the Suez debacle put him off. A conscientious middle-class progressive unsympathetic to socialism, he was exactly the kind of person that the Liberals were hoping to draw away from the Conservative Party, and his victory was a very bad blow for Macmillan's prospects.

Amory's first budget in April, far from being the sensational vote-winner for which the Prime Minister had been hoping, was instead extremely cautious, introducing only the most minor changes. During 1958 the British economy grew by only 0.4 per cent, the lowest rate since the war, and unemployment crawled past 2 per cent towards a total of 600,000.[141] As far as Macmillan was concerned, this made it imperative for Amory to take the brakes off: 1959 would be an election year and rising unemployment would be very difficult to square with his promises of consumer prosperity. Harrod told Macmillan that he should run 'a thumping Budget deficit to stop recession', and throughout late 1958 and the early months of the following year Macmillan bombarded his Chancellor with similar demands. The Treasury's cautious advice was grumpily brushed aside. When Amory sent him a paper on 27 October pointing out the limitations of using public investment to stimulate growth, Macmillan even scribbled on it: 'This is a *very bad paper*. Indeed, a disgraceful paper. It might have been written by Mr Neville Chamberlain's ghost.'[142]

This constant pressure finally produced its reward. In April 1959 Amory introduced precisely the kind of expansionary pre-election budget that the Prime Minister wanted, although, as Macmillan noted, 'he got rather tired at the end of his 2 hrs speech and we thought he was going to faint'.[143] Income tax was cut from 43.5 to 38.75 per cent; purchase tax was cut by a sixth; investment allowances were restored; and 2d was taken off a pint of beer. All of this amounted to a tax giveaway of some £360 million, even more generous that Butler's pre-election spree of 1955.[144] As the economist Samuel Brittan put it, Amory had unveiled 'the most generous Budget ever introduced in normal peace-time conditions'.[145] The Prime Minister and his backbenchers were delighted, but even Amory himself was worried that he might have gone too far. *The Economist*, too, wondered whether the budget would turn out to be 'the harbinger of economic expansion or merely of another autumn crisis'.[146]

As it turned out, the slump that Macmillan had feared never materialised. Instead the economy grew by 4 per cent in real terms during 1959, a dramatic contrast with the stagnation of 1958, and unemployment fell dramatically. Production was on the increase; more people were buying on credit than ever before; the high streets were awash with cars, televisions, washing machines and all the glittering panoply of consumerism.[147] At the same time, prices appeared to be stable, so Macmillan could privately exult that he had 'brought off the double'. The very night that he wrote those words, however, Amory came alone to dinner. Macmillan recorded:

> He seemed rather low. I believe it is partly because he lives this strange hermit life and (unless he remembers) hardly eats . . . He is

very sensitive and very conscientious and rather a man to worry. He is now worried about . . . generally having had a too reflationary Budget.[148]

Amory was right to worry. Economic conditions had already been improving anyway, and his expansionary budget had triggered an unsustainable boom. He had given away far too many tax concessions, and, as he recognised within a month, he had been wrong not to stand up to Macmillan's demands for generosity.[149] Little of this, however, was apparent to contemporary commentators, who were instead impressed by the manifestations of consumer affluence evident in the street and the home. On 1 July, Henry Fairlie wrote in the *Daily Mail*:

> What [the people] see are all the gleaming evidence of a society which is out on a spree: a Stock Exchange behaving more like a Casino than ever; extravagant parties and expensive cars; refrigerators, washing machines and gadgets piling up in the kitchen. Luxuries become necessities, necessities being forgotten.[150]

Two months later, after Macmillan had called the election, *The Times* reported: 'People are prosperous; prices are steady; unemployment is low.'[151] This was exactly what the Prime Minister had wanted. But, as his Chancellor feared, the costs of such an extravagant boom would haunt the Conservative Party for years to come.

When Macmillan called the general election in September 1959, he had been in power for two-and-a-half years. He had successfully disposed of the Suez issue and had established himself as a politician of global importance, having rebuilt British bridges to Washington, co-operated with the Americans in sending troops to Lebanon and Jordan in the summer of 1958 and pulled off a high-profile visit to Moscow the following February. The Tories' fortunes were already improving even before Amory's expansionary budget, not least because in July 1958, Iain Macleod as Minister of Labour had taken on the London bus drivers in a direct confrontation over pay and forced them to accept a wage increase five times smaller than their original demand. The struggle was a personal triumph for Macleod, of course, but it was also the first time since the war that a government had directly taken on one of the major unions, in this case the TGWU, and won. For both Tory Party members and many middle-class voters, it was an indication of a newfound self-confidence and vigour, and most observers agreed that it was 'the moment when their fortunes turned'.[152] From the summer of 1958, the government's opinion-poll ratings began to improve; according to Gallup, voters were impressed with the consumer boom, the low interest rates, Macmillan's personal demeanour and his strong stand against militant trade unionists in the TGWU and anti-Western elements in Lebanon and Jordan.[153] Labour, meanwhile, were perceived as divided, uncertain and afraid to stand up to trade union demands; with Gaitskell having built his appeal around the issue of economic management, the recovery had rather punctured his balloon. Nor did the party seem to have a new message for the supposed age of affluence; many people still associated Labour with nationalisation, devaluation and austerity.[154]

The summer of 1959 was the warmest anyone could remember: one long, hazy, cloudless day followed another, teenagers lazed in the sunshine listening to Cliff Richard, and in high streets across the nation the consumer boom was in full swing. Since 1952 the number of cars on the roads had doubled, and in 1959 alone 200,000 new motorbike licences were issued, a record.[155] In *Left, Right and Centre*, a political comedy shown in cinemas that summer, a Labour campaigner insists that 'Toryism means unemployment; poverty; destitution; starvation; despair,' but the film undermines his case by panning across a row of houses, each with its own brand new television aerial. Ordinary voters are simply uninterested in politics; they are too busy reading the *News of the World*, listening to the pop singer Tommy Steele, or watching *Spider Men from Mars*.[156] The film was not far off the mark. All the economic indicators appeared to favour the incumbent government: consumer spending and output were high; unemployment, inflation and bank rate were low; and the average weekly wage had almost doubled since 1951.[157] One in three voters confidently expected their material circumstances to improve in the next few years; only one in twenty thought that they might become poorer.[158] 'The sun is shining down on Britain's packed beaches in the first hot summer since 1955,' explained *The Economist*, 'and in an atmosphere of easy holiday contentment the literally floating voter feels no burning desire for a change.'[159]

The Conservatives had originally thought about basing their re-election drive around the themes of 'Opportunity' and 'Responsibility'. But with all the talk now about affluence and prosperity, they adopted a different approach, spending a record half a million pounds on a poster campaign to

promote their new message: 'Life's better with the Conservatives. Don't let
Labour ruin it.'[160] Their election handbook boasted: '*The Standard of Living* is
higher today than ever before in our history. It is no accident that today the
British people are earning, eating, producing, buying, building, growing and
saving far more than ever they did under a Socialist Government.'[161] One
poster showed a mother, father and son cheerfully washing their modest
Austin A35 car, while a younger boy plays on his tricycle in the background.
Another, decorated with the face of a hearty, well-fed worker, carried the
caption:

> Six Conservative years have brought big improvements all round. Life's
> better in every way than it was. He and his wife are both clear about
> that. So many more things to buy in the shops. More money to buy
> them with too. The kids are coming along well at school. In fact in his
> view a pretty encouraging outlook for all of them. Well, what's so spe-
> cial about that? Aren't there millions these days who are just as well
> fixed? You bet there are.[162]

Meanwhile, Macmillan, ebullient and self-assured, was the star of the show.
In November 1958 the cartoonist Vicky had drawn him as 'Supermac', flying
through the air in Superman's costume, with a giant 'No. 10' emblazoned
on his tunic. The cartoon was meant to be critical; the caption read: 'How to
Try to Continue to Be Top Without Actually Having Been There'.[163] But the
moniker stuck, as a tribute to Macmillan's presentational skills and the new-
found health of the economy. Macmillan had smartened up his image: he
now wore expensive Savile Row suits rather than the old baggy trousers he
had once favoured, had trimmed his old-fashioned moustache and had paid
a dentist to fix his lopsided teeth. He was calm, authoritative and masterful,
Supermac incarnate, running almost 20 per cent ahead of Gaitskell in the
opinion polls.[164] 'He looks what he is – very aristocratic,' one working-class
voter told an interviewer. 'He's had a jolly good education and he's very
wealthy. I've always thought that showed itself. It's a good thing in a Prime
Minister.'[165]

Perhaps one of Macmillan's few obvious weaknesses was his inability to
adjust to the new medium of television, which made its first significant
political appearance in the 1959 campaign. Television was thought to exercise tremendous power over an audience's opinions; when the networks
won the right to cover the Rochdale by-election in February 1958, another

Vicky cartoon portrayed a stereotypical dumb blonde asking her husband: 'How did people know who to vote for before they had TV, dear?'[166] Macmillan had already made a joint television appearance with President Eisenhower when the latter visited Britain at the end of August, and this was thought to have gone down well with the public.[167] However, the first official party political broadcasts were not a triumph. When the Chief Whip, Edward Heath, sat down to watch his party's first broadcast, he thought it was 'absolutely catastrophic':

> It was meant to be a report on our term in office and there was Mr Macmillan sitting very comfortably in an armchair with his senior Cabinet colleagues around him. And Harold said, 'Well now, Rab, I think we've done very well, don't you?' And Rab said, 'Oh yes, we've done awfully well, particularly the things I've been doing.' And Iain Macleod then said, 'Yes, well, I've done awfully well and we've all done very well indeed.' After we'd had a quarter of an hour of this we were driven absolutely up the wall. And the next programme was just as bad.[168]

At least Macmillan managed to project himself more successfully than Gaitskell, who always came over as rather wooden and patronising. Labour's broadcasts were famously slick, thanks largely to the enthusiastic efforts of the young 'Wedgie' Benn, the party's technological whizz-kid and media expert. But Gaitskell had never really came to terms with the new medium, and in the end it was Benn himself, rather than his leader, who was the real star of Labour's television campaign.[169]

Given the prosperity of the day, the result of the election was probably a foregone conclusion. Even so, Labour started the campaign well with a series of promises to raise pensions and increase economic growth. Gaitskell made a bad blunder, however, when he claimed that a Labour government would be able to spend more on social provision without raising income tax. There then followed a chorus of Tory claims that he was trying to bribe the electorate and 'auctioneering for votes' with reckless promises; not that Macmillan had dreamed of bribing the voters, of course, when he persuaded Amory to cut taxes in April.[170] The momentum now swung decisively in favour of the Conservatives. Despite his Labour sympathies, Vicky even produced a cartoon showing Gaitskell draped in a bath-towel and Macmillan running off with a workingman's clothes, his Labour adversary shouting angrily after him: 'Wot? ME trying to pinch YOUR clothes? Cor, it's obvious they're mine, ain't it?' Gaitskell, as the image made clear, was the emperor who had lost his clothes, no matter who was responsible.[171] At a time when most voters were feeling optimistic and self-satisfied, it would have taken flair and imagination to put the theatrical Macmillan on the defensive, but Gaitskell's brand of earnest sobriety could not compete. Even so, on the last Sunday before voting day, Gallup still had the parties at neck and neck, but late on 8 October Gaitskell was given the shattering news that the Conservatives not only had won but had even increased their majority from sixty to a hundred.[172] They took over 49 per cent of the vote and 365 seats, compared with Labour's 44 per cent and 258 seats. And as for the Liberals, their long-desired electoral breakthrough never materialised; although they doubled their share of the vote, 5.9 per cent and six seats was hardly a sensational tally.[173]

'That all went off rather well,' remarked Harold Macmillan on television after the extent of the Conservatives' victory had become clear.[174] But in the Labour camp all was gloom and despair. Many activists thought that it was the most shattering defeat for more than twenty-five years.[175] The young Roy Hattersley, who had fought and lost the hopeless seat of Sutton Coldfield, listened miserably to Gaitskell's concession speech late on election night. The Labour leader insisted that 'the flame of democratic socialism still burns bright', but to Hattersley, 'the fire had almost gone out'. 'I put away my huge red and yellow rosette', he wrote, 'without feeling very much confidence that I would ever wear it in a winning campaign.'[176]

Labour had now lost three successive general elections with a shrinking share of the vote, and the party's own review of the election concluded: 'We were defeated by prosperity: this was without doubt the prominent factor.'[177] Since prosperity was expected to last, this meant that the party was in serious trouble. In 1960 the political scientist Samuel Beer wrote an article for *Political Quarterly* entitled 'Democratic One-Party Government for Britain?', and a year later Professor John P. Mackintosh ended his book *The British Cabinet* with the prediction that 'the Labour Party is unlikely to return to power and that the government of the country will remain in the hands of the Conservatives for the foreseeable future'.[178] In *Must Labour Lose?*, an apparently authoritative survey of working-class voters, Mark Abrams and Richard Rose argued that as working-class homes had been transformed by appliances, televisions and consumer goods, so even manual workers were turning into middle-class Conservatives. Eight out of every ten working-class voters now owned a television; three in ten owned a washing machine; and many were beginning to make down-payments on a fridge or a car.[179] Abrams and Rose found that young people between eighteen and twenty-five were particularly likely to identify with the Conservatives: they thought that Macmillan's party represented 'skilled craftsmen, middle-class people, forward-looking people, ambitious people, office workers and scientists'.[180] Since prosperity was expected to last well into the sixties, the Labour Party had no choice but to reinvent itself for the age of affluence; if it failed to do so, they wrote, it was likely to end up on the wrong side of 'a permanent and continuing swing' towards Conservatism.[181]

Some of the old firebrands of the left urged an all-out attack on the culture of materialism. 'This so-called affluent society is an ugly society still,' Bevan thundered at that year's party conference. 'It is a vulgar society. It is a meretricious society. It is a society in which priorities have gone all wrong.'[182] But most of his younger colleagues recognised that there was no point harking back to the austere socialist earnestness of the thirties. As one defeated Labour candidate explained mournfully, the Red Flag and the union banner might make his blood tingle, but 'they get no answer in tingling blood in the suburbs of London'.[183] On the Sunday after the election, Gaitskell hosted a meeting for his friends and allies in his Hampstead house. One participant suggested revising the Labour Party's constitution and the deletion of Clause Four's reference to public ownership; another proposed changing the party's unfashionable name to the 'Reform' or 'Radical' Party. 'We were too closely tied to a "working class" that no longer exists,' wrote the leader's close friend Patrick Gordon Walker in a summary of the discussion.[184] The next morning, the *Daily Mirror* appeared for the first time since 1945 without its crusading socialist slogan 'FORWARD WITH THE PEOPLE!' Instead, the paper's new masthead announced: 'The accent is on Youth, the accent is on Gaiety.' A few months later, belatedly acknowledging the new values of its readers, the *Mirror* introduced a City page for the first time.[185]

'The class war is over,' Macmillan triumphantly remarked after his re-election victory, 'and we have won it.'[186] For the Prime Minister, the 1959 election had been a tremendous personal victory. Supermac was at his peak, his popularity apparently assured. As one Conservative MP recalled, it was 'the sudden genius of the new Prime Minister that clinched it' and his 'lively confidence which took the electorate by storm'.[187] But many commentators also recognised that the election had been won by affluence more than by any individual politician. An apocryphal story had it that Lord Poole, one of Macmillan's campaign managers, would spend his Saturdays driving out from his country estate into Watford, where he would watch the suburban shoppers wandering through the new supermarkets or signing hire-pur-chase forms in television and washing-machine showrooms, nod contentedly to himself, and then drive home again.[188] 'Most electors', said the News Chronicle, 'did indeed believe that they had never had it so good.'[189] A cartoon in the Spectator shortly after the election summed up the general impression. Macmillan is sitting in his Downing Street study; around the table are also sitting a car, a washing machine, a refrigerator and a television. 'Well, gentlemen,' he says contentedly, 'I think we all fought a good fight.'[190]

4

THE AFFLUENT SOCIETY

Since George Orwell published *The Road to Wigan Pier* in 1936, Wigan has changed from barefoot malnutrition to nylon and television, from hollow idleness to flush contentment.

Encounter, June 1956

Cheap suits, red kitchen-ware, sharp shoes, iced lollies,
Electric mixers, toasters, washers, driers . . .

Philip Larkin, 'Here' (1961)

In 1956 more than a million people crowded into Olympia, in Hammersmith, for the latest *Daily Mail* Ideal Home Exhibition, an annual celebration of domesticity, home-making and commercialism. Inside there were mock houses and flats, kitchens and bathrooms, tables and chairs, cookers and washing machines, vacuum cleaners and televisions. The kitchen manufacturers Berg showed off their latest innovation, the 'break-fast bar'. Cintique exhibited a special chair for the lady of the house, with a high seat and angled back 'to give really comfortable support while knitting or sewing'. A special display to celebrate the *Daily Mail*'s jubilee, entitled 'Sixty Years Back and Sixty Years Ahead', traced the changes in women's fashions and domestic life since 1896, and a House of the Future designed by the radical architects Alison and Peter Smithson gave visitors a glimpse of the plastic space age to come. And above the milling thousands in the Grand Hall there towered a mock-French château containing special National Trust displays of Famous English Homes, an enormous expression of the exhibition's main theme: 'An Englishman's Home is his Castle.'[1]

For many people in 1956, however, these visions of gleaming televisions and shiny new houses bore little relation to their own daily lives. In many cases, home meant a narrow, cramped Victorian terraced house, thrown up in haste during the industrial expansion of the previous century along-side hundreds of identical others. These terraces stretched in long, cold lines down the hillsides of Sheffield or Bristol and along the canals of Manchester and Birmingham, and from them each morning emerged the hordes of weary men and women whose labour drove the nation's industrial growth. Each house looked much like the next: meanly claustrophobic, crowded with shouting children, bare and poor, often with no garden, hedge or wall. The better ones might have a bay window and a patch of grass, but no more. Every day their inhabitants looked out across a sea of slate roofs towards what one geography textbook of the early fifties called 'a dreary scene of tall chimneys, black smoke, old slag heaps, railway lines and neglected waste'.[2]

Daily life in a terraced house in 1956 was a struggle against three foes: darkness, cold and dirt. Although 86 per cent of households were wired for electricity, the wiring was often unreliable and even dangerous, and many families chose to install only a few power points, or even make do with just lighting.[3] For the other 14 per cent, typically in remote rural areas, there was no electric light to pierce the gloom of the household, only the dull glimmer of gaslight. As one Cornishman recalled, the lack of light meant that his family cooked on a Cornish range, warmed themselves by an open fire, went to bed early and read by candlelight. 'Of course, there was no light in the bathroom,' he later told an interviewer, 'so if you wanted a bath in the evening you had to take a candle up, and if there was too much steam the candle went out.'[4] Even with electricity, many houses were bitterly cold and dangerously damp. Most were heated by coal fires, usually in one room only; since the other rooms were so cold, families clustered in the room with the fire, the doors tightly closed to prevent draughts. 'We did everything in one room and that was the room with the fireplace in it,' remembered one North Wales woman. 'The fireplace not only heated you, it boiled your water, it cooked your food, it was where you had your bath, it was the main hub of the house.'[5] But heat produced dirt. In the streets of manufacturing and mill towns, coal smoke poured from the fireplaces of hundreds of terraced houses to mingle with the black clouds belching from factory chimneys. Coughs and colds were common; dirt clung to the walls and to clothing. In winter children skipped or played football through a thick, pungent black fog, 'just like a dirty sticky cloud', according to one woman from Lancashire.[6]

With dirt came disease, increasingly rare after the war but a potent threat nonetheless. Sanitation was often rudimentary: in 1950, a survey found, nearly half of all homes had no bathroom.[7] Many families had to share an outdoor toilet with others from the terrace; the lucky ones had their own, hidden behind the house in a dingy little shed, and at night they would have to dash across the yard carrying a lamp or candle. In the countryside, the contents would often be buried in the garden. Social decorum still prevailed: one woman remembered that her family would replace their usual squares of newspaper with tissue papers whenever visitors arrived.[8] As for washing, most working-class families relied on one sink for their daily ablutions and bathed once a week in a tin bath, heated by gas burners or filled with water warmed from the coal fire. In *Light in the Dust*, her evocative memoir of Black Country life in the post-war years, Jo-Mary Stafford recalled that her mother would wash her and her siblings every night from a bowl of soapy water, standing them on a table in front of the fire.[9] Friday night, however, was bath night. When it was particularly cold, she wrote, 'mom would light the fire underneath the washing-boiler in the corner of the "back-kitchen", to warm the water in the boiler; then she would let the fire go out and dunk us in there, one at a time, the others waiting their turn in front of the gas stove'. On warmer evenings, however, a large tin bath was produced, as in many other working-class houses across the country. Usually the members of the family bathed one after the other, topping it up with pans of hot water, but the bathwater inevitably became ever cloudier and dirtier, so that the last bather effectively wallowed in the family dirt. In the Stafford household, Jo-Mary and her two sisters bathed all at once before their two younger brothers inherited the 'mucky water'. The coal tar soap with which they were rubbed was, for Jo-Mary, one of the distinctive smells of life in the 1950s, mingling with the steam, soot and polish that clung to the air of their little council house in Walsall.[10] Even the nation's capital, as one visitor reported, was 'scarred and dingy', a vision of 'rubble, greyness, smog, poverty, garish whores on the streets in Soho, trams still running along Kingsway, tramps sleeping on the Embankment and under the Arches'.[11] At the beginning of the fifties, then, Britain was still a country in which millions of people shared a toilet with their neighbours, in which many young married couples were forced to live with their parents, and in which few people had ever laid eyes on a television set. It was a country of conservative habits poised on the brink of exuberant affluence and irrevocable change.

For many observers, the real turning point between the immediate austerity of the post-war years and the rampant consumerism of the sixties came around 1954, when the last of the food rations was lifted.[12] Contemporary witnesses remarked on the suddenness of the changes that swept across Britain in the mid-fifties. 'Almost at once,' wrote Harry Hopkins, 'affluence came hurrying on the heels of penury. Suddenly, the shops were piled high with all sorts of goods. Boom was in the air.'[13] It was as though the British consumer, having been held in the blocks in interminable agony, had suddenly been propelled headlong down the track towards prosperity. The rush for affluence was further spurred by the relaxation of hire-purchase controls in August 1954. In the next twelve months, consumer expenditure rose by around 8 per cent, and spending on durable goods like televisions and refrigerators by 10 per cent.[14] Such was the demand that in the summer of 1955 shopkeepers in Birmingham were reporting three-month delays in supplying home electrical goods, four months for furniture and a year for cars.[15] But, despite such hitches, the boom showed little sign of slackening. By 1957, British shoppers were spending some £1004 million on durable goods; three years later, this figure had risen to £1465 million, an increase of 45 per cent.[16] Between 1950 and 1959, average consumption per head was to rise by 20 per cent, as large an increase in just nine years as there had been in the entire inter-war period.[17] And by the end of the decade the self-proclaimed age of affluence was in full swing. 'When did you last hear the word austerity?' asked *Queen* magazine in September 1959. 'This is the only time you will see it in this issue.'

> Have you woken up? Do you know you are living in a new world? You are half-aware of it, perhaps. You don't use words like ersatz or economy label. You don't even say credit squeeze. But here we are, 20 years after the war started, in an age better than any even our grandfathers can remember, for all their grumblings. Better, in fact, than any in the history of the world. Material, yes, but pleasant. You are richer than ever before. You are spending more than you have ever done. Our hope is that you realise it and enjoy it. We don't want you to miss it. Don't wait until years after to realise you have lived in a remarkable age – the age of BOOM.[18]

But, for all its razzmatazz, the consumer boom of the late 1950s was not an unprecedented economic revolution.[19] Rather, it was the resumption of a trend that had been interrupted by the Second World War. If anything, for middle-class Britons it was the austerity of the war years that had been anomalous, not the affluence of the following decade. Consumerism and advertising had long been dynamic forces in British society. In the nineteenth century, for example, the rapid expansion of Victorian industrial capitalism had been accompanied by a frenzy of advertisements, publicity stunts and unsolicited telegrams to trumpet the virtues of mass-produced foods and luxuries: Lipton's tea, Cadbury's chocolate, Beecham's medicines, Quaker porridge oats and so on. The Boer War was effectively sponsored by the Bovril company, which took out full-page newspaper advertisements to proclaim the important role of beef extract in fortifying the army, supplied special news bulletins to high-street customers in return for Bovril labels, and offered a free print of the Relief of Ladysmith in exchange for special Bovril tokens. Even the 1920s and 1930s, belying their reputation for depression and despair, had been marked by growing affluence, leisure and aspirational materialism. In affluent pockets like the south-east and the Midlands, the revival of the economy after 1933, especially in 'new' industries producing cars, pharmaceuticals and electrical appliances, had stimulated the growth of a genuine consumer society.[20]

Indeed, it makes little sense to try and understand the social changes of the fifties without first considering the consumer boom of the thirties. It was in the thirties, for example, that prototypical teenage consumers began spending their wages on dances, clothes, records and day trips. It was in the thirties that many families first enjoyed the benefits of electricity, with nearly 800,000 households a year being added to the network at the end of the decade. And it was in the thirties that middle-class consumers first became familiar with radios, vacuum cleaners, cookers, electric irons and family cars. Credit was readily available; by 1939, two-thirds of more expensive goods, like furniture and appliances, were bought on hire-purchase. Suburban housing estates of semi-detached mock-Tudor houses, 'fit for heroes to live in', were being built in stretches of ribbon development; chain stores like Sainsbury's and Marks and Spencer provided almost every town in the country with mass-produced foodstuffs and clothing; newspaper advertisements trumpeted the attractions of everything from clothing to cigarettes; and people entertained themselves with coach tours to seaside resorts and private drives into the countryside.[21] At the end of his *English Journey* in 1933, J. B. Priestley argued that two older versions of England – 'the country of the cathedrals and minsters and manor houses and inns'; and the 'industrial England of coal, iron, steel, cotton, wool, railways; of thousands of rows of little houses all alike' – were both being replaced by a third, 'new England' that anticipated the affluent society of the 1950s:

> This is the England of arterial and by-pass roads, of filling stations and factories that look like exhibition buildings, of giant cinemas and dance-halls and cafes, bungalows with tiny garages, cocktail bars, Woolworths, motor-coaches, wireless, hiking, factory girls looking like actresses, greyhound racing and dirt tracks, swimming pools, and everything given away for cigarettes and coupons. If the fog had lifted I knew I should have seen this England all round me at the northern entrance to London, where the smooth wide road passes between miles of semi-detached bungalows, all with their little garages, their wireless sets, their periodicals about film stars, their swimming costumes and tennis rackets and dancing shoes.[22]

By 1956, most middle-class couples in post-war Britain could readily afford a record player, a camera, a vacuum cleaner, or a new settee and chairs for their front room. Even working-class families, especially in the south and Midlands where unemployment was minimal, found themselves in Priestley's 'new England': they listened to their own wireless powered by mains electricity, regularly visited the cinema, ate tinned or processed food, heated and lit their homes with gas and electricity, and in some cases drove their own small cars.[23] One American journalist described the new British manual worker in 1957:

> He moved to a New Town or a housing estate from a slum or near-slum . . . He is living in what to him is comparative luxury: a living-room, a clean and, by British standards, modern kitchen. There is a bedroom for the children and a modern bath and toilet. He can walk or cycle to work and, if the weather is fine, he comes home for lunch. In the evening there is the 'telly' or the football pools form to be filled in . . . It is a quiet life, but to our subject a satisfactory one.[24]

Similarly, in Alan Sillitoe's novel *Saturday Night and Sunday Morning* (1958), the protagonist Arthur Seaton reflects on his father's life in working-class Nottingham:

The old man was happy at last, anyway, and he deserved to be happy, after all the years before the war on the dole, five kids and the big mis-erying that went with no money and no way of getting any. And now he had a sit-down job at the factory, all the Woodbines he could smoke, money for a pint if he wanted one, though he didn't as a rule drink, a jaunt on the firm's trip to Blackpool, and a television-set to look into at home . . . The thousands who worked there [at the bicycle factory] took home good wages. No more short-term like before the war, or getting the sack if you stood ten minutes on the lavatory reading your Football Post – if the gaffer got on to you now you could always tell him where to put the job and go somewhere else. And no more running out at din-nertime for a penny bag of chips to eat with your bread. Now, and about time too, you got fair wages if you worked your backbone to a string of conkers on piece-work, and there was a big canteen where you could get a hot dinner for two-bob. With the wages you got you could save up for a motor-bike or even an old car, or you could go on a ten-day binge and get rid of all you saved.[25]

This phenomenon was what contemporaries called the 'affluent soci-ety', and its fundamental economic basis was the steady rise of average earnings after the Second World War. In 1950 the average weekly wage was £6 8s; by 1959, it had almost doubled to £11 2s 6d. At the same time, the stan-dard rate of income tax had fallen from over nine shillings in the pound to less than seven shillings.[26] Rising wages in themselves were no novelty; what was new, however, was the experience of full employment, a startling con-trast with the dole queues of the thirties. Between 1948 and 1970, the number of registered unemployed touched 2 per cent only eight times.[27] Workers, especially if young and single, had greater freedom to move from job to job, whether for higher wages or simply to satisfy their own desire for change. And competition for labour naturally resulted in higher wages; even industrial working-class workers took home enough money to afford little treats and luxuries.[28] Many factory workers were, as one of their number later put it, 'quids in'. 'I was getting taxis about,' he recalled. 'I mean, a pound would buy you a bloody good night out. You could proba-bly have eight or nine pints of beer and twenty fags and a couple of tanners for the juke box.'[29]

The other basic premise of the consumer boom was the availability of cheap and dependable electricity. According to a new set of regulations issued in 1950, all new homes required correct ring mains and standardised power sockets, and an improved mains network guaranteed a reliable supply, as well as 'the joy of better light, of warmth and the power to make easier work of life's chores', as one advertisement put it.[30] By the early 1960s, electrification had been extended to even the most remote rural villages, and, with their power supply in place, families could think about saving for the new household appliances that promised so much. Spending on household items increased by a staggering 115 per cent during the decade.[31] The *Financial Times* found that in barely two years, from September 1957 to November 1959, the number of households owning a car had risen by 25 per cent, with even bigger increases in the ownership of televisions (32 per cent), washing machines (54 per cent) and refrigerators (58 per cent).[32] Just as in the United States, where the consumer boom had come earlier and with more effect, competition with friends and neighbours increased the pressure on families to buy the latest appliances, especially in middle-class suburbia. The classic study of an English suburb by Peter Willmott and Michael Young, based on a series of interviews in the London borough of Woodford in the spring of 1959, captures the everyday jealousy of middle-class life in the late fifties:

> 'As soon as next door knew we'd got a washing machine', said a husband, 'they got one too. Then a few months later we got a fridge, so they got a fridge as well. I thought all this stuff about keeping up with the Jones's was just talk until I saw it happening right next door.'[33]

The Hornby family, living in a pre-war semi-detached house in the lower-middle-class suburb of Neasden, was typical. 'We were the first family in our street to have a car and also the first family in our street to have a television set,' Lesley Hornby, a teenager during the late 1950s, proudly recalled.[34] Even poorer manual workers, especially in the affluent south of England, shared in the consumer competition. A labourer's wife in Woodford complained: 'Whatever the others have got, the people next door want as well. We get a new Hoover, so she's got to have one. Another neighbour's got a new studio couch, so she's got one – and she's still paying for it.'[35]

As the example of the Woodford woman suggests, the acquisitive rivalries of affluence were at least as strong among women as they were among men. The housewife had become a recognisable middle-class stereotype in the 1920s and 1930s, but it took the pressures of the consumer society, the Cold War and the return of women to domesticity after the wartime experience to turn the idealised housewife into the 'kitchen goddess'. A skilful cook, dedicated mother and committed cleaner, the kitchen goddess was the mistress of her technological environment, modern and glamorous, dynamic and efficient, effortlessly controlling the new technological appliances of the consumer society. Indeed, housework was generally seen not as domestic drudgery but as the essential framework of family life and an occupation in which a woman could take pride. It was the housewife, after all, who was responsible for the respectable appearance of the home, for the cleanliness and tidiness of the rest of the family and even for the dinner parties that played such a large role in suburban social life. And since she was expected to assume the lead role in the kitchen, it was often the housewife who was the focus of consumer activity.[36] 'It is not an exaggeration to say that [the] woman as purchaser holds the future standard of living in this country in her hands,' explained the educationalist John Newsom. 'If she buys in ignorance then our national standards will deteriorate.' Education, he thought, would guide working-class girls towards middle-class standards; with the right education, they would reject the 'aesthetically inept' and turn the houses of the national workforce into temples of the 'fitting and beautiful'.[37] 'In her function as a consumer, an immense amount of a woman's personality is engaged,' Mary Grieve, editor of *Woman*, told an advertising conference in 1957. 'Success here is as vitalizing to her as success in his chosen sphere to a man.'[38]

Advertisers and salesmen therefore tended to appeal not to husbands but to wives, manipulating both their hopes for material success and their fears of looking inferior compared with their contemporaries. Hoover, for example, proclaimed that their products were 'saving millions of housewives from hard, wearisome drudgery', and illustrated the claim with pictures of cheerful young housewives in high heels casually vacuuming the floor or washing their laundry in their bright, open new houses.[39] It was not always the same story, however, in appliance showrooms. Many employed female demonstrators to persuade shoppers of the worth of unfamiliar appliances, and these demonstrators were encouraged to concentrate on husbands, not wives. The husband was still thought to control the family purse-strings: indeed, well into the late sixties, some working-class housewives in northern England and Scotland still asked their husbands' permission before spending money on themselves.[40] As one demonstrator remembered: 'If a woman came in with her husband we would try to attract his attention because we knew that he was going to pay the bill at the end of the day . . . You had to get a sisterly fellow feeling with the wife, but at the same time you were also being a little seductive to the husband and suggesting that if he was a real man he was going to see that the woman in his life was well looked after.' It was, she recalled, 'a technique which always seemed to work'.[41]

The supreme object of a housewife's ambition in the late 1950s was a washing machine, hitherto a rare luxury. It was not surprising, given the tedious drudgery of washing laundry by hand, that most women ranked a washing machine as their single preferred purchase, despite the fact that they cost six weeks' average wages and were often less than reliable. Hotpoint's machine was even called 'The Liberator' in a bid to appeal to the exhausted housewife.[42] By 1955, 17.5 per cent of households owned a machine, a figure rising to 29 per cent three years later and 60 per cent in 1966.[43] For many families, the delivery of the washing machine was a memorable moment of tremendous excitement. 'I can remember the arrival of our first automatic washing-machine,' one girl told an interviewer some twenty years later. 'It was a Bendix and it had to be bolted to the floor, because it shook so much when it was spin-drying. The first time [my mother] used it, we all sat around and watched our clothes going around and around through the glass port-hole at the front.'[44]

One consequence of the ubiquity of such machines was an increase in the sales of washing powders, the first of which became available in 1950. The cut-throat competition between brands like Tide, Surf, Daz and Omo for such a rapidly expanding market explained the £7 million spent annually by advertisers on campaigns that emphasised freshness and purity.[45] The rivalry between the electricity and gas boards was similarly intense; both exhibited their products in their own high-street showrooms, and both also mounted travelling showrooms to reach consumers in rural areas. They even employed rival television cooks: while Fanny Cradock explained the virtues of gas cooking, Marguerite Patten demonstrated the potential of electricity. Since affluence was relatively new to many shoppers, however, their first concern was often the cost, and advertisers emphasised the efficiency and economy of their products. The Presto pressure cooker, for example, promised 'perfectly cooked meals and *lower fuel bills* . . . Why not get your Presto today? It will soon pay for itself by the enormous amount of fuel it saves.'[46]

To prevail in the ferocious competition for consumers' allegiance, manufacturers invested more and more in advertising, spending four times as much on publicity in 1960 as they did in 1947.[47] Even old-fashioned products were expensively relaunched in order to address the new anxieties and ambitions of men and, especially, women in the consumer age. In one magazine advertisement, readers were presented with the comic-strip tale of Jean and Jimmy, a typical middle-class couple of the fifties. Jean, we learn, is becoming 'dull and listless' and a 'dead weight' at parties; her marriage seems 'to be breaking up', and a tricky dinner party is looming. Like many similar advertisements of the day, this is the story of a married woman who is failing to live up to the standards of her husband and her peers; it is even given the title: 'The wife they didn't want'. By choosing the right product, however, she is able to win back her husband's affection, the admiration of their friends and her general social standing. In Jean's case, her husband consults a doctor who suggests that 'she's not getting the right kind of sleep'. He tells a relieved Jimmy: 'I suspect that all your wife needs is a cup of Horlicks at bedtime.' The Horlicks does the trick: Jean duly cooks a splendid lemon meringue pie, just as her husband likes it, and a dinner guest declares: 'Wonderful cook, wonderful woman. You're a lucky man, Jimmy!' 'Don't I know it!' replies Jimmy, telling himself in an italicised bubble: '*What a difference in Jean since she was put on Horlicks!*'[48]

Horlicks was just one among many products jostling for attention in an increasingly competitive and multinational marketplace. Confronted with a barrage of advertisements, many consumers found it difficult to tell one washing powder from another. The *New Statesman* even published a cartoon showing an old man staring glassily at the swirling patterns displayed by one of the new consumer delights. 'No, grandpa,' a girl tells him, 'that's the washing machine, not the television.'[49] Indeed, for many observers the bewildering range of products available was matched only by the devious trickery of the advertisers employed to sell them. On a visit to the United States in 1954 J. B. Priestley had coined the term *admass*: 'the creation of the mass mind, the mass man'. Admass man was blinded by the dazzling array of consumer goods offered by the consumer society, his senses dulled by the bland rapidity of modern communications and the pervasive pressure of advertising; he lived, thought Priestley, in a mechanical, superficial, conformist world, where 'people would cheerfully exchange their last glimpse of freedom for a new car, a refrigerator, and a TV screen'.[50] Many British consumers actually shared some of Priestley's fears about the new world of mass advertising, not least because many of the most recognisable products were provided by American manufacturers like Hoover, Heinz, Colgate or Gillette, and sold by American advertising executives. The Association for Consumer Research, later renamed the Consumers' Association, finally produced a guide for shoppers confused by the competing messages of advertisers but nevertheless keen to embrace the consumer society. Launched in 1957, *Which?* promised to conduct objective, comparative tests that would unmask flawed or overpriced products, and it was soon selling 300,000 copies a month. But even the Consumers' Association, which was the fastest-growing organisation of the sixties and boasted some 430,000 members by 1967, was itself based on an American prototype.[51]

Many people bought their new consumer goods on credit, taking advantage of attractive hire-purchase arrangements designed to encourage consumption. Hire-purchase was ideally suited to the aspirational nature of post-war consumerism, appealing to the materialistic daydreams of shoppers rather than to the values of respectability. According to a survey by the Oxford Institute of Statistics, at least a third of the more affluent working-class and lower-middle-class families were in 1953 buying durable goods on hire-purchase, as were a further 13 per cent of households headed by 'managers and technical workers'.[52] By 1956 half of all television sets and one-third of vacuum cleaners were being bought on hire-purchase credit. The contemporary writer Harry Hopkins reported that in his Oxford Street flagship shop the chairman of Great Universal Stores had opened a special lounge where hire-purchase customers could relax on 'contemporary settees' and watch large-screen televisions while the contracts for their furniture were drafted and signed. In 1947 Great Universal had made a profit of some £1.5 million; by 1957 that figure was more like £21.5 million. 'The whole nation', the chairman triumphantly informed his stockholders in 1958, 'has taken to buying nearly everything on the instalment plan.'[53]

Perhaps the most reliable indicator of consumer confidence, however, was the enthusiasm with which people rushed to take out mortgages and invest in their own homes. Building societies alone paid out over £544 million in 1960, representing an unparalleled 326,125 new mortgages.[54] One letter to *The Times* complained that this 'scramble in hire-purchase finance' was bound 'to entice more and more excursionists into the alluring but unhealthy Never-Never Land', a world in which they were 'persuaded by persons whom they do not know to enter into contracts that they do not understand to purchase goods they do not want with money they do not have'.[55] But the boom showed no sign of relenting. By the 1960s, the *Daily Mail*, always a barometer of middle-class opinion, was running a weekly financial supplement examining the claims of competing mortgages, overdrafts and life insurance packages, as well as discussing various kinds of stocks and shares. Even the *Mirror*, as we have seen, followed suit, providing its working-class readers with a City page with advice on investing all those saved earnings.[56]

Despite this welter of advice, many consumers were soon parted from their money by their less scrupulous fellows. By the early 1960s, rival mail-order companies like Colston, Duomatic and John Bloom's Rolls Razor were competing to offer household appliances at extremely cheap prices and with generous credit arrangements. At its peak, the Rolls Razor company sold six thousand Rapide washing machines a week and commanded almost a third of the market. Bloom had become a millionaire in just two years, at the age of twenty-eight, through the deceptively simple strategy of selling his washing machines cheaply and aggressively by direct-mail marketing. He ran advertisements presenting himself as 'Britain's youngest self-made industrialist' and the head of the 'Give-the-Housewife-Something-Extra-Movement', and turned himself into the personification of the opportunities of affluence.[57] He was even considered sufficiently respectable to have lunch with the Queen.[58] Unfortunately, disaster was not far around the corner. Bloom's competitors slashed their prices and in 1964 his company collapsed, leaving him to face prosecution and a fine of £30,000. The same newspapers that had once built up his myth as a self-made genius now solemnly proclaimed him a tragic example of materialistic hubris. 'Here was an ambitious young man', said the *New Statesman*, 'who grew up in the opportunity state and absorbed its atmosphere of unrestrained commercialism almost in the schoolroom . . . He has been taught to believe that the best employment for agile brains was to make a million before you were thirty . . . and he did it.'[59]

A more serious illustration of the potential for deception was the case of the self-styled Dr Emil Savundra, a notorious bogeyman of the mid-sixties. Savundra was a Ceylonese businessman and an experienced swindler who established in 1963 the Fire, Auto and Marine Insurance Company, an enterprise which claimed to use one of the world's most advanced computer systems to provide British motorists with cheap car insurance. Indeed, the company boasted that its rates bettered those of any competitor and that its computers could generate a policy in six seconds. Such publicity proved successful, and the benefits for Savundra were impressive. He funnelled large sums of the policyholders' money from Fire, Auto and Marine into a merchant bank in Liechtenstein that he himself had established, and then personally borrowed the money from the bank on extremely generous terms. By 1965 he was spending £13,000 a year in Harrods alone, running five Rolls-Royces, and lavishing money on a string of prostitutes; not for nothing did he triumphantly call himself 'God's own lounge lizard turned swindler'.[60] At the same time, he was ordering his staff to limit payments on insurance claims to £10,000 a week, a sign that all was not well with the scheme. In June 1966, after the publication of a book alleging wrongdoing at Fire, Auto and Marine, Savundra resigned from the company, and it promptly collapsed, leaving 45,000 unpaid claims and 400,000 customers without insurance. Despite the close attention of the newspapers, it turned out that the fraud laws were not sufficiently robust to secure a conviction.[61]

Savundra would probably have escaped justice altogether had it not been for his own outrageous self-assurance. At the beginning of 1967, the current-affairs television show *The Frost Programme* ran a thinly disguised sketch attacking Savundra's behaviour during the collapse of Fire, Auto and Marine. Savundra's response was to telephone the producers, congratulate them, and cheerfully accept their tentative invitation to appear on the show a week later. So it was that in February 1967 he duly appeared at the studios, full of what David Frost called 'towering self-confidence', and proceeded to insult an audience packed with his own victims, including widows whose husbands had been killed in car accidents and who were now left without insurance. Savundra beamed on as Frost described his depredations, agreed with the statement 'It's all fun to you, isn't it?', and when challenged by the furious widows, smoothly remarked: 'I am not going to cross swords with the peasants.' In one of the most vividly remembered television moments of the decade, Frost, barely able to conceal his contempt, asked 'one last question': 'You can look at these people here, widows, widowers, whoever they are, and you can feel, "I have no legal responsibility. And I have signed a piece of paper, and I have no moral responsibility either."' When Savundra nodded vigorously and replied, 'Right,' Frost then briefly apologised to camera and walked straight off the set in disgust.[62] This extraordinary confrontation reaped an instant reward; that very evening the Director of Public Prosecutions told the Fraud Squad to find some grounds to charge Savundra. At the ensuing trial the exotic, unrepentant financier collapsed in the dock on several occasions and had to be restrained from haranguing his own counsel, but was eventually sentenced to eight years in prison.[63]

If affluence brought new opportunities for entrepreneurs like Bloom and swindlers like Savundra, it also confirmed the attractions of the established chain stores of the thirties. In 1956 the changing patterns of consumer expenditure were officially recognised by the retail price index, which replaced old staples like sugar lumps, rabbits, candles and turnips with camera films, telephone rentals, dog food and nylon stockings. By the mid-sixties, the list had swollen to include sliced bread, fish fingers, jeans and scooters, all representative of the rapid transformation of everyday aspirations. In fact, high-street chain stores like Boots, W. H. Smith, Burton's and Woolworths had never been so prosperous, and the economic growth of the post-war years strengthened rather than threatened their control. In 1961 the chain stores accounted for 28 per cent of all retail sales; ten years later, the corresponding figure was 37 per cent. Many independent shopkeepers were finding it progressively harder to keep afloat; the chain stores, however, had never been more profitable or more popular.[64]

As wages and living standards increased, so did public interest in fashion, and the development of synthetic fabrics and cheap, colourful dyes encouraged shoppers to invest in bright new clothes for the affluent age. Women bought fuller, more colourful dresses; even men were tempted to abandon their old, heavy serge suits for lightweight jackets, blazers and slacks. There were few families in the country, except perhaps for the most isolated, who never visited one of the nearly three hundred outlets of Marks and Spencer for clothing and linen, and the company's profits quadrupled in the decade after 1948. Sir Simon Marks spent over half a million pounds annually on a large research and development department to predict the trends in everyday clothing before his competitors. His distinctive stores were designed to provide a sense of cool space and 'democratic good manners', an environment fit for 'doctor's wife and docker's wife', as one contemporary writer put it.[65] By contrast, fashionable boutiques like Mary Quant's shop Bazaar, which opened in Chelsea in 1955, remained exclusive enclaves for the rich and well connected; despite the classless rhetoric that surrounded such establishments, dockers' wives were rarely in evidence.[66]

The most important high-street innovation of the boom years was the supermarket. Until the 1950s, most housewives relied on a succession of daily or weekly home deliveries by milkmen, grocers' vans or boys on bicycles, having issued an order the day before if they wanted anything particular.[67] Food was kept covered in wire mesh on the shelves of a darkened pantry or larder situated on the cooler side of the kitchen, meaning that the housewife needed to make regular visits to the shops in order to replenish her perishable goods, a ritual of queue after queue in the butcher's, the baker's, the greengrocer's and so on, which though time-consuming and irksome inevitably strengthened a sense of local community. One woman later recalled that her mother 'went shopping every day – twice a day, sometimes', often for extremely small purchases like 'half an onion, or one apple'.[68] Shopkeepers and their assistants were often known by name to most of their customers, and in both villages and towns individual corner shops supplied the street with staple foods and gossip, the kind of shop nostalgically celebrated in the Ronnie Barker comedy *Open All Hours* some twenty years later. As one housewife put it: 'It was where you went to catch up with what was happening in the street. I was in there virtually every day, I'd always pick up something on the way home.'[69] It was this sense of intimacy that was lost with the arrival of supermarkets, although the vast majority of consumers evidently preferred the greater variety offered by the new leviathans.

The fifties were boom years for self-service stores and supermarkets. In 1947, according to one estimate, there were only ten self-service stores in the country. By 1956, there were three thousand; by 1962, there were twelve thousand; and by 1967, there were twenty-four thousand. Most of these shops, however, were too small to count as genuine supermarkets in the airy American manner. Britain's first real supermarket is generally held to have been a branch of Sainsbury's in Croydon, which in 1950 introduced 'Q-less' shopping as a response to the privations of austerity. Thick sheets of Perspex left over from the manufacture of bombers protected fresh food displays from flies and inquisitive children, and perishable foods were kept in refrigerated cabinets. By contrast, the supermarkets of the affluent fifties were much more luxurious establishments. It was expensive to build and equip a new supermarket in the desired clean, functional style: construction costs might reach £100,000, not to mention the cost of piling it high with goods. But, since each outlet could expect some twenty thousand customers a week, the endless ring of the cash registers more than compensated for the original outlay.[70] In 1960, there were 367 supermarkets in Britain; seven years later, there were nearly three thousand.[71] Although customers regretted the demise of their local shops with their homely atmosphere, they admired the efficiency, convenience and variety of the new stores. 'The vastness, the choice, you had everything there,' one woman recalled of the Bristol Co-op. 'There was all this fresh fish on display like Harrods, a counter with all the cheeses from around the world like you've never seen before in a corner shop, all this beautiful fruit from around the globe.'[72]

As the fifties progressed, the weekly expedition to the supermarket began to replace the daily trips to the corner shop or the village high street, especially if housewives enjoyed the luxury of a refrigerator. Even so, many families were reluctant to change either their purchases or their daily diet. One interviewee, a small boy in the 1950s, told Alison Pressley forty years later:

> If you asked me what I had for dinner on the first Monday in 1950 and last Friday in 1959, I would be able to tell you. Because Sunday was a beef joint, with a monumental, plate-size Yorkshire pudding filled to the brim with gravy; Monday was cold beef and Tuesday was beef stew. Wednesday was sausages and mash; Thursday was rabbit pie. Friday was fish . . . and Saturday was sandwiches, eaten on the run before the football match or the cricket.

This was fairly typical. Other children of the fifties interviewed for a different project remembered similar routines, beginning with a roast on Sunday and cold leftovers the next day and differing only in minor particulars, maybe with liver and bacon or faggots replacing some other staple dish. 'Tuesday would be bubble and squeak,' one Lancashire woman recalled, 'Wednesday was market day so there'd be something like boiled ham, Thursday was sausages and Friday was fish and chips.'[73] They were the fortunate ones; another interviewee reported only eating one meal throughout the fifties, 'mince and mashed potatoes, with stewed apple and custard for pudding'.[74]

All the same, the affluence of the post-war years naturally introduced gentle alterations to the standard menu. Chicken, for instance, had previously been a relative luxury, reserved for Christmas or Easter; now, cheaper and more readily available, it began to rival beef, lamb and pork on Sunday dinner tables and a total of twenty million broiler chickens was sold during the 1950s.[75] But it was, above all, convenience that was central to the marketing of food during the period, and precisely the same appeal that encouraged housewives to buy washing machines and electric irons was used to promote the refrigerator and the sliced white loaf. 'There's room inside to take a banquet', declared the advertisement for a New English Refrigerator. 'You can do your week's shopping in a day . . . here is the refrigerator to give you a fresh interest in food, more fun and more leisure.'[76] Convenience foods, processed or canned and ready to be reheated, had first become popular in the inter-war years; indeed, the food-processing industry had been one of the success stories of the 1930s.[77] This trend continued in the late fifties, with pre-war favourites like baked beans and tins of salmon or pineapple encountering new rivals in the shape of frozen foods: initially frozen peas, and then, from 1955 and to great excitement, frozen fish fingers.[78] Sales of frozen foods doubled between 1955 and 1957, and then doubled again in the following three years. By the end of the decade even little corner shops boasted their own freezers packed with fish fingers, frozen chips, peas and ice cream.[79]

So, despite the fact that British families were consuming more fresh foods – milk, eggs, cheese, meat and vegetables – than ever before, they were also drawn to the flashy modernity of convenience foods. In 1963 even the magazine *Good Housekeeping* yielded and gave its approval to such happy innovations as Batchelor's boil-in-the-bag curries, tinned steak and kidney pies, prepared meat in papier-mâché trays, and the delightful 'pizza in a bag'.[80] The most popular convenience food of all was the humble and perfectly square sliced white loaf, an innovation that proved tremendously popular with housewives who had been, as one put it, 'forever hacking at a loaf with a half-blunt knife'. By the end of the 1960s no fewer than forty-two million sliced white loaves were being sold a year. Another contender was the tea bag, launched in 1952 and vigorously marketed by Tetley's with great success, so that by the sixties it commanded three-quarters of the national tea market. Self-conscious sophisticates might drink instant Nescafé, introduced in 1960; children preferred fizzy drinks, or 'pop', another success story from the inter-war years and one that acquired new lustre with the popularity of new brands like Tizer, Vimto and Irn-Bru (all initially marketed as health drinks), and American imports such as Pepsi and Coca-Cola. Although tea was still widely recognised as the national drink, even as a symbol of national identity, it no longer went unchallenged.[81]

The crowning glory of the affluent household was not the television, the fridge or even the washing machine; it was the car. The 'motoring revolution', like many other developments associated with the affluent society, was based on pre-war trends. In 1919 there had been just 100,000 private cars on British roads, almost exclusively driven by the wealthy; twenty years later there were two million, supported by an infrastructure of by-passes, car parks, traffic lights, pedestrian crossings, transport cafés and roomy new roadside pubs.[82] Indeed, motorised transport had an enormous impact on British society between the 1920s and the 1970s. It brought dramatic changes to the British landscape, both in towns and in the shires; it promised new social and career opportunities; and it widened geographical horizons, exposing people to parts of their own country that would otherwise have been merely names on a map. The car allowed youngsters to escape the limiting world of their local communities, and suburban families to escape into the fresh air of the countryside; and it represented the increasing privatisation of leisure, with families preferring to amuse themselves alone rather than rely on the local community to provide entertainment, as had been the case in the world of charabancs and works outings.[83]

The car was a symbol not merely of affluence but of status. One woman recalled of her childhood in Lancashire during the early 1950s that the family car was treated 'just like the Crown Jewels', coming out only 'once a week, on a Sunday. Dad would take us all out for a spin, then wash it and put it in the garage again.'[84] At this point a car was still a relative luxury, but by 1960 some 28 per cent of households had one, rising to 37 per cent in 1965 and 45 per cent in 1969. While most men might aspire to drive a Vauxhall, a Humber or a Jaguar, they were more likely to drive one of the cheaper family cars, perhaps a Ford Popular, an Austin Seven or a Morris Minor.[85] Long journeys on Britain's narrow, winding roads remained something of an ordeal, with frequent traffic jams, and safety was still a serious concern, since there were no speed limits on country roads and no seat belts. But the car's attractions were irresistible. In 1955 there were 3.6 million; in 1965 there were nearly 9 million, crowding the often cramped and winding roads through town and countryside.[86] And as car ownership increased, so its potential as a democratising force became more obvious. 'Once I acquired a car,' one Cornishman recalled, 'out came the map and we were able to go places that we'd only dreamed of before . . . it was possible to go to the Lake District and Scotland, it was like going to a foreign land. You were seeing things that you'd read about in a book.'[87]

Meanwhile the railways, hitherto so important to the social and economic life of the nation, fell into steep decline. At the beginning of the fifties they had still been making a profit, but by 1960 British Railways showed a loss of £68 million, slumping to £104 million in 1962. A year later the head of the British Transport Commission, Dr Richard Beeching, announced his plan to dismantle 5000 miles of track, close 2359 local stations and get rid of 160,000 jobs in seven years.[88] Since many people were sentimentally attached to the railways as the symbol of Victorian enterprise, this scheme provoked fierce public opposition, but it went ahead anyway. Public transport in rural areas was slashed to the bone, with the burden being shifted on to the roads, and few historians now have much time for Beeching's cuts. 'It all meant a vast change in the quality of British life', one observer later wrote forlornly, 'with crumbling railway embankments shorn of rails and sleepers and overcrowded roads epitomising the disappearance of the heritage of the Industrial Revolution that had made Britain great.'[89]

Contemporary observers associated the affluent society above all with suburbia, but, as far as many intellectuals were concerned, this was far from a compliment. Middle-class families had been moving from the cities into the suburban fringes ever since the early nineteenth century, providing plenty of material for writers who mocked the suburbs and their bourgeois inhabitants as intellectually narrow, cautious, conformist, materialistic and, above all, boring.[90] At the end of the thirties, one commentator wrote:

> Which of us, on hearing that a person is 'suburban', does not instantly conjure up an over-eager half-sir who talks of 'the wife' and . . . mows a ridiculous lawn on Sunday afternoons, while his wife, saying 'pleased to meet you', sets out 'the preserves' on a d'oyley before her whist party? And the fact that in these days of high taxation and monstrous rents the suburbs are just as likely to house an eminent professor of Greek and a deposed monarch . . . makes no difference at all, and probably never will.[91]

To their critics, the 'appalling monotony, ugliness and dullness' of Slough, Wimbledon and Letchworth were antithetical to traditional British ideas of the organic, localised and hierarchical community.[92] The suburban experience was blamed for the depressing meaninglessness of modern life: a doctor writing in the *Lancet* in 1938 even identified a condition he called 'sub-urban neurosis', a sense of rootless fear, insecurity and isolation.[93] In George Orwell's novel *Coming Up for Air*, published the following year, the lower-middle-class narrator George Bowling grumbles about the festering frustration of his suburban environment: 'the stucco front, the creosoted gate, the privet hedge, the green front door. The Laurels, the Myrtles, the Hawthorns, Mon Abri, Mon Repos, Belle Vue . . . Just a prison with the cells all in a row. A line of semidetached torture-chambers where the poor little five-to-ten-pound-a-weekers quake and shiver, every one of them with the boss twisting his tail and his wife riding him like the nightmare and the kids sucking his blood like leeches.'[94]

As suburbs and New Towns spread across the countryside in the decades that followed, from Scotland to the south coast, the anti-suburban con-tempt of the intellectuals reached a new peak of intensity. To novelists like Angus Wilson or Penelope Mortimer, or to the playwright John Osborne, 'suburban' meant base, cheap, commercial, venal, heartless, mediocre, materialistic, unimaginative and banal; indeed, as the critic D. J. Taylor remarks, it is startling to discover 'the degree of hatred which invests the use of a word like "suburban" in the English novel of the 1950s and 1960s . . . It is as though moral worth were attainable only by people living in city ten-ements or on blasted heaths.'[95] The suburban ring fifteen miles from the centre of London was the fastest-growing area in the country, and in 1955 the *Architectural Review* warned: 'By the end of the century, Great Britain will consist of isolated oases of preserved monuments in a desert of wire, con-crete roads, cosy plots and bungalows.'[96] This was what the architect Iain Nairn called 'a universal subtopia, a mean and middle state, neither town nor country . . . a universal condition which spreads both ways from sub-urbia'.[97] In a society where many intellectuals felt deeply uneasy with the social and economic changes of affluence, the apocalyptic idea of 'subtopia' quickly caught on, and the Ministry of Housing found itself continually replying to charges that it was turning Britain into an enormous subtopian desert.[98]

At the end of the decade, suburbia was as disreputable as ever. In 1957 two sociologists working at the new Institute of Community Studies, Peter Willmott and Michael Young, published a survey of the working-class dis-trict of Bethnal Green which became a bestseller under the title *Family and Kinship in East London*. Bethnal Green, they found, was 'not so much a crowd of individuals – restless, lonely, rootless – as an orderly community based on family and neighbourhood groupings'. The implication, and the lesson drawn by many of the readers who flocked to buy the subsequent Penguin edition, was that middle-class suburbia could never match Bethnal Green's organic networks of families and friends, and was therefore doomed to be a wasteland of solitude and insecurity.[99] It was little accident that at the same time that Willmott and Young were celebrating the old-fashioned virtues of Bethnal Green's narrow streets, hospital psychiatrists in Crawley New Town were diagnosing 'Crawley neurosis', an 'emotional disturbance' supposed to be affecting women who found it difficult to cope with the transition from the warmth and bonhomie of inner London to the cold, lonely world of the New Town.[100]

As Willmott and Young later discovered, however, the condition of 'suburban blues' was little more than a snobbish myth. Although a small minority of housewives initially found it difficult to make friends in their new surroundings, sociological surveys consistently found that people were very happy with their suburban lives.[101] In one sample of 166 working-class respondents who had moved out of the centre of Birmingham, sixty-six were 'very glad' to have moved, thirty-two were 'quite glad', eleven were 'rather sorry' and thirty-six were 'very sorry'.[102] In 1956, questioning a group of Oxford families who had been moved from the poor district of St Ebbe's to the new Barton estate, a sociologist found that barely one in ten now had a good word for St Ebbe's. 'It's like heaven after what we've been used to,' one man said of his new estate. 'People today don't know of the times when we had to live in old broken down houses because we could afford nothing better. But today we are given nice little houses to live in.'[103]

The classic study of suburban life at the end of the decade was *Family and Class in a London Suburb*, another survey carried out by Willmott and Young between 1957 and 1959. The suburb in question was the borough of Wanstead and Woodford, a hitherto anonymous borough of some 61,000 people in Essex. Like many of the rural villages of Surrey and Essex, Woodford had been transformed in the nineteenth century by the railway and then in the inter-war years by arterial development, and its old identity as a farming community had been lost in the conversion to a modern commuter village.[104] Even further east into Essex, rural villages connected to Liverpool Street for the first time by the newly electrified Eastern Region lines were attracting developers keen to build new estates of detached commuter homes. What Woodford offered, then, was a fairly typical and unexceptional slice of suburban life, and for the two sociologists it proved fertile territory.[105]

Wilmott and Young originally expected to find that the 'warmth and friendliness' that they had found in Bethnal Green had no equivalent in a middle-class commuter suburb, where the people were supposed to be frustrated, selfish and lonely.[106] But what they discovered was precisely the opposite. 'People in the suburb', they concluded, 'are on the whole friendly, neighbourly and helpful to each other. They attend churches and clubs together, they entertain friends and neighbours in their homes, they like (or at any rate they profess to like) their fellow-residents.'[107] Some of their 1149 respondents, particularly among the older generation, did regret the transformation from village to suburb; one old resident complained that the hedges and trees were gone, and that the traffic and high buildings made it impossible to hear the church bells.[108] But the incontrovertible fact was that the world of the suburban middle classes was no less cheerful or contented than that of inner London. Barely a tenth of those interviewed thought their neighbours were 'standoffish'; most found them 'easy to get on with'. A certain Mrs Sankey explained: 'They're very friendly around this district', and a Mrs Noble remarked: 'There's a very friendly spirit. I think it's a wonderful community in this part.' As the authors noted: 'This in contradiction to a fashionable stereotype of the suburb — anxious, footloose migrants, somehow keeping themselves to themselves and yet up with the Jones's. The people of Woodford felt they belonged to a friendly, helpful community almost as unanimously as the people of Bethnal Green.'[109]

What was more, it turned out to be the municipal housing estate of Bethnal Green that was more unfriendly to newcomers, even after they had been there for five or six years. 'The kind of people who move into the suburb', the survey reported, 'mostly into houses of their own, seem to have no difficulty in getting to know each other and making friends.' Mrs Jackson remembered that the day she moved in, 'the lady opposite — whom I'd never seen before in my life — told the milkman to leave a pint of milk and call back at dinner-time to see what we wanted'. Mr Matthews proudly reported that his wife 'endeavours to entertain new people whenever they arrive. If anyone new comes to live on this estate, they're invited to one of her coffee evenings.' Walking the dog, taking the children to school and the daily routine of shopping all provided an opportunity for newcomers to meet and befriend their suburban neighbours.[110] The people of the British suburb, the very people who most epitomised the affluence and materialism of the fifties, were not quite the peripatetic, envious neurotics of sociological myth. Certainly they were ambitious, and despite their different backgrounds were 'more and more striving to earn more and spend it on the same things, in and around the home and the little car that goes with it'. Yet the result was not neurosis, but apparent contentment with the reality of suburban domesticity, 'the little province within it where husband and wife exercise their joint dominion'. As one housewife remarked:

> I often feel at the end of the day that all my efforts have been of no avail. I remember all the polishing and cleaning, washing and ironing, that will have to be done all over again, and like many other housewives I wish that my life could be a little more exciting sometimes. But when the evening fire glows, when the house becomes a home, then it seems to me that this is perhaps the path to true happiness.[111]

*

For all the exciting possibilities of the affluent society, popular culture in the middle 1950s was surprisingly similar to entertainment before the Second World War. Leisure time had been increasing for decades, thanks to shorter hours, paid holidays, smaller families and longer life expectancy, and the growth of the cinema, broadcasting, national sport and national newspapers meant that Britain was moving from a network of often isolated cultures based on class and region towards 'a more uniform and homogeneous society, partaking of an increasingly common culture'.[112] The British read more newspapers and periodicals than any of their American or European counterparts with the exception of the Swedes. They preferred national publications to regional ones, and they liked them written in a chatty, conversational style that horrified foreign observers used to the sententious self-importance of *Le Monde* or the *New York Times*. But this evidently made commercial sense: indeed, the British devoured nearly twice as many newspapers per head as their American cousins, despite the fact that American papers were much bigger.

The most popular daily paper was the *Daily Mirror*, which at the end of the fifties was selling almost five million copies a day, keenly followed by the *Express* (4.3 million), the *Mail* (2.6 million), the *Herald* (1.4 million) and the *Telegraph* (1.2 million).[113] The *Mirror*'s recipe for success, carefully nurtured by its chairman Cecil Harmsworth King and its editor Hugh Cudlipp, was a heady brew of 'bite-sized news, crime, sensationalism, astrology, sentiment, social conscience and sex', and it appealed predominantly to working-class readers.[114] By contrast, the *Express* was a more self-consciously respectable paper, and it was also the paper that best captured the attitudes and aspirations of Macmillan's affluent middle-class electorate. Sunday newspapers, meanwhile, were even more popular: nowhere in Europe or the United States was there a publication to match the *News of the World*, with its 6.6 million readers, or even the *People* (5.5 million), the *Sunday Pictorial* (5.4 million) or the *Sunday Express* (4.5 million). If we add to that the enormous weekly sales of the *Radio Times* and *TV Times*, which reached tens of millions, not to mention other magazines and cheap paperbacks, then it is clear that the British were indeed, as McKibbin suggests, a 'people of the book'.[115]

The most popular and important recreation of all was the trip to the cinema; as one historian puts it, 'going to the pictures was the country's principal extra-domestic leisure activity, and in the degree to which it was practised England had no peer'.[116] The 'dream palace' had caught the public imagination before the Second World War as a haven of cheap escapism from the rigours of the Depression, and it was also the model of the new mass culture that was beginning to unite different classes and regions, with the same films 'as likely to be shown near Land's End as near John O'Groats'.[117] By the end of the war there were nearly five thousand cinemas across the United Kingdom, of which the largest were closely tied to American studios. ABC picture houses, for example, were owned by Warner and MGM, and the Odeon and Gaumont cinemas were linked, through the Rank film empire, to Twentieth Century Fox.[118] The principal attraction of the picture house, as in the thirties, was to find a temporary release from daily pressures. 'The cinema was pure escapism, you could lose yourself in it,' one Bristol woman, who attended up to four times a week, recalled. 'It was uplifting, it was a different lifestyle. And when you came out you treated yourself to a bag of chips on the way home.'[119] At the beginning of the fifties it was calculated that the average Englishman or woman went to the pictures twenty-eight times a year, representing a tenth of the total global audience and, per capita, the highest proportion in the world.[120] Children, meanwhile, attended the cinema in overwhelming numbers. Nine children in every ten made regular visits, with more than five going at least once a week. Saturday morning matinees showed cartoons and gentle adventure stories, and special children's cinema clubs arranged demonstrations of hula-hoops, yo-yos and other childhood crazes. In 1955, more than a million children attended a weekly cinema club.[121]

Much of British social life and leisure in the years after the war was organised around similar clubs, especially in middle-class areas like the suburb of Woodford where many residents were relatively new to the neighbourhood. For decades the British had been notorious for their love of clubs; a well-known French quip from the late nineteenth century had it that if two Englishmen were stranded on a desert island, their first move would be to form a club.[122] Church youth clubs, for example, were a popular source of entertainment for older children and teenagers during the fifties, irrespective of their religious convictions. 'It was terribly innocent,' recalled one regular visitor, 'but we had fabulous times there, just sitting about nattering about or playing badminton, cards or table tennis.'[123] Youth clubs might lay on lemonade, sandwiches and biscuits, organise dances and competitions, or arrange educational excursions and weekend outings. They were also notoriously conservative: as late as 1960, a youth club leader in Huddersfield with six years' experience was dismissed for allowing his charges to play billiards, table tennis and darts and listen to rock and roll music. Modern entertainments like these were evidently not considered proper. Instead, as the County Youth Service explained, 'the teenagers should be encouraged to take part in handicrafts, classical music and could enter the drama festivals we organise'.[124]

This emphasis on order and organisation had its parallel in adult social life, which was structured along similar lines. In a survey of Banbury in the late fifties, Margaret Stacey found that seventy-one voluntary associations, not including formal religious and political bodies, competed for the allegiance of twenty thousand townspeople. These clubs varied 'from a sweet pea society to a rugger club, from university lectures to tropical fish keeping, from charitable organizations to trade unions', neatly stratified along recognisable class lines.[125] This was not unusual: the official guide to Woodford boasted of its 'wealth of organizations and amenities devoted to the development of every aspect of social life', and listed a total of 142 different clubs and associations in an area of 61,000 people.[126] These included women's clubs like the Women's Institute, the Women's Gas Federation, the Townswomen's Guild, the Young Wives' League and the Women's Section of the Conservative Party, without counting informal knitting or coffee circles. Men might belong to the golf club, the bowls club, the Conservative Club, the Essex Bee-Keepers Association or the Rotary Club; couples could join the Parent–Teacher Association, the tennis or badminton club, or church clubs; and those with particular interests might be tempted by the

Floral Arrangements Group, the Monkhams Singers, the Knighton Players, the Snaresbrook Ladies Hockey Club, the Archery Association or the Snaresbrook Riding School.[127]

Clubs were a means not merely of meeting new people but of ordering and controlling social life; they varied in their formality, from the casual intimacy of a coffee circle to the careful hierarchies of the Women's Institute, which in Woodford boasted a drama group, a choir, a reading group, a Shakespeare circle, a produce group, a handicrafts section and an icing class.[128] Most social surveys of the period suggested that the affluent middle classes were much more likely to join clubs and associations than their poorer neighbours.[129] Over half of the middle-class respondents to the Woodford survey were members of clubs, with over a third attending regularly; by contrast, two-thirds of the working-class interviewees had not joined clubs, whether for reasons of time, expense or simply a more informal attitude to sociability.[130]

All the same, there were still plenty of working-class clubs. Most mining villages and industrial communities boasted a selection of brass bands, and although bowls was regarded as an old man's game, it was nevertheless extremely popular. When Brian Jackson visited Huddersfield in the late fifties, he calculated that it had thirty-three different bowling clubs and some five thousand regular players, which meant that bowls was by far the most popular participatory sport in the town.[131] Millions of men still went to a working men's club at lunchtime or in the evening for a pint and a game of dominoes; most clubs organised coach trips to the races or a seaside resort, and many now made provision for women and children, too. 'The clubs remain as organizations of working men,' wrote Brian Jackson, 'embodying, strengthening and passing on their style of living. They are little touched by the mass media, little noticed by the upper sections of society.' But with more than two million members at the end of the sixties, the working men's clubs played a vital and enduring role in the lives of the British working classes.[132]

Despite the enduring popularity of working men's clubs, people drank less. Beer production had been steadily falling since the Edwardian era; fewer people considered themselves pub regulars, and even on a Saturday night no more than 15 per cent of the adult population visited their local public house. As the range of alternative entertainments expanded, so the position of the pub became ever weaker. People gambled, watched football, cricket or boxing, played bowls, golf or tennis, went motoring, cycling or walking, read or played board games at home, and, above all, went to the pictures or to the dance hall. In 1957 a Gallup poll found that almost nine in ten people had listened to the radio in the previous week, while two in three had watched television. Knitting, gardening, needlework and reading were similarly popular, and in 1962 a survey suggested that three in every four households took the trouble to fill in a weekly football pools coupon.[133]

These were overwhelmingly private pleasures, and the pioneering market researcher Mark Abrams devoted a BBC radio talk in November 1959 to 'The Home-Centred Society', arguing that the domestication of leisure was also marked by the 'domestication of the husband'.[134] No fewer than thirty thousand pubs closed down between 1939 and 1962, and those that remained open were struggling to attract a different kind of customer. Many developed 'lounge bars', dining rooms, games rooms and beer gardens to attract younger couples, women and families, and new establishments tended to be built on suburban fringes or along major roads rather than in working-class city neighbourhoods.[135] The obvious parallel was with the decline of the church; an opinion poll on Sunday observance found that while two in three people had listened to the radio and one in two had watched television, only one in seven said that they had gone to church.[136] Religious belief remained fairly constant in the post-war years: polls found that about half of the population believed in life after death, the divinity of Christ and the Virgin Birth, and three-quarters believed in a supernatural God.[137] Religious observance, however, was a different matter, and Protestant church membership in particular was in steep decline. Like their old rivals, the pubs, Britain's churches did not find the affluent society a happy hunting ground.[138]

For the leisure industry, on the other hand, the combination of spare time and rising wages was a great blessing. At least one million people regularly amused themselves with various kinds of self-assembled boats, creating 'a whole bobbing world of small boatery on rivers, coastal waters, lakes, reservoirs and gravel pits'. Two million, especially men and teenage boys, spent their weekends by rivers and lakes in the solemn pursuit of fish, and more than a hundred thousand regularly bought the *Angling Times*.[139] Local amateur dramatic societies flourished, and Birmingham alone boasted nearly two hundred. There were nearly three thousand amateur football teams taking the field in Sunday leagues; five million people went dancing every week and patronised five thousand dancing schools, 450 Palais,

Locarnos and Meccas and two thousand informal dance halls.[140] Speedway was a popular spectator sport, second only to football; it attracted six million observers annually and boasted a track in almost every large town. In cities like Birmingham and Coventry, where the motorcycles were actually manufactured, there was tremendous interest in the thrilling speed and excitement of speedway races.[141] Men played darts, kept pigeons, watched dog racing and tended their vegetables; women danced, sang, knitted, and read. Writing in 1957, the cultural critic Richard Hoggart noted that there were some 250 regular periodicals devoted to hobbies and entertainments, from *Angler's News* and *Popular Gardening* to *Bird Fancy* and *Cycling*. 'There are two on the breeding of pet fish,' he reported, 'seven on domestic pets and cage-birds, one on bell-ringing, ten on aspects of fishing, several cycling papers and dog papers, and almost two dozen on general aspects of hobbies and handicrafts.'[142]

Even the increasing popularity of pets reflected a trend already under way before the war, when the growing importance of domesticity had combined with better housing and higher income and launched something of a pet boom. Working-class households had their whippets and pigeons; middle-class families, with bigger houses and gardens, could afford bigger dogs or cats. After the war no family was complete without some domestic animal or bird. In 1957, according to Hoggart, there were almost half a million pigeon-fanciers in the country, organised in a thousand Homing Clubs and racing their beloved birds every weekend.[143] The number of pedigree dogs doubled between 1945 and 1960, and the Tailwaggers' Club boasted a million members, each with a badge proclaiming the dog's rank as a Staff Sergeant, Corporal or Private. Supermarkets stocked bright and cheery ranges of dog and cat food with snappy names like Wow, Woof, Kit-e-Kat and Pussikin; in the mid-fifties, the pet food industry enjoyed an annual turnover of £10 million, and had reached £23 million by 1962.[144] The fashionable pets of the 1950s, though, were tropical fish and caged birds. Middle-class families were already able to keep goldfish in garden ponds; the increasing popularity and availability of the aquarium, however, allowed poorer households to keep fish of their own. Budgerigars were especially popular, maintained in elaborate, if restrictive, cages in lavish style. In the ten years after the war the budgerigar population of Britain grew tenfold, reaching six million in 1956; there were even more budgerigars than dogs. Budgerigars, unlike dogs, were liable to escape at any moment, and Hopkins remarked that a 'poignant feature of the suburbs' was the omnipresence of mournful, tattered notices appealing for the return of a family favourite.[145] But cats held on to their pre-eminent position in the domestic jungle: one in five families had a dog, and one in four a bird; but one in every three retained the services of a cat.[146]

Hobbies and diversions thrived during the fifties and sixties because there was more free time. Indeed, one in four people told Gallup's interviewers that they were 'sometimes at a loss what to do' with all their spare time, and only two in five said they would like more time off work.[147] The two-day weekend was almost universal, and in 1959 a study found that ninety-nine out of a hundred industrial companies offered their workers two weeks' paid holiday.[148] It was hardly surprising, then, that the holiday industry was booming as never before. This was the heyday of the traditional seaside resort, of piers, postcards and Punch and Judy. Railway stations in July and August were often packed with hundreds, even thousands, of people waiting for a train to the coast.[149] In working-class areas, it was still common for an entire community to decamp en masse to the seaside, where whole streets might commandeer a stretch of the beach, and most people tended to return to the same boarding house, year after year. Southend and Brighton attracted holidaymakers from London; Rhyl and Weston-super-Mare were perennial favourites in the West Midlands; and Skegness and Mablethorpe drew visitors from eastern England. Further north, people from the textile towns of Lancashire and the north-west headed for Blackpool; families from Yorkshire went to Scarborough and Whitby; and Glaswegians made for resorts like Saltcoats on Scotland's west coast. Class distinctions played their part, too. On one coast, Scarborough was regarded as much more genteel than Bridlington; on the other, Southport and Morecambe generally attracted wealthier visitors than did the great working-class Mecca, Blackpool, which already had a reputation for noisy high jinks and sexual excess. This was all part of its appeal: throughout the fifties and early sixties, Blackpool was easily the most popular resort in the country, regularly attracting a phenomenal seven million visitors a year.[150]

The only real competition with the seaside resorts in the mid-fifties came from organised holiday camps, many of which had first begun to attract large numbers of holidaymakers in the 1930s. Many people preferred the structured ethos of the camps to the more chaotic world of the seaside, and by the late fifties the most famous organisation, Butlin's, ran nine camps and catered for sixty thousand guests (or 'campers') a week.[151] 'You Make New

Friends At Butlin's – Where You Will Meet the Kind of People You'd Like to Meet', declared one advertisement from the era, showing a bronzed Adonis inspecting a beaming beauty at the edge of the swimming pool.[152] Indeed, like the seaside resorts, holiday camps were widely regarded as excellent places for romantic adventure, and Friday nights in the ballroom were notorious for their sexual frolics and jealous brawls. But the camps' real selling point was their range of entertainments, organised by Redcoats, Bluecoats and Greencoats in an unrelenting timetable of competitions and activities. Campers could choose from a timetable that might include bingo, billiards, ballroom dancing, swimming, cabarets and sack races, and there were prizes for everything from Holiday Princess and Lovely Legs to Knobbly Knees and Shiniest Bald Head. Philishave sponsored a Shaver of the Week competition, while Rizla offered a prize for the best Cigarette Roller. Although the general tone of compulsory bawdiness evidently went down well with most campers, a minority considered that there was a thin dividing line between the holiday camp and the prison camp. As one account puts it: 'If you didn't like team spirit, then you were in the wrong place.'[153]

Both the seaside resorts and the holiday camps of the fifties preserved a tradition of working-class variety that otherwise seemed to be disappearing from British cultural life. The music halls had never recovered from the licensing restrictions of the Great War and the competition from the cinema. Some of the biggest halls, such as the Holborn Empire, had been destroyed in the Blitz, although the *Stage Year Book* estimated in 1949 that there were still over three hundred Hippodrome or Alhambra variety theatres and music halls in England and Wales, with eighty-nine in London.[154] George Formby and Gracie Fields were still household names, but they were growing old. Both had consciously emphasised their roots in working-class industrial England; they reflected a long tradition of proletarian bawdiness, which united performers and audience in the same love of costumes, jokes and song, the same wry political cynicism and the same cheerful and vigorous patriotism.[155] Most contemporary observers thought that their world had passed. 'The music hall is dying,' wrote the playwright John Osborne, 'and with it, a significant part of England. Some of the heart of England is gone; something that once belonged to everyone, for this was truly a folk art.'[156] But reports of the death of music hall were greatly exaggerated. Not only did resorts like Blackpool and Margate still put on variety shows to entertain working-class holidaymakers, but most towns had annual Christmas pantomimes that repeated many of the old routines. Above all, radio, television and film comedy preserved the stereotypes and customs of the Edwardian performers, so that, even twenty or thirty years later, popular entertainments like the *Morecambe and Wise Show*, *The Two Ronnies* or the *Carry On* films had all the bawdy vigour and colour of pre-war music hall. Indeed, the title of one television show, *Sunday Night at the London Palladium*, made explicit this link with the Edwardian past. Even in popular music the legacy of the music hall lived on, reflected later in the sixties in the songs of the Beatles, the Kinks and their imitators.[157]

The new stars of post-war British entertainment were to be found not in the music hall but in the cinema. So enfeebled was the domestic film industry by comparison with the giants of California that a series of attempts between 1947 and 1950 to restrain the American juggernaut, whether by import duties or by quotas, ended in ignominious failure, and British film-makers were under tremendous pressure to imitate their American counterparts.[158] One example of the new kind of star was the buxom Diana Dors, promoted in the mid-fifties as the British answer to Marilyn Monroe. Born Diana Fluck in Swindon in 1931, she broke through to fame and fortune in *Lady Godiva Rides Again* (1951), which became notorious when the American censors objected to the film's alleged bawdiness and demanded that her navel be covered for transatlantic projection. For a brief period in the mid-fifties, Dors was seen as a viable alternative to the glamorous stars of Hollywood; in 1956 she was the country's highest-paid film star and was voted the Variety Club's Personality of the Year. Her appeal, which swiftly evaporated after she moved to California and became involved in a string of turbulent affairs, was founded on what Raymond Durgnat called 'the happy rendezvous of old vulgarity and new affluence'.[159] Her cheeky, friendly working-class persona struck a chord with many ordinary audiences; she was not that different, after all, from Formby or Fields. What *was* different, though, was that Dors reflected the new aspirational materialism of the 1950s rather than the comfortable conservatism of the music hall. She was brash, brassy and bottle-blonde, and her ambition for wealth and celebrity embodied an exuberance that in the mid-fifties seemed more properly American than British. So the temporary success of Diana Dors as a self-consciously Americanised film star emphasises the influence in the early fifties not only of Hollywood films and fashions, but also of idealised ideas of American affluence, freedom and social mobility.

Few people doubted the influence of American fashions on impression-able British cinemagoers. As one librarian put it: 'I do sit and sigh for the kind of clothes Ginger Rogers and Lana Turner wear and would also be influenced by the Hollywood home with the pretty curtains and marvellous kitchens if Mr Dalton [her husband] would let me be.'[160] A study of teenage girls in 1953 noted 'the amazing extent to which the minutiae of the clothes and hair arrangements of an American actress may affect the spending habits of a child in a mining village in Durham or a girl in a tenement in central London'.[161] The American servicemen stationed in Britain during the war, with their glossy magazines, swing music, cigarettes and chewing gum, had left an indelible impression, and in the following decade American influence seemed to have reached its peak. As Harry Hopkins put it a few years later:

> From hula-hoops to Zen Buddhism, from do-it-yourself to laun-derettes or the latest sociological catch-phrase or typographical trick, from Rock 'n' Roll to Action Painting, barbecued chickens rotating on their spits in the shop windows to parking meters, clearways, bowling alleys, glass-skyscrapers, flying saucers, pay-roll raids, armoured trucks and beatniks, American habits and vogues now crossed the Atlantic with a speed and certainty that suggested that Britain was now merely one more offshore island.[162]

In the spring of 1948, for instance, with London gripped by austerity, no fewer than three new Broadway musicals in *Bless the Bride*, *Oklahoma!* and *Annie Get Your Gun* opened in the West End, eclipsing their British rivals and capti-vating over two million people over the next few years. Given the success of conventional dramas like *A Streetcar Named Desire* and *Death of a Salesman*, it appeared that 'in theatrical terms at least Britain was now on the way to becoming the 49th State'.[163]

Some younger intellectuals equated the United States with modernity, democracy and affluence, and adored all things American with a passion that approached fawning idolatry. 'The very air of America', enthused the critic Bernard Bergonzi, 'seems more highly charged, more oxygenated, than the atmosphere in England.'[164] But they were in a minority and, even though most ordinary people enjoyed American entertainments, they gen-erally disliked Americans themselves. During the war, the American forces stationed in Britain had been regarded with deep suspicion. In 1942, Gallup had found that the Soviet Union was almost three times as popular as the United States, and even after the onset of the Cold War ordinary Britons frequently expressed their contempt for their American allies.[165] According to a Mass Observation survey a few years later, most people thought of Americans as oversized children, being 'immature emotionally and intellectually . . . boastful and flamboyant, bad mannered and full of intolerance to any minority group'.[166] Indeed, visiting Americans were often amazed by their frosty reception. The London correspondent of the magazine *Newsweek* estimated that one in three Englishmen was 'more or less antagonistic to anything that came from America, from Buicks to businessmen', and in June 1953 a feature in the *New York Times Magazine* warned visitors to London to expect anti-American feeling 'in Conservative as well as Labour circles', 'the popular press' and 'the theatre where any jibe at an American raises a laugh'.[167]

Anxieties about Britain's declining influence abroad and the pace of social and economic change at home had become mixed up with resentment of American political and cultural success, and the anti-American incidents that followed the Suez crisis in 1956 were not isolated aberrations. Harold Nicolson, for instance, thought in 1945 that anti-American sentiments were 'dangerous and quite useless'; but eight years later he complained: 'Gradually they are ousting us out of all world authority. I mind this, as I feel it is humiliating and insidious . . . they are decent folk in every way, but they tread on traditions in a way that hurts.'[168] This kind of attitude had a distinguished pedigree, and by the late fifties the debate about what critics called 'Americanisation' was an old and rather clichéd one. Often they were really arguing about the changing values of the affluent society rather than about Americans and American products themselves. It was no accident that the patron saint of anti-Americanism was George Orwell, socialist, tea-drinker and distinguished veteran of the Eton Wall Game. In 1946, for instance, Orwell had even complained that the 'English Murder' was being driven out by the brutal violence of American imports, with all their tawdry overtones of 'dance halls, movie palaces, cheap perfume, false names and stolen cars'.[169]

What Orwell and his successors really resented was that, whereas the war had left Britain tired and battered, it had invigorated American capitalism, turning it into a strident, vulgar, commercialised threat to British identity and traditions. 'Death to Hollywood,' John Maynard Keynes famously declared at the end of the war, and even the sympathetic Harry Hopkins wrote that the arrival of American film stars and comedians in London in the austere forties 'left a curious, indefinably unpleasant after-taste'.[170] For these critics, to be Americanised was to be uniform, materialistic, selfish and, of course, suburban. In his book *The American Invasion* (1962), Francis Williams warned that 'what too often moves across the world in the wake of American money and American know-how is what is most brash and superficial'.[171] By contrast, many commentators were proud that the British were so conventional, seeing this as a useful corrective to the flashy, taste-less emphasis on change that was associated with American culture. The sturdy common sense of the British worker, rooted in a sense of commu-nity, tradition and restrained good taste, was therefore contrasted with the 'neurosis, criminality and demoralization' that inevitably came from the 'competitiveness' and 'intense mobility strivings' attributed to American society.[172]

Even the British diet, to the disgust of some older commentators, was showing signs of creeping Americanisation. Dining at a restaurant was con-sidered a luxury in the fifties, and choices were limited to hotel dining rooms, department-store restaurants, Lyon's Corner Houses for tea, or working-class cafés serving egg and chips. The standard was rarely very high: in John Wain's novel *Living in the Present* (1955), 'platefuls of twice-inferior food' are the usual fare:

> They had even given up crossing out from the menu the dishes that were 'off'; but . . . Edgar . . . knew by long experience that there would be, at this hour, nothing 'on' but corned-beef rissoles, a spoonful of greens boiled to rags and tasting of soda, and perhaps a chunk of waxy ice-cream to follow . . .
>
> London was full of places like this; so were the provinces; while as for the country towns and villages, they did not rise even to this parody of communal feeding.[173]

This was not as unfair as it might appear. In 1951 the left-wing journalist Raymond Postgate had launched the *Good Food Guide*, the first shot in a furi-ous onslaught against the 'intolerable' and 'dreadful' food served in British restaurants. British diners, he said, should cultivate the appearance of being 'suspicious, after a lifetime of suffering'.[174] In an age when television chefs like Philip Harben, Marguerite Patten and Fanny Cradock were winning loyal audiences keen to shrug off the culinary privations of wartime, few people had a kind word for the catering industry. Postgate's fellow critic Egon Ronay even suggested that 'what they do in Wales could be called gastronomic rape, except that they don't seem to derive any pleasure from it'. The 1957/8 edition of the *Good Food Guide* described a typical evening meal: 'Soup from an American tin. Soggy steak from the Argentine. Synthetic cream and tinned Empire fruit. Tinned coffee'. Even worse was to be found in one West Country restaurant:

> Grapefruit cut in segments which were put back with all the pith left in, sour but heavily sugared. Minestrone which was some sliced vegetable in coloured water. Scampi, the Mediterranean fish but still tough and tasteless, served with 'mayonnaise' poured from a bottle into a sauceboat round the corner. Roast beef, cut thin, overcooked to brownness, lying in weak beef-extract gravy . . .[175]

Despite the growing popularity of Italian and Chinese food in some metropolitan circles, it was American food that represented the first significant and widespread alternative to the standard fare, exploiting the belief of British teenagers in particular that all things American embodied style, glamour and luxury. In 1954 the first Wimpy bar opened within a Lyon's Corner House, and for the next fifteen years or so Wimpy was synonymous with American cuisine, serving grilled hamburgers, Knickerbocker Glories and milkshakes to young people waiting at tables adorned with the trademark Wimpy ketchup bottle, disguised as a plastic tomato. Teenage affluence meant that Wimpy could cater for a new kind of customer eager to emulate the heroes of American films; as the managing director explained: 'We realized that we were attracting an entirely new clientele – young people.' By 1969, indeed, there were 460 outlets in the country, with nine in Oxford Street alone.[176] Wimpy was just one of a series of well-known chains that succeeded by recasting American formulas for a British audience. In 1958 the first Little Chef, an eleven-seater snack bar based on the principle of the American diner, opened outside Reading, offering hearty breakfasts to tired travellers and capitalising on the rapid increase in car ownership. The formula worked perfectly, and by the end of the century Little Chef was the largest roadside chain in the country.[177]

Elsewhere, steakhouses on the American model proved attractive to British customers keen on the idea of steak, chips and peas accompanied by a cheap bottle of wine, especially since the rationing of meat in the early

fifties meant that steak was perceived as a treat, even an indication of affluence. The most popular steakhouses were Berni Inns, the creation of the
brothers Frank and Aldo Berni, Italian immigrants who originally owned
a string of cafés and restaurants in the West Country. Their first outlet was
a converted Bristol coaching inn, the Rummer Inn, which opened in 1953
with heavy red velvet hangings and dark wooden furniture. Berni Inns
broke with convention in several ways. They offered a limited, cheap
menu, costing under eight shillings, which in its classic form consisted of
prawn cocktail, a half-pound steak and chips, Black Forest gâteau or
cheese, and a medium sherry; they dispensed with the need for trained
chefs, using only a deep fryer and a grill; and they cut laundry costs by
using place mats rather than tablecloths. By the late sixties there were over
a hundred more, often in old inns renovated for the purpose like the Mitre
in Oxford or the New Inn in Gloucester, and in 1962 the company was
floated on the Stock Exchange.[178] Steakhouses were not merely popular
and profitable, though; they were also fashionable. When the budding
promoter Andrew Loog Oldham wanted to impress the American record
producer Phil Spector in the early 1960s, he took him to lunch at the
Angus Steak House in Soho.[179]

It was no accident that Oldham took his guest to Soho, for the area
around Wardour, Dean and Frith Streets had long enjoyed a reputation for
bohemianism. In the seventeenth and eighteenth centuries, groups of immigrants had poured into its narrow streets, and this gave the area an air of
cosmopolitan diversity that it never lost. In the years before the Second
World War, Soho became well known for its swing and jazz clubs, clustered
among the French and Italian restaurants and delicatessens of Frith and
Dean Streets.[180] J. B. Priestley recorded 'the glimpses of foreign interiors, the
windows lined with outlandish foodstuffs, Chianti flasks and bundles of long
cheroots; the happy foolish little decorations; the dark faces; the girls leaning out of the first floor windows'.[181] And in the early 1950s Soho and
Fitzrovia were popular destinations for upper-class writers, artists and self-
conscious bohemians, and Peter Vansittart's memoir of London in this
period brings together characters like Dylan Thomas, Philip Toynbee and
Francis Bacon in a fog of cigarette smoke, alcohol and arch conversation at
little venues like the Colony Room or Bertorelli's Restaurant.[182] But, for
younger visitors, Soho in the fifties meant cosmopolitanism, sex and, above
all, coffee bars. One young man from Acton, who first visited Soho in the
late fifties, wrote:

I loved the feel of Soho. The cheeses, and the ravioli, and the wine in the windows of the big Italian grocers' shops. The smell of fresh-ground beans from the Algerian coffee stores. The shops with French sausages, and Greek sweets, and Hungarian chicken livers, and Swiss chocolates.

It was fascinating to walk along the pavement through this medley of all nations. To see newspapers and magazines on sale in a dozen different languages and watch the waiters from the Indian, Chinese and Italian and Turkish restaurants gathered on the corners out of hours.

Every other doorway seemed to be a coffee bar. And, into Soho every day, drifted the young hopefuls with their guitars, all hoping to get a night's work or a week's work from the owners of these coffee bars.[183]

The coffee bar was emblematic of youth culture in the late fifties, reflecting the trend of increasing affluence and projecting the values of elusive sophistication. Tea, not coffee, was the national drink, and there was a Lyon's Tea House or Corner House on every high street, so the appeal of coffee was rooted in its Continental unfamiliarity.[184] There is no better illustration of coffee's exoticism than in the film *The Rebel*, released in 1960 and starring Tony Hancock as a frustrated suburban drudge yearning for a new life as a Continental artist. In one scene, the weary Hancock stumbles into a trendy new London coffee bar, decorated in bright red plastic and boasting an array of modernist chairs and rubber plants. He is by some distance the oldest customer; instrumental rock and roll of the Shadows type is playing on a jukebox, and he is watched with bored suspicion by the waitress (the pneumatic Liz Fraser). The following dialogue ensues:

HANCOCK: A cup of tea please, dear.
WAITRESS: We don't do tea, only coffee. Expresso or cappuccino.
HANCOCK: All right then, I'll have a white one with no froth.
WAITRESS: No froth?
HANCOCK: I don't like froth!
WAITRESS: That's half the attraction! You must have froth!
HANCOCK: I don't want any froth! I want a cup of coffee! I don't want to wash my clothes in it!
WAITRESS: I've never heard of anybody who didn't want froth!
HANCOCK: Well you have now! One white coffee, no froth!

These instructions are received with outrage by the owner of the shop, a man with a Cockney accent, a bristling moustache and a distinctly Mediterranean look, who mutters: 'Eight hundred quid's worth of frothing machinery!' and shakes his head. Needless to say, the coffee, when produced, turns out to be a disappointment.[185]

The development of coffee bars in post-war Britain owed a great deal to the entrepreneurship of Italian immigrants, tens of thousands of whom poured into the country during the immediate post-war years.[186] In 1951, according to the census, there were 38,000 Italians in Britain; ten years later, there were 87,000.[187] Around Old Compton Street and in the narrow streets of Soho there clustered a group of new Italian restaurants offering inexpensive food in exotic surroundings; most, like Amalfi, Presto or Pollo, were decorated in the bright new Contemporary style, their gleaming chrome and plastic furnishings a tribute to the cultural optimism of the day.[188] Although Soho had long been famous for its pubs and coffee houses, it is difficult to imagine the coffee bar taking off in quite the same way without the presence of such a large Italian community keen to establish itself in British life.[189] One other antecedent, meanwhile, was the milk bar, conceived as a meeting place where affluent adolescents could meet and share non-alcoholic drinks, and modelled on an Australian prototype. Britain's first milk bar was opened on Fleet Street in 1935 by an Australian businessman, and it swiftly found a market; within a year, there were over four hundred throughout the country, reflecting not only the growth of leisure but also the decline of the pub among younger consumers. By the fifties, the terms 'milk bar' and 'coffee bar' were used as synonyms, despite their different heritage; the differences between the two were generally in name only.[190]

The first true coffee bars, like the Moka bar in Frith Street, the Heaven and Hell in Old Compton Street or the Kaleidoscope in Gerrard Street, were established, unsurprisingly, in areas of Italian concentration.[191] The Moka bar, which opened in 1952, was the first to have one of Achille Gaggia's shiny new espresso machines, which pumped hot water through the coffee to produce a smoother drink sold in Britain as 'expresso'. The basic design of the typical coffee bar was simple enough: a pine bar, behind which steamed one of Gaggia's clattering machines; a series of little plastic tables at which the customers sipped their little glasses of coffee; a dancing area, or an area for a singer in the evenings; and, of course, a jukebox to play the new hit singles. Rubber plants were also a popular addition, and completed the decoration for the coffee-bar set in *The Rebel*.[192]

This template was copied across the country, and soon coffee and milk bars from London to Glasgow were catering for impoverished students and musicians as well as the newly affluent. As one patron recalled, they were 'the first places where you could hang about for an evening, spend a shilling on a coffee, go in at nine and come out at eleven, and nobody bothered you, nobody said you had to have a second cup of coffee'.[193] In the centre of Walsall, for instance, the 'young office set' gathered for 'coffee and cream buns' at the Clover Milk Bar; in Abingdon, there was the Mousehole, under the town hall, where local teenagers would 'sit there drinking frothy coffee and looking with indescribable envy at the Teddy boys and girls who played the juke box'; and in Sunderland there was the Bis Bar, where on a Saturday morning 'anybody who was anybody went there, wearing a sheepskin jacket'.[194] By the end of 1957, there were over a thousand such establishments, all hoping to capture a certain European sophistication. As Harry Hopkins put it, 'one dallied not over the once-inevitable slab-cake and iced pastries but over *Apfelstrudel*, Danish pastries, cheese-cake, chocolate *torte*, dispensed by sophisticates in swinging skirts and large brass ear-rings or black-jersied gamines with Audrey Hepburn hairdos'.[195]

In the context of the early fifties, the appeal of the coffee bars is easy to understand: during a period of introspective austerity, they represented an elusive ideal of modernity and cosmopolitanism.[196] Even the very name 'expresso' coffee implied speed and sophistication. The coffee bars also reflected a wider enthusiasm for all things Continental and especially all things French and Italian, evident in everything from scooters to films and from dress to diet. In 1953, for example, the young Terence Conran opened his first Soup Kitchen restaurant off Trafalgar Square, selling soup, bread and cheese, apple flans and coffee from what he claimed was only the second expresso machine in London. This venture, he later recalled, was directly inspired by his 'first trips to France and Italy' in the early fifties which had opened his eyes 'to a different way of doing things – a less pretentious way of life, in which pleasure was often derived from simple things done well. Good earthenware pots, solid saucepans, salads dressed in olive oil and a squeeze of lemon juice, huge plates of pasta hungrily devoured.' At the same time, he was running his own small furniture-making business, and would deliver small pieces 'strapped to the back of my Vespa', an Italian motor scooter.[197]

Possession of a scooter, perhaps a Lambretta GT200 or a Vespa GS160, was an indication not only of wealth but also of sophistication, since they were associated with the grace and worldliness of the Italians. This 'Italianisation' of style reflected both dissatisfaction with British austerity and also the age-less desire to attain some remote, romantic ideal of erudition and elegance. The fashionable young things of the late fifties were, although they little knew it, following in a long tradition, from the Continental tastes of the Hanoverians to the Grand Tour of the late eighteenth century and the Italian enthusiasms of the Victorians.[198] Perhaps it was no coincidence that just as France and Italy had once been the models for wealthy socialites in the eighteenth century, so France and Italy were now the models for the affluent young of the fifties. Glasses of expresso coffee and scooters were simply two modern examples of this phenomenon. Budding sophisticates brandished the translated novels of Albert Camus, Jean-Paul Sartre or Françoise Sagan, as they queued at independent picture houses for the latest subtitled films from Federico Fellini or French New Wave directors like Truffaut, Resnais and Godard.[199] Young men dreamed of stylish and volup-tuous European sirens like Sophia Loren, Claudia Cardinale and Gina Lollobrigida; young women copied the low-cut tops, tight sweaters and expansive skirts of Brigitte Bardot or the gloves and headscarf of Princess Grace of Monaco.[200]

The popularity of French and Italian fashions at the end of the 1950s owed much to the fact that communications between Britain and the Continent had improved a great deal over the previous decade. British air-lines introduced their first cheap 'Tourist' charter flights in 1952, and curious middle-class holidaymakers were, slowly but surely, beginning to abandon their traditional seaside haunts for the charms of the Riviera or the Costa Brava. Travel agencies offered package deals to Spain, Italy or the Alps, while special air-conditioned coach tours were laid on for the more cautious. By 1958, two million people were travelling abroad for their holidays, almost twice the number before the Second World War.[201] In 1960, holidaymakers could spend two weeks in Majorca for 39 guineas, while a fortnight's break in San Remo came to 44 guineas. A ten-day coach tour of the Swiss Alps, meanwhile, cost 51 guineas, and a fifteen-day tour of Rome, Florence, Venice and Capri cost 65 guineas. These were considerable sums, but not beyond the reach of the middle classes, and the destinations on offer were infinitely more glamorous than Skegness or Scarborough.[202] 'It was like going to the moon,' one woman recalled. 'Nobody had ever been to France for a holiday where we lived. They all went to Blackpool. They'd never heard of anyone going abroad except in a war. They made us so worried that we made a will the day before we left.'[203] Most of these early visitors fancied themselves as intrepid explorers in a bewilderingly Continental landscape; when Kingsley Amis took his family to Portugal in 1955, he noted the 'British tourists honking their horns and waving excitedly at the sight of another GB plate on the road'.[204] But what he called 'the domain of the few' was gradually becoming 'the domain of the many', especially when holidaymakers discovered that their money went much further in Italy or Spain. In 1960, some 3.5 million people went abroad on holiday: in later years, they would be joined by millions more.[205]

In 1956 the president of the Scarborough Hotels Association, Harry Lund, used the association's annual meeting to launch a furious attack on what he called 'the garlic and olive oil gang of the press and radio'. By this, Lund said, he meant 'those writers, usually women', who belittled 'bacon and eggs and the incomparable meats and vegetables of England' while praising 'starch-laden Continental breakfasts and main meals consisting of dollops of spaghetti with a little tomato sauce'.[206] In fact, most visitors to the Continent in the late fifties viewed foreign food with a combination of suspicion and horror, and there were plenty of stories of British children being violently sick on their first exposure to garlic or pasta. When eighty Derbyshire miners arranged an expedition to Riccione on the Adriatic, they took their own cook with them, as well as their own beer, but afterwards reported that 'wine and spaghetti are not all bad'.[207] Tastes were changing, and perhaps the most enduring legacy of the so-called Italianisation of the mid-fifties was in the middle-class kitchen. Although most people were slow to abandon their beloved roast beef or fish and chips, affluent consumers were beginning to flirt with French and Italian recipes, which were widely regarded as lighter, healthier and more sophisticated than the traditional favourites.

In 1950 Elizabeth David, an upper-middle-class bohemian from a landed Conservative family who had lived in France, Italy, Greece and Egypt, published *A Book of Mediterranean Food*, which was widely regarded as a breakthrough in British cookery writing. Twelve months later, another bestseller followed, entitled *French Country Cooking*. 'Lift up your eyes to the continent,' she advised her readers, 'and take an interest in exotic ingredients.'[208] Many recipes, like 'Turkish Stuffing for a Whole Roast Sheep' or 'Partridge Seasoned with Greek Mountain Herbs', were pure escapism, aimed at readers sick of the austerity of the Attlee years. As David admitted, she did not 'seriously expect that many of my readers will try stuffing a sheep, or even cooking a hare for seven hours: those recipes are included for sheer pleasure'.[209] Indeed, some of the essential ingredients were simply unobtainable: few people in the early fifties had large quantities of cream, eggs and bacon to spare, and even fewer knew where to find langoustines, garlic, olive oil, pasta, courgettes, peppers, aubergines or anchovies.

But within a few years, as affluence began to make its mark, readers were becoming more familiar with Continental products, and David felt able to drop her famous lists of recommended substitutes. 'So startlingly different is the food situation now as compared with only two years ago', she wrote in the 1955 edition of *A Book of Mediterranean Food*, 'that I think there is scarcely a single ingredient, however exotic, mentioned in this book which cannot be obtained somewhere in this country, even if it is in one or two shops.'[210] Slowly but surely, as Britain entered the sixties, aspirational middle-class housewives began introducing David's recipes into their culinary repertoire, proudly presenting them to guests in expensive, mock-Provençal earthenware bowls alongside bottles of cheap red wine; and within twenty years, David had become an institution, the personification of the affluent cosmopolitanism of the fifties and sixties. When she died in 1992, the *Guardian* declared: 'It is no exaggeration to say that for middle-class British people of the second half of the century, she did more to change their way of life than any poet, novelist or dramatist of our time.'[211]

Indeed, the examples of coffee bars, scooters and Mediterranean food give the lie to those commentators who see Britain in the fifties as a society trapped between the grey ruins of cultural conservatism and the tawdry pleasures of Hollywood and Manhattan. Not only did many people cheerfully keep up the traditions they had inherited from their parents and grandparents, but despite their nativist prejudices they also found themselves drawn to their old European rivals. Just as wealthy elites had once admired the elegant fashions of the Continental courts, so by the late fifties the British middle classes were cooking French recipes, wearing Italian outfits and copying Scandinavian designs. British youngsters, listening to the latest Elvis Presley hit on the local jukebox, were just as likely to sip an expresso as they were to drink a milkshake. Teenagers might well dream about cruising along the highways of California in a Cadillac; but they might equally well picture themselves zipping through the streets of Rome on a Vespa, or even gliding down the byways of London in a Jaguar.

In his history of Western Europe and the United States in the sixties, Arthur Marwick calls Britain 'an empty vessel in the realm of cultural creation', dismissing its 'philistine' record in high art as well as its 'derivative and second-rate' popular culture.[212] It is true that at this stage, British cultural life had not really been transformed from the patterns of the thirties and forties. But although British popular culture was conservative, drawing on decades of tradition and convention, it was also hearty and vigorous, adequately reflecting the values and interests of the nation. For all the novelty of Berni Inns, coffee bars and *French Country Cooking*, what was really remarkable about everyday life in the affluent fifties was the dogged fondness with which many ordinary people, in towns and suburbs across the country, held on to their traditional habits and hobbies. While perhaps half a million people might buy the biggest-selling single of the week, four times that many would head off that weekend to the nearest river or canal for a spot of fishing. While there were a thousand coffee bars, there were three times as many amateur football teams, five times as many cinemas or dancing schools, and six thousand times as many domestic budgerigars. Britain in the age of affluence, then, was a country as much of the old and the middle-aged as it was of the young. It was a world of anglers, knitters and amateur footballers, poised to confront the new cultural challenges of the 1960s.

5

THE PROVINCIAL ALL-STARS

I HATE anybody who does anything UNUSUAL at all.

Philip Larkin, 1946

Huggett's writing a book that's to go a long way for finding out the Truth, but it'll take him years to write because it's not only religion he's taking in but philosophy. So he works in this shipping office, but he has poems published and he's got all these followers – The Crowd they're called.

Angus Wilson, 'A Bit off the Map' (1957)

On 5 May 1941, in the porter's lodge of St John's College, Oxford, a tall, bookish undergraduate called Philip Larkin was idly reading the notice-boards when his tutorial partner spotted the name of an old school acquaintance and reported: 'He's a hell of a good man . . . He shoots guns.' Larkin did not understand this remark until later that afternoon, when they saw 'a fair-haired young man' coming down a nearby staircase. Larkin's friend pointed his right hand like a gun at the newcomer and 'uttered a short coughing bark to signify a shot':

The young man's reaction was immediate. Clutching his chest in a rictus of agony, he threw one arm up against the archway and began slowly crumpling downwards, fingers scoring the stonework. Just as he was about to collapse on the piled-up laundry, however . . . he righted himself and tottered over to us.

'I've been working on this,' he said as soon as introductions were completed. 'Listen. This is when you're firing in a ravine.'

We listened.

'And this is when you're firing in a ravine and the bullet ricochets off a rock.'

We listened again. Norman's appreciative laughter skirled freely: I stood silent. For the first time I felt myself in the presence of a talent superior to my own.[1]

The young man's name was Kingsley Amis, and his meeting with the dazzled Larkin marked the beginning of the most important relationship in post-war British letters.[2] In his often unsympathetic biography of Larkin, Andrew Motion suggests that his poetry 'transcends his time rather than merely encapsulating it: he is one of the great poets of the century . . . [His poems] speak directly to most people who come across them. He makes each of us feel he is "our" poet.'[3] As for Amis, D. J. Taylor puts it well:

> In the end, any discussion of dominant names and traditions takes us back to Kingsley Amis . . . The fact remains that no discussion of the post-war novel can journey very far without acknowledging Amis's enormous importance . . . in any discussion of the link between intellectual and political life in post-war England, Amis is a figure of monstrous symbolic interest.[4]

'It would be difficult', concludes Harry Ritchie, 'to overestimate the importance of Amis' literary career in the fifties . . . a career of challenges and controversies involving essential literary, cultural and social issues of the time.'[5]

In the decades that followed the First World War, British letters had enjoyed a stunning period of intellectual intensity and innovation, confirming the reputations of older writers like E. M. Forster and D. H. Lawrence and thrusting to prominence bright new Modernist talents such as Virginia Woolf and T. S. Eliot. In the weary aftermath of the Second World War, however, there was only silence. The salons of literary London seemed sunk in 'disappointed expectancy', writes Amis' biographer Eric Jacobs, 'like people waiting at a station platform when the train did not arrive at the time expected or, when it did, failed to disgorge any glamorous passengers'.[6] For the ageing mandarins of the literary scene, the silence merely confirmed what they already suspected. Political consensus, materialism and introspection were the hallmarks of the new age, and were necessarily inimical to artistic innovation. The numbing conformity and the bleak pessimism of the atomic age had succeeded the horrors of war; there was no longer a place for wit, style or humour. The literary institutions of the thirties were closing down: the Left Book Club, the highbrow series *Penguin New Writing* and Cyril Connolly's little magazine *Horizon* all ground to a halt between 1948 and 1950.[7] Shortly afterwards, a commentator in the *New Statesman* lamented that 'five years after the war there is still no sign of any kind of literary revival; no movements are discernible, no trends'.[8]

By the early 1950s, war-weariness and austerity had yielded to suburban contentment and economic affluence, and still the critics saw no sign of the desired cultural revival. In 1952, for example, the *Times Literary Supplement* predicted 'a difficult and confusing decade', dominated not by meteoric literary talents but by the gloom of 'A Generation in Search of Itself'.[9] For the members of the old literary establishment, like Connolly, Philip Toynbee, John Lehmann and Elizabeth Bowen, the bright lights of Modernist experiment seemed to have been forever dimmed.[10] Across the board observers claimed that British culture was characterised by a stultifying conformity and traditionalism reflecting the complacent, materialistic consensus of the nation's politics. Britain was, they argued, hidebound by class, struggling under the weight of its imperial history, tired, dreary and conformist. 'Is the Novel Dead?' asked a series of articles in the *Observer* in 1954.[11] And the veteran writer J. B. Priestley wondered where, 'in the Madame Tussaud's of the national consciousness, are the men of letters?'

> Or, for that matter, the other kind of creative artists? Name ten, widely known and highly regarded, under fifty years of age. Who and where are the massive talents, the towering personalities, the men of genius? Who represents us abroad as we ought to be represented – by the English mind blazing with art and throwing a light on the world we all share – and not by the assistant secretary to the Department of Drains, the vice-chairman of the Busybodies Association, the Secretary of the Society of Stuffed Shirts?[12]

*

Kingsley Amis and Philip Larkin were born in 1922, five months apart, and grew up in suburban south London and Coventry respectively. Both were lonely children, both were of lower-middle-class stock, and both were educated at local grammar schools.[13] The sense of belonging to the suburban middle classes was extremely important to both men. Amis later complained rather facetiously that being born 'the child of the urban or suburban middle classes' was 'a sad fate': he had been denied not only the 'brisk introduction to sex behind the coal tips' enjoyed by the working classes, but also the possibility of 'a fructifyingly bad time at Eton' among the wealthy. Instead, he was condemned to live with 'constant anxieties about decorum'.[14] Drawn together at Oxford through well-matched interests, temperaments and backgrounds, the two men parted company thereafter. Amis served in the Second World War as a signals lieutenant, returned to Oxford to finish his degree and was appointed to a lectureship at Swansea in 1949. Larkin, however, failed his army medical because of his poor eyesight; he took a First in English in 1943 and became a librarian, first in Wellington in Shropshire, then at universities in Leicester and Belfast; and then, from 1955, at the University of Hull.[15]

One of the remarkable legacies of the relationship between Amis and Larkin was the enormous stash of letters they exchanged, often several a month, for almost forty years. This was, above all, an epistolary friendship: Amis never visited Larkin in Hull, and was never really encouraged to do so.[16] The letters were full of double entendres, smutty jokes, parodies of despised authors, sexual anecdotes and schoolboy humour. 'I feel very depressed this evening,' Amis writes in June 1947. 'I feel from time to time a slight excess of sexual energy without object, not even towards masturbation, and not even – I think – towards very young girls. I feel as if I am on the threshold of some new and fearsome perversion that is going to burst into my conscious mind with the force of a mastodon's fart. Do you ever feel like that?'[17] Three years later, he thanks Larkin for a present:

> Thanks for that dirty magazine. I found the drawings horrible, and the letterpress spoke piercingly to me of my normality. I did quite like the schoolgirl bits, but this punishment idea *doesn't appeal to me*, any more than all this stuff about old women and heavy make-up and shoes and corsets and long hair and horses. I like corsets. I like long hair. I even like heavy make-up sometimes. But no more than I like bread and butter and marmite.[18]

But, for all the banter, the correspondence was artistically rewarding, and the two men exchanged not only ideas for future books, but also poems and extracts from their novels. Amis himself admitted that Larkin read and made important alterations to the early drafts of his first novel, tentatively entitled *Dixon and Christine*.[19] It was inspired by Amis' impressions of university life in Leicester, where Larkin was then working as the librarian; the central character Dixon was named after the street on which Larkin lived; and the character of the fearsome Margaret Peel was modelled on Larkin's lover Monica Jones.[20] 'I'm afraid you are very much the ideal reader of the thing,' Amis wrote not long before publication, 'and chaps like you don't grow on trees, course not.'[21]

Like many bright young men of their generation, Amis and Larkin also shared an obsessive interest in traditional jazz music. Amis would devise imaginary jazz bands of literary or historical figures, like 'Big Ben Jonson and his Tribesmen (actually Jonson fronting Donne's Metaphysicals)', an ensemble boasting talents like 'Andy Marvell (bass)' and 'Jack Donne, pno' and playing hits such as 'Volpone Drag' or 'Scholastic'.[22] Or he might prefer 'some really early stuff (early New Orleans pre-electric recordings)' such as 'OLLY CROMWELL and his ROUNDHEAD WASHBOARD BAND' performing their hits 'Revolutionary Blues' and 'Hittin' the Rump', with vocals written by Blind John Milton.[23] Both Larkin and Amis had first become interested in jazz music during the late thirties, and like many intelligent, middle-class grammar-school boys of their generation, they saw jazz both as a rebellion against the cultural elitism of the public schools and as a cherished cultural artefact to be protected against the ravages of post-war innovation. Larkin was introduced to jazz music by a schoolfriend and soon became addicted: not content with banging away on his own drum kit, he bought, listened to and analysed American recordings by the likes of Louis Armstrong and Sidney Bechet 'for hour after hour'.[24] Amis' passion was slightly less intense, but still powerful. Like his friend, he had picked it up from dance music on the wireless as a schoolboy; it had the 'added recommendation' of being opposed by his parents and other older people.[25] He arrived at Oxford a confirmed enthusiast, if not quite a disciple of Larkinesque dedication. Larkin would introduce him to new records, and the two young men would spend hours together listening to them, occasionally leaping around the room in enthusiasm, or playing tunes on a piano in an Oxford pub.[26]

To Amis, jazz was at first 'one more indisputably good thing, along with films, cricket, science fiction, the wireless and all that'. But for Larkin, he remembered, 'the music was a preoccupation, a passion, as it was for numbers of his and our friends and as it soon became for me'.[27] Their tastes were extremely traditional: Armstrong, Ellington, Beiderbecke, the white Chicagoans and so on.[28] Like so many other educated British aficionados of the post-war years, they reacted with contempt and horror to the innovations of modern jazz. Various enemies, Amis lamented, 'were moving in on our jazz, my jazz, from different directions': ruthlessly pretentious innovators like Charlie Parker and Miles Davis; growing audiences who encouraged excessive exhibitionism and improvisation; the designers of long-playing records, which destroyed 'the concentration and concision' of the old 78rpm records; most unforgivably, 'jazz critics, journals, university courses came along and helped to kill it with respectability'.[29] Such antagonism was not unusual: when the popular British musician Johnny Dankworth played modern jazz at the Beaulieu jazz festival, the crowd reacted with angry boos and jeers.[30] Larkin was equally bitter, and devoted much of his book *All What Jazz* to the subject. By trying 'to be different and difficult', he wrote, Parker and Davis had disappeared into 'exaggerated musical non-sequiturs'; they and their followers, the 'beret-and-dark-glasses boys', had turned the ordinary pleasures of jazz into 'chaos, hatred and absurdity'. This was an inevitable consequence of the slide into Modernism, which diverted audiences 'only by being more mystifying and more outrageous: it has no lasting power. Hence the compulsion of every Modernist to wade deeper into violence and obscurity: hence the succession of Parker by Rollins and Coltrane.'[31]

Amis was the first of the two men to make an impact on the British literary scene, and he did it in part through the radio. Both men were friends with yet another middle-class scholarship boy and St John's man, John Wain, a dentist's son from the Potteries.[32] In the words of another Oxford contemporary, the poet Al Alvarez, Wain saw himself 'as a mixture of Dr Johnson, George Orwell and J. B. Priestley, a plain man full of common sense, a plain-speaker who had no truck with pretension'.[33] He was also a fellow jazz enthusiast, like Amis seeing it as a form of rebellion against parental authority. In his novel *Strike the Father Dead* (1962), Wain's hero explains that his father had 'given me the idea, without actually saying it in words, that playing or listening to jazz was a disreputable act, something like masturbating'.[34] Although Wain was initially a good friend of Amis and Larkin, and enjoyed considerable success as a novelist, poet and academic, he was always rather looked down on by them. Amis reported that although Wain was a jazz fan, a drinker and a fine storyteller, 'his walking-stick, among the able-bodied surely a warning sign in the same category as facial hair, and a tendency to tweed hats, made me uneasy'. Larkin, meanwhile, held Wain's work in very low esteem. 'Isn't England a marvellous free, open country?' he once exclaimed to Amis.

Take a fellow like old John Wain, now. No advantages of birth or position or wealth or energy or charm or looks or talent – nothing, and look where he is now. Where else but in England could a thing like that happen? You know, a few years ago I think he got to be Professor of Poetry at Oxford. Just imagine.[35]

All the same, Amis recognised that it was Wain who, on the evening of 26 April 1953, first brought him to public attention. Wain, then a lecturer at Reading, had been offered the task of presenting a series of radio broadcasts on contemporary literature under the title *First Reading*, replacing a similar series by the highbrow grandee John Lehmann. These would be broadcast on the Third Programme at monthly intervals to an audience of some 100,000 listeners.[36] He began his first programme with a description of the new writers he wanted to promote, and this opening salvo announced the flavour of the new literary generation: 'They are suspicious of anything that suggests sprawling or lack of discipline. They are keenly aware of belonging to a tradition; not only the tradition of the last thirty years, but the longer tradition that stretches away behind, and with which the more recent discoveries will have to be put into perspective.'[37] This barely veiled attack on literary Modernism was followed by the first piece of new writing: an extract from Kingsley Amis' unpublished debut, now renamed *Lucky Jim*. The fifteen-minute scene came from one of the novel's more famous episodes. The hero Jim Dixon, a disaffected and dishevelled young lecturer in medieval history at a provincial university, is staying at his professor's house after a nightmarish evening of play-readings and folk song, during which Dixon has surreptitiously plundered the professor's drinks cupboard. The extract that Amis read for the broadcast described the aftermath: Dixon wakes with a fearsome hangover to discover that his cigarette has burnt holes in the bedclothes, blankets, a valuable rug and the bedside table, and endeavours haplessly to disguise the evidence by shaving the rug with a razor and, rather misguidedly, cutting larger holes in the bedclothes.[38]

Many literary-minded listeners were deeply offended by Amis' material, especially in the context of the attack on Modernism that had preceded it. The *New Statesman*, for instance, gave the programme an extremely hostile review, and the controller of the Third Programme remonstrated with Wain about the choice of material.[39] As it turned out, Wain was sacked as editor of the show after just six programmes, and replaced by Ludovic Kennedy.[40] As for *Lucky Jim*, it was finally published in January 1954 and was an instant success. The flavour of the book is best expressed by Amis himself:

> University shag. Provincial. Probably keen on culture. Crappy culture.
> Fellow who doesn't fit in. Seems anti-culture. Non-U. Non-Oxbridge.
> Beer. Girls. Can't say what he really thinks. Boss trouble. Given chores.
> Disaster. Boring boss (a) so boring girl (b). Nice girl comes but someone
> else's property. Whose? etc.[41]

Most reviewers were very impressed: *The Times* thought that the novel was 'genuinely comic'; the *Spectator* called it 'a very funny book'; and *Punch* declared that it was 'extremely amusing'.[42] Sales were excellent: within twelve months there had been sixteen impressions, an American version had been published, and a total of around twelve thousand copies had been sold.[43] By the time of its fortieth anniversary, the novel had been translated into twenty languages, selling millions of copies, had been made into a film, had been extended into a television sitcom, and had been republished as a Penguin Twentieth-Century Classic. Posterity had transformed Amis' novel from a disgruntled young lecturer's brilliantly funny debut into a milestone in modern literary history.[44]

Above all, *Lucky Jim* was controversial. For many conservative literary figures it seemed to encapsulate not only the new lower-middle-class challenge to Modernist orthodoxy, but also the degrading effects of the post-war welfare state. Evelyn Waugh complained in 1955 about the 'new wave of philistinism with which we are threatened by these grim young people coming off the assembly lines in their hundreds every year and finding employment as critics, even as poets and novelists'.[45] An editorial in the semi-literary periodical *Encounter* a year later agreed: in a society 'where the majority receive almost equal shares', there was no defence against the 'spreading grey of suburbs' and 'sacrifice of quality' that *Lucky Jim* was supposed to reflect.[46] Dixon, said Colm Brogan in the *Spectator*, was 'a loafer, a sycophant, a vulgarian who has taken advantage of State bounty to secure a university post when he is mentally and morally unfit to be a school janitor. If Redbrick has many like Lucky Jim, that institution may be written off.'[47] Dixon was also the victim of a remarkable denunciation in the *Sunday Times* from the octogenarian writer Somerset Maugham, an expression of total contempt not merely for Amis' protagonist, but also for the entire suburban world that he had come to represent. Maugham thought that *Lucky*

Jim was a 'remarkable novel', because it had captured with perfect accuracy the world of the 'white collar proletariat':

> They do not go to the university to acquire culture, but to get a job, and when they have got one, scamp it. They have no manners, and are woefully unable to deal with any social predicament. Their idea of a celebration is to go to a public house and drink six beers. They are mean, malicious and envious. They will write anonymous letters to harass a fellow undergraduate and listen in to a telephone conversation that is no business of theirs. Charity, kindliness, generosity are qualities which they hold in contempt. They are scum. They will in due course leave the university. Some will doubtless sink back, perhaps with relief, into the modest class from which they emerged; some will take to drink, some to crime, and go to prison. Others will become schoolmasters and form the young, or journalists and mould public opinion. A few will go into Parliament, become Cabinet Ministers, and rule the country. I look on myself as fortunate that I shall not live to see it.[48]

For the old literary lions, a novel should be all about upper-class elites, aesthetic ideals and political engagement, and Jim Dixon therefore seemed a baffling and repulsive character. As Amis' friend Anthony Powell later remarked, 'in certain quarters *Lucky Jim* was looked on quite simply as a shower of brickbats hurled by half-educated hooligans at the holiest and most fragile shrines of art and letters, not to mention music'.[49] And unfortunately for Amis, few reviewers bothered to make the distinction between Dixon and his creator. V. S. Pritchett, for instance, called Amis 'brashly, vulgarly, aggressively insensitive . . . a literary Teddy Boy'.[50] J. H. Weightman in the *Times Literary Supplement* noted that the book had 'spread the impression that Redbrick is peopled by beer-drinking scholarship louts, who wouldn't know a napkin from a chimney-piece and whose one idea is to end their sex starvation in the arms of a big-breasted blonde', but conceded that if this was an autobiographical portrait, 'Amis would presumably have long since lost his job, and rightly so'.[51] Even some seven years later, after Amis had moved to teach at Cambridge, the eminent critic F. R. Leavis remarked: 'Peterhouse can't expect to be taken seriously about anything now that it's given a fellowship to a *pornographer*.'[52] And decades afterwards, more self-consciously highbrow writers still failed to see the merits of Amis' work. In A. S. Byatt's novel *Still Life*, for instance, which is set in the fifties, *Lucky Jim*'s 'elementary school antics' are chronicled with incredulous distaste: 'There was a nice girl, whose niceness consisted of big breasts and a surprising readiness to find the lunatic Dixon attractive and valuable, and a nasty woman who was *judged* for bad make-up and arty skirts as well as for hysteria and emotional blackmail.'[53]

Amis' approach was not entirely unprecedented. John Wain's novel *Hurry On Down*, published the previous year, had an equally disgruntled middle-class hero, Charles Lumley. Both Wain and Amis were also indebted to a third writer, 'William Cooper' (H. S. Hoff), whose novel *Scenes from Provincial Life* (1950) had inaugurated the vogue for middle-class anti-heroes contemptuous of the highbrow intellectual culture that surrounds them. Amis later wrote that 'very few books have appealed to me as strongly' as did *Scenes from Provincial Life*: for one thing, there was the provincial setting of trams, market stalls, schoolrooms and teashops, a world away from the exotic or metropolitan worlds of Modernist fiction; most important, however, 'was that Joe Lunn, its hero, was just like me (and just like, I imagine, tens of thousands of other young men all over these islands)'.[54] What he took from Joe Lunn's experience was what he then reproduced in his own novels: the primacy of ordinary daily concerns over grand passions or world events. In Cooper's book, as Malcolm Bradbury pointed out, 'the day-to-day world of provincial life, the problems of love-affairs and jobs and local pleasures, eventually become far more important than history', so that the overall impression is of 'appreciative realism, a lyrically comic celebration of the ordinary over the extraordinary, the day-to-day over the grand march of history'.[55]

Much of the comedy of Amis' novel derives from the accumulation of mundane little misdemeanours: Dixon steals a bottle of port, destroys his bedclothes, writes insults in the steam on his bathroom mirror, impersonates strangers on the telephone, sends threatening anonymous letters, and so on. And Dixon himself is resolutely *ordinary*: he lacks any exceptional or heroic qualities and indeed often behaves in a selfish, petty or cowardly, if amusing, way. For example, he is described as 'hating' an old lady for wearing a particularly egregious hat.[56] Again, this reflects the provincial, middle-class background of the book, and indeed of fiction in general after the war. Blake Morrison notes that post-war heroes 'are rarely outstanding individuals', but are flawed, awkward, even cowardly.[57] But the comedy does not derive simply from the farcical situations into which

Dixon digs himself. It also develops, as with older English comic writers like Wodehouse or Waugh, in Amis' writing itself: his easy combination of post-war slang with high style, or the way in which the personalities of the more despicable characters are revealed in their ludicrous use of language. And it derives from the basic premise of the novel: the gulf between Dixon's frustrated inner life, his pent-up anger at the cultural snobbery of Professor Welch and his minions, and the necessity of presenting a polite and co-operative front. The only way that Dixon can cope with his frustration is by a series of boyish pranks, notably the array of faces he pulls behind Welch's back, from the grimaces of a Chinese mandarin or a Martian invader to his impersonations of Edith Sitwell or 'Sex Life in Ancient Rome'.[58]

There is no doubt that *Lucky Jim* was a work of tremendous influence. As D. J. Taylor remarks, if the success of a novel can be judged by 'the number of people who have tried, however unconsciously, to imitate it . . . then *Lucky Jim* must stand as one of the most successful novels of the post-war era'.[59] The *New Statesman*'s reviewer Walter Allen noted in January 1954 that Amis' hero, 'the intellectual tough, or the tough intellectual', could stand for an entire generation: 'He is consciously, even conscientiously, graceless. His face, when not dead-pan, is set in a snarl of exasperation.' This new hero, according to Allen, was sensitive above all to pretentiousness: 'at the least suspicion of the phoney he goes tough'. As for his origins: 'The Services, certainly, helped to make him; but George Orwell, Dr Leavis [ironically, given his scorn for Amis] and the Logical Positivists – or, rather, the attitudes these represent – all contributed to his genesis.'[60] So *Lucky Jim* was not merely an excellent comic novel in its own right; it was also emblematic of a post-war literary trend, known to commentators as 'the Movement', encompassing a fondness for middle-class provincial settings, the rejection of Modernism, cosmopolitanism and the avant-garde, and a mood of 'rationalism, realism, empiricism'.[61] More than any other novel of its day, it showed that it was possible to win popular and critical acclaim by writing about the ordinary lives of ordinary people in the new Britain of the 1950s.

In August 1954 the *Spectator* journalist Anthony Hartley, a great supporter of the new literary generation, tried to capture the qualities that made its members such a breath of fresh air. Amis, Larkin, Wain and their friends were, he said, '"dissenting" and non-conformist, cool, scientific and analytical', although they were in danger of pushing their ordinary, sober style 'to

.[62] Two months later, the magazine's literary editor J. D.
.ne name for the Amis group: 'this new Movement of the
.e old 'cold-bath Marxists' of the thirties were incapable of dealing
.ie reality of post-war affluent Britain:

> The bus service has made the village into a suburb; the gaunt moorland
> produces a glittering factory; the angry slagheaps sink and melt greenly
> into the landscape, and the long dull High Street flowers with the black
> tulip of Montague Burton, the Tailor of Taste.

Britain was 'a changed place', and tastes were changing too. The readers of
'Kafka and Kierkegaard, Proust and Henry James' belonged to an outdated
age: the new writers of the Movement preferred George Orwell and Robert
Graves. They were, according to Scott,

> bored by the despair of the Forties, not much interested in suffering,
> and extremely impatient of poetic sensibility, especially poetic sensibil-
> ity about 'the writer and society' . . . The Movement, as well as being
> anti-phoney, is anti-wet: sceptical, robust, ironic, prepared to be as com-
> fortable as possible in a wicked, commercial, threatened world which
> doesn't look, anyway, as if it's going to be changed much by a couple of
> handfuls of young English writers.[63]

The lively correspondence in the weeks that followed both praised and
attacked the idea of a middle-class, ambitious, aggressive literary Movement.
Evelyn Waugh felt moved to write to the magazine, as did a young
postgraduate student called Malcolm Bradbury.[64] One writer, the poetry
critic G. S. Fraser, noted the centrality of anger, 'an irascible temperament',
to contemporary literary success. 'It is a genuine novelty', he remarked, 'to
give the irascible appetite an intellectual respectability.'[65]

Some historians have since argued that the idea of the new Movement
was a fraud, a journalistic fiction designed to assuage anxieties about cultural
decline, imperial retrenchment and creeping Americanisation.[66] Amis himself disliked the idea of being lumped into a Movement. 'What a load of
bullshit all that was in the *Spr* about the new movt., etc.,' he wrote to Larkin.
'Useful up to a point, but the point is nearly here, I feel; someone should tell
old GSF to pipe down a little before people think he's buggering all our
arses.'[67] But if the Movement is narrowly defined to include Amis, Larkin

and their close friends and contemporaries, then there is no doubt that there *was* a genuine literary faction reflecting the feelings and ideas of a particular group of lower-middle-class intellectuals. Indeed, the nine writers generally taken to form the core of the Movement – Amis, Larkin, Wain, Robert Conquest, Donald Davie, John Holloway, Elizabeth Jennings, Thom Gunn and D. J. Enright – published their materials together in two anthologies, *Poetry of the 1950s* (1955) and *New Lines* (1956).[68] This inner group was identifiable enough for Conquest to name the 'Poet' class of space cruisers after its members in his science-fiction novel *A World of Difference*.[69] Amis even devised a jazz band, 'Jack Wain and the Provincial All-Stars' in November 1953:

Wain (tpt, voc) directing Phil Larkin (clt), 'King' Amis (tmb), Don Davie (alto), Al Alvarez (pno), Tommy Gunn (gtr), George 'Pops' Fraser (bs), Wally Robson (ds).

Drop me off at Reading / Up the country
Lay your racket / Things ain't what they used to be
It's the talk of the town / How'm I doing hey, hey.[70]

'There's no doubt, you know,' he wrote to Larkin a few months later, after they had appeared together on a radio programme, 'we are getting to be a movement, even if the only people we like apart from ourselves are each other.'[71]

In January 1956 the *Observer* supplied a facetious but surprisingly accurate 'identikit' of the ideal Movement writer:

Born: Coketown 1925. Parents: lower-middle class. Educated: local council school grammar school and university (after three years' military service). Married. One or two children. Occupation: civil servant/journalist/lecturer/minor executive. Politics: neutralist. Ambition: to live well. Interests: people, money, sex. Worries: money, sex. Enthusiasms: Orwell, jazz, Dr Leavis, old cars. Antipathies: Dylan Thomas, provincial culture, European novels. Future: indefinite.[72]

Four of the nine core members of the Movement had indeed grown up in provincial industrial towns; six had been to grammar schools; four were scholarship boys at Oxford or Cambridge; and five taught at provincial universities at some stage. It was no accident that their attitudes and ambitions were often those of middle-class provincial England, or that they cast themselves as the opposition to the pretentious, upper-class literary elites of the past.[73]

As Kingsley Amis saw it, what united the Movement writers was their common aim 'to write *sensibly*, without emotional hoo-ha'.[74] They wrote about everyday things in a fairly conservative, formal style, and shied away from literary experiment, excessive sentimentalism and elaborate metaphors. 'Nobody wants any more poems on the grander themes for a few years,' Amis explained, 'but at the same time nobody wants any more poems about philosophers or paintings or novelists or art galleries or mythology or foreign cities or other poems.'[75] His friend Larkin, for example, prided himself on speaking to the ordinary reader about familiar things and experiences: in 'The Whitsun Weddings', for example:

> The fathers with broad belts under their suits
> And seamy foreheads; mothers loud and fat;
> An uncle shouting smut; and then the perms,
> The nylon gloves and jewellery-substitutes . . .[76]

Some critics irritated Larkin by calling his work 'commonplace'.[77] But, as his enduring popularity suggests, Larkin had perfectly captured what Al Alvarez called 'post-war provincial England in all its dreariness'.[78] Few writers could have evoked the 'cut-price crowd' of industrial Hull in the early sixties as well as Larkin in 'Here':

> residents from raw estates, brought down
> The dead straight miles by stealing flat-faced trolleys,
> Push through plate-glass swing doors to their desires –
> Cheap suits, red kitchen-ware, sharp shoes, iced lollies,
> Electric mixers, toasters, washers, driers.[79]

The anti-Modernism of the Movement writers reflected a wider change in British intellectual culture in the fifties and sixties, a retreat from the earnestness and self-importance of preceding decades. Writers like Wain and Amis preferred to follow the example of George Orwell, who had patented the persona of the grumbling socialist with conservative cultural instincts.[80] Like Larkin, Orwell detested highbrow idealism and eccentricity, 'all that dreary tribe of high-minded women and sandal-wearers and bearded fruit-juice drinkers who come flocking towards Socialism like blue-bottles to a dead cat'; and like Amis, he held up in contrast the ideal of the 'ordinary decent person'.[81] At the same time, the Movement drew on a general contemporary enthusiasm for intellectual pragmatism. The leading literary critic of the fifties, F. R. Leavis, was well known for his preference for rigorous formalism over woolly romanticism.[82] Even the 'official' English philosophies of the day, the ordinary language philosophy of J. L. Austin and the logical positivism championed by A. J. Ayer, emphasised the analytical and the empirical rather than the metaphysical and the highbrow. 'The philosopher', Ayer wrote in his book *Language, Truth and Logic*, 'has no right to despise the beliefs of common sense.'[83]

To Amis, the upper-class intellectuals of the thirties had been self-indulgent, fraudulent and 'worthless'.[84] D. H. Lawrence, for example, fell foul of Amis for vaunting himself as the prophet of superior feeling. 'And what are we to do, all the rest of us, the mass?' Amis asked sarcastically. 'Can we become superior too? Hardly, because it's all a matter of feeling, you see.'[85] Instead of writing for the ordinary reader, Lawrence and his ilk had wallowed in pretentious intellectualism, 'torrid images' and 'grand meaning'.[86] Larkin agreed with his friend's diagnosis. English poetry, he wrote, had been taken away from 'the general reader' by 'the aberration of Modernism', 'the emergence of English as an academic subject', and 'the culture-mongering activities of the Americans Eliot and Pound'.[87] As far as the two friends were concerned, 'culture-mongering' in the Modernist manner was the province of the foreign, the pretentious and the unattractive. In the novel *I Like It Here* (1958), Amis' protagonist remarks that a 'far from wholehearted devotion to the pursuit of girls had sometimes struck him as a kind of selection-board requirement for writers and artists'.[88] 'It's nice to have a pretty girl with large breasts', Amis once remarked, 'rather than some fearful woman who's going to talk to you about Ezra Pound and hasn't got large breasts and probably doesn't wash much.'[89]

In the novels of Wain and Amis, the earnest 'intellectual' is usually a pretty contemptible figure, and very rarely one with large breasts. In Wain's novel *Hurry On Down*, the character of the bohemian Froulish functions as a mocking parody of the Modernist intellectual, a ludicrous poseur who claims his literary masters are 'Dante, Spinoza, Rimbaud, Boehme and

Grieg', and whose book begins with the elliptical and unpromising lines: 'A king ringed with slings, a thing without wings but brings strings and sings. Ho, the slow foe!'[90] But the quintessential intellectual is the loathsome Bertrand Welch in *Lucky Jim*: 'a tall man wearing a lemon-yellow sports-coat, all three buttons of which were fastened, and displaying a large beard which came down further on one side than on the other, half-hiding a vine-patterned tie. Dixon guessed with surging exultation that this must be the pacifist painting Bertrand.'[91] Unusual clothes, berets and other eccentric pieces of headgear, affected speech, of course beards: these are the indications of an intellectual at work. Bertrand's brother, 'the effeminate writing Michel', who appears only in the final scene of the novel, is similarly suspicious: 'a tall pale young man with long pale hair protruding from under a pale corduroy cap'.[92] And Margaret, the neurotic blue-stocking with whom Dixon is at first involved, is an instantly recognisable intellectual, wearing 'a sort of arty get-up of multi-coloured shirt, skirt with fringed hem and pocket, low-heeled shoes, and wooden beads'.[93]

Against these despicable figures is set the resolutely 'normal' Jim Dixon. His forthcoming academic article is called 'The Economic Influence of the Developments in Shipbuilding Techniques, 1450 to 1485'; he ponders its 'niggling mindlessness, its funereal parade of yawn-enforcing facts, the pseudo-light it threw on non-problems'.[94] He is staggered when a friend asks him if it is any good: 'Good God, no. You don't think I take that sort of stuff seriously, do you?' Indeed, he only ever became a medieval historian because 'the medieval papers were a soft option in the Leicester course'.[95] It is Dixon's utter contempt for both his own subject and the academic milieu that provides much of the comedy of the novel. He reviles Professor Welch's love of classical music, shuddering at 'a violin sonata by some Teutonic bore' or 'some skein of untiring facetiousness by filthy Mozart'.[96] People in the Middle Ages, he thinks, were 'nasty', 'self-indulgent', 'dull', 'miserable', 'bad at art' and 'dismally ludicrous'.[97] Not for nothing is the climax of the novel Dixon's famously disastrous, drunken public lecture on 'Merrie England', a lecture he reads at one point 'with a sarcastic, wounded bitterness': 'Nobody outside a madhouse, he tried to imply, could take seriously a single phrase of this conjectural, nugatory, deluded, tedious rubbish.' The final words of the lecture are his crowning assault on the affected values of the provincial intellectual elite: 'the home-made pottery crowd, the organic husbandry crowd, the recorder-playing crowd, the Esperanto . . .' – and then he passes out.[98]

Jim Dixon is the classic example of what Amis and his friends called the 'chap', the decent, ordinary, suburban, beer-drinking man, generally content with his lot in the affluent society. The chap cared little about fine wines, painting or the theatre; he was more interested in typical grammar-school enthusiasms like jazz and science fiction.[99] In the early fifties, both jazz and science fiction had anti-elitist, suburban connotations, and new writers like Amis and Robert Conquest were keen to elevate them above more highbrow fare. Both Amis and Conquest wrote science-fiction stories and edited a series of science-fiction anthologies. The magazine *Amazing Science Fiction*, Amis claimed, 'will, at least in a good month, contain as much that is genuinely imaginative and coherent as, say, what is averagely available in the *London Magazine*', the latter being one of the most prestigious intellectual 'little magazines'.[100] Other approved tastes included, perhaps incongruously, a taste for pornography, of which Larkin and Conquest were dedicated connoisseurs, sending each other recommendations and cuttings. Conquest even played an elaborate practical joke on Larkin, sending him a letter supposedly from the Vice Squad warning him of a forthcoming prosecution. The terrified Larkin went so far as to visit his solicitor, at which point Conquest relented and confessed the truth.[101] An enthusiastic practical joker, Conquest also gained great pleasure from publishing an article in the academic journal *Critical Quarterly* entitled 'Christian Symbolism in *Lucky Jim*', claiming that Dixon's drunken escapade in the Welch household was a re-enactment of the Crucifixion, and citing such authorities as Mrs Joyce Hackensmith, author of the seminal book *The Phallus Theme in Early Amis*.[102]

In February 1957 the *Daily Worker* cast an eye over Amis' second novel *That Uncertain Feeling*. 'Kingsley Amis', remarked the reviewer, 'is as much a part of the world of 1957 as television, rock 'n' roll and the FA Cup.'[103] Indeed, more than any other member of the putative Movement, it was Amis who was most courted by newspaper editors, television interviewers and gossip columnists. Much of this attention, especially in magazines like the *New Statesman* and *Spectator*, reflected the urgent need of literary commentators to find a genuine British movement that would stand comparison with contemporary writers in France and the United States. But the most unexpected literary phenomenon of the fifties could hardly have been more different from the middle-class insularity of the Movement. In May 1956, three weeks after the first performance of John Osborne's play *Look*

Back in Anger, a young man called Colin Wilson published *The Outsider*, his
first book. The result was a sensation: ecstatic reviews, enthusiastic sales and
hundreds of column inches praising the new literary meteor. Just two
months after *The Outsider* had reached the shelves, the *Daily Mail* remarked
that it had been welcomed with 'the most rapturous reception of any book
since the war'.[104] And yet, as events were to prove, Colin Wilson's was a very
strange story indeed.

Wilson was much younger than the Movement writers. He had been
born to working-class parents in Leicester in 1931, and had never been to
university. After leaving school at sixteen, he wandered through a bewildering succession of jobs, including being a laboratory assistant, a farmhand,
a navvy and a hospital porter, and amused himself by flirting with various
forms of radical politics and reading as much philosophy and literature as he
could find.[105] However, Wilson knew in his bones that he was unlikely to
remain a navvy or a hospital porter for very long. 'Ever since I was nine or
ten years old, I had been convinced that I was a "genius", and destined for
great things,' he later recalled.[106] Indeed, despite the literary vicissitudes of
the next few decades, this extraordinary conviction never deserted him.
Contemporaries like Kingsley Amis and John Osborne might have been self-
confident, but they were as nothing compared with Wilson. As he modestly
explained to an interviewer in the mid-1980s: 'I suspect that I am probably
the greatest writer of the twentieth century.'[107]

Wilson's genius initially went unrecognised, and his early years in
London were drab rather than dramatic. After two trips to France, during
which he fell under the spell of Continental existentialism, he decided to
write his own philosophical masterpiece and, while living in a sleeping bag
on Hampstead Heath, took himself off during the daytime to the Reading
Room of the British Museum, where he toiled away on his great work, a
supernatural novel about Jack the Ripper. He had acquired a similarly
bohemian friend in Stuart Holroyd, a bright boy from Bradford with literary aspirations. Holroyd was very taken with his mentor's enormous
self-belief: for instance, despite the fact that Wilson was as yet unpublished,
he 'would assert of other writers that they were fools or mediocrities and
claim that he was the greatest living English writer, but he was not at all
condescending'. In the flesh, however, Wilson was not a very impressive
figure: as Holroyd put it, he 'retained something of the look of the school
"swot": high brow, thin mouth, small eyes behind thick glasses, short back
and sides haircut; and when he moved or shook hands he did so jerkily, as

one not quite at ease with his body'.[108] Neither was his daily life very exciting: every morning he awoke on the heath, packed up his sleeping bag, bought a mug of tea at a busman's café, and cycled to the British Museum. His great break, however, came when he fell in with the novelist Angus Wilson, who was then working as assistant superintendent of the Reading Room and encouraged him to send his masterpiece to a publisher.[109]

The manuscript that Wilson junior eventually sent to the publisher Victor Gollancz was actually another book entirely, a work of vaguely mystical literary commentary tentatively called *The Pain Threshold*. Gollancz was an impressionable man who had turned to religion after a nervous breakdown some years previously; he bought the rights to the book, now renamed *The Outsider* in imitation of Camus, and ordered an optimistic print run of five thousand copies.[110] Even before the book was published, Gollancz had persuaded the *Evening News* to run a story on Wilson with the headline 'A Major Writer – and He's 24', and the very same literary elite that had been offended by the levity of Amis and the Movement rushed to congratulate Wilson on a stunning debut.[111] Cyril Connolly, the very embodiment of the London literary establishment, wrote in the *Sunday Times* that Wilson had 'produced one of the most remarkable first books I have read for a long time'; while in the *Observer* Philip Toynbee announced that this 'truly astounding' work was 'an exhaustive and luminously intelligent study of a representative theme of our time'.[112] Appearing a fortnight after the first production of *Look Back in Anger*, which had already caused a stir on the London stage, the book was an immediate bestseller. The first print run of five thousand copies was sold out on the day of publication, and twenty thousand more copies were sold in the next six months. Wilson himself was reported to have made the princely sum of £20,000 within a year.[113] Suddenly he was a celebrity, his book flying off the shelves, his telephone ringing non-stop with requests for interviews and his name rarely out of the gossip columns.[114] 'Not since Lord Byron woke up and found himself famous', wrote one excited reporter, 'has an English writer met with such spontaneous and universal acclaim.'[115] How, and why, had Wilson done it?

The success of *The Outsider* was largely a question of timing. For one thing, it exploited a limited interest in intellectual circles in French existentialism and American bohemian writing, which were then fashionable in the more highbrow coffee bars of Soho. Wilson's argument was basically a mishmash of Nietzsche, Sartre, Camus and dozens of other writers and philosophers, thrown together with frenzied enthusiasm. The Outsider, he argued, was a man who rejected the banal conformity of ordinary life; freeing himself from the constraints of conventional thought, he must 'find his way back into daylight where he can know a single undivided Will, Nietzsche's "pure will without the troubles of intellect"'.[116] The book teemed with allusions to, and misquotations from, European authors: in the first chapter alone, Wilson cites Barbusse, Keats, Lawrence, the Kabbala, Wells, Eliot, Schopenhauer, Spengler, Kierkegaard, Hegel, Nietzsche, Sartre, Camus and Hume, among others. A typical paragraph tells us that Blake, Kierkegaard, Nietzsche and Dostoyevsky 'held basically the same beliefs'. 'The differences that seem to separate them', says Wilson, 'are only differences of temperament (imagine Blake's reaction to Kierkegaard's *Diary of the Seducer*, or Nietzsche's to Dostoyevsky's *Life of Father Zossima*!); the basic idea is the same in all four.'[117] One minor flaw, however, was his inability to quote accurately. As one indignant correspondent pointed out in the *Times Literary Supplement*, a sample of 249 lines of Wilsonian prose revealed 82 major and 203 minor errors: at least one mistake per line.[118] This might have been excusable but for the fact that the book was pitched at a level that Humphrey Carpenter likens to 'a first-year undergraduate essay'.[119] This is actually being pretty generous: Harry Ritchie is perhaps nearer the mark when he calls it 'puerile pontification masquerading as analytical expertise', a 'callow', 'weird' and 'fatuous polemic' in which Wilson tries to 'show off how many books he has read . . . to conceal the absence of any coherent development in the argument, indeed, the absence of any argument whatsoever'.[120]

The stunning reception of *The Outsider* is better explained by the prejudices of its readers than by the content of the book itself. As Ritchie points out, the reviewers who liked Wilson's book and promoted his cause, like Cyril Connolly, Philip Toynbee, Edith Sitwell and John Lehmann, tended to be members of precisely that older literary avant-garde that Amis and Wain despised.[121] Self-consciously highbrow critics like Toynbee and Connolly were keen to find evidence of a British literary revival: first, to assuage their fears about the onset of Americanisation and commercialism; second, to assure themselves that, despite the decline of British imperial power, the country was still an intellectual and aesthetic superpower; and finally, to put forward a suitably serious alternative to the upstart philistines from the provinces. Toynbee's review of *The Outsider* even carried the title 'Unlucky Jims'.[122] Everything about Wilson's book seemed to meet their criteria for acceptance. He was very young, unknown and of working-class family, so he could be presented as a contemporary alternative to the Amis tendency. He was not shy of addressing vast metaphysical themes, which was just the sort of thing these old Modernists liked; he liked to throw in all sorts of arcane literary references; he was keen to show off his obsessive reading. He adored Modernism and Romanticism, presented himself as a bohemian genius, and made no secret of his contempt for the ordinary masses. For the old literary elite, therefore, he was 'a sensational prodigy who had beaten the French at their own game' and had made metaphysical speculation fashionable again.[123] Indeed, Cyril Connolly was so pleased to see what Wilson was doing that, as he later admitted, he had not even bothered to read the book; he simply thought it 'deserved a good review'.[124] As one article in the *Evening News* put it: 'It has been feared that the Welfare State has killed the thoughtful man by too much kindness, seducing him from the wholehearted pursuit of the meditative ideal. Thank God, it hasn't.'[125]

Wilson's rather unconventional opinions meant that he was, at first, a hit with the journalists and feature writers dispatched to interview him. 'I have just met my first genius,' wrote Daniel Farson in the *Daily Mail*. 'His name is Colin Wilson.'[126] Unfortunately, fame quickly went to Wilson's head and his public pronouncements became ever more bizarre. In an article for the *Daily Express* on 14 September 1956, for instance, he insisted that death was perfectly avoidable: it was merely a question of will. 'People die because they want to,' he wrote. 'And why do people die? Out of laziness, lack of purpose, of direction.'[127] Equally ill-advised, perhaps, was the great man's decision two months later to denounce Shakespeare for having a 'thoroughly second-rate mind'.[128] The writer Peter Vansittart recalled an appearance by Wilson at the ICA, where he announced: 'Man's enemies are herd-values, triviality, the weight of mental inertia, stale ideas and irrelevant history; escape is in self-realization, self-mastery, to expand luminous moments of vision and insight into authentic freedom.' During the question period, a bizarre exchange ensued when a middle-aged woman stood up and asked Wilson: 'I have a beautiful home and a well-kept garden, a loving husband and two friendly and well-behaved boys. We have saved and made sacrifices to afford them an excellent education. We enjoy simple things, and go abroad to see places of historical interest. So please tell me, in all seriousness, where I have gone wrong.' Wilson then rose, 'a man of wrath', and stormed:

You . . . you're the worst of the lot! Unspeakable! A mainstream criminal! Of course you enjoy simple things, you're incapable of anything
else. Your house is garbage, your garden a midden and a swamp, your
husband is Gordon FitzHomo and your children are dung. Their school
should be prosecuted. You're the dregs of the country, barely conceivable in your enormity and it's appalling that you were ever conceived.
When you nerve yourself to go abroad, black flags are run up and the
port authorities hold their noses.[129]

This was not an untypical performance. Whereas the Movement writers
generally celebrated the ordinary world of suburban affluence, Wilson
detested it. 'Our civilisation', he insisted, 'is an appalling, stinking thing,
materialistic, drifting, second-rate.'[130]

Not surprisingly, self-proclaimed defenders of the ordinary like
Kingsley Amis hated *The Outsider*. 'One of the prime indications of the sickness of mankind in the mid-twentieth century', Amis wrote in the *Spectator*,
'is that so much excited attention is paid to books about the sickness of
mankind in the mid-twentieth century.' The average Outsider was precisely
the kind of person that Amis despised; as he explained:

He will have a private income or a patron: the incidence of
Outsiderism among builders' foremen or bookies' runners must be
low. He is likely to be unmarried and without family ties . . . He tends
to amorality, feeling that a spot of murder or child-rape may come in
handy as a means of asserting his Will, escaping from the prison of
thought, etc., and he is totally devoid of humour. Now it is quite conceivable that chaps like that may really be 'society's spiritual dynamo',
but I judge it unlikely.

The ideal remedy for 'Outsiderism', said Amis, involved 'ordering up
another bottle, attending a jam session, or getting introduced to a young
lady'. As for Wilson's ostentatious learning, he caustically remarked: 'Here
they come – tramp, tramp, tramp – all those characters you thought were
discredited, or have never read, or (if you are like me) had never heard of:
Barbusse, Sartre, Camus, Kierkegaard, Nietzsche' and so on.[131] Of course, it
was implausible that Amis, a university lecturer in literature, had never
heard of them: the point was that he thought it pretentious and affected to
throw their names around like confetti at a wedding. This provoked an

interesting exchange between the two young meteors. Amis reported to Robert Conquest:

> Had an incredible letter from Capitaine C. Wilson of the Légion Étrangère (?). Pattern extracts: 'I'm not personally unamiable . . . this anti-culture stuff gets you nowhere . . . I believe I represent a new trend in English literature . . . not having time myself, I persuaded my girl-friend to read your 2 books and tell me what she thought . . . your fault seems to me to be the same as Auden's . . . I feel you'd better know the worst . . . I have a lot of things I want to establish – vital things for the course of modern history – and knocking you and other misplaced fig-ures off their pedestals will be the first step.'

'Good stuff, eh?' Amis wrote. 'I give him 2 years before paranoia closes over his head.'[132] His own reply to Wilson can only be imagined: he reported to Philip Larkin that it had been 'written with a fountain pen' on Wilson's letter, which he then posted back to the sender.[133]

Satisfaction for Amis was not long in coming. The first serious blow to Wilson's reputation came in February 1957 after a strange contretemps involving the parents of his girlfriend Joy Stewart, who came across one of his diaries and were shocked by what they claimed was its pornographic content. Wilson later tried to explain that they were notes for his 'research', but the offended Stewarts were having none of it. On the evening of 19 February, they burst unexpectedly into Wilson's flat, Mr Stewart brandish-ing a horsewhip and shouting the immortal lines: 'Aha, Wilson, the game is up! We know what's in your filthy diary!'[134] The story inevitably found its way into the newspapers. 'Horsewhip Threat to "Outsider" Wilson', the Daily Mail excitedly announced.[135] Mr Stewart told the press that Wilson's diaries had been the 'ravings' of a madman, all 'sadism and murder', and Wilson himself handed copies over to the Mail in order to dispel the accu-sations.[136] This was a disastrous mistake: few writers could have survived the revelation that they habitually wrote things in their diary like:

> The day must come when I'm hailed as a major prophet . . .
>
> I must live on, longer than anyone else has lived . . . to be eventually Plato's ideal sage and king . . .
>
> I *am* the major literary genius of our century . . . the most serious man of our age.[137]

As Mr Stewart put it, the game was up. Wilson's second book, *Religion and the Rebel*, was published in October 1957 and took his work to a new level. 'A man is more alive than a cow,' he opined at one point, 'just as a cow is more alive than a tree.'[138] This time the reviewers were less easily taken in. 'Deplorable . . . inferior . . . a vulgarizing rubbish bin,' said Philip Toynbee, while other critics called it 'highly embarrassing', 'half-baked Nietzsche' and 'a mixture of banality and incomprehensibility'. The 'most serious man of our age' had become what one *Manchester Guardian* commentator called 'a ridiculous figure', and next to his photograph *Time* magazine gleefully printed the caption: 'Egghead, scrambled'.[139] When Wilson and his two acolytes, Stuart Holroyd and Bill Hopkins, decided to voice their sympathy for the veteran fascist Sir Oswald Mosley, his cause was well and truly sunk.[140] Angus Wilson, who had once promoted his protégé's work, now mercilessly caricatured his pretensions, and in his short story 'A Bit off the Map' there appeared the character of 'Huggett', a 'thin', 'pale', 'feeble' young man, who venerates 'Love and Leadership' rather than 'democracy and freedom and stuff that . . . just gets in the way of real thinking'.[141]

But, even without his humiliation in 'A Bit off the Map', Colin Wilson's career as a popular philosopher was effectively doomed. His name gradually disappeared from the newspapers, and he retreated to a Cornish cottage to churn out an interminable series of books on the occult, aliens and serial killers, publishing 108 books in all by the end of the century. As one commentator puts it, his career was 'noteworthy for an unshakeable devotion to the spurious and the half-baked', and his investigations of alien encounters, astral ambassadors and intergalactic mysteries were 'tackled with all the thoroughness and the insight promised by *The Outsider* – none'.[142] Rather touchingly, Wilson nevertheless retained his faith in his own genius. More than forty years after the publication of *The Outsider*, he told a sceptical Humphrey Carpenter:

> Obviously I'm pretty talented, pretty clever – I'd be stupid if I didn't recognise that. And it strikes me that in five hundred years' time they'll say 'Wilson was a genius', because I'm a turning point in intellectual history. The problem of pessimism is lying across our contemporary culture like some giant log, and somebody had to come along and shift it. And I think that's what I've done, and one day that achievement will be recognised.[143]

Wilson had enjoyed such stunning temporary success because his book caught a particular mood and answered two needs: first, for a young British writer who could be compared with the European existentialists; and second, for a self-consciously intellectual rival to set against the bluff pragmatism of Amis and the Movement. Harry Ritchie has even argued that, with his ponderous seriousness, lank, floppy hair and polo-necked fisherman's jumper, Wilson defined 'a new literary image', the bohemian, high-minded Outsider. Before he came on the scene, 'there was no fixed image of young arty types'; now you could hardly move for polo-necks in the expresso bars of Fitzrovia.[144] By 1956 some coffee bars had already been claimed by groups of prototypical young 'beatniks' (although the word itself had yet to be invented): well-educated, middle-class men and women, often art students, often devotees of jazz or folk music, bored with their comfortable suburban lives and keen to embrace the supposed authenticity of American beat writers like Jack Kerouac or French existentialists like Sartre and Camus.[145] One habitué recalled 'those folk places, full of people with beards and unkempt clothes, wearing berets, carrying folders of their artwork, having poetry readings'.[146] These real-life Bertrand Welch figures were precisely the kind of people to whom Wilson's writing appealed; but in rejecting the world of suburban ordinariness they were also precisely the kind of people that Amis and Larkin most despised. As Larkin put it in July 1946:

> I HATE anybody who does anything UNUSUAL at all, whether it's make a lot of MONEY or dress in silly CLOTHES or read books of foreign WORDS or know a lot about anything or play any musical INSTRUMENT . . . or pretend that they believe anything out of the ordinary that requires a lot of courage, or a lot of generosity, or a lot of [self-control] to believe it – BECAUSE THEY ARE USUALLY SUCH SODDING NASTY PEOPLE THAT I KNOW IT IS 1000–1 THAT THEY ARE SHOWING OFF – *and they don't know it* but *I know it*.[147]

While Colin Wilson's literary career had already fizzled out by the beginning of the sixties, Kingsley Amis and Philip Larkin would be fixtures on the British intellectual landscape for decades to come. Although post-war literature spanned a broad and irreducible spectrum, their brand of conservative pragmatism caught the mood of the period much better than Wilson's pseudo-Continental abstractions. Indeed, in an age of increasing

American and European influence, the Movement can easily be seen as an aggressive, patriotic backlash. The old highbrow intellectuals had never concealed their admiration for all things French: the critic Raymond Mortimer, for instance, decorated the dining room of his Bloomsbury flat with French newspaper cuttings, while Cyril Connolly told the *Sunday Times* that his hobbies included 'Latin poetry, underwater swimming, claret, Sèvres porcelain and uncommon pet-animals'. As Ritchie remarks, 'the pretensions of the Welches seem unassuming by comparison'.[148] But, like George Orwell, middle-class writers like Larkin and Amis had little time for the 'Europeanized' cultural elitists who took 'their cookery from Paris and their opinions from Moscow'.[149] According to the poet Al Alvarez, they saw literary Modernism as 'a plot by foreigners . . . to divert literature from its true purpose; and their business was to get it back on its traditional track'.[150] If Britishness was good enough for the ordinary chap, they thought, it should be good enough for intellectuals too.

Larkin admitted to a profound 'hatred of abroad'. 'I wouldn't mind seeing China if I could come back the same day,' he remarked. 'I hate being abroad.'[151] Amis was not far behind. 'Being abroad seems compounded of the dull and the frightful,' he wrote to Larkin from Portugal in 1955.[152] On a trip to France, he somehow managed to enjoy himself but still complained: 'Why can't they talk English like everyone else?'[153] In Amis' novel *I Like It Here* (1958), the hero Garnett Bowen dislikes snobbery, Bloomsbury, London and, above all, 'abroad'. Italy, he muses, is full of 'all those rotten old churches and museums and art galleries'.[154] At the end of a long stay in Portugal, he reflects on how he hates 'all that sun', 'all those buildings', 'all that air of maturity, lack of nervousness and doubt, devotion to serious shouting argument or dedicated gaiety . . . all those revving motor-bikes, all those touts, all that staring'.[155] Safely back in England, he admits that the Portuguese were 'as decent as you'd find anywhere', but unfortunately 'the place is located abroad and the people are foreigners', so they can't understand one another or make friends. Ultimately, going abroad is merely 'as much an evasion as looking at the telly, only more expensive and you can't stop it when you want to and go to the pub'.[156]

These feelings were not inspired by any great hatred of Europeans themselves. Instead, as Amis admitted, they were rooted in his deep resentment of the cosmopolitan intellectual elites of the thirties and forties. In *I Like It Here*, Garnett explains that:

he had a long history of lower-middle-class envy directed against the upper-middle-class traveller who handled foreign railway officials with insolent ease, discussed the political situation with the taxi-driver in fluent *argot*, and landed up first go at exactly the right hotel, if indeed he wasn't staying with some *contessa*, all cigarette-holder and *chaise-longue*, who called him by a foreign version of his Christian name. He tried it over: Garnetto, Garnay, or rather Guhghr-nay. Later, he mused, they went off and dined, exquisitely and *madly* cheaply at – that's right, a little place one or other of them happened to know about, where – yes, you could get the best *merluza rellena al estilo de toro* in Valencia.[157]

Public schoolboys like Cyril Connolly might be up to ordering local specialities in exotic restaurants, but ordinary chaps like Garnett and Amis found the whole experience intimidating and uncomfortable. Indeed, throughout Amis' fiction, European sympathies are an unmistakable indication of pretentiousness and moral turpitude. In *Lucky Jim*, his hero delights in the news that Michel Welch has 'made himself ill by stuffing himself with filthy foreign food of his own preparation, in particular, Dixon gathered, spaghetti and dishes cooked in olive oil'.[158] When the Welch family organise a reading of a play by Jean Anouilh, Dixon bitterly mutters: 'Why couldn't they have chosen an English play?'[159] He even fantasises about tying Professor Welch in a chair and 'beating him about the head and shoulders with a bottle until he disclosed why, without being French himself, he'd given his sons French names'.[160] This animus did not mellow with time. Even forty years later, when Amis wrote *The King's English*, his guide to English usage, he advised his readers that when pronouncing the word 'liqueur', 'any attempt to say lee-cur in a Frenchified way is a useful wanker-detector'.[161]

Class anxieties of this kind were rarely far from the surface of British fiction in the late 1950s, and Amis confessed that he deeply resented the fact that 'things like novels in England . . . had been the preserve of what we'll call the public school upper classes'.[162] Jim Dixon, he said, was 'supposed to be the son of a clerk', the first in his family to go to university, a man 'who has seen, throughout his life, power and position going to people who (he suspects) are less notable for their ability than their smooth manners, their accents, the influence they or their fathers can wield'.[163] In Larkin's novel *Jill*, the Midlands-born hero travels down by train to Oxford white with fear at entering a new world, even eating his sandwiches in the toilet to avoid being watched by the other passengers.[164] But although class was a burden to scholarship boys like Amis, their aim was not to tear down social distinctions but to win acceptance for themselves and recognition for their own suburban values. When Dixon is becoming involved with the pretty, well-heeled heroine Christine, the hysterical Margaret snaps: 'You don't think she'd have you, do you? a shabby little provincial bore like you.'[165] Dixon's triumph, however, is that she *does* have him, and through the beautiful, well-bred Christine he is able to clamber up the ladder into the life of upper-middle-class London. Movement fiction never quite condemns upper-middle-class life outright: even if metropolitan intellectuals are scorned, their rich patrons are celebrated, their values are preserved, and the old cultural institutions are respected.[166]

Although Larkin had always been on the political right, Amis had once been a member of the Communist Party, and in 1957 described himself as 'an elderly young intellectual, perhaps with connections in the educational and literary worlds and left-wing sympathies'.[167] In *Lucky Jim* there are signs of his old political commitments. Dixon's enemies are all conservatives: the fearsome Margaret sings at the local Conservative club, and Bertrand Welch proclaims that 'the rich play an essential role in modern society'. Dixon himself is a vague Labour supporter; as he puts it: 'If one man's got ten buns and another's got two, and a bun has to be given up by one of them, then surely you take it from the man with ten buns.'[168] In general, however, British writers of the fifties shied away from overt political cheerleading, and some historians attribute this to the climate of the early Cold War, which restricted political debate, and the prevailing domestic political consensus, under which a fog of ideological apathy seemed to have settled over British letters.[169] In a 1957 essay for the Fabian Society, Amis explained that there were simply no great causes left: 'no Spain, no Fascism, no mass unemployment . . . No more millions out of work, no more hunger-marches, no more strikes; none at least that the rebel can take an interest in, when the strike pay-packet is likely to be as much as he gets himself for a review of Evelyn Waugh or a talk about basset-horns on the Third Programme'.[170] In *I Like It Here*, Amis has his hero reflect on the 'trivial insularity' of British politics, an 'endemic drabness [that] would no doubt be dissipated, Bowen reckoned, if the Tories could actually be witnessed in the course of jubilation over something or other to do with capital gains, if Labour could arrange to televise a *bona fide* very fat man occupied in watering the workers' beer'.[171]

Amis might be perceived by the likes of Somerset Maugham as a threat to decency and social order, but his politics really reflected the ambiguous relationship of the lower-middle-class intellectual with the prevailing post-war consensus. His mild attachment to socialism struggled with a distaste for emotional idealism; and his contempt for social snobbery vied with a pervasive sense of complacency. He opposed the government during the Suez crisis, but was nevertheless repelled by the 'vile old sick-and-tired' clichés he heard at a protest meeting.[172] Even given the political quiescence of the late 1950s, it was odd for a self-proclaimed socialist to write that 'the best and most trustworthy political motive is self-interest' and to denounce 'the professional espouser of causes, the do-gooder, the archetypal social worker'.[173] This kind of apathy was not very far from unashamed conservatism, and certainly approached it during the following decade. In *Girl, 20* (1971), Amis' withering portrait of the sixties, the hero proves indifferent even to charges of imperialism, racism and fascism. His incredulous accuser asks:

'Don't you think that's a bloody serious accusation, to call you a fascist?'

'No, I don't. Nor a communist or a bourgeois or anything else. I just don't care about any of that, you see.'

He looked at me in pure amazement. 'But these are some of the great issues of our time.'

'Of your time, you mean. The great issue of my time is me and my interests, purely musical. Can we go indoors now?'[174]

For many historians, the conservatism of British literature in the late fifties and sixties was closely connected to the rise of the Amis–Larkin generation. Of course this can easily be overstated. British fiction was so wide-ranging and diverse that no single trend completely dominated. Although many writers did concentrate on realistic descriptions of everyday life, attracting a great deal of attention in the late 1950s, others were experimenting with new techniques often borrowed from their Continental contemporaries: moral allegory, for example, or fantasy, or myth. In 1954, for instance, the year in which Amis made his literary debut, two very different writers in William Golding and Iris Murdoch also published their first novels. Muriel Spark's first novel *The Comforters* (1957) was a particularly arresting example of the more experimental style: published during the boom years of social realism, it plays with the conventions of novelistic form, with one character literally disappearing when she is no longer needed and another character showing a disconcerting awareness that she is a character in a novel.[175] And Murdoch, Golding, John Fowles and Anthony Burgess, not to mention the likes of Mervyn Peake, C. S. Lewis and J. R. R. Tolkien, were among other writers of the late fifties whose work defied the idea that down-to-earth realism swept all before it.[176]

And yet it was Amis and Larkin, at least in the eyes of the press, who set the tone for the late fifties. It was Amis, not Colin Wilson or William Golding or J. R. R. Tolkien, who was seen as the spokesman for the new generation and the literary voice of the affluent society. While American and Continental writers flirted with existentialism, absurdism and general bohemianism, their British counterparts were widely regarded as middle-class, anti-Modernist, nostalgic, introverted and politically uncommitted. This was not only a rebellion of the grammar schools against the highbrow elites; it was also the renewal of a native tradition of 'common sense', the bluff English provincial beer-swilling 'chap' standing up against the effeminate, Frenchified metropolitan coffee-drinking intellectual. Old traditions of scepticism and empiricism were thought to run deep. As one rather unsympathetic critic puts it, behind all this was 'a kind of defiant little Englandism, a reaction against the cult of foreign experimentalism . . . and an assertion that the English fictional tradition provided all the nourishment that was needed to rejuvenate the novel'.[177] And the Movement also exerted a powerful influence on the writers of subsequent generations. David Lodge, for example, wrote that *Lucky Jim* and the other novels of the period found a ready audience among his generation 'who came of age in the 1950s, especially those from lower-middle-class backgrounds who found themselves promoted into the professions by educational opportunity, but remained uneasy with, and critical of, the attitudes and values of the social and cultural Establishment'.[178]

By the late fifties, British literature seemed to have been transformed from a moribund backwater into an exciting, even glamorous world of colourful characters, simmering feuds and generous royalties. For many commentators, the fictional character 'Jim Dixon' had become the representative of affluent Britain itself: pragmatic, irreverent, down-to-earth and vaguely ambitious. In the first issue of *Universities and Left Review*, published in 1957, Stuart Hall and David Marquand solemnly picked apart Jim's political preferences in an attempt to gauge the mood of the electorate, and at the height of CND's popularity a few years later, the historian A. J. P Taylor announced that 'it was Lucky Jim who marched to Aldermaston, some thousands of him'.[179] By this point, however, the media had found a new label for Amis and his contemporaries, borrowed from the publicist of John Osborne's new play *Look Back in Anger*. Osborne barely knew either Amis or Wilson, but that seemed a trifling irrelevance. On 26 July 1956 the *Express* described the three writers as 'Angry Young Men', and two months later the same newspaper announced: 'A bright, brash and astonishingly bitter new crop of Angry Young Men has pushed up into the London scene this year: writing books and plays bristling with fresh if feverish ideas and opinions.'[180] Amis, who had been less than ecstatic at the idea of being lumped into the Movement, hated the idea of the Angry Young Men, which he thought was 'a phantom creation of literary journalists'.[181] But he was fighting a losing battle. In December 1956, the *Daily Mail* reflected on 'The Year of the Angry Young Men', and in August 1957 another paper mocked the three 'professional AYM . . . Kingsley Aimless, Colic Wilson and John Heartburn'.[182] A new wave of middle- and working-class writers, like Arnold Wesker, Shelagh Delaney, John Braine and Alan Sillitoe, was on the brink of literary fame and fortune. Complacency and conformity were out; almost overnight, anger was in.

6

THE NEW WAVE

The Northerner is a dreamer and a maker of films. He abolished insipid dialogue such as 'Anyone for tennis?' and replaced it with biting, incisive lines
such as 'Would you like a cup of tea?'

That Was The Week That Was (1963)

For many people living in the mill towns of Yorkshire, among the mining
valleys of South Wales or beside the shipyards of the Clyde, life in the late
fifties went on as it always had, a weary routine of little money and hard
work. In town after town, wrote one observer at that time, the visitor
trudged through 'street after regular street of shoddily uniform houses
intersected by a dark pattern of ginnels and snickets (alleyways) and
courts; mean, squalid, and in a permanent half-fog; a study in shades of
dirty-grey, without greenness or the blueness of sky'.[1] These were places
where the affluent society was little more than a mirage. Far away from
the trim suburbs of genteel England and the shiny showrooms of busy
high streets, the world of the working-class north seemed barely
changed:

Rough sooty grass pushes through the cobbles; dock and nettle insist
on a defiant life in the rough and trampled earth-heaps at the corners
of the waste-pieces, undeterred by 'dog-muck', cigarette packets, old
ashes; rank elder, dirty privet, and rosebay willow-herb take hold in
some of the 'backs' or in the walled-off space behind the Corporation
Baths. All day and all night the noises and smells of the district –
factory hooters, trains shunting, the stink of the gas works – remind
you that life is a matter of shifts and clockings-in-and-out. The children
look improperly fed, inappropriately clothed, and as though they could
do with more sunlight and green fields.[2]

Poverty had not disappeared. For Jo-Mary Stafford, a working-class girl growing up in Walsall, it meant 'hunger and cold', no light in the bedroom, meals of dried egg and Spam, 'shivering around a tiny flicker of flame' from a scrap of coal, thin and threadbare second-hand clothes and a trip to the School Clinic to redress under-nourishment.[3] It meant perfunctory washing and the ubiquitous stench of urine, dung, soot, tar and sewage.[4] There were, according to one estimate, seven hundred elderly people in prosperous Brighton at the end of the decade who lived on just toast and tea, unable to afford a cigarette or a beer because of the desperate struggle to keep down their costs.[5] Many of the poor lived in houses barely fit for human habitation, a legacy of the shattering destruction of the Second World War that, even a decade later, still cast a shadow over British housing. Even though successive governments poured money into new estates and new towns, some families were forced to live in battered shells. One woman later recalled her rooms with a shudder. 'The whole house was crumbling. Every time you shut a door hard a bit of the ceiling fell down. Big mushrooms the size of breakfast plates grew up the walls, and if you cut them down in a few days they grew back again. There was a hole in the bedroom floor a foot square where the rats had gnawed away.' There was, of course, no bathroom.[6]

Estimates of the total number that lived in poverty inevitably varied according to the criteria used. After studying social conditions in York, Seebohm Rowntree calculated that the proportion living in poverty had fallen from 18 per cent in 1936 to a mere 1.5 per cent in 1950, and an editorial in *The Times* declared that Britain had achieved a 'remarkable improvement – no less than the virtual abolition of the sheerest want'.[7] But not all observers agreed with this optimistic picture. In 1958 the sociologist Peter Townsend argued that, despite the prosperity of the Macmillan years, large groups of people were still living in poverty: the old, the widowed, the sick and disabled, and so on, reaching an estimated total of some seven million people.[8] In the early sixties a series of new surveys argued that since the official subsistence scales were both harsh and unrealistic, more people than the authorities admitted were in fact living below the poverty line.[9] In 1965 a comprehensive study compared household incomes with Ministry of Labour surveys to conclude that in 1960 no less than 14 per cent of the population had been living in poverty, confirming Townsend's figure of seven million people. According to this analysis, that figure included three million people who lived in families where the father's wage was inadequate to cover basic needs, either because it was simply too small or because there were too many children; over two million people who were poor because they were elderly; and hundreds of thousands more in single-parent families, families where one parent was disabled or sick, or families where the father was unemployed. Almost a third of all those in poverty were children under fifteen, two million in all.[10]

However poverty was defined, hardship and inequality clearly persisted in many parts of Britain in the late 1950s. Despite the welfare state and the prosperity of the decade, Britain was still a profoundly unequal society. Of the nation's private wealth, according to *The Economist*, more than four-fifths was owned by a mere 7 per cent of taxpayers. Indeed, nearly 90 per cent of the population owned less than 4 per cent of the national wealth.[11] At the end of the decade the *Financial Times* observed that, in the families of manual workers where the father's income fell below £350 a year, barely 1 per cent owned a car, 2 per cent a refrigerator, 11 per cent a washing machine, and 34 per cent a television.[12] And these were precisely the families that suffered most from the backbreaking drudgery of hard labour. As one account puts it, to be working class meant 'performing manual work, most usually under arduous, uncongenial or just plain boring circumstances', and returning home exhausted, dirty and bruised every evening: the same routine, hour after hour, day after day, with little chance of escape, little access to the entertainments of the affluent, and little hope of bequeathing a better future to one's children.[13]

The problem of poverty had occupied researchers and social reformers for decades, and, although the discipline of sociology really became established in Britain during the post-war years, a long series of social surveys and studies had been pouring forth since the Victorian years.[14] In the fifties, however, sociology was more fashionable than ever, boosted by two other developments: the growth of mass marketing and the Butskellite consensus. Mass marketing was vitally important in an expanding consumer society, and the techniques of social observation honed during the thirties were now developed further by market-research experts eager to sell televisions or detergent. 'Attitude measurement', 'opinion sampling' and 'consumer profiling' were, it appeared, the keys to commercial and even political success in the consumer-driven world of the 1950s.[15] The political consensus, meanwhile, meant that many bright, committed young men and women, uninspired by the apparent timidity of Butskellism, poured their political enthusiasm into other areas like CND or social and cultural studies.[16]

At the heart of sociological research in Britain was the London School of Economics, an expanding institution in the 1950s and 1960s, where the subject had a special appeal to students with strong progressive commitments and from modest family backgrounds. Two LSE scholars stood out: David Glass, the outstanding British expert on demography, and Edward Shils, an intellectually powerful American theorist. When sociology departments were established in the 1950s and 1960s at provincial universities like Leeds, Nottingham and Birmingham, their students were recruited to fill the new posts, eventually carrying the discipline into Oxford and Cambridge. The future Oxford sociologist A. H. Halsey was a typical pioneer; most of them, he recalled, were lower-middle-class and working-class young men who had won scholarships to grammar schools, were committed Labour supporters, were disgusted by the Suez affair and the Soviet invasion of Hungary, and were fervently opposed to the kind of old-fashioned snobbery that persistently denigrated their subject. Since social theory had European and American roots, it was automatically regarded by many academics in more conventional subjects with a great deal of suspicion; each new theory that crossed the Atlantic, from David Riesman's ideas about Organization Man and the Lonely Crowd to Marshall McLuhan's Global Village, provoked both moans of passion from the enthusiasts and groans of exasperation from the sceptics.[17]

The popularity of social science also affected other disciplines: in history, for example, young researchers from Asa Briggs and Hugh Trevor-Roper to E. P. Thompson and Eric Hobsbawm addressed social and political issues far removed from the dry world of constitutional or legal history. Traditional historians might complain that the subject was being debased from an art into a pseudo-science, and deplore the rise of subjects like 'The Economic Influence of the Developments in Shipbuilding Techniques, 1450 to 1485', but the intellectual momentum was with the social scientists, who in the following decades took their inquiries into subjects as diverse as the family structures of east London, the language of nursery rhymes, the voting patterns of general elections, and the spending habits of teenagers.[18] The Institute of Community Studies in Bethnal Green, which had been founded in 1954 by Richard Titmuss and Michael Young, both LSE sociology graduates, produced a stream of reports examining British society in the brave new world of the welfare state. Their surveys of individual areas, such as the report on suburban Woodford quoted earlier, were rich in the kind of personal details likely to attract general readers. Many reports were published for a mass audience in the form of Pelican paperbacks and Penguin Specials, and between 1961 and 1980 there were no fewer than fourteen Penguin editions of the first Wilmott and Young survey, *Family and Kinship in East London*.[19] The literary influence of social science had never been greater, and the most influential work of all was Richard Hoggart's book of social and cultural criticism, *The Uses of Literacy*.[20]

There is little doubt that *The Uses of Literacy*, an examination of Northern working-class culture published in 1957, was one of the most significant books of its period. Its author was an English lecturer in the adult education department at Hull, but, unlike Philip Larkin, Hoggart was of working-class stock. Born in 1918, he had been brought up by his grandmother in a working-class district of Leeds, won a scholarship to grammar school and another scholarship to Leeds University, and then served in Italy during the war before moving into teaching. Unlike the Movement writers, Hoggart had known hardship and want at first hand. He was impatient with middle-class intellectuals who romanticised the working class; the common images of the poor as 'rough and unpolished, but diamonds nonetheless', 'charitable and forthright', and 'possessed of racy and salty speech, touched with wit, but always with its hard grain of common sense', struck him as tired and inaccurate, blurred through 'the cosy fug of an Edwardian music hall'.[21] Similarly, he also disliked the 'part-pitying and part-patronising' Marxist or socialist stereotypes of the 'noble savage' oppressed by circumstance, 'the betrayed and debased worker' whose faults were 'entirely the result of the grinding system that controls him'. Instead, his ambition was to depict working-class men and women as they really were, without the cloying filter of sentiment.[22]

The first chapters of *The Uses of Literacy* describe the sights and smells of the industrial neighbourhood, the infinite variety of the people who live there and the often strained family relations behind the closed doors of their terraced houses, evoking a strong sense of poverty and hardship unique in academic discussions of culture. The world of working-class England that Hoggart describes is the real world of '"dog-muck", cigarette packets, old ashes', far from the drawing-room comedies of the West End or the cosy common rooms of the Movement.[23] 'The tiny house', he writes of his childhood, 'was damp and swarming with cockroaches; the earth-closet was a stinking mire in bad weather'. One of the most striking scenes is when his mother, having bought herself a little treat, 'a slice or two of boiled ham or a few shrimps', bursts out 'in real rage' when her little children pester her to share it.[24] But this homogeneous, warm, close-knit routine of working-class life is slowly being chipped away by affluence and education, and the honest, organic popular culture that Hoggart grew up with is being eroded by the cheap fictions peddled by advertisers and mass-market journalists. True, prosperity and education can in many ways represent freedom and opportunity; but he also argues that they result in the fragmentation of a society that was somehow more genuine and more 'solid': 'the steam-and-soda-and-hashed-meat smell of wash-day, or the smell of clothes drying by the fireside; the Sunday smell of the *News of the World*-mingled-with-roast-beef', for instance.[25]

Hoggart's emphasis on the innate decency of old-fashioned working-class life both drew on the legacy of older writers like George Orwell and shared something of the anti-modernism of Amis and the 'chaps' of the Movement.[26] Despite their differences, Hoggart, Amis and Larkin were all grammar-school boys intent on storming the citadels of exclusive high culture; they were all proud of their relatively modest backgrounds; and they all extolled the values of ordinariness and decency, using words like 'healthy', 'genuine' and 'honest' (as had Orwell and Leavis) to describe something that they liked.[27] One major difference, however, was Hoggart's contempt for modern mass culture, and *The Uses of Literacy* mounted a passionate attack on the excesses of consumerism in the late 1950s. He complains that 'to be old-fashioned is to be condemned' as 'stuffy and probably laughable . . . unknowing, old and prudish' when the old habits are much more genuine than the constant 'looking to the future' and 'the glorification of youth'.[28] His central argument is that modern mass entertainment is 'full of a corrupt brightness, of improper appeals and moral evasions'.[29] Mass culture gives the working classes cheap, sensationalist entertainment, enervating, dulling and eventually destroying their sense of taste; meanwhile, the working-class environment itself is being torn up and replaced by the cheap glitter of affluence, what Hoggart calls 'shiny barbarism'.[30] The most striking example is popular music and its public appreciation. On the one hand, Hoggart paints the picture of the old-fashioned working-class pub, a blind man playing familiar tunes on the piano, the drinkers merrily singing along to the ballads they know so well.[31] On the other, he gives us his famous indictment of the 'juke-box boys' revelling in the 'nastiness' and 'glaring showiness' of their 'modernistic knick-knacks'. Their 'harshly lighted' milk bars are full of desperate young men in their late teens, nursing cheap cups of tea and staring blankly 'across the tubular chairs' at the jukebox, listening to songs which are 'almost all American'.

> Compared even with the pub around the corner, this is a peculiarly thin and pallid form of dissipation, a sort of spiritual dry-rot amid the odour of boiled milk. Many of the customers – their clothes, their hairstyles, their facial expressions all indicate – are living to a large extent in a myth-world compounded of a few simple elements which they take to be the American dream.
>
> They form a depressing group . . . they have no aim, no ambition, no protection, no belief.[32]

For what was essentially a carefully argued book of social and cultural criticism, *The Uses of Literacy* proved very popular with readers, being reprinted thirteen times in twenty years.[33] Despite Hoggart's stated intentions, his depiction of the warmth and decency of the working-class household and the rugged authenticity of working-class social life further confirmed the established popular image of the working classes. This image owed much not only to Orwell but also to Dickens and the Victorian sentimentalists, perhaps even to Shakespeare and Chaucer; at its core, according to the cultural historian Robert Hewison, was 'a sense of the personal, the concrete, the local: it is embodied in the idea of first, the family, and second, the neighbourhood'.[34] Hoggart, like so many writers in the post-war years, was animated by a powerful sense of nostalgia, but his specific role was to focus that nostalgia on the world of the working-class North, fuelling an interest that would be further developed by the New Wave authors in the late fifties, like Alan Sillitoe or Stan Barstow, and eventually by the television series *Coronation Street*, which was first broadcast by Granada barely three years later.[35] Indeed, the longevity of *Coronation Street* ultimately made it the most popular and influential development of the working-class realism of the late fifties.[36]

The other important legacy of *The Uses of Literacy* was Hoggart's depiction of modern mass culture as shallow, destructive and debased, an analysis closely linked to the arguments of similar critics who opposed American influence.[37] Since commercial culture was supposed to be American in origin, it was all the easier for traditionalists to revile it. In 1951 the northern broadcaster Wilfred Pickles, a popular voice on BBC radio, drew a powerful contrast between American modernity and decent British working-class tradition:

> Walking under the glare of the neon signs and the dazzle from the cinemas, pin table saloons and those chromium corridors where young men in broad jackets and loud ties sip coffees with their Americanized girl friends, I thought for a moment of the men down the pit at Brodsworth and Atherton. They would be on the night shift now in that black underworld that is so much cleaner than London.[38]

Often this kind of nostalgic traditionalism went hand in hand with political opposition to the United States. A few months after the publication of Hoggart's book, the Marxist cultural critic Raymond Williams published *Culture and Society*, his influential study of English literary culture since 1780. Williams remarked that 'the smart, busy, commercial culture' gave him 'violent headaches whenever I passed through London and saw underground advertisements and evening newspapers'.[39] Like Hoggart, he was a working-class boy who had won a scholarship to grammar school, and he went on to win another scholarship to Cambridge, where he joined the Communist Party. Like Hoggart, he had been influenced by the Cambridge critic F. R. Leavis and he invoked 'authentic' culture as an antidote to commercialism and the consequences of laissez-faire capitalism.[40] And like Hoggart, he saw affluence as a cultural threat, and he deplored the influence of American mass culture. 'At certain levels', he remarked, 'we are culturally an American colony.'[41]

Writers like Williams and Hoggart stood out because they directed their intellectual energies into the study of working-class society and culture. Not all commentators could keep up with them: one reviewer even managed to write about '*The Uses of Culture* by Raymond Hoggart'.[42] At the same time there was a vogue for the depiction of working-class life on the stage, the page and the screen, often described as the British 'New Wave' or 'kitchen sink' drama. This was a literary phenomenon quite distinct from the Movement of Amis and Larkin, despite the efforts of contemporary journalists to lump them all together as 'angry young men'. New Wave writers were not part of the same provincial network of friends and colleagues that made up the so-called Movement, and rather than chronicling the frustrations of middle-class scholarship boys making their way in the affluent society, the New Wave writers were interested, like Hoggart, in the old world of the industrial working class, the world of Northern terraces, poverty and violence. What brought the New Wave together was a series of common themes and interests: a focus on the working class; aggressive attitudes to sex and women; a deep suspicion of modernity and mass culture; intense cultural nativism; a persistent strain of nostalgia, particularly for the Edwardian period; and a curious combination of indeterminate anger and political apathy. The idea of 'anger', in fact, ran through much New Wave writing, but it was never accompanied by any clear political programme. Anger had not been a very powerful emotion in the work of the Movement: although Jim Dixon was disgruntled, he was rarely openly angry. By contrast, it was the anger of the New Wave that first struck contemporary observers, and the most obvious example of this came in the theatre.[43]

After the war there was a general surge in interest in the stage. There were new academic periodicals devoted to the theatre, like *Theatre Notebook* and *Plays and Players*, and there was a rapid growth in applications to the major drama schools like RADA, LAMDA and the Central School of Speech and Drama.[44] The theatre was still a minority interest, and only one in every two hundred people attended regularly. But, as the historian Alan Sinfield points out, the theatre in the late 1950s not only became the focus of great press attention, it also became the subject of passionate cultural and social commentary, so it therefore took on a historical importance beyond its immediate appeal to an audience.[45] Since the theatre could no longer aspire to the massive popularity of the cinema, its audience was associated more than ever with intellectual eminence and respectable gentility. The West End was dominated by powerful impresarios like the legendary 'Binkie' Beaumont, who preferred proven commercial success to artistic experimentation.[46] But to prominent critics like Harold Hobson and Kenneth Tynan, Binkie and his contemporaries were guilty of a timid emphasis on predictability and nostalgia rather than on the challenging or the contemporary. Tynan had become the *Observer*'s theatre critic in 1954 at the age of just twenty-seven and thought that the West End was typified by an overemphasis on the drawing-room social comedy, a world 'almost exclusively concerned with the problems and pleasures of the upper-middle class . . . presented in a style of polite naturalism by actors whose performance was gentlemanly and unhistrionic'.[47] 'Apart from revivals and imports,' he declared, 'there is nothing in the London theatre that one dare discuss with an intelligent man for more than five minutes.'[48]

Tynan's principal target was the most successful playwright of the day, Terence Rattigan. During the course of the fifties there was scarcely a single month in which one of Rattigan's plays was not being presented on the London stage; both *Separate Tables* and *Ross* ran for over seven hundred performances, and *The Deep Blue Sea* for over five hundred.[49] Rattigan openly admitted that he wrote for a self-consciously conservative audience, a putative 'Aunt Edna', 'a nice, respectable, middle-class, middle-aged, maiden lady, with time on her hands and money to help her pass it, who resides in a West Kensington hotel'. She was, he said, 'a hopeless lowbrow', but she knew what she liked.[50] The invention of Aunt Edna made Rattigan an easy target for critics like Tynan, who accused him of pandering to the gentility of a wealthy public. In the drawing-room drama, Tynan claimed, 'the inhabitants belong to a social class derived from romantic novels and partly from the playwright's vision of the leisured life he will lead after the play is a success – this being the only effort of imagination he is called on to make'.[51] This was hardly fair; Rattigan had never meant to imply that he wrote to suit Aunt Edna's prejudices, and had argued that she should gently be pushed towards new ideas and attitudes.[52] Far from being unemotional, his plays in fact owed their appeal to the depiction of middle-class characters struggling to contain intense feelings. This conflict between emotion and reserve, between a barely suppressed secret life and the demands of public stoicism, lay at the heart of many of his plays, from *After the Dance* to *Separate Tables*, and was rooted in Rattigan's own struggle to conceal his homosexuality.[53] By the early sixties, however, this approach had become deeply unfashionable: two new Rattigan plays in 1960 and 1963 were forced to close early, and after 1963 he was absent from the West End stage for seven years.[54]

In fact, the conservatism of British theatre in the early fifties has been rather exaggerated. Harold Pinter later remarked that Rattigan was 'a writer of great sensibility and intelligence and perception and I think he was very hard done by by Tynan'.[55] As Charles Duff puts it in his rehabilitation of the era, 'the standard of the individual acting was high, and . . . its playwrights knew more about the human heart and wrote with greater literacy than many of their successors of the late 1950s and 1960s'.[56] Nevertheless, the impression of staid conformity was hard to shake, and for all the undoubted skill of dramatists like Rattigan and J. B. Priestley, they hardly represented a break from the styles of the thirties, and neither did they really reflect the new concerns of the post-war age. Harold Hobson noted in the *Sunday Times* that while the newspapers were full of 'war, insurrection, industrial unrest, political controversy, and parliamentary behaviour', on the stage 'all echo of these things is shut off as by sound proof walls'.[57] Rounding up the best plays of 1954, Anthony Hartley commented in the *Spectator* that he was 'appalled by the lack of standards' among British writers. 'It is not easy', he wrote, 'to recall one English play in this last year which even suggested that there might be a new playwright behind it . . . The English stage is passing through a singularly barren period.'[58]

The obvious contrast was with the theatre in the provinces, part of a general flowering of the arts in the British regions outside London. Thanks to the provision of generous subsidies from the Arts Council, repertory theatre was booming, and by 1960 there were forty-four companies in England alone, not to mention companies in Scotland, Wales and Northern Ireland, and countless little local theatres and amateur groups spread across the country.[59] Regional theatres, like the Belgrade Theatre in Coventry, the Cambridge Arts Theatre or the Liverpool Royal Court, were often keen to support innovative styles of drama, and kitchen-sink writers like Arnold Wesker, Bernard Kops and Shelagh Delaney made their initial impact in the provinces.[60] But the London stage, too, was beginning to change, not least through the influence of Continental writing. European dramatists like Eugene Ionesco, Samuel Beckett and Bertolt Brecht all had plays performed in London between March 1955 and August 1956, and they had a tremendous impact on younger writers and actors. All three broke radically with the conventions of drawing-room drama and encouraged writers to experiment with new styles of presentation, and between them they sketched out the path to take British drama into the sixties.[61]

The influence of writers like Ionesco and Brecht was particularly marked on companies like the agitprop group Theatre Workshop, which had been founded by two radical actors, Ewan MacColl and Joan Littlewood, in 1945 and was based on street theatre, improvisation, ensemble playing and didactic Marxist politics.[62] But although Theatre Workshop had been experimenting with new techniques for more than a decade, it was a younger group, the English Stage Company, which was most associated with the new drama of the late fifties. It was established at the Royal Court theatre in Sloane Square in 1955 with the avowed purpose of performing new English plays and contemporary imports from abroad. The artistic director was George Devine, an experienced actor and acting coach with his roots in the experimental theatre of the thirties, and his deputy was Tony Richardson, twenty-seven years old, a television director and yet another lower-middle-class scholarship boy.[63] The twenty-two young actors in the first company, among whom were Joan Plowright, Robert Stephens and Alan Bates, were paid less than half the West End average, but they were a talented bunch. Indeed, the Royal Court trained some of the most success-ful British stage performers of the post-war era: Alan Howard, Steven Berkoff, Glenda Jackson, Jeremy Brett, Rita Tushingham, Frank Finlay and Richard Briers all acted with the company during its early years.[64] The com-pany got off to a poor start, however, when its first play, *The Mulberry Bush* by the novelist Angus Wilson, received mixed reviews and failed to attract large audiences.[65] The second presentation was to be Arthur Miller's play *The Crucible*, a dependable Broadway hit; with the third, they needed another success. Devine and Richardson had trawled through over seven hundred scripts sent in response to their advertisement when they found one they liked, sent in by a struggling repertory actor living on a houseboat near Chiswick. They offered the author £25 for the option on it, and arranged to meet on his houseboat.[66]

The play in question had gone through a series of different working titles like *My Blood is a Mile High, Man in a Rage, Angry Man* or *Farewell to Anger*, but its author finally settled on *Look Back in Anger*. His name was John Osborne, and he was a frustrated provincial actor from a lower-middle-class background who had left school at eighteen, undergone National Service and worked as a journalist before embarking on his dramatic career. Although it was not his first play, it was unquestionably his breakthrough.[67]

The first performance of *Look Back in Anger* took place on 8 May 1956, a date often regarded as a milestone in British cultural history. It was directed by Tony Richardson, and starred Kenneth Haigh, Mary Ure and Alan Bates in the three main roles of Jimmy, Alison and Cliff.[68] There can be little doubt that when the curtain rose on the first night, some audience members were shocked by what they saw: a grimy, claustrophobic attic flat somewhere in the Midlands, crammed with battered old furniture. As the play begins, the character of Alison stands at stage left in front of an ironing board, working her way through a pile of clothes, while Jimmy and Cliff read the Sunday papers. The action never moves from the cramped little flat (too small even to have its own kitchen sink), and the plot follows the marital fortunes of

Jimmy and Alison Porter, with the main interest lying in Jimmy's various temper tantrums and tirades of boredom and frustration. The play ends with Alison and Jimmy reconciled after a period of separation during which she has lost their baby.

This was subject matter very different from the content of a play by Rattigan or Coward, and not everybody liked it. Rattigan himself remarked after the première that the play should have been called: 'Look, Ma, how unlike Terence Rattigan I'm being.'[69] Many of the early notices were poor. One reviewer commented that Jimmy Porter was 'a character who could only be shaken into sense by being ducked in a horse pond or sentenced to a lifetime of cleaning latrines'; the *Evening News* described the play as the 'most putrid bosh'; and the *Evening Standard* thought that it had 'the stature of a self-pitying snivel'.[70] The *New Statesman*'s reviewer, however, was impressed by the modernity of the piece, which he thought captured 'the authentic new tone of the Nineteen-Fifties, desperate, savage, resentful and, at times, very funny'. Jimmy Porter, he wrote, spoke with 'genuinely the modern accent – one can hear it no doubt in every other Expresso bar, witty, relentless, pitiless and utterly without belief . . . Don't miss this play. If you are young, it will speak for you. If you are middle-aged, it will tell you what the young are feeling.'[71] Both Harold Hobson and Kenneth Tynan wrote good reviews, the latter being especially enthusiastic:

> *Look Back in Anger* presents postwar youth as it really is, with special emphasis on the non-U intelligentsia who live in bed-sitters . . . All the qualities are there, qualities one had despaired of ever seeing on the stage – the drift towards anarchy, the instinctive leftishness, the automatic rejection of 'official' attitudes, the surrealist sense of humour . . . the casual promiscuity, the sense of lacking a crusade worth fighting for and, underlying all these, the determination that no one who dies shall go unmourned . . .
>
> I agree that *Look Back in Anger* is likely to remain a minority taste. What matters, however, is the size of the minority. I estimate it at roughly 6,733,000, which is the number of people in this country between twenty and thirty . . . I doubt if I could love anybody who did not wish to see *Look Back in Anger*. It is the best young play of the decade.[72]

Tynan's identification of *Look Back in Anger* with the supposed frustrations of youth became an important part of the myth of the Angry Young Men in the late fifties and early sixties. The term itself came from the title of Leslie Paul's book *Angry Young Man* (1951), which was actually about the shattering of socialist illusions during the thirties, but the Royal Court press officer borrowed the title in an attempt to impress journalists, telling them that Osborne was 'a very angry young man'.[73] The label stuck, and came to encompass not merely Osborne, but also those other writers of the mid-fifties perceived to be both young and challenging established institutions, especially John Wain, Kingsley Amis and Colin Wilson. 'Anyone in Britain who has anything to say about the Angry Young Men had better say it quickly,' wrote John Holloway in late 1957: 'the field is now trampled over so often, it is rapidly becoming contaminated.'[74] This new literary icon was almost always a man, and there were all sorts of explanations for his emergence, ranging from dissatisfaction with consensus politics to the rise of the lower-middle classes.[75] In retrospect, however, the Angry Young Men never really existed, except as the loosest and most general stereotypes. Middle-class newspapers like the *Daily Express* and the *Daily Mail*, which loved to repeat the cliché that there was some sort of surging movement of Angry Young Men, were indulging in a fundamental distortion of their subjects' real beliefs. Osborne, Amis and Wilson barely knew one another, wrote very different kinds of things, and had very little time for each other's work, so there is not much sense in lumping them all together in some army of the angry. As Harry Ritchie's definitive study of the phenomenon, *Success Stories*, puts it, the notion of the Angry Young Men was 'completely unjustified': despite all the contemporary column inches wasted on the intricacies of the movement, the truth was that it was no more than a press officer's invention.[76]

The first performance of *Look Back in Anger* was, according to its author, 'a rather dull, disappointing evening', yet it remains probably the best-known British cultural moment of the fifties.[77] The play became, as one writer puts it, 'an *event*', taking advantage of the interest of the newspapers in entertainment and culture, as well as the expansion of television audiences and the creation of a commercial channel. On 16 October, responding to the publicity for Osborne and his play in the metropolitan press, the BBC broadcast an extract from the Royal Court production; on 28 November, the entire play was shown on ITV to an even wider audience. Television exposure of this kind was something that no pre-war dramatist could have anticipated; it boosted box-office takings at the Royal Court from £900 to £1700 a week, and it made Osborne himself a household name.[78] Once an unemployed actor ensconced on a houseboat, he was said to have made £20,000 from the play by the end of the year.[79] He was also taken as the voice of a new generation. As one observer put it:

> It is a matter for special remark that Mr. Osborne alone should have captured the young imagination and with it the fisher-sweatered noctambules from Espresso-land, the *jeunes-mariés* from Knightsbridge, the bed-sitter *avant-garde* from Bayswater and Notting Hill. Almost the worst thing about the English theatre is that it has lacked for so long the support of the young intelligentsia. Audiences are apt to look as discreetly silver-haired as if they had been furnished by a casting agency themselves.[80]

Within six years it was widely accepted that Osborne's play marked an irrevocable and revolutionary shift in post-war British culture. In *Anger and After*, a history of modern British theatre published in 1962, John Russell Taylor explained that 'the whole picture of writing in this country' had been transformed overnight, 'and the event which marks off "then" decisively from "now" is the first performance of *Look Back in Anger*'.[81] Before that moment, he insisted, the outlook had been 'fairly grim'; but 'then, on 8 May 1956 came the revolution . . . No-one can deny that *Look Back in Anger* started everything off.'[82] Robert Hewison agrees, arguing that in the context of the Butskellite consensus, dissent could only be expressed in cultural terms. According to Hewison: 'Allowances must be made for coincidence and the distortions of publicity, yet something did happen in 1956 to change people's perceptions of their culture and their society.'[83]

It is hard to know how Hewison comes to his conclusion that 'people's perceptions' of their society had been changed by the cultural events of 1956. In political terms there seems to have been little change, since the Conservative government then in place was handsomely re-elected three years later. In cultural terms, meanwhile, it is worth remembering that the theatre was a minority interest unlikely to have had much effect on the lives of millions of people much more comfortable with bowls, gardening and the *Daily Mirror*. Even in purely theatrical terms, it is dubious whether Osborne's play was really very revolutionary at all. 'I never quite understood the definition or the description of John Osborne as a revolutionary writer, you know, part of a revolution in the English theatre,' Harold Pinter later remarked.[84] While Osborne presented conventional characters in a realistic setting, directed with down-to-earth simplicity, writers like Beckett and Brecht had defied almost all the conventions of the British stage. Only the shabby setting and Jimmy Porter's vehemence made *Look Back in Anger* remarkable.[85] Osborne himself later admitted that it was 'a formal, rather old-fashioned play'.[86] Most theatre historians now agree that *Look Back in Anger* was not really a revolution after all, that the theatre of the early fifties was actually much more satisfying than the drama of the New Wave, and that other New Wave plays were more daring than *Look Back in Anger* anyway.[87]

One obvious example was Osborne's next play, *The Entertainer*, first performed in April 1957 and written as a vehicle for Britain's most famous and most successful actor, Laurence Olivier. Like many established actors of the war years, Olivier was worried that his courtly style might be going out of date; he could not play romantic leads any longer, and was stuck in a series of West End Shakespeare revivals. 'I was going mad,' he recalled, 'desperately searching for something new and exciting.' After watching *Look Back in Anger*, he met Osborne backstage and asked him: 'Do you think you could write something for me?'[88] The result was the role of the music-hall comedian Archie Rice in *The Entertainer*, a collaboration that not only allowed Olivier to reinvent himself as an adventurous, versatile performer, confident with new drama as well as the classics, but also conferred unexpected respectability on Osborne and the theatrical New Wave.[89] Whereas *Look Back in Anger* had been ultra-naturalistic, *The Entertainer* played with the conventions of the music hall, moving from the flamboyant theatricality of Archie's exaggerated routines to the realism of the off-stage scenes with the Rice family. The play has the structure of a music-hall evening, with thirteen numbers, an overture and two intermissions, but the use of music-hall techniques also reflects the deep nostalgia of the piece.[90] Osborne wrote in the introduction to the script of the play: 'The music hall is dying, and with it a significant part of England. Some of the heart of England has gone; something that once belonged to everyone, for this was truly a folk art.'[91]

Unlike its predecessor, *The Entertainer* was explicitly concerned with the state of the nation as a whole: just as Archie's desperate routines fail to mask the decline of the music hall, so the country's leaders, off-stage, drag a decaying Britain into the Suez crisis to defend the national honour. The Rice family, tired and bitter, sunk in apathy in a mouldering seaside resort, represent Osborne's conception of a nation in terminal decline, 'a powerful metaphor for a country that on the one hand is benefiting from increasing affluence but on the other has alienated so many of its inhabitants through class barriers, a collective sense of disenfranchisement and an unacknowl-edged international impotence'.[92] Archie himself, the deeply flawed hero of the play, struggles to conceal his own misery with a series of ill-judged and blasé jokes; at the end of the play, his son Mick having been killed in the Suez landings, his music-hall routine finally collapses and he leaves the stage a broken figure. Contemporary critics loved *The Entertainer*. The role of Archie, wrote Kenneth Tynan, was 'one of the great acting parts of our age'. Harold Hobson thought that in the final ten minutes Olivier had reached 'the extreme limits of pathos. You will not see more magnificent acting than this anywhere in the world.'[93] In his history of the British stage, Dominic Shellard calls it 'one of the most unforgettable acting performances of post-war British theatre'.[94]

The Entertainer cemented the reputation of Osborne, Olivier and the Royal Court. It was not, however, typical of the New Wave that washed over the London stage in the late 1950s. Most of these new plays fell under the head-ing of 'kitchen sink' drama and reflected the intellectually fashionable interest in working-class life typified by the books of Hoggart and Williams. The phrase 'kitchen sink' captured the grim and often shabby realism of their settings; it had originally been coined in the early fifties to describe the vogue for sombre, realist paintings by the likes of Jack Smith, Derrick Greaves and John Bratby.[95] The realist plays usually had one central char-acter, like Jimmy Porter, around whom the action revolved. They were set in a single enclosed space, often a cramped and shabby living room in the provinces, such as Manchester in *A Taste of Honey* (Shelagh Delaney, 1958), or 'a typical lower-middle-class detached house in an industrial town in the North' in *Billy Liar* (Keith Waterhouse and Willis Hall, 1960). Their focus was resolutely on the private, the domestic and the mundane; there was little enthusiasm for ambitious political statements in the late fifties.[96] As the *Spectator*'s theatre critic Alan Brien put it in September 1959:

> The settings have been unfamiliar – a Midlands attic, an Irish brothel, a new housing estate, a Soho gambling-shop, a Bayswater basement. The characters have been misfits and outcasts exiled in the no-man's-land between the working class and the middle class. The dialogue has also been eloquent, bawdy, witty and concrete. The basic kick of the whole movement has been the feeling that the play was written last weekend, the exhilaration of listening to talk alive with images from the newspapers, the advertisements, the entertainments of today.[97]

Many were not very 'angry' at all; indeed, there is a case for arguing that *Look Back in Anger* was the only really angry play, and that there was more anger in contemporary novels and films than on the stage. 'Gritty' would perhaps be a better term than 'angry'.[98]

The grittiness of kitchen-sink drama owed much to the working-class origins of the various writers associated with it. Bernard Kops, who wrote *The Hamlet of Stepney Green* (1958) and *Goodbye, World* (1959), had been born to a working-class Jewish family in Stepney and left school at thirteen.[99] Arnold Wesker, the author of the Royal Court trilogy *Chicken Soup with Barley* (1958), *Roots* (1959) and *I'm Talking about Jerusalem* (1960), chronicling the development of an East End Jewish family, was the son of immigrant parents from Hungary and Russia and began his working life as a plumber's mate.[100] The most striking example was Shelagh Delaney, who was only nineteen when her first play *A Taste of Honey* was performed at the Theatre Royal in 1958. She had been born and raised in industrial Salford, failed her eleven-plus and attended a local secondary modern school, which she left at sixteen to work in an engineering factory. The story went that she saw a touring Rattigan play a year later, decided that she could do better herself, and came up with *A Taste of Honey*, which was then taken up by Theatre Workshop. The result was perhaps the least conventional of all the realist plays, not least because the Theatre Workshop group was much more given to experimental staging than was the English Stage Company. The characters in *A Taste of Honey*, moreover, were much more unusual than those in *Look Back in Anger*: Jo, the heroine, becomes involved with a black seaman who leaves her pregnant; she has no father, only a promiscuous mother who disappears to marry her rich lover; and her flatmate and closest friend is a homosexual young man.[101] The play was a great commercial success, running for over a year in both London and New York, and the film director Lindsay Anderson wrote a laudatory review applauding it as 'a real escape from the middlebrow, middle-class vacuum of the West End'.[102] Delaney was nicknamed 'the Françoise Sagan of Salford' as well as, predictably, 'an angry young woman'.[103] There were, in fact, very few angry young women: the actress who played Jo in the film version of *A Taste of Honey*, the strikingly gawky Rita Tushingham, was the only female performer to build a prominent career on the back of the new drama.[104] The New Wave was essentially a man's movement.

Most accounts of British culture in the post-war era have been extremely sympathetic to the new drama of the late 1950s, presenting it as a great working-class breakthrough.[105] Many of the kitchen-sink plays demanded working-class accents because they chronicled provincial working-class lives, and the success of Royal Court favourites like Kenneth Haigh and Alan Bates meant that young British actors no longer felt that they needed to cultivate an Oxford accent and upper-class drawl; instead, encouraged by the general interest in working-class realism, they emphasised authenticity, toughness and provincialism. The drawing-room manner of the great actors of the past, like John Gielgud and Ralph Richardson, seemed to many observers to be increasingly dated; the young actors of the sixties instead made a virtue of their humble origins. Albert Finney, for instance, was a Salford boy; Tom Courtenay came from Hull, Peter O'Toole from Leeds, and Michael Caine from South London.[106] This not only reflected a change in society as a whole, where regional accents were becoming increasingly acceptable, but also encouraged it. 'People weren't hindered by their accents any more, whether they were northern or Cockney or Antipodean or whatever – in fact an accent was an advantage,' one interviewee later told the writer Alison Pressley.[107]

Certainly provincial accents were much more acceptable in the fifties and sixties than they had been before the war, and they were much more common on stage and screen. But the fact remains that many people were still hindered by their accents, and even fifty years later surveys consistently found that strong regional accents, especially those of Liverpool, Birmingham and the West Country, were considered impediments to professional success. The actor Tom Courtenay, a rangy young man from Humberside and an icon of the early sixties, demonstrated a healthy scepticism about the claims of the demotic revolution. 'Take all this thing now about working-class actors and writers,' he remarked in 1961. 'It's simply a release of certain talents from that class . . . The real working class has nothing to do with the theatre today. The railway porter, the chap on the fish dock in Hull, they're not interested . . . Why should they be?'[108] Indeed, New Wave theatre appealed only to a small, well-educated minority of the public. More than half of the plays' directors and producers had been at Oxford or Cambridge, and a large proportion had attended public schools. Their audiences were certainly young: often more than 80 per cent were under thirty-five. But they did not represent a new class of theatre-goer, since up to a third were usually students and the majority of the rest had degrees, unlike the majority of the population.[109] 'We never appealed to the working class,' recalled the Theatre Workshop stalwart Harry H. Corbett. 'All I could ever see were beards and duffle coats every time I peered into the audience.'[110]

The fact was that the celebrated plays of the late fifties were rarely very popular with audiences. Most theatregoers still preferred the old-fashioned entertainments of the West End. Nostalgic musicals like *Salad Days* and *The Boy Friend*, which had opened in 1954 and 1955 respectively, could expect long and extremely lucrative runs.[111] In 1958, Binkie Beaumont mounted a spectacular production of *West Side Story*, and his production of *My Fair Lady* (1961–2) made a record profit of £138,381.[112] By contrast, at the Royal Court the audiences for the iconoclastic John Arden play *Serjeant Musgrave's Dance* (1959) filled barely a fifth of the auditorium, and during the first run of Arnold Wesker's play *Roots* the theatre was only two-thirds full.[113] Gross takings were sometimes a mere £19 for an evening performance and £6 for a matinee.[114] There was not much truth in Kenneth Tynan's claim that 'roughly 6,733,000 people', the entire population aged between twenty and thirty, would love *Look Back in Anger*. Most people showed very little interest in it at all. 'I've never heard such nonsense in my life,' remarked the working-class playwright Ted Willis. 'This is what a small section of young people were thinking, but it certainly isn't what six and a quarter million of our younger generation were thinking.'[115]

Indeed, unlike Rattigan and Beaumont, the producers of the New Wave often adopted an attitude of total contempt for their audiences, further distancing themselves from the expectations and values of ordinary theatregoers. Even the actors themselves were sometimes very reluctant revolutionaries; the theatrical knight Robert Stephens later recalled that during rehearsals for the Royal Court's pioneering production of Brecht's play *The Good Woman of Setzuan*, they were utterly baffled by the play's style and meaning. Stephens thought it 'a particularly dreadful production'.[116] The Royal Court's artistic director George Devine, however, admitted that he was simply not interested in pleasing his audience. During the première of Charles Wood's surrealist fantasy *Meals on Wheels* (1965), he said to John Osborne: 'They're hating it, aren't they?' According to Osborne, who had directed the piece, he was 'delighted because they were hating it for the right reasons, responding as we had anticipated'.[117] Still, the public's reaction was nowhere near as bad as the opprobrium that greeted Osborne's musical *The World of Paul Slickey*, which opened in May 1959 and was considered such a disappointment that 'a mob of about eighty people' from the audience chased its author down the Charing Cross Road before he sought refuge in a taxi. Osborne was unrepentant. The play's horrendous reviews were explicable because 'not one daily paper critic has the intellectual equipment to assess my work or that of any other intelligent playwright'. And reflecting on the reaction of the audience, he merely commented: 'It's a distinction to be booed by some people.' It was hardly surprising that, six weeks later, the play was taken off.[118]

While kitchen-sink plays inevitably reached only a limited audience, the fiction of the New Wave, especially when adapted for the cinema, appealed to a wider public. Like the plays of Wesker or Delaney, New Wave novels focused on the experience of provincial working-class life. In Malcolm Bradbury's words, it was 'anti-experimental and anti-romantic, anti-ideological and eminently realistic'. The fiction of Alan Sillitoe or Stan Barstow was rooted in the mundane world of ordinary everyday lives, concerned not with innovative literary technique but with rendering the experience and character of the working class in realistic terms. As Bradbury explains, its 'characteristic tale was the story of a working-class or lower-middle-class young man wandering, in a state of anguish and alienation, along a canal bank in Nottingham or Wakefield; its typical method was that of nineteenth-century reportorial realism'.[119]

Realistic fiction has often been identified as the dominant trend of British writing in the late fifties and early sixties, a successor to the lower-middle-class stories of Amis and Wain and an unprecedented literary rendezvous with the English working class.[120] But this picture is much too simple. British fiction was already such a broad church that it makes little sense to reduce it to one or two narrowly defined trends, and successful writers as diverse as William Golding, Iris Murdoch and J. R. R. Tolkien were quite happy to ignore the clichés of working-class realism. But it was 'anger', not allegory, that sold newspapers; and so the realist fiction of the New Wave, immersed in questions of character and depicting the conflict between tradition and cultural change in a working-class English environment, attracted more attention at the end of the decade than any other genre. There is no doubt that the novels and stories of Alan Sillitoe, David Storey, Bill Naughton, Philip Callow, Sid Chaplin and so on deserve to be treated together, as part of a specific movement. The similarities between them are extraordinarily striking, not merely because the protagonists have a confusing tendency to be called Arthur, but also because the central characters often face exactly the same emotional predicament, namely an involvement with an older, often married, woman. In each book, too, whether it be *Saturday Night and Sunday Morning* (Sillitoe, 1958), *The Day of the Sardine* (Chaplin,

1961) or *Going to the Moon* (Callow, 1968), the central character feels almost suffocated, not only by the narrow attentions of his close family, but also by the intimate, claustrophobic working-class culture of the North or northern Midlands. Compared with the fictional worlds of Wain, or Amis, or Angus Wilson, this is also a particularly violent world: fights are frequent, and in *This Sporting Life* (Storey, 1960) violence on and off the rugby field is one of the principal themes of the novel. Above all, there is a pervasive sense of frustration, insecurity, loneliness: the central characters often feel stifled by their environment, threatened by change or the expectations of others, dissatisfied with the drudgery of their lives but resigned to their inevitable lot.[121]

A good example, and one of the best realist novels, is Sillitoe's book *Saturday Night and Sunday Morning*. Arthur Seaton, a young lathe operator in a Nottingham bicycle factory, muses that all he wants is 'a good life: plenty of work and plenty of booze and a piece of skirt every month until I'm ninety'. At the same time, the novel tells us: 'He felt a lack of security. No place existed in all the world that could be called safe, and he knew for the first time in his life that there had never been any such thing as safety and never would be.'[122] This partly explains why Arthur is such a feisty, aggressive character, in and out of fights and women's beds. After a string of brawls, beers and amorous escapades, he decides to settle down with Doreen, a pretty young girl from a nearby estate. But, as the last paragraphs of the book make clear, he has not lost his pugnacious opposition to authority:

> And trouble it'll be for me, fighting every day until I die. Why do they make soldiers out of us when we're fighting up to the hilt as it is? Fighting with mothers and wives, landlords and gaffers, coppers, army, government. If it's not one thing it's another, apart from the work we have to do and the way we spend our wages. There's bound to be trouble for me every day of my life, because trouble it's always been and always will be.[123]

The main inspiration for *Saturday Night and Sunday Morning* was the life of Alan Sillitoe himself, who had been born in 1928 into a working-class Nottingham family and left school at fourteen to work in the Raleigh bicycle factory. Sillitoe joined the RAF after the war and finally established himself as a writer, living off his disability pension after contracting tuberculosis in Malaya. For a while he lived in Majorca, near another expatriate English writer, Robert Graves. 'I invented him,' Graves once told Kingsley

Amis. 'He used to live in Soller in the Fifties, writing I don't know what you'd call them, fantasies about imaginary countries set in no particular period. I told him, "Alan, nobody wants that sort of stuff. Write about the life you know in Nottingham."'[124] Sillitoe himself denied that his book had any great political purpose; like Hoggart, he was interested in cultural rather than economic deprivation, although since he had been in Majorca he did not read Hoggart's book until after writing *Saturday Night and Sunday Morning*. Arthur Seaton, he told the *Daily Worker*, was 'an individual and not a class symbol'. 'My main concern', he explained, 'was to show that, while in one sense a certain section of those who worked in factories had their earthly bread, they by no means had been shown any kind of worthwhile spiritual bread.'[125]

Yet *Saturday Night and Sunday Morning* does not dwell on the issue of poverty. The novel is set in the early fifties, during the Korean War, at a time when British manufacturing and the bicycle industry in particular were thriving on the export trade. Arthur and his friends do not consider themselves badly off. At one point he muses:

> The thousands who worked there took home good wages. No more short-term like before the war, or getting the sack if you stood ten min-utes on the lavatory reading your Football Post – if the gaffer got on to you now you could always tell him where to put the job and go some-where else.[126]

Another very successful realist novel, *A Kind of Loving*, published in 1960, leaves a similar impression. Its author, Stan Barstow, was the son of a West Yorkshire coal miner, a grammar-school boy who started work in an engi-neering firm at the age of sixteen and began in the fifties to have some short stories broadcast by the BBC. *A Kind of Loving* is set in a thinly disguised ver-sion of his home town of Dewsbury, but again there is a greater sense of affluence and change than of poverty and stagnation. Victor Brown, the protagonist, is the son of a miner and grew up in a traditional working-class environment, but his sister is a teacher, and his younger brother wants to become a doctor. Victor himself is an engineering draughtsman, ambitious and interested in culture. He falls for Ingrid, a typist in the office named after the Hollywood film star Ingrid Bergman; they go out, but he soon tires of her bottomless enthusiasm for television and game shows. However, by this time she has become pregnant and they feel compelled to get married, despite the fact that he evidently does not love her.[127] The novel is a poignant examination of the pain facing young people in such a situation, as well as a powerful demonstration of the way in which the old working-class morality stifles Victor's ambition in the bright world of affluence and social mobility.[128]

The contrast between tradition and affluence was typical of much New Wave fiction. Keith Waterhouse's novel *Billy Liar* (1958), for instance, is set in the fictional Yorkshire town of Stradhoughton, but Billy Fisher, a young clerk and the central character, is contemptuous of local journalists who praise its 'sturdy buildings of honest native stone, gleaming cobbled streets, and that brackish air which gives this corner of Yorkshire its especial *piquancy*'. The high street, according to Billy, 'was – despite the lying reminiscences of old men like Councillor Duxbury who remembered sheep-troughs where the X-L Disc Bar now stands – exactly like any other High Street in Great Britain'.[129] He meets his friends at Stradhoughton's fashionable coffee bar, the Kit-Kat, recently converted from a thirties milk bar:

> The Kit-Kat was another example of Stradhoughton moving with the times, or rather dragging its wooden leg about five paces behind the times . . . The Kit-Kat was now a coffee bar, or thought it was. It had a cackling espresso machine, a few empty plant-pots, and about half a dozen glass plates with brown sugar stuck all over them. The stippled walls, although redecorated, remained straight milkbar: a kind of Theatre Royal backcloth showing Dick Whittington and his cat hiking it across some of the more rolling dales.[130]

Although provincial and certainly frustrated, Billy Fisher is not really working-class at all: he is the son of a local small businessman who owns his own haulage firm, and like Arthur Seaton and Victor Brown, he is affluent enough to afford drinks and entertainments. Like Arthur, too, he is something of an anti-hero. Arthur is violent and sleeps with his friends' wives. Billy is an incorrigible liar, and as one critic puts it, 'a [nasty] piece of work, who behaves abysmally to his various girlfriends, treats his family with contempt and is indirectly responsible for his grandmother's death'.[131] Keith Waterhouse, meanwhile, had a background remarkably similar to those of Sillitoe and Barstow. Like Richard Hoggart, he had been brought up in Hunslet, Leeds; he was the son of a greengrocer, left school at fifteen and began work as a sweeper in a cobbler's shop. The central characters in New

Wave fiction clearly owe a great deal to the early lives of their creators; indeed, it seems plausible that at a time when there was a minor vogue for exploring the fading world of traditional working-class life, the authors themselves were well aware of the potential rewards for mining the imaginative seams of their native North.

New Wave fiction was extremely popular at the end of the 1950s, and made a good deal of money for its authors, not least because the rapid expansion of the paperback market was steadily widening their commercial horizons. It was also a godsend for the beleaguered British film industry. The heyday of the British cinema had been in the late forties and early fifties, when attendances reached their highest-ever level and British directors like David Lean, Michael Powell, Emeric Pressburger and Carol Reed were in their pomp.[132] As incomes and home-ownership levels were increasing, so families preferred to spend their earnings on domestic improvements and household goods. Since more women were heading out to work, the attendance at matinee presentations was in rapid decline. Worst of all, the diversification of leisure meant that consumers could choose from a range of alternatives, and the domestic pleasures of the television in particular undermined the appeal of the pictures.[133] Total admissions reached their peak of 1635 million in 1946; by 1956, this was down to 1101 million, and by 1963, it had reached a feeble 357 million.[134] Of the 4500 cinemas open in Britain in 1950, some 1550 had closed ten years later.[135] The years 1957 and 1958 were especially bad; the powerful Rank chain was forced to amalgamate its two Odeon and Gaumont circuits and made three hundred workers redundant, temporarily postponing four films being shot at Pinewood Studios.[136] One further problem was that it was primarily the older members of the audience who were staying away, preferring to spend their money on washing machines or nights in with the television. By the end of the decade, young people between the ages of sixteen and twenty-four made up nearly half of the regular weekly audience, as well as a quarter of those who came about once a month.[137] Clearly this was a new audience that needed something different from the old family fare, but what?

The studios' initial response to the long decline of the 1950s was to fall back on the Second World War. More than a hundred war films were produced between 1945 and 1960.[138] The most successful, *The Dam Busters*, was based on a 1951 bestseller by Paul Brickhill describing a daring bombing raid against the Moehne and Eder dams in Nazi Germany's industrial heartland. 'Perhaps this story will reassure those who are dismayed by the fact that the

British and their allies are outnumbered in this not too amicable world,' wrote the author.[139] Most of the war films, however, were not a success. An article in the *New Statesman* in 1958 complained:

> A dozen years after the Second World War we find ourselves in the really quite desperate situation of being, not sick of war, but hideously in love with it . . . while we 'adventure' at Suez, in the cinemas we are still thrashing Rommel . . . The more we lose face in the world's councils, the grander, in our excessively modest way, we swell in this illusionary mirror held up by the screen. It is less a spur to morale than a salve to wounded pride; and as art or entertainment, dreadfully dull.[140]

Clearly the vogue for war films was partly intended to alleviate anxieties about declining British power and prestige abroad, as well as trying to recapture the old community spirit of the Blitz. One successful war film director, Lewis Gilbert, admitted that they were 'a kind of ego trip, a nostalgia for a time when Britain was great'.[141] In fact the better films of the fifties quietly subverted the myths of the Second World War. *The Cruel Sea*, *The Dam Busters* and *The Bridge on the River Kwai* all broke with the myth of wartime consensus by showing dissent in the ranks, as well as the experience of suffering, injury and death. They were more realistic and gripping than their predecessors; but, all the same, making more and better war films was not the answer to the plight of the cinema.[142]

The first signs of dissatisfaction with studio conventions came in the form of the Free Cinema movement. Free Cinema's guiding spirit was Lindsay Anderson, an Oxford-educated upper-middle-class Scot who thought that contemporary British films were 'snobbish, anti-intelligent, emotionally inhibited, wilfully blind to the conditions and problems of the present, dedicated to an out-of-date, exhausted national ideal'.[143] Working-class culture, he argued, provided the antidote to the numbing conformity of bourgeois life, but:

> The number of British films that have ever made a genuine try at a story in a popular milieu, with working-class characters all through, can be counted on the fingers of one hand. This virtual rejection of three-quarters of the population of this country represents more than a ridiculous impoverishment of the cinema. It is characteristic of a flight from contemporary reality.[144]

Like Richard Hoggart, Anderson fell back on the vocabulary of healthy authenticity to describe his objectives: Free Cinema would be 'vital, illuminating, personal and refreshing'; it would rejoice in 'freedom, in the importance of people and in the significance of the everyday'.[145] Anderson and a group of other budding directors, including the future New Wave luminaries Tony Richardson and Karel Reisz, made a series of cheap experimental pictures that they exhibited in six programmes at the National Film Theatre between 1956 and 1959. Their debt to Hoggart was great: in Anderson's film O Dreamland, for example, there is exactly the same condemnation of the degenerate cultural habits of the working class as we find in The Uses of Literacy.[146] But the overall impact of Free Cinema was pretty limited. Although it provided useful experience for directors like Anderson, Reisz and Richardson, it looked very pallid in comparison with the contemporary art cinema in countries like France or Sweden, and it found little favour with audiences.[147] Very, very few working-class viewers ever saw the Free Cinema films, and in the long run their influence on British cinema was much smaller than that of the new television plays of the late fifties and early sixties, many of which were much more daring than anything in the cinema. And although the Free Cinema movement offered a good example of the frustration of many younger, artistically minded directors, it could not compare with the widespread popularity and public effect of films like the first New Wave picture, Room at the Top.[148]

Room at the Top, adapted from a novel by John Braine and directed by Jack Clayton, was released in January 1959 and immediately caught public attention, not least for its groundbreaking depiction of sex. Advertisements proclaimed that it was 'A Savage Story of Lust and Ambition', and in the context of the cosy world of Ealing comedies it felt like a complete break with the past. 'This seems a film', wrote Penelope Houston in Sight and Sound, 'which can only be summed up in the special context of our present-day cinema . . . It has the impact of genuine innovation: a new subject, a new setting, a new talent.'[149] The Daily Express's reviewer hailed 'a British film which [has] at long last, got its teeth into those subjects which have always been part and parcel of our lives, but have hitherto been taboo subjects on the prissy British screen – male ambition in all its ruthlessness, and sex in all its earthy compulsion', while in the Saturday Review Arthur Knight wrote:

One feels that a whole new chapter is about to be written in motion picture history . . . I can say for myself that the only shock I felt was the shock of recognition, the shock of recognising ordinary, tawdry people on the screen in an extraordinarily bitter, adult drama, and the shock of realizing how rarely this has happened before.[150]

The film did very good business: many cinemas were sold out, and it ended the year as the fourth most popular film of 1959.[151] Doubtless this owed much to its sexual content; the film had only been granted an X certificate after protracted negotiations with the censors.[152] British film producers, however, recognised a winner when they saw one, and by the end of the year most of the widely known New Wave plays and novels had been signed up for adaptation into films.[153] Room at the Top had, said one writer, 'put an X in Yorkshire'.[154]

John Braine was a lower-middle-class Yorkshire grammar-school boy and former librarian. He was certainly not an angry young man; instead, he was driven by intense material ambition, and when he published Room at the Top in 1957 he struck gold. The novel sold 34,000 copies in hardback and a further 125,000 copies in a book club edition, as well as being serialised in the Daily Express. It earned its author £10,000 in its first two months alone, a fortune considering that as a librarian he had usually earned £600 a year.[155] Braine was suddenly rich, and he loved it, rapidly throwing up a new job as a librarian in Wakefield and moving to a large new house in the Home Counties. He explained to an interviewer: 'What I want to do is to drive through Bradford in a Rolls-Royce with two naked women on either side of me covered in jewels.'[156] 'He would like it to be known', reported the Express, 'that he couldn't be less angry.'[157]

Braine's political leanings were unusual for a fashionable writer of the late 1950s and no doubt played a large part in determining the themes of the novel and subsequent film. He had begun work on Room at the Top in the more austere circumstances of 1952, and the materialistic longings of his novel reflected a time when naked women and jewels were in short supply.[158] The plot concerns Joe Lampton, a handsome young man from the bleak little Yorkshire town of Dufton who moves to the city of Warley to work in the city accountant's office. Unlike other protagonists of the New Wave, Joe is aggressive, materialistic and fiercely ambitious. 'He is a beast and his story is the autobiography of a cad,' commented a reviewer in the Observer. 'He is a ruthless rather than an angry young man: any anger he has is the driving force of his ambition.'[159] Joe becomes involved with an older married woman, Alice Aisgill, and a naive young girl called Susan

Brown, the daughter of the richest manufacturer in the city. Susan becomes pregnant; he agrees to marry her, and her father offers him a well-paid job. When Alice hears the news, she kills herself, and the novel ends with Joe being rescued from a remorseful drunken binge by friends who tell him, 'Nobody blames you,' to which he replies: 'Oh my God . . . that's the trouble.'[160] The story has something of the nineteenth-century American rags-to-riches fable, but it also reflects the enthusiastic materialism and mobility associated with the late fifties. Instead of being about anger, or even envy, it is really a tale of ambition.[161] 'I was going to the Top,' Joe tells us in the first scene of the novel, and he later tells a friend: 'I always go straight for what I want.'[162] As he watches a rich couple, he muses: 'I wanted an Aston-Martin, I wanted a three-guinea linen suit, I wanted a girl with a Riviera suntan – these were my rights, I felt, a signed and sealed legacy.'[163]

Joe sees the world as a collection of price tags and brand names. Looking down on the city from the hills above, he sees 'Wintrup the jeweller with the beautiful gold and silver watches that made my own seem cheap, Finlay the tailor with the Daks and Vantella shirts and the Jaeger dressing gown, Priestley the grocer with its smell of cheese and roasting coffee, Robbins the chemist with the bottles of Lenthéric after-shave lotion and the beaver shaving brushes'.[164] Women to Joe are commodities like any other, to be acquired just like watches or shirts. This is particularly emphasised in the film version; when Joe starts telling his relatives in Dufton about Susan, his aunt remarks: 'I ask you about the girl and all you tell me about is her father's brass.' His uncle, too, is suspicious: 'Sure it's the girl you want, Joe, not the brass?'[165] In the novel, when Joe finally has sex with Susan she is presented as a passive commodity to be seized without compunction. Joe tells her: 'I love you, you silly bitch, and I'm the one who says what's to be done. Now and in the future.' She struggles, and then:

> I shook her as hard as I could. I'd done it in play before, when she'd asked me to hurt her, please hurt her; but this time I was in brutal earnest, and when I'd finished, she was breathless and half-fainting. Then I kissed her, biting her lip till I tasted blood. Her arms tightened round my neck and she let herself fall to the ground. This time she did not play the frightened virgin; this time I had no scruples, no horizon but the hot lunacy of my own instincts.[166]

Afterwards, Susan gives 'a low gurgling laugh . . . full of physical content-ment' and tells him: 'You hurt me and you took all my clothes – look, I'm bleeding here – and here – and here. Oh Joe, I love you with all of me now, every little bit of me is yours.'[167]

As another New Wave writer, Stan Barstow, put it, the success of *Room at the Top* was an inspiration 'for a generation of writers from the North of England', spurring each one 'to use as the basis of his art the regional work-ing-class life he knew from the inside'.[168] And, as an adaptation of a bestselling book, it set the trend for Britain's cinematic New Wave, which now turned to literary or theatrical originals for inspiration.[169] The next big success came in October 1960. *Saturday Night and Sunday Morning* was made by Woodfall Films, a new company set up by Tony Richardson and John Osborne, and directed by Karel Reisz. Although its advertising budget was a fraction of the West End average, the film took £100,000 in London alone and shot straight to the top of the box-office charts. It was the third biggest box-office hit of 1961, and this windfall was what allowed Richardson to begin working on his next projects, *A Taste of Honey* and the Oscar-winning sixties landmark, *Tom Jones*.[170] It was also great news for Alan Sillitoe; until then, sales of his book had been sluggish, but now it flew off the shelves, becoming one of the first five million-selling paperbacks in Britain.[171] Once again, negotiations with the censors were called for to obtain even an X cer-tificate, and older viewers were shocked by the anti-authoritarianism, realism and sexual frankness of the film.[172] Before the opening credits have even begun to roll Arthur Seaton (Albert Finney) tells the audience, 'What I'm out for is a good time. All the rest is propaganda,' and the fact that the film showed working-class characters *enjoying* their sexual escapades did not always go down well. Warwickshire County Council banned the film from cinemas throughout the county, although in Birmingham they were over-ruled by the city council.[173] Lieutenant-Colonel John Cordeaux, a Nottingham Conservative MP, was indignant that the film maligned his constituents:

It undoubtedly creates an impression that the young men of our indus-trial towns are a lot of ill-behaved, immoral, drunken Teddy Boys . . . The principal character could hardly be less typical of the young men of Nottingham . . . We produce as good a type as anywhere in the coun-try, who work the best of their ability from Monday morning to Saturday noon. Many work through the weekend as well.[174]

New Wave films were now the flavour of the season. Tony Richardson directed versions of *Look Back in Anger* (1959), *The Entertainer* (1960), *A Taste of Honey* (1961) and *The Loneliness of the Long Distance Runner* (1962). John Schlesinger made *A Kind of Loving* (1962) and *Billy Liar!* (1963); Bryan Forbes made *The L-Shaped Room* (1962); and Lindsay Anderson directed *This Sporting Life* (1963). Like the original works on which they were based, these films were remarkably similar. All were organised around one central character who was meant to hold the audience's attention: in both *Saturday Night and Sunday Morning* and *The Loneliness of the Long Distance Runner*, he delivers his thoughts in interior monologues; and in both *The Loneliness of the Long Distance Runner* and *This Sporting Life*, his past life is described through subjective flashbacks. In both *Look Back in Anger* and *The Entertainer* the main character has an extramarital affair but returns to his wife. In both *Room at the Top* and *Saturday Night and Sunday Morning*, the main character is punished for his infidelity in a drunken brawl and finally agrees to get married. In both *Room at the Top* and *A Kind of Loving*, the main character marries his girlfriend only after she has become pregnant, while in *Saturday Night and Sunday Morning* the character of Brenda returns to her cuckolded husband after she herself has been impregnated by her lover.[175]

So many films, released in such a short space of time: very quickly they all began to blend into one enormous working-class blur. After April 1962, when *A Kind of Loving* was released to appreciative audiences, the demand for provincial realism was exhausted.[176] As Alexander Walker puts it, 'familiarity bred not contempt, but lack of interest'.[177] To make matters worse, a different and more enduring British hero was introduced the same year, and one who exuded far greater glamour and sex appeal: James Bond, appearing in the guise of Sean Connery in *Dr No*. Bond not only drew on some of the themes of the New Wave; as we will see later, he also surpassed it.

When *The Loneliness of the Long Distance Runner* came out in the autumn, its undoubted merits were overlooked amid the general exhaustion with its subject. *The Times*, for instance, remarked that it was 'very much in the fashion', but added: 'Nevertheless, it would be a pleasant change if all this elaborate apparatus of mockery at the expense of the existing order of things were put into action on behalf not of discontented youth, the spoilt darlings of the age, but of the ill, the solitary, the virtuous old.'[178] *Private Eye* ran a merciless lampoon on the film adaptation of 'Stan Blister's little-known novel *A Waste of Living*', the story of 'the latently homosexual professional lacrosse player Arthur Sidmouth and Doreen, the girl who watches sympathetically from a bar stool in the film's opening shots as Arthur vomits up his half-pint of ginger shandy'.[179] A year later, on the appearance of *Billy Liar!*, the *Guardian*'s reviewer wrote that the film *should* strike audiences with its 'convincing realism':

> But it doesn't. One reason is that in some ways we've seen it all before – 'A Taste of Loving on Saturday Night at the Top'. We've seen the dreary town, Billy's useless defiance, the office where he works and the men who bully him. We've seen his girlfriends and his parents and we have a pretty good idea of what they are going to say next.[180]

Even the scriptwriters of *Billy Liar!*, Keith Waterhouse and Willis Hall, participated in the mockery, writing a sketch for the satirical television programme *That Was The Week That Was* entitled 'What is a Northerner':

> A Northerner is a scrap of humanity moulded by God in his own image, swathed in a cloth cap and set down in the Metropolis . . . He showed the world that beneath their simple cotton frocks even mill girls are stark staring naked.
> The Northerner is a dreamer and a maker of films. He abolished insipid dialogue such as 'Anyone for tennis?' and replaced it with biting, incisive lines such as 'Would you like a cup of tea?' . . . Beneath every Northern watch-chain is a Southerner screaming to be let out.[181]

What was particularly unfortunate was that the later New Wave films were much more technically innovative than their predecessors. *The Loneliness of the Long Distance Runner*, for example, broke with the conventions of realism and employed a series of light-hearted cinematic tricks: a Chaplinesque speeded-up chase, jump-cuts and montage sequences, and a freeze-frame final image.[182] *Billy Liar!*, unlike its predecessors, used the full width of the cinemascope screen and cut from scenes of intense naturalism to the fantasy scenes of Billy's own imagination. It occupied an uneasy middle ground between the social realism of the late fifties and the swinging fantasy popular in the mid-sixties, between the kitchen sink and the stylish pad.[183] Indeed, the least successful New Wave film, Lindsay Anderson's adaptation in 1963 of David Storey's novel *This Sporting Life*, was probably the best. Arthur Machin (changed in the film to Frank Machin, since the cinema was suffering from a surfeit of characters called Arthur) is a violent and inarticulate factory worker (changed in the film, again, to a miner), a rugby league player, a womaniser and a bully. He is, as one critic puts it, 'arrogant, boorish, vengeful': he hits one of his own players to get an opponent sent off, and 'his attitude to women is simply disgusting'.[184] But the novel is generally regarded by literary scholars as more satisfying than its rivals. Storey brilliantly evokes the grim, shattering physicality of the rugby field and the factory, and the presentation of the novel through the limited outlook of its aggressive hero is very carefully managed.[185] Similarly, Anderson's film, although extremely gloomy and violent, carries more of a punch than most films of the sixties.[186] Karel Reisz thought it was 'the most completely achieved of the "New Wave" films, because the most passionately felt and ambitious'.[187] Unfortunately, the New Wave's moment had passed, and it was not a commercial hit.

Whether the New Wave represented a breakthrough in British cinema remains debatable. It was never entirely dominant: audiences continued to enjoy American films as well as domestic comedies, thrillers and science-fiction films.[188] And it did not succeed in halting the long-term decline in cinema admissions, nor the collapse of the British film industry. Some scholars, like the Open University duo of Anthony Aldgate and Arthur Marwick, are full of admiration for its achievements. Marwick in particular commends New Wave cinema for its social criticism and satire, its frank depiction of working-class life and its stylistic innovation; of course, this fits nicely with his general thesis about the cultural revolution of the sixties.[189] But other historians have suggested that some of this praise goes too far: Peter Woollen even claims that British filmmakers merely 'fetishized the second-rate novels of regionalists, realists and reactionaries'.[190] It is certainly not true that the working classes had never previously been portrayed on film in a respectful light; nor is it the case that British cinema had never previously confronted social problems. In the 1930s and 1940s the comedies of George Formby and Gracie Fields, designed specifically for northern working-class audiences, had presented northern working-class characters in heroic lead roles. A more honest depiction of sex, meanwhile, was already evident in the early fifties in X-rated films like *Knave of Hearts* (René Clément, 1954), which not only experimented with using hand-held cameras but also anticipated the New Wave's scenery of low, rainy urban skies and the New Wave plot device of an amoral clerk wooing a succession of attractive women: other potential sexual forerunners include *I Am a Camera* (1955), *The*

'ow good it is to hear the British Lion's roar!' Newspaper headlines on the Suez crisis,
October 1956. *(Godden/Getty Images)*

'Working for Peace.' A London policeman inspects Sir Anthony Eden's election posters, May 1955. *(Bettman/Corbis)*

An Egyptian boy watches as British tanks advance through the ruins of Port Said, November 1956. *(Hulton-Deutsch/Corbis)*

Full steam ahead: Harold
Macmillan at a London fair, 1962.
(Hulton-Deutsch/Corbis)

The illusion of unity:
George Brown, Hugh Gaitskell
and Harold Wilson pose for
photographers, early 1960s.
(JamesGriffiths/Getty Images)

Housewives chat while sweeping their front steps in Dundee, 195
(Murray/Getty Images)

Boys in a communal toilet in the Frank Street area of Liverpool, 1957.
(Hopkins/Getty Images)

Brave new world: a group of women and children watch the demolition of the Gorbals slum district in Glasgow, 1962. Behind them, work on a new high-rise tower block is under way.
(Drysdale/Getty Images)

Shopping in the household goods department of Selfridge's department store on Oxford Street, 1955. *(Murray/Getty Images)*

'I don't want any froth! I want a cup of coffee! I don't want to wash my clothes in it!' The interior of a London expresso bar, 1955. *(Hulton-Deutsch/Corbis)*

The bright lights of the supermarket, early 1960s.
(Evening Standard/Getty Images)

A honeymooning couple relax in the coffee bar of Billy Butlin's Ocean Hotel, Saltdean, Sussex, 1957.
(Tracey/Getty Images)

'Fellow who doesn't fit in. Seems anti-culture … Beer. Girls.' Kingsley Amis in Swansea, June 1956. *(Farson/Getty Images)*

'I suspect that I am probably the greatest writer of the twentieth century.' Colin Wilson, wrapped up in his sleeping bag, reads on Hampstead Heath, 1956. *(Kauffman/Getty Images)*

John Osborne in the fog, 1958, looking mor moody than angry. *(Aarons/Getty Images)*

Flesh Is Weak (1957) and *My Teenage Daughter* (1956), none of which, sadly, were quite as exciting as the titles might have suggested.[191]

While historians tend to exaggerate the impact of the New Wave, they also often ignore the cheap 'social problem' films made from about 1950 onwards. These were fairly conventional in style, but concentrated on working-class and juvenile characters, addressing problems like race and sexuality in mundane factory and housing-estate settings. As Marcia Landy argues, they reflected contemporary concerns about crime, the family, schools, capital punishment, immigration and juvenile delinquency, often returning to the central idea of authority and order coming under attack.[192] Some of the subjects were surprisingly daring. There were dozens of films about teenage misbehaviour, like *The Blue Lamp* (1950), *Cosh Boy* (1953) and *Violent Playground* (1958); there were films about the Teddy Boys like *The Angry Silence* (1960) and *Flame in the Streets* (1961); there were films about racial violence like *Sapphire* (1959); there were splendidly titled films about prostitution called *The Flesh Is Weak* (1957) and *Passport to Shame* (1959); and there was even a film about rape and child molestation entitled *Don't Talk to Strange Men* (1962).[193]

Indeed, ten years before the climax of the New Wave, working-class and marginal characters were being played by a different group of young actors: Richard Attenborough, Dirk Bogarde, Diana Dors and Joan Collins.[194] And even while the New Wave was in full swing, plenty of other genres, from crime to science fiction, were being reinvigorated by a similar spirit of frankness and realism.[195] The obvious explanation for the neglect of these films is that, unlike the New Wave efforts, they had no lofty artistic aspirations, and were not dressed up with didactic pseudo-intellectual rhetoric. In this context, the great claims made for the New Wave begin to look rather hollow. It is simply not accurate to claim that it was terrifically innovative, and it is revealing that the British New Wave produced not one film or director of genuine international standing to set alongside the products of Italian, Swedish, French or even American studios during the same period.[196] Humphrey Carpenter, a bright teenage schoolboy during the early sixties, later recalled that most of his contemporaries had never seen films like *Room at the Top*; they preferred to watch television.[197]

Like the Movement, the New Wave can be seen as a reassertion of 'British common sense' and 'feeling' against Continental affectation and intellectualism.[198] At the very beginning of *Look Back in Anger*, Jimmy Porter throws the newspaper down and complains: 'I've just read three whole columns on the English Novel. Half of it's in French.'[199] He is pleased to read that a Vaughan Williams concert will be broadcast on the radio, though: 'Well that's something, anyway. Something strong, something simple, something English.'[200] And in his autobiography, Osborne pulls no punches:

> The literary and academic classes seemed to have been tyrannized by the French. The 'posh papers' every Sunday blubbered with self-abasement in the face of the bombast of the French language and its absurd posture as the torch-bearer of Logic, which apparently was something to which no one in these islands had access.[201]

Many writers, including Osborne himself, had similar concerns about the influence of the United States. 'I must say,' muses Jimmy, 'it's pretty dreary living in the American Age – unless you're an American of course. Perhaps all our children will be Americans.'[202] In *Hurry On Down*, John Wain's hero winces at the 'cheap smartness' of his girlfriend's brother Stan: 'He talked a different language, for one thing; it was demotic English of the mid-twentieth century, rapid, slurred, essentially a city dialect, and, in origin, essentially American.' And he smokes 'a cheap American-style cigarette', an immediate sign of moral turpitude.[203] And in *Billy Liar*, too, there is the comic spectacle of Billy's friend Arthur singing in a dance hall in an American-cut suit and a fake American accent, which becomes 'so pronounced that it was difficult to understand what he was singing about'.[204]

One obvious contrast between the Movement and the New Wave was the latter's greater concentration on the sights and sounds of the industrial North. In *Room at the Top*, for instance, we find ourselves in 'the chilly bedroom with its hideous wallpaper and view of mill-chimneys and middens, the bath with its peeling enamel, the scratchy blankets', and in *Saturday Night and Sunday Morning* we see the 'trade-marked houses, two up and two down, with digital chimneys like pigs' tits on the rooftops sending up heat and smoke into the cold trough of a windy sky'.[205] But this was not necessarily an enormous novelty, and as Eric Hobsbawm points out, it was hardly surprising that a society based on mass domestic consumption became dominated by its biggest market, in other words, the industrial working class.[206] With traditional working-class values apparently under threat from social and economic change, images of the working-class North were the ideal antithesis to the dreaded 'shiny barbarism' of modernity. What George Orwell called a 'sort of Northern snobbishness' had deep cultural roots, and in *The Road to Wigan Pier* he had analysed the clichés in which 'the Northerner has "grit", he is grim, "dour", plucky, warm-hearted and democratic', both more honest and more natural than the 'fat and sluggish' southerners.[207]

The biting Yorkshire winds, the intimacy of crowded pubs and football terraces and the cosiness of the family living room were all invoked by Orwell's successors as implicit criticisms of the lazy new world of affluence.[208] As Raphael Samuel puts it, the North 'offered itself as an idiom for the degentrification of British public life. In place of an effete Establishment it promised a new vitality, sweeping the dead wood from the boardrooms, and replacing hidebound administrators with ambitious young go-getters'.[209] Indeed, the politician who dominated British life in the sixties took great pains to present himself as a pipe-smoking Yorkshireman who relaxed at home in a sweater and slippers watching *Coronation Street*. Harold Wilson even told one interviewer:

> I don't do much socializing and my tastes are simple. If I had the choice between smoked salmon and tinned salmon I'd have it tinned. With vinegar. I prefer beer to champagne and if I get the chance to go home I have a North Country high tea – without wine.[210]

Throughout the New Wave, modern commercial entertainments are brash, gaudy and superficial, in contrast to the rugged, authentic masculine values of the old working-class culture. In *The Entertainer*, the old music-hall veteran Billy Rice complains that the local pub has installed a television set: 'Now who do you think would want a television in a pub? Blaring away, you can't hear yourself think.'[211] Similarly, in the film of *Saturday Night and Sunday Morning*, Arthur Seaton's father is shown perpetually slumped in an armchair watching his television, and Arthur tells him a story to distract him: 'This fellow got his hand caught in a press. He didn't look what he was doing. Of course, he's only got one eye; he lost the sight of the other looking at telly day in day out.'[212] Indeed, affluence itself is contemptible. In the film of *The Loneliness of the Long Distance Runner*, the death of Colin's father means an unexpected windfall for the rest of the family, and they rush out on a shopping spree, falling in and out of shops in a montage intercut with images of silver stars in a parody of television commercials. When they return home, Colin (Tom Courtenay) grudgingly accepts his share of the loot and retreats upstairs to his dead father's bedroom, where he stares long and hard into the mirror and then quietly sets fire to a pound note, express-ing his revulsion at the materialism of his family.[213] The stage directions in the play of *Billy Liar* explain that the Fisher household is full of furniture 'in dreadful taste – as are also the plastic ornaments and the wall plaques with which the room is overdressed'; there is, of course, a television, as well as a 'flashy cocktail cabinet'.[214]

The deep suspicion with which most New Wave writers regarded afflu-ence and cultural change helps to explain their protagonists' extraordinarily aggressive treatment of women. In *Look Back in Anger*, Jimmy Porter snarls at his wife:

> I want to stand up in your tears, and splash about in them, and sing. I want to be there when you grovel. I want to be there. I want to watch it, I want the front seat. I want to see your face rubbed in the mud – that's all I can hope for. There's nothing else I want any longer.[215]

He complains that 'she has the passion of a python. She just devours me whole every time . . . She'll go on sleeping and devouring until there's nothing left of me,' and tells his friend Cliff that 'there's nothing for it, me boy, but to let yourself be butchered by the women'.[216] He warns the character Helena that he has 'no public school scruples about hitting girls. If you slap my face – by God, I'll lay you out!'[217] Indeed, throughout the novels and films of the New Wave, women are frequently the victims of lies, treachery and verbal and physical abuse.[218] In *Saturday Night and Sunday Morning*, Arthur Seaton is sleeping with two married women, but tells himself:

> If ever I get married . . . and have a wife that carries on like Brenda and Winnie carry on, I'll give her the biggest pasting any woman ever had. I'd kill her. My wife'll have to look after any kids I fill her with, keep the house spotless. And if she's good at that I might let her go to the pic-tures now and again and take her for a drink on Saturday. But if I thought she was carrying on behind my back she'd be sent back to her mother with two black eyes before she knew what was happening.[219]

'Women get in the way of a man's thinking,' Colin Wilson solemnly told his bohemian acolytes, 'particularly so-called intelligent women with their bright chatter.'[220] John Osborne agreed. 'I don't like a too-knowledgeable woman,' he wrote in December 1957. 'I feel it is against her sex.'[221] And in an appreciation of the American playwright Tennessee Williams, he went even further. Women, he said, 'all cry out for defilement . . . The female must come toppling down to where she should be – on her back.'[222]

The explanation for all this lies in the identification of supposedly feminine values with modernity and mass culture. Women were closely identified with the new affluent society because its products – washing machines, cookers, televisions to entertain the housebound mother – seemed to benefit working-class women more than their husbands, who were more likely to pursue interests outside the home. Women, not men, bought the household's bed linen, soap, detergent, medicines, toothpaste and toothbrushes, and often even the husband's razor blades.[223] The critic D. E. Cooper wrote in 1970 that the New Wave writers were really opposed to 'the effeminate society', defining effeminacy as 'the sum of those qualities which are supposed traditionally, with more or less justice, to exude from the worst in women: pettiness, snobbery, flippancy, voluptuousness, superficiality, materialism'.[224] Indeed, according to John Osborne, Britain's problems were caused by the domination of 'feminine' values: passivity, conformism, self-obsession and the absence of 'imaginative vitality'.[225] In the film of *Saturday Night and Sunday Morning*, for example, it is Arthur's fiancée who wants to move into a new house on an estate. 'I want a new one with a bathroom and everything,' she says enthusiastically. Arthur, by contrast, is unimpressed; indeed, the final image of the film shows him throwing a stone towards the new estate.[226]

After reading *Look Back in Anger*, Noël Coward mused: 'I wish I knew why the hero is so dreadfully cross and what about?'[227] Indeed, it is difficult to identify exactly what the 'anger' of the New Wave amounted to. Introducing Jimmy Porter, the original angry young man, the text of *Look Back in Anger* notes: 'To be as vehement as he is is to be almost non-committal.'[228] But Jimmy's anger is never directed at anything in particular, and there is nothing particularly terrible about his life to explain his state of mind. As one critic puts it, 'it is hard to understand why someone should be angry about having nothing to be angry about'.[229] Certainly the passion of the New Wave had very little to do with political or economic inequality. Most New Wave heroes are supremely non-idealistic; they look down on their working-class contemporaries, feel alienated from their families, and are desperate to cut themselves loose. The New Wave hero is the only sane man in a decadent world, and he typically exploits his circumstances and his fellows for all they are worth. Raymond Williams called this the 'fiction of special pleading', and the critic Kenneth Allsop even remarked in 1958 that the New Wave represented 'a new romantic tradition which is sanctifying the bully as hero' and 'a cult of fascism'.[230] Indeed, in many instances the anger of the New Wave really meant a combination of personal ambition and a vague resentment at a changing society. As Gilbert Phelps neatly puts it: 'One has the feeling that they beat against the doors not in order to destroy them, but in the confident hope that if they made enough fuss they would be let in.'[231]

Political radicalism in the New Wave is the dog that did not bark. While railing against what they saw as the smug inertia of the fifties consensus, the new writers did not present any committed, coherent alternative to it, and their political impact was minimal. Many called themselves socialists, but they could only explain their socialism in the most vague and negative terms. Arnold Wesker said that it meant 'a definite and humane attitude to the world and people around me'. Joan Littlewood defined it as 'that dull working class quality, optimism'.[232] John Osborne thought it was 'an experimental idea, not a dogma: an attitude to truth and liberty, the way people should live and treat each other'.[233] There is very little working-class solidarity in the literature and films of the New Wave: instead, the working classes are splintered by sexual tensions, individualism, selfish personal quarrels and the breach between skilled and unskilled workers.[234] None of the New Wave heroes is committed to a political cause or to a workers' organisation. Arthur Seaton, for instance, rails contemptuously against both the 'big fat Tory bastards in parliament' and also 'them Labour bleeders', who 'rob the wage packets every week with insurance and income tax and try to tell us it's all for our own good'.[235] Angry at the thought of being called up to fight in Korea, he thinks to himself:

> What did they take us for? Bloody fools, but one of these days they'd be wrong. They think they've settled our hashes with their insurance cards and television sets, but I'll be one of them to turn round on 'em and let them see how wrong they are . . . Other faces as well: the snot-gobbling gett that teks my income tax, the swivel-eyed swine that collects our rent, the big-headed bastard that gets my goat when he asks me to go to union meetings or sign a paper against what's happening in Korea. As if I cared![236]

The most famous expression of this same apathy comes in *Look Back in Anger*. Jimmy Porter complains: 'Nobody thinks, nobody cares. No beliefs, no convictions, and no enthusiasm.' But he himself admits:

> I suppose people of our generation aren't able to die for good causes any longer. We've had all that done for us, in the Thirties and the Forties, when we were still kids. There aren't any good, brave causes left. If the big bang does come, and we all get killed off, it won't be in aid of the old-fashioned grand design. It'll just be for the Brave New-nothing-very-much-thank-you. About as pointless and meaningless as stepping in front of a bus. No, there's nothing for it, me boy, but to let yourself be butchered by the women.[237]

The irony is that there were plenty of 'good, brave causes' in the fifties to which an idealistic young man might have dedicated himself: these were, after all, the years of the H-bomb, the early Cold War and the often bloody retreat from Empire.[238] Indeed, despite all its vehemence, masculine aggression and working-class 'authenticity', the New Wave illustrated not the weakness but the resilience, indeed the genuine contentment, of the post-war consensus. At the end of *A Kind of Loving* Victor comments: 'What it boils down to is you've got to do your best and hope for the same. Do what you think's right and you'll be doing like millions of poor sods all over the world are doing.'[239] And so, as the fifties gave way to a new decade, the New Wave reflected not poverty and inequality, but affluence and apathy; it sought not to build a new Britain, but simply to lament the disappearance of an old one.

7

THE WAR GAME

Nowadays all I write about in this diary is boys boys boys, I had better change the subject. I wonder if World War III is on the way, it certainly seems like it, doesn't it? The future is like a great gloomy cloud looming ahead that will swallow us up.

Schoolgirl's diary, late 1950s

What can we do from a practical point of view in the event of a nuclear attack? Well, the first golden rule to remember about hydrogen warfare is to be *out* of the area where the attack is about to occur – get right *out* of the area because that's the danger area, where the bombs are dropping. Get right out of it – get right out of it – if you're out of it, you're well out of it; if you're in it, you're really in it.

Beyond the Fringe (1961)

On 5 December 1962, the former US Secretary of State Dean Acheson, one of the most respected American experts on foreign policy and President Kennedy's designated special adviser on NATO affairs, was speaking to a conference at the West Point Military Academy. His address was, in general, uncontroversial, except for three sentences that found their way into every newspaper in Britain and, for many observers, encapsulated the decline in the nation's international reputation:

Great Britain has lost an empire and has not yet found a role. The attempt to play a separate power role – that is, a role apart from Europe, a role based on a 'Special Relationship' with the United States, a role based on being the head of a 'Commonwealth' which has no political structure, or unity, or strength and enjoys a fragile and precarious economic relationship – this role is about played out. Great Britain, attempting to work alone and to be a broker between the United States and Russia, has seemed to conduct a policy as weak as its military power.[1]

Harold Macmillan was not pleased to hear such sentiments from such a senior and revered figure in the American diplomatic elite, and he confided angrily to his diary that Acheson was 'always a conceited ass'.[2] Part of Macmillan's personal appeal to the British public was as the nostalgic embodiment of Edwardian grandeur, and his very first television address as Prime Minister, more than five years before, had been a deliberate attempt, in the aftermath of Suez, to reiterate Britain's credentials as a dynamic and influential international power. There was no need, he said, for 'defeatist talk', for 'Britain has been great, is great, and will stay great, provided we close our ranks and get on with the job.'[3]

Since Britain had emerged on the winning side in the Second World War without having been invaded and occupied by the Germans, and had also largely avoided the kind of overseas humiliations suffered by other European empires like the French and Dutch during the next ten years, many Britons from ministers to miners were understandably reluctant to accept that the age of international supremacy had long since passed. When a united Great Britain football team defeated the Rest of Europe XI in the 'Match of the Century' at Hampden Park in May 1947, the magnitude of the 6–1 scoreline struck most native observers as supremely appropriate.[4] Ernest Bevin, the Foreign Secretary and the gruff patriotic bulldog of the Labour Party, told the Commons in the same year:

> His Majesty's Government do not accept the view that we have ceased to be a Great Power ... We regard ourselves as one of the powers most vital to the peace of the world and we still have our heroic part to play. The very fact that we have fought so hard for liberty, and paid such a price, warrants our retaining this position.[5]

Like Churchill, Bevin saw Britain as a nation apart, its international importance resting on the fact that it stood at the intersection of three circles: the United States, Europe and the Commonwealth. In this view, which dominated British public life for decades afterwards, Britain was more than merely another small European country: its links with the dominions and colonies of the Empire and with its great Atlantic cousin elevated it to a position of rare influence in world affairs.[6] It therefore seemed perfectly natural that, as a great power, Britain shouldered international responsibilities, from governing the imperial colonies and possessions in Africa, Asia and elsewhere to guarding the frontiers against global Communism. Even in 1964,

Harold Wilson imagined the borders of the nation flung across the planet. 'Our frontier', he said defiantly, 'is on the Himalayas.'[7]

Since most Britons clung to the idea that their country was still a great world power, they were not immediately drawn to the schemes of European co-operation and integration that attracted so many admirers in France, West Germany and elsewhere in the early fifties. The Europeans, as Roy Denman puts it, were 'a bombed out, defeated rabble', at best inept cowards and at worst genocidal monsters, whereas Britain was the country that had stood alone against Hitler.[8] Rather than steer Britain towards a strong European alliance, therefore, British leaders on both left and right preferred to emphasise their links with the Commonwealth and the United States and to downplay their affinities with the perfidious French and hateful Germans.[9] But ideas about European integration had been floating around British intellectual circles for decades. Respected thinkers like William Beveridge, Harold Laski, Arnold Toynbee and Friedrich von Hayek had all toyed with European federalist schemes, and in 1943 Winston Churchill had sketched out designs for a 'Council of Europe' with a common market and unrestricted flow of goods and individuals.[10] In a much reported speech in Zurich in 1946, hailed as the greatest man in Europe, he insisted that the peoples of the Continent, including the British, must unite in 'a regional structure called, as it may be, the United States of Europe', and two years later he amplified his ideas at the first Congress of Europe in The Hague.[11] Clement Attlee, his Labour rival, was markedly less enthusiastic. In 1967, when old and frail, Attlee was asked to address a group of anti-European Labour backbenchers, and obliged with a characteristically terse speech that captured the sentiments of many of his fellow citizens: 'The Common Market. The so-called Common Market of six nations. Know them all well. Very recently this country spent a great deal of blood and treasure rescuing four of 'em from attacks by the other two.'[12]

Attlee's sentiments found favour with both the officials of the Foreign Office and his own Labour colleagues. In 1947, when negotiations began on the subject of a Western European customs union, both the Foreign Office and the Cabinet were staunchly opposed to the idea.[13] Any hopes of killing the plan soon evaporated, however, and in 1951 six nations (France, West Germany, Italy, Belgium, the Netherlands and Luxembourg) signed the Treaty of Paris establishing a single coal and steel authority and pledging to eliminate tariffs and work towards a common labour market. But, for Attlee

and his ministers, the projected Coal and Steel Community was an economic challenge to British industry and a potential intrusion on British
political sovereignty. 'Political federation', they worried, might be the result,
spelling the end for their projects to build a socialist Jerusalem through
nationalisation and full employment.[14] The Labour Party's National
Executive made their feelings felt in a dismissive statement drafted by Denis
Healey and disingenuously entitled *European Unity*:

> Britain is not just a small, crowded island off the Western coast of
> Continental Europe. She is the nerve centre of a worldwide
> Commonwealth which extends into every continent. In every respect
> except distance we in Britain are closer to our kinsmen in Australia and
> New Zealand on the far side of the world than we are to Europe. We are
> closer in language and in origins, in social habits and institutions, in
> political outlook and in economic interest.[15]

The Conservatives who took the reins of power from Attlee in 1951 were
no less hostile towards schemes of European union. Churchill's sympathy
for integration had largely faded; he was old and his attentions were dominated by the war against Communism in Korea and the demands of the
Cold War. The tone was set by Anthony Eden, a man who spoke French and
some German, enjoyed European culture and had a reputation for inter-
nationalism, but who also harboured a deep distaste for idealistic projects of
supranational unity. For Eden, Britain's affinities stretched much further
than Paris or Bonn; as his biographer puts it, he essentially 'did not consider
Britain to be a European nation'.[16] In January 1952, he told an audience in
New York that 'Britain's story and her interests lie far beyond the continent
of Europe'. Her 'family ties' in every corner of the globe made it impossible
'to join a federation on the continent of Europe. This is something which we
know, in our bones, we cannot do.'[17] Like his Labour rivals, Eden was simply
more interested in the Commonwealth and Empire than he was in
Continental Europe. For most of their generation, and for many of their
successors, Britain was a great international power, not a second-tier
European one. According to Cabinet minutes, when Harold Macmillan suggested in 1952 that it might be wise to contemplate some links with the Coal
and Steel Community or the projected European Defence Force, the right-
wing grandee Lord Salisbury reminded him that Britain was 'not a
continental nation, but an island power with a Colonial Empire and unique

relations with the independent members of the Commonwealth'.[18] There is little reason to doubt that most ordinary Britons agreed with Salisbury's argument. European integration was given little attention in the national press in the early fifties; no major politicians devoted themselves to the European cause; and the issue played no significant part in the elections of 1951 or 1955. Organisations dedicated to European unity were thin on the ground until the end of the decade, and even then the European issue was not one that galvanised the majority of voters.[19]

When, in July 1955, the foreign ministers of the Coal and Steel Community assembled in Sicily to discuss widening their association into a general economic association based on free trade, the unrestricted movement of capital and labour and a single market, the British reaction was spectacularly unenthusiastic. The Belgian Foreign Minister, Paul-Henri Spaak, flew to London to encourage Rab Butler to attend, but his idealism met its match in Butler's indifference, which verged on distaste. 'I don't think I could have shocked him more, when I appealed to his imagination,' Spaak commented, 'than if I had taken my trousers off.'[20] In the event, Russell Bretherton, a mere under-secretary at the Board of Trade, was sent to be Britain's representative at the Messina talks, an unmistakable indication of indifference and contempt. Legend has it that near the end of the conference Bretherton rose to his feet to address the delegates:

> The future treaty which you are discussing has no chance of being agreed; if it was agreed, it would have no chance of being ratified; and if it were ratified, it would have no chance of being applied. And if it was applied, it would be totally unacceptable to Britain. You speak of agriculture which we don't like, of power over customs which we take exception to, and of institutions which frighten us. *Monsieur le président, messieurs, au revoir et bonne chance.*

With that, Bretherton is supposed to have picked up his briefcase and walked out of the conference room.[21]

Unfortunately the story is almost certainly untrue, and it actually seems that Bretherton issued some blandly prevaricating statement and then, disappointingly, remained exactly where he was.[22] Even so, when the Six signed the Treaty of Rome two years later, creating exactly the kind of Economic Community that Spaak had proposed, the British were notable by their absence. The Mutual Aid Committee, a Whitehall body set up by the Treasury to examine the case for European integration, had concluded that it was undesirable for Britain to join. The Common Market would, it concluded, weaken Britain's links with the Commonwealth and overseas possessions; it would inhibit global free trade, while Britain was a global trading power; it would expose British industries to European competition; and it would promote further political integration and even Continental federalism, which the public were bound to abhor.[23] The Common Market would therefore go ahead without Britain at its heart; it was a decision that would reverberate for decades to come.

The refrain often heard from British politicians in the 1950s was that European integration would damage the country's 'family ties' with the Commonwealth. 'That is our life,' Eden insisted; 'without it we should be no more than some millions of people living on an island off the coast of Europe, in which nobody wants to take any particular interest.'[24] The rationale for the Commonwealth was that it preserved imperial ties by democratic, consensual means, gathering the old colonies beneath the umbrella of British prestige. When Macmillan took office in 1957, the 'Club' was still made up of Britain and the old dominions: Canada, Australia, New Zealand and South Africa. Three independent Asian nations in India, Pakistan and Ceylon had joined them, and Ghana was shortly to become the first African member.[25]

For nostalgic Conservative imperialists, the Commonwealth played a central part in their international outlook, supposedly preserving the Anglo-Saxon heritage and accomplishments of the old imperialists and offering protection and encouragement to the new post-colonial states of Africa and Asia. In the Labour movement, too, support for the Commonwealth was a sign of ideological virtue, denoting a commitment to help the post-colonial nations fight against poverty, racism and misgovernment. The Commonwealth, said one Labour MP, was 'one of the great progressive manifestations in the history of mankind', and its success was dear to the hearts of much of the British left.[26] As late as September 1961 a Gallup poll found that, when asked whether Europe, the Commonwealth or the United States was most important to Britain, 48 per cent chose the Commonwealth, 19 per cent the United States and only 18 per cent Europe. Old affections died hard.[27]

But the idea that the Commonwealth could preserve British power and prestige was a fantasy. Canada had already been drawn into a close trading relationship with the United States; Australian businessmen were beginning to look towards the expanding markets of south-east Asia; and the Indians were moving into closer association with the Soviet Union.[28] More and more British exporters, meanwhile, were finding customers in the expanding consumer markets of Western Europe; by contrast, the independent nations of Africa and Asia were hardly likely to encourage British imports at the expense of their own developing industries. Even as an economic entity, the Commonwealth was increasingly irrelevant.[29]

When Macmillan kissed hands as Prime Minister in 1957, he was acutely aware that Britain's most important political and cultural relationship was the alliance with the United States. It was always an uneasy liaison: while the British admired American power and were eager to share in its benefits, they were also suspicious and resentful of overweening transatlantic influence. Not merely did the decade since the end of the Second World War demonstrate the military and political supremacy of the United States in the Western world, it also brought a flood of American films, books, comics, records, television programmes, linguistic expressions and fashions. To some, American culture was the very model of glamour, classlessness and modernity, promising a brave new world of affluence; to others, it was the epitome of flashy, degraded materialism, threatening to drown British identity in a flood of cheap stockings. As Harry Hopkins put it in 1964, there was a sense that Britain was 'now merely one more offshore island'.[30] The events of the Suez crisis had made it painfully clear that, as an official inquest into the affair put it, 'It was the action of the United States which really defeated us . . . This situation with the United States must at all costs be prevented from arising again.'[31] But British politicians had to strike a careful balance; while the public saw the Americans as their natural allies and supported the NATO alliance, they disliked the idea of being stooges to Uncle Sam. In his first television broadcast as Prime Minister, for example, Macmillan assured his audience that, although the Atlantic alliance was as strong as ever, there was no danger of the British becoming 'satellites'.[32]

During his period in Downing Street, Macmillan was scrupulously careful to maintain close relations with the White House, and not to embark on ambitious overseas ventures without first consulting President Eisenhower, or, from 1961, John F. Kennedy. The Anglo-American partnership was to have priority over all other considerations, including relations with France, West Germany and the rest of Europe.[33] Macmillan was, after all, the son of a Midwestern heiress; having worked closely with Eisenhower and the Americans during the war, he was convinced that he knew how to manage the Anglo-American relationship. In 1944 he had explained to the Labour politician Richard Crossman:

> We, my dear Crossman, are Greeks in this American empire. You will find the Americans much as the Greeks found the Romans – great, big, vulgar, bustling people, more vigorous than we are and also more idle, with more unspoiled virtues but also more corrupt. We must run [Allied Headquarters] as the Greek slaves ran the operations of the Emperor Claudius.[34]

The analogy was not a promising one, not least since it implicitly acknowledged the vast gulf in power and resources between the 'vulgar, bustling' Americans and their weary British allies. The Greek cities under the Roman Empire, lazy provincial backwaters of scant importance, bore little relation to the cultural and political powerhouses of the age of Pericles. It was an unfortunate parallel; it is dubious whether the Prime Minister really pictured himself as a eunuch slave.

There is little doubt, however, that Macmillan was genuinely fascinated by the idea of the 'special relationship' and the problem of maintaining it in an age of European integration. 'One of our basic reasons why we could not integrate with Europe was our desire to maintain a special relationship with the United States,' he wrote to Selwyn Lloyd in December 1959. 'Just what does that mean? Is the pattern changing – will the Six replace us as the major ally of the United States?'[35] Lloyd, having taken soundings from his Foreign Office advisers, replied two days later:

Our Special Relationship with the USA
It does exist. It means preferential treatment for us in discussion and in certain types of knowledge (nuclear, intelligence, etc.). It gives us considerable influence on United States policy.

We ceased to be on an equal basis with the United States and USSR when we gave up the Indian Empire. We have been in retreat since . . . I do not believe size or physical military power will decide the future.

But even if it is so we must prevent the Six supplanting us as the principal influence on United States policy. (I admit our special relationship might end when Eisenhower and Herter go, but I rather doubt it.) To achieve this, we need to play in the game both as pro-Europeans and pro-Atlantic community.[36]

The special relationship undoubtedly meant more to British politicians, Labour as well as Conservative, than it did to the Americans; after all, the British had much more to gain from an alliance with a stronger partner.[37] Did it really amount to anything beyond the exchange of a few secrets, the occasional nuclear deal and British co-operation in American military adventures during the late fifties and early sixties? If there were important, tangible results for Britain, they are hard to find. Britain was not at the end of the sixties noticeably richer or more powerful than France or West Germany because of its special relationship with its old wartime associate.[38] American planners were also frequently irritated by Britain's claims to an independent role in the world; life would be much easier, they thought, if only the British would dismantle their empire and accept their inevitable position as part of an integrated European alliance. As Senator Pat McCarran commented in 1950: 'The fact is that in spite of the many policies which the United States has in common with the United Kingdom, despite the great good will which the two nations have for each other, the British objectives with respect for European integration are fundamentally opposed to those of the United States.'[39]

And yet many officials on both sides of the Atlantic were happy to testify to the ease of working within the Anglo-American relationship. The State Department official George Ball, a frequent critic of British pretensions, nevertheless recorded that there was indeed an indefinable affinity between the two nations, based as much on language and culture as on shared aims and policies. The peoples of the two countries, he wrote,

> to an exceptional degree . . . look out on the world through similarly refracted spectacles. We speak variant patois of Shakespeare and Norman Mailer, our institutions spring from the same instincts and traditions, and we share the same heritage of law and custom, philosophy and pragmatic *Weltanschauung* . . . starting from similar premises in the same intellectual tradition, we recognize common allusions, share many common prejudices, and can commune on a basis of confidence.[40]

In cultural terms, Britain and the United States were undoubtedly exceptionally close during this period, and the transatlantic popularity of the Beatles, James Bond, British actors and the fashions of Swinging London suggest that this was more a case of genuine exchange than the American 'cultural imperialism' that some scholars identify.[41] The peoples of the two countries certainly perceived one another differently, no doubt largely because the imbalance of power between them was now so great. Opinion polls taken in Britain during the late 1950s and early 1960s consistently put popular approval of the United States at around 60 per cent, occasionally fluctuating as high as 70 per cent or as low as 50 per cent after a particular incident like a summit or diplomatic disagreement. In other words, about one in three of the British public, if asked, registered disapproval of the United States.[42] By contrast, American polls recorded widespread affection for the British: one survey in 1965, for example, found that the American public, by an overwhelming margin, thought of the British as their closest and most reliable allies. Britain, they agreed, was still the fourth most influential country in the world, behind the two great superpowers and Communist China.[43]

The Anglo-American relationship after the Second World War was essentially a Cold War alliance. Even before Germany had been defeated, Churchill, Roosevelt and Stalin had begun to disagree about the future of Central and Eastern Europe, and within two years of the death of Hitler their divisions had hardened into a state of explicitly declared ideological and military antagonism. Since Britain and its European neighbours were exhausted by the ordeal of the war, it fell to the United States and Soviet Union to lead the rival armed camps on either side of the Iron Curtain. In the summer of 1945, few people in Britain could even contemplate the possibility of entering another international conflict so soon after the sacrifices of the last one, but within three years Ernest Bevin had persuaded his exhausted countrymen that British participation in the Cold War, under American leadership, was a desperate necessity. As Lord Bullock puts it, the public at large agreed with Bevin that:

> there was a real danger of the Soviet Union and other Communists taking advantage of the weakness of Western Europe to extend their power. We know now that this did not follow, but nobody knew it at the time. This was a generation for whom war and occupation were not remote hypotheses but recent and terrible experiences. The fear of another war, the fear of a Russian occupation, haunted Europe in those years and were constantly revived – by the Communist coup in Czechoslovakia, by the Berlin blockade, and the outbreak of war in Korea in 1950 which produced near-panic in France and Germany.[44]

The peace that settled over mainland Britain after the collapse of the Third Reich was therefore an insecure one; with the Red Army entrenched in Central Europe and American air bases dotted across eastern England and West Germany, the people of Britain could have little confidence that world war would not once more tear their lives apart. And while the mood of the Second World War had been a kind of black, sardonic determination, that of the Cold War was very different: fears of infiltration and subversion, suspicions of treachery and espionage and the supreme terror of nuclear holocaust all contributed to a heavy sense of dread, an insecurity that hung over the fifties and sixties and could never be entirely forgotten.[45]

Bevin's accomplishment was to resurrect the Anglo-American partnership that had performed so well against the Nazis and to make it the cornerstone of the anti-Communist alliance that would contest the Cold War. In June 1950, when North Korea invaded its southern neighbour, almost a hundred thousand British servicemen were sent to East Asia and the Labour Cabinet shifted its priorities from welfare spending to rearmament. This was a commitment not merely of minds and money but also of blood: one thousand British fighting men died in the fight for Korea.[46] By the end of the war, the North Atlantic Treaty Organization (NATO) had been welded into an integrated European fighting force, pledged to defend the frontiers of Central Europe against a potential invasion by the Red Army. The Attlee and Churchill governments agreed to commit four divisions and a sizeable air force to the defence of mainland Europe, a military undertaking that cemented Britain's place as the United States' chief partner and trusted ally.[47] But, even if the British were important partners in the North Atlantic alliance, they were nevertheless unquestionably junior partners, subordinate to their American cousins.

In 1946, Attlee and President Truman had concluded a deal allowing the United States to establish a series of air bases in East Anglia for the deployment of their atomic bombers in a European emergency, and military planners in both countries henceforth assumed that in the event of war they would be automatic allies. Seven years later, President Eisenhower gave permission for the deployment of complete nuclear warheads in the British air bases. From this point onwards, there was to be a permanent American nuclear presence on British soil. No other two countries in the Western alliance had such a close military relationship, although it was very clearly an unbalanced one.[48] The readiness of British negotiators to hand over the bases is best explained by their abiding fear of Soviet attack. From the very beginning of the Cold War it had been clear that, since Britain was the United States' closest European ally, it would in the event of war be one of the Soviet Union's principal military targets.[49] As a Foreign Office paper admitted in January 1950, however, the establishment of the American bases in eastern England made it doubly certain that in the event of nuclear war, Britain would be in the Soviet firing line. Since the Russians had successfully tested an atomic weapon in 1949, much earlier than predicted, the danger of Soviet nuclear attack was therefore both genuine and terrifying. British security could be guaranteed, according to the report, only by an overwhelming American nuclear deterrent. In short, the Americans must never be allowed to withdraw their nuclear umbrella. 'The primary aim of our foreign policy', the paper concluded, 'must be to keep the United States committed to Europe.'[50]

The Cold War was not merely a struggle for territory and technological advantage; it was also a battle for the allegiance of ordinary citizens, both at home and in the colonies. Since Britain escaped the kind of brutal slaughter visited upon the peoples of Korea, Vietnam, Cambodia, Angola, Afghanistan and elsewhere, most civilians experienced the Cold War only as an ideological and cultural contest. In a radio broadcast in July 1950, Attlee advised his audience to 'be on your guard against the enemy within'. 'Our fight', he said, 'is not only against physical but against spiritual forces.'[51] Hostility to Communism in Britain had deep roots: between 1918 and 1921, for example, there had been persistent fears of Communist subversion and revolution. It was common during the post-war period to blame Communist or Trotskyite infiltration of the trade unions for particularly bitter or prolonged outbreaks of industrial unrest.[52] In June 1966, for instance, Harold Wilson controversially blamed a seamen's strike on 'a tightly knit group of politically motivated men'; everybody knew that he meant Communists.[53] Recent research in the Moscow archives suggests that Communist militants in the trade unions were indeed being directed and funded by Soviet officials, so perhaps such claims were not so far-fetched.[54]

All the same, domestic Communism was never a serious threat to the British body politic. The Security Service, known as MI5, had by the mid-fifties collected no fewer than 250,000 files on Communists and their fellow travellers, suggesting that more than one in two hundred people were regarded as subversive. The great majority of these files, however, covered not party members but Communist sympathisers, most of whom had no doubt flirted with radical ideas when young only to abandon them later in life.[55] The

Communist Party itself was, in the words of one historian, 'little more than a narrow sect . . . an isolated pariah', having suffered a sorry decline from its pre-war heyday.[56] In the early 1950s it boasted fewer than forty thousand members, one in four of whom left the party in disillusionment in 1956 after the official revelation of Stalin's crimes and the Soviet invasion of Hungary. A small number of these apostates later formed the core of the British New Left, a notable example being the historian E. P. Thompson, who with John Saville edited the radical magazine *The Reasoner* and was actually expelled from the party because of his attitude towards the events of 1956.[57] Another historian, Eric Hobsbawm, was equally appalled by the attack on Hungary but chose to remain in the Communist Party even though he knew that it could have 'no long-term political future'.[58] The party's general secretary, Harry Pollitt, once told him that he would have liked a direct telephone link to Moscow. 'He thought that the party was an army of messenger boys,' Hobsbawm later recalled, 'while those who worked in the intellectual professions realised that we had to try to think things through on our own.'[59]

Despite the weakness and irrelevance of the domestic Communist Party, anti-Communism was still a significant force in cultural and political life, although it was never anything like as strong as the fervent anti-radicalism to be found in the United States, and had by the sixties lost much of its popular appeal. During the early and middle 1950s, the spirit of intellectual Butskellism held sway, self-satisfied, consensual and socially conservative. It was no coincidence that one of the most respected highbrow periodicals of the day, the magazine *Encounter*, was edited by two staunch Cold Warriors in Stephen Spender and Irving Kristol and was supported by a Parisian anti-Communist organisation, the Congress for Cultural Freedom, which was itself financed by the CIA.[60] Cultural support for the Cold War in Britain was not, however, dependent on the wiles of American intelligence; plenty of British intellectuals already had strong anti-Communist sentiments and were eager to express them. Many had themselves been members of the party during the thirties and approached the task of fighting Communism with the same zeal that they had once devoted to its propagation.[61]

The Cold War also had its place in popular culture, not least in the novels and films devoted to the theme of espionage that became popular in the early 1960s. Many of these works, however, were designed for light entertainment rather than education and instruction; it is doubtful whether audiences took the anti-Communist message of, say, the James Bond films very seriously, especially by comparison with the more realistic films celebrating the victory over Nazism that were popular during the fifties. There was a brief vogue for films on the themes of subversion and espionage in the early fifties; unfortunately, most of these pictures were shoddily plotted and made, and they had little box-office impact.[62] Indeed, since the cinema was the most popular form of mass entertainment in post-war Britain, it is revealing that so few films treated the perils of the Cold War with great seriousness or depth.[63]

If there was one outstanding Cold War film of the fifties, it was *High Treason* (1951), written and directed by the iconoclastic and talented Boulting brothers, both Liberals. The plot follows the efforts of a group of Communist plotters to take over Britain's power stations at the precise moment that a Soviet invasion will be launched from mainland Europe. As Raymond Durgnat observes, the conspirators are a motley crew of deluded progressives and cynical Communist agents predictably drawn from the textbook of paranoid populism: they include a pacifist, a cat-loving and therefore clearly homosexual bachelor, two admirers of avant-garde music, a well-bred Labour MP with a taste for rare vases, 'assorted burly doctors', Kenneth Griffith and 'various bespectacled duffle-coated characters who read books obsessively but are too impractical to handle guns': historians, perhaps? The front for their efforts is, not surprisingly, a college of further education, where they meet to ponder the class struggle and discuss 'bourgeois deviation' or 'democratic discipline'.[64] In the words of the historian Marcia Landy, the film is 'exemplary in dramatizing the postwar condition as one of cynicism, opportunism, threat, and the loss of the collective and patriotic ethos of the war years. The film exudes a sense of paranoia, a preoccupation with the misapplication of power and authority.'[65] Similar themes, as we will see, recurred later in the period in the novels of John le Carré, particularly *The Spy Who Came In from the Cold* (1963) and *The Looking-Glass War* (1965), although le Carré's works eschewed the militant and slightly ridiculous anti-Communism of *High Treason*. In fact, the film's box-office performance was pretty feeble; most filmgoers, it seemed, were put off rather than attracted by its political didacticism.[66]

Mainstream political culture in Britain was generally hostile to radicalism and Communism throughout the fifties and sixties. The phenomenon of aggressive domestic anti-Communism was, however, much more apparent on the left than on the right, especially during the early years of the Cold War when the fears of renewed war in Europe were greatest. In 1948 the Labour Party prohibited any co-operation with the Communists and expelled several left-wing members, and a year later the TGWU dismissed nine officials who were sympathetic to the Communist Party and prohibited Communists from holding union posts or serving as delegates.[67] But it would not do to exaggerate the British red scares of the late 1940s and early 1950s. By comparison with the paranoid purges of McCarthyism on the other side of the Atlantic, this was all pretty small-scale stuff and was generally limited to the Labour Party and the unions. While in the United States the full power of the federal state was dedicated to the search for Communists and subversives, most historians agree that hostility to Communism in the corridors of Whitehall was tempered by a genuine respect for civil liberties as well as the unwillingness of senior civil servants to disturb the cosy, cloistered world of administrative secrecy through which they had risen.[68]

Although MI5 was entrusted with the task of 'vetting' candidates for important civil service appointments, this arrangement turned out to be less than comprehensive, stifled by a lack of funds, personnel and political will. Sir Arthur de la Mare, the head of internal security at the Foreign Office, later recorded that their own vetting system was a 'farce': he was given the services of only five interviewers, so that in a week they could manage no more than a feeble ten reports at the very best.[69] The so-called civil service purges that began in 1948 were mild to say the least. In the United States, where security purges began at a similar date, almost ten thousand federal officials were dismissed after being investigated as Communists, while fifteen thousand more resigned while inquiries into their political affiliations were still continuing; all were publicly named. The British parallel is both instructive and rather ludicrous. According to the calculations of Richard Thurlow and Peter Hennessy, no more than thirty-five civil servants were dismissed after investigation, with a further twenty-five resigning and about eighty-eight being transferred to safe, non-sensitive employment within the civil service. None of these men and women was publicly identified by the state.[70]

Why was there no British equivalent of the McCarthyism that swept through American society in the 1950s? The simple answer is that anti-Communism was never terribly important in Britain. Although the film *High Treason* was striking for its dark paranoia, it was something of a one-off; neither political nor popular culture was deeply penetrated by the kind of intense anti-Communist populism that was so powerful in the United States. For one thing, the tribulations of life in the rubble and austerity of Britain under Attlee were too exhausting for ordinary citizens to spend their evenings wondering whether Doreen's new boyfriend might be a Communist. As a character remarks in Pamela Hansford Johnson's novel *A Summer to Decide* (1948), the common man was 'too busy coping with the daily problems of his rationed life, and trying to see a clear road for his own future' to worry about internal security.[71] What was more, the British had just spent six shattering years working and fighting together against the menace of Nazism, and the dream of national unity still carried considerable force. They had also spent much of the war being encouraged to salute the brave example of Joe Stalin's boys in the Red Army; they were, therefore, much slower than the American public to enter into the spirit of the Cold War, and remained much less enthusiastic anti-Communists.

The fact was that it was the American experience, not the British, that was the aberration. In Italy and France, where there were sizeable and important Communist parties that could conceivably have posed a genuine threat to internal security, there was no great panic about internal security either.[72] To take a later example, when in October 1957 the Soviet Union dispatched its *Sputnik* satellite into orbit, shattering the complacent belief of the Western powers in their own scientific superiority, there was an almighty fuss in the United States about the Communists having soared ahead in the technological struggle. Macmillan, always a worrier by temperament despite his phlegmatic reputation, wrote to Eisenhower asking: 'what are we going to do about these Russians? . . . This artificial satellite has brought it home to us what formidable people they are, and what a menace they present to the outside world.'[73] A month later the Soviet scientists sent up another *Sputnik*, with the dog Laika in it, and Macmillan mournfully noted in his diary:

> The Russians have launched another and larger satellite (with a little 'dawg' in it) which has created much alarm and despondency in US. The English people, with characteristic frivolity, are much more exercised about the 'little dawg' than about the terrifying nature of these new developments in 'rocketry'. Letters and telegrams were pouring in tonight to No. 10 protesting about the cruelty to the dog.[74]

Laika, sad to report, did not return in one piece.

One further reason that anti-Communist hysteria never really gripped the people of Britain was that they associated it with their American allies, about whom popular feeling was always ambiguous. There were plenty of examples of cultural anti-Americanism in Britain during the late fifties and early sixties, from muttered remarks in the plays of John Osborne to exasperated tirades in newspaper editorials. One Polish exile based in London complained that the United States was 'disliked, feared and sneered at with a unanimity that was remarkable'.[75] A survey of Oxford and Manchester students in 1962 found that the image of the United States was 'not very favourable . . . a basically adolescent, materialistic, slightly hysterical society, run primarily by Big Brother, a society exerting great pressure for conformity with little real freedom of thought, a society which can easily run amok or behave in an unpredictable way'.[76] British public opinion was consistently suspicious of American bellicosity: during the Korean War, for example, more than one in three people were still critical of American policy and one in five blamed the United States, not the Soviet Union, for the heightened state of tension.[77] In the summer of 1961, during the crisis over the erection of the Berlin Wall, a survey found that while 71 per cent of Americans were willing to contemplate fighting for Berlin, only 46 per cent of the British public were similarly inclined, and a tiny 9 per cent of the French.[78] And when in October 1962 Macmillan was informed by the American ambassador that the Soviet Union had installed missile sites in Cuba, he told him that 'he was going to have considerable trouble with the Commons and with the British public because there was great suspicion in England at that time that the United States exaggerated the Castro threat. The pictures satisfied him, but might be regarded as a bit of fakery unless somehow they could be shown to the British public generally.'[79]

   This belief that Americans were guilty of anti-Communist 'exaggeration' and 'hysteria' therefore inhibited British politicians from copying the techniques of red-baiting on the scale of McCarthyism; it was dubious anyway whether there was any great electoral advantage in doing so. It was the Labour Party, not the Conservatives, who borrowed most from American anti-Communism. This was not necessarily a great innovation, since in the thirties Labour had expelled members for being associated with Marxist groups, and neither was it really comparable to McCarthyism, since Labour leaders never adopted the same wheedling tones of populist resentment. As for the Conservatives, their dislike of the Soviet Union and domestic radicalism was beyond question, but their dislike of insurgent populism and American cultural values was not far behind, so they were never really caught up in the enthusiasm for anti-Communist purges.[80]

   A Whitehall committee set up to examine the case for positive vetting reported in 1950 that the procedures in the United States, including FBI investigations, loyalty oaths and ruthless dismissals of security risks, were certainly 'extremely elaborate', but also concluded that 'any such procedure would be repugnant to British thinking'.[81] Since the obsession with treachery and subversion was contained in the security services and did not seep into general political culture, positive vetting remained rudimentary, and internal security measures were extremely mild compared with those across the Atlantic. McCarthyism was therefore condemned on all sides as 'a disreputable form of politics', the result of what Thurlow calls 'a conscious decision to maintain civility in public life' and 'a profound belief in the administrative virtues of secrecy, which in the hands of a dedicated, reliable and trustworthy elite had created an efficient government machine which had strengthened democracy and the rule of law in Britain'. Ironically, given Whitehall's problems with leaks and moles, there was probably a greater need for rigorous security measures in Britain than in the United States. A British version of McCarthyism, however, was perceived as a greater threat to national harmony and administrative efficiency than the possibility of a few upper-class traitors in the corridors of power; no draconian action was therefore ever taken.[82]

Although anti-Communism in Britain was never as widespread or as intense as in the United States, official government support for the Cold War rarely wavered. As a self-proclaimed great power, albeit one quite clearly in military and political decline, Britain had the duty of standing shoulder to shoulder with the Americans against international Communism, and Macmillan was desperate to see the British acknowledged as important and influential participants in the diplomatic games of the time. In July 1959, when there was talk of the two superpowers conducting summit negotiations without the United Kingdom, the Prime Minister was horrified, confiding to his diary:

My own position here will be greatly weakened. Everyone will assume that the 2 Great Powers – Russia and America – are going to fix up a deal over our heads and behind our backs. My whole policy – pursued for many years and especially during my Premiership – of close alliance and co-operation with America will be undermined.

People will ask, 'Why should UK try to stay in the big game? Why should she be a nuclear power? You told us that this would give you power and authority in the world. But you and me have been made fools of. This shows that Gaitskell and Crossman & Co. are right. UK had better give up the struggle and accept, as gracefully as possible, the position of a second-rate power.'[83]

The British did attend the Paris summit in 1960, although future meetings between Kennedy and Khrushchev, for example, or Nixon and Brezhnev, took place without British participation. Macmillan certainly never publicly acted as though Britain were anything less than a world power of the first rank, one great coup being his visit to Moscow in 1959, where he strolled cheerfully about in plus-fours hailing bemused Russians with the greeting 'Double-gin!' and at one stage sporting an astounding twelve-inch-tall white Finnish hat, a relic of the Soviet–Finnish War of 1940 and perhaps not the most sensitive choice of headgear.[84]

On a more serious note, Macmillan shared the commitment of his predecessors to holding the line against international Communism in Britain's colonial possessions and on the Rhine. The most protracted example was the war against the Communist Malayan Races' Liberation Army, the so-called Malayan Emergency, which dragged on from 1948 until 1960 and demanded the commitment of tens of thousands of British and Commonwealth troops in an intensive jungle war that in some respects anticipated the American war in Vietnam in the following decade. By 1960 the British had prevailed, with General Sir Gerald Templer establishing a series of ruthlessly policed 'new villages', using helicopters and jungle platoons to eliminate rebel resistance and cutting deals with friendly local nationalists. As in Korea and the colonial conflicts in Kenya, Cyprus and Aden, national servicemen formed part of the British troop commitment, but fortunately relatively few lives were lost, although the same was not true for the Malayan peoples.[85] Another overseas adventure inspired by Cold War considerations was the deployment in 1958 of two thousand British paratroopers to bolster King Hussein of Jordan against threats of invasion from Egypt and Syria. On this occasion, no shots were fired, but Macmillan was confident that the episode had helped to restore Britain's reputation in the area and ward off Soviet-inspired subversives. American marines had been sent to the Lebanon at the same time, and it turned out that Macmillan had been pestering Eisenhower with a typically grand scheme not only to occupy Lebanon and Jordan but also to launch Anglo-American invasions of Syria and Iraq.[86]

With British regular troops and special forces not only serving overseas in colonial bases but also being sent to flashpoints like Aden, Kuwait and the Yemen, it was easy to maintain the notion that the United Kingdom was still a power of international importance. All of these enterprises, however, required both manpower and money at a time when successive Chancellors were hoping to trim expenditure on defence. British military resources were not inexhaustible. From 1951 onwards, when Aneurin Bevan and Harold Wilson walked out of Attlee's Cabinet in protest at the decision to introduce dental and ophthalmic charges to pay for an enormous rearmament programme, it had been evident that the country could not afford both a generous welfare state and the military infrastructure of a global superpower. Indeed, thanks to the Korean War, what had been a balance of payments surplus of £307 million in 1950 had become a deficit of £369 million the following year, and some historians see this as a missed opportunity to concentrate on a sustained boom in industry and manufacturing for export.[87] In 1958, more than 100,000 British troops, a seventh of the entire armed forces, were still stationed in the Middle and Far East, and three years later the unanticipated combination of the Berlin and Kuwait crises meant that the government had once again to call up the reserves.[88] Defence spending until the mid-sixties accounted for around £1500 million a year and between 7 and 10 per cent of GNP, a higher proportion than anywhere else except the Soviet Union and United States. There can be little doubt that the costs of maintaining a global role severely inhibited industrial investment and contributed to the balance of payments deficit, since so many valuable sterling reserves were being poured into foreign economies.[89] The bill for the four infantry divisions stationed in West Germany cost at least £70 million, while the 44,000 Germans employed by the British Army accounted for another £30 million.[90] In his survey *Anatomy of Britain*, Anthony Sampson reported that the British government had spent £1554 million on defence in 1958, which worked out as £30 per head of population. France, by contrast, spent £1180 million (£26 per head), West Germany £529 million (£10) and Italy £359 million (£7). Britain, he noted, spent three times as much on defence as it did on education; one new aircraft carrier cost the same as five Universities of Sussex; and the annual budget for the Royal Air Force was the equivalent of the entire gross national product of Ghana.[91]

In the decade before the Second World War, British scientists, not least in the Cavendish laboratory in Cambridge, had led the way in researching nuclear fission, and in 1931 two British scientists, John Cockcroft and E. T. S. Walton, successfully developed the particle accelerator that would allow them to split the atom. British scientists, too, had been involved in developing the atomic bombs that were dropped by the United States on Hiroshima and Nagasaki in 1945. However, the wartime Quebec Agreement that allowed for nuclear collaboration between the two allied powers was superseded in 1946 when the American Congress prohibited any exchange of nuclear secrets. This was a bad blow for British plans to develop an atomic bomb of their own; to produce fissile material for a nuclear warhead demanded an enormous, and expensive, industrial infrastructure that an impoverished country could barely afford.[92] A small Cabinet committee had already approved the construction of a secret plutonium plant at Windscale in Cumbria, and in October 1946 it met again to discuss spending even more money on a gaseous diffusion plant. Several ministers, including the Chancellor, criticised the costs involved, apparently winning the support of Attlee himself. Ernest Bevin then made a decisive intervention:

> No, Prime Minister, that won't do at all. We've *got* to have this . . . I don't mind for myself, but I don't want any other Foreign Secretary of this country to be talked at, or to, by the Secretary of State of the United States as I just have, in my discussions with Mr Byrnes. We've got to have this thing over here, whatever it costs . . . We've got to have the bloody Union Jack on top of it.[93]

The secret British nuclear programme therefore went ahead; there was no public debate or official admission that such an enterprise had begun, and the £100 million in costs was hidden away in the defence estimates.[94] Three scientists, William Penney, John Cockcroft and Christopher Hinton, were in charge of developing the British bomb, and by autumn 1951 they had produced enough plutonium for a test in the Monte Bello Islands, off the coast of Western Australia. According to legend, Churchill, now back in Downing Street, had two telegrams ready: 'Thank you, Dr Penney' for failure, and 'Well done, Sir William' for success. He sent the second one.[95]

It soon transpired that an atomic fission bomb was not enough. In November 1952 the Americans tested their first thermonuclear hydrogen bomb in the Pacific, a weapon immensely more destructive than the A-bomb that the British had developed. The Soviet hydrogen bomb was just a year behind. Lord Plowden, then the chairman of the Atomic Energy Authority, was summoned to see the Prime Minister with a report on the potential costs of developing and building a British equivalent, and he later recalled:

> I went to see Churchill in his room in the House of Commons after lunch, and when I'd explained what the effort necessary would be, he

paused for a time, and nodded his head, and said in that well-known voice of his, 'We must do it. It's the price we pay to sit at the top table.' And having said that, he got up and tied a little black ribbon round his eyes, and lay down on his bed in his room, and went to sleep.[96]

In the summer of 1954, the Cabinet agreed to plough more resources into the construction of a British thermonuclear capability. One obvious justification was the perceived need to deter a Soviet nuclear strike. A Ministry of Defence report explained that in a future war 'the United Kingdom – the nerve centre of European resistance – would be extremely vulnerable to nuclear attack [and] there is not in sight any air defence system which could protect us effectively . . . In short, possession by the West of the nuclear weapon is at present a real deterrent. Overwhelming and immediate retaliation with it is our only reliable defence.' Britain could not afford simply to rely on the United States to provide a nuclear umbrella; if that were withdrawn, the thinking went, then the country would be defenceless against Soviet assault.[97] A second justification, however, was what Churchill had called the price 'to sit at the top table'; in other words, only the H-bomb would convince the Americans of Britain's continuing influence and relevance. This eagerness to impress the White House no doubt partly explains why the first British hydrogen bomb test on Christmas Island in November 1957 was actually a fraud organised to conceal the fact that early tests had been disappointing. The H-bomb that was supposed to have been tested was, it later turned out, an unusually large atomic bomb supplemented with hydrogen fuel.[98] Public opinion, meanwhile, strongly favoured the British deterrent: 60 per cent approved of a British atom bomb in 1952, and 58 per cent backed the government's decision to build an H-bomb in 1955. There was little sign at this stage of the bitter controversies that were to erupt later in the decade.[99]

The Labour governments of the late forties and early fifties were much keener spenders on defence than their Conservative successors. Throughout 1957, Peter Thorneycroft was arguing from 11 Downing Street for drastic cuts in government expenditure, and, given the popular commitment to the welfare state, defence was clearly one area in which savings could be made. The White Paper issued by the Minister of Defence, Duncan Sandys, on 4 April 1957 was therefore a political landmark in that it openly admitted the need for Britain, hitherto a self-proclaimed international and imperial power, to cut back its armed forces at a time when the two global superpowers were spending vast sums on their own weapons. Financial pressures were not the only considerations in the drafting of the White Paper; recent developments like the increasing importance of NATO, the contraction of the Empire and the advances in thermonuclear technology were all taken into account.[100] For some years the more far-sighted civil servants had been pushing for reform; as one later put it, 'an awful lot of the collar work had been done before [Macmillan and Sandys] came into office'.[101] Nonetheless, it took a powerful and ruthless political operator to push through changes of the magnitude envisaged in the White Paper. Duncan Sandys was entirely the right kind of person: hard, obstinate, a hatchet man who had seen action in the Second World War and still felt the pain from a serious leg wound. He was certainly unpopular with the service chiefs, who fought bitterly with him over his projected cuts; on one occasion he even came to blows with the hero of Malaya, Field Marshal Sir Gerald Templer.[102] Macmillan called him 'a very tough man – he wouldn't have any nonsense . . . and was – quite simply – good at any job you gave him to do'; one of his civil service advisers thought he was 'remorselessly logical . . . like a mincing machine'.[103]

Sandys' report was a pivotal moment in the post-war evolution of Britain as a military power, and in Alistair Horne's words 'the most radical change ever made in peacetime'.[104] Although Britain would still maintain bases across the globe, from Aden to Singapore, the armed forces were to be cut from almost 700,000 men to just 375,000 over the next five years. National Service was to be abolished, so that by the end of 1962 the armed forces would consist only of regular volunteers. British forces in West Germany were to be reduced from 77,000 to 64,000, the last four Royal Navy battleships would be scrapped, and home defence would be slashed to the bare minimum; there could be no effective defence, after all, against nuclear attack. Although this would only save some £78 million in the next year, over several years the savings would be considerable.[105] These plans were followed with impressive fidelity. By 1965, British forces had indeed been reduced to fewer than 400,000 men, and total defence spending was down to 7 per cent of GNP.[106] Meanwhile, British defence planners were to concentrate on an offensive nuclear deterrent, with only a small, mobile and highly trained conventional force maintained for non-nuclear combat. So Sandys reaffirmed 'the commitment to nuclear weapons as the most effective deterrent to war . . . on this basis large conventional forces are not required . . . We believe that the British people will agree that the available resources of the nation should be concentrated not upon preparations to wage war so much as upon trying to prevent that catastrophe from ever happening.'[107]

The premise of this entire exercise, therefore, was that the British could develop and deploy their own thermonuclear deterrent that would make it impossible for the Soviet Union ever to contemplate an invasion of Western Europe. 'If Russia were to launch a major attack even with conventional forces only,' explained a less celebrated White Paper published in the following year, the West 'would have to hit back with strategic nuclear weapons. In fact the strategy of NATO is based on the frank recognition that a full-scale Soviet attack could not be repelled without resort to a massive nuclear bombardment of the sources of power in Russia.'[108] The fear in Whitehall was that at some future point the Americans might revert to their old isolationist ways; in that case, Britain had to have an independent deterrent of its own. 'However close we were to the US and however tied they were to us by alliances,' recalled Sir Richard Powell, a senior civil servant at the Ministry of Defence, 'one could not rule out circumstances in which they might go isolationist.'[109] What was more, possession of a nuclear deterrent was thought to ensure a place for Britain at the 'top table'. An internal report of late 1957 explained that its purposes were:

(a) To retain our special relation with the United States and, through it, our influence in world affairs, and, especially, our right to have a voice in the final issue of peace or war.

(b) To make a definite, though limited, contribution to the total nuclear strength of the West – while recognising that the United States must continue to play the major part in maintaining the balance of nuclear power.

(c) To enable us, by threatening to use our independent nuclear power, to secure United States co-operation in which their interests were less immediately threatened than our own.

(d) To make sure that, in a nuclear war, sufficient attention is given to certain Soviet targets which are of greater importance to us than to the United States.[110]

For many observers, the possession of nuclear weapons meant that Britain had every right to be considered a great power. In 1958, for example, Sir

Winston Churchill's dissolute and outspoken son Randolph, himself a failed politician, announced: 'Britain can knock down twelve cities in the region of Stalingrad and Moscow from bases in Britain and another dozen in the Crimea from bases in Cyprus. We did not have that power at the time of Suez. We are a major power again.'[111] 'It's OUR H-Bomb!' read the headline in the *Daily Express* the morning after the first Christmas Island test.[112] This was not any nuclear deterrent; it was an independent, *British* deterrent. A few days before the publication of Sandys' White Paper, Hugh Gaitskell declared that the Labour Party was no less dedicated to nuclear independence. 'Our party', he said, 'decided to support the manufacture of the hydrogen bomb . . . because we do not think it is right that this country should be so dependent . . . upon the USA.'[113]

The irony was that the British deterrent was not independent of the Americans at all. Not only had the supposed H-bomb test at Christmas Island been an elaborate deception, but the loudly proclaimed independence of the British deterrent was also itself a fiction. In May 1957, Eisenhower and Macmillan had reached a deal whereby Thor intermediate ballistic missiles, built in the United States, would be stationed at bases in Britain. These missiles, carried by British Vulcan bombers, were to propel atomic warheads against the Soviet Union if war broke out, but, to Macmillan's dismay, they were to be controlled not from London but from Washington.[114] From 1958, moreover, the Americans agreed to restore a degree of 'nuclear sharing' with their British allies, though in truth this was not so much collaboration as patronage, with British scientists eagerly accepting delivery not only of technical secrets but also of fissile material.[115] One British guided missile, Blue Steel, was developed and then abandoned. Duncan Sandys, meanwhile, was a keen proponent of a British long-range surface-to-surface rocket called Blue Streak, which, it was hoped, would offer a more advanced means of launching nuclear warheads into the Soviet Union than the antiquated V-bombers. By February 1960, thanks to Sandys' efforts, some £60 million had been spent on developing Blue Streak, but at this point it was becoming painfully clear that it was already out of date. As a Ministry of Defence report put it, if the Soviet generals pre-emptively fired their missiles at the British rocket silos, they 'could wipe out Blue Streak without any possibility of reply'. Blue Streak was accordingly, and embarrassingly, cancelled, leaving Sandys looking rather silly.[116] From the Labour benches in the Commons, Harold Wilson could not resist a dig at his expense:

We all know why Blue Streak was kept on although it was an obvious failure. It was to save the Minister's face. We are, in fact, looking at the most expensive face in history. Helen of Troy's face, it is true, may only have launched a thousand ships, but at least they were operational.[117]

Macmillan would have been well advised at this point to abandon the pretence that Britain could be an independent nuclear power. Millions had been wasted on two unusable rockets, the American Thor missiles were themselves rapidly becoming out of date, and the whole charade was doing nothing but damage to national self-esteem. Instead, in a desperate attempt to regain some credibility and an implicit acknowledgement of Britain's status as a nuclear client, he arranged in March 1960 a new deal with the United States to buy the long-range Skybolt missile. Since Skybolt was fired from the air, this would not only give the RAF Vulcan bomber fleet a new lease of life, but would also avoid the problem of the vulnerability of ground silos. Admittedly, even when the formal deal was signed in September there were already rumours that the American development of Skybolt was not going well, but Macmillan was confident that the missile would be delivered on time.[118]

As part of the deal, Macmillan agreed that the US Navy could use the Holy Loch on the Firth of Clyde as a Polaris submarine base. However, not only was the Holy Loch disturbingly close to major population centres in western Scotland, but the Americans made no commitment to consult their British counterparts before using their Polaris fleet in anger, an act which would quite probably bring utter devastation to the British Isles. Macmillan soon realised his error and wrote to Eisenhower suggesting that their agreement had been 'a serious mistake':

It would surely be a mistake to put down what will become a major nuclear target so near to the third largest and most overcrowded city in this country. As soon as the announcement was made Malinowsky [the Soviet defence chief] would threaten to aim his rockets at Glasgow and there would be not only the usual agitation of the defeatists and pacifists but also genuine apprehension among ordinary folk. But a more immediate difficulty is that a city of this size inevitably contains large numbers of people who would be quick to take the opportunity of making physical demonstrations against us both.[119]

Eisenhower refused to abandon the deal, and Macmillan's predictions of popular dissatisfaction were indeed justified. Campaigners for unilateral disarmament, Scottish nationalists, environmentalists and other groups all vigorously condemned the decision, while in both the press and the Commons there was much outrage at the fact that the British government had no control over the American nuclear weapons.[120] Not only was this a public-relations disaster, it also provided a powerful demonstration that British military independence was not quite all that Macmillan claimed.

In the end, the Skybolt deal proved if anything an even bigger and more humiliating debacle than the development of Blue Streak. British missiles, it seemed, were inseparable from failure. As Bernard Levin put it in 1970:

> They became a dreadful symbol of the country's erratic attempts to move into the future, a paradigm of national impotence as the thrusting rocket failed to take off, failed to achieve its intended climax, blew up in mid-course, or found itself being withdrawn for reasons outside anyone's control . . . It seemed that the country simply could not get a rocket off the ground.[121]

British planners should have paid closer heed to the rumours that Skybolt was not proving an unmitigated success. In December 1962, the Kennedy administration announced that it was cancelling Skybolt after all: tests had not gone well, $500 million had been wasted, and there was little point throwing good money after bad. As the Foreign Secretary, Lord Home, put it, this was 'a pretty good shock. We'd set a lot of store by its success, and the success had been advertised, and it was widely known that the government set a lot of store by it; so it was a shock, undoubtedly.'[122] Macmillan, meanwhile, was furious. An Anglo-American conference in Nassau was scheduled for 18 December, and he told his ambassador in Washington that if the Americans did not offer 'a realistic means of maintaining the British independent [sic] deterrent, all the other questions may only justify perfunctory discussion, since an "agonising reappraisal" of all our foreign and defence [plans] will be required'.[123] In the words of the historian Nigel Ashton: 'It was as though the Greek who had thought himself to be quietly running the Roman Empire had for the first time realised that the governing characteristic of his condition was slavery.'[124]

Contrary to myth, Kennedy and Macmillan had an uneasy relationship, not least because they disagreed about Britain's role in the North Atlantic alliance.[125] To the Americans, the British insistence on nuclear independence was an annoying distraction that both alienated their allies in France and West Germany and ruined their own plans for a united European force under American command. Not only was the American Secretary of Defense, Robert McNamara, continually complaining that the British deterrent was 'unnecessary', but Kennedy himself noted that it would be best 'for the British in the long run to phase out of the nuclear deterrent business since their activity in this field is a standing goad to the French'.[126] But since the nuclear deterrent had been presented to the British public as the key to international influence and national security, it was hardly likely that any Prime Minister would acquiesce in such a scheme, especially at a point in 1962 when the government's popularity was flagging. Macmillan arrived at Nassau determined to persuade the Americans that a multilateral, European deterrent was no alternative; what he wanted, and finally obtained through various histrionics from a reluctant Kennedy, was the opportunity to buy advanced Polaris missiles, which were fired from nuclear submarines.[127] In this respect, then, the Nassau summit was a triumph for Macmillan's diplomacy. By winning Polaris, he had actually emerged with a better weapon than Skybolt ever promised to be; by comparison, the French found it tremendously difficult to build their own submarine deterrent from scratch. Since Britain had therefore obtained preferential treatment, this was widely recognised as a powerful symbolic demonstration of the survival of the Anglo-American special relationship.[128] However, the deal also served to alienate the French at a point when Macmillan needed President de Gaulle's goodwill for his application to join the Common Market. Not for the last time, therefore, a British Prime Minister had chosen to emphasise the special relationship with the United States rather than the potential links with Europe.

The significance of Nassau was that it was, as one historian writes, 'the triumph of a nuclear mendicant rather than of a serious independent contributor to the West's combined nuclear profile'.[129] Polaris was a good deal, but it was by no stretch of the imagination an independent British deterrent. The nuclear fleet would be, at American insistence, assigned to NATO unless Britain's 'supreme national interests' were at stake; what these might be was never defined.[130] The *Express*, the newspaper that five years before had excitedly welcomed 'OUR H-Bomb', now announced 'The Sell

Out', insisting that 'the public will accept nothing less than our own nuclear deterrent'. The *Telegraph*, meanwhile, complained that the supply of Polaris was dependent on continuing American goodwill, and therefore gloomily concluded 'that Britain has had very much the worst of the bargain'. 'Macmillan's Nuclear Folly' thundered the headline in the *Daily Herald*.[131] In fact the arrangement was even more weighted in favour of the Americans than the newspapers realised. According to the government, the British would design and manufacture their own nuclear warheads to use on the Polaris underwater missile system. British scientists had in 1958 been handed a carbon copy of the American warhead design, so even here they were dependent upon foreign scientific research.[132] As both the Holy Loch decision and the Skybolt fiasco indicated, Britain was, in military terms, little more than a client state. The most important nuclear decisions were made not in Whitehall or Westminster but in Washington, DC. Millions had been squandered in an effort to prove that Britain could have an independent nuclear deterrent; what had been produced by the early sixties, however, was a British deterrent almost entirely dependent on the whims of American politicians and officials. This was not the bomb 'with the bloody Union Jack on top of it' at all.

The Nassau conference took place just two months after the international crisis in which the world came closest to a third world war: the controversy over the Soviet missiles in Cuba in October 1962. Macmillan's biographers often like to claim that the Prime Minister and the British ambassador to Washington played important roles in the missile crisis.[133] In fact their influence was, in the grand scheme of things, at best minimal and at worst entirely irrelevant. Kennedy's National Security Adviser later remarked that the British role was 'not very important', and the tape transcripts of American meetings and transatlantic telephone calls make it very clear that this was an American–Soviet confrontation in which British officials played miniscule cameo parts.[134] Britain was, quite simply, no longer a great power, and the independent deterrent about which so much had been claimed did *not* in fact provide Macmillan with an influential role in deciding whether the world would descend into nuclear war. There is no doubt that British forces would have seen action if the crisis had not been peacefully resolved, and little doubt either that the country would itself have been a target. Bobby Robson, an RAF navigator, later recalled sitting in his Vulcan bomber at the end of a Lincolnshire runway. 'If the hooter had gone,' he told Peter

Hennessy, 'we would have gone. It would not have mattered whether it was for real or an exercise. Nobody would have given it a second thought. We were doing a job. I never heard a conversation on the rights and wrongs of dropping a nuclear bomb.'[135] A Vulcan squadron commander at the same base, RAF Waddington, remembered that he and his crew were on permanent stand-by in a flight hut twenty yards from their bomber; they could have been airborne within ten minutes.[136] Among the public at large, there was widespread horror that the world appeared to be sliding towards a nuclear holocaust. Protesting crowds assembled in most large towns during the last days of October, and there were several arrests for obstruction. Not everyone lost their cool, however; a group of Sheffield students spotted the opportunity for a practical joke and produced newspaper placards with the headline: 'War Declared, Official'; sadly they were suspended by the university's characteristically humourless authorities.[137]

The shock of the Cuban missile crisis, like the furore over Holy Loch and the regular discussions of defence policy in the newspapers and on television, focused popular attention on the potential horrors of a nuclear war. It was clear from British tests in the Pacific, as well as the evidence of Hiroshima and Nagasaki, that the consequences of a nuclear explosion would be apocalyptic, from the intense blinding light of the initial blast to the radioactive fallout that could hang over an affected area for years to come. The twenty-two thousand British servicemen, fourteen thousand Australians and five hundred New Zealanders who witnessed the initial tests in the late fifties were themselves given inadequate protection against residual radiation, and in many cases the effects were lethal.[138] One sapper in the Royal Engineers recalled that he was ordered simply to sit on the beach of Christmas Island, wearing 'a jungle green hat and white cotton overalls' and jam his fists into his eyes, but when after the blast he opened his eyes slightly, he could see the bones of his hands illuminated through his skin. 'The noise was deafening, like a thousand horses thundering towards you,' he explained. 'The man next to me broke down and cried.' In the same year an RAF squadron leader, Eric Denson, was allegedly ordered to fly through the mushroom cloud after a test on the island so that government scientists could observe the effects of radiation. He spent forty minutes in the air, was physically sick immediately on landing, and was plagued by ill health and depression thereafter, finally committing suicide in 1976.[139]

To his credit, Macmillan played a key role in the test-ban agreement of

August 1963, by which Britain, the United States and the Soviet Union committed themselves to the suspension of atmospheric nuclear testing. France and China, less creditably, did not sign the treaty.[140] Tests on chemical weapons, however, continued at the Chemical Defence Experimental Establishment at Porton Down, where one airman, Ronald Maddison, died in 1953 after a nerve-gas experiment. Several other servicemen later claimed that they had been told the tests were for a cure for the common cold, and allegations that volunteers had been used as human guinea pigs dogged the establishment for decades to come.[141] In October 1957, meanwhile, a major fire at the Windscale nuclear reactor in Cumbria, built to provide plutonium for the nuclear-weapons programme, resulted in the contamination of the surrounding area, with winds blowing the radioactive cloud back onto the English mainland and the government being forced to destroy milk produced within 200 miles of the stricken reactor. The official line, as Macmillan explained to his Cabinet, was that such an accident was 'improbable'.[142] A report into the incident by the nuclear scientist Sir William Penney was promptly buried and all copies destroyed. Several dozen people at the very least are estimated to have died prematurely because of the leak, which was much worse than the more celebrated American meltdown at Three Mile Island in 1979.[143]

Such was the destructive power of the new military technology that even government officials could not be entirely sure of the consequences of a nuclear strike, especially as radioactive fallout could conceivably linger for generations thereafter. An internal report in 1953 estimated that if evacuation plans worked correctly, five million people, principally women, children and the elderly, would be sent to the countryside, with another four million streaming out of the cities on their own initiative. Even in this scenario, if the Soviet Union attacked Britain with atomic bombs of the kind dropped on Nagasaki, then 1.4 million people would immediately be killed and another 800,000 seriously injured. London would be hardest hit, followed by Birmingham; heavy casualties were also expected on Merseyside, on Clydeside and in Manchester.[144] After the first Soviet hydrogen bomb tests, however, these predictions were hastily revised. According to a civil service report in 1954:

A bomb dropped on London and bursting on impact would create a crater ¾ mile across and 150ft deep and a fire-ball of 2¼-miles diameter. The blast from it would destroy the Admiralty Citadel [a stone signals centre next to the Mall] at a distance of one mile. Suburban houses would be wrecked at a distance of 3 miles from the explosion, and they would lose their roofs and be badly blasted at a distance of 7 miles. All habitations would catch fire over a circle of 2 miles radius from the burst.[145]

One H-bomb dropped on London alone would probably kill four million people; if the Soviet Union launched a full-scale, pre-emptive night attack on the country as a whole, nine million people would die in the initial blasts and a further three from short-term fallout, while at least four million more would be severely injured or disabled. One in three people would be either dead or too badly wounded to work for reconstruction.[146]

If these figures were terrifying, so too were the gloomy prognostications of Sandys' Defence White Paper in 1957 when it came to discussing the provisions for national nuclear defence:

It must frankly be recognised that there is at present no means of providing adequate protection for the people of this country against the consequences of an attack by nuclear weapons. Though in the event of war, the fighter aircraft of the RAF would unquestionably take a heavy toll of enemy bombers, a proportion would inevitably get through. Even if it were only a dozen, they could with megaton [hydrogen] bombs inflict widespread devastation.[147]

Macmillan was no more optimistic. In November 1956, when still Chancellor of the Exchequer, he noted that there was little point spending money on military preparations for a future world war, since 'we cannot hope to emerge from a global war except in ruins'.[148] The deterrent, he thought, was enough. British nuclear strategy at the beginning of the sixties was based on a so-called '30–40 cities' approach; military planners expected that if their sixty hydrogen bombs were successfully fired from the V-bomber fleet, then they would kill about eight million Soviet citizens and injure eight million more. By the end of the decade, the plan was that Polaris missiles would be fired from Britain's three nuclear submarines at thirty cities in the USSR, probably killing a similar number of people.[149] One odd consequence of the development of Polaris was that from the early seventies all British Prime Ministers were compelled to write sealed instructions for the submarine commanders in case contact was lost for several days during wartime. One of the final tests, touchingly, was the transmission of Radio Four's *Today* programme; if it could not be found and the other tests suggested that Britain had indeed been destroyed, then the commanders were ordered to open the instructions and act accordingly, the various possibilities being to put themselves under American command, to attack the Soviet Union, to take refuge in Australia or New Zealand, or simply to use their own judgement.[150]

Civil defence preparations in Britain were pretty feeble, as in truth they were in most comparable countries.[151] Government plans in 1962 provided for the evacuation of nearly ten million women and children from nineteen major cities to the countryside, but it is hard to imagine such an operation proceeding smoothly amid the panic of impending nuclear attack.[152] The Third World War never took place, in the twentieth century at least, but it is possible to reconstruct what British officials in the 1960s thought might happen if it did. In October 1968, for example, the Ministry of Defence produced a speculative scenario describing the potential domestic security problems in the event of a drift to war. As the Cuban missile crisis had shown, there was likely to be considerable civil unrest, and the student protests of the late sixties were clearly at the forefront of their minds. During the opening period of international tension, there were expected to be widespread peace demonstrations and marches by anarchist and Communist groups, as well as nationwide strikes that could make it more difficult to mobilise British military forces. Once fighting had actually begun in Central Europe, according to the scenario, 'the public would by now be even more aware that the nation was possibly on the threshold of nuclear attack. Evacuation of likely target areas might already have started spontaneously if not officially. Anti-war action might spread and involve considerable numbers of normally stable and law-abiding people.' At this point small numbers of Soviet agents were likely to begin sabotage and subversion campaigns, meaning that police resources would be even more overstretched. During the fifth stage, the 'Period of Nuclear Exchange and its Immediate Aftermath', 'millions of homeless, bewildered people would need rudimentary shelter and sustenance. Looting of food stocks and other essential supplies, the blocking of essential routes by refugees, the seizing of property, all these problems on a mammoth scale could overwhelm the surviving police resources.' Assuming that Britain was not occupied by Soviet forces, the weeks and months after the nuclear strike were likely to be extremely difficult for the security forces, bringing a 'long term battle for survival . . . Crucial struggles are likely to arise over securing sources of food and other essential commodities together with the means of transporting them by sea and air.' As many as 200,000 soldiers would have to be deployed throughout the country to help the police keep order.[153]

Britain would now be in the grip of a nuclear winter, with most major cities and industrial conurbations destroyed by Soviet attack and as many as twelve million people dead. Millions more would be suffering from radiation burns and the effects of the explosions, and the overworked medical authorities would probably have to turn away those who were likely to die anyway. Stockpiles of food, medicines and equipment would be guarded from looters by Territorial Army reserves. The very air would be irradiated; agriculture would be sterile; the countryside would be a medieval, ghostly world of famine, homelessness and isolation.[154] Government plans provided for Britain after the nuclear apocalypse to be divided into twelve regional baronies of 'wretched and desperate survivors', centred on the regional seats of government at Catterick, York, Preston, Cambridge, Dover, Reading, Salcombe, Brecon, Kidderminster, Armagh, Edinburgh and Nottingham.[155] The Prime Minister and his War Cabinet, the Cabinet Secretary, the Chief of the Defence Staff, various intelligence, defence and communications officials and a host of clerks and support staff would all be huddled in the bleak underground command bunker 'Turnstile', hollowed into the southern Cotswolds near Corsham. Their wives and families, however, would all have been left above ground, in many cases to die.[156] Each of the twelve regional fiefs was in principle to be autocratically governed from a subterranean control centre by a designated Cabinet minister with the title of Regional Commissioner, who was to be assisted by an Army District Commander and the Regional Director of Civil Defence. In practice, however, the alternative, post-apocalyptic Britain of the late sixties and seventies, ravaged by terror, sterility and starvation, would no doubt have been ruled under martial law by those armed soldiers and policemen who were still alive.[157]

Although this nightmarish vision of a degenerate Britain after a third world war was never realised, it was hardly surprising that many ordinary people in the fifties and sixties lay awake at night worrying about nuclear Armageddon. As Anna desperately exclaims in Doris Lessing's novel *The Golden Notebook*, published in the year of the Cuban missile crisis: 'I don't want to be told when I wake up, terrified by a dream of total annihilation, because of the H-bomb exploding, that people felt that way about the cross-bow. It isn't true. There is something new in the world.'[158] The rapid development of nuclear weapons, the secretiveness of the nuclear industry, the unvoiced rumours about chemical testing and the thrilling mystery of the space race were all reflected in the popular culture of the time. Both utopian and dystopian fiction had deep roots in English literature, and twentieth-century authors like Wells, Forster, Huxley and Orwell had already won great acclaim for their fantasies of technological progress or totalitarian despair. In the years after Hiroshima and Nagasaki, however, it became even more fashionable to explore the possibilities of nuclear disaster, world war and environmental destruction. It was no coincidence that in *Lord of the Flies* (1954), William Golding's fable of 'the fallen nature of man', the marooned schoolboys are being evacuated to Australia after the beginning of a nuclear war. Their own savagery on the island is a limited but striking reflection of the wider human slaughter of a third world war.[159]

Dozens of other British writers, as well as hundreds of Americans, were drawn to the subject of mankind after a nuclear or environmental apocalypse, and in almost all cases the prognosis was extremely gloomy. Most authors speculated that post-apocalyptic society would be a new Dark Age, cold, barbaric and violent, rejecting technology and social equality and regressing to man's primitive urges and origins. A good example was John Bowen's play *After the Rain* (1958), a powerful story of superstition, ritual and sacrifice and a reworking of the biblical myth of the Flood set 'two hundred years after the Rain of 1969'.[160] In another post-apocalyptic work, L. P. Hartley's anti-egalitarian novel *Facial Justice* (1960), the only remnant of the past is the tower of Ely Cathedral, standing alone on a flat, bleak plain. 'In the New World,' we are told, 'there was no frost, no soft spring mornings – the war had swept them away, along with all the other changes of climate, temperature and season; they had this uniform, perpetual March, with an east wind that indeed grew keener towards evening and a grey sky which the sun never quite pierced.'[161]

If there was one literary genre above all that reflected popular fears of the Cold War, it was science fiction. Perhaps this was hardly surprising: on both sides of the Atlantic, hundreds of people, transfixed with the excitement of the arms and space races, claimed that they had seen unidentified spacecraft or mysterious otherworldly visitors, and for a time UFO-spotting became a craze in its own right.[162] Many of the central themes of post-war British science fiction had already been anticipated by writers like H. G. Wells: the discontent with contemporary society; the possibility of national degeneration; the alienation of the individual; the confrontation with the disturbing

Other; the reworking of biblical myths like the Adam and Eve story; and the final destruction of the human race.[163] In the years after the Second World War, the appetite for science fiction along these lines reached its peak. Talented British and American writers like Ray Bradbury, Kurt Vonnegut, John Wyndham, Brian Aldiss and Arthur C. Clarke all enjoyed critical praise as well as healthy sales, and their credibility was further improved by the praise of Kingsley Amis, whose analysis *New Maps of Hell*, published in 1960, was one of the most influential critical assessments of the genre.[164]

Post-war science fiction, at least in Britain, was frequently concerned with issues of individual identity and alienation, no doubt appealing to readers who felt their own individuality was threatened in a changing world of corporations, cities and consumerism. The most popular British science-fiction writer of the fifties, John Wyndham, was most renowned for his novels *The Day of the Triffids* (1951), *The Kraken Wakes* (1953) and *The Chrysalids* (1955), all of which embrace the apocalyptic theme. In *The Day of the Triffids*, the population of the world is blinded by laser beams dispatched from satellites in space (anticipating *Sputnik*); humanity is then destroyed by the Triffids, an alien species of intelligent plants. An earlier version of the story, intriguingly, described the Triffids as having originated in the Soviet Union; the Cold War was clearly on Wyndham's mind. *The Kraken Wakes*, meanwhile, describes how the blasts of American and Soviet nuclear tests rouse a terrible underwater monster, the Kraken, which then acquires atomic weapons of its own and melts the polar ice caps, drowning mankind beneath the consequent floods.[165] And in *The Chrysalids* Wyndham echoes the themes of Aldous Huxley's book *Ape and Essence*: the human race, blighted by a nuclear war, has regressed into religious tribalism, believing that the 'Tribulation' was a divine punishment for the arrogance of their forefathers, while their children are born as physically deformed mutants or telepaths and banished to the wilderness.[166]

All of these books, with their themes of the natural order being overturned by the misuse of technology, proved very popular with the public; not only did they address the topical concerns of the Cold War, but they also looked back to the values of Wells and his contemporaries. Like J. R. R. Tolkien, Wyndham extolled the values of nature, community and family rather than industry, progress and science. Families and friendships in Wyndham's books become tighter when tested against the horrors of the future; not for nothing did Brian Aldiss call him the master of 'the cosy catastrophe'.[167]

Wyndham's success in the middle 1950s proved an inspiration to other writers, who now realised that through popular science fiction they could both address the social and political concerns of the time and reach a wide and enthusiastic reading public. During the next two decades there followed a veritable deluge of stories of alien invasions, floods and famines, nuclear disasters and post-apocalyptic nightmares. Many authors were clearly inspired by the atrocities of the Second World War, the death camps and the bombing of Japan to delve deep into the problem of human evil in the twentieth century. In John Griffiths' novel *The Survivors* (1965), the hero survives a Chinese nuclear attack by hiding down a Cornish mine shaft, finally emerging after the invaders have died of radiation sickness. On his way to the mine he watches society collapse: two men ambush a Mini, kill the two adults inside and drive off 'as though the screaming children in the back seat did not exist'. In the shelter itself he observes 'the veneer of civilisation . . . begin to wear thin', and at the end of the novel he muses: 'We've survived the holocaust and all the dangers it brought. It remains to be seen if we can survive ourselves.'[168] Similarly, in 1964 Brian Aldiss published his own excellent vision of post-apocalyptic England, *Greybeard*, in which the two central characters embark on a journey to the sea through a medieval landscape of isolated towns and river villages. The history of the country's collapse slowly emerges: in 1981 'that deliberate act men called the Accident', spreading radiation sickness across the countryside; then the detonation of British and American nuclear weapons in space to contaminate the entire world; then the assumption of power by an autocratic coalition in 2005; and finally, by 2030, when the story takes place, the government of Britain by local chieftains in little childless communities divided by roaming wild animals, flooded valleys and mutated vegetation.[169]

By the end of the decade, meanwhile, the post-apocalyptic trend had even spread to children's fiction. The writer John Christopher, for example, had originally won acclaim for his novel *The Death of Grass* (1966), in which an agricultural experiment accidentally destroys all grasses and grains in the world and society collapses into an anarchic struggle for food supplies. Christopher then became something of a specialist in the genre, regularly wiping out millions of people in nuclear holocausts, enormous earthquakes, alien invasions, crop mutations, a tilt in the Earth's axis and so on. Many of these books, however, were written specifically for younger readers: popular examples were the Tripods trilogy (1967–8), set in a medieval, rural Britain far in the future, ruled by the alien Tripods; and the Sword of the

Spirits trilogy (1970–2), again set in a medieval English landscape, but in this instance after a nuclear holocaust that has left the population genetically damaged and bitterly antagonistic to all machines and technology. These novels were enduring successes with British children during the following decades, playing to their love of adventure and fantasy but also exploiting the fear of science and technology that had by the early 1970s seeped deep into popular culture. Even at the end of the century they were still popular choices in libraries and schoolrooms, despite their nightmarish post-apocalyptic settings. 'John Christopher', wrote one commentator in the late 1990s, 'has probably killed more people than any other author in history.'[170]

Given the financial struggles of the British cinema during the post-war years, it was hardly surprising that directors and producers eagerly welcomed the science fiction of the day. Cinematic depictions of science fiction and horror frequently equated modern life with personal alienation and social disintegration; science itself, as in the Frankenstein myth, was the enemy.[171] A popular example was *The Quatermass Experiment* (1955), which was written by the playwright Nigel Kneale and had a great influence on the Hammer horror films as well as television programmes like *Doctor Who*. Professor Quatermass (Brian Donlevy), a selfish and deluded scientific genius, inevitably American, sends a rocket into space to collect an alien fungus, which when brought back to Britain transforms one of the astronauts into a homicidal half-plant and then occupies Westminster Abbey while preparing to launch its spores into the atmosphere to take over the planet. The villainous fungus is eventually defeated when every power station in the land pours its electricity into the Abbey, but Quatermass himself, like so many mad scientists, remains unrepentant. The film is more than a pulp shocker; it articulates real social concerns, from the dangers of the space race and atomic testing to the hubris of scientific experimentation in the age of the Cold War.[172]

The sequel, *Quatermass II* (1957), presents an implicit criticism of the secrecy and detachment of the British political and scientific establishment, exploiting popular fears that the modern world has passed beyond the understanding and control of ordinary people. On this occasion, Professor Quatermass is a far more sympathetic figure, using his scientific expertise to unmask and foil a terrible conspiracy based, slightly implausibly, just outside Carlisle. Various Cabinet ministers, eminent scientists, police chiefs and civil servants, it transpires, have been taken over by a dastardly alien intelligence; meanwhile, an enormous industrial complex supposedly devoted to creating synthetic food to solve the world's problems of famine is actually being used to store a black acidic slime on behalf of the invaders. Despite the participation of Sid James, the effect of the film is extremely eerie, especially the atmospheric location shooting at the futuristic Shell refinery at Milford Haven. Indeed, with its cast of politicians and officials secretly being controlled by the alien intelligence, its themes of subversion and conspiracy, and its fears of scientific experimentation and technocratic secrecy, *Quatermass II* was the quintessential paranoid picture of the fifties.[173]

Films of this kind, eliding the boundaries between horror and science fiction, playing on Cold War concerns about dehumanisation and scientific arrogance, were ubiquitous in the post-war decades, providing a cheap and popular alternative to the New Wave realism then popular with newspaper critics, art-house aficionados and budding academics. In 1961 there was *The Day the Earth Caught Fire*, in which two simultaneous H-bomb tests throw the world off its axis and into a collision course with the sun.[174] In 1962 there was a cinematic version of *The Day of the Triffids*, opening with arresting images of the people of Britain blinded by a meteor shower: we see a sightless air stewardess, for example, calming her distraught passengers with soothing lies, only to discover that the pilot too is literally flying blind, desperately reading his instruments with his fingers through broken glass.[175] And two years later there were two notable examples of the genre: *The Earth Dies Screaming* and *Village of the Damned*. The former, directed by the Hammer stalwart Terence Fisher, portrayed a *Triffids*-style alien invasion with even greater panache, beginning with a tremendous sequence showing the impact of an alien gas attack on everyday British life: cars and trains crash, planes plummet to the earth, commuters keel over at railway stations . . . and finally, enter the robots, marching ominously down country lanes.[176] *Village of the Damned*, meanwhile, adapted from Wyndham's novel *The Midwich Cuckoos*, had a good claim to be the most frightening film of all: alien invaders secretly impregnate all the fertile women in a quiet, bucolic English village, and nine months later a group of frightening blonde children with piercing eyes and strange manners are born, with predictably terrifying results.[177] Most of these films were derided by contemporary reviewers and film historians; nevertheless, they usually made more than enough money to cover their production costs, and clearly appealed to a substantial audience at a time when the British film industry in general was beginning to slide towards disaster.

Few of the science-fiction films of the fifties and sixties were explicitly critical of the Cold War or war in general. There were nevertheless signs towards the end of the fifties that popular culture was beginning to reflect a renewed scepticism about war, reviving critical instincts that had lain dormant since 1939. Films like *The Dam Busters* and *The Cruel Sea* depicted the tensions within the British ranks as well as the shattering impact of injury and death; indeed, Alec Guinness' performance in *The Bridge on the River Kwai* (1957) functioned as a brilliant critique of the stereotype of the upright, strict, unimaginative British officer.[178] Between 1956 and 1963, meanwhile, two teenage amateurs, Kevin Brownlow and Andrew Mollo, were busy making *It Happened Here*, an extraordinary film acted almost entirely by volunteers which undermined the national myths of the Second World War by depicting life in an occupied Britain under the Nazis, complete with fake newsreels, native fascist collaborators played by genuine supporters of the extreme anti-Semitic right, and brutal partisans who execute their prisoners in cold blood.[179] The demands of realism and the pressures of the atomic age meant that it was now easier to present war as an unglamorous, dirty, bloody undertaking, and at the turn of the decade, three different films, *Yesterday's Enemy* in 1959, *The Long and the Short and the Tall* in 1960, and *The Valiant* in 1962, all depicted British forces torturing enemy prisoners in wartime. A particularly striking scene in *Yesterday's Enemy* shows the friendly sergeant (Gordon Jackson) saying to an old, bewildered Burmese man, 'Come on dad, over here,' and then ushering him before the firing squad.[180]

Anti-war and anti-imperial sentiments were also increasingly common in the theatre, the most celebrated example being *Oh! What a Lovely War*, an imaginative revue first performed by Joan Littlewood's Theatre Workshop company in 1963. Both critics and audiences loved the play, demonstrating that an anti-war message was not incompatible with critical and commercial success in the early sixties.[181] By the end of the decade, it was acceptable for the National Theatre to present productions as violently critical of war and nationalism as Charles Wood's plays *Dingo* and *'H', or Monologues at Front of Burning Cities*, both of which presented British soldiers as selfish, violent bullies. Even the great Victorian soldier–adventurers were not immune from criticism: *'H'* portrays Havelock's relief of Lucknow as a bloody rampage, and in 1969 the novelist George MacDonald Fraser published the first of his tremendous Flashman books, purporting to tell the true story of the Empire from the point of view of the cowardly, caddish villain of Thomas Hughes' nineteenth-century classic *Tom Brown's Schooldays*.[182]

All of the examples given above were ultimately acceptable because they did not pose a serious threat to the commitment of the nation to the Cold War. Science fiction might have voiced widespread anxieties about the enterprise, but it did not channel them into aggressive dissent. But, as the country's political leaders well knew, popular culture was easily capable of undermining the consensus that governed foreign policy. In April 1965 the BBC director Peter Watkins spent four weeks shooting a pseudo-documentary about the effects of a nuclear strike, *The War Game*, planned for broadcast at the end of the year. Watkins was an extremely talented filmmaker who liked to use non-professional actors, hand-held cameras and natural lighting to give his films the appearance of complete documentary realism. His first television project, *Culloden*, had been shown in December 1964 and was a frighteningly authentic and controversial re-enactment of the defeat of the Jacobites in 1746, complete with plenty of blood and misery. Audience research suggested that it had had a 'tremendous anti-war impact', and one senior BBC executive thought that Watkins had so much talent that he could 'make films in the same sort of way that Mozart could compose music when he was four'.[183] Watkins was fascinated with warfare and violence, and even before *Culloden* was shown he had approached his Corporation bosses with the project to make a film about Britain in a nuclear war. He wanted, he said, 'to make the man in the street stop and think about himself and his future'.[184] The result, a black and white film lasting just forty-seven minutes, was probably the most controversial the BBC had ever produced.[185]

The War Game covers a period of four months or so, from the initial diplomatic tension when Chinese troops intervene in the Vietnam War to the final escalation over Berlin and the outbreak of global nuclear war. In Watkins' projected future, it is NATO that strikes first, launching a nuclear strike on the Soviet Union; all the audience see, however, are the effects in one town, Rochester in Kent, when the Russians hit back. During the early stages of the international crisis, the cameraman struggles through crowds of refugees arrived from London and billeted on local residents on military orders. Most people, however, are convinced that there will be no war but make feeble preparations anyway. One poignant sequence has a proud householder giving the cameraman a tour of his 'bombproof' home, with its futile little bomb shelter in the garden, and brandishing a shotgun, determined to fight off any neighbours intruding into his shelter. The entire film is shot in the style of a documentary, with simple, hand-held black and white photography, extremely naturalistic acting and calm, dry narration;

there would be no reason for an uninformed viewer to imagine that it was at all fictional, were it not for the fact that no such war had ever happened. When the Soviet rockets land, the initial effect of the strike is rendered simply by overexposing the film so that it flashes into brilliant white negative, and by showing the sets and the hand-held camera shaking under the impact. All the usual British myths about national courage and determination disintegrate during the next few days: hospitals are choked with the dead and dying; exhausted policemen round up and shoot the seriously injured and terminally ill. There are food riots; people carry arms; civil order collapses and is replaced by a mixture of anarchy and martial law. In the closing scenes, the flat voice of the narrator tells us: 'It is now more than possible that what you have seen happen in this film will have taken place before 1980'; finally the film ends with images of people's faces staring at the camera, hungry, tired, desperate and ill.

The War Game pressed home its point with tremendous power; not only was it the most unsettling film ever made about nuclear warfare, it had a good claim to be among the most disturbing films of any kind. 'At this distance,' says the narrator dispassionately, 'the heat wave is sufficient to cause melting of the upturned eyeball'; on screen, a child's eyeball is seared by the effect of the blast many miles away. Later in the film, there is a brief close-up of a bucket used to collect wedding rings, the only way to identify the scorched bodies of the dead; in another scene we see a ruined building being used as an improvised furnace to destroy the hundreds of corpses left in Rochester after the attack.

This was strong stuff; too strong for the BBC. Despite all the effort that had gone into making it, The War Game was not broadcast. There have been frequent allegations of political pressure to ban the film, and certainly government officials were very unenthusiastic after watching the film in privately arranged screenings, but even without any direct pressure it is very unlikely that the Governors of the BBC would have agreed to the transmission of such a programme. Lord Normanbrook, the chairman of the Governors, had previously been Cabinet Secretary and head of the civil service; he later commented that he wished he had stopped the film being made in the first place. The truth is that no political pressure was necessary; even Watkins' own colleagues on the editing and directing staff of the BBC seem to have agreed that he had gone too far, and the Daily Sketch's headline 'Brilliant – But It Must Stay Banned' captured a general consensus.[186] In November 1965, the BBC announced that the film would not be shown because it was 'too horrifying for the medium of broadcasting' and might disturb 'children, the very old or the unbalanced'. The film appeared only in art houses and at private screenings arranged in anti-war circles until finally the BBC agreed to show it to a mass audience in 1985.[187]

The BBC's anxiety about *The War Game* reflected the belief that anti-war sentiment was a real threat to the security of the nation. In 1968, as we have seen, the Ministry of Defence was worried that anti-war activism might interfere with the country's military preparations.[188] In 1945, polls suggested that one in five Britons disapproved of the bombing of Hiroshima and Nagasaki, and in the twelve years thereafter opposition to the nuclear arms race gathered momentum. In 1950, for example, a hundred Cambridge scientists petitioned the government not to follow the United States in developing a hydrogen bomb, and three thousand pacifists met at Trafalgar Square to commemorate Hiroshima Day. In 1954 a million signatures were collected for a petition calling for a world disarmament conference; there were frequent ructions within the Labour Party over the issue of disarmament; and in 1957 two Quaker activists sailed into the nuclear test zone near Christmas Island – too late for the tests, admittedly, but with an enormous amount of publicity nonetheless.[189] The great breakthrough for the peace cause, however, came later that year, in November, when the venerable socialist playwright J. B. Priestley published an article, 'Britain and the Nuclear Bomb', in the *New Statesman*. It was a swashbuckling call to arms against the 'nuclear madness' that had gripped the world. 'There is no real security in it,' he wrote of the British deterrent, 'no decency, no faith, hope nor charity in it . . . If there is one country that should never have gambled in this game, it is Britain. Our bargaining power is slight; the force of our example might be great.' He concluded:

> Alone we defied Hitler – alone we can defy this nuclear madness into which the spirit of Hitler seems to have passed, to poison the world . . . The British of these times, so frequently hiding their decent, kind faces behind masks of sullen apathy or sour, cheap cynicism, often seem to be waiting for something better than party squabbles and appeals to their narrowest self-interest, something great and noble in its intention that would make them feel good again. And this might well be a declaration to the world that after a certain date one power able to engage in nuclear warfare will reject the evil thing for ever.[190]

The editor of the *New Statesman*, Kingsley Martin, was promptly deluged by a torrent of letters delighted that so eminent a cultural figure had voiced what many people had been afraid to say themselves, and a lively correspondence followed. Martin then had the idea of a meeting to establish a mass movement against nuclear weapons, and in January 1958 a variety of individuals, Quakers, novelists, politicians and churchmen, from the Bishop of Chichester to the socialist firebrand Michael Foot, assembled at the flat of Canon John Collins of St Paul's Cathedral to set up a new body, the Campaign for Nuclear Disarmament, or CND.[191]

The immediate success of CND can largely be explained by its timing. It was just over a year since the fiasco of the Suez crisis and the shock of the Soviet invasion of Hungary; many easy assumptions about international affairs, on both left and right, had been badly shaken, and some people had been terrified that the Suez crisis might escalate into a nuclear confrontation between East and West. In April 1957 the Sandys White Paper had openly admitted that there was 'no means of providing adequate protection for the people of this country against the consequences of an attack by nuclear weapons', and that 'widespread devastation' would be the result of a third world war.[192] In recent months increasing publicity had been given to the fact that American planes carrying hydrogen bombs were patrolling the skies above the United Kingdom; in May 1957 Macmillan and Eisenhower had reached their deal to install four Thor missile bases in East Anglia; and in November newspapers had reported the first British H-bomb test at Christmas Island. Many people, especially those with anti-American inclinations, were becoming tired of Macmillan's indulgence of Eisenhower's nuclear whims.[193] The left, meanwhile, was in ferment: many younger dissenters, having walked out of the Communist Party after the invasion of Hungary, still nursed their dissatisfaction with mainstream British politics and the values of the Labour Party and were keen to find a forum to express their dissatisfaction. In the spring of 1957, four young Oxford radicals, Stuart Hall, Gabriel Pearson, Raphael Samuel and Charles Taylor, founded the *Universities and New Left Review*, later to merge with E. P. Thompson's magazine and become the *New Left Review*, the house periodical of the British New Left. Across Britain thousands of pale, duffel-coat-clad students were hunched in coffee bars over their copies of Jean-Paul Sartre and Jack Kerouac, their ears ringing with the sound of jazz music and their eyes smarting from the smoke of a hundred Gauloises as they gloomily pondered the iniquity of the world. The ideas and personnel that drove CND already existed; they merely needed an institutional focus through which they might be expressed.[194]

The stated aim of CND was, as Priestley later wrote, to persuade the government and people of Britain to abolish nuclear weapons 'whatever other nuclear powers may decide . . . [and so] set other nations an example by deliberately challenging the hysterical fear that is behind the arms race'.[195] The first public meeting, held on 17 February 1958 in Central Hall, Westminster, attracted an audience of over five thousand, far in excess of that which had been predicted. Canon Collins spoke, along with Priestley, Bertrand Russell and the irreverent Oxford historian A. J. P. Taylor, who made the greatest impact of the evening when he calmly listed the projected effects of a thermonuclear explosion: so many miles of fires and fallout, charred bodies, horrendous injuries, cancers for years to come. At last Taylor stopped pacing about the stage, turned directly to the audience and demanded: 'Is there anyone here who would want to do this to another human being?' No one spoke. 'Then why are we making the damned thing?' The meeting broke up amid considerable enthusiasm, and part of the crowd, perhaps a thousand strong, marched down to Downing Street where they stood shouting 'Ban the Bomb!' and 'Murderer!' until the police arrived with dogs.[196]

This was the first step in a national crusade. During its first year of existence, CND organised a wide variety of marches, demonstrations and public meetings across the country, usually, as one might expect, in middle-class or metropolitan areas. By early 1959 there were over 270 different branches of the movement and twelve regional organising committees, concentrated around London and Manchester in the south-east and north-west of England, and in Scotland.[197] Support for CND in Scotland had been given a boost by Macmillan's reluctant deal with the Americans to allow them the use of the Holy Loch base for their Polaris submarines. Scottish membership was therefore, in the words of two CND activists, 'more widely based, more representative of the people in general, and therefore . . . more working class in character'; disarmament marches north of the border tended to be less precious and bookish than in England.[198] The campaign attracted an impressive list of left-wing intellectuals and celebrities: as well as Priestley, Russell, Taylor and Martin, CND boasted the endorsement of Benjamin Britten, Michael Tippett, E. M. Forster, Barbara Hepworth, Henry Moore, Peggy Ashcroft, Doris Lessing, John Osborne, Arnold Wesker, Robert Bolt,

Lindsay Anderson, Kenneth Tynan, Iris Murdoch and so on.[199] It was run, however, by a small minority, a 'self-appointed committee of "big names"' who resisted pressure from local offices to set up a more democratic structure. Canon Collins, Priestley and his wife Jacquetta Hawkes, Foot, Martin, Taylor and their friends enjoyed their regular little meetings, which were so informal that Taylor's wife, though not actually a member of the committee, used to turn up even when her husband was away.[200] This was one of the most glaring weaknesses of the movement; the tension between the executive committee and the regional offices would prove a serious problem a few years later.

The highlights of CND's efforts were the annual Aldermaston marches, three-day walks over Easter from Trafalgar Square to the village of Aldermaston, just outside Slough, where the marchers glowered at a nuclear research establishment from behind the wire perimeter fence. As with many such enterprises, the first march in Easter 1958 later became shrouded in myth, but it was far from the tremendous success that was subsequently claimed. The journalist and CND organiser Mervyn Jones later recalled that the weather was atrocious, 'with bitter cold and incessant rain' which then turned to snow. The crowd at Trafalgar Square at the outset had been 'quite a good' one, 'though short of filling the Square', but by the second day, according to Jones, the march was in danger of falling apart:

> It hadn't occurred to anybody that the CND big-shots were expected to do any marching; those pictures of the Canon in his cassock, Michael Foot with his stick and dog, and Jacquetta Hawkes in her splendid red hat were taken in subsequent years . . . The march therefore had a pleasantly amateurish flavour, and hardly anybody was over 25 years old. But we were few, sadly few. At the Peggy Bedford [Inn, at Cranford] I counted 300, and some dropped out or hitched lifts during the miserable afternoon. There was a serious question of whether the march was going to peter out.

The following day the *Sunday Express* ran a story about 'celebrities' who had endorsed the march and then failed to turn up, so on the final Monday morning, after a good deal of telephoning around, a large contingent of the 'big-shots' descended on Slough for the final stage of the march. By this point the crowd had swollen again to some four thousand, but those who had stuck it out for the full 45 miles were less than impressed with the latecomers. 'I wish they'd stop telling us how splendid we are,' one young woman whispered resentfully to Jones during the speeches.[201] The march had, nonetheless, been very effective in attracting the attention of the media, and was repeated every year until 1965 with great success. The direction of the route was changed, so that the walk finished with a rally at Trafalgar Square instead of a demonstration in a sodden field near Slough, and in 1959 the finale attracted 20,000 people, rising to 75,000 in 1960 and 100,000 in 1961. No such demonstrations had been seen in the capital since VE night, and, if that were not enough, the campaign's celebrity organisers even remembered to turn up.[202]

By the time of the second Aldermaston march in 1959, it was evident that CND had a powerful appeal to certain groups of young people. At least four in ten of the marchers that year, according to one informal survey, were under twenty-one, and in subsequent years the proportion was thought to be higher.[203] Most teenagers were not CND supporters; it had little appeal in Britain's industrial heartland, and those who did march tended to be students 'conforming to the values of their middle-class radical families', as Marwick puts it.[204] It is notable, however, that in no university were the majority of the students CND supporters; it remained a minority pursuit, linked in the public imagination with Continental philosophy, jazz and folk music, and Fair Isle sweaters.[205] For the jeans-and-sweater types, in other words those middle-class students who thought of themselves as 'beatniks', CND quickly became a popular social diversion as well as a political commitment; as one writer put it in the *Spectator* in January 1960, it was 'a tremendous stimulation of ideas and arguments and witticisms and friendships and love affairs'.[206] Concerts and plays were performed in church halls along the Aldermaston route, and those kinds of popular music that appealed to students were unsurprisingly popular, namely trad jazz, skiffle and folk music. As one activist wrote: 'The jazz revival and the rise of CND were more than coincidental; they were almost two sides of the same coin . . . At any jazz event a liberal sprinkling of CND badges, and perhaps even leaflets and posters, would be in evidence; conversely, at every CND demonstration live jazz music set the tempo for the march.'[207] Skiffle, or do-it-yourself, primitive jazz, was also popular among the CND marchers, but by the early sixties folk music, always favoured by political radicals, was becoming the defining sound of the Aldermaston marches.

All of these tastes, from blue jeans to folk songs, identified the CND supporters as a small, specific group; most young people did not share them. The quintessential example of the CND-supporting student was a man called Dixie Dean, sadly not the peerless striker of Evertonian legend but a disaffected young fellow from north London. Several decades later he explained:

> I just couldn't stand the look of the life in front of me. I knew the world was coming to an end. The nuclear holocaust was very real and we knew it was going to happen ... I was offered a scholarship to Cambridge University, which was pretty special then, but I turned it down. What was the point when we were all going to die? Our parents couldn't understand us because we were really the first teenagers to reject society. We certainly couldn't be bothered to explain to them what we were feeling.

Those who like stereotypes will be delighted to hear that, on being called up for his National Service, Dean fell out with his superiors over the issue of his beard. 'I cared about my beard,' he recalled; 'it was my beat symbol, it was what made me me and not one of them ... They did shave my beard off and I felt I'd lost a bit of me.' The first thing he did on leaving the RAF was to join a CND march, although whether the beard had returned is unclear. Predictably enough, he later became a university lecturer.[208]

Like so many single-issue campaigns that catch the imagination, CND was an alliance of conscience uniting a myriad of different constituencies: socialists, pacifists, environmentalists, Quakers, anarchists, Scottish nationalists, folk singers and the rest.[209] There was a dedicated Christian subgroup, the CCND, and prominent religious activists like Canon Collins were regularly spotted on CND platforms or leading marches and vigils.[210] One other common factor was a strong anti-Americanism: the United States was seen as belligerent, materialistic and racially repressive, even if jazz music was popular among the younger marchers. In one pamphlet, for instance, A. J. P. Taylor wrote that the Americans were not even reliable allies: 'They accumulate so-called allies, satellites, whose real function is to serve as hostages and to be sacrificed on the outbreak of modern war.'[211] Like their successors twenty years later, CND activists fervently believed that the American military should be kicked out of their British bases. The CND crusade was also stridently anti-parliamentary; like so many middle-class reform movements, it regarded party politics as a grubby exercise in compromise and cowardice. In the *New Statesman* article that first provoked the enthusiasm of late 1957, Priestley wrote that MPs were 'surrounded by an atmosphere of power politics, intrigue, secrecy and insane invention' and 'more than half barmy'.[212] At the Westminster meeting in February 1958, the crowd 'applauded disparaging references to the Labour party as happily as they applauded rude remarks about the Tory government'; at subsequent rallies, too, those speakers who attacked politicians as deluded or, better still, wicked received the loudest reception.[213]

This anti-political tendency was made all the easier because Gaitskell and the Labour Party seemed to be floundering between 1957 and 1960, not only because of their internal battles over nationalisation and disarmament but also because Gaitskell himself had supposedly lost touch with the socialist roots of the Labour movement. One Vicky cartoon showed him as a pollster asking a housewife: 'Which party would you like Labour to resemble?', another as the manager of 'Labour Stores', with signs in the window reading 'Gigantic sell out' and 'Socialist principles practically given away'.[214] In the morally austere world of CND, Gaitskell's social life and background also counted against him; his fondness for dinners, dances and dalliances in Hampstead was well known. A. J. P. Taylor remarked in 1957 that the difference between the Conservative and Labour parties 'is the difference between Eton and Winchester'; when Gaitskell finally won his party battle against the unilateral disarmers, a furious Taylor wrote to the *Guardian* mocking him as the man who had led Labour to 'staggering' success in 1951, 1955 and 1959.[215]

CND, therefore, was a typical anti-political movement of the educated, the affluent and the disaffected, a movement rooted in the leafy suburbs of the middle classes, not in the slums or council estates. Most of the protesters also opposed the death penalty, apartheid, immigration restrictions and the monarchy; it was revealing that the younger marchers tended to have the strong support of their parents.[216] One report in the *Daily Mail* characterised the Aldermaston marchers as 'the sort of people who would normally spend Easter listening to a Beethoven concert on the Home Service, pouring dry sherry from a decanter for the neighbours, painting a Picasso design on hard-boiled eggs, attempting the literary competitions in the weekly papers, or going to church with their children. Instead they were walking through the streets in their old clothes.'[217] Working-class faces were very few and far between, and, according to one survey, there were more clergymen and university lecturers in the organisation's membership than there were unskilled manual workers.[218] CND supporters were part of what Michael Frayn called 'the Britain of the radical middle-classes – the do-gooders; the readers of the *News Chronicle,* the *Guardian* and the *Observer;* the signers of petitions; the backbone of the BBC. In short, the Herbivores, or gentle ruminants, who look out from under the lush pastures which are their natural station in life with their eyes full of sorrow for less fortunate creatures, guiltily conscious of their advantages, though not usually ceasing to eat the grass.'[219] Thirteen of the original nineteen members of the CND executive were already listed in *Who's Who*; it was, as Taylor admitted, 'a movement of eggheads for eggheads'.[220]

Paradoxically these eggheads still believed, like Macmillan, that Britain was a great power capable of leading the world by the sheer force of example. J. B. Priestley's *New Statesman* piece had presented Britain as a Churchillian beacon to the world and the repository of supreme moral authority, and in *Tribune*, effectively the house newsletter of the Labour left, Michael Foot insisted:

> It would be hypocritical to surrender our own bomb and merely be content to shelter behind somebody else's. But it would not be immoral to abandon our own bomb and seek the best diplomatic means to ensure that others did the same. The power of example might be one of the best ways of securing that end . . .
>
> Indeed, I still believe – as I am convinced a growing number of people throughout the country will believe – that Britain's readiness to renounce the weapon which we all regard as an invention of the devil could capture the imagination of millions of people in many lands.[221]

CND pamphlets advertising the Aldermaston marches carried a similar message. 'If you believe that Britain must lead, march with us, make your protest, "do your bit",' one exhorted its readers. 'For four days . . . let Britain lead the world!' As the young Labour revisionist David Marquand put it, CND was for the left 'the last brave hope of British nationalism'.[222] But it was a vain hope, and one that depended upon a grossly inflated perception of British importance. There was very little evidence to suggest that if Britain renounced the bomb, then the United States, the Soviet Union, France or China would follow suit; in truth, such a prospect was extremely unlikely indeed. Twenty years later, Taylor admitted that they had 'made one great mistake which ultimately doomed CND to futility. We thought that Great Britain was still a great power whose example would affect the rest of the world. Ironically we were the last Imperialists.'[223]

The Campaign for Nuclear Disarmament, like so many moralistic single-issue crusades, was faced with one central dilemma. Should the disarmers work through the existing institutions of the Labour Party, or should they campaign for independent, anti-nuclear parliamentary candidates? Opinions were divided. Taylor, for instance, greatly disliked the idea of being subsumed within the Labour Party, but other members of the executive committee who had perhaps a deeper emotional investment in the Labour movement, like Kingsley Martin and Michael Foot, thought that the only way to succeed was by capturing the party.[224] Labour members had been quarrelling over the issue since the mid-fifties, and to keep the peace Gaitskell had been forced to come up with a temporary fudge, in which he supported the British bomb but suggested that testing be temporarily suspended pending an appeal to the other nuclear powers to stop their own tests. It was, he confided to a friend, 'an almost impossible subject for us', because it exposed the fault lines between a middle-class tradition of moralistic non-conformism and a working-class tradition of bullish patriotism.[225]

The announcement in 1957 that Britain was manufacturing a hydrogen bomb only made matters worse. At the party conference that October, there were no fewer than 127 motions calling for disarmament of some kind, backed in the main by the party's left wing, the Bevanites. For this group, disarmament had assumed a kind of transcendent importance: since they had so little to offer on domestic issues, they could use it to draw a firm line between themselves and the more conservative leadership. Various impassioned speeches were delivered, including one from a young Anthony Wedgwood Benn in which he dismissed the case for disarmament and pleaded with the party 'not to run round chasing after moral leadership'.[226] The climax, though, was the intervention of Aneurin Bevan himself, the great Welsh orator, who stunned his own followers with a slashing attack on the nuclear disarmers. If the disarmament resolution were passed, he said, then the conference would simply be sending 'the next Foreign Secretary, whoever he may be, naked into the conference chamber'. They would be creating 'a diplomatic shambles . . . you call that statesmanship? I call it an emotional spasm.'[227] The resolution failed. But Bevan had destroyed his own relationship with many of his former allies, including

Foot, regarded by many as his protégé and designated political heir. On one occasion in 1959, when the CND crusade was in full swing, he went to Foot's house after a reception at the Polish Embassy for a few drinks of reconciliation, but they fell to arguing about the bomb again and the evening turned sour. It ended with Bevan, according to Foot's biographer, 'bellowing at Michael, "You cunt! You cunt!"' before seizing one of Foot's prized Sheraton chairs and hurling it violently to the ground, where it smashed.[228] A year later, after a valiant but futile battle against cancer, Bevan was dead.

By the time of Bevan's death in 1960, the unilateralist movement in the Labour Party, buoyed by the public success of CND, was in full cry once again. In the aftermath of the severe defeat in the 1959 election, Gaitskell had been drawn into an ill-judged and debilitating attempt to rewrite the party constitution, notably Clause Four, with its emphasis on public ownership and implication of indiscriminate nationalisation. But few party activists shared his enthusiasm for breaking with the commitments of the past, and his humiliating defeat left him vulnerable to attack from the left.[229] A 'new mood of political protest' was fermenting within the Labour movement. Attlee had retired, Ernest Bevin and Aneurin Bevan were dead, and the older, more conservative union leaders who followed Bevin's line on foreign policy were themselves being shunted aside by younger men with little patience for compromise or conciliation.[230] The most prominent example was Frank Cousins, the painfully earnest new boss of the Transport and General Workers. Anthony Sampson described him in 1962 as 'a tall, erect man with swept-back grey hair, a long stride, and a beak-like nose between heavy spectacles ... proud, temperamental, capable of swift changes from charm to prickly suspicion'.[231] As Edward Pearce puts it, Cousins was 'decent, pedestrian, honourable, not clever and in a moaning sort of way left-wing'.[232] On foreign policy, although Cousins was not quite sure what he *did* stand for, one thing was certain: he did *not* stand for the nuclear foreign policy of Gaitskell and his allies.

When, after the announcement of the Skybolt deal in early 1960, Gaitskell once more refused to renounce the nuclear deterrent, it was clear that matters were heading for some sort of showdown. On 1 March forty-three MPs, led by that inveterate intriguer Richard Crossman, abstained on an official Labour defence motion. A month later, 75,000 people turned out on the final day of the Aldermaston march, and many trade unionists and party members jumped to the conclusion that unilateral disarmament was the wave of the future. In May the national committee of the AEU, the second largest union, voted to support the CND cause. By mid-summer it was evident that the union block vote gave the unilateralists a majority of almost a million votes at the forthcoming party conference, which would no doubt be bolstered by most of the constituency party votes. The fact that well over 80 per cent of Labour supporters in the country supported the British bomb seemed to be neither here nor there, and Gaitskell's own survival was now in question.[233] Anthony Wedgwood Benn, a supposed Gaitskellite who had been raised above most of his generation, was already eyeing further promotion under a new leader; he was, noted Crossman, 'full of gaiety and excitement and also pretty clear that Gaitskell couldn't last very long'.[234]

But Gaitskell was not yet prepared to give in. He remained convinced that the experience of the thirties demonstrated the dangers of excessive moralism or pacifism.[235] His own attitude was that Britain should consider giving up the national, independent deterrent but still remain within the Western alliance. To walk out of NATO, as CND, Foot and the rest wanted, was sheer folly: it would lead not to global disarmament and good cheer on all sides, but to the collapse of the anti-Communist alliance and Soviet ascendancy in Europe. In purely domestic terms, meanwhile, it would bring a crushing and inevitable electoral defeat: two-thirds of the electorate, after all, remained implacably opposed to CND. The unilateralists, he thought, were deluded zealots, drunk with their own rhetoric, blind to the realities of the Cold War and Britain's own lack of influence within it.[236] In short, Gaitskell would rather lose the leadership than abandon his principles. 'G has the seeds of self-destruction in him – he almost wants to destroy himself,' wrote his worried friend Patrick Gordon Walker after a meeting on 12 May. 'I said at one point that he had a death wish. He is becoming distrustful and angry with his best friends and wants to take up absolute and categorical positions that will alienate all but a handful.'[237]

In the opening week of October the party conference met at Scarborough. The mood was rancorous, with CND crowds outside the hotel shouting 'Ban the Bomb! Gaitskell must go!'[238] It was clear, simply by counting the union block votes, that the leadership was doomed to a heavy defeat in the defence debate; the real question, therefore, was how Gaitskell would react. On 5 October, after several days of tension and horse-trading, the debate began. Cousins spoke at length in support of the unilateralists and gave a typical rambling performance. The crux of the matter, as presented by Gaitskell's allies, was this: should NATO give up nuclear weapons even if the Soviet Union kept them? And if not, should Britain leave the North Atlantic alliance? Cousins' conclusion was woolly to say the least: 'When I am asked if it means getting out of NATO, if the question is posed to me as simply saying, am I prepared to go on remaining in an organisation over which I have no control, but which can destroy us instantly, my answer is Yes, if the choice is that. But it is not that.'[239] There followed a notable intervention by Denis Healey, the rising bruiser of the Labour right, in which he scornfully pointed out that Khrushchev was no pacifist and reminded the conference that 'he boasted that when he was a boy, he used to kill cats by swinging them round by the tail and breaking their heads open against a wall . . . He is not a man who is going to respond to a lead on nuclear disarmament.'[240] And then, just before three, Gaitskell rose to make the speech that would define his political career.

He had not slept the previous night, and had written his peroration at four in the morning. On this speech depended his survival as Labour leader, and perhaps even the electoral survival of his party. At first he sounded tired and nervous, but gradually he began to gather pace and confidence, carefully picking over the intricacies of the unilateralists' case. Did they really think that, if NATO abandoned nuclear weapons, the Soviet Union would follow suit? 'Are we really so simple', he demanded, 'as to believe that the Soviet Union, whose belief in the ultimate triumph of communism is continually reiterated by their spokesmen, are not going to use the power that you put into their hands?' Then he turned to the issue of the leadership and the party itself. Most MPs, he pointed out, were 'utterly opposed to unilateralism and neutralism. So what do you expect them to do? Change their minds overnight?' Then, to a chorus of shouting and booing from the floor, he continued:

> Supposing all of us, like well-behaved sheep, were to follow the policies of unilateralism and neutralism, what kind of an impression would that make on the British people? . . .
>
> I do not believe that the Labour Members of Parliament are prepared to act as time servers. I do not believe they will do this, and I will tell you why: because they are men of conscience and honour . . . I do not think they will do this because they are honest men, loyal men, steadfast men, experienced men, with a lifetime of service to the Labour Movement.
>
> There are other people, too, not in Parliament, in the Party who

share our convictions. What sort of people do you think they are? Do you think we can simply accept a decision of this kind? Do you think we can become overnight the kind of pacifists, unilateralists and fellow travellers that other people are? How wrong can you be? As wrong as you are about the attitude of the British people.

At the words 'fellow travellers' the noise from the floor redoubled in intensity. 'In a few minutes,' Gaitskell continued, 'the Conference will make its decision. Most of the votes, I know, are predetermined and we have been told what is likely to happen. We know how it comes about.' Perhaps, he said coldly, the system 'by which great unions decide their policy before even their conferences can consider the Executive recommendation, is not really a very wise one or a good one'. And then he reached the climax:

> I say this to you: we may lose the vote today and the result may deal this Party a grave blow. It may not be possible to prevent it, but I think there are a great many of us who will not accept that this blow need be mortal, who will not believe that such an end is inevitable. There are some of us, Mr Chairman, who will fight and fight and fight again to save the Party we love. We will fight and fight and fight again to bring back sanity and honesty and dignity, so that our Party with its great past may retain its glory and its greatness.[241]

Gaitskell sat down to an ovation. He had delivered one of the most celebrated pieces of political rhetoric in post-war British history; he had reinvigorated his own leadership and the anti-unilateralist wing of the party; and he had finally thrown off his own reputation as a dull, colourless trimmer. He did lose the debate, but by a margin far, far smaller than had been expected. 'As he spoke,' recalled the CND secretary sadly, 'you could feel the Constituency Party votes falling like heavy rain around you . . . It was a hollow victory.'[242] In the *Daily Herald* Harold Hutchinson wrote: 'He turned what looked like an exultant triumph for his enemies into the hollowest of paper victories . . . It was the greatest personal achievement I have ever seen in politics . . . Everyone in that hall knew that if there had been a straight vote of the delegates Gaitskell would have won overwhelmingly.'[243] Gaitskell's own position was safe; at the end of the year he easily defeated, indeed crushed, a characteristically opportunistic leadership challenge from Harold Wilson, and during the following twelve months he prepared his revenge against the unilateralists.[244] At the end of October a group of tal-ented young MPs like Anthony Crosland, Roy Jenkins, Bill Rodgers and Patrick Gordon Walker, all supporters of Gaitskell and the nuclear deter-rent, had launched the Campaign for Democratic Socialism; by the following spring it had the allegiance of more than forty MPs and an impressive collection of peers and trade unionists. At the 1961 conference, backed by five of the big six unions, Gaitskell's position was endorsed by three to one. He stood as the unquestioned master of his party; and CND's attempt to turn the Labour Party into its own parliamentary wing, the vehi-cle for a single-issue crusade overburdened with righteousness but short on reason, had failed.[245]

The peak of CND's popularity came in the late spring of 1960, when 100,000 people attended the climax of the Aldermaston march and the trade unions were tumbling into the unilateralist camp. The organisation had more than four hundred different branches, and its monthly magazine *Sanity* was reaching some 45,000 readers.[246] Even then, however, CND never man-aged to translate public anxieties about nuclear war into support for its own position. In 1958, according to a Gallup poll, four in every five Britons thought that less than half of the population of the country would survive a nuclear attack.[247] But if CND did have an effect on popular attitudes, it was a very small one. Support for unilateral disarmament rose from 25 per cent in April 1958 to 33 per cent in April 1960, but this was a brief moment of very moderate success that it was never able to recapture.[248] By the end of the year the movement was already beginning to fall apart, principally over the issues of direct action and civil disobedience. There were sit-down protests at an RAF rocket base at Swaffham and the Atomic Weapons Research Establishment at Foulness, and in October the Committee of 100 was formed to direct a campaign of nationwide civil disobedience. The members of the Committee of 100 tended to be young celebrities from the worlds of literature and theatre rather than the veteran socialists and journalists prominent in CND: they included such luminaries as Lindsay Anderson, John Osborne, Arnold Wesker, John Braine and Shelagh Delaney, and their leading performer was the octogenarian philosopher Bertrand Russell, who had resigned from the presidency of CND after a row with its other guiding spirits.[249]

A harsh verdict might therefore be that the point of the Committee of 100 was really to arrange outings and day-trips for the stars of the British New Wave; it was far less effective than, say, the sit-down protests popular with civil rights workers and anti-war protesters in the United States during the sixties. One great weakness was that, by comparison with police forces elsewhere, the British police were restrained in their handling of the demonstrators. When Bertrand Russell led several thousand people to a sit-down protest outside the Ministry of Defence on 18 February 1961, the police took no action, to Russell's evident displeasure; and as he began to nail a list of demands to the Ministry door, the door suddenly opened to reveal a civil servant who handed the dumbfounded philosopher a roll of Sellotape instead. The following morning, a disgruntled Russell complained that he did not want 'forever to be tolerated by the police. Our movement depends for its success on an immense public opinion and we cannot create that unless we raise the authorities to more action than they took yesterday.'[250] Arrests were made at subsequent protests, but never on a sufficient scale to disturb public opinion.[251] By the end of the year, many of the leading figures in the movement had lost heart, tired of the bickering and the acrimony, and the campaign never recovered from the schism over direct action. 'Having nationally lost its impact,' observed one veteran activist, 'the move-ment turned to vent its wrath on internal battles.'[252]

CND never really seized the imagination of the majority because, although people did worry about the Cold War and the threat of nuclear annihilation, they did not worry enough to devote their lives to a crusade against it. At the same time, it is unlikely that a movement so closely asso-ciated with upper-middle-class dissenters and student bohemians could ever have won the allegiance of Britain's working-class voters. By the early sixties, with Britain dependent on American military patronage and technology, it was clear that whatever the British did would have little influence on the rest of the world. As the Cuban missile crisis unfolded, it become obvious to all but the most ardent CND die-hards that the issue of the British nuclear deterrent was utterly irrelevant to the prospects of a third world war. 'If we threw away our bombs,' asked A. J. P. Taylor, 'who'd notice?'[253] And in 1963 the conclusion of the test-ban agreement meant that one of CND's strongest cards, the issue of atmospheric nuclear testing, had suddenly been removed.[254] But the truth was that the movement's potential had always been severely limited and its ultimate influence was therefore extremely slight. When Gallup asked people in 1959 to predict what might have hap-pened by 1980, a mere 6 per cent of respondents thought that an atomic war was likely, compared with 41 per cent who thought it probable that 'Russia and the West will be living peacefully together'.[255]

Just as the British people were too busy worrying about the problems of austerity to have much time for anti-Communist purges, they were also too busy thinking about the economy, taxation, nationalisation, crime, immigration and the problems of affluence to have much time for foreign policy. According to a survey at the end of 1959, a time when CND was on the march, only one person in fourteen listed the international situation, the Cold War or the bomb among their major political concerns.[256] In the general election of 1964, meanwhile, a tiny 7 per cent of the electorate named defence policy as the most important issue of the contest; indeed, the Labour leader only gave three speeches on defence during the entire election campaign: one supporting the deterrent, and two, in Portsmouth and Chatham, calling for more investment in the Royal Navy.[257] The prospect of nuclear war frightened people in much the same way as the prospect of death or bereavement frightened them; for most, it was something to think about while lying awake in the dead of night, but not something to have in mind when, say, buying a hat, eating a pie or watching a football match. What CND demonstrated, then, was not the great public concern about the international scene but the great public indifference to it. For all the fuss about the special relationship, or banning the bomb, or Skybolt, or nuclear testing, or the madness of modern science, it ultimately turned out that to most ordinary people there were a lot of better things to worry about.

THE END OF EMPIRE

We're all out for good old number one
Number one's the only one for me!
Good old England, you're my cup of tea,
But I don't want no drab equality . . .
Those bits of red still on the map
We won't give up without a scrap
What we've got left back
We'll keep – and blow you, Jack!

John Osborne, *The Entertainer* (1957)

COOK: Prince Philip has recently returned from Africa where he has been
    celebrating the independence of Kenya . . .
MILLER: I was there in a symbolic capacity.
COOK: What were you symbolising?
MILLER: Capitulation. Mind you, of course, I was very well received. Mr
    Kenyatta himself came to the airport to greet me and shook me very
    warmly by the throat as I got off the plane.

Beyond the Fringe (1963)

One fine morning in the late summer of 1956, a Royal Navy troopship
pulled away from the harbour at Southampton, bound for Korea. One of its
passengers was John Wells, a National Serviceman with the rank of second
lieutenant in the Royal Sussex Regiment, and years later the voyage was still
vivid in his memory:

From Southampton, we went down through the Bay of Biscay, and
stopped at Gibraltar, with the Union Jack flying. We then went across
the Mediterranean without stopping, and through the Suez Canal,
just before the Suez crisis, and the next stop was Aden, with the Union
Jack flying. Then we went to Colombo, with the Union Jack flying;
then we went to Singapore, with the Union Jack flying; Hong Kong,

the same; and we just didn't stop where there wasn't a British presence. And it just seemed perfectly natural. There was no sense of
colonial shame.[1]

The journey that Wells made in the summer of 1956 was one that millions
of British boys and girls had already made in their schoolroom imaginations.
In every corner of the land, children were taught to venerate the supreme
sacrifice of Wolfe at Quebec, or Nelson at Trafalgar, or Gordon at Khartoum.
History books teemed with military and imperial heroes like the Duke of
Wellington, Florence Nightingale and Sir Robert Baden-Powell. When Lord
Annan looked back at his schooldays during the twenties, he concluded that
the Empire was 'ever present in the mind of my generation':

> In the two minutes' silence one tried hard to think of the million dead
> of the British Empire. From time to time as a special treat a silent film
> of the raid on Zeebrugge was shown to frenzied cheering. Our history
> lessons resounded with the names of Havelock and Outram and the
> infamous deeds of Suraj ad-Doulah and the Nana Sahib who are now
> heroes to Indian schoolchildren; and what the masters omitted was
> taught in the novels of Henty whose heroes in *With the Allies to Peking*, in
> *The Dash for Khartoum* or *Through the Sikh War* can ride a hundred miles on
> horseback, scale a hill fort, capture a dacoit and his band and never
> shrink from shedding blood.[2]

The foundations of the British Empire had been laid in the seventeenth
and eighteenth centuries, when a succession of wars against the Dutch and
the French transformed the power of the British state, leaving a powerful
institutional legacy in the Bank of England, the City of London, a mod-
ernised national fiscal structure and a ruthless, efficient apparatus for
making war by land and sea. The acquisition of an overseas empire was a
good way of building a communal British identity, and the campaigns of the
eighteenth century, which left explorers, soldiers and administrators in
every part of the globe and ships on every sea, provided the ideal means to
unite the mutually suspicious English and Scots. The imperial enterprise
was also a money-spinner of unprecedented proportions: in fact, it is hard
to understand why the British Empire was so ruthlessly successful without
grasping the sheer acquisitiveness of its founders, forever searching for markets and trade routes and opportunities for plunder.

There were less commercial motivations, too: the Empire was acquired
not as part of a careful and considered grand design, but in an often disorganised and hotchpotch fashion, reflecting the changing values of traders
and officials. Some colonies were valuable mainly as strategic outposts for
the global campaign against the French and other European rivals. Others
were acquired in a fit of missionary zeal, reflecting the earnest religiosity, not
untainted with racial prejudice, of the Victorian imperialists.[3] Whatever
their motivations, there can be little doubt that the British handled the
imperial enterprise with unmatched vigour and drive. Throughout the
eighteenth and nineteenth centuries, the political situation at home was relatively orderly, calm and stable, which meant that unlike, say, the French,
they could plough their resources into expansion overseas. Britain itself provided an ideal island base: politicians could steer clear of costly
entanglements on the European mainland and concentrate on sea power
and a strategy to link their far-flung commercial outposts under the protection of the Royal Navy.[4] 'Britannia Incorporated', one popular historian
calls the British state in the late eighteenth century: an enormous business
concern with ambitions for profitable expansion overseas.[5]

Despite losing their thirteen American possessions in 1783, the British
barely looked back. By 1920 they had amassed two hundred colonies and lost
none. British power held sway over more than one-fifth of the world's
entire land surface, from the northern wastes of Canada to the islands of the
South Seas. One in four of the world's population lived and died under the
Union Jack.[6] Not only did the ministers of George V, the King–Emperor,
control more than 11 million square miles of the planet's surface, they also
governed the lives of more than 410 million people: Indians and Africans,
Arabs and Australians, Canadians, West Indians and Malayans.[7] Other
European countries might have colonial possessions of their own, but
Britain's imperial pre-eminence was unquestionable. The Empire was far
larger than any of its competitors; it was far more diverse; it generated far
more income; and it was far more powerful.[8] In 1938, when the young
Enoch Powell flew to Sydney to take up the university chair in Greek, his
plane made almost twenty stops between Crete and Indonesia. Only one, he
recalled, was not under British rule. 'Alexandria, the Lake of Galilee,
Habbaniya, Basra, Abu Dhabi, Mekran, Karachi, Jaipur, Allahabad,
Calcutta, Akyab, Rangoon, Penang, Singapore – one was witnessing the
ubiquity of a power on which the sun had not yet set. I saw; I felt; I
marvelled.'[9]

Powell was an especially intense example of the kind of Englishman in whose imagination the Empire always loomed large. Indeed, just like Protestantism or the monarchy, the Empire played a central part in the way the British understood their own nation and its place in the world.[10] According to P. J. Marshall:

> There cannot be the slightest doubt that empire was a major compo-
> nent in British people's sense of their own identity, that it helped to
> integrate the United Kingdom, and to distinguish it in the eyes of its
> own citizens from other European countries. Empire reinforced a hier-
> archical view of the world, in which the British occupied a
> pre-eminent place among the colonial powers, while those subjected to
> colonial rule were ranged below them in varying degrees of supposed
> inferiority.[11]

The imperial subjugation of supposedly inferior races, from Singapore to Jamaica and from Gibraltar to South Africa, strengthened the self-image of the British people as hard-working, godly and effortlessly superior.[12] It provided a political and strategic parallel to the success of British indus-try; it ensured there were ready markets for British goods; it offered plentiful opportunities for ambitious young men to build careers, for-tunes and reputations in exotic locations; and it introduced into British life a host of new foods, customs, words, ideas and experiences.[13] Growing up in the West Midlands during the late fifties and early sixties, the his-torian David Cannadine had 'the vague impression that there was a greater Britain, somewhere beyond Birmingham and beyond the seas, that had sent its representatives to London to join the queen in Westminster Abbey, and that this was how things always had been and always would be'.[14] When the Queen paid a state visit to India in 1961, Cannadine's primary school teacher encouraged the class to make a map to mark her royal progress – despite the fact that India had been inde-pendent since 1947. The classroom already boasted one fine example of imperial cartography: 'a large world map on which the British Empire was coloured red, as in those days it invariably was'. True, this great map was rather out of date, showing the Empire at its height between the wars rather than the crumbling Empire of Macmillan's day, but it was still 'an extraordinary vista of earthly dominion for a Birmingham boy of nine or ten to behold'. And these visions of far-flung dominion were not left behind at the classroom door; at home, too, there were constant reminders of Britain's imperial inheritance:

> There was lamb and butter from New Zealand, tea from India, choco-late from Nigeria, coffee from Kenya, and apples, pears and grapes from Africa. My mother went to a dressmaker named Miss Halfpenny, who was Canadian, and her house was full of souvenirs of her homeland: postcards of Niagara Falls, craftwork by Indians, and so on. And I played with toys that were identified as 'Empire Made' – an explicit acknowl-edgment that the empire still existed, but a euphemism for the fact that such goods inevitably originated in Hong Kong.[15]

The kitchen cupboard was a treasure trove of imperial memories: Assam and Darjeeling tea, Demerara sugar and Jamaican ginger cake, Lamb's Navy rum and Bombay Sapphire gin. And, although its trademark illustration of African servants carrying huge bars of the soap aloft was dropped during the mid-sixties, Cusson's Imperial Leather retained its position as the most pop-ular soap in the country.[16]

Even at its territorial zenith in the early years of the twentieth century, however, the British Empire was always an incoherent, even insecure con-struction, more of a muddle than a monolith. Its faraway possessions were bound together by the most fragile of threads, and its administrators could never ignore the threat of colonial rebellion.[17] It was also dubious whether it had any real administrative or institutional coherence. Not only was the Empire governed by no fewer than four competing departments, the Foreign, Dominions, Indian and Colonial Offices, but it also included territories that were utterly different in population, eco-nomic development and political structure. Canada and Australia, for example, were independent settler states in all but name, but many African and Asian colonies were governed by committee in Whitehall. This ramshackle, disorganised collection of colonial possessions was not run according to any blueprint or master-plan; instead, policy was impro-vised and eternally flexible. Neither was it held together by the imposition of military might. British resources were so thinly stretched across the globe that an empire based on the sword alone was simply impossible. Imperial policy was less an exercise in military valour than a ceaseless search for local collaborators and mutually convenient arrangements; colonial administrators governed by working with native elites, not by suppressing them. On the continued success of these local arrangements, therefore, would depend the survival of the British Empire in the twentieth century.[18]

As early as the late 1890s, British politicians and commentators had worried that the Empire might be entering a new stage of terminal decline. Not only were domestic industrialists beginning to fall behind their German and American competitors, but even the Royal Navy was losing its supremacy on the high seas. There was, however, plenty of life left in the Empire. Despite the economic troubles that followed the First World War, it seemed to recapture some of its old vigour, and in Africa, for instance, white settlement and colonial organisation seemed to be expanding.[19] During the Second World War, most British politicians expected that victory would mean the restoration of the Asian and Middle Eastern colonies that had been lost to the troops of the Axis. 'Let me make this clear in case there should be any mistake about it in any quarter,' insisted Churchill in November 1942. 'We mean to hold our own. I have not become the King's First Minister to preside over the liquidation of the British Empire.'[20]

At the end of the war, despite Britain's financial indebtedness and the election of a crusading Labour government, the Empire lived on. Its position had undoubtedly weakened under the pressures of war, but nobody was writing its obituary just yet: indeed, a Cabinet committee concluded that it would be 'a matter of many generations' before most colonies were ready 'for anything like full self-government'.[21] Even when India and Pakistan became independent in 1947 it was far too early to write off the Empire, and few historians now think that it was doomed even at the beginning of the 1950s. If the British maintained their close relationship with the United States, reinvigorated their economy and recaptured their old self-confidence, there was no reason to imagine that the decline would be anything but endlessly protracted.[22]

By the middle of the fifties, there were even grounds for quiet confidence. The Empire had been rebuilt after the ordeal of the war; the threat of international Communism had been largely contained; and the new spirit of devolved government, an 'empire of partnership' pioneered in the Gold Coast and other West African colonies, appeared to be working well.[23] Far from the Cold War marking the end of the British Empire, it seemed to breathe new life into it. During the war, many American politicians had gleefully proclaimed the collapse of European imperialism, but, as we have seen, they now acknowledged the value of the Empire as a bulwark against the spread of Communism, at least for the moment. In Malaya, where a third of the world's tin and much of its rubber was produced, the United States encouraged Britain to stand firm against the threat of Communist rebellion and Chinese subversion. The British military bases at Cyprus, Aden and Singapore had never seemed so important.[24] When the Conservatives regained power in 1951, their manifesto proudly proclaimed their intentions:

> To retain and develop the great and unique brotherhood of the British Empire and Commonwealth is a first task of British statesmanship . . . The Conservative Party, by long tradition and settled belief, is the Party of the Empire. We are proud of its past. We see it as the surest hope in our own day. We proclaim our abiding faith in its destiny. We shall strive to promote its unity, its strength and its progress.[25]

Britain, insisted a Commonwealth Office paper in 1956, was 'still in its own right a very great power'.[26]

But just four years later the position looked very different. In 1960, at the east end of the crypt of St Paul's Cathedral, the Chapel of the Order of the British Empire was finally dedicated after years of wrangling.[27] The irony was that the Empire itself had never seemed closer to total collapse. During the next few years, in one colony after another, the Union Jack was lowered for the last time. British political control was surrendered; British military power was in retreat; and even British cultural and commercial influence were under threat. When Macmillan became Prime Minister in 1957, no fewer than forty-five different countries were still governed by the Colonial Office, but during the next seven years Ghana, Malaya, Cyprus, Nigeria, Sierra Leone, Tanganyika, Western Samoa, Jamaica, Trinidad and Tobago, Uganda, Zanzibar and Kenya were all granted their independence. By 1964 the overseas population governed from London had fallen to scarcely fifteen million people. There could be no disguising the fact that the age of Empire was over.[28]

For some observers, both at the time and afterwards, there was a very simple, one-word explanation for the collapse of the British Empire: nationalism. Hundreds of thousands of ordinary people, subjugated for far too long, had at last cast off the shackles of imperialism and demanded their freedom to govern their own affairs. Enfeebled by war and economic

decline, and unable to quell the nationalists' protests, the British had eventually, grudgingly, granted them independence.[29] But few modern
historians still believe that the Empire was simply undermined from below
by heroic resistance movements. Nationalism certainly did pose a challenge
to the British administrators, but in most colonies it was disorganised,
divided, often incompetent, and sometimes easily bought off. In some places
there simply was no 'nationalism' as we would recognise it; in others,
indigenous leaders were more worried about defending their social position
against the masses than they were about leading them to independence.
Unlike the French in Indochina and Algeria, or the Portuguese in Angola
and Mozambique, the British did not give up their power after a long struggle against armed rebels: in fact, open rebellion against British rule was both
immensely risky and extremely rare. Only in two possessions, Palestine and
Aden, was imperial influence thrown off after a mass rebellion. In
Tanganyika and Uganda, meanwhile, the British pushed native leaders
towards independence even more quickly than the Africans themselves
expected. Although there is little doubt that the efforts of local nationalists
played a part in the end of British rule, there is equally little doubt that this
is not the whole story.[30]

From the British point of view, one of the central figures in the astonishing collapse of imperial power between 1956 and 1963 was Harold
Macmillan. Although he cultivated the appearance of an Edwardian relic
in order to assuage popular fears of national decline, Macmillan was, in
many respects, more progressive than his Conservative contemporaries. It
was Macmillan, for instance, who wrote that the key to electoral victory
was 'to keep the Tory party on *modern* and *progressive* lines', and one obvious
way of doing that was to distance himself from the reactionary elements in
his party who saw the Empire as the touchstone of Conservative
integrity.[31] He had little sentimental attachment to the Empire; all the evidence suggests that he was much more interested in Britain's links with
the United States and Western Europe. When he became Prime Minister in
1957, he had never visited black Africa and never been further south than
Casablanca, Algiers and Cairo; it was no accident that one of his first major
decisions was to demand an 'audit of empire' in terms of 'profit and loss'.[32]
Far from exciting his emotional sympathy, the white settlers in Kenya and
Rhodesia instead reminded him of the 'retired colonels in the golf club
and their ladies', whose right-wing prejudices he had opposed before the
war. Even though he had been a mere spectator when Churchill and

Baldwin argued about Indian self-government in the thirties, he was well aware of the arguments for gradual decolonisation. Indeed, as his biographer points out, Macmillan had even suggested in 1942 that the Kenyan farms might be bought by the Crown and developed into state companies for the benefit of both black and white, a proposal that would have horrified many of his eventual Cabinet colleagues.[33] He was no anti-colonial idealist, of course, and frequently referred to black Africans as 'childish' or 'children', but few Conservatives were better suited to manage the end of empire.[34] In a working day that might involve discussions with Kennedy about nuclear technology and de Gaulle about European integration, Macmillan almost certainly regarded the intricacies of colonial disengagement as a tedious distraction to be wound up as quickly and smoothly as possible.

The other central figure on the British side was Iain Macleod, whom Macmillan appointed Colonial Secretary after the 1959 election. Several commentators thought that Macleod's victory over the striking bus drivers in July 1958 had been the turning point in the government's road to re-election, and this was his reward. The son of a doctor from the Western Isles, he was widely regarded as the most promising, as well as the most liberal, of the new generation of middle-class Conservatives. Harold Macmillan noted in his diary that Macleod was a typical Highlander, 'which means that he is easily worked up into an emotional mood; it also means that he is proud and ambitious. But he has great qualities – a soaring spirit and a real mastery of public speaking.'[35] Some of this was romantic waffle: while certainly impulsive, eloquent and ambitious, Iain Macleod was a Highlander by descent only, not by breeding. Instead he had been born in the Yorkshire town of Skipton and was sent to public school in Edinburgh. He was an undistinguished scholar, even after he arrived at Cambridge, and was more interested in rugby, cricket and card-playing than in the higher pleasures of the intellect or imagination. During his early twenties, at a stage when many of his political contemporaries were immersing themselves in classical literature or European politics, Macleod was playing bridge for money and spending his winnings on wine, women and the turf. But he did have one or two significant qualities, such as a remarkable capacity to learn poetry by heart, which he used to show off as a kind of parlour game. He was also a brilliant gambler and card-player; while at Cambridge he founded the varsity bridge match and captained the team against Oxford. Not only did he play bridge for England in his early twenties, he also made more than ten times the average annual wage, tax-free. His political style would always be that of the professional gambler: cool, calculating, but always ready to take the bold leap forward if the odds were promising.[36]

Macleod's political career might have ended before it had begun. One night in 1941, while based with the Duke of Wellington's Regiment in Kent, he spent several hours in a local pub before drunkenly returning to barracks, where he accosted his superior officer, a close friend, and incoherently demanded to play stud poker. When his friend refused and retired to his own bedroom, Macleod got out his service revolver, fired several shots at the door, and then broke it down with a piece of furniture before collapsing over the threshold. This sort of behaviour, which his friend providentially forgave the next morning, could have ruined his political prospects, but the story never got out.[37]

In 1946, Macleod left the army and joined the Conservative Research Department, where he formed part of a famous intellectual trio with two other young men, Enoch Powell and Reginald Maudling. Macleod and Maudling in particular were great friends; both were liberal, One Nation Tories who supported the welfare state and the mixed economy, and both also shared a fondness for expensive cigars, generous whiskies and long lunches. Their middle-class background and progressive outlook meant that they had little in common with the Conservative old guard, and as successive Colonial Secretaries in the early sixties, they played vital roles in the dissolution of the Empire.[38] Both entered the Commons in 1950, but Macleod's biggest break came two years later, when his famous parliamentary demolition of Aneurin Bevan brought him to the attention of Winston Churchill.[39] From that point onwards he was marked as a coming man, and in 1959 Macmillan made him Colonial Secretary, replacing the huge, charismatic Alan Lennox-Boyd. It was, Macmillan recognised, 'the worst job of all', but he wanted a young, dynamic minister who would 'get a move on [in] Africa'.[40]

The great shadow that hung over the Empire in the late fifties was the legacy of the Second World War. Until 1939, British imperial administrators had, with relative success, pursued a pragmatic, moderate policy of appeasing colonial discontents and working closely with local collaborators. But, as the imperial historian John Darwin explains, during the war and its immediate aftermath they were forced into a policy of dynamic economic development that upset many of the delicate balances they had worked so hard to create.[41] In the desperate austerity of the 1940s, the colonies were seen less as fragile possessions to be held in trust than as economic assets to be milked for all they were worth. Administrators who had spent most of their careers cautiously guarding the equilibrium of their colonies now devoted their energies to cash crops, marketing boards, monopolies, rationing and 'Grow More Food' campaigns. In Africa, for example, colonial production was diverted into food and raw materials that could be sent to Britain as cheap imports or sold for valuable dollars on the open market. The sum of £40 million was invested in a disastrous attempt to grow groundnuts in Tanganyika, while a massive poultry farm in the Gambia yielded neither eggs for the British breakfast table nor benefits for the local workers.[42] Within several years it was clear that these enterprises, which had been designed for European rather than African purposes, had seriously disrupted the close relations between the British and their old local allies. It was this new 'development' imperialism, then, that most explains the alienation of African elites from their British governors in the years after the war. In south-east Asia, meanwhile, the links between administrators and collaborators had already been broken by the brutal Japanese conquests of 1941 and 1942; rebuilding those bridges, in the context of the Cold War and economic austerity, was an immensely difficult undertaking. The new pressures of the crusade against international Communism meant that in the Middle East, too, British officials were suspicious and heavy-handed towards local dissidents when the situation demanded subtlety and accommodation. When resistance flared, whether in Malaya or the Gold Coast, Kenya or Nyasaland, Britain's straitened economic circumstances meant that there was not enough money either to pay off the local troublemakers or to send in enough troops to quell the disturbance.[43] And even if Macmillan's government had possessed both the money and the resolution to fight for the colonies, the defence reforms introduced by Duncan Sandys in 1957 meant that there was simply not enough manpower to do so.[44]

Very few politicians in the late fifties, however, had any inclination to fight for the colonies. Some historians attribute this to a growing sense of popular revulsion at the very idea of imperialism. Richard Weight, for instance, thinks that there was a widespread rejection of 'imperial identity' during the fifties, and suggests that it was particularly (and predictably) marked among the young.[45] But there is no evidence for this at all. Neither is there much evidence that, as R. F. Holland suggests, middle-class voters resented the cost of Britain's imperial entanglements as a distraction from the welfare state and the new commitments of the affluent society.[46] It is certainly true that British trade with the colonies and the Commonwealth was in steep decline; by contrast, domestic manufacturers and businessmen were increasingly keen to cultivate links with their European counterparts.[47] But did this really mean that they were beginning to turn against Britain's obligations to the colonies? Instead of promising to wind up the Empire, as might have been expected if the electorate was turning against it, both major parties constantly assured their voters that they intended to stick to the task. Indeed, when conscripted National Servicemen were sent off to Malaya, Cyprus and Kenya, there was almost no public outcry at all. For all Macmillan's talk of presenting the Conservatives as a modern, progressive outfit, he was always more concerned about reassuring the reactionary wing of his own party than the minority of anti-imperialist critics to his left. Even at the 1959 election, at the height of the post-war imperial crisis, colonial issues were strikingly unimportant.[48]

It was not public opinion that inhibited Macmillan and his ministers from armed intervention in the colonies; rather, it was the example of what had happened when other European countries tried to suppress discontent by force. Anyone who thought that colonial problems could be solved by the application of brute military might had only to look south to North Africa, where the French were still engaged in a grinding, bloody and ultimately humiliating attempt to maintain their position in Algeria. When Macleod took over as Colonial Secretary, therefore, the Algerian experience served as a powerful warning not to stand in the path of history.[49] The French themselves had already learned their lesson: by the end of 1959, de Gaulle had not only offered self-determination to Algeria but had also promised independence to any French colony that requested it. And if France, the old rival, was committed to withdrawal from Africa, that made it almost impossible for Britain to justify holding firm, especially since the British colonies were much more politically and economically developed than their French neighbours.[50]

Six months later the pressure became even more intense. For several months discontent had been simmering in the Congo, an enormous and potentially wealthy Central African territory that had been systematically mismanaged and looted by its Belgian owners. In January 1960, following de Gaulle's example, the Belgians suddenly threw up their hands and announced that they would leave in six months. By the late summer the

Congo had collapsed into anarchy and civil war. The Congolese army mutinied; European settlers were raped and murdered; the rich copper province of Katanga declared its independence; and the country generally fell victim to the competing ambitions not only of rival local politicians but also of the Belgians, the Americans and the Soviet Union. Since the Congo shared frontiers with British colonies in Uganda, Tanganyika and Northern Rhodesia, there could be no more graphic or troubling illustration of the dangers of colonial misjudgement. Macmillan, who was well aware that the conflict was taking on a Cold War dimension, wrote melodramatically in his diary that 'civil war in Africa might be the prelude to war in the world . . . it has a terrible similarity to 1914. Now Congo may play the role of Serbia.'[51] Even in December 1961 he was fretting that Kenya 'might prove another Congo'.[52]

Between 1958 and 1961, therefore, the British found themselves under unprecedented and irresistible pressure to put their colonial affairs in order. 'We must also recognize', Macleod advised his Cabinet colleagues in January 1961, 'that pressure from the United Nations, now that Belgium and France are dropping out as Colonial powers, will increasingly concentrate on us.' The demands of the Cold War made matters even worse: the Soviet Union was keen to extend its influence into Africa and Asia, and Macleod knew that they could not afford to drive the colonies into the Communist camp by ignoring or repressing their grievances. The trick, he thought, was to keep to a moderate pace of change, 'not as fast as the Congo and not as slow as Algiers'.[53]

This was not, as is sometimes suggested, part of a deliberate, enlightened plan to lead the colonies to the sunlit uplands of independence; instead, it was a desperate, improvised attempt to adapt to the pressure of events both in the colonies and in the wider world. But as concessions were made, so the pace of change increased still further, and the government found itself being pushed towards granting independence much more quickly than had ever been anticipated. In January 1959, for instance, a conference of governors hammered out a provisional schedule for change in East Africa, with Tanganyika set for independence in 1970 and Uganda and Kenya to follow in 1975. In the event, the momentum of events in the Congo and elsewhere meant that all three actually gained their independence within the next four years.[54] Ironically, this sort of outcome had already been predicted by a Colonial Office paper in 1955, which noted that the very fact of constitutional development was likely to increase the pressure on the Empire:

This process cannot now be halted or reversed, and it is only to a limited extent that its pace can be controlled by the United Kingdom Government . . . In the main, the pace of constitutional change will be determined by the strength of nationalist feeling and the development of political consciousness within the territory concerned. Political leaders who have obtained assurances of independence for their people normally expect that the promised independence will be attained within their own political lifetime; and if they cannot satisfy their followers that satisfactory progress is being maintained towards that goal, their influence may be usurped by less responsible elements.[55]

The dismantling of the Empire was less an act of cheerful colonial philanthropy than a grudging recognition of political reality. 'Most of the horses have already bolted', remarked an official in March 1961, 'and a number are already so far out of the stable that they cannot be pushed back in again.'[56] Many officials thought that the pace of change was too fast but acknowledged that they simply had no choice, as Macmillan discovered when he talked to the Governor-General of Nigeria:

I said, 'Are these people ready for self-government?' and he said, 'No, of course not.'

I said, 'When will they be ready?' He said, 'Twenty years, twenty-five years.'

Then I said, 'What do you recommend me to do?' He said, 'I recommend you to give it to them at once.'[57]

*

As Iain Macleod was to discover, however, this was not quite as easy it sounded. Although there were plenty of problems in Cyprus, Malta and the Middle East, the greatest challenge was in Africa. Across the continent the bonds of empire were badly fraying, and in those East and Central African territories where white settlers and native Africans lived side by side, like Kenya and Rhodesia, the crisis was particularly acute. 'The Africans cannot be dominated permanently (as they are trying to do in South Africa) without any proper opportunity for their development and ultimate self-government,' Macmillan noted at the end of 1959. 'Nor can the Europeans be abandoned. It would be wrong for us to do so, and fatal for African interests.'[58]

In Kenya, for example, where 30,000 white settlers and more than 120,000 Asians lived alongside five million black Africans, the government seemed likely to be damned whatever it did. The relatively simple policy of part-nership and gradual independence, which had worked to calm local discontents in the Gold Coast and Nigeria, was thought likely to founder on the rock of settler intransigence. For the white population, concentrated in the White Highlands and deeply embedded in the political and commercial life of the country, black majority rule was unacceptable. What made the situation even more delicate was that the potential for bloodshed had already been well demonstrated during the Mau Mau emergency between 1952 and 1956, when the disruptive impact of post-war development pushed sections of the Kikuyu peasant community into violent rebellion. Dealing with the emergency was expensive, in money, manpower and lives. As many as 100,000 Kikuyu were imprisoned and interrogated in specially built 'rehabilitation' camps. Hundreds were hanged or shot by the British secu-rity forces while trying to escape, and beatings and torture were common. By the end of the emergency more than fourteen thousand Africans and ninety-five whites had been killed.[59]

Quite apart from the human and financial costs of the struggle, the Mau Mau crisis and its repressive aftermath provided terrible publicity for both the reputation of Britain abroad and the reputation of Macmillan's gov-ernment at home. In March 1959, eleven African prisoners were beaten to death by their guards at the Hola detention camp, provoking a public outcry at home, an immediate government inquiry and bitter exchanges in the House of Commons. Some Conservatives insisted that the victims deserved no better, since as African terrorists they were no more than 'sub-human'. But, for their younger, middle-class colleagues, the 'Hola massacre' was characteristic of a muddled, reactionary approach to colonial affairs. As Enoch Powell passionately insisted in the Commons:

It is argued that this is Africa, that things are different there. Of course they are. The question is whether the difference between things there and here is such that the taking of responsibility there and here should be on different principles . . .

We cannot say, 'We will have African standards in Africa, Asian stan-dards in Asia, and perhaps British standards here at home.' We must be consistent with ourselves everywhere.

All Government, all influence of man upon man, rests upon

opinion. What we can do in Africa, where we still govern and where we no longer govern, depends upon the opinion which is entertained of the way in which this country acts and the way in which Englishmen act. We cannot, we dare not, in Africa of all places, fall below our own highest standards in the acceptance of responsibility.[60]

The *Telegraph* thought this was 'a great and sincere speech'. Mark Bonham Carter, a Liberal, told Powell that it was 'by far the most impressive, the most intellectually convincing and the most moving speech' he had heard in the chamber; and the Labour backbencher Denis Healey called it 'the greatest parliamentary speech I ever heard' with 'all the moral passion and rhetorical force of Demosthenes'.[61]

Having been a fiercely passionate champion of empire in his youth, Powell was now one of the most articulate spokesmen for a new, post-colonial brand of Conservatism. He thought that Britain should pull back not only from the African colonies but also from all its bases east of Suez. As far as he was concerned, Britain's days of imperial might were over. 'That phase is ended,' he remarked in 1961, 'so plainly ended that even the generation born at its zenith, for whom the realisation is the hardest, no longer deceive themselves as to the fact . . . That power and that glory have vanished.' It was time, he thought, for Britain to come 'home from distant wandering'.[62]

Powell's old friend from the Conservative Research Department shared his belief that there was no point hanging on to the relics of imperial glory. Macleod had even less attachment to the Empire than did Macmillan; when he became Colonial Secretary in 1959, he had never set foot in one of the colonies.[63] On racial and colonial matters, he was probably the most liberal figure in the Cabinet. In May 1959, even before moving to the Colonial Office, he wrote to Macmillan: 'Black Africa remains perhaps our most difficult problem as far as relationships with the vital middle voters [are] concerned. It is the only one in which our policies are under severe criticism and for example the only one on which we are regularly defeated at the universities.'[64] Given the ease of the Conservative re-election campaign a few months later, it appears that Macleod was exaggerating his case. But his deep personal convictions were never in doubt. As he recalled afterwards, he had, like his Cabinet colleagues, been 'shocked and horrified' by the deaths at the Hola camp. It was, he said, 'the decisive moment when it became clear to me that we could no longer continue with the old methods of government in Africa and that meant inexorably a move towards African independence'.[65]

When Macleod took over, he already faced a tricky situation. Thousands were in detention in Kenya; Nyasaland was effectively being run as a police state by the Governor; and unrest was simmering everywhere from Rhodesia to Cyprus. The old days of the early fifties, of reasonably amicable partnership with local leaders in the Gold Coast or Nigeria, seemed far away. But Macleod was determined to cut through the tangled knot, principally by accelerating the transition to full independence, even in colonies where there were substantial white populations. It was a policy bound to bring him into conflict with the right wing of his own party, but Macleod was a tough character and, in the words of Denis Judd, 'without question the most radical and hard-headed Conservative' to occupy the Colonial Office since Joseph Chamberlain.[66] In October 1961, addressing a sceptical audience at the Conservative Party Conference, Macleod insisted:

I believe quite simply in the brotherhood of man – men of all races, of all colours, of all creeds. I think it is this that must be in the centre of our thinking.

And now what lies ahead in this event? It is perhaps strange to an English and to a Welsh audience to quote the greatest of our Scottish native poets, but nobody has put this in simpler or finer words than Burns:

It is coming yet for a' that,
That man to man the whole world o'er,
Shall be brothers for a' that.

And this is coming. There are foolish men who will deny it, but they will be swept away; but if we are wise then indeed the task of bringing these countries towards their destiny of free and equal partners and friends with us in the Commonwealth of Nations can be a task as exciting, as inspiring and as noble as the creation of empire itself.[67]

Beneath the soaring rhetoric, Macleod's basic premise was, as he put it, 'blindingly simple . . . and that is that if you give independence in West Africa you cannot deny it in East Africa just because there is a white settler community there'.[68] By the time he was moved from the Colonial Office, shortly after his 'brotherhood of man' speech, he had already laid down a strategy of swift and relatively painless withdrawal across the board. In 1960, Somaliland,

Cyprus and Nigeria became independent; in 1961 they were joined by Sierra Leone, the British Cameroons and Tanganyika. In 1962, following Macleod's pattern, Jamaica, Trinidad and Tobago and Uganda all won independence, and they were followed in 1963 by Malaysia, Zanzibar and Kenya, and in 1964 by Nyasaland and Northern Rhodesia, which became Malawi and Zambia. It was, according to one eminent authority, 'one of the most remarkable, and swift, decolonisation experiences ever undergone by any colonial power'.[69] Macleod admitted to the party conference in 1961 that he had set an almost reckless pace of change; but the cases of Angola, Algeria and South Africa suggested that 'confronted with this choice, as one would never hope to be, there is probably greater safety in going too fast than in going slow'.[70]

The example of South Africa was well chosen. Its racial affairs had been governed since 1948 by the system of apartheid, but by the early sixties the former dominion was becoming an international pariah. British public opinion had been shocked by the Sharpeville shootings in 1960, and although some right-wing elements of the Conservative Party strongly supported the apartheid regime, the One Nation liberals certainly did not. In January 1960 Harold Macmillan undertook a long tour of Britain's possessions in Africa, visiting Ghana and Nigeria before heading south to Nyasaland and South Africa. This tour was instrumental in building Macmillan's image as the great friend of African independence, and when he arrived in Cape Town to speak to the South African Parliament, he issued an unashamed endorsement of decolonisation that shocked much of his audience and remains his most famous speech, as well as his boldest:

> Ever since the break-up of the Roman Empire one of the constant facts of political life in Europe has been the emergence of independent nations. They have come into existence over the centuries in different forms, with different kinds of Government, but all have been inspired by a deep, keen feeling of nationalism, which has grown as the nations have grown . . .
>
> Today the same thing is happening in Africa, and the most striking of all the impressions I have formed is of the strength of this African national consciousness. In different places it takes different forms, but it is happening everywhere. The wind of change is blowing through this continent, and, whether we like it or not, this growth of national consciousness is a political fact. We must all accept it as a fact, and our national policies must take account of it.

Macmillan knew that many of his listeners were appalled by Britain's readiness to wind up the Empire in Africa. But the rush to independence was, he said, 'the only way to establish the future of the Commonwealth and of the Free World on sound foundations'. What was more, he hoped to build a colour-blind world in which 'individual merit and individual merit alone is the criterion for a man's advancement, whether political or economic'. In case any of his South African listeners had missed the point, he added:

> As a fellow member of the Commonwealth it is our earnest desire to give South Africa our support and encouragement, but I hope you won't mind my saying frankly that there are some aspects of your policies which make it impossible for us to do this without being false to our own deep convictions about the political destinies of free men to which in our own territories we are trying to give effect. I think we ought, as friends, to face together, without seeking to apportion credit or blame, the fact that in the world of today this difference of outlook lies between us.[71]

Despite the diplomatic language, the South Africans treated Macmillan's speech as an appalling slur. Hendrik Verwoerd, the Prime Minister, replied that there were 'problems enough in South Africa without your coming to add to them', and later accused him of 'appeasement of the black man'.[72] Macmillan, meanwhile, sent the Queen a letter on his return deploring 'the rigidity, and even fanaticism, with which the Nationalist Government in South Africa have pursued the apartheid policy' and told her that it had created 'a dangerous, even ominous situation in that country'.[73] A year later, after an argument about its racial policies, South Africa left the Commonwealth and began the long march into international isolation.

Explicitly distancing himself from the apartheid regime allowed Macmillan to reach out to moderate opinion in Africa and to assert his own progressive credentials at home. In one part of Africa, however, his words did not go over well, and that was the Central African Federation. Of all the colonial problems that Britain faced in the sixties, that of the Federation was probably the most intractable. It had been established by Churchill's government in 1953 as an extremely convoluted union of two colonies, Nyasaland and Northern Rhodesia, with the self-governing territory of

Southern Rhodesia. Of the three, Nyasaland was largely black and agricultural; Northern Rhodesia was rich in copper, cobalt and other industrial raw materials, and had about 75,000 white settlers; and Southern Rhodesia, again more agricultural, had a large and well-organised white population of some 220,000.[74] They had been yoked together in a federal union largely because the government did not really know what to do with the Rhodesian white nationalists, but by the time Macleod took over the Colonial Office it was clear that the Federation was not working.

In Nyasaland and Northern Rhodesia black leaders were agitating for secession and independence, but the settlers of Southern Rhodesia were keen to cling on to the mineral wealth of the North. White society in Southern Rhodesia was not a model of racial enlightenment. When the BBC executive Hugh Carleton Greene visited the colony to advise on their broadcasting system, he discovered that black and white MPs were forbidden to dine together at Parliament House in Salisbury. One factory manager proudly told him: 'I had a friend from Northern Rhodesia down here the other day who said what a relief it was to see a really good flogging again. He told me: "You know, up in Northern Rhodesia, if you raise your hand against one of these chaps, he drags you off to the police station."' The *New Statesman* reported in 1956 that a white settler who flogged his servant to death had been sentenced to spend a year in prison, the same sentence as a black man who stole sixteen shirts.[75] With cheap African labour and cheap raw materials from the North, Southern Rhodesia was booming, and its representatives were furious at the prospect of being sold out by their colonial masters. 'Britain's not bloody well going to make us live under a bunch of fucking monkeys,' one recent arrival from Scotland remarked in 1963. 'Look at South Africa, that's how to fix them.'[76]

As in Kenya, the tension between settlers and natives had already spilled over into violence: in March 1959 the security forces in Nyasaland had launched an unwarranted and violent crackdown on black dissidents, killing fifty-one people and throwing dozens more into prison. The repression in Nyasaland, which was severely criticised in a subsequent report by the High Court judge Sir Patrick Devlin, was also acutely embarrassing for Macmillan's government. Although he rejected Devlin's conclusions, Macmillan was beginning to recognise that something had to change in Central Africa.[77] In October 1959 the Treasury official Burke Trend reported that the Federation was in a mess. It had 'been imposed against the wishes of the Africans', and their opposition to it remained 'absolute and universal'.

Although Nyasaland and Northern Rhodesia might be able to make their own way in relative tranquillity, this was not true of Southern Rhodesia, where the atmosphere was 'unhappy', characterised by 'a selfish preoccupation with the maintenance of the white man's complete social dominance'.[78]

Instead of moving quickly and firmly to bring the Federation to an end, however, Macmillan dithered. Negotiations between the Commonwealth and Colonial Offices and the various local and federal representatives dragged on for the next three years and not until March 1963 was the Federation finally ditched. Immediately the Southern Rhodesians demanded their independence. This created a serious dilemma for Macmillan's Cabinet: while they were eager to wash their hands of all responsibility for Rhodesian affairs, they could hardly be seen to grant independence to a colony where the African majority was manifestly oppressed by a tiny white elite. Rab Butler, who had taken over responsibility for Central African affairs, suggested that since Rhodesian independence seemed inevitable, one way or another, it might be best to let them seize it themselves without British approval. 'It would be better', he told his colleagues, 'that they should be seen to do so by a unilateral action which will be unprecedented in the history of the progressive transfer of power to former dependencies.' Macmillan, meanwhile, simply put off making a decision.[79] In the end, and especially by comparison with his colonial policy in general, the situation in Rhodesia was one of the great failures of his administration. After wasting months and years worrying about the intricacies of the Federation, he came no closer to solving the Central African problem; instead, he merely passed it on to his successors, who were to find it equally intractable.[80]

British policy towards the Empire in the post-war years was governed by what one historian calls 'a kind of colonial Butskellism'.[81] There were occasional differences between the two parties, and Gaitskell certainly seemed keener on the idea of decolonisation than did Macmillan, but there was no real sense of a partisan divide on the issue. There were those, nevertheless, who felt that the dismantling of the Empire was a lamentable act of cowardice and betrayal. 'The good old imperialism', wrote Noël Coward in 1956, 'was a bloody sight wiser and healthier than all this woolly-headed, muddled, "all men are equal" humanitarianism, which has lost us so much pride and dignity and prestige in the modern world.'[82] Coward simply could not understand why decolonisation was happening, and poured out his resentment against the culprits in works like the novel *Pomp and Circumstance* (1960):

> The Samolans are a mild and temperamentally cheerful people; they are uninterested in politics and sensible enough to realise that they are perfectly happy under the aegis of the British . . . The present agitation, by the Labour Party at home, the Russians in Moscow, the Americans in Washington, and the Samolan Socialist National Party here, for Samolo to break free from British rule and achieve dominion status has very few supporters in the whole Samolan archipelago.[83]

Coward's argument that an essentially happy Empire had been betrayed by subversives and weaklings at home found plenty of echoes in the sixties and after. In Simon Raven's novel of Indian independence, *Sound the Retreat* (1974), a similarly disillusioned British sergeant major remarks that 'as things are nowadays, these bloody wogs only have to open their mouths and dribble, and everyone in the world's on their side against us. No one wants to know the truth of it. They're just for the wogs and against us – and so are half of our own people, come to that.'[84]

These kind of sentiments found a voice in Macmillan's critics on the right of the Conservative Party, who were often linked by blood or finance to the settler communities in Kenya and Rhodesia. There were few white settlers who did not feel personally abandoned by Macmillan and Macleod. 'We've been thoroughly betrayed by a lousy British government,' one Kenyan farmer fumed in 1962. 'We'll throw in our allegiance with somebody who's not prepared to pull the bloody flag down.' Some had fled Britain in order to escape the Attlee government, but now found the post-war consensus catching up with them. Others, like the farmer in Kenya, simply could not stand the idea of being ruled by blacks. 'I'm not a missionary,' he remarked. 'I hate the sight of the bastards.'[85] The settlers had close links not only with Conservatives in both Houses of Parliament but also with the City, the armed forces and the aristocracy, and when they felt threatened the reverberations were invariably felt in London.[86] Both the *Express* and the *Telegraph* frequently gave voice to complaints that decolonisation was going too quickly, but the settlers' chief spokesman was the Marquess of Salisbury, who had been instrumental in Macmillan's elevation to the premiership in 1957. Within three months Salisbury had resigned from the Cabinet in protest at the release of the Cypriot nationalist leader Archbishop Makarios, and he went on to become a frequent and bitter critic of the government's decolonisation policy.[87]

Salisbury was also the first patron of the Monday Club, which was formed by ten Conservative MPs in November 1961 and named after 'Black Monday', the day of Macmillan's Cape Town speech. The Monday Club had the explicit aims of opposing Macmillan's policy in Africa and fighting for a more right-wing brand of Conservatism; as time went by, it also became a vehicle for anti-immigration sentiment.[88] The other organisation for those who bemoaned the loss of the Empire was the League of Empire Loyalists, which had been founded in 1954 and was rather more eccentric. The League was particularly popular with returned expatriates, embittered colonial veterans and retired colonels in the stereotypical mould; its adversaries included African and Asian nationalists, immigrants, Jews, Harold Macmillan, the modern Conservative Party and the United Nations: an impressive list. Its energies were largely expended in irrelevant stunts and punch-ups of various kinds, a typical example being in November 1961 when a member of the League threw the entrails of a sheep wrapped in a copy of *The Times* at the Kenyan leader Jomo Kenyatta, who was visiting London for talks with the government. No lasting harm was done, except to the sheep.[89]

Above all, the government's right-wing critics hated Iain Macleod. Not only had Macleod presented himself as the personal champion of colonial liberalism, he also struck his opponents as intellectually arrogant, impatient and overbearing. While he usually got on well with black African national-ists, he often had trouble hiding his contempt for the leaders of the white settlers. In a letter to Macmillan about the white Rhodesian United Federal Party, for instance, he wrote: 'There really is no measuring the bottomless stupidity of their members here and in all three territories.'[90] Many con-servative observers thought, not necessarily inaccurately, that he had consciously taken the side of the black nationalists against their white rulers. Barely four months after Macleod had taken over at the Colonial Office, the Governor-General of the Central African Federation told his friend Lord Home that there was 'already considerable' antagonism in white society towards the new Colonial Secretary, and that right-wing sentiment was 'hardening because of the impression given by Macleod that "you can do anything provided your face is black"'. Macleod, he thought, 'must at least appear to be open-minded'.[91] The Federation's Prime Minister, Roy Welensky, had a particular dislike for Macleod, rooted in an unfortunate disagreement over music. Welensky had very traditional tastes and liked listening to light opera, but when invited to Macleod's house for dinner one evening he was horrified to find his host listening to the mordant, anti-nuclear songs of the American satirist Tom Lehrer. It was an inauspicious moment, and by the end of 1960 Welensky had told the Marquess of Salisbury that Macleod was 'the most sinister influence in the British Cabinet today'.[92] The constant rows with the settlers' leaders did no little harm to Macleod's image among his fellow Conservatives. In January 1961 the *Daily Express*, which frequently championed the settlers' cause, even called Macleod 'the most calamitous Colonial Secretary in History'.[93]

Two months later Macleod found himself the victim of an attack from Lord Salisbury in the House of Lords that even made mocking reference to his past as a professional card-player. The 'main responsibility' for the difficult relations between Britain and Rhodesia, Salisbury claimed, 'must rest on the present Colonial Secretary . . . I believe he has adopted, especially in his relationship to the white communities of Africa, a most unhappy and a wrong approach. He has been too clever by half.'

> I believe that the Colonial Secretary is a very fine bridge player . . . It is not considered immoral and or even bad form to outwit one's opponents at bridge. On the contrary, the more you outwit them within the rules of the game, the better player you are. It almost seems to me as if the Colonial Secretary, when he abandoned the sphere of bridge for the sphere of politics, brought his bridge technique with him . . .
>
> The Europeans [in Kenya] found themselves completely outwitted, and they were driven, if I may revert for the last time to the bridge metaphor, to think that it was the nationalist African leaders whom the Colonial Secretary regarded as his partners, and the white community and the loyal Africans that he regarded as his opponents in the game he was playing.[94]

Macleod was, according to his biographer, deeply upset by this attack. The charges of being 'too clever by half' and of playing the political game with the skill and cunning of a professional bridge-player did lasting harm to his reputation within the solidly anti-intellectual Conservative Party, and this helps to explain why, despite his talents, Macleod was not considered a serious short-term contender for the party leadership in the early sixties.[95]

By the autumn of 1961, even the Cabinet colleagues who worked with

Macleod on colonial issues, like Lord Home and Duncan Sandys, had fallen out with him: not only were they much more conservative than he was, they also agreed that he was 'too clever by half'.[96] Macmillan, too, eventually became sick of dealing with a Colonial Secretary who was unpopular with many party activists and frequently threatened to resign whenever his liberal initiatives were blocked. In October 1961 he finally moved Macleod to the post of party chairman and replaced him with Reginald Maudling, whom he thought 'very clever, a little lazy; and a trifle vain. But I believe that if he buckles down to it he will do *very* well.'[97] Maudling, however, turned out to be just as liberal as Macleod, albeit with a more amiable, emollient manner. Within months Macmillan was privately complaining that his new Colonial Secretary was '*plus noir que les nègres*, more difficult and more intransigent than his predecessor. He threatens resignation . . .'[98] So Macmillan's hopes for an easier life were dashed; the momentum towards the end of the Empire could not be checked, and Macleod's work went on.[99]

'England as a great power is done for,' Evelyn Waugh wrote in his diary in 1946. 'The loss of possessions, the claim of the English proletariat to be a privileged race, sloth and envy, must produce an increasing poverty . . . until only a proletariat and a bureaucracy survive.'[100] As one colony after another won independence in the late fifties and early sixties, it seemed that Britain was indeed doomed to become a nation in decline. Many observers traced the beginning of the rot to the independence of India and Pakistan in 1947: not only had the South Asian Raj been the most glittering of all the jewels in the British crown, but its evaporation also meant the loss of India's army, its natural wealth and its superlative strategic position. In subsequent years, plenty of British writers invested the end of empire in India with a deep, almost spiritual significance. In Osborne's play *Look Back in Anger*, the character of Colonel Renfrew reflects sadly:

> At the time, it looked like going on for ever. When I think of it now, it seems like a dream. If only it could have gone on for ever. Those long, cool evenings in the hills, everything purple and golden. Your mother and I were so happy then. It seemed as though we could have everything we could ever want. I think the last day the sun shone was when that dirty little train steamed out of that crowded, suffocating Indian station, and the battalion band playing for all it was worth. I knew in my heart it was all over then. Everything.[101]

The independence of India and the humiliation of Suez were powerful blows to the old dreams of national pre-eminence and imperial dominion. It was the collapse of the Empire between 1958 and 1963, however, that really confirmed the impression that the nation was in serious decline. Whatever Macmillan might tell his television audiences, the idea of decline had taken root among intellectuals on left and right and in the popular media, and it would be extremely hard to shift.[102] Literary representations of the Empire's final years, like Anthony Burgess' gloomy 'Malayan trilogy' (1956–9), were weighed down with the sense that not only the imperial ideal but also the nation itself was worn down and weary.[103]

Film studios might still be churning out war films by the dozen, but they were also beginning to produce comic pictures like *Carlton-Browne of the FO* (1959), showing British officials as anachronistic buffoons struggling to cope with the modern post-colonial world. 'That's frightfully slack!' says Terry-Thomas, confronted with some new evidence of administrative incompetence. Indeed, Selwyn Lloyd reportedly considered the film a splendid satire on his own officials.[104] By the early sixties, the Britain of the cinema was more *The Mouse That Roared* (1959) than the lion of old.[105] And since politicians and commentators had for so long associated the Empire with national greatness, it was not surprising that when it began to collapse many people felt nothing but a cold pessimism. What, after all, was left, but life on a wet, windswept collection of islands in the North Atlantic? 'At the bottom of his heart', George Orwell had written in 1937, 'no Englishman . . . does want [the Empire] to disintegrate':

> For, apart from any other consideration, the high standard of life we enjoy in England depends upon our keeping a tight hold on the Empire, particularly the tropical portions of it such as India and Africa . . . The alternative is to throw the Empire overboard and reduce England to a cold and unimportant little island where we should all have to work very hard and live mainly on herrings and potatoes.[106]

The great fear among many commentators on the political right was that, since the Empire was the key to Britain's unique identity, its dissolution overseas would mean inevitable repercussions at home. As the Conservative politician Leopold Amery put it in 1943, the Empire was 'the translation into outward shape, and under ever varying circumstances, of the British character and of certain social and political principles, constituting a definite British culture or way of life which, first evolved on British soil, has since been carried by our people across all the seas'.[107] What David Cannadine calls the 'ornamentalism' of the Empire had long emphasised its role as the supreme incarnation of British conservatism and continuity. It was 'about antiquity and anachronism, tradition and honour, order and subordination; about glory and chivalry, horses and elephants, knights and peers, processions and ceremony, plumed hats and ermine robes . . . about thrones and crowns, dominion and hierarchy, ostentation and ornamentalism'; and it therefore helped to bolster, both at home and abroad, the impression that Britain was a settled, ordered and conservative society.[108]

But with the collapse of the Empire that social order appeared itself to be under threat. In 1959 the young Tory journalist Peregrine Worsthorne published an influential article suggesting that the end of Britain's imperial greatness might have devastating consequences at home. 'The Right', he argued, 'is acutely aware that the kind of Britain it wishes to preserve very largely depends on Britain remaining a great power.' It was inevitable that 'a social system that seemed right and proper while it produced a nation capable of leading the world will look very different when that nation is in decline'. What, for instance, was 'the point of maintaining a Queen–Empress without an empire to rule over?' 'Everything about the British class system', he concluded, 'begins to look foolish and tacky when related to a second-class power on the decline.'[109]

Despite the warnings of commentators like Worsthorne and the outrage of conservatives like Lord Salisbury, the reaction of the general public to the end of empire was one of almost total indifference. Elsewhere, in Portugal or in France, the process of decolonisation caused deep social division and political conflict. In Britain there was no great national trauma or soul-searching; indeed, it appears that, as with the nuclear issue, most people simply could not care less. The League of Empire Loyalists never became a serious mass movement, and colonial policy was never an important issue in any post-war general election.[110] The obvious explanation for this striking indifference is that ordinary voters had never been very bothered about the Empire in the first place: there were always more important domestic issues to worry about. In his essay on his 'imperial childhood' in post-war Birmingham, David Cannadine acknowledges that he was more interested in the Empire than were most of his contemporaries. But he admits that even he was not 'drenched' in the imperial experience, that 'the imperial dog sometimes did bark in the night, but not very often, and not very loudly, and, while I heard the bark, I never saw the dog'.[111] It seems likely that most people either were unaware that the dog was barking at all, or simply regarded it as one of the more boring and irrelevant quirks of British life.

Doubtless this owed much to the fact that imperial affairs were both unfamiliar and complicated; even Macmillan remarked that the 'Cyprus Tangle' was 'one of the most baffling problems which I can ever remember'.[112] It is extremely unlikely, therefore, that most ordinary people, opening their daily newspaper or switching on their new television, could remember the difference between KAU, KANU and KCA, or between the Northern and Southern Rhodesian constitutions, or between one Somaliland and the other. As H. G. Wells had once remarked, nineteen out of twenty people knew as much about the British Empire as they did about the Italian Renaissance; and in 1906 Lord Milner had complained that 'one must unfortunately explain to these d–d fools why we want an Empire, and it pinches one in dealing with the methods of maintaining it'.[113]

An opinion poll taken in 1947, just before India and Pakistan became independent, found that three-quarters of the British public did not know the difference between a dominion and a colony, and half could not name a single British possession. One man even nominated Lincolnshire as a possible colony.[114] Indeed, whatever historians like Correlli Barnett and Richard Weight might think, this public indifference to the intricacies of empire was not something particularly new, and neither was it part of some popular backlash against Britain's imperial mission. Most ordinary voters were not particularly embarrassed by, or unsympathetic to, their imperial inheritance. Instead, like their parents and grandparents, they simply knew very little about it and cared even less. With this in mind, it becomes easier to understand why they were so unperturbed when it passed into history.[115]

It is also worth remembering that in many ways the British public had seen it all before. Far from being sudden or unexpected, the liquidation of the Empire in Africa and Asia looked like the latest stage in the long evolution of Britain's role overseas. Decolonisation was a complicated process with its roots deep in the nineteenth century: Canada, Australia, New Zealand and South Africa, for instance, had already been transformed from colonial possessions to self-governing dominions linked to the motherland through the Commonwealth. During the twenties and thirties, Conservative Party politics had been dominated by long and convoluted debates about Indian self-government and the future of the Empire, so for anyone who had ever glanced at a newspaper even the end of British rule in India was no great surprise. Macmillan himself had played his part in the arguments of the thirties, and his presence in Downing Street was the ideal symbol of this continuity. Indeed, one of his chief political assets was his ability to present the radical transformation of the Empire as though he were a trusted mechanic merely giving the old machine a much-needed over-haul.[116] It helped, of course, that most of the colonies retained their important economic and military links with Britain. The 'audit of empire' prepared for Macmillan in 1957 had made the point that 'the economic interests of the United Kingdom' might be better served by decolonisation rather than repression, and so it proved.[117] Those companies that had invested in the developing world were confident that their assets would be safe under the new regimes, and in many respects, the end of the formal, institutional Empire did not affect the profitable and unequal relationship between Britain and the colonies. Only later, during the sterling crises of the late sixties, did British economic influence in Asia and Africa really begin to diminish.[118]

In his public statements on colonial policy, Macmillan liked to talk a great deal about the Commonwealth. Although Empire Day was renamed Commonwealth Day in 1958 as part of a campaign to sell the institution to the British public, it remained in many ways a political and economic irrelevance. At Suez the British had made no effort to consult or even warn their Commonwealth colleagues, and in subsequent years many of the new members vigorously disagreed with British policy and even swung towards the Soviet Union. Macmillan was undaunted: for three years, beginning in 1959, the government sponsored 'Commonwealth Week', during which a touring exhibition would be presented to the people of fifteen different cities. It was not a success: people had even less interest in the Commonwealth than they did in the Empire.[119] But the role of the Commonwealth in easing the transition from empire should not be under-estimated. It was presented to the public not as a rather limp-wristed substitute for imperial glory, but as its inevitable and laudable culmination: a writer in the *Observer*, for example, claimed that it was 'a logical outcome of our own development'.[120] It was, the Queen told an audience in Ghana in 1961, 'a group of equals, a family of like-minded peoples whatever their differences of religion, political systems, circumstances and races, all eager to work together for the peace, freedom and prosperity of mankind'.[121] On both sides of the political divide it was seen as a vital psychological 'shock-absorber' or 'painkiller', preserving the illusion of Britain's international importance and reassuring the public that they still had much of which to be proud. And as a self-consciously benevolent and multi-racial institution, it delighted idealistic do-gooders on the left just as much as it appeased nostalgic imperialists on the right; indeed, its very mention drew just as many cheers in Labour circles as among Conservatives.[122]

The longevity of the Commonwealth, which even at the beginning of the twenty-first century was still going strong, helped to bolster the impression that British decolonisation had been 'transacted over tea in an atmosphere of sweetness and light'.[123] As early as 1954, the writer Arthur Koestler had remarked that the British Empire was 'dissolving with dignity and grace. The rise of this empire was not an edifying story: its decline is.'[124] The politicians who had actually presided over the dissolution, on both left and right, were keen to support Koestler's rose-tinted version. In 1960, delivering the Chichele Lectures in Oxford, Clement Attlee proudly told his audience that only Britain had 'voluntarily surrendered its hegemony over subject peoples and has given them their freedom'. Negotiations with the colonies, he claimed, had involved 'a talk round the table between friends'; he could never recall 'a division of opinion on racial grounds'.[125] Macmillan, meanwhile, would brook no talk of surrender; instead, he liked to present the British retreat as the triumphant fulfilment of a long-conceived design. When Khrushchev accused him at the United Nations of being an 'imperialist', Macmillan gestured around the hall:

> Gentlemen, where are the representatives of these former British territories? Here they are, sitting in this Hall. Apart from the older independent countries, Canada, Australia, New Zealand, South Africa – here are the representatives of India, Pakistan, Ceylon, Ghana, Malaya. Here, here in this Hall. In a few days' time, Nigeria will join us . . .
>
> Who dares to say that this is anything but a story of steady and liberal progress?

At this point, an irate Khrushchev removed his shoe and began banging it on the table in an attempt to interrupt. Macmillan stopped, glanced up from his text and said coolly: 'Mr President, perhaps we could have a translation, I could not quite follow.'[126]

Macmillan would have been pleased to know that many modern historians share his verdict on his own achievements, and the withdrawal from empire in Africa is generally seen as his greatest accomplishment, a triumph of 'remarkable dignity and skill'.[127] Whether this reputation is completely deserved is a different matter. British decolonisation, after all, was not an entirely painless process: in many places, African protesters lost their lives or their liberty, and the record of the British forces in Kenya and Nyasaland, to take two examples, was nothing to be very proud of. Macmillan and Macleod are often fêted as champions of colonial freedom, but, as John Darwin points out, it was not always obvious that they 'had any clear idea of where they were going'. To many African politicians, 'white and black alike, they appeared weak and vacillating, not resolute and clear-sighted'.[128] They were not necessarily visionaries, and no doubt Macmillan would have happily hung on to the colonies had it been possible. Instead, they managed to muddle through a very difficult situation, reluctantly acknowledging the new realities of the post-war order when necessary.

Still, it would not do to be too harsh: the fact remains that, when compared with their imperial rivals, the British divested themselves of their Empire with startling ease. The Portuguese, for example, fought two savage and interminable wars in Angola and Mozambique which dragged on for so long that the domestic regime itself finally caved in. The Belgian experience of withdrawal from the Congo, meanwhile, was hardly a happy one. And in France the repercussions of the end of empire included a long and bloody war in Algeria, the collapse of the Fourth Republic, an attempted military coup and a terrorist campaign by the Algerian settlers. In this context, the British retreat from empire looks strikingly peaceful. There was no equivalent of the wars in Algeria or Mozambique, and neither did the experience of decolonisation threaten domestic stability. Even the partition of India and Pakistan in 1947, which cost hundreds of thousands of Asian lives, left surprisingly few scars on the national consciousness, and was perceived in some quarters as a triumph of enlightened liberalism. There was, therefore, no great post-imperial trauma in Britain: instead, politicians and public alike congratulated themselves on the enduring traditions of pragmatism and flexibility that had helped them to avoid the reactionary excesses of their erstwhile imperial rivals.[128]

Many historians are keen to argue that, in the wake of empire, Britain was itself a 'successor state', adjusting to the realities of a new world position, its national identity profoundly transformed and its old institutions crumbling before a new mood of post-imperial irreverence.[130] It is certainly true that, in the long run, the end of the Empire made a difference to the way the British saw themselves and their place in the world; even so, this kind of analysis feels rather overheated. It was material prosperity that powered the social changes of the sixties, not the end of empire; indeed, most ordinary citizens would have scoffed at the thought that their lives had been changed by its passing. For all the talk of decline, the immediate domestic effects of decolonisation were extraordinarily limited. As one eminent historian puts it, the disappearance of the Empire and Britain's treasured world role, 'the stuff of political rhetoric since time-out-of-mind, left scarcely any visible political traces and cast no serious shadow over the viability of British institutions'.[131] The ceremonies that marked the independence of the African colonies were reported in Britain not as days of infamy and disaster, but as colourful carnivals brimming with optimism and good cheer.[132] Indeed, some commentators suggested that, after all the fuss, nothing had really changed. Enoch Powell, for example, told an audience in 1964 that 'the continuity of [English] existence was unbroken when the looser connections which had linked her with distant continents and strange races fell away'.[133] But he was wrong. Despite the dissolution of the Empire, Britain's cultural links with the wider world remained as strong as ever; and, instead of disappearing into far-flung obscurity, the 'strange races' of Powell's speech were at that very moment building new homes in the towns and cities of Britain itself.

9

THE NEWCOMERS

Would you let your daughter marry a black man?

Daily Express, 18 July 1956

Few subjects were as controversial and emotive during the late fifties and sixties as immigration. The arrival of workers and families from the West Indies, South Asia and East Africa left an indelible mark on British life, from the appearance of towns and cities to the cadences of British poetry, the beat of British music and the spice of British cooking. The way in which the British viewed the outside world could never be quite the same after they had accepted into their midst thousands of newcomers from overseas, and similarly, the easy assumption that Britishness itself was a matter of racial inheritance was no longer acceptable in a multi-racial society.

But for all the attention understandably given to immigration, the simple and indisputable fact is that in the twentieth century Britain was more accurately a nation of *emigrants*. From the late Victorian period right up until the last years of the following century, more people left the United Kingdom than arrived in it. Britain was, in short, 'a net exporter of people'. The exception was the short period between 1958 and 1962, when tens of thousands of immigrants arrived from the Caribbean and the Indian sub-continent in order to beat the restrictions in the planned Commonwealth Immigrants Act. If we look at the wider picture, however, the British experience is better represented by Ford Madox Brown's Victorian painting *The Last of England*, showing a mournful couple being carried away across the Channel to exile, than by the famous photographs of bewildered West Indians holding their suitcases at Tilbury Dock.[1]

For most of the emigrants, the attraction was the opportunity to build a better, more prosperous life in North America, southern Africa, Australia or

New Zealand. In 1950 alone, thirteen thousand people left Britain for a new life in the United States; ten years later twenty thousand followed them, and ten years after that the annual figure was fourteen thousand. Many of these people were not the desperate, poor emigrants of Victorian myth, but were instead well-educated, skilled professionals attracted by higher wages and living standards, so there was much talk about a 'brain drain' to the old colonies.[2] Others preferred the old-fashioned lifestyle of white settlers in Africa, where they could gather on the veranda at sundown with their gin and tonics and copies of the *Daily Telegraph* and mourn the passing of good old England. Between 1945 and 1955, the white populations of Northern and Southern Rhodesia increased from 5000 and 80,000 to over 60,000 and 200,000 respectively. Many of these people were middle- or upper-middle-class Britons who found life in Attlee's austere new world intolerable; the African colonies, with their sun-kissed villas and busily expanding cities of Salisbury, Lusaka and Nairobi, seemed to offer a new life of freedom, leisure, prosperity and status.[3] To take a fictional example, in Ian Fleming's short story 'Octopussy' (1966), we are told that the crooked Major Dexter Smythe, the quintessential example of middle-class flight, disappeared to the Caribbean after the war with his wife 'in one of the early banana boats heading off to Kingston, Jamaica, which they both agreed would be a paradise of sunshine, good food and cheap drink and a glorious haven from the gloom, restrictions and Labour government of post-war England'.[4]

Although the plain fact was that emigrants were more numerous than immigrants, this did not make a great impression on those politicians and activists at the forefront of the campaign against Commonwealth immigration in the 1960s. And for all the talk of immigration as an unprecedented and remarkable challenge to existing notions of national identity and the traditions of national life, it was also a plain fact that Britain had a long experience of receiving foreign newcomers, whether European, Jewish, black, Indian or Chinese. A country that had established its reputation and wealth on seaborne trade could hardly have avoided the presence of foreign ambassadors, sailors, traders, servants and slaves. From the seventeenth century onwards there had been considerable and increasing Irish and Jewish communities, especially in London. Black faces were not entirely unknown, whether as sailors in port towns, or domestic servants, or even exotic pets.[5] In the eighteenth century, as Britain became more tightly bound into the New World plantation, slave and trading networks, so there gathered small groups of black Africans in British cities and seaports like London, Bristol, and Southampton, and individual areas like Tiger Bay in Cardiff or Bootle in Liverpool had their own small black communities by the end of the eighteenth century. Black boxers, musicians or prostitutes became minor local celebrities, and it was fashionable for artistic gentlemen like Samuel Johnson or Sir Joshua Reynolds to have a black manservant.[6]

By 1800 the black community in Britain's cities and ports was about ten thousand strong, with additional smaller pockets of Indians and Chinese, and within three decades or so it had doubled in size.[7] Throughout the following century the Indian influence on British life, thanks to the Raj, was particularly strong, leaving its mark in words like *pyjamas*, *bungalow*, *dungarees* and *pukkah*, or in the pseudo-Mughal splendour of the Brighton Pavilion, or in the carpets and rugs in well-to-do Victorian homes.[8] It was not unusual to see Indian students strolling through late Victorian and Edwardian London, notable examples including Gandhi, Jinnah and Nehru. Indeed, London at the beginning of the twentieth century was a heady mixture of different nationalities, colours and languages, from black sailors and Indian students to Germans, Poles, Russians, Arabs and Jews, especially in poorer areas like Stepney, Canning Town or Spitalfields. The most notorious of all immigrant groups, the Chinese community in Limehouse, probably never numbered more than five hundred people; even so, its cafés, gambling dens, shops, restaurants, clubs, Tong hall and Chinese school were famous across Edwardian Britain.[9]

The United Kingdom was, therefore, a multi-racial society well before the Second World War. In one detective story of the 1920s, the hero comments on 'the Asiatic and African faces that one sees at the windows of these Bloomsbury boarding houses' in Upper Bedford Place and casually remarks that they must be an overflow from an exhibition at the British Museum.[10] The cook who worked on the SS *Empire Windrush* from Jamaica to Tilbury in 1948 later recalled: 'Where I come from, Custom House in Cardiff, seen it all before. We had coloured living in Custom House for years and years. Indian seamen used to walk past my house regular, you know. I was brought up seeing that. It didn't worry me.'[11] Some black entertainers were regarded as fashionable during the twenties and thirties, especially if they played in jazz bands or worked as nightclub entertainers. They were, however, few in number and were limited to roles that played up their exoticism or supposed wildness; while a black minstrel might be acceptable, a black Hamlet was unthinkable.[12] Outside the clubs and theatres, life could be tough. The small communities of black and Indian sailors in ports like Cardiff and Bristol were often regarded with intense suspicion by their neighbours; so not only did they live in overcrowded conditions with little chance of social and economic mobility, but they were also subject to the casual racism of the day.[13] One black writer in the early years of the century observed:

> In the low class suburbs a black man stands the chance of being laughed at to scorn until he takes to his heels . . . pray even now you never meet a troupe of school children just from school. They will call you all sorts of names, sing you all sorts of songs. Pray also that you never encounter a band of factory girls just from their workshop. Some of these girls will make fun of you by throwing kisses at you when not making hisses at you while others shout 'Go wash your face, guv'nor', or sometimes call out 'nigger, nigger, nigger'.[14]

The arrival of the SS *Empire Windrush* with almost five hundred Caribbean migrants at Tilbury Dock on 22 June 1948 is often taken to mark the beginning of black immigration into Britain. In fact there were already at least 75,000 black and Asian citizens living in Britain, most being British born and bred.[15] Still, the arrival of the *Empire Windrush* is an iconic moment in the history of immigration and has served ever since as a symbol of the determination of black migrants to build a new life in post-war Britain. The boat left Kingston on 8 June 1948 with 492 passengers, each of whom had paid a fare of £28 10s for the chance to cross the Atlantic to the 'mother country'. This was, for most West Indians, an extraordinary investment: the future mayor of Southwark, Sam King, remembered that his family had been compelled to sell three cows to raise his fare. Eighteen stowaways, unable to raise the fare, were also lurking about the boat. On arrival at Tilbury, the newcomers were at first fed and housed in deep shelters on Clapham Common and then were taken to the nearest labour exchange in Brixton in order to find work.[16]

This was not an organised transfer of labour from the colonies; all the evidence suggests that Attlee's government, rather than actively conniving in the process, was taken by surprise and rather bemused by the arrival of so many Caribbean migrants. But it did not try to stop the immigrants; instead, as the boat drew ever closer, various paternalistic bureaucrats spent weeks worrying about the problems of work and accommodation for the new arrivals.[17] There was some talk in the Cabinet of moving the immigrants on to Kenya, but eventually it was agreed that emergency measures should be taken to welcome them to Britain. When eleven Labour backbenchers wrote to Attlee complaining that 'an influx of coloured people . . . is likely to impair the harmony, strength and cohesion of our public and social life and to bring discord and unhappiness among all concerned', he calmly replied that it would be 'a great mistake to take the emigration of the Jamaican party to the United Kingdom too seriously' and that there was no question of ditching the tradition that all British subjects were 'freely admissible to the United Kingdom'.[18] The press, meanwhile, treated the occasion more as a diverting oddity than as a threat. The day after the landing, the *Daily Express* reported:

> Oswald M. Denniston – the first of 430 job-hunting Jamaicans to land at Tilbury yesterday morning from the trooper *Empire Windrush* – started a £4-a-week job last night. Wrapped in two warm blankets to keep warm, he settled in as night watchman of the meals marquee in Clapham Common, SW, where 240 of the Jamaicans are staying in deep wartime shelters. All of them sat down to their first meal on English soil: roast beef, potatoes, vegetables, Yorkshire pudding, suet pudding with currants and custard. A bed and three hot meals will cost them 6s.6d a day. Most of the Jamaicans have about £5 to last them until they find work. Oswald Denniston, 35-year-old sign painter, got his job after making a speech of thanks to government officials. He called for three cheers for the Ministry of Labour and raised his Anthony Eden hat. Others clapped. Panamas, blue, pink and biscuit trilbys, and one bowler were waved.[19]

The *Windrush*, however, was not a one-off. Within a few months other boats like the *Orbita* and the *Georgic* had also unloaded hundreds of West Indian passengers at the London docks.[20] It is hard to imagine economic migration to Britain on this scale occurring before the mid-twentieth century, when improvements in mass communications and long-distance transport meant that it was relatively easy to move from Jamaica or Barbados to Britain.[21] But this explains the means, not the motivation. Another factor was the weakness of the Caribbean economy, which had been savaged by a brutal hurricane in 1944 and was struggling to adjust to the new realities of post-war trade. Unemployment was high, and many young men evidently felt that there was little future for them at home. At the same time, the opportunities for seasonal employment in Florida and the southern United States were about to be curtailed by the immigration controls of the McCarran–Walter Act (1952). Had the American borders remained open, it is improbable that West Indian migrants would have arrived in Britain in such numbers, rising from three thousand in 1953 to thirty thousand in 1956 and sixty-six thousand in 1961.[22]

Thousands of men from the West Indies had already been to Britain. They had served in the British imperial forces during the Second World War, where they had been well trained, well paid and given assistance with their board and lodging. It was hard to return to the backbreaking, threadbare and authoritarian world of the islands after the excitement of, say, London at the height of the struggle against Nazi Germany. 'Life in the Caribbean', as one account puts it, 'seemed slower, smaller and poorer than it had before, with even fewer opportunities for advancement or self expression, and governed by the same oppressive structure of imperialist control.'[23] For many of these men, therefore, the chance to escape the unemployment of the islands and test themselves again in Britain was hard to turn down. One Jamaican who worked for a banana grower before making the voyage to Britain in 1949 explained: 'If you could make a few shillings for yourself, then you're alright, but if you couldn't make it, it was very hard. See, so that's the reason why I said to myself, I don't want to stop here to grow old and, you know, I want to travel and make something . . .'[24] As a character in the novel *The Emigrants*, published by the Barbadian immigrant George Lamming in 1954, puts it: 'Every man want a better break.'[25]

The key factor in explaining the wave of West Indian immigration in the 1950s, however, is the British economy's desperate need for cheap labour. The revival of the economy and the government's emphasis on full employment meant that by 1949 there were already severe labour shortages; a Royal Commission reporting in that year suggested that the country needed to attract 140,000 immigrants a year in order to meet the demands of capital, even though 'large-scale immigration' was still considered 'both undesirable and impracticable'.[26] The Commonwealth offered an obvious labour pool, and under the terms of the 1948 British Nationality Act, all Crown subjects were automatically entitled to British citizenship, no matter if they had been born in Singapore or Stevenage.[27] Attlee's Home Secretary, James Chuter Ede, told the House of Commons that the 'coloured races' were 'men and brothers with the people of this country', with every right to common citizenship.[28]

By the middle of the following decade, it was clear that the Act had created an inexhaustible supply of cheap labour for the booming British economy, and employers were quick to seize the benefits. In 1956, for example, the London Transport Executive reached an agreement with the Barbadian Immigrants' Liaison Service, whereby several thousand men and women from Barbados were loaned the money for their passage to Britain, which they then repaid out of the wages they received from London Transport. Similar agreements were reached with organisations in Trinidad and Jamaica, while the British Hotels and Restaurants Association also began recruiting workers from Barbados. These cosy arrangements were 'well greased' by the steamship and airline companies, which stood to make a healthy profit from ferrying immigrant workers from the Caribbean.[29] The largest block of these sponsored workers, the Barbadians brought over by London Transport and British Railways, amounted to some 4500 people between 1955 and 1961.[30] Although this was only a fraction of the total influx in the fifties, it was a very visible fraction, and illustrated the point that, despite the complaints of anti-immigration activists about 'invading' hordes, many thousands of West Indian workers had been *recruited* to come to Britain by some of the biggest corporations and organisations in the land.

By the late fifties, such was the demand for low-skilled and low-paid work in British industry that the influx had increased to 36,000 immigrants per annum. Every two years, therefore, a number equivalent to the total non-white national population in 1951 was arriving in Britain, and by 1961 the black and Asian population had risen to 337,000.[31] Immigration also reached high levels because of political decisions taken in Washington and London: not only the McCarran–Walter Act, but also the Commonwealth Immigrants Act, which was passed by the Macmillan government in 1962 and introduced strict controls on immigrants from the Commonwealth. It was no accident that the new legislation coincided with a period of rising unemployment and violent anti-immigrant agitation. From 1962 onwards, preference would be given to skilled workers, the assumption being that these would originate from the white Commonwealth countries, or those contracted to a named employer.[32]

News of the pending Commonwealth Immigrants Act quickly reached the Caribbean and South Asia, and, predictably enough, there was a great rush to arrive in Britain before the bill became law. In the eighteen months before the passage of the Act, more immigrants poured into Britain than had arrived in the whole of the previous five years. In 1961 alone, 49,000 people arrived from India and Pakistan, 66,000 from the Caribbean and a further 21,000 from Hong Kong, Cyprus and elsewhere, making it the largest mass migration in modern British history.[33] After 1962, immigration was more tightly curtailed and the numbers of unskilled young men dropped off dramatically. But that did not mean that immigration ceased: far from it. The arrivals in the middle and later sixties tended to fall into two groups. First, there were the dependants of the original migrants of the fifties: wives, children and so on. Second, there were the Asian refugees expelled by Jomo Kenyatta and Idi Amin from East Africa in the late sixties and early seventies: for example, the Kenyan Asians, who arrived in large numbers in 1967 and 1968.[34] By 1971, according to the national census, there lived in Britain well over 650,000 people who traced their origins to the West Indies, India or Pakistan, almost ten times the total non-white population of the United Kingdom twenty years earlier. Of these, 265,000 had come from the Caribbean islands; 241,000 from India, and 128,000 from Pakistan and Bangladesh.[35]

All these groups were themselves divided by lines of class, age, gender and region, and generalisations are difficult. Among the West Indians, for instance, there was a distinction between the original migrants, who tended to be skilled or semi-skilled workers from urban backgrounds, and the newcomers who arrived in the late fifties and after, who were more likely to be unskilled, poorer migrants from rural areas. Distinctive island identities and rivalries were still strong, too: the Trinidadians were said to be 'gay', the Jamaicans 'touchy and flamboyant' and the Barbadians 'dull and hard working'. 'Big islanders' were thought worldlier, and therefore less trustworthy, than 'little islanders', who 'wrote off Jamaicans as bullies'. Other distinctions, for example between the light-skinned and dark-skinned, or between evangelical Christians and Rastafarians, also ensured that this was far from a homogeneous community.[36] The West Indians were, at least at first, an overwhelmingly young male group: of the Caribbean migrants who arrived in 1953, for instance, only one in four was a woman.[37] By the late sixties, however, the balance had shifted, and the 1971 census found that in London there were more West Indian women than men. Since three-quarters of these women were young and single, having migrated for the same reasons of economic ambition as the men, they therefore represented what the historian Jerry White calls a 'specially fertile group'; so within the next few decades, the black population of Britain rose more quickly than the population in general.[38]

Whereas most Caribbean migrants arrived during the 1950s, the majority of the Indians and Pakistanis who came to Britain did so during the following decade, driven by demographic pressures in their native lands and attracted by the opportunities to build better lives for their families.[39] Although the South Asian communities lacked an iconic moment to match the docking of the *Empire Windrush*, they could at least point to two areas of London where Pakistanis and Indians had been settling before the great rush of the early sixties. In Spitalfields, in the East End, a community of Sylhettis from East Pakistan (later Bangladesh) had been established even before the war, with shops and institutions of their own, and a network of East Pakistani villages, called *Londoni*, would send migrants to the area in return for cash remittances back home.[40] The second area was Southall in west London, the first major suburban immigrant community. According to legend, the personnel officer of Woolf's Rubber Company had served with men from a Sikh regiment during the war and formed a very high opinion of them. When he ran out of workers willing to spend their days in the intense heat of the firm's Southall factory, he sent out to the Punjab for his old comrades, and the company even bought houses near the factory so the Punjabis would have somewhere to live until they could afford places of their own. Other factories in Southall copied his example, and as early as 1957 there was a local branch of the Indian Workers' Association and the Indo-Pakistan Cultural Society, with a Sikh temple being built two years later.[41]

As with the Caribbean migrants, the Indians and Pakistanis were also divided among themselves. There were, for example, two major groups of Pakistanis: those from Mirpur in the west, and the Sylhettis from the east; and, while all were Muslims, they had little else in common, not least because their languages were so different. The Indians, meanwhile, were divided into a Sikh majority and a smaller Hindu community, with no little tension between the two groups.[42] Again, as with the West Indians, men greatly outnumbered women. Until 1962, there were about six Pakistani men to every one woman; among the Indians the ratio was more like two to one.[43] Women and children classified as dependants under the 1962 Commonwealth Immigrants Act tended to arrive later in the sixties and seventies. These family reunions could be joyous occasions; on the other hand, since the men had already established roots and relationships in Britain, there was also ample scope for misunderstanding and disappointment.[44]

Three other significant and visible immigrant communities in post-war Britain were the Chinese, the Maltese and the Cypriots. There had been small Chinese communities in London and the major ports, as described earlier, since the nineteenth century. By the early 1900s, as they became more secure and ambitious, some Chinese seamen opened laundries in the East End, and the first Chinese restaurant in Liverpool was already up and running before the outbreak of the First World War. After the Communist Revolution in 1949, Hong Kong had come under immense population pressure from the influx of refugees and several thousand people chose to make the voyage to Britain, so by the sixties there were at least fifty thousand ethnic Chinese throughout the country, not just from China and Hong Kong but also from Singapore and Malaysia.[45] Migrants from the Maltese islands, usually young men escaping the poverty and strict Catholic morality of their little Mediterranean country, were especially prominent in the forties, and settled mainly in London, where their numbers reached about 4000 in the late fifties. The Cypriots, however, arrived later, fleeing the violence of their ill-starred island, and tended to be couples and families rather than single men. By 1966, there were about 75,000 Cypriots in London alone, and some areas of Holloway and Harringay had become little pockets of Cyprus with their clubs, greengrocers, banks and travel agencies.[46]

Until the Second World War the black and South Asian communities of Britain had been tightly concentrated in specific areas of London, in seaports and near universities. During the 1950s the focus of migrant settlement began to shift northwards and inland, to the great old industrial powerhouses of Lancashire and the West Midlands. The mill and manufacturing conurbations were prospering in the fifties, if only temporarily, because the British victory in the war meant they were perfectly placed to benefit from an export drive.[47] At the same time, however, their population was falling as affluent workers chose to move south or to the suburbs, so the demand for cheap labour was high. Most immigrant workers, therefore, were immediately attracted to these areas because unskilled or semi-skilled jobs were so readily available. Although by national standards these were very low-paid jobs, they were understandably attractive to migrant workers from the impoverished Caribbean or rural Pakistan. In Lancashire and West Yorkshire, Indian and Pakistani immigrants worked the unpopular night shifts in the roaring textile mills. In the West Midlands, the Pakistanis worked as labourers and the Indians toiled in the furnaces, foundries and rolling mills. In the capital, the West Indian community worked as labourers or for London Transport, and in the major urban hospitals across the country, West Indians were employed as porters, cleaners and kitchen staff. From the very beginning, therefore, Commonwealth immigrants were concentrated in ill-paid jobs and in declining areas.[48] They had little alternative but to look for housing in the poorer, dilapidated parts of towns, precisely those areas where crime rates and anxieties about labour competition would already be very high. Contrary to anti-immigrant myth, it was not the influx of newcomers that caused particular neighbourhoods to decline into ragged disrepair; instead, it was the very shabbiness and cheapness of these areas that made it possible for them to live there. Local people were often offended that immigrant groups lived in dense concentrations, but this was entirely predictable, as the geography of immigrant settlement in, say, the United States would suggest. It was natural for migrants to want to live near family and friends or those with whom they had strong cultural, linguistic and religious ties; but equally, they were often prevented from leaving these areas by housing discrimination and the aggressive suspicion of local people.[49]

This pattern first became apparent during the heyday of Caribbean immigration in the mid-1950s. In 1953, there had been fifteen thousand West Indians in London and eight thousand in Birmingham. Manchester and Nottingham had about two thousand black citizens each, and there were smaller communities in towns like Liverpool, Bristol and Wolverhampton. Five years later, however, the picture had changed dramatically. In most major cities the black population had doubled, and in the capital it had increased to forty thousand. The most striking increase, though, was in Birmingham, where the West Indian community had grown almost fourfold, largely because the Midlands manufacturers needed cheap labour.[50] Communications between the West Indian communities in Britain and their kinsfolk in the Caribbean were extremely effective: whenever new jobs became available, word would be sent back to the islands, and migrant workers would arrive within about three months armed with the addresses of the friends with whom they intended to stay. West Indian immigrants essentially tried to recreate their family, village and island networks, so that by the late fifties any newcomer would know that Jamaicans lived in Clapham and Brixton, Trinidadians in Notting Hill, Dominicans and St Lucians near Paddington, St Vincentians in High Wycombe, Nevis islanders in Leeds and Leicester, and so on.[51] All these areas had efficient transport links and cheap, readily available, if rather scruffy, housing, often shared late Victorian properties, since no one worker could afford to rent more than a single room. The various Caribbean communities were also spread across wide areas, even within the major cities like London and Birmingham. There was no tightly concentrated and delineated black ghetto in Britain that was even vaguely comparable with the situation in American cities. As early as 1958, for example, West Indians already lived in all but two of the twenty-eight metropolitan boroughs of inner London.[52] This was not, however, the case with the Indian and Pakistani immigrants that followed during the sixties. These groups tended to settle in specific suburbs rather than inner cities, and for cultural reasons were much more densely concentrated. Spitalfields and Southall were, as we have seen, already popular with East Pakistanis and Punjabis respectively, and the latter in particular became renowned for its dense concentration of Sikh immigrants. East African and Bangladeshi Asians fleeing the turmoil of their homelands in the late sixties and early seventies tended to settle in or near existing Asian communities, for understandable reasons, and so suburban areas of London like Neasden, Wembley and Norwood became extremely popular with Asian workers.[53]

In Britain as a whole the pattern was extremely inconsistent. Twenty years after the arrival of the *Empire Windrush*, almost half of the black and Asian population lived in London, with a further fifth in the West Midlands and the rest scattered throughout the larger cities or industrial towns of central and northern England. Bradford and Rochdale, for instance, had disproportionately large Pakistani populations, while Wolverhampton was a popular destination not only for Caribbean migrants but also for both Indians and Pakistanis. By contrast, very few black or Asian workers settled in rural Wales or Scotland, East Anglia or the West Country. Since these areas were predominantly agricultural, there was little demand for cheap unskilled labour.[54] In the more popular immigrant neighbourhoods, however, their presence was unmistakable. Edinburgh, Glasgow and Bedford all had their Italian areas, and some streets of London might have been transplanted from Cyprus. Moss Side in Manchester, formerly a middle-class Victorian suburb, had by the sixties acquired the nickname of the 'Black Belt'; similarly, Nicholson Street in the Gorbals, Glasgow, was known as the 'Burma Road' because it had attracted so many Indians and Pakistanis. In these centres of immigrant settlement, whether suburbs like Southall in London or Handsworth and Balsall Heath in Birmingham, or mill towns

like Bradford and Huddersfield, there sprang up all manner of establishments specifically aimed at the migrant community: travel agents, banks
and grocers; clothes, jewellery and record shops; cinemas, restaurants, cafés
and clubs.[55] All of this was not especially remarkable; immigrant communities everywhere, like the Italians or the Irish in Boston and New York,
establish similar institutions. Nonetheless, even some sympathetic British
observers found visiting the immigrant areas to be extremely disconcerting.
The sociologist Sheila Patterson, for instance, visited Brixton in May 1955
and recorded her impressions:

> As I turned off the main shopping street, I was immediately overcome
> with a sense of strangeness, even of shock. The street was a fairly typi-
> cal South London side-street, grubby and narrow, lined with cheap
> cafés, shabby pubs, and flashy clothing-shops. All this was normal
> enough. But what struck one so forcibly was that, apart from some
> shopping housewives and a posse of teddy boys in tight jeans outside
> the billiard hall, almost everybody in sight had a coloured skin. Waiting
> near the employment exchange were about two dozen black men,
> most in the flimsy suits of exaggerated cut that, as I was later to learn,
> denoted their recent arrival. At least half of the exuberant infants play-
> ing outside the pre-fab day nursery were *café noir* or *café au lait* in
> colouring. And there were coloured men and women wherever I
> looked, shopping, strolling, or gossiping on the sunny street-corners
> with an animation that most Londoners lost long ago . . . [I] experi-
> enced a profound reaction of something unexpected and alien.[56]

*

The newcomers who arrived at British docks and airports during the fifties
and sixties inevitably made their mark on national society and culture. It is
important to remember that this was not simply a case of a homogeneous
society being radically transformed from a drab monoculture into a multi-
cultural paradise. Britain was already a nation of immigrants, with many
thousands of black and Asian citizens as well as Continental Europeans and
others. Since Britain was a trading nation and an imperial power, it was
natural that its national culture should already be a mixture of native traditions and cosmopolitan borrowings, as the example of the English
language, with its splendid mongrel vocabulary of Scandinavian, German,
French and even Indian words, might suggest. That said, the influx of so

many Caribbean and South Asian Britons was bound to have a cultural impact, whether it be on British music, art, literature, language or behaviour.

Of all the areas of British life affected by the migrants, none was so quickly or visibly transformed as the nation's diet. Even those Britons who resented the newcomers as unwelcome invaders were often converted to the delights of their cooking. In the first edition of the *Good Food Guide*, published in 1951, just eleven of the 484 restaurants listed outside London were dedicated to foreign food, and only one of them served food from outside the European continent.[57] In the three decades that followed, the establishment of Chinese and Indian restaurants reflected the increasing wealth of those communities and also furthered the cause of multi-racial co-operation, as native white Britons learned to appreciate the tastes of their new neighbours. At the same time, it is implausible that Chinese and Indian cuisine would have taken off to such an extent had it not been for the fact that affluent Britons were eating out more and more, not merely as a break from cooking themselves, but also as a form of entertainment. Such was the demand for exotic tastes, in fact, that many Chinese immigrants came to Britain in the fifties and sixties specifically to work in the catering trade, before then moving into business for themselves.[58]

According to the historian Colin Holmes, the first recorded Chinese restaurant was established in Forfar Street, Liverpool at the turn of the century.[59] The acknowledged pioneer of Anglo-Chinese cuisine, however, was Chung Koon, a ship's cook who married an English girl, settled in London and opened Maxim's in Soho in 1908. Maxim's appealed to a relatively wealthy, bohemian crowd, and it was thinly disguised as the eponymous establishment in Anthony Powell's novel of literary London between the wars, *Casanova's Chinese Restaurant* (1960). But Chung Koon had few competitors, and not until after the Second World War did the taste for Chinese food begin to spread across the country and into middle- and working-class areas. In 1958, Chung Koon's son John opened the first really upmarket Chinese restaurant, the Lotus House in Soho, catering to Chinese diplomats and businessmen on expense accounts, and its great popularity suggested that there was an expanding market for exotic cuisine at cheaper prices. By bringing unskilled immigrants over to work long hours in the kitchens, Koon was able to keep costs to a minimum, and at the same time he borrowed the takeaway principle from traditional fish and chip shops. Having launched the first takeaway in Queensway in 1958, he then persuaded

Butlin's to open a Chinese kitchen in every holiday camp, offering a simple menu of chicken chop suey and chips. This was a masterstroke: the families who stayed at Butlin's were predominantly working and lower-middle class, and, having acquired a taste for the exotic while on holiday, they were keen to repeat the experience at home. By the end of the 1960s, therefore, Chinese cooking had been converted from a bohemian taste into a mass-market experience, and cheap Chinese takeaways had been opened in most major towns, from the Empire Palace in Chelmsford to the New Happy Gathering in Station Street, Birmingham and Ping On in Deanhaugh Street, Edinburgh. Not all customers were equally adventurous, of course, so most establishments found it necessary to serve fish and chips as well.[60]

The success of Chinese entrepreneurs with their inexpensive restaurants and takeaways proved an inspiration for other immigrant communities, notable examples including the Cypriots and the South Asians. The most remarkable success story was the enormous popularity of Indian food, with the numbers of restaurants escalating from a few hundred in 1960 to twelve hundred in 1970 and a staggering ten thousand by the end of the century.[61] Elements of Indian cuisine were actually already established in Britain before the Second World War, thanks mainly to the British imperial experience in the subcontinent from the eighteenth century onwards. The first recipe for 'currey' in English, for instance, was published in *Glasse's Art of Cookery* in 1747, and in 1861 Mrs Beeton included no fewer than fourteen curry recipes in her *Book of Household Management*.[62]

The first recorded Indian restaurant of the twentieth century was the Salut e Hind in Holborn in 1911, but the most influential establishment opened in Regent Street seven years later. Veeraswamy's Indian Restaurant, the first South Asian restaurant aimed at British diners, was a great success, especially among soldiers and officials who had served in India and nick-named it their 'curry club'. It also functioned as a training school for Indian cooks and restaurant staff, many of whom were sailors who had settled in England. Such was its success that before the Second World War the first South Asian chain had been established by the Bahadur brothers, with Taj Mahal restaurants in Oxford, Brighton and Northampton and Kohinoor restaurants in London, Cambridge and Manchester. As with Chinese cook-ing, the popularity of Indian restaurants owed much to the development of eating out as a leisure activity for the middle classes, and during the fifties and sixties hundreds of new establishments were set up throughout Britain and especially in areas of high South Asian settlement. Manchester, Glasgow and many southern English towns all had Indian restaurants before 1939, while Birmingham had to wait until 1945 and Bradford and Cardiff until the 1950s.[63]

Restaurant ownership generally followed the lines of local settlement. In Southall, the centre of the Sikh community in Britain, most restaurants were owned by Punjabis, but in the rest of the capital, and in southern England generally, Bangladeshi restaurants predominated. In Birmingham and the West Midlands, the restaurant business was divided between Bangladeshis and Pakistanis; in the major Northern cities like Manchester and Bradford, the restaurateurs were Pakistani, Kashmiri or North Indian; and in Glasgow, the eating establishments were almost entirely Punjabi. In fact, despite all the talk of an Indian restaurant boom, more than three-quarters of the restaurants were owned by Sylhetti villagers from Bangladesh, and to call them all 'Indian', therefore, was useful but inaccurate shorthand. Menus were inexpensive, filling and often rudimentary; many people enjoyed the exotic atmosphere but still preferred to eat egg and chips rather than strange, spicy food. Khan's Curry Centre in Stockport, for example, offered a basic choice of 'Plain, Madras and Biriyani Curry Dishes' with chicken, beef, prawn, scampi or egg, as well as either roast or fried chicken and chips, all priced at between five and seven shillings.[64]

As for the curries themselves, they often bore little relation to what was actually eaten in the South Asian subcontinent. The very word *curry* is almost never used in India, and its etymology remains uncertain. As far back as the eighteenth century, Britons had already developed their own recipes for curry, usually a thick sauce with spices, almonds and raisins, and a curry powder made from coriander seeds, cayenne, cardamom, turmeric, ginger and saffron had been commercially available since 1780. Not only were South Asian cooks compelled to offer chicken and chips during the 1950s and 1960s, but they also had to satisfy customers' demands for thick, creamy curries of this traditional kind. Two other innovations were the development of tandoori dishes and the creation of chicken tikka masala, supposedly the most popular of all British national dishes by the end of the twentieth century. Veeraswamy's was the first institution to serve tandoori chicken in Britain in 1959, and by the early seventies most Indian restaurants in the country had installed enormous brick-walled *tandoors* to the apparent delight of their customers. Chicken tikka masala, meanwhile, is a dish entirely unknown in South Asia and is essentially a mixture of chicken tikka pieces with a rich, creamy and colourful sauce, moderately spiced but not hot. An enormous army of competing Bangladeshi chefs have advanced claims to be recognised as the inventor of chicken tikka masala; perhaps it is best to steer clear of this potential scholarly minefield and conclude simply that the dish was developed during the late 1960s as a means of marrying British tastes with Indian culinary traditions.[65]

The popularity of Chinese and Indian cooking during the sixties is one of the obvious success stories of post-war immigration. It is easy, however, to underestimate the difficulties and unhappiness that many newcomers encountered when they came to Britain. The Trinidadian novelist Samuel Selvon recorded the daily hopes and disappointments of his fellow West Indians in his book *The Lonely Londoners* (1956), the title of which itself suggests the insecurity of migration and settlement. Most immigrants had never before been compelled to think of their own colour as a badge of identity; many had never even thought of themselves as 'black' but instead defined themselves by their village, island or region of origin; but they were now physically identifiable as strangers in a country where most people regarded black and brown people as inherently inferior.[66] As if that were not dislocation enough, most migrants originally came from poor rural areas.[67] Once in Britain, however, they were concentrated in urban areas that could hardly have been more unlike their home villages and where the landscape, the social conventions and the cultural life of the local community were totally different from what they were used to. Whereas the economies of the Caribbean islands, say, had been based on agriculture, cottage industries and handicrafts, the industrialised society of post-war Britain, with its mines and mills and factories, was a bewildering experience. West Indian immigrants brought with them the 'pardner' system of saving and drawing capital, by which a group of people would all regularly contribute money to a communal pool and then take turns at drawing a 'hand' from it. As one account observes, this was 'a model of social organisation which depended on a high level of personal knowledge, mutual trust and friendship', but it offered rural immigrants a valuable support system in an urban, industrial society where it was easy to feel anonymous, confused and isolated.[68]

Even skilled migrant workers found themselves stuck in tedious manual jobs. Labour shortages in the NHS meant that doctors and nurses could quickly find work, but more than half of all immigrants in the mid-fifties were compelled to settle for jobs that did not make full use of their skills.[69] One man who moved from Pakistan to Nottingham in 1962 later recalled that he went from being a customs inspector to a British Railways cleaner; eventually he gave up and went into business for himself. He explained:

> I knew I wasn't going to get any better jobs. I had seen qualified people – BA, MA, LLB, people who had been teachers, barristers – and not one of them got proper work. They were labourers, bus conductors, railway cleaners and so on. The jobs we got were always the worst, even if we were educated people who could read and write much better than the people who were in charge. They knew I had been an inspector of Customs, but that didn't matter.[70]

Another man, a Sikh who left Nairobi for Walthamstow in 1958, considered himself very fortunate to have landed the job of a postman and was struck by the erudition of his colleagues:

> After me a number of very well-educated Indians, mainly teachers, started to come and work at the Post Office. There were soon five or six of us, and they would all be talking about their qualifications – 'I've got a degree in this, I've got a degree in that' – and all of us were postmen. I was the only one without a degree. Their degrees were useless here, their careers were ruined – they couldn't follow them up.[71]

Generalising about the immigrant experience is, of course, tremendously difficult, but it is clear that many people were simply not prepared for the experience of loneliness and insecurity that came with moving to an industrialised, urban European country like Britain. Tryphena Anderson, a Jamaican woman who landed in Liverpool in 1952 and ended up working as a nurse in Nottingham, found that 'you weren't a person, you were a darkie':

> I wish I could be back home so bad it hurts, tears came into your eyes, because you missed the sort of freedom and companionship that you used to have, you know, with your own kind. One day I was on a bus, and I was upstairs and I was at the corner of Parliament Street, and I saw a black man. Although I was used to the very small community, I just felt, if only this bus would stop, I would get off it and just run and hug him, and find out, you know, where he came from. Because you feel lost, you know.[72]

Others did find it easier to make friends in the white community. Mike Phillips recalled that his Caribbean mother happily spent her days chatting to her colleagues in a sewing workshop, a German refugee couple and an Irish woman. 'Sometimes I went to meet her when she had something to carry home', he wrote, 'or when I was passing at the right time, and walking home, I used to listen to her talk with a feeling of surprise. She had never, in my experience, talked so much and so freely . . . She laughed a lot, too . . . Later on, thinking about her, it struck me that I'd probably never seen her so happy as in those times when her life was changing so much.'[73]

Tryphena Anderson's experience of being relegated from a 'person' to a 'darkie', however, was all too common. English or British xenophobia was as old as national identity; even during the Middle Ages, the English were notorious for their dislike of foreigners who visited their island kingdom.[74] Many modern historians, following the arguments of Edward Said in his influential book *Orientalism*, agree that the British built their imperial identity by contrasting their own virtues with the supposed wickedness, indolence, infantilism and corruption of their subjugated colonial peoples.[75] Racial stereotypes were central to the British outlook during the heyday of the Empire, and by the end of the nineteenth century not only was it perfectly acceptable to refer to Indians and Africans as 'wogs' and 'niggers', but biological racism had itself become a carefully codified scientific convention.[76] The superiority of the white Anglo-Saxon was, even in the middle of the twentieth century, taken as read; indeed, the assertion of a common racial identity was one way for British politicians to reach across class boundaries and appeal to different constituencies.[77] Racial prejudices often lurked behind the most self-consciously noble of imperial ideals. Even the Labour Chancellor Hugh Dalton described the colonies in 1950 as 'pullulating poverty stricken, diseased nigger communities', and one British serviceman sent to South Asia recalled his sergeant major's advice that 'wogs were very weedy and if we hit one we should not hit too hard in case we killed him'.[78] In Paul Scott's novel of the Empire in India, *The Birds of Paradise* (1962), the young narrator's father tells him that they are like the Romans in Britain, teaching the natives to rule themselves. The boy is pleased with the analogy, because 'the Romans were fine fellows'. But later in the novel his Roman nobility slips and prejudice resurfaces. Challenged by the son of a rajah, he angrily and sincerely shouts back: 'I can lick you any time, because I'm British and you are only a wog.'[79]

So although popular tradition in the twentieth century held that Britain was a uniquely tolerant and welcoming haven for foreign refugees from poverty, oppression and persecution, the fact was that immigrants were usually the objects of suspicion, prejudice and contempt.[80] Just as in the United States, British racist campaigns often reflected deeper insecurities about sexual inferiority and miscegenation; as early as the thirties the Anti-Slavery League had been agitating for restrictions on black immigration on sexual and biological grounds.[81] What was more, most Britons had been educated to believe that they were simply superior, and it was therefore difficult for them to accept black or Asian competitors for jobs and housing. There had been frequent anti-Chinese riots in ports like Cardiff and Liverpool during the early years of the century, and in the late 1940s the Maltese community had been popularly condemned as vicious pimps and gangsters.[82] Well before the peak of Commonwealth immigration, many hotels, restaurants, dance halls and landlords operated a discreet colour bar: in 1948, for example, a West African lecturer at London University won an apology from Rule's Restaurant in Covent Garden after he was barred from dining there.[83]

Thanks to the popularity of films and novels about the experience of empire and the reliance on imperial history in schools, it is extremely likely that almost all native Britons had strong preconceptions about black and Asian immigrants. Residual affection for the old colonies remained a considerable force in shaping public opinion: as late as 1956, opinion polls still suggested that more than two-thirds of the population supported the principle of unrestricted entry for Commonwealth citizens, although this was to fall in subsequent years.[84] At the same time, many members of the British public were strikingly ignorant about the newcomers and their homelands. One Jamaican student was constantly asked how many wives he had by Londoners astonished to find that he spoke English, and a Jamaican bus conductor had his hair patted so often for luck by his passengers that he feared going bald. The East Pakistani community in Spitalfields, meanwhile, was nicknamed 'Little Singapore'.[85] 'Of course,' one Huddersfield man told an interviewer, 'since this Mau Mau business we've got something against the Jamaicans. We're not so keen on them.'[86] This kind of ignorance often came as a shock to immigrant workers who had been told time and again that the British were a wise and benevolent people; but what was even more shocking was the strength of racial prejudice among white Britons. The sociologist Sheila Patterson explained in 1963:

A coloured skin, especially when combined with Negroid features, is associated with alienness, and with the lowest social status. Primitiveness, savagery, violence, sexuality, general lack of control, sloth, irresponsibility – all these are part of the image. On the more favourable side, Negroid peoples are often credited with athletic, artistic and musical gifts, and with an appealing and childlike simplicity which is no way incompatible with the remainder of the image.[87]

The very speech of Caribbean immigrants was regarded as 'careless', 'babyish' and 'slovenly', and despite the fact that the British were notorious for their refusal to learn foreign languages, the inability of immigrants to speak perfect, idiomatic English was seen as comical or suspicious.[88] During the fifties, West Indians were thought to be more intelligent and industrious than Indian and Pakistani immigrants, partly because they were perceived to have more 'English ways'. Civil servants praised Caribbean workers for their 'skilled character and proven industry', but South Asians were described as 'lazy . . . feckless individuals who make a beeline for National Assistance'.[89]

Among the public at large, almost all immigrant groups were viewed with considerable suspicion and hostility. British racial prejudice of the fifties and sixties often reflected sexual insecurity and fears of drugs, and, like the Maltese during the forties, black and Asian immigrants were often presented as cunning, unscrupulous sexual predators bent on the conquest of white women. A female social worker in Brixton explained to Sheila Patterson: 'Local people don't like the coloured men's attitude to women. You can't go along certain streets, even in broad daylight, without every second one making remarks and suggestions, whether you look the type or not. And local people say they are getting more noisy and aggressive as the numbers go up.'[90] Miscegenation was, of course, seen as the ultimate taboo. 'If you don't stop doing that, I'll run away with a black man,' one mother used to tell her naughty children.[91] In the film *Flame in the Streets* (1961), a young woman appals her mother by announcing that she plans to marry a black teacher. The violence of the mother's reaction is even more intense than the aggression of the Teddy Boys whose attack on the immigrant community marks the climax of the film. 'I'm ashamed of you,' she shrieks. 'When I think of you and that man sharing the same bed . . . It's filthy . . . disgusting . . . It makes my stomach turn over . . . I want to be sick.'[92]

Racial discrimination in the late fifties obviously drew on British cultural traditions that represented non-white peoples as simple, bestial, cunning, indolent, sexually voracious, unreliable, dirty and aggressive. White Britons complained that the newcomers stuck together and did not mix with local people, but, given the persistence of racial prejudice, this was hardly surprising. There were also genuine cultural differences between the different communities that gave rise to further hostility. Immigrants were criticised for their flashy clothes, extravagant friendliness, exuberant behaviour and pungent cuisine. Caribbean settlers in particular were associated with drug-taking, boisterous parties, loud music and sexual wantonness; in part this simply reflected differing attitudes to public and private space and the difficulties of adjusting to a cramped urban environment where privacy and domesticity were prized above all. As Mike and Trevor Phillips have pointed out, however, the fact that there were so few West Indian women among the first immigrants meant that there was a large pool of young single men, freed from the constraints of wives and mothers that had hitherto controlled their social behaviour.[93] By the end of the decade, nearly forty thousand immigrants were arriving a year, and since they were concentrated in poor, working-class communities, this only intensified the competition for jobs and accommodation.

It was in housing, in fact, that racial discrimination was most evident, not least because cheap housing was in such short supply after the devastation of the Blitz. In the London housing market, discrimination was the norm, and it was perfectly common to see the phrases 'No Coloureds' or 'Whites Only' in newspaper advertisements or on cards posted on newsagents' noticeboards. In 1953, a survey revealed that almost 85 per cent of London landladies would not let rooms to students who were 'very dark Africans or West Indians', and a similar survey in Birmingham found only fifteen out of one thousand people prepared to let rooms to non-white immigrants.[94] Cecil Holness, a Jamaican motor mechanic and a married man, saw a note in a shop window advertising a room, telephoned the landlady and immediately went to the house. The door was opened by a 'frightened' woman who told him:

'Oh, I'm so sorry. You are just five minutes late. The room is taken.'
So I said to her, I said, 'Madam, do you see that telephone kiosk down there?' She said, 'Yes.' I said, 'That's where I was phoning from and I did not see anyone come to your door like that.'
So she paused for a while and said, 'Well, I don't want black people.'

I said, 'Why not say so?' I said, 'You'd have saved me all that trouble of making all my own way here.' She said, 'We don't want any black people.' I say, 'You should have let me know.' I said, 'It's your place. I can't force you to let me rooms.'[95]

Official sources did not bother to deny that discrimination existed. The Ministry of Labour leaflet *How to Adjust Yourself in Britain* (1954) even explained to immigrants: 'You may be refused because you are coloured. You must expect to meet this in Britain.'[96] But most people, unlike the landlady in the anecdote quoted above, were reluctant to admit that they were prejudiced. The Caribbean writer A. G. Bennett complained in 1959:

Since I come 'ere I never met a single English person who 'ad any colour prejudice. Once, I walked the whole length of a street looking for a room, and everyone told me that he or she 'ad no prejudice against coloured people. It was the neighbour who was stupid. If we could only find the 'neighbour' we could solve the entire problem. But to find 'im is the trouble! Neighbours are the worst people to live beside in this country.[97]

Two years later, a sketch in *Beyond the Fringe* mocked the same phenomenon. 'Excuse me, I am from the London School of Economics and I am looking for lodgings for students,' says Jonathan Miller. 'I'm sorry,' replies Alan Bennett, 'I don't take coloured people, but don't think it's because of what the neighbours say; it's me, I am prejudiced.'[98]

Even when an immigrant worker had found a room, he then faced the problem of overcharging. Black tenants were usually charged more than their white contemporaries even though they were sharing a single room with other occupants. Where a white man might pay £1 a week, a black worker would pay £2, and in 1955 cases were reported of six Caribbean men paying 25 shillings each to share a single room.[99] Cecil Holness recalled:

You move around a lot because people didn't give you a lot of time. You say thirty bob a week, somebody would come and say two pounds. And, of course, when your wages is about five or six pounds a week, to pay two pounds, that's a lot, so you've got to go around and look, because in those days, it's either two or three of you in a room, in those days, as a black man, it's very hard to get a room, you wouldn't get one. They always put on the board, 'Black – Niggers not wanted here,' on the board, you know, these boards out there, 'No Niggers', or 'No Colour', things like that. So it's very hard to get a room.[100]

In fact the newcomers almost always found somewhere to bed down, if only temporarily. In 1955 a survey of West Indian immigrants in London found that more than two-thirds had 'no trouble finding housing when they arrived', and almost half were satisfied that their rent was reasonable. Many migrants were also beginning to think of buying their own houses, and some set themselves up as landlords for their fellow newcomers. But even here, conditions were cramped, dirty and unsanitary, and overcharging was rife. 'Colour premiums' charged when immigrants tried to buy properties might add £50 or £100 to the purchase price of a house, and Caribbean and Asian families were usually confined to the same poor, shabby areas.[101] One white Brixton woman told Sheila Patterson: 'Our street is getting "hot" – the blacks are beginning to move in and we'll have to sell while the going's good.'[102] A Gallup poll in September 1958 suggested that only one in ten people would move house if 'coloured people' came to live next door. On the other hand, when asked if they would move if 'coloured people came to live in great numbers in your district', 28 per cent said they would definitely move, another 28 per cent said they might do so, and 44 per cent said they would not. 'White flight' was not simply a matter of prejudice, since many householders believed that the threat posed by immigrants to local property prices left them with no choice but to move to a different area. Nevertheless, it is hard to deny that racial prejudice played its part.[103]

Discrimination on racial grounds was also common in employment and public entertainment. Since mass immigration was a comparatively recent phenomenon, there was little legal provision for breaking down racial inequities. In Nottingham, for example, the local labour exchange treated black and white applicants entirely separately and assumed that immigrants were fit only for unskilled, manual jobs.[104] There was an unofficial colour bar on British Railways platforms, where jobs were reserved for white porters and officials only. Some pubs and dance clubs also tried to institute a colour bar, although local magistrates almost always disapproved and threatened to withdraw their licence if the bar was not dropped. In February 1958, a Mr Das Gupta, an Indian student, vociferously complained when he was refused entry to the Scala Ballroom in Wolverhampton even though the ballroom presented entertainment by black singers and musicians. A spokesman for the Scala explained: 'The rest of the people in the ballroom just don't want to know coloured people.'[105] When the singer Adam Faith published his autobiography in 1961, he recalled that he had received a letter from a Maori girl asking whether there was 'a colour bar in your fan club', since she was a 'real-gone teenager'. Faith assured his readers that there 'certainly is no colour bar, and there never will be', but the very fact that she thought that there might have been a colour bar is revealing enough.[106] It takes little imagination to picture the frustration and unhappiness of those who were forced to put up with such treatment. One schoolboy of West African origin later recalled that in Forest Gate, London, 'there were certain roads I couldn't go along, like round the Romford Road. I'd be pelted with bricks and bottles. "Get out, blackie, nigger, nigger, nigger."'[107] 'You felt surrounded all the time, in those days,' remembered Rudy Braithwaite, a Barbadian osteopath. 'You felt that you were an intruder and, truly, you were a foreigner. You did not belong, but you had to bear it.'[108]

    Violence against immigrants was not unknown. In May 1948 a crowd of 250 young men stoned a house in Birmingham where a group of Indians had been living, and during the August bank holiday of the same year there were street brawls between Caribbean and Irish workers in Liverpool. There was an especially nasty outbreak in July 1949, when a mob of one thousand white men besieged a group of blacks in a hostel in Deptford Broadway for several nights. Seven years later, in Camden Town, two houses were set on fire as a gang of whites tried to force Caribbean families out of their homes.[109] The most violent episodes, however, took place in 1958 in Nottingham and North Kensington, London. There were four major areas of West Indian settlement in the North Kensington area in the late fifties: Kensal New Town, Notting Dale, Golborne and Notting Hill. Most were clustered around the northern Portobello Road and to the east of Ladbroke Grove, an area often described, with slight inaccuracy, simply as Notting Hill. This was not a pleasant area; it had been sinking into crime, decay and prostitution long before the *Empire Windrush* arrived at Tilbury, and its poor white population lived to a much lower standard than most working-class Londoners. It was quite simply a slum, stinking with dirt and disease and infested with rats and litter, its large Victorian houses crammed to the seams with ill-paid or unemployed workers and their families. Most of the men who lived there worked for the railways, London Transport or the Post Office, while the women had domestic jobs in cafés and hospitals. Affluent workers moved out of the area as quickly as they could, and there were considerable populations of Polish and Irish workers as well as West Indians. Within one house there might be twenty people, all sharing one bathroom and kitchen in dreadful conditions. One resident, for instance, recalled growing up with 'nineteen children and eleven grown-ups in nine rooms'. There was no bathroom; two families had to cook on the landing; and there was only one toilet for thirty people.[110] Crime was rife among the crumbling houses; for one thing, the area lay at the end of a long strip of prostitution that ran from Soho to Shepherd's Bush. On one evening in November 1958, the police counted seventy-three prostitutes on the short stretch of Holland Park Avenue running through Notting Hill.[111] Not only was the area inadequately policed, but it also attracted a transient population of 'floating' workers, single men who moved from house to house across London to find employment. It was hardly surprising that it was such a violent and insalubrious place.[112]

Life in Notting Hill and the surrounding areas was dominated, as one historian puts it, by 'poverty, rootlessness, violence and crime'.[113] The attraction of the area to Caribbean immigrants was simply that it was cheap; at the same time, the notoriously unscrupulous landlord Peter Rachman, a Polish refugee who owned several dozen properties in the area, had let it be known that he was quite happy to let to black workers and their families. As the numbers of migrants arriving in Britain increased, so did the flow into Notting Hill. Competition for housing was fierce; under the 1957 Rent Act, landlords were permitted to evict long-standing tenants of unfurnished rooms in order to install furnished lettings, which in prac- tice meant that white tenants at controlled rents were making way for immigrants at exorbitant ones. If tenants refused to leave, Rachman usu- ally sent in a gang of wrestlers and boxers to persuade them to think again. Once he ripped the roof off one of his houses to force the old tenants to depart; on another occasion, the tenants fought back by 'sawing up a stair- case and electrifying it with metal fittings' to stop his thugs from evicting a frightened couple.[114] Most of his houses were appallingly overcrowded and in a state scarcely fit for human habitation; one report in *The Times* described the 'pitifully small room' where a tearful young woman lived with her husband:

There was no water, except for a cold tap in the backyard down three flights of dark rickety stairs. The one lavatory for the 11 people in the building was too filthy to use. Cooking facilities had to be shared. The house was rat-infested and the walls so ridden with bugs and beetles that the girl was afraid to replace the ancient wall-paper which helped to some extent to keep them from crawling into the room.[115]

'It was filthy, it was smelly, it was freezing cold in the winter and all we had for curtains was an old blanket,' remembered one man who arrived from Jamaica in 1961. 'We complained but nothing was done. And if you fell behind on the rent, men would come round with dogs to frighten you. We were terrified of the dogs.'[116] But for many immigrants, it was Rachman or the street. 'When doors slammed shut in your face and accommodation agencies code-marked your name as "undesirable"', Terri Quaye bitterly recalled twenty years later, 'a room could always be found by Rachman – with all the perks which ghetto housing brings – humiliation, despair and anger.'[117]

Since most of the black newcomers were young men, their social lives were predictably boisterous: dozens of informal basement shebeens, blues and ska clubs and gambling dens could be found in the network of streets around Ladbroke Grove and Westbourne Park. 'It was a wild life,' recalled one young Trinidadian:

> The police didn't take kindly to it. A lot of things made them annoyed. The music was too loud. They didn't like blacks, period, gathering in any kind of situation, and the selling of drinks which was outside the law, because you couldn't get a licence. So you had to break the law . . . The police used to regularly raid them, kick their boxes in, kick their speakers in, but that aggravated the blacks no end and gave them the determination to persevere and the whole police hatred came out of that.[118]

Not only were Caribbean immigrants the victims of crime, they were also occasionally themselves the perpetrators. In Ladbroke Grove, for instance, there were simmering battles between gangs of Dominicans, St Lucians and Trinidadians, and by the end of the decade rival black gangsters were running prostitution and drugs rings reaching from Notting Hill down to Park Lane.[119] In the Rachman houses, white prostitutes and West Indian men often lived together, an open affront to the guardians of white sexual morality. The involvement of Caribbean men in the prostitution racket therefore strengthened the existing stereotypes that associated immigrants with uncontrolled, predatory and subversive sexuality. To make matters worse, the North Kensington area was also a favourite haunt of the extreme right. Organisations like the British League of Ex-Servicemen and Women or the Union for British Freedom were organised from addresses in the neighbourhood; there were frequent, although ill-attended, public meetings; and it was common to see painted slogans like 'Keep Britain White' or 'KBW', 'Niggers Go Home' and 'Niggers Leave Our Girls Alone'.[120]

By the late fifties, 'nigger hunting' was on the increase. Teddy Boys, the teenage folk devils of the mid-fifties and the heirs of youthful delinquents like the nineteenth-century scuttlers and razor boys, were often associated with violence against immigrants, even though most of their aggression was directed at rival Teddy Boy gangs with whom they fought for territory.[121] Rudy Braithwaite was reading a book on the London Underground one evening when a gang of Teddy Boys came down the carriage:

> And once they'd got to me, of course, all the indigenous people got up, because some of them were elderly people and they were frightened. And two of them sat next to me, one on either side. And the first one went, 'Nigritta, Nigritta, Nigritta, Nigritta, Nigritta, Nigritta.' And the other one went, 'Catch a nigger by the toe, when he hollers let him go.' That's what they were saying. And I just went on reading the book. And then they got up, and one fellow put his hand on my head – like that – and they went on, up the tube, terrorising whoever they could.[122]

The racial disturbances of the summer of 1958, which many contemporary observers blamed on the Teddy Boys, began in earnest on 23 August in the St Ann's area of Nottingham. The city was suffering a slight recession, with several factories having closed down as it adjusted to an economy based on light engineering, and the St Ann's area was regarded as particularly poor and unattractive. According to a report in *Tribune* that September, it was a neighbourhood of 'small, cooped-up terrace houses with decaying brick-work, broken windows and inadequate sanitary arrangements . . . second-hand furniture shops, fish and chip shops, pubs, pawnbrokers'. In the crowded, 'decaying, crumbling air' of the district some two thousand West Indian immigrants were the targets of casual, occasional violence from gangs of white teenagers; indeed, there was even an unofficial curfew since black citizens caught walking through the streets late at night were liable to be attacked by self-styled 'nigger hunters'.[123] On 23 August, a Saturday night, a fight broke out as a pub was closing and a group of black men succeeded in putting seven of their white adversaries in hospital. An eighth casualty, a policeman, was run over by a car in the general mêlée. Within hours news of the affray had spread throughout the area and a mob of over a thousand white men and women had assembled with razors, knives and bottles, bent on attacking any West Indians that they could find. Fortunately there were relatively few casualties: only eight more people were injured, and none killed, and after several nights of tension the disturbances petered out.[124]

Both St Ann's and North Kensington were poor, dilapidated, areas; both had a mixed population of immigrants and poor whites; both were notable for 'gang fighting, illegal drinking clubs, gambling and prostitution'; and both had 'a large proportion of frightened and resentful residents'.[125] Racism alone does not explain the disturbances; they were as much a product of poverty and despair as they were a reflection of racial prejudice. In St Ann's, white gangs had attacked one another when they could not find black victims on whom to vent their aggression. Similarly, crime and disaffection in the North Kensington area predated the arrival of several thousand West Indian immigrants. By 1958, however, the resentment of the local population was being expressed above all in terms of racial prejudice, thanks not least to the efforts of right-wing organisations like Sir Oswald Mosley's Union Movement. Television also helped to popularise the racist idiom; by covering the St Ann's disturbances in great depth, television reporters drew public attention to the issues of racial conflict and public violence and unwittingly presented the events as models for emulation.[126] There were numerous reports of simmering tension in London following the events at St Ann's, and on Sunday 24 August the Metropolitan Police stopped several cars of young white men heading to west London with malice aforethought. One car contained a group of nine 'nigger hunters' aged between seventeen and twenty, mainly from Notting Dale and the White City estate. They were carrying a knife, several table and chair legs, a car starting-handle and a couple of iron street railings, and had already attacked five Caribbean men in

Shepherd's Bush and Ladbroke Grove. This should have been a warning of events to come.[127]

Between 24 August and the following Saturday the situation in North Kensington was quiet, the simple reason being that many people were too busy at work to worry about starting a mass brawl. At around midnight on 30 August, however, scuffles broke out in the streets of Notting Dale, the smallest of all the West Indian communities in the area, and therefore the easiest for young whites to attack.[128] Crowds of up to four hundred men laid siege to Caribbean homes with milk bottles, iron bars and knives, eventually being repelled by the police and their own exhaustion. The following night the violence was even worse, as gangs roamed the streets of the area listening for the telltale music of West Indian parties and then attacking the houses with bricks, knives and now even petrol bombs. Many of the perpetrators were young working-class men who had come to the area especially to cause trouble, while white residents came out of their houses to watch, cheer and point out potential targets. According to *The Times*, a kind of running commentary and encouragement was being provided by groups of older men singing racist songs and shouting 'Keep Britain White'.[129]

Since it was a bank-holiday weekend, the fighting did not end on Sunday evening, but instead continued for two more nights, the last flurry coming on Tuesday 2 September. On both the Monday and the Tuesday, mobs of several thousand people were reported wandering the streets of Notting Hill and Notting Dale, indiscriminately hurling milk bottles and petrol bombs and hunting for immigrant victims. The reporter for the local *Kensington News* captured the scene:

> As I turned into Bramley Road I saw a mob of over 700 men, women and children stretching 200 yards along the road. Young children of ten were treating the whole affair as a great joke and shouting, 'Come on, let's get the blacks and the coppers. Let's get on with it.' In the middle of the screaming, jeering youths and adults, a speaker from the Union Movement was urging his excited audience to 'get rid of them' (the coloured people). Groups of policemen stood at strategic points carefully watching the 'meeting' while police cars and Black Marias waited round the corner.
>
> Suddenly, hundreds of leaflets were thrown over the crowd, a fierce cry rent the air and the mob rushed off in the direction of Latimer

Road, shouting 'Kill the niggers!' Women grabbed their small children and chased after their menfolk. Dogs ran in among the crowds barking. Everywhere there was riotous confusion . . .

Within half an hour the mob which had by now swelled to uncontrollable numbers had broken scores of windows and set upon two negroes who were lucky to escape with cuts and bruises. Women from the top floor windows laughed as they called down to the thousand strong crowd, 'Go on boys, get yourself some blacks.' As the crowd swung into Blenheim Crescent milk bottles rained down from tenement buildings where coloured men were sheltering. Accompanied by a dozen bottles, down came a petrol-bomb in the middle of the mob. One eighteen-year-old youth was led away with blood streaming from a head wound.[130]

The most dramatic single incident of the riots involved a black student, Seymour Manning, who took refuge in a greengrocer's shop from a group of pursuers. According to the *Manchester Guardian*, a moment later 'the shopkeeper's wife . . . appeared in the doorway, locked the door behind her, and turned to face the trio of toughs'. A crowd quickly assembled in front of the shop, shouting 'Lynch him!' and demanding that the greengrocer's wife give up their victim, but with the assistance of a housewife friend and 'a boy in his teens', this redoubtable woman fended off the besieging forces until the police arrived to escort Manning to safety.[131]

After Tuesday 2 September, the passions of the riots were largely spent, although there were sporadic scuffles on the fringes of the district and in areas like Shepherd's Bush and Paddington for a few more evenings. There had been, fortunately, no fatal casualties, a striking contrast with the riots in American cities during the sixties with which the Notting Hill disturbances are often compared. Some 140 people were arrested, most of whom were clearly white aggressors, but some of whom were West Indians who had responded to provocation or were caught carrying weapons for their own protection; a small minority were whites who had actually been defending their black neighbours.[132] Many of the white rioters did not in fact live in Notting Hill or Notting Dale, but had come from places like Tottenham, Acton, Barnes, Hayes and Greenford; in other words, there were many suburban youths who had made the trip especially to join in the carnage. The *Kensington News* reported that 'gangs of hooligans from all over London came to join in. They came on foot, by train, bus, motorbike, car and lorry, shouting, "Alright boys, we're here."' The youths on motor-bikes or in cars, the report continued, 'toured the district looking for coloured people. When they found them they went back to tell their friends.'[133]

The press generally chose to interpret the riots in the context of the con-temporary obsession with teenage delinquents. *The Times* noted that the arrested youths had given up a collection of 'flick knives, stilettos, razors, bicycle chains, choppers, a club and a carving knife', the first four of which were already associated in the popular imagination with everyday teenage violence.[134] Working-class adolescents, apparently more affluent, sexually active and self-confident than ever before, were during the late fifties equated with aggression and social conflict, and so the stereotype of the delinquent hooligan became an easy scapegoat for the events of August and September. Few commentators blamed poverty, working-class white cul-ture or the circumstances of immigration and settlement for the disturbances; instead, almost all observers attributed the riots to hooligans and Teddy Boys, even though the Teddy Boy fashion had by 1958 long passed its peak. An editorial in the *Daily Mirror* declared that the riots had been the responsibility of 'white hooligans . . . spineless louts and bully boys, with their razors and broken bottles', while a front-page cartoon showed Hitler's ghost addressing a 'racialist thug' in full Teddy Boy regalia. 'Go on, boy,' the late Führer is saying. 'I may have lost the war but my ideas seem to be winning.'[135]

In the aftermath of the Notting Hill riots, many black activists recog-nised that self-defence had to become a priority, and West Indian vigilante groups were established to patrol the area or to escort black London Transport employees who worked very late hours. During the next few years, a multitude of support groups and political organisations sprang up among the Caribbean community, reflecting their renewed determination to fight for their place in British society.[136] Another indication of the new interest in racism and race relations was the foundation of the Institute for Race Relations in 1958, which became, at least for the media, the spearhead of the fight against racism for the following decades. Barely a month after the Notting Hill disturbances, the institute published a report on *Colour in Britain* by James Wickenden, the implicit purpose being to look more deeply into the causes of the riots than the press was prepared to do. Wickenden's conclusion was that the circumstances of immigration, rather than hooliganism, racism or the migrants themselves, were ultimately to blame. What he called the 'disease' of racial violence was caused not by 'the presence of coloured people in Britain but hostile reactions to their presence'. He went on:

> It does appear that the danger lies where a concentration of immigrants has formed too quickly for an area's capacity to absorb them. Where this occurs there has been violence and the danger of violence and hostility will always be present. As a short-term measure it is therefore surely desirable to keep the number of immigrants to a level which can be absorbed. This applies both to the country as a whole and to particular areas. But the restriction should not come from Britain.[137]

Although Wickenden's analysis was liberal and well-meaning, it was unrealistic to think, as he did, that the problems of immigration would be eased as long as the Caribbean governments legislated to restrict the number of immigrants entering Britain. As for all the talk of immigrants exceeding 'a level which can be absorbed', there is no doubt that Wickenden's motives were tolerant and anti-racist; all the same, his vocabulary was an ominous foretaste of the rhetoric used to attack immigration in the late sixties.[138] Most ordinary people now thought that the British government should take action to restrict the flow of immigrants. In June 1961 a Gallup poll found that 67 per cent supported government restrictions; a further 6 per cent thought that all immigrants should be barred from entry, while 21 per cent wanted the current laissez-faire system to continue.[139] The Cabinet felt under considerable public pressure to act, and Andrew Fountaine, the founder of the National Front, somehow got hold of Macmillan's private telephone number and used to ring him up to suggest various anti-immigration schemes. 'He'd pick up the receiver', Fountaine recalled, 'and as soon as he heard it was me, pretend he was the butler.'[140] It was not an issue that greatly fascinated Macmillan; his biographer estimates that he devoted ten times as many hours to the Central African Federation as he did to immigration. All the same, at the end of 1961 the Cabinet gave their support to the Commonwealth Immigrants Bill, and from May 1962 immigrants from the Commonwealth were only allowed in if they already had an employment contract or had certain specific skills. Hugh Gaitskell was not alone in denouncing what he called 'cruel and brutal anti-colour legislation'. *The Times* was also vociferous in its criticism of the bill, and it seemed to many observers that black immigrants were themselves being stigmatised for the racism of their fellow citizens. But, whatever the merits of the case, the result was clear: the era of unrestricted immigration was over.[141]

One happier consequence of the 1958 race riots was the organisation the following year of a West Indian carnival in St Pancras Town Hall, an expression of solidarity and pride that by the mid-sixties had evolved into the Notting Hill carnival. Despite occasional problems with crime, the carnival had within two decades become London's most colourful and dynamic public celebration as well as a symbol of multi-racial harmony.[142] Another immediate consequence was that thousands of West Indian immigrants chose to return to the Caribbean. In most years, only 150 made the return journey, but in 1959 there were over 4500.[143] This perhaps slightly gives the lie to the emphasis of Mike and Trevor Phillips on the 'renewed sense of confidence' felt by West Indians after the riots. Certainly many Caribbean migrants felt that they had been drawn together by the experience and that a shared identity as black West Indians had overtaken the old, divisive island loyalties. In the years after 1958 there was a stronger sense of mutual allegiance and communal Caribbean tradition, expressed particularly in support for the West Indies cricket team.[144] Meanwhile, many white social workers, politicians and local citizens made a great effort to convince the migrant settlers of their good intentions; during the riots themselves, a journalist for *The Times* 'saw a white man deliberately cross the street to shake hands with a coloured fruit vendor who was terrified'.[145] On the other hand, the area also became a magnet for racist and fascist agitators like Mosley's Union Movement activists. The 'Keep Britain White' crowd were often to be seen on the street corners of Notting Hill in the months after the riots, although Mosley's very poor performance as a parliamentary candidate for North Kensington in 1959, where he lost his deposit, demonstrated the limits of his appeal.[146] The brutal murder in May 1959 of a young Antiguan carpenter, Kelso Cochrane, by six white youths demonstrated that fear, intimidation and racist bullying were still lamentable elements of the immigrant experience; the Metropolitan Police, meanwhile, discounted any racial motive for the murder and never caught the killers.[147]

The Notting Hill riots are often seen as a landmark in the history of British race relations, a jarring, visceral demonstration of white racism and a spur to black solidarity, organisation and self-awareness. From 1958 onwards, West

Indians increasingly saw themselves as a united, self-conscious cultural and ethnic group, defiantly facing down the challenge of white aggressors. For many white Britons, meanwhile, the disturbances drew their attention to issues of race and discrimination as never before. The inexpensive 'social problem' films, in which liberal writers and directors examined contemporary social issues like crime, delinquency and the family, now switched their attention to racism and immigration. Like the newspaper reports on the Notting Hill riots, these films usually associated racism with teenage crime, thereby addressing two fashionable and 'dangerous' issues at once. The film *Winds of Change* (1961), for example, deals with racism among the Teddy Boys, perhaps rather belatedly given that there were very few Teddy Boys left in 1961. The central character, a teenage delinquent played by Johnny Briggs, is obsessed by the idea of racial miscegenation: in fact, the first revelation of his racial prejudice comes when he watches a young Caribbean man chatting up a white woman in a coffee bar.[148]

The most successful example of this sub-genre, though, was Basil Dearden's film *Sapphire* (1959), an explicit response to the events in St Ann's and North Kensington. The plot follows an investigation by a benign police inspector into the murder of a promiscuous student of mixed race called Sapphire; as it turns out, she was killed by the mother of her white fiancé, a conventional British housewife, in order to save her son from the shame of miscegenation. The film is set in Notting Hill, and it takes great care to present the local West Indian community in a positive light. So the inspector meets a series of respectable, middle-class black characters, such as a wealthy barrister and an eminent doctor, as well as the petty criminals who inhabit the local Tulips club. Inter-racial relationships are presented with sympathy: one black character, a polite and pleasant young man played by Earl Cameron, is shown backing out of a liaison with a friendly white girl because he doubts it will work in the circumstances, despite their mutual enthusiasm.[149] However, the most striking scene makes it very clear that the filmmakers had not abandoned the old cultural association between blackness and unbridled, animalistic passion. At one point the detectives descend into the underworld of the Tulips nightclub, where they watch an attractive young woman, apparently white, dancing with frenzied enthusiasm among a group of black men to bongo music. The club's owner explains that she is of mixed race, and therefore cannot suppress her natural urges when the music begins: 'She's a lilyskin . . . you can always tell . . . once they hear the beat of the bongo.' The film then cuts to a rapid montage as the tempo of the music increases: shot after shot of the dancing woman, her black partner and other black dancers, culminating with a series of rapidly edited low-angle shots of the dancer's gyrating thighs beneath her twirling skirt intercut with close-ups of the bongo drums.[150] Despite the anti-racist intentions of the film, therefore, black men and women were still associated with exotic music, suggestive dancing and ferocious passion, stereotypes that had deep roots in British culture and would take a long time to die out.

As if the West Indians of Notting Hill did not have enough difficulties of their own, in the early sixties they also had to endure the enthusiastic attentions of London's bohemian set. Newspaper reports of the 1958 riots spread the word of North Kensington nightlife across London and southern England: readers lapped up the stories of basement clubs, drinking and gambling dens, blues and jazz record shops, and the rest. For various disaffected, affluent, self-styled cultural dissidents, the lure of the Notting Hill area was the appeal of the exotic, an environment in which they could pride themselves on their anti-racism, dabble in marijuana and Caribbean music, and pretend that they were just like the American Beat poets that they idolised.[151] As one bohemian writer, Barry Miles, later put it:

> The hip society in Notting Hill in those days was basically very involved with the West Indians. They were the only people around who had good music, they all knew about jazz and ska and bluebeat. They also smoked rather good dope. That was the classic excuse in court if anyone got busted: 'Where did you get it from?' 'I bought it from a black man in Notting Hill.'[152]

Whether this was a different or more mature attitude to that exemplified by the bongo dancing scene in *Sapphire* must remain very doubtful: certainly the identification of West Indians with drugs, free love and loud parties seems both partial and patronising. Middle-class white bohemians idolised the Caribbean men of Notting Hill for their exotic lifestyles and ready supplies of marijuana, and self-consciously fashionable revellers, including at one point Princess Margaret and her husband as well as Stephen Ward and Christine Keeler, would frequent the Rio Café on Westbourne Grove. The sights of Notting Hill, wrote Monica Dickens in 1961, included:

Fairies, tarts, coffee-bar weirdies, unwashed geniuses, juvenile delinquents, old ladies living and dying under sheets of newspapers on the
benches by the playgrounds. Drunks and thugs and Maltese pimps, all
living cheek by jowl with people like you who are madly normal, and
people who are madly chic . . .[153]

Some luminaries of the bohemian scene moved specifically to live in the
area, but as one local black activist put it, this was the classic example of the
'white nigger' syndrome: essentially an inverted stereotyping whereby
Caribbean immigrants were celebrated by their white admirers for their cultural rebelliousness, innate authenticity and sexual freedom.[154] It certainly
seems very unlikely that the identification of black men with 'smoking
enormous spliffs', as Barry Miles would have it, eased their integration into
a culturally conservative society.[155]

Of all the white middle-class bohemians who embraced Caribbean culture as the antithesis of British banality, the most influential was the
novelist Colin MacInnes, who, in his trilogy *City of Spades* (1957), *Absolute
Beginners* (1959) and *Mr Love and Justice* (1960), tried to show that the uninhibited spirit of West Indian culture and the classless authenticity of
affluent British teenagers were combining to build a new and better society.
Since MacInnes was in his fifties, and was the son of the novelist Angela
Thirkell, the grandson of Sir Edward Burne-Jones and the cousin of Stanley
Baldwin, it is not clear that he was a great expert on either youth culture
or classlessness. He was the quintessential self-declared outsider, a homosexual who felt ill at ease in genteel society and called himself 'an "English",
London-born, Australian-reared Scot'.[156] While more conservative journalists saw immigrants, teenagers, record shops, scooters and coffee bars as
symptoms of a general national and moral decline, undermining traditional authority and importing pernicious American values, MacInnes
celebrated them precisely because he was so disaffected. Black immigrants,
he wrote in 1958, 'represent the New English of the last half of our century:
the modern infusion of that new blood which, according to our history-
books, has perpetually re-created England in the past and is the very reason
for her mongrel glory'.[157]

MacInnes' attitude to West Indians was well expressed in the novel *City
of Spades*, which is partly narrated by Montgomery Pew, the assistant welfare
officer of the Colonial Office. Pew does not accept his predecessor's verdict
that the black man is 'still, deep down, a savage' and throws himself into the

study of immigrant lives in London. But is Pew's conclusion so very different? When he says that they 'bring an element of joy and fantasy and violence into our cautious, ordered lives', he is simply repeating the stereotype of the black man as the noble savage, authentic, simple and primal.[158] For Pew, as for MacInnes, the 'innocence and wisdom' of the newcomers therefore represents an implicit challenge to the weary, cynical sophistication of white British society.

The second novel of the trilogy, *Absolute Beginners*, is usually taken as the emblematic text on British youth culture, the bohemian Notting Hill scene and the links between the fashionable rich and West Indian immigrants in the late fifties and early sixties. The narrator, an unnamed sixteen-year-old would-be photographer, potters through the coffee bars and jazz clubs of Soho and Notting Hill in the weeks leading up to the North Kensington riots. For a teenager, he is remarkably self-assured and all-knowing; his friends are other teenagers like himself, bohemian dissidents and Caribbean migrants of all ages, while the remainder of the population, that banal and contemptible mass from Glasgow shipbuilders and Rhondda miners to Norfolk farmers and City stockbrokers, are smugly dismissed as 'conscripts' and 'squares'. As the critic Alan Sinfield notes, the teenage hero has no calls on his time, 'money problems miraculously disappear, and he has no difficulty meeting interesting and important people', the impression being that 'if you listen to jazz, dress snappily and stay cool, then the rest of it needn't bother you'.[159] The style of the book is fragmentary and episodic; the narrator is not merely implausible but also downright irritating; there is little distinction between the narrator's viewpoint and MacInnes' own preconceived opinions; and the whole thing comes over as a relatively feeble pastiche of *The Catcher in the Rye*.[160]

Despite all this, the account of the riots in Notting Hill (fictionalised here as 'Napoli') and the narrator's shocked reaction to them both carry considerable power. At first, he refuses to accept that public racist violence is even conceivable, such is his faith in his native land: 'They'd never allow it! The adults! The men! The women! All the authorities! Law and order is the one great English thing!' When the disturbances begin, however, his attitude changes:

> 'I don't understand my own country any more,' I said to her. 'In the history books, they tell us the English race has spread itself all over the

dam world: gone and settled everywhere, and that's one of the great, splendid English things. No one invited us, and we didn't ask anyone's permission, I suppose. Yet when a few hundred thousand come and settle among our fifty millions we just can't take it.'[161]

After he has watched the street violence himself, the narrator rides down on his Vespa scooter past the BBC building at White City. By now the riots have driven him to question his own faith in his fellow countrymen, and in England:

And I looked at it and thought, 'My God, if I could get in there and tell them – all the millions! Just take them across the railway tracks, not a quarter of a mile away, and show them what's happening in the capital city of our country!' And I'd say to them, 'If you don't want that, for Christ's sake come down and stop it – every one of you! But if that's what you do want, then I don't want you, and for me, it's good-bye England!'[162]

By the end of the novel he has made up his mind to leave Britain for good and make a new life overseas. Standing at the airport, however, he feels his resolve weakening when through the London drizzle he sees a new group of African immigrants descending from an aeroplane, and in the final passage of the novel he goes out to welcome them in a scene of mingled optimism and sadness:

Some had on robes, and some had on tropical suits, and most of them were young like me, maybe kiddos coming here to study, and they came down grinning and chattering, and they all looked so dam pleased to be in England, at the end of their long journey, that I was heartbroken at all the disappointments that were there in store for them. And I ran up to them through the water, and shouted out above the engines, 'Welcome to London! Greetings from England! Meet your first teenager! We're all going up to Napoli to have a ball!' And I flung my arms around the first of them, who was a stout old number with a beard and a brief-case and a little bonnet, and they all paused and stared at me in amazement, until the old boy looked me in the face and said to me, 'Greetings!' and he took me by the shoulder, and suddenly they all burst out laughing in the storm.[163]

MacInnes' novels present a view of immigrants that at times comes close to condescension: all the talk about 'grinning and chattering', the emphasis on the natural wisdom and exuberance of black people and the rather patronising implication that the union of teenagers and immigrants represents a unique force for good in the grey adult world of Britain in the fifties. Black and Asian immigrants, it appeared, could not be men and women like any other; they were either demonised as the incarnation of violence, degeneracy and disorder or lauded as the embodiments of virtue and authenticity.

But the British immigrant experience could not be reduced to a few easy stereotypes. The effects of decolonisation and immigration were to make Britain, like the newly independent nations of Africa and Asia, a post-colonial nation in which nationality was conferred not by ethnic or racial identity but by common citizenship. As many immigrants found, this was not easy for many indigenous Britons to accept; indeed, immigration became one more symbol of a changing modern world in which pre-war assumptions were increasingly outmoded. For thousands of Caribbean, Indian, Pakistani, Maltese and Cypriot settlers, the reality of immigration was not a bohemian fantasy of music, drugs and parties, but a grinding slog of hard work, grubby surroundings and everyday prejudice. After such a struggle, they were entitled to feel as British as anyone else.

10

I'M ALL RIGHT, JACK

We do not and cannot accept the principle that incompetence justifies dismissal. That is victimisation.

I'm All Right, Jack (1959)

What sort of an island do we want to be? . . . A lotus island of easy, tolerant ways, bathed in the golden glow of an imperial sunset, shielded from discontent by a threadbare welfare state and an acceptance of genteel poverty? Or the tough, dynamic race we have been in the past, striving always to better ourselves, seeking new worlds to conquer in place of those we have lost, ready to accept growing pains as the price for growth?

Michael Shanks, *The Stagnant Society* (1961)

In 1959 the most successful film at the domestic box office was not, for once, a Hollywood production. In seventeen weeks one British comedy attracted more than two million people to cinemas across the country, while in New York it ran at the art-house Guild Theater for four months and broke the house box-office record.[1] In early September, when Harold Macmillan went up to Balmoral to ask the Queen for a dissolution of Parliament and a general election, she arranged that they should spend the evening watching a special projection of the chart-topping film.[2] It was called *I'm All Right, Jack*, and its unexpected star, rewarded ahead of Laurence Olivier and Richard Burton with the British Academy award for the best British actor of 1959, was a young man called Peter Sellers.

Born in 1925 to theatrical parents, Sellers grew up with a talent for mimicry and improvisation. As an army entertainer during the Second World War, he would horrify his fellow performers by dressing up in a squadron leader's uniform and sneaking off to conduct unexpected inspections of RAF bunkhouses elsewhere in the camp. One Christmas Eve he even impersonated an air commodore and inveigled his way into the officers' mess, where he deflected difficult questions by muttering: 'Sorry, old boy, must-n't say. Intelligence, you know.'[3] From May 1951 he had been a member of the Goons, the enormously popular troupe of radio surrealists who proved such an inspiration for future comedians; but his real ambition was to be a star of the silver screen. One obvious problem was his chronic unreliability. When he appeared in his first stage play, *Brouhaha*, in 1958, he quickly fell out with his fellow actors because he refused to give the same performance night after night. He might ad-lib dialogue; he might enter from an unex-pected angle; he might be wearing something as outlandish as a bright pink suit; he might start chatting to the front row of the audience. On one occa-sion he even turned up drunk from a cocktail party and told the audience: 'I'm sloshed, but I know my lines. I may not be able to say them all. But do you want me to carry on – or will I get the understudy in?'[4] A brilliant, inse-cure and self-destructive man, Sellers was not content to be merely another talented improvisational comedian. Instead, he was determined to turn himself into the equal and successor of his hero, the actor Alec Guinness, and after a few cameo appearances in the mid-fifties he had at last been given the ideal role to make his dreams a reality.

In January 1959, Sellers had signed a five-picture deal with the brothers John and Roy Boulting, whose films included *Brighton Rock*, *High Treason*, *Lucky Jim* and *Carlton-Browne of the FO*.[5] As committed supporters of the Liberal Party, they represented a particular kind of disaffected, high-minded middle-class politics, antagonistic towards Conservative materialism but suspicious of socialism and the trade unions. According to John Boulting, their films represented 'a plea for the rights of the individual as against the Establishment, authority, society and all the things that are totally imper-sonal'; and in their successful comedies of the fifties, the brothers drew an explicit contrast between the hypocrisy and materialism of post-war British society and the declining values of established religion, traditional moral-ity and social duty.[6] Perhaps the best early example of this approach was the film *Private's Progress*, a wry satire on materialism and selfishness which was dedicated 'to all those who got away with it'. And since *Private's Progress* had been a minor box-office hit on its release in 1956, it made excellent com-mercial sense for the Boulting brothers to reunite its cast, which included Ian Carmichael, Richard Attenborough and Terry-Thomas, for a sequel, *I'm All Right, Jack*.[7]

The satirical intent of their new film was evident merely from the title. *I'm All Right, Jack* was a sanitised version of a common working-class saying of the day, 'Fuck you, Jack, I'm all right'.[8] It was planned as a comedy about modern labour relations, mocking both the corruption of the employers and the selfishness of the workers, and one of the central roles, a comical trade union leader called Fred Kite, was earmarked for the ambitious young Peter Sellers. At first Sellers turned the part down; he complained that he 'couldn't see the laughs' and thought the whole thing fairly unfunny.[9] Finally, after hours of argument, he agreed to give it a try, and began to develop Kite's character by working on his voice, a dull, clipped, self-important monotone. He also had his hair sheared to the scalp, wore a Hitler moustache and a shapeless, baggy suit, and walked in a comically robotic waddle.[10]

The Boultings had partly based the character on a shop steward in the Electrical Trades Union who worked at the film studios, and Sellers himself drew on a particular example for inspiration:

> There was a trades-union official I used to know at one of the studios. 'I've seen 'em all come and go, you know,' he'd say. When I came off the set: 'you was 'avin a bit of fun today, I seen you . . .'; then: 'Why don't you come along 'ome one night and meet the wife?' He was the type who always had about six pencils in his breast pocket; or else he rushes about with a little notice board in his hands and a list of names on a sheet of paper fastened on with paper clips – I'm sure it's completely useless.[11]

As the Boulting brothers later recalled, the enthusiasm of the watching studio employees at an early screen test hinted at the appeal of the Kite character:

> Suddenly there was a gale of laughter, a round of applause from the workers who . . . were savouring something they'd never dreamed of hearing – their own shop stewards turned into figures of outrageous fun . . .
>
> And this is an extraordinary coincidence: it also happened that, as we were filming, a seven-man union delegation was waiting to take issue with us on some perfectly petty point or other, led by the very man Peter was taking off. Of course they completely failed to recognize themselves – or their leader – in his performance. They even joined in the applause.[12]

Once convinced of the comic potential of Fred Kite, Sellers became increasingly obsessed with the character. He walked to the canteen at lunch with Kite's waddle, held his cutlery as Kite might have done, and even made pompous and foolish small talk as he 'heard' Kite doing. Even at this relatively early stage in his career, he was convinced that he had been 'possessed' by the character he was playing, and later in his life he liked to claim that Peter Sellers was nothing more than an empty vehicle for the self-expression of his 'tenants'. 'I do not exist,' he told Kermit the Frog in 1978. 'There used to be a me, but I had it surgically removed.'[13]

I'm All Right, Jack is widely regarded as one of the most entertaining and historically illuminating British films of the post-war era. It begins with a pre-credits sequence set in a genteel London club on VE Day. A servant goes to wake 'old Sir John', a doddering club stalwart (Sellers, heavily disguised), to tell him that the war is over at last. Change is in the air, as a disembodied narrator explains: 'Look hard, for this is the last we shall see of Sir John . . . a solid block in the edifice of what seemed to be an ordered and stable society. There goes Sir John – on his way out.' Victory will bring 'a new age, and with that new age a new spirit', and this is immediately captured by an image of a soldier celebrating atop a lamppost, grinning into the camera and unexpectedly turning his V-for-victory sign around into a gesture of brazen contempt for the audience. The film's theme, sung by the fifties pop star Al Saxon, makes the message of the new order even more explicit:

> I'm all right, Jack, I'm okay,
> That is the message for today.
> So, count up your lolly, feather your nest,
> Let someone else worry, boy, I couldn't care less.
> You scratch my back; I'll do the same for you, Jack,
> That is the message for today.[14]

The film's central character, Stanley Windrush (Ian Carmichael), is a naive, well-meaning neophyte, baffled by his encounters with lazy, materialistic workers and corrupt, conspiratorial bosses. The plot of the film follows his efforts to find a job in the cutthroat world of post-war Britain, where his impeccable breeding and generosity of spirit are not assets but handicaps. He finally ends up as an unskilled manual worker at the arms factory run by his uncle Bertram; not entirely coincidentally, his uncle is planning an enormous fraud based on a convoluted arms sale to an Arab

employers are bad, the workers are little better. To
y arrive for work at the very last minute, spend most
bout and playing cards, and are ready to down tools at
ity; when Stanley appears to be working too hard, they
e him. To the personnel officer Major Hitchcock, played
stic suavity by Terry-Thomas, they are 'stinkers', 'rotters' and
'an abs   hower'; and as a time-and-motion inspector (John Le Mesurier
on fine form) remarks: 'The natural rhythm of the British worker is neither
natural, rhythmic, or much to do with work.' Hitchcock agrees: 'We've got
chaps here who could break out in a mild sweat simply by standing still.'

Most of Stanley's fellow workers are fairly anonymous figures, but there
is one notable exception: Fred Kite, the head of the works committee. Kite's
attitude is captured in his first few scenes, when he marches across the yard
to accuse Major Hitchcock of 'jeropadising [sic] the safety of employees' by
employing such a blundering ass as Stanley. Hitchcock nods wisely: 'This
man must be sacked immediately.' But this, of course, runs against all Kite's
principles. He asks to 'withdraw and consult', and then returns with their
message: 'We do not and cannot accept the principle that incompetence justifies dismissal. That is victimisation.' So Stanley is allowed to stay on; indeed,
as an 'intellectual', he is taken under Kite's wing and even moves into his
house as a lodger. In the evenings he is compelled to listen to Kite's political opinions, expressed in supremely pompous and ludicrous style.

Kite is a masterpiece of vanity, snobbery and frustrated respectability, and
in Sellers' hands he dominates the film. He loves reading about the Soviet
Union and treasures the works of Lenin; he would love to visit the country,
he says with touching banality, to see for himself 'all those cornfields and
ballet in the evening'. 'Russia, Russia, it's all we ever get in this house,' complains his irate wife. In Stanley, however, Kite has at last found a captive
audience. 'I see from your particulars you was at college in Oxford,' he
remarks, offering Stanley another glass of his Australian burgundy. 'I was up
there meself. I was at the Balliol summer school in 1946. Very good toast and
preserves they give you at tea time, as you probably know.'[15]

I'm All Right, Jack owed much of its success to its matchless comic cast.
Sellers was in sparkling form; Carmichael and Terry-Thomas were at the
height of their careers; and even the smaller parts were played by talented
stalwarts like Margaret Rutherford, Irene Handl and Kenneth Griffith, not
to mention Malcolm Muggeridge, playing himself. But the popularity of
the film also reflected the fact that it expressed widespread doubts about

the virtues of affluence and modernity. The Boulting brothers, as good Liberals, were equally scornful of the employers and the trade unions for their 'tendency to think of people not as human beings but as part of a group, a bloc, a class'. 'Nowadays there seem to be two sacred cows – Big Business and Organised Labour,' they explained in the *Daily Express*. 'Both are deep in an organised conspiracy against the individual – to force us to accept certain things for what they are not.'[16] The 'brave new world' of consumerism is gently but relentlessly exposed in *I'm All Right, Jack* as a corrupt new world of materialism, selfishness and social disintegration. At the outset, the narrator tells us: 'Industry, spurred by the march of science in all directions, was working at high pressure to supply those vital needs for which the people had hungered for so long.' But when Stanley sets out to get a job in industrial management, he soon finds out what these 'vital needs' are: Num-Yum chocolate bars, Detto washing powder (the 'new black whitener') and the armaments manufactured by his uncle. Although the scenes in the Num-Yum and Detto factories are dominated by broad slapstick, the Boulting brothers are still making a serious point about the degeneracy of post-war society: not for nothing do they carefully reproduce the irritating billboards, jingles and slogans of modern commercialism.[17]

The climax of the film, meanwhile, is set in the supremely modern surroundings of a television studio, where Malcolm Muggeridge is hosting a debate about the industrial unrest that has afflicted the armaments factory. Stanley has just been handed a great bag of cash as a bribe to keep his mouth shut, but he nevertheless decides to make a futile last stand on behalf of the old values, angrily denouncing both 'the phoney patriotic claptrap of the employers' and 'the bilge about workers' rights'. 'Wherever you look,' he cries in frustration, 'it's a case of "Blow you, Jack, I'm all right."' Then he produces the bag, delves into it, and holds up a pile of pound notes. 'These are the only facts that interest anybody in this dispute. This is what they all want. This is *all* they want! Something for nothing!' And as he throws the money up into the air, the studio audience, the panellists and the film crew rush from their seats to grab as many banknotes as they can for themselves, hurling punches left and right, smashing the cameras and the lighting equipment, and scrabbling desperately to get their hands on the cash. Stanley's point could hardly have been better proved. But it is Stanley who is blamed for the fracas and hauled up before a magistrate, while the conspirators escape scot-free. There is no place for an honest and virtuous individual in the modern world of consumerism, greed and special interests. By the final scene of the film, he has taken refuge in a nudist colony. Only here, in an artificial pastoral paradise of thatched cottages and rural quiet, can he at last escape the materialism of the modern world, with its ugly factories, jeering jingles and rampant corruption.[18]

While some reviewers, notably in *The Times* and the *Express*, liked the film, more highbrow critics did not detect much distinction in *I'm All Right, Jack*.[19] It was intellectually fashionable to celebrate working-class authenticity and grit, not to laugh at the pretensions of proletarian self-improvement. For critics on the political left, *I'm All Right, Jack* was an unpardonable assault on the values of the Labour movement: to satirise the unions at all was bad enough, but to use them as the basis for a cheerful, crowd-pleasing farce was disgraceful.[20] There was certainly some truth in the charge that the unions came out of *I'm All Right, Jack* rather worse than the employers, but this was almost entirely down to the performance of Peter Sellers, who ensured that the scenes of dishonest union officials and indolent workers lingered longer in the mind than those of the bosses' corruption.

Certainly it was much gentler than a second film about trade union excesses, *The Angry Silence*, which was released the following year. The makers of this film, Guy Green (director), Bryan Forbes (writer and producer) and Richard Attenborough (star and producer), were younger than the Boulting brothers and more critical of union excesses. *The Angry Silence* was therefore a labour of love rooted in political conviction, and many contributors deferred their salaries to keep down the budget.[21]

The Angry Silence is set in an industrial factory, and its central character is Tom Curtis (Attenborough), a strong-willed worker who refuses to join an unofficial strike and is persecuted by his old friends on the shop floor. As the film makes clear, he is perfectly justified; the strike has in fact been conjured out of nothing by a conspiratorial shop steward at the behest of a mysterious, sinister left-wing organisation. With its depiction of radical agitators at work, seeking to foment chaos and division, *The Angry Silence* occasionally comes close to red-baiting paranoia, and it is a much more aggressive, gritty and pessimistic film than *I'm All Right, Jack*. The strikers become a violent, unruly mob; Curtis' son is smeared with tar by his schoolfellows; and Curtis himself is eventually set upon and beaten by a gang of Teddy Boys employed by the strikers, losing the sight of one eye. The workers are here portrayed as even more apathetic, stupid and intolerant than in the Boultings' film, and the appeal to old-fashioned British individualism is much stronger. The hero has a foreign wife, for instance; all he wants to do is to carry on earning money so that he can build a better home for his young family. 'I'm the hero as much as they are!' he exclaims at one point. According to the screenwriter, Bryan Forbes, the message of the film was that 'that *everybody has the right to be different* and that any attack on this right must be resisted by thinking people'.[22]

The Angry Silence was extremely well crafted and acted, and it was no surprise that the conservative press was full of praise. *The Times*, for instance, called it 'a film of rare quality and impressive realism', telling the story of 'real people caught in a situation not of their making'. 'This is not a biased film,' the review concluded. 'It tells its story honestly and with understanding. It has about it the clear ring of truth.'[23] Many trade unionists, however, were appalled by its content, and the *Daily Worker* called it 'a lying travesty . . . vicious, ugly and cruel'.[24] In Ipswich, where the film had been shot, the producers even arranged a special screening to mollify four hundred local union members who had appeared as extras, and Richard Attenborough triumphantly reported that there had been 'not one breath of criticism'. It was not, he insisted, 'an anti-trade union film'; it was 'critical, not of the trade union movement, but of certain aspects – apathy, mob-violence and subversion'.[25] Letters columns swelled briefly with correspondence debating the merits of the film: the general secretary of the Association of Cinematograph, Television and Allied Technicians wrote to *The Times* with the news that 'many trade unionists, including a number in the film industry, consider *The Angry Silence* an anti-union film'; and a staff tutor in Trade Union Studies at the University of London declared that most union members thought it was 'basically anti-trade union and anti-working class, dramatizing an incident that is not typical . . . the fact that it is a well-made and well-acted film is therefore all the more dangerous and distorting'. He suggested that perhaps, by way of recompense, its producers might consider making a film about the life of Ernest Bevin.[26]

The great success of *I'm All Right, Jack* and the mild controversy surrounding *The Angry Silence* reflected a wider debate at the beginning of the sixties about the strengths and weaknesses of British trade unionism. Many middle-class observers blamed the unions and the 'British worker' for the travails of the national economy. 'The working class is wrongly named', one company director told Peter Wilmott and Michael Young, 'because they don't work at all, judging by what happens in our firm.' The wife of another Woodford businessman agreed. 'The workers don't pull their weight,' she explained. 'I'm going by all those men I see leaning on their shovels. If they can get out of working they will.'[27] Such sentiments were of course rooted in a long tradition of hostility to working-class militancy stretching back into the nineteenth century. There was no doubt, however, that they had been intensifying during the course of the 1950s. In the immediate aftermath of the Second World War, British industrial relations had, in a comparative context, been rather good. Government ministers and leading trade unionists agreed that workers should be encouraged to join a union, but that the state had little place intervening in the workplace to settle disputes between employers and unions. Not only were the unions attracting more members, but the conditions of full employment meant that they also enjoyed an unusually strong bargaining position. Walter Monckton, the Conservatives' first post-war Minister of Labour, understandably struck a note of benevolent co-operation with union leaders rather than challenge them head-on.[28] 'There is now so much work to be done and so little unemployment,' admitted one plumber in 1951, 'so if the boss rattles at you or threatens you with the sack you can just up and leave . . . The working people are better off and the bosses have lost a lot of their grip.'[29]

By 1962 there were just over nine million trade union members in Britain, all but half a million of whom were affiliated to the TUC.[30] Most were motivated by a mixture of political conviction, social solidarity and personal economic advantage. Since 1953 the unions' relationship with the ruling Conservative government had been steadily worsening: there had been strikes by engineering workers, dockers, busmen, printers and railwaymen, and industrial unrest was edging towards levels reminiscent more of the thirties than the forties. The statistics for strikes in the fifties make interesting reading. Between 1945 and 1954, there were, on average, 1791 strikes a year, involving 545,000 workers and resulting in the loss of 2,073,000 working days. Between 1955 and 1964, meanwhile, the average had risen to 2521 strikes a year, involving 1,116,000 workers and 3,889,000 lost working days. For Arthur Marwick, these figures indicate that strike activity was 'remarkably constant'; on the other hand, the same figures have also been used by more conservative observers to illustrate the point that strikes were steadily increasing and swallowing up more and more workers and production time. Certainly most contemporary observers were struck by the growth of industrial unrest rather than its continuity.[31] Another way of looking at the same phenomenon, however, is to examine British strike activity in an international context. Between 1951 and 1962, these were the average figures for days lost annually to strikes per thousand workers in the mining, manufacturing, construction and transport industries in the major industrial democracies:

USA	1185
Italy	780
Canada	649
Japan	579
Belgium	501
Australia	462
France	391
UK	272
West Germany	77
Sweden	53 [32]

'Britain is not, contrary to frequent impressions, a country very prone to strikes,' wrote Anthony Sampson in 1962.[33] The misfortunes of the British economy at the time could not, therefore, be blamed on militant industrial action. Indeed, in their election propaganda two years later, the Conservatives boasted of their success in keeping strike levels lower 'than any other major industrial country in the free world except Western Germany'.[34]

So why was it that the British trade union movement had acquired such a reputation for militant unruliness by the beginning of the 1960s? One answer was that it had become a convenient scapegoat for middle-class resentment. Since the end of the war, working-class incomes had steadily risen; meanwhile, technological and cultural changes were chipping away at old social conventions and boundaries. As the self-declared representatives of the workers, then, trade union leaders could easily be blamed for economic underperformance or disquieting social developments. What was more significant, however, was that although the *number* of strikes was not, in an international context, especially remarkable, the *kind* of strikes was unquestionably changing. Anthony Sampson noted that union leaders had great 'difficulty in keeping and controlling their members'. 'Most unions since the war', he observed, 'have been challenged by "wildcat strikes" and rebellious shop-stewards.'[35]

From the mid-fifties onwards it was clear that a gulf was emerging between the prosperous, well-fed union leaders and their rank-and-file members. As the union officials became ever wealthier, fatter and more complacent, so many ordinary members came to feel that their economic grievances were better represented by their own unpaid shop stewards: hence the resonance of a character like Fred Kite. 'It is the shop-stewards who collect union dues at the factories, recruit new members, and enforce the factory agreements,' wrote Sampson; 'the T and G has 25,000 of them, and altogether there are said to be 200,000 – more shop-stewards than soldiers.'[36] In the car industry, for instance, aggressive and dynamic campaigning by the shop stewards had enabled them to build up powerful personal organisations on the shop floor. The new disputes of the late 1950s were often unofficial, localised affairs, organised by the shop stewards rather than union bosses and provoked by internal union disagreements or rivalries between skilled and unskilled workers. At Ford's Dagenham plant, for example, there were 235 work stoppages in two years, culminating in the notorious 'bell ringer' strike of 1957. Most had been called without any discussion or negotiation of any kind, and the shop stewards were later accused by a court of inquiry of running 'a private union within a union, enjoying immediate and continuous contact with the men in the shop, answerable to no superiors and in no way officially or constitutionally linked with the union hierarchy'.[37] At the same time, a new generation of more militant union leaders, closer to the shop stewards in spirit and outlook, was emerging to take the place of solid old warhorses like Ernest Bevin and Arthur Deakin, the most prominent example being Frank Cousins, the head of the TGWU from 1956, the champion of unilateral disarmament and the whingeing bogeyman of the conservative press. Cousins, like many other younger leaders of the late fifties, had little time for accommodation or wage restraint.[38]

This new, more aggressive style of trade unionism found little favour with middle-class observers or the conservative press. Opinion polls taken in the months before the 1959 election suggested that public opinion favoured a harder government line on 'unofficial strikes', and since the Labour Party was closely associated with the union movement, it was bound to suffer in public esteem.[39] A month after the election, an editorial in *The Times* suggested that 'for the first time the Labour Party's association with the organized workers counted against it in the minds of liberal-minded men and women':

No longer were the unions pictured in the public mind as the defenders of the underdog, but rather as his persecutors and oppressors. The organized workers, it seemed, sent men to Coventry, rushed into strikes without justification and without consideration for other workers, attacked the livelihoods of those who refused to join them, fought each other for jobs, and wangled their own elections for office. If this was the power behind the Labour Party, then the voters wanted none of the Labour Party.

This picture, the writer admitted, was 'a distorted one', but 'lapses from virtue have been becoming more common', and union leaders had shown their 'complacency and weakness' in dealing with the 'little bullies and petty Napoleons' on the shop floor.[40]

Films like *I'm All Right, Jack* and *The Angry Silence* did little to correct the impression that 'petty Napoleons' were at work on factory floors across the land. The problem for union leaders was that as the economy began to struggle in the 1960s, so it became easy to blame the alleged excesses of the shop stewards, and hence the movement itself, for British weakness. One trade union official even admitted that he was interested more in the welfare of his members than in the general prosperity of the nation:

> We were not meant to be public servants to guard the interests of the nation. We were appointed to protect our members and to further their interests within the framework of the law. Does anyone ask the employer to have the national interest in mind instead of the interest of his firm? It is all right having the national interest in mind but we are not the right people to have it.[41]

It was perhaps not surprising, then, that as the economy lurched from boom to bust in the early sixties, many analysts pinpointed the short-sighted selfishness of the unions as a central element in British economic decline. The most notable was the industrial editor of the *Financial Times*, Michael Shanks, who was extremely impressed by the success of centralised planning in Eastern Europe and Scandinavia and in 1961 published an unlikely paperback bestseller, *The Stagnant Society*, calling for the immediate modernisation of British economic life. 'The unions', he wrote, 'are too often proving themselves the natural allies of the forces of stagnation and conservatism in industry – and not those of expansion and dynamism.'[42]

They had allowed themselves to become sucked into 'unofficial strikes, demarcation disputes between unions, restrictive practices, breaking of freely-negotiated agreements and refusal to abide by the agreed disputes procedure, victimization of non-unionists and minority groups within unions, Communist infiltration [and] election irregularities'. And instead of embracing technological progress and the growth of the affluent society, they stood in its way, refusing to face a post-industrial future:

> The smell of the music hall and the pawnshop clings to them, and this more than anything else alienates the middle classes and the would-be middle classes from them. To be a trade unionist is to align oneself with those at the bottom of the social ladder at a time when the predominant urge is to climb it . . . At a time when the class structure is more fluid than ever before and the industrial worker enjoys a hitherto undreamed-of prosperity and security, the trade unions continue to express a way of life which is in many ways out of date.[43]

The unions must, in Shanks' view, reform themselves to 'harness the winds of change rather than resist them'. They must work more closely with employers, civil servants and ministers; they must develop a more democratic and accountable organisation; and they must look abroad, to the Low Countries, Scandinavia and the United States, for inspiration rather than keep their eyes fixed doggedly on their shoes. That way, he thought, they could build a new, aggressive, 'radical union movement' for a new age of economic expansion.[44] But, as he noted in a postscript six months after he had finished his book, they showed no signs of doing so. 'We shall pay for it', he wrote sadly, 'before we are much older.'[45]

Shanks' analysis of the 'stagnant society' hit a nerve precisely because, ever since the 1959 election, the economy had been in something of a mess. The generosity of Derick Heathcoat Amory's budget in April 1959 had undoubtedly helped to win the election for the Conservatives, but within a month of making his budget statement, Amory was gloomily warning Macmillan that he had given too much away.[46] Macmillan, of course, was a dedicated expansionist: as far as he was concerned, his Chancellor could never be too generous. Amory, however, was more sensitive than Macmillan to the inflationary pressures that would result from a short-lived boom, and he was also acutely conscious that excessive government indulgence might well have unpleasant consequences for the balance of payments and the stability of sterling. Even during the election campaign, he confessed to his Treasury advisers that he would have to bring in a much more austere budget in 1960 to deflate the economy; but, as they pointed out, to reverse direction so soon after the election would 'hardly look seemly'. Two days after the election, the anxious and conscientious Amory told Macmillan that he would like to step down as Chancellor, but he nevertheless was persuaded to stay on to prepare one more budget.[47]

By the beginning of 1960 a disquieting pattern was already clear. Television sets, cars, scooters, transistor radios, advertising jingles and billboards: Britain seemed awash with the colourful paraphernalia of the consumer society. In the month of November 1959 alone, imports had risen by 7 per cent, with most of the new spending going on foreign consumer goods, and the trade gap had widened by an additional £10 million.[48] Between January and December 1959, imports had increased by 10 per cent, but exports by a mere 4 per cent. The pace of economic expansion meant greater and greater pressures on resources and demands for labour, but as unemployment fell, so the unions demanded higher and higher wage increases. Far from restraining government spending, as Thorneycroft and his allies had demanded, Macmillan had approved some £750 million in additional government expenditure since their resignations, and he was now compelled to offer the railway unions a 5 per cent pay increase to prevent a crippling strike.[49] The Prime Minister's attentions were monopolised in the months after the election by foreign policy, notably the Paris summit in December and his famous tour of Africa in January and February 1960. When he returned, however, it was to be confronted by 'a great log-jam of problems', and especially a Chancellor who was 'worried – almost nervously so – about inflation'.[50] On 23 February Macmillan was sent a Treasury memorandum warning that if the boom continued, 'we cannot exclude the possibility of a payments crisis in the autumn'; and three days later, he had a gloomy meeting with Amory and the Governor of the Bank of England, both of whom, he observed, were 'very pessimistic' about the prospect of 'inflation, too much imports, balance of payments difficulties, loss of gold and dollar reserves, etc. etc. – the same old story. So they want violent disinflationary measures and a fierce Budget (£100 million extra taxation).'[51]

Typically, however, Macmillan was dead against such an austere approach; deflation was not in his vocabulary. On 27 February he sent Amory a long letter explaining why:

Following the Budget of last year and the Election of this autumn, a deflationary Budget would either be very foolish or very dishonest. Unless it is supposed that we would be thought very modern and up-to-date, like those young ladies who oscillate daily between the stimulant and the tranquillizers, the new Progressive Conservatism will turn out to be a policy of alternation between Benzedrine and Relaxa-tabs. I do not like it at all.

For these reasons I still think that you should consider a *stand-still Budget* . . . A gentle squeeze may be right, but it cannot be sensible to cheer the economy on vigorously one moment and then push it violently back the next.[52]

The Prime Minister was beyond persuasion; when Amory sent him a Treasury paper explaining why the budget ought to be 'mildly deflationary and not merely standstill', he dismissed it as 'a very weak document . . . so ill-written as to be almost unintelligible'. Amory had to be dissuaded from resigning there and then, but the fact that he had already decided to leave 11 Downing Street for personal reasons meant that he found it difficult to resist Macmillan's ceaseless pressure.[53] So it was that on 3 April he presented a budget much closer to Macmillan's 'stand-still' model than the austerity recommended by the Treasury, with only very mild tax increases and little to excite economic commentators, or indeed the general public. Even so, Labour spokesmen still pointed out the contrast with the exaggerated optimism of 1959. Harold Wilson, for instance, accused the government of 'lurching from semi-depression to boom and back again'.[54] As the trade figures showed no signs of improvement, so Amory was finally forced to introduce hire-purchase restrictions, and a sense of unease began to swirl through Conservative circles. Bob Boothby warned Macmillan of the 'impression, now rapidly gaining ground, that there is a total lack of assurance and decision at the Treasury. The hand may be on the tiller. But it is becoming clearer every day that it doesn't know where the hell it is steering.'[55]

Amory finally resigned at the end of June, exhausted but relieved finally to be rid of his burdens, and went off to a life of distinguished retirement as a businessman and High Commissioner for Canada. In the last months, Macmillan wrote to the Queen, he 'had lost his buoyancy and resilience and entered into a permanent quietism more suitable to a monastery than to the busy life of every day. I do not say he was defeatist. He just seemed overwhelmed.'[56] His replacement would be a rather more cheerful figure. There were three promising candidates in the Cabinet, David Eccles, Iain Macleod and Reginald Maudling, and each might have been expected to bring to the Treasury a new dash of vim and vigour after the gloom of Amory's last days.[57]

Instead, Macmillan picked Selwyn Lloyd, a man with no intellectual interest in economics and little experience of economic management; it was an unmistakable sign that, after his battles with Thorneycroft and Amory, the Prime Minister was now determined to run the Treasury from 10 Downing Street. Even Lloyd himself, who many felt had been very lucky to emerge from the shambles of Suez with his political career still intact, confessed that he 'knew nothing about the job'.[58] *The Times* spoke for many when it suggested that Lloyd was 'moving to a sphere with which he has been wholly out of touch'; but, as Edmund Dell remarks, he was 'a staff officer, not a man of ideas', and a loyal staff officer was precisely what Macmillan was looking for.[59] There was also a slight whiff of controversy about Lloyd's replacement at the Foreign Office, the Commonwealth Secretary Lord Home, who was both rather obscure and, of course, a hereditary member of the Lords rather than an elected MP. The Labour leadership argued, very effectively, that Home's promotion illustrated the unrepresentative, anachronistic tendencies of the Conservative Party, and, as with Lloyd, the august editorial column of *The Times* pronounced the appointment unsatisfactory. Home, it argued, had 'not been highly tested in the offices which he has held hitherto, and to the country at large his career will seem to have been insufficiently distinguished to warrant his elevation to the post of Foreign Secretary'.[60] In fact, Home proved an extremely competent Foreign Secretary, popular not only in Washington but in most chancelleries of the world, and in this instance at least Macmillan's judgement had not let him down. Although few observers could have guessed at the time, it would prove one of his more momentous appointments.[61]

From July 1960 onwards, the domestic fortunes of Macmillan's government lay in the hands of Selwyn Lloyd, ever the lonely, pliable monkey to the Prime Minister's organ grinder. His strengths as a politician – clubbable bonhomie, dependability, honesty and loyalty – were not necessarily those of an effective Chancellor, especially at a moment when the economic situation demanded imagination, conviction and sheer skill. Macmillan, however, entertained high hopes of success. 'I was glad to find him in capital form,' he recorded in September 1960, 'full of confidence, buoyant, and with many practical ideas. A great contrast to the last few months of poor Don Quixote, his predecessor.'[62] In truth, Lloyd was out of his depth: according to the Treasury official Alec Cairncross, he had 'no knowledge of economic theory' and was 'shy and rather diffident in discussing matters with experts, and at the same time distrustful of would-be experts. He stuttered more than any Minister I have ever known and was given to taking up the time of his officials in long meetings to draft speeches and memoranda.' Certainly there was no sign that he approached his new responsibilities with any firm economic convictions of any kind, and it was far from clear that he was going to be anything more than a front man for Macmillan's expansionist instincts.[63]

In a climate of economic ease, this might not have been a problem; unfortunately for Lloyd, the economy was rapidly sliding out of control. In October 1960 the trade figures were more alarming than ever, with the gap having widened from £76 million to £122 million in a matter of weeks, and to make matters worse, the government had also to deal with a crippling series of strikes in the docks and the car and construction industries.[64] If the balance of trade did not improve, it seemed entirely likely that the pound would come under severe pressure sooner or later. Yet as far as Macmillan was concerned, no obvious solution presented itself. After the Cabinet had discussed the economic situation for over two hours at the end of November 1960, he confessed that it was 'really baffling. We are borrowing short and lending long; exports are stable or falling; imports leaping up – yet the £ is strong and money – some "hot", some genuine investment (e.g. Ford) – keeps coming in. "Everyone believes in Britain – except the British."'[65]

The early months of 1961 did not bring much relief. There was more industrial unrest, as 160,000 Post Office workers spent a month on work-to-rule after their demand for a 4 per cent pay increase was rejected, and the dockers walked out yet again. As an internal report by the Conservative Research Department pointed out, the government was extremely fortunate that the Labour Party had been too busy fighting among themselves about disarmament and Clause Four to mount a sustained attack on the evident failure of Macmillan's economic policy. Even so, the report continued: 'The existing armoury of economic weapons – Bank Rate, hire-purchase restrictions, credit squeezes – is admittedly deficient. Yet apart from the introduction of special deposits last year, we have tried out no new ones and, much *more* important, we have done nothing visibly to examine the problems and search for new ones.'[66] In March, after the revaluation of the West German mark, international speculators launched a new raid on sterling, and Macmillan forlornly noted that in one day alone they had lost £67 million. Many commentators now suggested that the pound would have to be devalued, and even Macmillan's perennially optimistic adviser Roy Harrod agreed that they had to do something to puncture the over-heated boom, restrain imports and stabilise the balance of payments. The outlook, another adviser privately admitted, was 'very bad, and there does not seem to be any idea as to how to meet the situation. I suppose there are only three courses: (1) Devaluation. (2) Import controls. (3) Significant expansion of world trade in which our exports could play their part.'[67]

As it turned out, however, Lloyd's budget for 1961 did little to address the situation, being mostly concerned with inventing new tools of economic management in the form of 'regulators' to adjust indirect taxes and National Insurance contributions without the necessity for a new budget.[68] Since the trade figures did not immediately show any great improvement, the pressure on sterling did not abate. On 28 June, Lloyd finally sent his col-leagues a message of despair: 'The pressures on the economy both from without and within are becoming increasingly dangerous . . . the situation is more serious than at any time during the past ten years.' For two years, he explained, they had been running a trade deficit, and 'a succession of adverse balances of this duration is unprecedented in our post-war experience'. He had therefore decided to cut government spending and squeeze domestic demand to reduce imports, while at the same time it was imperative to halt the growth of wages and salaries.[69] Just like Peter Thorneycroft over three years previously, he found that this prospect did not fill his Cabinet col-leagues with great enthusiasm, and, yet again, each member battled to save his own pet spending projects. This time, however, the Chancellor had the reluctant backing of his Prime Minister, not least because the situation seemed so much worse than the winter of 1957, and on 25 July Lloyd was able to present a new 'little budget' to the Commons. Deflation was the order of the day: purchase taxes were raised by 10 per cent, bank rate was increased to 7 per cent, and government spending and bank lending were tightly curtailed. What was more, he also announced a 'pay pause' until March 1962: there would be no wage increases in the public sector, and he hoped that private businesses would follow his example.[70]

Lloyd's deflationary shock package was, according to The Economist, 'the biggest immediate cut in demand that has been deliberately imposed by a

British government on any single afternoon on peacetime history'.[71] It was also a clear admission that Macmillan's economic policy since 1959 had been an abject failure: this was 'stop–go' with a vengeance. Nobody likes austerity, and Labour immediately shot into a five-point advantage in the Gallup opinion poll, their first lead for three years.[72] The pay pause was especially controversial. Lloyd's justification was that incomes had risen by 8 per cent during the previous twelve months, although productivity had increased by a mere 3 per cent. Labour MPs, however, were distinctly unimpressed, shouting 'Resign!' at him during his statement, and Macmillan's press secretary observed that the measures had 'the most universally critical Press that I can remember for any government proposals'.[73] *The Times* announced that the task of economic stabilisation was not merely 'beyond' Selwyn Lloyd, but 'beyond any Chancellor of the Exchequer':

> Britain's economy has been sick for years. The malady has outstayed all too many Chancellors. They come; they apply their nostrums at some feverish moment; they declare the patient will now recover; they go. Before the public have had time to know much about their successor the trouble starts all over again . . . Every British Government since the war has funked the consequences of really fighting inflation. It is hard to believe that at long last Britain has come to the turning point.[74]

Both politically and economically, the pay pause was a fiasco. Astonishingly enough, Lloyd had not bothered to consult the trade unions beforehand, and their leaders were furious at the prospect of an immediate wage freeze. Many industries had automatic wage increases built into their workers' contracts, so that their pay would increase in line with the retail price index, while in others compulsory pay arbitration was in operation. As Richard Lamb points out, neither employers nor unions were about to ignore these agreements merely to placate the Treasury, and, since unemployment was so low, businessmen tended to recruit and keep workers by offering them superior jobs at higher rates of pay, so it was hardly in their interests to conform to the pay pause. The government did not even have statutory powers to enforce the freeze, so when the electricity workers were awarded a generous pay increase in November 1962, the inadequacy and futility of the measures were exposed for all to see. Wage inflation and the price index both continued to rise after July 1961, and it is hard to disagree with Lamb's judgement that 'the

Government failed miserably with their pay pause'.[75] What was perhaps even worse was that the freeze was manifestly unfair, penalising public sector workers but not the privately employed, and therefore the most lasting effect of Lloyd's measures was to alienate that same middle-class professional constituency on which Conservative fortunes depended. 'The Pay Pause', noted a miserable Macmillan in March 1962, '. . . has offended dons, schoolmasters, school-teachers, Civil Servants, clerks, nurses, public utility workers, railwaymen and all the rest.'[76]

For many observers, there was an obvious solution to the misfortunes of the economy: planning. Michael Shanks, for example, was much taken with the interventionist corporatism thought to be so successful in Scandinavia and France, and in *The Stagnant Society* he extolled the virtues of 'joint consultation' and 'industrial democracy', both in individual factories and in the country as a whole.[77] The French example was particularly fashionable, largely since economic growth across the Channel had overtaken that in Britain, and even many Conservatives thought that a domestic equivalent of the Commissariat Général du Plan might represent the answer to Lloyd's problems. The Federation of British Industry had recently been converted to the virtues of Gallic planning, while Macmillan himself, having argued passionately for centralised planning in the thirties, was also instinctively sympathetic towards such an arrangement.[78] On 25 July, Lloyd told the Commons that he was 'not frightened' of 'the controversial matter of planning', and declared that he hoped to establish a National Development Council to set long-term goals for the British economy. The following day, he explained:

I envisage a joint examination of the economic prospects of the country stretching five or more years into the future . . . Above all, it would try to establish what are the essential conditions for realising potential growth. That covers, first, the supply of labour and capital, secondly, the balance of payments conditions and the development of imports and exports, and thirdly, the growth of incomes. In other words, I want both sides of industry to share with the Government the task of relating plans to the resources likely to be available.[79]

Several senior members of the Cabinet were less than impressed by the new spirit of corporatism, arguing that it violated the traditional Conservative faith in competition and economic freedom. Indeed, the Thatcherite right-wingers of the seventies and eighties later liked to cite Macmillan's experiment with planning as the quintessential example of woolly, weak-kneed One Nation bureaucracy.[80]

The centrepiece of the experiment was the National Economic Development Council (the NEDC, known as 'Neddy'), which first met on 7 March 1962, consisting of six industrialists, six trade unionists, two independent experts and three Cabinet ministers. Most of its members arrived at the first meeting panting for breath; in an unpromising omen, the lift in their building on the Embankment had broken down. They were a distinguished bunch: among those around the table at that first meeting were the bosses of Dunlop, Boots, Ferranti, the British Transport Commission and the National Coal Board, as well as the heads of the Transport and General Workers, the Amalgamated Engineers, the National Union of Railwaymen and the TUC.[81] Unfortunately the NEDC never had the bureaucratic resources extended to its French counterpart, and its achievements were, as one historian puts it, 'infinitesimal': its reports went unread and unheeded, its predictions were laughably optimistic and its effects on industrial policy were entirely negligible.[82] Planning alone was no panacea: contemporary admirers of the NEDC might have done well to note that of Britain's major industrial competitors, the Americans, the West Germans and the Italians all produced impressive growth figures with little resort to centralised planning of any kind. As Edmund Dell points out, it was an 'extraordinary misunderstanding' of the nature and potential of economic planning to imagine that, merely by meeting every now and again for a few hours and issuing a series of quasi-papal encyclicals, a handful of the great and the good could rescue the British economy. What was perhaps even more extraordinary was that, despite its manifest irrelevance, such a 'burden and a bore' was not actually abolished until the last decade of the century.[83]

The deflationary measures of July represented an unpleasant shock to an electorate becoming ever more enamoured of the attractions of consumerism; since the pay pause and the NEDC were such clear failures, it was not surprising that Selwyn Lloyd's personal popularity sank to the lowest level of any Chancellor since the war. Barely three in ten voters approved of his austerity package, and as domestic demand began to fall, so public esteem for the government fell with it.[84] By the end of 1961, meanwhile, Hugh Gaitskell was generally acknowledged to have vanquished his critics within the Labour Party and had reinvented himself as an assertive and dynamic leader, so the Conservatives could no longer shelter behind the divisions of their opponents. In October Macmillan asked Butler to step aside as chairman of the Conservative Party, thinking that younger and more aggressive salesmanship from Iain Macleod might help to restore his fortunes, but presentation alone could not mollify the underlying public dissatisfaction with the government. As 1961 gave way to 1962, still the gloomy economic figures poured in. The justification for Lloyd's harsh measures had been that they would put the economy back on its feet, but recovery was still elusive. The trade gap for January 1962, for instance, was some £67 million, while production and retail sales figures showed little sign of recovering from their slump of the previous year. Middle-class hostility to the pay pause was still running high, and even on the Conservative back-benches there were murmurs that 'Supermac' had lost his touch.[85]

On 14 March 1962 the voters took their revenge in sensational fashion, when the Liberals overturned a Conservative majority of 14,760 and won the Orpington by-election by 7885 votes. Orpington was a prosperous, leafy, sub-urban seat on the south-eastern fringes of London, next door to the Prime Minister's own constituency of Bromley. Even though the government had been floundering for months, and the Liberals had already shown flickers of revival among the middle classes, nobody had predicted that Macmillan would be handed such a devastating rebuke. The Conservative candidate, Peter Goldman, was the brightest star of the Conservative Research Department and tipped by many for high office, but it was the Liberals' pop-ular candidate Eric Lubbock who took the seat. For *The Times*, the result was 'the most severe blow that the Conservatives have suffered since they returned to office in 1951'.[86] This was no aberration: at Blackpool the Tories only just clung on to a safe seat against a Liberal surge, while in Middlesbrough East they were driven into third place behind Labour and the Liberals. All in all, the Conservative share of the vote fell by more than a fifth in eight by-elections that spring. When the *Daily Mail* conducted a nationwide opinion poll immediately after Orpington, the results were so staggering that the newspaper decided not to publish the poll for fear of ridicule. The Liberals, incredibly, led with 35.9 per cent, while Labour were on 30.5 per cent and the Conservatives on 27.4 per cent. A few days later, NOP confirmed the general picture, giving the Liberals 33.7 per cent, Labour 33.5 per cent and the Conservatives 32.8 per cent.[87] Even if some Conservatives were heartened that Labour had still not managed to put together a commanding lead, others felt that a Liberal revival among middle-class voters was potentially even more damaging, especially if the electorate decided to vote tactically against the government. Macmillan put on the usual show of unflappability, but privately he was appalled. 'We have been swept off our feet by a *Liberal* revival,' he wrote in his diary ten days after Orpington. Even a month later, he was still worried: 'Conservative party gets weaker and the Liberals eat into our position like rats . . . They are voting Liberal to give the Government a smack in the eye.'[88] More intimations of disaster followed. In April the Liberals won 27 per cent of the vote at Stockton-on-Tees and 25 per cent at Derby North; on 6 June, in Derbyshire West, a weak Liberal candidate took second place ahead of Labour and came within 1200 votes of winning the seat entirely.[89]

As the press saw it, 'Orpington Man' was on the march. 'Orpington', said *The Times*, 'is a suburb filled with middle-class people whose wages have not kept up with inflation, who have been given no Schedule A relief, who are buying houses a little beyond their means and who are having to pay higher interest on their mortgages . . . a perfect constituency for protest votes by those classes of electors who have gained least from the affluent society in the past few years.' In the suburbs of Middle England, the newspaper explained, 'the lower middle-class have found Conservative visions of a property-owning democracy frustrated as Bank rate soars, taking mortgage interest rates up with it'.[90] These voters tended to be young men and women who had migrated from industrial, working-class areas in search of affluence and respectability in the expanding suburbs: in other words, the very same group that had supposedly abandoned Labour for good in the election of 1959. These were precisely the people who had gained the most from the boom of the late fifties, but with high mortgage costs and outgoings they were also the people who stood to lose the most from Selwyn Lloyd's economic blundering. Under their dynamic, thoughtful young leader, Jo Grimond, the Liberals had successfully transformed themselves from an eccentric pressure group into a respectable outlet for middle-class resentment, but the real threat to Macmillan came from a reinvigorated Labour Party. By the summer of 1962, the Liberal tide had peaked; Labour were once again riding high at the top of the polls, and Gaitskell looked and sounded like a Prime Minister in waiting. Labour strategy was now based on appealing to the material self-interest of the 'new' clerical and technical middle classes, and the party leadership was moving towards the rhetoric of 'white heat', technology and modernisation, carefully designed to strike a chord with Orpington Man, the aspirational suburban voter at the heart of the affluent society.[91]

In the meantime, Harold Macmillan was not a happy man. Lloyd's strict deflationary package had not merely thrown the economy into a jarring and uncomfortable reverse, it had also sent the Conservatives tumbling in the opinion polls, and they could ill afford to remain in third place for long. His 1962 budget, less than a month after the Orpington by-election, was a severe disappointment to many Conservatives hoping for crowd-pleasing measures. Tax concessions were carefully balanced with tax rises: while purchase tax was cut on cars, televisions and washing machines, it was increased on soft drinks, sweets and ice cream, a public relations blunder of the utmost foolishness. Even the Chancellor's own sister commented gleefully: 'Well, well! Taxing the poor children's pocket money!'[92] Many in the Cabinet felt that it was already time for Lloyd to relax the brakes and allow the economy to expand once again, but, since he did not agree, the budget only made it through Cabinet after a difficult and dispiriting argument. In fact, consumer demand was not rising, as Lloyd and his Treasury aides had assumed, but was steadily falling; rather than encouraging a modest recovery, therefore, the budget instead merely pushed up unemployment.[93]

Like so many Chancellors before and since, Selwyn Lloyd became the chief scapegoat. In truth the performance of the government as a whole had been fairly incompetent ever since the 1959 election, but the Orpington result had put tremendous pressure on Lloyd to come up with something special, and this he had manifestly failed to do. Macmillan had by now already decided that he would like to hold the next election at the end of 1963, and he had come up with a recovery plan of his own. Treasury officials used to joke that Macmillan's motto was 'When in doubt, reflate,' and as usual they were right. According to Macmillan's scheme, Lloyd would prepare the ground for a new expansionist boom, while the threat of inflation would be kept under control by a government incomes policy applicable to both public and private employees and closely linked to productivity. This was all very well in theory, but, as Lloyd and his advisers pointed out, there was no guarantee that such an incomes policy would be effective; and if it failed, as was quite likely, then there was a terrible risk of rampant inflation and renewed payments crises. Macmillan was not pleased that his 'very bold' plan had met with such a 'chilly' response. Lloyd's job was to do his master's bidding, not to think for himself, yet here he was, 'making too much of the dangers of inflation'.[94]

It was against this background of general disillusionment that

Macmillan's senior colleagues began pressing him to prepare a Cabinet reshuffle. Another potentially humiliating by-election, at Leicester North-East, was scheduled for 12 July, and both the party chairman Iain Macleod and the Chief Whip Martin Redmayne encouraged Macmillan to recast his government before the parliamentary recess in order to regain some credibility with the electorate.[95] In fact, Macmillan had already had a conspiratorial lunch with Rab Butler on 21 June to discuss shuffling his pack. According to Macmillan's diary, Butler thought that:

> the present grave political position is due entirely to the bad handling of the economic problem (or rather its bad presentation) by the Chancellor of the Exchequer and the Treasury. He felt that drastic action was necessary to save the situation. This means the problem (an immense human and political problem) of replacing the Chancellor of the Exchequer.[96]

The idea of sacking Lloyd, his faithful political Passepartout, certainly appealed to Macmillan. Not only was the Chancellor making trouble over the future direction of the economy, but he was also a political liability, unpopular both on the Tory benches and in the country. 'Selwyn – of whom I am very fond and who has been a true and loyal friend since I became PM – seems to me to have lost grip,' Macmillan wrote on 8 July. 'He is, by nature, more of a staff officer than a commander. But lately, he seems hardly to function.' Still, if sacrificing the dependable, amiable Lloyd was the way to save his government, then so be it:

> If (as I must) I decide that he must go, *when* and *how*? It will be personally terrible and I shrink from it. It will be said to be a 'panic' measure. I will be accused of gross 'disloyalty'. Yet all those I trust – Alec Home, Norman Brook, Chief Whip – agree that it is right. I am to talk with him on Thursday [12 July] and try to give him fore-warning in a nice way, with a view to the changes (which should be on a large scale) being announced at the end of the Session (August 3rd).[97]

Unfortunately, Macmillan's scheme never went to plan. Butler, characteristically, could not keep his mouth shut. On 11 July, during a typically convivial lunch with Lord Rothermere and a group of executives from the *Daily Mail*, he gleefully confided that Lloyd was facing the sack. Among those present was the paper's lobby correspondent, and on the following morning, the very day that Macmillan was supposed to be breaking the news to Lloyd and also the day of the Leicester North-East by-election, the *Mail* ran a front-page scoop, 'MAC'S MASTER PLAN', with the news that Lloyd was to be replaced and the government entirely reshuffled.[98]

What followed was a disaster of the most spectacular proportions, the infamous 'Night of the Long Knives' from which Macmillan's government never really recovered. By mid-morning on 12 July, not only had the news that 'Rab has blabbed' flashed around Westminster and Fleet Street, but it had also overshadowed a tense Cabinet meeting during which Macmillan awkwardly denied any responsibility for the rumours. Even at this stage, it seems, the Chancellor did not suspect what was to follow. Just after four that afternoon, however, Macmillan's principal private secretary and close confidant Tim Bligh appeared in the doorway of Lloyd's office in the Treasury, 'ashen pale and stammering more than usual'. According to Lloyd, Bligh announced nervously: 'The PM wants to see you at six this evening. We have always been good friends, and I must warn you it is about the reshuffle.' 'Does he want me to go?' Lloyd asked in stunned horror. 'Yes,' Bligh replied.[99] Two hours later, still in a state of shock, Lloyd presented himself in Admiralty House, the Prime Minister's temporary residence while 10 Downing Street was being renovated. What followed was, as Macmillan himself recorded, 'a terribly difficult and emotional scene', lasting for the best part of an hour.[100] Macmillan was not offering his loyal ally an alternative job; he was sacking him outright after years of close collaboration and companionship. Lloyd pointed out that the sudden move smacked of 'panic', that a radical reshuffle might be better delayed until the Orpington storm had fully passed, and that if he was dismissed, then the public might well ask why 'the old man' had not gone too. Macmillan tried to mollify him by suggesting that he might like to make some money in the City. Lloyd flatly said that he had no interest in doing so. Macmillan offered him a peerage. Lloyd turned it down. After forty-five minutes of this painful charade, the Chancellor left, utterly distraught.[101]

But instead of going home, to the empty silence of his bachelor flat, Lloyd went to the smoking room of the House of Commons and poured his troubles out to two of his closest parliamentary friends: John Hare, the Minister of Labour; and Nigel Birch, the waspish former Financial Secretary who had never forgiven Macmillan for their clash over inflation at the end of 1957. Birch, who immediately spotted the opportunity to strike at his former adversary, thought that Hare should resign in protest, but Hare refused. So Birch contented himself with writing an elegant letter to *The Times*, to be printed the following Saturday morning:

> Sir,
>
> For the second time the Prime Minister has got rid of a Chancellor of the Exchequer who tried to get expenditure under control.
>
> Once is more than enough.
>
> Yours truly,
> Nigel Birch[102]

With Hare's refusal to resign in sympathy, the drama of the Thursday evening came to an end, leaving Macmillan safely tucked up in Admiralty House and Lloyd drowning his sorrows among friends in the Commons. Early on Friday morning, however, Macmillan had an unpleasant surprise: a telephone call from his Foreign Secretary, Lord Home, with the information that Lloyd had encouraged Hare to resign from the government. Macmillan was always, despite his outward show of amiable self-confidence, an anxious, jittery man, and he jumped to the conclusion that Lloyd was planning some sort of parliamentary coup against him. 'All this confirmed in me the need for speed,' he wrote later.[103] The Cabinet had to be purged immediately: all the changes that he had been pondering for weeks must be rushed into one day. The result was political butchery. As one backbencher later put it: 'Ministers who later on during the afternoon were to be sacked were still continuing to dictate memoranda and hold meetings in Whitehall, quite clearly under the illusion that they were continuing safely in office.'[104] Although Macmillan tried to sweeten the pill in most instances with the offer of a peerage or some similar honour, reading from notes prepared for him by the faithful Bligh, many of them could hardly believe what was happening.[105]

The first head to roll was that of Lord Mills, Minister without Portfolio, who went quietly enough. John Maclay, the Scottish Secretary, was next, and he too caused little trouble. Then came Harold Watkinson, the Minister of Defence, who thought that Macmillan was on the verge of collapse:

> I found the PM alone, but with Tim Bligh, his Principal Private Secretary, hovering around. Harold Macmillan looked tired and

distressed. In emotional terms he told me that the Government was in crisis. He painted a picture of a political situation that was beyond my wildest dreams and his forebodings of Ministerial revolt, centred upon Selwyn Lloyd, did not seem to me to make sense . . . Selwyn, who was a friend of mine, was not of the stuff of which rebels are made.[106]

Watkinson was quite right: the idea that Lloyd could be behind any such conspiracy was laughably implausible. Macmillan was not, however, in the mood for a debate; and Watkinson was out. Two more ministers remained to be dismissed before Macmillan could retire to the relative sanctuary of a Buckingham Palace garden party scheduled for that afternoon. One was Lord Kilmuir, the Lord Chancellor, an old friend, neighbour and fellow Guardsman who had helped to secure the succession for Macmillan in 1957. Kilmuir's personal life was little better than Macmillan's: his wife was openly living with a fellow peer, and his ceremonial office was a welcome consolation to a lonely old man. When Macmillan announced that he was to be sacked, Kilmuir was appalled. The Prime Minister, he thought, had lost 'both nerve and judgement'; he himself would have given a cook more notice than Macmillan had given him. But then, as Macmillan later pointed out, it was much easier to get a good Lord Chancellor than a good cook.[107] There was little love lost between them from that day onwards. 'He was always a "beta minus",' Macmillan snapped, 'the stupidest Lord Chancellor ever . . . hopeless in Cabinet – that's why I got rid of him.'[108]

The last victim was David Eccles, the Minister of Education, whom Macmillan asked to go back to his old job at the Board of Trade. Eccles refused; he had been drifting around the middle order for too long, and the only alternative job he would accept was that of Chancellor of the Exchequer. He was regarded by most of his colleagues as a serious, heavyweight figure, and as a talented self-made businessman would probably have made an effective and independent Chancellor. What was more, as Alistair Horne points out, he idolised Macmillan as 'the politician he most admired and . . . a friend who would not let him down'.[109] Macmillan, however, thought that Eccles was 'frightfully bumptious' and had 'a very high opinion of himself'; he did not want an independent Chancellor, no matter how well qualified. So Eccles was out, too; as he later put it, he had been 'sacked with less notice than a housemaid'.[110]

Macmillan had sacked a third of his Cabinet: it was 'an act of carnage unprecedented in British political history'. He had been pondering a reshuffle for weeks, but on 13 and 14 July he badly miscalculated. Certainly the dismissal of so many old friends and colleagues was not something he enjoyed, and according to Horne he was even physically sick between meetings.[111] His reputation as the 'unflappable' political master was destroyed, and Selwyn Lloyd reflected the feelings of millions of voters when he contemplated his old colleague's 'utter ruthlessness, and his determination to retain power by the sacrifice of even his closest friends'.[112] Indeed, Macmillan's treatment of Lloyd, a man who had faithfully stood by him through thick and thin, was perhaps the most striking aspect of the entire business. In the words of Lloyd's biographer:

> Whatever the political expedience, however urgent the necessity, Harold Macmillan treated Selwyn in a most shameful and personally wounding manner. The man who was privy to all his counsels was unceremoniously and ungratefully despatched to an intended political oblivion. It was the unworthiest moment of Macmillan's entire premiership.[113]

Happily for Lloyd, an unimaginative but essentially decent man, it was not quite the end of his political career; indeed, in 1971 his popularity in the House helped him to win the office of Speaker. At the time, however, the abrupt end of his Treasury stewardship struck many observers as a turning point in the fortunes of the Macmillan government. Gaitskell put down a motion of censure in the Commons, hoping to make hay from Macmillan's difficulties, and in the ensuing debate he taunted the Prime Minister by wondering aloud why he had dismissed only seven ministers. One Conservative backbencher declared that Macmillan should be congratulated because 'he had kept his head when all about were losing theirs', which provoked great gales of mocking laughter, and the rising star of the Liberals, Jeremy Thorpe, elegantly applied the knife with his famous quip: 'Greater love hath no man than this, that he lay down his friends for his life.'[114]

All in all, the Night of the Long Knives dealt a devastating blow to Macmillan's public image, and it severely weakened his popularity in the country. The last Gallup poll published before the purge, on 11 July, had found 47 per cent of the public satisfied with Macmillan's leadership and 39 per cent dissatisfied. In the next poll, published on 20 July, only 36 per cent counted themselves as satisfied, while 52 per cent were dissatisfied, a stunning personal decline without recent precedent.[115] Nigel Birch's cold, withering letter to *The Times* caught the general mood, and even the Conservative newspapers were staggered by what the *Telegraph* called 'the Stalinist scale of the purge'. Supermacbeth, it appeared, had taken the place of Supermac, and the headlines in the Sunday newspapers, such as 'HIS OWN EXECUTIONER' and 'MAC THE KNIFE', made ominous reading. Whether Macmillan could long survive seemed extremely unlikely; as one paper now put it: 'FOR MAC THE BELL TOLLS'.[116]

11

TV WITH AUNTIE

Television is at last given the real freedom of the air. The event is comparable with the abolition of the law that kept motor-cars chugging sedately behind a man carrying a red flag.

Now it's the 'go' signal, the green light for TV, too – with no brake on enterprise and imagination.

TV Times, 22 September 1955

I hardly ever see a television programme. Now, that is not just the stock boast of those who like to feel intellectually superior. On the contrary, I say it with a feeling of resentment and deprivation. Not for me the joys of Half Hours with Hancock. No Dixon. No Maigret. No Chislebury. No Lone Ranger. No Lennie the Lion. It isn't actually that we can't afford a set at Number 10, but the trouble is my employers never actually give me an evening off!

Harold Macmillan, November 1961

In January 1960 the BBC newsletter *Ariel* welcomed the arrival of a new Director General to lead the national broadcaster into the sixties. Hugh Carleton Greene, said *Ariel*, was 'One of Us'. The brother of the novelist Graham Greene, he had previously run the wartime German service, the Overseas Service and then the News and Current Affairs Department, and was a lover of cricket, beer and women, who worked his way through three wives at a time when divorce was still regarded as rather suspicious.[1] As the *Daily Star* put it, he was 'the best kind of Uncle – the kind who isn't stuffy, prefers chuckles to a frown; wants his nephews and nieces to treat serious things seriously, but doesn't wish to spoil anyone's fun'.[2] As far as Greene was concerned, the moral didacticism of the BBC's old days was out; he wanted to cultivate a new mood of creativity, innovation and enthusiasm that would turn the Corporation into the mirror of Britain in the 1960s. He later explained:

I wanted to open the windows and dissipate the ivory-tower stuffi-
ness ... which still clung to some parts of the BBC. I wanted to
encourage enterprise and the taking of risks. I wanted to make the BBC
a place where talent of all sorts, however unconventional, was recog-
nized and nurtured, where talented people could work and, if they
wished, take their talents elsewhere, sometimes coming back again to
enrich the organization from which they had started. I may have
thought at the beginning that I should be dragging the BBC kicking
and screaming into the Sixties. But I soon learnt that some urging,
some encouragement, was all the immense reserve of youthful talent
in the BBC had been waiting for, and from that moment I was part of
a rapidly flowing stream.[3]

By the time Greene took over at the top, the BBC was not merely a
national institution but a powerful and definitive expression of national will
and character. It had been founded as a public company in the early twenties by a group of radio companies and in 1927 was issued with a royal
charter giving it a monopoly of broadcasting in Britain for seventy years and
establishing a Corporation run by a board of Governors and a Director
General. It quickly became one of the most successful cultural institutions
in the country. With guaranteed funding from a mandatory licence fee, and
privileged access to a captive market, it enjoyed resources and opportunities
unmatched anywhere else in the world, and within a few years it was being
semi-seriously bracketed with 'Parliament, Monarchy, Church and the Holy
Ghost'.[4] By the end of the Second World War, it had become 'an additional
established church, a source of authority over the language, an arbiter of
national taste, a national musical impresario and a re-invigorator of national
drama and song'.[5] People trusted the BBC: 'it strove to be the mirror of the
nation, and the nation accepted it'.[6]

The didactic ethos of the Corporation was encapsulated in the words of
its first Director General, John Reith: 'Give the public slightly better than it
thinks it likes.' Reith was an engineer and a Presbyterian Scot, a man of stern
moral principle and clipped, reserved bearing, and ran the BBC with iron
control until 1938. It was Reith who decided that all radio announcers
should be anonymous, and Reith who in 1925 commanded that his radio
presenters, most of whom were former public schoolboys and Oxbridge
men, should wear evening dress when on the air.[7] The voice of Reith's BBC
was that of upper-class, southern England; indeed, more than any other

institution, it was the Corporation that determined the tone and accent of 'standard English' in the twentieth century.[8] Long after Reith had departed, his influence lingered on in the corridors of the Corporation. John Osborne complained that it produced 'a staff of highly trained palace lackeys with graveyard voices, and a ponderous language stuffed with Shakespearean and semi-Biblical echoes'. One of Reith's assistants explained: 'He was Queen Victoria, Genghis Khan, Leonardo, rolled into one. He was Headmaster, Field-Marshal, Permanent Secretary, Commoner, Captain of the Ship, Father wielding a cane, a baton, a pen, a telephone, a secretary with an effortless ease . . . Around him we were all dwarfs.'[9]

The centrepiece of Reith's BBC was the radio. Even during the 1950s, many BBC executives saw television as a trivial diversion from the serious business of radio, and the *Radio Times* reflected this by printing television listings as a four-page supplement after the long radio schedules. One anecdote told of a BBC mandarin bumping into an old producer friend in the bowels of Broadcasting House. 'I thought you were dead,' he is supposed to have said. 'Ah, gone to television? Well, it's the same thing.'[10] While television was still the province of a minority, radio could claim to be a genuinely national medium, with coverage reaching every corner of the British Isles and offering something for everybody from dukes to dustmen.[11] The sound of the radio was therefore an integral part of British life in the fifties and sixties; many people conducted their daily lives with the voice of the BBC constantly murmuring in their ears. As one man later put it: 'The radio was on all the time, it was part of the background of family life, something we all shared. We'd sit down to Sunday lunch and end up eating in silence because we were all concentrating on what was happening on the radio.'[12]

Listeners could choose between three stations; whereas Reith had advocated mixing 'high' culture and light entertainment together, post-war radio programming divided the stations on cultural lines. The Home Service, perceived as middlebrow, offered news, plays and lectures; the Light Programme, which had evolved from the General Forces Programme in wartime, presented popular music, comedies and soap operas; and the Third Programme consisted of classical music and self-consciously 'high' culture. The explicit assumption was that this tripartite system represented a 'cultural pyramid' and would inexorably draw the listener towards the pinnacle that was the Third Programme. As the post-war Director General Sir William Haley explained in a lecture in 1948:

The pyramid is served by three main Programmes, differentiated but broadly overlapping in levels and interest, each Programme leading on to the other, the listener being induced through the years increasingly to discriminate in favour of the things that are more worthwhile . . . The listener must be led from good to better by curiosity, liking, and a growth of understanding. As the standards of the education and culture of the community rise so should the programme pyramid rise as a whole.[13]

Of the three post-war networks, the real success story was the Light Programme at the base of the pyramid, which attracted about two-thirds of listeners. The formula initially established in the forties proved an extremely successful and long-lasting one, and many of the individual programmes devised during those years ran continuously for several decades. The tone of the Light Programme was domestic, middle-class, feminine and individual, aimed like so many other cultural phenomena of the period at affluent women whose daytime hours were filled with household chores.[14] *Housewives' Choice*, for example, attracted over seven million regular listeners during the hour just after breakfast when many women were readying themselves for their household duties; similarly, *Woman's Hour* won a loyal and enduring following and continued to be broadcast into the twenty-first century. For toddlers and young children there was *Listen with Mother*, broadcast just after lunch and always beginning with the famous lines: 'Are you sitting comfortably? Then I'll begin.' For older children, there was *Children's Hour* at five o'clock, or the drama serial *Dick Barton: Special Agent*, which appealed to boys in particular and reached audiences of up to fifteen million. The most popular music programme was *Family Favourites*, which played records requested by the audience themselves; as the title suggested, it was not thought likely that the musical tastes of parents and children would be particularly different. The various radio comedies, meanwhile, demonstrated the wit and diversity of British comic traditions, from the surreal anarchy of *The Goon Show* to the working-class humour of *Take It from Here*, which starred Dick Bentley and June Whitfield as the hapless couple Ron and Eth, or the melancholy wit of *Hancock's Half Hour*.[15]

The most successful programme of all, however, had its origins as an educational vehicle for farmers, designed to inform them of new agricultural methods and to help them respond to the challenges of rationing. *The Archers* was first devised in 1950 as 'a farming *Dick Barton*', an 'everyday story of country folk' with an explicit didactic function and set in the village of Ambridge in the fictional Midland county of Borsetshire.[16] Not until 1972, in fact, was its educational role finally abandoned. Given its background and purpose, the popularity of The Archers was extremely impressive: within five years it had reached a peak audience of twenty million people. Not only did the programme's domestic focus suit the mood of the times, but it also exploited the romantic rural longings of British audiences, not least among urban listeners. The BBC's publicity for the show described Ambridge as 'a gentle relic of Old England, nostalgic, generous, incorruptible and (above all) valiant. In other words the sort of British community that the rootless townsman would like to live in and can involve himself in vicariously.'[17] The Archers continued to thrive for decades afterwards, suggesting that rural nostalgia was a continuing force in British cultural life; by the time it celebrated its fiftieth anniversary, the programme had become an institution in itself, reflecting the moods and tastes of its loyal middle-class audience.

The Third Programme, meanwhile, the intended pinnacle of the BBC's cultural pyramid, was nowhere near as popular. Its avowedly elitist, high-minded programmes, including classical music, plays and lectures, were undoubtedly of an extremely high quality, but they simply did not win over audiences. Three years after its launch in 1946, listeners to the Third Programme accounted for an underwhelming 1 per cent of the radio audience, and they continued to fall rather than rise, finally sinking beneath the measurable level to under 36,000 people.[18] The 'cultural pyramid' project was clearly a failure, in that listeners preferred to stick with the Light Programme or Home Service rather than move up to the Third Programme, and by the mid-fifties BBC executives were discussing cutting its output as a prelude to further reorganisation. This provoked a predictable outcry from that minority devoted to the network, and in March 1957 a Third Programme Defence Society was established, which organised letters to The Times in its support signed by such luminaries as Bertrand Russell, T. S. Eliot and Albert Camus.[19] The cultural gulf between such characters and the general public was summed up well by a Punch cartoon in April 1957, which showed a woman in sensible shoes and a bearded man with a beret soliciting signatures for a petition under a banner reading 'Hands Off the Third Programme'. At her door stands a bewildered housewife who explains: 'I'm not worried – we don't listen to Luxembourg no more since the commercial telly started.'[20] As it happened, the Third Programme was never abolished, despite the fact that it was far from popular and hardly cost-effective; instead, its hours were cut and its daytime service was relaunched in 1957 as Network Three, finally being incorporated into the new Radio Three in 1967.[21]

The BBC had begun broadcasting to a television audience in 1936, but the service was promptly closed down on the outbreak of war and only restored in June 1946. Television was still tightly circumscribed well into the following decade, and the BBC only broadcast from three in the afternoon on weekdays and from five on Sundays. Indeed, in the immediate post-war period, the audience consisted of a mere 25,000 middle-class households in the London region; not until 1949 and 1951 was the television service available in the Midlands and the North of England, let alone the more distant regions of the United Kingdom.[22] At this stage, television was little more than a curiosity, since programmes were primitive, the coverage patchy and the reception unreliable. One academic later recalled cycling three miles to a friend's house as a boy in 1951 to watch his new black-and-white set; the experience struck him as 'quaint and cosy . . . looking at a little box of tricks you might see at a fairground side-show'.[23] Early attempts to televise sport were not entirely successful; after watching the 1952 Boat Race, one viewer recorded in his diary: 'This was a ludicrous performance, television-wise. The cameras died in an explosive series of blinding flashes; for sound we were transferred to the Light Programme commentary; their launch ran out of petrol. TV did produce a blurred and bad picture of the finish, but that was about all.'[24] Most programmes at this stage were little more than rehashes of the shows transmitted before the war: indeed, some of the presenters, like Jasmine Bligh and Joan Gilbert, were the same. As for television drama, only very slowly was a specific televisual style being developed; most televised plays were 'simply photographed stage dramas'.[25]

The expansion of television over the course of the following decade was extraordinary. In 1949, after all, two-thirds of the population had never even laid eyes on a television set, let alone owned a working model.[26] The event that converted the public at large to the attractions of television was the Coronation in 1953, the first royal event to be televised at such length and with such ceremony and care. The number of licence-holders doubled overnight, from one and a half million to nearly three million, and many of those who had rented television sets especially for the big day were so impressed that they decided to keep them. Estimates of the viewing audience varied from twenty million to twenty-seven million, which in any case marked a national record, and there were plenty of anecdotes about dozens of people huddling in one sitting room to watch the only set in the street. According to a conservative estimate from the BBC, eight million had seen it in their own homes, ten million in the homes of friends or neighbours, and two million more in pubs, clubs and cinemas.[27] Twelve million more, meanwhile, had listened to the event on the radio; but, as the experience of the Coronation suggested, radio's position as the senior partner was under threat.[28] In the next seven years, television strengthened its hold, especially after the introduction of a second, commercial channel in 1955 and the expansion of television reception to cover almost the entire country in the final two years of the decade.[29] A brief look at the figures for licence-holders tells the story. In 1951 there had been 764,000 combined television and radio licences; in 1955 there were over four million; and in 1960 there were over ten million.[30] By this point, 72 per cent of the population had access to both ITV and the BBC, and the £4 licence fee seemed a better investment than ever.[31]

Television ownership reached a natural peak at the end of 1964, when there were thirteen million sets in use and almost total coverage had been assured. Within the space of a few years, television had been transformed from a minority interest, a mere novelty even, into the cornerstone of an evening's entertainment and the following morning's banter. It was no longer a luxury; it had become a social necessity.[32] The dramatic expansion of television was in itself indicative of working-class affluence in the late fifties; at the same time, as Robert Hewison puts it, it also represented 'a massive change in the way the working classes entertained themselves'.[33]

For one thing, it evidently marked a new stage in the domestication of culture and entertainment. Where once men had spent their evenings in the pub with their friends and workmates, they might now stay in with their wives and children to watch the television. Television was one factor in a general 'return to the home' in the post-war years, part of a broad process in which the family was exalted as the cornerstone of social and political life. Not surprisingly, the development of television came as an unwelcome shock to those in the worlds of film and provincial theatre, who saw their already shaky position decline still further. It was no coincidence that, at the same time that television was booming, attendance at football matches, in pubs and in cinemas was entering a period of steady decline.[34] By the winter of 1957–8, one unremarkable Sunday evening found nearly half the adult population clustered around the 'box', and a year later, another survey found that 60 per cent of British adults were watching television every day for an average of five hours in winter and three and a half hours in summer.[35] Magazines in the late fifties printed recipes for 'TV dinners' that families could eat from their laps to avoid missing their favourite programmes, and there was even a brief vogue for modern plastic trays, like the 'Tea-V-Tray' or the 'Armchair Tray', to make eating in front of the television easier.[36]

The set itself, the focus of so much attention, was neatly presented as just another piece of household furniture. In middle-class households, it stood quietly in the corner, often hidden behind mahogany or walnut double doors in a tall cabinet. The screen, meanwhile, was tiny by the standards of subsequent decades, only nine or ten inches across. Turning on the television during much of the day produced little more than 'restful silence or . . . restful Mozart'; after all, programming only began at three in the afternoon and five on Sundays, paused between six and seven for the so-called 'toddlers' truce', designed to persuade small children that the programmes were over so that they could be put to bed, and stopped for good at half-past ten. Since programmes did not always run to the precise time allotted, there were also occasional 'interludes' between them, when the screen might show 'a windmill turning, horse ploughs ploughing, waves breaking eternally on the rocks, a potter's wheel revolving hypnotically, calmingly or maddeningly, according to the temperament of the viewer'.[37] The mood was one of gentle didacticism. In Peter Lewis' words:

> The programmes themselves were also of a blandness that it is hard to recapture. There was about them a strong flavour of evening classes run by a well-endowed Workers' Education Institute: cookery lessons from the TV chef, the goatee-bearded Philip Harben; gardening hints from the TV gardener, the venerable Fred Streeter; 'Music for You' – nothing too demandingly classical – conducted in a black tie and introduced with an ingratiating few words by Eric Robinson . . . Live entertainment consisted mainly of stultifyingly dull continental cabaret artists, Slav acrobats, Czech jugglers, dancers in clogs, boots and lederhosen without the command of English to risk a joke even if they knew one.[38]

The cosy world of BBC television received its first major shock in 1955, with the launch of ITV, a controversial commercial television channel established by the 1954 Television Act and funded by advertising breaks between the programmes.[39] The launch of the new channel was anticipated by months of news stories about the 'defection' of BBC performers and presenters to commercial television, the first shots in decades of struggle between the two channels. The 'Gala Opening' of ITV on 22 September 1955 imitated the BBC's emphasis on tradition and prestige: champagne was served at the Mayfair Hotel, state trumpeters blew a fanfare at a white-tie banquet in the London Guildhall, and Sir John Barbirolli conducted the Hallé Orchestra in a performance of Elgar's *Cockaigne Overture*. Just after eight o'clock, forty-five minutes after the station had begun transmission, there came the first advertisement, extolling the virtues of 'tingling fresh' Gibb SR toothpaste, followed by more 'commercials' for chocolate and margarine.[40] The advertisements themselves were regarded as an intriguing novelty. 'A charming young lady brushed her teeth,' Bernard Levin reported to his curious readers in the *Manchester Guardian*; 'while a charming young gentleman told us of the benefits of the toothpaste with which she was doing it.'[41]

The evening was most remembered, however, not for anything ITV had shown, but for the BBC's response. Only 190,000 homes could receive the new channel on its opening night; by contrast, the biggest audience of the evening, accounting for over nine million people, was tuned in to *The Archers* and listening in horrified disbelief to the news of Grace Archer's death in a stable fire. Indeed, it was the death of Grace Archer, a ruthless masterstroke on the part of the BBC, that captured the following day's headlines, rather than the new channel. 'Radio Fans wept as Grace Archer died,' reported the *Mirror*. 'Why did Grace have to die?' lamented the *News Chronicle*. Even *The Times* felt moved to print a short report on what some commentators regarded as the 'murder' of a much loved character.[42] The furore over Grace's death both indicated the continuing appeal of radio – no television audience could compete with the nine million who listened to the Light Programme that night – and presaged a difficult first year for the new commercial channel. Only four of the proposed regional companies had been established by the time the channel began broadcasting, and they lost a combined £11 million during their first eighteen months.[43] One major problem was that the new service was not yet available outside London and the south-east. ITV did not reach the Midlands until the following February and the North of England until May, while Scotland had to wait until August 1957, South Wales until January 1958, and eastern England and Northern Ireland until the end of 1959.[44]

Once fully established, however, the commercial channel began to win audiences over, and advertising revenue mounted accordingly. In 1956, the first full year of ITV, advertisers had spent some £13 million on television commercials; by 1960, this had reached £76 million, and rose to £93 million a year later. By this point commercial television had proved to be exactly the 'licence to print money' that had been predicted, and the companies were making annual profits of 130 per cent. Norman Collins, a former BBC executive who had become an early recruit to the ITV cause, admitted that there was something 'immoral' about their profits; his own investment of £2250 had turned into £500,000.[45] It is worth noting the unwelcome consequences for newspapers, which depended for their survival on a steady income from advertisers: evening papers in particular were badly hit, since readers were deserting them for the pleasures of the television, and picture magazines like *Picture Post*, *Illustrated* and *Everybody's* found that, with their advertisers turning to ITV, survival was impossible. By 1959, just four years after its launch, ITV's advertising revenue was greater than that of all of the Fleet Street newspapers combined.[46]

Clearly the novelty of advertising was not in itself sufficient to lure television audiences away from the BBC. What made ITV distinctive, and so successful, was that it promised a new kind of programming: modern, snappy, international and classless. 'Viewers will no longer have to accept what is deemed best for them,' promised the first issue of the *TV Times*, the listings magazine for commercial television. 'The new independent television planners aim at giving viewers what viewers want – at the time viewers want it.'[47] The informality of the new station was epitomised by a new breed of younger 'newscasters', the most famous being Robin Day, who appeared on camera and spoke in a more relaxed, familiar style than the clipped tones associated with the BBC. A few early attempts to impress viewers with Shakespeare, history and classical music were quickly abandoned; only Granada, which served northern viewers, stood out for its highbrow ambition and dedication to showing what it called 'items of unusual or topical interest and special programmes of intellectual or cultural value'.[48] Instead, most ITV networks offered programmes that tried to copy the light, fast, amusing style of entertainment that working-class audiences already enjoyed in music halls and variety shows. A show like ATV's *Sunday*

Night at the London Palladium, which ran extremely successfully from 1955 to 1967, was self-consciously traditional both in its title and in its presentation of old-fashioned comedy and variety acts; similarly, *The Adventures of Robin Hood*, which ran for four years from 1955, drew on the patriotic legend of the medieval outlaw to great popular acclaim.[49]

A second aspect of ITV's appeal was its reliance on imported American programmes, which were often slicker and more expensive than their British counterparts and proved extremely popular with working-class and lower-middle-class audiences, despite the horror of many cultural critics. The ITV network began screening *I Love Lucy*, *Dragnet* and *Gunsmoke* within a year of its launch, and by the end of 1956 the BBC and ITV were between them showing no fewer than twelve American comedy series, introducing transatlantic comedians like George Burns, Jack Benny, Bob Hope and Phil Silvers to British sitting rooms.[50]

The programme most associated with ITV in its early years, however, was the quiz show, a format copied from the United States where it had been both enormously successful and, after the revelations of quiz-rigging and corruption, unexpectedly controversial. Quiz shows like *Double Your Money* and *Take Your Pick* were relatively cheap to make and made few demands on the viewer; for millions of exhausted families at the end of a long day, they were the ideal evening entertainment. While American contestants could win tens of thousands of dollars, however, or even a Cadillac as a consolation for losing, British contestants took home rather more modest rewards: some kitchen furniture, say, or a new refrigerator. 'Who wrote Mendelssohn's *Spring Song*?' ran one infamous question; the lucky winner in this case was rewarded with five years' worth of nylon stockings.[51] Another popular show, *Opportunity Knocks*, successfully combined the slick Americanism of the quiz show with the old variety tradition and the talent competitions familiar to viewers from clubs and holiday camps; presented by the smooth Canadian host Hughie Green, with his casual mid-Atlantic drawl, it pulled in twenty-five million viewers at its peak.[52]

The populist emphasis of ITV programmes during the late fifties was, in terms of the broadcasting world, a genuine innovation; even though the network drew on older conventions of working-class entertainment from music halls to working men's clubs, it also presented itself as modern, informal and glamorous, qualities typically associated with all things American. By the end of 1957, the early months of struggle were a distant memory and commercial television commanded 72 per cent of the national audience share.[53] Unlike the Governors of the BBC, the executives who ran the various ITV companies had little interest in education, didacticism or appearing genteel, and their programmes were better equipped to address specific regional and class audiences than those of a Corporation acutely conscious of its prestigious national role. Few of the ITV executives had any great qualms about the populism of their output. 'You don't necessarily make more money in television if you provide a better product,' commented Sidney Bernstein, the head of Granada.[54] 'Let's face it once and for all,' insisted Roland Gillet, the Controller of Associated Rediffusion. 'The public likes girls, wrestling, bright musicals, quiz shows and real-life drama. We gave them the Hallé orchestra and . . . visits to the local fire station. Well, we've learned. From now on, what the public wants, it's going to get.'[55]

Not surprisingly, many commentators associated ITV with little more than cheap working-class populism, and in many middle-class households it was regarded as common and vulgar, especially when set against the politeness and tradition of the BBC. One Berkshire woman later remembered: 'We weren't allowed to watch ITV. My mother was a teacher, and she thought it would rot our brains.'[56] This was not particularly unusual: one middle-class woman told an interviewer that it was 'cheap entertainment' and 'a dreadful waste of time'. 'I didn't want the boys to get used to watching it,' she explained, 'so I used to ban it. It seems funny now, but I just didn't think it was a worthwhile way for them to spend time, but I know that they used to watch it when my back was turned, or at friends' houses.'[57] The process also worked in reverse. 'In my Secondary Modern School,' a London schoolteacher reported, 'to watch the BBC is regarded as "sissyfied" behaviour.'[58] As for the press, it was largely bitterly hostile to the new network. Even before its launch, there had been a committed campaign against the introduction of a commercial channel, uniting the Labour Party, university vice-chancellors, the Archbishop of York and assorted other clergymen, peers and notables. Lord Reith, defending the BBC monopoly, had even likened commercial television to 'smallpox, bubonic plague and the Black Death'.[59]

Within a year of the ITV launch, the criticism was deafening. The *Spectator* called the channel 'a monument to fraud and a daily reminder of the worthlessness of political promises', and the *Daily Express* published an editorial demanding that the government 'write ITV off as an experiment that went wrong' and 'hand the wavelength over to the BBC'.[60] The most savage attack came from a review in the *Manchester Guardian* in April 1956 by the young Bernard Levin. Some ITV programmes, he allowed, were 'neutral', such as the weather forecast or national anthem; others were even 'programmes which people of intelligence and taste might be able to watch for two hours a week without actually feeling ill'. The great majority, however, were either 'ordinary trash' or simply 'not fit to be fed to the cat'.[61]

Clearly much of this antagonism towards ITV reflected a wider sense of unease at the forces of Americanism, commercialism and corrosive modernity that were thought to be undermining British cultural traditions. For many commentators, television itself was culturally pernicious, irrespective of whether the provider was the BBC or ITV. In many cases this simply reflected financial self-interest, since television threatened to eat into the profits of theatres, cinemas, pubs and the like.[62] By the late fifties, however, it was evident that television was a serious cultural force that demanded thoughtful attention; as the *New Statesman* put it, it could not be dismissed 'as a vulgar or ephemeral craze'.[63] Even so, hostility towards the medium in intellectual quarters was slow to fade. One survey quoted abstainers who thought that it had 'killed civilised conversation'; it was cited in divorce proceedings and blamed for ills as diverse as children's nightmares, typists' errors and juvenile street crime. Doctors examined conditions like 'TV Neck', 'TV Crouch', 'TV Dyspepsia' and the curious 'TV Stutter'; dentists warned that children who watched from the floor, their chins cupped in their hands, were giving themselves buck teeth.[64] The Oxford don Sir Maurice Bowra quipped: 'All television corrupts and absolute television corrupts absolutely.'[65] Many on the left were even more hostile than their contemporaries on the intellectual right. In his Fabian essay *Labour in the Affluent Society*, Richard Crossman observed that the 'commercialized media of mass communications' had been 'systematically used to dope the critical faculties' of the electorate.[66] Tom Driberg, meanwhile, wrote that television viewers were 'completely passive', wandering around vacantly and mumbling 'infantile ditties in honour of *cornflakes in the morning* or *brightness women want*'.[67]

This kind of analysis drew heavily on Richard Hoggart's book *The Uses of Literacy*; as explained earlier, left-wing cultural commentators like Hoggart and Raymond Williams as well as the luminaries of the New Wave were united in their contempt for the 'shiny barbarism' and 'anti-culture' of the television age. For Williams, television was the centrepiece of 'a synthetic culture, an anti-culture, which is alien to almost everybody, persistently hostile to art and intellectual activity, which it spends much of its time misrepresenting, and given over to exploiting indifference, lack of feeling, frustration, and hatred. It finds such common human interests as sex, and turns them into crude caricatures or glossy facsimiles.'[68] This was by no means an unusual stance; indeed, among British intellectuals in the late fifties, it was rare to find anyone to defend the values of television except for unashamed populists like Kingsley Amis. Doris Lessing, for instance, wrote that television had invaded and destroyed traditional working-class culture:

> Before, when the men came back from work, the tea was already on the table, a fire was roaring, the radio emitted words or music softly in a corner, they washed and sat down at their places, with the woman, the child, and whoever else in the house could be inveigled downstairs . . . They all talked . . .
>
> And then . . . television had arrived and sat like a toad in the corner of the kitchen. Soon the big kitchen table had been pushed along the wall, chairs were installed in a semi-circle and, on their chair arms, the swivelling supper trays. It was the end of an exuberant verbal culture.[69]

As Anthony Hartley noted in 1963, this critique of television was rooted in the outrage of the intellectuals that their romanticised image of working-class values had been repudiated by the working classes themselves. 'Instead of holding discussion groups or organizing amateur theatricals,' he wrote, 'the English working classes have been reading women's magazines and comics or watching television – and commercial television at that. What is worse, they have appeared positively to enjoy doing so.'[70]

The Pilkington Committee, which was established by the Macmillan government on 13 July 1960 to discuss the future of broadcasting, the roles of the BBC and commercial television, and even the possibility of a third channel, partly reflected similar cultural attitudes. There were twelve members, with an average age of forty-nine. Not one could be said to reflect the views of what the *News of the World* called the 'man and woman in the street'.[71] The chairman was Sir Harry Pilkington, a successful businessman and director of the Bank of England, but the most prominent and articulate member was none other than Richard Hoggart, who might have been expected to be instinctively hostile to commercial television.[72] This indeed proved to be the case. Hoggart's own wife admitted that he was happy to watch documentaries 'when he has nothing better to do', but in general 'a whole fortnight might go by without him turning on the set'.[73] His contempt for the values of ITV was already on record, published in *Encounter* earlier that year. Watching ITV's evening programmes, he wrote, had convinced him that they were trying to 'push' society 'towards a generalised form of life . . . whose texture is as little that of the good life as processed bread is like home-baked bread'.[74]

Hoggart was considered the most influential figure on the committee, and its report in the summer of 1962 was greeted with identical headlines in the *Sunday Times* and the *Observer*: 'Going the Whole Hoggart'.[75] The report noted that many people felt 'that the way television has portrayed human behaviour and treated moral issues has already done something and will in time do much to worsen the moral climate of the country'. This disquiet, it concluded, was 'mainly attributable to independent television and largely to its entertainment programmes'. The committee further noted that these programmes were too often made with 'the object of seeking, at whatever cost in quality or variety, the largest possible audience; and that, to attain this object, the items nearly always appealed to a low level of public taste'.[76] ITV, then, came out of the report very badly indeed, and the committee recommended that the Independent Television Authority be given a more active regulatory role, supervising the programming of the various regional companies and selling advertising time itself. Meanwhile, the BBC, which had spent months carefully lobbying the committee, emerged triumphantly unscathed, its position as 'the main instrument of broadcasting' explicitly confirmed. Above all, it was authorised to begin immediate preparations to provide a third television channel, the future BBC2.[77]

In the competition between populism and elitism, the Pilkington Committee had struck a major blow on behalf of the latter. *The Economist*, in an article entitled 'TV with Auntie', declared 'the worst has happened', and complained that British audiences were 'subjected to this compulsive nannying over everything they want to see and hear'.[78] 'Pilkington tells the public to go to hell,' announced the *Mirror*, and in his *Sunday Pictorial* column the Labour MP Woodrow Wyatt parodied the tones of the committee's 'tiny handful of pretentious prigs':

You 'trivial' people, to borrow the Pilkington Committee's favourite phrase. How dare you prefer watching commercial television to looking at what Auntie BBC so kindly provides for you? . . . The ITV programmes are 'naughty' and 'bad' for you. They are produced by ordinary men and women who like the same things as you do . . . Pilkington is out to stop all this rot about you being allowed to enjoy yourself . . . You trivial people will have to brush up your culture.[79]

The mandarins of the BBC, however, were delighted, as was the venerable Lord Reith, while T. S. Eliot wrote an enthusiastic letter to *The Times* in praise of Pilkington.[80] BBC2 itself was conceived as a kind of testament to the values of Richard Hoggart and the Pilkington Committee; according to Corporation plans, the new channel would offer television programmes 'for those people who are interested in the *uncommon* denominators – not the common ones like Dixon or Bootsie or Snudge'.[81] BBC2 was not actually launched until 1964, when a rather ominous accident ruined its opening night: an explosion at Battersea Power Station cut all electricity to central London and threw the Lime Grove studios into darkness. Even George, a kangaroo hired as the mascot for the opening night, ended up trapped in the Lime Grove lift. As it happened, there was still power at Alexandra Palace, and those viewers who did have power were treated to intermittent news announcements and stand-by records.[82] The audiences for the new channel were slow to grow, but gradually BBC2 established itself in the national consciousness, not least thanks to the impact of an ambitious twenty-six-part documentary source, *The Great War*, which was broadcast from May 1964 and widely regarded as the finest historical documentary of the era.[83]

By this point, the BBC itself was in the throes of change. The stunning success of ITV's populist approach obviously posed a serious threat to the Corporation, and even before the Pilkington report the BBC's counterattack was under way. For one thing, it was obvious that television had supplanted radio as the centrepiece of British broadcasting. The turning point came between 1957 and 1960. In 1957, licences just for radio were still more numerous than combined television and radio licences, but within three years there were nearly twice as many combined licences as radio ones.[84] Radio programmes were losing listeners at a rapid rate. Between 1955 and 1960, the audience for *The Archers* fell from twenty-three million to barely ten million, while there were equally alarming declines in the fortunes of *Friday Night Is Music Night* (from twelve and a half million to five million) and *Saturday Night Theatre* (from fourteen million to four million).[85]

Television evidently represented the future, and the BBC needed an urgent riposte to its commercial competitor if it were not to be left behind for good. This came in the form of five new programmes introduced in the late fifties as an attempt to update the image of the Corporation and lure viewers back from ITV. One was *Tonight*, an informal, genial magazine programme, which was presented from 1957 by the amiable Cliff Michelmore and succeeded in luring nine million viewers during the old 'toddlers' truce' teatime hour. *Monitor*, meanwhile, an arts programme launched in 1958, was not aimed at large audiences, but was a kind of cultural flagship for the early sixties, presented by Huw Wheldon and broadcasting reports on everything from Elgar and Betjeman to Amis and circuses. Of the 'magazine' programmes, however, none was more prestigious than *Panorama*, which ran once a week and was regarded as perhaps the most serious and incisive current affairs programme in the world. Such was the respect for its host Richard Dimbleby that even a spoof item about harvesting spaghetti from trees, shown on April Fool's Day 1957, was taken entirely seriously by a significant part of the audience. Two more programmes completed the revamped line-up of the late fifties: *Face to Face* and *This Is Your Life*. *Face to Face*, which was launched in 1959, could easily claim to be the most innovative and compelling interview programme of its time. The interviewer, John Freeman, was never seen; the camera focused exclusively on the faces of the guests, showing their every flicker and expression in unforgiving detail. Most of the interviews were shown live, and guests spanned the breadth of British culture in the early sixties, from Evelyn Waugh and Bertrand Russell to Albert Finney and Adam Faith. On one memorable occasion, when asked about the death of his mother, the notoriously rude *What's My Line* panellist Gilbert Harding burst into tears in front of the implacable, unwavering stare of the camera.[86] On a lighter note, *This Is Your Life* first appeared in 1955, based on an American model, and ran successfully for decades to come, with audiences around the thirteen-million mark.[87]

What these five programmes had in common was not merely their popular success or their timing, but also their flavour, which combined modernity and even deft informality with the kind of dignity and professionalism that viewers already associated with the BBC. The mood at the Corporation was one of change; few people still thought that the old programmes of the early fifties would be able to compete with ITV. Television drama, for example, was in a state of transition: while literary adaptations like *Lorna Doone*, *Framley Parsonage*, *Little Dorrit* and *Anna Karenina* were staples of the Sunday-evening schedules, the BBC was also keen to encourage new writing talent, including playwrights such as Ted Willis, John Mortimer and Johnny Speight.[88] By the end of the decade, the BBC had managed to staunch the haemorrhage of viewers to commercial television with a characteristic mixture of innovation and tradition. Its most popular programmes during 1959 and 1960 were, interestingly enough, not American imports but British shows, notably comedy series like *Hancock's Half Hour* and *Charlie Drake*, the reassuring police serial *Dixon of Dock Green*, *The Billy Cotton Band Show*, the quiz show *What's My Line?*, the science-fiction drama *Quatermass and the Pit* and, most popular of all, sports programmes like *Sportsview*.[89] No generalisation would be able to capture adequately the tastes of the British public in the late fifties; there was an appetite for everything from sport and variety shows to classical drama and hard-hitting documentaries, and while viewers liked to feel that they were being offered modern, exciting fare, they also sought the comfort of familiar faces and themes.

The recovery of the BBC in the last years of the fifties set the scene for the following decade, a period during which the Corporation would reach perhaps the height of its prestige and accomplishment. If there was a guiding spirit of television in the new era, it was Hugh Carleton Greene, who was determined to drag 'the BBC kicking and screaming into the Sixties'.[90] As Asa Briggs, the official historian of the Corporation, puts it, Greene 'never wished to be standing still – even for a moment'. He had, he said, 'a duty to take account of the changes in society, to be ahead of public opinion, rather than always to wait upon it'.[91] Predictably enough, this proved a controversial stance, and Greene made his fair share of enemies, most notably Mary Whitehouse. Many people liked to think of the BBC as a national institution, a repository of tradition and old values, immune to the whims of fashion. Throughout the history of the Corporation, changes in programme schedules or content periodically provoked angry responses from militant sections of the audience, as had already been the case with the Third Programme. The abolition of *Children's Hour* in March 1964 was a famous example from Greene's tenure; even though the programme seemed extremely dated, the decision to scrap it provoked angry protests from national and provincial newspapers, veteran broadcasters and both Conservative and Labour MPs, the latter proving particularly vehement.[92] The confrontation of old and new was epitomised by the contrast between Greene and Lord Reith, who in private became one of his most vehement critics. By 1963 Reith was complaining in his diary that the BBC had 'utterly discarded everything I did'; a year later, he wrote:

The dignity of the BBC has utterly departed . . . Hugh and I [are] fundamentally in complete opposition of outlook and attitude. I lead, he
follows the crowd in all the disgusting manifestations of the age . . .
Without any reservation he gives the public what it wants; I would not,
did not and said I wouldn't.[93]

Perhaps Greene's most significant achievement was the recruitment of
a new head of Television Drama, a Canadian producer called Sydney
Newman who had, at forty-five, moved to Britain in 1958 to run *Armchair
Theatre*, ABC's Sunday night drama flagship.[94] *Armchair Theatre*, which at this
stage relied mainly on adaptations of well-known authors like F. Scott
Fitzgerald and Oscar Wilde, inherited a large audience from the show that
preceded it, *Sunday Night at the London Palladium*, and the aim was to retain as
many viewers as possible without sacrificing the programme's commitment to quality and seriousness. Newman's skill lay in drawing on the
themes of New Wave theatre and fiction, especially the emphasis on working-class realism, and combining them with an innovative, more
cinematic approach to television drama. His aim was to persuade audiences
'that the working man was a fit subject for drama, and not just a comic foil
in middle-class manners'.[95] At the same time, he was convinced that 'great
art has to stem from, and its essence must come out of, the period in which
it is created'.[96]

During the next few years, Newman turned *Armchair Theatre* into the pre-
eminent example of British television creativity, recruiting ambitious
American directors like Philip Saville and Ted Kotcheff to work with material by a stream of talented young British playwrights: Harold Pinter, Clive
Exton, Giles Cooper and Alun Owen.[97] In many ways, the programme was
simply the television equivalent to the New Wave boom in the cinema; plays
like Alun Owen's trilogy *No Trains to Lime Street* (October 1959), *After the Funeral*
(April 1960) and *Lena, O My Lena* (September 1960) presented realistic contemporary events in a fluid, mobile style that broke with the static camera
techniques of the early fifties.[98] British settings and themes were being presented using techniques borrowed from American television, which at this
stage was more technically advanced and innovative. Considering the serious nature of much of the material, the viewing figures were impressive,
often exceeding ten million. Most famously, *Armchair Theatre* provided a great
opportunity for the young Harold Pinter, whose play *A Night Out* was
watched by 6.4 million people when broadcast in April 1960. Pinter's most

acclaimed play, *The Caretaker*, opened in London the following month and some commentators later suggested that its commercial success owed much to the fact that audiences were already familiar with his work from *Armchair Theatre*.[99] Indeed, Pinter himself remarked that *The Caretaker* would have to run continuously in the theatre for over thirty years to come close to the audience that *A Night Out* had attracted in one evening on television.[100]

Newman moved to the BBC from ABC in April 1963, an important coup in the Corporation's efforts to revive its feeble viewing figures. His arrival was reported in the press much like the recruitment of a star footballer from a rival team. 'BBC signs ITV "dustbin" man,' read the headline in the *Daily Mail*, alluding to Newman's faith in kitchen-sink drama.[101] But he was more than a dustbin man. He was also interested in presenting older plays through modern eyes, and he set to work reorganising the BBC drama group into three different sections dealing with series, serials and individual plays, as well as developing new programmes like *Doctor Who*. On joining the BBC he sent his producers a printed card to hang in their offices, reading 'Look back not in anger, nor forward in fear, but around with awareness'.[102]

For most observers, Newman's principal achievement was *The Wednesday Play*, which built up a regular audience of between eight and ten million viewers for what were often challenging and controversial dramas that were eventually regarded as classics of the genre. Hugh Carleton Greene specifically asked Newman to introduce the fast and realistic style of American drama and theatre and to address controversial social and moral issues, and told him on his appointment: 'You've managed to collect writers like Harold Pinter, Alun Owen, Clive Exton and Bill Naughton for your *Armchair Theatre*. They got their start on BBC Radio. I want you to get them back – and find all the new ones you can.'[103] Newman did as requested, and gave his writers and directors unprecedented freedom to develop their own ideas. 'I said I want you to concentrate on the turning points of British society,' he later recalled. 'I gave them the money and left them alone. And so *Cathy Come Home* and *Up the Junction* – all those real breakthroughs.'[104] In 1964 he explained his philosophy at length for the BBC Board of Governors:

Pre-marital intercourse has increased enormously since World War II; homosexuality and abortion have become subjects for parliamentary debate and legal concern. The Labour Party is totally responsible and so are the unions, the divorce rate has gone up, the relations between management and labour, parent and child, worshipper and minister, England and the World – all these are food for the hungry and aware playwright.[105]

There is no doubt that *The Wednesday Play* marked a high point in terms of sheer quality of writing and direction. Between October 1964 and 1967 the team produced plays by, among others, John Betjeman, Alun Owen, Simon Raven, David Mercer, John Hopkin, Nell Dunn, Jim Allen and Dennis Potter. Particular highlights included Potter's two plays *Stand Up, Nigel Barton* and *Vote, Vote, Vote for Nigel Barton* (1965); Dunn's gritty play *Up the Junction* (1965), which was directed by Ken Loach; and, above all, *Cathy Come Home* (1966), a powerful discussion of homelessness by Jeremy Sandford and again directed by Ken Loach with gripping documentary realism. These particular plays were indeed controversial, because they tackled social and political issues with uncompromising frankness and realism, and the public tended to assume that the entire series was similarly hard-hitting, although in fact there was a wide range of styles and subjects.[106] What is true, however, is that most plays were shot in a startlingly naturalistic style, often not far removed from documentary realism, not least because the development of new lightweight 16mm film cameras made location filming much easier and cheaper. At the same time, as directors increasingly recorded their plays on film rather than shot them live, they felt able to use more expansive cinematic techniques and stylistic tricks, so that there was a gradual shift from the pre-eminence of the writer to that of the director, the most obvious example being the prominence of Ken Loach from 1965 onwards.[107] That audiences of eight million or so, and twelve million in the case of *Cathy Come Home*, were tuning into to watch such plays was both a tribute to the producers and a source of great concern to moral campaigners, most notably Mary Whitehouse, who thought that *The Wednesday Play* was obsessed with issues of sex, violence and degradation. As Whitehouse's biographers put it, the programme became identified with a realistic style that some viewers found extremely disturbing: 'The shift in emphasis was a little more than a move from the drawing room to the kitchen: it was a bus ride across town to the council estates and working-class slums, to peroxide hair and bags under the eyes, to violence of language and mind, and above all to manifest sexuality.'[108]

While it would be going too far to claim that *The Wednesday Play* set the tone for the BBC's vast output, its spirit of uncompromising realism, which it had inherited from the New Wave of the late fifties, was characteristic of many BBC dramas and comedies of the same period.[109] One striking example of the naturalistic style was *Hancock's Half Hour*, which was also among the first, and wittiest, sitcoms produced in Britain. It was written by two young scriptwriters, Ray Galton and Alan Simpson, rather than by a team as was the practice in the United States, and first appeared on the radio in October 1954 before transferring to television two years later. The producer of the radio series observed in a BBC memorandum that the 'comedy style' would be 'purely situation[al]', and explained: 'We shall try to build Tony as a real life character in real life surroundings. There will be no "goon" or contrived comedy approaches.'[110]

Hancock's Half Hour charted the recurring disappointments of the irritable, lugubrious but permanently hopeful Anthony Aloysius St John Hancock of 23 Railway Cuttings, East Cheam, a setting described in a BBC press release as 'a street of terraced Victorian houses . . . the buildings are quite ugly and so are most of the residents'.[111] His eponymous character was a middle-aged bachelor, permanently frustrated by the gulf between his own pretentious aspirations and the glum drudgery of reality, and the choicest comic moments often came in his exasperated rants to his friend Sid James. After 1957 the minor roles were filled by straight dramatic actors rather than comedians, and the innovative camera style, employing frequent close-ups, allowed the comedy to flow naturally from Hancock's own range of expansive facial expressions.[112] Some episodes, especially later ones such as 'Twelve Angry Men', 'The Bed Sitter' and 'The Blood Donor', are rightly regarded as peaks of British television comedy, but, despite the fact that they drew a handsome audience share (over 30 per cent), Hancock himself was unsatisfied, and after several failed attempts to break into film and an unsuccessful series for ATV, he took his own life in 1968.[113]

A more enduring example of the new style of television realism was a soap opera called *Florizel Street*, created for Granada in 1960 by a working-class Lancastrian writer, Tony Warren. As Warren put it in a memorandum to his Granada bosses, the purpose of *Florizel Street* was to explore 'the driving forces behind life in a working-class street in the north of England' and 'to entertain by examining a community of this kind and initiating the viewer into the ways of the people who live there'.[114] So the show was set in one terraced back street in the fictional north-western town of Weatherfield, and the plan was to shoot thirteen episodes with twenty-two characters. The original title was dumped shortly before transmission, allegedly because a tea lady at the Granada studios remarked that it sounded like the name of a toilet cleaner. The producers were torn between *Jubilee Street* and *Coronation Street*; in the end, it was the latter which had the right ring of working-class patriotism. But when the first edition appeared on 9 December 1960, the reaction of the press was not encouraging: the *Daily Mirror*'s reviewer, for instance, found it 'hard to believe that viewers will want to put up with continuous slice-of-life domestic drudgery two evenings a week' and called the show 'a boob in programme planning'.[115] Nonetheless, *Coronation Street* gradually established a following. Within six months, the remaining regional companies who had not originally chosen to show it had agreed to do so, and by October 1961 it had become the most popular programme in the country, with over twenty million regular viewers.[116]

Granada advertised its new soap opera as 'life in an ordinary street in an ordinary town', and one reason for *Coronation Street*'s success was that it was a perfect fit with the mood of the moment.[117] The opening titles, with their mournful music and establishing shots of long terraced streets, imparted a sense of regional identity and working-class community that resonated with viewers for whom such things were threatened by mobility and affluence, while the anachronistic setting of the programme, a world of local shops, cobbled streets and cosy Northern living rooms, seemed almost a direct reproduction of the scenes in *The Uses of Literacy*. Indeed, many of the details of working-class life that Hoggart had described were faithfully duplicated in *Coronation Street*: the absence of political debate and indifference to the world of work; the warm, enveloping matriarchal families; the nostalgia for bygone days; the preference for common sense rather than cleverness, and so on.[118] Some left-wing cultural critics objected to the cosy working-class world depicted in the programme. A review by Clancy Sigal in the *New Statesman* in January 1962, for example, described it as 'a lie from start to finish if it is supposed to represent any recognisable aspect of life' and 'false in its avoidance of class tensions . . . alive between shop-keepers and residents in the north', not to mention its avoidance of political questions or depictions of the workplace. By channelling the working-class solidarity of its viewers into banality and 'harmlessness', Sigal angrily concluded, '*Coronation Street* gently rapes you.'[119]

False or not, *Coronation Street* evidently went down extremely well with working-class audiences. The first episodes were broadcast live without editing, so the actors needed to be on their very best form, and in fact the programme's success owed much to the quality of the early scripts and performances. The most striking characters were women: the prim land-lady Annie Walker (Doris Speed); the prurient street gossip Ena Sharples (Violet Carson, complete with hairnet); and the Street's scarlet woman Elsie Tanner, damned as 'no better than she ought to be' and played by Pat Phoenix. Both Carson and Phoenix were old music-hall performers rather than theatrical actresses, and there was initially a strong strain of traditional working-class comedy in *Coronation Street*.[120]

The first episode also introduced the character of Ken Barlow (William Roache), a bright, ambitious university student who was supposed to rep-resent the tension between the restless ambitions of the young and the narrow horizons of the old working class. He complains, for example, that his father always drinks tea with his evening meal, and at one point is hor-rified to discover that his middle-class student girlfriend has been roped in to help his father and brother repair a bicycle on the living-room floor. Barlow was, in other words, a kind of exaggerated fictional embodiment of the social tensions described by the likes of Richard Hoggart and Raymond Williams, and the obvious expectation was that, as the sixties progressed, he would eventually fly the nest for better prospects elsewhere, probably London. In the event, William Roache had no desire to forfeit a regular income, and forty years later Ken Barlow was still there – having lived, rather implausibly, in eight different houses on the same street.[121]

Throughout all this time, *Coronation Street* remained one of ITV's most suc-cessful programmes and outlived a number of imitators. The most successful of these was *Crossroads*, an ATV production set in a motel near Birmingham and first screened in 1964; although the acting and the sets were widely regarded as little better than abysmal, the viewing figures were surprisingly strong, touching nearly eighteen million at their peak.[122] *Coronation Street*, however, was thought by most observers to be well written and performed. It is also likely that audiences remained loyal because the vision of a warm, intimate regional community, huddled in the familiar landscape of a terraced street, tapped an apparently unquenchable vein of nostalgia in British culture.

The BBC's most successful attempt to introduce a self-consciously modern, realistic style into a long-running series was not a soap opera but the police series *Z Cars*, which like *Coronation Street* was set in working-class north-western England and was first broadcast in 1962. What made *Z Cars* particularly novel was the fact that the BBC already made one police series, *Dixon of Dock Green*, which had been running since 1955. The success of *Dixon of Dock Green* is often underrated, and many television historians prefer to concentrate on the greater realism of *Z Cars*, but in fact *Dixon* ran for a much longer period, regularly attracting over fourteen million viewers to its 434 episodes and only ending in 1976.[123]

The contrasts between *Dixon of Dock Green* and *Z Cars* reveal an interesting shift in the way that the British public viewed its police force. Until the fifties, the British policeman had been portrayed in popular stories and films as 'a bumbling simpleton who habitually licked the stub of his pencil, was respectful to the Squire and left the investigation and solution of serious crime to brilliant, educated amateurs like Sherlock Holmes and Lord Peter Wimsey', as the *Dixon* scriptwriter Ted Willis put it.[124] The police were depicted as comic buffoons for two reasons: first, because it helped to defuse the long-standing bitterness towards them in some sections of the working class; and, second, because the policemen themselves were usually working-class, and convention dictated that middle-class culture showed working-class characters as incompetent blunderers.[125] The character of PC Dixon, however, marked a break with this image and established a new stereotype of the policeman, a reassuring personification of 'continuity, tradition and service'.[126]

Dixon of Dock Green was a gentle, comforting series about a kindly and authoritative policeman who knows everyone on his beat and stands for the 'nation-as-family', as one historian puts it.[127] The central character, the bluff police constable George Dixon (Jack Warner), revived a part that Warner had already played in the film *The Blue Lamp*, an Ealing production which had not only won the British Academy Award for the best film of 1950 but also proved the biggest British box-office hit of the year.[128] From 1957, the theme song was written by Jack Warner himself: its title, 'Just an Ordinary Copper', summed up the ethos of the programme, and his catchphrase, 'Evening, all,' became a kind of shorthand for the image of the policeman as a friendly, avuncular figure.[129] Dixon was the very incarnation of an idealised Britishness: he liked gardening and fishing, he played darts, and like any decent Englishman, he preferred tea to coffee and beer to wine. In one episode shown in 1958, the character was awarded a British Empire Medal for gallantry, and a widow then sent Warner the ribbon of a BEM that her late husband, a policeman, had won for bravery during the Blitz. 'My husband', she wrote, 'was similar to the character you portray, loved by everybody, tough when need be, but with not enough push to be made a sergeant . . . To me, Dixon is real.'[130]

The popular enthusiasm for the humble bobby was no myth. Geoffrey Gorer's survey of English attitudes in 1950 found that three people out of four expressed 'an enthusiastic appreciation for the English police' and saw the policeman as a model of polite and plucky behaviour.[131] Compared with the situation on the Continent, the admiration of the British for their supposedly clumsy, honest and dependable policemen was a fascinating oddity, even though it seems likely that the unarmed British police were indeed more benign than many of their European counterparts.[132] As Clive Emsley puts it, the policeman had become a symbol of national character and 'the personification of an idealized image of the English legal system – impartial and functioning with solemnity and clockwork regularity'.[133]

The sudden surge of respect for the police force after the Second World War probably reflects the fact that the old class antagonisms were subsiding and being replaced with a stronger sense of the nation as the united family that had come through the horrors of wartime. Most of the series' viewers were enjoying greater affluence and security than they had ever known; Dixon himself would probably have been the son of a worker and, as the romanticised personification of working-class gentility, had 'thoroughly imbibed all that is best, firmest and most sensibly liberal in middle-class attitudes'.[134] He was quite simply the ideal fictional character to represent the values of the Butskellite consensus. It is worth noting that Ted Willis, the character's creator, had working-class roots and was a strong Labour supporter who worked as a speechwriter for Harold Wilson in two election campaigns; the values of working-class respectability that Willis celebrated in *Dixon of Dock Green* were very similar to those that Wilson himself tried to project with his pipe, slippers and fondness for *Coronation Street*.[135]

By the early sixties, however, the popular image of the police was changing. Many policemen did live up to the example of the fictional PC Dixon; others, inevitably, did not. In 1963 the press reported the case of Harold Challenor, a sergeant in the Metropolitan force who hated Italians and other immigrant groups, had abused, assaulted and falsely imprisoned the West Indian test cricketer Harold Padmore, and had planted bricks on political demonstrators and then charged them with the possession of offensive weapons. Challenor was quickly compelled to retire from the force and declared unfit to stand trial, but his case evidently reminded many people that there was a gulf between the fictional policemen of *Dixon of Dock Green* and the policemen they often encountered in their daily lives.[136] According to an opinion poll taken in the same year, over 40 per cent of the public believed that the police took bribes, while a third thought they used unfair means to get their information and a third also thought that they distorted evidence in court.[137] Already a grittier image of the police force had begun to emerge in British cinema, especially in thrillers informed by the realism of the New Wave. In films like *Beyond This Place*, *Hell Is a City*, *The Criminal* and *Never Let Go*, all released between 1959 and 1963, the force was depicted as a tougher, more working-class institution, locked in a violent struggle with the criminal underworld.[138]

Z Cars was created in 1962 by Troy Kennedy Martin, Elwyn Jones and John McGrath both as a way of expressing these new attitudes to the police and as a reflection of the modern, realistic style of Hugh Carleton Greene's BBC. As with *Coronation Street*, the intention was to use a particular television genre, the cops-and-robbers story, to explore the lives of a Northern, working-class community. John McGrath later explained: 'The series was going to be a kind of documentary about people's lives in these areas and the cops were incidental – they were the means of finding out about other people's lives.'[139] The BBC's publicity for the new series made very clear its function as a social documentary confronting the problems of urban life in the sixties. 'Life is fraught with danger for policemen in the North of England overspill estate called Newtown,' the *Radio Times* told its readers. 'Here a mixed community, displaced from larger towns by slum clearance, has been brought together and housed on an estate without amenities and without community feeling.'[140] Newtown was based on Kirby, just outside Liverpool (which the series called 'Seaport'), and the general atmosphere reeked of New Wave naturalism: gritty black and white photography, familiar Northern locations, working-class characters and everyday situations. 'We placed a conscious emphasis on narrative-society, real and recognizable, but *in motion*,' recalled McGrath. 'No slick tie-ups. No reassuring endings, where decency and family life triumphed.'[141]

The programme benefited from the advice of the Lancashire police force, whose senior officers liked the idea of a realistic series exploring the real problems they faced, and the credits for the first episode acknowledged the 'valuable assistance' of the Lancashire Police, another indication of the series' realism.[142] This episode, 'Four of a Kind', begins, like *The Blue Lamp* twelve years previously, with the shooting of a policeman on the beat. The Newtown police react by sending out crime patrols in the radio cars Z-Victor 1 and Z-Victor 2, occupied by the four toughest constables they can find: the Scottish rugby player Jock Weir, the Lancastrian Bob Steele, the

Ulsterman Bert Lynch and the Yorkshireman Fancy Smith. Supervising operations by VHF radio from the station are the irascible Detective Superintendent Charlie Barlow and his calm, faithful deputy, Detective Sergeant John Watt. As well as establishing the characters and situation, the episode also features a pub brawl, a subplot about teenage runaways, and the appearance of an escaped axe-wielding lunatic. Most controversially, the programme also addresses the domestic problems of the policemen themselves: Sergeant Watt's wife has left him because of the demands of his job, and an argument between Bob Steele and his wife leaves her with a black eye.[143]

The episode attracted nine million viewers, but it also lost the support of the police force. The *Guardian* quoted an educational psychologist who thought that, while the programme was made with 'all-round excellence', its 'vivid visual presentation of sexual perversion' could damage the mental health of any children watching. This included, the newspaper noted, 'a criminal's implied seduction of his sister-in-law; a woman in bed with a man other than her husband; the beating up of a pregnant woman; a sex maniac dragging a girl into bushes; and a lot more "so called real life stuff"'. The Chief Constable of Lancashire demanded that the series be cancelled, since his men had reacted to it with 'disgust . . . almost to a man', while one of the Chorley Crime Patrol told reporters: 'It was awful. We all thought it made us look fools. And our wives thought it made them look fools too.'[144] On the other hand, the *Bolton Evening News* considered that the *Z Cars* policemen had simply 'looked like a set of hearty North-country lads':

> One wonders if the county force is not making too heavy weather of it all. Admittedly the social and domestic background of the men seen in this programme is made up of somewhat rougher strands than is the domestic background of someone like Dixon of Dock Green. But then social backgrounds in the North do tend to be robust.[145]

The BBC had to drop the screened acknowledgement to the Lancashire constabulary, but the series was not cancelled. Within eight weeks its viewing figures had risen from nine million to fourteen million and in the following year they peaked at nearly seventeen million, making it the Corporation's most popular drama series, although it is interesting to note that at the same time the ratings for *Dixon of Dock Green* remained steady at thirteen million, suggesting that many viewers still preferred nostalgia and reassurance to grittiness and realism. Only *The Black and White Minstrel Show* and *Steptoe and Son*, of which more elsewhere, were consistently attracting more viewers to the BBC.[146] Within a year the critic of the *New Statesman* was enthusing that *Z Cars* gave 'such a superb picture of men at work' that 'one could switch on week after week merely for the pleasure of joining the gang'.[147] Although the policemen had originally been intended to be 'incidental' to the focus on the wider community, the show now revolved around their own relationships.[148] By 1965, however, the ratings had begun to slip behind *Dixon* and the programme was overhauled, with the characters of Barlow and Watt transferring to a new series about regional crime squads, *Softly, Softly*. The public appetite for police dramas was evidently inexhaustible: *Softly, Softly* itself ran for ten more years, while, confusingly, the name *Z Cars* was revived in 1967 with a largely new cast, this new incarnation surviving until 1978.[149]

Z Cars provides probably the best example of the way the BBC tried to reinvigorate its image to face the challenges of commercial television and address the new issues of the sixties. It drew on the legacy of New Wave cinema and kitchen-sink drama, not least through its recognisable Northern setting, and it was the first successful BBC drama series to feature working-class characters with distinctive regional accents. Unlike *Dixon of Dock Green*, it was scripted and edited in a fast-moving, fragmented style, took great care to present its studio footage as realistic, and also incorporated location filming to heighten the contemporary feel.[150] Unlike *Dixon*, it did not deliver a moralistic message at the end of each episode, and the producers paid close attention to modern police procedures; indeed, the story went that Troy Kennedy Martin first had the idea for the programme when listening to the police waveband and being struck by the difference between modern police work and the fictional accounts on television.[151] Dixon was a genial policeman walking his regular beat in a quiet, settled East End community; the *Z Cars* characters, by contrast, used modern technology and radio-equipped squad cars to move around the insecure communities of a new town haunted by domestic and juvenile crime, a setting of brutalist tower blocks and social deprivation. Like *Coronation Street*, *Z Cars* reflected the trend for realism, but it also went further. While *Coronation Street* was rooted in a nostalgic vision of a traditional Northern urban environment, the producers of *Z Cars* were more interested in exploring the changes that social mobility, economic decline and working-class affluence were bringing to

Northern towns. *Z Cars* was also a useful vehicle to address social issues from
which other programmes recoiled: teenage delinquency, extramarital sexuality, domestic violence and so on, all of which were related not so much
to personal wickedness as to the problems of poverty and insecurity in a
changing urban world. At this level, it was more than a passing entertainment; it was a window on to the society of the sixties.[152]

In the New Wave novel *Saturday Night and Sunday Morning*, the central character, Arthur Seaton, feels nothing but contempt for the populist innovation
that dominates his contemporaries' lives:

> Television, he thought scornfully when she had gone, they'd go barmy
> if they had them taken away. I'd love it if big Black Marias came down
> all the streets and men got out with hatchets and go into every house
> and smash all the tellies. Everybody'd go crackers. They wouldn't know
> what to do. There'd be a revolution, I'm sure there would.[153]

Much as the New Wave writers disliked the influence of television, the fact
was that by the early sixties it had become by far the most important cultural medium in the country. Thanks to the success of *Z Cars* and the
notoriety of *The Wednesday Play*, the BBC had at last recaptured both the creative initiative and public attention from commercial television, with other
series like *Steptoe and Son* and *Dr Finlay's Casebook* also regularly pulling in tens
of millions of viewers. ITV, meanwhile, had little cause to despair. *Coronation
Street* remained enormously popular, and shows like *Sunday Night at the London
Palladium* and *Opportunity Knocks* appealed to the same kind of working-class
audiences that had once delighted in the merriment and spectacle of the
music halls. As the 1960s progressed and New Wave realism fell from fashion, new, more fantastic programmes emerged to capture the loyalties of
a mass audience, like *The Avengers* or *Doctor Who*. Later in the decade, shows
like *The Forsyte Saga*, *Civilisation*, *Monty Python's Flying Circus* and *Dad's Army* followed in their turn, attracting enthusiastic audiences and admiring press
coverage.

In their various ways, all of these programmes reflected different aspects
of British culture and society in the sixties, from working-class realism to
scientific utopianism and from swinging gaiety to romantic nostalgia. Above
all, it was from television that the majority of the British public now drew
their entertainment, and through television that they understood the world

beyond their immediate experience. Before the war relatively few ordinary people had travelled widely, and some never left their home towns at all, so their horizons were shaped largely by conversational anecdotes and stories in the popular press. Thanks to the television, however, entirely new vistas were opened up: in travel programmes, for example, the sights of Bangkok could be brought into the living rooms of Bolton. Viewers were able to participate, albeit passively, in their national culture as never before, and just as *That Was The Week That Was* encouraged millions of viewers to laugh at the inadequacies of the Macmillan government, so *Ready, Steady, Go!* brought pop music and fashion into the living rooms of teenagers across the country.

Like the car and the wireless before it, the television transformed the mental landscapes of ordinary viewers: where once their experiences might have been confined to the narrow streets of their neighbourhood, now the BBC and ITV conjured up worlds almost beyond their imagining. Political and cultural events that would once have reached the public second-hand, through newspapers, now reached them directly, through the television. In 1953, millions had been able to watch the Coronation; three years later, they had watched Eden's address to the nation on Suez and ITV's broadcast of *Look Back in Anger*. As the sixties unfolded, they would be able to see for themselves the Beatles performing their latest hits, England winning the World Cup, and Harold Wilson and Edward Heath competing for political authority. From the new towns of the North to the wide green spaces of Wembley, the events of the 1960s would be played out on national television before an audience of millions.

THE TEENAGE CONSUMER

Television and Pools and Space Robots, that was all the children of today thought about.

Angus Wilson, 'Higher Standards' (1957)

'That's enough, Darbishire.' Mr Wilkins turned back to the rabbit-fancier. 'You illiterate nitwit, Jennings, can't you see that your essay's miles away from the subject? It's a perfect example of – er – of –'
  'Juvenile delinquency, sir?' suggested Darbishire.

Anthony Buckeridge, *Jennings Goes to School* (1950)

On 14 April 1950, a new weekly comic paper for children appeared in Britain's newsagents. The *Eagle* was slick, colourful and smartly produced, and its first page told the story of 'Dan Dare, Pilot of the Future', described 'racing to the rescue of Rocket Ship No. 1 trapped by the silicon mass on the fringe of the Flame Lands'. It was an immediate success. More than 900,000 copies of the first issue were sold, and sales continued to rise towards a peak of two million in the mid-fifties. Dan Dare in particular became a children's favourite, exploiting the popular fascination with rocketry, space exploration and technology in the atomic age.[1]

But it was not merely the self-conscious modernity of the *Eagle* that explained its success. Unlike its competitors, the *Eagle* had an overt moral message. Its creator was an Anglican vicar, the Reverend Marcus Morris, who deplored the success of American comics in the depleted post-war market. For Morris and many other parents and teachers, American 'horror comic books' were a source of moral corruption.[2] The American comics, Morris wrote, were certainly 'skilfully and vividly drawn, but often their content was deplorable, nastily over-violent and obscene, often with undue emphasis on the supernatural and magical as a way of solving problems'. His dream was to create a 'paper which would be the natural choice of the child, but, at the same time, would have the enthusiastic approval of the parent and the teacher'.[3]

The character of Dan Dare was originally called Lex Christian, a fighting parson in the slums of the East End. Lex Christian then evolved into a flying priest, the Parson of the Fighting Seventh, and finally became the Pilot of the Future. As a square-jawed pilot in the International Space Fleet, he represented the wartime stereotype of the dashing English flying ace updated for a young audience. He was more overtly moralistic than most British heroes; there was none of the casual aggression of Bulldog Drummond or James Bond, but instead an emphasis on compassion and conciliation.[4] The comic placed a heavy emphasis on patriotism and moral uplift. Morris wrote a weekly Editor's Letter dispensing moral advice, and many of the other writers and illustrators were committed Christians, notably Chad Varah, the founder of the Samaritans. There were cartoon lives of imperial heroes like Nelson and Montgomery, and there were comic strips based on the lives of St Paul ('The Great Adventurer') and even Christ ('The Road of Courage'). This moral seriousness made the Eagle stand out from the silly high jinks of its American rivals, but it did not dent its appeal. In fact, the Eagle was a good example of the way in which old notions of patriotic duty and Christian service were reinvigorated rather than abandoned after the war; although Dan Dare's adventures take place in the far future, he retains the services of a batman and the International Space Fleet is identifiably a British hierarchical organisation. The millions of children who read the Eagle during the fifties and sixties were presented with an image of Britain as a conservative Christian country enjoying an unparalleled history of decency and valour.[5]

The phenomenal success of the Eagle in the fifties and sixties was closely tied to its overt Christianity. Middle-class parents generally distrusted comics as vulgar, subversive and American; by contrast, the Eagle was reassuringly conservative and respectable. During the early fifties the Comics Campaign Council and the National Union of Teachers waged an implacable campaign against American 'horror comics', with their shocking tales of grave-robbers, monsters and flesh-eaters. This crusade had originally been inspired by British Communists keen to attack American cultural influence, but its roots were kept very quiet, and the campaigners won support across the political divide. The Labour MP Horace King, for instance, denounced the comics as 'all that is worst in America', while his Conservative counterpart Sir Hugh Lucas-Tooth condemned them as 'crude and alien'.[6] 'It is not only American comics that should be banned,' thundered Picture Post in

1952, 'but also many of the other false practices that have been imported into this country. The sooner that we return to a sane British way of life (built on traditional lines) the better for this great nation.' Readers must 'act now, before the moral values of our young people have become perverted by this degraded and degrading substitute for healthy enjoyment'.[7]

The result of all this pressure was the Children and Young Persons (Harmful Publications) Act of 1955, effectively prohibiting the sale of the offending American imports.[8] Even after the Act was passed, however, comic-reading was still seen as rather suspicious: since comics were identified with the working classes, it was not unusual for middle-class children to be told that they were unsuitable or common. 'My parents thought I should be reading a real book, not looking at pictures,' recalled one woman, whose parents compelled her to return the *Bunty* annual to the shop.[9] Another recalled that she was allowed *Girl*, 'but I looked down on *Bunty* because my parents did'.[10]

Despite all the complaints, comics in general thrived during the late fifties and sixties. Boys eagerly devoured the stories of courage and dedication presented not merely in the *Eagle* but also in comics like *Swift*, *Lion* and *Tiger*, the latter offering stories of the star footballer Roy of the Rovers. War comics like the *Victor*, *Commando* and *Valiant*, with their tales of plucky Tommies and sadistic Huns, sold half a million copies apiece. In fact most comics projected a conservative, hierarchical view of the world: authority might be temporarily defied, but dissidence and rebellion were always punished in the end. The *Beano* and *Dandy*, which showed unruly children thumbing their noses at authority, were probably the most controversial of all comics; however, even characters like Dennis the Menace inevitably ended up being outwitted and humiliated by their adult adversaries.[11]

Girls were not expected to enjoy the belligerence of *Tiger* or the rowdiness of the *Dandy*. Instead, they chose from a range of comics and magazines like *Girl*, *Girl's Crystal*, *School Friend* and, from 1958, *Bunty*, with stories of school escapades, intrepid girl investigators, policewomen, air nurses and historic heroines like Elizabeth I or Helen Keller.[12] After the age of thirteen or fourteen, however, girls typically moved on to 'older' magazines that tapped their interest in romance, consumerism and popular music. Between 1955 and 1957 three popular girls' magazines, *Romeo*, *Mirabelle* and *Valentine*, made their first appearances, soon to be joined by *Boyfriend*; the titles themselves reveal their emphasis, although some parents regarded them as 'common'.[13] 'The keynotes of VALENTINE', proclaimed an editorial in the first issue, 'are Romance . . . Youth . . . Excitement! Romance which lies deep in the heart of every girl. Youth which makes her fresh and lovely – glad to be alive and to be loved. Excitement which comes from the thrill of music, dancing and song.'[14]

Most of the articles in magazines like these concerned pop and film stars of the day: there were features on 'the love secrets of your favourite stars', interviews with Cliff Richard talking about his 'dream girl', and so on. These publications, with their advertisements for clothes, cosmetics, engagement rings and even an insurance society offering schemes for single women to save for their weddings, exploited the increasing affluence of adolescent girls in the later fifties. In other words, they functioned as consumer guides, and it was no coincidence that they appeared at exactly the same point that *Which?* was winning over adult readers keen to share in the delights of the affluent society. But of course they also had another function that *Which?* certainly did not share, that of advising their teenage readers on how to manage their budding love lives, so there were plenty of tips on looking good, attracting boys, conducting romances, and, of course, firmly drawing the line before things got out of hand. Only in 1963, when it published a special supplement on birth control, did *Which?* come anywhere near this kind of territory.[15]

Although magazines like *Valentine* presented themselves as fashionable guides to the new world of teenage consumerism, they actually carried a relatively conservative moral message. As one observer noted in 1965, their stories were generally celebrations of 'the virtue of things as they are, of the apparently dull boyfriend, of the small town against the sickly delights of the big city. The predominant moral tone is of the importance of respect and consideration for others, without any strict reliance on delivered principles.'[16] By the mid-sixties, however, they were looking rather old-fashioned. *Honey*, launched in April 1960 and then impressively revamped in 1961, offered a more buoyant, light-hearted approach, and it was followed in January 1964 by two new magazines, *Jackie* and *Fabulous*, with a stronger emphasis on fashion and sexuality. *Valentine* and *Boyfriend* soon collapsed, and the circulation of *Mirabelle* fell from over 500,000 in 1956 to 175,000 in 1968.[17] It was the misfortune of such publications that their readers quickly grew up and moved on; subsequent generations frequently demanded something entirely different.

Children born in Britain after the Second World War were fortunate to be brought up in a rich and stable European country, free from civil unrest, hunger and extreme deprivation. They were also more fortunate than their parents, who had endured two gruelling world wars as well as the misery of the Depression. The British birth rate had been falling steadily since the late nineteenth century: a woman married in the 1880s would have had four or five children, but already in the 1920s this had fallen to two.[18] Towards the end of the Second World War there came a brief rally, no doubt connected with the enthusiasm of impending victory and the eventual reunion of husbands and wives after long enforced separations, and the rate peaked at almost twenty-one births per thousand in 1947. But this was not a sustained phenomenon: although the birth rate had picked up, there was no real 'baby boom' in Britain. Family sizes were small, especially among the middle classes, and even working-class birth rates were falling.[19] Children were healthier and fitter than ever before; there was little reason to fear child mortality, and in 1950 infant mortality fell below thirty per thousand for the first time. From 1948 onwards, almost all children drank a third of a pint of free school milk; they were heavier, taller than ever, and reached puberty much more quickly.[20] Women were also keener than before to limit the size of their families, whether by sexual abstinence, induced abortion, *coitus interruptus* or artificial birth control, specifically rubber sheaths and diaphragms.[21] Children were expensive; the raising of the school-leaving age meant they had to be supported for longer before they went out to earn money themselves. For middle- and upper-class families, meanwhile, the high costs of private education and domestic servants meant that it was increasingly preferable to lavish love, attention and income on just one or two children rather than three or four.[22]

Most anecdotal evidence suggests that the majority of parents were gentler and more liberal with their children than their own parents had been with them. The American paediatrician Benjamin Spock's *Common Sense Book of Baby and Child Care*, which was first published in New York in 1946 but did not reach Britain until 1955, was extremely popular with British parents and encouraged them to adopt a more relaxed, tolerant and demonstrative manner with their children.[23] This new approach was summarised by the parenting specialist of *Housewife* magazine in April 1952, who explained that 'firmness is one of the least useful attitudes of a good parent and certainly not nearly so important as sympathy, understanding, patience and skill'.[24] This change was even reflected in a vogue for more adventurous names, recognising the child's status as an independent individual: rather than being named after their parents or grandparents, as had once been the norm, boys and girls were often given supposedly classless or American names: Christopher, Matthew, Gary and Adrian; or Marilyn, Carol, Jacqueline and Gloria.[25]

Only one in five married women went out to work in 1951.[26] It was widely believed that constant maternal love was essential for preserving a child's mental health and forming his or her character. The other particularly influential childcare book in the fifties, the paediatrician John Bowlby's bestseller *Child Care and the Growth of Love* (1953), insisted that adolescent delinquency was the fault of working mothers who had neglected their children and permanently damaged their psychological wellbeing. For Dr Bowlby, it was 'essential for mental health . . . that the infant and young child should experience a warm, intimate and continuous relationship with his mother'. Separation would bring 'acute anxiety, excessive need for love, powerful feelings of revenge, and arising from these, guilt and repression'. 'The mother of young children', Bowlby explained, 'is not free, or at least should not be free, to earn.'[27] Some women disagreed; the young Margaret Thatcher argued in 1954 that if a mother had 'a powerful and dominant personality, her personal influence is there the whole time', and that a break from family duties prevented her from becoming 'a little impatient'. 'I am sure', she insisted, 'that it is essential both for her own satisfaction and for the happiness of her family that she should use all her talents to the full.'[28] Most, however, followed Bowlby's recommendations. Since families were smaller and few couples relied on nannies or servants, the relationship of mother and child was probably stronger than ever before.[29]

Many working-class children continued to spend most of their spare time playing communal games like football, hopscotch, marbles and conkers outside in the street as their parents had in their time. For middle-class children, however, play was increasingly located indoors and either individual or concentrated within the family, a consequence not only of more indulgent styles of parenting but also of the increasing comfort and space of most homes as well as the increasing levels of traffic in urban and suburban streets. Indeed, it was not unusual to hear adults lamenting that their children were being ruined by the abundance of the modern world. 'Nowadays toys are so beautiful that it is hard to impose . . . a sense of necessity on a child,' wrote the novelist Margaret Drabble in 1965. 'If I don't assemble the jigsaws and put the wooden fire engines together again nobody does, and moreover nobody cares . . . In short, I worry that my children will be spoiled, and not because of my wicked indulgence, but because of the delightful affluence in England today.'[30]

It was certainly increasingly common for children to receive lavish presents, especially in more affluent families; even working-class parents now made considerable efforts to celebrate birthdays and Christmas and bought new toys for their children. In more comfortable households, children no longer needed to earn money delivering newspapers or running errands for local shopkeepers: instead, they received weekly pocket money from their parents, usually contingent on good behaviour.[31] This money was spent on toys of the child's own choice: the possession of toys was an important part of the child's status among his fellows. Toys were, however, strictly regimented by gender. Boys were expected to buy toys that reflected interests beyond the home, transport, adventure and so on, whereas girls' toys supported their identity as the domesticated, maternal housewives of the future. The extremely successful series of Matchbox model vehicles, founded by two former Royal Navy sailors and an army engineer, caught children's attention in 1953 when they sold a million models of the Coronation coach.[32] Like Dinky or Corgi models, Matchbox cars were designed to exploit boys' fascination with action and speed, and a similar formula ensured the success of Scalextric racing cars, first produced in 1952 and electrified four years later, allowing them to be raced around a specially designed track.[33]

Military toys were popular too. Boys could buy toy soldiers to re-enact the glories of the world wars as well as the imperial conquests of the nineteenth century, and from 1952 they could also repeat the country's finest hour with glued Airfix models of RAF fighter planes. Football was brought in from the street to the living-room table in the form of the Subbuteo table football kit, through which boys could themselves plot the fortunes of heroes like Tommy Lawton or Billy Wright. Hornby electric train sets were particularly prized, and, as they became more affordable in the fifties, most middle-class boys could hope to have their own. One later recalled that he would submit every birthday and Christmas a 'carefully researched' list of his desired additions. The pressure to keep up with one's contemporaries, however, was just as great among the train-set fraternity as it was among suburban homeowners:

I spent much of my young schooldays dreaming about my train set, making up timetables, pretending I was driving this little train, it seemed so exciting at the time. And there was real competition amongst boys as to how big your train set was and what engines you had. I didn't have as big a set as some of my classmates so I lied to keep up with them. The problem was I couldn't invite them back to our house and have them up to my room because they'd realise then that I'd been lying.[34]

The conventional boy's trinity of speed, battle and travel was supplemented by a modern innovation: science. Like ray guns, toy robots and flying saucers, chemistry sets became popular with boys during the fifties, although their interest usually lay in producing pungent smells and dramatic explosions rather than furthering the cause of scientific inquiry.[35]

As with model aircraft and train sets, chemistry sets were designed specifically for boys: it was not considered likely that girls would find them interesting. Gender lines were tightly drawn not only in schools, where girls were prohibited from playing boys' games and discouraged from being too academically ambitious, but also in the home.[36] One woman remembered that she loved playing with train sets but had to 'beg and plead' with the boys to borrow them: 'As a girl I had no chance of ever getting one of my own. This was understood implicitly – it never even occurred to me to ask for one.'[37] Girls' toys, then, included dolls and dolls' houses, nurses' uniforms, hula-hoops (an example in 1958 of one of the first toy crazes) and cookery sets. The development of dolls during the 1960s reflected both the increasing sophistication of plastics and the importance of foreign influence on children's toys. The glamorous American Barbie doll was introduced in the early sixties to great interest, and in 1963 British manufacturing responded with Sindy, advertised as 'the free, swinging, grown-up girl, who dresses the way she likes'. Lego arrived from Denmark in 1960, and six years later the American plastic soldier GI Joe was renamed Action Man and introduced into Britain.[38]

By this point children's toys were beginning to reflect the increasing importance of television in their lives. The BBC ran *Children's Hour* programmes between five and six, and between 1950 and 1956 they gradually introduced a cast of popular characters like Muffin the Mule, Andy Pandy, the Flowerpot Men, Rag, Tag and Bobtail, and the Woodentops.[39] By the late fifties children's programmes were becoming more ambitious, not least because of the competition between the BBC and commercial television; both Sooty and Sweep, who made their debut in 1953, and Paddington Bear,

who appeared in 1958, commanded considerable audiences throughout the sixties. In 1958 the BBC also launched their supremely successful programme *Blue Peter*, which was designed to wean older children away from ITV with a mixture of 'toys, model railways, games, stories and cartoons'. With its badges and stationery it tried to make viewers feel that they were part of the programme, and for the remainder of the century it continued to educate and inform as well as entertain.[40]

By the end of the sixties, with television now an essential part of most children's lives, toy manufacturers could hope to exploit the popularity of successful programmes. There were popular board games based on shows like *The Magic Roundabout* and *Basil Brush*, plastic dolls inspired by futuristic puppet shows like *Stingray* (1964), *Thunderbirds* (1965) and *Captain Scarlett* (1967), and above all, an extremely successful range of toys based on the series *Doctor Who*.[41] The semi-robotic Daleks first appeared in the BBC's new science-fiction series at the end of 1963, and proved a popular sensation. Woolworths sold over a million Dalek badges, for example, over Christmas 1964, and the following year the BBC issued licences for another ninety Dalek-themed products, from clockwork model Daleks to Dalek suits and astro-ray Dalek guns.[42]

Like their parents, many British children structured their social lives around a network of hobbies and clubs. 'Everyone in the world had to have a hobby in those days,' one child of the era later recalled. 'I could never understand the attraction of stamp collecting but we did it, simply because everybody did it.'[43] Children might collect stamps or birds' eggs, go bird-watching, tend their own little patch of the family garden, note down bus or train numbers, or keep scrapbooks. One woman later recalled that at school they were encouraged to keep scrapbooks on members of the royal family: in her case, oddly enough, Lady Mountbatten.[44] For every hobby there existed a national club or organisation, and children could compare their own collections against the achievements of others. The *I-Spy* books, for example, devised by a retired headmaster who called himself Big Chief I-Spy, encouraged children to think of themselves as Indian braves spotting different varieties of cars, birds, aircraft, animals, signposts and so on. By the late 1950s half a million children were enlisted members of the I-Spy tribe.[45]

'Spotting' various phenomena was an extremely popular exercise: the physical mobility afforded by cars and holidays meant that children were able to record the sights of different parts of the country, or even of different countries. The most enduring example was train-spotting. Boys (very rarely were spotters girls) would travel to distant railway stations with their fathers to collect rare train numbers; some men would travel up to 300 miles a week in search of a particular number. The Locospotters' club claimed 82,000 members in 1952 and the *ABC Locomotives* books sold over fifty thousand copies a year. During the fifties train-spotting grew to such a proportion that at Clapham Junction, a busy and therefore popular venue, spotters were herded into a wire cage at the end of the platform. Train-spotters were even temporarily banned from Crewe, the most popular spotters' destination of all, after a series of accidents, and in 1952 seven spotters were arrested at Derby station and fined for trespass.[46] In the sixties, however, train-spotting began to lose some of its allure; thanks to Dr Beeching's ruthless cuts, thousands of rural stations and halts had been shut down, and much of the fun had evidently gone out of the spotting game.[47]

Many organisations did not exist to promote a common interest or hobby, but offered membership of the club itself as their sole rationale. *Girl* magazine, for example, promoted the 'Girl Adventurers': applicants sent off a postal order for one shilling and sixpence, and were promised in return 'a delightful brooch' and a membership card with the club rules: enjoy life, work for the common good, be kind to animals, help others, and so on. Although girls could contact pen pals through the club and enlist on Walking and Cycling Tours, it is hard not to conclude that this was a shilling and sixpence ill spent.[48]

The most popular organisation of all was the Scouting movement, which had been founded in 1908 by Colonel Robert Baden-Powell as a typically Edwardian expression of imperial solidarity and emphasised duty, obedience and 'purity'. The scout swore 'to do my duty to God and the Queen', and was advised in the Scout Law to remain loyal to the monarch and his officers, 'and to his parents, his country and his employers. He must stick to them through thick and thin against anyone who is their enemy or even talks badly of them.'[49] Like many organisations, from the Boys' Brigade to the Salvation Army, the Scouts were dressed in uniforms and organised on quasi-military lines. But none of this seemed to put off children in the post-war era, who were eager to enjoy the vigorous outdoor activities promised by the movement. The historian Richard Weight comments rather snidely that after 1960 'membership went into decline as young Britons discovered that pop music was more exciting (and often safer) than bivouacking in national parks with middle-aged men'; but, sadly for Weight, this is not at all true.[50] At the end of the Second World

War, the Scouts and their various affiliated groups like the Cubs, Brownies and Girl Guides claimed some 471,040 members; in 1955, there were 511,010; and by 1970, there were 539,340.[51] Evidently this is not explicable merely in terms of parental pressure: despite the regimentation, many children clearly looked forward to events like the annual summer camps and Christmas parties.

Children's fiction generally reflected this emphasis on the collective rather than the individual. It was now an industry in its own right: as children became more literate with the expansion of the national education system, so the possibilities for children's authors widened accordingly. The undisputed queen of children's fiction, despite the opprobrium in which she was held by many progressive-minded teachers, remained Enid Blyton. Her Famous Five and Secret Seven stories, in which a secret children's club foils a succession of dastardly villains, illustrated the collective ethos of post-war children's fiction. A similar example was the Lone Pine series by Malcolm Saville, chronicling the adventures of wartime evacuees in rural Shropshire. As with toys, gender stereotypes abounded. Books like Elsie Oxenham's Abbey Girls series, Elinor M. Brent-Dyer's Chalet School tales, or Noel Streatfeild's ballet stories were aimed specifically at girls, and any boy seen reading them in public would have risked endless teasing from his fellows. The ninety-eight Biggles books by Captain W. E. Johns were another example of how pre-war characters and situations survived the transition to post-imperial Britain: in this case, Biggles, Algy, Ginger and company were successively involved in the First and Second World Wars, a series of colonial wars in the fifties and sixties and finally a number of operations for Interpol and the Secret Service. These were unmistakably books for boys: female characters appear only rarely and usually take the form of deadly enemy spies or helpless victims. Some children's stories, however, were read and enjoyed by both sexes. Arthur Ransome's sailing stories, from *Swallows and Amazons* onwards, were still deservedly popular during the fifties and sixties, and Richmal Crompton produced twelve more of her splendidly funny William books during the fifties and sixties, updating them for the space age with titles like *William and the Moon Rocket* and *William and the Space Animal*.[52]

School stories of all kinds met with great success. The most popular school stories tended to be those set in boarding schools, despite the fact that most children had never seen the inside of such an institution, and it is often argued that these were therefore tales of hierarchy and tradition imposed on unwilling children by their elders. The obvious explanation for the success of boarding school stories is that they reflected some aspects of the reader's existence (classroom situations and so on), while adding an element of the unfamiliar. The boarding school setting also nicely disposed of the heroes' parents, always a necessity in successful children's fiction.

The quintessential school stories of the fifties were Anthony Buckeridge's twenty-five books about two eleven-year-old schoolboys called Jennings and Darbishire, whose classes were presided over by the wise Mr Carter and harangued by the irascible Mr Wilkins. The supreme achievement of this genre, however, was still the inimitable Billy Bunter, 'the Owl of the Remove', an enormously fat, vain boy forever expecting the arrival of his postal order, whose escapades at the Edwardian boarding school Greyfriars continued to entertain both children and adults long after the death of his creator Frank Richards.[53] By the early sixties, new authors were beginning to challenge the dominion of these established figures. Michael Bond published his first Paddington Bear book in 1958; Rosemary Sutcliff produced a string of rollicking historical adventures; and the fantasy writer Alan Garner won the attention of older children with books like *The Weirdstone of Brisingamen* (1960) and *Elidor* (1965).[54] All the same, there is little doubt that most British children in the period grew up reading much the same kind of books that had been read by middle-class children during the twenties and thirties. Many of these stories reflected the mores of an older age: the attitudes to women and foreigners in the Biggles books, for example, surely seemed odd in the context of the late sixties, and in the work of several authors black characters are depicted as either infantile or contemptible. The tension between the undoubted quality and appeal of much of the writing and the equally undoubted anachronism of the attitudes presented continued to divide adult readers for decades to come. Children, however, did not seem to mind.

Most children were educated under the framework of the 1944 Education Act, the handiwork of the Conservative reformer Rab Butler.[55] This had established a tripartite system, built on the confusingly diverse legacy of British education in the nineteenth and early twentieth centuries. Children attended local primary schools from the age of five until they were eleven or so, at which point they were deemed ready for examination and sat the eleven-plus papers. If they were part of a successful minority, they went on to a grammar school and studied academic subjects of a fairly conventional kind until the age of fifteen; if not, they were sent to a secondary modern school, teaching similar subjects but not always with very successful results. The third alternative was the technical school, teaching purely vocational subjects: this never had any great prestige, and numbers soon collapsed. Fully comprehensive schools were very rare indeed; at the beginning of the fifties, there were fewer than twenty throughout England and Wales.[56]

There is no doubt that successive Labour and Conservative governments were deeply committed to state education: between 1947 and 1958, spending on education doubled in real terms and increased as a proportion of the national income by 75 per cent.[57] The problem was that although the Butler Act was, as Nicholas Timmins concludes, 'a mighty creation', it did not turn out to be a lasting answer to the country's educational needs.[58] The central flaw, which lay as much in the implementation of the Act as in the legislation itself, was the balance between grammar and secondary modern schools. Ambitious parents were desperate for their children to go to grammar schools rather than the secondary moderns, but, since grammar schools were now free of charge and open to all classes, the only way in was through the eleven-plus. This therefore took on enormous importance, and wealthy parents were happy to pay tutors to coach their children for the examination, meaning that in the early fifties the middle-class domination of grammar schools actually rose rather than fell.[59]

Many middle-class children were under tremendous pressure to pass the eleven-plus. 'We'd been building up to it for ages,' one schoolgirl in the early sixties later recalled. 'For years it had been impressed upon us at school how important the whole thing was. I felt that if I didn't get through this exam and do well, then I would never do anything with my life.'[60] Another girl remembered:

> My parents were frightfully middle-class so it would have been a disaster not to pass the eleven-plus. I was terrified of failing. I remember on the day of the exam I got home and as a special treat my mother let me have fish fingers, which I was usually never allowed as she saw them as working-class food.[61]

She passed, so the fish fingers were well deserved. But between 75 and 80 per cent did not, and the sense of disappointment was often hard to shake. In a BBC documentary shown in 1962, a worried mother laments her daughter's 'failure' in front of the headmaster. 'I hardly think that "failed" is the right word, Mrs Kitchen,' he says smoothly. 'You see, what happened is that Janet took a test so we could find out what school suited her best. She would have failed the test if she had been selected for the wrong school and so if she has been selected for the right school, she has really passed the test.' At these words Janet looks pleased; her mother, less easily fooled, remains downcast.[62]

The framers of the Butler Act had expected a small minority of only 15 per cent to go to grammar schools: since the overwhelming number of pupils would attend secondary moderns, the intention was that they would never be seen as a poor relation. Butler himself later wrote that it was 'important to ensure that a stigma of inferiority did not attach itself to those secondary institutions . . . which lacked the facilities and academic prestige of the grammar schools'. Conditions in the schools, he thought, ought to be 'broadly equivalent', and he welcomed the idea of combining different types of school on one site, which he saw as anticipating 'the comprehensive idea'.[63]

But the system in the fifties and sixties did not turn out as Butler had planned, and in terms of educational opportunity a place at a secondary modern was not far short of a catastrophe. 'To have been consigned to the limbo of the secondary modern is to have failed disastrously,' wrote the journalist Peter Laurie in 1965, 'and very early in life.'[64] In 1960, two in every three state-educated twelve-year-olds attended a secondary modern. The vast majority were encouraged to leave at fourteen or fifteen, since they were considered to have no future in higher education, and almost none went on to university. By comparison, well over half of the grammar-school pupils were still in school at seventeen, and most of these went on to university.[65] The average grammar school had three times the resources of the average secondary modern, and usually had the pick of the best teachers. As Correlli Barnett puts it, for all the success of the grammar schools, the secondary modern 'was to remain in the eyes of parents and children alike a mere educational settling-tank for academic failures'.[66]

Children in poor urban or remote rural areas were usually the least well served; for many, failure to reach grammar school was almost inevitable. There were wide regional and class variations: whereas fewer than 10 per cent of children in Gateshead and Sunderland attended their local grammar schools, the corresponding figure in Westmoreland was well over 40 per cent.[67] A survey of the Nottingham inner city district of St Ann's between 1966 and 1968 found that junior school children there were 'intellectually handicapped': they 'seldom had any idea about play with paints, water, sand or clay'; they 'had almost no experience of pencils, pictures or books'; and in consequence 'they lacked the prerequisites of reading ability'. The researchers worked out that a mere 1.5 per cent of the district's school population attended grammar schools; in a neighbouring middle-class suburb, however, the figure was more like 60 per cent. Interestingly, when these results were published, the researchers were banned from further research in the education office, and a local alderman declared that 'bearded nits' from the university should 'stay out of St Ann's'.[68]

Most grammar schools were devoted to the ideals of middle-class respectability, and their pupils were taught to see themselves as an elite. In one survey of sixteen-year-old grammar-school girls in West Yorkshire, the girls frequently fell back on words like 'decent', 'educated' and 'sensible' to describe the kind of boys they wanted to meet; one girl even thought that since most of her fellow teenagers were 'not as clean as they should be', 'policemen ought to have the right to wash people's faces and necks'.[69] Not surprisingly, those working-class children who reached grammar schools were often bewildered by the experience, despite the unquestionably excellent facilities on offer. They were expected by the teachers to abandon their old friends and discouraged from joining clubs in their own neighbourhoods, and many working-class girls, who tended to think of themselves as more mature than their middle-class counterparts, found the regulations of grammar-school life extremely trying. Bright working-class pupils were often faced with a stark and unpalatable choice: if they accepted the middle-class ethos of the school, they would be abandoning the values of their families and friends.[70] One working-class girl, attending a grammar school in Huddersfield, wrote that her old friends 'dwindled away, until my band of friends only included those from this school and from the church I attended'.

> Problems did not come from my friendships, but from within the family. Quarrels with my parents usually arise from the fact that other children are earning their living at my age – why can't I be more thoughtful. Usually the replies are – you sent me to grammar school and I can't help you a lot because of my homework . . .
>
> Grammar school taught me to read widely, yet at the expense of my parents. I thought an evening could not be spent in a pleasanter way than doing my homework and then reading – and not joining in conversation.

Her cultural values, she recognised, had changed a great deal since she won her grammar-school place:

> In early adolescence when I was with my non-grammar school friends I was well satisfied with detective novels or a 'funny' film and 'pop music'; but now I have learnt to appreciate finer things such as real music and more subtle entertainments. Previously I had to go to a cinema for my entertainment but walks and hikes give me more thrills.[71]

Yet for all its problems, a grammar-school education undoubtedly opened up opportunities to a minority of working-class pupils about which their contemporaries could only dream. 'We have built up a new middle class,' the headmaster of Manchester Grammar School proudly told a BBC interviewer in 1958. 'We are building it up now, a new middle class of technologists, and where is that coming from? It is coming from the grammar schools, inevitably from the grammar schools, so in a way the grammar schools are really the spearhead of the movement of social mobility.'[72]

The 5 per cent of children who did not attend state schools were educated privately, with their parents paying large sums for tuition and often for boarding expenses. Although private education concerned only a minority of children, this remained a disproportionately influential and important minority. The survival of the public schools at all was something of a surprise. Between the wars they had suffered from a crisis both in their finances and in their reputation, with eminent old boys like Robert Graves and Graham Greene attacking their antiquated philistinism, bullying and homosexuality. Both Butler and Churchill initially imagined that the public schools would have to be substantially reformed and perhaps even integrated into the state system.[73] The difficulty of managing the transition, however, coupled with the opposition of much of the Conservative Party, meant that the plan was never implemented, and an opportunity was missed.[74] After the war, the public schools recovered from the crisis of the thirties. Overseas officers and diplomats often sent their children to boarding schools, but the real boost came from middle-class families whose children had failed the eleven-plus and who were determined not to condemn their offspring to a secondary modern. Curiously enough, then, the Attlee government ended up benefiting the public-school system rather than scrapping it, and admissions rose by some 20 per cent.[75]

The most famous public schools were the nine establishments examined by the Clarendon Commission of 1861: Eton, Harrow, Rugby, Westminster, Shrewsbury, Charterhouse, Winchester, St Paul's and Merchant Taylors'. Other schools, often of more modern foundation, like Marlborough, Cheltenham, Malvern and Clifton, were also well thought of. It would be a mistake to imagine that these were all genuinely upper-class institutions; many attracted the children of the professional middle classes. According to Ross McKibbin, perhaps only four or five could claim to be really aristocratic: Eton, Harrow, Westminster and Winchester certainly, and possibly Charterhouse and Ampleforth.[76] All the same the public schools were considered the ideal training ground for the national elites of the future. In 1955, over half of Eden's first Cabinet and another fifth of all the Conservative backbenchers had been to Eton. More than a third of the entries in the 1961 edition of *Who's Who* had been educated at public schools, with Eton claiming a sixth of the entire total. The education provided by these schools was, therefore, of national importance, even if only a tiny fraction of the population attended them.[77]

Many schools had changed little for decades, and placed a high premium on leadership, loyalty, hierarchy and tradition. Pupils were reminded that they were a social elite by their physical detachment from their families and towns and by the high fees paid by their parents. As McKibbin puts it: 'They tended to see the working class only in their subordinate role – as people who carried your baggage or from whom you might buy a railway ticket. Even the lower middle class was largely unknown to them.'[78] The clearest example of their separation from society was the individual argot that developed in each school, which in isolated institutions became virtually a language in its own right, often revolving around sexual and specifically homosexual slang.[79] Although the misery of such institutions is perhaps a little exaggerated, many boarders did find it a gruelling experience. A new arrival at Wellingborough, for instance, sharing a dormitory with nineteen others, wrote disconsolately that 'the floors were bare and the bathroom had just two tiny tubs for all twenty boys'.[80] Another pupil later recalled: 'You had to have a cold bath every morning. The junior house was a kind of Nissen hut, and the prefects would stand in the bathroom and make sure you put your shoulders under the water.'[81]

In 1960, some 35 per cent of all public schoolboys went on to university, compared with only 27 per cent of boys from grammar schools.[82] The university system was divided into four informal divisions: first, the ancient universities of Oxford and Cambridge; second, the colleges of the University of London; third, the large provincial 'redbrick' universities founded in the late nineteenth and early twentieth centuries, like Manchester, Liverpool and Birmingham; and fourth, the smaller redbrick universities in towns like Reading and Exeter.[83] There had been only fifty thousand full-time students in 1939, but during the war there came a chorus of calls to expand student numbers and provide the country with a better-educated workforce. The Barlow Committee report on scientific manpower (1946) noted that science was more important than ever to the nation's future: radar had helped to win the Battle of Britain; penicillin had saved thousands of lives; and the power of the atomic bomb had transformed both warfare and diplomacy. 'Never before has the importance of science been so widely recognised,' the report explained, 'or so many hopes of future progress and welfare founded upon the scientist.'[84]

Throughout the decades that followed, politicians and social commentators endlessly repeated the mantra that the country's economic future depended on the expansion of higher education in order to train hundreds of young scientists, linguists, engineers and inventors. The consequent increases in government grants to universities and state scholarships to students meant that numbers rose more than ever before, transforming the British higher education system. By 1951 there were 84,000 students, and in 1958 the total reached 100,000. Most of this growth came in the redbrick universities, which saw their student numbers rise by some 130 per cent. There were two new universities, based on existing colleges at Nottingham (1948) and Southampton (1952); there was also one entirely new institution, the University College of North Staffordshire, which opened in 1950 and was later to become the unlovely Keele University.[85]

However, higher education was still in many ways a traditional world. Much of the post-war expansion came not in the sciences, as had been hoped, but in the arts: only one in a hundred students was on a course in applied science.[86] The bias towards the arts was especially strong at Oxford and Cambridge, which retained their historic prestige as centres of excellence and training-grounds for the national elite. Student journalism, theatre or politics at Oxford or Cambridge were still regarded as the most effective routes to a career on Fleet Street, at the BBC or in the Commons. It was at Oxford and Cambridge, moreover, that bright grammar-school boys from Alan Bennett and Tony Richardson to Harold Wilson and Edward Heath were given the opportunities to pursue careers closed to their parents. For some students, the traditionalism and ritual of Oxbridge came as a shock. Dennis Potter, an undergraduate at New College, Oxford, wrote a scathing indictment of the strange world of 'cavalry twill and cut-glass accents'.[87]

The deficiencies of the British education system were a favoured target of reformers whenever the country's political and economic fortunes seemed at low ebb. In the early 1960s, for example, with the Conservative government beginning to flounder, the call of expansion was taken up once again. Arthur Koestler spoke for many other commentators, especially in the Labour Party, when he blamed Britain's economic problems on an 'outdated education system . . . which perpetuates the iniquities of the past'.[88] 'Where are all the Young Men Going?' asked the *Daily Mirror* in 1963. 'Young talent has been or is being wasted and frustrated. Brainpower, vital to Britain's future, has been and is being wasted.'[89] Educational expansion was, as Jim Tomlinson accurately puts it, a 'panacea', a painless cure that would supposedly end the nation's economic troubles at a stroke.[90] Noël Annan later explained the argument: 'Turn on the tap and the next generation would be more productive as well as better educated. The more dons there were the higher production would rise because of the spin-off from fundamental to applied research and from that to industry.'[91] By the early sixties, moreover, the 'baby bulge' generation of children born in 1945 and shortly thereafter were beginning to think about going to university, and it was clear that there were not nearly enough places to satisfy them. The result was the Robbins Committee, appointed by Macmillan to review the provision of higher education, which advised him in 1963 that 'when we compare published plans for future developments, many other countries are far ahead of us. If, as we believe, a highly educated population is essential to meet competitive pressures in the modern world, a much greater effort is necessary if we are to hold our own.'[92]

Robbins recommended that the government guarantee a place in higher education 'for all those who are qualified by ability and attainment to pursue them and wish to do so', and he also suggested targets of 50 per cent more students by 1967 and 250 per cent more by 1980. With both political parties desperate to prove that they were democratic, progressive and committed to technological innovation, few critics questioned the premise that the welfare state should be expanded to fund three years' further study for all, although the economic benefits of such largesse were never definitively established.[93] Eleven more universities, then, were established during the remainder of the decade: Sussex, East Anglia, York, Essex, Kent,

Warwick and Lancaster in England; and Strathclyde, Stirling, Heriot-Watt and Dundee in Scotland. There were new research councils, funding boards, business schools, student unions and a centralised application system, and all of this meant spending more money. In 1956 the University Grants Committee disbursed £3.8 million; in 1963, it was paying out more than £30 million.[94]

The most significant innovation was the introduction of the polytechnics in the 1960s, a second tier of thirty-two higher institutions designed to compensate for the universities' weaknesses in scientific and vocational subjects. As with Butler's technical schools, they were expected to become centres of excellence attracting bright people to study advanced technology; and as with Butler's technical schools, they represented an opportunity not taken. The polytechnics were encouraged to compete with traditional universities, concentrating their efforts on awarding degrees for three-year courses rather than offering shorter, more technical courses of training. The local authorities that controlled them often saw them not as high-class technical colleges, but as budding universities, so as Noël Annan puts it:

> The polys should have concentrated all their efforts on applied science and have been geared to make British industry more productive, more inventive, more competitive. Instead, starved by sixth-form specialization of applicants wanting to study science and technology, they taught art subjects, and colleges of fine art were often ordered to become part of them.[95]

Indeed, for all Robbins' fine words, the British education system remained defiantly biased towards the arts rather than the sciences. While lecture halls were crowded with languages or history students, gleaming new engineering and physics laboratories lay empty and silent. Twenty years after the Robbins report, arts and humanities students still easily outnumbered their scientific counterparts, and only a tiny proportion of women chose to study scientific subjects, an imbalance that was hotly debated but never truly understood.[96]

Art colleges were the third element in the British higher education system, and an important one at that: indeed, there were more art schools per head in Britain than anywhere else in the world.[97] The various art colleges and design schools scattered across the country usually attracted working-class or lower-middle-class students who, while not academically outstanding, might have some glimmers of creativity. Entrance standards were less than exacting, and often the courses were relatively flexible and undemanding, so art colleges became, as George Melly put it, 'the refuge of the bright but the unacademic, the talented, the non-conformist, the lazy, the inventive and the indecisive'.[98] 'The thing was you were bombarded with a lot more than just a set syllabus,' one earnest young man later recalled. 'You had this thing called "Liberal Studies" and the people that taught it were often very interesting . . . The fact that we were technically being trained to design ceramic pots or books or theatre sets was irrelevant.'[99]

Art colleges were therefore perceived as centres of imagination and cultural exchange; the typical art student in the early sixties was thought to be a serious-minded young man in a black polo-neck or duffel coat, perhaps carrying a pile of books or jazz records or CND flyers under his arm, no doubt on his way to the nearest coffee bar for an expresso and a look at some Sartre. In Iris Murdoch's novel *The Bell* (1958), Dora, the central character, is a typical lower-middle-class art student who spends her meagre pocket money on 'big multi-coloured skirts and jazz records and sandals'.[100] It was in the art schools that relatively uncommercial kinds of music, like modernist jazz or, initially, rhythm and blues, first took hold, and the general ease of art-school life meant that there was plenty of time for aspiring musicians to form and rehearse bands of their own. Indeed, since so many pop musicians, designers and artists of the mid-sixties studied at art colleges, their importance in the youth culture of the sixties can hardly be overstated.[101]

The final rite of passage for most teenagers in the fifties was the experience of National Service, 'half adult boarding school, half lunatic asylum', as one young conscript later called it.[102] It had been introduced by the National Service Act in 1947 with support across the political parties, and conscripts began arriving in the armed forces two years later. Under the terms of the Act, all eighteen-year-old men were liable to spend eighteen months in the services, extended to two years after the outbreak of the Korean War; even after discharge they had to remain for the following four years in the military reserves, liable for immediate recall to the colours in case of emergency.[103] Once eighteen, the conscript would have to report for an army medical; then, a few weeks later, the postman would bring a plain brown envelope with the instruction to report to barracks. Every fortnight

some six thousand young men were called up, and by the time the last
National Serviceman was discharged in 1963 a total of two and a half million
young men had been conscripted.[104]

There was, of course, a long national tradition of opposition to standing
conscript armies: however, the circumstances of the late 1940s were
unusual. British forces were tightly stretched across the globe, with the
British Army of the Rhine still occupying part of West Germany and British
garrisons in Austria, Palestine, Aden, Cyprus, Singapore, Hong Kong and
various other colonial outposts. What was more, the threat of war with the
Soviet Union and the Communist bloc was a very real one, and the shadow
of appeasement meant that no politician wanted to risk appearing complacent. Finally, National Service was seen as an experience that would
promote unity across economic and regional divisions: the united spirit of
wartime would be reproduced by fostering patriotism and common effort,
and young men would spend two good years working hard for the Empire
rather than idling in back-street pubs with their friends. The Minister of
Labour, Walter Monckton, explained in 1953 that conscripts encountered 'as
good a comradeship as they are likely to get anywhere. They generally benefit a great deal in health and physique and put on weight. They have an
opportunity of travel certainly in Britain and possibly overseas.'[105] The official guide for new conscripts promised the new arrivals that they would
have a tremendous time:

> It is in truth an education in itself – the finest in the world: quite apart
> from the training and instruction the National Service man will
> receive, he will meet and live with men drawn from all classes of soci-
> ety, of all trades, of all standards of education, and of various religious
> and political faiths ... Discipline is the foundation of the army ...
> Discipline starts with the individual and there is nothing debasing about
> it: quite the reverse.[106]

After their mandatory five weeks of basic training, some young men
found themselves in empty army barracks in the provinces polishing their
kit and marching up and down squares. Others fought against nationalist
guerrillas in Malaya, Kenya or Cyprus, and almost four hundred were killed
in action.[107] For some it was two years of grinding regimentation, drabness
and misery; for others it was a liberating opportunity to see the world and
fulfil dreams of service. The future satirist John Wells spent his time in the

Royal Sussex Regiment, and sailed for Korea in 1956, where he discovered a world worthy of Gilbert and Sullivan:

> There had been a ceasefire, and all we had to do was patrol, and we had taken all the regimental silver, and the band, and even in temperatures well below freezing the band played during dinner, and we all wore full Number One Mess Kit, and we entertained the Americans and Swedes and French, and afterwards there was tremendous pride in showing these other United Nations forces how British officers whiled away the evenings.

The after-dinner entertainments, in which Wells played a prominent role, consisted of playground games and cabaret impressions of American generals.[108] Not all servicemen, though, had such an eccentric experience. The military campaigns of the fifties were not always popular among those compelled to fight: one conscript, for instance, said that he felt 'increasingly distressed' by having to defend the 'injustice' of empire in Malaya; another, who fought in Korea, complained that he 'never really understood' why he was there.[109]

In general, men served grudgingly, because they did not want to let down their country or their families, not because of any great enthusiasm. After interviewing hundreds of conscripts, a government committee reported in 1955: 'Our overwhelming impression is that, with few exceptions, the National Service man regards his . . . period of service as an infliction to be undergone rather than a duty to the nation.'[110] The general drudgery and authoritarianism of military life, not to mention the danger of being killed or wounded, shocked many young men, especially those with intellectual aspirations: the writer Karl Miller, for example, recalled National Service as 'interlarded with scenes of horror and desolation'.[111] One Glaswegian corporal, after two years working in the Scottish pits, insisted: 'Compared to the Army, the Scottish coal mines were a warm, profoundly moving and satisfying way to live.'[112] Of course, the military lifestyle, with its emphasis on regimentation and obedience, was entirely inappropriate for many men. Others enjoyed it, though; as one conscript put it, 'most of us *did* feel proud to be part of an army which had only recently won the war'.[113] Another liked the fact that he had spent his time 'in a complete cross-section of the population, and got to know boys from Newcastle or Glasgow or whatever who'd had pretty hard upbringings'.[114] A Welsh signalman thought two years' discipline helped men to grow up:

> My service taught me self-confidence, taught me comradeship, under-standing of my fellow men, discipline and appreciation of my home and parents. I returned to Caernarvon a very responsible adult. I had come across quite a few hoodlums from the bigger cities, but the Army soon knocked them into shape and they left their National Service far better citizens than when they entered it.[115]

National Service was abolished as part of the massive defence cuts announced by the Macmillan government in April 1957. As Duncan Sandys explained in his Defence White Paper, British military strength would henceforth be based on a small, technologically advanced professional army, not on the systematic conscription of thousands of reluctant young men.[116] The last call-ups went out at the end of 1960, and the last conscripts left the army in 1963. Most young people regarded military service as a regrettable intrusion and simply resumed their lives afterwards as though nothing had happened, although the satirists of the early 1960s frequently drew on their experience for comic material.[117]

Since conscription was widely disliked, it was an easy and safe target for those eager to criticise the state of the nation. Young writers like David Lodge and Leslie Thomas, for instance, lampooned the stultifying regimentation and anachronism of military life in their respective novels *Ginger, You're Barmy* (1962) and *The Virgin Soldiers* (1966).[118] The most popular examples of army satire, however, were two notable films: *Private's Progress* (1956) and *Carry On, Sergeant* (1958). *Private's Progress* debunks the military myths of the forties: when an education officer tells the cadets, 'We need to get a clear picture of the sort of world we're all fighting for,' they react with utter boredom and apathy. Perhaps most revealingly, they even skip their duties in order to watch the film *In Which We Serve*, a wartime classic.[119] In *Carry On, Sergeant*, meanwhile, the comedy is gentler but no less impudent. William Hartnell plays a gruff but good-natured sergeant major training his last group of conscripts before retirement, among them such comic stalwarts as Kenneth Williams, Charles Hawtrey and Kenneth Connor, as well as Bob Monkhouse as the young romantic hero. The film was much less bawdy than those that succeeded it in the *Carry On* series, but it was a box-office hit nevertheless. This owed much to the unpopularity of army life among young cinema audiences: anything that mocked the tedious rituals of the parade ground was likely to strike a chord with young men in particular.[120]

The idea of National Service never entirely disappeared. Some Conservatives later lamented its abolition and suggested that it had contributed to the rise in crime during the sixties and seventies. Since the increasing crime rates were already apparent before National Service was abolished, this argument holds little water.[121] Still, for decades to come, nostalgic commentators suggested that military service might provide an answer to the problems of Britain's young. For, just as military conscription was falling from favour, a new image of youth was becoming alarmingly prominent: the image of the teenager.

In the opening scene of Colin MacInnes' novel *Absolute Beginners*, the teenage hero sits with a friend in a fashionable rooftop café and looks back on the late fifties:

> This teenage ball had had a real splendour in the days when the kids discovered that, for the first time since centuries of kingdom-come, they'd money, which hitherto had always been denied to us at the best time in life to use it, namely, when you're young and strong, and also before the newspapers and telly got hold of this teenage fable and prostituted it as conscripts seem to do to everything they touch. Yes, I tell you, it had a real savage splendour in the days when we found that no one could sit on our faces any more because we'd loot to spend at last, and our world was to be our world, the one we'd wanted and not standing on the door of somebody else's waiting for honey, perhaps.[122]

Reading many memoirs and histories of British life in the sixties, one could be forgiven for thinking that the country was inhabited entirely by young men and women between the ages of, say, sixteen and thirty. Both Arthur Marwick and Jonathon Green devote great chunks of their books to teenagers and youth culture. According to Green, 'the prevailing ethos [of the sixties] was a desire to oust the adult world'.[123] Marwick, meanwhile, argues that the period was characterised by 'the rise to positions of unprecedented influence of young people, with youth culture having a steadily increasing impact on the rest of society'.[124] Even the normally sober Marxist historian Eric Hobsbawm agrees: 'Youth was the name of the secret ingredient that revolutionized consumer society, and western culture.'[125]

It is certainly true that young people were given more prominence by the media in the sixties than they had been in, say, the forties; indeed, the problem of 'youth' was one of the issues of the day. It is also beyond question that young people were more affluent than before, more economically independent and influential, and that a network of manufacturers, retailers and publications was developing to meet that demand. On the other hand, millions of people, quite obviously, were not young at all, did not think of themselves as fashionable or exciting, and ploughed on with their lives cheerfully indifferent to the youth culture of the day. Those individuals with genuine power over the lives of their contemporaries, like politicians, businessmen and union leaders, were not young, and neither were most voters. Nor did the young people of the late fifties and sixties themselves constitute a united body of opinion or a cohesive social force: they were divided by class, region, political opinion, personal inclination, and of course from one another by age. A sixteen-year-old schoolgirl in 1958 would be twenty-eight in 1970, probably married with a child, and, unless she was particularly affluent or well educated, not likely to be especially sympathetic to the values of the sixteen-year-olds of 1970.

Although it would be foolish to neglect youth culture entirely, or to pretend that it lacked any historical significance at all, it is worth bearing two points in mind. First, the millions of people who passed through adolescence in the late 1950s and 1960s should not all be judged by the antics of a wealthy and well-educated minority, by the posturing of the most radical, by the violence of the most disaffected or by the promiscuity of the most wanton. The teenagers of the sixties, after all, were also the estate agents, loss adjusters and car-park attendants of the seventies. Second, it should not be forgotten that young people formed merely one demographic group among many. To concentrate exclusively on their experience, to ignore the contribution to British life made by millions of apparently nondescript people in their forties or fifties or sixties, gives a distorted picture of the period. All too often writers suggest that young people were somehow more visionary, more exciting and more righteous than their elders, that their 'revolution' was, in Green's breathless words, 'a period of unprecedented intensity, the height of the party as it were, a glorious mêlée into which would be poured all the energies, all the creativity, all the hopes of a generation who foolishly but genuinely believed that they could change the world'.[126] But that serves only to appropriate the history of the period on behalf of a minority; the reality was rather different.

The Lord Mayor of London demonstrates a 'jukebox of NATO tunes' at a NATO exhibition in Hyde Park to a delighted Lord Hailsham, 1957. *(Fox Photos/Getty Images)*

CND on the march, 1961, 'a movement of eggheads for eggheads'. *(Hulton-Deutsch/Corbis)*

West Indian immigrants at Victoria Station, 1956. *(Hulton-Deutsch/Corbis)*

Children at a Christmas party thrown at Holland Park Comprehensive to encourage racial integration, 1958. *(Miller/Getty Images)*

d Kite (Peter Sellers) leads his men out on strike in *I'm All Right, Jack* (1959). He had
rned his militancy at the Balliol College summer school in 1946: 'Very good toast and
serves they give you at tea time, as you probably know.' *(Scherschel/Getty Images)*

cast of *Hancock's Half Hour* in rehearsal, 1956: *from left*, Kenneth Williams,
y Hancock, Bill Kerr and Sid James. *(BBC/Corbis)*

The Evans family gather around their television set in the new town of Harlow, Essex, 1958
(Martin/Getty Images)

Teenage girls on the hills above a Northern mill town, 1957; the photograph was taken for
a feature in the *Picture Post* entitled 'The Truth About Teenagers'. *(Hardy/Getty Images)*

Saturday night at the dance hall, Birmingham, early 1950s. *(Hardy/Getty Images)*

Jazz in the caves: a jazz band plays during a party in Chislehurst Caves, Kent, 1957. *(Pace/Getty Images)*

The entertainer: Lonnie Donegan on stage, early 1960s.
(Blackman/Getty Images)

Billy Fury, probably Britain's best rock and roll singer of the early sixties. Born Ronald Wycherley, he was a keen bird-watcher.
(Evening Standard/Getty Images)

'Is this boy too sexy for television?' Cliff Richard rehearses with Hank Marvin of the Shadows, November 1962. His jumper certainly was too sexy for television.
(McCabe/Getty Images)

The *Beyond the Fringe* team: *from left*, Alan Bennett, Peter Cook, Dudley Moore and Jonathan Miller, early sixties. *(Newell Smith/Getty Images)*

Richard Ingrams, Christopher Booker and William Rushton, apparently hard a work on the lates issue of *Private Eye*, March 1963 *(Pratt/Getty Images)*

The teenager was a modern invention, and an American invention at that. While it encompasses both the pubescent and the adolescent, the word also carries the implication of affluence and independence. It was first used in the United States in the late 1930s to describe boys and girls between the ages of ten and twenty, who were both more physically mature than their predecessors and also more economically important.[127] Recent research on Manchester in the same period suggests that, in well-to-do areas, teenage consumers were becoming increasingly powerful even before the Second World War: taking part-time jobs, spending their earnings on records, clothes and dances, and breaking free of parental controls.[128] But the term *teenager* itself only became popular in Britain during the fifties, when it was used to describe a group that was wealthier and more economically conspicuous than ever before. The general economic contentment of the Macmillan era was important, of course, but there were also other factors: the demographic 'bulge' of teenagers in the late fifties; their concentration in towns and suburbs rather than isolated rural villages; the development of mass media like the radio and television; the expansion of education; and the fact that Britain was enjoying a period of relative peace after the tribulations of the two world wars.[129] Adolescents had more free time. There were school holidays for those still in education, for example, or paid holidays for those at work. The development of kitchen appliances meant that girls were no longer expected to spend hours helping their mothers with the housework, and the abolition of National Service in 1960 gave most teenage boys two extra years of freedom.[130]

'The distinctive fact about teenagers' behaviour is economic,' wrote Peter Laurie in 1965; 'they spend a lot of money on clothes, records, concerts, make-up, magazines: all things that give immediate pleasure and little lasting use.'[131] The *Daily Mirror* began in the late fifties to run a teenage page, with tips and anecdotes about romance, growing up and, above all, entertainments, clothes and desirable purchases.[132] There were three loose groups of young people with money to spend: first, young earners, often in married couples, between the ages of perhaps eighteen and twenty-five; second, students at university; and third, boys and girls still at school.[133] In Mark Abrams' influential surveys *The Teenage Consumer* and *Teenage Consumer Spending in 1959*, for example, teenagers were defined as unmarried young people between fifteen and twenty-five; marriage was thought to mark an important transition from youth to adulthood. As Abrams saw it, there were more than five million teenagers in Britain at the beginning of 1960, commanding almost 10 per cent of the population's total personal income.[134] Male teenagers, he calculated, spent 71s 6d (more than £3) a week, while girls spent 54s. In total, then, young people spent some £830 million a year, an increase in real terms of over 50 per cent since the last years of the thirties. True, this was only 5 per cent of all consumer spending in Britain, but the important thing was that it was concentrated in certain areas. Teenagers did not spend their money on food, consumer durables or housing: instead, they lavished it on luxuries and entertainments.[135] The Albemarle Report on British teenagers in 1960 noted:

> Much of the spending is clearly – and naturally – on goods designed to impress other teenagers (e.g. dressing up) or on gregarious pursuits (e.g. coffee-bar snacks). This is spending which is, to an unusually high degree, charged with an emotional content – it helps to provide an identity or to give status or to assist in the sense of belonging to a group of contemporaries.[136]

Mark Abrams worked out that British teenagers in 1959 spent 20 per cent of their money on clothes and shoes; 17 per cent on drinks and cigarettes; 15 per cent on sweets, snacks and soft drinks and in cafés; and the rest, just under half of the total, on entertainment of various kinds, from cinemas and dance halls to magazines and records. Many of these markets had come to depend on teenage spending. Teenagers bought over a third of all bicycles and motorbikes, for example. Their purchases accounted for nearly a third of the markets for cosmetics, film admissions and public entertainments in general. And young people accounted for more than 40 per cent of the markets for records and record players.[137] This was not, then, the same as adult spending: the teenage consumer was different. Teenagers looked for products that were 'highly charged emotionally', that offered something different from what their parents liked, and that carried connotations of excitement and modernity. As Abrams suggested, this partly explained the allure of American products and styles. British manufacturers, he thought, had been slow to adapt to the demands of the new market:

> Post-war British society has little experience in providing for prosperous working-class teenagers; the latter have, therefore, in shaping their consumption standards and habits, depended very heavily on the one industrial society in the world that has such experience, i.e. the United States.[138]

It was, he wrote, '*distinctive teenage spending for distinctive teenage ends in a distinctive teenage world*'.[139]

The teenager was therefore a creation of affluence, and many older people found the image of the teenager as a carefree, profligate big spender to be a shocking rebuke to their own values of thrift and caution. 'Are We Turning Our Children Into Little Americans?' worried *Everybody's Weekly* in 1957.[140] Peter Laurie recorded:

> The *Sunday Graphic* in 1960 found a boy who could hang £127 worth of suits in his parents' back yard to be photographed, another who earned £5 a week and owned: five suits, two pairs of slacks, one pair of jeans, one casual jacket, five white and three coloured shirts, five pairs of shoes, twenty-five ties and an overcoat. A sixteen-year-old typist owned six dresses, seven straight skirts, two pleated ones, one overcoat and a mac, one Italian suit, one pair of boots, one of flat shoes and three of high heels. One eighteen-year-old drove a new car which he had bought for £800; many who earned something under £7 a week had motorbikes at £300. A hire purchase firm said they had 4,000 teenagers on their books and not a single bad debt.[141]

These were, needless to say, exaggerated examples: very few teenagers owned five suits. But for many teenagers, especially if they were in steady work, it was not unusual to spend money every weekend on entertainments and luxuries. 'Every week I'd buy at least two or three singles,' remembered one man from Coventry. 'I had so much money to spend, it's unbelievable looking back. There were so many well-paid jobs for teenagers connected with the car industry. I'd spend ten pounds every weekend on myself, on clothes, on going out, and, most of all, on music.'[142]

Two good examples of teenage affluence were Terry, a lorry driver's son from Acton, and Lesley, a lower-middle-class Neasden girl. Terry was born in 1940, and his recollections cover the late fifties; Lesley was born nine years later, and is remembering the early sixties. Both spent a great deal of time and money on their clothes. Terry explained: 'I paid for all my own clothes from the age of 12. I never wanted to ask my parents for money.' While still a schoolboy, he simultaneously had several paper rounds, worked as a newsboy selling papers outside a tube station, cleaned the workbenches in a nearby factory, and travelled as a baker's delivery van boy at weekends. He earned, he thought, at least 27 shillings a week.[143] Lesley's family, meanwhile, was more prosperous. She was given pocket money, and worked on Saturday's at a local hairdresser's, cleaning and tidying, sweeping the floor and washing the customers' hair: she earned about thirty shillings, plus another pound or so in tips. To Lesley, this was a small fortune. Most of it went on clothes: she had been fascinated by clothes and fashion since she was a small child, and had made her own clothes from the age of thirteen. By her early teens Mod fashion was in full swing, and she recalled that the key thing was to be 'with it', to look exactly the same as the older girls who were seen as trend-setters. One Saturday night, for instance, she noticed that the seventeen- and eighteen-year-old girls were all wearing skirts that came down to their ankles and chiffon 'granny blouses' decorated with cameo brooches. Lesley and her friends promptly decided that they ought to be wearing exactly the same kind of outfits, and so the next week, her pocket money jangling in her purse, she went with her best friend to C&A. They returned with two chiffon blouses, Lesley's in royal blue and her friend's in brown: they did not want to look like identical twins, after all. Even years later, she remembered proudly that although the sleeves and 'Peter Pan' collars were transparent, the rest of the blouse was lined in satin. As for the skirts, they were too expensive, so Lesley and her friend had to make those themselves.[144]

Both Terry and Lesley had enough money to choose their own possessions and entertainments. Terry 'was paying off instalments on more than £100 worth of gear' before he had even left school, including a record player and 'a super bicycle' that had cost him about £28 each. The door-to-door salesman that his family dealt with was, he wrote, 'so impressed with my spending that he let me have my own card, instead of putting my purchases down on the family card!'[145] He left school at fifteen and worked as a messenger boy in a television studio. Within a year he could afford to buy a second-hand motorbike, a BSA 250, and from then on he threw himself into skiffle music.[146] Lesley, on the other hand, was more interested in keeping up with the latest fashions than in simply accumulating material possessions. For her, 'the great thing was to follow the pack', and the culmination of the week's preparations was the ritual of the dance hall on Saturday night.[147]

'The real dynamo behind the teenage revolution', observed Peter Laurie, 'is the anonymous adolescent girl from twelve to sixteen, nameless but irresistible.' Teenage girls not only bought magazines like *Valentine* and *Honey* but also represented the major market for clothes, make-up and records, and it was no accident that most pop stars in the late fifties and early sixties were good-looking young men groomed to appeal to a female teenage audience.[148] Dancing, too, remained an immensely popular entertainment for working-class and lower-middle-class girls, who would spend much of the week 'working out what we'd wear at the dance hall'.[149] The public display of dancing was especially important to many teenage girls: it was their big opportunity to show off their latest fashionable clothes, and their only chance to take the sexual initiative with boys. One Lancashire girl, for example, received ten shillings a week in pocket money, all of which went on a pair of new stockings, a ticket to the Wigan Embassy Ball-room or the Bolton Palais, a drink of lemonade, and the bus fare home.[150]

Although Lesley was more affluent than many girls of her age, her tastes were not so different, and the Saturday night trip to the dance hall was the climax of her week. Her routine, she later recalled, was always the same. First, she would settle down in front of the television just after five o'clock to watch *Doctor Who*; then she would head upstairs for a bath, before dressing and carefully applying her make-up; and then she would go out. Her first trip to the dance hall always stuck in her mind. With two friends, Jennifer Read and Ellen Chard, she had planned an expedition to the Kingsbury Ritz, the other side of Wembley from her suburban home. She could even remember what she had worn that evening: a grey pinstripe pinafore dress which reached down to the middle of her calf at a time when most skirts tended to stop just short of the knee. For make-up she had bought white lipstick from Woolworth's and had applied a heavy layer of mascara around her eyes. Her friends, meanwhile, were similarly attired and made up: the point was to look the same. However, when the three Neasden girls arrived at the dance hall, they were too excited and frightened to go in. Lesley remembered being particularly intimidated by the sight of 'grown-ups' loitering outside and the spectacle of girls cheerfully chatting to boys leaning on their scooters. Giggling nervously, she and her friends retreated towards the station, and only after they had calmed their nerves by applying yet another layer of mascara did they summon up the courage to return.[151] In fact, dance halls were nothing new; the mothers and even grandmothers of the teenagers of the fifties and sixties had often patronised them before the war. For all Lesley's interest in the latest fashions, her pleasures were in fact little different from those of older generations: her own parents had met while dancing at the Cricklewood Palais.[152]

The individual cases of Terry and Lesley illustrate a general rule that teenage girls were more interested in fashion than were boys, and much more interested in dancing. The second notable difference concerns the issue of pocket money. Lesley's father was a skilled carpenter who could afford to give his daughter several shillings a week. Terry's father, however, was a lorry driver who could afford no such luxury; his son later wrote that money 'didn't exactly flow round our household'.[153] This minor economic disparity points to wider variations of class and economic opportunity which meant that teenagers never formed a united, homogeneous group. During the fifties and especially the sixties, a great deal of misleading tosh was written about the supposed classlessness of youth. The *Daily Mail*, for example, claimed that the 'new after dark citizens of Soho' were 'typists, nurses, factory workers' as well as 'students, dreamers, bank clerks'.[154] Colin MacInnes, whose novels tried to capture the spirit of London youth culture at the turn of the decade, was another to emphasise the classlessness of young people. In *Absolute Beginners*, the smug teenage narrator has an argument with his elder half-brother and dismisses any talk of class loyalty:

> 'You poor old prehistoric monster,' I exclaimed. 'I do *not* reject the working-classes, and I do *not* belong to the upper-classes, for one and the same reason, namely, that neither of them interest me in the slightest, never have done, never will do. Do try to understand that, clobbo! I'm just not interested in the whole class crap that seems to needle you and all the tax-payers – needle you all, whichever side of the tracks you live on, or suppose you do.'
>
>   He glared at me. I could see that, if once he believed that what I said I really meant, and thousands of the kiddos did the same as well, the bottom would fall out of his horrid little world.
>
>   'You're dissolute!' he suddenly cried out. 'Immoral! That's what I say you teenagers all are!'[155]

It was easy for the middle-aged, well-born MacInnes to dismiss the importance of class. But the fact remains that class was still a significant force in teenagers' lives as well as a source of division between them. The market-research pioneer Mark Abrams noted that working-class girls spent much less money than their middle-class counterparts; on the other hand, working-class boys, who were likely to have left school and started work, spent more than middle-class boys, many of whom remained in school and then went on to university.[156] The teenage boy, defined by his economic habits, was a working-class or lower-middle-class phenomenon. He left school at fifteen, earned his living in an often tedious, ill-paid job, and until getting married spent his money on relatively cheap commodities like records and radios, precisely the kind of products that would appeal to young men who were not especially wealthy and never expected to be. Those boys still studying, whether at private or grammar schools, were likely to listen to different kinds of music (jazz, classical or folk) rather than the rock and roll beloved of working-class youth. They were less likely to go to dance halls, and more likely to go to art cinemas. They were more likely to go abroad on holiday than to Blackpool. Although they liked clothes and fashions, music and entertainment, they liked different kinds; they were likely to end up in very different jobs, paid at very different levels, and to lead very different lives. There was no such thing as the classless teenager.[157]

Since teenage culture was working-class rather than classless, its most visible manifestations, from dance halls and jukeboxes to motorbikes and pop singers, were associated with young working-class men. This no doubt explains why teenage culture and the issue of 'youth' in general became identified in the 1950s with social deviance, violence and delinquency. But was this any great novelty? As early as October 1949 the *Daily Mail* had been running letters attacking modern teenage delinquents: as one disgruntled reader put it:

> Teenagers are pampered with high wages, first-class working conditions and excellent facilities in education. Their outlook is centred in trashy books and films. The boys are hoodlums in embryo, defiant and uncouth, while the girls are brazen and unrefined. A rigorous period of military training might make men and women of them, if they had the courage to face it.[158]

In fact the history of teenage misbehaviour went back much further than the 1940s. The very term 'hooligan' was first used in 1898 after drunken working-class boys ran amok in London over the August holiday; as an Irish term, it implicitly identified such behaviour as un-English.[159] Late Victorian writers associated hooliganism with the period of life between leaving school and reaching formal maturity at twenty-one: it was seen as a product of the noxious, corrupting world of the city, in contrast to the healthy simplicity of the countryside.[160] And the concept of delinquent youth also owed something to the simple fact that young people do tend to be more energetic, irreverent and sexually precocious than their elders expect. It has always been common for the middle-aged to forget how they themselves behaved when young, and to imagine that standards have irretrievably fallen since those happy days.[161]

Even before the consumer boom of the mid-1950s, young men and rising crime had become closely linked in the public imagination. Almost as soon as the war had ended in 1945, attention had switched to the enemies at home: spivs, burglars and juvenile delinquents. Rising crime figures, no doubt largely explained by the transition from the common determination of wartime to the cheerless hardships of peace, seemed to suggest that Britain had won the war overseas only to face a major crime wave at home. There were more than twice as many recorded crimes against the person in 1951 as there had been in 1938, and three times as many rapes. During the hard years of austerity the stories circulated of a butcher who slept in his shop with a loaded revolver for two weeks to protect his Christmas turkeys, or a small boy who sneered at his arresters: 'You can't touch me, mate. I'm under eight.'[162]

The real 'folk devils' of the fifties, however, were the Teddy Boys. In his novel *Hurry On Down* (1953), John Wain describes a group of young men:

> Knots of youths were standing about, on the steps, inside the vestibule, on the pavement outside. Most of them wore blue or brown suits and shoes with pointed toes; but here and there was one with a loud tweed jacket and flannels, with broader shoes sometimes in suede. The ones in blue or brown suits had their hair swept into shiny quiffs, stiff with grease, above the forehead; the others had theirs brushed smoothly back, with no parting, or cut off entirely except for a thin covering of scrub, some three-eighths of an inch long . . . Those who had violent-coloured shirts on, to make them look like their own conception of Americans, stood with their jackets unbuttoned and hanging a long way open. There were no corresponding knots of girls.[163]

This was an early and reasonably reliable description of the Teddy Boy style: extravagant sideburns and long, greased hair, swept up in a quiff; colourful shirts and suits worn with bootlace ties; tapered drainpipe trousers and bright socks; brothel-creeper shoes or smart pointed black boots.[164] It had originated among wealthy, upper-class young men in the late forties, 'slightly narrowed trousers, a velvet collar here, a brocade waistcoat there': reminiscent of Edwardian style, it was a brief, low-key male equivalent of the flamboyant New Look fashion that had enraptured young women of means after 1947.[165] Within a year or two it had seeped across the Thames and been taken up by gangs of young men in working-class South London: from that point onwards, the wealthier 'Edwardians' abandoned the look and it became, in the words of the *Daily Sketch*, 'the uniform of the dance hall creepers'.[166]

By early 1954, the phrase 'Teddy Boy' had been coined to describe the working-class Edwardians, and the uniform had spread from London to the provinces.[167] It was expensive: the suits themselves cost about £20, and given the cost of the various accessories, from the thick crêpe brothel creepers to the enormous quantities of grease required to discipline his hair, a Teddy Boy might spend the best part of £100 on his outfit.[168] This was, in the context of the times, a shocking amount of money for a working-class youth to spend on clothes. 'I am consumed with curiosity to know where the Teddy Boys find the money to indulge their rather nostalgic taste for Edwardian dress,' wrote an indignant Lady Child of Chobham Park House, Surrey, to the *Express* in 1954. 'Do their parents produce the not-insignificant sum or has the Welfare State taken on yet another lighthearted commitment?'[169] Even more shocking was the association of the Teddy Boys with violence. They became notorious after a young man called Michael Davies was convicted of a brutal murder on Clapham Common in 1953: the press noted that 'he took great pains to look like a dandy' and spent all his money on '"gay dog" clothes'.[170]

From this point onwards, it was common to identify Teddy Boys as vicious young toughs armed with flick-knives, the very stereotype of the juvenile delinquent.[171] In April 1954, for instance, two gangs clad in 'Edwardian dandy suits with velveteen collars and drainpipe trousers' fought on the platform of St Mary Cray station in Kent after a night at the dance hall.[172] A young man from sedate Tunbridge Wells later remembered: 'Nine times out of ten the trouble started over a girl. You'd get two gangs of Teds at a dance and somebody would fancy somebody else's girlfriend. I always went tooled up. I'd have a bicycle chain and fish hooks behind my lapels so that if someone grabbed hold of me they'd get stuck and I could just bang them.'[173] Not surprisingly, many people were appalled by the phenomenon. One boy from Darlington recalled that he had to buy his Teddy Boy equipment in bits and pieces and hide it around the house: if his parents had discovered it, he would have been thrown out.[174] A writer billed as a 'family doctor' explained to the readers of the *Evening News* that the delinquents were literally diseased: they were 'all of unsound mind in the sense that they are all suffering from a form of psychosis. Apart from the birch or the rope, depending on the gravity of their crimes, what they need is rehabilitation in a psychopathic institution'. They were forced into crime, he thought, because of their simple 'desire to do evil': not only were they afflicted by 'a degree of paranoia, with an inferiority complex, they are also *inferior* specimens apart from their disease'.[175]

'In terms of English teenagers,' wrote Nik Cohn in 1971, 'Teddy Boys were the start of everything.'[176] Jonathon Green agrees: 'the Teddy Boys must be credited with starting . . . "the whole teenager epic"'.[177] It was the Teddy Boys, they argue, who were responsible for the equation of teenagers with violence, and the Teddy Boys who pioneered the display of 'exhibitionist plumage' by working-class youngsters to identify themselves as a distinct group.[178] Perhaps. But were the Teddy Boys really without antecedents? They certainly had contemporaries: the *Halbstarken* in West Germany, the *Skinnuttar* in Sweden, the *Blousons Noirs* in France, and even the *Stilyagi* in the Soviet Union.[179] In many ways they were simply successors to the aggressive young men of the thirties and forties, the 'razor boys', 'cosh boys', 'wide boys' and spivs of London and other big cities.[180] As the example of the late Victorian hooligans suggests, the sight of working-class youths drinking and fighting in public was nothing new. Even their appearance was no great innovation. Young people in provincial towns had been dressing themselves in extravagant uniforms for decades. In the late nineteenth century, observers commented on the phenomenon of 'scuttlers' in Northern slum towns, 'a minor menace' that resulted in pitched street battles between rival gangs of youths. The scuttler wore 'the union shirt, bell-bottomed trousers, the heavy leather belt, pricked out in fancy designs with a large steel buckle and thick, iron-shod clogs. His girl friend commonly wore clogs and shawl and a skirt with vertical stripes.'[181] In his history of hooliganism, Geoffrey Pearson notes the 'striking continuities' across the centuries: 'the same rituals of territorial dominance, trials of strength, gang fights, mockery against elders and authorities, and antagonism towards "outsiders" as typical focuses for youthful energy and aggressive mischief'.[182] Razor boys, hooligans, scuttlers: all these groups were not so unlike the Teddy Boys of the early fifties, and not so very different from the gangs of subsequent decades either.

The Teddy Boys themselves, meanwhile, were a relatively short-lived phenomenon. By 1955 many young people were inhibited from dressing in Edwardian finery because of the public outcry; at the same time, others, especially in London and southern England, were turning to new fashions, above all the smart, chic 'Italian' look that was the precursor of the Mod style of the mid-sixties. Second-hand Teddy Boy suits were said to be on sale at an open market in Hertfordshire, rejected by the new trend-setters of the mid-fifties.[183] Some writers have identified Teddy Boys with rock and roll music: Green calls it 'their favourite music' and declares that 'the way in which a musical style could set one aside from the acceptable mainstream was established by these neophyte teens'.[184] But this is not really true. By the time rock and roll really became popular with young people, in late 1956 and 1957, the Teddy Boy style was already falling from grace. The Teddy Boys were a phenomenon of the very early fifties, the years of austerity, rather than the affluence of the Macmillan era. When Elvis Presley's first number one 'All Shook Up' reached the top of the British charts in July 1957, the Teddy Boys' moment had already passed.[185]

The gradual disappearance of the Teddy Boys in the late 1950s did not mean the end of the panic about teenage delinquency. Statistics for juvenile crime were rising steadily. Between 1955 and 1961, the number of boys between fourteen and seventeen convicted of serious offences more than doubled, with a similar increase among young men from seventeen to twenty-one.[186] Teenage convictions overall doubled between 1955 and 1959.[187] This did not actually mean that there was a vast number of delinquent teenagers: in 1958, for example, only twenty-one teenagers in every thousand were in trouble with the police, and there were only two juvenile convictions a day in London.[188] All the same, the post-war period was one of consistently rising crime. In 1955 just under six thousand violent crimes were committed in Britain; in 1960 there were almost twelve thousand; and in 1970 there were twenty-one thousand.[189] Improvements in statistics, and perhaps an increased awareness of and sensitivity to crime, cannot explain away these figures. Indeed, exactly why crime, especially juvenile crime, increased so quickly is difficult to explain. Perhaps the Second World War had contributed to family instability; perhaps the hostility of the authorities to young people provoked a violent reaction; perhaps the temptations of affluence were too much for young men in ill-paid, hopeless jobs; perhaps, as Marwick says, civic loyalty and respect for rules had never been as high as people liked to believe.[190]

What is certain is that the juvenile delinquent became a metaphor for the supposed collapse of standards throughout society as a whole, and people became extremely sensitive to teenage high jinks and misbehaviour. The occasional disturbances at cinemas during presentations of *Rock Around the Clock*, for example, were described as 'scenes of depravity' and 'a relaxing of all self-control'.[191] At the Elephant and Castle, one of the first centres of Teddy Boy activity, two thousand youths were reported to have brawled on the streets like some uncontrollable barbarian horde. In fact what happened was that some cups and saucers were thrown and two policemen injured, and the result was nine arrests and a few £1 fines.[192] It was widely imagined that teenagers carried flick-knives, which they might produce at any moment to maim some innocent passer-by. If they did carry them, it was only to use on one another. But the flick-knife was a symbol of the depravity of British youth in the affluent society, and was given extra credence by the involvement of young white working-class men in the Notting Hill race riots of August 1958.[193] 'Years ago, not so many years ago, it used to be thought un-English and despicable for a man to produce a knife during a fight,' commented the *Daily Mirror*. 'Now, alas, it seems that the production of a knife is thought by young men to be merely an earnest of manhood.'[194] In the spring of the following year the *Mirror* launched a campaign to educate parents about the dangers of 'the flick knife craze', encouraging them to persuade their teenage children to surrender their weapons. 'Ban This Thing,' read one headline: 'Week after week in this country people are being threatened and wounded and – sometimes – killed.' No parent could afford to be complacent: 'Are you sure your SON hasn't got a knife?'[195]

This atmosphere of moralistic panic was reflected in some of the minor British films of the era, especially the cheap 'social problem' films addressing contemporary public concerns. In the late fifties British audiences were treated to a considerable number of films about teenage delinquency, from *No Trees in the Street* and *Violent Playground* (both 1958) to *And Women Shall Weep* (1960) and *Some People* (1962). Many, in keeping with the general suspicion of affluence and consumerism among artists and writers, linked the disaffected violence of the young to the degenerate, lazy prosperity of the age. In *No Trees in the Street*, written by the playwright Ted Willis, a benign, Labour-supporting policeman wrests a flick-knife from a cowardly teenage delinquent and lectures him about the hard days of the thirties when there were 'no trees in the street', the implication being that few teenagers realise how lucky they are.[196] In *Some People*, meanwhile, a church choirmaster (Kenneth More) tries to rehabilitate three rebellious bikers by allowing them to practise music in the church hall and encouraging them to enlist in the Duke of Edinburgh Award Scheme. The film begins with a montage of images of affluence: records, televisions, washing machines, jewellery, advertisements reading 'Enjoy immediate delivery' and 'Credit with dignity'. The three youths have bought their motorbikes on hire-purchase: they are not poor, deprived or unemployed, but merely aimless, dulled by commercialism and mass entertainment. They are not inherently evil: modern society is at fault.[197] And in *Violent Playground*, too, the violent young Johnny, played by David McCallum, is not so much underprivileged as frustrated and directionless. He is introduced to us in full Teddy Boy regalia, throwing stones to the sound of a pop soundtrack. Pop music is used throughout as the accompaniment to violence: later in the film, Johnny abandons his good intentions to reform by throwing off his jacket, turning up his radio and dancing feverishly with his friends. Listening to pop music does not necessarily equate to violence, but it forms part of the same corrupt, commercialised modern world.[198]

At the end of *Violent Playground*, after Johnny has finally been imprisoned, the chief inspector muses:

> Haven't we had enough of these crazy, mixed-up kids who go around bullying and ganging up on people, beating up old ladies? . . . I'm a policeman. I've got respect for the law. I know it isn't fashionable. But let's spare a thought for the old lady. Not just for the old lady but you and yours. I'm tired of tough-guy fever . . . sick and tired of it.[199]

Outrage at the misdemeanours of the young was concentrated particularly in the more conservative parts of society, and above all in the Conservative Party itself. As Home Secretary, Rab Butler already had personal experience of youthful misbehaviour: in February 1958, while delivering the Rectorial Address to the students of Glasgow University, he had been bombarded with flour and tomatoes in an extremely humiliating scene. Butler himself remained on the platform, calm as ever, covered in flour and sodden with fire extinguisher foam. But he disappointed party members by the nonchalance of his reaction. 'I understand youth. I have children of my own and I like to feel I haven't lost touch,' was not quite the fiery condemnation that the Conservative faithful was expecting.[200]

At their party conference later that year, Tory activists submitted twenty-eight separate resolutions relating to crime and punishment. Butler wryly remarked that they were pretty 'bloodthirsty', and struggled to find 'one out of the 28 which is at least moderate'.[201] He managed temporarily to appease the fury, and then the following spring published a White Paper, *Penal Practice in a Changing Society*. Young offenders would, he promised, receive a 'short, sharp shock' in new, purpose-built detention centres, while more serious delinquents would be sentenced to a period of up to three years in a borstal.[202] This was another disappointment, though, for party

activists who thought that juvenile offenders deserved more physical retri-
bution. A Home Office conference on delinquency in 1959 was dominated by
voices complaining that young people were too sexually adventurous and
needed a dose of corporal punishment to keep them in order.[203] But judi-
cial flogging and birching had been abolished in 1948, and Butler, a decent
and civilised man, had little inclination to restore it. The newspapers were
predictably furious: a cartoon in the *Express* in November 1960 showed three
youths with Italian haircuts and winkle-picker shoes, carrying a cosh, a
chain and a razor, making good their escape after assaulting a middle-aged
man. Butler, in the form of a policeman carrying a report entitled 'No More
Birching', is consoling the victim: 'Bad luck, Sir! Never mind – if I catch the
scoundrels, I'll give them a tap on the head with this report!'[204] Perhaps he
preferred the strategy adopted by the decent, working-class mother in the
film *And Women Shall Weep*, released the same year. Realising her teenage son
is a vicious, cowardly murderer, she hurls a cup of tea in his face to disarm
him, and gallantly hands him over to the police for punishment.[205]

Butler's relatively unruffled approach to the problem of delinquency
was echoed in February 1960 by the findings of a Ministry of Education
report on the English and Welsh youth service, generally known as the
Albemarle Report. The government had appointed a committee in
November 1958, chaired by the philanthropist Diana, Countess of
Albemarle, to look into the problems of young people and state provision
for them; it was no coincidence that this came at the peak of the controversy over flick-knives and teenage violence, and barely three months after
the Notting Hill race riots.[206] One problem, the report conceded, was that
of the 'bulge' of children born in the immediate aftermath of the war,
which meant that in 1964 there would be one million more teenagers over
fifteen than in 1958.[207] The committee also accepted that young people
posed a bigger social problem than ever before, talking of 'a new climate of
crime and delinquency' and of crime as being 'very much a youth problem'. Teenagers, the report argued, were reacting to the rapid changes in
the post-war world 'in ways which adults find puzzling and shocking'.
Delinquency was not merely the product of individual wickedness: 'the
"problems of youth"', the committee explained, 'are deeply rooted in the
soil of a disturbed modern world'.[208]

Group and club activities were, as we have seen, extremely popular in the
post-war period, and the report suggested that group activities would give
'opportunities for challenges of all sorts to the young'. These challenges

would 'satisfy the sense of achievement for which all hunger and which so many have failed to find in school or at work'. The upshot of all this, in short, was the need to expand the youth service for the modern world, pouring money into new facilities and training new staff, and developing new, modern techniques of dealing with teenagers' problems. Young people needed to be 'trained' in how to be good citizens; they needed to be given concrete aims and challenges; and they needed to be encouraged to work in co-operative association with other members of society.[209]

These conclusions met a relatively enthusiastic reception: the *Mirror*, for example, greeted the report with the headline 'Scandal of Our Youth Service', and praised its call for action.[210] Spending on the youth service did indeed increase in the following decade: the number of full-time youth workers doubled, and the government spent some £28 million on three thousand building projects.[211] Despite all these well-intentioned efforts, however, many of the activities put on to divert the young seemed bizarre to say the least. In 1962 the London Union of Youth Clubs, 'seeking to mould the citizens of tomorrow', sent a hundred teenage girls on an 'initiative test' to spend the night at sea on a ship full of sailors. The point of this exercise was never entirely clear, but it takes little imagination to speculate that that the evening did not unfold quite as the youth service would have wished. A year later, the National Guild of Teenagers prohibited its members from playing bingo, attending late-night jazz clubs, reading *Lady Chatterley's Lover*, seeing *Saturday Night and Sunday Morning* or *Room at the Top*, and even from visiting Brighton. According to Peter Laurie, the Guild also frowned upon 'walks in parks, fields or woods' as well as 'visits to roller skating rinks, brothels or air raid shelters', an incongruous collection of potential destinations. As he aptly concluded, 'the lunatic fringe of the establishment was still at work'.[212]

Although it addressed the problems of crime and delinquency, the Albemarle Committee did not regard young people as a mob of violent, disaffected rebels, but praised their 'good sense, goodwill, vitality and resilience'.[213] In 1967 this verdict was echoed by the Latey Report, which found young people to be literate, well educated and independent, and recommended lowering the voting age to eighteen.[214] The fact is that the vast majority of teenagers were nowhere near as unconventional, as rebellious or as colourful as some historians suggest. Until the mid-sixties British teenagers were actually regarded as rather stolid and unexciting compared with their American or European counterparts.[215] 'The Young of the 1950s', wrote one twenty-three-year-old woman in 1954, 'are no longer young: they are pre-maturely middle-aged.' They were no longer 'Bright Young Things', but 'responsible, sober citizens'.[216] Commenting on the furore over the play *Look Back in Anger* in 1956, *The Times* remarked that young people 'sometimes put on almost too serious a face. There is about the young man a suspicion of a whisker.'[217] Four years later, Mark Abrams concluded that young people between eighteen and twenty-four were 'more likely to be Conservative than Labour'.[218] As for the Albemarle Report, it listed all the usual clichés about young people, that they were 'a generation of teenage delinquents', had 'rejected family life', were 'featherbedded by the Welfare State', had 'no moral values' and so on, but found them to be entirely erroneous. There was in young people a streak of 'potential idealism', but their abiding characteristic was a 'healthy scepticism'.[219] Throughout the post-war period, in fact, British teenagers showed a marked reluctance to become involved in politics of any kind, and a withering disdain for radical idealism. 'It's all a big skive, in't it?' remarked one fifteen-year-old from Huddersfield. 'All those takeover bids and that, all this yammer about old age pensioners and the bomb. Nobody really cares, do they? I mean, if they did, they'd do something about it.'[220]

University students, meanwhile, were both disproportionately middle-class and exceedingly conservative. They were, wrote the sociologist Michael Young in 1963, 'in danger of becoming cautious adults at twenty'.[221] There was so little discontent on British campuses that one observer concluded in 1964 that students were 'a negligible political force' best characterised by the word 'servility'; there was 'no prospect' of students leading a rebellion against the conventions of the day.[222] Far from being ardent admirers of American society and culture, many students shared the anti-American suspicions of their elders. According to the 1962 survey quoted earlier:

> [Among students] the image of the USA is not very favourable. It is the image of a basically adolescent, materialistic, slightly hysterical society, run primarily by Big Brother, a society exerting great pressure for con-formity with little real freedom of thought, a society which can easily run amok or behave in an unpredictable way. Its excessive influence on Britain is rather resented and many are afraid that what America is today Britain may become tomorrow.[223]

Young people were, in short, never much of a threat to the conventions of British life. They were neither as radical nor as violent as many observers feared: the great majority, like the examples of Terry Nelhams and Lesley Hornby given above, were more interested in pottering about making a little extra money for entertainments and clothes than they were in knifing their neighbours or saving the world. When Brian Jackson went to hear a brass band rehearse in Huddersfield in the early sixties, he observed that two cornet players were under twenty-five and wore fashionable 'pop clothes' and sleek Mod haircuts; both, however, seemed perfectly happy to spend their Sundays playing alongside their elders. Most of the Huddersfield bands recruited new members through family connections; there was little evidence, therefore, of any generation gap.[224] Even during one of the most frenzied bouts of moral panic about teenagers' behaviour, during the rock and roll disturbances of September 1956, *The Times* noted that most young people were much more conservative than the stereotype suggested, and gave the unexpected example of bird-watching. It reflected well on the people of Great Britain that 'so many young men and boys – and girls too – should be content to spend almost the whole of their leisure time in such worthwhile occupations as bird-watching'. Indeed, the article explained, in field clubs across the nation the 'best work in this respect is done by young people'.[225]

At one level, the moral panic of the late fifties reflected a genuine concern about rising crime and the increasing visibility and self-confidence of working-class teenagers. Since health care was better after the war than before it, young people were certainly bigger and more mature than ever before, and this inevitably meant that they became sexually active earlier. In September 1958 the *Mirror* ran a series entitled 'The Beanstalk Generation', discussing how children were growing up faster than ever, both physically and emotionally. The first article, by the New Wave writer Keith Waterhouse, was called 'Our Children Are Changing' and described a teenage girl who had clearly 'matured early': although only thirteen, she had worn a bra for a year and tights for two years; she curled her hair, wore lipstick and high heels, and went out on dates.[226] The Albemarle Report, too, commented:

> today's adolescents are taller and heavier than those of previous generations, and they mature earlier . . . it appears certain that puberty is occurring earlier, and that the large majority of young people now reach adolescence, as determined by physical changes, before the age of 15.

This obviously had implications for sexual behaviour: several observers told the committee that young people now had 'considerable surplus energy which their work, and most of the more easily available facilities for leisure, do not always satisfy'.[227]

Thanks to the rising crime statistics and the faster physical development of modern teenagers, the moral panic did have a genuine factual basis. Teenage crime *was* increasing, and teenagers *were* more sexually mature than before. However, all the scholarly surveys of the era agreed that teenage sexual behaviour was surprisingly chaste.[228] 'All in all,' wrote Peter Laurie in 1965, 'it is astonishing how few teenagers are sexually experienced.'[229] Indeed, it is unlikely that statistical increases in teenage crime and sexual maturity entirely explain the heated controversies of the late fifties. A more intriguing possibility is that rebellious teenagers were turned into 'folk devils' by the media and the police. According to the sociologist Stanley Cohen, teenagers formed 'subcultures' like the Teddy Boys or the Mods, groups which were united by their particular fashions or musical tastes and which rejected the values of mainstream society. The creation of moral panics, according to this argument, was society's way of disciplining these groups and enforcing conformity.[230] This explanation captures the extent to which the media exaggerated the misbehaviour of groups like the Teddy Boys, but it is also too schematic, too implacably rooted in its dualistic view of a monolithic mainstream culture ruthlessly repressing the joyous subcultures of youth. As Andrew Blake points out, most teenagers did not reject the values of social conformity.[231] Lesley Hornby and her friends at the Kingsbury Ritz, for example, certainly formed a subculture of a kind, but it was one that accepted the norms and conventions of adult society.

Perhaps a better explanation of the panics of the fifties lies in what youth came to represent. The sociologist Bryan Wilson wrote in 1959 that the affluent young were 'without background, education and information necessary to the cultivation of stable tastes . . . They are exposed in innumerable ways to commercial exploitation, and induced to pay high prices for the merely novel and ephemeral.' So, he argued, people had become 'confused about their norms, values, tastes and standards'.[232] Behind the problems of young people, therefore, lay the real problem: the affluent society. Indeed, in 1958 one Halifax church newsletter explicitly drew the link between teenage wrongdoing and the changing values of the adult world:

If young people tend to be dishonest it is because many of them have had a rotten example from their parents.

If they are lazy, it is because older people have taught them the art of doing five hours' work for eight hours' pay.

If they grow up with an irreverence for sex it is because they have heard sex dirtied and degraded by the conversation of their elders.[233]

A Home Office report on teenage behaviour published in October 1960 agreed. Delinquency was simply the consequence of social and economic change. There had been 'a material, social and moral revolution' since the beginning of the century and although life was now easier and more secure than ever, 'the future of mankind may seem frighteningly uncertain'. It was this 'fundamental insecurity', the report concluded, which lay behind teenage crime.[234]

The 'problem' of youth, in other words, was not self-contained, but instead became a symbol of the wider problems of British society in a period of economic and social transition. As one critic puts it: 'Youth was . . . a powerful but concealed *metaphor* for social change: the compressed image of a society which had crucially changed in terms of life-style and values.'[235] In the social problem films of the period, the issue of juvenile deviance represents wider anxieties: the decline of traditional authority, the instability of the family, the break-up of settled communities, the uneasiness of class identities; in other words, the impact of affluence, education and mobility on the settled conventions of life. We have already seen that many people in the fifties were suspicious of American cultural imports, of mass entertainment and popular culture, of the effects of prosperity and mobility on traditional customs and communities. For many people, the teenager was simply the personification of all these concerns: a figure who represented modernity, energy, sexuality and ambition. Rather than teenage subcultures representing a genuine attempt to challenge the values of mainstream culture, what had happened was that people had projected on to the teenager their own fears about the modern world. For the fact was that teenagers were not really a threat at all: like Terry and Lesley, the majority were instead ambitious, fashionable and cheerfully conservative.

13

ROCK AND ROLL BABIES

More than a Furlong to the West, my Ear was beguiled in so tempting a Fashion by the mellifluous Sounds proceeding from a basement Saloon situate at No. 100 that I could not forbear to allow my Feet to carry me Thither. O Happy pedal Error! . . . there I descried the noble Countenance and dignified Mien of that Pillar of metropolitan diurnal Entertainment, Mr Acker Bilk, bending to his artistic Will the Intricacies of his Clarionet.

Publicity leaflet for Acker Bilk, 1958

Groups are out; four-piece groups with guitars particularly are finished.

Dick Rowe, 1962

One evening, towards the end of the 1960s, the *New Statesman* columnist Alan Watkins was invited to appear on a television chat show. Afterwards, in the studio's hospitality area, Watkins was chatting to the American bandleader Bill Haley when another of their fellow guests 'loped purposefully across the room' towards them.

'Mr Haley,' he said, 'may I shake you by the hand? Powell is the name, Enoch Powell.'

'Why sure, go ahead,' Haley said.

This action having been performed to mutual satisfaction, they talked with equal affability for a few minutes. Later I asked Powell:

'Why did you want to shake Bill Haley's hand, Enoch?'

'Why did I want to shake Bill Haley's hand?' Powell replied, for one of his conversational tricks was to repeat the question before answering it, if indeed he ever came round to doing so. 'Surely the answer must be obvious. He is the most influential character of our age.'[1]

American entertainers wielded tremendous influence over British popular culture in the 1950s and 1960s. But this was not necessarily any great novelty. In the late Victorian era, British popular songs and dances, plays and music halls had eagerly borrowed from their American equivalents, just as the Americans had from them.[2] In the twenties and thirties Noël Coward and Ivor Novello drew on Broadway innovations in their plays and songs, and transplanted Broadway musicals by the likes of Cole Porter, Irving Berlin and George Gershwin proved popular additions to the West End stage.[3] Indeed, British audiences generally gave a keen welcome to transatlantic innovations, from the ballads and nonsense songs of the Edwardian era to the ragtime and jazz of the inter-war years.[4] Benny Goodman's appearance in London in 1949 had provoked a burst of enthusiasm for swing, and jazz music was also becoming increasingly popular, boosted during the war by the broadcasts of the American Forces Network.[5]

At the same time, many British musicians and critics regarded American dancing styles as immoral and swing or jazz music as dangerously redolent of blacks and New York intellectuals. The guardians of ballroom dancing, for example, developed during the inter-war years a 'Modern English Style' to resist American innovations, while the Musicians' Union established a dance-band section in 1930 to exclude American performers from British bands, and struck a 'needletime' agreement with the BBC to restrict the amount of American material that would be played on the wireless.[6] Unfortunately the enthusiasm of British audiences for new American styles could not successfully be contained, as was evident in the dance halls of the late forties and early fifties. British musical culture was not merely a pale shadow of an American model; moments when the crowd would break, cheering and clapping, into classics like 'Oh, the Hokey Cokey' reaffirmed the lasting affection for native British songs. But it was true that most dance bands were modelled on the Glenn Miller or Tommy Dorsey bands, and most singers copied Frank Sinatra rather than, say, George Formby. Frequent battles over jitterbugging and jiving, dances imported from the United States during the post-war years, reflected the combination of suspicion and excitement with which American innovations were regarded.[7] A few years later, similar struggles were being waged over the routines that accompanied rock and roll. One Staffordshire man would head to his local village hall every Saturday night, despite the weekly arguments over proper dance routines:

There were notices everywhere saying 'No Jiving or Bopping' and they even employed a local heavy called Rubber Belly to keep order. Well, me and my girlfriend, we were amongst those who loved doing all the new rock 'n' roll routines, but there were lots of others who just wanted to do the quickstep. We weren't going to stop, so when the music started half the floor are doing the quickstep and the other half are jiving. People were getting clouted round the ears with the flailing arms of the rock 'n' rollers. And if old Rubber Belly caught you he'd catch you by the scruff of the neck and march you out of the hall. 'No jiving or bopping,' he'd say. You wouldn't be let back in and sometimes you couldn't go in next week either.[8]

Yet popular music in the immediate post-war years was marked more by conservatism than by innovation. It was only one element in a wider national repertoire, and just like any other cultural product it reflected differences of age, class and region. Different British audiences enjoyed colliery brass bands, church choirs, Gilbert and Sullivan recitals, light classical orchestras, nonsense and novelty songs, folk ballads, American swing and jazz music, romantic crooners, and so on.[9] The fact that most of these musical forms dated from before the war, and in many cases from the nineteenth century, suggested not only that British audiences were resistant to change but also that this was still a market for adults rather than teenagers. In terms of sales, meanwhile, the dominant trends favoured swing, big-band music, American or pseudo-American crooners, and romantic ballads, bought by affluent consumers on 78rpm gramophone records.[10]

Increasing record sales were based not merely on consumer affluence but also on technological innovation. In 1948, Columbia had introduced the long-playing twelve-inch 33rpm disc, or LP, and in the same year RCA Victor developed the seven-inch 45rpm single. These new vinyl records required new equipment, but were smaller and offered superior sound quality. By 1955, British consumers were buying over four million 45rpm singles a year; by 1960, they were buying fifty-two million; and by 1963, sixty-one million.[11] These sales figures also reflected the increasing importance of the song in its own right, rather than as an accompaniment to dancing, so that the domestic and individual pleasure of listening to songs on a gramophone was gaining at the expense of the public and communal pleasure of the dance. Dance bands were badly hit by the arrival of the jukebox in British coffee bars and clubs in the early fifties, which provided contemporary music more cheaply than a band of musicians and also drew attention to the individual merit of the song itself.[12] Band musicians were not alone in being affronted by the new technological competitor, and many observers saw the jukebox as a symbol of crass American commercialism. The working-class *Daily Mirror*, for example, captured the blend of insecurity and patriotism with which many people greeted American innovations when in 1954 it printed a photograph of a demure couple enjoying a cup of tea. The caption read: 'What the British Think of the Yanks: We dislike the fun you make about our domestic habits, the way you despise us for being dull. A cup of tea is more enjoyable to us than the garish delights of the juke box.'[13]

Until 1952 the popularity of a record was determined by sales of its sheet music, reflecting the importance of public performance rather than private entertainment. On 14 November 1952, however, the *New Musical Express*, which had recently been relaunched for a teenage market, printed its first Top Twelve chart. The Top Twelve was modelled on the American *Billboard* charts but was idiosyncratically determined by the magazine's publisher Percy Dickins and his staff telephoning fifty-three record shops in the major cities and asking for their most popular singles.[14] It was only the most successful of several competing charts; although not entirely accurate, it nevertheless gave a reasonably reliable impression of the conservatism of British musical tastes in the mid-fifties. The first number one was 'Here in my Heart', a romantic number by the Italian-American crooner Al Martino; the chart had come too late for Vera Lynn, whose 'Auf Wiedersehen Sweetheart' had been a monumental success on both sides of the Atlantic for much of the year. The next few weeks reflected the hold of transatlantic ballads on the British market, with strong showings by Bing Crosby, Rosemary Clooney and Nat 'King' Cole; their only challengers were orchestral pieces like Mantovani's version of 'White Christmas', a December number one.

For the next four years or so the charts reflected a balance between American crooners, orchestral pieces and British sentimental ballads. War-weary audiences evidently appreciated the reassuring sound of comfortable voices and a familiar style. American singers like Dean Martin and Perry Como were closely associated with wealth, luxury and glamour: the precocious Andrew Loog Oldham, who bought his first record, a Perez Prado single, in 1955, reported that he was 'transported for a few minutes to glamorous movie sets inhabited by *femmes fatales* and white dinner-jacketed could-be villains'.[15] Mantovani repeated the success of 'White Christmas' with top-ten orchestral successes like 'Moulin Rouge' and 'Swedish

Rhapsody', both in 1953, and Eddy Calvert matched him with trumpet pieces like 'Oh Mein Papa' and 'Apple Blossom White'. Among British artists, David Whitfield's sentimental style ensured hits for such ballads as 'Cara Mia' and 'Santa Natale' in 1953 and 1954. Even at this early stage it was obvious that exposure on the radio was essential for chart success. The independent Radio Luxembourg began its *Top of the Pops* show in 1952 to coincide with the *NME* chart, and the BBC Light Programme already ran an immensely popular programme of its own, *The Billy Cotton Band Show*. British artists like Alma Cogan and Lita Roza were thought to owe their prominence to Cotton's programme. Cogan's string of hits included 'Little Things Mean a Lot', 'I Can't Tell a Waltz from a Tango', 'Twenty Tiny Fingers' and 'Never Do a Tango with an Eskimo', while Roza had a memorable number one in April 1953 with the novelty ballad 'How Much Is that Doggy in the Window'.[16]

If many older people had been suspicious of the jukebox in the early fifties, they were even more affronted by the success of rock and roll after 1954. Its origins lay far from British shores, in the spread of the jagged, gritty African-American blues of the Mississippi Delta to urban nightclubs in expanding cities like Memphis, Tennessee during the American boom of the 1940s. It was in Memphis in the sweltering summer heat of 1953 that the young Elvis Presley first made an impression on the record producer Sam Phillips, and Presley's historical importance, not to mention his popularity, lay in his ability to take a musical style associated with Southern blacks and present it to white audiences without losing either the intensity or the perceived authenticity attributed to black performers. Presley was not the first white artist to try this trick; Frankie Laine and, especially, Johnny Ray had both enjoyed success in the American and British charts with songs that sounded to many listeners like black recordings. His success lay instead in his versatility: his ability to combine the blues with 'hillbilly' country music and more conventional pop ballads in order to introduce a white middle-class audience to different musical forms.[17] But, although Elvis was the American performer that most British listeners came to associate with the development of rock and roll, he was not the first to make an impression. The first genuine rock and roll record in fact entered the charts in December 1954 in the form of Bill Haley and the Comets' 'Shake, Rattle and Roll'. It was also Haley who recorded the first rock and roll single to top the British charts, when 'Rock Around the Clock' became number one in November 1955.

The phrase 'rock and roll' is usually attributed to the American disc jockey Alan Freed, who used it in 1954 as the title of his New York radio show: 'Hello, everybody, yours truly, Alan Freed, the old king of the rock and rollers, all ready for another big night of rockin' and rollin', let 'er go!' In fact, he did not coin it himself: it was black slang for sexual intercourse, and had been used as far back as 1922 by the blues singer Trixie Smith. As used by Freed, the phrase really worked as slang for rhythm and blues: 'it was just another euphemism for black music'.[18] Rock and roll music, simply put, was black music played for white audiences. Above all, it was a triumph of marketing. As one music historian writes: 'rock and roll from the start was manufactured with the help of a variety of technological gimmicks, propped up with electronic prostheses, and then disseminated, in more or less controlled contexts, through every available mass medium: radio, recordings, film, television, newspapers . . . [and] a large and growing cast of managers, publicists, directors, arrangers and a new breed of audio fixers, able to airbrush away almost any sonic blemish'.[19] 'Rock Around the Clock' was a very good example of this process. A song commissioned especially for the dumpy, middle-aged Haley by an ambitious Philadelphia impresario, it had initially failed to impress American audiences and only became famous after the impresario persuaded the producers of the teenage film *Blackboard Jungle* to play it at high volume over their opening titles. The success of this wheeze on both sides of the Atlantic led in turn to a new film, itself titled *Rock Around the Clock* in order to exploit teenagers' familiarity with the song. The film was eminently forgettable; what counted were the nine songs by Haley and his Comets, accounting for half of the running time.[20]

Haley's band first toured Britain in the spring of 1957, playing in large, crowded venues like the Dominion Theatre on Tottenham Court Road, where one teenage music fan later bitterly recalled his disappointment at the 'paltry thirty-five minutes from this fat, kiss-curled housewife from the middle of America, the uncle you never wanted, Bill Haley'.[21] But six months earlier, when *Rock Around the Clock* was released in British cinemas in September 1956, the reaction had been rather different. According to the press, wherever the film was shown, young working-class audiences would leap up and try to dance to the songs, provoking violent confrontations with cinema managers and policemen. The manager of one cinema in Croydon was sprayed with a fire extinguisher when he attempted to restrain the dancing hordes, and the pattern was repeated even in small towns, like

Colne in Lancashire. 'It was a great atmosphere and everybody was jiving in the aisles,' one enthusiast remembered. 'And we started doing things we shouldn't have done. We were tearing seats off, ripping off covers and throwing stuff into the air. And they said that's it, everybody out, and they closed the cinema down. It was just too exciting for words.'[22]

The exaggerated reaction of the newspapers encouraged more teenagers to emulate their contemporaries, so that the vandalism soon became something of a ritual. When the film opened in Manchester, for instance, the *Daily Mirror* reported: 'A thousand screaming, jiving, rhythm-crazy teenagers surged through the city last night, sweeping aside police cordons and stopping traffic,' and quoted a police spokesman who solemnly announced: 'Nothing like it has ever been seen in the city.'[23] Yet it would not do to overstate the threat to social order of the so-called 'rock and roll riots', and it seems fairly clear that the exaggerated, colourful accounts of looting and rapine had a mildly self-fulfilling effect. Not every cinema in the country was invaded by mobs of frenzied berserkers; the young, middle-class Andrew Oldham, for one, watched the film in 'the primly sterile Haverstock Hill Odeon with twenty or so uptight patrons who tutted and shifted in their seats, while I quietly tore a gash in mine'.[24] When the excited fifteen-year-old John Lennon went to see the film in Liverpool, 'to his disappointment, no riot happened. There was just this fat man in a tartan jacket with a kiss curl on his forehead.'[25]

All the same, the experience confirmed the opposition of traditionalists to American culture in general and rock and roll in particular. Since rock and roll was associated both with blacks and with sexual abandon, the intense opposition of conservative commentators was hardly surprising. In May 1956, for instance, the jazz and swing magazine *Melody Maker* launched a fierce attack on the new craze:

Comes [*sic*] the day of judgement, there are a number of things for which the American music industry, followed (as always) panting and starry-eyed by our own, will find itself answerable to St. Peter. It wouldn't surprise me if near the top of the list is 'Rock-and-Roll' . . . Viewed as a social phenomenon, the current craze for Rock-and-Roll material is one of the most terrifying things to have happened to popular music . . . The Rock-and-Roll technique, instrumentally and vocally, is the antithesis of all that jazz has been striving for over the years – in other words, good taste and musical integrity.[26]

The national press was not far behind. On 4 September 1956 the *Daily Mail* commented that rock and roll was 'sexy music. It can make the blood race. It has something of the African tom-tom and voodoo dance.'[27] The following morning the same paper ran an apocalyptic front-page editorial entitled 'ROCK AND ROLL BABIES'. 'It is deplorable,' the *Mail* warned its readers. 'It is tribal. And it is from America. It follows ragtime, blues, dixie, jazz, hot cha-cha and the boogie-woogie, which surely originated in the jungle. We sometimes wonder whether this is the Negro's revenge.'[28] Even the Bishop of Woolwich wrote to *The Times* on 13 September calling for *Rock Around the Clock* to be banned. It was not in itself pernicious, he explained, but had unfortunately provoked scenes of depravity: 'The hypnotic rhythm and the wild gestures have a maddening effect on a rhythm-loving age group and the result is a relaxing of all self-control.'[29]

There was also considerable antipathy to Elvis Presley, who broke into the British charts during the same period, first with 'Heartbreak Hotel' in May, and then with 'Blue Suede Shoes', 'Hound Dog' and a succession of other hits. 'Lo these many times have I heard bad records, [but] for sheer repulsiveness coupled with the monotony of incoherence, "Hound Dog" hit a new low in my experience,' wrote *Melody Maker*'s reviewer on 10 October. 'There must be some criteria left, even in popular music. If someone is singing words, one surely has the right to demand that the words are intelligible?'[30] As in the United States, critics were alarmed by the sexual suggestiveness of Presley's performances. One schoolgirl recalled that her classmates 'were allowed to bring in our own records for the last day of term', which in itself was an indication of the affluence of the pupils, 'but there was a ban on Elvis. You could have Pat Boone, but you couldn't have Elvis.'[31] But in many cases parental disapproval made Presley and his ilk even more attractive to British adolescents. One Liverpool woman 'never got a minute's peace. It was all Elvis Presley, Elvis Presley, Elvis Presley.' Eventually she wearily told her nephew: 'Elvis Presley's all very well, John, but I don't want him for breakfast, dinner *and* tea.'[32]

Neither Bill Haley nor Elvis Presley would have been so successful had it not been for wider developments within British society and culture. For one thing, they would never have sold so many records had it not been for the new affluence of British teenagers. Not only did teenagers in the late 1950s constitute an increasingly powerful economic group, but they also exhibited much more passion for popular music than did their elders: in 1954, for example, a survey suggested that nine out of ten London teenagers liked listening to records. Since teenagers were becoming more and more afflu-ent, they were able to buy more and more records, and so by the middle of the 1950s it was already obvious that teenage tastes were beginning to dom-inate the market.[33] The commercial success of the *New Musical Express* was a case in point. Originally a newssheet about jazz and big-band music, it had been relaunched in March 1952 by Percy Dickins and Maurice Kinn as the first publication dedicated to teenage pop music, and their innovation in publishing the first Top Twelve was the central part of their strategy to exploit the teenage market.[34] 'If somebody was in the charts,' Kinn later recalled, 'that was our signal to give the people what they wanted. We went for stars in the hit parade, as opposed to being a poor man's *Melody Maker*, making big stories [out of] the fourth trombone change in Teddy Cox's Orchestra.'[35] Occasionally the *NME* miscalculated: in 1956, for instance, the reviewer of Elvis Presley's record 'Heartbreak Hotel' concluded: 'If you appreciate good singing, I don't suppose you'll be able to hear this disc all through.'[36] Overall, however, the strategy was a success. Between 1955 and 1958, *Melody Maker*'s sales fell from 107,000 to 99,000, while the circulation of the *New Musical Express* rose from 93,000 to 122,000.[37] From the mid-fifties onwards, the appeasement of teenage tastes usually meant commercial success.

At the same time, the market in general was rapidly expanding. Almost every household, with the exception of the very poor, could afford a gramo-phone, and in 1960, as we have seen, British consumers were buying more than twelve times as many 45rpm singles as they were in 1955.[38] Thanks to affluence and technological innovation, music was simply more accessible than it had been in previous decades, with a corresponding increase in choice for the consumer.[39] As the critic Ian MacDonald has pointed out, lis-teners often enjoyed popular music for a combination of entirely different reasons. Some, probably a minority, were attracted by the content of the lyrics; larger numbers placed a greater emphasis on the sound of the music itself, or on the cultural associations of the performers, 'the attitudes, the clothes, the moves, the atmosphere'.[40] Both Haley and Presley owed their success more to the innovations of their sound and style than to their rel-atively conventional lyrics. Indeed, it seems likely that during the decades that followed, many, if not most, ordinary consumers judged musical acts as much by the cultural and social values they projected as by the lyrical meaning or musical skill of their productions.

But the overall success of popular music during the post-war years cannot be gainsaid. By the end of the sixties, it was ubiquitous: not only was music played in churches, concert halls, recital rooms, pubs and restaurants, it was also carried into almost every home in the land by televisions and radios. There were more opportunities to perform, too, since teenagers stayed in school for longer before joining the job market, and the universities provided large and enthusiastic student audiences. It was hardly surprising, therefore, that the period between 1956 and 1970 should be so closely identified with the development of a new kind of popular music for an expanding and expectant audience.

The success of rock and roll music and its derivatives depended upon a booming nationwide network of radio programmes, music magazines, jukeboxes, record shops and coffee bars. As early as the late thirties, observers had commented on the adolescent habit of leaving the radio on to provide a background soundtrack to their daily lives, and the invention of the transistor meant that in the 1950s radios were cheaper and smaller than before.[41] The single greatest force in national musical life was still the BBC, not only through its thirteen orchestras and promenade concerts, but also through its ability to promote a record or an artist on the radio. Although the Light Programme played a hit parade of ballads and band music, the Corporation had little enthusiasm for the new popular music of the late fifties, and the irksome government restrictions on 'needletime' meant that it was impossible to broadcast extensive pop music programmes anyway.[42] Instead, teenage audiences tuned in to Radio Luxembourg, which by the late fifties was playing six hours of new material a night, as well as a Top Twenty based on sheet-music sales. Indeed, Radio Luxembourg was considered so influential that record companies even paid for fifteen-minute slots to promote their latest rock and roll releases.[43] For many teenagers, it was their principal means of access to the new musical culture. 'I remember lying in the dark,' recalled one aficionado, 'listening to Radio Luxembourg, and feeling as though I suddenly belonged to a worldwide conspiracy, a movement.'[44]

By the end of the 1950s, television was rapidly overtaking the radio as the principal means of mass communication. Television producers were relatively quick to gauge the potential of popular music, and television shows therefore played an important part in popularising new musical acts and fashions. The first programme dedicated to pop music was ITV's *Cool for Cats*, which began at the end of 1956 and consisted simply of dancers performing rather unenthusiastically to the sound of the latest records. The real pioneer, however, was the BBC's live show *Six-Five Special*, which first went out on 16 February 1957, the same evening that the BBC scrapped the 'toddlers' truce' between six and seven. Since it originally devoted sections to sport, comedy and classical music, *Six-Five Special* was not at first planned as a pop music programme, but it was certainly aimed at a teenage audience. Throughout its two-year run, the show featured rock and roll, skiffle, folk, blues and jazz music, testifying to the diversity of youthful tastes in the late fifties. The co-producer and co-presenter, Jo Douglas, was only twenty-nine, and her fellow presenter Pete Murray was a former disc jockey. The opening exchange between the two was, in the words of Asa Briggs, 'meticulously, if appallingly, scripted' to create the right impression of fashionable informality:

> MURRAY: Welcome aboard the *Six-Five Special*. We've got almost a hundred cats jumping here, some real cool characters to give us the gas, so just get with it and have a ball.
> DOUGLAS: Well, I'm just a square it seems, but for all the other squares with us, roughly translated what Peter Murray just said was 'we've got some lively musicians and personalities mingling with us here, so just relax and catch the mood from us'.[45]

The spontaneous and self-consciously exuberant tone of the show struck many viewers as something of a breakthrough for the national broadcaster. 'Yes, it was BBC, not ITV,' the *Birmingham Mail*'s reviewer reminded his readers. 'Just the kind of thing, in fact, that you might have expected from ITV.'[46]

The general air of slapstick evidently went down well with the teenage public: *Six-Five Special* attracted more than ten million viewers and commanded considerable influence in the music industry. Its power to introduce new acts to a national audience was without parallel, and its producers were bombarded with offers from the managers and record companies.[47] Older viewers, however, were not always impressed. In February 1958 a Conservative Party agent told an audience of Young Conservatives that the BBC, besotted with the 'scatter-brained' teenagers who watched *Six-Five Special*, were giving the impression that 'the youth of today were only interested in rock 'n' roll and wore nothing but jeans and sweaters, and spent their leisure beating time to "pop music"'.[48] Even the BBC's own Deputy Director of Television Programmes complained two months later that there were 'too many girls who wore very abbreviated skirts, and several who wore practically no skirts at all', adding: 'I know how kids feel and act, and I sympathise with them, but they must not be allowed complete licence.'[49]

Still, the success of *Six-Five Special* was a clear lesson for network executives. ITV responded in June 1958 with a punchier show of its own, *Oh Boy!*, based on the appeal of two domestic rock and roll stars, Marty Wilde and Cliff Richard, and the BBC then came up with two new programmes, *Dig This!* and *Drumbeat*.[50] Finally, in June 1959, the BBC hit on a lasting winner, *Juke Box Jury*, which lasted well into the following decade. The formula was simple: a panel of four musicians or celebrities passed judgement on the latest new releases, proclaiming them a Hit or a Miss. The show itself was a clear Hit, and by 1961 it was attracting more than twelve million viewers, both adults and teenagers.[51]

By the late fifties, therefore, the commercial potential of popular music was greater than ever before. Not only was there a ready market of teenage consumers with disposable incomes of their own, but there was already a solid infrastructure of magazines, charts, radio broadcasts and television programmes to support the music industry. What was not clear at this stage was the form that the music of the sixties would take, and in fact the sheer diversity and unpredictability of British tastes meant that the path from Bill Haley and Elvis Presley to the Beatles and the Rolling Stones was neither smooth nor inevitable. Rock and roll music never entirely overwhelmed the British public, and older styles of popular music, from brass bands to ballads, continued to claim listeners for decades afterwards. The singles charts continued to reflect the more conservative tastes of older record purchasers; for example, between Haley's 'Rock Around the Clock' in November 1955 and Presley's 'All Shook Up' in July 1957 there came a string of chart-topping records by familiar performers like Winifred Atwell, Dean Martin, Kay Starr and Doris Day. Indeed, by the end of the decade rock and roll looked like a fad that had run its course, and most informed observers thought that it would play little part in the soundtrack of the 1960s.

The most unlikely pretender to mass-market success at the turn of the decade was folk music, which was closely associated with CND, bohemianism and the radical left. Although folk music did not make many appearances in the higher reaches of the *NME* charts, that did not mean that it was without cultural influence. The folk revival of the late 1950s was part of the general wave of interest in working-class culture and the 'forgotten' regions of the North and Midlands that also produced works like Hoggart's *The Uses of Literacy*, Williams' *Culture and Society* and E. P. Thompson's *The Making of the English Working Class* (1963), as well as the plays, novels and films of the New Wave. The stereotypical folk aficionado was, by and large, a paid-up member of the same 'home-made pottery crowd, the organic husbandry crowd, the recorder-playing crowd, the Esperanto [crowd]' that is assailed by Jim Dixon at the end of Kingsley Amis' novel *Lucky Jim*.[52] The ethos of the movement was a blend of committed Marxism and intense cultural nostalgia; most enthusiasts were contemptuous of the sleek, commercialised culture of the modern world, and their passion was often accompanied by a lot of talk about moral seriousness, personal authenticity and political solidarity.[53] The quintessential folk revivalist of the day was Ewan MacColl, a working-class Marxist born in Salford of Scottish parents, who had helped to establish Theatre Workshop in east London and could often be seen in London folk clubs singing unaccompanied, with one hand cupped over an ear to help him judge the pitch.[54] As far as he was concerned, the only 'authentic', 'honest' music was that of the downtrodden miners, fishermen, sailors and labourers of Britain's past. In his book *The Singing Island*, MacColl explained that the unaccompanied voice was the purest form of musical expression; fiddles and flutes were acceptable, but guitars and banjos were intolerable. Showbusiness of any kind was certainly not on.[55]

In 1959 Ralph Vaughan Williams and A. L. Lloyd noted with approval that folk music was having some success among committed young people in the 'youth hostels, city pubs, skiffle cellars, even in the jazz clubs' of many major cities.[56] MacColl, on the other hand, was not pleased to see the authentic purity of his beloved folk music contaminated by the commercial intrusions of jazz and skiffle. Not only did skiffle recruits bring acoustic guitars, they played American music and often proved resistant to his stern Marxism. The danger, he told *Melody Maker* in 1961, was that they would take folk song 'so far away from its traditional basis that in the end it is impossible to distinguish it from pop music and cabaret'. He was determined 'to give top traditional singers a platform where they will be protected from over-commercialisation'. Skiffle, as he saw it, was 'mercenary': the answer was a Critics Group and a series of 'policy clubs' to protect the radical purity of genuine folk music.[57] Unfortunately for the earnest MacColl, despite his efforts to promote 'authentic' folk song on BBC radio and in London clubs, it never really caught on. As Ian MacDonald puts it, the folk revival was 'an ideological fiction' that exaggerated both the authenticity of its own music and the supposed artificiality of the popular music that it despised.[58] Far from appearing authentic, folk traditions struck most ordinary observers as insufferably precious, and as Richard Weight puts it, the plain fact was that audiences in the fifties and sixties simply 'did not respond to earnest celebrations of the Tolpuddle Martyrs by men and women in Aran sweaters with a hand clasped over one ear'.[59]

Unlike MacColl and the folk purists, many musicians drew little distinction between skiffle, folk music, traditional jazz and American blues. Skiffle had originated in the early 1950s as an offshoot of Ken Colyer's revivalist New Orleans jazz band, and was inspired by 'rent' music from the American South. In the inter-war years, impoverished black tenants, struggling to pay their rent, had thrown parties at which they played improvised music on instruments made from broomsticks, washboards and general household articles.[60] When revived in the fifties, skiffle was more commercial, more exuberant and more eclectic than either jazz or folk; one early press release described it as 'light-hearted folk-music with a jazz slant and a very definite beat – normally sung to a background of guitars, bass and drums only'.[61] Since skiffle musicians drew from both jazz and folk musicians, and rarely took themselves very seriously, they were therefore much more likely to woo an uninitiated audience looking for uncomplicated entertainment. As one early reviewer noted in July 1953, Ken Colyer's band was almost as famous for its skiffle interludes as its jazz set:

> The Skiffle Group which takes over during the intervals at the London Jazz Club is obviously going to be the success of the year. It's getting so that more people flock to the Club for the interval than for the rest of the session . . . If you don't believe that this kind of music could be a draw in London – and I don't blame you for doubting – drop in and feel the electric atmosphere that builds up during Lonnie Donegan's version of 'John Henry' or Ken Colyer's 'How Long'.[62]

Of these first skiffle musicians, easily the most famous and commercially successful was Lonnie Donegan. A Glaswegian by birth, he had been brought up in the East End of London and played the banjo and guitar for a string of revivalist jazz bands. His real break came in 1954, when he recorded four skiffle songs with the Chris Barber Jazz Band for their new LP, *New Orleans Joys*. The album sold sixty thousand copies in its first month, an unprecedented success for a debut album by a British jazz band, and the potential of skiffle was obvious. One of the four tracks, the classic blues song 'Rock Island Line', was then released as a 45rpm single to a spectacular reception. It sold three million copies in six months, more than fifty times the sales of the album from which it was taken; it reached number one in the British chart, largely on the back of its teenage sales; and it was the first British record to reach the Top Twenty of the American *Billboard* chart. British imports had never been very successful with American audiences, but 'Rock Island Line' was different. Not only did Donegan sing with a nasal American accent, but the song was performed by a rhythm section of double bass, kitchen washboard and banjo similar to that associated with the original skiffle music of the twenties and thirties.[63] 'Donegan', as one writer remarked a decade afterwards, 'was indeed the first British artist who managed to sell musical coals to a transatlantic Newcastle'; he would be the first of many.[64]

With his reedy, adenoidal voice and unconventional looks, Donegan was an unlikely celebrity, but after the success of 'Rock Island Line', there could be no doubt about his star status. In 1956 he signed a solo contract with Pye Records, and over the next few years his single releases spent a total of 321 weeks in the charts, including thirty-one Top Thirty hits and three number ones. He was not merely the first British musician to fight his way into the rarefied heights of the American charts; he was also the first musician to introduce post-war British audiences to the folk-blues of the Depression years. Many of his early releases were imitations of iconic blues artists like Huddie 'Leadbelly' Ledbetter and Lonnie Johnson, in honour of whom Donegan had changed his own Christian name, and he also recorded Cajun and Appalachian country songs, Negro spirituals and slave hollers.[65] And yet it would not do to paint Donegan as a pale transatlantic imitation. His contempt for rock and roll was legendary: in September 1956 he informed *Picturegoer* magazine that rock was merely 'a gimmick'. 'Like all gimmicks,' he explained, 'it is sure to die the death. Nothing makes me madder than to be bracketed with those rock 'n' roll boys.'[66] On one occasion, riled by his insults, the British pop star Tommy Steele was even driven to throw a bucket of water over Donegan during a live television broadcast.[67]

Indeed, Donegan owed his success to domestic musical traditions as well as American influences. Two of his three number-one records, 'Cumberland Gap' and 'Putting On the Style', were American folk classics, but his third, which reached the top of the chart in 1960 within a week of its release, was the music-hall staple 'My Old Man's a Dustman'. Another hit, 'Does Your Chewing Gum Lose Its Flavour', was a comic novelty number, barely distinguishable from the parodies performed by Peter Sellers in the guise of 'Lenny Goonigan'. Donegan was no rebel; he was a national icon in the lovable variety tradition. 'I've always wanted to be an entertainer,' he told an interviewer shortly after his initial breakthrough. 'I never minded much exactly in what form. But I always knew I could do it.'[68] His air of cheerful amateurism, so different from the brooding earnestness of his American models, went down well with children and families. He appeared in pantomimes and variety revues, and in 1966 he recorded 'World Cup Willie', the official World Cup song. 'In retrospect,' wrote George Melly four years later, 'he sounds more like George Formby than Huddie Ledbetter.'[69]

Like so many British cultural icons of the 1950s and 1960s, Donegan appealed to a wide audience because he presented the perfect balance of American innovation and domestic tradition. He was therefore the ideal front man for the skiffle boom of the late fifties, a craze that went far beyond the narrow, strict, almost scholarly attractions of folk music and revivalist jazz. The first skiffle audiences, with their beards, woolly jumpers and chequered shirts, were not easy to distinguish from the admirers of folk music.[70] But the sheer informality of skiffle meant that, unlike folk music, it reached out to thousands of young amateurs in provincial towns and suburbs, and the skiffle craze therefore represented the first stage in a transition from professionalism to amateurism.[71] Skiffle succeeded because anybody could play it, and in the affluent society of the late fifties, middle-class boys could afford to equip themselves with the basic instruments and perform themselves. A guitar was expensive, costing perhaps £10 or so, but its associations with Elvis Presley meant that it was also alluringly glamorous. 'Rock 'n' Roll GUITARS – Professional Style – SENT FOR 5/-' ran one advertisement. 'FREE! Beginners' Guitar System. STRUM IMMEDIATELY!'[72] Even those teenagers with limited means could participate: a primitive bass could be made from an inverted tea chest or washtub, broom handle and string, while a simple metal washboard and thimble provided the percussion. 'By the summer of 1957,' recorded Harry Hopkins, 'it seemed hardly possible to move more than a mile or two in urban England without coming upon some little band of troubadours on a suburban street corner,

under a railway arch, in pub or coffee bar, below pier or promenade, confidently "doing it themselves" on guitar, domestic washboard and
double-bass made from tea-chest and clothes prop.'[73]

Many young enthusiasts spent hours practising in their bedrooms before
venturing out to play at Saturday Teenage Shows at the local cinema,
church fêtes, wedding receptions or youth club dances.[74] *Woman* magazine
carried advice for worried mothers on the ideal outdoor skiffle party,
Kellogg's Rice Krispies promised a free 'skiffle whistle' in every pack, and the
Daily Herald and the *People* sponsored skiffle competitions in Butlin's holiday
camps.[75] The beauty of skiffle was that it was such a broad church. Skiffle
groups could play anything from rock and roll to folk music, and there were
plenty of regional variations. On Merseyside there was a brief vogue for sea
shanties; in Birmingham skiffle was supposedly closer to jazz; and in the
West Country groups like the Avon Cities Skiffle Group and the Satellites
incorporated rural folk traditions rooted in the world of Morris dancing.[76]
In Acton, the young Terry Nelhams and his fellow messenger boys 'mem-
orised every note' of Donegan's records and formed a band called the
Worried Men. Terry himself later recalled that during their boys' club concerts he 'used to sing as close as I could to Lonnie Donegan's style'.[77] At
Quarry Bank Grammar School in Liverpool, the Quarry Men not only
copied Donegan's songs but also practised recent hits by Elvis Presley and
other American stars for performance in ballroom competitions, parish
churches and youth club 'hops'. They even had a formal visiting card, proclaiming that they played country, western, rock 'n' roll and skiffle, and
were 'open for engagements'.[78] By contrast, Little Boy Blue and the Blue
Boys, a group of three friends from Dartford Grammar School, were
inspired by black American musicians like Howlin' Wolf, Dale Hawkins and
Chuck Berry. The Dartford boys, unlike the Quarry Men, never quite had
the courage to take their music to the masses; they preferred to play only to
the drummer's mother, who presciently told their singer that 'he'd got
something special'.[79]

For many entrepreneurs, skiffle was good business, and a small network
of music and record shops catered for devotees who wanted to delve more
deeply into American jazz and blues music. The first skiffle clubs, meanwhile, were established in London in 1955, and were exclusive affairs.[80]
Audiences at these early clubs tended to be of the folk persuasion: black
jumpers, beards and sandals were *de rigueur*. By the end of the decade, however, skiffle was the province of a mass audience rather than a narrow sect.

'In the past few weeks', the *Daily Mail* reported in April 1957, 'a new world has sprung up in the sleazy back streets. A new world of young people set in the network of skiffle parlours, jazz joints, rock 'n' roll basements . . . These new after dark citizens of Soho are typists, nurses, factory workers. They are students, dreamers, bank clerks.'[81] These audiences, younger and more catholic than the original skiffle aficionados, frequented Soho establishments like the Cat's Whisker, the Skiffle Cellar, Heaven & Hell, and above all, the 2-Is Coffee Bar in Old Compton Street.[82] The origins of the 2-Is were modest enough: it was opened as a coffee bar by two Australian wrestlers in April 1956, almost immediately began haemorrhaging money, and was serendipitously rescued that summer when Wally Whyton and the Vipers, one of the most popular skiffle bands of the era, began regular performances in the tiny basement. Within weeks of their debut long lines of teenagers were queuing to pay their shilling entrance fee, and although the official capacity was only eighty people, every night the owners crammed several hundred devotees into the cramped and sweaty cellar. It was not only the most famous club in the country, wrote one enthusiast; it was 'the hub of all skiffle'.[83]

In November 1957 the owners of the 2-Is were paid the ultimate compliment when the BBC took over the premises for a live edition of *Six-Five Special*.[84] By this point, however, the era of 'pure' skiffle was already over. Many early fans had begun to lose interest in the finer points of pre-war folk songs, and even Lonnie Donegan had quietly dropped the very word 'skiffle' as part of his move towards the musical mainstream. Not only were there plenty of orchestral versions of skiffle hits, there was even a Christian skiffle record, *Pops with a Purpose*, by Canon E. C. Blake and the Twentieth Century Church Light Music Group, and although Donegan never lost his interest in American folk music, he had already begun to churn out comedy records and music-hall staples.[85] Instead of challenging the musical tastes of British consumers, therefore, both skiffle and rock and roll were being subsumed within them. Although many amateurs continued to strum their guitars in clubs and bedrooms up and down the country, public attention had switched back to the traditional glitz and glamour of showbusiness. Like their rock and roll rivals, skiffle musicians in the late fifties were generally perceived as conventional stars rather than dangerous subversives, and, just as before, the market was dominated by a few carefully groomed stars who appealed both to teenagers and to their elders. 'If you were game enough to learn two or three chords on a guitar and dye your hair blond,' wrote one observer, 'you could stand up on the stage and earn a lot of money.'[86] This was not, perhaps, the spirit of the first skiffle musicians, but it was certainly the spirit of the intermingled skiffle and rock and roll worlds by the end of the decade. 'The World Famous 2-Is Coffee Bar, Home of the Stars', proclaimed a neon sign above the entrance to skiffle's most celebrated venue.[87]

The 2-Is owed its reputation as 'Home of the Stars' to two or three young singers who had made the leap in the late 1950s from obscure amateurs to teenage icons and British alternatives to Elvis Presley. Some had begun their careers as rock and roll performers, others as skiffle musicians, but in truth the distinction was largely meaningless. The pioneer was Tommy Hicks, a nineteen-year-old working-class boy from Bermondsey who was first presented to the public as Tommy Steele, the British Elvis, in 1956. Steele's commercial performance was not especially impressive: his debut single, 'Rock with the Caveman', reached number thirteen, and he only recorded one number one, 'Singing the Blues', in January 1957. His impact, however, could not be measured in sales alone. As George Melly sees it, Steele's breakthrough was 'the first British pop event', by which he means that it was the first post-war cultural development that depended almost entirely on the 'cosmopolitan working-class adolescents' who were in the future to dominate the audience for pop music and culture.[88] It was relatively easy for working-class teenagers to identify with Steele: he once admitted that until his musical career took off he had never been to the West End, despite the fact that the bus to Piccadilly ran past his front door.[89] Steele was also the first domestic star to excite real passion among his teenage followers, and the scenes at his concerts anticipated the shrieking bedlam that greeted the Beatles in 1963. Donegan's fans listened to their idol in thoughtful silence, but Steele's almost drowned him out. 'At certain ritual gestures – a dig with the foot, a violent mop-shake of the head,' noted Colin MacInnes, 'the teenagers utter a collective shriek of ecstasy. Tommy has sent them!'[90]

Like so many popular musical acts of the century, Steele was closely controlled by his managers, John Kennedy and Larry Parnes, a wily pair who circulated the myth that they had discovered him singing at the 2-Is.[91] As far as Parnes and Kennedy were concerned, affluent adolescent girls represented the key to the teenage record market, and over the next few years they recruited a string of young men from coffee bars, variety shows and talent contests to serve as the new Tommy Steele or Elvis Presley. The great majority of the male stars of the late fifties and early sixties came from what Parnes called their 'stable', and they followed the rigid formula developed to promote Steele. The first step was 'a homely Christian name coupled to an abstract surname suggestive of a force of nature or, to be more exact, descriptive of their properties' sexual potential': so among Steele's successors were Marty Wilde, Vince Eager, Tommy Quickly, Duffy Power, Rory Storm, Johnny Gentle and Dickie Pride. Once the name had been chosen, the aspiring young star was spruced up, dressed in flashy clothes and given a suitably fashionable blow-dried haircut. He was presented to the public on television programmes like *Six-Five Special* or *Oh Boy!*, and he recorded a series of singles, which were either cover versions of American hits or imitations written by Lionel Bart. Finally he was taken on tour around the country, milking his transitory moment of fame and performing not only in theatres and cinemas, but also in town halls, dance halls and rural corn exchanges.[92]

The most talented product of Parnes' stable was probably Billy Fury, whose chart career lasted from 1959 until 1965. An unemployed tugboat hand from Liverpool, his real name was Ronald Wycherley and his break came when he managed to sneak his way into Marty Wilde's dressing room after a concert at Birkenhead. Parnes was impressed by what he heard and offered Wycherley a place in the show under the new moniker of Billy Fury. His first single, 'Maybe Tomorrow', immediately reached the Top Twenty, while his debut album, *The Sound of Fury* (1960), is considered 'Britain's finest example of the rockabilly genre'.[93] Fury had written all the songs himself, which was very unusual for a Parnes artist. More typically, he dressed in a lurid gold outfit and provoked extreme reactions among his female devotees. Like most of his fellow stars, Fury was discouraged from speaking too much; Larry Parnes feared that his strong Liverpool accent would alienate middle-class audiences.[94]

The two most enduring stars associated with the new pop music of the late fifties, however, were not part of Parnes' troupe. The first, and by far the most successful British musician of the entire post-war era, was Harry Webb, who was born in 1940 and spent his teenage years in suburban Hertfordshire. Like so many performers of the day, Webb first formed a skiffle band after falling under the spell of Bill Haley and Elvis Presley and in the summer of 1958 he managed to secure a booking at the 2-Is, a deal with EMI and a regular slot on the ITV show *Oh Boy!* His group, the Drifters, was eventually renamed the Shadows in order to avoid confusion with another group across the Atlantic, while Webb himself took the name Cliff Richard. His first single with the Shadows, the unusually catchy 'Move It', was an instant success, reaching number two in the charts, but the real secret of

Richard's appeal was in his stage persona. Not only was he better looking than many of his competitors, he was also able to combine the polish of the old variety stars with the sheer energy of an Elvis Presley, and his appeal to teenage girls in particular was unmatched by his rivals. Many older observers, however, deplored his 'indecent, short-sighted vulgarity'. 'His violent hip-swinging was revolting, hardly the performance any parent could wish her children to see,' insisted the *NME*'s reviewer shortly after Richard's debut on *Oh Boy!* 'He was wearing so much eyeliner he looked like Jayne Mansfield. If we are expected to believe that Cliff was acting naturally, then consideration for medical treatment may be advisable.' For parents worried by tales of teenage promiscuity, Cliff Richard initially looked like a serious menace to their daughters' purity. 'Is this boy too sexy for television?' asked an agitated *Daily Sketch*.[95]

But, as one critic noted, by 1959 Richard was becoming safe rather than sexy, 'less of a threat than a promise'. He had already recorded two number-one singles and appeared in two films, and was inexorably moving, as had Tommy Steele before him, from rock and roll into showbusiness. 'His erotic twitching turned into a bent-kneed shuffle,' remarked George Melly, 'not so much a sexual courtship dance as a suggestion that he'd wet himself; and his dance material became soppier and soppier.'[96] Although Richard's brand of pop ballads quickly lost favour with the rock critics of the sixties, he never lost his hold on the affections of the British public. Between 1960 and 1969 his records spent longer in the *NME* singles charts than those of any other artist, and he had more chart hits than the Beatles and the Rolling Stones combined. Even in the last decade of the century he was not only a knight of the realm and one of the most famous Christians in the country; he was still, almost incredibly, a chart-topping musician.[97]

Cliff Richard's only serious rival in the late 1950s was Terry Nelhams, a young messenger boy from Acton. Nelhams began his career in the stereotypical manner: a teenage skiffle band; a stint at the 2-Is, where he was filmed by the cameras of *Six-Five Special*; and then a regular slot on *Drumbeat*. Like Cliff Richard, he owed much of his success to the television producer Jack Good, and it was Good who suggested Nelhams' new name, Adam Faith.[98] Originally Faith affected the stern, aggressive image that was thought to denote rock and roll authenticity, but his great breakthrough came after he abandoned it in favour of a much gentler, friendlier style that ensured his popularity not only with suburban teenage girls but also with 'do-gooders, youth leaders and teachers'. 'Fathers and mothers all over the country could rest assured that such a boy would bring the girl back home again at ten o'clock as instructed,' wrote one commentator, 'still polythene-wrapped and untouched by human hand.'[99] By Christmas 1959 Faith's single 'What Do You Want', produced by the composer and arranger John Barry, was number one and selling fifty thousand copies a day. Although he tried to sound American, Faith could never quite disguise his Acton accent, and the result was a rather strange hybrid, epitomised by his verbal trademark, the pronunciation of 'baby' as 'by-a-bee'. Still, with John Barry toiling away behind the scenes, he released eleven more Top Ten hits within the next five years and then made a remarkably successful transition into acting.[100]

What distinguished Faith from his peers was not the quality of his singing: in fact, when asked to sign a compilation of his hits in 1983, he shook his head and said: 'Who buys this crap? The best British rock and roll record was "Move It"! Do you think I even came close to that?'[101] Instead, he appealed to audiences because he was unusually articulate, honest and engaging. While performers like Billy Fury were effectively barred from talking in public, Faith defied his advisers in December 1960 by appearing on the prestigious BBC interview programme *Face to Face*. That he stood up to the relentless interrogation of the host, John Freeman, surprised many viewers; what struck others as even more surprising was that he admitted to liking Sibelius, Dvořák and Tchaikovsky, as well as the novels of Aldous Huxley and J. D. Salinger. In its way, this was probably a bigger contribution to the culture of the early sixties than Faith's music. 'The public was surprised that a working-class pop star could talk,' he reflected many years later. 'Whether I said anything intelligible or not, I don't know.'[102]

What all the pop stars of the late 1950s had in common was that they neatly bridged the gap between the novelty of American rock and roll and the surviving British traditions of variety and showbusiness. Teenagers tended to identify the United States with glamour, vigour and cultural innovation, so it made sense for aspiring stars to imitate American models. In most cases the young singers began their careers by emphasising their American credentials, gradually abandoning the pretence as they moved from a teenage market to an older one. Cliff Richard, for one, sang his first hit 'Move It' in a strong American accent and continued to imitate American intonation throughout his career; similarly, the disc jockeys in most pirate radio stations were encouraged to develop a kind of mid-Atlantic drawl, the most obvious example being Tony Blackburn.

Since in some quarters the creeping spread of American culture was equated with national decadence and decline, it was not surprising that the transatlantic affectations of the new stars displeased some observers. In December 1957, for instance, Colin MacInnes published the influential essay 'Young England, Half English', reflecting on his experience at a Tommy Steele concert:

> In his film or when, on the stage, he speaks to his admirers between the songs, his voice takes on the flat, wise, dryly comical tones of purest Bermondsey. When he sings, the words (where intelligible) are intoned in the shrill international American-style drone. With this odd duality, his teenage fans seem quite at ease: they prefer him to be one of them in his unbuttoned moments, but expect him to sing in a near-foreign tone: rather as a congregation might wish the sermon to be delivered in the vernacular, and the plainsong chanted in mysterious Latin.

As MacInnes saw it, singers like Steele had won the struggle for fame and fortune 'at the cost of splitting their personalities and becoming bi-lingual: speaking American at the recording session, and English in the pub round the corner afterwards'. With Americanisation so deeply entrenched, he wondered whether the English would in the future be considered 'a people in any real sense at all'.[103]

What critics like George Melly and Colin MacInnes overlooked, however, was the indisputable fact that most pop and rock stars of the fifties and sixties were the inheritors not only of American styles and traditions, but of native, British ones as well. During Tommy Steele's heyday in 1956, for example, his managers promoted him by sending him out to perform in civic halls and variety theatres, and they certainly did not consider him above appearing in Christmas pantomimes, as Buttons in Cinderella in 1958, for instance, or even a triumphant performance as Humpty Dumpty in Liverpool in 1961.[104] MacInnes himself commented that Steele was 'every nice girl's boy, every kid's favourite brother, every mother's cherished adolescent son'.[105] By the end of the decade, pop music was generally thought 'safe': after interviewing Cliff Richard, one Daily Mirror journalist concluded that he was 'a very nice kid indeed . . . trembling lips, wiggle and all'.[106] Rock and roll was even considered a fit subject for a spoof record by Terry-Thomas and his Rock 'n' Roll Rotters, 'A Sweet Old Fashioned Boy', notable for occasional interjections by the inimitable lead singer like 'Dig those crazy sounds, Daddio' and 'See you later, alma mater'.[107]

For George Melly, this was all part of a general 'prettiness' and 'castration' of British popular music in the late fifties, destroying its potential to move towards the kind of American blues that Melly evidently associates with masculinity, authenticity and so on.[108] But this is to misunderstand the essence of pop music in the late 1950s. It was never, at heart, especially subversive, and most singers actually saw pop music as a route to the stage or televised variety shows. In Adam Faith's autobiography, *Poor Me*, published in 1961, the inside cover describes him not as a pop star, singer or musician, but as 'one of today's greatest stage personalities'. The photographic inserts show him playing golf in a Pringle sweater, riding a horse and shaking hands with the Queen Mother. And his answer to the question: 'What's been the highspot of your career so far?' sums up the conservatism of the entire book:

> I don't have to think before I answer that question. There's only one highspot as far as I'm concerned. That's the night that I was included among the stars honoured to appear before the Queen and Prince Philip at the 1960 Royal Variety Performance at the Victoria Palace . . .
>
> He [Prince Philip] put on that famous quizzical smile of his and almost winked at me.
>
> 'This isn't your usual garb, is it?' he said humorously. And, suddenly, I felt as proud as Punch, because it meant that at least I was known to him from TV or the papers.
>
> I went home in a daze that night, saying to myself, 'Terry Nelhams, for an ordinary kid from Acton, you haven't done so badly for yourself, mixing with Royalty!'[109]

By the time that Faith's autobiography reached the shops, most observers thought that rock and roll was on its last legs. Most of the popular American rock singers of the late fifties, like Buddy Holly, Chuck Berry and Jerry Lee Lewis, were no longer recording. The two most popular artists of 1960 and 1961, judged on sales, were Cliff Richard and Elvis Presley, but both had been effectively tamed to appeal to an older audience. Teenagers might still swoon at the sound of Cliff Richard and Adam Faith, but in truth their music was already approaching the territory of the family-oriented ballad. Even Presley, the great pioneer of rock and roll, was no longer considered subversive: in truth, he had become little more than a bombastic Italianate crooner with aspirations to be the next Frank Sinatra. This general impression of clean-cut, rather bland professionalism was reinforced not only by the two most successful singles of the period, 'Cathy's Clown' by the Everly Brothers and 'Runaway' by Del Shannon, but also by the presence further down the charts of female vocalists like Shirley Bassey and Helen Shapiro as well as novelty performers like Rolf Harris and Ken Dodd. From the perspective of 1961, the rock and roll boom looked like a lucrative gimmick that had reached the limits of its potential. Most of the brooding young performers who had emerged out of the skiffle craze were moving on to showbusiness, theatre and films; most of the carefree sixteen-year-olds who had screamed at the sight of Tommy Steele in 1956 were now hard-working twenty-one-year-olds with jobs and families. True, in 1961 there was still a teenage market, but it seemed extremely implausible that the new generation would be seduced by the same kind of music that had captivated their elders five years previously. There would always be a new fad; but there was no reason to imagine that any of them would ever last any longer than had rock and roll.[110]

By the beginning of 1962, most record executives agreed that rock and roll music and its derivatives were destined to be remembered only as quaint relics of the late fifties. On New Year's Day, for instance, the young executive Mike Smith went to Decca's West Hampstead studio to hear an audition by four aspiring rock and roll musicians from Liverpool. He had little hesitation in turning them down; as far as Decca were concerned, rock was, in commercial terms, 'dead'.[111] Later that year, in an obituary for the music of the fifties, the BBC producer and disc jockey Brian Matthew commented that rock had simply fallen victim to its own sudden and transitory popularity:

> When the 'experts' announced that rock was dead a lot of us yelled that they were wrong. But in a sense, you know, they were half right. That's to say the immense popularity of the simplest thump and crash form of beat music was on the wane. Mammoth package shows with 'star-studded' bills of nonentities, with one howling hooligan following another, bawling undecipherable lyrics to indistinguishable tunes, no longer had the mesmeric impact they had had, as more than one 'get-rich-quick' promoter found to his cost. What had been exciting in its early stages soon became boring. Here was a real case of familiarity breeding contempt.[112]

Already, Matthew noted, publishers and managers were looking for 'signs of the next craze'. 'You may remember', he explained, 'that we were told frequently and loudly not long ago that rock was dead and next in line would be the calypso – but it wasn't! Then they tried again with cha-cha, and for a while when Tommy Dorsey's "Tea for two cha-cha" was a tremendous hit it looked like this might be it – but it wasn't!' Instead, he advised his readers, 'the way things are at the moment it looks as though the sixties may well come to be labelled the ten years of Trad'.[113]

The prediction that trad jazz would be the soundtrack to the 1960s might look supremely ill judged, but at the time it seemed both sensible and plausible. Jazz music had, after all, been very popular with middle-class intellectuals and students from the mid-thirties onwards, although its rather antiquarian, scholarly air prevented it from conquering the growing teenage market.[114] The first jazz aficionados had little access to live music, since the Musicians' Union bitterly resisted the infiltration of American musicians, and were therefore more interested in listening to records in private, and then discussing them with other enthusiasts, than in dancing to them.[115] The music appealed in particular to what the historian Eric Hobsbawm, who wrote a pseudonymous jazz column for the *New Statesman*, called 'the world of the grammar school and public library': young lower-middle-class men, ambitious and bookish, keen to carve out a cultural life of their own away from the sneers of the public schools and the wealthy.[116]

Indeed, there always remained an unmistakable earnestness about jazz audiences, and they were often associated with progressive political causes. One survey of Huddersfield in the early sixties found that that the local Jazz Club appealed to 'boys and girls from working-class homes who went to grammar school': bright and well educated, they nevertheless wanted to kick against the self-consciously respectable atmosphere of their school environment.[117] 'It was a special voice that we all latched on to', wrote John Osborne, 'because it was exotic and it was powerful, and it was completely different from the kind of life that we knew at the time.'[118] And the trumpeter Humphrey Lyttelton observed that his club attracted in particular the serious young men and women who attended art colleges and adored modern fiction, not least because the improvisational aspects of jazz offered a respite from the daily grind. 'They didn't want to be regimented', he remembered, 'and all the things like clothing at the club, the do-it-yourself dancing, dance styles and things, arose I think from the fact that people didn't want just to be told what to do.'[119]

By the beginning of the fifties, a rift had opened up within the British jazz community between on the one hand the various revivalist camps, for whom 'authentic' jazz had ground to a halt before the war, and on the other those who embraced the more intricate and self-consciously sophisticated harmonies of modern New York bebop. For the revivalists, the attraction of jazz was in its non-commercial exclusivity. Discussion was more important than dancing; Eric Hobsbawm observed that true enthusiasts would never dance, but instead 'stand or sit by the bandstand, soaking in the music, nodding and smiling at one another in a conspiracy of appreciation, and tapping their feet'.[120] Humphrey Lyttelton recalled that when he first played in front of dancing crowds at the Feldman Swing Club in the late forties, 'the regular jazz buffs who used to come along and sit through the thing thought this was absolute heresy'.[121] Their great adversaries were the new breed of jazz modernists, the cerebral, dark-suited admirers of the experimental styles of Charlie Parker and Miles Davis. These arguments, petty though they might seem, were played out in the new clubs of post-war London: the Feldman Swing Club, the Marquee, the Flamingo and Cy Laurie's Jazz Club.[122] One of the most long lived, Ronnie Scott's, which generally featured modern rather than Dixieland jazz, opened in 1959 and became something of a Soho institution. Unlike most rival clubs, it had a licensed bar, and Scott boasted that this made it 'the first British jazz club on American lines'.[123]

From the beginning, some critics associated jazz clubs with licentiousness and drugs. Club 11, where young performers like Ronnie Scott and Johnny Dankworth played modern jazz in a dingy basement on Carnaby Street, had been forced to close in 1950 after a police raid. 'It left me filled with resentment of the police', declared an indignant RAF servicewoman arrested in the raid, 'because I was accused of possessing a low moral standard, fraternising with "buck niggers", and the likelihood of becoming a drug addict.'[124] And yet jazz also had its respectable side. Lyttelton, the most famous of all British jazz musicians, was an Old Etonian, a former Grenadier Guardsman and a cartoonist for the *Daily Mail*: he was therefore a safe choice to present the BBC's regular jazz broadcast, *Looking at Jazz*, from October 1950. Lyttelton was, moreover, one of the few jazz musicians in the early fifties who tried to bridge the gap between revivalists and modernists, a gap that he had himself helped to create when he offended the purists by including a saxophonist in his Oxford Street band.[125]

Yet whatever their internal disagreements, most jazz devotees were united in their contempt for rock and roll, the music of the teenage working classes. Indeed, their sense of educated exclusivity was strengthened rather than diluted by the emergence of rock and roll as a commercial rival. 'To us in the jazz world', wrote George Melly, 'it seemed a meaningless simplification of the blues with all the poetry removed and the emphasis on white, and by definition inferior, performers . . . Why should anyone prefer this unsubtle, unswinging, uncoloured music to the real thing?'[126] Behind this rhetoric, however, lay a history of collaboration. Jazz musicians had often played vital roles in the explosion of teenage popular music of the late fifties, and the arcane divisions between folk, blues, jazz, skiffle and rock and roll were not always easy to distinguish. The first skiffle group had, after all, originated as an offshoot from Ken Colyer's Dixieland jazz band, and trained jazz players were in great demand to play in the backing bands supporting Larry Parnes' blue-eyed boys.[127] In this context, the breakthrough of revivalist and 'trad' jazz to nationwide fame was perhaps not such a surprise; and many revivalist musicians were nicely positioned to take advantage when it came.

Until the beginning of 1961, Dixieland jazz was regarded as little more than a minority taste.[128] Its breakthrough came when Brian Matthew, the presenter of the Light Programme's Sunday-morning show *Easy Beat*, decided to adopt it as an alternative to rock and roll. 'We had been running for considerably over a year on a diet of rock, a sprinkling of folk music, and pop records', he later recalled, 'and quite suddenly the show needed a vigorous "shot in the arm".' His solution was to promote a minor trad jazz group, Kenny Ball's Jazzmen, for the first four editions of 1961, and the result was a triumph. 'The band made a colossal impact,' he explained, 'our audience increased by leaps and bounds, and Kenny's contract was increased until he eventually stayed on the show for seven months without a break.'[129] Now, boosted by the patronage of the BBC and the gradual decline of rock and roll, trad jazz began to take off. Ball's single 'Midnight in Moscow' was simultaneously number two in Britain and number one in the United States, a sensational achievement, and his next two British releases also made the Top Ten. The Temperance Seven, an outfit who wore Edwardian outfits and specialised in twenties dance music, recorded a number-one hit with their very first single, 'You're Driving Me Crazy'. Suddenly, quite unexpectedly, Dixieland jazz bands were all the rage.[130]

The greatest beneficiary of the trad craze, however, was the flamboyant Acker Bilk, a clarinettist and bandleader from rural Somerset who was always immaculately turned out in a striped Edwardian waistcoat and a bowler hat. The 'Bilk Marketing Board' made sure that he was always billed as 'Mr Acker Bilk', and his publicity usually read like an elaborate pastiche of a Victorian advertisement, complete with excruciating puns and parodies: 'An Acker A Day Keeps The Bopper Away', 'There IS No Substitute for Bilk', or 'Spinna Disca Bilka Day'.[131] His jaunty music apart, Bilk's great selling point was his exaggerated rustic background. As one sceptical observer saw it, 'the public was asked to accept a cider-drinking, belching, West Country contemporary dressed as an Edwardian music-hall "Lion Comique", and playing the music of an oppressed racial minority as it had evolved in an American city some fifty years before. More surprisingly they did accept it. Acker was soon a national idol.'[132] In 1959, his punning single 'Summer Set' had reached number five, but his greatest triumph came in 1961 with the triumph of 'Stranger on the Shore', an instrumental piece which had been written for his daughter but became the theme of a children's television programme. It spent a record-breaking fifty-five weeks in the British singles chart, peaking at number two, and twenty-one weeks in the American chart, where it reached number one in May 1962. As one commentator puts it, Bilk was 'quite possibly the only man to top the American charts wearing a bowler hat and a striped waistcoat'.[133] And when a compilation album, *The Best of Ball, Barber and Bilk*, reached the top of the British LP chart in 1962, traditional jazz seemed to be sweeping all before it.

What was most surprising about the trad jazz boom was that it seemed so completely unsuited for commercial success. Jazz enthusiasts were conventionally seen as rather intense, shabby figures. They clustered in dingy clubs, as Peter Lewis puts it, 'in their Fair Isle knitted sweaters and their duffel coats, with submissive girls in tow, heavy pipes clamped in jaw and the air of thoughtful acolytes observing time-honoured rites'.[134] In the spring of 1962 George Melly went to an all-night 'trad ball' at the Alexandra Palace, and afterwards reported in the *New Statesman*:

> The audience were dressed almost without exception in 'rave gear'. As the essence of 'rave gear' is a stylised shabbiness, the general effect was of a crowd scene from a biblical epic. To describe an individual couple, the boy was wearing a top hat with 'Acker' printed on it, a shift made out of a sugar sack with a CND symbol painted on the back, jeans and no shoes. The girl, a bowler hat with a CND symbol on it, a man's shirt worn outside her black woollen tights.[135]

The period of trad jazz's greatest commercial success was also the period when CND was at its height, and for a time jazz was seen as the music of the disarmament movement, eventually giving way to folk in the mid-six- , ties. CND badges and leaflets were liberally distributed at jazz venues, and in the early 1960s jazz musicians used to play impromptu concerts during the Aldermaston marches.[136] At the same time, the trad performers themselves were hardly glamorous figures. While Cliff Richard, Adam Faith and their imitators had been dashing, handsome characters in their late teens, most of trad's household names were men in their thirties and forties. Even Acker Bilk, the most charismatic of the Dixieland musicians, looked comic rather than compelling with his bowler hat and goatee beard. And yet, for a time, the unpretentious look and style of the jazz musicians was a strength rather than a weakness. Their Edwardian dress not only served to distinguish them from the clichés of teenage rock and roll, it also appealed to a deep vein of nostalgia in British popular culture. Audiences who loved American music and American associations could enjoy the sound of the Dixieland revival; but audiences who disliked and distrusted transatlantic cultural influences could take solace in Bilk's exaggerated rural Englishness. The music might be American, but trad jazz was a peculiarly British phenomenon.

By 1962, when Brian Matthew published his book *Trad Mad*, it was reasonable to imagine that traditional jazz would have a firm foothold in the charts for the foreseeable future. 'Trad jazz is indestructible', wrote Eric Hobsbawm in the *New Statesman*, 'because it is today the basic dance-music of British juveniles.'[137] The BBC ran a television series devoted to trad jazz entitled *Trad Fad*, and almost every week trad bands appeared before twenty million viewers on *Sunday Night at the London Palladium*. In the film *Band of Thieves*, Acker Bilk pulled off a series of dashing diamond heists, while Richard Lester's film *It's Trad Dad* offered audiences the opportunity to watch Bilk, Kenny Ball, Chris Barber, and the Temperance Seven, as well as dozens of other stars of the day, performing on the big screen.[138] 'With the continually increasing interest in jazz and the ever-growing number of young people, I think we'll be in business for some considerable time,' remarked the bandleader Terry Lightfoot.[139] As far as Matthew was concerned, trad jazz had begun to take over the place in teenagers' hearts once reserved for rock and roll. He explained:

There is not much room for refinement or an intellectual approach with trad: we are concerned with the basic, even crude, gaiety of human nature, and it runs the whole gamut from tremendous gaiety to abject misery. Trad shouts when it is happy, and moans when it is low. It laughs when anything tickles its fancy and cries when anything touches its heart. And this gets back to what I said at the beginning of this book about why people are finding trad jazz so entertaining: it reflects everyday life in dramatic terms.[140]

Had trad reached the limit of its potential? Kenny Ball, for one, thought not: instead, trad music's appeal would grow as bands tackled different kinds of instrumentals. 'I would say that there is no peak, as such, to be reached,' he said confidently. 'Trad will broaden . . . Trad will last as long as it swings.' Brian Matthew agreed. 'I feel confident that he will be around for a long time to come,' he told his readers, 'as will all the other people we have met in this book. The top men of trad are entertainers, and they are really going to set their seal on this decade.'[141]

One bright morning in August 1960 a battered cream and green Austin van set off from Liverpool to Hamburg. The trip had been organised by Allan Williams, a stocky, black-bearded Welshman who owned a little Liverpool coffee bar called the Jacaranda and managed a number of local skiffle and rock and roll groups. His fellow passengers on the long journey from Liverpool to London, from London to Newhaven, across the water to Holland, and overland to Hamburg, included his wife, his brother-in-law, his West Indian business partner 'Lord Woodbine', and five nervous young musicians for whom he had recently obtained a booking in a Hamburg nightclub. The group had chopped and changed in the last few years, but now they had a more settled line-up: John Lennon, vocals and guitar; Paul McCartney, vocals and guitar; George Harrison, lead guitar; Stuart Sutcliffe, bass; and Pete Best, drums. Sutcliffe, at twenty, was the oldest; Lennon and Best were both nineteen; McCartney was eighteen; and Harrison, the baby of the group, was only seventeen. None of them had ever been abroad before, and Lennon had only acquired his passport a few days before they were due to depart. They had all been packed off by their families with old-fashioned suitcases and bags of clothes and keepsakes, and Williams had advanced them £15 to buy some new tennis shoes and black sweaters from Marks and Spencer. Young George Harrison was clutching a tin of home-made scones that his mother had given him for the journey. Only one family member had come to see them off: Stuart Sutcliffe's mother, who had quietly followed her son to the Jacaranda and stood in a shop doorway, crying to herself as the van, with its crude paper sign 'THE BEATLES' pulled away down the street towards unimaginable fame and fortune.[142]

Liverpool was well known in Britain as a gloomy, fog-bound city of docks, ships, and crumbling Victorian splendour. It was an imperial port in terminal decline, with a famous tradition of salty music-hall comedy, an impenetrable dialect and a distinctive working-class flavour.[143] The apprehensive young men who set off for Hamburg in the late summer of 1960 were not, however, poor working-class Liverpool lads. Although they later chose to play up their proletarian backgrounds, this was a convenient but misleading myth. John Lennon, effectively the founder of the group, spent his childhood in a mock-Tudor villa called 'Mendips', facing on to the golf course in the leafy, respectable suburb of Woolton. His uncle and aunt, who owned the house and looked after him, also owned the collected works of Winston Churchill and an impressive collection of Royal Worcester dinner plates, and they even employed a gardener.[144] 'I lived in the suburbs in a nice semi-detached place with a small garden and doctors and lawyers and that ilk living around, not the poor slummy kind of image that was projected,' he admitted in 1980. 'I was a nice clean-cut suburban boy.'[145]

John's Aunt Mimi disapproved of his Beatles friends, as was typical in a society intricately interlaced with class distinctions. Although she regarded George Harrison as a 'low type' because he worked at weekends as a butcher's errand boy, his childhood had also been reasonably comfortable. Harrison's father drove a Corporation bus and the family lived in a new council house, but George wanted for very little: his mother even lent him the money to buy a £30 guitar when he was in his mid-teens.[146] Paul McCartney's family also lived in a council property, but they too were hardly poor; thanks to the housing crisis of the fifties, it was not necessarily unusual for middle-class families to live in rented council houses. When Paul was thirteen they moved to a little semi-detached house in the district of Allerton, not far from Lennon's home in Woolton. As he later remembered, his mother wanted to get the family 'into a slightly posh area so that perhaps some of the posh might rub off on us . . . In fact, it was quite a middle-class area where we were, but they'd built a council estate in the middle of all the posh houses, much to the chagrin of the local residents.'[147] Paul's parents were, like so many people in the post-war period, intensely ambitious for themselves and their son. His mother wanted him to be a doctor; his father hoped that he would become 'a great scientist, a great university graduate'. Jim McCartney took the solidly middle-class *Daily Express* and encouraged his son to study crosswords and build up his 'word power'. McCartney junior followed his father's example: he passed his eleven-plus, won a place at the oldest grammar school in the city, the Liverpool Institute, and was almost always chosen as the head boy of his form.[148] As for the other members of the Beatles, both Stuart Sutcliffe and Pete Best were from respectable lower-middle-class backgrounds. Only Richard Starkey, the drummer later recruited under the name of Ringo Starr, had a genuine claim to working-class origins.

There was nothing particularly unusual about the Beatles' teenage enthusiasm for rock and roll music. In the 1930s Jim McCartney had been the leader of the Jim Mac Jazz Band, playing dance music in his spare time at social clubs and works dances; he still loved to play the old tunes on his piano, so to some extent music was in young Paul's blood. Paul used to sing himself to sleep at night, but began clamouring for a guitar after seeing Lonnie Donegan in concert at the Empire Theatre, Liverpool. John Lennon, meanwhile, had first been converted by the sound of Elvis Presley when he was fifteen, but was similarly inspired by Lonnie Donegan's hit 'Rock Island Line' to form a band of his own with a shifting group of friends from Quarry Bank Grammar School.[149] At this early, pre-McCartney stage there was nothing special about them at all: they banged away at various skiffle and rock and roll numbers and used to enter skiffle competitions at the big local ballrooms. Like so many teenagers of the late fifties, they tried to copy the music of their favourite American artists: Presley, Buddy Holly, Chuck Berry, Gene Vincent and others. The quality of their performances, however, can perhaps be gauged by the fact that one group that often beat them included 'as its chief attraction a midget named Nicky Cuff, who actually stood on the tea chest bass while plucking at it'.[150]

On Saturday 6 July 1957 the Quarry Men were booked to play at the St Peter's Parish Church fête in Woolton. It was a warm, sunny afternoon, perfect for an ordinary, traditional summer fête. The band of the Cheshire Yeomanry led a procession through the streets, and floats of Scouts and Guides, Cubs and Brownies, Morris dancers and schoolchildren in fancy dress all followed in their wake. In the field behind the church a makeshift stage had been set up, surrounded by stalls selling home-made cakes and sweets, fruit and vegetables and hardware, and sideshows like bagatelle, hoopla and shilling-in-the-bucket. Just after four, as the Quarry Men started playing a selection of skiffle standards and recent hits, the fifteen-year-old

Paul McCartney wandered into the field. A schoolfriend had told him about Lennon's group and, while he was keen to see what they were made of, he was even keener to see if there were any pretty girls at the fête. Lennon was on stage, singing 'Come Go with Me', a recent hit by the Dell Vikings; unfortunately, he had struggled to transcribe the words from the radio, so where the original version read: 'Come go with me, don't let me pray beyond the sea,' Lennon was singing: 'Come go with me, down to the penitentiary.' Still, despite this inauspicious beginning, McCartney hung around until the stage was cleared for the highlight of the afternoon, a display by the City of Liverpool police dogs, and the boys moved to the nearby church hall. The requisite introductions were then made, and McCartney, whose musical expertise was at this point far ahead of anything the Quarry Men could offer, confidently demonstrated his Gene Vincent and Little Richard impersonations, borrowing a guitar and reeling off lyrics and chord changes from memory. Lennon, despite being more than a year older, could not help being impressed. Later that evening the boys all trooped down to the pub for an illicit drink, and then went their separate ways.

At the time, nobody could possibly have guessed the importance of the meeting. Sparks of creative inspiration did not immediately fly, and although McCartney's ability impressed the Lennon group, they disliked his air of casual self-confidence. A week later, however, McCartney was out cycling when he bumped into one of Lennon's friends and heard that he was officially invited to join the band. And so, on 18 October, at the Conservative Club in Norris Green, McCartney and Lennon took the stage together for the first time.[151]

The Quarry Men were never the same again after McCartney joined the group. Although Lennon was still the leader in 1957 and 1958, there was no doubt that McCartney was their most accomplished musician. One of the reasons that he had not immediately been invited to join the group, in fact, was that the Quarry Men suspected that he was simply too good for them.[152] Like Lennon, he was passionate about guitars, and the two spent hours together at McCartney's house practising their chord changes. The new member was a relentless perfectionist, constantly striving to improve not only his own performance but also the general sound of the band, and one by one Lennon's old schoolfriends dropped out. Over the next couple of years, while Lennon and McCartney were finishing school, the Quarry Men went through various incarnations, always scraping a concert here and there at birthday parties, youth club hops and church events. At one point they were called Johnny and the Moondogs; at another, the Rainbows; and when John and Paul played as a duo, they called themselves the Nurk Twins.[153] By 1959 they were at last beginning to settle on a line-up. George Harrison, a pale, serious boy whom McCartney had met years before on the bus to school, had been tagging along with them for months and would occasionally sit in when another member failed to turn up; gradually, through sheer persistence and grim hard work, he played his way into the heart of the group. The other new addition was Stuart Sutcliffe, a talented young painter whom Lennon had befriended, and indeed idolised, at the Liverpool College of Art. Unlike the earnest Harrison, Sutcliffe had little or no musical talent, but since his bohemian style appealed to Lennon's more rebellious instincts he was persuaded to invest in a bass guitar and join the band.[154]

Unfortunately the Quarry Men were not very successful, and as 1958 became 1959 and then 1960, they secured fewer and fewer bookings. In their self-consciously 'arty' black crewneck sweaters and tennis shoes they looked very different from the groups that played with Cliff Richard or Adam Faith; their stage presence was frenetic rather than cool; and they did not even have a regular drummer. In the first three months of 1960 they did not have a single engagement. In March, after attracting the attention of Allan Williams at the Jacaranda coffee bar, they began to think about changing their name. They needed something catchy, like Buddy Holly's Crickets; Sutcliffe jokingly suggested 'beetles', and they settled on the Beatals. Two months later, Williams persuaded them to change it to Long John and the Silver Beetles. Lennon disliked the sound of Long John, but the Silver Beetles stuck. In May they called themselves the Silver Beats; in June they were the Silver Beetles again; in July the Silver Beatles; and finally, for the trip to Hamburg, they acquired the services of their friend Pete Best on drums and renamed themselves the Beatles.[155]

When the five Beatles arrived in Hamburg, on the evening of 17 August 1960, they were not the only expatriate British group in the city. Dozens of other 'beat' groups, playing amateurish skiffle and rock and roll, made similar journeys. The British market was extremely crowded, and most of the more lucrative venues preferred to take on bands playing trad jazz, no doubt because they attracted a more affluent crowd. So British bands were brought over to the Continent in order to entertain bored American servicemen stationed in West Germany and sailors in ports like Hamburg, Amsterdam and Copenhagen. In Hamburg alone the curious punter might expect to see Dave Lee and the Staggerlees from Cornwall; the Loving Kind from Kent; the Shades Five from Kidderminster; the Nashville Teens from Weybridge; or the Hellions from Worcestershire.[156] The only real alternative, especially after the trad jazz boom began in 1961, was to stay at home and play in seaside holiday camps: Ringo Starr, for example, spent most of this period playing at Butlin's. For those who did go to the Continent it was very far from being an easy life: the pay was poor, the hours were long and the accommodation was frequently appalling. As one veteran later put it:

> When the group, giddy and stiff, finally reached its destination, they might find themselves unloading outside an auditorium plusher than the most salubrious hall they'd ever worked in Britain. The accommodation provided, however, may have sickened pigs: cramped, dingy rooms still full of the previous tenants' litter and sock-smelling frowziness; naked light bulbs coated with dust; improvised ash-trays and piss-pots; lumps of brittle plaster falling from walls so mildewed that it was as if they were covered with black-green wallpaper; not enough old camp beds to go round; waking up shivering to open-mouthed snores and the drummer breaking wind before rising to shampoo his hair in the club lavatory.[157]

The Beatles' experience of playing in Hamburg was entirely typical. They were based in the St Pauli district, a neon warren of alleys alive with the noise of bars, brothels and nightclubs, and they played at Bruno Koschmider's Indra club, a cramped, dingy cellar that doubled as a strip joint. They were put up in an immensely dirty set of rooms, perhaps better described as cubbyholes, just behind the screen in a cinema across the street, and they washed in a basin in the cinema toilets. Allan Williams and his wife had to buy blankets for them, and Williams felt a twinge of guilt that he had committed his charges to such a life of grime. The five Beatles had travelled with high hopes, but this was a very different world from the London Palladium or even the 2-Is. The Indra's clientele usually consisted of prostitutes and their customers: on the Beatles' opening night there were no more than half a dozen people watching listlessly from the audience. On stage, the British boys played in a motionless, miserable huddle, while Williams encouraged them from the bar and Koschmider shouted: 'Mak show, boys! Mak show, Beatles!'[158]

And yet, somehow, they got used to it. They had to play for four and a half hours on weekdays, and six on Saturdays and Sundays, and before long word was spreading that Koschmider had picked up an exuberant, entertaining outfit, who made up in volume for what they lacked in class. Indeed, they were so loud that the neighbours complained, and in October 1960 Koschmider moved them to a bigger and better club, the Kaiserkeller. There they played for fifty-eight nights in tandem with Rory Storm and the Hurricanes, another Liverpool group with the friendly Ringo Starr on drums. In November, however, the West German police happened to check George Harrison's passport, noticed that he was only seventeen and therefore too young to be playing after midnight, and deported him forthwith. The Beatles had already fallen out with Koschmider and had signed with a rival club manager, but when McCartney and Best went back to pick up their belongings from their cinema lodgings, they were accused of trying to burn the place down and deported in their turn. Penniless and despondent, the others followed the next day.[159]

Although the Beatles did return to Hamburg in the following two summers, performing at the Top Ten Club in 1961 and the Star Club in 1962, it was their first visit that was later elevated to the status of myth. There is no doubt that their stint in the German port had a powerful effect on their style and sound, but it would not do to exaggerate it: many other groups, after all, had similar experiences, and when the Beatles returned to Liverpool they found themselves in the doldrums once again. For all of them, however, it was certainly an experience that broadened their personal horizons, as was only natural given that they were inexperienced young men who had never before left the country. The atmosphere of Hamburg itself, the neon, the booze and the whores, was certainly something new. As one account puts it:

They saw the women who grappled in mud, cheered on by an audience tied into a protective communal bib. They visited the Roxy Bar and met ravishing 'hostesses' with tinkling laughs and undisguisably male biceps and breastbones. Two streets away where a wooden fence forbade entry to all under 18, their companions steered them through the Herbertstrasse, past red-lit shop windows containing whores in every type of fancy dress, all ages from nymphet to scolding granny, smiling or scowling forth, gossiping with one another, reading, knitting, listlessly examining their own frilly garters or spooning up bowls of soup . . .

Everything was free. Everything was easy. The sex was easy. Here you did not chase it, as in Liverpool, and clutch at it furtively in cold shop doors. Here it came after you, putting strong arms round you, mincing no words; it was unabashed, expert – indeed, professional.[160]

When the Beatles left Hamburg, they were unquestionably a far more mature outfit. After coping with the rowdy German audiences, they were louder, punchier and more self-confident, 'a charismatic powerhouse', as Pete Best put it.[161] They also left with a new look inspired by the style of the West German art-school set. During their first visit, Stuart Sutcliffe had acquired a German girlfriend, an aspiring young photographer called Astrid Kirchherr. She was what many Germans called an *Exi*, part of a bohemian, cerebral crowd who loved to read French existentialism, dress in black leather and pretend they were on the Left Bank. It was Kirchherr and her friends who first persuaded the Beatles to abandon their scruffy image and dress like good *Exis*, in smart black leather jerkins; and it was Kirchherr who first persuaded Sutcliffe to give up his greasy Teddy Boy haircut and cut it in a short fringe brushed forwards across the brow, the prototype of the famous 'mop top'.[162] The Beatles might still be far from exceptional, but they had already come a long way from the Woolton church fête.

At the end of 1960, Stuart Sutcliffe decided to take up painting full-time and stayed in Germany with Kirchherr. The rest of the band divided their time between stints in Hamburg and a steady flow of engagements in Liverpool, although they were paid very little and seemed nowhere near a national breakthrough. Part of the problem was that Fleet Street, the BBC and the leading record companies were losing interest in rock and roll, and the charts were correspondingly dominated by old-fashioned ballads and trad jazz. 'You don't seem to have the same kind of rhythm groups that we have in the States,' commented the visiting Roy Orbison in June 1962, 'and I'm sure that is what the kids want: strong, beaty rhythms that make them jump.'[163] And yet there were still plenty of groups like the Beatles in Northern cities like Liverpool; so many, in fact, that it was extremely difficult to be noticed. Live 'beat' music was still popular in clubs because it was loud, cheap and relatively easy to play; trad jazz bands, by contrast, required considerable expertise to sound anything like the popular bands of the moment.

In February 1961 the Beatles secured their first booking at the Cavern, a jazz club that had only recently converted to rock and roll, but there were plenty of rival bands and venues. According to most estimates, the

Merseyside area boasted some four hundred beat groups, and the Beatles found themselves contending with popular rivals like the Searchers, the Merseybeats, the Beatcombers, the Big Three, the Four Jays and the Undertakers, as well as Faron and the Flamingos, Kingsize Taylor and the Dominoes, Dale Roberts and the Jaywalkers, Steve Day and the Drifters, and Gerry and the Pacemakers.[164] On a typical weekend evening, a popular group might begin playing at a ballroom, dash across town to perform a set at another venue, and then end up at a nightclub like the Cavern or the Iron Door to play their loudest favourites well into the small hours.[165] The beat scene even had its own fortnightly newspaper, *Mersey Beat*, launched in July 1961 with details of hundreds of venues and little articles on the lives of the most popular groups. The first issue had a print run of five thousand copies; it sold out within a few days.[166]

One of the most enduring myths associated with the rise of the Beatles is that the Merseybeat scene was 'unique': that Liverpool, because of its effervescent local traditions and its status as a port city importing goods and ideas from across the Atlantic, was somehow predestined to produce the most popular British group of the era.[167] This is a gross exaggeration. The amateur beat boom of the early sixties was more a product of national teenage affluence than of legendary local traditions. Low unemployment, high wages and cheap credit meant that it was relatively easy for youngsters to afford a guitar, a drum kit or an amplifier, or perhaps just an evening's entertainment in a local nightclub. Liverpool certainly boasted an enormous number of beat groups as well as its own music paper; but so did dozens of other cities across the nation. Sheffield's rock and roll fans, for instance, could read *Top Star Special*; in the Midlands there was *Midland Beat*; and even in Torquay there was *South-West Scene*. Liverpool had the Cavern and the Iron Door; but Manchester could point to the Oasis, the Three Coins and the Kingfisher, Newcastle had Club-A-Go-Go and Guys and Dolls, and Glasgow had the Lindella Club and the La Cave Club.[168]

There was nothing unique about the Liverpool beat circuit. In 1961 alone thousands of similar groups were banging away all over the country, usually conforming to the four- or five-man formula and often with identical names denoting novelty, glamour or adventure. They might be called after American Indian tribes, legendary monsters, playing cards, precious stones, types of storms, cars, cats, space rockets or outlaws, and hundreds were compelled to put the word 'Blue' before their name in order to distinguish themselves from some identically named rival. At least five well-known performers boasted the surname 'Storm' – Jerry, Rory, Robb, Ricky and Danny – and there were two different groups of Stormers. In Rotherham alone there were three separate sets of Dominoes; in the West Midlands there were three groups of Fortunes; and only the true connoisseur could tell the difference between the Blue Jays, the Four Jays, the Jaymen, the Jaywalkers and the Jaybirds.[169] Most provincial towns, so often neglected by historians of the sixties, boasted groups of their own in 1961 and 1962. In Weston-super-Mare, for instance, the Winter Gardens ran a weekly 'Teenbeat Night' at which the star attractions were Ricky Ford and the Cyclones. On Thursday nights in Worcester the 'Ot Spot played host to the Cossacks and the Jaguars. In Hereford the Four Aces regularly played at the Hillside Ballroom. Not everybody was keen on the enthusiastic amateurs; jiving was still banned in many rural venues, and Gloucester Town Council banned the Sapphires from ever returning to the Guildhall because of the offensively tight trousers worn by their lead singer Rodney Dawes.[170]

The Beatles' regular venue was the Cavern on Mathew Street, a stone's throw from Liverpool's decaying docks. Eighteen stone steps led down from a grubby hatchway underneath the warehouse at No. 10 to three connected brick-vaulted tunnels, with a stage in the central tunnel. There was nothing glamorous about the Cavern: it was, in the words of one visitor, a 'sodden oven in a ravine of lofty warehouses'.[171] While the Beatles were playing, a thin sheen of condensation would form on the barrelled ceilings, dripping steadily down the brick walls onto their electrical equipment: on one occasion, it touched a naked wire, fusing the lights and an amplifier. Visitors could hardly miss the rotting, pervasive stench of damp, drains, disinfectant, sweat and cheap perfume. But it was popular. At lunchtimes, when the Beatles and other bands often played, the local warehouse workers would watch in bemusement as queues of office girls and shop assistants waited outside to hand over their shilling entrance fee, their stiletto heels clacking on the Victorian cobbles.[172] Plenty of different groups played there, but with their smart leather outfits, stage confidence and sheer volume the Beatles made the strongest impression. In his first column for *Mersey Beat*, in August 1961, the Cavern's MC Bob Wooler called them 'the biggest thing to hit the Liverpool Rock and Roll set up in years'. The real attraction, he thought, was the 'mean, moody magnificence' of the handsome drummer Pete Best, but overall they were 'rhythmic revolutionaries' and a genuine 'phenomenon'. 'Such are the fantastic Beatles,' he mused. 'I don't think anything like them will happen again.'[173]

If Wooler's readers had glanced further down the same page, they would also have seen a brief article on the latest record releases by the manager of NEMS, an electrical store and record shop in Whitechapel Street. Brian Epstein, twenty-six, was a smart and successful businessman of respectable, middle-class Jewish stock. After dropping out of RADA in his early twenties, he had returned to Liverpool to work for the Epstein family's retail business. He spent most of his time turning the NEMS electrical store into Liverpool's leading record shop, paying close attention to the tastes of his newly affluent customers. He took care to appear dapper and charming; as one old associate put it, he was 'a handsome but slight young man with a patrician air about him . . . usually dressed in a hand-tailored suit, Turnbull and Asser shirt, and a silk foulard about his neck. His imperious manner and elegant dress made him seem older than he was.'[174] But Epstein was also a fundamentally unhappy and insecure man. He drank too much, drove too fast and was regularly drawn into clandestine, unsatisfying homosexual encounters with working-class men. He had once been arrested and fined for immoral behaviour; on another occasion, in a public toilet in Derby, he was attacked and robbed by a man who later tried to blackmail him. By the autumn of 1961, he was bored with his provincial existence and was vaguely looking around for a ticket to an alternative life. The Beatles provided the answer.[175]

According to his own recollection, Epstein first saw the Beatles play one afternoon in November 1961. A week or so earlier, a local boy called Raymond Jones had come into NEMS to ask for 'My Bonnie', an amateurish single that the Beatles had recorded in Hamburg. Not only had Epstein never heard of the single, he had never even heard of the group, and he scribbled on his notepad: 'The Beatles – check on Monday.'[176] When he made some inquiries, he discovered that the unknown band was scheduled to play on 9 November at the Cavern, just 200 yards from his shop. He made the necessary arrangements, and at noon on the 9th he made his way down the cobbles of Mathew Street towards the stone steps. It was a routine lunchtime at the Cavern: a boisterous crowd in the damp, dingy cellars and the clash of the Beatles' guitars ringing around the barrel vaults. Epstein's success at NEMS meant that he was an important figure in the local music world, and the MC was even moved to announce: 'We have someone rather famous in the audience today.'[177] But Epstein looked out of place among the young throng in his dark, tailored suit, and was beginning to regret his decision to come. Then he took note of the band on stage, and was immediately impressed:

It was pretty much of an eye-opener, to go down into this darkened, dank, smoky cellar in the middle of the day, and to see crowds and crowds of kids watching these four young men on stage. They were rather scruffily dressed, in the nicest possible way, or, I should say, in the most attractive way: black leather jackets and jeans, long hair of course. And they had a rather untidy stage presentation, not terribly aware, not caring very much what they looked like. I think they cared more even then for what they sounded like. I immediately liked what I heard. They were fresh and they were honest, and they had what I thought was a sort of presence and, this is a terribly vague term, star quality.[178]

When Epstein got back to his shop, he told one of his assistants that 'they were wonderful, just wonderful. The music was the best he had heard of any beat group, loud and crazy and driving, and they were so much fun to watch, there was something infectiously happy about them.'[179] Over the next few weeks, he watched them play again at the Cavern and made more discreet inquiries around town. Finally, at the beginning of December, he invited them to NEMS and offered to become their manager. Just over a month later, the contract was signed. Epstein would take a quarter of their gross receipts; but, first, he had to get them a record contract.[180]

Epstein's version of his meeting with the Beatles leaves something to be desired. It is simply not plausible that a businessman who prided himself on his knowledge of local musical tastes would not have heard of the Beatles before November 1961. Every single issue of *Mersey Beat* had carried an article about the Beatles, and they had been featured on the front cover of the second issue. Not only did NEMS sell dozens of copies of the magazine, but Epstein himself was one of its columnists, and some witnesses later claimed to have seen him at previous Beatles appearances. In short, the story about Raymond Jones and 'My Bonnie' was merely a convenient and entertaining myth devised by their wily manager during the band's heyday in the mid-sixties.[181] That said, the result was still the same: the Beatles ended up with a flamboyant manager who was determined to turn them into national stars and bent on securing a major recording contract. Indeed, it was the Beatles' great good fortune that they were taken up with a manager of Epstein's vision, drive and apparent self-assurance. One of his first vital decisions was to clean up the boys' image. If they wanted to be taken on by a big record company, they had to look professional and

reliable. They must turn up on time; they must play an agreed programme; they must not shout or swear at the crowd; they must not eat,
drink or lark about on stage. Their black leather *Exi* jackets and jeans were
out, despite the protests of John Lennon. Instead, from March 1962, they
wore smart grey lounge suits from Burton's, with velvet collars and thin
lapels.[182]

In order to woo record company executives, Epstein prepared a brief
letter extolling the virtues of his new clients. 'These four boys, who are
superb instrumentalists, also produce some exciting and pulsating vocals,'
he wrote. 'This is a group of exceptional talents and appealing personalities.'[183] It was certainly true that, thanks to their deafening appearances at
the Cavern and elsewhere, the Beatles commanded the support of a considerable local fan base. In January 1962 *Mersey Beat* printed the results of a
poll to determine the most popular local group of the previous year, and
the Beatles came top, followed by Gerry and the Pacemakers, the Remo
Four, Rory Storm and the Hurricanes and Kingsize Taylor and the
Dominoes.[184] Many fans found it extremely frustrating that none of their
favourite bands had been able to break through to national acclaim.
'London, Take A Look Up North,' a headline in the magazine begged a
month later.[185]

The basic problem was that the national commercial climate of 1962
was not very sympathetic to groups playing American rock and roll. The
Beatles' audition with Decca on New Year's Day 1962 was a case in point.
Their material was indicative of the musical trends of the day: a mixture of
pseudo-Cockney vaudeville, revamped rock and roll hits of the fifties, and
a couple of songs that Lennon and McCartney had written themselves. It
was not a particularly impressive selection, and neither was it very well
played: the Beatles were too nervous for that. Although Decca's decision
to turn them down was later seen as a disastrous blunder, the truth is that
in the circumstances their verdict was entirely sensible. All the evidence of
the charts suggested that ballad singers and trad jazz bands, not rock and
roll bands, represented the music of the future. As Decca's head of A and
R (artists and repertoire), Dick Rowe, explained to Epstein: 'Groups are
out; four-piece groups with guitars particularly are finished.'[186] What was
more, in the stark emptiness of the studio the Beatles' musical limitations
were cruelly exposed. McCartney was palpably anxious, Lennon seemed
permanently distracted, Harrison's vocals occasionally veered off-key and
Best's range appeared extremely limited.[187] Epstein bitterly told the Decca

executives that one day his boys would be 'bigger than Elvis Presley', but in January 1962 there was no reason for an unbiased observer to share his optimism. The other record labels that he approached – Pye, Philips, Columbia and HMV – did not even give the Beatles an audition. 'You've got a good business, Mr Epstein,' one executive said, trying to be kind. 'Why not stick to it?'[188]

The Beatles' difficulties in securing a record contract are often cited as evidence of the incompetence and conservatism of British record companies in the early sixties. At the time, however, they were a markedly inferior band compared with the Fab Four that would conquer the charts two years later. Even their biggest fans could not possibly have predicted in January 1962 how much they would develop in later years, and their success was certainly not inevitable. Playing at the Cavern or in Hamburg day after day was not especially satisfying, and, of all the members of the band, it was Stuart Sutcliffe who seemed to have made the most sensible decision when he chose to stay in Germany as a painter. They were not getting any younger and could hardly expect to maintain their popularity in Liverpool indefinitely; indeed, the pop historian Alan Clayson suggests that, had they failed to strike a record deal within the next twelve months, they would probably have lost their local pre-eminence to younger groups like the Mojos or the Downliners Sect.[189] For every beat band that tasted success, there were hundreds, if not thousands, of failures, compelled to choose between a life of ageing obscurity or an alternative career. Since many chart observers thought that there was no future in groups anyway, the Beatles would not have been the only group to lose heart; and there were plenty of examples of budding musicians who gave up in the early sixties only to watch from the sidelines as their old colleagues went on to unexpected glory.[190] John Lennon was exactly the same age as Cliff Richard, Adam Faith and Billy Fury, but while they had already been household names for at least two years, he had never known real success. So it was only natural for the members of the group to be losing faith in their own endeavours, and the Beatles had already come close to splitting up in October 1961, when Lennon and McCartney bunked off to Paris for a break without telling Harrison and Best.[191] As it turned out, matters were smoothed over. But the stark truth is that had it not been for the sheer coincidence of the Beatles' encounters with Brian Epstein and George Martin, they would surely have remained just another transitory and ultimately unsuccessful skiffle band.

The Beatles owed their eventual deal with Parlophone Records to a stroke of very good fortune. On 8 February 1962, Brian Epstein took a tape of their audition material into a booth at the Oxford Street branch of the HMV record chain, where for £1 an engineer would transfer it to an acetate disc. The engineer preparing the acetate told him that it was 'not at all bad' and suggested that he take it upstairs to Syd Coleman, the head of EMI's publishing company. Coleman liked it too, and advised Epstein to arrange a meeting with the head of A and R at Parlophone Records, an EMI subsidiary.[192] When Epstein arrived five days later, he was shown in to see a man he later described as 'a stern but fair-minded housemaster': the elegant, courteous and consummately suave George Martin.[193] In fact, Martin came from a relatively humble background in North London, but his gentlemanly bearing and manners often led visitors to imagine that blue blood ran through his veins; his superiors at Parlophone joked that he was 'very twelve-inch'.[194] A trained piano and oboe player, he had studied at the Guildhall School of Music before being taken on by Parlophone. Since it was only a minor element of the EMI empire, Martin rarely handled the big stars. Instead he spent the late fifties working on light orchestral records, jazz and classical pieces, although his most notable accomplishments were comedy records by popular entertainers like Peter Ustinov and Peter Sellers, as well as live recordings of performances by the casts of *Beyond the Fringe* and *That Was The Week That Was*. In 1962 Martin was regarded as the head of a 'junk' label, but, as events were to prove, this eclectic musical background was actually the ideal preparation for working with a band as unconventional and imaginative as the Beatles in their heyday.[195]

As luck would have it, George Martin was already looking for a pop act of his own and did not immediately reject the Beatles, although he was not exactly enthusiastic. 'Frankly, the material didn't impress me,' he wrote afterwards, 'least of all their own songs. I felt that I was going to have to find suitable material for them, and was quite certain that their songwriting ability had no saleable future!' Still, he thought some of the guitar playing was fairly good, and he did like McCartney's vocals. The band also had 'an unusual quality of sound, a certain roughness that I hadn't encountered before': the legacy of Hamburg, no doubt.[196] On the evening of 6 June, the Beatles came down to the Abbey Road studios in St John's Wood for an audition. Epstein, remembering the New Year's Day debacle at the Decca studios, wisely but disingenuously told the band that the contract was already in the bag, and they were more confident this time. Martin spent much of the session sipping tea and eating biscuits in the canteen; there was no need, he reasoned, to be on hand merely for 'four berks from Liverpool'. At ten o'clock, when recording had finished and he had heard some of the material, he sat down with the exhausted group in the control room and gently told them where they were going wrong. Then he asked if there had been anything they had been unhappy with. 'Well, for a start,' said a dead-pan Harrison, 'I don't like your tie.'[197] Fortunately Martin had a sense of humour, and the meeting continued with everyone in good spirits. John Lennon was a passionate admirer of Spike Milligan and Peter Sellers, and the revelation that Martin had worked with them immediately elevated the producer to heroic status. 'The next fifteen to twenty minutes', Martin recalled, 'was pure entertainment. When they left I just sat there saying, "Phew! What do you think of that lot then?" I had tears running down my face.'[198]

The Beatles had their contract at last. One final change, however, remained to be made before they could launch their drive for national recognition. Even at their very first meeting, George Martin had decided that the drummer, Pete Best, was not up to scratch. The problem was that many of the band's admirers on Merseyside saw Best as their principal asset, a brooding, handsome icon whose drums were often positioned at the front of the stage to appeal to girls in the audience.[199] But Martin was adamant, and the other three members of the group were sufficiently ambitious to contemplate Best's departure with relative equanimity. On 15 August, after playing in a lunchtime engagement in Chester, Best gave Lennon a lift home in his car and asked what time he should pick him up the next evening. Lennon said coldly, 'Don't bother,' and quickly walked away. The following day, Epstein called Best in to his office at NEMS and told him: 'The boys want you out of the group. They don't think you're a good enough drum-mer.' Best was stunned. 'It's taken them two years', he said in disbelief, 'to find out I'm not a good enough drummer.'[200]

Such was the ruthless world of showbusiness; the Beatles had sacked Best with little more compunction than Harold Macmillan showed when dis-missing Chancellors. Many of the Beatles' fans were appalled, despite the immediate recruitment of another local drummer to replace him. Petitions flooded into the *Mersey Beat* offices, and when they played at the Cavern three days later the concert was ruined by chants of 'Pete Best for ever – Ringo never!' Harrison was even sporting a particularly fine black eye, administered by one of Best's female admirers during scuffles at the entrance to the club.[201] Still, the new drummer was unquestionably a musical improvement. The son of a barmaid and a bakery worker, Ringo Starr had spent several years playing for Rory Storm and the Hurricanes, knew the members of the Beatles well, and had a wider range than did his predecessor. His philosophical, self-effacing and good-humoured personality was ideally suited to a group in which three overbearing egos were already competing for attention, and over the next eight years it was often Ringo who kept his colleagues' spirits high and their feet on the ground. The most underrated of the Beatles, he was also in many ways the most immediately likeable.[202]

The swift dismissal of Pete Best left little doubt that, for all their cheeky irreverence, the Beatles were an intensely ambitious group of people. Despite their experiences in Hamburg, they also had surprisingly conservative cultural tastes. In February 1963, for instance, the *NME* made them the subject of its 'Life-lines' questionnaire feature, and the results suggested that they were not especially different from thousands of other young men of their age and background. John Lennon and George Harrison nominated tea as their favourite drink, and all but Lennon chose Brigitte Bardot as their favourite actress; he nominated Sophia Loren. All but Ringo Starr nominated 'girls' among their hobbies; instead Ringo chose 'night-driving, sleeping, [and] Westerns'. There were also already signs of a taste for whimsy: McCartney's personal ambition was 'to have my picture in the *Dandy*', while Starr's dislikes were 'onions and Donald Duck'. And even in such a rudimentary exercise there were glimpses of the distinctive personalities of the four men. McCartney's professional ambition was musical: 'to popularise our sound'. Lennon's was more mercenary: 'to be rich and famous'. Both McCartney and Lennon mentioned their love of songwriting, although only Lennon described himself as an author of 'poems and plays'; and only Lennon could have entered under 'dislikes' the words 'Stupid people'. Rather more touchingly, Starr's favourite songwriters were Burt Bacharach and 'McCartney and Lennon', while his personal ambition was simply 'to be happy'.[203] As for George Harrison, his answers were the shortest and least revealing of all, but perhaps his defining trait became apparent a year later when the Beatles visited New York and he told an interviewer that his ambition was 'to retire with a whacking great pile of money'.[204]

The undisputed 'leader' of the group at this stage was still John Lennon, who was also the only remaining member from the line-up that had played at the Woolton church fête in July 1957. He was the most aggressive and outspoken of the four Beatles, as well as the only member with his own microphone, to stage right. McCartney and Harrison had to share a microphone, to stage left. Ironically, George Martin originally planned to install McCartney as leader and vocalist because of his stronger voice, but this idea never took off. As far as the public was concerned, Lennon in 1962 and 1963 had founded and 'led' the group, while even McCartney, despite his talents, deferred to his older colleague in interviews and recording sessions.[205] The personality differences between the two men that were to divide their fans for decades to come were already strongly apparent, and it is unlikely that they would have become teenage companions had it not been for their shared musical obsession. Where Lennon was blunt, caustic and rebellious, McCartney was emollient, easy-going and dependable. In Hamburg Lennon gobbled down amphetamines as if there were no tomorrow, but McCartney generally stuck to beer.[206] McCartney himself later mused:

> People always assume that John was the hard-edged one and I was the soft-edged one, so much so that over the years I've come to accept that . . . [But] John, because of his upbringing and his unstable family life, had to be hard, witty, always ready for the cover-up, ready for the riposte, ready with the sharp little witticism. Whereas with my comfortable upbringing, a lot of family, a lot of people, very northern, 'Cup of tea, love?', my surface grew to be easy-going. Put people at their ease. Chat to people, be nice, it's nice to be nice.[207]

In spite of their differences, the two men made a formidable partnership; indeed, it was probably the fact that their temperaments were so different that made them such a creative team. They had begun writing together as teenagers in the late summer of 1957. Lennon would come over to McCartney's house in Allerton, and they would sit in the living room with their guitars and an old school notebook. 'I would write down anything we came up with,' McCartney remembered, 'starting at the top of the first page with "A Lennon–McCartney Original". On the next page, "Another Lennon–McCartney Original". All the pages have got that. We saw ourselves as very much the next great songwriting team.'[208] Although some sources claim that they produced as many as two hundred songs during this early period, this seems very unlikely indeed: in reality, only two dozen or so have been identified.[209] McCartney himself admitted that although they would 'try and persuade people that we had about a hundred songs before "Love Me Do"', the truth was that 'it was more like four – less than twenty, anyway'.[210] What was more, far from seeing themselves as the next great songwriters, they evidently had very little confidence in their own output, and were more used to playing other people's material. Only under pressure from George Martin, especially after the success of their first releases, did the two men begin to write with greater fluency and self-confidence.[211]

The important thing now was to score an initial hit, no matter how modest, and then move on quickly; commercial success was all about momentum. One single would lead to another, they might then be able to record an EP record, then an LP, then go on tour, and so on. Yet, for all the support of George Martin and Parlophone, success was by no means guaranteed, especially since beat groups were still not considered very fashionable. In the first published chart of the year, the top five positions were held by Cliff Richard and the Shadows, Elvis Presley, Frank Ifield, Rolf Harris and Duane Eddy. And in the *NME*'s annual readers' survey, published in January 1963, the top six acts were Elvis Presley, Cliff Richard, Frank Ifield, the Shadows, Acker Bilk and Billy Fury. The Beatles, who had released their first single three months earlier, finished in joint 111th place with Mike Berry, the Clyde Valley Stompers and Norman Vaughan, and nobody was predicting great things for any of them. Even in the 'British Small Group' table the Beatles were not particularly popular:

1.	Shadows	45,951
2.	Tornados	15,051
3.	John Barry Seven	2292
4.	Acker Bilk	2025
5.	Kenny Ball	2025
6.	Peter Jay/Jaywalkers	843
7.	Temperance Seven	747
8.	Beatles	735
9.	Sounds Incorporated	732
10.	Joe Brown's Bruvvers	684

According to the poll, the Shadows were more popular than all the other groups added together; only the Tornados were even vaguely comparable.[212]

Both the Shadows and the Tornados were guitar-based instrumental groups, and they had made their name backing Cliff Richard and Billy Fury respectively. The Shadows were by far the most popular group in Britain between 1960 and 1963: indeed, they were probably the only group that had any genuine pretensions to stardom. Their first instrumental hit, 'Apache', had been number one for six weeks in 1960, and four more chart-topping singles followed. Some critics now see their success as a symptom of the decline of British popular music in the early sixties, the argument being that instrumental music only thrived because of the failings of vocal artists.[213] But in many ways their influence has been underrated, and although the Beatles sounded very different from the Shadows, they did build on their achievements. Not since Lonnie Donegan had any British musician done as much to popularise the guitar as Hank Marvin, the Shadows' lead guitarist.[214] And as Alan Clayson argues, the band's line-up also established the balance of pop and rock groups for the next two decades. From the Shadows onwards, the basic line-up of a rock group consisted of three guitarists (lead, rhythm and bass) and a drummer. Keyboard, brass and woodwind players were only used occasionally, and although some groups with keyboards and horn sections did continue, like the John Barry Seven and the Jaywalkers, they were really too unwieldy to be viable. Even the Beatles' new smart appearance had been inspired by the Shadows: in putting the Beatles into shiny grey suits from Burton's, Brian Epstein had simply been copying the example of the most popular guitar group in the country.[215]

The first track that the Beatles recorded with George Martin was 'How Do You Do It', an undemanding, breezy number already written by Mitch Murray. Martin was, quite correctly, convinced that it had the potential to be a big hit, but the Beatles disliked it. Instead they preferred 'Love Me Do', which had been written by Paul McCartney in 1958 when he was just sixteen. With its harmonica sound and open harmonies, 'Love Me Do' was something a little different: the band thought of it as 'bluesy' and Martin was persuaded that its stark simplicity would stand out from the usual chart material.[216] In September 1962 he told a meeting of EMI label chiefs that Parlophone was about to put out a single by a group called the Beatles. Most of the other executives thought that it was another of his comedy records, and one even asked: 'Is it Spike Milligan in disguise?' 'I told them, "I'm serious,"' Martin later recalled. '"This is a great group, and we're going to hear a lot from them." But nobody took much notice.'[217] In the event, 'Love Me

Do' came out on 5 October. Its performance was solid, if not spectacular: a peak chart position of seventeenth was not bad for a debut single, even though George Martin himself was privately disappointed.[218]

By the New Year the Beatles had already recorded their next single, 'Please Please Me'. Originally written by John Lennon, it was a brooding ballad in the style of Roy Orbison, but George Martin suggested that Lennon and McCartney add a harmonica introduction, speed the song up and rearrange it for harmonised voices. After the final take, he pressed the intercom button in the control room and calmly said into the microphone: 'Congratulations, gentlemen. You have just made your first Number One.'[219] As MacDonald remarks: 'That he was right is less remarkable than that someone of his age and background should have understood music as new and rough-hewn as The Beatles' well enough to see that emphasising its quirks would improve it.' Indeed, the changes to 'Please Please Me' were a good example of Martin's pivotal importance. He was an accomplished musician and producer in his own right, but, more importantly, his experience with comic and novelty records meant that he handled his protégés with an iconoclastic tolerance that no other producer in Britain could match.[220] And if the Beatles had any doubts about his judgement, these were now triumphantly allayed. On 16 February, while the Beatles were plodding across the snow-bound countryside supporting Helen Shapiro on a nationwide tour, they heard the news that 'Please Please Me' had soared to number two in the charts. Then, on 2 March, just as winter's grip was beginning to slacken, came the best news of all. The Beatles, sixty-eight long months after the Woolton church fête, had finally made it to number one.[221]

It would have been only natural at this point for the Beatles to stop and savour the moment. But what marked them out from many of their rivals was that their initial achievement simply spurred them to work even harder, and the sensational scandals and political dramas of the next nine months were therefore played out against a soundtrack of successive Beatles hits. In May their third single, 'From Me to You', also went to number one, where it remained for seven weeks. In the same month their first album, *Please Please Me*, recorded in one gruelling twelve-hour marathon, reached the top of the LP charts. John Lennon and Paul McCartney had written half of the songs themselves, which was unusual in a debut album and reflected their growing confidence under George

Martin's tutelage. As he pushed them for new material, so the two men wrote at an even faster pace and with greater professionalism. They had become, in the words of one critic, 'a firm, businesslike partnership, taking their writing craft seriously, intent on not merely staying competent at it but getting better all the time'.[222] 'Please Please Me' had been their first mature composition, and for the next six months or so Lennon and McCartney worked together at a furious pace, 'one on one, eyeball to eyeball', as Lennon later put it. This 'fifty–fifty' collaboration was something of a new development, but it did not last; by the end of 1963 they were both writing independently again, and the last genuine bar-by-bar collaboration, 'Can't Buy Me Love', was recorded in March 1964.[223] It was only at this point that their songwriting credit was changed from 'McCartney–Lennon' to 'Lennon–McCartney'. Despite the predictable ridicule that greeted McCartney's attempts to change it back forty years later, 'McCartney–Lennon' had in fact been the original credit. It was a mark of the sheer competitiveness of the partnership, and of Lennon's fundamental insecurity when challenged by McCartney's increasing productivity in the summer of 1963, that it had ever been changed in the first place.[224]

By the middle of 1963 the phenomenon of 'Beatlemania', with its crowds of screaming teenage fans, enormous record sales, regular television appearances and admiring newspaper coverage, was already under way.[225] Much of this can be attributed simply to the popular appeal of the Beatles themselves, who were regularly producing hits of unsurpassed quality and consistency. But it is also notable that from the very beginning the Beatles were treated remarkably sympathetically by the media, especially when compared with, say, the Rolling Stones. Their first appearance in the national press, an *Evening Standard* interview by Maureen Cleave in January 1963, set the tone for what followed:

> The Beatles made me laugh immoderately, the way I used to laugh as a child at the *Just William* books. Their wit was just so keen and sharp – John Lennon's especially. They all had this wonderful quality – it wasn't innocence, but everything was new to them. They were like William, finding out about the world and trying to make sense of it.[226]

In fact the press, had they chosen, could probably have destroyed the Beatles' career almost before it had begun. The members of the band smoked and drank with abandon, casually took their pick of their female devotees, and generally behaved in a manner likely to horrify most of their fans' parents. They bickered among themselves and, when on tour, did not always conceal their disdain for playing the same material night after night.[227] On 18 June, at McCartney's twenty-first birthday party, Lennon violently attacked the Cavern's master of ceremonies Bob Wooler, an old friend of the group. Wooler was so badly injured that he was later sent a payment for damages. His offence had been to intimate that the close relationship between Lennon and Brian Epstein was more than a platonic friendship, and indeed it did seem strange to some people that Lennon had gone on holiday with Epstein to Spain that summer rather than spend time with his wife Cynthia and baby son, or even go away with the other three band members. All the same, there was only one brief piece in the *Daily Mirror* three days afterwards, and the rest of the press simply ignored the story.[228]

The truth was that there was no market for a scandal involving the Beatles, because the front pages were already full of far better scandals involving the Macmillan government, Soviet spies and teenage callgirls. As so often in their career, and by accident rather than design, the Beatles' timing was perfect. At the precise moment when the crooked, weary self-indulgence of the Establishment had never been more manifest, the band's northern accents immediately associated them with honesty, dynamism and authenticity. Northerners, and Lancastrians in particular, had for years been presented by working-class entertainers as plain-speaking, independent and warm-hearted types, and the Beatles fell nicely into the same category. They were the heirs of George Formby and Albert Finney as well as Elvis Presley and Chuck Berry.[229] 'Who are the Beatles?' asked the *Daily Mirror* in September. 'They are pleasing to look at, friendly of manner . . . [They prefer] tea and cakes rather than Dry Martini with a twist of lemon.'[230] The country might be sinking into the gutter, dragged down by Americanisation, aristocratic decadence and political corruption, but the Beatles proved that four ordinary lads from Liverpool, with all the decent virtues of their provincial environment, could still woo an audience better than any jumped-up crooner straight off the flight from New York. The *Evening Standard* explained:

The Beatles are the first people to make rock 'n' roll respectable . . . They have won over the class snob, the intellectual snob, the music snob, the grown ups and the husbands . . . They appeal to the family, they appeal to the nation. Liverpool and the North are fiercely proud and now the rest of England has taken them over.[231]

Even the Beatles' designated characteristics – Lennon's dry wit, McCartney's boyish good looks and Harrison's shyness – worked in their favour, cementing the impression of old-fashioned simplicity. 'Ringo is not the world's most inventive drummer,' commented George Melly of the band's fourth member, 'but he *is* lovably plain, a bit "thick" as a public persona, and decidedly ordinary in his tastes. He acts as a bridge, a reassuring proof that the Beatles bear some relation to ordinary people.'[232] The Beatles, in other words, were ideal cultural icons for an era in which Harold Wilson – another Northern grammar-school boy – was catching the public imagination with his attacks on the 'aristocratic cabal' that was mismanaging the nation's affairs.[233] In some ways, then, Beatlemania was a deliberate media creation, a matter of coincidental timing as much as musical ability. And once the majority of Fleet Street editors had decided to promote the Beatles as the innocent antithesis to the corruption of the Conservative government in the summer of 1963, it was extremely difficult for anyone to disagree. 'You *had* to write it that way,' remarked one correspondent afterwards. 'You knew that if you didn't, the *Sketch* would and the *Express* would and the *Mail* and the *Standard* would. You were writing in self-defence.'[234]

In January 1963 Lennon had announced: 'We all want to get rich so that we can retire. We don't want to go straight or get to be all-round entertainers.'[235] It was the Beatles' good fortune to be breaking into the charts at a time when the record market, and therefore the scope for immense commercial success, was never greater. The obvious example was the case of Frank Ifield, an Australian singer notorious for his falsetto yodelling, who in late 1962 and early 1963 became the first artist to release three consecutive number-one singles. What was more, his first number one, 'I Remember You', had itself been the first single to sell more than a million copies in England alone.[236] What distinguished Ifield from his predecessors was not that he was a better singer; it was that he was appealing to a bigger, more visible and more enthusiastic teenage market. 'CALL THEM SPENDAGERS!' began the *Daily Mirror*'s latest investigation into teenage spending, published on 2 October 1963. There were, the writer estimated, some five and a half million teenagers in Britain, spending an annual total of £1000 million and buying fifty million records a year.[237] Overall record sales had increased by more than twelve times in the preceding eight years, and the annual turnover of the pop industry now reached over £100 million a year.[238] The national press now paid far more attention to popular music and teenage tastes than before; even the *Telegraph* was about to begin printing the weekly Top Ten.[239] In this context, Beatlemania looked rather like an accident waiting to happen. True, in the late fifties there had been frenetic bursts of enthusiasm for Bill Haley and Elvis Presley, but by 1963 the potential for a new British act to inspire widespread popular devotion and sell millions of records was simply much greater. Had the Beatles not broken through, it is plausible that some other group might have done so instead.

The Beatles' other great advantage was that they appeared to offer their listeners something new. To begin with, they were a guitar group in a market swollen with solo singers. Until the beginning of 1963, vocalists had been much more popular than groups. Trad jazz bands led by the likes of Acker Bilk and instrumental guitar bands such as the Shadows had occasionally challenged Elvis Presley and Cliff Richard for commercial supremacy, but the singers had generally come out on top with material written by professional songwriters. Indeed, Richard had just enjoyed his most successful year yet, with another number one, two number twos, several film appearances and multiple outings on television variety shows and at almost every major theatre in Britain.[240] And yet, although the head of Decca had famously dismissed guitar groups as 'finished' in January 1962, there were signs even before 'Please Please Me' made it to number one that audiences were becoming tired of single vocalists. 'Groups are in!' announced the *NME* on 15 February 1963, adding that 'record fans are growing tired of the insipid droning of the solo voice'.[241]

By the end of the year, the momentum clearly lay with electrically amplified guitar groups like Gerry and the Pacemakers, the Dave Clark Five and the Beatles themselves. What was more, most of these new groups wrote their own music and wanted to make their own decisions about their look, sound and direction. Their success therefore marked the climax of the amateur spirit that had animated the booms in skiffle and beat music at the turn of the decade. As Ian MacDonald puts it:

> What was different about 1963 and the decades which followed was that the balance of power in deciding the direction and content of pop music began to shift from a corps of professionals – managers,

songwriters, producers, publishers, record executives, radio station pro-
prietors and record shop owners – to a body of young amateurs whose
connection with the industry's audience was as close as could be: these
young amateurs *were* that audience cast in proto-professional form.[242]

In the *NME* readers' survey at the end of 1962 the top six acts had been
Elvis Presley, Cliff Richard, Frank Ifield, the Shadows, Acker Bilk and Billy
Fury. Only Ifield was a newcomer, and he was really a teenage heartthrob in
the old style. Even in the 'small group' section of the same poll, six of the
seven groups that finished above the Beatles had already been nationally
well known for two years or more.[243] The Beatles, by contrast, were barely
known at all outside the Liverpool circuit, and therefore seemed to be pioneering an entirely new sound. For the dedicated fans of older acts like Cliff
Richard, this was an unwelcome innovation. 'Are you going to let Britain's
king of talent be beaten by a flash-in-the-pan group like the Beatles?' one
correspondent implored her fellow fans in the *NME* on 5 April.[244] Cliff himself was less than impressed with his new rivals and their 'five year old
music'. 'All they've done is revert to rock 'n' roll,' he explained to the *Daily
Mirror*. 'We've played the whole thing down, the screaming and the raving.
The Beatles have stoked the whole thing up again . . . Their stuff is real
homemade music. Anybody who can shout can be a Beatle.'[245] At the same
time, he recognised that there was no sense in fighting them on their own
territory; he was better off sticking to ballads and family material. 'We are
not going to contest the beat groups,' he admitted in November. 'We'll carrying on doing what we are doing until the public stops buying our
records.'[246] In his case, they never did.

To their old rivals on the beat circuit, the public perception of the
Beatles as groundbreaking pioneers was an irritating myth. '[They] have
nothing new about their sound,' the producer Joe Meek complained to
Melody Maker in May 1963. 'Cliff Bennett and the Rebel Rousers have been
doing the same thing for a year, and so has Joe Brown.'[247] George Harrison
himself admitted that their music was 'typical of a hundred groups in our
area. We were lucky. We got away with it first.'[248] But this also worked to
their advantage: what many beat fans found inspirational about the Beatles
was that they were only the most accomplished representatives of the kind
of people who played similar music in cities and towns the length and
breadth of Britain. By Christmas, even the unlikeliest town had its own
guitar group with a loyal coterie of fans convinced that their heroes, given

the chance, could be just as big as the Beatles. The West Midlands were a case in point. Coventry boasted the Sorrows, Cheltenham had the Talismen, and Henley-in-Arden produced Ken Jackson and his Strangers. In the pubs of Birmingham there was some talk of the Solihull Sound as a challenger to Merseybeat, although sadly neither the Applejacks nor the Rinki-Dinks quite caught the public's imagination and the Solihull Sound disappeared into obscurity.[249] An equally unfortunate end awaited the Tewkesbury Sound when the Severnbeats discovered that success in Gloucestershire did not necessarily lead to global stardom. Still, there was no harm in trying. The Andover Sound might appear a contradiction in terms, but when the Troggs secured their first number one in 1966, Hampshire was vindicated.[250]

Liverpool, meanwhile, was the flavour of the month. In some ways this was a development of previous trends; the novels and films of the New Wave, for instance, had already strengthened the association of Northern culture with values like vigour, authenticity and imagination. Nobody, however, could have predicted at the beginning of 1963 that the decaying port of Liverpool would become fashionable. But the media and the record companies had every reason to embrace the Mersey Sound, for Brian Epstein's record as an impresario was simply stunning. As soon as the Beatles had reached number one, everything he touched turned to gold. In March, his second group, Gerry and the Pacemakers, reached number one with their debut, 'How Do You Do It', the very song that George Martin had initially pressed upon the Beatles. In June, Billy J. Kramer and the Dakotas had a debut number one with 'Do You Want to Know a Secret', a song written by Lennon and McCartney. In July, Gerry and the Pacemakers topped the chart again with 'I Like It'. In August, Billy J. Kramer recaptured the top spot with 'Bad to Me', another Lennon–McCartney composition. In November, Gerry and the Pacemakers were back at number one with 'You'll Never Walk Alone'. In twelve months, Epstein, a virtual unknown at the beginning of the year, had been responsible for no fewer than eight number ones. At one point, his artists even held the top three places in the chart, an achievement unmatched in the history of pop music.[251]

By July, when another Liverpool group, the Searchers, made it to number one with 'Sweets for My Sweet', almost every record company executive in Britain was desperate to find a beat band of his own, preferably complete with mop-tops and Scouse accent. Any Merseybeat band without a record contract by the end of the year was clearly doing something wrong. Kingsize Taylor signed with Decca; the Undertakers and the Chants signed with Pye; the Merseybeats went with Fontana; and both Faron's Flamingos and Rory Storm and the Hurricanes found a home at Oriole. Even Pete Best secured a deal with Decca, the company that had turned down the Beatles now signing up the man the Beatles had themselves rejected.[252] Poets like Roger McGough and Brian Patten found themselves the unexpected beneficiaries of the vogue for all things Liverpudlian.[253] Television camera crews trudged down Mathew Street to the Cavern, looking for the secrets of the Beatles' success, and the distinctive slang used by the city's teenagers – *gear*, *fab*, *endsville* and so on – was taken up by young fans across the country. McCartney recalled seeing the script of their first film, *A Hard Day's Night*, which had been entrusted to the kitchen-sink playwright Alun Owen. Owen had them saying words like *neb* and *grotty*, which he claimed were local colloquialisms, even though McCartney admitted they were words 'none of us used'. Still, the Beatles played along. They knew what the public wanted.[254]

On 26 June, killing time before their evening performance at the Majestic Ballroom in Newcastle, Paul McCartney and John Lennon sat in their hotel room, smoking and talking 'in the afternoon daylight'. McCartney had an idea for a song that would recast the clichéd lyric 'I Love You' in the third person, and the two men began scribbling some notes on a piece of paper. The next day was a day off, and they finished the new song in McCartney's family home in Liverpool, before a less than appreciative audience:

> We sat in there . . . just beavering away while my dad was watching TV and smoking his Players cigarettes, and we wrote 'She Loves You'. We actually finished it there because we'd started it in the hotel room. We went into the living room – 'Dad, listen to this. What do you think?' So we played it to my dad and he said, 'That's very nice, son, but there's enough of these Americanisms around. Couldn't you sing, "She loves you. Yes! Yes! Yes!"' At which point we collapsed in a heap and said, 'No, Dad, you don't quite get it!'[255]

For all Jim McCartney's objections, the Beatles' lyrics and melody were working together better than ever. When the song was finally recorded, on 1 July, the result was refreshingly exuberant. Indeed, the famous 'yeah, yeah, yeah' refrain became the band's trademark for the next couple of years; for many European teenagers they were known simply as the Yeah-Yeahs, and in France pop was nicknamed *yé-yé* or *yeh-yeh* music. Demand for the new single was already so great that in the next four weeks Parlophone produced more than a quarter of a million copies, largely to fulfil advance orders, and when 'She Loves You' was released on 23 August it went straight to number one, their third successive chart-topping hit. It would become the biggest-selling single of their career. For a group that had been virtually unknown nine months before, this was a tremendous accomplishment, and it would not be their last.[256]

14

LIVE NOW, PAY LATER

BRITAIN BOTTOM OF THE CLASS.

The Guardian, 9 April 1962

Old mac, he's hed of Skool as if you didnt kno . . . it doesnt look as if hes going to be Hed of Skool much longer wotever he do.

Private Eye, 15 June 1962

In the aftermath of the Night of the Long Knives, Harold Macmillan's political prospects had rarely seemed less encouraging. Only one in three voters was satisfied with his leadership, and the vultures of Fleet Street were beginning to circle. In private, as he took himself off for the parliamentary recess in August 1962, Macmillan told a friend that although 'it was a terribly painful job to make these recent changes, I am more and more convinced that I was right not to shrink from my duties'. He was physically exhausted: his hands were 'very stiff' and his eyes were 'deteriorating – stupidly'. Nonetheless, he remained defiant in the face of adversity, adding: 'I hope to still be able to see – and kill – a few grouse'. Politically, too, he was still clinging obstinately to life, and when he returned to London after a few weeks' rest, he had recaptured his enthusiasm for the job. It was time, he felt, for the government to roll up their sleeves, set 'an expansionist course', and begin the long march back to electoral popularity.[1]

Carried away by the rush to condemn 'Mac the Knife', contemporary critics often overlooked the fact that Macmillan's purge had paved the way for an influx of fresh new faces in the Cabinet: Keith Joseph at Housing, Edward Boyle at Education, and William Deedes as the new Minister of Information, for instance. If the Night of Long Knives had left the Prime Minister looking a rather old, isolated figure, it had also ushered in a brighter, more imaginative line-up than his previous team. Rab Butler later mused that it was 'one of the strongest young Cabinets of the century'.[2] The most important figure would be the new Chancellor. As early as 19 April, Tim Bligh had sent Macmillan a minute suggesting that after Lloyd left the Treasury they should appoint 'the right sort of man, young, tough, imaginative, politically strong and publicly articulate'.[3] The obvious candidate, and the eventual selection, was Reginald Maudling, who immediately became the popular front-runner to replace Macmillan when he retired as party leader.

At forty-five, Maudling was relatively young, but he already had the reputation of an intellectual heavyweight who could quite happily give elegant and incisive speeches about economics from a few scribbled notes on the back of an envelope; the Labour MP Douglas Jay thought that he had 'by far the best economic mind, together with Gaitskell, in the House of Commons in the thirty years I was a Member'.[4] Articulate and supremely self-confident, Maudling was an upper-middle-class scholarship boy who became most famous for his open love of a very good life. Nobody in Westminster could fail to know that 'Reggie' 'liked a good lunch'.[5] The political journalist Alan Watkins noted:

> Unlike Iain Macleod, who was a member of White's club, he did not aspire to the Tory *beau monde*. He was solidly bourgeois and highly intelligent. He liked good wine, whisky and Havana cigars. He was not, however, at all fussy. I once asked him, in Annie's Bar, what sort of whisky he liked. 'Large ones,' he replied.[6]

In his memoirs, Maudling cheerfully admitted that as a child he had been 'the fattest boy in the school'; that he had spent much of his Oxford career consuming 'vast quantities of beer'; and that despite his first-class degree he had been 'of a rather lazy disposition, and not a meticulous scholar in any sense at all'. Travelling around the world by cruise liner after leaving Oxford, he spent one 'very pleasant evening' drinking with the crew in a Buenos Aires nightclub, before waking 'rather stiff and uncomfortable on the floor of the second mate's cabin'. 'Unfortunately,' he noted ruefully, 'it was the wrong ship.'[7]

Despite this early misfortune, Maudling had no intention of giving up his pursuit of earthly pleasure. As a promising junior minister, he once spent a morning closeted with his advisers 'conducting a scientific analysis of the relative merits of various vintage ports', before sauntering down to the Commons front bench. Some time passed, and his concentration began to drift. 'Gradually I became aware that something was amiss,' he later recalled. 'I opened one eye cautiously trying to pretend that I had been awake all the time, only to hear some Member putting to the Chair as a Point of Order, "Mr Speaker, is it in order for the Minister of Supply to snore so loudly that we cannot hear Sir Gerald Nabarro?"'[8] Even after he had been appointed as Macmillan's new Chancellor, Maudling seemed to cultivate an impression of general loucheness. One contemporary profile noted that 'at important conferences his habit of sitting slumped in a chair and the permanent blue shadow across his heavy chin combined to suggest that instead of sitting up all night working on government briefs, he had just wandered in from watching a floor-show in a night-club'.[9] At one point, Maudling later recalled, he also took to wearing 'a light-blue dinner jacket which I had recently acquired and of which I was rather proud'. When his Chancellor turned up to an important dinner in the new jacket, Macmillan took one look at him and said coolly: 'Ah, Reggie, playing the drums at the 400 Club again tonight, I see.' Maudling never wore it again.[10]

With his boundless affability and frank materialism, Maudling seemed the ideal choice to guide Britain into economic recovery and the Conservatives to victory in the next election. Within a few months of his appointment, in fact, he was being bombarded with advice from both 10 Downing Street and the popular press to 'stop dawdling' and take action to reflate the stagnant economy. Unemployment was steadily rising, and both output and demand were still disappointingly low. The Chancellor yielded at the beginning of October, releasing special deposits and cutting bank rate, and the following month he reduced purchase tax on cars from 45 per cent to 25, as well as adding a further £100 million to the package in investment incentives. All of these measures amounted to the equivalent of a shilling off income tax, and when more reflationary steps followed in the New Year, Maudling's expansionist commitments seemed unassailable.[11] Even this, however, was not enough for Macmillan and those commentators who demanded a faster and faster rate of growth with little heed for the potential dangers of inflation, as if to compensate for the national gloom that followed the worst winter weather in more than a hundred years. In Macmillan's eyes, the forthcoming budget must be the centrepiece of the Conservatives' campaign for re-election the following year. 'The Budget should be a great national plan for expansion,' he wrote to his Chancellor on 22 February. 'This would give

great local encouragement as well as the feeling of a national forward movement.'[12] Four days later, he wrote again: 'The Budget and all that goes with
the Budget will be the key to the success or failure of the Government, the
Party and in my view of the country's effort over the next period . . . The
whole country is waiting for what is called a lead.' What he wanted, in short,
was 'a national campaign for expanding the economy', supported by loans
from foreign banks and the IMF. If there was a danger of a balance of payments crisis, Macmillan suggested that they could forestall it by such
imaginative measures as import controls, selling off their overseas invest-
ments (the dollar portfolio) and even allowing the pound to float freely on
the exchange markets. With these mechanisms in place, he thought that
Maudling could afford to give away some £400 million in tax cuts, an enormous injection of spending power into the economy that would certainly
unleash a period of breakneck growth.[13]

Maudling was a gambler by temperament, but even he recognised that
Macmillan's figure of £400 million was far too high; as his Treasury advisers pointed out, the consequences would probably be an overheating
economy and rampant inflation, meaning that Maudling would then
have to raise taxes and interest rates again in 1964, just before the anticipated election. Instead, they settled on tax cuts of £260 million, consisting
largely of personal allowance increases and tax reductions in the lower
income bands in order to encourage everyday consumption.[14] These were
unveiled in Maudling's budget on 3 April 1963, which its author admitted
was 'designed on an ambitious scale' and became known in the press as the
'Maudling Experiment' or the 'Dash for Growth'.[15] The fundamental
premise for Maudling's approach was that only by rapid and dynamic economic growth could Britain break out of the tedious cycle of boom and
bust, stop–go fiscal policy and eternal payments crises; and if that growth
were sustained, then inflation would not become a problem. As Edmund
Dell explains:

> According to the theory predominant among politicians of all parties,
> faster growth was the answer to inflation and, by reducing unit costs,
> it was the key to successful exporting and hence to solving the balance
> of payments constraint . . . There would be a virtuous circle. The
> British economy in spate would, perhaps after an anxious interval, con-
> tain inflation by satisfying the desire for an expanded standard of living,
> and balance the nation's payments through surging exports.[16]

So income tax was cut, state spending was increased, and there were plenty of measures to encourage more and more investment. 'The theme of this Budget', Maudling told the Commons, 'is expansion: expansion without inflation, expansion that can be sustained.'[17] This was not merely audacious pump-priming; it was electioneering of the most blatant kind, and most Conservative backbenchers were delighted. And yet if Maudling was criticised, it was for not having been generous enough. 'Damn the torpedoes,' quipped *The Economist*, 'half speed ahead.'[18] James Callaghan, the Shadow Chancellor, commented: 'In my view, the Chancellor has been too cautious,' and called for a more 'sudden spurt' before settling down to growth of 4 per cent or so. Two of the most celebrated brains on the Labour benches, Anthony Crosland and Roy Jenkins, agreed that Maudling had been too parsimonious: Crosland said that he had 'acted on the cautious side', while Jenkins condemned his 'half-hearted approach to expansion'.[19] When the true consequences of Maudling's generosity became clear a year or so later, they could hardly claim to occupy the moral high ground.

The most visible result of Maudling's dash for growth was a new, exuberant wave of consumer spending, the fruits of which could be found in homes and garages across the country. It was no accident that, while Reginald Maudling was poring over figures in the Treasury, the Beatles, James Bond and Mary Quant were becoming household names across the nation. Throughout the fifties and sixties, as we have seen, British families bought cars and television sets, fridges and washing machines, new houses and foreign holidays, telephones and paperbacks and records and clothes, all the paraphernalia of a society becoming increasingly focused on consumerism as an activity and a source of self-definition. By 1964, after thirteen years of Conservative economic management, annual consumer expenditure had in real terms doubled. But Maudling's period at the Treasury certainly marked the high noon of consumer spending, not least because his tax cuts effectively amounted to a wage increase of 2 per cent for the average worker.[20] Indeed, between 1959 and 1964 the real wages of manual workers alone increased by some 19 per cent. The proportion of homeowners increased from 37 per cent (1959) to 44 per cent (1964). In both cases, the real increases had come under Maudling's economic stewardship rather than those of Amory or Lloyd. During Amory's last year at the Treasury, there were more than five million motor vehicles on the roads; when Maudling finally left the building, four years later, there were almost nine million. Hire-purchase was more popular than ever, and by

1964, nine-tenths of all households owned an electric iron and a television set; three-quarters owned a vacuum cleaner; half owned a washing machine; and a third owned a fridge.[21]

Even before Maudling's dash for growth began, critics were worried that Britain was sinking into a morass of avarice and selfishness. At the beginning of 1960, for instance, the *New Statesman* had declared:

> Few tears will be shed for the fifties. Cynical, meretricious, selfish, the decade made the rich richer, the poor poorer. To the advanced countries of the West it brought unprecedented prosperity, achieved largely at the expense of the vast and growing proletariats of Africa and Asia . . .
>
> The Tories imprisoned homosexuals and prostitutes – and pacifists. But they allowed the striptease joint and the drinking club to multiply . . . They made Britain into a windfall state, a national casino with loaded dice; and when violence and dishonesty increased they clamoured for the birch.[22]

This was not the only expression of unease with the ambitious materialism of what the *Guardian* called the 'bingo age'.[23] Michael Shanks complained that the 'spirit of 1960' was 'the Janus-face of the semi-affluent society, with its cars and washing machines on the "never-never", its gossip column heroes and Soho strip clubs, its feverish pursuit of a prosperity it can never really bring itself to believe in'.[24] Macmillan himself seemed to have lost his grip on the electorate's affections: no longer the symbol of national recovery after Suez, he had become, in Gaitskell's scornful words, 'the great architect of complacency and the materialistic outlook'.[25] Indeed, the Prime Minister's famous words about never having it so good were increasingly being associated with indolence and indifference rather than prosperity and progress. No less a figure than the Archbishop of Canterbury, Geoffrey Fisher, called the famous phrase a 'dreadful' excuse for 'a smug contentment which ignores the peril of our own situation and the appalling conditions of people in other countries'.[26] Even the Conservative journal *Crossbow* grumbled in 1962 that the affluent society was 'a vulgar world whose inhabitants have more money than is good for them . . . a cockney tellytopia, a low grade nirvana of subsidised houses, hire purchase extravagance, undisciplined children, gaudy domestic squalor, and chips with everything'.[27]

When the first major cinematic dissection of modern consumerism was released in the same year, its very title seemed to capture the spirit of the age: *Live Now, Pay Later*. Based on a novel by Jack Trevor Story, it tells the story of Albert Argyle (Ian Hendry), a slick hire-purchase 'tally boy' who sells furniture to bored housewives and occasionally wheedles his way into their beds as well as their purses. Like his customers, Albert is deep in debt, but only rarely does he acknowledge the shabbiness of merry-go-round materialism. 'There's two hundred thousand consumers in this town, and they're all waiting for you, just you,' says Mr Callendar, his employer. 'Yeah,' Albert replies, 'to con them into buying a whole load of stuff they don't need and can't afford.' Callendar is unimpressed: 'There's a nasty little streak of honesty in you, Albert. You want to watch that . . . it's bad for business.' There could hardly be a more cynical vision of Reginald Maudling's affluent Britain, awash with money and populated by promiscuous women, greedy entrepreneurs, fraudulent estate agents and grasping shopkeepers. Even the local vicar touts a collecting box labelled 'Pay Now – Live Later'.[28]

Live Now, Pay Later was a fitting motto for the Maudling experiment. By the end of the year it looked likely that the economy was growing too quickly, and that the old problem of the balance of payments was likely to rear its ugly head. In presenting such a munificent budget, Maudling had assumed that higher output would eventually promote a higher volume of exports and hence counterbalance the inevitable tide of imports, but this did not appear to be happening. Instead, his tax concessions and recent wage rises meant that British consumers were lavishing millions on foreign imports, and the current account deficit was sliding further and further into the red. Maudling had not broken out of the stop–go cycle; in truth, he had merely exacerbated it.[29] In February 1964 he was compelled to raise bank rate to 5 per cent, and in his second budget, two months later, he admitted that 'the combination of an increased capital outflow with a deterioration of the current account will mean a worsening of the overall balance of payments this year'. Some observers were now urging him to apply the brakes and impose tax increases of between £200 and £400 million to stabilise the economy; but, ever the optimist, Maudling shied away from such unpleasant medicine. 'The best judgement I can make', he told the House, 'is that if taxation is increased in this Budget by about £100 million . . . I should be doing enough to steady the economy without going so far as to give a definite shock to expansion.'[30] Yet again it was not enough: the trade figures published in July 1964 showed that imports were continuing to pour into the country while export levels were actually sinking. The annual balance of payments deficit was now estimated to have widened to £600 million; by October, when the government finally faced the electorate, it had apparently stretched to a crippling £800 million.[31]

'We went for expansion', Maudling wrote in his memoirs, 'quite deliberately, with our eyes open, recognizing the dangers.'[32] The dash for growth had been based on the eschatological hope that although in the short term imports would outstrip exports, in the long run the investment engendered by his largesse would promote exports to such an extent that the balance of payments problem would be solved once and for all.[33] But what Maudling had done was to inject £200 million in purchasing power into the economy at a point when, as it eventually emerged, recovery was already beginning anyway. He had no incomes policy through which inflation might be kept under control, and he had severely underestimated the looming threat of a balance of payments crisis. Maudling was a consummate gambler; the Treasury official Alec Cairncross later reflected that he 'took risks with the balance of payments in the hope of a breakthrough in economic growth in which he had little faith; and delayed – in the event abandoned – action of any kind to check an obvious boom in 1964, comforting himself with the thought that if necessary, the pound could be allowed to float'.[34] But not only had the Chancellor lost his bet, he had not even made it for the right reasons: throughout his time at the Treasury, he had always kept one eye firmly on the Tories' election prospects. The truth was that he had gambled with the nation's finances in order to win the general election for Macmillan and then put himself in pole position to succeed him in a year or so. Edmund Dell sums it up well:

> Maudling persisted with his breakthrough policy in 1964, despite the evidence that it was going wrong, because he had an election to win and was not averse to the cynical exploitation of the opportunity he found in the Treasury's earlier support and in the feeling, by no means confined to politicians, that *something* had to be done about the performance of the British economy . . .
>
> The idea of breakthrough by precipitate expansion was one that only businessmen, politicians in a hole and their friends in the economics profession could possibly claim to believe. There was also, in

Maudling's attitude, an element of carefree, romantic, cavalier defiance. If the world insisted on confining the British economy within a straitjacket entitled the balance of payments, he would show that, like Houdini, he could break free.[35]

Maudling's manifest intelligence and cheerful, whisky-swilling bonhomie made him one of the more immediately appealing politicians of the sixties, but his dash for growth had been little short of an utter disaster, 'the ultimate example of a combination of politics, ignorance, and hubris on economic management'.[36] When he left the Treasury in 1964, he bequeathed to his successor an estimated shortfall of £800 million in the balance of payments, the deepest such deficit in British history. And as it turned out, Houdini's failed attempt to break free from the straitjacket would overshadow British politics for the remainder of the decade.

The Conservatives had been re-elected in 1959 as, above all, the party of prosperity and sound economic stewardship. At first glance, the statistics for the five years of their next administration suggest that this reputation was well deserved. Between 1959 and 1964 economic growth was, on average, just under 4 per cent a year, an impressive figure when compared with other periods of modern British history. Even during the stagnation of 1962, the economy still expanded by 1.3 per cent: there were no recessions or real 'stops', despite all the talk of stop–go. Wages and living standards steadily rose; unemployment remained extremely low at an average of 1.8 per cent; and the inflation rate, too, was reassuringly low at an average of 3 per cent. Most people not only experienced a rising standard of living but also benefited from the transformation in their daily lives that consumerism brought: the opportunities afforded by a car, for example, the liberating impact of a washing machine, or the educational possibilities of books and television programmes.[37]

This does not, however, tell the whole story; indeed, comparison with other Western European countries of similar size suggests that the prosperity of the late fifties and early sixties occurred despite Conservative economic management, not because of it.[38] Indeed, there was at the same time a strong and justified sense that Britain was falling behind her competitors. Between 1951 and 1964, real national income grew in West Germany by 5.6 per cent, in Italy by 5.4 per cent, in France by 5 per cent, in the Netherlands by 4.3 per cent, and in Britain by 2.6 per cent.[39] In the same period total production in Britain increased by 40 per cent, a rate that looks rather less healthy when compared with corresponding increases of 100 per cent in France, 150 per cent in West Germany and Italy and 300 per cent in Japan.[40] 'Britain', Roy Harrod told Macmillan after an IMF meeting in October 1961, 'is now universally regarded as a country of very low growth.'[41]

The stereotypical excuse that Britain's competitors were starting from a lower base because of the destruction of the war makes little sense. Britain's comparatively stronger position in 1945 gave her an excellent advantage and a chance to grow at a faster rate.[42] Not only was Britain's growth rate extremely disappointing, but her trading position, in which so many national hopes had been invested for so many years, was also in steep decline. Again, British exports increased during the fifties and early sixties by some 29 per cent, a superficially impressive statistic that dwindles into insignificance compared with the rates for France (86 per cent), West Germany (247 per cent), Italy (256 per cent) and Japan (378 per cent).[43] As we have already seen, Britain's competitive position had been declining ever since the late nineteenth century, and some further decline after the Second World War was no doubt inevitable; but, even so, the rate of decline in the fifties and sixties was extremely worrying to observers aware how important exports were to the balance of payments and the economic health of the nation. In 1950 Britain commanded 25 per cent of the world's trade; by 1962, this had ebbed away to some 15 per cent. By comparison, the West Germans, starting from a weak and battered industrial base, had streaked ahead, increasing their own share from 7 per cent to 20 per cent in the same period. It was little wonder that so many old servicemen cursed German efficiency.[44]

For most contemporary commentators, then, there could be little doubt that British exporters had become much less competitive than their European rivals. True, unemployment was low, wages were high and living standards were booming, but all the talk, especially on the left, was of economic decline.[45] Some commentators blamed strikes, wage inflation and high labour costs, arguing that the intransigent militancy of the trade unions made it impossible for exporters to compete with their foreign counterparts; but, as we have already seen, the British unions were actually less militant than their French, Italian or Japanese brethren, and only marginally more militant than West German workers.[46] Others, especially those already unsympathetic to the Empire and Britain's world role, argued that the cost of keeping British troops in bases stretching from the Mediterranean to the Far East contributed to the persistent problems with the balance of payments; but while it was certainly true that it was expensive and difficult to have both guns and butter, this does not fully explain why the British struggled by comparison with, say, the French, who during the 1950s had fought two costly wars in Indochina and Algeria.[47] A more convincing contemporary explanation for British competitive weakness was that the successive governments from Attlee to Macmillan had failed to encourage modernisation and industrial investment, so that British industry in the fifties and sixties remained stuck in the patterns of the thirties. Instead they were distracted by what Edmund Dell called 'the imperial tradition in industrial policy', devoting their energies to relatively unproductive fields like nuclear energy and aerospace technology that were supposed to support British claims to global leadership.[48]

Britain enjoyed an extremely favourable trading position in the late forties and early fifties, as we have seen. Unfortunately this only bred complacency and the assumption that, since profits were pouring in, there was little need to change. Yet the fact was that the British model of capitalism was in urgent need of an overhaul. American and European managers and businessmen were often better educated than their British counterparts; their industries were tougher and leaner; and they were keener to embrace new technologies and working practices. In Britain, both company managers and elected politicians hesitated to push through the kind of reorganisation and reform that would rebuild industry and business on the successful lines of their rivals in the United States, West Germany and, increasingly, Japan. But as Andrew Gamble explains, 'no such new beginning was made':

> Low investment was . . . the key problem, and it was the failure of British companies and British governments to create the kind of climate for large-scale investment and rapid increases in productivity that was striking. Few British industries adopted the kind of organisational practices which were developed by their competitors to overcome restrictive practices on the shop floor and make investment pay. The failure was more a failure of management than of the work-force.[49]

During the Macmillan years, investment had been half-hearted, sporadic and unimaginative, while at the same time, thanks to full employment, rising public expectations and pressure from the unions, labour costs were increasing: hence the problems with productivity and insufficient exports. At the same time, since domestic consumer demand was high, Britain was importing more and more finished and semi-finished manufactures, and so when Amory or Maudling 'went for growth', the inevitable consequences were a deficit in the balance of payments and international pressure on the pound, followed with tedious predictability by a deflationary package and economic stagnation. This stop–go cycle can largely be blamed on the inability of successive Conservative Chancellors to stand up to Macmillan's political demands; it also contributed to Britain's relatively weak rates of productivity and output.[50] As a self-declared if rather simplistic Keynesian, Macmillan saw the economy as a machine to be manipulated by politicians. 'The real truth is that both a brake and an accelerator are essential for a motor car,' he explained; 'their use is a matter of judgement but their purpose must remain essentially the same – to go forward safely; or, in economic terms, expansion in a balanced economy.'[51]

Even if this were true, the problem was that the Conservatives had an unhappy knack of applying the accelerator and the brake at the worst possible times.[52] It was not inevitable that British industry should become so uncompetitive in the early sixties: more modernisation and investment would surely have ensured higher productivity and greater export sales. Stop–go economic management, however, made it extremely difficult to make and execute plans for investment and expansion, and in the long run British industry gained little from the artificial, short-sighted booms stoked up by successive Chancellors. When political self-interest collided with economic prudence, the former usually emerged victorious. Too often, then, the economic policies of the Macmillan government had been based on what Michael Pinto-Duschinsky called 'bread and circuses': the sacrifice of long-term economic reinvigoration for short-term popularity and brief, wild bursts of consumer enthusiasm.[53] It was no coincidence that in 1955, 1959 and 1963, in each case just before an election, the brakes were removed; and it was a sad indictment of Conservative mismanagement that on each occasion boom turned very quickly to bust.

It did not escape some observers that while British growth was stuttering, the countries of the Common Market were becoming ever more competitive. Between 1960 and 1964, gross domestic product per head increased in Britain by 2.2 per cent. In the five countries at the core of the Common Market (West Germany, France, Italy, Belgium and the

Netherlands), it grew by an intimidating 5.2 per cent.[54] 'The market of the future was growing next door, across the Channel', writes Hugo Young, 'and the figures were already telling, there for all to see.' By the beginning of 1962, nearly two-fifths of all British exports went to Western Europe, but only a third, and a dwindling third at that, to the Commonwealth. Neither the old dominions nor the new post-colonial states of the developing world could offer markets as enticing as those of the Six, not least because the consumer economies of Western Europe were so much richer and more developed than those of post-colonial Africa and Asia; moreover, many post-colonial countries were understandably keen to build up their own industries rather than rely on British exports. In this context, the decision to stand aside from the Treaty of Rome was probably the single most important mistake of the post-war years, dwarfing any of the blunders made by Macmillan's various Chancellors.[55] Even in the early sixties, some politicians on both sides of the partisan divide regarded Britain's failure to join the Six as a blunder of tragic proportions. The Continental economies appeared to be growing at a much faster rate than the domestic economy, and to observers like George Brown and Edward Heath the obvious conclusion was that it would be better to be trading at the heart of Europe than isolated at the periphery. 'By bringing Western Europe together', Brown explained, 'we should provide a domestic market of some 300 million people and be associated with countries whose economies are in many ways complementary to ours. That would give us an economic base big enough to stand up to anything the Americans or the Russians can do industrially.'[56]

George Brown was the quintessential example of the post-war politician for whom Europe was not only an economic panacea but also a glorious ideal. In his view, Europe was the key both to economic success and to the preservation of world order against unchecked American capitalism and ruthless Soviet Communism. 'The British people have done many things in history,' he wrote, 'but the moral and cultural inheritance behind our achievement comes from Western Christendom, which belongs to Europe as a whole. The Dutch, the French, the Germans, the Belgians, the Luxemburgers and the Italians see as clearly as we should that we share a common culture and a common heritage, and they see more readily than some of us are willing to see that we face a common danger.' Perhaps only Edward Heath could match Brown's intellectual attachment to the European dream, but since Brown was a much more voluble and passionate individual, for sheer messianic fervour he was surely unrivalled:

I am convinced that Britain's role is in Europe, that it is a powerful role, an influential role and one which will pay us great dividends in every way. This is what makes so much of the argument about the Common Market frustrating and irrelevant. It is not the price of butter which in the end really matters – it's the size, stability, strength and political attitude of Europe that matters. We have got to have a new kind of organization in Europe. We *must* succeed in this, and our children's children will wonder what on earth all the argument about the Market was about: to them it will be so natural a part of the scene as not to be visible. If we don't succeed, I doubt if there will be much of a Britain for our children's children.[57]

This kind of rhetoric put Brown in a minority: opinion polls and surveys during Macmillan's administration suggested that the general public were either hostile or indifferent to the European Economic Community across the Channel.[58] In September 1957, Gallup found that 39 per cent of respondents had never heard of the Common Market, and of those who had, only 35 per cent knew that France was a member, while 20 per cent thought that Britain had already joined.[59] Senior politicians like Rab Butler professed themselves 'bored' by the issue, but in truth they were becoming increasingly worried that the success of the Six would leave Britain marginalised in Europe.[60] In 1957 and 1958 the Macmillan government had tried to persuade the members of the Common Market to accommodate a wider free trade association of eleven other countries led by Britain: this scheme aimed, therefore, at a European Free Trade Association (EFTA) of seventeen members. This was a fairly blatant manoeuvre to undermine the strength and unity of the Six, and it was not therefore particularly astonishing that de Gaulle vetoed the proposal in December 1958.[61] In Westminster and Whitehall, meanwhile, the patriotic self-confidence and complacency of the early fifties were quickly draining away, leaving only a vague sense of resentment and self-pity. In March 1959, for example, Reginald Maudling, who as Paymaster General had been in charge of the EFTA negotiations, wrote to Macmillan:

The fact is the French do not want us in Europe at all. The Community of the Six has become a Paris/Bonn axis, with Paris at the moment the dominating partner on the basis of Adenauer's personal policy. The other four countries are no more than satellites . . .

In these circumstances the need for some positive action to hold together our friends outside the Six seems to be growing. The recent discussions among officials have shown an encouraging degree of interest in an alternative free trade area, not only in Scandinavia but also among the Swiss, Austrians and Portuguese . . . I remain convinced that if we were to reject the idea of forming some alternative association with our friends outside the Six we should be left without a friend in Europe and we should thoroughly deserve such a fate.[62]

The result, finally ratified in Stockholm in November 1959, was an 'EFTA of the Seven', a loose association of Britain, Sweden, Norway, Denmark, Austria, Switzerland and Portugal based on a common commitment to promote economic growth and eliminate non-agricultural tariffs.[63]

EFTA never caught the British imagination. Since its members were economically weaker than the Six, it was never really likely that it would assuage the political and economic anxieties of Whitehall and Fleet Street. Its markets were much smaller than those of the Six: only 90 million people, many of them rural, were covered by EFTA, compared with the 120 million in the heavily urbanised Common Market. 'For the first time since the Napoleonic era,' Macmillan gloomily told his Foreign Secretary barely a month after the ratification of the EFTA treaty, 'the major continental powers are united in a positive economic grouping, with considerable political aspects, which, though not specifically directed against the United Kingdom, may have the effect of excluding us both from European markets and from consultation in European policy.' He was even worried that the Six might 'replace us as the major ally of the United States', and wondered why it was 'so difficult to make the United States realize that the Six which they support for the sake of European political unity is in fact (because of the economic threat to the United Kingdom and others) a threat to European unity'.[64] The success of the Six was clearly weighing heavily on Macmillan's mind. In July 1960 he scribbled in his diary:

Shall we be caught between a hostile (or at least less and less friendly) America and a boastful, powerful 'Empire of Charlemagne' – now under French but later bound to come under German control? Is this the real reason for 'joining' the Common Market (if we are acceptable) and for abandoning (a) the Seven (b) British agriculture (c) the Commonwealth? It's a grim choice.[65]

Whereas British politicians in the early 1950s had spurned the advances of European politicians, they now shuddered at the thought of exclusion. What made matters worse was that their neighbours had so visibly thrived without them; there was no guarantee, then, that they would even welcome a British application to join. As early as January 1959 a report from James Marjoribanks, an official at the Embassy in Bonn, explained that unless the British could come to some arrangement with the Six, they faced a future of falling exports and economic decline. 'Our position would be changed from the biggest market, and the second largest exporter of manufactured goods to Europe, to a member of what would be very much a second eleven scattered round Europe,' the report concluded. Even worse, it was already clear that it would be extremely difficult to gain admittance to the industrial markets of the EEC. 'I think it is vitally important', Marjoribanks added, 'for us all to rid ourselves of the feeling that the Six cannot do without us . . . The consequences for them of the United Kingdom being excluded are far less than the consequences for the United Kingdom of being shut out of Europe.'[66]

Little more than five years after haughtily snubbing the overtures of their neighbours, therefore, British officials were already contemplating the difficulties of an application to join them. By the beginning of 1961, a belated British application was clearly in the offing. Macmillan himself had once been a committed opponent of the Common Market, but since the mid-fifties British military power and international influence had undergone a rapid transformation. The Suez crisis had destroyed any moral credibility the British still enjoyed in the developing world, while the Empire was unravelling almost by the month. The reduction of internal tariffs within the Common Market made British exclusion even more painful, and given the perennial problems with sterling and the balance of payments, it made little sense to stay out. In May 1960, the Treasury mandarin Sir Frank Lee submitted a report on the European issue to the Prime Minister. Lee felt that the EEC and EFTA were likely to drift further apart rather than come together, with inevitable consequences for British exports to the markets of the Six. In 1953, only 10 per cent of British exports had gone to the Six; by 1960 the corresponding figure was more like 16 per cent. The Common Market, not the Commonwealth, represented the future of British trade.[67] Not only were several distinguished economists, like Lord Plowden and Lord Robbins, strongly in favour of joining, but many industrialists and businessmen had also expressed a keen interest; even prestigious publications like *The Economist* and the *Financial Times* were enthusiastic. Like Marjoribanks, however, Lee noted that the process would not now be easy:

> We shall not get the solution which we want on the cheap. There is nothing to show that we are desperately needed in Europe – e.g. to oppose German hegemony in support of the French. That has become the way of illusion. Therefore we shall have to be prepared to pay for the sort of settlement we want – in political terms or in terms of inconvenience for or damage to some of our cherished interests – the Commonwealth, domestic agriculture, our tariff policy, perhaps indeed our political pride and sense of self-reliance.[68]

Lee's report emphasised above all the economic case for European integration. At the same time, however, Macmillan was coming under great pressure from the United States to abandon the divisive EFTA experiment and combine with the Six to form a strong, united bulwark in Western Europe against Soviet Communism. Macmillan had been stunned by Eisenhower's enthusiastic support for the Common Market, and when Kennedy moved into the White House in January 1961, the British were disappointed to find in him another keen advocate of European integration.[69] Isolation from a Franco-German–American axis was unthinkable for a nation of Britain's self-proclaimed greatness: indeed, some historians have argued that the decision to apply to the Six was ultimately motivated by questions of prestige and power rather than trade and economics. As far as Macmillan was concerned, Britain's change of heart was rooted in power politics, above all his desire to play the learned Athenian statesman to Kennedy's dynamic Roman commander. As we have seen, he was determined to maintain the so-called special relationship; in this context, applying to the Common Market was simply the price that he had to pay for Kennedy's continued friendship. European integration, then, was not so much a way of coming to terms with the decline of British power as a way of ensuring its survival. There was no profound change of heart, and no great reassessment of Britain's destiny and its place in the world.[70]

The Cabinet spent months agonising over the decision, but by July 1961 Macmillan had won over the majority of his colleagues to the cause of integration. Of all his senior colleagues, only Maudling, who had a personal stake in the survival of EFTA, remained unconvinced.[71] On 22 July the Cabinet agreed in principle to make a formal application to join the

Common Market, and on 2 August Macmillan rose to put the case to the House of Commons. In one of the most finely judged speeches of his career, he strove to allay the concerns of his suspicious backbenchers. Many saw the Commonwealth as an enduring symbol of international prestige and imperial history, and were concerned that European integration would undermine it; to them, Macmillan addressed his closing remarks:

> To sum up, there are, as I have said, some to whom the whole concept of our working closely in this field with other European nations is instinctively disagreeable. I am bound to say that I find it hard to understand this when we have accepted close collaboration on other more critical spheres. Others feel that our whole and sole duty lies with the Commonwealth. If I thought that our entry into Europe would injure our relations with and influence in the Commonwealth, or be against the true interest of the Commonwealth, I would not ask the House to support this step.
>
> I think, however, that most of us recognise that in a changing world if we are not to be left behind and to drop out of the main stream of the world's life, we must be prepared to change and adapt our methods. All through history this has been one of the main sources of our strength.[72]

The anticipated opposition among Conservative backbenchers never materialised; only one voted against the government, and fewer than thirty abstained.[73] This was perhaps surprising, since the decision to open negotiations with the Common Market was, in the words of Richard Lamb, 'one of the most important political turning points of the twentieth century'.[74] Macmillan's new-found enthusiasm for the Common Market suggested that the days of global empire and Anglo-Saxon union had passed into memory, leaving Britain as a small, if influential and industrially powerful, island kingdom on the fringes of north-western Europe. But his strategy was to persuade the party and the public that British entry into Europe did not mean a decline in national power and greatness, and he therefore sought to downplay the significance of his decision. In a Conservative pamphlet published later in the year, for example, he assured his readers:

> We in Britain are Europeans. That has always been true, but it has now become a reality which we cannot ignore. In the past, as a great maritime

Empire, we might give way to insular feelings of superiority over foreign breeds and suspicion of our neighbours across the Channel . . . [but] we have to consider the state of the world as it is today . . .

It is sometimes alleged that we would lose all our national identity by joining the European Community . . . I myself believe that the bulk of public opinion in this country . . . is firmly against the extinction of separate national identities and would choose a Europe which preserved and harmonised all that is best in our different national traditions.[75]

The European project, for Macmillan and millions of his countrymen, was hardly a thrilling release from the shackles of parochial national history; rather, it looked like a regrettable but necessary enterprise designed to restore and reaffirm British national greatness. Even the senior members of the government were less than totally enthusiastic about the forthcoming negotiations, and their attitude has been well described as 'nervous', 'negative' and 'apologetic'.[76] Public support for the European adventure peaked at an unimpressive 53 per cent in December 1961, falling to 47 per cent and then 36 per cent in May and June 1962. By December 1962, as the negotiations neared their close, a mere 29 per cent of the public favoured joining the Common Market, and then only 'if the government decided it was in Britain's interest'. Younger and more affluent voters, especially white-collar professionals, were more likely to favour entry; the bulk of the manual working classes, however, counted themselves among the two-thirds who were opposed, undecided or indifferent. Farmers were almost unanimous in their opposition, the trade unions were ambivalent, and many old Bevanites distrusted the Six as a club for capitalists and Catholics.[77]

In September 1962 the Conservative Party chairman Iain Macleod advised his Cabinet colleagues: 'Agents report increasing distrust of foreign political connections and indeed of foreigners, and report fears that we are going to be "taken over", "pushed around", "outvoted", "forced into the Common Market to serve American interests" or "to surrender our independence to 'Frogs and Wogs'".' As he saw it, 'thoughtful anxieties about the extent to which British sovereignty, traditional institutions and forms of government would be eroded' were not actually very important in determining public opposition to the European enterprise. Instead, what drove suspicion of Europe 'both amongst the working class and amongst those of the middle-class who are opposed, is a sort of patriotism (or its negative counterpart, xenophobia)'.[78] This kind of opposition was often closely associated with a sentimental attachment to the Commonwealth, and by implication the national greatness implicit in Britain's imperial traditions. 'We must not join Europe,' declared the intensely conservative Viscount Montgomery of Alamein in June 1962:

> I stand for the British Commonwealth with the Queen at its head . . . There is only one race under Heaven which could stand between the Western world and utter destruction. That is the British race to which we belong – united by close ties of blood, speech and religion the world over . . . Let the Mother of Nations gather her children about her to the call of common kindred; do not let her cast away the affection of her offspring. Let her grasp the hand of her children and draw them closer to her – rather than desert them. Thus will the ancient heart be warmed and inspired – a heart which is beating today just as firmly as ever it did in the days of Trafalgar and Alamein.[79]

The paradox of British policy towards the Six in the early 1960s was that, although Macmillan and his colleagues were themselves no more than half-hearted converts to the European ideal, they still represented the most pro-European group in British political life.[80] The Labour leadership was certainly not pressing Macmillan to take a more enthusiastic line. George Brown, admittedly, was very keen on Europe, and so were bright young Gaitskellite revisionists like Roy Jenkins and Anthony Crosland, not least because their own cultural tastes inclined towards the cosmopolitan.[81] They were, however, very much a minority, and most Labour backbenchers shared the old suspicions of Clement Attlee and Ernest Bevin. The most passionate anti-European speech in the Commons debate in August 1961, for instance, came from a Labour veteran, Lynn Ungoed-Thomas, who called the government's proposal 'alien to the mind of this country' and 'ruinous to our Commonwealth connection'. 'Right from its earliest days', he insisted, '– the days of Wellesley, of Cornwallis, of Warren Hastings – there has been as a continuous thread amongst the best of our people the conception of the Empire as being a trust to develop into a Commonwealth of all our peoples, including the coloured peoples.'[82] Harold Wilson agreed. 'If there has to be a choice,' he declared, 'we are not entitled to sell our friends and kinsmen down the river for a problematical and marginal advantage in selling washing machines in Düsseldorf.'[83] Even Hugh Gaitskell shared many of these concerns. Although no Little Englander, he was an intensely patriotic, even old-fashioned man who found it difficult to abandon the nationalist fantasies of great power and empire. 'English sausages, how I missed them in Vienna!' the young Gaitskell exclaimed eagerly at lunch the day he returned from studying in Austria.[84] In his eyes, Britain's global responsibilities were never in serious doubt, and he was never seized by the pan-European idealism that animated one or two of his younger colleagues. 'Whether you or I like it or not, the thing is there,' he told a Commonwealth audience in July 1962. 'In many ways I cannot help regretting it . . . although I see the advantage of Franco-German understanding.' The subject was, he thought, 'a bore and a nuisance'.[85]

In April 1962, Roy Jenkins had arranged a dinner meeting between Gaitskell and the European visionary Jean Monnet, which unfortunately turned out rather like the meeting between Rab Butler and Paul-Henri Spaak seven years previously. Jenkins himself admitted that he had 'never seen less of a meeting of minds'.[86] 'One must have faith,' the miserable Monnet said at the end of the dinner. 'I don't believe in faith,' Gaitskell replied coldly. 'I believe in reason, and there is little reason in anything you have been saying tonight.'[87] Even though he acknowledged that Britain would one day join the Six, his cultural patriotism made it difficult for him to be very enthusiastic about any such development; what was more, he also knew that the European project was not popular among the Labour rank and file. Many party members, he recognised, saw it as the end of 'an independent Britain . . . sucked up in a kind of giant capitalist, Catholic conspiracy, our lives dominated by Adenauer and De Gaulle, unable to conduct any independent foreign policy at all'.[88] Opposing the European application would allow Gaitskell to shore up his fragile standing on the left of the party, and on 21 September, in a national television broadcast, he argued that the Six were expecting the British to scrap their existing preferential trading system in return for 'promises, vague assurances and nothing more'. Entry into the Common Market on such bad terms, he thought, meant 'the end of Britain as an independent nation; we become no more than "Texas" or "California" in the United States of Europe. It means the end of a thousand years of history; it means the end of the Commonwealth . . . [to become] just a province of Europe.' It was ridiculous to expect the British people 'in a moment of folly, [to] throw away the tremendous heritage of history'.[89]

Two weeks later, at the Labour conference at Brighton, Gaitskell returned to the attack, giving one of the great exhibitions of political rhetoric with which he was later associated in party legend. He made no apology for repeating the themes of his broadcast. Membership of the Common Market meant 'the end of Britain as an independent European state . . . the end of a thousand years of history'. As for Macmillan's suggestion that the complicated economic arguments in favour of entry could hardly be understood by the ordinary, benighted voter, Gaitskell dismissed it with suitable contempt: 'What an odious piece of hypocritical, supercilious, arrogant rubbish this is!'[90] At the end of the speech, wave after wave of adoring applause broke over the conference dais. Gaitskell had never been more popular with his party's left. 'All the wrong people are cheering,' remarked his wife Dora.[91]

Meanwhile the negotiations for British entry were already under way. The British team was led by the former Chief Whip, Edward Heath, now deputy to Lord Home at the Foreign Office. It was an excellent choice. Heath might appear stolid and dour, but he was a cultivated man and a committed European. As a student, he had visited the Third Reich, watched a Nuremberg rally from a seat close to Hitler's box and shaken hands with Himmler and Goebbels at a Nazi soirée. He had come back to Britain a committed opponent of appeasement, and fought with distinction in France and the Low Countries before returning to Nuremberg as a fascinated spectator at the war crimes trials. He recalled in 1977:

> As I left the court, I knew that these evil things had been beaten back and their perpetrators brought to justice. But at what a cost. Europe had once more destroyed itself. This must never be allowed to happen again. My generation could not live in the past; we had to work for the future. We were surrounded by destruction, homelessness, hunger and despair. Only by working together had we any hope of creating a society which would uphold the true values of European civilisation. Reconciliation and reconstruction must be our tasks. I did not realize then that it would be my preoccupation for the next thirty years.[92]

For Heath, the decision to apply for Common Market membership was, as he told his fellow negotiators in 1961, 'a great decision, a turning point in our history'.[93] His handling of the Brussels talks was, by all accounts, masterful. Farm support, tariffs and quotas, zinc and lead, tea and butter, sterling balances and cashew nuts: the mind-numbing intricacies of the negotiations offered the ideal platform for his blend of meticulous, powerful seriousness. Both in

Westminster and across the Channel his stock rose with every long night he spent haggling in the smoke-filled committee rooms of Brussels.[94] One of his Foreign Office aides later wrote that Heath's performance 'was surely extraordinary. He put into his task an immense amount of devoted work and showed remarkable energy, drive and stamina. His mastery of the very complex subject matter of the negotiations was complete.'[95] An official from the Ministry of Agriculture agreed: Heath was 'an outstanding leader', with 'complete mastery' of the talks.[96]

Still, the negotiations were far from easy. They dragged on and on and on, bogged down in interminable arguments about the Common Agricultural Policy, Commonwealth trade and the technicalities of economic harmonisation. Far more troubling, however, was the intense suspicion with which the leaders of France and West Germany, Charles de Gaulle and Konrad Adenauer, viewed the British application. Britain, the German Chancellor told his friend de Gaulle, was 'like a rich man, who has lost his property but does not realise it'.[97] Indeed, the diplomatic relations between these two men and Macmillan were frequently strained to breaking point. In May 1959, for instance, Macmillan denounced the Chancellor in his diary as 'vain, suspicious and grasping', devoted to 'a great campaign of vilification of Her Majesty's Government and especially of me'. A month later, he recorded: 'De Gaulle will not play with me or anyone else. Adenauer is half-crazy'; and a few weeks after that: 'De Gaulle and Adenauer are just hopeless. Adenauer because he is a false and cantankerous old man.'[98] These personal jealousies and suspicions did not disappear with time; instead, if anything, they intensified. The most serious threat came from de Gaulle, whose resentment of the Anglo-American special relationship, in which he, like Macmillan, placed much credence, appeared to deepen with every passing day. On 1 December 1962, Heath wearily reported from Brussels that the French, anxious to protect their farmers and manufacturers, were still being difficult. An angry Macmillan wrote that night: 'The *French* are opposing us by every means, fair and foul. They are absolutely ruthless. For some reason they *terrify* the Six – by their intellectual superiority, spiritual arrogance, and shameful disregard of truth and honour.'[99]

Two weeks later, locked in talks with de Gaulle in the spectacular setting of Rambouillet, Macmillan had an unpleasant shock. Instead of mellowing, the French President had become more intransigent. Britain, according to de Gaulle, had not yet thrown off its old ties to the United States, and Macmillan had failed to convince him that he was prepared to be a good

European rather than an Atlantic stooge. France was currently the senior partner among the Six, but, as de Gaulle also pointed out, if Britain joined the Common Market then the French position would be automatically weakened. Macmillan was, according to de Gaulle's own account, on the verge of tears. Why had the French allowed the talks to drag on for so many weary months if they were opposed to the British application all along? 'This poor man,' de Gaulle condescendingly told his Cabinet a few days afterwards, 'to whom I had nothing to give, seemed so sad, so beaten, that I wanted to put my hand on his shoulder and say to him, as in the Edith Piaf song, "*Ne pleurez pas, milord.*"'[100]

On 14 January 1963, at a press conference in the grand surroundings of the Elysée Palace, de Gaulle put an end to Macmillan's faint hopes. 'England is insular,' he remarked, 'bound up by her trade, her markets, her food supplies with the most varied and often the most distant countries . . . In short, the nature and structure and economic context of England differ profoundly from those of the other states of the Continent.' Should Britain be allowed to join the Six, 'in the end there would appear a colossal Atlantic community under American dependence and leadership which would soon swallow up the European Community'. He had therefore decided to veto the British application.[101]

There is little doubt that the ostentatious reluctance, domestic bickering and general half-heartedness associated with Macmillan's application had made it much easier for de Gaulle to knock it down. It would have been much better if Macmillan had pressed for an early resolution to the talks, before de Gaulle was secure enough at home to exercise his veto. It would also have been much more sensible to apply for entry immediately after the 1959 election, when Macmillan's popularity and prestige were at their height and when the French President's personal position was still uncertain.[102] Having missed that particular boat, Macmillan made matters worse in December 1962 by ignoring the likely consequences of his meeting with Kennedy in Bermuda. He would have been better advised to wait until after the end of the European talks before squeezing the Polaris deal out of the Americans; in the event, the Polaris agreement only confirmed all de Gaulle's suspicions of Anglo-Saxon conspiracy.[103]

Even so, the responsibility for the collapse of the application ultimately lay with de Gaulle, not with Macmillan. Even during their first discussions on the subject in 1961, de Gaulle had hinted to the British Prime Minister that he was reluctant to admit the United Kingdom to the Common

Market as long as its Atlantic and Commonwealth links remained so strong. Well before the Polaris deal it looked very likely that de Gaulle would veto the application, and in fact it was probable that he would always have done so, provided that he commanded enough domestic polit-ical strength to get away with it.[104] Given the long wartime and post-war association of the two leaders, Alistair Horne is surely right to conclude that 'Macmillan was treated monstrously by de Gaulle, from whom he personally deserved better things'.[105] Had de Gaulle been more accom-modating, the recent history of both Britain and Europe would no doubt look very different.

The news of the veto was greeted by no great outpouring of grief in Britain. 'Glory, glory, Hallelujah!' exclaimed the *Daily Express*. 'It's all over; Britain's Europe bid is dead. This is not a day of misery at all. It is a day of rejoicing, a day when Britain has failed to cut her throat.'[106] In fact, most people were not rejoicing, but instead shared the feelings of the playwright Harold Pinter, who remarked: 'I have no interest in the matter and do not care what happens.'[107] In Brussels, meanwhile, Edward Heath took the fail-ure of the negotiations in which he had invested so much effort with dignity and equanimity. At the final meeting of the negotiating teams on 29 January, amid high emotion, he insisted that this must be merely a tempo-rary setback. It was nonsense that the British were 'not European enough': 'There are many millions in Europe who know perfectly well how European Britain has been and are grateful for it.' He and his countrymen, he vowed passionately, would not give up:

And so I would say to my colleagues: they should have no fear. We in Britain are not going to turn our backs on the mainland of Europe or on the countries of the Community. We are a part of Europe by geog-raphy, tradition, history, culture and civilisation. We shall continue to work with all our friends in Europe for the true unity and strength of this continent.[108]

When Heath had finished, the ministers and officials of the five non-Gallic members of the Community lined up to shake his hand, while the French Foreign Minister stood aside in awkward embarrassment. Three of the min-isters had tears in their eyes, and the female interpreters were reaching for handkerchiefs to hide their own emotion. As the first historian of the talks concluded: 'Mr Heath had earned more respect and admiration from his

European colleagues than had any British minister concerned with European questions since the end of the war.'[109]

As for Macmillan, he presented a relatively composed front to the nation in a televised address the following evening. 'A great opportunity has been missed,' he admitted, but it was all the fault of the misguided French:

> What has happened has revealed a division. France and her Government are looking backwards. They seem to think that one nation can dominate Europe and, equally wrong, that Europe can or ought to stand alone. Europe cannot stand alone. She must co-operate with the rest of the Free World, with the Commonwealth, with the United States in an equal and honourable partnership. That is why we in Britain need to stand by the Atlantic Alliance.[110]

In private, though, Macmillan was distraught. De Gaulle's veto, coming just months after Orpington and the Night of the Long Knives, had capped a long year of troubles. 'All our policies at home and abroad are in ruins,' he wrote in his diary. Heath had done his best, for 'no one could have been a better negotiator and Ambassador – but French duplicity defeated us all'.[111] A similar mood of fatalistic gloom had overtaken his faithful deputy. Rab Butler privately noted his agreement with the verdict of the journalist James Margach that 'the engine had fallen out of the entire government strategy'. A few weeks later, indiscreet as ever, he told Anthony Wedgwood Benn: 'You know, the Common Market breakdown was a much bigger shock for us than you chaps realised.'[112] Macmillan's foreign policy was certainly in tatters, but the collapse of the European application also dealt a severe blow to his plans for economic renewal and electoral revival. 'The shattering thing about the French veto was not merely that the nation and the Prime Minister had been humiliated in the eyes of the world,' wrote the Conservative journalist Patrick Cosgrave. 'The application to join the EEC represented Macmillan's only hope of breaking out of a cycle of decline at home.'[113] The head of the Conservative Research Department, Michael Fraser, later admitted:

> Europe was to be our *deus ex machina*. It was to create a new contemporary political argument with insular socialism; dish the Liberals by stealing their clothes; give us something *new* after 12–13 years; act as the catalyst of modernisation; give us a new place in the international sun.

It was Macmillan's ace, and de Gaulle trumped it. The Conservatives never really recovered.[114]

By the time of de Gaulle's veto in January 1963, Macmillan was an increasingly lonely, frustrated and misunderstood figure. His government had never really found its feet after the heady days of the 1959 election; rather than soaring triumphantly towards a prosperous future, it seemed to have spent the last three years struggling from disaster to disaster. The Prime Minister in particular, with his exaggerated, Edwardian mannerisms, hooded gaze and languid drawl, looked more like a relic of the fifties than a symbol of the bright new sixties. His three Chancellors since the election had hardly covered themselves in glory. Butler had been a relative success at the Home Office, introducing a series of liberal measures to reform the laws on charities, licensing hours and gambling, and to improve the condition of Britain's antiquated prisons. Although a private opponent of the death penalty, he had never fought hard for its repeal, and neither had he accepted the Wolfenden Committee's recommendation that he decriminalise homosexual behaviour.[115] Indeed, Butler, too, looked more and more old-fashioned, a relic from the days of Chamberlain and Churchill who had somehow survived into the age of washing machines and pop music. By contrast with the performance of his successor, however, his record was positively glorious. Henry Brooke, who replaced him at the Home Office after the Night of the Long Knives, was widely considered the most incompetent senior minister since the war. A series of public relations blunders culminated in the decision in 1963 to deport the Nigerian chief Enahoro, despite the fact that he faced imprisonment and possible execution for subversion. Bernard Levin remarked, harshly but not unfairly, that Brooke made 'in a mercifully short term of office a series of decisions unequalled for their pig-headedness, it is safe to say, by any of his predecessors'.[116] His ham-fisted approach to security issues was emblematic of a government becoming widely regarded as anachronistic, befuddled and generally incompetent.

In April 1962 the *Guardian* reported a new low in the nation's fortunes:

BRITAIN BOTTOM OF THE CLASS

Britain economically came bottom of the class in the annual report published here tonight by the Secretariat of the United Nations Economic Commission for Europe. Britain has the 'sorry distinction of being the only Western country whose volume of national output was practically unchanged from the previous year', and is 'the one country where the employment situation has seriously deteriorated'.[117]

Few commentators in the early sixties were prepared to dispute the proposition that Britain was indeed 'bottom of the class', and as the Macmillan government stumbled from boom to bust, books and articles poured forth dissecting the 'state of England' or 'What's Wrong with Britain'. It was no accident that the boom in such books coincided with the expansion of the paperback industry and the reading public, as described earlier; it was also no accident that they were produced at a time when the British Empire was unravelling, the economy was stuttering and traditional values and ways of life were thought to be under threat from rampant affluence and materialism.

Sociology, as we have seen, was a growth area in the late fifties, but now the style and vocabulary of empirical, scholarly social analysis were being appropriated by popular commentators and used to dissect the imagined backwardness of British politics and industry.[118] Highbrow periodicals like *Encounter* and the *New Statesman* appeared almost obsessed by the themes of national anachronism and decline, and in 1963 the American magazine *Newsweek* remarked that the British had 'been wallowing in an orgy of self-criticism as relentless as the one which swept the US after the launching of the first *Sputnik* in 1957'.[119] Michael Shanks' manifesto *The Stagnant Society*, with all its talk of antediluvian labour relations, inefficient and timid management and complacent, nepotistic governing elites, was only the most obvious and influential example, and sold over sixty thousand copies in 1961.[120] Hoping to cash in on the mood of introspection, Penguin even ran a series of short non-fiction titles under the title *What's Wrong With . . . ?*, and October 1962 saw the launch of the journal *New Society*, dedicated to exploring Britain's social and economic malaise.[121] The economist Andrew Shonfield published a tract suggesting that cutting the overseas defence burden and investing instead at home would help to revive the flagging British economy; and in successive years Anthony Sampson produced his enormous *Anatomy of Britain*, Anthony Hartley published *A State of England*, and Nicholas Davenport analysed *The Split Society*.[122]

By September 1963 the stream of complaints, laments and recommendations had become a torrent. *The Economist* reflected:

In the gloom of this summer some uncomfortable memories have been stirring. Twenty-five years ago friends abroad were blaming Britain for going to sleep in the face of the enemy. Now they not only accuse Britons of wanting to contract out of the cold war. They also say that Britain is badly governed, badly managed, badly educated and badly behaved – and the striking thing is that more Britons are saying the same, more stridently still. Every summer visitor to London has been hit between the eyes by this passionate soul searching. All the political parties are going into their annual conferences with plans . . . to put Britain right by bringing it up to date; each promises that, like a detergent, it will wash whiter. The British have become, suddenly, the most introspective people on earth.[123]

'Bringing it up to date': this was the central theme of the 'What's Wrong with Britain?' critics. They might disagree about the intricacies of trade union legislation or civil service reform, but they all poured scorn on the record of the Conservative governments since 1951, and they all contrasted British inadequacies with the successes of rivals like Sweden, West Germany, France and even Bulgaria. In the words of Anthony Sampson, Britain was 'a country that doesn't believe in anything and is confused about its direction'.[124] Like his fellow critics, he saw 'modernisation' as the answer. Britain, the assumption ran, was endemically and fatally backward; the country must be dragged kicking and screaming into the modern, scientific, classless world of the 1960s.[125]

Among the most striking examples of this genre was a collection of essays with the ominous title *Suicide of a Nation?*, based on a special issue of *Encounter* in July 1963. All the usual suspects were on show, including Arthur Koestler (who edited the book), Henry Fairlie, Malcolm Muggeridge, Michael Shanks, Andrew Shonfield, John Grigg and Cyril Connolly. The political parties, industrial management, the unions, the workers, the class system and the public schools all came in for the predictable bashing. The image on the dust-jacket was a parody of the royal coat of arms, a mangy, bloodshot lion and an ostrich with its head buried in the sand, and the colours of the design were in Bernard Levin's words 'a particularly cruel parody of red, white and blue, consisting of a central band of white flanked by a strip of the palest, most faded blue, and a bilious, bloodless pink'.[126]

Koestler set out the argument of the book in his introduction. The

British were 'riveted on the past', their 'gaze turned backward and inward'. They laboured under an 'anachronistic class structure' and an 'out-dated educational system, out-dated in almost every respect'. 'The cult of amateurishness,' he complained, 'and the contempt in which proficiency and expertise are held, breed mediocrats by natural selection: the too-keen, the too-clever-by-half, are unfit for survival and eliminated from the race in which the last to pass the post is winner.'[127] The most striking passage, though, came from the pen of Malcolm Muggeridge, who mounted a withering attack on the backwardness of his native land and pointed an accusing finger directly at the Prime Minister:

> Each time I return to England from abroad the country seems a little more run down than when I went away; its streets a little shabbier; its railway carriages and restaurants a little dingier; the editorial pretensions of its newspapers a little emptier; and the vainglorious rhetoric of its politicians a little more fatuous. On one such occasion I happened to turn on the television and there on the screen was Harold Macmillan blowing through his moustache to the extent that 'Britain has been great, is great, and will continue to be great.' A more ludicrous performance could scarcely be imagined. Macmillan seemed, in his very person, to embody the national decline he supposed himself to be confuting. He exuded a flavour of moth balls. His decaying visage and somehow seedy attire conveyed the impression of an ageing and eccentric clergyman who had been induced to play the Prime Minister in the dramatized version of a Snow novel put on by a village amateur dramatic society.[128]

Macmillan was, increasingly, a weary and frustrated man. From the Night of the Long Knives onwards, he had begun to complain more and more often about drowsiness, physical fatigue and back pain.[129] He was in his late sixties and beginning to feel his age. As Muggeridge's indictment suggests, the Prime Minister was also an increasingly easy target for satire and criticism, associated not with national renewal but with profligacy, corruption, ineptitude and repression. His personal ratings had failed to improve from the debacle of the Night of the Long Knives, and by-election results consistently illustrated the unpopularity of the Conservative Party. For all Reginald Maudling's largesse, the unemployment figures were still disturbingly high: over 500,000 in the autumn of 1962, and over 800,000 in the

New Year.[130] The satirists, from Peter Cook and Dudley Moore to David Frost and *Private Eye*, were circling. Christopher Booker's parliamentary sketches in the *Eye*, written in the Molesworth style under the name of Eric Buttock, lampooned the musty, public-school flavour of the Macmillan government:

> Old mac, he's hed of Skool as if you didnt kno, hav been studying the press with grate interest during the parst few dais. he hav been very woried about staing on as Hed of Skool and wondring how he could do it . . . it doesnt look as if hes going to be Hed of Skool much longer wotever he do.[131]

Old Mac had become emblematic of a general sense of national decline. The erosion of British colonial power, the decline of industrial competitiveness, the persistence of unofficial strikes and sterling crises: all contributed to the impression that, far from leaping ahead into the gleaming future of the 1960s, Britain was stuck in the past. Yet even Macmillan himself recognised the need to project a more modern, dynamic image. At the end of October 1962 he noted that it was time for 'a blue print for modernising Britain against which the Government's actions can be judged and to which people will respond', and a few weeks later he established a small 'steering group' to co-ordinate the modernisation programme.[132] On 6 December he presented to the Cabinet a paper entitled 'Modernisation of Britain', in which he suggested that the government devote its energies to encouraging technological development, rapidly increasing productivity and economic growth in the more backward regions of the British Isles. 'We have now reached a stage in our post-war history where some more radical attack must be made on the weaknesses of our economy, both productive and structural,' he began. 'We face a situation in which the conditions of trade are becoming increasingly competitive and our commercial rivals increasingly better equipped to compete with us, while our own economy remains sluggish and "patchy".' Whether the European negotiations succeeded or failed, 'Britain needs to be brought up to date in almost every sphere of life.'[133]

By December 1962 the Labour Party had moved into a nine-point lead in the opinion polls. Hugh Gaitskell's strident opposition to the European application had done his popularity no harm at all. 'Mr Gaitskell is now at the peak of his command of the Labour movement,' wrote James Margach in the *Sunday Times* after the party conference. 'Labour . . . for the first time in years seemed to have overcome its obsessional complex about its inner self, appearing more outward-looking and healthy.'[134] Richard Crossman, one of Gaitskell's most persistent critics within the party, remarked in the New Year that 'one of the most fascinating developments of 1962 was the almost invisible transfer of the nation's confidence, from the man with real power in Downing Street to the man with Shadow power in the Opposition. This has made Hugh Gaitskell one of Labour's main electoral assets.'[135] More than half of all voters thought Gaitskell an impressive leader of his party; as his old friend Frank Pakenham put it, he led 'a Party more united than at any time since 1945–7, poised and prepared for victory, a Moses on the verge of the promised land'.[136]

In June 1962, on a trip to Battersea, Gaitskell had complained of feeling unwell and for a few moments lost consciousness before recovering and driving himself back to the Commons. For the next few months, like his great rival in Downing Street, he struck friends as tired and ill, not least because he worked phenomenally hard. He also suffered from rheumatic pains in his shoulder which he attributed to a tennis injury. On 15 December, after the House had risen for the recess, he went into hospital with what he thought was persistent flu, and emerged again just before Christmas, confident that he would eventually be better. On 3 January 1963, however, he went back into hospital with what appeared to be a severe viral infection affecting both his lungs and his heart. There was no need for alarm: his condition seemed serious but not life-threatening, and so his deputy, George Brown, saw no need to return to London from Manchester; nor did his close rival Harold Wilson break off a tour of the United States.

Within the next week, however, Gaitskell deteriorated. He had lupus erythematosus, an extremely rare immunological disease for which no cure was known. By the beginning of the third week of January he was in extreme danger, 'listless and rambling', according to his biographer, murmuring childhood songs and seeing apparitions on the wall of his hospital room. On 17 January he underwent emergency kidney surgery, but his body was struggling to cope with the onslaught of the disease, and on the evening of the following day, quite suddenly, he died.[137] He was just fifty-six, and his death was an immense shock to the general public, most of whom had known he was seriously ill for barely a week. Within the Labour Party, and especially on the right of the party, the news came as a staggering blow. Roy Jenkins, for instance, later remembered that although he was worried about his friend and mentor, 'it did not seriously occur to me that he was about to die'. The *Daily Express* telephoned him in New York and asked for a tribute. Jenkins felt too upset to give them one. 'Harold Wilson, who is in New York, was able to give us one without difficulty,' said the reporter disappointedly. 'Yes,' Jenkins snapped with bitter sarcasm, 'but you have to remember that he was very fond of Gaitskell.' The incident, he wrote, 'expressed both my shattered dismay and my revulsion from the prospect of a Wilson leadership, a succession to the man I loved and revered . . . by the man who had stood against him two years before'.[138]

Gaitskell's unexpectedly early death was a contingency that no one could have foreseen. As his obituaries agreed, he died at the cruellest possible moment, when his popularity was at its peak and he stood ready to take over the reins of government.[139] 'Probably no party leader since Parnell has enjoyed [such] unquestioning dominance,' wrote Iain Macleod the day after Gaitskell died. The Labour leader, he thought, 'looked, sounded and was set to be the Prime Minister of England'.[140] If Gaitskell had lived, modern political history might have been very different. The standard judgement is that of his biographer, Philip Williams: Gaitskell, whose personal popularity outstripped that of his party, would have won the 1964 election by a wide margin and governed as a self-confident, dynamic and effective leader.[141] The historian David Marquand, a former Labour MP, even calls him 'the Social Democrat as Hero', a man 'who probably would have become a great reforming Prime Minister'. And yet the stereotype of 'the best Prime Minister we never had' is too simplistic. Gaitskell had his weaknesses: intolerance, inflexibility and the persistent impression of aloof detachment from the ordinary voters he sought to inspire. Even though his competence and suitability for the highest office were never in doubt, Gaitskell was too intellectually combative to be the kind of wily, cynical operator who wins elections and jealously clings on to power. He might well have been popular with the majority of the voters, but his very name aroused considerable opprobrium in many quarters of his own party. He might well have proved a cool and thoughtful leader of the nation, but could he have held together his own movement under the pressures of the mid-sixties?[142]

In the end, speculation is pointless. Within days, if not hours, of Gaitskell's death, his erstwhile colleagues were jockeying for the succession.

On 14 February, Harold Wilson defeated George Brown by 144 votes to 103 and was duly elected leader of the parliamentary Labour Party. Wilson was a bright, cunning Yorkshireman, keen to present himself as the incarnation of a new, progressive, technocratic Britain; for Harold Macmillan, reeling under the impact of economic stagnation, endless security scandals and the mockery of the satire boom, he was not a welcome opponent. By the middle of March 1963, Labour's lead over the government stretched to fifteen points. Not since 1945 had the Conservative Party been in such terrible trouble; and it was about to get worse.[143]

A GANG OF LOW SCHOOLBOYS

The aim of the Establishment is to run the country.

Queen, August 1959

It was satire, wasn't it? Mucky jokes. Obscenity – it's all the go nowadays.

That Was The Week That Was (1963)

In the aftermath of the Coronation in 1953, the British monarchy enjoyed a long honeymoon of popular acclaim, and the years that followed were a rare period of contentment and security for the royal family. They still had their critics, but these were few in number. Elizabeth II worked hard to perfect the blend of 'ritual splendour, an appearance of domesticity, and ubiquity' that had ensured the success of her more esteemed predecessors, like Victoria and George V.[1] The Crown both represented 'ordinary', humble virtues, with its emphasis on a happy, united family, and aspired to stand for something rather more transcendent: not only the glory of empire, but also the continuity of British history. Although its political influence was waning, the monarchy continued to command popular loyalty through a careful combination of timeless splendour and modest homeliness: the magazine *Twentieth Century* praised 'the quick commonsense of the Queen, and the shrewd modernity of the Duke of Edinburgh' which both made them the ideal modern parents and also gave the entire nation 'a sense of family'.[2]

At the beginning of the sixties, one admiring historian declared that the Queen 'was the subject of adulation unparalleled since the days of Louis XIV'.[3] This was perhaps rather exaggerated. Richard Hoggart suggested that most working people gave little thought to the monarchy; they harboured no real resentment towards it, but they were not excessive royalists, either. To most working-class newspaper readers, the Crown was a vague symbol of patriotism, while the royal family itself was really a collection of individual celebrities, certainly more interesting than the country's leading politicians, but not necessarily more exciting than, say, the Hollywood film stars of the day.[4] Elizabeth II herself was a rather remote figure, very much the daughter of George VI. In public she was always carefully formal, with only two visible expressions: a fixed smile and a look of melancholy solemnity. According to intimates, she had a wry sense of humour and even showed flashes of temper, but these never revealed themselves in public, where she exercised iron control over her feelings and appearance, perhaps partly as a way of masking shyness and anxiety.[5] So, while Elizabeth made daily appearances in the newspaper headlines, her personality was largely concealed from her subjects, and at the same time that the monarchy was being presented as the incarnation of modernity, a heavy fog of conservatism and complacency hung over Buckingham Palace.[6]

The glamour of royalty was represented not by the monarch but by her closest companions, her sister Princess Margaret and her husband Prince Philip, Duke of Edinburgh. Unlike other members of the royal household, Philip was frustrated by the emphasis on ritual and tradition, and keenly felt his lack of status and responsibility. During the fifties and early sixties he was by far the most interesting member of the family, perceived as a manly, modern character with interests in industry and technology, a sort of domesticated James Bond. He was, wrote Harry Hopkins in 1964, '"international", apparently classless, informal, totally unpompous'.[7] While the Queen had been in 1952 the first British monarch to travel to London in an aeroplane, her husband went one better by being the first person to take off from Buckingham Palace lawn in a helicopter. She was comfortable with the staid conservatism of the court she had known as a child; he, on the other hand, breezed in 'like a breath of fresh air', as one courtier put it. Unlike most of the Queen's advisers, Philip believed that the institution should be immediately overhauled to bring it closer to the experience of her subjects, but the refusal of her courtiers to see sense baffled him. 'He was always asking, "What am I doing here? Why am I here?"' one of his friends recalled.[8]

There was a precedent for Philip's uneasy position: the experience of Prince Albert, the German consort to Queen Victoria who had thrown himself into the cause of science and industry. Philip initially responded in the same way; after all, he was already the President of the British Association for the Advancement of Science, and had addressed its members in 1951 on the subject 'The British Contribution to Science and Technology in the Past

Hundred Years'.[9] During the following decade, he made a great effort to visit research centres, scientific institutions and centres of industry, and frequently called for more investment in science and technology so that Britain would become one of the most modern industrial powers in the world. When he flew a prototype Comet, the world's first passenger jet, on a visit to de Havillands, the *Picture Post* reported that this was 'no royal chore', but evidence that 'he wants to see for himself how Britain goes to it'.[10] 'He will galvanise British industry,' opined the *Sunday Dispatch* in 1955, '. . . to get Britain back on her feet.'[11] Whether his efforts had any actual effect is in fact extremely dubious. His influence was more strongly felt within the Palace itself, where he introduced regular lunch parties to which commoners as well as aristocrats were invited, and generally tried to have the more rigorous court ceremonial relaxed. Even here, however, he never made the impact that he hoped for, and nor did he really succeed in playing the influential role of a latter-day Prince Albert, although he did help his wife with her speeches and broadcasts. Despite his brusque manner with journalists, however, his public image remained at this stage extremely favourable.[12]

By the early sixties, Philip was best known for having 'courageously set himself up as the chief critic of British complacency', as Anthony Sampson put it in 1962. His public statements were becoming increasingly unguarded and his exasperation with national decline ever more obvious. 'It's no good shutting your eyes and saying "British is best" three times a day after meals and expect it to be so. We have to work for it by constantly criticising and improving,' he declared in 1956. Two years after that he was quoted attacking 'the frustrations of a pettifogging bureaucracy' and 'the slow poison of bad industrial relations', comments which also reflected his political conservatism. By October 1961, there could be no disguising British competitive decline, and he made his most notorious intervention:

> Just at this moment we are suffering a national defeat comparable to any lost military campaign, and what is more, self-inflicted . . . The bastions of the smug and the stick-in-the-mud can only be toppled by persistent undermining . . . Gentlemen, I think it is about time we pulled our fingers out.[13]

Although statements like these annoyed many British industrialists, they did not appear to inflame the general public; if anything, the reverse was true. In 1960, Mass-Observation reported that the Duke of Edinburgh was felt 'to signify a *continuation of the Coronation* trend: that is, to be *seen* to exist and *felt* to belong'. One respondent summed up the feelings of many: the Duke was 'not so snobby as some of the others'. According to a poll of teenagers in the *Mirror* two years later, he was 'TOP OF THE ROYAL POPS', and well into the following decade he often finished top of national popularity polls.[14]

Philip was not alone in his frustration at the conservatism of Buckingham Palace, and the first, tentative signs that the royal family's honeymoon with the public was drawing to an end came in the space of a few months at the end of 1957. The first blow fell in August, delivered by John Grigg, Lord Altrincham, in the magazine *National and English Review* of which he was both proprietor and editor. Altrincham was a Tory peer and a committed monarchist who knew the court well, but, as he explained in his article, he was not impressed with what he had seen. He was especially contemptuous of the royal entourage, 'people of the tweedy sort, a tight little enclave of British ladies and gentlemen', who had trapped the monarch within their cloying embrace. 'All this', he wrote, 'would not have been good enough for Elizabeth I!' If this was not bad enough, Altrincham then turned to the monarch herself. She was popular enough for the moment, but that was largely attributable to her tender years. But when she had 'lost the bloom of youth', her reputation would depend much more on her own personality. Unfortunately, he thought, her style of speaking was 'frankly "a pain in the neck"', and like her mother, 'she appears to be unable to string even a few sentences together without a written text'. And then, the supreme insult:

> George V . . . did not write his own speeches, yet they were always in character; they seemed to be a natural emanation from and expression of the man. Not so the present Queen's. The personality conveyed by the utterances which are put into her mouth is that of a priggish schoolgirl, captain of the hockey team, a prefect, and a recent candidate for Confirmation. It is not thus that she will be enabled to come into her own as an independent and distinctive character.[15]

For a peer of the realm to attack the Queen in print as 'priggish' and a 'pain in the neck' was, in August 1957, a sensation. At first the BBC refused to carry the story altogether, despite the fact that both cinema newsreels and ITN bulletins were giving it their full attention. Although the *National and English Review* was a fairly obscure publication, the choicest extracts were reprinted in the national press under headlines like 'Peer's Strange Attack on the Queen'. A few commentators supported him, notably in the *New Statesman*, but most reacted with outrage. Writing in the *Daily Mail*, Henry Fairlie excoriated Altrincham for 'daring to pit his infinitely tiny and temporary mind against the accumulated experience of centuries'; the *Sunday Times* accused him of caddishness and cowardice for attacking someone who could hardly answer back; the *Observer* sacked him as a columnist; and the town of Altrincham itself disowned him.[16] In the following issue of *National and English Review*, Altrincham himself published a letter from one furious woman who spoke for many. 'What a cowardly bully you are!' she wrote. 'I can well imagine what a beastly specimen you were at your preparatory school – the sort who hit boys smaller and weaker than yourself, no doubt.'[17] Within Buckingham Palace, although the older courtiers were generally disgusted by Altrincham's behaviour, some of the younger palace aides were pleased to have the opportunity for debate. The Queen's assistant private secretary, Martin Charteris, told Altrincham: 'This is the best thing that has happened in my time,' and later recalled that while the Queen, understandably, disliked the article, he thought that 'there was something of great importance in what John Grigg said . . . we were a bit stuffy, you know'.[18]

The climax of the affair came when Altrincham was leaving Television House after an interview by Robin Day. In full view of the television camera, an elderly buffer called P. K. Burbidge, a member of the extremely conservative League of Empire Loyalists, stepped forward and smacked the peer across the face, shouting: 'Take that, from the League of Empire Loyalists!' Of course, this made a splendid story for the newspapers. 'Smack! Lord A. Gets His Face Slapped', read the main headline in the *Mirror* the following morning.[19] At his trial Burbidge told the Chief Metropolitan Magistrate that he 'felt it was up to a decent Briton to show resentment'. He was fined twenty shillings, although the magistrate agreed that 'ninety-five per cent of the population of this country were disgusted and offended by what was written'.[20] Indeed, Altrincham's critics were not confined to Fleet Street and the Empire Loyalists; he received one letter that apparently read as follows:

Altrincham, if we ever see you in the street, we'll do you in. We ain't no law-abiding boys and we don't hold with this police stuff but you

go too flamin' far when you critisise our Queen who does more good
than you if you lived to be 500. She's a grand lady and you bloody
well know it.

Yours,

Eight (loyal to the Queen) Teddy Boys[21]

As the Altrincham affair suggested, the monarchy in the fifties had
become so closely associated with the national–imperial ideal that criticism
of it was, for some people, simply intolerable. The fact remained, however,
that the conservatism and narrow introversion of the royal family did irritate
many commentators, and Altrincham's article only marked the beginning of
the controversy. Two months later, a second storm erupted over an article by
Malcolm Muggeridge in New York's *Saturday Evening Post*. Unlike the relatively
obscure if well-heeled Altrincham, Muggeridge was one of the most distinctive and controversial characters of post-war British journalism. During the
thirties he had been a Marxist, but after a visit to the Soviet Union he publicly
recanted and became a zealous anti-Communist. In the summer of 1957 he
had just finished a stint as editor of the gently satirical magazine *Punch*, but
was better known to most people as a gnomish and controversial television
interviewer, 'Telly Mugg' or the 'pop Socrates', who asked pointed questions
in an unpredictable if dandyish manner. As his sympathetic biographer puts
it: 'For many, he was "the man you love to hate", but many more simply
hated him.'[22] He was perhaps the country's best-known sceptic, but at the
same time many viewers found him both irritating and unremittingly negative, a 'gargoyle', a 'clown' and 'a pathological hater'.[23]

Muggeridge had already written one piece on the monarchy, an article
for the *New Statesman* in September 1955 entitled 'Royal Soap Opera' in which
he had remarked how extraordinary it was to idolise the royal family, 'to put
them above laughter, above criticism, above the workaday world', to turn
them into untouchable celebrities instead of the human members of a
useful and historic institution:

There are probably quite a lot of people – more than might be supposed – who, like myself, feel that another newspaper photograph of
the Royal Family will be more than they can bear. Even Princess Anne,
a doubtless estimable child, becomes abhorrent by repetition. Already
she has that curious characteristic gesture of limply holding up her
hand to acknowledge applause.[24]

At the time, few people took any notice; the country was in confident mood, and there was little of the anxiety about national decline that became so evident after Suez. In October 1957, however, the *Saturday Evening Post* ran a revised and expanded version of the same piece to coincide with a royal visit to the United States and Canada. Perhaps unfortunately, the article was given the headline 'Does England Really Need a Queen?', and the *Post* released a copy of it to the British press before its own edition had even reached American newsstands, with predictable results.[25] Like Altrincham, Muggeridge deplored the fact that the court had become the focus for so much 'snobbishness', and thought its emphasis on the tweedy upper class 'obsolete and disadvantageous in the modern world'. But much of his argument was taken out of context: where he had attacked the argument that the Crown was 'a drain on the British taxpayer', for example, he was quoted in London newspapers as having said that it was exactly that. He also noted that the upper classes were more likely to criticise the monarchy than the working classes (as the Altrincham example might suggest), remarking: 'It is duchesses, not shop assistants, who find the Queen dowdy, frumpish and banal.' In Britain, however, it was Muggeridge himself who was credited with such sentiments.[26]

Although the gist of the article was similar to the one he had published in 1955, on this occasion, with the Altrincham affair only a month or two old and national pride still smarting from the Suez fiasco, the reaction was very different. The fact that the Queen's tour of North America had passed off extremely successfully despite the appearance of Muggeridge's essay did not mitigate the public outrage that a British journalist could stoop so low as to mock his country in the American press. The attitude of the *People* was typical; it condemned the article as 'a diatribe . . . ruthless, shocking, patronizing, gruesome'.[27] If anything, Muggeridge became even more of a public whipping boy than had Altrincham, no doubt because many people already intensely disliked him. A group of schoolboys burned an effigy of Muggeridge outside Sandringham, a man spat in his face while he was taking a walk on Brighton beach, and the vicar of Cholsey in Berkshire announced that Muggeridge had 'a face it would be most satisfying to poke – the sort of face one just wishes to flatten out'. When he travelled to Edinburgh, he was met at the station by a crowd chanting 'God Save the Queen' and 'No Mercy for Muggeridge'. His house in Sussex was vandalised and his garage and barn covered with obscene slogans in yellow paint by the League of Empire Loyalists.[28] His career suffered, as well as his property: he was sacked by the *Sunday Dispatch*, which had only just signed him as a weekly columnist, and, like Lord Altrincham, he was temporarily banned from appearing on the BBC.[29] Perhaps most disturbingly there were the letters, some of which contained the usual excrement and razor blades, while others exulted in the fact that Muggeridge's son Charles had been killed in a skiing accident the previous year. 'The world is better off now he has gone: what about joining him?' one correspondent asked.[30]

Both Altrincham and Muggeridge eventually recovered from the scandal that had engulfed them. Many of their critics assumed that the outraged reaction to their articles had discredited their views completely, but this was not the case. Not only did the younger members of the Queen's staff privately agree with their sentiments, but Prince Philip, the leading proponent of modernisation from within the family itself, welcomed the chance to push for change.[31] The most enduring result of this new mood was the end of the Queen's resistance to giving a television broadcast on Christmas Day, as opposed to the usual radio address that had been the norm since George V began the tradition in 1932. Her grandfather had taken surprisingly easily to the wireless, while her shy and nervous father had found it something of a trial. As for the Queen, she was initially reluctant to move from radio to television, where her every hesitation would be mercilessly displayed, and both the royal household and the BBC spent weeks planning the big occasion to minimise any accidents. The final draft of the speech was written by Prince Philip himself, ever eager to be involved in his wife's career, and the producer was compelled to pluck up his courage and advise the Queen that she was pitching her voice too high and over-emphasising every word. As it turned out, try as she might, the Queen could not avoid sounding extremely aloof and stilted during her first broadcasts; only after a great many editions did she begin to relax and sound natural, although her accent still struck many viewers as strange and anachronistic. All the same, the 1957 Christmas broadcast was a resounding success, watched by over sixteen million people, and in many households it became something of a festive ritual.[32]

In the long term, the controversies of 1957 hinted at the re-emergence of an older critical spirit, keen to identify the weakness and complacency of national elites and institutions. But, as far as many people at the time were concerned, it had been a short-lived storm in a tea-cup. No doubt many other potential critics of the monarchy were reluctant to risk the same opprobrium as had befallen Altrincham and Muggeridge, and they inspired few immediate imitators. Most newspapers treated the monarchy with solemn reverence, although the *Manchester Guardian* looked down, rather disdainfully and predictably, on the royal family's unsophisticated cultural and intellectual tastes.[33] Critical discussion was also hard to find because there was very little political purpose in it; while Conservatives strongly identified with the monarchy, most working-class Labour MPs, like their constituents, enjoyed royal ritual and had been brought up to respect the institution.[34] 'The monarchy in Britain is established and safe,' commented one observer in the *New Statesman* in January 1960; 'indeed, the age of mass-communication has brought it a degree of popularity which would have seemed inconceivable even to the Victoria of the Jubilee.'[35] This was probably true: in 1961, a record audience of nearly half of the population watched or listened to the Queen's Christmas broadcast.[36] Two months later, looking forward to the tenth anniversary of the Queen's accession, the *Observer* commented:

> Public criticism of the person of the Queen is unheard, and in private it is usually a signal of a consciously daring arrogance. Virtually no one in public life comes out and declares himself a republican and it is doubtful that any political career would at present survive such a declaration.[37]

*

In October 1957, at the same time that Malcolm Muggeridge's article on the monarchy was stirring up a fuss on both sides of the Atlantic, London's bookshops took delivery of a collection of essays entitled *Declaration*. It was edited by Tom Maschler, a young and ambitious editor at MacGibbon and Kee who had decided to bring together 'a number of young men and widely opposed writers who have burst onto the scene and are striving to change many of the values which have held good in recent years'. As Maschler's gushing introduction put it, the eight authors – Doris Lessing, Colin Wilson, John Osborne, John Wain, Kenneth Tynan, Stuart Holyroyd, Bill Hopkins, Lindsay Anderson – were people who would 'mould our tomorrow'.[38] Six of the eight need no introduction, while the two more obscure contributors, Hopkins and Holroyd, were self-styled existentialists and geniuses in the Wilson mould. Two other fashionable writers of the moment who refused to participate were Iris Murdoch and Kingsley Amis. Amis, although still nominally a socialist, was full of scorn for the venture and the subjects suggested by Maschler. 'I hate all this pharisaical twitter-ing about the "state of our civilisation",' he wrote, 'and I suspect anyone who wants to buttonhole me about "my role in society".'[39] Not only did Maschler reprint this refusal in the introduction to the book, but two of the contributors, Lessing and Anderson, also attacked Amis in their essays. 'Amis reveals himself as a coward, too scared to take any stand at all,' wrote Lindsay Anderson. 'Socialism as a positive ideal, involving definable human values, apparently means nothing to him . . . One can only wonder why he continues to vote Left: through a lingering, irrational, shame-faced human-ism, I suppose.'[40]

To many readers the book offered less a coherent argument than a hotchpotch of wildly different ideas linked by a nominal sense of bitterness against contemporary Britain. The most overtly political contributions were those by Lessing and Anderson, both of whom openly stated their attachment to socialism. Tynan was rather more sceptical about the poten-tial of political radicalism in a society dominated by consumerism and celebrity; Osborne and Wain steered clear of party politics; and Wilson, Hopkins and Holroyd were operating in some mysterious ether of warmed-over existentialism and sub-Nietzschean philosophising. But they were all agreed on two counts. First, they accepted the premise that Britain was in decline and entering a period of cultural disintegration. 'If there is one thing which distinguishes our literature, it is a confusion of standards and the uncertainty of values,' wrote Lessing. 'I believe that our civilization is in decline, and that Outsiders are a symptom of that decline,' declared Wilson. Second, they all agreed on the cause: the moral and political inad-equacies of their elders, the cultural critics who had dominated British letters in the forties and fifties and the old men who had governed the nation since the war.[41]

Beyond that, however, there was very little agreement. The three bohemians clearly constituted a bizarre faction of their own. Colin Wilson muttered darkly about the coming 'evolution of a higher type of man . . . hardly less than superman', while Hopkins forecast 'the end of pure rationalism as the foundation of our thinking' and Holroyd called for an end to 'the myths of democracy and representative government'.[42] To many readers, these kinds of opinions were not far removed from the exal-tation of fascism, and in *Declaration* itself Kenneth Tynan called their authors 'young *Führers* of the soul'.[43] Indeed, it was hardly surprising, given their apparent admiration for both Oswald Mosley and Hitler, that the three geniuses found it difficult to retain the respect of their contemporaries. John Osborne contemptuously dismissed Hopkins and Holroyd as Wilson's 'two altar boys', and like Wilson they were swiftly condemned to lives of crushing anonymity, their appearances in the early issues of *Penthouse* notwithstanding.[44] Meanwhile Doris Lessing, the oldest contributor at thirty-eight and the most politically committed, devoted her essay to the dangers of mass culture, complaining that 'working people get their view of life through a screen of high-pressure advertising, sex-sodden newspapers and debased films and television', while the middle-class papers were 'debilitated by a habit of languid conformity which is attacking Britain like dry rot'. The task of the writer, she believed, was to cry out against 'the pettiness and narrowness' of British life.[45] Both John Wain and Kenneth Tynan based their contributions around the issue of snobbery. Wain attacked the nepotism of the 'smart magazines' that dominated literary London, a typical preoccupation of a Movement writer. Tynan was unsurprisingly absorbed by theatrical questions and complained that British drama was still governed by the 'assumption that there are still people who live in awe of the Crown, the Empire, the established Church, the public schools and upper classes'.[46] Whether this was still true in 1957 was dubious, since the vogue for kitchen-sink drama was well under way, but his implied criticism of the great national institutions was in itself something of a novelty.

The two most provocative essays were those by Lindsay Anderson and John Osborne. Anderson was only just beginning to build his reputation as the pioneer of Free Cinema, and he used his essay to launch an attack on national cinema for being 'metropolitan in attitude, and entirely middle-class'. It was, he thought, symptomatic of a nation that was drab and dull by comparison with the Continent. Returning to Britain after a trip abroad was, he said, 'always something of an ordeal':

> It isn't just the food, the sauce bottles on the café tables, and the chips with everything. It isn't even saying goodbye to wine, goodbye to sunshine . . .
>
> For coming back to Britain is also, in many respects, like going back to the nursery. The outside world, the dangerous world, is shut away: its sounds are muffled . . . Nanny lights the fire, and sits herself down with a nice cup of tea and yesterday's *Daily Express*, but she keeps half an eye on us too.[47]

As Arthur Marwick suggests, the language of the piece is just as revealing as its message: very few of the ordinary working-class Britons that Anderson extolled were in the habit of making trips to Europe, and even fewer were familiar with Nanny.[48] Still, the argument was powerful enough, and the striking image of modern Britain as a deceptively cosy, old-fashioned world of open fires and cups of tea was common to other writers in the late fifties, C. P. Snow being a good example.[49]

More striking still was the language used by John Osborne in his essay 'They Call It Cricket', the most controversial of the lot. Osborne shared the same very vague political convictions as many of his peers, but much of the article was an attack on the dramatic and literary critics who wrote 'sneering and parochial' articles in the weekend reviews: they were 'deluded pedants', 'fashionable turnips' and 'death's heads of imagination and feeling'. Further abuse was then hurled at other respectable figures: the bishops of the Church of England, for example, who had 'repeatedly ducked' issues like poverty, the atomic bomb and South Africa, and were little more than 'bewigged old perverts at Assizes'.[50] Where Osborne really hit his stride, though, was his attack on his countrymen's adoration for the monarchy, 'that fabulous family we love so well – the Amazing Windsors!' It was, he thought, the 'National Swill':

> The leader-writers and the bribed gossip-mongers only have to rattle their sticks in the royalty bucket for most of their readers to put their heads down in this trough of Queen-worship . . . My objection to the royalty symbol is that it is dead: it is the gold filling in a mouthful of decay . . . It distresses me that there should be so many empty minds, so many empty lives in Britain to sustain this fatuous industry; that no one should have the wit to laugh it into extinction, or the honesty to resist it.[51]

Osborne's essay attracted little of the outrage that had greeted Muggeridge's much more innocuous article published in the same month, although the directors of the Royal Court, where the launch party for *Declaration* was scheduled to be held, wanted to dissociate themselves from his outburst and the party was moved to a basement club instead.[52] Even so, the phrase 'the gold filling in a mouthful of decay' stuck, not least because it so perfectly captured the current sense of frustration at national decline.[53]

Declaration enjoyed respectable sales, selling about 25,000 copies to the domestic market and being translated into several languages, so Tom Maschler was very pleased with his product.[54] On the other hand, the reviews were pretty awful. Daniel Farson, a reviewer sympathetic to the young intellectuals of the late fifties, wrote in *Books and Bookmen* that it was 'conceited and remote', 'a complete failure . . . as a statement of any real significance or permanence'. Henry Fairlie, writing in *Tribune*, was baffled why the authors presented themselves as socialists when there was 'no doubt what their protest is about. They resent the fact that Britain is no longer a Great Power. They don't like being Little Englanders.'[55] In the *Observer*, Angus Wilson thought that the content of the book was 'trivial', but that somehow it expressed a general mood of pessimism and frustration:

> We are all waiting for something great to turn up. And in our discontent we are often led to speculate whether England's artistic death does not reflect a wider sterility in the social and political structure of the country. To have voiced this gnawing fear . . . is surely the real achievement of the Angry Young Men as a group. Much of their picture is pure myth but it responds to our present discontents.[56]

If John Osborne had escaped serious controversy for his attack on the monarchy in 1957, he had not long to wait. He had made it his business to cultivate 'a freelance indignation' unfettered by any great ideological commitments; as one commentator puts it: 'Name a topic, any topic . . . and he would lambast it.'[57] In 1961 he published a splenetic 'Letter to My Countrymen' in the pages of *Tribune*, a vituperative rant that perfectly caught his resentment at the banality and complacency of British life in the post-imperial age:

> This is a letter of hate. It is for you, my countrymen. I mean those men of my country who have defiled it. The men with manic fingers leading the sightless, feeble, betrayed body of my country to its death. You are its murderers, and there's little left in my own brain but the thoughts of murder for you . . .
>
> There is murder in my brain and I carry a knife in my heart for every one of you. Macmillan and you, Gaitskell, you particularly . . .
>
> . . . You are MY hatred. That is my final identity . . . I think it may sustain me in the last few months. Till then, damn you, England. You're rotting now, and quite soon you'll disappear.[58]

This time Osborne had all the attention he could want; with the economy in the doldrums and the Empire in a state of collapse, anxiety about the state of the country was running high and conservatives were quick to defend the national honour. Shortly afterwards Osborne, who was nominally married to the young actress Mary Ure (Alison in *Look Back in Anger*), took a girlfriend for a country weekend in Hellingly, Sussex. Not only did Osborne find the house surrounded by the press, but he was also amused to see a posse of elderly residents waving placards:

DAMN YOU OSBORNE
HELLINGLY WANTS MARY URE
ENGLAND'S ANGRY OLD MEN OBJECT[59]

Declaration was just one among many tracts published during the Macmillan years to lament the decline of national prestige and competitiveness and to find a scapegoat in the anachronistic, snobbish, conspiratorial political elite that was thought to be running the country. As early as 1953 and his novel *Hurry On Down*, John Wain had articulated the frustration of the outsider through the thoughts of Charles Lumley: 'The network everywhere: no, a web, sticky and cunningly arranged. You were either a spider, sitting comfortably in the middle or waiting with malicious joy in hiding, or you were a fly, struggling amid the clinging threads.'[60] In the same year, a new term for the 'network', or what the radical campaigner William Cobbett had once called 'the THING', caught on. 'The THING gets hold of you, even if you kick against it,' wrote A. J. P. Taylor in the *New Statesman*. 'The Establishment draws in recruits from outside as soon as they are ready to conform to its standards and become respectable. There is nothing more agreeable in life than to make peace with the Establishment – and nothing more corrupting.'[61] Taylor had first coined the term 'the Establishment' two years previously, but in 1955 it was taken up by the conservative journalist Henry Fairlie, who used it in the *Spectator* to describe the 'matrix of official and social relations by which power is exercised'. 'The "Establishment"', he explained, 'can be seen at work in the activities of not only the Prime Minister, the Archbishop of Canterbury and the Earl Marshal, but of such lesser mortals as the Chairman of the Arts Council, the Director-General of the BBC and even the editor of *The Times Literary Supplement*.'[62] Above all, Fairlie blamed the Establishment for protecting the Soviet spies Guy Burgess and Donald Maclean, both of whom had been educated at public schools and Cambridge but had defected to Moscow in 1951. For many commentators, the reluctance of the Foreign Office to admit their departure until 1955 provided a telling illustration of official incompetence and nepotism. The *Daily Herald* demanded 'a little more fresh air in the place' and 'fresh minds whose schooling was irrelevant'; the *Sunday Express* complained that the Foreign Office officials had failed to 'realise that this isn't an old-school-tie society'.[63]

The Suez crisis, predictably enough, had only increased the criticism. The idea of an undemocratic, impenetrable and incompetent political elite provided a useful excuse for national humiliation and a focus for the unsystematic anger and resentment of younger critics who were disillusioned with socialism but still disliked the Conservative government and felt excluded from power and influence. At the height of the crisis, for example, the literary scholar F. R. Leavis wrote in the *Listener* that the Establishment could be defined as 'those who have the institutional positions and the power in the institutional system, and, by all the signs, stand solidly together'.[64] A year later, *Twentieth Century* magazine published a special issue with contributions from the likes of A. J. P. Taylor and Philip Toynbee, asking: 'Is There a Power Elite?' According to Toynbee, there certainly was: an intellectual and political elite, recruited from the major public schools and the universities of Oxford and Cambridge and then propelled smoothly into positions of influence. The English upper class, he argued, had not really been displaced during the Attlee years because 'the *social* power of that class was almost untouched, and will remain so until a genuine social revolution has been accomplished here'.[65] In 1958, ITV made a short documentary on the subject, with Lord Boothby and Lady Violet Bonham Carter as expert witnesses and Paul Johnson as chief advocate for the prosecution. *The Times* even ran a notorious advertising campaign to try and exploit the public fascination with the idea of an elite: 'Top People Take *The Times*'.[66]

It would be tempting to dismiss all this as the slightly hysterical search for a national scapegoat, but in fact there was a good deal of truth in the accusations. In 1962, according to one analysis, the descendants of just four Victorian peers (Devonshire, Lansdowne, Abercorn and Marlborough) included the Prime Minister, the Foreign Secretary, the Lord Chancellor and six other government ministers, the British Ambassador to the United States, the Governor of the Bank of England and his predecessor, seven directors of the largest merchant banks and the owners of *The Times*, the

Observer and the *Daily Mail*. The best way to enter the Establishment, as Lord
Annan observed years later, was by birth or, failing that, by 'knowing somebody'.[67] The literary intellectuals of the thirties and forties, many of whom
were still influential in the 1950s, had in many cases known one another as
children. Cyril Connolly, Cecil Beaton and George Orwell, for instance, had
all attended the same prep school.[68] Not for nothing is Annan's retrospective look at public affairs during his lifetime called *Our Age*: it was still natural
in the fifties for a small group of men who grown up together to feel that
they defined and directed politics and letters in Britain. They had the same
education, spoke in the same accents and understood the same allusions.
This was not, however, an entirely closed world; grammar-school boys who
made it to Oxford or Cambridge could clamber aboard provided that they
were bright and adaptable:

> The manners of Our Age were public school manners; and it was easier
> to be accepted if you adopted their manners, dressed like them, spoke
> with their accent and learnt their language and jokes. The grammar
> school boy who came up to sit for the scholarship exams with fountain
> pen clipped into his breast pocket, in school blazer or with the collar of
> his open-necked shirt worn outside the coat, would change the way he
> dressed in order to conform.[69]

A glance at Oxford during the late thirties suggests that Annan was
right. A timid young Harold Wilson arrived at the small college of Jesus in
1934, and one year later another grammar-school boy, Edward Heath, came
up to Balliol, by tradition the most intellectually powerful and politically
influential of the Oxford colleges, as an organ scholar. Heath went on to
become president of the Balliol Junior Common Room, and his successor
was a boy from Bradford Grammar School called Denis Healey. Two years
later, the Balliol presidency was occupied by a young Roy Jenkins, whose
closest friend, Anthony Crosland, was a student next door at Trinity. The
college on the other side of Balliol from Trinity is St John's; it was there, in
1941, that another grammar-school boy, Philip Larkin, first spotted the
name of Kingsley Amis on a list in the porter's lodge.

     While these are just some of the more famous examples of Oxford grad-
uates who came to dominate British life and letters in the fifties and sixties,
there were plenty of much more anonymous cases. Between 1948 and 1956,
no less than half of the recruits to the higher levels of the civil service had

been to Oxford, and a further third had been to Cambridge. Half of all the new appointments had studied classics or history; just one in a hundred had studied science. While the Civil Service Commissioners were keen to encourage applicants from grammar schools, even writing a congratulatory letter to their headmaster every time a candidate was accepted, they were unperturbed by the emphasis on Oxford and Cambridge. 'It's partly that the best people are creamed off to Oxbridge at sixth-form level,' one explained to Anthony Sampson, 'but also that the life at Oxford and Cambridge gives people wider interests and more developed ideas – at the other universities so many students have never even left home.'[70] Not only were the two major universities disproportionately favoured, but certain colleges within them were especially successful at sending their boys to fill senior positions in the civil service. Between 1956 and 1961, for example, twenty-seven senior positions were filled by graduates of New College, Oxford; twenty-six by men from King's, Cambridge; and twenty-five by Balliol men. During the same period, precisely one position went to a man who had been educated at a comprehensive or secondary modern school.[71]

The most successful Oxford and Cambridge graduates, especially if they showed themselves reliable and orthodox, could expect to hold 'a multitude of public appointments', so while the Establishment certainly contained members of the royal family and the court, the editor of *The Times*, the Director General of the BBC and so on, it also included rather blander figures like Lionel Robbins and Cyril Radcliffe.[72] Robbins was an economist and professor at the LSE; at various points he was chairman of the boards of the *Financial Times* and the National Gallery and president of the British Academy, and he also sat on the boards of the Tate Gallery, the Royal Opera House and the Royal Economic Society. Radcliffe, meanwhile, had been director general of the Ministry of Information during the war, supervised the drawing of the partition lines between India and Pakistan and Greek and Turkish Cyprus, chaired one inquiry into monetary policy, two inquiries into taxation, and three inquiries into security, and was the chairman of the trustees of the British Museum and a member of the Court of the University of London. Robbins was a life peer; Radcliffe was a law lord.[73] Yet what made the charges of conspiracy even harder to dispel was that so many of these men were so anonymous. The editor of *The Times*, Sir William Haley, had previously been the Director General of the BBC. Two more prestigious positions it is difficult to imagine; all the same, astonishingly, Sir William was so little known that in the late fifties a journalist managed to interview him under the impression that he was Bill Haley, the bandleader and rock and roll pioneer.[74]

Not surprisingly, given the level of popular interest in the idea of an Establishment in the fifties and sixties, it played a considerable part in several novels of the period, especially those which tried to give an expansive picture of society through the device of a cycle, or *roman fleuve*. The most successful was Anthony Powell's series *A Dance to the Music of Time* (1951–1975), which was the object of great praise by many literary critics and has a good claim to be the supreme fictional achievement of the period. His narrator and hero, Nicholas Jenkins, moves effortlessly but with wry detachment through a world of privilege and power: he attends a prestigious public school (obviously Eton), goes up to Oxford, moves in the intellectual world of the thirties, serves in the army during the war (the highlight of the sequence) and then is on hand to observe the social changes of the fifties and sixties. The cycle often turns on coincidences and chance meetings with friends from school or college, but of course such things were highly plausible in the world in which Jenkins (and Powell, who went to Eton and Balliol) moved; the old-boy network is here very much a reality.[75] There is a similar emphasis in Simon Raven's sequence *Alms for Oblivion* (1964–1976), which is much more overtly comic but also less detached: in Raven's works, gentlemen usually turn out to be cads, self-interest and cynicism rule, but the patrician shits who inhabit its pages are still invariably more interesting and worthwhile than their bland and conniving middle-class contemporaries.[76] While Powell is content to observe the Establishment in action, and occasionally to subject it to apparently mild but actually incisive ridicule, Raven is much keener to expose, and wallow in, its various indecencies, with a bawdier but less satisfying effect.

The image that writers in the fifties and sixties used most frequently to represent the Establishment was that of the 'corridors of power', which was the title of a novel by C. P. Snow in 1964. Snow himself described the corridors of power in an evocative passage in the *Listener* in 1957:

> The most characteristic picture of modern power is nothing at all sinister. It is no more or less remarkable than an office – I mean, an office building. Office buildings are much the same all over the world. Down the corridor of one of these offices, of any of them, a man is walking briskly. He is carrying a folder of papers. He is middle-aged and well-preserved, muscular and active. He is not a great tycoon but he is well

above the model of his particular ladder. He meets someone in the corridor not unlike himself. They are talking business. They are not intriguing. One of them says: 'This is going to be a difficult one' – meaning a question on which, in a few minutes, they are going to take different sides. They are off to a meeting of a dozen similar bosses. They will be at it for hours. This is the face of power in a society like ours.[77]

Like so many other writers, Snow was fascinated by power and its trappings, and the exercise of power from within the British Establishment was the theme of his vast novelistic sequence *Strangers and Brothers* (1940–1970), which focused on 'the struggles of the committee room' from the beginning of the Great War to the end of the sixties.[78] Each book examines a cloistered, successful, masculine and exclusive environment, from the law courts and the common rooms of Cambridge to the laboratories of a research establishment and the numberless corridors of Whitehall. The protagonist is Lewis Eliot, a provincial outsider who rapidly rises through the Establishment, moving through the Inns of Court to Cambridge, the country houses of the aristocracy and the boardrooms of big business, and is welcomed into a rich Anglo-Jewish family. In the Second World War he joins the civil service and works at a top-secret atomic research centre; he is knighted, becomes a senior government adviser, and finally becomes a government minister in the mid-sixties.[79] The model for Eliot was, very obviously, Snow himself, whose career moved along similarly smooth lines, from his childhood in Leicester to his Cambridge fellowship, civil service work in the war, stint as a Civil Service Commissioner with responsibility for scientific recruitment, and post as Parliamentary Secretary at the Ministry of Technology in the first Wilson government from 1964 to 1966.[80] Throughout his books two images proliferate: first, the image of a warm, cosy room with the curtains drawn against the night and a fire roaring in the grate; second, the same scene observed from without by an outsider who can see only the glimmer of light through windows that remain firmly closed. On the one hand, we experience the feeling of success and acceptance that comes with admission into the Establishment; on the other, we sense the frustrated ambitions of the outsider who can only stare through the night at the lit windows.[81]

Not all of those who discussed the Establishment in the late fifties shared Snow's admiration for it. Criticism of the Establishment seems to have become something of a rite of passage for younger intellectuals, and well before the advent of the television satirists of the sixties there was a healthy climate of argument and national self-criticism. In August 1959, the fashionable magazine *Queen* ran a satirical piece purporting to be 'The Establishment Chronicle & Nepotists' Gazette', a school newsletter based on the *Eton Chronicle*, claiming William Haley as its editor and Kenneth Clark as its art director. The arms of the Establishment bear the motto: 'Qualify, Compromise, Arrange', and the Club rules include the following:

1. The aim of the Establishment is to run the country.
2. Membership is restricted to those either in a position of direct power or able to wield great personal influence . . .
7. Power is all important, but must only be exercised in the following ways: –
    (a) through front men, puppets and 'the faceless ones'
    (b) through nominees, trustees and lawyers
    (c) by pure cash
    (d) by glimpses of social advancement.
8. Power may be discreetly misused for the following purposes: –
    (a) to cover up mistakes
    (b) to provide for one's family
    (c) to preserve law and order
    (d) to keep Selwyn Lloyd in office.[82]

The centrepiece of the article is a double-page photograph of the Establishment, their faces superimposed on a photograph of an Etonian boarding house, with the names given from left to right in good old-fashioned school style, so we get the likes of L. Mountbatten, E. Waugh, T. Eliot, E. Heath, I. Berlin, W. Haley and so on, with H. Macmillan in the centre, next to the cups and prizes won. Overleaf there is a report of the last Debating Society meeting, which supposedly discussed the motion 'All power is delightful but absolute power is absolutely delightful', and there is also a note regretting that the Establishment has 'lost touch with the following old boys: – G. Burgess, D. Maclean, A. Eden, G. Glubb, O. Mosley, A. Alanbrooke, A. Head'.[83]

The cynical tone with which the 'Establishment Chronicle' ridiculed the Prime Minister and assorted other eminent figures anticipated the mockery usually associated with the satire boom of Macmillan's final years. A few weeks later, Hugh Thomas published *The Establishment*, an edited collection of essays covering everything from the public schools and the army to the City of London and the BBC. Thomas, just twenty-seven, had resigned from the Foreign Office in protest at the time of the Suez crisis; something of a loner, he was 'a classically discontented very bright young man', according to one profile.[84] His intention in publishing the book, he later recalled, was to draw attention to the fact that 'the most sensitive institutions in England were dominated by the same anachronistic master class'.[85]

Essentially *The Establishment* was a rather more serious alternative to *Declaration*, written by a slightly older group of contributors who spanned the political spectrum from left to right. The novelist Simon Raven contributed a chapter on the army; the economist and future Labour peer Thomas Balogh wrote on the civil service; Henry Fairlie discussed the BBC, and so on. As in *Declaration*, there was no real agreement between the various authors, although Thomas declared in his introduction that if the 'resources and talents of Britain' were to be 'fully developed and extended', then there was 'no doubt that the fusty Establishment, with its Victorian views and standards of judgement, must be destroyed'.[86] As Henry Fairlie himself pointed out, however, the term 'Establishment' had by now become so debased that to most people it really meant 'those in positions of power they happen to dislike most'. In Fairlie's eyes, the Establishment amounted to nothing: there was no network of elites controlling Britain, but simply a vast nothingness at the centre of British political life, representing, he thought, the emptiness of the Butskellite consensus.[87]

The fact that the term 'Establishment' remained vague and undefined, and that its popularity reflected the anxiety of British intellectuals after Suez rather than any wider groundswell of revolution in the shires, did not prevent it from becoming one of the clichés of the next few years. There were so many attacks on the old-boy network between 1957 and 1964 that it seemed that any journalist searching for a theme was dusting down the Establishment, propping it up and then aiming a few weary punches in its general direction.[88] The historian Jim Tomlinson rightly dismisses much of this stuff as 'Mickey Mouse sociology', but at the time both publishers and readers had a hearty appetite for more of the same, and one book in particular stands out.[89]

In 1962, a particularly bad year for Macmillan and the Conservatives, the *Observer* correspondent Anthony Sampson published his *Anatomy of Britain*, a comprehensive attempt to analyse the political and social networks that dominated British life, drawing closely on the work of the 'What's Wrong with Britain' critics. In a telling phrase in the introduction, Sampson explains that his intention is 'to offer myself as an informal guide to a *living museum*, describing the rooms and exhibits as I found them'.[90] His themes are the struggle between meritocracy and aristocracy; 'the conflict between professionals and amateurs'; 'the proliferation of committees; the prevalence of sons-in-law; the obscuring of ends by means; the pressure of conformism; the difficulties of combining democracy with efficiency; the conflict between old, protected, semi-feudal values and aggressive competition and salesmanship'. There is, he says, 'no point in disguising' the fact that 'a loss of dynamic and purpose, and a general bewilderment, are felt by many people, both at the top and the bottom in Britain today'. True, he admits that Britain is still the most 'civilised and humane country, and the happiest to live in', but it is quite clear from the introduction alone that he has found it backward, inefficient, unambitious and nepotistic.[91]

Sampson's analysis of the Establishment in *Anatomy of Britain* is much more sophisticated than those found in books like *Declaration* and even *The Establishment*. As he notes, a simple dichotomy between 'We' and 'They' is nothing more than a 'mirage'. The ruling elite is 'not at all close-knit or united':

> They are not so much in the centre of a solar system, as in a cluster of interlocking circles, each one largely preoccupied with its own professionalism and expertise, and touching others only at one edge – an image depicted symbolically on the endpapers of this book; they are not a single Establishment but a ring of Establishments, with slender connections. The frictions and balances between the different circles are the supreme safeguards of democracy. No one man can stand in the centre, for there is no centre.[92]

But this does not mean, however, that the idea of a ruling elite is merely a myth. A chart halfway through chapter three makes this very obvious: it shows how, for example, the family connections of the Duke of Devonshire encompass the Prime Minister, the Attorney General, the Secretary for War, the owners of *The Times* and *Observer*, the Ambassador to Washington, and even President Kennedy. The connections of the Duke of Marlborough, meanwhile, include the Foreign and Commonwealth

Secretaries, the chairmen of Lazards, Guinness and Courtaulds, the owner of the *Daily Express* and the Deputy Governor of the Bank of England.[93] Over the course of his 638 pages, Sampson builds up a picture of inefficiency and amateurism that he attributes to the legacy of the Victorian age, when so many of the institutions he studies were established. Among other things, he condemns the 'irrelevant façade' of Whitehall pageantry and secrecy, the facelessness and irresponsibility of modern bureaucracy, where 'the will of people dissolves in committees', and above all, 'the old English ideal of the amateur'.[94]

The ideal of the amateur, according to Sampson, remains one of the most attractive aspects of British public life, but it epitomises the failings of the current Macmillan government. Britain is stagnating in an old world of family connections and complacent assumptions of superiority, while across the Atlantic the Kennedy administration is inaugurating a new environment of professionalism, dynamism and efficiency:

> In particular, the hereditary Establishment of interlocking families, which still has an infectious social and political influence on the Conservative party, banking and many industries, has lost touch with the new worlds of science, industrial management and technology, and yet tries to apply old amateur ideals into technical worlds where they won't fit . . .
>
> The menace of the British Conservative nexus, it seems to me, lies in the fact that it has retreated into an isolated and defensive amateur world, which cherishes irrelevant aspects of the past and regards the activities of meritocrats and technocrats as a potential menace.[95]

In sum, Britain has become 'astonishingly uncommercial' and its people have 'lost their dynamic, are sunk in complacency, are far too snobbish, and have carried on a pattern of relationships that is disappearing elsewhere in the world'.[96] The country must rid itself of 'the club-amateur outlook', and turn with wholehearted enthusiasm to a new breed of meritocratic experts, scientists, managers and technicians to carry it into the 1960s.[97]

Sampson's analysis was well timed, since it appeared at a time when Macmillan's government was struggling badly in opinion polls and by-elections; it accordingly drew a great deal of praise from critics on all sides, prompting him to issue several revised versions over the next few decades.[98] The argument that scientific modernisation had the potential to reverse

Britain's decline was a popular refrain of the day, not least among some factions in the Labour Party, and formed the core of Harold Wilson's appeal to the electorate in 1964. It also provided an intellectual backdrop for the satirists of the early sixties; if anything united this disparate crowd, it was the idea that Britain was being steered into decline by a gang of complacent, snobbish, weary, anachronistic old men. In his comprehensive account of the satire boom, Humphrey Carpenter suggests that it is best understood as a short-lived rebellion against the conformity, drabness and formality of the fifties.[99] There is some truth in this, of course, but the satire of the sixties was also dominated to a great extent by exactly the same themes of snobbish anachronism and scientific modernity that were being developed by contemporary writers to explain national decline after Suez. The reason that the satirists won such acclaim between 1960 and 1963 was that they expressed ideas that were already current in public debate and familiar to their audiences. They were controversial not because the ideas themselves were new – often their ideas were reminiscent of books like *Declaration* that had been published years previously – but because this was the first time that they had been developed on television for a mass audience, rather than an audience of intellectuals. So while the central premise of the satirists struck a chord because it was already so familiar to many viewers, their irreverent style, and the form in which they developed it, did represent something new: a combination of serious political criticism and juvenile irreverence, played out under the aegis of one of the most respected institutions in the country, the BBC.

The satire boom of the early sixties was more than just a television phenomenon. But satire reached its greatest audience, and caused the most controversy, when it was televised; had it not been for the rapid development of televised entertainment since the mid-fifties, especially after the arrival of Hugh Carleton Greene, the satirists would never have enjoyed such success or renown. The satire boom also drew on a long history of irreverent comedy, from Hogarth to Dickens. Working-class culture, far from being bluff and primitive, had elements of baroque and even grandiloquent eloquence, and working-class comedians often delighted their audiences with their dark, biting humour and elaborate linguistic panache.[100] Most people liked to believe that the British sense of humour was unique, not least in the fact that it was often self-directed. Continental Europeans were mocked for their blunt and obvious sense of humour, while

Americans were usually regarded as being almost entirely humourless. In one book published on the eve of the Second World War, *The English Genius*, it was argued that the true patron saint of England was 'not St George, but Sir John Falstaff . . . we are the most civilised people in the world, the reason being that we are the most humorous people in the world'. Just after war had been declared, the *Listener* observed: 'Bravery of the devil-may-care variety is not peculiar to the English. Where we do differ from other peoples is in our natural capacity for laughing at ourselves . . . And this is an attitude that in the days to come will stand us in good stead. Whatever other noises will assail our ears, it is safe to predict that the sound of English laughter will not cease to echo around the world.'[101] No doubt the British capacity for self-mockery is often overstated, but the sustained success of television comedies like *Dad's Army* and *Fawlty Towers* in the sixties and seventies suggests that British audiences did have a hearty appetite for laughing at the failings of their own country.

The obvious comic forerunners for the satirists of the early sixties were the radio comedians known as the Goons – Spike Milligan, Peter Sellers Harry Secombe, and, initially, Michael Bentine – who delighted audiences during the years of austerity. Indeed, the success of the Goons gives the lie to those who would paint the early fifties as nothing more than a period of 'strict formalism', 'a dull and cliché-ridden popular culture' and so on.[102] First broadcast in May 1951, the show soon claimed almost two million listeners and did not come to an end until 1960, long after Bentine had departed and by which time Sellers had become a successful film actor.[103] Even the Goons, despite their taste for the anarchic and the surreal, drew on existing traditions of British comedy: nonsense songs, catchphrases, puns, schoolboy juvenilia, silly voices, and the practical jokes of the Crazy Gang.[104] The general tone of the show was anarchic in the extreme, and audiences never quite knew what to expect, although the repetition of catchphrases and familiar comic stereotypes delighted the boys and young men who tended to make up most of the audience. Popular characters included Major Bloodnok (Sellers), formerly of the Rajputana Rifles, decorated for having emptied the dustbins during a battle; Hercules Grytpype-Thynne (Sellers), the supreme aristocratic cad; and Neddy Seagoon (Secombe), a good-natured, incompetent bungler.[105] The most successful characters, like Major Bloodnok, were often caricatures of stereotypical national heroes, and according to Sellers' biographer Roger Lewis, the *Goon Show* can be seen as a surrealistic reaction to the violence and suffering of the war, which all four men had seen at first hand. Many episodes were devoted to parodies of war films or pastiches of the tales of nineteenth-century imperial heroism that the team had read as boys before the war, and the show took an attitude of exuberant ridicule towards the Empire and British national institutions.[106] Jonathan Miller, one of the satirical pioneers of the sixties, recalled with affection a scene in which Major Bloodnok is stranded on the Northwest Frontier, doubled up with diarrhoea, the very antithesis of the cool British imperial officer. As Miller saw it, the show was 'a send-up of British imperialism' and 'did an enormous amount to subvert the social order'. Like most of his fellow satirists, he was an enthusiastic fan of the Goons as a schoolboy, and drew on their anarchic inspiration when developing material of his own.[107]

The first major element in the satire boom was *Beyond the Fringe*, a professional revue assembled by the assistant director of the Edinburgh Festival in January 1960 to perform at the Festival at the end of that summer.[108] It was not an undergraduate revue, as is often thought. Of the four performers, two (Alan Bennett and Jonathan Miller) were twenty-six, while Dudley Moore was twenty-five and Peter Cook, who had just finished his studies at Cambridge, was twenty-two. They were an odd bunch. Alan Bennett was the son of a Yorkshire butcher, a very shy young man who had won a scholarship to Oxford to read history and was now researching the reign of Richard II while working as a junior lecturer at Magdalen. Jonathan Miller, by contrast, was a much more self-confident character, born into a talented and successful London Jewish family; he played the giraffe to Bennett's mouse. He had read medicine at Cambridge and was working in the pathology department of the hospital at University College, London, but he was also increasingly well known as a comedian, having appeared in the Cambridge Footlights and on television. The two younger men, Dudley Moore and Peter Cook, later won international renown as a double-act, but at this stage they did not know one another at all. Moore was the son of an electrician and a typist from a Dagenham council estate; although he was extremely short and had a deformed left leg and clubfoot, his puckish manner made him very attractive to women, as he discovered as an organ scholar at Oxford and then as a freelance jazz pianist and entertainer. Cook was very different, a tall, gawky, brilliantly funny man from an upper-middle-class background, educated at Radley and Cambridge, where he appeared in the Footlights and then in a West End revue.[109] All four, then, were highly talented and intelligent; two were from upper-middle-class backgrounds, and two from the upper fringes of the working classes. All four had experience of comedy that relied upon verbal cleverness, impersonations and improvisation, while Moore was also an exceptionally talented musician. Despite being younger than the others, Peter Cook contributed most to the original script that they prepared for Edinburgh.[110]

The team took to the stage for the first time in Edinburgh on 22 August 1960, and at first drew little critical attention. Their audience figures, however, were very encouraging, and by the end of the week there were long queues at the box office for returns.[111] Most newspapers gave the revue little attention, but a young critic called Peter Lewis, later the author of a thoughtful book on the 1950s, wrote an enthusiastic review for the *Daily Mail*, calling it 'the funniest, most intelligent, and most original revue to be staged in Britain for a very long time'.[112] Whereas other productions confined themselves to theatrical jokes and gossip and oblique references to sex, the *Beyond the Fringe* team were eager to show off their verbal dexterity and interest in issues beyond the stage, including politics and even philosophy. Since the humour largely depended on the quality of the script, they had done away with the usual trappings of the revue: flashy decorations, chorus girls and the rest, and appeared in cardigans and grey flannels, the typical casual dress of bright young men in the early sixties, on a bare stage. This was not entirely original: American comics had already pioneered a plainer style of presentation, notably Mort Sahl, whose records were by then available in London.[113]

Peter Lewis' review in the *Daily Mail* emphasised not only the sheer novelty and intelligence of the show but also its biting irreverence, which, as he recalled later, had left him 'absolutely astonished': 'They take to the stage for 90 minutes with grey sweaters, four chairs, and a piano, and proceed to demolish all that is sacred in the British way of life with glorious and expert precision.'[114] The revue began by mocking the convention of playing the National Anthem before public theatrical performances: when Dudley Moore came on stage and began playing on the piano, the audience stood up, only to discover that this was the beginning of the first sketch, in which the pianist is unmasked as a Russian because he is playing the anthem 'while sitting down'. Immediately afterwards, the other three cast members tried to persuade Moore to blow raspberries at Khrushchev and make approving grunts about Macmillan, but of course he insisted on doing the opposite, thereby poking fun at the Prime Minister in an amusing, undidactic way. Other sketches included a parody of the patriotism of newspapers like the *Mail* and *Express*, and a monologue by Alan Bennett purporting to be a pro-South African middle-class reactionary. Towards the end of the show came Bennett's most famous monologue, a spoof sermon delivered by a rambling, woolly Anglican vicar, nominally based on the unpropitious text: 'My brother Esau is a hairy man, but I am a smooth man.'[115]

The real highlight, though, and easily the most striking sketch in the show, was Peter Cook's impersonation of a party political broadcast by a doddering Harold Macmillan:

> Good evening. I have recently been travelling round the world on your behalf and at your expense, visiting some of the chaps with whom I hope to be shaping your future. I went first to Germany, and there I spoke with the German Foreign Minister, Herr . . . Herr and there, and we exchanged many frank words in our respective languages; so precious little came of that in the way of understanding . . . I then went to America, and there I had talks with the young, vigorous President of that great country, and danced with his very lovely lady wife. We talked of many things, including Great Britain's role in the world as an honest broker. I agreed with him, when he said that no nation could be more honest; and he agreed with me, when I chaffed him, and said that no nation could be broker.[116]

The impersonation of living public figures was extremely rare in British comedy in the fifties, and that made Cook's sketch all the more powerful. Rather than caricaturing Macmillan, he merely delivered a careful impression, which he himself, 'a great Macmillan fan', thought was 'extremely affectionate'.[117] As Carpenter notes, the theme of the monologue was Britain's impoverishment and decline, and the comparison of the 'young, vigorous' President and the decrepit Prime Minister was hardly a flattering one. Michael Billington, another young theatre critic, later recalled that he once asked the *Beyond the Fringe* team: 'What are you really attacking, what's your gripe?' 'Complacency,' they replied.[118]

The reaction of the Edinburgh audiences, as well as the enthusiasm of the show's producers, persuaded the four performers to agree to a revival the following year in Cambridge and Brighton, with the possibility of a

London run thereafter. The revue was twice as long this time, with a great deal of new material having been added, and some of this proved more controversial. Two sketches were particularly memorable and nicely illustrate the preoccupations of their creators. The first was a lecture by Peter Cook, playing a Civil Defence volunteer discussing the measures to deal with nuclear war:

Now, we shall receive four minutes' warning of any impending nuclear attack. Some people have said, 'Oh my goodness me – four minutes? – that is not a very long time!' Well, I would remind those doubters that some people in this great country of ours can run a mile in four minutes.[119]

The other sketch concerned the Second World War, a slightly risky undertaking given that many people in 1961 perceived the war as an untouchable symbol of national pride, unfit for criticism or mockery. Called 'The Aftermyth of War', it consisted of a series of dialogues or monologues, all lampooning the clichés of the war films of the fifties. One memorable example was an exchange between two British officers: a bewildered Perkins, played by Jonathan Miller, and his clipped, unsmiling superior, played by Peter Cook:

COOK: War's not going very well, you know . . . War is a psychological thing, Perkins, rather like a game of football. You know how in a game of football ten men often play better than eleven?
MILLER: Yes, sir.
COOK: Perkins, we are asking you to be that one man. I want you to lay down your life, Perkins. We need a futile gesture at this stage. It will raise the whole tone of the war. Get up in a crate, Perkins, pop over to Bremen, take a shufti, don't come back. Goodbye, Perkins. God, I wish I was going too.
MILLER: Goodbye, sir – or is it *au revoir*?
COOK: No, Perkins.[120]

More controversial, however, was a monologue by Alan Bennett parodying the film *Reach for the Sky*, the story of the air ace Douglas Bader. Bennett even entered the stage like Bader, with ostentatiously stiff legs (Bader had lost his legs in a flying accident) and a pipe clenched between his teeth, and then delivered a short speech recalling his experiences as 'one of the Few'. One Sunday, he said, 'we got word that Jerry was coming in – over Hastings, I think it was'.

> I could see Tunbridge Wells, and the sun glinting on the river, and I remembered the last weekend I'd spent there with Celia that summer of '39, and her playing the piano in the cool of the evening. Suddenly, Jerry was coming at me out of a bank of cloud. I let him have it, and I think he must have got me in the wing, because he spiralled past me out of control. As he did so – I will always remember this – I got a glimpse of his face, and, you know – he smiled. Funny thing, war.[121]

The humour here lay not in wordplay, but in the exaggeration of the conventions familiar from the films of the fifties: Celia, Tunbridge Wells, 'Jerry' and the general tone of manly understatement. Mockery of the Second World War, though, was not universally acceptable. While this new material had gone down very well in Cambridge, it did not prove a hit in Brighton, where audiences were older, more conservative and more easily offended. Alan Bennett recalled that 'the seats were going up like pistol shots throughout the performance, so that, come the curtain, there were scarcely more people in the audience than there were on the stage'.[122] It was, said the local theatre critic, 'vaguely indecent for twenty-year-olds to be making fun of Battle of Britain pilots'.[123] But the controversy that surrounded the show was not too great, and this was probably the worst review the team ever received. It is easy to exaggerate the conservatism of British audiences, and although the war routines did not please the burghers of Brighton, they did not damage the show's long-term future.

When *Beyond the Fringe* finally opened in London in May 1961 it proved a considerable hit, attracting sell-out audiences and generally enthusiastic reviews. Pearson Philips in the *Daily Mail*, for instance, called it 'a sensation . . . Between them they carve up a clutch of sacred British institutions – the National Anthem, the "Few", Civil Defence, Mr Macmillan and the Church of England'.[124] Of course, if these institutions really had been 'sacred', then a conservative newspaper like the *Daily Mail* would hardly have applauded the performance. As we have seen, the themes of national decline, anachronism and snobbery were already well-trodden ground by 1961. They had not, however, been expressed in the theatre before with such directness and humour, and some critics like

Kenneth Tynan were barely able to restrain their excitement. 'Future historians may well thank me', Tynan solemnly wrote as he prepared to give a detailed rendition of the first sketch, 'for providing them with a full account of the moment when English comedy took its first decisive step into the second half of the twentieth century.'[125] Some of the team, notably Jonathan Miller, thought that Tynan had gone too far. Miller did not think of their material as being really satirical at all; Bennett thought it was more a matter of 'observation' than satire; Moore disclaimed any satirical intent and called it merely 'good fun'; and Peter Cook would admit only that 'certain parts of it were satirical'.[126] All the same, they evidently drew great inspiration from the mood of the day, and with Hugh Gaitskell or Harold Wilson as Prime Minister, it is hard to see *Beyond the Fringe* having quite the same political edge. Audiences loved it, and the show ran night after night until September 1966, although the original quartet had departed in 1962 for an equally triumphant run on Broadway and then for other pursuits.[127] Macmillan himself, ever the genial Edwardian grandee, went to see the show, as did the Queen in February 1962, prompting a backstage row about Alan Bennett's refusal to drop the word 'erection' from one of his lines.[128]

The success of the show also provided a boost for Peter Cook's long-cherished ambitions of opening a cabaret club in London along the lines of the satirical clubs that existed in West Germany. In October 1961 these plans reached fruition with the opening of The Establishment on Greek Street in Soho, 'London's first satirical night-club', according to the *Daily Mail*.[129] The club secretary later commented that their target was 'the blandness and patronizing condescension of the Macmillan years', and this was exactly the line that Cook himself adopted at the club's press launch. The sketches, he told reporters, would be aimed at targets 'from Macmillan to Macmillan . . . It will not necessarily be left-wing . . . But because the Conservatives are . . . in power, it will, of course, be easier to attack what is there. Attacking the Labour Party at the moment seems a bit like robbing a blind man.'[130]

The club initially did very well, and boasted a talented regular cast of young performers in John Bird, John Fortune, Jeremy Geidt and Eleanor Bron, although the extravagant promise that the *Beyond the Fringe* team would always be on hand turned out to be something of a pipedream. As the only woman working in a world of young men, Eleanor Bron naturally stood out, and she also introduced routines that focused more on issues of sex and class than the political or literary emphases of *Beyond the Fringe*. As a private club, The Establishment did not have to undergo the strictures of the Lord

Chamberlain's pen, and its material was much more daring than that presented by the *Beyond the Fringe* team. The first sketch on its opening night was a parody of the Crucifixion, in which the pretensions of a middle-class Christ are continually being mocked by the two Cockney thieves, complaining for example about 'that bint down there washing your feet'. There was a monologue delivered by God ('How do you do. My name is God and I'm here tonight because I'm omnipresent'), there was a sketch mocking Coventry Cathedral, which had just been built as a symbol of post-war reconciliation, and there were plenty of jokes about subjects from capital punishment to masturbation.[131]

Satire, or what passed for it, was fashionable. Not only was *Beyond the Fringe* playing to crowded audiences night after night, but The Establishment had sold over four thousand subscriptions before it had even opened. On the first night on 5 October 1961, according to John Wells:

> Television arc lights blazed above the crush, rich girls in diaphanous dresses wriggled and squealed in the crowd, their rock-jawed escorts bellowing above the din. 'Hello, Jeremy! You going to Antonia's thrash on Thursday?' Satire was in, and they were damned if they were going to miss a second of it.

So many people tried to get in that the doors had to be wedged shut, leaving an angry queue of frustrated members standing in the road. Inside, as Wells recalled, the atmosphere was not unlike that of Berlin in the thirties, except that 'the harsh clatter of fascist jackboots' had been replaced by the sound of 'the elastic-sided boots affected at that time by the go-getting jet set'.[132]

Although The Establishment did well for a time, it suffered from three problems. First, while satire was 'in', it could quite easily go 'out' at short notice, and once satire had been brought to the masses through television, the club lost its social cachet. The club was also very badly managed and some members of staff were alleged to be 'borrowing' large sums of money that were never quite returned. Finally, it fell prey to the local Soho protection rackets, so that by the beginning of 1964 it was effectively being run by gangsters. Whether it could have survived anyway is doubtful, the potential audience for satire having fallen away by that point.[133]

A more enduring product of the brief vogue for satire at that time, with which Peter Cook also became involved, was the magazine *Private Eye*. At the beginning of the decade the only vaguely satirical publication with a mass-market appeal was *Punch*, which was particularly renowned for the quality of its cartoons, but its humour, the stuff of upper-middle-class dentists' waiting rooms, was much more genteel and undemanding than in its mid-Victorian heyday.[134] By contrast, *Private Eye* was aimed at a younger and more irreverent audience. It was edited by a group of young men who had first met as pupils at Shrewsbury School, one of the more prestigious and old-fashioned public schools: Richard Ingrams, William Rushton, Christopher Booker and Paul Foot, as well as John Wells, another former public schoolboy who had fallen in with Ingrams and Foot at Oxford.[135]

The first issue of the magazine appeared with perfect timing at the end of October 1961, just after the opening of The Establishment club, although this was a complete coincidence and the two institutions had little in common. While The Establishment largely reflected the fashionable discontents of the day, *Private Eye* struck a note of iconoclasm and even misanthropy. Its early editions owed most to Ingrams, Booker and Rushton, but all three were at heart more conservative than the cast of The Establishment. There was in fact something of a minor feud between the two groups. Both *Beyond the Fringe* and The Establishment had cast members from lower-middle-class backgrounds, while the tone of *Private Eye* was unmistakably that of a public school. At one point, the various factions assembled for 'Satirical Lunches', but these proved a disaster:

> The Establishment group, state and scholarship-Cambridge educated, thought the *Eye* lads were greedy, ambitious and supercilious . . . The *Eye* contingent found the Establishment boys and girls flint-hard, down-market, even threatening . . . The *Eye* people . . . gloried in boozing, braying and throwing up in pubs . . . The Establishment team . . . worked, drank coffee, discussed F. R. Leavis, and played poker for relaxation.[136]

Between Jonathan Miller and Richard Ingrams, meanwhile, there simmered a long-running dispute. Miller thought that Ingrams was a 'leather-elbowed thug' whose magazine was opposed to sensitivity and sincerity of any kind; Ingrams denounced Miller as the epitome of the 'pseuds' that he despised so much.[137] Even within the *Private Eye* team itself there were all sorts of quarrels. Christopher Booker wanted a more serious magazine of political satire and criticism, while Ingrams and Rushton were thinking of a more anarchic, Goonish publication. Booker had been brought up in the Liberal tradition; Ingrams was a Conservative voter but self-declared socialist; and Rushton's politics were a strange mixture of Conservatism and anarchism. In 1963 Booker was ousted from the editor's chair in a palace coup and replaced by Ingrams, although he continued to write for the magazine afterwards.[138]

The tone of *Private Eye*, unlike that of *Beyond the Fringe* and The Establishment, was not very closely tied to the fashionable critique of snobbery, anachronism and national decline, and probably this helps to explain why the magazine survived beyond 1964 while the other satirical institutions of the time collapsed. On the other hand, since its beginnings were humble, it probably would not have lasted beyond a few months had it not been for the fact that there already existed a receptive audience keen to snap up anything associated with satire. The first issue could not have been produced without the generosity of another Oxford friend of the team, Andrew Osmond, and was indubitably an amateur production, stapled together in a Kensington house on yellow paper. There were only about four hundred copies, and they were sold, according to Ingrams, 'in fashionable restaurants like Nick's Diner and cafés like the Troubador where bearded CND men gathered to listen to folk songs'.[139] Not only was it produced in a Kensington villa, it was aimed at the public schoolboys who frequented the cafés and bars of South Kensington and who might be expected to understand the writers' sense of humour. For a long time, in fact, the writers of the *Eye* made it clear that they considered lower-middle-class mores inherently funny: the suburb of Neasden, for example, was used as shorthand for banality and mediocrity, while tedious and commonplace views were usually ascribed to Sid and Doris Bonkers.[140]

Only slowly did the magazine acquire a reputation for incisive humour and, eventually, investigative journalism. Word of mouth was its greatest ally, although its cause was also helped by an enthusiastic review in the *Observer* in February 1962, which noted that, while 'engaging', the *Eye* was 'almost impossible to obtain except at a few eccentric shops and at 28 Scarsdale Villas, Kensington'.[141] By June the following year, however, the circulation figures were looking rather healthier at around fifteen thousand a fortnight, and the publishers even had an offer for the magazine from another Old Salopian, the young entrepreneur Michael Heseltine, which they declined. It was instead Peter Cook who bought the magazine, in concert with his business partner Nicholas Luard, in the summer of 1962.

From this point on, the fortunes of the magazine improved still further, especially as Cook was naturally funnier than either Ingrams or Booker. A familiar cast of recurring characters was assembled, including Sir Herbert Gusset and Lunchtime O'Booze, and the *Eye* also recruited new contributors of the quality of Ralph Steadman and Spike Milligan. By the time of its first anniversary in October 1962, sales had reached a new high of 46,000 a fortnight.[142]

'The satire industry is booming,' reported the *Observer* in July 1962:

Following the recent merger of *Private Eye*, the fortnightly lampoon, with The Establishment night-club in Soho, the club are now preparing to extend their empire. They plan, among other things, to open a New York branch; to produce a *Private Eye* strip-cartoon book (published by Weidenfeld) for Christmas; to start a restaurant in London made of converted railway carriages, satirizing British Railways food; and to launch a weekly shilling magazine about entertainment, called *Scene*.[143]

There was indeed a tour of New York by the cast of The Establishment, as well as a short-lived magazine called *Scene*, but sadly the British Railways restaurant never saw the light of day.[144] One scheme that did get off the ground, however, was an idea mooted by the young BBC producer Ned Sherrin: a televised satirical programme. With the BBC locked in bitter competition with ITV and keen to promote itself as young and modern, the attractions of satire were obvious. Sherrin had been working on the light-hearted magazine show *Tonight* and his original intention was to produce 'a new sort of revolutionary programme . . . a mixture of News, Interview, Satire and Controversy' and 'an experimental two-hour mixture of conversation, satire, comedy, debate and music'.[145]

Sherrin's idea seemed a perfect fit with the ambitions of the BBC in the sixties, and in July 1962 he recorded a pilot for the new show, *That Was The Week That Was*. It was not a success: the BBC executives were unimpressed with the Establishment team of Bird, Fortune, Geidt and Bron, around whom Sherrin had planned to build the show, and the programme ran for a numbing two and a half hours, so the studio audience found it understandably difficult to maintain their interest. However, when the BBC management heard that one of the commercial companies was planning a satirical show of its own, they agreed to a second pilot, this time without the Establishment team and with a different group of writers. When that proved more successful, Sherrin was given a starting date at the end of November.[146]

The first edition of *That Was The Week That Was* (or *TW3*, as it was known) came on air at 10.50 on the night of 24 November 1962 with a burst of atonal music which eventually blended into Millicent Martin's trademark theme song, which always began, 'That was the week that was; it's over, let it go', and then broke into a series of lines chronicling the events of the last seven days. The look of the show was startling: just as *Beyond the Fringe* had broken with the conventions of theatrical revue by presenting four men in cardigans on an empty stage, so *TW3* broke with convention by its very lack of polish. As George Melly put it: 'Sherrin virtually invented the new TV brutalism: the scaffolding, the sound booms blatantly probing towards the speakers instead of jerking guiltily out of sight when picked up accidentally, and especially the cameras roaming round like purposeful Martians: the machinery as part of the spectacle it's responsible for.'[147] What was more, when seated behind the long desk that formed the centrepiece of the set, many of the performers evidently thought they were safe to read their scripts openly, and on various occasions they even delivered their lines to the wrong camera.[148] This was, of course, part of the charm of the show: its very clumsiness, when set against the slickness of so much television entertainment, became a novelty and a virtue. The sketches themselves were rather less sensational: a spoof of by-election coverage; a sketch about the army becoming involved in politics; a song parodying the hit 'Love and Marriage', but changing the lyrics to 'Love before Marriage'; and so on.[149]

Viewers who had also seen *Beyond the Fringe* were unlikely to think this especially groundbreaking or witty stuff, and as with *Private Eye* it took some time for the writers to find their feet. The expectation was that the show would attract only 'a fringe metropolitan audience' not unlike the clientele of The Establishment or the readers of the *Eye*.[150] But the fact was that most viewers had never seen *Beyond the Fringe*, been to The Establishment or read *Private Eye*, although many had heard of them, and the early viewing figures took Sherrin and his team by surprise. Almost four million people saw the first edition, rapidly rising to eight million within a few weeks as word spread, and the show reached its peak of popularity in April 1963 when the ratings hit twelve million, a tremendous achievement for a programme broadcast so late in the evening.[151] The first reviews, all of which agreed that the programme was indeed satirical, were also excellent: the *Sunday Telegraph*, of all newspapers, thought it was 'without reservations . . . brilliant', praised the spirit of 'intelligence and dislike' and called it 'as lethal as a gun'.[152] According to the *Daily Sketch*, only five viewers had rung the BBC to complain, while eighty-three had telephoned their congratulations.[153]

As *TW3* attracted more public attention, so it attracted more and better writers, and the quality of the scripts showed a marked improvement. Two talented stalwarts who had been working with Sherrin since the second pilot were Keith Waterhouse and Willis Hall, the writing team behind the West End version of *Billy Liar*, which was by then being adapted into a New Wave film.[154] Such was the appeal of the new show that ideas poured in from dozens of bright young writers, including Malcolm Bradbury, Jack Rosenthal, Alan Plater, Christopher Booker, Peter Shaffer, John Braine, Dennis Potter, David Nobbs and even Kenneth Tynan. On some occasions the list of writing credits might stretch for as many as thirty names, which was extremely unusual for a British television programme.[155] The names most associated with *TW3*, however, were those of the performers, almost all of whom were unknown before the show began. The chief presenter was a twenty-three-year-old cabaret performer and Cambridge graduate called David Frost, whose talents lay in introducing and linking the items rather than in his wooden acting skills. Among the other performers were William Rushton, moonlighting from *Private Eye*; two talented young actors in Kenneth Cope and Roy Kinnear; the gangling Lance Percival; Timothy Birdsall, a cartoonist; and Millicent Martin, probably the most experienced of them all, an accomplished singer and actress. As Percival recalled it, they were encouraged to let people think that they were 'bright young things from university', but in fact Frost was the only one with a degree, and they did not usually mix socially with him.[156] In a category of his own was Bernard Levin, an extremely opinionated journalist in his thirties who also had a degree, from the LSE. Levin's function was to provoke debate by attacking people or institutions that he disliked, and he performed this task with gusto.

The real star was Frost, who had been handed the greatest responsibility and yet had never appeared on television until he presented *TW3*. Most reviewers emphasised the novelty of his voice, which departed from BBC convention by being neither the upper-middle-class accent of southern England nor a recognisable regional accent, but instead what they called 'cheeky', 'classless' or 'nasal'. It sounded rather as though Frost was pitching his voice somewhere in the mid-Atlantic, combining the casual cadences of

American English with his own naturally adenoidal tone, not unlike the pop singers and disc jockeys of the mid-sixties.[157] He was the son of a Methodist minister who had been moved regularly from parish to parish across the English counties, and was educated at grammar school and Cambridge, where his suburban accent came in for a good deal of mockery. After one cabaret performance, an Old Etonian went up to Frost and congratulated him in all seriousness on 'that wonderfully silly voice', only to discover that it was Frost's own.[158]

What was really striking about Frost, though, was his extraordinary ambition: at the Societies Fair at the beginning of his undergraduate career, for instance, he saw that two of the largest stalls were for the arts magazine *Granta* and the Cambridge Footlights, and set his heart on running both.[159] Christopher Booker, a contemporary at Cambridge and fellow luminary of the satire boom, thought that Frost's rise to fame was 'freakish and unreal', but allowed that the signs were there at university. So assiduously did Frost work to get ahead that according to Booker 'he soon became a kind of affectionate joke', despite the fact that his cabaret routines were blatantly borrowed from Peter Cook, the main Cambridge star of the time. Once when the Footlights team arrived in Great Yarmouth for a performance, they were staggered to see that the posters read: 'DAVID FROST presents The Cambridge Footlights', even though Frost was then only a very junior member of the group.[160] Although the rotund *Private Eye* contributor William Rushton also appeared on *TW3*, the attitude of the *Eye* to Booker's old university colleague was less than enthusiastic. He was branded 'The Bubonic Plagiarist', and Peter Cook later lamented that his worst mistake was to have once saved Frost from drowning.[161]

In many ways, *TW3* was no great novelty. It was not as clever as *Beyond the Fringe*, not as fashionable as The Establishment club, and not as acerbic as *Private Eye*. Even Christopher Booker admitted that although there was some 'witty and original' material, 'much of it was amateurish, juvenile and completely stereotyped in attitude'.[162] Indeed, as early as the end of January 1963 the *Evening Standard*'s reviewer presciently remarked:

> *That Was The Week That Was* is . . . already beginning to go damp. Last Saturday's programme was one of the worst yet. It was too long, too self-consciously clever and, worst of all, neither very funny nor biting . . . It has been grossly overrated, and the oldest jokes gilded with praise simply because they are new to television.[163]

The real difference between *TW3* and the other products of the satire boom was simply that *TW3* attracted a much larger and more diverse audience than the others could ever hope for; and what was more, it was produced by the BBC, still a symbol of national dignity despite the new climate of the sixties. As *TW3* became more successful, so it became more daring, and therefore more controversial. To take one example, Bernard Levin's tirades were always likely to antagonise someone, whatever the subject. In the third edition, shown on 8 December 1962, his target was not a group but one man, the hotelier Charles Forte, who sat smiling awkwardly while Levin denounced his company as 'lazy, inefficient, dishonest, dirty, complacent, exorbitant – but disgusting just about sums it up' and called the catering at London Airport, for which Forte was responsible, 'a national disgrace'. As some reviewers noted, Forte was barely allowed to get a word in edgeways and the confrontation ended without him even having a chance to defend himself, which seemed unfair whatever the alleged faults of his catering business.[164] A week later Levin greeted a group of farmers with the words 'Good evening, peasants,' although in this case the farmers went on, in most people's eyes, to win the day. In April 1963, meanwhile, a member of the audience dashed on to the set and punched Levin on the jaw: revenge for a bad review that Levin had given the man's wife, an actress.[165] All of this was enthralling rather than shocking; like Malcolm Muggeridge, Levin became a television personality whom many viewers understandably hated but still found irresistible.

The greatest controversy stemmed from those sketches that mocked national institutions like the monarchy, the armed services and the Church of England. As early as 10 December 1962, the *Daily Mail* – the newspaper that had lavished such praise on *Beyond the Fringe* – complained that in the edition broadcast two days previously, 'RELIGION was mocked – a small harmony group of Cardinals sang "Arrivederci, Roma" . . . THE PRIME MINISTER was insulted – one of his TV recordings was distorted'.[166] Evidently what was acceptable in the confines of a theatre, among upper-middle-class audiences, was intolerable on public television. Worse was to follow. The edition on 15 December, for example, lampooned Britain's declining international status: one sketch depicted the American Secretary of Defense, Robert McNamara, telling his British counterpart: 'We in America have always had the highest respect for British craftsmanship – you make the buttons, we'll press them.'[167]

The most controversial item of the first series, meanwhile, appeared on 12 January 1963, and was called the 'Consumer Guide to Religion'. It was a monologue, delivered by David Frost, in which each religion was tested as though it were a washing machine being assessed by *Which?* Judaism, for instance, was 'the oldest religion we tested' and offered 'membership of the oldest club in the world . . . and we particularly liked the guarantee of Eternal Life'. Catholicism, meanwhile, offered excellent security, with Christ having 'undertaken personal responsibility for the consumer's misdemeanours. This gives extra support. And the confessional mechanism is standard; it operates as an added safety-factor to correct running mistakes, making Salvation almost foolproof.' Protestantism, Islam and Buddhism came in for similar analysis, while Communism was criticised because 'its Chief Prophet appears to have no background in the industry at all'. The Church of England, needless to say, was recommended as the best buy, 'a jolly little faith for a very moderate outlay'.[168]

As soon as the sketch had finished, the BBC began receiving telephone calls, more than for any other item that ran on *TW3*. There were 246 complaints, a record, and also 167 calls of appreciation. Most newspapers criticised it; the *Daily Express*, for example, was incredulous that a man's religion could be 'mocked' in this way. One vicar on the Isle of Man remarked that if Britain was really a Christian country then people would 'storm the BBC building and make it drop this horrible programme', while the Bishop of Swansea wrote to Hugh Carleton Greene denouncing the sketch as in 'deplorable bad taste, and gratuitously offensive to many viewers'. The item certainly damaged the image of *TW3* within the BBC, especially as senior executives noted that the edition in general had been both longer and weaker than usual. 'In a satirical programme of this sort one is continually walking the tightrope and sometimes one falls off,' Greene replied to the Bishop. 'I personally agree this was a fall.'[169]

By the time the first run of *TW3* ended in April 1963, the series had reached its peak audience of twelve million. At the end of the last edition, Roy Kinnear, playing a bewildered suburban viewer, commented: 'It was satire, wasn't it? Mucky jokes. Obscenity – it's all the go nowadays.'[170] The *People* greeted the end of the run with relief: 'Goodbye to a Gang of Low Schoolboys'. In his parish magazine, meanwhile, another vicar was expounding on the vices of the cast, calling Millicent Martin 'a repulsive woman' and Bernard Levin 'a thick-lipped Jew boy'.[171] There can be little doubt that at least a significant minority found *That Was The Week That Was* highly offensive, especially when it mocked religion. Mary Whitehouse, at this stage merely an obscure housewife but subsequently to become famous in her own right, thought that it was 'the epitome of what was wrong with the BBC – anti-authority, anti-religion, anti-patriotism, pro-dirt and poorly produced'.[172] The letters that the Corporation received on the subject of *TW3* usually ran in favour of the show by two to one, but it is worth noting that telephone calls, which were easier to make than letters are to write, ran heavily against the show, often literally jamming the BBC switchboard. According to Asa Briggs, complaints about the programme typically came from Scotland and provincial England, with some criticising it, reasonably enough, for a perceived metropolitan bias.[173]

The programme did return on air on 28 September, by which time both Macmillan's government and the nation's attention were gripped by scandal. However, BBC executives were not now prepared to give the *TW3* producers the freedom they had once enjoyed. For one thing, they were forbidden from overrunning, which was always a problem for an undisciplined live show like *TW3*, and the Controller of Programmes publicly warned Sherrin against including 'smut', even though there had been very few references to sex in the first series.[174] As it turned out, the second series of *TW3* was something of a damp squib. One of the show's own writers, Dennis Potter, wrote in the *Daily Herald* that 'the shock was gone', the jokes about Macmillan were 'predictable' and 'there was an almost cosy air of self-congratulation'.[175] Even Ned Sherrin thought that the new series was 'dull . . . stilted and self-conscious', as though they were all trying too hard to emulate the success of the first run.[176] The real problem was that the first series had a novelty value for most viewers that the second could never hope to recapture. In those circumstances, the show could retain its audience only by maintaining a very high level of writing and performance, but even at its peak it had always been somewhat patchy. Even worse, the effect of the sensational scandals that unfolded during the summer of 1963 meant that *TW3* was bound to look rather tame by comparison; it was almost impossible to parody a political system that had already descended into an orgy of rumours, revelations and resignations.

When Macmillan's premiership came to an end, the programme's central target had suddenly been removed at a stroke, and its response to the elevation of Sir Alec Douglas-Home was ill-judged to say the least. On 19 October, David Frost delivered a monologue dressed as Benjamin Disraeli during which he attacked Home's 'bleak, deathly smile' and concluded: 'You have always drifted with the tide – the tide of appeasement, the tide of Suez . . . You have foreseen nothing. You are qualified only to do nothing.'[177] This was the first time that any BBC programme had been so openly critical of a sitting prime minister, or so blatantly partisan, and it proved the most offensive item in the show's history.[178] The audience was not impressed: while there were more than six hundred telephone calls of protest, there were only sixty of support, far fewer than there had been for the 'Consumer Guide to Religion'.[179] If the piece had been genuinely funny, that might have made a difference, but it was perceived only as insulting. Even before this broadcast, the BBC Board of Governors and General Advisory Council had both been unsympathetic to TW3, not only because it brought unwelcome controversy to the doors of the Corporation, but also because they thought it was running out of steam. On 10 October, for instance, the Governors expressed their 'anxiety' at the staleness of the new series, and two weeks later one of the members of the Advisory Council called it 'offensive, undergraduate, potentially venomous, increasingly humourless and creating too many difficulties'.[180] The Disraeli monologue crystallised all the problems that TW3 was causing the Corporation: while the programme had offended many viewers and stirred up trouble in the press, it seemed to be lacking the zip of the first series.

On 7 November, Hugh Carleton Greene finally told the Governors that the show had become 'a gigantic red herring, diverting attention from the real achievements of the BBC and prejudicing judgements of broadcasts on important but difficult social themes'. It was showing 'a perceptible decline in vitality', and, given that 1964 would be an election year, it seemed sensible to take the show off the air and spare the BBC the controversy that it would be bound to provoke. The decision to drop it was Greene's own; this was not a case of the Governors pulling the plug on a show that he supported.[181] Nor was the decision the result of political pressure: in fact, Macmillan had advised his Postmaster General, Reginald Bevins, who oversaw national broadcasting, that he should 'not, repeat not, take any action' against the programme.[182] Bevins, who was in agreement, reported that most Conservative backbenchers were actually 'hostile to the thought of any interference'.[183] While it is true that the BBC's Charter was due for renewal, and that the Corporation was reluctant to antagonise the government in such circumstances, the fact remains that TW3 was cancelled because it had run out of ideas and was losing support in the press and in the country, not because it was censored by 'reactionaries' at the BBC, as some accounts have it.[184] While some commentators affected outrage, and Harold Wilson, not surprisingly, 'deplored' the decision to drop a programme that had savagely attacked his opponents, the *Guardian* observed that just as 'satire came in as a craze, like boots for women', it was 'probably about to go out, much as boots will go out next year'.[185] The remaining six editions of the show were fairly unspectacular, the lowlight being a lachrymose, crawling tribute to President Kennedy on the night of his assassination. The *Private Eye* stalwart Paul Foot accurately described it as 'sickeningly sycophantic' and the Kennedy edition strikes even the sympathetic Humphrey Carpenter as 'a belated attempt to save *TW3* from the scaffold'.[186] It failed, needless to say, and after thirty-seven episodes *TW3* ended on 28 December 1963.

For many of the performers of *TW3*, like Kenneth Cope and Roy Kinnear, the show marked the beginning of a long and successful acting career. Of all the satirists, though, it was David Frost, whose stint as presenter and public face of the programme had made him a household name, who enjoyed the greatest renown and public success. The initial signs were not particularly encouraging: a new satire show that he presented for the BBC called *Not So Much a Programme, More a Way of Life* attracted only a third of the *TW3* audience and was cancelled in April 1965. The difference between Frost and his colleagues, however, was that his ambition and drive seemed limitless, more than compensating for the fact that he was a much less talented performer. William Rushton even claimed to have seen a folder inside Frost's briefcase marked 'Airport Quips', prepared so that he would sparkle when waylaid by reporters at international airports.[187]

The most famous example of Frost's ambition was a breakfast that he arranged at the Connaught Hotel in Mayfair on 7 January 1966, where, to the stupefaction of the press, the guests included the Prime Minister, the Bishop of Woolwich, the fashionable spy novelist Len Deighton, the philosopher A. J. Ayer, the newspaper barons Cecil King and David Astor, the social campaigners Lord Longford and Lord Soper, the publisher Robert Maxwell, the chairman of EMI and various television executives. Of those invited, only Paul McCartney, with a characteristic flash of good sense, failed to appear. Melon and grapefruit, eggs, bacon and kidneys, coffee, toast and marmalade, and finally caviar and champagne were all served. It was, said Frost casually, 'a chance for a few friends who don't always meet to gather and chat'.[188] For his former *TW3* colleague Christopher Booker, however, it was 'an impertinent stunt', and an example of the power of television to blur the distinction between genuine importance and hollow celebrity.[189]

In terms of Frost's career, the breakfast was a triumph, putting him right back in the headlines after a lean period during which he seemed in danger of sinking into obscurity. His next show, *The Frost Report*, a blend of sketches and chat, was more of a success, propelling Frost back into the bosom of the public and introducing new talents like John Cleese, Michael Palin, Terry Jones, Ronnie Barker and Ronnie Corbett. By the end of the decade he owned a large house in Knightsbridge, hosted interview shows on both sides of the Atlantic simultaneously and was one of the biggest shareholders in London Weekend Television, which had captured the London weekend franchise in 1967.[190] More than any other individual, it was Frost who had grasped the potential of television to create celebrities and success stories of its own. He had, remarked Malcolm Muggeridge's wife Kitty, 'risen without trace'.[191]

The 'satirical vogue' was quick to disappear. By the end of 1964, *TW3* was only a memory, The Establishment had become little more than a front for Soho racketeers, and the original *Beyond the Fringe* team had performed for the last time together in New York. Even *Private Eye* was struggling: its sales had dropped by almost three-quarters since the heady summer of 1963, although the continued support of Peter Cook kept it afloat.[192] Jonathan Miller had begun to move into arts programming and directing for the stage; Alan Bennett was trying to combine the careers of actor and academic; Dudley Moore had thrown himself into acting; and Cook was concentrating on the *Eye*.[193] All went on to enjoy considerable success, and the 'Pete and Dud' routines later performed by Cook and Moore in *Not Only . . . But Also* elevated them to the status of television icons.[194]

At the beginning of 1965, however, satire seemed defunct. Of its four institutions – a stage revue, a club, a television series and a magazine – three were no longer in existence, and the fourth had fallen back on cartoons, investigative reporting and surreal wit rather than genuine political criticism. One obvious reason for the collapse of the satire industry, then, was that it was only very small, relied on the talents of a few bright performers, and could not sustain itself after they ran out of steam. The likes of Jonathan Miller, Alan Bennett and David Frost never thought of themselves merely as satirists; like many of their colleagues, they had ambitions in very different fields and were keen to pursue them at the earliest opportunity. When they moved on, there were few performers of equal talent or drive to succeed them.

What was more, satire had become identified with fashion; and fashion changes. By 1964, audiences were bored of watching earnest, witty young men with crumpled cardigans and Oxbridge degrees making jokes about the Conservative Party or the Church of England. As the *Guardian* had observed, satire was bound to fall out of favour as inevitably as trad jazz and duffel coats.[195] Politics had also changed a great deal since the first performance of *Beyond the Fringe* in August 1960. The satire boom had been closely tied to the themes of the Establishment debate, but by 1965 there appeared little point in harping on the old themes of anachronism and snobbery now that there was a new Prime Minister who promised to bring the 'white heat' of 'the scientific revolution' into British government.[196] Michael Frayn, a Footlights veteran, *Guardian* columnist and close friend of Alan Bennett, perceptively noted in 1963 that 'to go *on* mocking the so-called Establishment has more and more meant making the audience not laugh at themselves at all, but at a standard target which is rapidly becoming as well-established as mothers-in-law'.[197] The satire boom, quite simply, had run its course.

For all the praise lavished by historians and critics on the satirists of the early sixties, the truth is that most of their material was cosily predictable. Many of their jokes, instead of being satirical, were really examples of either political partisanship or good-humoured wit, and rather than attacking the prejudices of their audiences, the satirists tended to confirm them. As Hewison observes, the satirists had grown up within the very institutions that most epitomised the old order, and their satire was ultimately 'stifled by the indulgence of its targets'.[198] Jonathan Miller later insisted that he and his colleagues were all 'very comfortably off and doing very nicely': they had 'nothing to complain of', and were very far from being genuine satirists.[199] In one edition of *TW3* shown in January 1963, for instance, there were only two items that could even loosely have been described as satirical, while most were typical of the kind of friendly, good-humoured revues that had been popular in the fifties.[200] Certainly the subversive or shocking elements of the satire boom have been grossly exaggerated.[201]

It is also worth remembering that the audience for satire in the early sixties did not, by and large, include the most disaffected and excluded members of British society. Malcolm Muggeridge commented in 1962 that The Establishment was crowded with 'hard hearts and coronets', *Private Eye* 'sells like hot cakes outside the Ritz' and the *Beyond the Fringe* performers 'survey in their appreciative audiences the living targets of their wit'.[202] The

Establishment club was initially extremely fashionable among the wealthy young things of the capital; even after the novelty had worn off, it was 'a middle-class night out', as John Fortune put it, where suits and dresses were the norm. This was an affluent, comfortable and self-confident audience; it was revealing that one woman shouted angrily, 'That's not what you're here for,' when a sketch poked fun at anti-nuclear campaigners.[203] As for *TW3*, although it reached a much wider audience than any of the other institutions of the satire boom, it still appealed to viewers who were disproportionately middle-class. According to an analysis of the viewing figures in February 1963, less than two-thirds of its audience was working-class, an extremely low rate for a programme of comedy and light entertainment: so while over a quarter of the entire British upper-middle class watched the show, less than 20 per cent of the working classes did so.[204]

Humphrey Carpenter even suggests that the satire boom had a 'reactionary' thrust, mocking 'not so much . . . a corrupt and enfeebled old order deserving destruction as . . . the old guard pathetically trying to modernize itself in the age of television and rock 'n' roll'.[205] The members of the *Beyond the Fringe* team had made their mark at the oldest and most prestigious universities in Britain, while *TW3* was created by a disaffected Conservative in Ned Sherrin and presented by an ambitious self-seeker in David Frost. *Private Eye*, meanwhile, was edited by a group of former public schoolboys who hated the modernity of the sixties and in many cases ended up as waspish political conservatives. As an *Observer* report noted in 1962, the *Eye* was funny, but its satire was not very 'deep': there was 'a certain Oxbridge cosiness' and no sense of 'heartfelt disgust at society'.[206] Certainly there was no sense of political progressivism: Labour politicians, for example, were described as venal and cynical, while anti-nuclear protesters were personified in the character of Ted Snivel, who calls the police 'murdering Fascist swine' after he bruises his ankle at a demonstration.[207] Instead, *Private Eye* was scornful of the entire business of politics, part of its general 'amused contempt for almost everything', which for more earnest readers, such as Jonathan Miller, smacked of public-school philistinism.[208] As Carpenter puts it, the mood of the *Eye* was well summarised in the issue of 6 April 1962: '*Private Eye* says, "Balls to the lot of them."'[209]

Some conservative critics later suggested that the satire boom of the sixties marked the end of deference and decency in British culture.[210] But this overestimates the impact of the satirists. Only *That Was The Week That Was*, the most derivative and restrained of all the instruments of the satire boom, reached a mass audience, and its real heyday lasted a very brief five months or so. The *Beyond the Fringe* performers, who were unquestionably the most talented of all the personnel of the satire industry, said themselves that their target was 'complacency': they had no interest in tearing down established morality, patriotism or anything else. David Frost later wrote that the *TW3* team consisted of 'Exasperated Young Men': not even angry, but merely irritated at the failings of British politics in the late fifties.[211] Indeed, the satire boom makes most sense as an expression of very similar concerns to those voiced in the Establishment debate of the late fifties and early sixties: the same frustration at national decline after Suez, the same weariness with the evasions of the Macmillan government, the same yearning for an alternative to the old-fashioned, complacent Conservatives who were thought to be running the country aground. In the election of 1964, almost all the satirists were hoping that Harold Wilson would defeat Sir Alec Douglas-Home, and *Private Eye* even put up William Rushton as a 'Death to the Tories' candidate in Douglas-Home's constituency, where he attracted a disappointing forty-five votes.[212] With the Conservatives defeated, the satirists lost their principal opponents and much of their verve, and by the time Harold Wilson took charge of 10 Downing Street, the focus of national attention had already begun to shift away from the blunders of the late fifties to the exciting possibilities of the mid-sixties.

THE SECRET AGENT

There are moments of great luxury in the life of a secret agent.

Ian Fleming, *Live and Let Die* (1954)

We have arrested a spy who is a bugger and a minister is involved.

Director of Public Prosecutions, September 1962

On 5 October 1962, *Dr No* opened at the Pavilion Cinema in London. Its producers, Albert R. Broccoli and Harry Saltzman, did not have high hopes of success. When they had privately shown their first James Bond film to an audience of cinema distributors a few weeks previously, the reaction had not been enthusiastic. 'Well, all we can lose is 950,000 dollars, Harry,' one man commented to Saltzman. 'It simply won't work in America,' said an executive at United Artists, convinced that they had a flop on their hands. 'Connery will never go over.'[1] The first reviews, meanwhile, were far from encouraging. '*Dr No*: no, no,' wrote the *Spectator*'s critic. 'Too inept to be as pernicious as it might have been.'[2] Some admitted that the film made for diverting entertainment, but few were impressed by Sean Connery's interpretation of the James Bond character. The *New Statesman* described him as 'an invincibly stupid-looking secret service agent', while the *Monthly Film Bulletin*, which called the film 'tame', thought Connery was 'such a disappointingly wooden and boorish Bond that the film's touches of grim humour go for less than they need'.[3]

As it happened, however, the film was serendipitously timely. It was adapted from one of Ian Fleming's more fantastic Bond yarns, the story of a freakish scientific mastermind working for the Soviet Union and undermining the American test rocket programme from his futuristic base off the coast of Jamaica. If nothing else, it proved a welcome contrast to the gritty, introspective New Wave realism ubiquitous in previous months, and quickly began to attract audiences. When a real Cold War crisis involving missiles in the

Caribbean began to unfold just two weeks into the film's run, James Bond's reputation for modernity and relevance was assured. The coincidence of the Cuban missile crisis did not in itself explain the success of *Dr No*, but it certainly helped.[4] By the end of the year, the film had become the second-highest-grossing British film of 1962, behind Cliff Richard's musical *The Young Ones*; far from losing its costs, it had made them back on the strength of the British receipts alone.[5] Young audiences in particular were transfixed, above all by the self-conscious modernity of the film. 'The only movies we'd seen were war pictures, or drawing room comedies, or westerns,' recalled the future James Bond actor Timothy Dalton, then an adolescent schoolboy in Derbyshire, 'and here was something up-to-date and really terrific.'[6]

The subject of espionage had long maintained a powerful grip on the British imagination. There had been moral panics about spies and subversion, whether German or Bolshevik, both before and after the First World War, and the stereotype of the enemy within, the malignant secret agent or the dastardly traitor, provided a comforting scapegoat for international pressures and domestic unease. Fears of spies and subversives were often really displaced anxieties about the general decline of British prestige and power, or anxieties about the pace of social changes at home and the threat they seemed to pose to the assumptions of middle-class spy-story readers.[7] The spy story, then, had proved an excellent vehicle to carry popular resentments, and it was no surprise that the social changes of the post-war world found their expression in a new generation of spy stories in print and on celluloid. James Bond was the emblem of modern affluence, living a life of conspicuous consumption, luxury and sexual licence, surrounded by first-class airline tickets, champagne bottles and Turkish cigarettes. One step removed was Len Deighton's hero Harry Palmer, the bespectacled, cheeky face of lower-middle-class ambition, living in a world of supermarkets, coffee bars and Italian restaurants. But, when the optimism of the early sixties began to pall, readers did not have to look far for a cold dissection of national decline: the bright technological optimism of James Bond looked thin and false beside the grey, shadowy depths of John le Carré, with his tired, disillusioned, unhappy men sunk in a world of moral ambiguity and seedy boarding houses. To the enthusiastic audiences of *Dr No*, the sixties might well offer a reassuring future of national self-assertion, consumerism and hedonism; but to the audiences who emerged three years later from *The Spy Who Came In from the Cold* there seemed little guarantee that the future would be anything other than grey and bleak.

The resonance of spy stories in the early 1960s owed much to the fact that the issue of espionage was simply more relevant than ever before. For most British onlookers, the Cold War was, as Peter Hennessy puts it, 'a specialists' confrontation, not a peoples' conflict', to be fought out in humming laboratories and secret back rooms. Such were the technological demands of the nuclear arms race that spies were credited with tremendous capabilities. According to Michael Herman, the former secretary of the Joint Intelligence Committee: 'The Cold War was in a special sense an intelligence conflict . . . Never before in peacetime have the relationships of competing power blocks been so influenced by intelligence assessments. Never before have the collection of intelligence and its denial to the adversary been such central features of an international rivalry.'[8] Intelligence, espionage, infiltration and betrayal were closely associated with the global battle against Communism from the very outset, and fears of Red treason appeared to be vindicated as early as January 1950, when Dr Klaus Fuchs, the head of theoretical physics at the Harwell atomic research establishment in Oxfordshire, was arrested and sentenced to fourteen years' imprisonment for passing nuclear secrets to the Soviet Union. Fuchs' information then led the American authorities to arrest a Jewish Communist couple, Julius and Ethel Rosenberg, who were later executed for treason, and when, just months after Fuchs' arrest, yet another supposed traitor, the senior American official Alger Hiss, was imprisoned for perjury following an extremely murky series of allegations, it seemed that the wildest fantasies of Communist espionage were not so far removed from the truth.[9] For British observers, however, all this was merely a foretaste of the controversy to come.

At dusk on Friday 25 May 1951, Donald Maclean, the head of the American department of the Foreign Office, was celebrating his thirty-eighth birthday. A nervous, introverted man, known for breakdowns and bouts of hard drinking, he was preparing for a quiet dinner with his wife when a car pulled up in the drive of his ramshackle house on the North Downs. When the occupant emerged, Maclean introduced him to his wife as Roger Stiles, 'a colleague from the Foreign Office', and invited him to stay for dinner. As soon as the birthday meal was over, Maclean said calmly to his wife: 'Mr Stiles and I have to keep a pressing engagement, but I don't expect to be back very late. I'll take an overnight bag just in case.' He did not return that night, or the next day, or the next. His wife Melinda waited by the telephone all weekend, frantic with worry, and then finally, tearfully, telephoned the Foreign Office on the following Monday morning. Her husband and the mysterious Mr Stiles had simply disappeared. In fact Maclean and Stiles had immediately driven south to the coast, not north to London, and had boarded the late-night ferry from Southampton to St Malo. Early the following morning, a taxi took them from St Malo to Rennes, where they caught the express train to Paris. Then they went to ground. On the night of 6 June, two reassuring messages were handed in at a post office near the Paris Bourse, one for Maclean's wife, and one for his mother. 'Had to leave unexpectedly,' read the first. 'Terribly sorry. Am quite well now. Don't worry darling. I love you. Please don't stop loving me.' By this point, however, Maclean was not in Paris. He had already been moving, from Paris to Zurich and then from Zurich to Prague; and from Prague he would later make one last journey to his ultimate destination: Moscow.[10]

Maclean was a committed Communist and a spy. The man who called himself Roger Stiles, meanwhile, was in fact Guy Burgess, a flamboyant, hard-drinking diplomat who had been Maclean's close friend and homosexual lover when they were students together at Trinity College, Cambridge in the 1930s. Burgess, too, was a spy. He had, like Maclean, been recruited by the Soviet NKVD, the forerunner of the KGB, at Cambridge, where both men had been members of the exclusive, decadent Apostles club, which was notorious for attracting well-born Marxists. Both had been educated at prestigious public schools, and both were extremely well connected, moving easily through the metropolitan cultural elite and counting literary icons like Stephen Spender and Cyril Connolly among their casual friends.[11] This information, however, did not immediately reach the public. Although the British Security Service realised within days of their flight that Burgess and Maclean had defected to Moscow, they managed to keep the story quiet for four years. At last, in September 1955, the *People* printed the revelations of a KGB agent, Vladimir Petrov, who told the world that Burgess and Maclean had been recruited at Cambridge and that their flight had been arranged by the Soviet secret services.[12] It was a shattering blow to the British intelligence community, not least because the news provided excellent ammunition for those commentators who insisted that the weaknesses of British government could be attributed to the Establishment, the 'Power Elite' and what the *Sunday Express* called the 'old-school-tie society'.[13] The 'monstrous stupidity' of the Foreign Office, said the *Mirror*, was down to its staff: 'intellectuals, the Old School Tie brigade, long-haired experts and the people-who-know-the-best-people'.[14]

Maclean and Burgess were ideal targets for populist criticism. They were well born, expensively educated, socially exclusive and culturally sophisticated, precisely the kind of people who staffed the supposed Establishment. Indeed, Soviet intelligence strategy depended for its success upon the existence of the same old-boy network that A. J. P. Taylor, Henry Fairlie and other critics liked to claim dominated British society. As one historian puts it: 'Oxbridge life was as intimate as it was isolated, and teeming with secrets. Cut off from the rest of society, single sex, rigidly ruled, and abounding in all manner of personal and group loyalties, Oxford and Cambridge provided a silent training for spies from both camps.'[15] With their Cambridge education and public-school contacts, Burgess and Maclean could easily move from literary salons into secret Foreign Office meetings. To many observers, they had not merely betrayed their class, they had laid bare its social domination.

One central element in the mystique of Burgess and Maclean was that they had both been homosexuals at Cambridge. Like the public schools, the colleges of Oxford and Cambridge were sexually segregated, and it was popularly imagined, with considerable justification, that homosexuality was rife in such institutions. Noël Annan later wrote of the 'cult of homosexuality' that had flourished during his youth, and remarked that at Oxbridge during the thirties 'you could choose between joining the Comintern or the Homintern – unless, like Guy Burgess, you joined both'.[16] Many commentators in the post-war years therefore concluded that there was a clear and indisputable link between social exclusiveness, homosexuality, Marxism and treason.[17] 'There has for years existed within the Foreign Office service a chain or clique of perverted men,' thundered the *Sunday Pictorial* in 1955.[18] Two years later, when the civil service drew up the official guidelines for defining security risks, they included Communists and fascists, schizophrenics, religious fanatics, bankrupts, people 'living a very shady existence' and 'suspected homosexuals'.[19]

Indeed, homosexuality was often described in terms more suited to the analysis of a subversive cult. In 1955, for example, Lord Hailsham contributed an essay to *They Stand Apart*, a discussion of the 'problems of homosexuality', in which he described homosexuality as 'a proselytising religion . . . contagious, incurable and self-perpetuating', its converts being a 'potentially widely expanding secret society of addicts'. Just as Burgess and Maclean had been drawn into the circle of Communist treachery at Cambridge, so other young men were liable to be corrupted by their elders, and Hailsham warned that homosexuals were on the march, their ranks swelling with new recruits thanks to 'initiation . . . by older homosexuals whilst the personality is still pliable'.[20] As the *Scotsman* saw it ten years later, all homosexuals were potential traitors because 'by the nature of their disability [they] owe their primary allegiance to the homosexual group before any other authority or loyalty in their lives. Hence the connection between perversion and subversion.'[21]

Like Marxist treachery, homosexuality was associated in the popular imagination with literary and artistic elites, not entirely without good reason. As Lord Annan's memoir explains at some length, homosexuality had in the thirties become 'a freemasonry that reached into the upper echelons of the elite', an affirmation of aesthetic detachment and social exclusivity.[22] The younger literary figures of the fifties like Kingsley Amis, John Braine and John Osborne, whose social backgrounds were humbler than those of the poets of the thirties, tended to resent what they saw as the foppish homosexuality of their elders, and no doubt this helps to explain why New Wave writers were so aggressively critical of feminine values, affected aestheticism and homosexuals in general. From the late forties onwards, there were signs of a new self-confidence in metropolitan homosexual circles, with the establishment of homosexual gentlemen's clubs in London, Brighton and Blackpool.[23] To outsiders, however, the homosexual subculture could appear a closed and unnerving world of code words, surreptitious signals and clandestine meetings, not unlike the world of spies and informers. 'It is a secret world,' wrote John Vassall, a homosexual civil servant blackmailed into spying for the KGB, 'a kind of masonic society to protect oneself against mankind because they can be so cruel – especially in the Anglo-Saxon world.'[24]

Just like fears of espionage and subversion, fears of homosexuality had for decades been linked to wider anxieties about imperial decline and social unrest. As far back as the 1770s, Edward Gibbon had suggested that the Roman Empire had collapsed in part because of the 'degeneracy' of a 'servile and effeminate age', and more modern commentators described the prospect of British imperial eclipse in terms of immorality, corruption and perversion. Manly virtues had, it was supposed, built British power, and its decline was therefore explained as the degeneration of aristocratic manhood into sexual deviance and political radicalism.[25] 'Perversion is very largely a practice of the too idle and the too rich,' wrote the popular *Sunday Express* columnist John Gordon. 'It does not flourish in lands where men work hard and brows sweat with honest labour.'[26] Surveys in the mid-fifties, meanwhile, suggested that at least half the population considered homosexuality 'disgusting'. The physical expression of homosexual love was still illegal, and in most sections of society, with the notable exceptions of the theatre and the media, the admission of homosexuality was considered grounds for immediate dismissal and even prosecution.[27]

In the mid-fifties, official and public hostility to homosexuality sharply intensified. For one thing, the persistence of homosexuality jarred badly with the increased emphasis after the war on the health and sanctity of marriage and family life. What was more, the fact that London staged two enormous public set-pieces in the early part of the decade, the Festival of Britain and the Coronation, placed great pressure on the police to stamp out homosexual soliciting in parks and public toilets. Above all, there was an atmosphere of moral panic in which homosexuality became closely associated with national decline and political subversion. British internal security arrangements, always flimsy by comparison with those in the United States, looked embarrassingly shoddy after the defections of Burgess and Maclean, and the Conservative government were keen to show their American allies that they were indeed cracking down on security risks. In this context, the bogeyman of the homosexual became a vulnerable and convenient scapegoat for broader anxieties about national security.[28] 'In the general run,' commented one Conservative backbencher, 'the homosexual is a dirty-minded danger to the virile manhood of this country.'[29]

It was no coincidence, then, that the years immediately after the flight of Burgess and Maclean were also those of reinvigorated official persecution of homosexuals in Britain. As Lord Hailsham's article had made clear, many hostile observers were convinced that homosexuality was increasing to the point where it was becoming a tide of filth sweeping through the streets of London; the authorities must therefore act quickly to save young men from falling into the clutches of their depraved elders. In 1953 the Commissioner of the Metropolitan Police, Sir John Nott-Boyer, vowed to 'rip the cover off all London's filth spots', while the Home Secretary, Sir David Maxwell-Fyfe, later Lord Kilmuir, told the House of Commons: 'Homosexuals in general are exhibitionists and proselytisers and are a danger to others, especially the young.'[30] As he saw it, 'sodomistic societies and buggery clubs' were bound to foster a spirit of 'lying, cruelty and indecency', and with the help of a like-minded Director of Public Prosecutions, the austere Catholic Sir Theobald Mathew, the Home Secretary was determined to 'smash homosexuality in

London'.[31] Under the 1885 law that governed homosexual behaviour, 'any act of gross indecency' between two men, whether in public or in private, was punishable by imprisonment, and it was therefore not difficult to mount a sustained drive to improve the prosecution rate, not least through the use of handsome agents provocateurs working for the Metropolitan Police in public toilets. Prosecutions for homosexual offences had already risen fourfold in the 1940s, thanks largely to the crusading zeal of Sir Theobald Mathew, and between 1950 and 1954 the annual prosecution rate soared from 4416 cases to 6644.[32]

This orchestrated purge of metropolitan homosexuals went down well with the popular press, especially since this was a period of increasingly bitter struggles for circulation and advertising revenue, and therefore of ever greater sensationalism. Indeed, attacking 'perverts' was quite simply good for sales.[33] In the summer of 1952, for example, the *Sunday Pictorial* ran a three-part series under the title 'Evil Men' promising 'an end to the conspiracy of silence' about homosexuality in Britain. 'Most people know there are such things – "pansies" – mincing, effeminate, young men who call themselves queers,' the *Pictorial* explained. 'But simple, decent folk regard them as freaks and rarities.' Homosexuality, the newspaper warned, was 'a spreading fungus' that had infected 'generals, admirals, fighter pilots, engine drivers and boxers'. One article described with horrified glee 'a dirty café off Shaftesbury-avenue, where dozens of the most blatant perverts meet, calling each other by girls' names openly'.[34]

Although the anti-homosexual drive of the fifties eventually ran out of steam, popular hostility to the conspiratorial and subversive habits attributed to homosexuals remained strong throughout the sixties. By April 1963 the *Sunday Pictorial* had been renamed the *Sunday Mirror*, but it had not lost its crusading verve, producing a two-page guide for its readers entitled 'How to Spot a Homo'. Not unexpectedly, 'shifty glances', 'dropped eyes' and of course 'a fondness for the theatre' were all authoritatively identified as unmistakable signs of dangerous and deviant intentions.[35]

Although popular fears of left-wing subversion in Britain never reached the heights of American McCarthyism, that did not mean they were non-existent. In Burgess and Maclean, British commentators found the ideal symbols of Communist infiltration and moral decline. The popular imagination cast them, like all such traitors, as devious, perverted and unhealthy, representatives not of idealism but of degeneracy. By contrast, the loyal British secret agent was portrayed in a very different light: gallant, dashing and intrepid, the worthy heir of the adventurers of empire and the lions of the world wars. Five years after the flight of the Cambridge spies, newspaper readers were eagerly reading about a character who might have sprung from some cheap comic book for boys: Commander (Special Branch) Lionel 'Buster' Crabb, RNVR, GM, OBE. Crabb had won his honours as a navy frogman during the Second World War, diving into the Mediterranean to clear Italian limpet mines from sunken vessels, and then seems to have worked for Naval Intelligence as a kind of underwater secret agent, investigating sunken submarines, searching ships in Haifa harbour for mines planted by Jewish terrorists and in October 1955 secretly diving to examine the hull of the Soviet cruiser *Sverdlov*, a technologically sophisticated warship which was visiting Portsmouth for a naval review. The success of this mission encouraged Crabb's handlers in the security service to contemplate a second, even more audacious operation. In April 1956 the *Sverdlov*'s sister ship, the similarly advanced cruiser *Ordzhonikidze*, was due to arrive in Portsmouth, bringing the Soviet leaders Khrushchev and Bulganin for a state visit. According to the MI6 plan, Crabb was to dive into the Portsmouth waters and examine the hull of the *Ordzhonikidze* for sonar and mine equipment. It was, needless to say, an extremely risky undertaking: given that Khrushchev had arrived in Britain on the boat, it would be a diplomatic disaster if a British frogman were caught in the vicinity. The operation went ahead nonetheless. On 17 April, Crabb and his MI6 contact took rooms at a hotel in Portsmouth. The following day, the *Ordzhonikidze* docked in the Royal Navy yards, with two other Soviet destroyers moored alongside, and the Soviet leaders disembarked to begin their tour. In the evening, Crabb met a few old friends for a drink and then returned to his hotel. He was never seen again.[36]

Ten days later, under pressure from the press, the Admiralty released a brief statement explaining that Commander Crabb had been on 'a test dive . . . in connection with trials of certain underwater apparatus in Stokes Bay, in the Portsmouth area'.[37] This story did not fool anyone, especially when reporters discovered that the pages in the hotel register where Crabb and his contact, a Mr Smith, had signed in were mysteriously missing. The Soviet Union lodged a formal protest that a frogman had been seen diving near their warships, the government denied everything, and a secret internal inquiry reported that Crabb had indeed been on an unauthorised MI6 operation. Just over a year later, in June 1957, fishermen found a body on a sandbank in Chichester harbour. The corpse was certainly clad in Crabb's wetsuit, but, mysteriously, its head and hands had been severed.[38] The appearance of what appeared to be Crabb's body was the cue for all kinds of extravagant conspiracy theories. Popular rumour had it that Crabb was not dead at all, but instead had been captured by Soviet agents, taken back to Moscow and brainwashed into training KGB frogman teams. Other stories had Crabb as a commander in the Soviet navy under the name of Lev Lvovich Korablov, or commander of the Soviet Special Task Underwater Operational Command in the Black Sea fleet, or, more prosaically, Prisoner 147 in the Lefortovo prison in Moscow.[39]

The Crabb case, ostensibly at least, had all the elements of a successful spy thriller, and it was little surprise that it captured the public imagination. As an intrepid diving hero, decorated for his services in the war, Crabb seemed a splendid *Boy's Own* hero, whether incarcerated in some dreadful Soviet dungeon or proudly steering his warship through the Black Sea. Unfortunately, the truth was rather more mundane. Crabb was not quite the cool, square-jawed champion of public renown, but a miserable, unfit, middle-aged eccentric who smoked and drank heavily, was rumoured to be bisexual, and ostentatiously carried an ornate swordstick engraved with a golden crab. Not only was he probably too old for the *Ordzhonikidze* operation, but the whole enterprise was strictly unauthorised and badly planned from the start, while the fact that his MI6 handler had a heart attack the day before the dive hardly made matters easier. Precisely how and why Crabb died remains unclear. Harold Macmillan, then the Chancellor of the Exchequer, noted at the time in his diary that Crabb had been 'either killed by the Russians or drowned by misadventure – we don't know for certain'.[40] Some reports claim that he was probably shot in the head by a Soviet sniper after being spotted in the water, but, according to one senior MI6 officer, he probably died 'from respiratory trouble, being a heavy smoker and not in the best of health, or conceivably because some fault had developed in his equipment'.[41] This does not, however, explain what happened to his head and his hands; since neither respiratory trouble nor the action of the sea tends to sever heads, foul play remains a strong possibility.

Far from being a glamorous adventure, the Crabb affair could better be described as a shoddy operational blunder that not only suggested the perils of entrusting private citizens with sensitive enterprises but also illustrated the capacity of the British intelligence services to lapse into rank amateurism.[42] The Secret Intelligence Service, better known as SIS or MI6, had first been established in 1909 to collect evidence of German planning for an invasion of Britain, although within two decades it had switched its attentions to the Soviet Union, and militant anti-Communism remained the guiding spirit of the service for decades to come. The MI6 headquarters were in the suitably gloomy and forbidding surroundings of 54 Broadway Buildings, although in 1966 the service moved to Century House, an anonymous office block in Lambeth. Like its fictional counterparts, MI6 had its quirky traditions: the head of the service was always known as C, after its first chief, the one-legged Captain Mansfield Cumming, and, in deference to the first C, all his successors continued his practice of writing in green ink.[43] From the outest, there was a cheerfully amateurish public-school spirit about MI6 that continued to amaze American collaborators during the Cold War. On one occasion, a group of British and American intelligence officers met to discuss the difficulties of an operation to dispatch anti-Communist guerrillas into Albania, and the chief American spokesman later recalled:

After sitting round a table in a desultory fashion for an hour or two, one Englishman finally said, 'I say, why don't we get old Henry up here? He knows about this.' A day or two later Henry showed up from down in Sussex, and when the problem was put to him, he agreed to take on the task, although he said, 'This will wreak havoc with the garden, you know. Just getting it into trim.'[44]

For all the talk about gardens in Sussex, MI6 operations were in deadly earnest. In every country in the Communist bloc British officers ran extensive networks of agents and informants, many of whom contributed intelligence that was genuinely valuable to British planners and diplomats. The MI6 station in West Berlin, for example, boasted about a hundred officers and ancillary staff, dedicated to collecting political and scientific intelligence, gathering information on the Soviet and East German military forces, planning technical operations and penetrating the Soviet headquarters at Karlshorst.[45] The prize MI6 informant was Oleg Penkovsky, a colonel in Soviet military intelligence who handed over information about Soviet missiles, the personal style of Nikita Khrushchev and Soviet intentions in the Berlin and Cuban crises as well of reams of blueprints and documents shot on tiny Minox cameras, before he was detected and shot by the KGB in

1962.[46] Throughout the Cold War, British intelligence officers organised expeditions and operations that had something of the *Boy's Own* spirit about them: sending agents into the Ukraine or the Balkans, dispatching teams of elite special forces into Oman, or plotting to kill President Nasser with, so the MI5 agent Peter Wright later claimed, 'a cigarette packet which had been modified by the Explosives Research and Development Establishment to fire a dart tipped with poison'.[47]

As the Crabb debacle suggested, however, not all British intelligence officers took the trouble to secure political authorisation for their pet schemes, and nor were those schemes always well conceived and executed. By the end of the fifties a new C, the career MI5 officer Sir Dick White, had been installed at the head of the secret service, with instructions to cut down on the risky derring-do and generally clean up MI6's act.[48] Contrary to popular myth, the secret and security services never wielded immense clout in the corridors of Whitehall; as Richard Thurlow points out, by comparison with their counterparts in other Western European countries like France or Italy, and especially with the FBI and CIA across the Atlantic, their influence and standing were surprisingly low.[49] In fact, by the mid-sixties, morale in the British intelligence services had slumped to unprecedented depths, especially after the revelation of further spies in high places, notably the MI6 officers George Blake and Kim Philby and the Admiralty clerk John Vassall. Far from being the smooth, sophisticated and stylish organisation portrayed in popular bestsellers, MI6 was sunk in 'cynicism and weariness', with few major intelligence coups to its name after Penkovsky's execution by the KGB. Its senior officers were transfixed by the fear of further embarrassing scandals, its ranks were riddled with suspicion and speculation, and in Westminster and Washington its reputation had probably never been lower.[50]

As far as the general public was concerned, however, the affairs of the intelligence services were shrouded in impenetrable and fascinating mystery. Only rarely did intimations of British secret operations reach the breakfast table of the ordinary citizen, one example being the arrest in August 1962 of Colonel Penkovksy's British contact, a businessman called Greville Wynne, who was subsequently interrogated and tried by the Soviet authorities, exposed as a go-between for MI6 and sentenced to eight years in a Moscow prison. When, in 1964, Wynne was exchanged for a British traitor who had been caught spying for the Soviet Union, he maintained his cover as an innocent businessman with no interest in the intelligence world. Three years later, impressed by the public demand for spy stories of all kinds, he published an extremely colourful account of his secret past which predictably proved a great success. Like Buster Crabb, however, Wynne was a middle-aged alcoholic of dubious reliability, and ultimately an unpromising candidate for spy stardom.[51] By this point, real spies like Wynne were struggling to live up to the high standards set by a series of fictional secret agents whose impact on popular culture during the early sixties had been immense. Even the title of Wynne's autobiography, *The Man from Moscow*, imitated the style of the popular thrillers of the day: *The Man with the Golden Gun*, say, or *The Spy Who Came In from the Cold*. If any one individual defined the public image of the British secret agent fighting the clandestine Cold War, it was not Buster Crabb or Greville Wynne; it was Ian Fleming.

Ian Fleming was born in London in 1908. His paternal grandfather was a dour Scottish merchant banker; his father, a Conservative MP and country gent, was killed in the Great War when Ian was just eight. For the rest of his life the framed obituary of his father written by his friend Winston Churchill was one of Fleming's most treasured possessions. His early life was the typical chequered story of a younger son from the British upper classes: an indifferent education at Eton and Sandhurst, lacklustre spells at schools in Austria and Switzerland, failure in the Foreign Office examination, stints as a Reuters journalist and a stockbroker. His interests lay in gastronomy, cards and sex; as David Cannadine puts it in a fine essay, 'women came and went, attracted by his good looks, Etonian drawl, animal magnetism, cultivated air of mystery and (at least initially) rather cruel and arrogant charm'. At the same time, Fleming was manifestly a deeply unsatisfied man, and there clung to him 'an aura of wounded and solitary melancholy, of deep but usually latent romanticism that would also characterize the Bond books and give them much of their unique tone, conviction and appeal'.[52] As he himself admitted, James Bond was 'the author's pillow fantasy'. 'It's very much the Walter Mitty syndrome,' he told an interviewer in 1963; 'the feverish dreams of the author of what he might have been, bang, bang, bang, kiss, kiss, that sort of stuff.'[53]

During the Second World War Fleming found a niche in Naval Intelligence as personal assistant to the director, Admiral Sir John Godfrey. It was a job in which Fleming thrived, and he evidently loved the air of intrigue, the relationships with military and paramilitary types, the status associated with his rank of commander in the Royal Navy, and the opportunities to travel to places like Tangiers, Lisbon and Washington on intelligence business. At one level, therefore, the James Bond books reflected Fleming's nostalgia for those dashing days: life after the war as foreign manager for Kemsley Newspapers was rather more sedate, and he spent much of his time composing the Atticus gossip column for the *Sunday Times*, writing articles about underwater treasure hunters and smugglers, pursuing women and hobnobbing with friends like Noël Coward at his Jamaican retreat, Goldeneye.[54]

Fleming began to write the first Bond book, *Casino Royale*, in January 1952, partly because he was keen to emulate his elder brother Peter, a debonair and intrepid explorer who had just published his own satirical novel about the security services, and partly because he was being encouraged by his fiancée, the aristocratic society hostess Lady Ann Rothermere, whom he married later in the same year. It was not a very happy marriage; indeed, within four years she had become the mistress of Hugh Gaitskell and was to remain his lover until his death.[55] Within three months the book was finished, and it was published the following year by the London firm Jonathan Cape.[56] Fleming told a friend that it was a 'dreadful oafish opus', and even sent the manuscript to his publisher with a letter declaring that it was a 'miserable piece of work'.[57] In reality, though, he was rather proud of his creation, and explained in 1963:

> I am not an angry young, or even middle-aged man. I am not 'involved'. My books are not 'engaged'. I have no message for suffering humanity and, though I was bullied at school and lost my virginity like so many of us used to do in the old days, I have never been tempted to foist these and other harrowing personal experiences on the public. My opuscula do not aim at changing people or making them go out and do something. They are not designed to find favour with the Comintern. They are written for warm-blooded heterosexuals in railway trains, airplanes or beds.[58]

When *Casino Royale* reached the bookshops in April 1953, however, it was not an immediate success. The prestige of Jonathan Cape meant that it attracted reviews in upmarket periodicals like *The Times Literary Supplement* and the *Spectator*, both of which praised it as a lively, entertaining read, but there was little sign of a great popular rush to snap up Fleming's novel.[59] Royalties were disappointing, and in the United States *Casino Royale* was rejected by three publishers before being brought out, to enormous indifference, by Macmillan. For the next three years, although Fleming produced a book every year, the Bond books failed to trouble the compilers of the bestseller lists, and although a film deal with Sir Alexander Korda was mooted at one stage, it never materialised.[60]

The real breakthrough came in 1956, when *Casino Royale* was published by Pan as a cheap paperback. Sales of paperback books, designed for comfortable middle- and working-class readers, suburban book clubs and public libraries, were booming amid the affluence of the mid-fifties, and Pan were keen to challenge the dominance of Penguin. With their promise of intrigue, sex and violence, the James Bond novels were ideal weapons in the paperback war, and when in 1957 the *Daily Express* began running a comic-strip serial based on *From Russia with Love*, Bond paperback sales began to take off. Indeed, without the boom in paperback popular fiction, itself a consequence of wider social and economic developments, it is hard to see Fleming's books enjoying the phenomenal success that was eventually their lot.[61] In 1962 Bond finally reached the cinema thanks to the entrepreneurial vision of Broccoli and Saltzman, and the release of *Dr No* confirmed Bond's grip on the public imagination. Paperback sales of that title alone rose from 85,000 in 1961 to 232,000, 437,000, 530,000 and 476,000 in the next four years.[62] It can without exaggeration be said that James Bond was the publishing sensation of the sixties. In 1965 alone, for example, Bond books sold some twenty-seven million copies worldwide. Almost a third of all Pan paperback sales were James Bond titles, and of the first eighteen books to sell a million copies in Britain, ten were Bond books.[63]

For some critics, the success of Fleming's hero was a deplorable indication of public ignorance. In 1958 the journalist Paul Johnson wrote a furious review of *Dr No*, entitled 'Sex, Snobbery and Sadism', in the *New Statesman*:

> I have just finished what is, without doubt, the nastiest book I have ever read. I had to suppress a strong impulse to throw the thing away . . . There are three basic ingredients in *Dr No*, all unhealthy, all thoroughly English: the sadism of a schoolboy bully, the mechanical, two-dimension sex-longings of a frustrated adolescent, and the crude snob-cravings of a suburban adult . . . Mr Fleming has no literary skill . . . This seems to me far more dangerous than straight pornography. This novel is badly written to the point of incoherence.[64]

Fleming's biggest champion, meanwhile, was Kingsley Amis, for whom the Bond books, like science fiction, represented a virile populist rebuke to the Continental pretensions of the old literary elite. Indeed, in 1965 he even published the first critical study of the Bond series. Fleming's novels, according to Amis, were 'far more than simple cloak-and-dagger stories with a bit of fashionable affluence and sex thrown in'. Instead, they deserved to be ranked alongside popular classics of earlier generations, from Jules Verne to Conan Doyle. 'Ian Fleming', said Amis, 'has set his stamp on the story of action and intrigue, bringing to it a sense of our time, a power and a flair that will win him readers when all the protests about his supposed deficiencies have been forgotten.'[65] Perhaps this was a little excessive: after all, like so many popular bestsellers, the Bond novels depended for their success not so much on originality or finesse as on the repetition of reassuringly familiar episodes according to a tried and tested formula: card games, kidnappings, love scenes, chases and so on. As one American critic puts it:

> First there are opening scenes at Headquarters to give necessary background and to legitimize the hero with his institutional allegiance. The hero then travels and Fleming incorporates passages of local color. Arriving at the main scene of the action, the hero explores the ground and meets the villains. Then there are physical and/or psychological tests for the hero to undergo. Finally the hero eliminates or aids in the elimination of the villain.[66]

According to the Italian structuralist critic Umberto Eco, meanwhile, 'the reader's pleasure consists in finding himself immersed in a game of which he knows the pieces and the rules – and perhaps the outcome – drawing pleasure simply from the minimal variations by which the victor realises his objective'.[67]

What often attracted readers to the Bond books, then, was that they offered not the shock of the new but the comfort of the familiar. Since the Edwardian era, each generation had produced its own classic spy storytellers, from Erskine Childers and John Buchan to Somerset Maugham and Graham Greene, and each writer produced a different variation on the traditional formula of exotic foreign villains, plucky British heroes, thrilling pursuits and deadly violence.[68] The authors to whom Fleming was evidently most indebted were John Buchan and 'Sapper' (H. C. McNeile), who between them dominated the adventure-story market in the 1910s and 1920s. Ironically, in the very same year that *Casino Royale* first went on sale, the writer Richard Usborne published a book entitled *Clubland Heroes* bemoaning the fact that patriotic thrillers like those produced by Buchan and 'Sapper' had gone out of fashion.[69] The success of the Bond phenomenon, however, was to prove him wrong. Fleming had as a boy loved reading about the escapades of Richard Hannay and Bulldog Drummond, and in Bond he set out to create a modern but ultimately faithful recreation of the clubland hero. All three men shared what one American critic later called the 'Tory imagination' and therefore presented their readers with heroes that were models of physical stamina and moral courage as well as staunch lovers of tradition and empire, inevitably drawn to the struggle against immense worldwide conspiracies usually run by devious Continental boffins.[70]

Like Buchan, Fleming was effectively retelling 'schoolboy stories dressed up for adults', showing how British pluck and application would defeat international Communism just as surely as it had beaten the Kaiser and the Nazis.[71] Like 'Sapper', meanwhile, Fleming created a central character who saw himself as 'a sportsman and gentleman' but offended sensitive souls by his aggressive, even violent contempt for political deviants, plutocratic parasites and, above all, foreigners of all creeds and colours.[72] And as in so many classic adventure stories, Fleming's books appease the fantasies of their readers partly through the sheer accumulation of superlatives. Bond is something of a superman: 'the finest gambler' and the 'best shot' in the Secret Service, a walking gastronomic encyclopaedia, an expert on the wines of the world, a learned connoisseur of vintage cars, and a supreme seducer and lover. This is just as well, as David Cannadine has pointed out, because his adversaries are no less extraordinary. To take but four, Mr Big is 'the most powerful negro criminal in the world'; Dr No is 'one of the most remarkable men in the world' with 'the most valuable technical intelligence centre in the world'; Emile Largo 'had fought for Italy in the Olympic foils, was almost an Olympic class swimmer' and had 'nerves of steel, a heart of ice and the ruthlessness of a Himmler'; and Ernst Stavro Blofeld is 'the biggest crook in the world' with plans 'on the scale of a Caligula, of a Nero, of a Hitler, of any of the great enemies of mankind'.[73]

Fleming's books appealed to readers in the fifties and sixties partly because in James Bond he had invented a protagonist who reminded them of the fictional heroes of their youth. An anonymous reviewer in *The Times Literary Supplement*, for example, commented in 1953 that Bond reminded him of a 'somewhat more sophisticated' version of Bulldog Drummond.[74] According to Fleming, he chose for his hero 'the dullest name he could find', and christened him after the ornithologist James Bond, whose book *Birds of the West Indies* was lying on his coffee table at Goldeneye when he began writing in January 1952.[75] The character was, in many ways, a fictionalised and exaggerated version of Fleming himself. James Bond is an orphan: when he was eleven, his Scottish father, an employee of the Vickers arms company, and Swiss mother were killed in a climbing accident at Chamonix. He was educated with little distinction at Eton, where he was expelled for consorting with a maid, and Fettes; he left school and studied for a while in Geneva, like Fleming; finally, shortly before the war, he began working with the Secret Service and then moved into the Ministry of Defence for good.[76] In one scene in the early novel *Moonraker* (1955), Bond goes with M, the head of the Secret Service, to play cards at his club Blades, and wryly reflects on his own appearance:

> And what could the casual observer think of him, 'Commander James Bond, CMG, RNVSR', also 'something at the Ministry of Defence,' the rather saturnine young man in his middle thirties sitting opposite the Admiral? Something a bit cold and dangerous in that face. Looks pretty fit. May have been attached to Templer in Malaya. Or Nairobi. Mau Mau work. Tough-looking customer. Doesn't look the sort of chap one usually sees in Blades.
>
> Bond knew there was something alien and un-English about himself. He knew that he was a difficult man to cover up. Particularly in England. He shrugged his shoulders. Abroad was what mattered. He would never have a job to do in England.[77]

The parallels with Richard Hannay and Bulldog Drummond, both of whom also feel themselves to be outsiders in modern British society, could hardly be clearer. Bond even dresses in a self-consciously classic, timeless style: 'dark-blue single-breasted suit, white shirt, thin black knitted silk tie, black casuals', as though to make it absolutely clear that he stands outside and above the whims of passing fashion and the innovations of suburban modernity.[78] At one level, then, Bond is simply another of Richard Usborne's clubland heroes, a political and cultural conservative dedicated to protecting the world of luxury and convention represented by clubs like Blades.[79]

In itself this does not explain why the character appealed so much to readers in the sixties who were, after all, often fascinated by novelty and modernity rather than ritual and tradition. The success of Fleming's books also depended on the fact that far from being merely another well-bred clubman, James Bond could easily be seen as the representative of modernity and modernisation, less an imperialistic throwback than a sophisticated, classless hero of the scientific age and the Cold War. The Bond books are very firmly rooted in the post-war years, and like all successful spy stories, they tend to reflect the particular concerns of the day, functioning as what the critic Michael Denning calls 'cover stories . . . translating the political and cultural transformations of the twentieth century into the intrigues of a shadow world of secret agents'.[80] The context of imperial decline might have been thought unpropitious for a series of spy stories about a secret agent devoted to Queen and Empire, but Fleming's timing was perfect. Tired of hearing about imperial retreat and the grim realities of post-war retrenchment, the British middle classes were the ideal market for his reassuring fantasies of enduring power and influence.[81] As Kingsley Amis pointed out in 1965, James Bond was the incarnation of 'chauvinism at once smartened up and on its last legs', and the novels were 'a collective power-fantasy' in which the British Empire secretly endures thanks to the agents of the Secret Service. The partnership between Bond and the CIA agent Felix Leiter reflects the supposed special relationship between Britain and the United States, but, as Amis points out, Leiter is very much the subordinate: 'Bond is constantly doing better than he, showing himself . . . smarter, wittier, tougher, more resourceful, the incarnation of little old England with her quiet ways and shoe-string budget wiping the eye of great big global-tentacled multi-billion-dollar-appropriating America.'[82]

In *From Russia with Love*, Lieutenant-General Vozdvishensky of the Soviet Foreign Ministry explains to his colleagues that the Americans may have 'the biggest and the richest service among our enemies . . . but they have no understanding for the work'. By contrast:

> England is another matter altogether . . . Their Security Service is excellent. England, being an island, has great security advantages and their so-called MI5 employs men with good education and good brains. Their Secret Service is still better. They have notable successes. In certain types of operation, we are constantly finding that they have been

there before us. Their agents are good. They pay them little money – only a thousand or two thousand roubles a month – but they serve with devotion . . . Their social standing abroad is not high, and their wives have to pass as the wives of secretaries. They are rarely awarded a decoration until they retire. And yet these men and women continue to do their dangerous work. It is curious. It is perhaps the Public School and the University tradition. The love of adventure.[83]

Similarly, James Bond himself never doubts that the British are inherently superior to all other nations. The Russians are described as 'cold, dedicated and chess-playing', the Bulgarians are 'stupid and obedient' and the Koreans are 'the cruellest, most ruthless people on earth'. American negroes, meanwhile, are 'clumsy black apes'. And as so often in spy stories, the master criminals usually reflect the antagonisms and anxieties of international politics. Mr Big is a black American gangster; Dr No is an Oriental mastermind sprung from the pages of the Fu Manchu stories; even Sir Hugo Drax, who masquerades as a patriotic Englishman, is actually Graf Hugo von der Drache, a typically fanatical German nationalist.[84]

Fleming was, however, all too aware of the decline in Britain's international position since the publication of *Casino Royale* in 1953. In all the Bond books of the fifties, the hero's adversaries are either working for the Soviet secret service or, more typically, for SMERSH, 'the official murder organization of the Soviet government' with a particular animus against agent 007.[85] By 1961, however, Fleming had withdrawn Bond from the front line of the battle against international Communism, it no longer being plausible that the British were leading the way in the Cold War. From *Thunderball* onwards, Bond is pitted against SPECTRE, a gang of international terrorists led by the super-villain Ernst Stavro Blofeld, a more fantastic adversary but one better suited to the realities of the sixties.[86] This was not the only way in which the Bond books reflected their author's unease at national decline. He once claimed that he was 'a totally non-political animal', but in fact his attitudes were unwaveringly Conservative.[87] After the war, he thought, 'the liberal spirit got a little out of hand', and he intensely disliked the welfare state, upon which he blamed 'the increasing emphasis of our society not only upon materialism, but upon materialism *without effort*'.[88] In an essay in the *Spectator* in 1959, he complained that 'taxation, controls and certain features of the Welfare State' had 'turned the majority of us into petty criminals, liars and work-dodgers'.[89]

Bond moves, therefore, in a world delicately poised between the reassurance of tradition and the disquiet of change. Blades, M's London club in *Moonraker*, is the best example of the former, an oasis of Victorianism and a refuge from the trials of the modern world. 'If a member is staying overnight,' we are told, 'his notes and small change are taken away by the valet who brings the early morning tea and *The Times* and replaced with new money. No newspaper comes to the reading room before it has been ironed. Floris provides the soaps and lotions in the lavatories and bedrooms; there is a direct wire to Ladbroke's from the porter's lodge; the club has the finest tents and boxes at the principal race meetings, at Lords, Henley and Wimbledon, and members travelling abroad have automatic membership of the leading club in every foreign capital.' Bond reflects that Blades provides the 'luxury of the Victorian age'; it is probably the place in which he feels most at home, and is reintroduced in several later books.[90] Indeed, his image of Britain is entirely coloured by his Tory imagination. Later in the same novel, he goes for a stroll with the heroine Gala Brand on the cliffs of Kent, the cue for a lyrical passage describing 'the whole corner of England where Caesar had first landed two thousand years before', the 'carpet of green turf, bright with small wildflowers' sliding down to the 'sparkling blue of the Straits . . . a panorama full of colour and excitement and romance'.[91] Similarly, when Bond thinks about returning home at the end of *Dr No*, his mind 'drifted into a world of tennis courts and lily ponds and kings and queens, of London, of people being photographed with pigeons on their heads in Trafalgar Square, of the forsythia that would soon be blazing on the bypass roundabouts, of May, the treasured housekeeper in his flat off the King's Road, getting up to brew herself a cup of tea . . . of the first tube trains beginning to run, shaking the ground beneath his cool, dark bedroom'.[92]

But there is no escaping the pace of change. In the penultimate novel, *You Only Live Twice*, published in 1964, the Japanese spymaster Tiger Tanaka mocks Bond's patriotic pretensions, almost certainly articulating Fleming's own hostility to post-war society:

> You have not only lost an empire, you have seemed almost anxious to throw it away with both hands . . . When you apparently sought to arrest this slide into impotence at Suez, you succeeded only in stage-managing one of the most pitiful bungles in the history of the world . . . Your governments have shown themselves successively

incapable of ruling, and have handed over effective control of the economy to the trade unions, who appear to be dedicated to the principle of doing less and less work for more money. This feather-bedding, this shirking of an honest day's work, is sapping at ever-increasing speed the moral fibre of the British, a quality the world once so admired. In its place, we now see a vacuous, aimless horde of seekers after pleasure.

Bond angrily sticks up for his countrymen, no doubt sending a warm glow through Fleming's more patriotic readers:

Balls to you, Tiger! And balls again! . . . Let me tell you this, my fine friend. England may have been bled pretty thin by a couple of world wars, our welfare-state politics may have made us expect too much for free, and the liberation of our colonies may have gone too fast, but we still climb Everest and beat plenty of the world at plenty of sports and win Nobel Prizes. Our politicians may be a feather-pated bunch, but I expect yours are, too. All politicians are. But there's nothing wrong with the British people – although there are only fifty million of them.

Tiger nods approvingly; he was only teasing. 'Those are very similar to the words I addressed to my Prime Minister,' he says with a reassuring smile.[93]

The Bond books work so well as reflections of the sixties precisely because of this ambiguous attitude towards modern Britain. Even though their central character despises the indolent ease of the welfare state, the novels wallow in the consumerism of the affluent society. One major difference between the world of James Bond and the world of Bulldog Drummond, for example, is the ubiquity of sex in Fleming's novels. Paul Johnson's comparison with 'straight pornography' was a telling one. The Bond books were the first major thrillers, indeed the first major British best-sellers, in which sex was a central element of the plot, the hero's character and the books' publicity. In the critic Michael Denning's words, they were 'an important early form of the mass pornography that characterises the consumer society, the society of the spectacle, that emerges in Western Europe and North America in the wake of post-war reconstruction'.[94] The film critic Raymond Durgnat, with good reason, remarked that the Bond phenomenon represented a cross between the public school and *Playboy* magazine, which coincidentally first appeared in the same year as *Casino*

Royale.[95] There is plenty of sexual voyeurism, for example: Bond spies on Tatiana Romanova through a periscope in *From Russia with Love*, and again spies on a naked Honey Rider in *Dr No*, an experience he finds 'extraordinarily erotic'.[96] Sex is described in breathless, semi-pornographic prose: like his creator, Bond has no desire to be tied down in a lasting relationship, but simply lusts after the succession of stunning, and stunningly disposable, nymphets who cross his path, usually with exotic or even erotic names like Vesper Lynd, Pussy Galore, Honey Rider or Kissy Suzuki.[97]

In the world of James Bond, women are merely disposable consumer luxuries like any other, with the exception of his wife Tracy di Vicenzo, a neurotic and wayward young heiress who is killed off before she can spoil the hero's fun. 'Women were for recreation,' Bond thinks at one point in *Casino Royale*. 'On a job, they got in the way and fogged things up with sex and hurt feelings and all the emotional baggage they carried around. One had to look out for them and take care of them.'[98] Like his creator, then, and like many of the New Wave protagonists, he bitterly resents the changes in British society since the Second World War, and in this respect the Bond novels represent an angry reaction to the transformation in the public image and role of women, not least their increasing involvement in the labour market. The Secret Service is a man's world: a female M would be unthinkable, and the only women at MI6 headquarters are secretaries like Miss Moneypenny and Mary Goodnight. When in *Casino Royale* Bond's partner Vesper Lynd is kidnapped by the SMERSH agent Le Chiffre, he angrily reflects: 'These blithering women, who thought they could do a man's work. Why the hell couldn't they stay at home and mind their pots and pans and stick to their frocks and their gossip, and leave men's work for the men?'[99]

Often the very women that Bond finally seduces are earlier shown as uninterested in sex or even as lesbians. Bond's role is to restore them to their traditional function as the passive object of male sexual attentions.[100] In *Goldfinger* he encounters two lesbians, Pussy Galore and Tilly Masterson; one succumbs to his charm, the other dies. Homosexuality, for Bond and for Fleming, is part of the deplorable feminisation of post-war society, and, thanks to pushy women, men are losing their nerve and their identity:

> Bond came to the conclusion that Tilly Masterson was one of those
> girls whose hormones had got mixed up. He knew the type well and
> thought they and their male counterparts were a direct consequence

of giving votes to women and 'sex equality'. As a result of fifty years of emancipation, feminine qualities were dying out or being transferred to the males. Pansies of both sexes were everywhere, not completely homosexual, but confused, not knowing what they were. The result was a herd of unhappy sexual misfits – barren and full of frustrations, the women wanting to dominate and the men to be nannied. He was sorry for them, but he had no time for them.[101]

Fleming often casts Bond as the chivalrous romantic hero, leaping in to save the beautiful heroine from a dreadful fate, listening sympathetically to her tale of betrayal and abuse, and applying a good dose of 'tender loving care'. Contemplating his future wife Tracy, Bond feels 'a sweeping urge to protect her, to solve her problems, make her happy'.[102] Chivalry, however, is frequently overshadowed by cruelty. Bond is often described as having 'cruel' or 'cold' features: in *Casino Royale*, for example, his sleeping face is described as a 'taciturn mask, ironical, brutal and cold'.[103] Ian and Ann Fleming incorporated corporal punishment into their own sex life, and, as John Lanchester puts it, the novels are 'at heart a series of lavish beatings strung together with thriller elements'.[104] Bond is regularly beaten up and tortured, most famously in the first book, when his genitals are thrashed with a cane carpet-beater. 'Towards the end,' Fleming tells us, 'there came a wonderful period of warmth and languor leading into a sort of sexual twilight where pain turned to pleasure and when hatred and fear of the torturers turned to a masochistic infatuation.'[105]

But not only is Bond a frequent victim of sado-masochistic torture, he also likes to dish it out to his lady friends. In *Dr No*, he looks at Honey Rider, 'bright with desire', and 'unsteadily' tells her: 'Honey, get into that bath before I spank you.'[106] 'You will beat me if I eat too much?' Tatiana asks him jokingly in *From Russia with Love*. 'Certainly I will beat you,' Bond replies solemnly.[107] Five years after John Osborne had observed that all women 'cry out for defilement', Fleming had Vivienne Michel, the narrator of *The Spy Who Loved Me*, admit:

All women love semi-rape. They love to be taken. It was his sweet brutality against my bruised body that had made his act of love so piercingly wonderful. That and the coinciding of nerves so completely relaxed after the removal of tension and danger, the warmth of gratitude, and a woman's natural feeling for her hero.[108]

This is not an isolated example. In *Casino Royale*, Bond notes approvingly that Vesper Lynd's enigmatic, unfathomable personality means that 'the conquest of her body . . . would each time have the sweet tang of rape'.[109] And in *On Her Majesty's Secret Service*, Tracy tells him: 'Make love to me . . . Do anything you like. And tell me what you like and what you would like from me. Be rough with me. Treat me like the lowest whore in creation. Forget everything else. No questions. Take me.'[110]

There is, then, a startlingly aggressive side to Bond's treatment of women, one more in keeping with Fleming's reactionary anti-feminism and reminiscent of the violent hostility to women often present in the New Wave novels of the late 1950s. Just like *Room at the Top* or *Saturday Night and Sunday Morning*, Bond novels such as *Casino Royale* or *On Her Majesty's Secret Service* present their readers with a hero who treats women as disposable commodities and barely distinguishes between physical love and sadistic violence. It was surely no coincidence that all these books were published within a short period of about a decade; and no coincidence either that they were eagerly snapped up by male readers at a time when women were financially, socially and sexually more independent and assertive than ever.

If Fleming's treatment of women appears reactionary, his attitude towards other aspects of the consumer society reveals greater enthusiasm for post-war modernity. True, in *Thunderball*, Bond mocks the 'cheap self-assertiveness of young labour since the war' and complains about the youths who make twenty pounds a week and 'would like to be Tommy Steele'.[111] And similarly, in the film version of *Goldfinger*, Sean Connery comments that drinking champagne at room temperature would be 'like listening to the Beatles without earmuffs'. But Bond himself is very much a product of the affluent society, even if he had to wait until 1973 and the soundtrack of *Live and Let Die* to make his peace with Paul McCartney. Just as the Bond novels occasionally resemble pornography, so they also borrow the language and style of post-war leisure: sports writing, for instance, in the long descriptions of card games and golf matches; or the enthusiastic prose of travelogues and tourist brochures. Long-distance travel is described in meticulous detail and with evident relish; there are lengthy descriptions of journeys by car, train and aircraft, and sometimes luxurious journeys become crucial narrative set-pieces, examples being the fight on the Orient Express in *From Russia with Love* and the showdown aboard a BOAC jet airliner in *Goldfinger*.[112] When Bond reaches an exotic destination, it is common for an entire chapter to be devoted to an extended travelogue: in

Live and Let Die there is a long discussion of Haitian voodoo rituals, and in *You Only Live Twice* Fleming gives exhaustive descriptions of Japanese landscapes and customs. One critic has even suggested that Fleming consciously set his stories in the tourist 'pleasure periphery' of the Mediterranean, the Caribbean and South-East Asia: warm, exotic locations that were becoming increasingly popular during the fifties and sixties as holiday destinations for affluent American and British travellers and playgrounds where the wealthy could enjoy a lifestyle of sport, sex and gastronomy.[113]

James Bond's personal habits, which are described at enormous length, illustrate the extent to which Fleming's novels are in essence fictions of post-war consumerism. Bond wears tailored dark-blue suits or sleeveless dark-blue Sea Island cotton shirts and tropical worsted trousers. He uses Pinaud Elixir shampoo, reads Eric Ambler thrillers, plays golf and cards and drives a Mark II Continental Bentley. At various points he consumes Taittinger Blanc de Blancs Brut '43 and caviar, pink champagne and stone crabs, Lyon and Strasbourg sausage with Mâcon and Riquewihr, herrings and onion rings with schnapps and draught Löwenbräu, and so on. When Bond has dinner with M at Blades, the description of the meal takes up an entire chapter.[114] He certainly likes his food: breakfast alone, his 'favourite meal of the day', is an astounding ritual:

> It consisted of very strong coffee, from De Bry in New Oxford Street, brewed in an American *Chemex*, of which he drank two large cups, black and without sugar. The single egg, in the dark blue egg-cup with a gold ring round the top, was boiled for three and a third minutes.
>
> It was a very fresh, speckled brown egg from French *Marans* hens owned by some friend of May in the country. (Bond disliked white eggs and faddish as he was in many small things, it amused him to maintain that there was such a thing as the perfect boiled egg.) Then there were two thick slices of wholewheat toast, a large pat of deep yellow Jersey butter and three squat glass jars containing Tiptree 'Little Scarlet' straw-berry jam, Cooper's Vintage Oxford marmalade and Norwegian Heather Honey from Fortnum's. The coffee pot and the silver on the tray were Queen Anne, and the china was Minton, of the same dark blue and gold and white as the egg-cup.[115]

His favourite drink, of course, is a dry Martini: 'three measures of Gordon's, one of vodka, half a measure of Kina Lillet', shaken, not stirred, until it is ice-cold.[116] On one air journey from London to Istanbul in *From Russia with Love* he drinks two Americanos, two measures of ouzo, two dry Martinis and half a bottle of claret.[117] He also smokes no fewer than sixty cigarettes a day, a special high-nicotine blend of Balkan and Turkish tobacco made for him by Morlands of Grosvenor Street. It is little wonder that in 1961 M is compelled to send him to a health spa for two weeks of 'a more abstemious regime'.[118]

It is hard to think of a fictional character more enthusiastically and conspicuously dedicated to consuming both things and women. In his obsession with price tags and brand names, Bond recalls Joe Lampton, the hero of John Braine's novel *Room at the Top*, and Bond's easy, self-centred metropolitan lifestyle, free of interfering relatives and brimming with five-star hotels, Comet airliners, Morlands cigarettes and Tiptree jam, is exactly the kind of materialistic paradise to which Joe aspires.[119] Like John Braine, Fleming was much criticised for celebrating the vulgar values of mass consumerism, and, like Braine, his literary skills lay in 'the mastery of things rather than people', as Anthony Burgess once remarked.[120]

The same fascination with the products of the age of affluence was present in the early film versions of Fleming's books: one publicity still for *Dr No*, for example, showed Sean Connery, dressed in a made-to-measure shirt from Turnbull and Asser and a plain black silk tie, pouring a Smirnoff vodkatini while listening to music on the latest Dansette record player.[121] The Bond books can, in this context, easily be read as fantasies of modern consumerism; indeed, they can even be read as *guidebooks* to modern consumerism, instructing the affluent neophyte about the correct dress, food and drink, cars and hobbies. 'Red wine with fish,' comments Bond in the film of *From Russia with Love*, just after unmasking 'Captain Nash' as the SPECTRE assassin Red Grant. 'That should have told me something.'

As Denning suggests, the books even work as 'redemptions of consumption': golf, skiing, dry martinis and the rest are associated not with frivolous leisure, but with intrigue, glamour and international influence.[122] It was no surprise that James Bond became closely associated in the sixties with the American magazine *Playboy*, another quintessential emblem of the affluent society, or that the first glossy colour supplement issued with the *Sunday Times* in February 1962 should include a short James Bond story, 'The Living Daylights'.[123] For some observers, the success of James Bond was therefore another indication of the materialism and corruption of modern society. The literary critic Bernard Bergonzi complained in 1958 that the

Bond books had a sorry 'air of vulgarity and display', a 'strongly marked streak of voyeurism and sado-masochism' and a 'total lack of any ethical frame of reference'.[124] But for every detractor, James Bond had thousands and even millions of admirers. Hugh Gaitskell, rather ironically given his affair with Fleming's wife, remarked: 'The combination of sex, violence, alcohol and – at intervals – good food and nice clothes is, to one who leads such a circumscribed life as I do, irresistible.' And President Kennedy was said to count *From Russia with Love* among his favourite books.[125]

It was the modernity of James Bond that gave *Dr No* and its cinematic successors their appeal. The aspects of Bond's character that most recalled Bulldog Drummond – his ruthless cruelty, his aggressive xenophobia, his humourless stoicism – were toned down for film audiences, and instead he was presented even more explicitly as an emblem of the affluent society. As one analysis puts it: 'Functioning as a figure of modernisation, he became the very model of the tough abrasive professionalism that was allegedly destined to lead Britain into the modern, no illusion, no-holds-barred post-imperialist-age, a hero of rupture rather than one of tradition.'[126]

The decision to cast Sean Connery as Fleming's secret agent was itself highly revealing. Film distributors wanted a recognised star in the part, and Fleming himself suggested his friend David Niven, James Mason or Richard Burton. One other candidate, Roger Moore, was then appearing on television as the Saint; he would get another chance ten years later, with splendidly suave results. At this stage, however, Broccoli and Saltzman wanted an unknown who would have no associations beyond the world of James Bond.[127] Auditions and screen tests were held in the summer of 1961, and at the producers' request Fleming wrote a little summary of the role: 'He likes gambling, golf and fast motor-cars. He smokes a great deal, but without affectation. All his movements are relaxed and economical.' The official criteria continued: 'Competitors must be aged between 28 and 35; measure between 6ft. and 6ft. 1in. in height; weigh about 12st.; have blue eyes, dark hair, rugged features – particularly a determined chin – and an English accent.'[128] After long negotiations, and despite his Scottish burr, the obscure Connery was announced as the cinematic face of James Bond. The son of an Edinburgh truck driver; he had like so many young actors initially drifted from obscure job to job, working as a milkman, coffin polisher, merchant seaman and cement mixer before landing a series of small parts in forgettable films. He made an excellent impression, however, turning up in baggy trousers and loafers with a heavy five-o'clock shadow and amusing the producers with his easy, laconic manner. 'What impressed me', Saltzman later recalled, 'was that a man of his size and frame could move in such a supple way.' 'He looked like he had balls,' said Broccoli.[129]

Fleming himself was pleased with the choice, even if Connery's modest social background was very different from that of the literary Bond. 'Saltzman thinks he has found an absolute corker,' he wrote to a friend, 'a thirty-year-old Shakespearian actor, ex-Navy boxing champion, etc., etc., and even, he says, intelligent.'[130] Since Bond himself was half-Scottish and had attended an Edinburgh public school, and since Fleming was the grandson of a Dundee millionaire, Connery's gentle Edinburgh accent was not quite as incongruous as is often claimed. 'Not quite the idea I had of Bond,' Fleming later admitted, 'but he would be if I wrote the books over again.'[131] Not only did Connery look the part, with his cool charm and rugged masculinity, but he also worked very nicely as a link between the working-class realism of the New Wave films and the fantasy of the swinging sixties. Just like the literary Bond, Connery's version represented in many ways the final flourish of the New Wave; since audiences had read about his humble origins in breathless newspaper reports about the new films, it was easy for them to see him as an ordinary man moving upwards through a world of foreign travel, consumer luxuries and disposable pleasures. At the same time, the James Bond of the early films cannot easily be fitted into the British class system: while Connery's accent means that he is an unlikely member of the upper class, his knowledge of fine wines, smart clothes and exotic dinners means that he is something more than a working-class boy made good. He was not so much classless as unclassifiable: a professional, modern man equally at home in an underground laboratory or a gentleman's club. He was, in short, the ideal hero to appeal to audiences used to, but slightly weary of, the gritty working-class naturalism of New Wave cinema: less an angry young man, then, than a very satisfied one.

Just as the first Bond films softened the callousness of James Bond himself, so they also played up the more fantastic elements of Fleming's books. *Dr No*, as already noted, was one of the more implausible tales, although its relentless pace, comic-book villain and glamorous location were ideal for the screen. By contrast, *Casino Royale* had been a much bleaker and simpler book, with Bond little more than a passive victim tortured by the perverted Le Chiffre and, in the final pages, betrayed by his lover.[132] Although the success of the later Bond films ensured that tales of espionage eventually became associated above all with the fantastic, this was not at all the case during the fifties and sixties. Spy stories might be 'magical thrillers where there is a clear contest between Good and Evil with a virtuous hero defeating an alien and evil villain'; but they might also, as Denning observes, be much more serious, realistic affairs, 'existential thrillers' using the issues of secrecy and betrayal to explore wider questions of identity and morality.[133] The climate of the Cold War gave the subject of espionage greater relevance and sensitivity: it was no coincidence that more self-consciously literary authors like John le Carré and Len Deighton used the spy genre to make serious points about social change and national decline. In the novels of le Carré, for instance, there is no easy distinction between good and evil as there is in the Bond films and most of the Bond books. The exception was *Casino Royale*, a much bleaker vision of the Cold War. Bond is saved from torture only because of an internal dispute within SMERSH, and he bitterly complains afterwards in a chapter entitled 'The Nature of Evil' that 'when one's young, it seems very easy to distinguish between right and wrong, but as one gets older it becomes more difficult . . . The villains and heroes get all mixed up.' He even goes on: 'Of course, patriotism comes along and makes it seem fairly all right, but this country-right-or-wrong business is getting a little out-of-date . . . History is moving pretty quickly these days and the heroes and villains keep on changing parts.'[134]

This approach to spy fiction, which Fleming quickly abandoned, nevertheless played a central role in the development of spy culture in the early sixties.[135] For younger writers like Deighton and le Carré, who had been born at the beginning of the thirties and missed serving in the Second World War, the realistic style was both more intelligent and more rewarding than the extraordinary adventures of James Bond, and allowed them to build a reputation within the mainstream literary world.[136] Both were writing in the shadow of the defections of the Cambridge spies, and their novels are shot through with an atmosphere of suspicion and duplicity. At the same time, the cynicism and gloom of the realistic spy novels also captured the realities of British decline after Suez.[137] Both writers reflected the themes of the anti-Establishment commentaries of the late fifties and early sixties: whereas Fleming has nothing but praise for James Bond and his secret service colleagues, Deighton and le Carré portray the intelligence organisations as hidebound by prejudice and privilege, decaying bastions of amateurism in an increasingly professional world. *The Ipcress File* was published in 1962, and *The Spy Who Came In from the Cold* a year later; not only did they benefit from the general public enthusiasm for spy fiction that followed the publication of the Bond paperbacks, but both also caught the intellectual mood of the times, which was sharply critical of Macmillan's supposedly antiquated style of government and of the values of the British elite. Both books echoed the terse realism of New Wave fiction, and both used the corrupt and class-ridden world of the Secret Service as a metaphor for British decline since the Second World War. Like *Anatomy of Britain* or *Beyond the Fringe*, they mocked the antediluvian public-school values associated with Westminster and Whitehall; and in their fascination with national decline, they also antici-pated the hand-wringing 'condition of Britain' debate later in the decade.

The Ipcress File was the first novel of Len Deighton, a trained illustrator and photographer in his early thirties who had recently given up his job as the art director of an advertising agency. The very appearance of the book made it clear that this was not merely another Bond imitation: it begins, for instance, with a mock Cabinet Office memorandum in typewritten fount, includes appendices and footnotes with extracts from supposedly official publications, and is littered with the bureaucratic jargon of the secret agent's trade. This scholarly apparatus heightens the novel's air of realism; what is more, Burgess and Maclean even feature in the plot when at one point a civil servant explains that the villain, Jay, arranged their defection to the Soviet Union in 1951, dressing this up with all sorts of dates and bank account details. One of the names in the Maclean narrative is suppressed: a footnote explains, with mock scholarly authority: 'Name withdrawn from MS.'[138] The organisation for which the hero works, the WOOC(P), a little intelligence department struggling for survival in the Whitehall game, is nowhere near as glamorous and prestigious as Fleming's Secret Service. The WOOC(P) operates in surroundings M would hardly have tolerated: a couple of rooms in a Soho office block with a dirty door and cracked linoleum floors. Refreshment is provided not by the deferential staff of Blades, but by a secretary with a jar of Nescafé.[139] Much of the department's work is devoted to shoring up its own position against rival British govern-ment agencies and ensuring a decent budget for the following year, bureaucratic worries that never bothered James Bond.

Indeed, much of the effect of *The Ipcress File* depends on the extent to which it deliberately breaks with the Bond tradition. Although Bond is something of an outsider, he still shares and protects the values of the gen-tleman's club. Deighton's narrator, however, is unremittingly hostile to the status quo. 'What chance did I stand between the Communists on the one side and the Establishment on the other?' he asks himself at one point.[140]

Not only is the narrator very different from James Bond, he is also a walking rebuke to the nepotism, homosexuality and decadence of the Cambridge traitors. Unnamed in the books but called Harry Palmer in the subsequent film adaptations, he is a grammar-school boy from industrial Burnley who studied maths and economics at a provincial university. He has vague left-wing sympathies, reads the *New Statesman*, the *Daily Worker* and *History Today*, and spends much of the book trying to fiddle his expenses so that he can pay his bills. In some ways, then, *The Ipcress File* is the *Lucky Jim* of spy fiction: the story of a bright, disrespectful, impecunious provincial upstart who dislikes his elegant, well-bred superiors and keenly feels his social exclusion:

> Dalby tightened a shoe-lace. 'Think you can handle a tricky little special assignment?'
>   'If it doesn't demand a classical education I might be able to grope around it.'
>   Dalby said, 'Surprise me, do it without complaint or sarcasm.'
>   'It wouldn't be the same,' I said.[141]

While Bond parks his Bentley outside his rooms off the King's Road, buys his honey from Fortnum's and orders lavish banquets in expensive restaurants, Palmer has trouble getting taxis to come to his flat south of the river, shops at the supermarket and cooks his own meals. In the cinematic version of *The Ipcress File*, released in 1965, Palmer is played by Michael Caine as a cheeky Cockney, wearing thick glasses as if to symbolise his fallibility and banality. Even the design of the film is carefully contrived to look as different from the Bond pictures as possible: there are no massive, gleaming laboratories or underground bases, but merely the dull greys and greens and browns of London, and Palmer's boss works in a bare office with a camp bed, a table and a chair. No doubt the effect was easier to achieve since the production designer, Ken Adam, had also been responsible for the look of the first Bond films; he therefore knew exactly what to avoid.[142]

And yet, like Bond, Harry Palmer also reflects the values and enthusiasms of his day, specifically the Continental tastes of the affluent metropolitan middle class, and offers a little tour of the consumer society of the early sixties. Immediately on beginning his assignment, he wanders through Soho 'seeking excuses to delay; I bought two packets of Gauloises, sank a quick grappa with Mario and Franco at the Terrazza, bought a

Statesman, some Normandy butter and garlic sausage'. He then strolls into Lederers coffee house, 'one of those continental style coffee-houses where coffee comes in a glass'.[143] Indeed, the book's function as a kind of guide to gracious living is explicitly spelled out when the narrator takes his pretty assistant to lunch:

> In London with a beautiful hungry girl one must show her to Mario at the Terrazza. We sat at the ground floor front under the plastic grapes and Mario brought us Campari-sodas and told Jean how much he hated me . . . We ordered the Zuppa di Lenticchie and Jean told me how much this lentil soup reminded her of visits with her father to Sicily many years ago . . . We ate the Calamari and the chicken deep in which the garlic and butter had been artfully hidden to be struck like a vein of aromatic gold. Jean had pancakes and a thimbleful of black coffee without mentioning calories, and went through the whole meal without lighting a cigarette.[144]

There are, by contrast, very few slap-up dinners at fashionable Italian restaurants in the novels of John le Carré, the pen name of the writer David Cornwell. More than any other writer of the fifties and sixties, le Carré used the conventions of popular fiction to dissect the lies and hypocrisies of an enfeebled British elite struggling to come to terms with their fall from international pre-eminence. In his books, London is a city not of timeless gentlemen's clubs or painfully stylish Continental boutiques, but of dreary, ramshackle streets stretching endlessly away into the drizzle and fog. Le Carré was peculiarly well qualified to address such themes. He appeared the consummate insider, having been educated at Sherborne, Berne and Oxford and having spent two years teaching at Eton and five years in the Foreign Office. In truth, however, he never felt part of the inner circle of the British establishment. His father, Ronnie Cornwell, was a charming but utterly ruthless conman who served time in prisons all over the world, accumulated three wives and swindled a host of victims from the Panamanian ambassador in Paris to impecunious pensioners in country villages.[145] As a bright public schoolboy and budding Foreign Office mandarin, le Carré always knew himself to be an impostor devoted to 'clandestine survival – the whole world was enemy territory'. His entire education, he suspected, was based on the criminal ambitions of his father: 'His dream was that my brother should be a solicitor and I should be a barrister. And for that purpose he sent us into the gents' stream, the private education system, and we learnt the language, we learnt the manners, we learnt to be charming. But we went back to mayhem . . . This extraordinary contrast between my father's world and the world he wanted us to get into made us frontier-crossers the whole time.'[146]

For le Carré, then, duplicity and deceit were themes that ran throughout his entire life. His first two novels, *Call for the Dead* and *A Murder of Quality*, were published in 1961 and 1962 without attracting enormous public attention. Despite the fact that he was still a serving diplomat in the Foreign Office, le Carré was already developing the themes that would characterise his mature works: moral ambiguity, divided loyalties, the everyday betrayals and inhumanities of the Cold War. These reflected not only his unhappy personal history, but also the climate of suspicion that hung over Whitehall in the 1950s. *Call for the Dead*, for instance, is a depressing story about the apparent suicide of Samuel Feenan, an obscure Foreign Office clerk who is actually murdered by the East Germans when he discovers that they have recruited his own wife as an agent. As in *The Ipcress File*, real events intrude on the fictional plot: there are allusions to Fuchs and Maclean, and we are told that George Smiley, the intelligence officer investigating the case, had only returned to secret work because 'the revelations of a young Russian cipher-clerk in Ottawa had created a new demand for men of Smiley's experience', this being a reference to the defection of the Soviet clerk Igor Gouzenko.[147]

Defectors, double agents and moles play central parts in le Carré's novels of the sixties and seventies: identities and loyalties are consistently threatened by the pressures of the secret world. As one critic puts it, 'little remains stable' in the world inhabited by le Carré's characters: 'wives betray husbands, husbands destroy wives, friends betray friends, students reject teachers, individuals deceive themselves'.[148] For le Carré, the simple verities of the Bond books were positively dangerous, blinding their readers to the moral complexity of the struggle against global Communism. 'Bond on his magic carpet', he wrote in May 1966, 'takes us away from moral doubt, banishes perplexity with action, morality with duty. Above all, he has the one piece of equipment without which not even his formula would work: an entirely evil enemy . . . There is no victory in the Cold War, only a condition of human illness and a political misery.'[149]

George Smiley, le Carré's protagonist, is as different from James Bond as it is possible to imagine. On the very first page of *Call for the Dead*, his own wife calls him 'breathtakingly ordinary'. 'Short, fat and of a quiet disposition,' we are told, 'he appeared to spend a lot of money on really bad clothes, which hung about his squat frame like skin on a shrunken toad.'[150] In *A Murder of Quality* an old friend thinks of him as 'the most forgettable man she had ever met; short and plump, with heavy spectacles and thinning hair, he was the very prototype of an unsuccessful middle-aged bachelor in a sedentary occupation'.[151] Where Bond is unreflective, charming and hedonistic, Smiley is thoughtful, drab and withdrawn. Where Bond beds one beautiful woman after another, Smiley is a cuckold whose wife has an affair with a Soviet mole and eventually abandons him. As an intelligence officer he is, his creator admits, 'bloodless and inhuman':

> Smiley in this role was the international mercenary of his trade, amoral and without motive beyond that of personal gratification.
>
> Conversely, it saddened him to witness in himself the gradual death of natural pleasure. Always withdrawn, he now found himself shrinking from the temptations of friendship and human loyalty; he guarded himself warily from spontaneous reaction. By the strength of his intellect, he forced himself to observe humanity with clinical objectivity, and because he was neither immortal nor infallible he hated and feared the falseness of his life.[152]

The government body that employs him, the Circus, is unromantic, demoralised and mouldering, a soulless organisation shot through with doubt and disappointment. Without it, however, its officers' lives are meaningless. Smiley and his colleagues have little to live for but their work, and in le Carré's hands the Circus becomes a good example of the post-war fear of the individual being smothered by the dead hand of the institution. Since spy stories were, by the mid-sixties, being read by an increasingly middle-class, white-collar audience, the endless struggle for survival within the company was something with which readers would have been eminently familiar.[153] So le Carré, even more than Deighton, spends a great deal of time discussing the intricacies of bureaucratic politics and delicately illustrating the dangers of unthinking subservience to bureaucratic imperatives. The Circus was, he later wrote, 'a microcosm of all institutional behaviour, and the ever-repeated dilemma which overcomes individuals when they submit their talent for institutional exploitation'.[154]

There is even more jargon in le Carré's novels than in Deighton's: thus the reader is pitched into a world of lamplighters, wranglers, babysitters, scalphunters, ferrets, honeytraps and Cousins. So dominant is the institution that it has a vocabulary all of its own; not for nothing is it frequently likened by le Carré's narrators to a public school or a church.[155] In *The Looking-Glass War* (1965), a misguided and disastrous operation is launched purely so that a group of desperate, ageing men can preserve their independent agency in the Whitehall jungle. Their motivation, as le Carré explained in *Encounter*, 'lies not in the war of ideas but in their own desolate mentalities'; the enterprise is a shambles, the innocent, trusting agent is sent to certain death, and their Department is swallowed up anyway.[156] In the frantic final scenes, as the East German police tighten the net around his agent, the Department's chief is reduced to discussing 'the question of Registry' and the possibility of buying a new photostat machine, a vain and tragic attempt to block out the reality of failure.[156]

Although his skill as a novelist meant that he was likely to have enjoyed critical and commercial success whatever the circumstances, le Carré's renown was based above all on *The Spy Who Came In from the Cold*, a typically bleak book that was published months after the cinematic release of *Dr No* and was therefore well timed both to profit from the popular interest in espionage and to provide a stark corrective to the glamorous fantasy of James Bond. *The Spy Who Came In from the Cold* is an intricate story of defectors and show trials; for Michael Denning, 'with its cold, spare and cynical prose, beginning and ending at the Berlin Wall, it is one of the great war novels of the Cold War'.[158] The hero, the British agent Alec Leamas, is determined to avoid thinking about questions of principle or morality. When his East German interrogator, a utopian Marxist, asks him about the philosophy behind his dedication to the Circus, Leamas struggles to find an answer:

'What do you mean, a philosophy?' he replied; 'we're not Marxists, we're nothing. Just people.'

'Are you Christians, then?'

'Not many, I shouldn't think. I don't know many.'

'What makes them do it, then?' Fiedler persisted; 'they must have a philosophy.'

'Why must they? Perhaps they don't know; don't even care. Not everyone has a philosophy,' Leamas answered, a little helplessly.

Later, wearily, he simply says: 'I just think the whole lot of you are bastards.'[159]

This aversion to idealism runs right through the book. Near the beginning, Leamas listens to a little lecture from his chief, Control, that sums up the atmosphere of moral equivalence between the Communists and their Western adversaries:

> Of course, we occasionally do very wicked things . . . And in weighing up the moralities, we rather go in for dishonest comparisons; after all, you can't compare the ideals of one side with the methods of the other, can you, now? . . .
>
> I mean, you've got to compare method with method, and ideal with ideal. I would say that since the war, our methods – ours and those of the opposition – have become much the same. I mean you can't be less ruthless than the opposition simply because your government's *policy* is benevolent, can you now? . . . That would *never* do.[160]

By the closing pages of the novel, when Leamas realises that he and his lover Liz Gold, a harmless British Communist librarian, have been pawns in a fiendishly complicated and devious game to save their mole in East German intelligence, a former Nazi called Mundt, he angrily tries to explain to her the point of the whole grubby business:

> What do you think spies are: priests, saints and martyrs? They're a squalid procession of vain fools, traitors too, yes; pansies, sadists and drunkards, people who play cowboys and Indians to brighten their rotten lives. Do you think they sit like monks balancing the rights and wrongs? I'd have killed Mundt if I could, I hate his guts; but not now. It so happens that they need him. They need him so that the great moronic mass that you admire can sleep soundly in their beds at night. They need him for the safety of ordinary, crummy people like you and me . . .
>
> This is a war . . . It's graphic and unpleasant because it's fought on a tiny scale, at close range; fought with a wastage of innocent life sometimes, I admit. But it's nothing, nothing at all besides other wars – the last or the next.

When Liz answers that he and his kind are turning 'the humanity in people' into a weapon 'to hurt and kill', he shouts:

Christ Almighty! . . . What else have men done since the world began?
I don't believe in anything, don't you see – not even destruction or
anarchy. I'm sick, sick of killing but I don't see what else they can do.
They don't proselytise; they don't stand in pulpits or on party platforms and tell us to fight for Peace or for God or whatever it is. They're
the poor sods who try to keep the preachers from blowing each other
sky high.

'I hate it, hate it all; I'm tired,' he admits. 'But it's the world, it's mankind
that's gone mad. We're a tiny price to pay . . . but everywhere's the same,
people cheated and misled, whole lives thrown away, people shot and in
prison, whole groups of people and classes written off for nothing.'[161]

Like the other spy bestsellers of the sixties, *The Spy Who Came In from the Cold*
was adapted for the cinema, although its release in 1965 coincided with the
beginning of the 'swinging London' craze, a trend not conducive to the
popular success of an existential thriller shot in black and white.[162] The
acting is first-class, especially Richard Burton as the hard-drinking, cynical
Leamas and Oskar Werner as the sympathetic Marxist Fiedler. The American
director, Martin Ritt, ordered his team to avoid suggestions of glamour at
any cost, and his screenwriter later recalled that the performances were
'purposefully pared, pruned, damped, clipped and shorn of even the minor
histrionic affectations with which our actors thought to mirror nature'.[163]
In the cinematic climate of the day, which prized colour, novelty and general wackiness, this was not likely to produce a popular hit, although it did
make for an excellent film. Both the novel and the film explored much
deeper waters than most spy stories of the period; Malcolm Bradbury, for
one, thought that le Carré's works were not merely Cold War thrillers but
also provided 'an enquiry into the moral state of the nation . . . with a scope
that made them important interpretations of late twentieth-century sensibility'.[164] Indeed, bearing in mind his reliance on 'seedy landscapes,
depressed lives, failed loves, political and sexual faithlessness, divided loyalties, [and] moral and metaphysical guilt', le Carré stands comparison with
writers like Joseph Conrad and Graham Greene. Greene commented that
The Spy Who Came In from the Cold was the best novel about espionage he had
ever read, while the *Scotsman* thought that it stood 'quite alone, on a peak of
achievement so remote from contemporary writing in the genre that any
comparisons would be irrelevant'.[165] Le Carré would, in future decades, continue to win critical praise unmatched by any of his competitors. Whereas

the books of both Fleming and Deighton were firmly and unassumingly rooted in the political and cultural fashions of the fifties and sixties, le Carré's novels represented a genuine literary achievement, deserving a prominent place in any history of British writing since the war.[166]

By 1963 commentators were already beginning to talk of a spy craze in British popular culture. Not only had Deighton and le Carré attracted ecstatic reviews and sold thousands of books, but *Dr No* had been a huge box-office success in the United States, and in October a second Bond film, *From Russia with Love*, was released to the most lucrative opening week in British cinematic history.[167] Spies, it seemed, could not be kept out of the headlines. In 1961 the newspapers had gleefully reported the extremely colourful story of the Portland ring, when it transpired that two greedy Admiralty clerks had been passing secrets to the Soviet Union through a couple called Peter and Helen Kroger, who lived in a suburban bungalow in Ruislip and ran an antiquarian bookshop on the Strand. The Krogers were in reality the Cohens, a pair of American Communists, and in their house the police discovered a powerful radio transmitter, miniature cameras, cigarette lighters and torches with false compartments, letters in Russian and secret naval documents with details of anti-submarine technology and fleet orders. The head of the gang, meanwhile, purported to be a Canadian businessman called Gordon Lonsdale but was in fact a Soviet KGB agent called Kolon Molodi. All five were eventually given lengthy prison sentences, although Molodi and the Cohens were subsequently exchanged for Soviet prisoners.[168]

In May 1961, just months after their trial, another, far more spectacular scandal broke. This was the case of George Blake, a Jewish immigrant from the Netherlands who had joined the intelligence service during the Second World War and afterwards was posted to Seoul, where in 1950 he was captured by Communist forces during the Korean War. During his stint in a North Korean prison, Blake had apparently read *Capital* and concluded that he was on the wrong side; by the time he was released in 1953, he had enlisted as a double agent working for Soviet intelligence. During the next eight years, working in West Berlin and London with access to highly sensitive card-index files of agents and contacts, Blake systematically betrayed every single member of the British operation in Germany to the KGB, and at least forty people were thought to have died as a result of his treachery. He was finally unmasked by a defector from Polish State Security, but when

MI6 officers summoned him for questioning in April 1961 he evidently enjoyed explaining to his horrified interrogators just how clever he had been. 'Am I boring you?' he asked in the stunned silence after a particularly dramatic revelation.[169]

Blake's arrest was the first major step in a series of security scandals in the early sixties that severely tarnished the reputation not only of the intelligence services but also of Macmillan's Conservative government. Such was the extent of Blake's betrayal that Macmillan is supposed to have remarked, 'The government could fall over this,' when Sir Dick White, the head of MI6, told him the news. American pressure meant that there would have to be a trial, although the Prime Minister would have preferred Blake to be given immunity and the whole thing hushed up. As it was, the trial was conducted *in camera*, and the exceptionally harsh sentence of forty-two years in prison was agreed beforehand by the Prime Minister, the Attorney General and the Lord Chief Justice.[170] Blake served only five years of his sentence, because he managed to pull off one of the most daring escapes in modern British criminal history, further enhancing the popular mystique of the secret agent in the process. As a prisoner in Wormwood Scrubs he had been extremely well behaved, and the authorities allowed him to exercise right next to the walls despite the warnings of MI6 officers that he was bound to try and break out. An old Irish cellmate then smuggled into the prison an entire escape kit: a walkie-talkie, a camera, a car jack, wire cutters, and a makeshift ladder to be assembled from three lengths of clothesline and thirty steel knitting needles. In October 1966 Blake climbed over the wall, hid in a flat near the prison and was eventually smuggled across the Channel and into East Germany in a hidden compartment of a camper van. On arrival in Moscow, he was awarded the Order of Lenin.[171]

Harold Macmillan recognised, quite correctly, that the persistent spy scandals were doing his government's image no good at all. Since he was already perceived in some quarters as bumbling, amateurish and anachronistic, his failure to root out Soviet infiltrators was intensely embarrassing and tended to confirm the suspicions of his fiercest critics. He was far from pleased, therefore, when barely a year after the Blake trial yet another scandal threatened to break. In September 1962, he recorded in his diary:

> There has been another espionage case – and a very bad one – in the Admiralty. An executive officer, homosexual, entrapped by the Russian Embassy spies and giving away material (of varying value) for five or six

years. Only caught by the help of a Russian 'defector'. There will be another big row . . .[172]

When the head of MI5, Sir Roger Hollis, gleefully announced: 'I've got this fellow, I've got him!' Macmillan merely looked downcast. 'You don't seem very pleased, Prime Minister,' Hollis said. According to his own recollection, Macmillan replied:

No, I'm not at all pleased. When my gamekeeper shoots a fox, he doesn't go and hang it up outside the Master of Foxhounds' drawing room; he buries it out of sight. But you can't just shoot a spy as you did in the war . . . [There will be] a great public trial. Then the security services will not be praised for how efficient they are but blamed for how hopeless they are. There will then be an enquiry . . . There will be a terrible row in the press, there will be a debate in the House of Commons, and the Government will probably fall. Why the devil did you 'catch' him?[173]

The Orpington by-election, the Night of the Long Knives and the general woes of the economy had already sapped public confidence in the Conservatives, and Macmillan's fear that more security revelations could weaken their support still further was perfectly justified. By the early sixties, spies were not merely the incarnations of patriotism and consumerism; in the eyes of many observers, they also symbolised the greed, corruption and incompetence of the governing elite in general and the Conservative Party in particular. It was not by chance that in *The Ipcress File* the real villain turns out to be Palmer's own employer Dalby, the laconic, elegant civil servant and the quintessential insider. Like the public schools, Oxford colleges and gentlemen's clubs dissected in Sampson's *Anatomy of Britain* and lampooned in *Beyond the Fringe* and *That Was The Week That Was*, the secret agent and his world had become emblematic of Macmillan's affluent society. And even in September 1962, as Macmillan wearily prepared to contemplate yet another security scandal, the most damaging revelations of all were still months away.

The latest case had all the ingredients of a typical spy scandal, not least the taint of homosexuality and high living. 'We have arrested a spy who is a bugger and a minister is involved,' was how the Director of Public Prosecutions succinctly put it.[174] The traitor this time was John Vassall, a former cipher clerk in the British Embassy in Moscow who now worked in the Admiralty. The son of a clergyman, he was a socially insecure man who felt that his talents had never been properly rewarded. He was also a homosexual, and during his stay in Moscow he had managed to become the star performer in an orgy arranged and discreetly photographed by the KGB. One of the most important factors in his decision to betray his country, he admitted, was the sight of a shot of himself 'naked, grinning into the camera; naked, holding up a pair of men's briefs which must have been mine', and if that were not enough, the Russians also had photographs of him affectionately entwined with a man in Soviet military uniform.[175]

After Vassall returned to Britain in 1956, he regularly passed photographs of Admiralty documents to Soviet intelligence via a contact, 'Gregory', in return for about £700 a year, roughly as much as he was already earning as a civil servant. His career was prospering: he was promoted to the post of assistant private secretary to the Civil Lord of the Admiralty, the MP Thomas Galbraith, and then into the Military Branch of the Admiralty. Meanwhile, his extra income meant that he was especially well placed to benefit from the consumer boom of the late fifties. He took a flat in Pimlico at an annual rent of £500 which obviously would have been beyond his means were he not a spy; in 1959 alone he went on holiday to Capri and Egypt while most of his colleagues made do with British seaside breaks; and he was later reported by the *Daily Mail* to own 'nineteen suits, one hundred ties, twelve pairs of shoes [and] three dozen shirts' and to dine regularly at Simpson's.[176] Vassall was not merely a spy: he was a conspicuous consumer in the class of James Bond himself. In the heady atmosphere of the hire-purchase boom, however, nobody noticed. When the former Chancellor Peter Thorneycroft, now Minister of Aviation, was asked by Labour backbenchers why Vassall's behaviour had not drawn greater attention, he shrugged and said lightly: 'How many of us are living beyond our incomes?'[177]

Like Blake, Vassall was detected and arrested only because of the revelations of a defector from the Communist bloc. He was sentenced in late October 1962 to eighteen years in prison; but that was far from the end of the matter. For one thing, his homosexuality caused predictable excitement in the press. On 28 October the *Sunday Pictorial* carried an enormous headline, 'WHY I BETRAYED MY COUNTRY', above a suggestive photograph of an apparently naked Vassall reclining on a bed, and a week later the same newspaper suggested that Vassall had been a minor figure in a wider homo-sexual conspiracy.[178] A series of rather dubious reports claimed that Vassall was known as 'Aunty' to his colleagues, treated himself to expensive women's underwear and 'liked to spend the evening in the West End haunts of perverts'.[179] He was 'sick', according to one newspaper, which added for good measure: 'Men like Vassall don't want to be cured.'[180] A day after the first *Pictorial* scoop, the *Daily Mail* declared that the authorities had found 'a postcard sent during a holiday abroad to Vassall from a leading public figure', indicating 'a friendliness which one would not expect between a clerk and a senior colleague'.[181] The postcard, like forty-two other pieces of correspondence, was from Vassall's old boss at the Admiralty, Thomas Galbraith, Conservative MP for Glasgow Hillhead and son of Lord Strathclyde. In fact, as the *Annual Register* later put it, the letters contained 'nothing more damaging than the former Civil Lord's interest in his office carpets, crockery and paper clips', but to the frenzied press, the fact that they began with the tell-tale phrase 'My dear Vassall' was proof of a dread-ful pederasts' plot. The *Express* even used Galbraith's greeting as a headline of its own, despite the fact that it appeared a perfectly reasonable way to begin a letter to a man called Vassall. The unfortunate Galbraith had done absolutely nothing wrong and if anything it was he who had been pestered by his former employee; even so, under pressure from the Chief Whip, he felt compelled to resign.[182]

The Labour Party did not have a particularly creditable record in this affair, and its deputy leader George Brown, himself hardly a paragon of reli-ability, led the chorus of attacks on Galbraith and Macmillan.[183] Galbraith was, incidentally, eventually cleared by the Radcliffe Tribunal and restored to office. Macmillan's fury at the press, however, had reached its peak. With the Cuban missile crisis barely a month old, the Conservatives still flagging in the polls and the economy stubbornly refusing to improve, he was an anxious and frustrated man. During the Commons debate on the Vassall affair, he lashed out against 'those who pose as protectors of the public . . . [while] trying to destroy public reputations from motives of either spite or gain'. Bitterly, but not without reason, he continued: 'Fleet Street has gen-erated an atmosphere around the Vassall case worthy of Titus Oates or Senator McCarthy . . . a dark cloud of suspicion and innuendo.'[184]

Within six months, Macmillan had drawn blood. The Radcliffe Tribunal that he had established to investigate the affair summoned two journalists to give evidence about their sources for articles linking Vassall to the

Portland ring: the two men refused, and in March 1963 they were sent to prison for six and three months respectively.[185] Although it transpired that the reporters had largely based their stories on embellishments to other newspaper accounts, and were therefore protecting their own reputations by refusing to disclose their sources, Fleet Street reacted with undiluted outrage. Newspapers across the political spectrum rushed to condemn the verdict and the government's campaign against the press. 'Such is the path to dictatorship,' said the *Daily Sketch* sententiously. *The Times* even called for a change at the top. 'The country has moved enough towards a presidential form of government', its leader announced, 'to mean that only a change of Prime Minister will persuade people that they are looking at a new Ministry.'[186] Macmillan's position had already been weakened by two years of disappointment and drift; he had become the lampooned personification of a supposedly antiquated social system; and with the imprisonment of the two journalists, at the worst possible moment, he had made enemies of the press. 'Now,' writes his biographer, 'open war was declared.'[187]

SCANDAL

At this time too, the Chief of the Praetorian Guard, Sextus Profano, came under widespread suspicion for his admission in the Senate that he had been acquainted with Christina, a beautiful girl known to many of the great figures of society despite her lowly origins.

Private Eye, 5 April 1963

> There was a young girl called Christine
> Who shattered the Party machine;
> It isn't too rude
> To lie in the nude
> But to lie in the House is obscene.

Popular limerick, 1963

Nineteen-sixty-three began with Britain shivering through the worst winter for almost a century. From December until March, the entire country lay under a thick, silent blanket of snow. Milk bottles froze solid on the doorstep, the zebra at Whipsnade Zoo died from the cold, and the West Country was completely cut off.[1] There was little cheer in 10 Downing Street; it was not easy for Harold Macmillan to forget the shattering blow of de Gaulle's veto. A crippling electricians' strike in January rammed home the weakness of the national position, especially when a power cut suddenly threw a Cabinet discussion at Chequers into darkness.[2] The opinion polls offered little solace. Harold Wilson's honeymoon as the new Labour leader was in full swing, and by March Labour were running 17 per cent ahead of the Conservatives, their biggest lead since 1946. 'Gallup Poll continues unfavourable,' Macmillan gloomily recorded in his diary; '. . . nearly half the Conservatives think that I should retire.'[3] According to a sample taken by the *Sunday Telegraph*, almost two-thirds of all voters thought that he ought to resign.[4]

And yet it was never wise to write Macmillan off. His poll ratings might be weak, but his spirit was undimmed. By the late spring, the position of sterling was beginning to improve, production figures looked promising and unemployment was falling at last. Macmillan was convinced that, as in the late fifties, his political resurgence would come just in time to sweep to another election victory; and as in the late fifties, he was counting on an expansionist budget from his Chancellor to do the trick. Reginald Maudling had duly obliged, and so by the beginning of April the Prime Minister felt sufficiently confident to tell the annual lunch of the 1922 Committee that they were set fair for victory, under his command, in the next general election.[5] Throughout May the Conservatives began, slowly, inch by inch, to claw back Wilson's lead in the opinion polls.[6] Then, on 4 June, one of Macmillan's junior ministers resigned and the whole picture suddenly changed.

At the heart of the scandal that eventually engulfed Macmillan's government was a doctor called Stephen Ward. The son of a Hertfordshire vicar, educated at a minor public school, Ward had studied medicine in the United States in the thirties and was a qualified and respected osteopath. After returning to London, he had worked hard to advance his reputation in high society and by the late fifties he could claim an impressive list of clients. He treated Sir Winston Churchill, for example, on a dozen occasions, and was always happy to rattle off the names of clients like King Peter of Yugoslavia, Elizabeth Taylor and Ava Gardner, as well as a series of prominent politicians including Hugh Gaitskell, Duncan Sandys and Peter Thorneycroft. A fairly talented artist, Ward also specialised in sketching famous faces, and his own natural charm, as well as a willingness to please, meant that he was a popular figure in metropolitan high society. He was particularly friendly with Lord Astor, a wealthy aristocrat who enjoyed a louche existence at Cliveden on the border between Berkshire and Buckinghamshire, and regularly threw lavish weekend parties for his celebrity friends. From the mid-fifties onwards, Astor allowed Ward to rent Spring Cottage, a large mock-Tyrolean villa in the grounds of the Cliveden estate, where he would escape at weekends from the stresses of life pandering to the whims of Belgravia.[7]

Ward was certainly a charismatic character, smooth, sensitive and intelligent. It seems probable, however, that despite his eminent acquaintances he was actually a very lonely man. His marriage had collapsed in 1949 after six weeks, and like many men of his class and generation he often resorted to the services of prostitutes. His schoolboyish obsession with sex was, even when allowances are made for human nature, unusually intense.[8] He had a peculiar fascination for grooming young working-class girls, casting himself as something of a modern Henry Higgins. Indeed he prided himself on cultivating and collecting new specimens rather as a lepidopterist might collect butterflies: working-class or lower-middle-class women in their late teens or early twenties, usually with stereotypical, busty good looks, whom he would teach to walk, talk, eat and drink in the correct upper-class manner. Vicki Martin, a fashionable model of the early fifties, was the prototypical Ward girl: he had found her near Marble Arch, sheltering in a doorway from the pouring rain, a miserable hostess in a Mayfair nightclub, and had transformed her into the popular 'Golden Girl' of society gossip columns.[9] Some of the girls who emerged from the 'Ward production line' became models like Martin or found rich husbands; but most eventually regressed into obscurity.[10] Although the girls were occasionally trained in sexual technique, Ward rarely sought to become their lover himself, instead preferring to remain their friend and mentor. Some certainly did sell their services to his blue-blooded friends, but the stories of wild orgies on the Cliveden estate and outlandish bacchanalian parties in London drawing rooms are usually exaggerated. Ward did not make any money from the girls' activities; indeed, given that they generally lived in his flat, ate his food and even wore his ex-wife's old clothes, his hobby was probably as expensive as it was unusual. He was not a pimp or a procurer, but a Pygmalion.[11]

In 1959, Ward acquired a new girl, a seventeen-year-old showgirl from Murray's Cabaret Club in Soho called Christine Keeler. Keeler's background was very different from that of her new mentor: she had grown up in a converted railway carriage without hot water in Wraysbury, an unlovely village of bungalows and gravel pits near Staines in Middlesex. Hers was the predictable sad story of so many girls who ran away to London in their late teens: bored of school and alienated from her mother and stepfather, she was sleeping with airmen from a nearby American base by the age of fifteen, and at one point discovered she was pregnant. Abortion was of course still illegal, so she was forced to resort to 'all the usual things . . . gin and hot baths, castor oil and finally the horrible self-probing with the knitting needle'.[12] Eventually, in 1957, she packed in her job in Slough and moved to London, working as a shop assistant and modelling on the side. She was a slim, pretty brunette with long legs, and her attractions were indisputable. 'Though she's only fifteen, Christine Keeler is pretty enough to be a professional model,' read the caption to her first published pictures in *Tit-Bits* magazine in March 1958. 'But the idea doesn't occur to her because, quite frankly, she rather prefers animals to people, and her hobby is dog-, cat- or even bird-sitting . . . It's not surprising that pretty Christine's ambition is to have a large house full of animals or that her pet hates include cruelty to animals. Like any other young girl, or older girl for that matter, she loves dancing, the theatre, and gay parties.'[13]

Keeler would soon have plenty of opportunities for gay parties. In August 1959 she began working at Murray's, where she appeared in a topless revue in a lavish costume including high heels and feathers. The wealthy clientele, which often included considerable numbers of Americans and Arabs, liked to sit and drink with the girls between dances, and it is likely that Keeler, like many of the girls, often crossed the line between dancer and courtesan. She was, however, still very young and lonely, and it was not surprising that she welcomed Ward's attentions. During the next three years, Keeler moved in and out of his Marylebone flat as the mood took her. Ward may have trained and chaperoned her, but they were not lovers. Occasionally, when no boyfriend was on the horizon, she came down to the Cliveden estate to spend the weekend with him, and it was there, in July 1961, that she met Eugene Ivanov and Jack Profumo.[14]

Captain Yevgeny Ivanov, known to his British acquaintances as Eugene, had arrived in London in April 1960 as an assistant naval attaché at the Soviet Embassy. Unusually for a Soviet diplomat, the gregarious Ivanov spoke good English, regularly appeared on the party circuit and quickly won a reputation as a handsome, hard-drinking ladies' man. In January 1961 he met Stephen Ward at a lunch party at the Garrick Club, and the two men soon became fast friends. Ivanov regularly came over to Ward's flat for a drink and a game of bridge, and at weekends he would drive down to Cliveden to help Ward with his garden. They often discussed politics; Ward fancied himself as something of a radical, and they enjoyed some friendly but intense arguments about Soviet policy and international affairs.[15]

In fact, Ivanov was a spy working for Soviet military intelligence. MI5 and the Foreign Office had already seen through his cover, and as early as August 1961 there had been talk at the Cabinet table about using Ward's friendship with Ivanov as a clandestine communications channel to the Soviet leadership. During the Cuban missile crisis the following year, Ward and Ivanov themselves approached the Foreign Office with a scheme to act as intermediaries between London and Moscow; this did not, however, greatly appeal to Lord Home, the Foreign Secretary.[16]

The mysterious intricacies of the relationship between Ward and Ivanov have been relentlessly analysed by journalists and historians. While it seems probable that Ivanov cultivated Ward for his social contacts and access to political circles, it also appears that Ward's friendship with the diplomat was encouraged, and even perhaps directly inspired, by officers of MI5. Ward certainly does not seem to have been either a traitor or an unwitting dupe of Soviet intelligence. Keith Wagstaffe, a senior MI5 counter-intelligence officer, met Ward in June and July 1961 and again in May 1962 to discuss his relationship with Ivanov, and these meetings were even publicly admitted in Lord Denning's report into the Profumo affair in September 1963. There is no need to resort to conspiracy theories to explain these links; given that Ivanov had already been recognised as a Soviet spy, it was entirely natural for MI5 to contact his great friend Stephen Ward and explore the possibilities of using the osteopath as an intermediary. According to Anthony Summers and Stephen Dorril, however, Ward's first meeting with Ivanov had actually been organised by the Security Service as the first step in an operation to lure the Soviet officer to defect: a 'honeytrap', indeed, in which Ward's girls would be used as bait.[17] The exact details of this scheme remain very murky, and it seems far from certain that Ward really understood the significance of his contacts with MI5. That these contacts existed is, nonetheless, beyond dispute, and although the honeytrap scenario has not been proved beyond question, it remains an eminently plausible possibility.[18]

On Saturday 8 July 1961, the south of England was basking in something of a minor heatwave. Lord Astor was throwing a dinner party that night for about thirty friends; in the best tradition of Cliveden, a sprawling neo-Renaissance house set in sumptuous gardens and with a reputation for diplomatic intrigue, the guests included Ayub Khan, the President of Pakistan, as well as various Conservative MPs and aristocratic types. Meanwhile, in Spring Cottage, Stephen Ward was having a little soirée of his own with four friends from London, one of whom was Christine Keeler. It was still stiflingly hot, and since Ward had a standing invitation to use the Cliveden open-air pool just beyond the stables, he and his friends strolled over after dinner for a late-night swim. Spare swimming costumes were always available in the nearby changing rooms, but Keeler's did not fit properly; at Ward's laughing suggestion, she took it off and dived naked into the pool. In the main house itself, at about the same time, Astor's dinner party was breaking up, and a few guests, carrying brandy and cigars, ambled over with their host towards the pool, from where the sounds of splashing and laughter were drifting through the muggy night air. Astor and one of his guests, the Conservative War Minister Jack Profumo, were walking a little ahead of their wives and the rest of their party, deep in conversation; as they turned the corner to reach the pool, they were startled by the sight of a naked and embarrassed Keeler rushing to fetch her towel. Ward thought the spectacle hilarious, and threw her costume into the bushes, so she was left standing by the side of the pool, dripping wet and giggling awkwardly, clad only in a small towel. Astor and Profumo, both worldly types, thought the whole business very funny, and by the time their wives had caught up with them there was still a general air of harmless hilarity. 'It was totally innocent high jinks,' Lady Astor later recalled. 'You couldn't see that the girl had nothing on.' The party in dinner jackets and gowns were duly introduced to the party in swimming costumes and towels, and after Ward's friends had got dressed, they all wandered back up the main house for a few amiable drinks, whereupon Astor invited them all to a picnic lunch by the pool the following day.[19]

Late that night Keeler returned to London to pick up a couple more of Ward's girls, and the next morning the girls all drove back down to Cliveden for the picnic. Their driver was Eugene Ivanov, who had already arranged to visit Ward for the day and vaguely knew Keeler from visits to Ward's flat. Sunday was an even hotter day, and when they arrived the various guests were lazing around the pool, some eating, some swimming, some merely basking in the sunshine. Ivanov and the girls were welcomed into the party, and the Soviet spy even, famously, had a swimming race with the War Minister. The catch was that use of the legs was forbidden, but a gleeful Profumo cheated and won the race. 'That'll teach you to trust the British government!' he said jokingly to Ivanov. The Soviet agent, meanwhile, manifestly loved every minute of it. 'There it all was,' Ward wrote later, 'all his dreams come true. There was the Minister, the President of Pakistan, the Pakistan High Commissioner, duchesses, peers and even officials of oil companies.'[20] The atmosphere was friendly and playful; even the slightly incongruous mixture of the two groups seemed to work very well, and both Profumo and Ayub Khan took plenty of photographs of the occasion.

Early in the evening, as the sun was beginning to set, Ivanov and Keeler left to drive back to the capital. When they reached Ward's flat in Wimpole Mews, Marylebone, they went upstairs together and, according to Keeler, Ivanov opened a bottle of vodka. It had been a lazy, relaxing, happy day;

they were both in good spirits, and the evening ended with them falling into bed together. Ivanov, Keeler later wrote in awed tones, 'was a *man* . . . rugged with a hairy chest, strong and agile . . . There was a wild thrashing about, a real Russian romp! . . . He was just kissing me with all the power of a man in a frenzy of passion.'[21] As for Ivanov, he saw the episode in a rather less romantic light. Christine, he wrote, was 'a semi-literate, naïve provincial girl with loose morals . . . a dangerous creature, sly and treacherous . . . That devil of a girl could seduce anybody!'[22] But what Ivanov did not know was that, just before they had left the Cliveden party, his swimming rival Jack Profumo had asked Christine for her telephone number. 'Talk to Stephen,' she had replied. 'He has my number.'[23]

Although John Profumo was of aristocratic Italian stock, he had grown up in an atmosphere of English country gentility. His father, a successful barrister and committed Conservative, owned a large country house in southern Warwickshire, and so the young Jack moved easily through a world of house parties, village fêtes and hustings. He was educated at Harrow and Oxford, and by the time he was twenty-five had won a seat in the Commons. Like so many successful Conservative politicians of the fifties and sixties, he could point to a good war, having risen to the rank of colonel and won an OBE. Throughout the fifties he held a succession of junior ministerial posts, and in 1960 Macmillan made him Secretary of State for War, a job that was far less grand than it sounded, since the reorganisation of the defence departments meant that it was in reality a junior post under the Secretary of State for Defence. It was certainly not, whatever some accounts might claim, a Cabinet post.

Profumo was a popular, modestly successful but ultimately rather minor political figure. He was married to Valerie Hobson, an attractive and well-known actress of the forties and fifties, and this meant that he was a prominent figure on the Conservative circuit, but by no means was he a heavyweight. Observers did not credit him with extraordinary political talent or vision and he was not necessarily a candidate even for promotion to the Cabinet. Claims that he was a potential Prime Minister are very wide of the mark indeed: there were plenty of brighter and more successful candidates of his own generation, from Iain Macleod and Enoch Powell to Edward Heath and Reginald Maudling. He was an affable, breezy man, balding at the age of forty-six but still reasonably handsome, and popular on both sides of the House. As a young man, he had a reputation for spending his evenings dallying in London nightclubs, but there were no serious whispers of scandal. He was a typical young Tory officer MP of the fifties: dashing, amiable and well liked, but not, ultimately, a politician of great consequence.[24]

Profumo telephoned Keeler two days after the Cliveden weekend and asked to see her. He visited her at the flat in Wimpole Mews two or three times and they became lovers. If there were other people at Ward's flat, Profumo would take her for a drive in his red Mini; on one occasion he borrowed a black Bentley belonging to his friend John Hare, the Minister for Labour, and they drove in state through central London. Occasionally Profumo gave her presents, a cigarette lighter for instance, and on one occasion twenty pounds, but it would be wrong to see the affair as a simple matter of prostitution. It would equally be ludicrous to see the affair as some epic passion. Christine Keeler herself accurately described it as 'a very, very well-mannered screw of convenience'. Profumo was, it seems, attracted to Keeler because she was young (still nineteen), extremely pretty and a refreshingly extrovert diversion from the routine of ministerial office. As far as she was concerned, 'his ways appealed to me': he was polished, personable, wealthy and well connected. Once, in August, he took her to his sumptuous nineteenth-century terrace in Regent's Park, and she was thrilled to see the 'lovely rooms', the 'large ornamental animals', the jewellery and scrambler telephone.[25] The War Minister was taking risks, perhaps, but not enormous ones. Like many MPs of his generation, Profumo saw himself as 'set apart from others – the officer class as the new ruling class'. Adulteries and liaisons with prostitutes were certainly not unknown in the House of Commons, and there was nothing particularly unusual about his behaviour. Even if the affair were discovered, it was unlikely to be major news, and he would not necessarily lose his reputation as an officer and a gentleman.[26] Contrary to popular belief, he was not sharing Keeler with Captain Ivanov: most accounts agree that Ivanov slept with Keeler no more than once.[27]

Within a mere five weeks, anyway, Profumo's affair with Keeler was over. MI5 were, as we have seen, keeping Ivanov under close surveillance, and it did not escape their notice that both he and the War Minister were frequent visitors to Ward's flat. On 31 July, Sir Roger Hollis told the Cabinet Secretary, Sir Norman Brook, that given his responsibilities Profumo ought to be careful what he said to Ward, since it might well find its way to Ivanov and thence to Moscow. On 9 August, therefore, Brook duly called Profumo in and explained the situation to him. At this stage, the Security Service had no

interest whatsoever in Christine Keeler; it was the relationship between
Profumo, Ward and Ivanov that bothered them. Profumo, however, jumped
to the conclusion that Sir Norman Brook was giving him an indirect warning that it was imprudent to continue seeing Keeler.[28] He had no great
emotional commitment to her; they had, after all, only known one another
for a few weeks, and it was no hardship for him to call the affair off. They
were due to meet the following evening, so after leaving the meeting
Profumo scribbled a quick note to his lover. It would come back to haunt
him, although its contents were not especially revealing:

9/8/61

Darling,
In great haste and because I can get no reply from your phone –
Alas something's blown up tomorrow night and I can't therefore
make it. I'm terribly sorry especially as I leave the next day for various
trips and then a holiday so won't be able to see you again until some
time in September. Blast it. Please take great care of yourself and
don't run away.
Love J.
PS: I'm writing this 'cos I know you're off for the day tomorrow and I
want you to know before you go if I still can't reach you by phone.[29]

It seems clear, despite a few conspiracy theories to the contrary, that the
affair finished at this point, exactly a month and a day after Profumo and
Keeler had first met.[30]

And there the whole matter, apparently so inconsequential, might well
have ended. Profumo threw himself back into his work, and Keeler
returned to her life with Stephen Ward. She was bored and restless, and
began flirting with a new social scene entirely: the world of West Indian
immigrants. In October 1961, Ward and Keeler visited the Rio Café on
Westbourne Park Road to try and buy some marijuana; like many other
fashionable types in the late fifties and early sixties, they were drawn to the
drinking and gambling dens of Notting Hill because they associated the
area, and above all its immigrant population, with exoticism, adventure
and general raffishness.[31] Keeler went into the back of the café, by the toilets, and agreed to buy ten shillings' worth of 'weed' from a West Indian
loitering meaningfully in the vicinity. This man, who assumed that Keeler

was a prostitute, was keen on seeing her again and pressed for her telephone number; she agreed to meet him, provided that he brought 'a sister
for my brother', in other words a black girl to satisfy Ward's taste for the
unusual.[32]

Thus began Keeler's relationship with Aloysius 'Lucky' Gordon, an
unfortunate development not only for her but also for Jack Profumo and
Harold Macmillan. Gordon had been discharged from the army for
threatening an officer and deported from Denmark for violent assault;
not only was he unstable, he was also extremely aggressive and treated
Keeler very roughly indeed. By the beginning of 1962, fascinated by the
West Indian underworld, she had moved out of Wimpole Mews and was
moving from bedsit to bedsit, often with Gordon in tow. Their relationship was often strained: Keeler relied on Gordon for a constant supply of
marijuana, while he remained intensely jealous to the point of threatening her, on one occasion, with an axe.[33] She had become the very model
of the impressionable, wayward young white girl tempted into the supposedly violent and licentious world of immigrant dancing clubs. In 1964
a Home Office report noted that in Notting Hill 'heroin and hemp were
said to be available and coloured men were associating with white girls'.
Young people, the report observed, were 'in serious moral danger . . . It
requires a strong character and a secure home background with understanding parents to avoid contamination once the young person has
entered the club world.'[34] This kind of attitude often reflected racial anxieties rather than genuine realities, but it might have been written
specifically to describe Keeler's case. Since she had neither a strong character nor a secure background, she was particularly vulnerable to a bully
like Gordon, and to conservative commentators in the mid-sixties their
association provided the perfect example of the supposed moral and
sexual degeneracy of immigrant society.

In the summer of 1962 Keeler finally abandoned Lucky Gordon and took
up with another West Indian called Johnny Edgecombe. Gordon, however,
did not give up easily; the two men occasionally fought over her, and after
one brawl Gordon needed seventeen stitches to knife wounds on his face. In
December 1962, to complicate matters further, Keeler left Johnny
Edgecombe and temporarily moved back into Ward's flat in Wimpole Mews,
where she rejoined her friend Mandy Rice-Davies, another of Ward's girls
and the former lover of the slum landlord Peter Rachman. She was now
being pursued, therefore, not merely by Gordon but also by Edgecombe;

evidently her charms were irresistible. Edgecombe was hiding from the police in Brentford, worried that he would be sent to prison for slashing his rival's face, and in December he telephoned Keeler at Ward's flat and asked her to find him a solicitor. She refused and, to Edgecombe's fury, even said that she would testify against him herself.[35]

This was a serious mistake: Edgecombe was a hot-tempered man, and late on the morning of 14 December he appeared outside Ward's door touting an automatic pistol. He later explained that what had provoked him most was that Keeler threw a pound note down to him from one of the windows, a supremely dismissive gesture; with that, he attempted to break down the door, failed, and began wildly firing his pistol. Keeler and Rice-Davies telephoned Ward at his surgery; he called the police, and, since shootings were rare in a genteel part of London like Marylebone, a host of policemen and journalists descended on the Mews. Edgecombe was arrested and charged both with assaulting Gordon with a knife and with firing at the girls in Ward's flat.[36] This was the first time since her affair with the Minister of War that Keeler had become involved with the police; it was also the first time that she had come to the attention of the national press. 'GIRL IN SHOTS DRAMA' said the *Mirror*, and indeed it was a splendid little story for the popular newspapers: two pretty girls of dubious repute, a respected London osteopath, and West Indian immigrants running amok with knives and guns.[37] For Profumo, however, it was to prove a catastrophe.

Rumours of the brief affair between Profumo and Keeler had already seeped through Stephen Ward's social set, largely because Keeler herself was so childishly proud of her conquest.[38] In the August 1962 issue of the society magazine *Queen*, the gossip columnist Robin Douglas-Home, nephew of the Foreign Secretary, had published an item entitled 'Sentences I'd Like to Hear the End of', which ran, in full: '. . . called in MI5 because every time the chauffeur-driven Zils drew up at her *front* door, out of the *back* door into a chauffeur-driven Humber slipped . . .' This was supposed to be an allusion to the Ivanov–Keeler–Profumo triangle, although only a tiny handful of the magazine's readers could possibly have guessed.[39] In the aftermath of Edgecombe's arrest, however, Keeler lost her head and began spilling the details of her last eighteen months to anybody who would listen.[40] By the end of January 1963 she had told her story to at least four different confidants, including a solicitor friend of Stephen Ward and the detective sergeant investigating the Edgecombe case. Keeler also sold her story, and the letter from Profumo ending their relationship, to the *Sunday Pictorial* for £1000, although they initially held off from publication for fear of legal action. One of the *Pictorial* journalists then approached Stephen Ward for an interview, and he, realising that the secret was out, told Lord Astor and Profumo himself.[41]

Even though the affair was eighteen months old and had lasted a mere five weeks, Profumo was desperate to prevent the *Pictorial* running a story that might destroy not only his political career but also his marriage. At the end of January 1963, at a time when the government was distracted by de Gaulle's veto and the problems of the British nuclear deterrent, he approached the head of MI5, the Attorney General, the Chief Whip and various other prominent officials and asked them to stop the newspaper publishing Keeler's story.[42] All the time he denied that they had ever been lovers. When Martin Redmayne, the Chief Whip, said in exasperation: 'Well look, nobody would believe that you didn't sleep with her,' Profumo simply replied: 'Yes, I know they wouldn't believe it, but it happens to be true.' This went down very well, and the consensus was that Profumo must just wait for the story to emerge and then immediately sue for libel. If he had resigned at this early stage, the subsequent scandal would largely have been averted. It was Redmayne, however, who had compelled Thomas Galbraith to resign in the aftermath of the Vassall case, and he had little desire to administer such harsh treatment a second time based purely on the claims of a former showgirl. He therefore chose to accept Profumo's story and told him that there was no need either to talk to the Prime Minister or to worry about resigning.[43]

As for Macmillan himself, he knew about the allegations as early as 4 February, when he returned from a trip to Italy and read a private note from his close adviser John Wyndham, reporting a conversation with an executive of the *News of the World*:

> According to Mr Chapman-Walker Mr Profumo is alleged to have met this girl 'Kolania' through Lord Astor at Cliveden, where they chased her naked round the bathing pool.
>   According to Mr Chapman-Walker it is also alleged that:
> (i) 'Kolania' got into this company through the agency of a Mr Ward, who Mr Chapman-Walker described as a 'psychopathic specialist' of Wimpole Street;
> (ii) Mr Profumo, visiting 'Kolania' in Mr Ward's house, passed in the

passage the Russian Naval Attaché on his way out from 'Kolania';
(iii) 'Kolania' has two letters on War Office paper signed 'J' – although
it is not suggested that these letters are anything more than ones of
assignation.[44]

Again, if Macmillan had intervened at this stage then he might have avoided
the embarrassing shambles of the summer. Instead, he preferred to leave
matters to the Chief Whip, and therefore nothing was done.

From February 1963 onwards, at precisely the time that Macmillan was
hoping to rebuild the electoral fortunes of the Conservative Party, Keeler's
revelations were hanging over the government. The story had all the ingredients of a sensation, from Soviet espionage and sexual shenanigans in high
places to aristocratic parties and West Indian drug peddlers, and it could
hardly fail to leak out. By the beginning of the following month, most of
Fleet Street had heard the rumours and on 8 March Profumo had his first
chance to sue, when *Westminster Confidential*, an obscure newsletter stencilled
and delivered on subscription to two hundred devotees of political gossip,
became the first publication to print a version of the story:

THAT WAS THE GOVERNMENT THAT WAS!
'That is certain to bring down the Government!' a Conservative MP
wailed – 'and what will my wife say?'

This combination of tragedy and tragi-comedy came from the effort
of this MP to check with a newspaperman on the story which has run
like wildfire through Parliament.

The best-authenticated version is this: that two call-girls came into
the limelight as a result of the effort of a Negro to kill them for having
given him a venereal disease. This notoriety having made their calling
difficult, the two girls started selling their stories to the Sunday newspapers, the *Sunday Pictorial* and the *People* in particular.

One of the choicest bits in their stories was a letter, apparently
signed 'Jock' on the stationery of the Secretary for W+r. The allegation
by this girl was that not only was this Minister, who has a famous
actress as his wife, her client, but also the Soviet military attaché, apparently a Colonel Ivanov. The famous-actress wife, of course, would sue
for divorce, the scandal ran. Who was using the call-girl to milk whom
of information – the W+r Secretary or the Soviet military attaché – ran
the minds of those primarily interested in security.[45]

The story could hardly have been more explicit, and photostat copies of *Westminster Confidential* were soon being handed around the Commons lobbies. Both Profumo and the Attorney General agreed that its circulation was too small to justify a potentially messy libel action; the problem, however, was that the national press were inching ever closer to running the rumours themselves. 'I agree that for the moment Profumo can afford to ignore this publication,' the Attorney General wrote to one of Macmillan's advisers, 'but I feel it may become increasingly difficult for him to maintain his position much longer.'[46] The danger of exposure increased on 14 March, when Johnny Edgecombe's trial opened at the Old Bailey and it transpired that Keeler, the star prosecution witness, had fled to Spain with a friend of Ward's.[47] The following morning, the *Daily Express* ran the banner headline 'WAR MINISTER SHOCK' above an entirely erroneous story that Profumo had 'for personal reasons' offered to resign. One column away was a large photograph of Keeler together with the headline 'VANISHED OLD BAILEY WITNESS'.[48] Few readers would connect the two stories, but for those who had already heard the rumours the inference was plain. On 16 March, meanwhile, the *Daily Sketch* published an interview with Mandy Rice-Davies about the Edgecombe case in which Captain Ivanov's existence was publicly admitted for the first time, and on 20 March the *Daily Mail* again suggested that Profumo's resignation was imminent.[49]

What was imminent, however, was not Profumo's resignation but the belated public revelation of the story. The magazine *Private Eye* had by this point begun to find its feet and was reaching more than 10,000 readers a fortnight; the Profumo rumours offered an excellent opportunity to attract further public attention. On the afternoon of 21 March the latest edition broached for the first time the tale of 'gay fun-loving Miss Gaye Funloving', the missing '21 year old "model"':

'Parties'

One of Miss Funloving's close 'friends', Dr. Spook of Harley Street, revealed last night that he could add nothing to what had been already insinuated.

Dr. Spook is believed to have 'more than half the Cabinet on his list of patients'. He also has a 'weekend' cottage on the Berkshire estate of Lord *, and is believed to have attended many 'parties' in the neighbourhood.

Among those it is believed also attended 'parties' of this type are Mr. Vladimir Bolokhov, the well-known Soviet spy attached to the Russian Embassy, and a well-known Cabinet Minister.

RESIGNATION?

Mr. James Montesi, a well-known Cabinet Minister, was reported last night to have proffered his 'resignation' to the Prime Minister on 'personal grounds'. It is alleged that the Prime Minister refused to accept his alleged resignation. Mr. Montesi today denied the allegations that he had ever allegedly offered his alleged 'resignation' to the alleged 'Prime Minister'.[50]

That evening the House of Commons was scheduled to debate the question of the two journalists imprisoned for their role in reporting the Vassall case, and at least four Labour MPs had separately decided that this was the moment to strike.[51] Just before eleven, with the debate plodding towards an unremarkable conclusion, George Wigg rose to speak. A lugubrious, suspicious character, Wigg was obsessed with political mismanagement of the army and national security; although not a popular figure on the Labour back benches, he was a faithful servant, indeed a loyal bloodhound, to Harold Wilson.[52] He had initially got on rather well with Profumo, a fellow war veteran, but in November 1962 they had fallen out over the alleged disorganisation of the British army in Kuwait, and Wigg bitterly blamed the War Minister for making a fool of him in the House.[53] It seems that Wigg had got hold of the Profumo rumours in the early months of 1963 through another embittered character, John Lewis, a former Labour MP who had crossed swords with Stephen Ward during a messy divorce case. Christine Keeler had met Lewis at a Christmas party and very foolishly told him her story, not realising that Lewis hated Ward with a passion and would certainly use it to strike at his enemy if he could do so.[54] Two men with personal grudges, then, played central roles in the public revelation of the Profumo–Keeler liaison.

Wigg began with some words on the case of the imprisoned journalists, but soon switched to other matters:

There is not an Honourable Member in this House, nor a journalist in the Press Gallery, nor do I believe there is a person in the Public Gallery, who, in the last few days, has not heard rumour upon rumour involving

Honor Blackman and Patrick Macnee rehearse their roles as Cathy Gale and John Steed for the new series of *The Avengers*, October 1963.
(Keystone/Getty Images)

'Exterminate!' The Daleks invade London for a publicity photograph, early 1960s.
(McPhedran/Getty Images)

New Labour, New Britain: Harold Wilson in his room at the House of Commons, 1963.
(Keystone/Getty Images)

a member of the Government front bench. The Press has got as near as it could – it has shown itself willing to wound but afraid to strike . . .

That being the case, I rightly use the Privilege of the House of Commons – that is what it is given to me for – to ask the Home Secretary, who is the senior member of the Government on the Treasury Bench now, to go to the Dispatch Box – he knows that the rumour to which I refer relates to Miss Christine Keeler and Miss Davies and a shooting by a West Indian – and on behalf of the Government, categorically deny the truth of these rumours.

On the other hand, if there is anything in them, I urge him to ask the Prime Minister to do what was not done in the Vassall case – set up a Select Committee so that these things can be dissipated, and the honour of the Minister concerned freed from the imputations and innuendoes that are being spread at the present time.[55]

This was sensational stuff, and as Wigg spoke there were gasps of stunned recognition as Members struggled to rouse themselves from their late-night torpor and take in the impact of his words. Two more Labour Members, Richard Crossman and Barbara Castle, almost immediately backed Wigg's proposal to establish a select committee to investigate the story. One other speaker, the hearty Labour MP for Northampton, Reginald Paget, made a splendidly blimpish intervention. 'What do these rumours amount to?' he asked in bewilderment. 'They amount to the fact that a Minister is said to be acquainted with a very pretty girl. As far as I am concerned, I should have thought that was a matter for congratulation rather than inquiry.'[56]

Now that Wigg had forced the issue, it was clear that Profumo himself would be compelled either to admit or to deny the allegations. The next few hours were vital to the resolution of the affair, but they could hardly have been handled in a more inept fashion. Just before one-thirty in the morning, the debate ended and five senior Conservative ministers immediately huddled in the Attorney General's office to discuss the predicament. The five men were the Chief Whip, Martin Redmayne; the Leader of the House, Iain Macleod; the government's 'super public relations man', William Deedes; the Attorney General, Sir John Hobson; and the Solicitor General, Sir Peter Rawlinson.[57] One of Redmayne's junior whips was sent to Profumo's house in Regent's Park and roused the War Minister by banging on the door. Profumo had taken a sleeping pill and was still manifestly groggy, but just before three he arrived in Hobson's office with his solicitor to be presented with an ultimatum. Either he must resign instantly, or, if he were innocent, he must deny the charges forthwith.

It was a terrible dilemma for a man still half asleep and facing five expectant colleagues across a desk. William Deedes later reflected that they had presented Profumo with an impossible situation. They were 'in a desperate hurry', he admitted, but he had 'often wondered as one present at this extraordinary gathering whether in those circumstances I would instantly have owned up to the truth, the whole truth, and nothing but the truth. Later we were accused of being hoodwinked; but I think the charge against us is graver than that. We created circumstances which made the truth extremely hard to tell.'[58] Lord Denning, who later drafted a controversial report into the affair, agreed: to give such an ultimatum to a man torn from his sleep was 'most unfair', and the ministers should have waited until the following day and allowed him more time.[59] It was ludicrous to ask Profumo to sign his own political death warrant in such circumstances. Iain Macleod, who had conducted various romances of his own and, like Profumo, had insouciantly written letters to his mistresses on ministerial notepaper, was particularly blunt: 'Look Jack, the basic question is, "Did you fuck her?"'[60] The bleary-eyed Profumo was hardly likely to answer in the affirmative; if he resigned as a minister, even though he might retain his seat as an MP, there was no guarantee that his political career would ever recover.[61] He denied the allegations. Macleod immediately told the two law officers to draft a statement for Profumo to deliver in the Commons, as had already been agreed with the Prime Minister.[62] At eleven the following morning, after just two hours' sleep, Profumo duly rose from the front bench and read the statement to a packed House. He admitted knowing both Ward and Ivanov, and recalled having met Keeler 'on about half a dozen occasions at Dr Ward's flat, when I called to see him and his friends. Miss Keeler and I were on friendly terms. There was no impropriety whatsoever in my acquaintanceship with Miss Keeler.' If 'scandalous allegations are made or repeated outside this House', he added, 'I shall not hesitate to issue writs for libel and slander'.[63]

When, a few weeks later, Profumo sued the French and Italian magazines *Paris Match* and *Tempo Illustrato* for libel, winning minor damages, his unwavering denials seemed to have worked. 'He must be OK, he wouldn't perjure himself in court,' Dorothy Macmillan told her husband, who himself refused to believe that Profumo could possibly have lied to the Commons.[64]

Even the existence of the 'Darling' letter had been successfully explained away, as Macmillan confided to his diary:

> Profumo has behaved foolishly and indiscreetly, but not wickedly. His wife (Valerie Hobson) is very nice and sensible. Of course, all these people move in a raffish, theatrical, bohemian society, where no one really knows anyone and everyone is 'darling'. But Profumo does not seem to have realised that we have – in public life – to observe different standards from those prevalent today in many circles.[65]

Although the national press reported Profumo's denials relatively sympathetically, the rumours did not entirely disappear. At the end of March there were a couple of typically unfunny items about the story on *TW3*, with Millicent Martin delivering a monologue as a model in dark glasses ready to 'spill' her secrets if her income did not improve.[66] *Private Eye*, too, continued to print jokes hinting that Profumo's account was not perhaps the whole truth.[67] Far from Profumo's statement having put an end to the affair, his defence was unravelling behind the scenes. On 5 April Keeler admitted to the police that she had briefly been the minister's mistress. Stephen Ward, meanwhile, was evidently terrified that he would be dragged into a protracted and humiliating investigation, and therefore told both Wigg and Macmillan's private secretary that Profumo was lying.[68]

Wigg relayed this information to Harold Wilson, who now found himself with a difficult hand that he played extremely cleverly, discreetly concentrating on the espionage issue and gambling that the government's inaction would eventually give him the opportunity to strike. In fact the indefatigable Wigg had concluded that the Profumo affair was not really a serious security risk at all, especially since MI5 had had their eye on Ivanov the entire time.[69] Nonetheless, Wilson was determined to use the affair as a further illustration of the amateurish incompetence of the Conservative government where national security was concerned. On 9 April he wrote to Macmillan advising him that he had heard rumours that Ward was somehow mixed up with MI5, and on 27 May he went to see Macmillan and personally told him that Ward was 'a tool of Russian Communism' and that the entire Profumo–Keeler business might well pose a serious threat to national security.[70]

Macmillan breezily dismissed his rival's advice, although deep down he was extremely worried that the security issue was about to engulf his government once again. Two days after his meeting with the Labour leader, an agitated Prime Minister called in Sir Roger Hollis, the head of MI5, and asked him whether Wilson's allegations were true. He did not get the answer he wanted.[71] No, Hollis said, Ward was not a serious security risk; he was 'a pimp, not a spy'. On the other hand, he admitted, Keeler had claimed in her statements to the police that Ward wanted her to find out from Profumo when the Americans were likely to install atomic weapons in their West German bases, this information presumably being bound for Ivanov and Moscow.[72] The question of German armaments was certainly a sensitive one in the early sixties, but it is laughable to suggest, as some authors do, that Christine Keeler was some Mata Hari figure pumping the War Minister for information.[73] It was ridiculous to imagine that Keeler, a glorified teenage callgirl with absolutely no understanding of nuclear technology and Cold War diplomacy, could ever be the intermediary in an elaborate operation to discover NATO atomic strategy. But that, as far as Macmillan was concerned, was not the point. The problem was that, in the aftermath of the Vassall case, any link between the Profumo case and national security would be a disaster for his government's fragile standing in the country. And if Profumo had lied, as some senior figures in the party and on Fleet Street evidently still thought he had, then the Prime Minister would find himself in a terrible mess.[74]

Throughout his premiership, Macmillan had been a curious blend of nervous anxiety and jaunty insouciance. The latter was uppermost when, at the end of May, he disappeared to Scotland for a ten-day holiday, leaving instructions for the Lord Chancellor, Lord Dilhorne, to look into the Profumo matter.[75] Meanwhile Profumo himself was also off on holiday, taking his wife to Venice during the parliamentary recess. He already knew that he was facing yet another interrogation when he returned, and when Dilhorne sent a cable to Italy asking Profumo to come back for their meeting a day earlier than planned, he evidently felt the walls closing in around him very quickly indeed. Ever since the last months of 1961, the War Minister had been jealously guarding the secret of his affair. The pressure from the newspapers, his colleagues and the Labour benches was now intense; he must have known, deep down, that the secret had to come out eventually. At last he decided, over dinner in Venice, to confess to his wife. Her immediate reaction has not been recorded; it is unlikely that she was overjoyed. The couple then decided to return to London early and, as she put it, 'face up to it'.[76] Since Profumo had knowingly misled the House of

Commons, there could be no illusions about the outcome. On 4 June, after a tense meeting with the Chief Whip during which he admitted his culpability, Profumo resigned, not merely as a minister, but also as a Member of Parliament.

Macmillan was still in Scotland when the news of Profumo's resignation reached him by telephone, but he did not think it sufficient cause to break off his holiday, proceeding with his planned outings to Iona and Gleneagles. Butler, who was standing in for him in London, was dumbfounded to hear that the Prime Minister was wondering 'whether we could not fight back' and that Macmillan could 'hardly believe that this was a major issue'.[77] Since the affair had been so protracted, and since it was now so closely associated not only with national security but also with the integrity and competence of the government, it was obvious to Butler that the consequences would be devastating. As it happened, the news of Profumo's resignation broke on 5 June, the very day that Lucky Gordon was to stand trial for assaulting Keeler in a minor incident outside a friend's flat in April. A coincidence more likely to increase public interest could hardly have been imagined, and Keeler herself added to the excitement when she arrived at the court that morning in a chauffeur-driven Rolls-Royce. With the press still absorbing the news about Profumo, Gordon provided a diversionary spectacle of his own by discharging his counsel halfway through the day and then becoming embroiled in a loud and emotional shouting match with Keeler during which he accused her of giving him venereal disease and she then burst into tears and stormed out of the courtroom.[78] On 8 June, meanwhile, Stephen Ward was arrested for living on the earnings of prostitution and detained in Brixton prison.[79]

The entire thing might have been scripted by Macmillan's worst enemies, and his absence in Scotland made it even more difficult for him to try and contain the momentum of the press coverage. The Sunday papers on 9 June did not make heartening reading. The *Sunday Telegraph*, usually so supportive of the Conservatives but already critical of Macmillan's enthusiasm for decolonisation in Africa, had come out against him. The *Sunday Mirror* printed a copy of the 'Darling' letter that Profumo had sent to Keeler in 1961. And the *News of the World*, most damagingly of all, published the first part of Keeler's 'confession' describing the events at Cliveden and her relationships with Ward and Ivanov, illustrated by a large and subsequently famous photograph of her sitting naked astride a fashionably modern chair.[80] The Prime Minister spent the morning closeted in his room with the newspapers, played golf in the afternoon with his wife, and took the sleeper train south in the evening. 'I do not remember ever having been under such a sense of personal strain,' he later wrote in his diary.[81]

'In the dawn of Monday 10 June,' the *Annual Register* recorded, 'Mr Macmillan emerged from his overnight sleeper at Euston and marched grimly down the platform. The toughest, bitterest week of his premiership was before him.'[82] Redmayne, the Chief Whip, had already submitted his resignation, but Macmillan refused to accept it. 'If you resign, I resign,' he told Redmayne, adding that they had 'nothing with which to reproach ourselves, except perhaps too great a loyalty'. Even Redmayne thought this 'a gross over-simplification of an appalling situation'.[83] His offer to resign was itself an admission of guilt: if he had done his job properly and kept a more careful track of Profumo's personal life, then the shambles might never have happened. Macmillan himself, however, was equally at fault. He and his aides had been almost incredibly casual and negligent in their handling of the affair, and it beggared belief that all of them had, despite all the evidence to the contrary, simply accepted Profumo's word.

Perhaps the key to the problem was that, in Redmayne's words, Macmillan 'found it distasteful' to contemplate the liaison of one of his ministers with a girl like Christine Keeler.[84] In later years, Macmillan liked to joke about the affair; he cheerfully told the BBC in 1973 that 'Profumo should simply have said, "Of course, I took a well-known courtesan to bed, and I cannot tell you how agreeable she was."'[85] At the time, however, this was certainly *not* his reaction. As his biographer points out, everyone who knew the Prime Minister agreed that 'it was all deeply repugnant to what was essentially puritanical in him, and personally painful to him'. Sex was not a subject that one broached with Harold Macmillan, and the intrusion of the press into private lives was something he greatly resented. One potential reason for this deep distaste was his guilt that Thomas Galbraith had been sacrificed so cheaply in the Vassall affair. More fundamental, however, was what Horne calls the 'Boothby factor'. Macmillan had never really recovered from the shock of discovering his wife's adultery with Robert Boothby, and the fact that their illicit relationship still continued while he remained personally abstinent meant that he instinctively shied away from masculine ribaldry about sex. According to Horne, the world of Profumo and Boothby, the world of the adulterer 'which comprised the half-heard, half-imagined sly innuendoes of the Commons Smoking Room and the St James's clubs . . . was a world to which, for the past thirty-odd years and

Ian Fleming, the creator of James Bond, looking appropriately debonair and mysterious. *(Tappe/Getty Images)*

Michael Cummings comments on the wave of sex and security scandals, *Daily Express*, 10 July 1963. 'It's all very well Maudling talking about youth,' Macmillan is saying, 'but I happen to be taking part in an X-certificate film.'

Stephen Ward poses with three of his girls: *from left*, Mandy Rice-Davies, Penny Marshall and Christine Keeler, early sixties. *(Express/Getty Images)*

Britannia and John Bull are horrified to see what they have become: Cummings in the *Express*, 24 July 1963.

Christine Keeler and Mandy Rice-Davies are mobbed by photographers as they leave the Old Bailey, 22 July 1963. *(Evening Standard/Getty Images)*

The Prime Ministers who never were: *from left*, Reginald Maudling, Quintin Hailsham and R.A. Butler at the Conservative party conference in Blackpool, October 1963. The leadership contest had not yet been decided, but they all look suitably miserable.
(Miller/Getty Images)

In the autumn tranquillity of his days while the golden leaves fall silently to the ground an old man, his faithful wife by his side, sits peacefully in the park happy in the knowledge of a lifetime's work well done, a country served and an old colleague stabbed ruthlessly in the back...

Private Eye reacts to the Conservative leadership contest, 1 November 1963.

'The leader has emerged, an elegant anachronism.' The new Prime Minister, Sir Alec Douglas-Home, on a shooting expedition, November 1963.
(Keystone/Getty Images)

The Beatles on stage at the London Palladium, 13 October 1963. *(Webb/Getty Images)*

'A cup of tea is more enjoyable to us than the garish delights of the jukebox.' The Beatles relax between rehearsals for the Royal Variety Performance, 4 November 1963. *(Hulton Archive/ Getty Images)*

"Gentlemen, can't we persuade you to become Conservative candidates—after all, you've never had it so good!"

Sir Alec Douglas-Home and Selwyn Lloyd attempt to recruit the Fab Four as Conservative candidates: Michael Cummings in the *Express*, 11 November 1963.

Sean Connery and his co-star Daniela Bianchi pose for photographers during the filming of *From Russia with Love* in Istanbul, 1963.
(Sunset Boulevard/Corbis)

more, Macmillan had resolutely closed his mind as well as his ears; and it went grievously against his nature to have to open both now, over Profumo'.[86] With its overtones of marital duplicity and betrayal, the Profumo case exposed psychological wounds that for Macmillan had never really healed. In this context, then, it was not so surprising that he handled it so badly.

Macmillan met his Cabinet two days after returning to London and secured their support for his management of the crisis.[87] It was much more difficult, however, to halt the momentum of journalistic speculation and public excitement, or to relieve the sheer pressure of events. The Commons was scheduled to debate the Profumo affair on 17 June, giving the Prime Minister very little time to prepare his defence or rally popular support. Harold Wilson was still playing it very coolly, ordering his Labour colleagues to keep off the airwaves and restrict their criticism to questions of national security, so there was no way that the Conservatives could pretend that this was a purely partisan matter.[88]

On 13 June, Lord Hailsham, the Lord President of the Council, sallied forth onto the BBC programme *Gallery* in a vain attempt to defend the government. If Macmillan were to fall, Hailsham would be one of the likely candidates to replace him, but his conduct on this occasion did not do him any favours. He appeared to have very little sympathy for his former colleague; indeed, he cast himself as the spokesman for what one commentator called 'the armies of Pharisees marching in their holy wrath'.[89] 'A great party', Hailsham blustered, 'is not to be brought down because of a scandal by a woman of easy virtue and a proven liar . . . It is intolerable for Mr Profumo in his position to have behaved in this way, and a tragedy that he should not have been found out, that he should have lied and lied and lied; lied to his family, lied to his friends, lied to his solicitor, lied to the House of Commons.' If he was hoping to defuse the security issue, he had a strange way of doing it. 'Of course there's a security problem,' he exclaimed. 'Don't be so silly! A Secretary of State for War can't have a woman shared with a spy!'[90]

This generally angry and uncharitable performance did not impress many observers. Bernard Levin commented that he had 'the air of a man who had entirely lost control of himself' and was not alone in thinking that the intensely religious Hailsham was possessed with 'such manic violence that those watching might have thought that he was about to go completely berserk'.[91] Hailsham's attempt to recast the Conservatives as the party of moral rectitude had been a manifest disaster, and the interview compounded a reputation for juvenile irresponsibility that was to cost him dear several months later. Profumo's own brother-in-law wrote to *The Times* noting that Hailsham 'could have shown some element of Christian charity in his denunciation of a man with a shattered life'.[92] The Bishop of Southwark suggested that Hailsham might like to consult a psychiatrist, and *Private Eye* gleefully asked: 'IS HAILSHAM MAD? . . . We are forced to conclude that he is not. He is simply a conceited, boring, anachronistic, deluded and arrogant old gentleman.'[93]

Throughout the week after Macmillan's return, Westminster was buzzing with rumours that the Conservatives might launch a palace coup against their leader. Enoch Powell was generally imagined to be sharpening his knife, although, as it turned out, he had already decided to back the Prime Minister.[94] Just before half past three on 17 June, with MPs packed into the Commons chamber and the public galley overflowing, Macmillan took his seat for the debate on the government front bench, looking nervous and pale. Harold Wilson walked in two minutes later, 'quietly predatory and carrying an ominous file'. Moments afterwards the Labour leader 'rose, paused to savour the hanging silence, and then began, in confident and incisive style': 'This is a debate without precedence in the annals of this House. It arises from disclosures which have shocked the moral conscience of the nation. There is clear evidence of a sordid underground network, the extent of which cannot be measured and which we cannot debate today because of proceedings elsewhere.'[95] It was immediately obvious that Wilson's usual flamboyant, knockabout wit had been put aside for the occasion; this was Wilson the serious forensic prosecutor, meticulously assembling his case and concentrating on the issue of national security. He pointed out that he had several times warned Macmillan of the danger that Ward's association posed to British security, and he reminded MPs that he had even told Macmillan about Ward's meeting with George Wigg, the record of which was 'a nauseating document, taking the lid off a corner of the London underworld of vice, dope, marijuana, blackmail and counter-blackmail, violence, petty crime, together with references to Mr Profumo and the Soviet attaché'. The Labour leadership, he neatly observed, had therefore known about the rumours for months; but they had 'decided that, although the documents in our possession were, in a sense, dynamite, and would have touched off such an explosion, it was our duty, as a responsible Opposition, to hand over all the information to the Prime Minister, who has first responsibility for security, and not to make public use of them'.[96]

And yet, he pointed out, the Prime Minister had not shown 'a corresponding sense of responsibility'; instead, his attitude had been: 'What has this to do with me?' When, he asked, had Macmillan first heard about the affair? Had MI5 told him about it, and if so, when?

> I believe the first the security services knew or even guessed about this very big security risk was when a Sunday newspaper told them a few months later. If this is true – the Prime Minister must be frank about this – this would imply that the £60 million spent on these services under the Right Honourable Gentleman's premiership have been less productive than the security services of the *News of the World*.
>
> So, though I personally acquit the Right Honourable Gentleman of foreknowledge or complicity in this matter – of course I do; of course we all do; I mean complicity in the misleading of the House – he cannot be acquitted of a grave dereliction of duty in failing to find out.

Wilson ended by turning back to the question of morality, and broadening the attack so that the Profumo affair became not merely a matter of security but an indictment of the degenerate moral tone of Macmillan's Britain. There was 'something utterly nauseating about a system or society which pays a harlot twenty-five times as much as it pays its Prime Minister, two hundred and fifty times as much as it pays its Members of Parliament, and five hundred times as much as it pays some of its ministers of religion'.

> What we are seeing is a diseased excrescence, a corrupted and poisoned appendix of a small and unrepresentative section of society that makes no contribution to what Britain is, still less what Britain can be. There are, of course, lessons to be drawn for all of us in terms of social policy, but perhaps most of all in terms of the social philosophy and values and objectives of our society – the replacement of materialism and the worship of the golden calf by values which exalt the spirit of service and the spirit of national dedication . . . The sickness of an unrepresentative sector of our society should not detract from the robust ability of our people as a whole to face the challenge of the future.[97]

When Wilson sat down, few onlookers doubted that he had presented his case quite superbly. Richard Crossman noted that it was 'better than I thought possible . . . really annihilating, a classical prosecution speech, with weight and self-control'.[98] Macmillan, meanwhile, had sat through the speech looking intensely miserable, and when he got up to respond it was immediately obvious that Macmillan the flamboyant Edwardian actor had been replaced by a much more plaintive, indeed feeble, figure. His strategy was, essentially, to beg for the sympathy of the House, and he opened with a rare admission of private emotion:

On me, as Head of the Administration, what has happened has inflicted a deep, bitter and lasting wound. I do not remember in the whole of my life, or even in the political history of the past, a case of a Minister of the Crown who has told a deliberate lie to his wife, to his legal advisers, to his ministerial colleagues, not once but over and over again, who has then repeated this lie to the House of Commons as a personal statement . . . and has subsequently taken legal action and recovered damages on the basis of a falsehood. This is almost unbelievable, but it is true.

'I find it difficult', he admitted, 'to tell the House what a blow this has been to me, for it seems to have undermined one of the very foundations on which political life must be conducted.' Turning to the detailed chronology of the affair, he denied absolutely that he had known about it before Profumo's resignation. He admitted that it was 'an extremely fair question' to ask why he had not interrogated the minister himself, but explained that he thought it would be easier for Profumo to talk to more junior figures, and that the alternative 'would have made it difficult, if not impossible for him to feel in future, however innocent he might have been, that he enjoyed my confidence'. The Vassall case and the resignation of Galbraith had, he confessed, been playing on his mind. As for the famous 'Darling' letter from Profumo to Keeler, Macmillan explained that according to Profumo 'in circles in which he and his wife moved it was a term of no great significance'. 'I believe that might be accepted,' Macmillan continued forlornly. 'I do not live among young people fairly widely myself.' The core of Macmillan's defence was that he had been no less in the dark than any member of the general public; he had not been kept well informed by the security services; and the Commons should, if anything, feel sorry for him. After an hour of excuses, he returned at last to the theme of his opening words:

I said at the beginning that it was my duty to act honourably, to act justly, and to act prudently. My colleagues have been deceived, and I have been deceived, grossly deceived – and the House has been deceived – but we have not been parties to deception, and I claim that upon a fair view of the facts as I have set them out I am entitled to the sympathetic understanding and confidence of the House and of the country.[99]

Macmillan sat down to rather perfunctory cheers from the Conservative benches. By his own insouciant standards, it had been a weak and defensive effort; although his frankness might have impressed some observers, it was certainly not clear that he had done enough to blunt Wilson's attack and dispel the doubts about his leadership. But it was not for his speech, or Wilson's, that the debate was to be remembered, nor for the vitriol directed from all sides at Christine Keeler, who was variously described as a 'dirty little prostitute', a 'harlot' and a 'little slut'.[100]

After the Liberal leader, Jo Grimond, had made a thoughtful but rather anodyne contribution, Nigel Birch, Macmillan's old back-bench critic, rose to speak. Time had not softened his acerbic style, tempered his intellectual independence or moderated his antipathy to the Prime Minister. Rumours had earlier associated Birch with an attempt to rally back-bench support behind Enoch Powell as a challenger for the leadership. Now he delivered a short, elegant speech laced with irony and neatly designed to tear down his leader's defences. It was not merely, as Simon Heffer says, 'the hammer-blow to Macmillan'; it was one of the great modern parliamentary demolitions.[101]

Birch began by coolly puncturing the balloon of self-righteousness that had swelled around Hailsham during his television broadcast, noting wryly that 'so many people have found some genuine happiness' in exploiting the miseries of their colleagues. Then he moved on to Macmillan's claim that he had simply taken Profumo at his word:

We know a deal more about Profumo than we did at the time of his statement, but we have all known him pretty well for a number of years in this House. I must say that he never struck me as a man at all like a cloistered monk; and Miss Keeler was a professional prostitute . . .

Here one had an active, busy man and a professional prostitute. Profumo had a number of meetings with her, and, if we are to judge by the published statements, she is not a woman who would be intellectually stimulating. Is it really credible that the association had no sexual content? There seems to me to be a certain basic improbability about the proposition that their relationship was purely platonic. What are whores about? Yet Profumo's word was accepted. It was accepted from a colleague. Would that word have been accepted if Profumo had not been a colleague or even if he had been a political opponent? Everyone, I think, must make his own judgement about that.

Macmillan, he said, had taken 'a colossal risk and a colossal gamble' in keeping Profumo in his government. It had not paid off; and he must therefore pay the price.

I absolutely acquit my Right Honourable Friend of any sort of dishonour. On the other hand, on the question of competence and good sense I cannot think that the verdict can be favourable.

What is to happen now? I cannot myself see at all that we can go on acting as if nothing had happened. We cannot just have business as usual. I myself feel that the time will come very soon when my Right Honourable Friend ought to make way for a much younger colleague. I feel that that ought to happen. I certainly will not quote at him the savage words of Cromwell, but perhaps some of the words of Browning might be appropriate in his poem on 'The Lost Leader', in which he wrote:

> . . . let him never come back to us!
> There would be doubt, hesitation and pain
> Forced praise on our part – the glimmer of twilight,
> Never glad confident morning again!

'Never glad confident morning again!' – so I hope the change will not be too long delayed.[102]

There followed a few more speeches, including a memorable assault by George Wigg on Hailsham, calling him 'a sinister saint' and 'a lying humbug', and then the House voted. Twenty-seven Tories abstained, and the government majority was down to sixty-nine – appropriately, some thought. Macmillan won the backing of his party, as it was always obvious that he would. But there could be no doubt that Birch had drawn blood, and that the Prime Minister was deeply, perhaps fatally, wounded.[103]

Macmillan left the Commons that evening looking 'bowed and dispirited'.[104] He privately told Butler that 'his heart was broken, although his spirit was still strong'.[105] The newspapers the following morning offered him little solace. 'Premier likely to resign soon' was the headline in the *Telegraph*; *The Times* had 'Macmillan unlikely to be leader in next Election', while the *Mail*'s headline read simply 'MAC: THE END'.[106] The American ambassador cabled Washington with the news that Macmillan's defence had been 'pitiable and extremely damaging'; he was now 'an electoral liability' and 'his replacement cannot be too long delayed'.[107]

All Macmillan's hard work to erode Labour's lead in the opinion polls had been undone at a stroke: the Conservatives had now fallen twenty points behind, fewer than one in four voters thought he should stay on as Prime Minister, and his personal popularity had reached the lowest level of any national leader since Neville Chamberlain.[108] Ever since Profumo's resignation almost two weeks previously, the press had been merciless in their pursuit of the wounded leader. 'Every part of the Profumo story', Macmillan later wrote, 'was used against the Government by an exultant Press, getting its own back for Vassall. The "popular" Press has been one mass of the life stories of spies and prostitutes, written no doubt in the office. Day after day the attacks developed, chiefly on me – old, incompetent, worn out . . .'[109] The most damning attack came from *The Times*, which had already called for change after the Vassall case. Sir William Haley, the paper's editor, spoke for many when he equated the grubby shenanigans of the Profumo affair with the decadent materialism of the affluent society under the Conservatives. 'It *Is* a Moral Issue' thundered the editorial on 11 June:

> Eleven years of Conservative rule have brought the nation psychologically and spiritually to a low ebb . . . The Prime Minister and his colleagues can cling together and still be there a year hence. They will have to do more than that to justify themselves . . .
>
> There are plenty of earnest and serious men in the Conservative Party who know that all is not well. It is time they put first things first, stopped weighing electoral chances, and returned to the starker truths of an earlier day.
>
> Popularity by affluence is about played out, especially when it rests on so insecure a basis. Even if the call had metaphorically to be for 'blood, sweat and tears', instead of to the fleshpots, they might be

surprised by the result. The British are always at their best when they are braced.[110]

Government ministers were furious. 'The Times', fumed Lord Hailsham during his infamous interview, 'is an anti-Conservative newspaper with an anti-Conservative editor.'[111]

What the Profumo affair had done was to concentrate the attentions of the press and the public on the issues of morality, security and sheer incompetence that had already been dogging Macmillan's government for at least two years. When the Sunday Times commented that the government had proved itself 'unalert to security dangers and indifferent to traditional moral standards', it explicitly linked middle-class anxieties about modern consumerism with their underlying fears of infiltration and subversion.[112] What was more, Mandy Rice-Davies' liaison with the late slum landlord Peter Rachman did not escape Macmillan's critics in the press. Eager to demonstrate the links between sexual excess, racial tension, public housing shortages and rising crime, the newspapers were quick to play up the links between 'Rachmanism' and the Profumo scandal. At the beginning of July both the Sunday Times and the Observer ran long exposés of Rachman's violent methods of intimidating his tenants and maximising his income, and on 15 July the latest edition of the BBC programme Panorama was devoted to an anatomy of Rachmanism.[113] In Punch the cartoonist Ralph Steadman portrayed the Profumo affair as a crumbling slum, 'the house that Jack spilt': on the bottom floor, the brothel crowded with girls and wine bottles; above, rooms of sinister spies and frightened black immigrants; at the top, a smirking slum landlord, chomping on a fat cigar and contemplating his profits. As Harold Wilson was keen to remind his audiences, the scandal was the ideal window on to a landscape of Conservative decadence and mismanagement.[114]

For the satirists, most of whom had established their careers by criticising the anachronism and materialism of the Macmillan government, the affair was a wonderful opportunity to redouble their attacks. The Conservatives' old election slogans, for instance, proved eminently suitable for revision. One Trog cartoon published in Private Eye captured the mood, showing Macmillan painting the latest Tory catchphrase on an advertising hoarding: 'WE'VE NEVER HAD IT SO OFTEN'.[115] 'Life's better under a Conservative' read the message of another Eye cartoon, while a spoof of Keeler's revelations in the News of the World, 'Macmillan Confesses', was illustrated with a Gerald Scarfe drawing of a busty, naked Macmillan posing in Keeler's famous chair-straddling position. 'Little did I foresee', read the breathless confession, 'how my Government was to become notorious through the world for its incompetence, laxity and vile corruption . . . And that eventually the little children would run through the streets, howling execration at my name and tweaking without mercy my already ludicrous moustache.'[116]

The magazine's sharpest comment on the affair, however, and one worth repeating at length, was Christopher Booker's pastiche of Edward Gibbon, 'The Last Days of Macmillan', which had been audaciously published as early as 5 April:

> By the early days of the year 1963, the twilight of the British Empire provided a sorry spectacle of collapse and decay on every hand . . .
>
> A strange mood walked abroad in Britain of that year, the eighth of the Emperor Macmillan. The ability and desire of the Emperor and his advisers to undertake the proper responsibilities of government seemed to have quite evaporated . . .
>
> After years of an uneasy indulgence, the people were restless and dissatisfied – a spirit which reached into all quarters of society . . . After his final defeat in the Gallic campaign, after the prolonged and tiring battle of Brussels upon which all his ambitions had been centred, the Emperor Macmillan himself lounged increasingly powerless at the heart of this drift and decay . . . Wild rumours flew nightly through the capital. Of strange and wild happenings in villas out in the country. Of orgies and philanderings involving some of the richest and most powerful men in the land . . .
>
> At this time too, the Chief of the Praetorian Guard, Sextus Profano, came under widespread suspicion for his admission in the Senate that he had been acquainted with Christina, a beautiful girl known to many of the great figures of society despite her lowly origins, and whose lover, a negro slave, had been sentenced to seven years in the sulphur mines for threatening to kill her in a fit of jealous revenge . . .
>
> All these happenings brought the capital into a frenzy of speculation that was far from healthy for the continued reign of Macmillan, and the scribes and pamphleteers were only the leaders and articulators of the widespread hostility and contempt aroused by the Government in the hearts of the great mass of the people.[117]

The writers of *Private Eye* were certainly not alone in associating Macmillan's government with moral decadence and sexual corruption. At a meeting of the 1922 Committee shortly after the Profumo debate, one Conservative backbencher caused uproar when he demanded that Macmillan resign in the next two weeks and added that there were 'too many pimps and prostitutes in high places'.[118] The Prime Minister was privately terrified that one more scandal might finish off his administration entirely.[119] Anthony Wedgwood Benn recorded in his diary that there were incessant rumours of 'more scandals to come'; whatever happened, 'if Mac can go on I think he will be massacred in the Election'.[120] Not surprisingly, most Labour MPs hoped that somehow Macmillan would struggle on; they had no wish to face a younger, fresher opponent like the affable and popular Reginald Maudling, who was now the favourite to take over. 'The important thing is to prevent them from having time to regroup under a new leader,' Benn noted on 18 June. 'All the papers this morning said that Macmillan was on the way out and so I wrote a paper for Harold, intended to suggest ways in which we could keep the pressure up and thus retain Macmillan or bring down the whole government.'[121] Wilson himself thought that the ageing incumbent was now Labour's greatest asset. 'The one thing I am really frightened of', he admitted privately, 'is Maudling.'[122]

This perhaps explains why, when a new scandal broke two weeks after the Commons debate, Macmillan managed to ride out the storm. This was not another tawdry affair of swimming pools and stolen assignations, but the stunning and serious revelation that Kim Philby, formerly the head of the Soviet section of MI6, had been unmasked as a KGB mole and had fled behind the Iron Curtain. Philby was the 'Third Man' in the Cambridge spy ring of the thirties, and had been instrumental in organising the defection of Burgess and Maclean in 1951. Unlike his comrades, he really did live up to the stereotype of the spy: although superficially hesitant and stammering, he was at heart cool, charming and calculating, a practised seducer and a very smooth operator indeed. Of the three men, he was the most effortless and effective spy, and the information he provided about British and American strategy during the Second World War and its immediate aftermath was beyond price.[123] From 1951 onwards there had been a careful hunt for the man who had tipped off Burgess and Maclean that the net was closing; a partially intercepted Soviet transmission had alluded to a 'ring of five [agents]', and the security services were desperate to find the Third, Fourth and Fifth Men.[124] What was especially embarrassing for Harold Macmillan, meanwhile, was that in November 1955 he had, as Foreign Secretary, denied on the floor of the House of Commons that Philby was the Third Man. Since Philby was at the time closely suspected by various members of both MI6 and the CIA, this had been an act of reckless folly, and Macmillan could now hardly avoid looking a credulous dupe.[125]

Philby had been working since the late fifties as a Middle Eastern correspondent for the *Observer*, but the net was closing all the time. In January 1963 an officer was sent out to Beirut to interrogate him, and after initially admitting his guilt, Philby then disappeared, later resurfacing in Moscow as a KGB consultant.[126] Although Philby had actually defected in January, the intelligence services and the government, desperate to avoid the inevitable scandal, managed to keep the news under wraps for several months, with the unfortunate consequence that it finally emerged on 1 July, when Macmillan was still entrenched in the depths of the Profumo crisis. Had the Labour leadership chosen to press home their advantage, it is possible that he might have been forced to resign; it is therefore revealing that Wilson readily yielded to Macmillan's private entreaties to underplay the issue and protect national security.[127] It was almost with disbelief that Macmillan recorded his debt to Wilson's 'high sense of responsibility . . . at a period when I was very hard-pressed'; but, of course, Wilson's behaviour makes perfect sense if he was indeed hoping to avoid the replacement of an old, unpopular adversary with a young, fresh one.[128] Given the mood of the times and the potential sensitivity of the Philby revelations, then, Macmillan was lucky to avoid a greater furore.

The Fourth Man was rapidly unmasked as the art historian Sir Anthony Blunt, a subtle, precious and ingratiating character who had long since won the trust of the royal family and been appointed Surveyor of the Queen's Pictures. Blunt had been suspected for many years, but was no longer considered a serious security risk since he had lost interest in Marxism and become absorbed in his artistic interests; indeed, he later proclaimed his 'abhorrence' of the Soviet system and became an admirer of Margaret Thatcher.[129] In April 1964, after numerous interrogations by MI5's tireless grand inquisitor William Skardon, he finally agreed to a deal whereby he would confess in return for immunity from prosecution, and his case was therefore buried until 1979, when he was publicly exposed by the writer Andrew Boyle and *Private Eye*.[130] As for Philby, his carefully cultivated persona of the debonair spy guaranteed him a prominent place among 'the immortals of the spy cult'.[131] According to his old friend and fellow agent Malcolm Muggeridge:

In the climate of ideological conflict, the spy is king. From Bulldog
Drummond to James Bond, from Kipling's Kim to Kim Philby is the
course our world has run. Philby, in other words, may be regarded as a
real-life James Bond. His boozy amours, his tough postures, his intelligence expertise, are directly related to the same characteristics in
Fleming's hero.[132]

Similar evocations of Philby the glamorous and even admirable traitor
were certainly not uncommon in the sixties and seventies. John le Carré, for
instance, was fascinated with the way in which Philby had insinuated himself into the heart of the British Establishment. 'Effortlessly he copied its
attitudes, caught its diffident stammer, its hesitant arrogance,' he wrote in
1977; 'effortlessly he took his place in its nameless hegemony.' He was 'of our
blood and hunted with our pack'.[133] In reality, however, Philby was a cold-
blooded, callous and domineering man, less a portrait of idealistic devotion
than a caricature of ruthless self-aggrandisement who sent scores of men to
their deaths. When he later learned the fate of one young Georgian agent
that he had betrayed, he dryly remarked: 'It was an unpleasant business, of
course . . . I knew very well that they would be caught and that a tragic fate
awaited them. But on the other hand, it was the only way of driving a stake
through the plans of future operations.'[134] It was typical of the man that,
once ensconced in Moscow, he threw himself into a new clandestine operation: the seduction of Donald Maclean's wife.[135]

Compared with the revelation that Philby had been a Soviet spy, the
Profumo scandal looked very trifling indeed. The intelligence services were
badly damaged by the ramifications of Philby's defection: indeed, MI5 was
nearly torn apart by the hunt for KGB moles, and the fact that several officers suspected their chief Sir Roger Hollis of being the Fifth Man meant that
the entire organisation was infected with suspicion.[136] To the ordinary
observer, however, the Philby affair did not seem so very different from all
the previous spy scandals. It certainly compounded Macmillan's general
misery and cemented the impression of corruption and incompetence in
high places. What made the Profumo scandal different, however, was the
explicit link between political corruption and sexual licence, a potent combination at a time when the government was deeply distrusted and sexual
mores were being widely discussed.

There had already been much controversy about the sexual behaviour of
teenagers and immigrants, the spread of pornography and birth control, the

publication of novels like *Lady Chatterley's Lover* and the changing status of women. Sexual frankness was closely equated with the developing consumer society; just as conservative commentators expressed their dissatisfaction with social change by attacking the appearance and attitudes of teenagers, so they used sexual issues to represent the alleged decline of post-war British society into materialism and vice.[137] 'The ease with which girls could pass from suburbia into the promiscuity belt of London was alarming,' noted one contemporary report. 'Christine Keeler and Mandy Rice-Davies might have been anyone's daughters.'[138] Unlike the Philby affair, therefore, the Profumo scandal might have been deliberately scripted to encompass a range of sensitive issues of the early sixties: espionage and subversion, sexual wantonness, unchecked materialism, the supposed exoticism and criminality of immigrant communities and the nepotism and ineptitude of the Conservative government.[139] Like all good scandals, it touched on public and private anxieties that had already been festering for years. During the second and third weeks of June, when the crisis was at its height, several observers made a telling comparison with the public hysteria of the seventeenth-century Popish Plot. Not for nothing did Macmillan scribble in his diary that 'a kind of Titus Oates atmosphere prevailed, with the wildest rumour and innuendo against the most respectable Ministers'. Altogether, he noted, 'partly by the blackmailing statements of the "call girls"; partly by the stories started or given by the Press; and partly (I have no doubt) by Soviet agents exploiting the position, more than half the Cabinet were being accused of perversion, homosexuality and the like'.[140]

Macmillan was not exaggerating, and, if anything, it is surprising that more ministers did not fall victim to the whirlwind of rumour and suspicion that swirled around Westminster in June and July 1963. On 21 June, Macmillan had asked Lord Denning to prepare a report on the 'security aspects' of the Profumo case, hoping to stem the 'flood of accusation and rumour'.[141] Denning's investigation, however, soon became bogged down in a bizarre world of sado-masochism, sex slaves and general debauchery. The columnist Bernard Levin recorded hearing from friends:

> that nine High Court judges had been engaging in sexual orgies, that a member of the Cabinet had served dinner at a private party while naked except for a mask, a small lace apron and a card round his neck reading 'If my services don't please you, whip me', that another member of the Cabinet had been discovered by police beneath a bush in Richmond Park

where he and a prostitute had been engaging in oral-genital activities and
that the police had hushed the matter up, that the Prime Minister . . .
had known about some, or all, of these matters but had taken no action,
and that a principal member of the royal family had been having sexual
relations with one, if not two, prostitutes in circumstances that would
have made exposure sooner or later inevitable.[142]

Far from drawing a discreet veil over the rumours, Denning in fact drew
attention to them in his report, solemnly ticking them off one by one: 'The
Cup of Tea', 'The Spaniard's Photograph', 'The Man in the Mask', 'The Man
Without a Head' and so on.[143] One particularly sensitive story concerned the
potential involvement of the royal family, and was largely created by the
Daily Mirror. Not only had Stephen Ward occasionally sketched the Duke of
Edinburgh, he had in the late forties and early fifties been part of the same
boozy, bawdy, masculine circle.[144] These links went unreported until 24
June when the *Mirror* dropped its somewhat disingenuous bombshell. An
enormous headline screamed, 'PRINCE PHILIP AND THE PROFUMO
SCANDAL', while, underneath, an article explained that 'the foulest
rumour being circulated about the Profumo Scandal has involved a member
of the Royal Family. The name being mentioned is Prince Philip.' Although
the article went on to admit, rather limply, that the story was 'utterly
unfounded', the dramatic headline alone ensured the Duke a prominent
place in Profumo gossip for the next few weeks, despite the fact that no evidence of his involvement in the scandal ever surfaced.[145]

As for the other rumours, most appear to have been fairly baseless. The
'man in the mask' story was a particularly sensational example. Both Keeler
and Rice-Davies claimed to have been taken by Stephen Ward to various bacchanalian Belgravia parties at which, as described above, a naked slave served
dinner dressed only in a black mask; according to popular gossip, this man
was in fact a senior minister. Lord Denning evidently decided that this was
worth investigating and actually interviewed both the hostess of the infamous parties and several guests, declaring himself satisfied that the girls had
indeed attended 'perverted sex orgies; that the man in the mask is a "slave"
who is whipped; that the guests undress and indulge in sexual intercourse
one with the other; and indulge in other sexual activities of a vile and revolting nature'. The trail eventually led to the man in the mask himself, who
told Denning that he was 'grievously ashamed of what he did', but, perhaps
disappointingly, he turned out not to be a Cabinet minister at all.[146]

One story, however, did pose a genuine threat to Macmillan's survival. For more than three years a particularly lurid legal case, in which the eleventh Duke of Argyll was attempting to divorce his errant wife, had been illuminating the Edinburgh courts, to the immense entertainment of newspaper readers across the nation. The Duke had already cited four different co-respondents, but his lawyers claimed that they could have picked any four from a cast of dozens. The case had reached its conclusion at the beginning of April, when Lord Wheatley delivered an epic summing-up lasting almost five hours during which he had described the Duchess as 'a completely promiscuous woman whose sexual appetite could only be satisfied by a number of men'.[147] There could hardly have been a more fitting example of the decadence popularly attributed to the ruling elite of Macmillan's Britain. What was more, during the Argyll proceedings the Duke's barrister had at one point produced a Polaroid photograph allegedly showing the Duchess, naked apart from a string of pearls, performing oral sex on an unidentified man at an orgy. It was impossible to recognise her lover for the simple reason that his head was not in the shot, although the rest of his unclothed body certainly was, and he therefore, rather unfairly, entered posterity as 'The Headless Man' or 'The Man Without a Head'. During the next two months the salacious details of the Argyll divorce became generally confused with the Profumo case, so by the beginning of June it was popularly agreed that the Duchess had been part of the same orgiastic set as Ward and Keeler. By the time of the Commons debate on the Profumo affair, Fleet Street gossip had identified the headless man as the Commonwealth Secretary, Duncan Sandys.[148]

Gossip alone was no great threat to Macmillan's premiership. The problem, however, was that although Sandys was certainly not the headless man, he *had* been having an affair with the Duchess; what was worse, he had also been something of a libertine in earlier days. When he heard that rumour placed him in the Polaroid photograph, Sandys decided that he had to resign, and indeed he came to a Cabinet meeting two days after the debate with his resignation letter already written. A second sex scandal following so quickly after the Profumo debate would have been a disaster for the government and probably fatal for the Prime Minister. In the event, Macmillan persuaded Sandys to reconsider, and they agreed that Lord Denning would address the issue in his report.[149] The stories, Denning concluded, 'were entirely without foundation'.[150] Privately, however, he was well aware that Sandys and the Duchess had been having an affair, as his own notes on the case attest.[151] Denning also felt compelled to write to Macmillan with the news that two additional rumours appeared to be true. One minister, whom Richard Lamb identifies as Ernest Marples, the Minister of Transport, had been carrying on with prostitutes; another, who remains anonymous, had attended a homosexual party three years earlier and 'there participated in homosexual conduct'. As with the full details of the Sandys–Argyll liaison, these stories were suppressed and did not appear in the final report.[152] What did make the report was the revelation that Sandys, who was not named, had submitted himself to a doctor for examination in order to prove that his 'physical characteristics' were not those of the headless man. Bernard Levin was not alone in finding it utterly extraordinary that 'almost exactly two-thirds of the way through the twentieth century, and in a country as advanced as Britain . . . a judge should have been obliged to ask a doctor to examine the penis of a politician'.[153]

If Denning had been more candid about the Sandys and Marples affairs in his report, it is likely that the Prime Minister would have been forced to resign. On the other hand, it is difficult to see why Denning felt it necessary to delve into every nook and cranny of the ministers' private lives. His brief was to examine the implications of the Profumo scandal for national security, but these relatively minor goings-on had nothing to do with the defence of the realm. There was, needless to say, nothing new about prominent politicians having turbulent or colourful love lives, from Asquith and Lloyd George to Gaitskell and Macleod. The difference in 1963 was that the press and popular opinion had been seized by a spirit of hysterical excitement about sexual misbehaviour, and instead of ignoring the phenomenon, the Macmillan government itself fell under its spell. Enoch Powell compared the mood to the South Sea Bubble, 'a collective state of mind' of 'credulity, alarm, excitement' that bore no relation to 'particular events'.[154] *Private Eye* printed a cartoon by William Rushton entitled 'Romantic England', showing a nondescript, bespectacled man peering nervously out from the Clapham omnibus at the orgy of debauchery and vice that surrounds him.[155] Even Tony Benn confided in his diary: 'This is quite mad. I am terrified that George Wigg will be made Minister of Security and given power over all our lives.'[156] Stories of Conservative sleaze were eagerly anticipated and exchanged: one particularly bizarre and trivial example, reported in the *Express* in July, was the case of the local party agent in Wokingham, who had ordered the teenage treasurer of the Young Conservatives to remove his trousers and be beaten with a fly-swatter after a disappointing report from Central Office. 'The trousers were removed without question', it was explained, 'because Mr Gillman [the treasurer] thought it was a test of character.'[157]

It seems hardly likely that most people took stories of this insignificance very seriously. The real problem, however, was that Macmillan himself, having already been personally hurt and betrayed by Profumo's admission of guilt, had been swept up in the hysteria of the press. Shortly after the Commons debate he called in Iain Macleod, the party chairman, and as the latter recalled: 'He was in a terrible state, going on about a rumour of there having been eight High Court judges involved in some orgy. "One," he said, "perhaps two, conceivably. But eight – I just can't believe it." I said if you don't believe it, why bother with an inquiry? But he replied, "No. Terrible things are being said. It must be cleared up."'[158]

While Macmillan was busy working himself into a lather about judges at orgies, the police investigation into the Profumo affair was winding towards its close. Lucky Gordon, whose unconventional if voluble defence had not saved him from conviction, had already been sentenced to three years' imprisonment.[159] On 22 July an even more sensational courtroom drama opened: the trial of Stephen Ward for living on the earnings of prostitution. Although it was very doubtful whether the charges could be made to stick, the police had evidently succumbed to the same excess of excitement and enthusiasm that animated the general public; they had interviewed almost 140 people, and questioned Keeler alone on thirty-eight separate occasions.[160] The proceedings were held at the Old Bailey, the explanation being that only such a grand venue could cope with the enormous press and popular interest. Scores of photographers jostled for position in the streets outside; crowds harangued the witnesses as they came and went; and hundreds queued for the public gallery. Both Christine Keeler and Mandy Rice-Davies testified against their former mentor, joining two other girls, Ronna Ricardo and Vickie Barrett, who admitted that they had worked as prostitutes. The jury were regaled with various accounts of orgies, whippings and general licentiousness, and the picture of Ward that emerged from the proceedings was distinctly unfavourable. The notion of a wealthy fifty-year-old man occasionally having sex with naive sixteen-year-old girls did not impress many observers, and the prosecuting barrister, Mervyn Griffith Jones, was not far off the mark when he branded Ward 'a thoroughly filthy fellow'.[161] On the other hand, the eight-day trial did not prove by any means that Ward had benefited from the earnings of his girls; in fact it appeared that quite the opposite had been the case: that in fact *they* had taken money from him. Still, thanks to a clever performance from Griffith Jones, who emphasised moral turpitude rather than financial gain, and an exceptionally hostile summing-up from the judge, it looked very likely that Ward would be serving a term in prison.

On 30 July the disgraced osteopath left the courtroom with the judge's summing-up still unfinished and spent the evening writing twelve letters, before taking an overdose of Nembutal sleeping pills. 'The horror, day after day at the court and in the streets,' he wrote in one of his suicide notes. 'It's a wish not to let them get me. I'd rather get myself – I do hope I haven't let people down too much. I tried to do my stuff.' He was found the following morning and taken to hospital in a deep coma; in the meantime, at the Old Bailey, the jury found him guilty on the two counts relating to Keeler and Rice-Davies. He never regained consciousness and died on 3 August.[162] At his funeral a week later, there were only six mourners. Twenty-one writers and artists, including John Osborne, Kenneth Tynan and Joe Orton, sent a wreath of white roses with the legend: 'To Stephen Ward, a victim of British hypocrisy'.[163] A rather different verdict, and one probably more in tune with public opinion, came from the *News of the World*, which called him 'a central figure of evil, a lying mischief-maker' who associated with 'lying whores, frightened scrubbers, irresponsible little tarts' and 'did not have the guts to face his nemesis'.[164] Certainly it suited the interests of Macmillan's critics in the artistic avant-garde to celebrate Ward as the representative of freedom and pleasure, brutally repressed by a puritanical political elite. But Ward was no martyr, whatever the weaknesses of his conviction. He had for years used his social connections to cultivate and exploit a succession of vulnerable young girls, many of whom were fleeing deprived or abusive backgrounds. Although he was cruelly deserted in the summer of 1963 by his upper-class friends and intelligence contacts, it seems ludicrous, not to say hypocritical, to remember him as a sacrificial victim when the real victims in the case were the girls he had trained.

Ward's unhappy death effectively marked the end of the Profumo scandal, and within weeks the newspapers had hit on a new subject to entertain the public: the story of the Great Train Robbery. At almost exactly the same moment, Macmillan's poll ratings began slowly to improve. He had ridden out the worst of the storm; indeed, by the end of June, the Conservatives had recovered much of the ground they had lost since Profumo's resignation. They were still well behind Labour, of course, but then they had been behind for months irrespective of this particular scandal. During July, when the Philby affair and Ward's trial were competing for attention, surveys suggested that the public mood was fickle and undecided. Labour still commanded a hefty lead, but it differed enormously from poll to poll, with NOP estimating it at 8 per cent and Gallup at 20 per cent; at the same time, there was a remarkably high proportion of 'Don't know' answers.[165]

The first week of August, however, brought good news for Macmillan. He had just returned from a trip to Moscow, where he had successfully negotiated a nuclear test-ban treaty that was to remain one of his finest diplomatic accomplishments, and as the public lost interest in Keeler, Ward and the motley cast of characters who had been entertaining them for months, so they also began to reconsider their hostility to the Conservatives. On 2 August the *Daily Mail* announced that Labour's lead had shrunk to 6 per cent, its lowest level for many months, and Macmillan jubilantly recorded the news as 'a tremendous swing back to us'.[166] He was, wrote his press officer Harold Evans, 'jauntily and firmly back in the saddle', his backbench critics silenced and the voters beginning once again to heed his appeals.[167] There was no new scandal to interrupt his comeback. On 17 September Denning finally produced his report. One paragraph criticised Macmillan and his ministers for failing to deal with Profumo earlier: but that was all. MI5 escaped censure, and the police were only mildly criticised for not having taken a complete statement from Keeler in the New Year. Even Harold Wilson privately remarked that 'there wasn't much in it', by which, Macmillan noted gleefully, 'he meant "not much in it for me"'.[168] The report was duly published by the Stationery Office, and such was the public interest that a mob assembled on the day of publication, fighting to get hold of a copy. More than 100,000 copies were allegedly sold in the first day alone, a record worthy of the most sensational paperback bestseller.[169] The style was unusually informal for a government report, and even the chapter headings evoked the world of cheap crime thrillers: 'Christine Tells Her Story', 'The Slashing and Shooting', '"He's a Liar"', 'Mr Profumo's Disarming Answer' and so on. There was, nevertheless, nothing very sensational in it. Macmillan was safe. 'All day long came messages of congratulation,' he recorded the day after it had gone on general sale.[170]

*

John Profumo never returned to politics after resigning his seat in June 1963. Instead he unfailingly shunned the limelight and became involved in social work, cleaning and washing up for three days a week at Toynbee Hall, an institution in East London for alcoholics, drug addicts and the homeless. In 1975 he became the chairman of the institution and was awarded the CBE for services to charity. If it was not the life he had once expected, it was nevertheless a useful, creditable and rewarding one. Christine Keeler, by contrast, did not lead a very happy existence after 1963; as one account puts it, her life was 'a trail of dole queues and broken marriages', council flats and recriminations.[171]

Many historians play down the importance of the scandal in which these individuals played the leading roles. Gilmour and Garnett, for example, call it 'utterly trivial', while Pimlott comments on its 'puzzling triviality'.[172] Other writers exaggerate its impact. Weight claims that it 'undermined conservative attempts to contain postwar affluence within a prewar moral framework' and destroyed the 'moral authority' of 'Britain's ruling elites'. 'Henceforth,' he writes, 'Britons would not care to be lectured about their sexual habits; nor would they welcome any attempt by the state to prevent these habits being freely enjoyed.'[173] But this is clearly nonsense. Most people's sexual morality did not in fact change a great deal between 1963 and 1970, while any attempt to quantify so woolly a concept as the 'moral authority' of the political elite is doomed to failure.[174] For much of the rest of the century, sexual behaviour remained restricted by legislation and custom, just as it was in other societies and in other periods; the Profumo affair did not therefore mark some startling transition to an age of self-indulgent freedom. Philip Larkin may, famously, have written that 'Sexual intercourse began / In nineteen sixty-three', but in this case he is not a very good guide.[175]

The importance of the Profumo affair was not that it brought a profound revolution in sexual habits and attitudes, and neither did it herald the end of deference. Instead, it brought to a head existing anxieties about post-war social and cultural change and crystallised the growing public discontent with the Macmillan government. It was not an isolated scandal; it was the last in a series of spy scandals, all of which had been related by contemporary observers to wider issues like homosexuality, materialism and political nepotism. *The Times*, for instance, treated this latest case as the final proof of the corruption and decadence of the affluent society, explaining on 4 July that it summed up the 'tawdry cynicism' of Macmillan's government. 'The kind of affluence that all too much of Conservatism has seemed to encourage', it argued, 'has been the pursuit of money for its own sake, the acquisition of wealth with the least effort and by whatever means are handiest, the jealous protection of capital gains at a time of firm control of wages, the rewarding of smartness instead of industry.'[176] The popular impact of the scandal, in short, was so great precisely because it appeared to confirm so dramatically everything that Macmillan's critics, from Labour frontbenchers to BBC satirists, had already been saying for months. Pimlott suggests that 'no real issue existed'; it might be more accurate to say that the 'real issue' behind all the colourful incident of the Profumo scandal was simply the state of the nation in the age of affluence.[177]

What this meant was that, with the election now just twelve months away, the government was still in deep trouble. For month after month the crisis had monopolised the attention of the Cabinet, and they had never really developed a new strategy after the humiliating shock of de Gaulle's veto. Rab Butler recorded privately that, despite their minor rally in the opinion polls, the party was 'in a very bad way'. 'It will be with the utmost difficulty', he wrote, 'that we will recapture the high ground.'[178] The Prime Minister, meanwhile, had survived, but he was badly wounded. Nigel Birch's quotation from Browning – 'Never glad confident morning again!' – was perhaps more appropriate than he realised. Macmillan was tired after almost seven years of hard work in Downing Street, and the succession of setbacks since the last election had drained his energy and self-confidence. The image of the doddery old Edwardian had always been something of a front, but by the autumn of 1963 many of his colleagues thought he seemed strikingly older, wearier and lonelier than before.[179] The references in Macmillan's diary to age and ill health become more frequent after July 1962, when he sacked so many old friends in the Night of the Long Knives. He was, he admitted later, beginning 'to get very tired . . . to lose grip . . . much more fatigue'; probably these were the early symptoms of the disease that was shortly to strike.[180] Not surprisingly, therefore, the calls coming from *The Times* and the *Sunday Telegraph* for him to step down were still playing on his mind. On 16 August he wrote that he was planning to spend a few days during his holiday thinking 'seriously and serenely, out of the turmoil of House of Commons and all the rest, about my own future'. The choice, as he saw it, was between 'a) *resigning* in week before Parliament meets – about October 22nd or so; b) going on and fighting election and saying so at Conference'.[181]

Macmillan spent the last two weeks of August relaxing in Yorkshire, but when he returned to London he had still not made up his mind. With his wife away in Scotland, he sat alone in Downing Street, brooding sadly on the drama of the summer and the uncertain future that awaited him. On 5 September he unburdened himself in his diary:

> . . . I cannot go on to an election and lead in it. I am beginning to feel that I haven't the strength and that perhaps another leader could do what I did after Eden left. But it cannot be done by a pedestrian politician. It needs a man with vision and moral strength – Hailsham, not Maudling. Yet the 'back benchers' (poor fools) do not seem to have any idea, except a 'young man'. Admirable as Maudling is, I doubt if he could revive our fortunes as well as Hailsham. (I sent H. to Moscow on purpose, to test his powers of negotiation etc. He did *very* well.)[182]

For the next few weeks, Macmillan vacillated, swinging first one way and then the other. He wrote to the Queen to tell her that he had not yet decided his future; he told Butler and Lord Home that he was thinking of retiring; and he went over the alternatives again and again in his diary. On 21 September, chatting to two close advisers at Chequers, he came to an 'irreversible decision' to retire just before the party conference in the second week of October; but then he began to have more doubts.[183] The Denning Report, which largely exonerated him of responsibility for the Profumo shambles, had set off a wave of affection for him in the Conservative shires, and at the same time the succession was looking increasingly complicated, with Maudling, the favourite for much of the year, losing ground to Hailsham and Butler. At the beginning of October Macmillan told his son Maurice that he was planning to retire, but the following night he lay awake thinking about the problems his resignation would cause:

> There are so many factors – the chief one being that there is *no* clear successor. But there is a growing wave of emotion in my favour, throughout the Party, especially the Party in the provinces. This will be evidenced at Blackpool. I have written the actual speech – leaving six or seven minutes at the end for the personal bit – to go or to stay? I *hate* the feeling that I shall be letting down all these loyal people. On the other hand, I shall probably be humiliated if I stay and people will say that failure has been due to the old limpet . . . [184]

Early on Monday 7 October he drove from his country house to London, still nowhere near a decision. His advisers assured him that the Cabinet would back him if he stayed, and both the Lord Chancellor and Chief Whip promised to champion his cause. In the afternoon he met the co-chairman of the party, Oliver Poole, and admitted that he was now beginning to think of staying after all. Macmillan explained that if he resigned it might look as though he was 'deserting' or giving in to a 'group of malcontents' with 'reactionary sentiments'; he would also, he thought, 'leave the Party in complete disarray', divided between the competing factions of Butler, Maudling and Hailsham. Later he met another group of senior colleagues, who confirmed that if he wanted to lead the party into the next election the Cabinet would stand by him. The balance had finally, decisively, tilted in favour of staying, and late that night Macmillan wrote in his diary that he was 'determined to inform the Cabinet that I had now decided to stay on and fight the General Election and to ask for the full support of my colleagues'.[185] He had not slept for two nights, but his mind, at last, was made up, and he retired to bed tired but satisfied. Little did he know that within a few hours, everything was to change.

THE MAGIC CIRCLE

In the autumn tranquillity of his days, while the golden leaves fall silently to the ground, an old man, his faithful wife by his side, sits peacefully in the park, happy in the knowledge of a lifetime's work well done, a country served and an old colleague stabbed ruthlessly in the back . . .

Private Eye, 1 November 1963

In the early hours of 8 October 1963, Macmillan awoke, gripped by 'an excruciating pain' in his bladder. 'I was seized by terrible spasms,' he wrote later, 'but no water emerged. Dorothy came to my help and got a doctor.' His regular physician, Sir John Richardson, was on holiday, but by four in the morning a locum, Dr King-Lewis, had been summoned and managed temporarily to relieve the Prime Minister's discomfort by inserting a device to drain water from his bladder. By breakfast time, however, the pain was even worse than before, and King-Lewis assured Macmillan that he would arrange for him to be seen immediately by Alec Badenoch, the most distinguished surgeon and urologist in the business.[1] Somehow Macmillan managed to dress, compose himself and stumble downstairs to the Cabinet Room, where his ministers were due to arrive at ten for their first full meeting in almost a month. So began what Anthony Howard calls 'one of the most dramatic days in the history of modern British Government', and the opening day of a ten-day crisis with a strong claim to be the most exciting political drama since the war.[2]

Macmillan's illness was very obvious to his ministers. At one point a Downing Street aide brought in a glass of milky medicine – although, since the Prime Minister was a notorious hypochondriac, this was not necessarily a sign of anything untoward. Still, he looked dreadfully pale and frail, and had to leave the meeting twice when the spasms became too much to bear. Butler was even moved to offer him a Valium.[3] At noon, Macmillan cut short the lengthy discussion and announced that he had made up his mind about his political future. He did not, however, express himself very clearly, no doubt because of the severe pain of his condition; so all that he actually said was that 'there has to be a decision and I shall announce it at Blackpool'. He then left the room, obviously still in great discomfort, to allow the Cabinet to discuss his decision. Lord Hailsham, as voluble and impulsive as ever, emotionally called after him: 'Prime Minister, wherever you go, you know our hearts go with you.' Most ministers were simply bewildered by these scenes, but, according to the Chief Whip, all except the character-istically unconventional Enoch Powell were agreed that Macmillan should stay on and that they would back him.[4] There was very little time for debate, however, for the purely practical reason that most of them were due to catch a special train at half past one from Euston to Blackpool for the party conference. Lord Dilhorne, the Lord Chancellor, added that if Macmillan did for some reason decide to step down, then he would be very happy to organise the soundings to find a successor, as his predecessor Lord Kilmuir had done in 1957. At that the Foreign Secretary, Lord Home, declared that since he would in no circumstances himself be a candidate, he would be glad to help. All of those present, therefore, assumed that Dilhorne and Home would be the umpires in any putative contest. None imagined that the Foreign Secretary might be a candidate after all: in the light of later events, his intervention was both a moral mistake and a tactical masterstroke.[5]

At this stage, Macmillan had no intention of going back on his plans, and still hoped to make his set-piece speech in Blackpool on Saturday 12 October, four days away. 'I had no reason to think (from what Dr. King-Lewis had said) that my trouble would be very serious,' he noted. 'He hoped that normal passing of water might be re-established in a few hours. Any treatment of a more radical character would be perhaps avoided or postponed.'[6] At lunchtime, however, Badenoch, the surgeon, made his entrance and imme-diately told the Prime Minister that he was suffering from inflammation of the prostate gland, probably caused by a benign tumour, and that he needed an early operation. Always a nervous man, Macmillan panicked, and by the late afternoon, when his personal physician, Sir John Richardson, arrived at Downing Street having thundered down from the Lake District at alarming speed, he had got it into his head that he could not carry on as Prime Minister. Horne suggests that Richardson's absence was crucial, since he might have persuaded Macmillan that he could continue in his duties after a short absence of 'three to four weeks'. Richardson himself later mused: 'Yes, if I had been there on that critical day, I think he would have gone on – there was absolutely no medical alternative, but the pass had already been sold.' Indeed, on 14 October he prepared a memorandum to that effect, suggesting that Macmillan could 'lead the party in six weeks time and . . . do the work of the Premier at Downing Street within a few days of his return'.[7] The implication of all this is that King-Lewis and Badenoch, two doctors unknown to Macmillan, had essentially terrified him into resignation; as the patient himself put it afterwards, he would have happily stayed on as Prime Minister 'if the doctors hadn't frightened me that it looked possibly "malignant"'.[8] This was, however, grossly unfair. Badenoch always took care to emphasise that the tumour was benign and that the Prime Minister could expect to recover his faculties, his vigour and his full capacity to govern. Macmillan did *not*, contrary to political myth, resign because his personal physician happened to be away at a crucial moment and because two overawed doctors exaggerated his condition. He resigned because he had been undecided for months, was now under sudden and enormous strain, and had therefore convinced himself to do so. Badenoch's son, himself a consultant urologist, wrote some twenty years later that his father had been struck by Macmillan's 'great relief that he had reason to leave the political crises that he faced. He termed this "an act of God".'[9]

By the early evening, by his own account in 'excruciating pain' and embarrassment, Macmillan was, quite understandably, swinging between the utmost gloom and the delusion that somehow he could still address the party conference at the weekend. At seven o'clock the three doctors met and agreed that he must go immediately to hospital for an operation in two days' time. Macmillan called his staff and his deputy, Butler, who had remained in London, into his study.[10] The Prime Minister was eccentrically dressed in a dressing gown with the colours of the Guards over pale-blue pyjamas and a scruffy brown cardigan, and was in a wild, melodramatic mood. Harold Evans, his press secretary, later remembered:

> I told him what I proposed to say in the announcement, and then posed the critical question I would have to answer, 'does this mean the PM will resign?' Was it unfeeling? Walking up and down by the windows, in the half-light of the table lamp, he threw up his arms in a dramatic gesture. 'Of course I am finished. Perhaps I shall die. You can say that it is quite clear that I shall be unable to fight the election.' I asked, did he *really* want that to be said? He said 'Yes,' and so I went away to rejig the draft.

Butler greeted the revelation with his usual lazy nonchalance. He 'seemed rather surprised', wrote Evans, 'and said surely this was going rather far, but shrugged his shoulders'.[11] Two hours later, having made his momentous decision, Macmillan left for the hospital. At ten the BBC reported the news of his forthcoming operation and the Cabinet Secretary ordered that all Prime Ministerial correspondence be sent to Butler. 'MAC IN HOSPITAL' declared the *Daily Mail* the following morning. Memories are, however, short in politics. Within a few hours, all the talk was not of the old leader in King Edward's Hospital, but of the increasingly hysterical scenes at the conference in Blackpool. The early-afternoon edition of the *Evening Standard* caught the mood: 'TORIES ON THE BOIL: CRISIS OVER THE LEADERSHIP HEADS FOR SHOWDOWN'.[12]

Macmillan himself spent the following day, Wednesday 9 October, tucked up miserably in bed in the hospital, writing up his diary and reading the first book of Samuel. His role in the drama, however, was far from over. Lord Home had not yet left for Blackpool with most of his colleagues, and that morning he paid a call to the stricken Macmillan. There was nothing particularly conspiratorial about his visit: the two men were old friends, after all, and Home was one of the Cabinet members closest in age to his leader. The discussion turned to Macmillan's intended resignation. He had already prepared a secret, draft letter to Butler, which he now showed to his Foreign Secretary:

SECRET AND PERSONAL
DRAFT LETTER TO MR BUTLER

As you know, I am going into Hospital for some weeks to have an operation for prostate trouble. This blow to my health has made me decide that I should, when I am well enough to see The Queen, resign my position as Prime Minister and Leader of the Party. I do not propose to announce this decision at this stage. But I should be grateful if you and any Ministers whom you care to consult would decide how best to apply this decision to resolving the problems which we have discussed, both in relation to the Party Conference at Blackpool and the succession.[13]

Home thought that the letter was a mistake: it would, he said, only encourage more and more feverish speculation. He had long been urging Macmillan to stand aside and make way for a younger man, and now he redoubled his efforts. Macmillan ought to announce his retirement immediately to the party conference. As it happened, quite by coincidence, Home was serving as the President of the National Union of Conservative and Unionist Associations: he could therefore carry a letter from the Prime Minister to the conference announcing the news. This idea went down very well, the secret letter to Butler was cast aside, and one of Macmillan's aides immediately set about preparing a draft letter for Home to read out on either Thursday or Friday. An apparently minor decision, this was in fact one of the central turning points of an exceptionally intricate political crisis. If Macmillan had waited until after the conference to announce his resignation, as his letter to Butler envisaged, then the whirlwind of political intrigue would have been centred on the Cabinet and the Commons, where Maudling and, in particular, Butler commanded considerable strength. With the announcement being made in the middle of a party conference already drunk with speculation, the effect was instead to turn the proceedings into 'the nearest British equivalent of an American presidential convention', which undoubtedly promoted the interests of the two peers, Hailsham and Home, who were both popular with the local associations. For Butler above all, this was an unfortunate development, and he later discreetly complained that Home had rushed 'a wounded and sick man to make such [an important] decision at such a febrile time'.[14]

In the meantime, the Imperial Hotel in Blackpool was rapidly becoming a bear-pit. Butler had arrived on Wednesday afternoon and, with unusual resolution, immediately insisted that as the acting Prime Minister he be put up in the grand suite booked for Macmillan. He then summoned the chief officers of the National Union and demanded that they invite him to address the annual rally on the forthcoming Saturday in lieu of the stricken leader. In the evening the other Cabinet ministers in Blackpool gathered in Butler's suite and were persuaded to agree that he could accept the invitation; very few of them, at this point, realised that Macmillan had taken the decision to resign, but it was already apparent that Butler was positioning himself to take over in the event of a vacancy.[15] Hailsham, one of the other obvious candidates for the succession, had already received a rapturous reception in the conference hall, but was still unaware of Macmillan's intentions. That evening, he delivered a bravura speech to a crowd in Morecambe, ending with the emotional message:

Some of us have been with Mr Macmillan since the beginning of his premiership in 1957. We love our political chief. Now that he has been stricken down by illness, our love and sympathy go out to him and Lady Dorothy all the more . . .

Harold, get well quick . . . And when we come back we will hand back to you a Government and a party in good order.[16]

In fact, Macmillan went under the knife the following morning. The operation was a complete success; but there was to be no retraction of his decision to resign.[17] Home was already bound, by aeroplane, for Blackpool with the Prime Minister's message in his pocket. For two days rumours had been swirling around the Imperial Hotel and the Winter Gardens, and by the time the Foreign Secretary arrived, late on Thursday afternoon, the central platform was packed with anxious party grandees. John Boyd-Carpenter, who was in the middle of delivering a convoluted speech about local government finance, was persuaded to yield the microphone, and donning a pair of old-fashioned half-moon spectacles, Home stepped forward to unleash his bombshell. He announced that he had visited the Prime Minister in hospital and had been asked to read out his letter 'as soon as I could after arriving in Blackpool'. Then, slowly, peering through his glasses, he read Macmillan's letter:

I should be very grateful if you would tell the conference assembled at Blackpool, of which you are President, how sorry I am not to be with them this week . . .

It is now clear that, whatever might have been my previous feelings, it will not be possible for me to carry the physical burden of leading the Party at the next General Election . . . Nor could I hope to fulfil the tasks of Prime Minister for any extended period, and I have so informed the Queen.

In these circumstances I hope that it will soon be possible for the customary processes of consultation to be carried on within the party about its future leadership.[18]

The assembled ministers on the dais sat in stunned silence. It was, Home remarked as he put down the letter, 'a moment of sadness and deep emotion for all Conservatives'.[19]

Now the race was on. As one reporter noted, the atmosphere of 'the canvassing, the hourly shifting in the betting, the mood of fatal self-induced excitement' was reminiscent of 'a fireworks display that gets bigger and better as it goes along, and in the end no one knew where to turn for certainty'.[20] The mixture of personalities concerned made it all the more exciting. 'There are three probable contenders in the succession,' insisted the outspoken backbencher Sir Gerald Nabarro: 'Mr Butler: donnish, dignified and dull. Lord Hailsham: ebullient, erudite and erratic. Mr Maudling: manly, matey and money-wise.'[21] According to a Gallup poll published in the *Telegraph* that morning, Butler was the choice of 14 per cent of the public, followed by Hailsham and Maudling, both on 10 per cent. Heath, Macleod, Selwyn Lloyd and Home brought up the rear, while almost half of the respondents admitted that they had no opinion. Conservative voters expressed a marginal preference for Hailsham (18 per cent) over Butler (15 per cent) and Maudling (11 per cent), with Home languishing (3 per cent).[22] The *Mirror*, meanwhile, was offering bookmakers' odds, with Butler the favourite at 6–4 on, Hailsham at 7–4, Maudling at 6–1 and Home at 10–1. As far as the country was concerned, it was a two-horse contest: as in 1957, Butler was the clear favourite, well ahead of Viscount Hailsham.[23]

As members of the House of Lords, neither Hailsham nor Home would have been plausible candidates for the leadership had not an entirely coincidental development forced a change in the law. In 1960, Anthony Wedgwood Benn had inherited the title of Viscount Stansgate from his late father, but, since he wanted to remain in the House of Commons, he simply refused to accept it. His Bristol seat was declared vacant; he contested the by-election anyway, and eventually won it back. After a long campaign by Benn and his allies, the government had finally passed the Peerage Act at the end of July 1963, allowing hereditary peers to disclaim their titles and stand for election to Parliament. Neither Hailsham nor Home had taken advantage of the change in the law, but both were now perfectly at liberty to do so. In the climate of 1963 it was unthinkable that the Prime Minister could sit in the House of Lords; it was only by the oddest of historical quirks, therefore, that Hailsham and Home were candidates at all.[24]

Quintin Hailsham had good reason to think himself Macmillan's preferred candidate. In September, as already explained, Macmillan had confided to his diary the opinion that the party needed 'a man with vision and moral strength – Hailsham, not Maudling', and he had been toying with the idea of Hailsham as his successor for several months before that.[25] According to Hailsham himself, Macmillan had actually called him in at the beginning of that very week and given him formal notification 'that he wished me to succeed him'.[26] What is beyond dispute is that on 9 October, lying stricken in his hospital bed, Macmillan had called in his son Maurice and son-in-law Julian Amery, both Conservative MPs, and ordered them to go north 'and make sure that they get Quintin in'. From the very beginning of the conference, then, Macmillan's emissaries were working behind the scenes for Hailsham.[27]

Hailsham was a mischievous, warm, dynamic man who often seemed to cultivate the image of a clown. As one commentator puts it, he left the impression of 'a slight derangement of temperament forever barring a clever man from being taken altogether seriously'.[28] This was based not merely on Hailsham's behaviour during the Profumo affair, but also his antics while chairman of the party, especially during the 1957 conference. On this occasion, he had delighted journalists by appearing on Brighton beach in the ludicrous apparel of a dressing gown, old-fashioned bathing suit, snorkel and flippers, and then diving into the sea; to make matters worse, he had then decided that it would be a good idea to swing a bell furiously over his head at the end of his conference address, accompanied by various quips about the bell tolling for the Labour Party. He later admitted that these incidents had done his career little good, since the press 'had positively revelled in representing me as an ambitious and self-advertising buffoon', forgetting what he called 'my serious academic background in politics, classics, ancient history, philosophy and law, [and] my devotion to my church and society'.[29]

At heart, indeed, Quintin Hailsham (originally Quintin Hogg) was a serious and intelligent man: a prize fellow of All Souls, a talented barrister, a civilised and progressive politician, and a committed Christian, as was revealed in two painfully frank volumes of autobiography.[30] Macmillan had a soft spot for Hailsham, who had discovered his first wife in bed with a French officer when he returned from the war, a situation not unlike the Prime Minister's own unhappy domestic arrangements. 'One of the finest men I knew,' Macmillan mused in later years, 'a big man, a great churchgoer, and an idealist. But he didn't always do himself justice; there was an excess of boyishness.'[31] He also recognised that the dynamic Hailsham, despite his occasional 'absurdities and posturings and emotions', was the one potential leader who could really compete with Harold Wilson. 'He belongs *both* to this strange modern age of space and science', Macmillan wrote, '*and* to the great past – of classical learning and Christian life.'[32]

In the excitement of the moment, Hailsham now let his natural zeal get the better of him. Julian Amery, recently arrived from his father-in-law's bedside, instructed him urgently to 'act at once', which tallied with the advice of close friends like Oliver Poole that he must immediately disclaim his peerage and declare for the leadership.[33] Shortly after Home's dramatic announcement to the conference, Hailsham was due to give the annual lecture to the Conservative Political Centre, a group which was meeting in the Winter Gardens and looking forward to a highbrow, thoughtful occasion. Hailsham duly arrived, in a state of considerable tension, and delivered a long prepared talk about Conservatism. Then, when replying to the vote of thanks, buoyed by applause and shouts from the audience of 'Declare yourself!' he veered abruptly from his script. 'I shall continue to serve the country honourably,' he proclaimed enthusiastically, 'but I wish to say tonight that it is my intention to disclaim my peerage.' At that the crowd started chanting 'We want Hailsham!' and in his own words, 'the whole audience, and the platform, went mad, standing, cheering and waving in the full light of the national television'. 'If I can find anyone to receive me as a candidate to stand for Parliament I shall do so,' he continued over the noise. The crowd began to sing 'For he's a jolly good fellow', and some surged chanting on to the streets of Blackpool, swept up by the enthusiasm of their candidate.[34] Exuberant, even raucous scenes of this kind were entirely unknown in the staid world of Conservative Party conferences. The press, of course, were delighted. 'ENTER MR HOGG' read the headline in the *Express*, while *The Times* carried the entire text of his speech.[35] Many influential older Tories, however, did not like it at all. On the platform that night, according to one account, 'Geoffrey Lloyd appeared livid; Keith Joseph embarrassed; Toby Aldington, William Rees-Mogg and Peter Goldman all embarrassed; Peter Thorneycroft supportive; Martin Redmayne, Chief Whip, stony and prefectorial, clearly not best pleased; Michael Fraser rather embarrassed.'[36]

What was more, on the following day, with Hailsham basking in the publicity of his reception, the perennially irresponsible and well-oiled Randolph Churchill pitched up from the United States with a consignment of specially printed badges, each bearing an enormous 'Q' for Quintin, which he distributed to friend and foe alike. 'He came up to my room and obligingly handed me some for my wife, myself and my friends,' Butler dryly recalled. 'These I consigned to the waste-paper basket.'[37] The business of the badges, at least, was nothing to do with Hailsham. What was a serious error, though, was his decision to feed his baby daughter Kate in full view of those friends, fellow delegates, journalists and photographers who gathered in his room on the Friday morning. 'Some odious people subsequently tried to make out that I did this only to advertise my candidature,' he angrily wrote afterwards, and many observers were indeed shocked by this apparently shameless bid for public sympathy. In fact it was an accident, necessitated by the cramped conditions of the hotel and the general confusion and chaos in his quarters.[38] In the context not only of the previous evening but also of Hailsham's past history of clowning and self-promotion and Randolph Churchill's ubiquitous and much-detested badges, it raised serious questions about his judgement and did his cause 'untold harm'.[39] Almost as soon as Hailsham's candidacy had been launched, support began leaking away, and by the end of the conference his star was sinking fast. 'Never discount the baby food', one senior Conservative remarked years later, 'as a factor in disqualifying Hailsham.'[40]

While Hailsham was busy feeding his daughter, another serious candidate, Reginald Maudling, was launching his own bid for the leadership. For a long time, ever since his promotion to the Treasury after the Night of the Long Knives, in fact, Maudling had been tipped as the most likely successor. In January the *Sunday Pictorial* had run an admiring profile of the 'man to watch': 'He is only 45. He is fast-talking, amiable, confident, un-pompous. He gets on well with everybody from TUC delegates to Treasury officials. He can stand up to the hottest attack in the House of Commons . . . He is one of the new middle-class conservatives.'[41] Had Macmillan fallen during the Profumo crisis, Maudling would probably have replaced him. 'Of course, I'd be very glad to serve under you, Reggie,' Butler told him at one point over the summer.[42] The genial Chancellor was the candidate the Labour leadership most feared, and he was also the candidate most popular with younger Conservatives in the Commons. But by the autumn, as Maudling himself admitted, his stock had somehow fallen 'for some reason which I could not quite discern'.[43] His own particular brand of effortless intellectual ease, which often came over as sheer indolence, was not quite of the kind to whip up the troops at party conferences, and many older Tories found it hard to see him as leadership material. He had already agreed on a 'non-aggression pact' with his old friend Iain Macleod: they would not run against one another, but would work together. On the morning after Hailsham's flamboyant declaration, Maudling was scheduled to address the conference. This was his great opportunity, and Macleod offered to help him with his speech. If Maudling could rouse the delegates to their feet with a barnstorming oration, then he might be a very compelling candidate indeed. 'For God's sake, give them time to clap,' Macleod advised, 'and when you get to your peroration, belt it out with all you've got.' He even sat next to Maudling on the platform to give him moral support, and, as the Chancellor stood up to speak, Macleod whispered: 'Go on Reggie, this is your chance.'[44]

The correspondent of the *Sunday Express*, who had already seen the speech, thought that it was 'a cracker':

> It was eloquent, moving and wise. It merited the adjective statesman-like . . . I feel that given the delivery it deserved it would have brought the conference to its feet and swept Maudling to the front in the leadership race . . .
>
> If only the delivery could have matched the words.
>
> But, alas, it fell abysmally below them.
>
> Handed to Churchill, or to Macmillan, or to Macleod, this text would have produced a fine speech. Maudling himself wrecked it.[45]

Maudling later admitted that he blew his chance.[46] He was not a natural orator, and on this occasion he spoke too quickly in a passionless monotone, never really managing to catch the audience's attention. *The Times* had little sympathy:

> With the economic tide flowing the Government's way at last, and with a personal incentive as great as any man could ask for, this was surely a moment for sounding the brass. Mr Maudling had left the mute stuck in his trumpet . . .
>
> The clapping started slowly, grew to a moderate volume, and there it stuck. In an effort to get the bandwagon moving, a few of Mr Maudling's supporters on the platform, and a sparse scattering in the body of the hall, jumped to their feet and cheered. But the bulk of the conference would not be budged. They stuck to their seats and damned the Chancellor with faint praise. One by one, the Maudlingites faltered and sat down.[47]

Iain Macleod, sitting in dumb horror on the platform, was fighting back tears of frustration and disappointment. 'How could Reggie do it?' he cried in despair afterwards.[48] In the full glare of the national media, the Chancellor had thrown away a marvellous opportunity, and, minutes after he had sat down, many of his supporters were reconsidering their options.

To make matters worse, he had also been eclipsed that morning by a candidate nobody expected: Macmillan's messenger, the Earl of Home, whose speech on foreign affairs was extremely well received. Unlike Maudling, Home sounded relaxed and poised, and his reward was the biggest ovation of the conference. 'I am offering a prize to any newspaper-man this morning', he began with a smile, 'who can find a clue in my speech that this is Lord Home's bid to take over the leadership of the Conservative Party.' 'Alec, you're lying!' one of his neighbours on the platform whispered.[49]

To the public outside the Winter Gardens, the sixty-year-old Lord Home was still something of an unknown quantity. Born Alec Douglas-Home, later Lord Dunglass and finally the fourteenth Earl of Home, he had been from his schooldays onwards a popular, responsible and strikingly unassuming figure. Cyril Connolly, an Etonian contemporary and a fellow member of the school society Pop, remembered:

> The other important Pop was Alec Dunglass, who was President and also Keeper of the Field and Captain of the Eleven. He was a votary of the esoteric Eton religion, the kind of graceful, tolerant, sleepy boy who is showered with favours and crowned with all the laurels, who is liked by the masters and admired by the boys without any apparent exertion on his part, without experiencing the ill-effects of success himself or arousing the pangs of envy in others. In the eighteenth century he would have become Prime Minister before he was thirty; as it was he appeared honourably ineligible for the struggle of life.[50]

Alec Home's family owned an idyllic estate, the Hirsel, in the Lowlands and had been mixed up in most of the more colourful episodes in Scottish history. Despite his privileged background and expensive education, he always thought of himself as a Lanarkshire man: he loved shooting and fishing on the family estates, presided over local Burns clubs and Boys' Brigades, and as a young man served as a territorial officer in the Lanarkshire Yeomanry.[51] To most observers, he seemed a man of integrity, decency and seriousness: not a very inspiring character, perhaps, but one who could be relied upon to play up and play the game, the 'invaluable all-rounder of the Eton eleven'.[52]

At the age of just twenty-eight Alec Douglas-Home was elected Conservative MP for Lanark, and in the Commons, too, he proved an invaluable all-rounder. During the late thirties, while Macmillan and Eden were wrestling with their consciences, Douglas-Home had served as the loyal, unquestioning parliamentary private secretary to Neville Chamberlain. The image of the amiable duffer with which he was later lumbered, however, was unfair: a man who compiled crosswords for *The Times* could hardly have been a half-wit.[53] Not for nothing did Macmillan remark to the Queen in December 1962 that 'Alec Home is steel painted as wood.'[54] For most of the early 1940s he had been confined to bed with an extremely grim case of spinal tuberculosis, and had to spend almost two years encased in plaster. This was, of course, a nightmarish experience, but one that evidently transformed Douglas-Home from a solid mediocrity to a man of greater psychological and spiritual strength.[55] It also gave him plenty of time for reading: not merely the predictable political biography, nineteenth-century history and classic realist fiction, but also, rather incongruously, works by Marx, Engels and Lenin. He remains the only British Prime Minister known to have read *Capital* from cover to cover, and when he later came to deal with Khrushchev and Gromyko, he enjoyed showing off his almost perfect recall of the *Communist Manifesto*.[56]

In 1951 Home succeeded to his father's earldom and entered the Lords, and after a stint as Commonwealth Secretary he was surprisingly and controversially promoted to Foreign Secretary. He remained a largely anonymous figure: on his appointment in June 1960, one newspaper even referred to him as the Earl of Rome.[57] But Home's qualities soon won over the doubters. Within a few months the *News of the World* noted admiringly that he had won 'golden, nay platinum, opinions among the Western world', and Andrei Gromyko thought that if he was not brilliant, he was still pleasantly 'mild-mannered' and 'civilised'.[58] He was best known for one ill-timed miscalculation. In an interview in the *Observer* published in September 1962, Home was asked if he ever thought of becoming Prime Minister. It was an unlikely prospect, he replied with a smile. 'When I have to read economic documents I have to have a box of matches and start moving them into position to simplify and illustrate the points to myself.'[59] It was a joke, of course, but it created the defining image of Home's subsequent career: the Bertie Wooster of Downing Street, frowning over his pile of matches. In the climate of the times, with all the talk about gentlemanly amateurs and scientific professionals, it was an unfortunate mistake indeed.

Macmillan's choice of Home rather than Butler to announce his resignation to the party conference was not necessarily an accident. Throughout
the summer and early autumn of 1963 the Prime Minister had been toying
between two younger men, Maudling and Hailsham, and inclining towards
the latter. On 9 October, when Home visited him in hospital, and even
before Hailsham's explosion of enthusiasm, he changed horses once again.
After Home had persuaded him to write his resignation announcement,
Macmillan wondered aloud whether Home himself might not be the ideal
successor; perhaps he could disclaim his peerage and declare himself available? Home, it seemed, was reluctant; but Macmillan pursued the idea.[60]
Why he did so remains a slight mystery: the most likely explanation is
simply that he had never been entirely satisfied with Hailsham as his successor and simply changed his mind at the last minute, preferring an older
colleague who had been a trusted adviser in the previous two years.[61] Home,
meanwhile, had been approached as early as July by several senior backbenchers and invited to consider himself a candidate to succeed Macmillan.
For bluff knights of the shires like Major John Morrison, Sir Charles Mott-
Radcliffe and Sir Harry Legge-Bourke, the thought of a moderniser like
Maudling or Hailsham taking over was unacceptable. They were 'good, solid
citizens, hangers and floggers, who deplored what had been done in Africa
and thought the Government had moved too far to the left at home'. 'We
can't go wrong with a shooting gent,' remarked Morrison, the chairman of
the 1922 Committee. Unknown to most observers, therefore, Home had
already agreed to run as their candidate in the event of an opportunity.[62] He
did put on a show of reluctance, both at Macmillan's bedside and at the conference, but as one account has it, 'the most distinguishing feature of a
reluctant candidate is that his candidacy is more real than his reluctance'.[63]
Throughout the conference, he was quietly receiving sympathetic visitors in
his hotel room, among them Lord Dilhorne, Duncan Sandys, John Hare,
Nigel Birch and Selwyn Lloyd: an impressive collection of supporters. Lloyd
in particular was a great advocate of Home's cause, but unlike Randolph
Churchill he did not undermine his candidate by the noisy distribution of
badges, preferring instead to drop a discreet word here and there. By the
Friday morning, Home and Lloyd had successfully recruited not only the
Lord Chancellor but also the Chief Whip.[64] While his rivals – Hailsham,
Maudling and Butler – were busily eliminating themselves, his undeclared
campaign was already gaining ground. His Cabinet colleagues, meanwhile,
did not believe the rumours. They had, after all, heard Home himself, just

three days previously, offer to be an umpire for the contest, as he had no intention to stand. 'Alec has told me that he is not a candidate,' Hailsham insisted to his friends. Macleod, meanwhile, told his parliamentary private secretary: 'Don't be bloody ridiculous. That's absolutely cuckoo. Alec told us in Cabinet he wasn't a runner.'[65]

As Home sat down from delivering his address on the Friday morning, commentators on the BBC's *Gallery* programme were already identifying him as 'the man who may be drafted into the premiership to break the deadlock between Mr Butler and Lord Hailsham', while the *Daily Mail* reported that 'the chandeliers rocked with the applause for the Earl Home, in crisp fighting form'.[66] The success of Home's speech, which was not in truth a particularly outstanding effort, was itself a telling development. As Roy Jenkins wrote later: 'A politician who is applauded without deploying rhetoric is like a comedian who provokes laughter without saying anything funny. Neither can fail to succeed.'[67] The obvious contrast was with Maudling, whose spectacular failure had effectively, and rather unfairly, destroyed his remaining chances of the succession. Hailsham's cause was failing. Butler, however, was still waiting in the wings.

Although most observers considered Butler the favourite, he was conscious that he had also been the favourite in 1957. It was not enough to trade on familiarity; he had never been a great performer at party conferences, and he needed to show that he was capable of dynamic, inspirational leadership. Like Maudling, Butler was pinning his hopes on one set-piece speech, in this case the leader's address to the Saturday morning rally that marked the end of the conference. He had inherited a draft from Macmillan's speechwriters, with which he tinkered to adjust it to his own rhythms and cadences, but felt confident enough to invite Home and his wife for lunch in his suite in the Imperial Hotel an hour or so before he was due to speak. While their wives were chatting away, Home casually dropped his bombshell. He thought Rab ought to know, he said, that he would be consulting his doctor when he returned to London. Butler, who had kept aloof from the conspiratorial intrigues of the previous two days, innocently asked why, and Home replied: 'Because I have been approached about the possibility of my becoming the Leader of the Conservative Party.'[68] Either this was a deliberate attempt to throw Butler off his stride, or, more likely, it was merely supremely tactless. As Home's biographer puts it, 'it is difficult to imagine a more unsettling piece of news for Butler to receive at what was already an anxious and nervous time for him'.[69] Since their wives were present, they could hardly start arguing about it, and the pressure on Butler became even more intense when they walked to the Winter Gardens and Home, introducing him to the audience, was greeted by enthusiastic applause. Butler's address was being covered live by the BBC, which kept cutting between the Winter Gardens and the afternoon's racing from Kempton Park; but the producers of *Grandstand* would have done better to stick to the horseracing. Butler's speech was better than Maudling's, but not by much. Home's news was a bad blow to his chances and his confidence, and he never really hit his stride. Declamatory rhetoric did not come easily to him as it did to Macmillan or Hailsham, and the crowd's applause at the end was perfunctory at best. At one point he was even heckled by a member of the League of Empire Loyalists; and as Butler paused to mop his brow and gather his thoughts, Alec Home, the President of the National Union and the invaluable all-rounder, intervened to restore order.[70]

The Cabinet left Blackpool later that afternoon, and the focus of the drama therefore moved to the capital. Sunday was a day of rest and reading the newspapers. 'It's Still Anyone's Guess,' insisted the *Sunday Mirror*.[71] Randolph Churchill was still confidently predicting a straightforward victory for Hailsham, but most columnists were no longer so sure.[72] The extremely conservative *Daily Telegraph* had already noted the existence of a 'Stop Quintin' movement and offered odds of 1000–1 on a Hailsham victory.[73] According to the *Observer* 'the general impression, as the Conservative party conference broke up, was that Lord Home, the Foreign Secretary, was the most likely successor'. The *Sunday Telegraph* advised its readers that the next Prime Minister would be either 'the Earl of Home, the compromise and universally acceptable but reluctant candidate: or Viscount Hailsham, backed by powerful groups in the party hierarchy, but with some bitter opponents among some back-bench MPs and Ministers'.[74] Maudling was clearly out of the running, but Butler still found strong support in some quarters, and remained the clear favourite at Ladbrokes. 'BUTLER'S THE MAN' read the headline of the *Daily Express* on Monday morning.[75] The public still favoured Butler first and Hailsham second, with the rest languishing far behind: on 16 October, two days before the end of the contest, an opinion poll commissioned by the *Express* put Butler on 39.5 per cent, Hailsham on 21.5 per cent, Maudling on 11 per cent and Home on 9.5 per cent. Among Conservative voters alone the margin between the top two was rather closer, but there could be little doubt that, despite all the drama of the conference, Butler was still the popular choice.[76]

Harold Macmillan had spent the last days of the week under heavy sedation, but by Sunday he was drifting back into full consciousness, and as he recovered his strength, so he also rediscovered his flair for intrigue. The following day, with most of the candidates for the succession lying low in London, he received the Chief Whip and Lord Chancellor at his bedside. Both Redmayne and Dilhorne were, he recorded, 'rather upset at the rather undignified behaviour of Hogg and his supporters at Blackpool':

> It wasn't easy for him, since whenever he appeared he was surrounded by mobs of enthusiastic supporters. But it was thought that he need not have paraded the baby and the baby food in the hotel quite so blatantly or talked so much at large. This is said (by both L.C. and Chief Whip) to be turning 'respectable' people away from Hogg. Nor need he have talked so much about giving up his peerage and going into the House of Commons at this stage . . . So Hogg (who really had the game in this hand) had almost thrown it away. But the movement against Hogg (on this account) had not gone to Butler or Maudling but to Home. The 'draft' Home movement was in reality a 'Keep Out' Butler movement. I was struck by the fact that both Lord C. and Chief Whip agreed on this analysis and both are, or were, supporters of the Hogg succession. Both are against the Butler succession on the ground that the party in the country will find it depressing.[77]

Both men, of course, had already been recruited to Home's cause: it was hardly surprising that their advice therefore favoured their own man. Macmillan was certainly sorry to hear about Hailsham's self-immolation, but, since he had already switched his own allegiance to Home before the conference began, he was relieved to hear that the Foreign Secretary was gaining ground. In the evening, meanwhile, Macmillan's son Maurice came to see him with the party chairman Oliver Poole. Neither saw Home as the favourite:

> They were both calm and firm. The unlucky coincidence of my physical breakdown with Blackpool conference had created rather a shambles. But the basic situation was the same – the party in the Country wants Hogg; the Parliamentary Party wants Maudling or Butler; the Cabinet wants Butler. The last 10 days have not altered this fundamental fact.[78]

Home had, admittedly, enjoyed a good conference. But he was still a long way short of being the favourite of the Cabinet, the Commons or the party at large. Macmillan had no intention of allowing this to interfere with his plans, or of surrendering control of the Conservative Party without ensuring that his own man stood ready to replace him. As in 1957, the Prime Minister was resigning due to ill health; once again, the monarch had the prerogative to choose her own new First Lord of the Treasury from the senior ranks of the Conservative Party. The difference was that this time Macmillan fully expected to control the process himself by recommending his preferred candidate to the Queen. His position as Prime Minister allowed him not only to draw up the rules and timetable for the contest, but also to judge its outcome and report the results to Buckingham Palace.[79] That evening, he prepared a memorandum for Butler to read at Cabinet the next morning, instructing the Lord Chancellor to sound out the Cabinet, the Chief Whip to canvass the other Conservative ministers and backbenchers, and Lords St Aldwyn and Poole to report on the views of the Lords and party activists. Dilhorne and Redmayne, both Home supporters, would act as Macmillan's lieutenants in the speedy accomplishment of his design.[80]

On Tuesday 15 October, Macmillan received a stream of visitors, much to the annoyance of the redoubtable hospital matron and his wife Dorothy. Butler pottered in to see him and agreed to present his memorandum about the soundings to the Cabinet that morning. There were no complaints; in Anthony Howard's words, 'no one seems to have realised the extent to which total control of the situation had been handed to a sick, if determined, outgoing Prime Minister with a major operation only a week behind him'. Most of the Cabinet, it appears, assumed that the process would take at least a week.[81] Macmillan also made a point of summoning each of the plausible candidates: not merely Butler, Home and Hailsham, but also Maudling, Macleod and Heath. Home, belying his reputation as an amiable, unambitious mediocrity, now took the opportunity to finish off one of his rivals. He explained 'his alarm at Hailsham's behaviour at Blackpool'. He had thought, he said, that Hailsham was merely a 'show-off', but he now believed that 'the person concerned was actually mad at the time'. Not content with casting doubt on Hailsham's mental health, Home twisted the knife even further. The British ambassador in Washington had, he claimed, personally telephoned him 'in a great state to say that if Lord Hailsham was made Prime Minister this would be a tremendous blow to Anglo-American relations and would in fact end the special relationship. It was believed that the ambassador had been talking to the President.'[82] The basis for this was Hailsham's performance at the nuclear test-ban talks in Moscow; it was, however, a ridiculous and unfounded allegation with no conceivable basis in fact. Hailsham's candidacy, which had been struggling to stay afloat, was nonetheless well and truly sunk.

That evening, Macmillan started work on a draft of his letter to the Queen, making it very clear that Home was his own choice and couching his praise in terms likely to appeal to the monarch:

> Lord Home is clearly a man who represents the old, governing class at its best and those who take a reasonably impartial view of English history know how good that can be. He is not ambitious in the sense of wanting to scheme for power, although not foolish enough to resist honour when it comes to him.
>
> Had he been of another generation, he would have been of the Grenadiers and the 1914 heroes. He gives that impression by a curious mixture of great courtesy, and even of yielding to pressure, with underlying rigidity on matters of principle. It is interesting that he has proved himself so well liked by men like President Kennedy and Mr Rusk and Mr Gromyko. This is exactly the quality that the class to which he belongs have at their best because they think about the question under discussion and not about themselves.[83]

The soundings on which Macmillan planned to base his recommendation were carried out on Tuesday afternoon and all of Wednesday. It was suspicious, to say the least, that the two most important figures in this exercise, Redmayne and Dilhorne, had both already agreed to support Lord Home. Many of their Cabinet colleagues later believed that they had tampered with the results in some way, and this has been borne out by most subsequent scholarship. Redmayne was the first to report, telling Macmillan that, of the MPs canvassed, Home had eighty-seven first-choice votes, Butler eighty-six, Hailsham sixty-five, Maudling forty-eight, Macleod twelve and Heath ten.[84] What was more, Redmayne said, Home had easily the most second-choice votes and also aroused the least opposition:

> I have carefully studied the quality of support given to these candidates. Maudling's is almost exclusively from the younger and more junior

element. That given to Home and Butler is more mature but Home's covers a far wider cross-section of the Party. I would describe the quality of Hailsham's backing as comparatively unimpressive.

Apart from Home's actual lead, I am impressed by the general good will shown towards him, even by those who give reasons in favour of other candidates, and I cannot fail to come to the opinion that he would be best able to secure united support.[85]

This was precisely what Macmillan wanted to hear, but it needs to be taken with a heavy pinch of salt. The party whips certainly knew that their chief favoured Home, and they phrased their questions to MPs accordingly, emphasising second preferences and opposition to individual contenders in order to strengthen the appeal of Home as a compromise candidate.[86] Their style is well illustrated by an exchange in Blackpool between Redmayne and Jim Prior, a nervous and relatively young MP:

'Who do you favour?'
'Reggie Maudling as first choice, but if not, Rab, of course.'
'Not Quintin.'
'Not Quintin.'
'Thank you very much.'
Then:
'By the way, what about Alec if he decides to stand?'
'I don't really know him, and in any case he's in the House of Lords.'
'So he's not a runner?'
'Well, we don't know yet, do we?'
'But if he does renounce?'
'I suppose he would be possible.'

Prior had 'little doubt that even at that early stage I was put down as an Alec supporter'.[87] This was not an isolated example: one account suggests that, regardless of their first preferences, many MPs were asked: 'If there is a deadlock between Rab and Quintin would you accept Alec Home?' Willie Whitelaw, then a junior minister, told the whips that he backed Butler. Then came what he considered a 'totally irregular' follow-up question: 'But if Alec Home was available, would you be prepared to support him?'[88] In this context, it seems reasonably certain that the figures were fixed.

Lord Dilhorne's results for the Cabinet, meanwhile, were even more sus-picious. These figures were crucial, because whoever was chosen as Prime Minister would need the trust and support of his senior colleagues. According to Dilhorne's notes, eleven members of the Cabinet (including the candidate himself) supported Home; four backed Maudling; three were for Butler, and two for Hailsham.[89] As one account puts it, these figures were certainly 'wildly inaccurate, [and] perhaps even wilfully dishonest'.[90] The liberal Edward Boyle, for example, was recorded as having voted for Home, but in fact his preference was for Butler. Iain Macleod, who bitterly attacked the figures, resigned from the Cabinet and claimed that he knew eleven ministers who had voted against Home, was *himself* recorded as voting for Home. Even Home's own authorised biographer thinks that this was 'inconceivable'.[91] Dilhorne also claimed that Hailsham 'was by no means certain that he would serve if R. A. Butler was chosen'. Again, this was non-sense. Hailsham had already told his friends at Blackpool: 'Rab is my favourite candidate.'[92] Either Dilhorne, who was rather deaf, had totally misheard, or he was being less than scrupulous. The Chief Whip was so con-fident of the right result, in fact, that he did not always bother to conceal his partisanship. When Freddie Erroll, the President of the Board of Trade, told him that he thought the next leader should be Reginald Maudling, Redmayne said calmly that he was too late: 'It's all arranged – it's going to Alec Home.'[93] He was right. As dusk was falling on Thursday 17 October, with all the results safely in, Macmillan telephoned Home and told him that he would formally be recommending his name to the Queen.[94]

It was a measure of Macmillan's skill as a political poker-player that very few of the Cabinet had any idea that the end of the drama was now so close. Butler had received a call that morning from the Lord Chancellor suggest-ing that the denouement was near, but, characteristically, he told nobody and simply carried on with his routine duties.[95] At breakfast, meanwhile, Iain Macleod's wife had passed on to her husband the rumour that the suc-cession was to be decided that afternoon. Eve Macleod had heard the story from her friend Lady Monckton, who had heard it herself from Dorothy Macmillan. Macleod had assumed that this item of gossip must mean that Butler, the favourite, was on the verge of victory.[96] Later that morning, he had a drink with Reginald Maudling and the two men decided to telephone Dilhorne and ask for a special Cabinet meeting to review the procedures for the succession. The Lord Chancellor refused. Butler might have called the Cabinet together and thereby taken the initiative, but Maudling and

Macleod lacked the authority. So, instead, they went off to lunch, chatting amicably about their prospects in a Butler government. 'It is an indication of the tightness of the magic circle on this occasion', Macleod later wrote bitterly, 'that neither the Chancellor of the Exchequer nor the Leader of the House of Commons [i.e. Maudling and himself] had any inkling of what was happening.'[97]

Shortly after lunch Macleod had a call from William Rees-Mogg of the *Sunday Times*. 'He told me that the decision had been made, and that it was for Home,' Macleod wrote later. 'He himself found this incredible, but he was utterly sure of his source.'[98] This, as far as he was concerned, was sensational and appalling news. At three o'clock he telephoned both Maudling and Enoch Powell, his oldest political friends. All agreed that Butler, their old chief at the Conservative Research Department, would be a much better choice than Home, who struck them as ignorant of domestic issues and ante-diluvian in his attitudes to the Commonwealth and the colonies. 'How can I serve under a man whose views on Africa are positively Portuguese?' Powell is supposed to have asked.[99] Macleod and Powell had been estranged for a long time; but, quite coincidentally, relations had been restored a week pre-viously. When Macleod telephoned, Powell was actually busy working a cartoon projector at his daughter's seventh birthday party: the cartoons were silent and he was supplying the various voices himself. He brought the pro-ceedings to a rapid conclusion and dashed over to Macleod's flat in Chelsea, where Reginald Maudling was already listening to the unexpected news.[100]

Many Conservative MPs, especially those from the left of the party, were extremely disappointed to hear the rumours that Home had got the nod. Anthony Royle, for instance, wrote that the news was 'greeted with dismay and amazement by us all. Whilst we all admired Alec Home as an hon-ourable and able man, no one really considered during the events of the past ten days that he either wished to be Prime Minister or would be chosen. As the Fourteenth Earl of Home . . . it was going to be difficult to fight a gen-eral election in 1964 under a man with a similar but more aristocratic background as Harold Macmillan's'.[101] There were even stories of distraught Tories telephoning Buckingham Palace that night to complain that Home was unacceptable.[102]

At the centre of what became called 'The Revolt in the Night' were Iain Macleod and Enoch Powell, who spent the night sitting by the telephone in the latter's house at South Eaton Place, surrounded by balloons and debris from Jennifer Powell's birthday party, determined to do whatever they could to block Home's candidacy. The two men had agreed with Maudling that they would all now back Rab Butler in an urgent attempt to stop Home. Maudling then headed off for a lavish black-tie dinner and rolled back, suitably refreshed, later in the evening with Freddie Erroll and Lord Aldington. In Putney, meanwhile, Lord Hailsham had been joined by his closest supporters, Julian Amery and Peter Thorneycroft, and the two groups were in constant contact. Hailsham, who was 'deeply shocked' and 'plainly much upset' by the news, spoke to Powell and agreed that he would withdraw his own claim in favour of Butler. The fact that both Maudling and Hailsham had now thrown their support to Butler meant that there was still hope, and the conspirators' strategy hinged on two things. First, they had to persuade Butler to stand firm and to resist the entreaties of Macmillan and Home; and second, they had to tell Home that he was simply not acceptable.[103]

The second part was the easier. Macleod and Powell telephoned Home, who was cloistered with some of his retinue, and told him that as a member of the Lords he could hardly claim to be the best leader for 'the modern Tory Party'.[104] Maudling, Hailsham and Butler, meanwhile, conducted themselves exactly as might have been predicted. Maudling, well fed and still dressed for dinner, lounged in apparently lazy indifference. Hailsham, by contrast, immediately rang Home to tell him that his nomination was 'disastrous' and 'the most awful thing I have ever heard'.[105] According to one of Hailsham's supporters:

> Finally he rang Butler, an exchange which differed from the other con-versations because Quintin kept on repeating aloud what Rab had just said, in the same way that barristers sometimes repeat the answer of a witness when they are particularly contemptuous of it.
>   'Oh, you were just dozing off, were you, my dear Rab?'
>   'You will take note of what I have said and possibly act on it.'
>   Finally Quintin said, 'You must don your armour, my dear Rab, and fight.' Regaining his armchair with difficulty (he had hurt his leg), Hailsham observed that everyone was running true to form. '[Powell] was open and definite, Reggie thought it "not a very good idea", and Rab was "taking note of my remarks".'[106]

While Hailsham was talking to Butler, the Chief Whip had arrived at Powell's house to confront the plotters. He tried to persuade them to accept

Home, and they refused; they tried to persuade him to back Butler, and he proved equally obdurate. After a long and heated argument, he left, agreeing to report their views to Macmillan and therefore to the Queen. Lord Aldington, who drove Redmayne back to Downing Street and correctly guessed that he might be less than reliable, telephoned the Queen's private secretary himself to report the dissent within the Conservative ranks. At last, well after midnight, the three young Turks rang Butler to assure him of their support. All night their old mentor had been fielding calls from supporters old and new, while his wife Mollie was begging him to stand firm and fight. Yet he was as inscrutable as ever; he simply thanked them for their kind words and added that Macmillan ought to be told of their feelings. With that, the 'midnight meeting' broke up. Maudling headed homewards to sleep off his dinner, and Powell drove Macleod back to his flat. In enlisting Hailsham to Butler's cause and warning Home of their opposition, they had done all they could. It was now by no means certain that Home would win the day: no fewer than seven ministers had promised that they would follow Butler to the back benches if he refused to serve under Home. 'Well, we have placed the golden ball in Rab's lap,' Macleod remarked to Powell on the drive into Chelsea. 'If he drops it now, he does not deserve to be Prime Minister.'[107]

Home himself had taken the calls from his opponents with calm courtesy. 'It looks rather smelly now, doesn't it?' said his worried wife Elizabeth. The candidate himself murmured: 'Well, I was quite prepared to come forward as the candidate to unify the party, accepted by everyone; but if it is said that my coming forward would split the Party, that is a different proposition.' The Lord Chancellor, who was listening, brushed the complaints aside: Home, he said, 'must pay no attention' and stick to his guns.[108] This was certainly Macmillan's attitude the following morning, when he was woken early to be told of the brewing revolt, and Home was dissuaded from any thoughts of withdrawing. At ten o'clock, Tim Bligh took Macmillan's letter of resignation to Buckingham Palace, and just over an hour later the Queen's car pulled up outside the King Edward VII Hospital.

The long-awaited meeting between the monarch and her former Prime Minister was, in Ben Pimlott's view, 'the most remarkable audience in modern monarchical history'.[109] Macmillan, still extremely frail and bedridden, was wheeled down to the hospital boardroom; he had put on a white silk shirt for the occasion, but as it was being worn over a battered brown pullover the effect was comic rather than dignified. His doctor noted: 'The poor man had to have a bottle in bed with him, a bell by his side, and Sister was outside the door, in case he needed help while the Queen was there. He took all this, as everything else, with supreme detachment and dignity. He was very pale and tense, and indeed unhappy.'[110] The Queen, meanwhile, struck Macmillan as 'deeply moved'; she spoke softly and unsteadily, and was obviously upset to be losing a trusted Prime Minister in such circumstances. He formally asked her if she wanted to hear his advice; when she said yes, he then began to read his memorandum recommending Home, to which she nodded agreement. 'I said that I thought speed was important and hoped she would send for Lord Home immediately – as soon as she got back to the Palace,' he recorded later. 'He could then begin to work. She agreed.'[111] An hour after she had come in, the Queen made her farewell and left, accompanied by her private secretary, Sir Michael Adeane, a short, rotund man clutching an enormous white envelope containing Macmillan's memorandum and looking 'like the Frog Footman'.[112] In the car on the journey to the Palace, Adeane reminded the Queen that she did not have to take Macmillan's advice. But it was never likely that she would ignore his recommendation: for one thing, she preferred Home to Butler herself. As one courtier later pointed out: 'Rab wasn't her cup of tea. When she got the advice to call Alec she thought "Thank God". She loved Alec – he was an old friend. They talked about dogs and shooting together. They were both Scottish landowners, the same sort of people, like old school friends.'[113] Back in the hospital, meanwhile, the Downing Street staff were saying farewell to the former Prime Minister for the last time, many of them, like Tim Bligh, weeping as they left. 'So ended my premiership,' Macmillan wrote slowly and sadly in his diary: '*January 11 1957–October 18 1963.*'[114]

After all the excitement of the previous two days, the denouement was swift and anticlimactic. Just after noon, Home received a message to go to the Palace, where he asked the Queen for time to see if he could form an administration. He then took possession of 10 Downing Street, which until that point had been Butler's temporary domain. This was a supremely symbolic moment, since the media immediately hailed him as Prime Minister, and this meant that it would be extremely difficult to dislodge him. 'He has got the loaves and fishes,' commented Lord Beaverbrook; 'there is no stopping him now.'[115] That afternoon, Home received his Cabinet colleagues. In the cold light of day, the passions of the midnight meeting had cooled, and the rebel ministers' nerve began to fail. Neither Butler nor Maudling immediately accepted Home's invitation to join his new administration; but neither refused point-blank, either. Hailsham, as might have been guessed from his excitable, unreliable personality, was beginning to waver. That evening, with Maudling having cancelled a special trip with his wife to a private showing of *From Russia with Love*, the four senior contenders held a 'quadrilateral' summit meeting. Hailsham's resolve, much to the barely concealed annoyance of Maudling, had now deserted him entirely. 'Quintin, having started the day by buzzing about like a fly in a bottle, simply capitulated,' Maudling commented a few months later.[116] Butler, ignoring the entreaties of his friends, was the next to give in. Early the following morning he accepted Home's offer of the Foreign Office. Within an hour, Maudling had heard the news and agreed to stay on as Chancellor. Only Macleod and Powell, the two ringleaders of the failed Revolt in the Night, stuck to their guns. Both refused to serve in Home's government, and returned to the back benches. Late on the morning of Saturday 19 October, Home was driven back up the Mall to Buckingham Palace to kiss hands and accept the Queen's invitation to become Prime Minister. It was an outcome that twelve days previously, when Macmillan had first been taken ill, nobody could possibly have foreseen.[117]

Home was an unexpected successor, but contrary to political myth, he was not a particularly inappropriate or unpopular one. Reginald Maudling remarked on the 'extraordinary affection' for Home among ordinary party activists, 'who regarded him as the sort of man they would like to be themselves: a good athlete; not brilliant but intelligent, a man of charm, integrity and balance'.[118] 'He had no enemies,' Peter Thorneycroft told Peter Hennessy years later. 'He was a natural compromise candidate.'[119] He was also the only contender with any real appeal to the right wing of the party, since Butler, Hailsham and Maudling were all identified with liberal tendencies towards mild reform at home and decolonisation overseas. For the landed gentry, conservative activists in rural constituencies and the nostalgic imperialists in groups like the Monday Club, Home was the ideal candidate. Five years later, he would have probably been too old for consideration; as it was, his timing was excellent. At the same time, the divisions between his more liberal opponents undoubtedly helped: most people expected the contest to be between Butler and Hailsham, and only at the very last minute did those two camps come together.[120]

But the real key to Home's unexpected victory was the weakness and indecision of Butler. 'In the end,' writes Richard Thorpe, 'Rab Butler made Alec Home Prime Minister, not Harold Macmillan.'[121] Unlike his colleagues,

Butler had kept aloof from the intrigues and plots of the final days; on the vital, fraught Thursday afternoon and evening, he had simply worked in Downing Street until six, then walked across Whitehall to his office for Central African affairs, and then been driven to the hotel where he and his wife were staying while their house was being redecorated. He had taken little interest in the frenzied telephone calls of the night, and had greeted the news of Home's invitation to the Palace with stoical equanimity.[122] As Hailsham put it, by agreeing to stand by him against Home, Butler's senior colleagues had effectively offered him the premiership 'on a plate'.[123] If he had refused to meet Home in No. 10 on the Friday afternoon, but had instead, in his capacity as Deputy Prime Minister, called a Cabinet meeting to discuss the succession, he might well have emerged victorious. By going to see Home like some supplicant invited to meet his new master, he forfeited the advantage.[124] Merely by refusing to serve, in fact, Butler would surely have prevented Home's elevation. If he had refused to join the government, then Maudling, Hailsham, Macleod, Powell and Edward Boyle would certainly have followed suit, making it impossible for Home to continue. 'We all understood that Alec could not form a government unless Rab agreed to serve,' explained Lord Charteris, then the Queen's assistant press secretary, 'and, if not, the Queen would have had to call for Rab.'[125]

Why, then, did Butler not act to secure the premiership for himself? His biographer explains:

> The sad truth was that, almost from the beginning, Rab succumbed to what appears to have been a fatal intimation of his own ultimate political defeat. Even before the end of July he was already conceding, 'To sum up the whole thing, it is not good thinking there is no life left if one is not elected Pope. One can always be a respected Cardinal.'

Throughout the leadership struggle, Butler 'showed a marked reluctance to exert himself': so marked, in fact, that it is almost impossible to imagine any of his colleagues, whether Maudling, Hailsham, Macleod or Heath, behaving in the same extraordinarily detached manner.[126] Only Butler, when implored by Hailsham over the telephone: 'Don your armour, my dear Rab!', could have replied: 'I was just dozing off . . . I take note of your remarks, but now I really must doze off.'[127] To be fair, he was in a very difficult position: by refusing to serve, he would have risked splitting the party and destroying the Conservatives' chances in the forthcoming general election. But in truth his inaction was largely a question of temperament and inclination. Enoch Powell later wrote that 'after years, after decades even, of patience and of waiting, there comes the moment to "draw sabre and charge". When the moment came to Rab, he turned his horse and trotted slowly away.'[128]

What aggressive young ministers like Powell and Macleod did not quite understand, though, was that the language and behaviour of the swashbuckling political adventurer did not come easily to Butler, the consummate insider. It was not in his character: as his colleague Reginald Bevins put it, Butler was, quite simply, 'temperamentally incapable of aggravating a crisis by refusing to serve'.[129] A thoughtful, popular and effective departmental minister, he lacked the ruthless, self-serving killer instinct that makes a successful party leader. 'One cannot alter one's nature,' Butler wrote later. 'I had always worked for the unity of the party and I did so on this occasion.'[130] To make matters worse, he was personally fond of Alec Home. 'You see, I had against me such a terrific gent,' he once remarked. 'If I had the most ghastly walrus I might have done something.'[131] Both men thought of themselves as gentlemen, and behaved accordingly in the aftermath of the contest. Friendship and political rivalry are not always completely incompatible. 'Never in my wildest dreams did I think that circumstances could ever conspire to bring me to hurt even in the tiniest degree one of my friends,' Home wrote privately to Butler three days after the end of the drama. 'And when, of all the people in the world, it had to be you, my misery was complete. I would like to say how deeply grateful I am for your loyalty and to express my unstinted admiration for your courage. Now that we have been put to the test, perhaps the most precious thing is that friendship and loyalty holds.'[132]

If there was little enduring bitterness between Butler and Home, the same could not be said of Butler and Macmillan. Twice Butler had been the favourite for the crown; twice he had been denied by Macmillan's machinations. 'The truth is', Iain Macleod famously and controversially wrote afterwards, 'that . . . from the first day of his premiership to the last, Macmillan was determined that Butler, although incomparably the best qualified of the contenders, should not succeed him.'[133] When Macleod wrote these words, in January 1964, they were assumed to be a gross exaggeration. Nonetheless, all the evidence suggests that, although Macmillan valued Butler as an able colleague and loyal deputy, he did everything he could to prevent his old friend and rival succeeding to the leadership. On the very day that Home's appointment as Prime Minister was confirmed, Macmillan grumbled in his diary that it was 'quite untrue that I wanted to "down" Rab'. Yet he continued: 'It *is* true that of the three [alternative contenders] I would have preferred Hailsham, as a better election figure. All this pretence about Rab's "progressive" views is rather shallow. His real trouble is his vacillation in any difficult situation. He has no strength of character and for this reason should *not* be P.M.'[134] Reflecting on the leadership battle a decade later, he mused: 'Rab is a backroom boy by nature: a marvellous chief of staff. [But] Macleod and Hailsham had the qualities of a commander.'[135] Macmillan had spent much of 1963 building up Hailsham, Macleod and Maudling for precisely this reason, so that in the event of a vacancy at the top there would be a younger, more dynamic man ready to take over. When, just before his illness, Macmillan told Hailsham that he wanted him to succeed, Hailsham asked in bewilderment: 'What about Rab? Surely he's the obvious successor?' 'On no account,' Macmillan allegedly replied. 'Rab simply doesn't have it in him to be Prime Minister.'[136]

Only Iain Macleod and Enoch Powell refused to serve under Home as Prime Minister, partly because they disliked his politics. As former members of the post-war Conservative Research Department, they both felt that a modern party leader ought to be more dynamic, innovative and imaginative than the cautious, old-fashioned, socially conservative Home. Powell was particularly agitated that Macmillan, having resigned his office, had then presumed to give the Queen advice.[137] More important, though, Macleod wrote afterwards, was the fact that 'for myself and Powell it had become a matter of "personal moral integrity"'.[138] As one friend put it, having told Home on the Thursday night 'that he was no good at all for Prime Minister, they could not simply fall into line and say, well now you've got it, yes, we think you are wonderful'.[139] To do him credit, Home appreciated that they had emerged with considerable though quixotic honour from the episode. 'Well I don't expect, Alec, you expect me to give you a different answer on Saturday from the one I gave you on Friday,' Powell said at their last meeting. 'I'd have to go home and turn all the mirrors round.'[140] Powell returned to the back benches, while Macleod accepted an offer to become the editor of the *Spectator*.

Neither would stay out of the headlines for long, but Macleod was the first to surface. On 17 January 1964, reviewing a glib and partial account of the leadership crisis by Randolph Churchill, he broke his vow of silence and launched what struck observers as an astonishing attack on Macmillan and the Conservative Party hierarchy. Entitled 'The Tory Leadership', the article was the highlight of that week's issue of the *Spectator* and later became famous for its indictment of the 'magic circle' that controlled the party and the political process. Macleod mocked Churchill's little book as 'Mr Macmillan's trailer for the screenplay of his memoirs'; it was, he suggested, tendentious, inaccurate and self-serving. Macmillan had manipulated the entire process to prevent the supremely qualified Butler from succeeding him, and he had been helped by an unholy alliance of the Lord Chancellor, the party whips and the backbench grandees, a tight and unaccountable 'magic circle' that had controlled events behind the backs of senior figures like the Chancellor and the Deputy Prime Minister. The conspirators constituted a closed social elite based on birth and breeding. 'Eight of the nine people mentioned in the last sentence', he remarked at one point, 'went to Eton.'[141]

The issue was a sell-out, and newspapers across the country rushed to reprint Macleod's remarks.[142] His allegations were hardly unfair, since Macmillan certainly had become dependent on a small group of older, right-wing friends and confidants, but they were immensely controversial. 'What a nasty piece of work you are,' one angry reader telegraphed to the *Spectator*. '. . . Thank God you're not Prime Minister.'[143] Ministers, backbenchers and ordinary activists were all shocked by his apparent disloyalty; invitations to meetings were cancelled; his constituency party executive passed a motion of censure; and only the younger MPs rallied round. 'That the beloved leader should be accused of meeting his crown by by-paths and devious crook'd ways, at the very moment when he was about to sally into the field,' wrote one commentator, 'seemed to the party a monstrous treason [when] touching protestations of loyalty were imperative.'[144] When his friend Humphry Berkeley accompanied a gloomy Macleod for a drink in the Commons Smoking Room, they were 'cut by every single person in the room'.[145]

Harold Macmillan, meanwhile, lived cheerfully on for another twenty-three years. The last two weeks of his premiership had been typical of the man and his administration: devious, theatrical and self-serving, though rarely without vision and droll intelligence. 'The country may well, some day, look back with regret to a man who knew how to give such style to the otherwise unglamorous politics of a prosperous Welfare State,' commented the *Spectator*.[146] For the historian John Turner, he 'had a broader vision than most leaders of the 1950s and 1960s, and greater courage in facing change . . .

he avoided many of the obvious pitfalls and rescued a little dignity from the wreckage. One man alone can do little more.'[147] Richard Lamb even calls him 'the most interesting and intelligent . . . [and] by far the best of Britain's post-war Prime Ministers'.[148]

Macmillan certainly was a sensitive, thoughtful and intriguing character, always ready with a classical or historical allusion; he dominated Parliament and his Cabinet, and rescued his party from the ignominy of Suez. But was he really as effective as these historians suggest? The affluence of the late fifties and early sixties was the consequence not of political decisions made in Downing Street, but of a long process of social change and economic development. Macmillan might have presided over the consumer boom, but he could take little credit for it. Although he had worked hard to restore Britain's international position after the debacle of 1956, nurtured the special relationship with the Americans and handled the realities of colonial retrenchment much more skilfully than many of his European counterparts, it was not clear that ordinary voters had gained an enormous amount from his determination to maintain a seat at the diplomatic top table. His policy towards the new European Economic Community was nothing if not a failure. Economic management, meanwhile, was little short of a shambles, especially considering Britain's competitive advantages and the prosperous mood of the times. Too often economic policy was determined by electoral considerations; Chancellors came and went; and bursts of breakneck growth were followed by periods of severe deflation as surely as autumn follows summer. Even Macmillan's authorised biographer calls his government from 1959 to 1963 'a series of disappointments of tragic proportions'.[149] By the end of the Macmillan premiership, the Conservatives had been in crisis for at least a year, the government appeared to be drifting lifelessly, and the only hope for re-election essentially lay in bribing the electorate with a recklessly generous budget. Despite his personal strengths, Macmillan himself was popularly associated not with prosperity, vision and progress, but with corruption, anachronism and stagnation. Few observers mourned his political departure; many were already looking forward to a general election and a new era.

His unexpected successor, now called Sir Alec Douglas-Home, met with a mixed reception in Westminster and Fleet Street. The *Sunday Times* greeted Home's appointment with a leader entitled 'Turning Aside from Progress', and the *Observer* thought that the Conservatives had decided to 'settle for second best. It is very doubtful whether he has the perception and imagination for effective statesmanship in a rapidly changing world.'[150] Most contemporary commentators shared Edward Pearce's verdict that Home was 'a one-subject technician garlanded with an Oxford fourth [actually a third], ignorant of economics, social policy or an atom of home policy, and sitting for the previous 13 years in the House of Lords'.[151] Even Home's aged mother, the Dowager Countess, told inquiring journalists: 'I am frankly very surprised. I thought it would be Mr Butler – he seemed to deserve it.'[152] Labour observers, meanwhile, were pleased and relieved that their opponents had chosen a little-known aristocrat rather than a younger, more progressive figure like Maudling or Macleod. Anthony Wedgwood Benn thought that Home would be 'a dud when it comes to exciting the electorate and Wilson will run rings round him'. 'It is incredible that such a thing has happened,' he wrote on 18 October. 'From the Labour Party's point of view he is much less dangerous than Maudling but I am disturbed that my battle should have paved the way for a Conservative peer to come back to the Commons as PM.'[153]

It was Macleod's 'magic circle' article, though, that really defined the image of Home and his promotion to the highest office. Harold Macmillan noted:

This, of course, just suits the press today, most of which loves to attack Eton and the aristocracy. It's all great nonsense, but it touches off the 'inverted snobbery' emotion wh. is very strong today . . . What harm this will do is hard to say. Our electoral prospects are *not* good – for natural and normal reasons, 13 years of power. But I'm afraid Macleod's article will do *some* damage. [154]

Home himself was furious with Macleod for breaking the sacred laws of party loyalty. Barely a year later, on the day he lost the premiership, he was angrily pacing up and down Selwyn Lloyd's flat at Buckingham Gate, cursing Macleod in language that might not have been expected from a former peer of the realm.[155] The real significance of Macleod's article was that it confirmed everything that the 'What's Wrong with Britain?' critics, the Labour leadership and the television satirists had been claiming for years. For those who had followed the Burgess, Maclean and Philby cases, or had read the novels of C. P. Snow and Anthony Sampson's book *Anatomy of Britain*, or had watched *Beyond the Fringe* and *TW3*, the elevation of Lord Home seemed simply another episode in the history of the inbred, incestuous, class-ridden elite that had controlled British politics and society after the war. From this perspective, Home could hardly have been a more unfortunate choice: a sixty-year-old Earl, largely unversed in modern economic thought and management, who owned two country houses in Scotland, fifty-six farms, three hundred acres of forest and more than fifty thousand acres of hill farmland. His entry in *Burke's Peerage* filled no fewer than three columns.[156] Not for nothing did one former minister, Reginald Bevins, later complain in his memoirs that the Conservative Party was 'a bad joke of democracy . . . led predominantly by a group of Old Etonians'.[157] The country *was*, it appeared, governed by a closed group of small-minded men, who really thought that the gleaming new Britain of Sean Connery and Paul McCartney could be governed by an aristocratic nonentity from Eton and Oxford.

Harold Wilson was unsurprisingly quick to pounce. On the very day that Home was confirmed in office, he attacked his promotion as yet another example of the 'Edwardian Establishment mentality' that was dragging Britain back:

> The message that has gone out to the world is that in 1963 the Government party in Britain selects its leader and the country's Prime Minister through the machinery of an aristocratic cabal. In this ruthlessly competitive, scientific, technical, industrial age, a week of intrigues has produced a result based on family and hereditary connections. The leader has emerged, an elegant anachronism.[158]

On the same day, the cast of *That Was The Week That Was* were in rehearsal for the evening's show. At the last minute, Christopher Booker and Ned Sherrin came up with a new sketch to form the centrepiece of the night's entertainment. This was the infamous Disraeli monologue, in which the Victorian statesman, played rather unconvincingly by David Frost, reads a letter to his successor. Quite apart from the consequences of the sketch for the future of the programme, it not only crystallised all the public doubts about Home's succession, it also set the scene for the confrontation between aristocratic nostalgia and scientific expertise that most people expected in the following year's election:

> My Lord:
>   When I say that your acceptance of the Queen's commission to form an administration has proved and will prove an unmitigated disaster for the Conservative Party, for the Constitution, for the Nation, and for yourself, it must not be thought that I bear you any ill will . . .

Your bleak, deathly smile is the smile today not of a victor – but of a victim. You are the dupe and unwitting tool of a conspiracy . . . of a tiny band of desperate men who have seen in you their last, slippery chance of keeping the levers of power and influence within their privileged circle . . .

You have always drifted with the tide – the tide of appeasement, the tide of Suez . . . You know little of economics, little of all the manifold, complex needs of a country that has become tired in a technological age, and nothing of the lives of the ordinary people who must now, without consent, submit as your subjects. You have foreseen nothing. You are qualified only to do – nothing.

The piece concluded with Frost dropping the Disraeli impersonation and saying to camera: 'And so, there is the choice for the electorate; on one hand Lord Home – and on the other hand Mr Harold Wilson. Dull Alec versus Smart Alec.'[159]

19

ON TO 1964

This is Britain in the autumn of 1963, slightly hungover, ready to be Spartan.
Out goes the hedonist, the aura of self-indulgence, the cult of inefficiency. In
comes the technocrat with clear eyes and clinical mind.

Queen, September 1963

We'll try to do everything we can to please you with the type of songs we
write and record next year.

Paul McCartney's Christmas message, December 1963

Sir Alec Douglas-Home's first few months as Prime Minister were far from
easy. On 8 November he won a seat in the Commons at the Kinross and
West Perthshire by-election, but his first appearance in the House was, as the
American ambassador wryly put it, 'rough going', with 'loud and long heck-
ling' from the Labour benches.[1] Home's working days were dominated by
foreign affairs: in November he flew to Washington for the funeral of
President Kennedy and talks with the new President, Lyndon Johnson, and
in December and January he was preoccupied by a new outbreak of communal strife in Cyprus and continuing negotiations with the Southern
Rhodesians. At home the outlook was bleak. Harold Wilson still enjoyed an
impressive lead in the opinion polls, and, for all Home's personal amiability,
he found it hard to shake the impression of being an old-fashioned public
school amateur, propelled into the highest office by the obscure workings
of the 'magic circle'.[2]

For many observers, not least his Labour opponents, the new Prime
Minister personified a vision of Britain that at the end of 1963 was passing
into history. On 31 October the *Evening Standard* published a Vicky cartoon
that perfectly captured the apparent clash between the modern values of
the affluent society and the anachronistic, grouse-shooting image of the
new Prime Minister. In the cartoon, Sir Alec, beaming vaguely under a

tweed cap, is standing awkwardly in the doorway of a back room in 10 Downing Street. Before him are four very sheepish men – Butler, Maudling, Hailsham and Heath – sitting around a table under an enormous banner reading 'Modernisation'. In the foreground, a book of Harold Macmillan's beloved Trollope has been confined to the waste-paper basket; instead, Butler is clutching a book entitled 'James Bond' and Hailsham is reading a volume labelled 'Science Fiction'. All four of the guilty men are peering uncomfortably out from beneath their enormous, exaggerated mop-top wigs. The message is plain: for all the efforts of his colleagues, the aristocratic Sir Alec is an embarrassing relic marooned in the new world of Bond and the Beatles.[3] Two weeks later, in the *Daily Express*, the cartoonist Cummings depicted Home crawling through crowds of teenage fans and policemen to reach the four young musicians in their matching grey suits, begging: 'Gentlemen, can't we persuade you to become Conservative candidates – after all, *you've* never had it so good!'[4]

There was no need to identify the band: by the end of 1963, anyone who read a newspaper knew all about the Fab Four and their devoted admirers. The *New Musical Express* explained to its readers:

> In the distant future, when our descendants study the history books, they will see one word printed against the year 1963 – Beatles! Just as convincingly as 1066 marked the Battle of Hastings, or 1215 the Magna Carta, so this year will be remembered by posterity for the achievement of four lads from Liverpool.[5]

By the autumn of 1963 the Beatles' pre-eminence was unchallenged. Since June they had been hosting their own regular BBC radio shows, *Pop Go the Beatles*, as well as recording, touring and generally cementing their popularity. At the beginning of September, 'She Loves You' was still top of the *NME* singles chart; their extended-play record 'Twist and Shout' was top of the EP chart; and their album *Please Please Me* was top of the LP chart. The two incidents that most attracted public attention, however, were their appearances on *Sunday Night at the London Palladium* on 13 October, and at the Royal Command Variety Performance on 4 November.

The ATV programme *Sunday Night at the London Palladium* was the most popular variety show on television, a traditional blend of comedy, music, acrobatics and competitions broadcast live from the theatre on Argyll Street. The act that topped the bill was frequently the most popular singing sensation of the moment, and so the Beatles' appearance – on the Sunday that followed the Conservative Party conference at Blackpool – was nothing unusual. What was unusual was the front-page coverage in the newspapers that followed. 'SIEGE OF THE BEATLES' read one headline: 'What a Sunday Night at the Palladium!' According to the *Mirror*, the 'police fought to hold back 1,000 squealing teenagers as the Beatles made their getaway after their Palladium TV show . . . A Police motorcade stood by as the four Pop idols dashed for their car. Then the fans went wild, breaking through a cordon of more than 60 Policemen.'[6] The *Express* agreed, although it thought that the mob of screaming girls was only five hundred strong, and amended the number of policemen to twenty.[7] In fact both versions were probably exaggerated: a photographer who accompanied the band to the theatre later recalled that they saw no more than eight girls, and a photograph printed in the *Daily Mail* showed McCartney leaving the theatre watched by one policeman and three girls.[8]

Three weeks later, however, the crowds that awaited the Beatles outside the Prince of Wales Theatre in Leicester Square were certainly no figment of an editor's imagination. Every year a few hundred people would gather outside the theatre to welcome the monarch to the Royal Variety Performance, but this time there were also several thousand fans, mainly female, as well as five hundred additional policemen to control them. As far as the Beatles were concerned, the engagement was both an honour and a challenge. An invitation to perform at the Royal Variety Performance was considered extremely prestigious, even if the Queen herself, about to give birth to Prince Edward, was absent. This was not an excited mob of impressionable teenagers, but 'a bejewelled and evening-suited adult audience', so it would be a real test of the Beatles' ability to reach across the generations.[9] It was one they passed with relative ease, cheerfully bashing out three songs to polite applause. The defining moment of the occasion, however, occurred just before their final number, the exuberant and driving 'Twist and Shout'. Lennon had already announced in the dressing room, much to the horror of Brian Epstein, that he was planning to ask the audience 'to rattle their fucking jewellery', and he now did precisely that, albeit with one minor alteration. 'For the last number I'd like to ask for your help,' he said coolly from the stage. 'Will the people in the cheaper seats clap your hands?' (Laughter.) 'And the rest of you, if you'll just rattle your jewellery.' (More laughter.) It was cheeky, but not too cheeky, and it worked.[10]

If there was one event that confirmed the Beatles' popularity with the general public, this was it. When ITV broadcast the tape of the concert a few days later, almost twenty-six million people tuned in to watch.[11] As far as the newspapers were concerned, meanwhile, the Beatles' reception meant that they had effectively been given the royal imprimatur. Every paper treated Lennon's remark about rattling jewellery as one of the great witticisms of the age. 'Night of Triumph for Four Young Men' was the verdict of the *Daily Mail*; 'Yes – the Royal Box was stomping.'[12] The headline in the *Mirror*, meanwhile, was simple: 'BEATLEMANIA!' Nine years before, the *Mirror* had dismissed 'the garish delights of the juke box'; now it turned its editorial column into a paean to the new national heroes:

YEAH! YEAH! YEAH!

You have to be a real sour square not to love the nutty, noisy, happy, handsome Beatles.

If they don't sweep your blues away – brother, you're a lost cause. If they don't put a beat in your feet – sister, you're not living.

How refreshing to see these rumbustious young Beatles take a middle-aged Royal Variety performance by the scruff of their necks and have them Beatling like teenagers.

Fact is that Beatle People are everywhere. From Wapping to Windsor. Aged seven to seventy. And it's plain to see why these four cheeky, energetic lads from Liverpool go down so big.

They're young, new. They're high-spirited, cheerful. What a change from the self-pitying moaners, crooning their lovelorn tunes from the tortured shallows of lukewarm hearts.

The Beatles are whacky. They wear their hair like a mop – but it's WASHED, it's super clean. So is their fresh young act. They don't have to rely on off-colour jokes about homos for their fun . . .

Youngsters like the Beatles are doing a good turn for show business – and the rest of us – with their new sounds, new looks.

Good luck Beatles![13]

Beatlemania was at its zenith. In the week following the Royal Variety Performance the *Daily Express* ran five front-page articles on the band, while the *Mail* devised a special logo of four mop-topped heads for all its Beatles stories. Just as with the Profumo scandal a few months previously, the press were happy to print almost any anecdote at all, no matter how trifling, and every day there seemed to be some new story. On 10 November it was reported that the first schoolboy had been sent home by his headmaster for turning up with a Beatle haircut. On 18 November, a vicar asked the Beatles to record 'Oh Come All Ye Faithful, Yeah! Yeah! Yeah!' for his Christmas carol service. On 19 November, two hundred girls in an Accrington cotton mill went on strike when their foreman banned them from listening to *Housewives' Choice* because they were liable to scream at the Beatles and lose interest in their work. On 20 November, there were questions in the House about the cost of the Beatles' police protection.[14] Two days later, the band released their second album, *With the Beatles*, for which 300,000 advance orders had already been placed. Its progression to number one in the LP chart was almost certain even before it reached the shops.[15] And on 29 November the new single came out, perfectly timed for Christmas. 'I Want to Hold Your Hand' entered the *NME* Top Thirty directly at number one.

Paradoxically, what fascinated the press so much about the Beatles was not so much their music as the reaction they provoked among their fans. The disturbances at the London Palladium might have been exaggerated, but there were too many such stories for them all to be invented. On 26 October, for example, tickets for a Beatles concert went on sale in Carlisle. The band had already appeared there earlier in the year, during their tour supporting Helen Shapiro. The public had been indifferent then; but now six hundred fans queued for thirty-six hours to buy their tickets. When the box office finally opened, the crowd surged forward so enthusiastically that the adjacent shop windows shattered and nine people had to be taken to hospital.[16] Much of the coverage, however, focused on the way in which teenage girls responded to their idols, which most observers described simply as 'hysteria'. While it was true that girls had screamed at pop stars before, they had never done so with such apparent intensity, and never had it made the front pages of the newspapers. In a way, this became self-fulfilling: the more that the press talked about hordes of screaming girls drowning out their heroes' music, the more likely it was that hordes of screaming girls would do precisely that. Many years later one fan told John Lawton:

It's very mysterious to look back on participating in that kind of mass hysteria. I screamed my head off. I cried and cried. I got tickets for the Hammersmith Odeon. It seemed very special to be able to get two tickets. I took a friend. It seemed very important to go with someone who was as crazy about them as I was. She was a little older than me – she was fifteen and wore make-up – which mattered . . . It was impossible to hear them. They were just a phenomenon on the stage. We had a banner that said 'JOHN' and had an enormous heart on it – we waved it as soon as the curtain went up. The whole theatre was full of banners. Everyone was on their feet and the screaming began. It was like a competition.[17]

Since there had already been several long debates in the press about teenage sexual precocity, it was no surprise that some commentators chose to interpret the girls' 'hysteria' as a sexual phenomenon. After the Beatles' concert at the Cambridge ABC on 26 November, so the story went, the seats were found to be wringing wet and the floor damp with puddles of urine.[18] It was 'painfully clear', wrote Dr David Holbrook in the *New Statesman*, 'that The Beatles are a masturbation fantasy, such as a girl presumably has during the onanistic act – the genial smiling young male images, the music like a buzzing of the blood in the head, the rhythm, the cries, the shouted names, the climax.' This was all too characteristic, he thought, of 'our age, that masses of people should be captivated and "sent" by the unconscious appeal of a masturbation fantasy image, exploited by the economic interests, through the new media of distraction such as television'.[19]

Most experts consulted by the media, however, were rather more circumspect: editors clearly liked the sexual angle but at the same time it was not wise to criticise Britain's beloved Beatles and their devotees. When the *Sunday Times* interviewed an unnamed medical consultant, he struck the perfect balance. 'You don't have to be a genius to see the parallels between sexual excitement and the mounting crescendo of delighted screams through a stimulating number like "Twist and Shout",' he said cautiously, 'but at the level it is taken, I think it is the bubbling, uninhibited gaiety of the group that generates enthusiasm.'[20] The *News of the World*'s resident psychologist thought that teenage Beatlemania was all about growing up:

This is one way of flinging off teenage restraints and letting themselves go . . . The fact that thousands of others are screaming along with her makes the girl feel she is living life to the full with people of her own age . . . this emotional outlook is very necessary at her age. It is also innocent and harmless.

The girls are subconsciously preparing for motherhood. Their frenzied screams are a rehearsal for that moment. Even the jelly babies
[which girls threw on to the stage] are symbolic.[21]

The general tide of approval notwithstanding, many people, especially
those over twenty-five or so, still found the attractions of the four mop-tops
extremely easy to resist. Some critics saw Beatlemania as the ugly face of the
affluent society, a combination of teenage delinquency, rampant sexuality
and soulless commercialism. Noël Coward, for instance thought that the
whole thing was simply 'a mass masturbation orgy'.[22] An editorial in the
Telegraph, greatly concerned at the prospect of youthful degeneracy, suggested that the Beatles' concerts were becoming reminiscent of Hitler's
Nuremberg rallies: 'The hysteria fills heads and hearts otherwise empty . . .
Is there not something frightening in whole masses of young people, all
apparently so suggestible, so volatile and so rudderless?'[23]

The fiercest enemy of Beatlemania was the journalist Paul Johnson,
whose contempt for teenage culture was equalled only by his unremitting
scorn for James Bond. As his regular readers in the *New Statesman* knew, he
was a man of wrath: Jonathan Miller once compared him with an explosion
in a pubic-hair factory.[24] For Johnson, the Beatles and their fans were, above
all, representatives of a decadent, materialistic modern world. In his most
vituperative attack, 'The Menace of Beatlism', he insisted that in his youth,
he and his friends 'would not have wasted thirty seconds of our precious
time on The Beatles and their ilk', but would have stuck with the likes of
'Milton, Wagner, Debussy, Matisse, El Greco, Proust'. Modern teenage culture, Johnson argued, was 'a collective grovelling to gods who are
themselves blind and empty'. 'Those who flock round the Beatles,' he thundered, 'who scream themselves into hysteria, whose vacant faces flicker over
the TV screen, are the least fortunate of their generation, the dull, the idle,
the failures.' Surveying the studio audiences on *Juke Box Jury* and *Thank Your
Lucky Stars*, he saw only 'a bottomless pit of vacuity . . . the huge faces bloated
with cheap confectionery and smeared with chain store make-up, the open,
sagging mouths and glazed eyes, the hands mindlessly drumming in time to
the music, the broken stiletto heels, the shoddy, stereotyped, "with-it"
clothes: here, apparently, is a collective portrait of a generation enslaved by
a commercial machine'.[25]

Whatever one thinks of his ferocious assault on teenage values,
Johnson was certainly right to point out that the Beatles were, above all,

a commercial phenomenon; and by Christmas their 'machine' was running more powerfully than ever. Thanks to Reginald Maudling's dash for growth, consumer confidence was booming once again; indeed, the economy was now growing even more quickly than the debonair Chancellor had anticipated.[26] The market for Beatles merchandise was consequently very healthy indeed, and in preparation for the Christmas rush, manufacturers churned out guitars, drums, posters, hats, bags, badges, shirts, jackets, socks, handkerchiefs, tea towels, mugs, ashtrays and jigsaw puzzles.[27] For £5 10s, the devotee could buy a 'Beetle Style Jacket', while an 'All-Plastic Record-Carrier', with a photograph of the band on the front, cost only 12/6. The Subbuteo company, more famous for its miniature football sets, offered fans the chance to buy for only 11/6 their own two-inch-high moulded Beatles figurines, complete with 'fabulous characteristic action and absolute realistic facial reproduction' as well as a 'stage set in gorgeous presentation box coloured blue, tangerine and silver'.[28] 'She'll love you in the MOD MOOD in the deluxe MERSEY BEAT WIG, the latest, greatest Party rave!' proclaimed one advertisement in the *Mirror*. 'Only 19/11d plus 2/1d p&p. Dad, dig this new mod fad. It's a gas!'[29]

No cultural trend in living memory had provoked such an avalanche of commercial enterprise. There were Beatles lockets with miniature group photographs inside; there were Beatles cakes shaped like guitars; there were Beatles airbeds, bedspreads and kitchen aprons.[30] The sales of Beatles jackets alone were enormous. 'Who could have forecast only a year ago', asked Edward Heath, the new Trade Secretary, 'that the Beatles would prove to be the salvation of the corduroy industry?'[31] On Christmas Eve a cartoon in the *Daily Mail* showed a sweet little girl praying by her bedside. The caption read: 'All I want for Christmas is a Beatle; failing that, a pair of kinky boots, a fab leather jacket, black tights and £500,000 for Oxfam.'[32]

Amid all the bags and wigs and badges, it was easy to overlook the staggering extent of the Beatles' musical success. Advance orders alone had been enough to propel 'I Want to Hold Your Hand' directly to the top of the chart, a position it still held on Christmas Day. The second spot, meanwhile, belonged to another Lennon–McCartney hit, 'She Loves You'. The Beatles also occupied the top two places in the album charts: indeed, the sales of their latest LP, *With the Beatles*, which reached almost a million, were enough to push it to fifteenth place in the *singles* chart as well. Three more records, the EPs 'Twist and Shout', 'Beatles' Hits' and 'Beatles' No. 1', were also selling

strongly enough to occupy places in the Top Thirty. None of their competitors, not Cliff Richard, not Billy J. Kramer, not Gerry and the
Pacemakers, came even close to matching their success. For thirty-seven
weeks out of fifty-two, George Martin had seen one of his own records at
the top of the chart, an achievement that would have seemed both incredible and impossible a year before.[33] In the *NME* readers' survey that
December, the Beatles were voted 'Top British Vocal Group' with more
votes than every other act put together.[34] In true showbusiness fashion,
they spent Christmas and the New Year at the Finsbury Park Astoria, appearing in an old-fashioned pantomime-cum-revue alongside Cilla Black and
Rolf Harris: predictably enough, every show sold out.[35] They even made an
appearance on the *Morecambe and Wise* show, singing 'Moonlight Boy' in blazers and straw boaters.[36] 'An examination of the heart of the nation at this
moment', remarked one commentator, 'would find the name "Beatles"
upon it.'[37]

Two days after Christmas, the group received their most unexpected
accolade from no less an observer than William Mann, the music critic of
The Times. For the first time, a reputable classical expert argued that the
Beatles' music was worthy of serious respect, and Mann's article, 'What
Songs the Beatles Sang . . .' remains probably the most famous and controversial piece of British music journalism since the war. He began with a
stunning assertion: Lennon and McCartney were nothing less than 'the
outstanding English composers of 1963'. Their music might appeal to
teenage admirers because of its 'sheer loudness', but 'parents who are still
managing to survive the decibels and, after copious repetition over several
months, still deriving some musical pleasure from the overhearing, do so
because there is a good deal of variety – oh, so welcome in pop music –
about what they sing'. He went on:

> Glutinous crooning is generally out of fashion these days, and even a
> song about 'Misery' sounds fundamentally quite cheerful; the slow, sad
> song about 'That Boy', which features prominently in Beatle pro-
> grammes, is expressively unusual for its lugubrious music, but
> harmonically it is one of the most intriguing, with its chains of pandi-
> atonic clusters, and the sentiment is acceptable because voiced cleanly
> and crisply. But harmonic interest is typical of their quicker songs too,
> and one gets the impression that they think simultaneously of har-
> mony and melody, so firmly are the major tonic sevenths and ninths

built into their tunes, and the flat submediant key switches, so natural is the Aeolian cadence at the end of 'Not a second time' (the chord progression which ends Mahler's *Song of the Earth*).

It was wrong, he suggested, to think of the Beatles as part of a long process of Americanisation: instead, Lennon and McCartney reflected a general revival of native British musical traditions, 'distinctly indigenous in character, the most imaginative and inventive examples of a style that has been developing on Merseyside during the last few years'.

> The autocratic but not by any means ungrammatical attitude to tonality (closer to, say, Peter Maxwell Davies' carols in *O Magnum Mysterium* than to Gershwin or Loewe or even Lionel Bart); the exhilarating and often quasi-instrumental vocal duetting, sometimes in scat or in falsetto, behind the melodic line; the melismas with altered vowels ('I saw her yesterday-ee-ay') and which have not quite become mannered, and the distinct, sometimes subtle varieties of instrumentation . . .
>
> These are some of the qualities that make one wonder with interest what the Beatles, and particularly Lennon and McCartney, will do next, and if America will spoil them or hold on to them, and if their next record will wear as well as the others. They have brought a distinctive and exhilarating flavour into a genre of music that was in danger of ceasing to be music at all.[38]

Mann's article left many readers either baffled or amused, including the Beatles themselves. Lennon later admitted that he had little idea who Mahler was, and thought that Aeolian cadences sounded like 'exotic birds'.[39] One or two observers, however, agreed with *The Times*' expert, and in the *Sunday Times* two days later the eminent ballet critic Richard Buckle even claimed that the Beatles were 'the greatest composers since Beethoven'.[40]

The one indisputable part of Mann's argument was the suggestion that the real challenge for the Beatles lay ahead, in the United States. As early as May 1963, the American singer Roy Orbison had predicted:

> The Beatles could be tops in America . . . These boys have enough originality to storm our charts in the US with the same effect as they have already done here in Britain, but it will need careful handling. You see,

they have something that's entirely new, even to us Americans, and
although we have an influx of hit groups at home at the present time,
I really do believe your own boys could top the charts as frequently as
they seem to be doing here.[41]

Many informed observers did not share Orbison's confidence. It was not
quite true that no British musical act had ever made the breakthrough into
the American market: Lonnie Donegan, Acker Bilk and the Shadows had all
enjoyed considerable success across the Atlantic. All the same, British rock
and roll was considered vastly inferior to its American equivalent, and even
Cliff Richard had made only one American tour, appearing half-way down
the bill to little effect. The Beatles' singles 'Please Please Me', 'From Me to
You' and 'She Loves You' had already been released on minor labels in the
United States, and none had managed to make it into the *Billboard* 'Hot 100'.
Even at the beginning of January 1964, most Americans had simply never
heard of them. The senior executive of Capitol, the American arm of EMI,
told George Martin: 'We don't think the Beatles will do anything in this
market.'[42]

And yet, by every conceivable measure of success, the Beatles had
nothing left to achieve in their home country; only worldwide recognition could possibly provide the spur to keep them writing and performing
at their peak. At the end of 1963, Brian Epstein managed to persuade
Capitol to release 'I Want to Hold Your Hand', and began planning a two-
week American tour in February. Three days into the New Year, Paul
McCartney told an interviewer that the group had been talking to 'an
American reporter who has been on tour with us and he says that the
thing to do is just to be natural'. 'America', said McCartney, 'is our biggest
challenge. It would knock us out to go over there and make good.'[43]

There is no doubt that in December 1963 the interest of the media in the
Beatles and their fans reached a peak of intensity rarely matched either
before or since. But it is also worth remembering that for every individual
who did buy a copy of 'I Want To Hold Your Hand', there were more than
fifty who did not. For one thing, some seven million people, especially
among the elderly, the sick and the unemployed, were still too poor to play
their full part in the breakneck consumerism of the Maudling experiment.[44]
What was more, even for the affluent, popular music was only one among
a number of possible consumer entertainments, and older people in

particular found plenty of other ways to spend their leisure time. Macmillan's Minister without Portfolio, William Deedes, had noted in a Cabinet report in May that 'leisure occupations may permanently shape [national] character, determine their contentment or otherwise with every-day life, and perhaps, in total, mould the image of the nation'. But, as his report found, the 'greatest British hobby' in 1963, measured in terms of popularity, was not rock and roll music or anything even vaguely like it. It was something much more mundane: gardening.[45]

Amid all the excitement of the early sixties, gardening reflected what people saw as the stable, enduring virtues of Britishness: quietness, patience, decency, tidiness. On an average Saturday morning in December 1963, up to a million people might rush out to buy the latest number-one record. But, at the same time, a staggering nineteen million looked forward to another day pottering about in the garden and nursing their flowerbeds through the winter.[46] The neat suburban garden was, at one level, a refuge from the changes of the decade; but it also reflected the increasing affluence and domesticity of family life in the post-war years. Four in every five British homes had a garden, and as more people found themselves able to afford their own home, so they liked to spend more time and money on their garden, tending their flowerbeds, mowing their lawns and building their patios.[47] Indeed, it was clear that instead of undermining popular enthusiasm for the simpler pleasures of life, the affluence of the seven years since Suez had reinforced it. And as home ownership increased, so did public interest in everything from flowerbeds and lawnmowers to do-it-yourself repairs and furnishings. In their survey of Woodford in the late fifties, Peter Willmott and Michael Young found middle-class husbands busy stripping paintwork, installing central heating, knocking down chimneys and planning extensions.[48] Sales of wallpaper, tools and specialist magazines were booming. In 1962 the BBC bought a derelict house of their own and, once a week, unleashed their resident expert Barry Bucknell to renovate it; within months he was reportedly receiving more fan letters than the entire cast of *Coronation Street*.[49]

Deedes' report on the popularity of gardening testifies to the unheralded stability of British social life as the country moved towards the middle of the sixties. Despite the seven years of rollicking consumer growth that marked the Macmillan years, old habits died hard. For all the money lavished on cars, telephones and even foreign holidays, many people were simply more interested in their gardens than in new-fangled innovations, and there were still plenty more amateur anglers than there were aspiring rock stars.[50] Indeed, if there was one pastime that seriously threatened the position of gardening, it was not performing or even listening to rock and roll music; it was another domestic diversion, watching television. By the end of 1963 there were more than twelve million sets in use, ensuring almost complete national coverage.[51] *That Was The Week That Was* might be facing the axe, but there was no shortage of other popular shows that both commanded public loyalty and reflected the move away from New Wave grittiness towards the high jinks of Swinging London. Realistic programmes like *Coronation Street* and *Z Cars* were still extremely popular, but two new attractions, *The Avengers* and *Doctor Who*, were already beginning to win audiences over to a more fantastic, elaborate and self-consciously modern approach.

The Avengers had been devised by Sydney Newman at ABC, and started life in 1961 as a subdued, realistic crime thriller, broadcast live in black and white. By the beginning of the third series in September 1963, however, the producers had started moving towards the more flamboyant style for which the programme subsequently become famous, and *The Avengers* began to appear regularly among the twenty most popular programmes on television, alongside such reassuring perennials as *Coronation Street*, *Dixon of Dock Green* and *Doctor Finlay's Casebook*.[52] The show also turned its two lead actors, Patrick Macnee and Honor Blackman, into minor stars of the mid-sixties. As the *TV Times* preview of the new autumn series reminded its readers, Macnee played John Steed, 'a charming man-about-town with a taste for Edwardian elegance in his clothes – jackets with cuffed sleeves and patent leather, Chelsea-style boots', while Blackman's character, Cathy Gale, was a woman of 'great beauty and intelligence, noted for her wide knowledge and wider acquaintances – and a passion for wearing leather clothes', as well as for her judo expertise.[53]

The Avengers clearly owed much of its appeal to the contemporary enthusiasm for James Bond and all things connected with espionage, but it also anticipated some of the cultural trends of the later sixties. The character of Cathy Gale in particular – bright, independent, sexy and self-confident – evidently struck a chord with audiences in 1963 and 1964. British women were increasingly asserting themselves outside the kitchen and the bedroom: even the Christmas season's bestselling toy, the Sindy doll, was sold as a 'free, swinging, grown-up girl'.[54] Launched earlier that year by Pedigree of Kent, Sindy was the sensation of the season, selling 200,000 dolls that Christmas, and plans were already afoot to give her a boyfriend, named Paul after Paul McCartney. British fashion, too, was becoming both more creative and more affordable, and it seemed only natural that Cathy Gale wore only the latest, trendiest designs. Her skin-tight, black leather outfits, which frequently drew the attention of reviewers and, no doubt, many male viewers, had been specially designed for the new series by Frederick Starke of the London Fashion House, and in October they were publicly exhibited at Les Ambassadeurs Club in Park Lane. Indeed, Macnee and Blackman even released a novelty single in the New Year, paying homage to her 'Kinky Boots'.[55]

The double act of Steed and Gale allowed *The Avengers* to strike a balance between patriotic tradition and swinging modernity, not so very different from the combination offered by James Bond or even the Beatles. This same blend of tradition and modernity was also evident in *Doctor Who*, which began life just when *The Avengers* was really becoming popular, the autumn of 1963, and inspired an even more dedicated following. *Doctor Who*, like *Z Cars*, was a perfect example of the dynamic new approach encouraged at the BBC by Hugh Carleton Greene and Sydney Newman.[56] The programme was devised by Newman and a group of BBC writers in order to fill the gap between *Grandstand* and *Juke Box Jury* on Saturday evenings and consolidate the BBC's grip on 'family' audiences. The aim was also to impress older children with a genuinely exciting, modern and popular series, especially as ITV serials like *Robin Hood* were already losing viewers. This emphasis on excitement was blended with a hint of the old Reithian worthiness, as Verity Lambert, the series' first producer, explained:

> I think Sydney . . . was trying to find something which took into account the new things that fascinated kids, like space and other planets, and certainly he felt that he wanted a programme which, while not necessarily educational as such, was one which children could look at and learn something from. In the futuristic stories they could learn something about science and in the past stories they could learn something about history in an entertainment format.[57]

Verity Lambert was, incidentally, the only female producer then employed by the BBC, and having worked in both the United States and

ITV she was able to inject the appropriate dose of populist enthusiasm into what might have been an unbearably worthy undertaking.[58] Thanks to its brilliant premise, a mysterious old man and his companions travelling through time and space in a machine disguised as a police telephone box, the series was able to adopt a number of different styles befitting an enormous range of settings, from ancient Troy to the far future. As the *Radio Times* put it in November 1963: 'They may visit a distant galaxy where civilisation has been devastated by the blast of a neutron bomb or they may find themselves journeying to far Cathay in the caravan of Marco Polo. The whole cosmos is in fact their oyster.'[59] True, *Doctor Who* often blatantly borrowed from popular children's fantasies like *Alice in Wonderland* or even the horror films of the day; but its emphasis on technology and science fiction also helped to attract an audience excited by the space race and the scientific advances of the sixties.[60]

When *Doctor Who* was first broadcast on 23 November, its producers took care to present their audience with an attractive blend of old and new. Three of the four regular characters were recognisably modern: two were teachers at a suburban London secondary school; and one was a teenage pupil, first seen listening in rapture to 'John Smith and the Common Men' on the radio. The fictional band, she explains, have just reached second place in the charts; in fact the position was then occupied by the Beatles' single 'She Loves You'.[61] The fourth character was her grandfather, the mysterious 'Doctor', played as an irascible old Edwardian gentleman by the familiar character actor William Hartnell. By the end of the opening episode, all four found themselves transported back in time to the Stone Age. This was perhaps not the best setting to emphasise the contemporary appeal of the new series, and the initial viewing figures of around six million were less than spectacular. Few observers would have predicted at this stage that the programme would become one of the longest-running television shows of all time; it hardly looked likely that it would last beyond 1964.[62]

Four days before Christmas, however, the producers struck gold. The show's second story, 'The Mutants', took the time travellers to a strange world in the distant future and introduced the race of monsters for which the series would become famous: the Daleks. The initial intention of *Doctor Who*'s producers had been to avoid 'bug-eyed monsters', but bug-eyed monsters were what the Christmas audience evidently demanded. The Daleks themselves, squat, mechanical pepper-pots that glided noiselessly down the steel corridors of their futuristic city, grating out the command 'Exterminate!' in their harsh metallic voices, immediately captured public attention.[63] By the second Dalek instalment, on 28 December, the ratings were already rising, and when the story ended in February they had reached 10.4 million. The Daleks were not just a hit; they were the television sensation of the season. Four in every five letters to the BBC's *Points of View* programme were about the Daleks, and the critic of the *Huddersfield Daily Examiner*, who had originally damned the programme, was among many who reversed their opinion:

> As for spine chillery . . . well, I take back what I said a few weeks ago about *Doctor Who* having got off to such a bad start it could never recover . . . Last Saturday, when, after the Dalek 'intelligence' had been lifted unseen from its robot and placed in a blanket on the floor, the episode closed with something very horrible indeed just beginning to crawl from under the blanket. So horrible was it, that I very much doubt whether I shall have the courage this evening to switch on to see what it was. Lovely stuff!.[64]

The success of the Daleks cemented the image of *Doctor Who* as a stylish, dynamic and, above all, *modern* series, albeit one liable to send children scurrying behind the sofa in excited terror. When the Daleks returned to the programme nine months later, this time mounting an invasion of Earth, once again the viewing figures lurched upwards, rising above twelve million for the first time.[65] 'My children introduced me to this series. I'm glad they did!' wrote one man in a BBC survey.[66] In fact, the programme almost immediately transcended its intended audience of older children and attracted a large adult following; subsequent research claimed that a third of the audience was between twenty and fifty. Anecdotal evidence about the readership of the Dan Dare comic strip in the *Eagle* had already suggested that futuristic adventures appealed to both adults and children, to 'Cabinet ministers along with Rhondda Valley schoolboys', and one medical scientist reported that his hospital staff would discuss every *Doctor Who* storyline in great detail.[67] All the same, children formed the bedrock of the audience, and in the months after the pepper-pots' first appearance, a stream of Dalek-related toys poured forth. Only the Beatles and James Bond inspired comparable quantities of cheap consumer merchandise. One writer later recalled the routine of a Dalek-dominated childhood:

Awake in bedroom decorated in Dalek wallpaper. Put on Dalek slippers (Furness Footwear Ltd) and go to bathroom to wash with Dalek soap (Northants Assoc for the Blind). Do daily exercises with inflatable Dalek (Scorpion toys) as punchbag before setting off to school sporting Dalek mini-badge (Woolworths) on jumper.

Once at school, meanwhile, he would steal surreptitious glimpses at his Dalek comics and books, eat Dalek sweet cigarettes, ponder buying Dalek records and slide-shows, and generally lose himself in visions of a Dalek future.[68]

Television's early critics had often assumed that the new invention would disastrously undermine the popularity of the written word. But, despite the enormous popular success of programmes like *Coronation Street*, *The Avengers* and *Doctor Who*, British publishing was flourishing as never before. There were ten million more new titles than in 1949, many of them cheap paperbacks aimed at the mass market. Penguin led the way, but Pan, thanks to their lucrative James Bond series, were not far behind.[69] Indeed, in 1963 the Christmas shopper was almost spoilt for choice, such was the range of new books. There was le Carré's novel *The Spy Who Came In from the Cold*, for instance; or Alistair MacLean's new bestseller *Ice Station Zebra*, in which a British scientist accompanying an American nuclear submarine to the North Pole saves his predictably brash companions from disaster. Anglo-American relations were also the subject of Kingsley Amis' latest book, *One Fat Englishman*, the satirical story of an grotesquely fat and predatory British publisher who travels across the United States insulting and molesting his hosts.

Perhaps the most surprising bestsellers of 1963, though, were three works of non-fiction that hinted at the social trends of the decade to come. Bishop John Robinson's book *Honest to God*, a controversial theological tract updating Christian beliefs for the technological age, sold over 300,000 copies within a year of publication and eventually passed the million mark.[70] Even more remarkably, Penguin turned Colin Buchanan's government report on *Traffic in Towns*, which called for the restructuring of city centres to cope with the enormous growth of car ownership, into an unlikely paperback bestseller. And, finally, there was *Great Dishes of the World*, a glossy collection of international recipes by the food critic Robert Carrier and the ideal Christmas present for the 'kitchen goddess' who dreamed of transforming

Solihull into Siena. At four guineas a copy, it was an expensive purchase, but few books were more popular in the affluent sixties, and over the next twenty years more than two million copies were sold.[71]

Above all, though, there was Bond. In the spring of 1963 Jonathan Cape had published Ian Fleming's latest novel, *On Her Majesty's Secret Service*, and this time they really pulled out all the stops. There had already been a staggering 42,000 advance orders for the new book, but nothing was left to chance. Life-size models of James Bond, complete with gun, were mounted in the bigger branches of W. H. Smith, and Cape even ran a competition to find the best Bond-themed bookshop window in the country.[72] It was worth it: many aficionados thought that *On Her Majesty's Secret Service* was one of Fleming's very best. No other Bond book came close to matching its shattering final paragraphs:

> Bond turned towards Tracy. She was lying forward with her face buried in the ruins of the steering-wheel. Her pink handkerchief had come off and the bell of golden hair hung down and hid her face. Bond put his arm round her shoulders, across which the dark patches had begun to flower.
>
> He pressed her against him. He looked up at the young man and smiled his reassurance.
>
> 'It's all right,' he said in a clear voice as if explaining something to a child. 'It's quite all right. She's having a rest. We'll be going on soon. There's no hurry. You see —' Bond's head sank down against hers and he whispered into her hair — 'you see, we've got all the time in the world.'[73]

In a gushing review, the *Sunday Times* declared that Fleming had created the ultimate 'culture-hero': 'James Bond is what every man would like to be, and what every woman would like between her sheets.'[74]

Like the Beatles, Bond was at the threshold of a four-year period of unsurpassed international popularity. *Dr No* had performed creditably, although not spectacularly, at the American box office in 1962, but its British success had been enough to guarantee a sequel.[75] *From Russia with Love* opened at the Odeon, Leicester Square, on 10 October 1963 and was another immediate sensation. The novel on which it was based was both more realistic and more gripping than *Dr No*, and the film was also an improvement on its predecessor. Connery had now settled comfortably into the lead role, and there was a more dynamic, crowd-pleasing mix of action and humour, including a garrotting, various gun battles, helicopter attacks and boat chases, a fight on the Orient Express and even a cat-fight between two gypsy women, shot and edited to create an impression of mesmerising speed. It was next to impossible to get hold of a ticket, and after seven days at the Odeon the film had taken £14,258 and broken the house record. By the end of the year, it had taken more than £800,000 and pulled ahead of *Tom Jones*, *The Great Escape* and *The Pink Panther* to become the highest-grossing film of 1963.[76] It was, said one enthusiastic film magazine, 'The Most Sensational Business in the History of the Film Industry'.[77] Even Reginald Maudling, who no doubt appreciated Bond's taste for high living, arranged a private screening during the Conservative leadership contest so that he could see what all the fuss was about, although, as we have seen, he was forced to cancel it.[78] That autumn, sales of the Bond books went through the roof. Pan sold 4.4 million Bond paperbacks in Britain alone, more than three times the figure for 1962, while the hardback edition of *On Her Majesty's Secret Service* accounted for another 75,000 sales. The film's soundtrack album made the LP chart and the title song, performed by Matt Monro, reached number twenty in the singles chart. James Bond could do no wrong; not for nothing did Ann Fleming take to calling her husband 'Thunderbeatle'.[79]

By contrast, the New Wave, which had once seemed so modern and so vibrant, now felt tired and old hat. In February 1963 *This Sporting Life*, which was actually one of the best New Wave films, was released to general indifference and a poor box-office performance. Audiences had, as the *Guardian* put it, 'seen it all before': they wanted colour, fantasy and excitement, not a miserable black and white film about a rugby league player.[80] But four months later the reception of *Tom Jones* was very different. The public loved it, the critics applauded it, and the Americans gave it the Oscar for Best Picture. Shot in a freewheeling, inventive style, it was buoyant and bawdy where *This Sporting Life* had been grim and gritty. It bombarded the audience with cinematic tricks and winks, and the star, Albert Finney, looked as though he were having a whale of a time, quite a contrast with his turn in *Saturday Night and Sunday Morning*.[81] As the Bond director Terence Young later put it, flamboyant films like *Tom Jones* and *From Russia with Love* now matched the public mood far better than anything the New Wave could offer. 'I think people were getting tired of the realistic school,' he explained, 'the kitchen sinks and all those abortions.'[82]

In the last true New Wave film, *Billy Liar!*, released in August, the confrontation between old and new was played out by the two lead characters. Billy, played by Tom Courtenay, is a disaffected provincial clerk who dreams of escaping to the capital but also fears to leave his Northern backwater: not so different, then, from Arthur Seaton, Arthur Machin or even Jimmy Porter. But his girlfriend Liz, played by Julie Christie, is a much more modern character: self-confident, sexy and independent, more like Cathy Gale or the glamour girls of Carnaby Street than the downtrodden women of the New Wave. In the final scene, Billy chooses to stay in his Northern town of Stradhoughton, but Liz boards the train for Swinging London. Billy clings to the past; Liz embraces the future. 'With Julie Christie,' wrote Alexander Walker, 'the British cinema caught the train south.'[83]

On the last day of 1963, the Labour MP Anthony Wedgwood Benn went out to a party at a friend's house before returning 'just before midnight where the boys and Melissa were welcoming in the New Year, twisting and shouting'. He wrote in his diary:

> The end of 1963 and what a year politically and personally! First the dead – Pope John XXIII, Kennedy and Gaitskell. The collapse of the Common Market application. The Profumo affair, and Macmillan's resignation. Now, Home versus Wilson and the fortunes of the Party are reversed. The year of the test-ban treaty and the end of Adenauer and the beginning of a new era . . .
>
> On to 1964 which will be the busiest and most important politically and personally. At the moment a Labour victory and with it a complete change in our lives seems certain too, though in what capacity I shall have to work I just don't know.[84]

One of the arguments of this book has been that historians have tended to exaggerate the extent and speed of change in Britain during the sixties, and to ignore the numerous cultural and political continuities that stretched back to the thirties or even beyond. And yet, as Reginald Maudling's dash for growth began to make itself felt in the second half of 1963, the pace of change had clearly quickened. In the final months of the year, there was an undeniable sense of what Benn called 'the beginning of a new era'. The initial novelty of post-war affluence was gradually fading: after all, nine in every ten households now had their own television set; and cars, private telephones, vacuum cleaners and even washing machines were becoming commonplace. The politicians of the late fifties had largely disappeared from the stage: Eden and Macmillan had resigned; Bevan and Gaitskell were dead; even Butler was now in the twilight of his career. In 1945 the British Empire had controlled the lives of more than 500 million overseas subjects; by the beginning of 1964, it governed fewer than 15 million. In the aftermath of the Cuban missile crisis, the tension of the Cold War had begun to ease. The nuclear powers had signed the test-ban treaty, and CND was rapidly haemorrhaging support. Jazz had surrendered its cultural cachet; the satire boom had lost its fizz; and the Angry Young Men were looking distinctly middle aged.

In *From Russia with Love*, or *With the Beatles*, or *Doctor Who*, or even Robert Carrier's expensive cookery book, the themes of British cultural life in the next few years were already becoming apparent. Audiences had a fresh appetite for novelty, fantasy and flair, and the country seemed on the threshold of a new era of modernisation, scientific progress and cultural self-renewal. New enthusiasms were beginning to attract the patronage of the affluent public, from foreign holidays to fashion. Duffel coats and Aran sweaters were looking terribly dated, but the heydays of Mods and Rockers, of mini-skirts and go-go boots, of space-age tunics and see-through dresses, were just months away. From the Highlands to Cornwall, aspiring bright young things had only to switch on ITV's new Friday-night flagship *Ready, Steady, Go!*, or just turn to their Sunday newspapers, to see the latest trends. The cover of the country's first colour supplement, launched by the *Sunday Times* in February 1962, had shown eleven photographs of a pretty girl in a grey flannel dress. On the inside, a caption gave the names of the model, the photographer and the designer, Jean Shrimpton, David Bailey and Mary Quant.[85] All three were on the verge of international celebrity. So too was Terence Conran, the designer and entrepreneur who at the end of 1963 was busily planning his latest venture, a new furniture and design store that he intended to set up in Chelsea with the name Habitat. Other canny designers were starting to open up their own boutiques, especially in one nondescript, battered stretch of Soho called Carnaby Street. In the suburbs of London, an obscure rhythm and blues group called the Rolling Stones was beginning to build up a following; and in Lancaster Gate, England's new football manager was planning his team's campaign for the World Cup.

One man above all was looking forward to the new year. At his party conference that October, Harold Wilson had confidently predicted that the old amateur values of the Conservatives would be consumed in the 'white heat' of the scientific revolution that was about to transform British society and industry for ever. 'In the Cabinet room and the boardroom alike,' he told his supporters, 'those charged with the control of our affairs must be ready to think and speak in the language of the scientific age.'[86] The audience cheered, the press loved it, and 'White Heat' became an almost immediate catchphrase for Labour's programme to modernise Britain. More than any other individual in the country, Wilson seemed the incarnation of the new dynamic, technological spirit of 'the jet-age', the herald of a new era of creativity and progress.[87] And as 1963 drew to a close, he was at the height of his popularity, eleven points clear in the opinion polls and, according to almost every political expert in the land, the likely winner of the forthcoming election.[88]

Barely three weeks into the New Year, two thousand Labour supporters trudged through the frost and fog of a Birmingham winter's evening towards the Town Hall and a vision of the future of Britain. On the platform stood Harold Wilson, the picture of cool, self-assured professionalism, and his opening words rang with confidence and vigour:

> I want to speak to you today about a new Britain and how we intend to bring home to our people the excitement there will be in building it.
>
> For 1964 is the year in which we can take our destiny into our own hands again.
>
> Since the war, the world has been rushing forward at an unprecedented, an exhilarating speed. In two decades, the scientists have made more progress than in the past two thousand years. They have made it possible for man to reach out to the stars, and to bring abundance from the earth. They have made it possible to end the dark ages of poverty and want, to take mankind forward to a future which our fathers could not have dreamed possible.

The people of Britain, he declared, were 'living in the jet-age', but they were still 'governed by an Edwardian establishment mentality'. It was time to change all that, to banish 'the chill frost of Tory leadership':

> This is the time for a breakthrough to an exciting and wonderful period in our history, in which all can and must take part. Our young men

and women, especially, have in their hands the power to change the world. We want the youth of Britain to storm the new frontiers of knowledge, to bring back to Britain that surging adventurous self-confidence and sturdy self-respect which the Tories have almost submerged with their apathy and cynicism.

'This is what 1964 can mean,' Wilson told his audience, his voice echoing around the grand old Victorian building:

A chance for change. More, a time for resurgence.
A chance to sweep away the grouse-moor conception of Tory leadership and refit Britain with a new image, a new confidence.
A chance to change the face and future of Britain.[89]

NOTES

All documentary references beginning PREM, HO, FO and so on are taken from the archives at the National Archives, formerly the Public Record Office, in Kew.

References to 'Benn diary' are taken from the two volumes of Tony Benn's diaries for the early 1960s: *Years of Hope: Diaries, Papers and Letters, 1940–62* (London, 1994) and *Out of the Wilderness: Diaries, 1963–67* (London, 1987).

PREFACE

1 Bernard Levin, *The Pendulum Years: Britain and the Sixties* (revised edition: London, 1977), p. 282.

2 *Observer*, 9 November 1960. The writer was Kenneth Tynan.

3 C. H. Rolph, ed., *The Trial of Lady Chatterley* (Harmondsworth, 1961), pp. 70–1; Cate Haste, *Rules of Desire: Sex in Britain: World War I to the Present* (London, 1994), pp. 178–80.

4 John Sutherland, *Bestsellers: Popular Fiction of the 1970s* (London, 1981), p. 35; Haste, *Rules of Desire*, p. 181; Stuart Laing, 'The Politics of Culture: Institutional Change', in Bart Moore-Gilbert and John Seed, eds, *Cultural Revolution? The Challenge of the Arts in the 1960s* (London, 1992), p. 85.

5 Levin, *The Pendulum Years*, p. 290.

6 *Observer*, 9 November 1960.

7 Arthur Marwick, *The Sixties: Cultural Revolution in Britain, France, Italy, and the United States, c.1958–c.1974* (Oxford, 1998), p, 146.

8 Quoted in the *Guardian*, 13 September 2000.

9 Christopher Booker, *The Neophiliacs: The Revolution in English Life in the Fifties and Sixties* (revised edition: London, 1992), p. 135.

10 Moureen Nolan and Roma Singleton, 'Mini-Renaissance', in Sara Maitland, ed., *Very Heaven: Looking Back at the 1960s* (London, 1988), p. 25.

11 Jonathon Green, *All Dressed Up: The Sixties and the Counter-Culture* (London, 1998), pp. ix, xiii.

12 Green, *All Dressed Up*, pp. xii–xiii.

13 David May quoted in Jonathon Green, *Days in the Life: Voices from the English Underground, 1961–1971* (Pimlico edition: London, 1998), p. 425.

14 Marwick, *The Sixties*, pp. 15–20, 805.

15 *Open Eye*, February 1998.

16 Marwick, *The Sixties*, p. 806.

17 Mary Whitehouse, *Whatever Happened to Sex?* (Hove, 1977), pp. 8–9.

18 Quoted in introduction to Moore-Gilbert and Seed, eds, *Cultural Revolution?*, p. 2.

19 *Daily Mail*, 29 April 1988.

20 Peter Hitchens, *The Abolition of Britain: The British Cultural Revolution from Lady Chatterley to Tony Blair* (revised edition: London, 2000), pp. 337–8, 369; *Guardian*, 20 July 2004.

21 Christopher Booker, *The Seventies: Portrait of a Decade* (Harmondsworth, 1980), p. 9.

22 Levin, *The Pendulum Years*, p. 78.

23 Jeffrey Richards, 'Imperial Heroes for a Post-imperial Age: Films and the End of Empire', in Stuart Ward, ed., *British Culture and the End of Empire* (Manchester, 2001), p. 137.

24 Eric Hobsbawm, *Age of Extremes: The Short Twentieth Century 1914–1991* (London, 1994), p. 319.

25 Marwick, *The Sixties*, pp. 733, 806.

26 Paul Ferris, *Sex and the British: A Twentieth-Century History* (London, 1993), p. 180.

27 *Guardian*, 8 October 1960; *Daily Telegraph*, 18 October 1960. On the press and the trial in general, see Tim Newburn, *Permission and Regulation: Law and Morals in Post-War Britain* (London, 1992), pp. 83–4.

28 Ferris, *Sex and the British*, p. 176; Griffith Jones quoted in the *Guardian*, 13 September 2000.

29 See HO 302/11, and Ferris, *Sex and the British*, p. 181.

30 Haste, *Rules of Desire*, pp. 181–2.

31 *New Society*, November 1969.

32 Green, *All Dressed Up*, p. xiii.

33 Quoted in Noël Annan, *Our Age: The Generation That Made Post-war Britain* (London, 1990), pp. 603–4.

34 Ken Coates and Richard Silburn, *Poverty: The Forgotten Englishmen* (Harmondsworth, 1970), p. 142.

35 *New Society*, 27 November 1969.

36 My italics. See Jann Wenner, ed., *Lennon Remembers: The Rolling Stone Interviews* (Harmondsworth, 1972), quoted in introduction to Moore-Gilbert and Seed, eds, *Cultural Revolution?*, pp. 3–4.

37 Green, *All Dressed Up*, p. 86.

38 Robert Hewison, *Too Much: Art and Society in the Sixties 1960–1975* (London, 1986), p. xiii; introduction to David Alan Mellor and Laurent Gervereau, eds, *The Sixties: Britain and France, 1962–1973: The Utopian Years* (London, 1997), p. 7; Hobsbawm, *Age of Extremes*, pp. 8–9, 257–86.

39 Marwick, *The Sixties*, pp. 7–8.

40 Marwick, *The Sixties*, p. 9.

CHAPTER 1: SUEZ

1 Robin Neillands, *A Fighting Retreat: The British Empire 1947–1997* (London: 1996), pp. 337–8.

2 Neillands, *A Fighting Retreat*, pp. 342–3.

3 Derek Hopwood, *Egypt: Politics and Society 1945–1990* (third edition: London, 1993), pp. 10–13; Denis Judd, *Empire: The British Imperial Experience from 1765 to the Present* (London, 1996), pp. 92–103.

4 FO 371/912219, 10 January 1951, quoted in D. R. Thorpe, *Eden: The Life and Times of Sir Anthony Eden, First Earl of Avon 1897–1977* (London, 2003), p. 490.

5 John Darwin, *Britain and Decolonisation: The Retreat from Empire in the Post-War World* (London, 1988), p. 113; Lawrence James, *The Rise and Fall of the British Empire* (London: 1994), pp. 560–2.

6 John Barry quoted in Eddie Fiegel, *John Barry: A Sixties Theme, from James Bond to Midnight Cowboy* (London, 1998), p. 34.

7 Neillands, *A Fighting Retreat*, p. 259.

8 Evelyn Shuckburgh, *Descent to Suez* (London, 1986), p. 29.

9 See Neillands, *A Fighting Retreat*, pp. 255–81.

10 Hopwood, *Egypt*, pp. 23–33.

11 See Jean Lacouture, *Nasser* (London, 1973).

22 Hopwood, *Egypt*, p. 78.

13 Selwyn Lloyd, *Suez 1956: A Personal Account* (London, 1978), p. 15.

14 See Hopwood, *Egypt*, p. 41.

15 Robert Rhodes James, *Anthony Eden* (London: 1986), p. 397.

16 See Rhodes James, *Anthony Eden*, pp. 397–8; Thorpe, *Eden*, pp. 426–7.

17 Mohammed Heikal, *Cutting the Lion's Tail: Suez through Egyptian Eyes* (London, 1986), p. 64.

18 Hopwood, *Egypt*, p. 43.

19 FO 371/121271, 5 March 1956.

20 See Hopwood, *Egypt*, pp. 44–7.

21 Anthony Gorst and Lewis Johnman, *The Suez Crisis* (London, 1997), p. 53.

22 Anthony Nutting, *Nasser* (London, 1972), p. 144; Hopwood, *Egypt*, p. 48.

23 Thorpe, *Eden*, p. 475.

24 Rhodes James, *Anthony Eden*, pp. 196–7; Thorpe, *Eden*, pp. 189–219.

25 Ian Gilmour and Mark Garnett, *Whatever Happened to the Tories: The Conservatives since 1945* (London, 1997), p. 127.

26 Rhodes James, *Anthony Eden*, p. 335.

27 Rhodes James, *Anthony Eden*, p. 403

28 Robert J. Wybrow, *Britain Speaks Out, 1937–87: A Social History as Seen through the Gallup Data* (London, 1989), p. 43.

29 *Yorkshire Post*, 7 April 1955.

30 Thorpe, *Eden*, p. 434.

31 Rhodes James, *Anthony Eden*, p. 408; Thorpe, *Eden*, pp. 437–41.

32 Rhodes James, *Anthony Eden*, p. 158.

33 Edward Pearce, *The Lost Leaders: The Best Prime Ministers We Never Had* (London, 1997), p. 5.

34 Thorpe, *Eden*, pp. 60, 104, 315, 338, 376–7.

35 Thorpe, *Eden*, pp. 384–7.

36 Quoted in Peter Hennessy, *Muddling Through: Power, Politics and the Quality of Government in Postwar Britain* (London, 1996), p. 211.

37 Kevin Jefferys, *Retreat from New Jerusalem: British Politics, 1951–64* (London, 1997), p. 41; Pearce, *The Lost Leaders*, pp. 81–9.

38 Gilmour and Garnett, *Whatever Happened to the Tories*, p. 87.

39 Samuel Brittan, *The Treasury under the Tories 1951–1964* (Harmondsworth, 1964), pp. 177–9; Kenneth O. Morgan, *The People's Peace: British History since 1945* (second edition: Oxford, 1999), pp. 122–3; Richard Holt, *Second Amongst Equals: Chancellors of the Exchequer since the Second World War* (London, 2001), p. 126.

40 Thorpe, *Eden*, pp. 456–7; John Turner, *Macmillan* (London, 1994), pp. 105–7.

41 *Daily Telegraph*, 3 January 1956; Thorpe, *Eden*, pp. 420, 459–61.

42 Jefferys, *Retreat from New Jerusalem*, p. 53.

43 Anthony Nutting, *No End of a Lesson: The Story of Suez* (London, 1967), pp. 34–5.

44 Nutting, *No End of a Lesson*, p. 32.

45 CAB 128/30, Cabinet Minutes, 27 July 1956.

46 *The Times*, 27 July 1956; Booker, *The Neophiliacs*, p. 115; Thorpe, *Eden*, pp. 481, 490.

47 Rhodes James, *Anthony Eden*, p. 481.

48 *Daily Mirror*, 30 July 1956.

49 *Daily Herald*, 28 July 1956.

50 PREM 11/1098, Eden to Eisenhower, 5 August 1956.

51 See Gorst and Johnman, *The Suez Crisis*, pp. 65–8.

52 See Rhodes James, *Anthony Eden*, pp. 478–520.

53 CAB 134/1216, 7 August 1956.

54 Noble Frankland, ed., *Documents on International Relations 1956* (Oxford, 1959), pp. 159–60.

55 PREM 11/1100, Eisenhower to Eden, 8 September 1956.

56 Gilmour and Garnett, *Whatever Happened to the Tories*, p. 112.

57 Rhodes James, *Anthony Eden*, p. 509.

58 James, *The Rise and Fall of the British Empire*, p. 580.

59 Rhodes James, *Anthony Eden*, p. 532.

60 Rhodes James, *Anthony Eden*, p. 523.

61 Rhodes James, *Anthony Eden*, pp. 520–1; Thorpe, *Eden*, p. 513.

62 Nutting, *No End of a Lesson*, p. 93.

63 Peter Clarke, *A Question of Leadership: From Gladstone to Thatcher* (London, 1992), pp. 219–21.

64 Lloyd, *Suez 1956*, p. 4.

65 Thorpe, *Eden*, p. 457.

66 Lloyd, *Suez 1956*, pp. 180–3; see also Clarke, *A Question of Leadership*, p. 222.

67 Gorst and Johnman, *The Suez Crisis*, p. 94.

68 CAB 128/30, Confidential Annex, 23 October 1956.

69 The British copy of the protocol was destroyed on Eden's orders. It has been reconstructed from French and Israeli sources and its authenticity confirmed by Sir Donald Logan, one of the British negotiators: see Keith Kyle, *Suez* (London, 1991), pp. 565–6.

70 Gorst and Johnman, *The Suez Crisis*, p. 98.

71 Edward Heath, *The Course of my Life: My Autobiography* (London, 1998), p. 169.

72 T236/4188, 'Measures to Protect Sterling', Bridges to Macmillan, 8 August 1956.

73 T236/4188, Bridges to Macmillan, 7 September 1956.

74 James, *The Rise and Fall of the British Empire*, p. 585.

75 CAB 128/30, Cabinet Minutes, 11 September 1956.

76 Peter Clarke, *Hope and Glory: Britain 1900–1990* (London, 1996), p. 260.

77 CAB 128/30, Cabinet Minutes, 25 October 1956.

78 Hopwood, *Egypt*, p. 53.

79 CAB 128/30, Cabinet Minutes, 30 October 1956.

80 PREM 11/1105, Eden to Eisenhower, 30 October 1956.

81 Gorst and Johnman, *The Suez Crisis*, p. 115.

82 *The Times*, 27 August 1956.

83 Booker, *The Neophiliacs*, p. 116.

84 Harry Hopkins, *The New Look: A Social History of the Forties and Fifties in Britain* (London, 1964), p. 446.

85 Asa Briggs, *The History of Broadcasting in the United Kingdom: Volume V: Competition* (Oxford, 1995), pp. 100–1.

86 Actually, Jean confesses that she found the rally 'rather boring': John Osborne, *The Entertainer* (London, 1957), pp. 17, 28.

87 Ben Pimlott, *The Queen: A Biography of Elizabeth II* (London, 1996), p. 255.

88 Mountbatten had previously supported military action, but as the months dragged on so he developed serious misgivings. See Piers Brendon and Phillip Whitehead, *The Windsors: A Dynasty Revealed, 1917–2000* (London, 2000), p. 147.

89 Benn diary, 1 November 1956.

90 Rhodes James, *Anthony Eden*, pp. 553–5.

91 Rhodes James, *Anthony Eden*, p. 558.

92 David Owen, *Time to Declare* (London, 1992), p. 40; and see Lawrence Black, '"The Bitterest Enemies of Communism": Labour Revisionists, Atlanticism and the Cold War', *Contemporary British History* 15:3, Autumn 2001, pp. 50–2.

93 Benn diary, 2 November 1956.

94 Benn diary, 4 November 1956. It is an interesting reflection of Benn's political priorities that he spent the day at Gaitskell's side rather than at the Trafalgar Square demonstration being addressed by Aneurin Bevan.

95 The speech is reprinted in Gorst and Johnman, *The Suez Crisis*, pp. 119–20.

96 Clarke, *A Question of Leadership*, p. 247.

97 Philip M. Williams, *Hugh Gaitskell* (Oxford, 1982), pp. 287–8.

98 Rhodes James, *Anthony Eden*, p. 555.

99 Neillands, *A Fighting Retreat*, p. 340. The idea that the British population had always unthinkingly united behind its forces overseas was, needless to say, not quite accurate.

100 Rhodes James, *Anthony Eden*, pp. 564–5.

101 Gorst and Johnman, *The Suez Crisis*, pp. 116–17.

102 *Observer*, 4 November 1956.

103 The quotations are from Rhodes James, *Anthony Eden*, p. 556; on Eden's calm, see Thorpe, *Eden*, pp. 522–3.

104 Lloyd, *Suez 1956*, pp. 206–7; Peter Lewis, *The Fifties* (London, 1978), p. 144.

105 Rhodes James, *Anthony Eden*, p. 556.

106 Rhodes James, *Anthony Eden*, p. 567.

107 CAB 128/30, Cabinet Minutes, 4 November 1956.

108 PREM 11/1177, Eden to Eisenhower, 5 November 1956.

109 Hopwood, *Egypt*, p. 55.

110 Neillands, *A Fighting Retreat*, p. 345.

111 Gorst and Johnman, *The Suez Crisis*, p. 133.

112 Rhodes James, *Anthony Eden*, p. 573.

113 Lloyd, *Suez 1956*, p. 209.

114 CAB 128/30, Cabinet Minutes, 6 November 1956. See also Alistair Horne, *Macmillan 1894–1956: Volume I of the Official Biography* (London, 1989), p. 440; Turner, *Macmillan*, pp. 118–19.

115 Rhodes James, *Anthony Eden*, p. 576.

116 J. W. Mallalieu, quoted in Lewis, *The Fifties*, p. 152.

117 Clarke, *A Question of Leadership*, p. 223.

118 CAB 128/30, Cabinet Minutes, 20 November 1956.

119 CAB 128/30, Cabinet Minutes, 28 November 1956.

120 Rhodes James, *Anthony Eden*, p. 585.

121 For the definitive discussion of Eden's health during the last months of 1956, see Thorpe, *Eden*, p. 544.

122 Fleming's house later gave its name to the seventeenth James Bond film, *GoldenEye*, released in 1995. Anthony Eden, however, did not feature in it. See Rhodes James, *Anthony Eden*, p. 582; Andrew Lycett, *Ian Fleming* (London, 1995), pp. 302–7.

123 *Manchester Guardian*, 24 November 1956.

124 Rhodes James, *Anthony Eden*, pp. 589–91.

125 Jeffreys, *Retreat from New Jerusalem*, p. 56.

126 Rhodes James, *Anthony Eden*, p. 592.

127 Thorpe, *Eden*, p. 503. The evidence of Eden's high standing in the opinion polls, although rarely acknowledged, is pretty overwhelming: see Wybrow, *Britain Speaks Out*, p. 48; Anthony King and Robert J. Wybrow, eds, *British Political Opinion 1937–2000: The Gallup Polls* (London, 2001), pp. 186–7.

128 On Eden's illness and resignation, see Rhodes James, *Anthony Eden*, pp. 595–601; Thorpe, *Eden*, pp. 545–8. Some historians, for example, Judd, *Empire*, p. 365, have argued that Eden was driven from office and that the explanation about his health was a mere cover. But there is absolutely no evidence for this.

129 Eden often presented the prize, a bottle of beer, at the daily boxing match held on deck. The young Prescott frequently used to win, revealing pugilistic skills that later surfaced during the 2001 election campaign. Indeed, he won so often that Eden took to presenting him with bottles of wine in the privacy of his cabin, so as not to annoy the other boxers. See Thorpe, *Eden*, pp. 553–5.

130 See Ben Pimlott, *Frustrate their Knavish Tricks: Writings on Biography, History and Politics* (London, 1994), p. 369.

131 Alan Sked and Chris Cook, *Post-War Britain: A Political History* (second edition: London, 1984), p. 133; Thorpe, *Eden*, p. 485.

132 For example, see Pimlott, *Frustrate their Knavish Tricks*, p. 372.

133 Hennessy, *Muddling Through*, p. 143.

134 Judd, *Empire*, p. 364.

135 See the excellent historiographical discussion in Gorst and Johnman, *The Suez Crisis*, pp. 166–9.

136 See Gorst and Johnman, *The Suez Crisis*, p. 166.

137 Lloyd, *Suez 1956*, p. 36.

138 PREM 11/1138, Eden memorandum, 28 December 1956.

139 Sked and Cook *Post-war Britain*, p. 136.

140 See the discussion in Darwin, *Britain and Decolonisation*, pp. 222–4.

141 *Executive Sessions of the Senate Foreign Relations Committee, Volume IX, 1957* (Washington, 1979), p. 91, quoted in Gorst and Johnman, *The Suez Crisis*, p. 157.

142 Emmet John Hughes, *The Ordeal of Power: A Political Memoir of the Eisenhower Years* (London, 1963), p. 217.

143 Thorpe, *Eden*, p. 560.

144 Pimlott, *Frustrate their Knavish Tricks*, p. 370.

145 King and Wybrow, eds, *British Political Opinion*, p. 325.

146 Peter Vansittart, *In the Fifties* (London, 1995), p. 200.

147 Evelyn Shuckburgh, quoted in D. J. Taylor, *After the War: The Novel and England since 1945* (London, 1994), p. 65.

148 Andrew Sinclair, *The Breaking of Bumbo* (London, 1959); see also Taylor, *After the War*, pp. 81–4.

149 Julian Amery, in 'The Move towards the Sandys White Paper of 1957', seminar held July 1988, Institute of Contemporary British History, 2002, <http://www.icbh.ac.uk/witness/sandys/>, p. 21.

150 See Hopkins, *The New Look*, p. 448.

151 Dilwyn Porter, '"Never-Never Land": Britain under the Conservatives', in Nick Tiratsoo, ed., *From Blitz to Blair: A New History of Britain since 1939* (London, 1997), p. 115.

152 Judd, *Empire*, pp. 365–71.

153 Taylor, *After the War*, p. 64.

154 *Sunday Times*, 30 December 1956.

155 Booker, *The Neophiliacs*, p. 119.

CHAPTER 2: BRITAIN IN 1956

1 Population details from Arthur Marwick, *British Society since 1945* (Harmondsworth, 1982), p. 36; Peter Hennessy, *Never Again: Britain 1945–1951* (London, 1992), p. 99; Norman Davies, *The Isles: A History* (London, 1999), pp. 957–8.

2 Anthony Sampson, *Anatomy of Britain* (London, 1962), p. 28; Hennessy, *Never Again*, p. 164.

3 On the population of London, see Jerry White, *London in the Twentieth Century* (London, 2001), pp. 43–4.

4 Arthur Marwick, *Class: Image and Reality in Britain, France and the USA since 1930* (London, 1980), p. 33.

5 George Orwell, 'The Lion and the Unicorn: Socialism and the English Genius', online at <http://www.k-1.com/Orwell/lion.htm>, last consulted 31 October 2002.

6 *Birmingham Mail*, 8 May 1945, quoted in Richard Weight, *Patriots: National Identity in Britain 1940–2000* (London, 2002), p. 106.

7 George Santayana, *Soliloquies in England* (London, 1922), p. 30. Note that Santayana, like many of the speakers cited elsewhere, referred to 'England' when it seems reasonably clear that he meant 'Britain'.

8 Robert Colls, *Identity of England* (Oxford, 2002), pp. 208–9.

9 Noël Coward, *The Lyrics of Noël Coward* (London, 1965), pp. 122–3.

10 Colls, *Identity of Britain*, pp. 82–3.

11 David Cannadine, *Class in Britain* (London, 2000), p. 1; *Times Literary Supplement*, 23 January 1998.

12 Cannadine, *Class in Britain*, p. 148.

13 Cannadine, *Class in Britain*, pp. 22–3.

14 Evelyn Waugh, 'An Open Letter to the Honourable Mrs Peter Rodd (Nancy Mitford) on a Very Serious Subject', in Nancy Mitford, ed., *Noblesse Oblige: An Enquiry into the Identifiable Characteristics of the English Aristocracy* (London, 1956), p. 79.

15 Marwick, *The Sixties*, p. 278.

16 Michael Kahan, David Butler and David Stokes, 'On the Analytical Division of Social Class', *British Journal of Sociology* 17:2, June 1966, pp. 124–30.

17 Ross McKibbin, *Classes and Cultures: England 1918–1951* (Oxford, 1998), p. 106.

18 McKibbin, *Classes and Cultures*, p. 177; see also the discussion of the affluent society later in this book.

19 Richard Hoggart, *The Uses of Literacy* (Harmondsworth, 1958), pp. 279–80; McKibbin, *Classes and Cultures*, p. 202.

20 See Marwick, *British Society since 1945*, p. 41.

21 Marwick, *British Society since 1945*, pp. 40–1; McKibbin, *Classes and Cultures*, pp. 45–6. But for a slightly different, historically specific definition, see Simon Gunn and Rachel Bell, *Middle Classes: Their Rise and Sprawl* (London, 2003), pp. 1–20.

22 McKibbin, *Classes and Cultures*, pp. 47–9.

23 Gunn and Bell, *Middle Classes*, pp. 71–3.

24 Gunn and Bell, *Middle Classes*, pp. 81–2.

25 McKibbin, *Classes and Cultures*, p. 66.

26 Peter Willmott and Michael Young, *Family and Class in a London Suburb* (London, 1960), pp. 22–3.

27 McKibbin, *Classes and Cultures*, p. 97; Colls, *Identity of England*, pp. 80–1.

28 Willmott and Young, *Family and Class in a London Suburb*, p. 23.

29 See Alison Light, *Forever England: Femininity, Literature and Conservatism between the Wars* (London, 1991).

30 J. R. R. Tolkien, *The Hobbit, or There and Back Again* (London, 1981), pp. 14–15.

31 Tolkien, *The Hobbit*, p. 16.

32 Alan S. C. Ross, 'U and Non-U: An Essay in Sociological Linguistics', reprinted in Mitford, ed., *Noblesse Oblige*, pp. 11–36.

33 Ross, 'U and Non-U', pp. 26–7.

34 Ross, 'U and Non-U', pp. 28–32.

35 Ross, 'U and Non-U', p. 34.

36 See Mitford, ed., *Noblesse Oblige*; and *Encounter*, September and November 1955.

37 McKibbin, *Classes and Cultures*, p. 37.

38 Nancy Mitford, 'The English Aristocracy', in Mitford, ed., *Noblesse Oblige*, pp. 43–4.

39 Waugh, 'An Open Letter to the Honourable Mrs Peter Rodd', p. 75.

40 Waugh, 'An Open Letter to the Honourable Mrs Peter Rodd', p. 73.

41 Ross, 'U and Non-U', p. 29.

42 Waugh, 'An Open Letter to the Honourable Mrs Peter Rodd', p. 76.

43 Waugh, 'An Open Letter to the Honourable Mrs Peter Rodd', p. 75.

44 Quoted in Humphrey Carpenter, *That Was Satire That Was: The Satire Boom of the 1960s* (London, 2000), p. 20.

45 John Betjeman, 'How to Get On in Society', in Mitford, ed., *Noblesse Oblige*, pp. 113–14.

46 McKibbin, *Classes and Cultures*, pp. 1–2. The novels of P. G. Wodehouse, Evelyn Waugh and Anthony Powell are an amusing guide to this upper-class lifestyle, especially in the 1920s and 1930s.

47 Hopkins, *The New Look*, p. 172; McKibbin, *Classes and Cultures*, p. 238.

48 Sampson, *Anatomy of Britain*, p. 18.

49 David Cannadine, *G. M. Trevelyan: A Life in History* (London, 1992), p. 159; for more on this, see David Cannadine, *The Decline and Fall of the British Aristocracy* (New Haven, 1990).

50 See Giles Worsley, *England's Lost Houses: From the Archives of* Country Life (London, 2002).

51 Peter Mandler, *The Fall and Rise of the Stately Home* (New Haven, 1997), p. 396; Weight, *Patriots*, p. 158; Andrew Rosen, *The Transformation of British Life 1950–2000* (Manchester, 2003), p. 45; David Cannadine, 'Conservation: The National Trust and the National Heritage', in Cannadine, *In Churchill's Shadow: Confronting the Past in Modern Britain* (London, 2002), pp. 224–43.

52 Sampson, *Anatomy of Britain*, p. 10; obituary, *The Independent*, 29 October 2002.

53 David Cannadine, *Ornamentalism: How the British Saw their Empire* (London, 2001), pp. 101–5; Simon Schama, 'The Domestication of Majesty: Royal Family Portraiture 1500–1850', *Journal of Interdisciplinary History* 17:1, Summer 1986, pp. 155–83, quoted in Pimlott, *The Queen*, p. 60; on the 'formula' for royal success, see Linda Colley, *Britons: Forging the Nation 1707–1837* (New Haven, 1992), p. 236.

54 Brendon and Whitehead, *The Windsors*, pp. 1–87. One historian famously noted that George V had his trousers 'creased at the sides, not front and back': see A. J. P. Taylor, *English History 1914–1945* (Oxford, 1965), p. 2.

55 Brendon and Whitehead, *The Windsors*, pp. 87–9, 122–3.

56 Brendon and Whitehead, *The Windsors*, pp. 88–9; see also Robert Rhodes James, *A Spirit Undaunted: The Political Role of George VI* (London, 1998).

57 Brendon and Whitehead, *The Windsors*, p. 121; McKibbin, *Classes and Cultures*, p. 4.

58 *Spectator*, 30 June 1990.

59 Rhodes James, *A Spirit Undaunted*, p. 210.

60 Pimlott, *The Queen*, p. 180.

61 Weight, *Patriots*, p. 211.

62 Pimlott, *The Queen*, pp. 24, 52–3.

63 Robert Lacey, *Majesty* (London, 1977), p. 121.

64 Pimlott, *The Queen*, p. 103; see also Brendon and Whitehead, *The Windsors*, pp. 125, 142–1.

65 Pimlott, *The Queen*, pp. 106–7.

66 Brendon and Whitehead, *The Windsors*, pp. 123–4; Pimlott, *The Queen*, pp. 67–8.

67 Pimlott, *The Queen*, p. 117.

68 Pimlott, *The Queen*, pp. 176–9.

69 Pimlott, *The Queen*, p. 207; Miriam Akhtar and Steve Humphries, *The Fifties and Sixties: A Lifestyle Revolution* (London, 2001), p. 134; Weight, *Patriots*, p. 234.

70 *Sunday Graphic*, 17 February 1952; John Campbell, *Margaret Thatcher: Volume One: The Grocer's Daughter* (London, 2000), pp. 94–6.

71 Richard Holt, *Sport and the British: A Modern History* (Oxford, 1990), pp. 278–9; Peter H. Hansen, 'Coronation Everest: The Empire and Commonwealth in the "Second Elizabethan Age"', in Ward, ed., *British Culture and the End of Empire*, pp. 57–72.

72 *Daily Express*, 3 June 1953; Weight, *Patriots*, p. 231.

73 Tom Fleming, ed., *Voices out of the Air: The Royal Christmas Broadcasts, 1932–1981* (London, 1981), pp. 73–4.

74 J. H. Huizinga, *Confessions of a European in England* (London, 1958), pp. 207, 209. On the talk of a new Elizabethan age in general, see Weight, *Patriots*, pp. 227–39.

75 Historians disagree about the numbers of war dead: for a useful comparison of the different estimates, see < http://users.erols.com/mwhite28/ww2stats.htm >.

76 Angus Calder, *The Myth of the Blitz* (London, 1991), pp. 30–1.

76 Roy Denman, *Missed Chances: Britain and Europe in the Twentieth Century* (London, 1996), pp. 182–4.

78 Annan, *Our Age*, p. 336.

79 *Daily Telegraph*, 7 July 1999.

80 Hennessy, *Never Again*, pp. 434–5. The phrase 'cenotaph culture' comes from Davies, *The Isles*, p. 899.

81 Paul Addison, *Now the War Is Over: A Social History of Britain 1945–1951* (London, 1985), p. 178; Hennessy, *Never Again*, p. 99; Clarke, *Hope and Glory*, p. 227–9.

82 Susan Cooper, 'Snoek Piquante: The Trials and Tribulations of the British Housewife,' in Michael Sissons and Philip French, eds, *Age of Austerity* (Oxford, 1989), p. 30.

83 Pearson Phillips, 'The New Look', in Sissons and French, eds, *Age of Austerity*, p. 121; Jim Tomlinson, 'Reconstructing Britain: Labour in Power 1945–1951', in Tiratsoo, ed., *From Blitz to Blair*, p. 89.

84 Cooper, 'Snoek Piquante', pp. 35–37.

85 Cooper, 'Snoek Piquante', p. 25.

86 Cooper, 'Snoek Piquante', p. 23.

87 Mrs Vera Mather, quoted in Addison, *Now the War Is Over*, p. 54.

88 Addison, *Now the War Is Over*, p. 54; Hennessy, *Never Again*, p. 308.

89 On the history of the Palace of Westminster, see A. N. Wilson, *The Victorians* (London, 2002), pp. 62–4; Cannadine, *In Churchill's Shadow*, pp. 3–26.

90 Sampson, *Anatomy of Britain*, p. 52.

91 On the House in the late fifties and early sixties, see Sampson, *Anatomy of Britain*, pp. 51–65.

92 Steven Fielding, *The Labour Governments 1964–1970: Volume 1: Labour and Cultural Change* (Manchester, 2003), p. 21.

93 Pimlott, *Frustrate their Knavish Tricks*, p. 237; Jefferys, *Retreat from New Jerusalem*, pp. 39–40.

94 *Observer*, 29 May 1955.

95 R. S. Milne and H. C. Mackenzie, *Marginal Seat: A Study of Voting Behaviour in the Constituency of Bristol North East at the General Election of 1955* (London, 1958), pp. 169–72.

96 See John Ranelagh, *Thatcher's People: An Insider's Account of the Politics, the Power and the Personalities* (London, 1992), pp. 48–50, which is very good on the different strands of twentieth-century Conservatism.

97 Sampson, *Anatomy of Britain*, p. 56.

98 Colls, *Identity of England*, p. 110.

99 Jefferys, *Retreat from New Jerusalem*, p. 168.

100 John Stevenson and Chris Cook, *Britain in the Depression: Society and Politics 1929–39* (London, 1994), pp. 110–42; McKibbin, *Classes and Cultures*, p. 530; Gilmour and Garnett, *Whatever Happened to the Tories*, p. 58.

101 Robert McKenzie and Allan Silver, *Angels in Marble: Working-Class Conservatives in Urban England* (London, 1968), passim.

102 David Marquand, *The Progressive Dilemma: From Lloyd George to Blair* (second edition: London, 1999), pp. 70–1.

103 Conservative Political Centre, *One Nation: A Tory Approach to Social Problems* (London, 1950); John Campbell, *Edward Heath: A Biography* (London, 1993), pp. 76–9; Robert Shepherd, *Iain Macleod: A Biography* (London, 1994), pp. 61–70.

104 Shepherd, *Iain Macleod*, p. 66.

105 Shepherd, *Iain Macleod*, pp. 284–5.

106 See Henry Pelling, *The Origins of the Labour Party 1880–1900* (London, 1954); Frank Bealey and Henry Pelling, *Labour and Politics, 1900–1906* (London, 1958).

107 Edmund Dell, *A Strange Eventful History: Democratic Socialism in Britain* (London, 2000); on the influence of the New Liberalism, see Marquand, *The Progressive Dilemma*, pp. 5–16.

108 Dell, *A Strange Eventful History*, pp. 26–7.

109 Marwick, *British Society since 1845*, p. 102.

110 George Brown, *In my Way* (Harmondsworth, 1972), p. 25.

111 Dell, *A Strange Eventful History*, pp. 20–1.

112 Milne and Mackenzie, *Marginal Seat*, pp. 169–72.

113 Kenneth O. Morgan, *Labour People: Hardie to Kinnock* (second edition: Oxford 1999), p. 5.

114 Marquand, *The Progressive Dilemma*, pp. 16–17; see also Dell, *A Strange Eventful History*, pp. 20–44.

115 Marquand, *The Progressive Dilemma*, p. 19.

116 Sampson, *Anatomy of Britain*, pp. 555–60.

117 Sampson, *Anatomy of Britain*, pp. 554–5.

118 See E. H. Phelps-Brown, *The Growth of British Industrial Relations* (London, 1959); H. A. Clegg et al., *A History of British Trade Unions since 1889* (Oxford, 1964); Henry Phelps-Brown, *The Origins of Trade Union Power* (Oxford, 1985).

119 Geoffrey Owen, *From Empire to Europe: The Decline and Revival of British Industry since the Second World War* (London, 1999), p. 433.

120 Owen, *From Empire to Europe*, pp. 432–3.

121 Sampson, *Anatomy of Britain*, p. 57.

122 See Morgan, *Labour People*, pp. 6–7; Dell, *A Strange Eventful History*, pp. 32–3.

123 Edward du Cann, *Two Lives* (London, 1995), pp. 43–4.

124 See Vernon Bogdanor, 'The Labour Party in Opposition, 1951–1964', in Vernon Bogdanor and Robert Skidelsky, eds, *The Age of Affluence* (London, 1970), p. 81; Dell, *A Strange Eventful History*, pp. 208–10.

125 Richard Crossman, 'Towards a Philosophy of Socialism', in Richard Crossman, ed., *New Fabian Essays* (London, 1952), p. 1.

126 Anthony Crosland, *The Future of Socialism* (London, 1956), pp. 79, 97, 99.

127 There was a very hostile review in *Tribune*, 5 October 1956. See Kevin Jefferys, *Anthony Crosland* (London, 1999), pp. 59–60.

128 Bogdanor, 'The Labour Party in Opposition, 1951–1964', p. 80.

129 Ben Pimlott, *Harold Wilson* (London, 1992), p. 174; Bogdanor, 'The Labour Party in Opposition, 1951–1964', p. 82.

130 Dell, *A Strange Eventful History*, p. 221.

131 Morgan, *Labour People*, p. 207; on Bevan in general, see John Campbell, *Nye Bevan and the Mirage of British Socialism* (London, 1987).

132 Alan Bullock, *Ernest Bevin: Foreign Secretary 1945–1951* (London, 1983), p. 77.

133 Ben Pimlott, ed., *The Political Diary of Hugh Dalton, 1918–40, 1945–60* (London, 1986), pp. 539, 650, 529; Morgan, *Labour People*, pp. 204–19.

134 Marquand, *The Progressive Dilemma*, pp. 109–22; Anthony Howard, *Crossman: The Pursuit of Power* (London, 1990), pp. 162–3.

135 Both quoted in Nicholas Timmins, *The Five Giants: A Biography of the Welfare State* (London, 1995), p. 113.

136 Quoted in Giles Radice, *Friends and Rivals: Crosland, Healey and Jenkins* (London, 2002), p. 98.

137 Williams, *Hugh Gaitskell*, pp. 16, 29–30.

138 Williams, *Hugh Gaitskell*, pp. 440–1.

139 Lord Hailsham, *A Sparrow's Flight: Memoirs* (London, 1990), p. 361.

140 See Williams, *Hugh Gaitskell*, pp. 20–37.

141 His most powerful sponsor was Arthur Deakin, the right-wing head of the Transport and General Workers: see Clarke, *A Question of Leadership*, pp. 249–50.

142 Williams, *Hugh Gaitskell*, pp. 238–43.

143 Sampson, *Anatomy of Britain*, pp. 100–1; Radice, *Friends and Rivals*, pp. 99–100.

144 Asa Briggs, *The History of Broadcasting in the United Kingdom: Volume V: Competition* (Oxford, 1995), p. 241.

145 Alistair Horne, *Macmillan 1957–1986: Volume II of the Official Biography* (London, 1989), p. 156.

146 Williams, *Hugh Gaitskell*, pp. 434, 249–52, 255–7.

147 Williams, *Hugh Gaitskell*, p. 155. There is some good stuff about the tribalism of Labour in the 1950s in Pimlott, *Harold Wilson*, pp. 173–5.

148 Clarke, *A Question of Leadership*, p. 240.

149 Dell, *A Strange Eventful History*, p. 200.

150 The phrase is from Douglas Jay, *Change and Fortune: A Political Record* (London, 1980), p. 221.

151 An example being Tony Benn: see Benn diary, 5 November 1957.

152 Paul Addison, 'The Road from 1945', in Peter Hennessy and Anthony Seldon, eds, *Ruling Performance: British Governments from Attlee to Thatcher* (Oxford, 1989), pp. 5–6.

153 See José Harris, *William Beveridge: A Biography* (Oxford, 1977), pp. 378–418; Chris Pierson, 'Social Policy', in David Marquand and Anthony Seldon, eds, *The Ideas That Shaped Post-War Britain* (London, 1996), pp. 141–5; Timmins, *The Five Giants*, pp. 11–62.

154 Timmins, *The Five Giants*, pp. 61, 135.

155 Hennessy, *Never Again*, p. 122.

156 Hopkins, *The New Look*, p. 166.

157 Hopkins, *The New Look*, pp. 138–9.

158 Timmins, *The Five Giants*, p. 207.

159 Anthony Howard, '"We Are The Masters Now": The General Election of July 5th, 1945', in Sissons and French, eds, *Age of Austerity*, pp. 18–20; Taylor, *After the War*, p. 26.

160 Howard, '"We Are The Masters Now"', p. 19.

161 R. A. Butler, *The Art of the Possible: The Memoirs of Lord Butler* (Harmondsworth, 1973), p. 134.

162 Michael Pinto-Duschinsky, 'Bread and Circuses? The Conservatives in Office, 1951–1964', in Bogdanor and Skidelsky, eds, *The Age of Affluence*, p. 61.

163 See Reginald Maudling, *Memoirs* (London, 1978), p. 45; Jeffreys, *Retreat from New Jerusalem*, p. 34; Roy Jenkins, *Churchill* (London, 2001), pp. 803–62. Peter Hennessy suggests that the 1951 election made less difference to national economic policy than any other twentieth-century election up to that point: *Never Again*, p. 427.

164 Pinto-Duschinsky, 'Bread and Circuses?', p. 72.

165 Quoted in Marwick, *British Society since 1945*, pp. 82–3.

166 *Observer*, 31 May 1953.

167 See two excellent short essays: Robert Skidelsky, 'The Fall of Keynesianism', and Peter Clarke, 'The Keynesian Consensus', both in Marquand and Seldon, eds, *The Ideas That Shaped Post-War Britain*, pp. 41–66 and 67–87. The best discussion of Keynes' economic ideas is Robert Skidelsky, *John Maynard Keynes: The Economist as Saviour 1920–1937* (London, 1992), pp. 537–624.

168 See *Employment Policy* (Cmnd 6527: London, 1944); Dell, *A Strange Eventful History*, pp. 104–8.

169 Butler, *The Art of the Possible*, pp. 148–9.

170 Elizabeth Durbin, *New Jerusalems: The Labour Party and the Economics of Democratic Socialism* (London, 1985), pp. 152–3. Durbin had been reading Hayek.

171 J. F. Wright, *Britain in the Age of Economic Management: An Economic History since 1939* (Oxford, 1979), p. 142.

172 Peter Oppenheimer, 'Muddling Through: The Economy, 1951–1964', in Bogdanor and Skidelsky, eds, *The Age of Affluence*, p. 119.

173 On Attlee and Whitehall, see Hennessy, *Never Again*, p. 380.

174 Sampson, *Anatomy of Britain*, p. 533. Note that the turnover figures refer to the financial year 1957–8.

175 Sampson, *Anatomy of Britain*, p. 533.

176 For example, Correlli Barnett, *The Audit of War: The Illusion and Reality of Britain as a Great Nation* (London, 1986).

177 Owen, *From Empire to Europe*, pp. 52–3.

178 Quoted in introduction, Bogdanor and Skidelsky, eds, *The Age of Affluence*, p. 8.

179 Barnett, *The Audit of War*, p. 304; see also Barnett, *The Lost Victory: British Dreams, British Realities, 1945–1950* (London, 1995); *The Verdict of Peace: Britain between her Yesterday and the Future* (London, 2001).

180 As expressed as a proportion of GDP: see José Harris, 'Enterprise and Welfare States: A Comparative Perspective', *Transactions of the Royal Historical Society* 40, 1990, pp. 175–95; Jim Tomlinson, 'Welfare and the Economy: The Economic Impact of the Welfare State, 1945–1951', *Twentieth-Century British History* 6:2, 1995, pp. 194–219.

181 Andrew Gamble, *Britain in Decline: Economic Policy, Political Strategy and the British State* (fourth edition: London, 1994), p. 109.

182 See, for example, Dell, *A Strange Eventful History*, pp. 139–40.

183 Peter Calvocoressi, *The British Experience 1945–75* (Harmondsworth, 1979), pp. 213–16.

184 See Alec Cairncross, *The British Economy since 1945* (Oxford, 1992), p. 5.

185 Addison, *Now the War Is Over*, p. 179.

186 There is a good short discussion of the value of sterling in Calvocoressi, *The British Experience*, pp. 86–88.

187 See Wright, *Britain in the Age of Economic Management*, pp. 160–1.

188 Gamble, *Britain in Decline*, p. 111.

189 Harold Macmillan, *Riding the Storm, 1956–59* (London, 1971), p. 199.

190 *The Economist*, 13 February 1954.

191 See Anthony Howard, *RAB: The Life of R. A. Butler* (London, 1987), pp. 203–4; Williams, *Hugh Gaitskell*, p. 213.

192 Butler, *The Art of the Possible*, pp. 162–3.

193 Philip M. Williams, ed., *The Diary of Hugh Gaitskell 1945–1956* (London, 1983), p. 307.

194 See Williams, *Hugh Gaitskell*, p. 213; Clarke, *Hope and Glory*, p. 245; Gilmour and Garnett, *Whatever Happened to the Tories*, p. 75. There is an interesting discussion of the differences between the Conservative and Labour economic strategies in Jefferys, *Retreat from New Jerusalem*, pp. 32–3.

195 Pinto-Duschinsky, 'Bread and Circuses?', p. 76; Oppenheimer, 'Muddling Through: The Economy, 1951–1964', p. 160; Anthony Seldon, *Churchill's Indian Summer: The Conservative Government, 1951–55* (London, 1981); Jeffreys, *Retreat from New Jerusalem*, p. 9.

196 Gilmour and Garnett, *Whatever Happened to the Tories*, p. 37.

197 Keith Middlemas, *Power, Competition and the State: Volume One: Britain in Search of a Balance, 1940–61* (Basingstoke, 1986), p. 267; Harriet Jones, 'New Tricks for an Old Dog? The Conservatives and Social Policy, 1951–1955', in Anthony Gorst, Lewis Johnman and Wm Scott Lucas, eds, *Contemporary British History, 1931–61: Politics and the Limits of Policy* (London, 1991), pp. 33–43; Timmins, *The Five Giants*, p. 170; Neil Rollings, '"Poor Mr Butskell: A Short Life, Wrecked by Schizophrenia"?', *Twentieth-Century British History* 5:2, 1994, pp. 183–205; Ben Pimlott, 'The Myth of Consensus', in Pimlott, *Frustrate their Knavish Tricks*, pp. 229–39; Jefferys, *Retreat from New Jerusalem*, p. 34.

198 Michael Fraser, contribution to 'British Politics 1945–1987: Four Perspectives', in Hennessy and Seldon, eds, *Ruling Performance*, p. 310.

199 Porter, '"Never-Never Land"', p. 106.

200 Jefferys, *Retreat from New Jerusalem*, p. 198.

201 Quoted in Dan Rebellato, *1956 And All That: The Making of Modern British Drama* (London, 1999), p. 15.

202 *Encounter*, April 1955.

CHAPTER 3: SUPERMAC

1 Howard, *RAB*, pp. 246–8.

2 Rhodes James, *Anthony Eden*, p. 599.

3 Howard, *RAB*, p. 246.

4 Howard, *RAB*, pp. 1–87; Pearce, *The Lost Leaders*, pp. 5–36.

5 See Howard, *RAB*, pp. 70–87.

6 See Turner, *Macmillan*, pp. 20–39; Dell, *A Strange Eventful History*, pp. 82–96.

7 Clarke, *A Question of Leadership*, p. 215.

8 Harold Macmillan, *The Middle Way: A Study of the Problem of Economic and Social Progress in a Free and Democratic Society* (Wakefield, 1978), pp. 109, 119; for a discussion of Macmillan's economic ideas, see Turner, *Macmillan*, pp. 25–37; Dell, *A Strange Eventful History*, pp. 82–3.

9 Alistair Horne quoted in Peter Hennessy, *The Prime Minister: The Office and its Holders since 1945* (London, 2000), p. 254.

10 James Margach, *The Abuse of Power* (London, 1978), pp. 116–17.

11 Horne, *Macmillan 1894–1956*, pp. 332–3; Clarke, *Hope and Glory*, pp. 241–2.

12 Pearce, *The Lost Leaders*, p. 95.

13 Quoted in Jefferys, *Retreat from New Jerusalem*, p. 55.

14 Kyle, *Suez*, p. 556.

15 Howard, *RAB*, pp. 240–1.

16 Howard, *RAB*, p. 241.

17 Pearce, *The Lost Leaders*, pp. 100–2.

18 Lord Kilmuir, *Political Adventure: The Memoirs of the Earl of Kilmuir* (London, 1964), p. 285.

19 Howard, *RAB*, p. 247.

20 Howard, *RAB*, pp. 246–7; Horne, *Macmillan 1957–1986*, pp. 3–5; Jefferys, *Retreat from New Jerusalem*, pp. 60–1; Heath, *The Course of my Life*, p. 179.

21 Jefferys, *Retreat from New Jerusalem*, pp. 60–1.

22 Butler, *The Art of the Possible*, p. 197; Rhodes James, *Anthony Eden*, pp. 599–600; Howard, *RAB*, p. 248.

23 Jefferys, *Retreat from New Jerusalem*, p. 61; Gilmour and Garnett, *Whatever Happened to the Tories*, pp. 128–9.

24 Pearce, *The Lost Leaders*, pp. 34–5, 104, 127.

25 Horne, *Macmillan 1957–1986*, p. xiii.

26 On the best-read Prime Ministers, see Clarke, *A Question of Leadership*, p. 224.

27 See Howard, *RAB*, pp. 210–13.

28 Horne, *Macmillan 1957–1986*, pp. 587–8; see also Horne, *Macmillan 1894–1956*, passim; and the excellent short essay in Clarke, *A Question of Leadership*, esp. pp. 211–14.

29 Richard Lamb, *The Macmillan Years 1957–1963: The Unfolding Truth* (London, 1995), p. 1.

30 Levin, *The Pendulum Years*, p. 199.

31 Pearce, *The Lost Leaders*, p. 101, quotes one of his senior civil servants on Macmillan's 'old man act'. One famous sketch by the left-wing cartoonist Vicky depicted him as Archie Rice, the crumbling, declining music-hall comedian from John Osborne's then fashionable play *The Entertainer*: see *Evening Standard*, 11 December 1958.

32 *The Economist*, 15 February 1958.

33 Howard, *RAB*, pp. 259–60.

34 Macmillan diary, 17 July 1952, quoted in Thorpe, *Eden*, p. 430.

35 L. A. Siedentrop, 'Mr Macmillan and the Edwardian Style', in Bogdanor and Skidelsky, eds, *The Age of Affluence*, pp. 17, 30; Elizabeth Wilson, *Adorned in Dreams: Fashion and Modernity* (London, 1988), p. 5.

36 Horne, *Macmillan 1957–1986*, p. 13.

37 John Barnes, 'From Eden to Macmillan, 1955–1959', in Hennessy and Seldon, eds, *Ruling Performance*, p. 116.

38 Horne, *Macmillan 1957–1986*, p. 12.

39 George Walden, *Lucky George: Memoirs of an Anti-Politician* (London, 1999), p. 58.

40 Quoted in Hennessy, *Muddling Through*, p. 220.

41 Horne, *Macmillan 1957–1986*, p. 154.

42 Quoted in Hennessy, *The Prime Minister*, p. 271.

43 Macmillan diary, 3 February 1957, quoted in Horne, *Macmillan 1957–1986*, p. 4.

44 Sir Freddie Bishop quoted in Hennessy, *Muddling Through*, p. 226.

45 Heath, *The Course of my Life*, p. 181.

46 Horne, *Macmillan 1957–1986*, p. 5.

47 *The Times*, 11 January 1957.

48 Hailsham, *A Sparrow's Flight*, p. 315.

49 See Horne, *Macmillan 1957–1986*, pp. 2–3; Jefferys, *Retreat from New Jerusalem*, pp. 63–4.

50 William Wallace, 'World Status without Tears', in Bogdanor and Skidelsky, eds, *The Age of Affluence*, pp. 207–8; Horne, *Macmillan 1957–1986*, p. 16.

51 Benn diary, 21 January 1957.

52 Sir Harold Nicolson, *Letters and Diaries: Volume III: 1945–1962* (London, 1968), p. 331.

53 Hansard, 16 May 1957; Horne, *Macmillan 1957–1986*, p. 18.

54 Howard, *RAB*, pp. 251–2.

55 Quoted in Anthony Sampson, *Macmillan: A Study in Ambiguity* (London, 1967), p. 121.

56 Horne, *Macmillan 1957–1986*, p. 7.

57 Clarke, *A Question of Leadership*, pp. 224–5.

58 Christopher Hollis, 'The Conservative Party in History', *Political Quarterly* 3, July–September 1961, pp. 219–20; see also David Childs, *Britain since 1945: A Political History* (London, 1979), pp. 96–7; Horne, *Macmillan 1957–1986*, pp. 8–9; Jefferys, *Retreat from New Jerusalem*, pp. 62–3.

59 Horne, *Macmillan 1957–1986*, p. 15.

60 Horne, *Macmillan 1957–1986*, p. 17.

61 Quoted in D. R. Thorpe, *Alec Douglas-Home* (London, 1996), p. 200.

62 *Queen*, 15 September 1959.

63 Macmillan, *Riding the Storm, 1956–59*, p. 199.

64 *The Times*, 22 July 1957.

65 The expression 'having it so good' was actually borrowed from the American labour leader George Meany.

66 See Horne, *Macmillan 1957–1986*, p. 65.

67 Brittan, *The Treasury under the Tories*, p. 180; Michael Pinto-Duschinsky, 'From Macmillan to Home, 1959–1964', in Hennessy and Seldon, eds, *Ruling Performance*, pp. 167–8; Holt, *Second Amongst Equals*, pp. 147–8.

68 Lamb, *The Macmillan Years*, p. 47.

69 Macmillan diary, 27 January 1959, quoted in Horne, *Macmillan 1957–1986*, p. 142.

70 Quoted in Lamb, *The Macmillan Years*, p. 52.

71 Horne, *Macmillan 1957–1986*, p. 140.

72 *The Economist*, 20 July 1957.

73 See Jefferys, *Retreat from New Jerusalem*, p. 58.

74 J. C. R. Dow, *The Management of the British Economy, 1945–60* (Cambridge, 1964), p. 94.

75 Edmund Dell, *The Chancellors: A History of the Chancellors of the Exchequer, 1945–90* (London, 1996), p. 211.

76 Dell, *The Chancellors*, p. 224.

77 On Birch and Powell, see Simon Heffer, *Like the Roman: A Life of Enoch Powell* (London, 1998), pp. 211–12.

78 Gilmour and Garnett, *Whatever Happened to the Tories*, p. 136

79 Gilmour and Garnett, *Whatever Happened to the Tories*, p. 135.

80 Shepherd, *Iain Macleod*, pp. 123–8; Jefferys, *Retreat from New Jerusalem*, p. 66.

81 Dow, *The Management of the British Economy*, p. 95.

82 See Dell, *The Chancellors*, pp. 227–8.

83 CAB 128/31, 'Memorandum by the Chancellor of the Exchequer', 30 April 1957.

84 Dell, *The Chancellors*, p. 227.

85 This was the scheme known as ROBOT, with which Butler had toyed earlier in the decade. See Dell, *The Chancellors*, p. 229; Gilmour and Garnett, *Whatever Happened to the Tories*, p. 138.

86 Horne, *Macmillan 1957–1986*, p. 67; Lamb, *The Macmillan Years*, pp. 48–9; Dell, *The Chancellors*, pp. 231–2.

87 Heffer, *Like the Roman*, p. 218.

88 Heffer, *Like the Roman*, pp. 212, 198.

89 Heffer, *Like the Roman*, pp. 6–8.

90 Heffer, *Like the Roman*, pp. 14–16, 35.

91 Heffer, *Like the Roman*, p. 77.

92 See Heffer, *Like the Roman*, pp. 952–3.

93 Heffer, *Like the Roman*, p. 140.

94 Annan, *Our Age*, p. 552–3.

95 See Heffer, *Like the Roman*, pp. 14–23.

96 Heffer, *Like the Roman*, p. 100.

97 Butler, *The Art of the Possible*, p. 143.

98 Dell, *The Chancellors*, pp. 231–2.

99 Dell, *The Chancellors*, p. 233.

100 Dell, *The Chancellors*, pp. 233–5; Heffer, *Like the Roman*, p. 222.

101 Lamb, *The Macmillan Years*, p. 47.

102 Heffer, *Like the Roman*, p. 224.

103 Heffer, *Like the Roman*, pp. 226–7.

104 Dell, *The Chancellors*, pp. 237–8.

105 Heffer, *Like the Roman*, pp. 227–8.

106 Macmillan diary, 22 and 23 December 1957, quoted in Horne, *Macmillan 1957–1986*, pp. 70–1.

107 Heffer, *Like the Roman*, p. 229.

108 CAB 128/31, Cabinet Minutes, 31 December 1957.

109 John Boyd-Carpenter, *Way of Life* (London, 1980), p. 50; see also CAB 128/32, Cabinet Minutes, 3 January 1958.

110 Lamb, *The Macmillan Years*, p. 51.

111 Macmillan diary, 6 January 1958, quoted in Horne, *Macmillan 1957–1986*, p. 71.

112 CAB 128/32, Cabinet Minutes, 5 January 1958.

113 Heffer, *Like the Roman*, p. 233.

114 Macmillan diary, 5 January 1958, quoted in Horne, *Macmillan 1957–1986*, p. 72.

115 Heffer, *Like the Roman*, p. 233.

116 Horne, *Macmillan 1957–1986*, p. 74.

117 Macmillan diary, 6 January 1958, quoted in Horne, *Macmillan 1957–1986*, p. 71.

118 Horne, *Macmillan 1957–1986*, p. 72.

119 *Daily Telegraph*, 8 January 1958.

120 Heffer, *Like the Roman*, pp. 234–5.

121 Ranelagh, *Thatcher's People*, p. 80.

122 Simon Heffer and Edmund Dell are notable examples.

123 Gilmour and Garnett, *Whatever Happened to the Tories*, p. 142.

124 See Shepherd, *Iain Macleod*, p. 133.

125 Quoted in Jefferys, *Retreat from New Jerusalem*, p. 71.

126 Shepherd, *Iain Macleod*, p. 132.

127 Alan Watkins, *A Short Walk down Fleet Street* (London, 2000), p. 75.

128 Hailsham, *A Sparrow's Flight*, p. 319; Heffer, *Like the Roman*, p. 236.

129 See, for example, the overblown argument in Gilmour and Garnett, *Whatever Happened to the Tories*, pp. 141–3, a ferocious attack on the monetarists.

130 Turner, *Macmillan*, pp. 235–6; Jefferys, *Retreat from New Jerusalem*, p. 73.

131 PREM 11/2306, Thorneycroft to Macmillan, 19 December 1957.

132 Hansard, 23 January 1958.

133 Quoted in Hennessy, *The Prime Minister*, p. 266.

134 On Amory, see Horne, *Macmillan 1957–1986*, pp. 139–40; Lamb, *The Macmillan Years*, p. 51; Dell, *The Chancellors*, p. 244.

135 Quoted in Lamb, *The Macmillan Years*, p. 52. On the economy in 1957–1958, see Pinto-Duschinsky, 'Bread and Circuses?', p. 69; Lamb. *The Macmillan Years*, pp. 51–2; Dell, *The Chancellors*, p. 245.

136 Macmillan to Amory, 5 March 1958, quoted in Lamb, *The Macmillan Years*, pp. 52–3.

137 Gilmour and Garnett, *Whatever Happened to the Tories*, p. 145.

138 Clarke, *Hope and Glory*, pp. 240, 408–9.

139 Lamb, *The Macmillan Years*, pp. 58–9; Gilmour and Garnett, *Whatever Happened to the Tories*, pp. 145–6.

140 Jefferys, *Retreat from New Jerusalem*, pp. 73–4; Horne, *Macmillan 1957–1986*, p. 88.

141 Jefferys, *Retreat from New Jerusalem*, pp. 75–6; Gilmour and Garnett, *Whatever Happened to the Tories*, pp. 146–7.

142 See PREM 11/2311; quotations are from Lamb, *The Macmillan Years*, pp. 55–6; Turner, *Macmillan*, p. 240.

143 Macmillan diary, 7 April 1959, quoted in Horne, *Macmillan 1957–1986*, p. 142.

144 Samuel Brittan, *The Treasury under the Tories, 1951–1964* (Harmondsworth, 1964), pp. 220–6; Jefferys, *Retreat from New Jerusalem*, p. 78.

145 Brittan, *The Treasury under the Tories*, p. 202.

146 *The Economist*, 11 April 1959.

147 Jefferys, *Retreat from New Jerusalem*, p. 78; Gilmour and Garnett, *Whatever Happened to the Tories*, p. 150.

148 Macmillan diary, 26 May 1959, quoted in Horne, *Macmillan 1957–1986*, p. 143.

149 Brittan, *The Treasury under the Tories*, p. 203; Dell, *The Chancellors*, pp. 250–3.

150 *Daily Mail*, 1 July 1959.

151 *The Times*, 9 September 1959.

152 Shepherd, *Iain Macleod*, p. 141; see also Horne, *Macmillan 1957–1986*, pp. 88–90; Jefferys, *Retreat from New Jerusalem*, pp. 74–5.

153 Lamb, *The Macmillan Years*, p. 59.

154 Gilmour and Garnett, *Whatever Happened to the Tories*, p. 149.

155 Clarke, *Hope and Glory*, pp. 254–5.

156 See John Hill, *Sex, Class and Realism: British Cinema 1956–1963* (London, 1986), p. 145; Marcia Landy, *British Genres: Cinema and Society, 1930–1960* (Princeton, 1991), p. 386.

157 Juliet Gardiner, *From the Bomb to the Beatles: The Changing Face of Post-War Britain* (London, 1999), p. 83.

158 Mark Abrams and Richard Rose, *Must Labour Lose?* (Harmondsworth, 1960), p. 45.

159 *The Economist*, 25 July 1959.

160 Jefferys, *Retreat from New Jerusalem*, p. 79.

161 Horne, *Macmillan 1957–1986*, p. 146.

162 Reprinted in David Butler and Richard Rose, *The British General Election of 1959* (London, 1960), p. 136.

163 *Evening Standard*, 6 November 1958.

164 Horne, *Macmillan 1957–1986*, pp. 144–5; Wybrow, *Britain Speaks Out*, p. 57.

165 Abrams and Rose, *Must Labour Lose?*, p. 88.

166 *Evening Standard*, 8 February 1958.

167 Horne, *Macmillan 1957–1986*, pp. 146–8; Michael Cockerell, *Live from Number Ten: The Inside Story of Prime Ministers and Television* (London, 1988), pp. 66–7.

168 Cockerell, *Live from Number Ten*, p. 70.

169 See Benn diary, 30 December 1958, 11 March 1959, 9 September 1959; Cockerell, *Live from Number Ten*, pp. 70–2; Briggs, *The History of Broadcasting in the United Kingdom: Volume V*, pp. 249–51.

170 Williams, *Hugh Gaitskell*, pp. 310–11.

171 Horne, *Macmillan 1957–1986*, pp. 151–2.

172 Williams, *Hugh Gaitskell*, p. 312.

173 Sked and Cook, *Post-War Britain*, pp. 158–9.

174 Cockerell, *Live from Number Ten*, p. 75.

175 Radice, *Friends and Rivals*, p. 111.

176 Roy Hattersley, *Who Goes Home? Scenes from a Political Life* (London, 1995), p. 23.

177 Quoted in Jefferys, *Retreat from New Jerusalem*, p. 82.

178 See Bogdanor, 'The Labour Party in Opposition, 1951–1964', p. 96. In fact, the extent of Macmillan's victory was wildly exaggerated. Labour had, after all, still won 44 per cent of the total vote, and, given the dynamics of the party system, all it would take for a Labour victory next time was a swing of three voters in every hundred. See *The Times*, 10 October 1959; Pinto-Duschinsky, 'Bread and Circuses?', p. 71.

179 Abrams and Rose, *Must Labour Lose?*, pp. 42–3; see also Stuart Laing, *Representations of Working-Class Life 1957–1964* (Basingstoke, 1986), pp. 3–30.

180 Abrams and Rose, *Must Labour Lose?*, pp. 47–58. For the counter-argument to this thesis, see J. H. Goldthorpe, D. Lockwood, F. Bechhofer and J. Platt, *The Affluent Worker: Political Attitudes and Behaviour* (Cambridge, 1968), which was then attacked in its turn by, for example, Ivor Crewe, 'The Politics of "Affluent" and "Traditional" Workers in Britain: An Aggregate Data Analysis', *British Journal of Political Science* 3:1, 1973, pp. 29–52.

181 Bogdanor, 'The Labour Party in Opposition, 1951–1964', pp. 95–6. There is a very good, and very sceptical, discussion of all this stuff in Jefferys, *Retreat from New Jerusalem*, pp. 156–9.

182 Quoted in Anne Perkins, 'What If Gaitskell, Not Bevan, Had Died in 1960?', in Duncan Brack and Iain Dale, eds, *Prime Minister Portillo, and Other Things That Never Happened* (London, 2003), p. 75.

183 Jefferys, *Retreat from New Jerusalem*, p. 162.

184 Quoted in Pimlott, *Harold Wilson*, p. 225; see Roy Jenkins, *A Life at the Centre* (London, 1991), pp. 128–9; Radice, *Friends and Rivals*, pp. 112–13.

185 Hopkins, *The New Look*, p. 453.

186 Sampson, *Macmillan: A Study in Ambiguity*, p. 165.

187 Martin Redmayne quoted in Horne, *Macmillan 1957–1986*, p. 152.

188 Pinto-Duschinsky, 'Bread and Circuses?', p. 77.

189 *News Chronicle*, 10 October 1959.

190 *Spectator*, 16 October 1959.

CHAPTER 4: THE AFFLUENT SOCIETY

1 Deborah S. Ryan, *The Ideal Home Through the Twentieth Century* (London, 1997), pp. 106–9, 113–16.

2 C. C. Carter and H. C. Brentnall, *Man the World Over* (Oxford, 1952), quoted in Hitchens, *The Abolition of Britain*, p. 92; Marwick, *British Society since 1945*, p. 22; Colls, *Identity of England*, pp. 243–4.

3 Akhtar and Humphries, *The Fifties and Sixties*, p. 80.

4 John Harris quoted in Akhtar and Humphries, *The Fifties and Sixties*, p. 80.

5 Jo Jones quoted in Akhtar and Humphries, *The Fifties and Sixties*, p. 78; Alan A. Jackson, *The Middle Classes 1900–1950* (Nairn, 1991), p. 78.

6 Eileen Cook quoted in Akhtar and Humphries, *The Fifties and Sixties*, p. 78.

7 Akhtar and Humphries, *The Fifties and Sixties*, p. 114.

8 Akhtar and Humphries, *The Fifties and Sixties*, pp. 114–15.

9 Jo-Mary Stafford, *Light in the Dust: An Autobiography 1930–1960* (Stourbridge, 1995), p. 33.

10 Stafford, *Light in the Dust*, pp. 25–6.

11 Stuart Holroyd, *Contraries: A Personal Progression* (London, 1975), p. 21; Timmins, *The Five Giants*, pp. 172–3.

12 Hennessy, *Never Again*, p. 112.

13 Hopkins, *The New Look*, p. 309.

14 Porter, '"Never-Never Land"', p. 112.

15 Hopkins, *The New Look*, p. 309.

16 Porter, '"Never-Never Land"', p. 119.

17 Hopkins, *The New Look*, p. 311.

18 *Queen*, 15 September 1959.

19 *Pace* Marwick, *The Sixties*, p. 8.

20 See John Benson, *The Rise of Consumer Society in Britain 1880–1980* (London, 1994), passim; Matthew Sweet, *Inventing the Victorians* (London 2001), pp. 38–56; Gunn and Bell, *Middle Classes*, pp. 38–43. Benson gives the common definition of a consumer society as one 'in which choice and credit are readily available, in which social value is defined in terms of purchasing power and material possessions, and in which there is a desire, above all, for that which is new, modern, exciting and fashionable', although he goes on to point out the weaknesses of the term (p. 4).

21 John Stevenson and Chris Cook, *Britain in the Depression: Society and Politics 1929–1939* (second edition: London, 1994), pp. 15–39.

22 J. B. Priestley, *English Journey* (London, 1997), pp. 321–5.

23 See John Morris, 'Technology, 1930–55', in Clive Bloom and Gary Day, eds, *Literature and Culture in Modern Britain: Volume Two: 1930–1955* (London, 1997), p. 235; Addison, *Now the War Is Over*, p. 200.

24 Drew Middleton, *The British* (London, 1957), p. 127.

25 Alan Sillitoe, *Saturday Night and Sunday Morning* (Paladin edition: London, 1990), pp. 26–7.

26 Gardiner, *From the Bomb to the Beatles*, p. 83.

27 John Westergaard and Henrietta Resler, *Class in a Capitalist Society* (Harmondsworth, 1977), p. 34; Gardiner, *From the Bomb to the Beatles*, p. 83.

28 Addison, *Now the War Is Over*, p. 176.

29 Quoted in Benson, *The Rise of Consumer Society*, p. 18.

30 Akhtar and Humphries, *The Fifties and Sixties*, p. 81.

31 Gardiner, *From the Bomb to the Beatles*, p, 88.

32 Porter, '"Never-Never Land"', p. 119.

33 Peter Willmott and Michael Young, *Family and Class in a London Suburb* (London, 1960), p. 99.

34 Twiggy Lawson, *Twiggy in Black and White* (London, 1997), p. 18.

35 Willmott and Young, *Family and Class in a London Suburb*, p. 100.

36 Benson, *The Rise of Consumer Society*, p. 71; Gunn and Bell, *Middle Classes*, pp. 68–71; Ina Zweiniger-Bargielowska, 'Housewifery', in Ina Zweiniger-Bargielowska, ed., *Women in Twentieth-Century Britain* (Harlow, 2001), p. 153.

37 John Newsom, *The Education of Girls* (London, 1948), pp. 102–3.

38 Gardiner, *From the Bomb to the Beatles*, p. 92. For more on women, housewives and kitchen goddesses, see the forthcoming sequel to this book.

39 Advertisement reprinted in Alison Pressley, *The Best of Times: Growing Up in Britain in the 1950s* (London, 1999), p. 13.

40 Benson, *The Rise of Consumer Society*, p. 186.

41 Joan Viveash quoted in Akhtar and Humphries, *The Fifties and Sixties*, p. 83.

42 Harris, Hyde and Smith, *1966 and All That*, pp. 148–9.

43 Akhtar and Humphries, *The Fifties and Sixties*, p. 84.

44 'Laura', in Cecile Landau, ed., *Growing Up in the Sixties* (London, 1991), p. 4.

45 Gardiner, *From the Bomb to the Beatles*, p. 92.

46 Advertisement reprinted in Akhtar and Humphries, *The Fifties and Sixties*, p. 91.

47 The figures are £114m in 1947 and £454m in 1960: see John Montgomery, *The Fifties* (London, 1965), p. 288.

48 Horlicks advertisement reprinted in Carpenter, *That Was Satire That Was*, p. 8.

49 Quoted in Marwick, *The Sixties*, p. 41.

50 J. B. Priestley, *Journey down a Rainbow* (London, 1955), p. 51; J. B. Priestley, *Thoughts in the Wilderness* (London, 1957), p. 122.

51 Lewis, *The Fifties*, p. 31; Harris, Hyde and Smith, *1966 and All That*, p. 12.

52 Middle-class families were more reluctant to embrace the new trend for hire-purchase, not merely because it emphasised their limited means, but also because it offended old ideas of middle-class thrift. See Hopkins, *The New Look*, p. 317.

53 Hopkins, *The New Look*, p. 317.

54 Porter, '"Never-Never Land"', p. 120.

55 *The Times*, 1 September 1958.

56 Levin, *The Pendulum Years*, p. 362; Brian Masters, *The Swinging Sixties* (London, 1985), p. 21.

57 Lawton, *1963*, pp. 282–3.

58 Masters, *The Swinging Sixties*, p. 20.

59 *New Statesman*, 24 July 1964.

60 According to one account, Savundra had once obtained girls from Stephen Ward, the society osteopath later embroiled in the Profumo scandal. Savundra was alleged to have told Ward that he had a partiality for blondes and redheads 'with long legs and very white skin'; these included Mandy Rice-Davies, another figure from the Profumo affair. See Anthony Summers and Stephen Dorril, *Honeytrap* (London, 1987), pp. 20, 84.

61 Willi Frischauer, *David Frost: A Biography* (London, 1971), pp. 135–6; Stuart Hylton, *Magical History Tour: The 1960s Revisited* (Stroud, 2000), pp. 167–9.

62 *The Frost Programme*, broadcast 3 February 1967; see also Frischauer, *David Frost*, pp. 136–8.

63 The trial threw up various strange allegations, including the claims that the Fire, Auto and Marine money had been used to buy a nudist colony at Hastings and that Savundra's co-defendant Stuart de Quincy Walker had been using a former German E-boat for smuggling: see Hylton, *Magical History Tour*, p. 169.

64 Harris, Hyde and Smith, *1966 and All That*, p. 51.

65 Hopkins, *The New Look*, pp. 95–6, 314–15.

66 Marnie Fogg, *Boutique: A Sixties Cultural Phenomenon* (London, 2003), pp. 20–7.

67 On daily deliveries, see Pressley, *The Best of Times*, p. 27.

68 Unknown interviewee quoted in Pressley, *The Best of Times*, p. 12.

69 Eileen Cook quoted in Akhtar and Humphries, *The Fifties and Sixties*, p. 106; see also Clarke, *Shadow of a Nation*, p. 90.

70 Hopkins, *The New Look*, p. 353; Benson, *The Rise of Consumer Society*, p. 41.

71 Harris, Hyde and Smith, *1966 and All That*, p. 51; Rosen, *The Transformation of British Life*, p. 150.

72 Irene Ranahan quoted in Akhtar and Humphries, *The Fifties and Sixties*, p. 106.

73 Eileen Cook and Maggie Stiles quoted in Akhtar and Humphries, *The Fifties and Sixties*, p. 106.

74 Unknown interviewees quoted in Pressley, *The Best of Times*, p. 19.

75 Akhtar and Humphries, *The Fifties and Sixties*, p. 99.

76 Gardiner, *From the Bomb to the Beatles*, p. 92.

77 Stevenson and Cook, *Britain in the Depression*, p. 15.

78 According to an apocryphal story, fish fingers were originally to be called 'frozen cod pieces' until a possible misunderstanding was spotted: see Akhtar and Humphries, *The Fifties and Sixties*, p. 107.

79 Hopkins, *The New Look*, p. 326.

80 Clarke, *The Shadow of a Nation*, p. 141.

81 John Burnett, *Liquid Pleasures: A Social History of Drinks in Modern Britain* (London, 1999), pp. 66–7; Akhtar and Humphries, *The Fifties and Sixties*, pp. 108–9.

82 John Stevenson, *British Society 1914–5* (Harmondsworth, 1984), p. 390.

83 On the transition from community holidays to individual leisure, see Miriam Akhtar and Steve Humphries, *Some Liked It Hot: The British on Holiday at Home and Abroad* (London, 2000), pp. 7–8.

84 Dorothy Robson quoted in Akhtar and Humphries, *The Fifties and Sixties*, p. 149.

85 Benson, *The Rise of Consumer Society*, p. 50; Akhtar and Humphries, *The Fifties and Sixties*, p. 155.

86 Marwick, *British Society since 1945*, p. 37.

87 John Harris quoted in Akhtar and Humphries, *The Fifties and Sixties*, p. 155.

88 Lamb, *The Macmillan Years*, pp. 431–42.

89 Horne, *Macmillan 1957–1986*, p. 252.

90 Jackson, *The Middle Classes*, pp. 34–5; Mark Clapson, *Invincible Green Suburbs, Brave New Towns* (Manchester, 1998), p. 24; Gunn and Bell, *Middle Classes*, pp. 27–31, 58–89.

91 Rachel Ferguson, *Passionate Kensington* (London, 1939), p. 25, quoted in Jerry White, *London in the Twentieth Century* (London, 2001), p. 35.

92 *The Times*, 1904, quoted in Edward Platt, *Leadville: A Biography of the A40* (London, 2000), p. 28; White, *London in the Twentieth Century*, pp. 35–6; Clapson, *Invincible Green Suburbs, Brave New Towns*, pp. 5–6.

93 Colls, *Identity of England*, p. 342.

94 George Orwell, *Coming Up for Air* (Harmondsworth, 1962), pp. 13–14.

95 Taylor, *After the War*, p. 45.

96 Quoted in Platt, *Leadville*, p. 208.

97 Iain Nairn, *Outrage* (London, 1955), p. 365.

98 Clapson, *Invincible Green Suburbs, Brave New Towns*, pp. 6–7.

99 See Michael Young and Peter Willmott, *Family and Kinship in East London* (London, 1957), esp. pp. 108–23; Laing, *Representations of Working-Class Life*, pp. 38–43; Clapson, *Invincible Green Suburbs, Brave New Towns*, p. 66. The quotation is from Willmott and Young, *Family and Class in a London Suburb*, p. 7.

100 Clapson, *Invincible Green Suburbs, Brave New Towns*, p. 138.

101 Catherine Hall, 'Married Women at Home in Birmingham in the 1920s and 1930s', *Oral History* 5:2, 1977, pp. 62–83.

102 June Norris, *Human Aspects of Redevelopment* (Birmingham, 1962), pp. 11, 27–8.

103 J. M. Mogey, *Family and Neighbourhood: Two Studies of Oxford* (Oxford, 1956), p. 74.

104 Willmott and Young, *Family and Class in a London Suburb*, pp. 13–20. The MP for Woodford at the time was still Sir Winston Churchill.

105 Akhtar and Humphries, *The Fifties and Sixties*, p. 65.

106 Willmott and Young, *Family and Class in a London Suburb*, p. 7.

107 Willmott and Young, *Family and Class in a London Suburb*, p. 112.

108 Willmott and Young, *Family and Class in a London Suburb*, p. 19.

109 Willmott and Young, *Family and Class in a London Suburb*, p. 91.

110 Willmott and Young, *Family and Class in a London Suburb*, pp. 92–3.

111 Willmott and Young, *Family and Class in a London Suburb*, p. 115.

112 Stevenson, *British Society 1914–45*, p. 381. In his book *Classes and Cultures*, on the other hand, Ross McKibbin suggests that even in the immediate post-war years English

life was characterised by a multiplicity of different, even antagonistic cultures divided above all by class. This is broadly persuasive, although it does seem likely that the popularity of the BBC and the national press, for example, helped to promote a more common culture after the Second World War.

113 Sampson, *Anatomy of Britain*, pp. 112–13.

114 Ruth Dudley Edwards, *Newspapermen: Hugh Cudlipp, Cecil Harmsworth King and the Glory Days of Fleet Street* (London, 2003), pp. 119, 201.

115 Sampson, *Anatomy of Britain*, pp. 112–113; McKibbin, *Classes and Cultures*, p. 503.

116 McKibbin, *Classes and Cultures*, p. 422. This quotation obviously refers to England, rather than to the United Kingdom; the same, however, applied to the Scots, the Welsh and the Northern Irish.

117 Stevenson, *British Society 1914–45*, p. 401.

118 Robert Hewison, *In Anger: Culture in the Cold War 1945–60* (London, 1981), p. 14.

119 Pat Dallimore quoted in Akhtar and Humphries, *The Fifties and Sixties*, p. 131.

120 McKibbin, *Classes and Cultures*, p. 419.

121 Akhtar and Humphries, *The Fifties and Sixties*, p. 132.

122 Quoted in Jeffrey Hill, *Sport, Leisure and Culture in Twentieth-Century Britain* (London, 2002), p. 130.

123 Unknown interviewee quoted in Alison Pressley, *Changing Times: Being Young in Britain in the '60s* (London, 2000), p. 63.

124 Peter Laurie, *The Teenage Revolution* (London, 1965), p. 43.

125 Margaret Stacey, *Tradition and Change: A Study of Banbury* (Oxford, 1960), pp. 75, 82–6.

126 *Wanstead and Woodford Official Guide* (1958–1959), p. 43, quoted in Willmott and Young, *Family and Class in a London Suburb*, p. 79. For other examples, see A. H. Birch, *Small Town Politics* (Oxford, 1959); Hill, *Sport, Leisure and Culture in Twentieth-Century Britain*, pp. 135–6.

127 Willmott and Young, *Family and Class in a London Suburb*, pp. 80–1.

128 Willmott and Young, *Family and Class in a London Suburb*, pp. 79–80.

129 See the studies of Derby and 'Squirebridge' quoted in Willmott and Young, *Family and Class in a London Suburb*, p. 82; and also the survey of Nottingham in the sixties in Coates and Silburn, *Poverty*, p. 113.

130 Willmott and Young, *Family and Class in a London Suburb*, p. 82.

131 Brian Jackson, *Working Class Community* (Harmondsworth, 1968), pp. 22–39, 106–10.

132 Jackson, *Working Class Community*, pp. 70–1.

133 Wybrow, *Britain Speaks Out*, p. 51; Sampson, *Anatomy of Britain*, p. 579. My maternal grandfather, for example, religiously completed his weekly pools coupons despite a general disapproval of gambling and a complete lack of interest in football.

134 *Listener*, 26 November 1959.

135 Sampson, *Anatomy of Britain*, p. 576; Stevenson, *British Society 1914–45*, p. 383. For an excellent description of a South Wales pub in the early fifties, where 'round glass-topped tables had replaced the old oblong plain-wood ones' and 'pink and green lino covered the wooden floor', see Kingsley Amis, *That Uncertain Feeling* (London, 1955), p. 69.

136 Wybrow, *Britain Speaks Out*, p. 49.

137 Very oddly, one in six of those who did not believe in God, and one in five of those

who did not believe that Jesus was divine, still believed in the Virgin Birth, suggesting immense confusion in many minds: Mass-Observation, *Puzzled People: A Study of Popular Attitudes to Religion, Ethics, Progress and Politics in a London Borough* (London, 1948), pp. 156ff.

138 Grace Davie, *Religion in Britain since 1945: Believing Without Belonging* (Oxford, 1994), pp. 78–9.

139 Sampson, *Anatomy of Britain*, pp. 579.

140 Hopkins, *The New Look*, pp. 430–1.

141 McKibbin, *Classes and Cultures*, p. 364.

142 Richard Hoggart, *The Uses of Literacy* (Harmondsworth, 1957), pp. 326–7.

143 Hoggart, *The Uses of Literacy*, p. 328.

144 Hopkins, *The New Look*, p. 333.

145 Hopkins, *The New Look*, pp. 332–3; for anecdotes about budgerigars, see Pressley, *The Best of Times*, pp. 38–9.

146 Sampson, *Anatomy of Britain*, p. 579.

147 Wybrow, *Britain Speaks Out*, p. 51.

148 Hopkins, *The New Look*, p. 430. He quotes a survey carried out by the Industrial Welfare Society in 1959.

149 Addison, *Now the War Is Over*, pp. 114–15; Akhtar and Humphries, *Some Liked It Hot*, p. 10.

150 Akhtar and Humphries, *Some Liked It Hot*, pp. 18–22.

151 Akhtar and Humphries, *Some Liked It Hot*, pp. 42–4.

152 Advertisement reprinted in Pressley, *The Best of Times*, p. 85.

153 Akhtar and Humphries, *Some Liked It Hot*, p. 43.

154 Cited in Stevenson, *British Society 1914–45*, p. 395.

155 Dominic Shellard, *British Theatre since the War* (London, 1999), pp. 28–9; Landy, *British Genres*, pp. 334–41, 352–4.

156 Osborne, *The Entertainer*, p. 7.

157 Andrew Blake, 'Popular Music since the 1950s', in Bloom and Day, eds, *Literature and Culture in Modern Britain: Volume Three*, p. 225.

158 It was Harold Wilson, as President of the Board of Trade, who was largely responsible for these rather shambolic efforts. See Pimlott, *Harold Wilson*, pp. 118–20.

159 Raymond Durgnat, *A Mirror for England: British Movies from Austerity to Affluence* (London, 1970), p. 55.

160 McKibbin, *Classes and Cultures*, p. 432.

161 Pearl Jephcott, *Rising Twenty* (London, 1953), pp. 62–3, cited in McKibbin, *Classes and Cultures*, p. 432.

162 Hopkins, *The New Look*, p. 454.

163 Hopkins, *The New Look*, p. 107.

164 Bernard Bergonzi, *The Situation of the Novel* (London, 1970), p. 62.

165 Wybrow, *Britain Speaks Out*, pp. 14, 21, 33 and passim.

166 Rosen, *The Transformation of British Life*, p. 149; David Reynolds, *Rich Relations: The American Occupation of Britain 1942–1945* (London, 1995).

167 *New York Times Magazine*, 14 June 1953; Fred Vanderschmidt, *What the English Think of Us* (New York, 1948), quoted in Hopkins, *The New Look*, p. 109.

168 Quoted in Weight, *Patriots*, p. 243.

169 George Orwell, 'The Decline of the English Murder', in Orwell, *Collected Essays, Journalism and Letters: Volume IV* (Harmondsworth, 1980), pp. 124–8.

170 Robert Skidelsky, *John Maynard Keynes: Fighting for Britain 1937–1946* (London, 2000), p. 295; Hopkins, *The New Look*, p. 109.

171 Francis Williams, *The American Invasion* (London, 1962), p. 12.

172 Dennis Wrong, 'The Functional Theory of Stratification' (1959), cited in Colls, *Identity of England*, p. 190. On Americanisation and its critics, see also Duncan Webster, *Looka Yonder! The Imaginary America of Populist Culture* (London, 1988), pp. 174–208.

173 John Wain, *Living in the Present* (London, 1955), quoted in Humphrey Carpenter, *The Angry Young Men: A Literary Comedy of the 1950s* (London, 2002), p. 86.

174 Raymond Postgate, ed., *The Good Food Guide 1951–1952* (London, 1951), p. 19.

175 Quoted in Clarke, *Shadow of a Nation*, pp. 138–139.

176 Akhtar and Humphries, *The Fifties and Sixties*, pp. 110–11.

177 See <www.littlechef.co.uk>.

178 Akhtar and Humphries, *The Fifties and Sixties*, pp. 110–11.

179 Andrew Loog Oldham, *Stoned* (London, 2000), p. 169. There is also a good literary example: when the innocent heroine of Kingsley Amis' novel *Take a Girl Like You* is taken by her boyfriend to a 'roadhouse' for dinner, she is extremely impressed by, for example, the 'dinner-mats with Old Master pictures on them, and a menu the size of the *Daily Mirror* each'. See Kingsley Amis, *Take a Girl Like You* (London, 1960), pp. 45–8.

180 Arthur Ransome, *Bohemia in London* (London, 1907); White, *London in the Twentieth Century*, pp. 104–8.

181 See J. B. Priestley, *Angel Pavement* (London, 1930).

182 Vansittart, *In the Fifties*, pp. 70–83, 130–52. The quintessential Soho bohemian is the character X. Trapnel in Anthony Powell's novel *Books Do Furnish a Room* (London, 1971). Trapnel, who carries a trademark death's-head stick, was supposedly modelled on the dandified Soho character Julian Maclaren-Ross, whom Vansittart captures 'in long camel-hair coat, with gloves and silver-topped cane' (p. 81).

183 Adam Faith, *Poor Me* (London, 1961), p. 16.

184 Jackson, *The Middle Classes*, pp. 248–53; Burnett, *Liquid Pleasures*, p. 66.

185 *The Rebel*, directed by Robert Day, was released in 1960 as an attempt to translate Hancock's television appeal into the cinema, but it did not really succeed. British audiences evidently expected different things from the small screen than they did from the pictures.

186 Colin Holmes, *John Bull's Island: Immigration and British Society, 1871–1971* (London, 1988), pp. 31, 51.*

187 Holmes, *John Bull's Island*, p. 214.

188 Lewis, *In the Fifties*, p. 136.

189 White, *London in the Twentieth Century*, p. 335.

190 McKibbin, *Classes and Cultures*, p. 187.

191 See Akhtar and Humphries, *The Fifties and Sixties*, p. 38; Gardiner, *From the Bomb to the Beatles*, p. 11.

192 Lewis, *In the Fifties*, p. 136.

193 Wally Whyton quoted in Tony Bacon, *London Live* (London, 1999), p. 25.

194 This was evidently before the sheepskin jacket became associated with football commentators in general and John Motson in particular. On Walsall, see Stafford, *Light in the Dust*, p. 171. Note that her selection of their favourite artists of the day suggests the conservatism of many young people's tastes in the period: 'Frankie Laine, David Whitfield, Lita Roza, Dickie Valentine, Alma Cogan'. On Abingdon and Sunderland, see unidentified interviewees quoted in Pressley, *Changing Times*, p. 63; Alan Clayson, *Beat Merchants: The Origins, History, Impact and Rock Legacy of the 1960s British Pop Groups* (London, 1995), p. 43.

195 Hopkins, *The New Look*, p. 460.

196 This is the explanation also offered by Hopkins, *The New Look*, pp. 459–60 and Hewison, *In Anger*, p. 59. Hewison calls the coffee bars 'bogus', but agrees that the emphasis on imported Italian espresso machines suggests an enthusiastic desire to copy the habits of the Continent as an alternative to the austerity of British life in previous years.

197 See Terence Conran, foreword to Gardiner, *From the Bomb to the Beatles*, pp. 7–9.

198 On the attractions of French and Italian culture, see Langford, *A Polite and Commercial People*, pp. 312–16; Colley, *Britons*, pp. 165–6; John Brewer, *The Pleasures of the Imagination: English Culture in the Eighteenth Century* (London, 1997), pp. 82–6, 204–7.

199 For instance, in Amis' novel *Take a Girl Like You* (1960), the fashionable young schoolteacher Patrick Standish runs a film society dedicated to showing pictures like the Italian neo-realist classic *Bicycle Thieves*: see Amis, *Take a Girl Like You*, p. 35.

200 There is a good discussion of this phenomenon in Gardiner, *From the Bomb to the Beatles*, pp. 108–9.

201 Hopkins, *The New Look*, p. 461.

202 Advertisements reprinted in Hylton, *Magical History Tour*, pp. 140–1.

203 Dorothy Isles quoted in Akhtar and Humphries, *Some Liked It Hot*, p. 84.

204 *Sunday Times*, 26 July 1981.

205 Lewis, *The Fifties*, p. 30.

206 *Manchester Guardian*, 11 December 1956.

207 Hopkins, *The New Look*, p. 463.

208 Lisa Chaney, *Elizabeth David: A Mediterranean Passion* (London, 1998), p. 347.

209 Quoted in Sutherland, *Reading the Decades*, p. 131.

210 Elizabeth David, *A Book of Mediterranean Food* (London, 1991), p. 1; Clarke, *Shadow of a Nation*, pp. 131–2.

211 Clarke, *Shadow of a Nation*, p. 146; see also Sutherland, *Reading the Decades*, pp. 19–20.

212 Marwick, *The Sixties*, pp. 35–6.

CHAPTER 5: THE PROVINCIAL ALL-STARS

1 Andrew Motion, *Philip Larkin: A Writer's Life* (London, 1993), pp. 54–5. The quotation is from Larkin's introduction to the Faber edition of his novel *Jill* (London, 1964), pp. 14–15.

2 Blake Morrison, *The Movement: English Poetry and Fiction of the 1950s* (Oxford, 1980), pp. 10–11.

3 Motion, *Philip Larkin*, pp. xix–xx.

4 Taylor, *After the War*, p. xxv.

5 Harry Ritchie, *Success Stories: Literature and the Media in England, 1950–1959* (London, 1989), p. 64: this is an indispensable survey of the Movement and the Angry Young Men.

6 Eric Jacobs, *Kingsley Amis: A Biography* (London, 1995), p. 165.

7 Laing, *Representations of Working-Class Life*, p. 60.

8 Quotations from Jacobs, *Kingsley Amis*, p. 165.

9 Ritchie, *Success Stories*, pp. 5–7.

10 On the literary establishment, see Ritchie, *Success Stories*, pp. 105–7.

11 Malcolm Bradbury, *The Modern British Novel* (London, 1993), p. xiii.

12 J. B. Priestley, quoted in George Scott, 'Time and Place', in Gene Feldman and Max Gartenberg, eds, *Protest: The Beat Generation and the Angry Young Men* (London, 1959), p. 270.

13 Amis's father worked for Colman's Mustard in London, Larkin's was the Coventry city treasurer. See Jacobs, *Kingsley Amis*, p. 20; Motion, *Philip Larkin*, pp. 6–7.

14 Jacobs, *Kingsley Amis*, p. 19.

15 For Amis, see Kingsley Amis, *Memoirs* (London, 1991); Jacobs, *Kingsley Amis*; Richard Bradford, *Lucky Him: The Life of Kingsley Amis* (London, 1991). For Larkin, see Motion, *Philip Larkin*.

16 Amis, *Memoirs*, p. 58. They did, however, continue to meet, but generally at neutral venues.

17 Amis to Larkin, 16 June 1947, in Zachary Leader, ed., *The Letters of Kingsley Amis* (London, 2000), pp. 134–5.

18 Amis to Larkin, 12 June 1950, in Leader, ed., *The Letters of Kingsley Amis*, pp. 231–4.

19 Amis, *Memoirs*, p. 57.

20 See Bradford, *Lucky Him*, pp. 77–98.

21 Amis to Larkin, 3 March 1953, in Leader, ed., *The Letters of Kingsley Amis*, pp. 310–12.

22 Amis to Larkin, 30 January 1947, in Leader, ed., *The Letters of Kingsley Amis*, pp. 111–12.

23 Amis to Larkin, 6 February 1947, in Leader, ed., *The Letters of Kingsley Amis*, pp. 113–14.

24 Motion, *Philip Larkin*, p. 21. For the account of another notable jazz aficionado building an eminent career in the same period, see Eric Hobsbawm, *Interesting Times: A Twentieth-Century Life* (London, 2002), pp. 225–7.

25 Amis, *Memoirs*, p. 65; see also Jacobs, *Kingsley Amis*, pp. 80–1.

26 Motion, *Philip Larkin*, pp. 56–7; Morrison, *The Movement*, p. 12.

27 Amis, *Memoirs*, p. 52.

28 Amis, *Memoirs*, pp. 52–3.

29 Amis, *Memoirs*, p. 67.

30 Lewis, *The Fifties*, p. 141.

31 Philip Larkin, *All What Jazz* (London, 1964), pp. 20–1, 27.

32 On Wain, see Carpenter, *The Angry Young Men*, pp. 38–45.

33 Al Alvarez, *Where Did It All Go Right?* (London, 1999), p. 136.

34 John Wain, *Strike the Father Dead* (London, 1962), p. 42.

35 On another occasion that stuck in Amis's memory, Wain asked him if he was 'working on anything at the moment', as though the indignant Amis were 'a mere part-timer':

> 'Yes,' I said.
>
> 'Oh. What is it?'
>
> Could it have been a monograph on the fauna of Kentucky? 'A novel,' I said with restraint, not adding 'actually' or 'called *Fuck You*'.
>
> John gave me a sly, old-pals' wink. 'Make it a good one this time, eh?' he said.
>
> 'I suppose that's what we're all trying to do,' I said, in an attempt to piss on him and sound humble at once.

For both these stories, see Amis, *Memoirs*, pp. 42–3.

36 Morrison, *The Movement*, pp. 42–43; Ritchie, *Success Stories*, pp. 11–15; Carpenter, *The Angry Young Men*, pp. 44–5.

37 Morrison, *The Movement*, p. 44.

38 See Kingsley Amis, *Lucky Jim* (London, 1954), pp. 61–6.

39 Wain explained: 'It is going to be a famous book some day.' See *New Statesman*, 18 July 1953; Kate Whitehead, *The Third Programme: A Literary History* (London, 1989) p. 200.

40 Morrison, *The Movement*, p. 46; Carpenter, *The Angry Young Men*, pp. 56–8.

41 Jacobs, *Kingsley Amis*, p. 144.

42 Ritchie, *Success Stories*, p. 67.

43 Note, however, that Victor Gollancz printed fewer copies than virtually any other major publisher, so this amounted to fewer books than one might imagine: see Jacobs, *Kingsley Amis*, p. 160.

44 Jacobs, *Kingsley Amis*, p. 162.

45 *Encounter*, December 1955.

46 *Encounter*, June 1956.

47 *Spectator*, 6 July 1956.

48 *Sunday Times*, 25 December 1954.

49 Quoted in Carpenter, *The Angry Young Men*, p. 70.

50 *New Statesman*, 20 August 1955.

51 *Times Literary Supplement*, 17 February 1956.

52 Amis, *Memoirs*, p. 217.

53 See Taylor, *After the War*, pp. 100–1.

54 *Observer*, 29 January 1961.

55 Bradbury, *The Modern British Novel*, p. 321. On Cooper's influence, see also Randall Stevenson, *The British Novel since the Thirties: An Introduction* (London, 1986), p.124; Bernard Bergonzi, *Wartime and Aftermath: English Literature and its Background, 1939–1960* (Oxford, 1993), pp. 141–2.

56 See Taylor, *After the War*, p. 76.

57 Morrison, *The Movement*, p. 171.

58 See Bergonzi, *Wartime and Aftermath*, p. 144; Bradbury, *The Modern British Novel*, p. 321; Bradford, *Lucky Him*, p. 78.

59 Taylor, *After the War*, p. xxi.

60 *New Statesman*, 30 January 1954.

61 Morrison, *The Movement*, p. 9; Ritchie, *Success Stories*, pp. 122–3.

62 *Spectator*, 27 August 1954.

63 *Spectator*, 1 October 1954.

64 See Ritchie, *Success Stories*, p. 20.

65 *Spectator*, 15 October 1954.

66 Steven Earnshaw, 'Novel Voices', in Bloom and Day, eds, *Literature and Culture in Modern Britain: Volume Three*, p. 53. John Hill similarly argues that the Movement was a journalistic myth: see Hill, *Sex, Class and Realism*, p. 21.

67 'GSF' refers to G. S. Fraser: see Amis to Larkin, 18 October 1954, in Leader, ed., *The Letters of Kingsley Amis*, pp. 404–7.

68 See D. J. Enright, *Poets of the 1950s* (Tokyo, 1955); Robert Conquest, *New Lines* (London, 1956); Morrison, *The Movement*, pp. 2–3. Blake Morrison's book is the definitive treatment of this subject.

69 Amis, *Memoirs*, p. 146.

70 Amis to Wain, 6 November 1953, in Leader, ed., *The Letters of Kingsley Amis*, pp. 340–3.

71 Amis to Larkin, 14 March 1954, in Leader, ed., *The Letters of Kingsley Amis*, pp. 374–8.

72 *Observer*, 1 January 1956.

73 Morrison, *The Movement*, pp. 56–7.

74 Amis to William Van O'Connor, 21 January 1958, in Leader, ed., *The Letters of Kingsley Amis*, pp. 525–6.

75 Bergonzi, *Wartime and Aftermath*, p. 161.

76 'The Whitsun Weddings', in Larkin, *Collected Poems*, pp. 114–16.

77 Charles Tomlinson, 'The Middlebrow Muse', *Essays in Criticism* 7, 1957, pp. 214–15; Motion, *Philip Larkin*, p. 343.

78 Michael Kirkham, 'Philip Larkin and Charles Tomlinson: Realism and Art', in Boris Ford, ed. *The New Pelican Guide to English Literature : Volume 8: From Orwell to Naipaul* (revised edition: London, 1998), p. 288.

79 'Here', in Philip Larkin, *Collected Poems* (London, 1999), pp. 136–7.

80 See Morrison, *The Movement*, pp. 130–1; Alistair Davies and Peter Saunders, 'Literature, Politics and Society', in Alan Sinfield, ed., *Society and Literature 1945–1970* (London, 1983), p. 24.

81 Orwell, *The Road to Wigan Pier*, p. 160. Note that the harassed lower-middle-class heroes of Orwell's novels, with their horror of 'the snooty "cultured" kind of books' described in *Keep the Aspidistra Flying* (1936), clearly prefigure characters like Joe Lunn and Jim Dixon: see Morrison, *The Movement*, pp. 73–4.

82 On Leavis and the Movement, see Morrison, *The Movement*, pp. 31–3; Bergonzi, *Wartime and Aftermath*, p. 171; Annan, *Our Age*, p. 434; Geoffrey Strickland, 'F. R. Leavis and "English"', in Ford, ed., *From Orwell to Naipaul*, pp. 166–83; Michael Bell, *F. R. Leavis* (London, 1988).

83 A. J. Ayer, *Language, Truth and Logic* (second edition: London, 1946), p. 51, quoted in Morrison, *The Movement*, p. 158; see also Michael Tanner, 'Wittgenstein and English Philosophy', in Ford, ed., *From Orwell to Naipaul*, p. 472. For the links between Ayer and the Movement, see Morrison, *The Movement*, pp. 158–9. Kingsley Amis wrote that he was 'always cheered by the sight of [Ayer] and his enormous nose', and also respected him as 'a great cocksman', 'remarkably keen on female company and good at acquiring it': see Amis, *Memoirs*, pp. 308–10. I am indebted to Martin O'Neill for his thoughts on these and other matters.

84 Ritchie, *Success Stories*, pp. 91–4.

85 Paul Fussell, *The Anti-Egotist: Kingsley Amis, Man of Letters* (Oxford, 1994), p. 68.

86 See the discussion of this poem in Morrison, *The Movement*, pp. 160–3: this argues that Amis' poem was in large part a rejoinder to the neo-romanticism of Dylan Thomas and his emulators in the late forties and early fifties.

87 Quoted in Motion, *Philip Larkin*, p. 345.

88 Kingsley Amis, *I Like It Here* (London, 1958), p. 68.

89 Ritchie, *Success Stories*, p. 102.

90 Wain, *Hurry On Down*, pp. 65–8.

91 Amis, *Lucky Jim*, p. 38.

92 Amis, *Lucky Jim*, p. 250.

93 Amis, *Lucky Jim*, p. 76.

94 Amis, *Lucky Jim*, p. 14.

95 Amis, *Lucky Jim*, p. 33.

96 Amis, *Lucky Jim*, p. 63.

97 Amis, *Lucky Jim*, p. 87.

98 Amis, *Lucky Jim*, pp. 226–7. Folk dancing and the celebration of a bucolic, pastoral 'Merrie England' of old-fashioned amateur entertainments had been favourites of the English heritage movement and the Arts Council during the 1940s: see Eric W. White, *The Arts Council of Great Britain* (London, 1975), p. 36. They were also the favoured pastimes of Amis' father-in-law, the inspiration for the character of Professor Welch.

99 Morrison, *The Movement*, p. 131. Note the affinities with the fiction of H. G. Wells, especially *Kipps* (1905) and *The History of Mr Polly* (1910), as well as the works of George Orwell.

100 *Books and Art*, October 1957: on science fiction, see Hewison, *In Anger*, p. 115.

101 See Motion, *Philip Larkin*, p. 266.

102 *Critical Quarterly*, Spring 1965, pp. 87–92.

103 *Daily Worker*, 12 February 1957, quoted in Ritchie, *Success Stories*, p. 74.

104 *Daily Mail*, 13 July 1956.

105 Ritchie, *Success Stories*, pp. 142–3; Carpenter, *The Angry Young Men*, pp. 94–100.

106 Carpenter, *The Angry Young Men*, p. 98.

107 Carpenter, *The Angry Young Men*, p. 197.

108 Holroyd, *Contraries*, p. 32.

109 Carpenter, *The Angry Young Men*, pp. 104–7.

110 Ritchie, *Success Stories*, pp. 143–4.

111 *Evening News*, 26 May 1956.

112 *Sunday Times*, 27 May 1956; *Observer*, 27 May 1956.

113 Hewison, *In Anger*, pp. 130–1, 136; Ritchie, *Success Stories*, p. 146.

114 Ritchie, *Success Stories*, pp. 144–6; Carpenter, *The Angry Young Men*, pp. 111–13.

115 Lewis, *The Fifties*, p. 166.

116 Quoted in Hewison, *In Anger*, p. 131.

117 See Colin Wilson, 'Country of the Blind', reprinted in Feldman and Gartenberg, eds, *Protest*, pp. 173–85.

118 *Times Literary Supplement*, 14 December 1956, quoted in Ritchie, *Success Stories*, pp. 154–5.

119 Carpenter, *The Angry Young Men*, p. 110.

120 Ritchie, *Success Stories*, pp. 160–3.

121 Ritchie, *Success Stories*, p. 175.

122 *Observer*, 27 May 1956.

123 Ritchie, *Success Stories*, p. 177.

124 Carpenter, *The Angry Young Men*, p. 168.

125 *Evening News*, 28 May 1956.

126 *Daily Mail*, 13 July 1956.

127 *Daily Express*, 14 September 1956.

128 Ritchie, *Success Stories*, p. 154.

129 Vansittart insists that he recalls Wilson's words 'more or less exactly': see Vansittart, *In the Fifties*, pp. 214–15.

130 Quoted in Hill, *Sex, Class and Realism*, p. 24.

131 *Spectator*, 15 June 1956.

132 Amis to Conquest, 20 June 1956, in Leader, ed., *The Letters of Kingsley Amis*, pp. 470–1.

133 Amis to Larkin, 25 June 1956, in Leader, ed., *The Letters of Kingsley Amis*, pp. 471–4.

134 Lewis, *The Fifties*, p. 167; Ritchie, *Success Stories*, p. 150; Carpenter, *The Angry Young Men*, pp. 168–9.

135 *Daily Mail*, 20 February 1957.

136 Carpenter, *The Angry Young Men*, p. 169.

137 *Daily Mail*, 23 February 1957.

138 Colin Wilson, *Religion and the Rebel* (London, 1957), quoted in Ritchie, *Success Stories*, p. 163.

139 Reviews quoted in Lewis, *The Fifties*, p. 168; Ritchie, *Success Stories*, pp. 156–7.

140 Ritchie, *Success Stories*, pp. 171–2.

141 Angus Wilson, 'A Bit off the Map', in *A Bit off the Map* (Penguin edition: Harmondsworth, 1968), pp. 16–17.

142 Ritchie, *Success Stories*, pp. 172–3.

143 Carpenter, *The Angry Young Men*, p. 197.

144 Ritchie, *Success Stories*, pp. 147–8.

145 See Green, *Days in the Life*, pp. 2–5. Sheila Rowbotham, *Promise of a Dream: Remembering the Sixties* (London, 2000), pp. 6–8, has a nice description of bohemian culture in Leeds, of all places.

146 Unknown interviewee quoted in Pressley, *Changing Times*, p. 19.

147 Bradford, *Lucky Him*, p. 88.

148 Ritchie, *Success Stories*, p. 108. These were very bad cases of what Arthur Koestler famously diagnosed as 'French 'flu', a disease to which British intellectuals are depressingly prone. See Arthur Koestler, *The Yogi and the Commissar* (London, 1945), p. 25.

149 See Orwell, 'My Country Right or Left', in *The Collected Essays, Journalism and Letters of George Orwell: Volume II* (Harmondsworth, 1970).

150 Carpenter, *The Angry Young Men*, p. 84.

151 Motion, *Philip Larkin*, pp. 26–7.

152 Amis to Larkin, 10 July 1955, in Leader, ed., *The Letters of Kingsley Amis*, pp. 433–8.

153 Amis to Larkin, 9 September 1956, in Leader, ed., *The Letters of Kingsley Amis*, pp. 476–8.

154 Amis, *I Like It Here*, p. 7.

155 Amis, *I Like It Here*, p. 133.

156 Amis, *I Like It Here*, pp. 156–7.

157 Amis, *I Like It Here*, p. 19.

158 Amis, *Lucky Jim*, p. 178.

159 Amis, *Lucky Jim*, p. 44.

160 Amis, *Lucky Jim*, p. 84.

161 Kingsley Amis, *The King's English* (London, 1997), p. 80.

162 Ritchie, *Success Stories*, p. 98.

163 Amis to William Van O'Connor, 6 January 1958, in Leader, ed., *The Letters of Kingsley Amis*, pp. 522–4.

164 Motion, *Philip Larkin*, p. 35.

165 Amis, *Lucky Jim*, p. 158.

166 Morrison, *The Movement*, pp. 68–85.

167 Kingsley Amis, *Socialism and the Intellectuals* (Fabian Society pamphlet: London, 1957), reprinted in Feldman and Gartenberg, eds, *Protest*, pp. 254–68.

168 Amis, *Lucky Jim*, p. 51.

169 See Hewison, *In Anger*, p. 121 and passim.

170 Amis, *Socialism and the Intellectuals*, pp. 260, 264.

171 Amis, *I Like It Here*, p. 80.

172 Amis, *Socialism and the Intellectuals*, p. 266.

173 Amis, *Socialism and the Intellectuals*, pp. 267–8.

174 Kingsley Amis, *Girl, 20* (London, 1971), pp. 16–17.

175 Muriel Spark, *The Comforters* (London, 1957).

176 Bergonzi, *Wartime and Aftermath*, p. 135; Ritchie, *Success Stories*, pp. 215–17; Bradbury, *The Modern British Novel*, pp. 280–1, 318–19.

177 Gilbert Phelps, 'The Post-War English Novel', in Ford, ed., *From Orwell to Naipaul*, p. 425.

178 *Guardian*, 15 June 2002.

179 Ritchie, *Success Stories*, p. 78; *New Statesman*, 2 January 1960.

180 *Daily Express*, 26 July 1956 and 4 September 1956.

181 *Encounter*, November 1968.

182 *Daily Mail*, 13 December 1956; *News Chronicle*, 13 August 1957.

CHAPTER 6: THE NEW WAVE

1 Hoggart, *The Uses of Literacy*, pp. 58–9.

2 Hoggart, *The Uses of Literacy*, p. 59.

3 Stafford, *Light in the Dust*, pp. 19–24.

4 Stafford, *Light in the Dust*, pp. 25–7.

5 Sinfield, *Literature, Politics and Culture in Post-war Britain*, p. 21.

6 Gina Spreckley quoted in Akhtar and Humphries, *The Fifties and Sixties*, p. 56.

7 Seebohm Rowntree and G. R. Lavers, *Poverty and the Welfare State* (London, 1951); and undated *Times* editorial, quoted in Coates and Silburn, *Poverty*, p. 14.

8 See Coates and Silburn, *Poverty*, p. 18.

9 For example, Richard Titmuss, *Essays on 'The Welfare State'* (London, 1958); Dorothy Cole, 'Poverty in Britain Today – The Evidence', *Sociological Review*, 1962, pp. 257–82; Richard Titmuss, *Income Distribution and Social Change: A Study in Criticism* (London, 1962).

10 Brian Able-Smith and Peter Townsend, 'The Poor and the Poorest', *Occasional Papers on Social Administration* 6, December 1965.

11 John Westergaard and Henrietta Resler, *Class in a Capitalist Society* (Harmondsworth, 1977), p. 43

12 Porter, '"Never-Never Land"', p. 22.

13 Marwick, *British Society since 1945*, p. 47.

14 See the bibliography in Stevenson, *British Society 1914–45*, pp. 473–84.

15 Ralph Glasser, *Gorbals Boy at Oxford* (London, 1988), p. 173, quoted in Colls, *Identity of England*, p. 64.

16 Hewison, *In Anger*, pp. 176–7.

17 For sociology in the fifties see Laing, *Representations of Working-Class Life*, pp. 31–58; Annan, *Our Age*, pp. 346–7; and on the expansion of sociology into the provinces, see Hewison, *In Anger*, pp. 176–7.

18 See Annan, *Our Age*, p. 348; Vansittart, *In the Fifties*, p. 102. The shipbuilding article is the paper on which Dixon is working in *Lucky Jim*.

19 Laing, *Representations of Working-Class Life*, pp. 37–8; Sutherland, *Reading the Decades*, p. 245; Clapson, *Invincible Green Suburbs, Brave New Towns*, pp. 65–6.

20 See Laing, *Representations of Working-Class Life*, pp. 31–81.

21 Hoggart, *The Uses of Literacy*, p. 15.

22 Hoggart, *The Uses of Literacy*, p. 16.

23 Hoggart, *The Uses of Literacy*, p. 59.

24 Hoggart, *The Uses of Literacy*, p. 48; Taylor, *After the War*, p. 110.

25 Hoggart, *The Uses of Literacy*, p. 39.

26 For example, see Orwell, *The Road to Wigan Pier*, pp. 102–5.

27 On Hoggart and Leavis, see Colls, *Identity of England*, pp. 363–4.

28 Hoggart, *The Uses of Literacy*, pp. 192–3.

29 Hoggart, *The Uses of Literacy*, p. 340.

30 Hoggart, *The Uses of Literacy*, pp. 202–3, 340.

31 Hoggart, *The Uses of Literacy*, pp. 149–66.

32 Hoggart, *The Uses of Literacy*, pp. 248–9.

33 Marwick, *British Society since 1945*, p. 128.

34 Hewison, *In Anger*, pp. 177–8.

35 Richard Dyer et al., *Coronation Street* (London 1981), p. 4.

36 Taylor, *After the War*, p. 111.

37 Gary Day, introduction to *Literature and Culture in Modern Britain: Volume Three*, p. 15.

38 Quoted in Colls, *Identity of England*, p. 311.

39 Raymond Williams, *Culture Is Ordinary* (London, 1990), p. 12.

40 Raymond Williams, *Culture and Society 1780–1950* (London, 1958); for cogent analyses of Williams' approach, see Laing, *Representations of Working-Class Life*, pp. 197–202; Maurice Cowling, 'Raymond Williams in Retrospect', *New Criterion*, February 1990; Colls, *Identity of England*, pp. 362–4.

41 Quoted in Hewison, *Too Much*, p. 12.

42 Ritchie, *Success Stories*, p. 57.

43 For a discussion of the differences between the Movement and their contemporaries working in theatre and film, see Morrison, *The Movement*, pp. 246–7.

44 Shellard, *British Theatre since the War*, pp. 17–18.

45 Alan Sinfield, 'The Theatre and its Audiences', in Sinfield, ed., *Society and Literature 1945–1970*, p. 173.

46 Shellard, *British Theatre since the War*, pp. 7, 33.

47 Hewison, *In Anger*, pp. 66–7; Dominic Shellard, *Kenneth Tynan: A Life* (New Haven, 2003).

48 Hewison, *In Anger*, p. 72.

49 Christopher Innes, 'Terence Rattigan: The Voice of the 1950s', in Dominic Shellard, ed., *British Theatre in the 1950s* (Sheffield, 2000), pp. 53, 55.

50 Terence Rattigan, *Collected Plays: Volume II* (London, 1953), pp. xx–xii.

51 *Observer*, 21 February 1954.

52 Rattigan, *Collected Plays: Volume II*, p. xvi.

53 See Dan Rebellato, *1956 and All That: The Making of Modern British Drama* (London, 1999), pp. 166–7; Innes, 'Terence Rattigan: The Voice of the 1950s', pp. 62–3.

54 Innes, 'Terence Rattigan: The Voice of the 1950s', p. 55. In fact, such was the reaction against Rattigan in the 1960s that he retreated into exile as a scriptwriter in Bermuda, where he died in 1977, six years after a belated knighthood. See Shellard, *British Theatre since the War*, p. 46.

55 'Harold Pinter's Recollections of his Career in the 1950s', in Shellard, ed., *British Theatre in the 1950s*, p. 75.

56 Charles Duff, *The Lost Summer: The Heyday of the West End Theatre* (London, 1995), p. xii.

57 *Sunday Times*, 30 March 1952.

58 *Spectator*, 7 January 1955.

59 John Russell Taylor, *Anger and After: A Guide to the New British Drama* (Harmondsworth, 1963), p. 126; Hewison, *In Anger*, p. 144; Shellard, *British Theatre since the War*, p. 6.

60 Shellard, *British Theatre since the War*, p. 87; Hewison, *In Anger*, p. 148.

61 Shellard, *British Theatre since the War*, pp. 37–8, 78.

62 Howard Goorney, *The Theatre Workshop Story* (London, 1981); Laing, *Representations of Working Class Life*, pp. 84–7; review of *Richard II* in *Sunday Times*, 23 January 1955.

63 Oliver Neville, 'The English Stage Company and the Dramatic Critics', in Ford, ed., *From Orwell to Naipaul*, pp. 250–2; Shellard, *British Theatre since the War*, pp. 47–9.

64 Shellard, *British Theatre since the War*, pp. 50, 81.

65 Taylor, *Anger and After*, pp. 19, 92.

66 Neville, 'The English Stage Company and the Dramatic Critics', pp. 252–3; Shellard, *British Theatre since the War*, p. 51; Carpenter, *The Angry Young Men*, pp. 119–20.

67 Taylor, *Anger and After*, pp. 37–8; Carpenter, *The Angry Young Men*, pp. 30–37, 114–20.

68 Masters, *The Swinging Sixties*, p. 132.

69 Carpenter, *The Angry Young Men*, p. 130. Rebellato, *1956 and All That*, p. 5, gives a slightly different version: 'Look, Ma, I'm not Terence Rattigan.'

70 Quoted in introduction to Sinfield, ed., *Society and Literature 1945–1970*, p. 4; Ritchie, *Success Stories*, p. 126. See also Shellard, *British Theatre since the War*, p. 54.

71 Taylor, *Anger and After*, p. 29.

72 *Observer*, 13 May 1956.

73 See Ritchie, *Success Stories*, pp. 26–7; Carpenter, *The Angry Young Men*, p. 130.

74 John Holloway, 'Tank in the Stalls: Notes on the "School of Anger"', *Hudson Review* 10:3, Autumn 1957, reprinted in Feldman and Gartenberg, eds, *Protest*, p. 307.

75 Holloway quotes articles by, for example, K. W. Gransden in *Twentieth Century*, March 1957, and Geoffrey Gorer, *New Statesman*, 4 May 1957: see Holloway, 'Tank in the Stalls', p. 308.

76 Ritchie, *Success Stories*, p. 207.

77 Quoted in Ritchie, *Success Stories*, p. 126.

78 Lacey, *British Realist Theatre*, pp. 3, 17; see also Shellard, *British Theatre since the War*, p. 57.

79 Hewison, *In Anger*, p. 136.

80 Derek Granger in *London Magazine*, December 1956, quoted in Hewison, *In Anger*, p. 146.

81 Taylor, *Anger and After*, p. 11.

82 Taylor, *Anger and After*, pp. 28, 37.

83 Hewison, *In Anger*, p. 139.

84 'Harold Pinter's Recollections of his Career in the 1950s', p. 71.

85 Shellard, *British Theatre since the War*, p. 70.

86 Taylor, *Anger and After*, p. 38.

87 See Shellard, *British Theatre in the 1950s*, p. 14; Rebellato, *1956 and All That*, p. 3.

88 Donald Spoto, *Laurence Olivier* (London, 1991), pp. 226–7. Osborne himself disputed this account: see Carpenter, *The Angry Young Men*, p. 149.

89 See the discussion in Shellard, *British Theatre since the War*, pp. 81–2.

90 Lacey, *British Realist Theatre*, p. 104; Shellard, *British Theatre since the War*, p. 82.

91 Osborne, *The Entertainer*, p. 7.

92 Shellard, *British Theatre since the War*, p. 83.

93 *Observer*, 14 April 1957; *Sunday Times*, 14 April 1957.

94 Shellard, *British Theatre since the War*, pp. 81–2.

95 These painters were famously championed by the Marxist art critic John Berger: see Hewison, *In Anger*, p. 156.

96 See Lacey, *British Realist Theatre*, pp. 68–9.

97 *Spectator*, 18 September 1959.

98 As argued by Lacey, *British Realist Theatre*, p. 7.

99 Taylor, *Anger and After*, p. 152.

100 Taylor, *Anger and After*, p. 131.

101 See Taylor, *Anger and After*, pp. 112–13; Shellard, *British Theatre since the War*, p. 70.

102 Laing, *Representations of Working-Class Life*, p. 89.

103 Marwick, *The Sixties*, p. 137.

104 See Alexander Walker, *Hollywood, England* (London, 1974), p. 123.

105 See, for example, Marwick, *The Sixties*, pp. 143–88, which discusses British New Wave theatre and (especially) film with undisguised adoration.

106 See Masters, *The Swinging Sixties*, p. 135.

107 Unknown interviewee quoted in Pressley, *Changing Times*, p. 11.

108 *Daily Express*, 2 November 1961, quoted in Walker, *Hollywood, England*, p. 127.

109 Sinfield, *Literature, Politics and Culture in Post-war Britain*, pp. 178–9.

110 Goorney, *The Theatre Workshop Story*, p. 99.

111 Carpenter, *The Angry Young Men*, p. 119.

112 Shellard, *British Theatre since the War*, pp. 85–6.

113 Neville, 'The English Stage Company and the Dramatic Critics', p. 256.

114 Rebellato, *1956 and All That*, pp. 109–110.

115 Quoted in Laing, *Representations of Working-Class Life*, p. 98.

116 Robert Stephens, *Knight Errant* (London, 1995), pp. 27–8.

117 Rebellato, *1956 and All That*, p. 112.

118 Ritchie, *Success Stories*, p. 61.

119 Bradbury, *The Modern British Novel*, pp. 315, 280.

120 Again, see Marwick, *The Sixties*, pp. 143–88, which focuses on New Wave writing almost to the exclusion of all else.

121 Taylor, *After the War*, pp. 111–15.

122 Alan Sillitoe, *Saturday Night and Sunday Morning* (reprinted edition: London, 1990), p. 183.

123 Sillitoe, *Saturday Night and Sunday Morning*, p. 219. Note the place of women in this list, which reflects the suspicion of wives and mothers that runs through much New Wave fiction.

124 Amis, *Memoirs*, p. 215; Ritchie, *Success Stories*, pp. 184–7.

125 *Daily Worker*, 28 January 1961, quoted in Hill, *Sex, Class and Realism*, p. 203.

126 Sillitoe, *Saturday Night and Sunday Morning*, pp. 26–7.

127 See Stan Barstow, *A Kind of Loving* (Harmondsworth, 1962).

128 Bergonzi, *Wartime and Aftermath*, p. 151.

129 Keith Waterhouse, *Billy Liar* (Harmondsworth, 1962), p. 23.

130 Waterhouse, *Billy Liar*, p. 44.

131 Taylor, *After the War*, p. 76.

132 See Anthony Aldgate and Jeffrey Richards, *Best of British: Cinema and Society from 1930 to the Present* (London, 1999), p. 153.

133 See Hill, *Sex, Class and Realism*, pp. 35ff.

134 Robert Murphy, *Sixties British Cinema* (London, 1992), pp. 102–3.

135 Hewison, *In Anger*, p. 151.

136 Walker, *Hollywood, England*, p. 68; Murphy, *Sixties British Cinema*, p. 104.

137 Aldgate and Richards, *Best of British*, pp. 185–6.

138 Lawrence James, *Warrior Race: A History of the British at War* (London, 2001), p. 722.

139 Sutherland, *Reading the Decades*, pp. 27–8.

140 *New Statesman*, 5 April 1958.

141 John Ramsden, 'Refocusing the People's War: British War Films of the 1950s', *Journal of Contemporary History* 33:1, January 1998, p. 37.

142 Durgnat, *A Mirror for England*, p. 83; Landy, *British Genres*, p. 176.

143 Lindsay Anderson, 'Get Out and Push', in Tom Maschler, ed., *Declaration* (London, 1957), p. 157.

144 Anderson, 'Get Out and Push', pp. 158–9.

145 Introduction to programme for *Free Cinema 3*, May 1957, quoted in Walker, *Hollywood, England*, p. 29 and Hewison, *In Anger*, p. 153.

146 See Murphy, *Sixties British Cinema*, pp. 11, 64–5; Erik Hedling, 'Lindsay Anderson and the Development of British Art Cinema', in Murphy, ed., *The British Cinema Book*, pp. 241–6.

147 Durgnat, *A Mirror for England*, pp. 127–8; Jackson, *Working-Class Community*, pp. 127–35.

148 See Durgnat, *A Mirror for England*, p. 129; Walker, *Hollywood, England*, p. 31; Murphy, *Sixties British Cinema*, p. 11.

149 *Sight and Sound*, Spring 1959, quoted in Hewison, *In Anger*, p. 154.

150 *Daily Express*, 3 April 1959, *Saturday Review*, 11 April 1959; see also Hill, *Sex, Class and Realism*, p. 191.

151 Murphy, *Sixties British Cinema*, p. 15.

152 See Anthony Aldgate, *Censorship and the Permissive Society: British Cinema and Theatre 1955–1965* (Oxford, 1995), pp. 33–47.

153 Hewison, *In Anger*, p. 154.

154 *Evening Standard*, 22 January 1959.

155 Sutherland, *Reading the Decades*, p. 35. After the film had been released the book sold another 300,000 paperback copies. See Marwick, *The Sixties*, p. 122.

156 Carpenter, *The Angry Young Men*, p. 160.

157 *Daily Express*, 23 May 1957.

158 Ritchie, *Success Stories*, p. 5.

159 *Observer*, 17 March 1957.

160 John Braine, *Room at the Top* (reprinted edition: London, 1991), p. 235.

161 Alexander Walker in *Hollywood, England*, p. 45, argues that the film is a story of envy, but, as Robert Murphy points out, Joe Lampton in the novel explicitly disavows envy as a 'small and squalid vice'. See Murphy, *Sixties British Cinema*, p. 14; Braine, *Room at the Top*, pp. 29.

162 Braine, *Room at the Top*, pp. 9, 42.

163 Braine, *Room at the Top*, p. 29.

164 Braine, *Room at the Top*, p. 196.

165 Quoted in Hill, *Sex, Class and Realism*, pp. 157–8.

166 Braine, *Room at the Top*, pp. 198–9. There is a nice analysis of this passage in Jonathan Dollimore, 'The Challenge of Sexuality', in Sinfield, ed., *Society and Literature 1945–1970*, p. 68ff.

167 Braine, *Room at the Top*, pp. 199.

168 Carpenter, *The Angry Young Men*, pp. 164–5.

169 So, as Alexander Walker argues, the British New Wave was much more derivative than, say, the French *nouvelle vague*: see Walker, *Hollywood, England*, p. 53.

170 Hill, *Sex, Class and Realism*, p. 45.

171 Ritchie, *Success Stories*, p. 189.

172 Aldgate, *Censorship and the Permissive Society*, pp. 94–9.

173 Walker, *Hollywood, England*, pp. 88–90.

174 *Daily Herald*, 6 February 1961, quoted in Hill, *Sex, Class and Realism*, p. 204.

175 See the excellent analysis in Hill, *Sex, Class and Realism*, pp. 133, 160.

176 On the reception of *A Kind of Loving*, see Walker, *Hollywood, England*, p. 120.

177 Walker, *Hollywood, England*, p. 128.

178 *The Times*, 26 September 1962.

179 Richard Ingrams, ed., *The Life and Times of Private Eye* (London, 1971), pp. 30–5.

180 *Guardian*, 13 August 1963.

181 David Frost and Ned Sherrin, eds, *That Was The Week That Was* (London, 1963), p. 11.

182 Most of these had been copied from the French *nouvelle vague* films of directors like Truffaut, Resnais and Godard. See the discussions in Walker, *Hollywood, England*, p. 128; Murphy, *Sixties British Cinema*, p. 24; Aldgate and Richards, *Best of British*, pp. 192–200; and Peter Hutchings, 'Beyond the New Wave: Realism in British Cinema, 1959–63' in Murphy, ed., *The British Cinema Book*, pp. 146–52.

183 See Lez Cooke, 'British Cinema: A Struggle for Identity', in Bloom and Day, eds, *Literature and Culture in Modern Britain: Volume Three*, p. 159.

184 Taylor, *After the War*, pp. 118–19.

185 See, for example, the analysis in Phelps, 'The Post-War English Novel', pp. 426–7.

186 See Anthony Aldgate, 'Defining the Parameters of "Quality" Cinema for "The Permissive Society": The British Board of Film Censors and *This Sporting Life*', in Anthony Aldgate, James Chapman and Arthur Marwick, eds, *Windows on the Sixties: Exploring Key Texts of Media and Culture* (London, 2000), pp. 37–69, a useful article despite its convoluted title.

187 Quoted in Walker, *Hollywood, England*, p. 175.

188 Hutchings, 'Beyond the New Wave', pp. 148–9.

189 Arthur Marwick, '*Room at the Top, Saturday Night and Sunday Morning*, and the "Cultural Revolution" in Britain', *Journal of Contemporary History* 19:1, 1984, pp. 148ff.

190 Peter Woollen, 'The Last New Wave: Modernism in the British Films of the Thatcher Era', in Lester Friedman, ed., *British Cinema and Thatcherism: Fires Were Started* (London, 1993), pp. 37–8. Hill, *Sex, Class and Realism*, p. 172, is more measured.

191 See Durgnat, *A Mirror for England*, pp. 193–4, and especially Philip Gillett, *The British Working Class in Postwar Film* (Manchester, 2003), which concentrates on the cinema of the late 1940s and early 1950s.

192 Landy, *British Genres*, pp. 48–9; Hill, *Sex, Class and Realism*, p. 59.

193 See Hill, *Sex, Class and Realism*, p. 67.

194 Landy, *British Genres*, p. 437.

195 Hutchings, 'Beyond the New Wave', pp. 150–1.

196 Hill, *Sex, Class and Realism*, p. 1.

197 Carpenter, *That Was Satire That Was*, pp. 308–9.

198 Rebellato, *1956 and All That*, pp. 143–5.

199 Osborne, *Look Back in Anger*, p. 2.

200 Osborne, *Look Back in Anger*, p. 11.

201 John Osborne, *Almost a Gentleman: An Autobiography, Volume II: 1955–1966* (London, 1991), p. 11.

202 Osborne, *Look Back in Anger*, p. 11.

203 Wain, *Hurry On Down*, p. 185.

204 Waterhouse, *Billy Liar*, p. 132.

205 Braine, *Room at the Top*, p. 96; Sillitoe, *Saturday Night and Sunday Morning*, p. 166.

206 See Eric Hobsbawm, *Industry and Empire* (Harmondsworth, 1969), especially chapter 13.

207 Orwell, *The Road to Wigan Pier*, pp. 98–9.

208 See Colls, *Identity of England*, pp. 186–8.

209 Raphael Samuel, *Island Stories: Unravelling Britain* (London, 1998), p. 165.

210 *Daily Express*, 8 November 1962, quoted in Pimlott, *Harold Wilson*, p. 267.

211 Osborne, *The Entertainer*, p. 22.

212 Quoted in Hill, *Sex, Class and Realism*, p. 153,

213 See Hill, *Sex, Class and Realism*, p. 154.

214 Quoted in Lacey, *British Realist Theatre*, p. 84.

215 Osborne, *Look Back in Anger*, p. 61.

216 Osborne, *Look Back in Anger*, pp. 36, 89.

217 Osborne, *Look Back in Anger*, p. 58.

218 See, on the one hand, Murphy, *Sixties British Cinema*, p. 33, and Aldgate and Richards, *Best of British*, p. 189; and on the other, Hill, *Sex, Class and Realism*, pp. 3, 25, and Cooke, 'British Cinema: A Struggle for Identity', pp. 146–8.

219 Sillitoe, *Saturday Night and Sunday Morning*, pp. 145–6.

220 Holroyd, *Contraries*, p. 65.

221 Ritchie, *Success Stories*, p. 52.

222 *Observer*, 20 January 1957.

223 Benson, *The Rise of Consumer Society*, p. 71.

224 D. E. Cooper, 'Looking Back on Anger', in Bogdanor and Skidelsky, eds, *The Age of Affluence*, pp. 257–8.

225 *Daily Mail*, 14 November 1957. See also Sinfield, *Literature, Politics and Culture in Post-war Britain*, pp. 79–81; and especially Rebellato, *1956 and All That*, pp. 156–223, which argues very strongly that the reaction against homosexuality was a powerful force in the theatrical New Wave of John Osborne and company. On the other hand, it is likely that Osborne himself was going through a homosexual phase when he was writing *Look Back in Anger*: see Carpenter, *The Angry Young Men*, p. 125.

226 The situation is slightly different in the novel: Doreen already lives on an estate, and tells him: 'I like living in them nice new houses. It's a long way from the shops, but there's plenty of fresh air.' Sillitoe, *Saturday Night and Sunday Morning*, p. 150.

227 Weight, *Patriots*, p. 303.

228 Osborne, *Look Back in Anger*, p. 2.

229 Rebellato, *1956 and All That*, p. 12.

230 Bergonzi, *Wartime and Aftermath*, p. 153; Kenneth Allsop, *The Angry Decade* (London, 1958), pp. 10, 194–5. See also Taylor, *After the War*, pp. 116–18; Rebellato, *1956 and All That*, pp. 31–2; Hill, *Sex, Class and Realism*, pp. 22–4, 56.

231 Phelps, 'The Post-War English Novel', p. 129.

232 Rebellato, *1956 and All That*, pp. 10–11.

233 Osborne, 'They Call It Cricket', p. 83.

234 Taylor, *After the War*, pp. 121–2.

235 Sillitoe, *Saturday Night and Sunday Morning*, pp. 35–6.

236 Sillitoe, *Saturday Night and Sunday Morning*, p. 132.

237 Osborne, *Look Back in Anger*, p. 89.

238 As argued in Rebellato, *1956 and All That*, p. 13.

239 Barstow, *A Kind of Loving*, p. 272.

CHAPTER 7: THE WAR GAME

1 *Guardian*, 6 December 1962; Douglas Brinkley, 'Dean Acheson and the "Special Relationship": The West Point Speech of December 1962', *Historical Journal* 33:3, September 1990, pp. 599–608.

2 Macmillan diary, 7 December 1962, quoted in Horne, *Macmillan 1957–1986*, p. 429.

3 Wallace, 'World Status without Tears', pp. 207–8; Horne, *Macmillan 1957–1986*, p. 16.

4 See Morgan, *The People's Peace*, p. 59.

5 Clive Ponting, *1940: Myth and Reality* (London, 1990) pp. 233–4.

6 See the chapters on Churchill and Bevin in Hugo Young, *This Blessed Plot: Britain and Europe from Churchill to Blair* (London, 1998), pp. 5–70.

7 Quoted in Davies, *The Isles*, p. 893.

8 Denman, *Missed Chances*, p. 184.

9 See Hennessy, *Never Again*, pp. 341–2; Alan S. Milward, *The Rise and Fall of a National Strategy 1945–1963* (London, 2002).

10 Young, *This Blessed Plot*, pp. 10–15.

11 Young, *This Blessed Plot*, pp. 16–22.

12 Hennessy, *The Prime Minister*, p. 173.

13 Quoted in Young, *This Blessed Plot*, pp. 37–8.

14 Dell, *A Strange Eventful History*, p. 189.

15 Dell, *A Strange Eventful History*, p. 187; Radice, *Friends and Rivals*, pp. 75–6.

16 Rhodes James, *Anthony Eden*, p. 350.

17 David Carlton, *Anthony Eden: A Biography* (London, 1981), pp. 310–11.

18 CAB 128/24, Cabinet Minutes, 13 March 1954.

19 Young, *This Blessed Plot*, p. 72; Horne, *Macmillan 1957–1986*, p. 35.

20 Denman, *Missed Chances*, p. 199.

21 Denman, *Missed Chances*, pp. 198–9.

22 Young, *This Blessed Plot*, pp. 93–4.

23 See T 233/433 and T 234/191.

24 Carlton, *Anthony Eden*, pp. 310–11.

25 See Judd, *Empire*, p. 367.

26 Hansard, 6 June 1962.

27 Rosen, *The Transformation of British Life*, p. 157.

28 Judd, *Empire*, p. 341; John Darwin, *Britain and Decolonisation: The Retreat from Empire in the Post-War World* (London, 1988), pp. 46ff.

29 See Young, *This Blessed Plot*, pp. 138–40, 156–8, 166.

30 Hopkins, *The New Look*, p. 454.

31 Quoted in Hennessy, *The Prime Minister*, p. 158.

32 Wallace, 'World Status without Tears', pp. 207–8; Horne, *Macmillan 1957–1986*, p. 16.

33 On Macmillan's determination to make the special relationship his priority, see Horne, *Macmillan 1957–1986*, pp. 21–3.

34 Horne, *Macmillan 1891–1956*, p. 160.

35 Macmillan to Lloyd, 11 December 1959, quoted in Lamb, *The Macmillan Years*, pp. 132–3.

36 Lloyd to Macmillan, 13 December 1959, quoted in Lamb, *The Macmillan Years*, p. 133.

37 On Labour's Americanism, see Peter Jones, *America and the Labour Party: The Special Relationship at Work* (London, 1997).

38 For a recent analysis of the special relationship during the early sixties, see Nigel Ashton, *Kennedy, Macmillan and the Cold War: The Irony of Interdependence* (London, 2002).

39 Quoted in Sked and Cook, *Post-war Britain*, p. 96.

40 George Ball, *The Discipline of Power* (London, 1968), p. 91.

41 On American cultural imperialism, see James, *Warrior Race*, pp. 733–4; Marwick, *The Sixties*, pp. 35–6.

42 C. J. Bartlett, *The Special Relationship: A Political History of Anglo-American Relations since 1945* (London, 1992), p. 80; see also Wybrow, *Britain Speaks Out*, p. 33 and passim.

43 Gallup poll, 17 March 1965, cited in Bartlett, *The Special Relationship*, p. 109.

44 Alan Bullock, *Ernest Bevin: Foreign Secretary 1945–1951* (London, 1983), pp. 844–5.

45 On the 'flavour' of the Cold War, see Tony Shaw, *British Cinema and the Cold War: The State, Propaganda and Consensus* (London, 2001), passim; Peter Hennessy, *The Secret State: Whitehall and the Cold War* (London, 2002), introduction.

46 On Britain in the Korean War, see Callum MacDonald, *Britain and the Korean War* (Oxford, 1990); Brian Catchpole, *The Korean War, 1950–1953* (London, 2000); Michael Hickey, *The Korean War: The West Confronts Communism, 1950–1953* (London, 2000).

47 Wallace, 'World Status without Tears', p. 192; Carl Watts, 'Britain and the Formation of NATO', *The Historian* 62, 1999, pp. 5–11; Don Cook, *Forging the Alliance: NATO, 1945–1950* (London, 1989).

48 John Baylis, 'American Bases in Britain: The "Truman-Attlee Understandings"', *The World Today* 42:8–9, August–September 1968, pp. 155–9; Hennessy, *Never Again*, p. 353; Bartlett, *The Special Relationship*, pp. 23–4.

49 Richard Thurlow, *The Secret State: British Internal Security in the Twentieth Century* (Oxford, 1994), p. xx.

50 Bartlett, *The Special Relationship*, p. 36.

51 Shaw, *British Cinema and the Cold War*, p. 35.

52 Thurlow, *The Secret State*, pp. 110–11, 290.

53 Pimlott, *Harold Wilson*, pp. 406–7; Francis Beckett, *Enemy Within: The Rise and Fall of the British Communist Party* (London, 1995), p. 191.

54 Thurlow, *The Secret State*, p. 290.

55 CAB 130/37, 'The Communist Party'; see also Hennessy, *The Secret State*, p. 79.

56 Thurlow, *The Secret State*, p. 280.

57 Rebellato, *1956 and All That*, p. 19; Meredith Veldman, *Fantasy, the Bomb, and the Greening of Britain: Romantic Protest, 1945–1980* (Cambridge, 1994), pp. 180–6.

58 Eric Hobsbawm, *Interesting Times: A Twentieth-Century Life* (London, 2002), pp. 210–11.

59 Eric Hobsbawm, *The New Century: In Conversation with Antonio Polito* (London, 2000), p. 159.

60 Hewison, *In Anger*, p. 60; Frances Stonor Saunders, *Who Paid the Piper? The CIA and the Cultural Cold War* (London, 2000), passim; Richard Aldrich, *The Hidden Hand: Britain, America and Cold War Secret Intelligence* (London, 2001), pp. 449–51.

61 See two splendid articles by Hugh Wilford: '"Unwitting Assets?" British Intellectuals and the Congress for Cultural Freedom', *Twentieth Century British History* 11, 2000, pp. 42–60; and 'Calling the Tune? The CIA, the British Left and the Cold War', *RUSI Journal* 146, February 2001, pp. 56–61.

62 Shaw, *British Cinema and the Cold War*, pp. 35–62.

63 Landy, *British Genres*, pp. 184–5; but see also Shaw, *British Cinema and the Cold War*, pp. 1–3, 193–6, which effectively puts the opposite case.

64 Durgnat, *A Mirror for England*, pp. 70–1. The best account of the film is in Shaw, *British Cinema and the Cold War*, pp. 61–5.

65 Landy, *British Genres*, p. 186.

66 Shaw, *British Cinema and the Cold War*, p. 45.

67 Black, '"The Bitterest Enemies of Communism"', p. 44; Hewison, *In Anger*, pp. 28, 30. On anti–Communism in the trade unions, see Joseph Melling, '"Red under the Collar?" Clive Jenkins, White Collar Unionism and the Politics of the British Left, 1947–65', *Twentieth Century British History* 13:4, 2002, pp. 412–48.

68 For the contrasting bureaucratic attitudes to internal security in the United States and Britain, see Thurlow, *The Secret State*, pp. 287–8.

69 Sir Arthur de la Mare, *Perverse and Foolish: A Jersey Farmer's Son in the British Diplomatic Service* (Jersey, 1994), pp. 99–100. On MI5, see Hennessy, *The Secret State*, p. 86.

70 *The Economist*, 5 June 1982; Thurlow, *The Secret State*, p. 294; Aldrich, *The Hidden Hand*, pp. 116–18, 383–4, 426–7.

71 Hewison, *In Anger*, pp. 24–5.

72 Thurlow, *The Secret State*, pp. 279–80, 307.

73 Macmillan to Eisenhower, 10 October 1957, quoted in Horne, *Macmillan 1957–1986*, p. 53.

74 Macmillan diary, 5 November 1957, quoted in Horne, *Macmillan 1957–1986*, p. 57.

75 Quoted in Stephen Dorril, *MI6: Fifty Years of Special Operations* (London, 2000), p. 495.

76 Ferdynand Zweig, *The Student in an Age of Anxiety: A Survey of Oxford and Manchester Students* (London, 1963), pp. 200–1.

77 George H. Gallup, ed., *The Gallup International Public Opinion Polls: Great Britain 1937–1975, Volume I* (New York, 1976), pp. 237–42, 269.

78 Quoted in Curtis Cate, *The Ides of August* (London, 1978), pp. 450–1.

79 Chester L. Cooper quoted in Horne, *Macmillan 1957–1986*, p. 365.

80 See Black, '"The Bitterest Enemies of Communism"', pp. 44–5; Thurlow, *The Secret State*, pp. 309ff.

81 Hennessy, *The Secret State*, p. 93.

82 Thurlow, *The Secret State*, pp. 108–9.

83 Macmillan diary, 26 July 1959, quoted in Hennessy, *The Prime Minister*, p. 264.

84 Horne, *Macmillan 1957–1986*, pp. 122–7; Michael Cockerell, *Live from Number Ten*, p. 64.

85 On Malaya, see Anthony Short, *The Communist Insurrection in Malaya, 1948–1960* (London, 1975); Matthew Jones, *Conflict and Confrontation in South East Asia, 1961–1965: Britain, the United States, Indonesia and the Creation of Malaysia* (Cambridge, 2001).

86 Horne, *Macmillan 1957–1986*, pp. 92–8; Lamb, *The Macmillan Years*, pp. 34–43.

87 Hennessy, *Never Again*, p. 415; James, *Warrior Race*, pp. 729–30.

88 Pinto-Duschinsky, 'From Macmillan to Home', p. 155; Sked and Cook, *Post-war Britain*, p. 165.

89 Clarke, *Hope and Glory*, p. 265.

90 Morgan, *The People's Peace*, p. 217.

91 Sampson, *Anatomy of Britain*, p. 252.

92 See Hennessy, *Muddling Through*, p. 102.

93 Quoted in Peter Hennessy, *Cabinet* (Oxford, 1986), pp. 126–7.

94 See Gowing, *Independence and Deterrence*, passim.

95 Hennessy, *Muddling Through*, p. 105.

96 Quoted in Hennessy, *Muddling Through*, p. 106.

97 Hennessy, *The Secret State*, p. 111.

98 John Baylis, 'The Development of Britain's Thermonuclear Capability, 1945–61: Myth or Reality?', *Journal of Contemporary British History*, 8:1, Summer 1994, pp. 159–74; Katherine Pyne, 'Art or Article? The Need for and Nature of the British Hydrogen Bomb, 1954–58', *Contemporary Record*, 9:3, Winter 1995, p. 579; see also Lorna Arnold and Katherine Pyne, *Britain and the H-Bomb* (London, 2001).

99 Wybrow, *Britain Speaks Out*, pp. 33, 41.

100 See 'The Move towards the Sandys White Paper of 1957', seminar held July 1988, Institute of Contemporary British History, 2002, <http://www.icbh.ac.uk/witness/sandys/>, pp. 18–25.

101 T. G. C. James, in 'The Move towards the Sandys White Paper of 1957', p. 23.

102 Sir Arthur Drew, in 'The Move towards the Sandys White Paper of 1957', p. 34; Horne, *Macmillan 1957–1986*, pp. 48–51.

103 Horne, *Macmillan 1957–1986*, p. 48; Sir Richard Powell, in 'The Move towards the Sandys White Paper of 1957', p. 25.

104 Horne, *Macmillan 1957–1986*, p. 49.

105 *Defence: Outline of Future Policy* (Cmnd 124: London, 1957).

106 Wallace, 'World Status without Tears', p. 215; Pinto-Duschinsky, 'From Macmillan to Home', p. 155.

107 *Defence: Outline of Future Policy*.

108 Quoted in Lamb, *The Macmillan Years*, p. 284.

109 Sir Richard Powell, in 'The Move towards the Sandys White Paper of 1957', p. 38.

110 Quoted in Hennessy, *The Prime Minister*, p. 113.

111 Sked and Cook, *Post-war Britain*, p. 143.

112 Lewis, *The Fifties*, p. 92.

113 Sked and Cook, *Post-war Britain*, p. 142; Williams, *Hugh Gaitskell*, pp. 296–7.

114 See Lamb, *The Macmillan Years*, pp. 284–5.

115 Andrew Pierre, *Nuclear Politics: Anglo-American Defence Relations 1939–1980* (London, 1981), p. 62.

116 Horne, *Macmillan 1957–1986*, p. 275; Lamb, *The Macmillan Years*, pp. 286–7.

117 *The Times*, 14 April 1960.

118 Horne, *Macmillan 1957–1986*, pp. 275–7; Lamb, *The Macmillan Years*, pp. 287–97.

119 Macmillan to Eisenhower, 24 June 1960, quoted in Lamb, *The Macmillan Years*, p. 290.

120 See Malcolm Chalmers and William Walker, *Uncharted Waters: The UK, Nuclear Weapons and the Scottish Question* (Edinburgh, 2001).

121 Levin, *The Pendulum Years*, p. 130.

122 Quoted in Hennessy, *Muddling Through*, p. 111.

123 Horne, *Macmillan 1957–1986*, p. 433.

124 Ashton, *Kennedy, Macmillan and the Cold War*, p. 132.

125 Early biographers of both men, as well as Macmillan himself, claimed the opposite, but archival evidence suggests they were being rather economical with the truth. See Lamb, *The Macmillan Years*, pp. 299, 342.

126 Kennedy was commenting on a National Security Council paper of 21 April 1961, quoted in Lamb, *The Macmillan Years*, pp. 297–8; see also Arthur M. Schlesinger, Jr, *A Thousand Days* (Boston, 1965), p. 723.

127 Horne, *Macmillan 1957–1986*, p. 438. In fact the British had their eyes on Polaris even when they were signing the deal for Skybolt: see Lamb, *The Macmillan Years*, pp. 296–7, 310–17.

128 Bartlett, *The Special Relationship*, p. 98.

129 Hennessy, *The Secret State*, p. 62.

130 Lamb, *The Macmillan Years*, p. 316.

131 *Daily Express, Daily Telegraph, Daily Herald*, all 22 December 1962.

132 Dorril, *MI6*, p. 159.

133 See, for example, Horne, *Macmillan 1957–1986*, pp. 362–85.

134 Oral history of McGeorge Bundy, John F. Kennedy Library, Boston, Massachusetts, quoted in Lamb, *The Macmillan Years*, p. 356. I am indebted to Andrew Preston, the dean of McGeorge Bundy scholarship, for discussions on this point. On Britain's general

insignificance in the missile crisis, see Ernest R. May and Philip D. Zelikow, eds, *The Kennedy Tapes: Inside the White House during the Cuban Missile Crisis* (London, 1997); Aleksandr Fursenko and Timothy Naftali, *One Hell of a Gamble: The Secret History of the Cuban Missile Crisis* (New York, 1997), among innumerable other publications on the subject.

135 Hennessy, *The Secret State*, p. 75. Amazingly, Robson also won twenty caps in mid-field for England and went on to coach Ipswich, England, PSV Eindhoven, Sporting Lisbon, Porto, Barcelona and Newcastle United, finally ending up with a knighthood: a varied career indeed. Or did he?

136 L. V. Scott, *Macmillan, Kennedy and the Cuban Missile Crisis* (London, 1999), p. 136.

137 *The Times*, 30 October 1962. Nothing changes!

138 See James, *Warrior Race*, pp. 739–42.

139 *Guardian*, 28 December 2001.

140 Horne, *Macmillan 1957–1986*, pp. 521–2; Turner, *Macmillan*, pp. 168–72.

141 *Guardian*, 19 November 2002.

142 CAB 123/31 Part II, Cabinet conclusions, 6 November 1957.

143 On Windscale, see Horne, *Macmillan 1957–1986*, pp. 53–4; Morgan, *The People's Peace*, pp. 179–80;

144 Hennessy, *The Secret State*, p. 128.

145 CAB 130/101, 12 March 1954.

146 Home Defence ministerial committee report, 1955, quoted in Hennessy, *The Secret State*, p. 137.

147 *Defence: Outline of Future Policy*.

148 Horne, *Macmillan 1957–1986*, p. 47.

149 Hennessy, *The Secret State*, p. 187.

150 Hennessy, *The Secret State*, pp. 191–3.

151 Switzerland, Norway and Sweden were the exceptions; evidently there is some correlation between blandness and civil-defence preparedness.

152 Hennessy, *The Secret State*, pp. 138–9; Hennessy, *The Prime Minister*, p. 136.

153 DEFE 4/232, 'Military Aspects of the Home Defence of the United Kingdom', 1 October 1968.

154 James, *Warrior Race*, p. 743.

155 Hennessy, *The Secret State*, pp. 159, 164.

156 Hennessy, *The Secret State*, pp. 171–8.

157 AIR 8/2376, 'UK Command Structure'; James, *Warrior Race*, p. 743; Hennessy, *The Secret State*, p. 140.

158 Patricia Waugh, *Harvest of the Sixties: English Literature and its Background, 1960–1990* (Oxford 1995), p. 211.

159 On *Lord of the Flies* and the Third World War, see Sinfield, *Literature, Politics and Culture in Post-war Britain*, p. 142.

160 See Paul Brians, *Nuclear Holocausts: Atomic War in Fiction, 1895–1984* (Kent, Ohio: 1987); Stevenson, *The British Novel since the Thirties*, pp. 117ff.

161 Bergonzi, *The Situation of the Novel*, p. 177.

162 Lewis, *The Fifties*, pp. 241–2; Shaw, *British Cinema and the Cold War*, pp. 126–7.

163 See Bernard Bergonzi, *The Early H. G. Wells: The Scientific Romances* (Manchester, 1961);

Norman and Jeanne Mackenzie, *The Life of H. G. Wells: The Time Traveller* (revised edition: London, 1987).

164 Brian Aldiss and David Wingrove, *Trillion Year Spree: The History of Science Fiction* (London, 1986).

165 Sutherland, *Reading the Decades*, pp. 40–1.

166 David Dowling, *Fictions of Nuclear Disaster* (London, 1987), pp. 63–4.

167 Tom Shippey, *J. R. R. Tolkien: Author of the Century* (London, 2000); Sutherland, *Reading the Decades*, p. 40.

168 John Griffiths, *The Survivors* (London, 1965), pp. 26, 81, 159.

169 See Dowling, *Fictions of Nuclear Disaster*, pp. 158–61.

170 Graham Nelson, 'Wells, Wyndham and ruined Earths', at <http://www.gnelson. demon.co.uk/tripage/genre.html>.

171 Shaw, *British Cinema and the Cold War*, pp. 119–20.

172 Landy, *British Genres*, pp. 410–11; Shaw, *British Cinema and the Cold War*, pp. 128–9.

173 Durgnat, *A Mirror for England*, p. 134; Shaw, *British Cinema and the Cold War*, pp. 130–1.

174 Murphy, *Sixties British Cinema*, p. 55. There is a fine website on all these films: see <http://www.hammerfilms.com/vaults/index.html>.

175 Durgnat, *A Mirror for England*, p. 150.

176 Murphy, *Sixties British Cinema*, p. 180.

177 Durgnat, *A Mirror for England*, p. 222.

178 Durgnat, *A Mirror for England*, p. 83; Landy, *British Genres*, p. 176.

179 Murphy, *Sixties British Cinema*, p. 86.

180 Durgnat, *A Mirror for England*, pp. 92–3.

181 Dan Rebellato, 'Look Back at Empire: British Theatre and Imperial Decline', in Ward, ed., *British Culture and the End of Empire*, pp. 73–4; Goorney, *The Theatre Workshop Story*, pp. 125–7; Lacey, *British Realist Theatre*, pp. 159–61.

182 On Charles Wood's plays, see John Russell Taylor, *The Second Wave: British Drama of the Sixties* (reprinted edition: London, 1978), pp. 65, 69. George MacDonald Fraser, it should be pointed out, was no anti-war campaigner, but that did not prevent him from writing some of the most splendidly entertaining novels of the period.

183 Briggs, *The History of Broadcasting in the United Kingdom: Volume V*, p. 531; Richard Cawston quoted in Paul Ferris, *Sir Huge: The Life of Huw Wheldon* (London, 1990), p. 182. See also S. J. Arrowsmith, 'Peter Watkins', in George Brandt, ed., *British Television Drama* (Cambridge, 1981), pp. 217–39.

184 Shaw, *British Cinema and the Cold War*, p. 137.

185 Joseph A. Gomez, *Peter Watkins* (Boston, Massachusetts, 1979), pp. 49–50.

186 *Daily Sketch*, 9 February 1966, quoted in Shaw, *British Cinema and the Cold War*, p. 139.

187 The controversy over the cancellation of the film is covered in Briggs, *The History of Broadcasting in the United Kingdom: Volume V*, pp. 533–5; Shaw, *British Cinema and the Cold War*, pp. 137–40.

188 DEFE 4/232, 'Military Aspects of the Home Defence of the United Kingdom', 1 October 1968.

189 John Minnion and Philip Bolsover, eds, *The CND Story* (London, 1983), pp. 11–13.

190 *New Statesman*, 2 November 1957.

191 Minnion and Bolsover, eds, *The CND Story*, p. 14; Masters, *The Swinging Sixties*, pp. 198–9; Mervyn Jones, *Michael Foot* (London, 1994), pp. 225–7.

192 *Defence: Outline of Future Policy*.

193 See Wallace, 'World Status without Tears', pp. 222–3.

194 Hewison, *In Anger*, p. 163; Veldman, *Fantasy, the Bomb, and the Greening of Britain*, pp. 180–6.

195 Minnion and Bolsover, eds, *The CND Story*, p. 15.

196 Adam Sisman, *A. J. P. Taylor: A Biography* (London, 1994), p. 274; Jones, *Michael Foot*, p. 227; Masters, *The Swinging Sixties*, pp. 200–1.

197 Wallace, 'World Status without Tears', p. 226; Minnion and Bolsover, eds, *The CND Story*, pp. 15–18.

198 Janey and Norman Buchan, 'The Campaign in Scotland', in Minnion and Bolsover, eds, *The CND Story*, pp. 52–3.

199 Wallace, 'World Status without Tears', p. 226; Sinfield, *Literature, Politics and Culture in Post-war Britain*, p. 239; Lewis, *The Fifties*, p. 99.

200 Sisman, *A. J. P. Taylor*, p. 309.

201 Mervyn Jones, 'Aldermaston 1958', in Minnion and Bolsover, eds, *The CND Story*, pp. 44–5.

202 Jo Richardson, 'Tea for 20,000', in Minnion and Bolsover, eds, *The CND Story*, pp. 45–7; Wallace, 'World Status without Tears', p. 222.

203 Minnion and Bolsover, eds, *The CND Story*, p. 27.

204 Marwick, *The Sixties*, p. 65.

205 Wallace, 'World Status without Tears', p. 226.

206 *Spectator*, 15 January 1960.

207 Ian Campbell, 'Music against the Bomb', in Minnion and Bolsover, eds, *The CND Story*, p. 115; see also Hewison, *In Anger*, p. 165.

208 Dixie Dean quoted in Akhtar and Humphries, *The Fifties and Sixties*, pp. 38–9.

209 In the short story 'Bingo Bans the Bomb', it even captures the allegiance of P. G. Wodehouse's ill-starred hero Bingo Little, who is dragged into a demonstration by the stunning Mabel Murgatroyd only to be arrested and publicly shamed on the front page of the *Daily Mirror*: see P. G. Wodehouse, 'Bingo Bans the Bomb', in *Plum Pie* (London, 1966).

210 Veldman, *Fantasy, the Bomb, and the Greening of Britain*, pp. 160–4.

211 Sisman, *A. J. P. Taylor*, pp. 275–6; see also Marwick, *The Sixties*, p. 65.

212 *New Statesman*, 2 November 1957.

213 Hewison, *In Anger*, p. 165; Wallace, 'World Status without Tears', p. 227.

214 Williams, *Hugh Gaitskell*, p. 329.

215 Sisman, *A. J. P. Taylor*, pp. 278–9. In fairness, Taylor's own life was hardly a model of moral rectitude.

216 See Frank Parkin, *Middle-Class Radicalism: The Social Bases of the Campaign for Nuclear Disarmament* (Manchester, 1968).

217 Quoted in Masters, *The Swinging Sixties*, pp. 202–3. On CND as part of a wider tradition, see Morgan, *The People's Peace*, p. 181.

218 Parkin, *Middle-Class Radicalism*, p. 17.

219 Michael Frayn, 'Festival', in Sissons and French, eds, *The Age of Austerity*, pp. 307–8.

220 *New Statesman*, 21 June 1958; Veldman, *Fantasy, the Bomb, and the Greening of Britain*, p. 133.

221 *Tribune*, 11 October 1957.

222 Veldman, *Fantasy, the Bomb, and the Greening of Britain*, p. 140.

223 A. J. P. Taylor, *A Personal History* (London, 1983), p. 227.

224 Wallace, 'World Status without Tears', p. 228; Sisman, *A. J. P. Taylor*, p. 278.

225 Williams, *Hugh Gaitskell*, pp. 296–7.

226 Jones, *Michael Foot*, p. 222.

227 Quoted in Williams, *Hugh Gaitskell*, p. 297.

228 Jones, *Michael Foot*, p. 230.

229 Williams, *Hugh Gaitskell*, pp. 314–44.

230 Morgan, *The People's Peace*, p. 139; Williams, *Hugh Gaitskell*, pp. 304–5.

231 Sampson, *Anatomy of Britain*, p. 95.

232 Pearce, *The Lost Leaders*, p. 175.

233 Williams, *Hugh Gaitskell*, pp. 336–47; *Daily Herald*, 4 October 1960.

234 Crossman diary, 12 May 1960, quoted in Williams, *Hugh Gaitskell*, p. 347.

235 Williams, *Hugh Gaitskell*, pp. 364–5.

236 See Gaitskell's NEC memorandum of 13 April 1960, quoted in Williams, *Hugh Gaitskell*, p. 339.

237 Quoted in Pimlott, *Harold Wilson*, p. 238.

238 Benn diary, 2 October 1960.

239 Williams, *Hugh Gaitskell*, p. 356.

240 Edward Pearce, *Denis Healey: A Life in our Times* (London, 2002), p. 216.

241 See *The Times* and *Daily Express*, 6 October 1960; Williams, *Hugh Gaitskell*, pp. 357–59.

242 Peggy Duff, *Left, Left, Left* (London, 1971), p. 191.

243 *Daily Herald*, 6 October 1960.

244 See Williams, *Hugh Gaitskell*, pp. 369–72; Pimlott, *Harold Wilson*, pp. 240–5.

245 Radice, *Friends and Rivals*, pp. 116–118; Clarke, *A Question of Leadership*, pp. 254–5; Childs, *Britain since 1945*, pp. 132–3.

246 Veldman, *Fantasy, the Bomb, and the Greening of Britain*, p. 117.

247 Minnion and Bolsover, eds, *The CND Story*, p. 15.

248 Minnion and Bolsover, eds, *The CND Story*, p. 17; Christopher Driver, *The Disarmers: A Study in Protest* (London, 1964), p. 99.

249 Minnion and Bolsover, eds, *The CND Story*, pp. 20–2.

250 Wallace, 'World Status without Tears', p. 243.

251 See Masters, *The Swinging Sixties*, pp. 206–10, a sympathetic account.

252 Frank Allaun, 'In with a Bang, Out . . .', in Minnion and Bolsover, eds, *The CND Story*, pp. 56–7.

253 *New Statesman*, 2 January 1960.

254 On the decline of CND, see Minnion and Bolsover, eds, *The CND Story*, pp. 27–8; Jones, *Michael Foot*, pp. 269–70; Sisman, *A. J. P. Taylor*, p. 310.

255 Wybrow, *Britain Speaks Out*, pp. 58–9.

256 Lewis, *The Fifties*, p. 102.

257 Wallace, 'World Status without Tears', p. 248.

CHAPTER 8: THE END OF EMPIRE

1 Quoted in Carpenter, *That Was Satire That Was*, p. 32.

2 Annan, *Our Age*, pp. 43, 53; see also Davies, *The Isles*, pp. 710–11.

3 For a full account, see Wm Roger Louis and Robin W. Winks, eds, *The Oxford History of the British Empire: Volume V: Historiography* (Oxford, 1999). See also Judd, *Empire*, pp. 1–17.

4 Gamble, *Britain in Decline*, p. 48.

5 Simon Schama, *A History of Britain: The British Wars 1603–1776* (London, 2001), p. 326.

6 J. A. Hobson, *Imperialism* (reprinted edition: London, 1961), p. 20.

7 Gamble, *Britain in Decline*, p. xiii; Davies, *The Isles*, p. 718.

8 Darwin, *Britain and Decolonisation*, p. 5.

9 Heffer, *Like the Roman*, p. 37.

10 See Colls, *Identity of England*, pp. 4–5.

11 P. J. Marshall, 'Imperial Britain', *Journal of Imperial and Commonwealth History* 23 (1995), p. 385.

12 See Edward Said, *Orientalism: Western Concepts of the Orient* (New York, 1978); and Edward Said, *Culture and Imperialism* (London, 1993). For a counter-argument, which holds that British imperialists often projected their own values on to their colonial subjects, rather than formed their values and identity in opposition to them, see David Cannadine, *Ornamentalism: How the British Saw their Empire* (London, 2001), esp. pp. 1–10.

13 Judd, *Empire*, p. 5.

14 Cannadine, *Ornamentalism*, pp. 183–4.

15 Cannadine, *Ornamentalism*, pp. 185–6.

16 See Colls, *Identity of England*, p. 99; Weight, *Patriots*, p. 286.

17 Judd, *Empire*, p. 10.

18 See John Gallagher and Ronald Robinson, 'The Imperialism of Free Trade', *Economic History Review* 6:1, 1953, pp. 1–15; Darwin, *Britain and Decolonisation*, pp. 30–1; John Darwin, *The End of the British Empire: The Historical Debate* (Oxford, 1991), pp. 3–4; D. George Boyce, *Decolonisation and the British Empire, 1775–1997* (London, 1999), pp. 18–19.

19 Darwin, *Britain and Decolonisation*, pp. 8, 33.

20 Jenkins, *Churchill*, p. 702.

21 John Gallagher, *The Decline, Revival and Fall of the British Empire* (Cambridge, 1982), pp. 142–3.

22 Darwin, *Britain and Decolonisation*, pp. 124–31; Boyce, *Decolonisation and the British Empire*, p. 267.

23 Darwin, *Britain and Decolonisation*, pp. 165–66; Boyce, *Decolonisation and the British Empire*, pp. 148–9.

24 Darwin, *Britain and Decolonisation*, pp. 69–166; and see Melvyn Leffler, *A Preponderance of Power: National Security and the Truman Administration in the Cold War* (Stanford, California, 1992); Short, *The Communist Insurrection in Malaya*, passim.

25 Quoted in Judd, *Empire*, p. 364.

26 Quoted in Boyce, *Decolonisation and the British Empire*, p. 177.

27 Cannadine, *Ornamentalism*, p. 100.

28 Gilmour and Garnett, *Whatever Happened to the Tories*, p. 154.

29 For a much more sophisticated account in this vein, see Henri Grimal, *Decolonization: The British, French, Dutch, and Belgian Empires, 1919–1963* (London, 1978).

30 Gallagher, *The Decline, Revival and Fall of the British Empire*, p. 73; Darwin, *Britain and Decolonisation*, pp. 18–19, 256–64; John D. Hargreaves, *Decolonization in Africa* (London, 1988), pp. 193–8; Darwin, *The End of the British Empire*, p. 104; Boyce, *Decolonisation and the British Empire*, p. 117.

31 Quoted in D. R. Thorpe, *Alec Douglas-Home* (London, 1996), p. 200.

32 CAB 134/1555, Macmillan to Salisbury, 28 January 1957, quoted in Tony Hopkins, 'Macmillan's Audit of Empire, 1957', in Peter Clarke and Clive Trebilcock, eds, *Understanding Decline: Perceptions and Realities of British Economic Performance* (Cambridge, 1997), p. 234.

33 Horne, *Macmillan 1957–1986*, p. 187; Graham Stewart, *Burying Caesar: Churchill, Chamberlain and the Battle for the Tory Party* (London, 1999), pp. 142–99.

34 Simon Ball, *The Guardsmen: Harold Macmillan, Three Friends, and the World They Made* (London, 2004), pp. 345–6.

35 Macmillan diary, 4 June 1961, quoted in Horne, *Macmillan 1957–1986*, pp. 183–4.

36 Shepherd, *Iain Macleod*, pp. 1–24.

37 Shepherd, *Iain Macleod*, pp. 29–30.

38 Shepherd, *Iain Macleod*, p. 43; on middle-class Conservatives and colonial policy, see R. F. Holland, *European Decolonization 1918–1981* (Basingstoke, 1985), pp. 208–9.

39 Shepherd, *Iain Macleod*, pp. 73–7.

40 Horne, *Macmillan 1957–1986*, p. 183.

41 Darwin, *The End of the British Empire*, p. 120.

42 Hargreaves, *Decolonization in Africa*, pp. 101–2.

43 Darwin, *Britain and Decolonisation*, pp. 44–59, 131–8; Hargreaves, *Decolonization in Africa*, pp. 97–109; Darwin, *The End of the British Empire*, pp. 45–46, 92, 118–20; Boyce, *Decolonisation and the British Empire*, pp. 138–9.

44 Judd, *Empire*, p. 369.

45 Weight, *Patriots*, pp. 286–7.

46 Holland, *European Decolonization 1918–1981*, pp. 200–20.

47 See Darwin, *The End of the British Empire*, p. 50; Judd, *Empire*, pp. 328–9, 370.

48 John Darwin, 'Decolonization and the End of Empire', in Louis and Winks, eds, *The Oxford History of the British Empire: Volume V: Historiography*, p. 547; Darwin, *Britain and Decolonisation*, p. 20; Boyce, *Decolonisation and the British Empire*, pp. 129–30.

49 Shepherd, *Iain Macleod*, p. 159.

50 Horne, *Macmillan 1957–1986*, p. 177; Darwin, *Britain and Decolonisation*, pp. 251–2.

51 Macmillan diary, 4 August 1960, quoted in Horne, *Macmillan 1957–1986*, pp. 207–8.

52 Macmillan diary, 19 December 1961, quoted in Horne, *Macmillan 1957–1986*, p. 414.

53 CPC (61) 1, 3 January 1961, quoted in Shepherd, *Iain Macleod*, p. 214; and see Darwin, *Britain and Decolonisation*, pp. 226–7.

54 Hargreaves, *Decolonization in Africa*, p. 165.

55 CO 1032/50, 'The Future of Commonwealth Membership', January 1955.

56 CO 1032/241, quoted in Boyce, *Decolonisation and the British Empire*, p. 187.

57 Horne, *Macmillan 1957–1986*, p. 190.

58 Letters of 22 August and 1 November 1959, quoted in Horne, *Macmillan 1957–1986*, p. 183.

59 Darwin, *Britain and Decolonisation*, pp. 183–9; Hargreaves, *Decolonization in Africa*, pp. 129–34; Judd, *Empire*, pp. 346–53; Boyce, *Decolonisation and the British Empire*, p. 220.

60 Heffer, *Like the Roman*, pp. 253–4.

61 Heffer, *Like the Roman*, pp. 254–5; Denis Healey, *The Time of My Life* (London, 1989), p. 146.

62 Heffer, *Like the Roman*, pp. 334–7.

63 Shepherd, *Iain Macleod*, p. 154.

64 Shepherd, *Iain Macleod*, p. 156.

65 Shepherd, *Iain Macleod*, p. 159.

66 Judd, *Empire*, p. 365.

67 Shepherd, *Iain Macleod*, pp. 254–5.

68 Shepherd, *Iain Macleod*, p. 162.

69 Boyce, *Decolonisation and the British Empire*, p. 196.

70 Shepherd, *Iain Macleod*, p. 254.

71 Horne, *Macmillan 1957–1986*, pp. 195–7.

72 Lamb, *The Macmillan Years*, p. 246; Levin, *The Pendulum Years*, p. 203.

73 Horne, *Macmillan 1957–1986*, p. 203.

74 Darwin, *Britain and Decolonisation*, p. 195; Hargreaves, *Decolonization in Africa*, pp. 134–8.

75 James, *The Rise and Fall of the British Empire*, p. 612; *New Statesman*, 30 January 1956.

76 *New Statesman*, 10 May 1963.

77 Horne, *Macmillan 1957–1986*, pp. 176–82; Lamb, *The Macmillan Years*, pp. 234–7.

78 PREM 11/2784, quoted in Lamb, *The Macmillan Years*, pp. 242–4.

79 CAB 128/37, Cabinet Minutes, 28 March 1963.

80 Even his greatest admirers criticise his handling of Rhodesia: see Horne, *Macmillan 1957–1986*, pp. 412–13; Lamb, *The Macmillan Years*, p. 272.

81 Morgan, *The People's Peace*, p. 129.

82 Graham Payn and Sheridan Morley, eds, *The Noël Coward Diaries* (London, 1982), pp. 348–9.

83 Noël Coward, *Pomp and Circumstance* (London, 1960), pp. 86–7, quoted in Cannadine, *In Churchill's Shadow*, p. 271.

84 Simon Raven, *Alms for Oblivion: Volume II* (London, 1998), p. 508.

85 *Sunday Times Magazine*, 3 June 1962; James, *The Rise and Fall of the British Empire*, p. 616.

86 Miles Kahler, *Decolonization in Britain and France* (Princeton: 1984), pp. 303–306; and see also Philip Murphy, *Party Politics and Decolonization: The Conservative Party and British Colonial Policy in Tropical Africa, 1951–1964* (Oxford, 1995).

87 Horne, *Macmillan 1957–1986*, pp. 36–9; Gilmour and Garnett, *Whatever Happened to the Tories*, pp. 133–4; Ball, *The Guardsmen*, pp. 333–7.

88 Dennis Kavanagh, *Thatcherism and British Politics: The End of Consensus?* (Oxford, 1987), pp. 191–2; Gilmour and Garnett, *Whatever Happened to the Tories*, pp. 157–8.

89 James, *The Rise and Fall of the British Empire*, p. 591; the sheep story is (appropriately!) in Lamb, *The Macmillan Years*, p. 228.

90 Quoted in Pearce, *The Lost Leaders*, p. 315.

91 Lord Dalhousie to Lord Home, 24 February 1960, quoted in Lamb, *The Macmillan Years*, p. 249.

92 Shepherd, *Iain Macleod*, pp. 204, 213.

93 *Daily Express*, 13 January 1961.

94 Shepherd, *Iain Macleod*, pp. 224–5; Ball, *The Guardsmen*, pp. 354–5.

95 Shepherd, *Iain Macleod*, pp. 226–7.

96 Shepherd, *Iain Macleod*, pp. 217–19; Lamb, *The Macmillan Years*, p. 224.

97 Macmillan diary, 3 February 1957, quoted in Horne, *Macmillan 1957–1986*, p. 407.

98 Macmillan diary, 10 January 1962, quoted in Horne, *Macmillan 1957–1986*, p. 408.

99 See Maudling, *Memoirs*, pp. 89–101.

100 Quoted in Bradbury, *The Modern British Novel*, p. 276.

101 Osborne, *Look Back in Anger*, p. 70.

102 Waugh, *Harvest of the Sixties*, p. 3; Colls, *Identity of England*, p. 143.

103 See Holloway, 'The Literary Scene', p. 65.

104 Shaw, *British Cinema and the Cold War*, pp. 174–5; Paul Wells, 'Comments, Custard Pies and Comic Cuts: The Boulting Brothers at Play, 1955–65', in Alan Burton, Tim O'Sullivan and Paul Wells, eds, *The Family Way: The Boulting Brothers and Postwar British Film Culture* (Trowbridge, 2000), p. 58.

105 *The Mouse That Roared* (1960) was a gentle comedy in the Ealing manner starring Peter Sellers.

106 Orwell, *The Road to Wigan Pier*, Part II, ch. 10.

107 Leopold S. Amery, *The Framework of the Future* (Oxford, 1944), quoted in Cannadine, *Ornamentalism*, p. 132.

108 Cannadine, *Ornamentalism*, p. 126.

109 Peregrine Worsthorne, 'Class and Conflict in British Foreign Policy', *Foreign Affairs* XXXVII, 1959, pp. 419–31.

110 Marwick, *British Society since 1945*, p. 107; Darwin, *Britain and Decolonisation*, pp. 229, 328; Darwin, *The End of the British Empire*, pp. 1–2. John Mackenzie calls this view a 'travesty', but is unable to find much evidence to prove that the public was anything other than indifferent: see John M. Mackenzie, 'The Persistence of Empire in Metropolitan Culture', in Ward, ed., *British Culture and the End of Empire* pp. 21–36.

111 Cannadine, *Ornamentalism*, p. 198.

112 Macmillan diary, 7 July 1957, in Horne, *Macmillan 1957–1986*, p. 100.

113 Quoted in Aldgate and Richards, *Best of British*, p. 20; Darwin, *Britain and Decolonisation*, p. 229.

114 James Morris, *Farewell the Trumpets: An Imperial Retreat* (London, 1978), p. 474; David Goldsworthy, *Colonial Issues in British Politics, 1945–61* (Oxford, 1971), p. 399.

115 See Correlli Barnett, *The Collapse of British Power* (London, 1972), pp. 19, 23, 53; Weight, *Patriots*, pp. 286–7; Darwin, *The End of the British Empire*, p. 13.

116 Sampson, *Macmillan*, p. 179.

117 CPC (57) 30 (Revise), 6 September 1957, quoted in Hopkins, 'Macmillan's Audit of Empire', p. 250.

118 In other words, the end of empire did not mean the end of colonialism, only a new, 'neo-colonial' form of exploitation: for more on this argument, see Judd, *Empire*, p. 366; Darwin, *Britain and Decolonisation*, pp. 244, 300–1, 329.

119 Weight, *Patriots*, p. 291.

120 *Observer*, 24 June 1956.

121 *Daily Telegraph*, 11 November 1961.

122 James, *The Rise and Fall of the British Empire*, pp. 556–7; Darwin, 'Decolonization and the End of Empire', p. 547.

123 Darwin, 'Decolonization and the End of Empire', p. 554.

124 Quoted in Booker, *The Neophiliacs*, p. 87.

125 Clement Attlee, *Empire into Commonwealth* (Oxford, 1961), pp. 1, 25–7.

126 Horne, *Macmillan 1957–1986*, p. 278.

127 Sked and Cook, *Post-War Britain*, p. 144; for similar verdicts, see for example Hargreaves, *Decolonization in Africa*, p. 198; Gilmour and Garnett, *Whatever Happened to the Tories*, p. 214.

128 Darwin, *The End of the British Empire*, p. 34.

129 Boyce, *Decolonisation and the British Empire*, pp. 2–3, 267–70.

130 For example, Cannadine, *Ornamentalism*, pp. 172–3; Weight, *Patriots*, passim.

131 John Darwin, 'The Fear of Failing: British Politics and Imperial Decline since 1900', *Transactions of the Royal Historical Society*, Fifth Series, 36, p. 29.

132 James, *The Rise and Fall of the British Empire*, pp. 607–8.

133 Address to the Royal Society of St George, 1964, reprinted in John Wood, ed., *A Nation Not Afraid: The Thinking of Enoch Powell* (London, 1965), p. 144.

CHAPTER 9: THE NEWCOMERS

1 Holmes, *John Bull's Island*, pp. 14–15.

2 Davies, *The Isles*, pp. 959–60.

3 Judd, *Empire*, p. 332.

4 Ian Fleming, 'Octopussy', in *Octopussy* (London, 1966).

5 Shamit Saggar, *Race and Politics in Britain* (London, 1992), p. 9.

6 Holmes, *John Bull's Island*, p. 8; Saggar, *Race and Politics in Britain*, pp. 12, 23.

7 See Ron Ramdin, *The Making of the Black Working Class in Britain* (Aldershot, 1987), p. 18; Folarin Shyllon, *Black People in Britain, 1555–1833* (London, 1977).

8 Judd, *Empire*, p. 423.

9 White, *London in the Twentieth Century*, pp. 112–14.

10 R. A. Freeman, *Famous Cases of Dr Thorndyke* (London, 1929), p. 941, quoted in Holmes, *John Bull's Island*, p. 31.

11 Arthur Coats quoted in Mike Phillips and Trevor Phillips, *Windrush: The Irresistible Rise of Multi-Racial Britain* (London, 1999), p. 53.

12 Holmes, *John Bull's Island*, p. 153.

13 See Holmes, *John Bull's Island*, p. 92.

14 A. B. C. Merriman Labor, *Britain through Negro Spectacles* (London, 1905), quoted in Judd, *Empire*, p. 211.

15 Saggar, *Race and Politics in Britain*, p. 66.

16 Phillips and Phillips, *Windrush*, pp. 50–71; Hennessy, *Never Again*, pp. 440–1.

17 Phillips and Phillips, *Windrush*, pp. 67–9.

18 CO 876/88, 5 July 1948; Kathleen Paul, *Whitewashing Britain: Race and Citizenship in the Postwar Era* (Ithaca, New York: 1997), p. 21.

19 *Daily Express*, 23 June 1948.

20 Holmes, *John Bull's Island*, p. 220.

21 Holmes, *John Bull's Island*, p. 279.

22 Holmes, *John Bull's Island*, p. 221.

23 Phillips and Phillips, *Windrush*, pp. 45, 51; see also Hennessy, *Never Again*, p. 440.

24 Lloyd Miller quoted in Phillips and Phillips, *Windrush*, p. 9.

25 George Lamming, *The Emigrants* (London, 1954), p. 37.

26 *Royal Commission on Population* (London, 1949), p. 125.

27 See Weight, *Patriots*, pp. 136–7.

28 Quoted in Stephen Brooke, *Reform and Reconstruction* (Manchester, 1985), pp. 125–6.

29 Holmes, *John Bull's Island*, pp. 221–2; Saggar, *Race and Politics in Britain*, p. 97.

30 Phillips and Phillips, *Windrush*, p. 121.

31 Saggar, *Race and Politics in Britain*, pp. 66, 98.

32 On the political pressures behind the Act, see Horne, *Macmillan 1957–1986*, pp. 421–3; Lamb, *The Macmillan Years*, pp. 410–21.

33 Marwick, *The Sixties*, p. 231; Phillips and Phillips, *Windrush*, p. 159.

34 Saggar, *Race and Politics in Britain*, p. 49.

35 Holmes, *John Bull's Island*, p. 226.

36 Sheila Patterson, *Dark Strangers: A Sociological Study of the Absorption of a Recent West Indian Migrant Group in Brixton, South London* (Harmondsworth, 1963), p. 376; Donald Hinds, *Journey to an Illusion: The West Indian in Britain* (London, 1966), p. 38.

37 Phillips and Phillips, *Windrush*, p. 124.

38 White, *London in the Twentieth Century*, p. 134.

39 Saggar, *Race and Politics in Britain*, p. 51.

40 White, *London in the Twentieth Century*, p. 138.

41 White, *London in the Twentieth Century*, pp. 138–9.

42 Holmes, *John Bull's Island*, p. 222.

43 Saggar, *Race and Politics in Britain*, p. 51.

44 Holmes, *John Bull's Island*, p. 225.

45 Holmes, *John Bull's Island*, pp. 53, 218–19.

46 White, *London in the Twentieth Century*, p. 137.

47 Holmes, *John Bull's Island*, p. 227; Saggar, *Race and Politics in Britain*, p. 53.

48 Holmes, *John Bull's Island*, p. 230.

49 Holmes, *John Bull's Island*, p. 285.

50 Statistics from Marwick, *The Sixties*, p. 231.

51 Phillips and Phillips, *Windrush*, pp. 124–5.

52 White, *London in the Twentieth Century*, pp. 134–6.

53 White, *London in the Twentieth Century*, p. 139.

54 Saggar, *Race and Politics in Britain*, p. 53; Holmes, *John Bull's Island*, p. 227.

55 Holmes, *John Bull's Island*, pp. 242, 285.

56 Patterson, *Dark Strangers*, p. 3.

57 See Postgate, ed., *The Good Food Guide 1951–1952*.

58 Holmes, *John Bull's Island*, pp. 218–19.

59 Holmes, *John Bull's Island*, p. 53.

60 See Holmes, *John Bull's Island*, p. 229; Rosen, *The Transformation of British Life*, p. 20. Weight, *Patriots*, p. 650, repeats an apocryphal and rather implausible story that the Chinese takeaway was invented in 1958 by none other than Cliff Richard.

61 Rosen, *The Transformation of British Life*, p. 20.

62 See *Mrs Beeton's Book of Household Management* (reissued edition: London, 2000).

63 See Peter and Colleen Grove, 'The History of the "Ethnic" Restaurant in Britain', online at <http://www.menumagazine.co.uk/book/restauranthistory.html>.

64 Menu reprinted in Hylton, *Magical History Tour*, p. 119. For recollections of visiting Indian restaurants in the fifties and sixties, see Pressley, *Changing Times*, p. 68.

65 See Peter and Colleen Grove, 'Is It or Isn't It? The Chicken Tikka Masala Story', online at <http://www.menumagazine.co.uk/book/tikkamasala.html>.

66 Colls, *Identity of England*, p. 152.

67 Saggar, *Race and Politics in Britain*, p. 54.

68 Phillips and Phillips, *Windrush*, p. 99.

69 See Weight, *Patriots*, p. 140.

70 Gulzar Khan quoted in Jonathon Green, *Them: Voices from the Immigrant Community in Contemporary Britain* (London, 1990), p. 200.

71 Bhajan Singh Chadha quoted in Green, *Them*, pp. 201–2.

72 Tryphena Anderson quoted in Phillips and Phillips, *Windrush*, p. 97.

73 Phillips and Phillips, *Windrush*, p. 148.

74 P. J. Marshall, 'Imperial Britain', lecture quoted in Judd, *Empire*, p. 430.

75 Colley, *Britons*, p. 369; see also Said, *Orientalism*, pp. 33–4.

76 Saggar, *Race and Politics in Britain*, pp. 19–20. For a different interpretation that instead emphasises class over race, see Cannadine, *Ornamentalism*.

77 Colls, *Identity of England*, pp. 133–5.

78 Pimlott, *Hugh Dalton*, p. 577; Neillands, *A Fighting Retreat*, p. 13.

79 See the discussion of the novel in Sinfield, *Literature, Politics and Culture in Post-war Britain*, p. 118.

80 On the tradition of tolerance, see Holmes, *John Bull's Island*, p. 67.

81 Holmes, *John Bull's Island*, pp. 156–7.

82 Holmes, *John Bull's Island*, pp. 80, 255; Saggar, *Race and Politics in Britain*, p. 34; Phillips and Phillips, *Windrush*, p. 105.

83 White, *London in the Twentieth Century*, pp. 128–9.

84 Saggar, *Race and Politics in Britain*, p. 98.

85 White, *London in the Twentieth Century*, p. 145.

86 Jackson, *Working-Class Community*, p. 1.

87 Patterson, *Dark Strangers*, pp. 212–13.

88 See Colls, *Identity of England*, p. 104.

89 Paul, *Whitewashing Britain*, p. 149.

90 Patterson, *Dark Strangers*, p. 237.

91 Unknown interviewee quoted in Pressley, *Best of Times*, p. 25.

92 Cooke, 'British Cinema: A Struggle for Identity', p. 150.

93 Phillips and Phillips, *Windrush*, p. 118; Weight, *Patriots*, pp. 140–1.

94 White, *London in the Twentieth Century*, p. 146; Weight, *Patriots*, p. 140.

95 Cecil Holness quoted in Phillips and Phillips, *Windrush*, pp. 90–1.

96 Ministry of Labour, *How to Adjust Yourself in Britain* (London, 1954), quoted in Colls, *Identity of England*, p. 138.

97 Quoted in Peter Fryer, *Staying Power: The History of Black People in Britain* (London, 1985), p. 375.

98 Carpenter, *That Was Satire That Was*, p. 111.

99 See White, *London in the Twentieth Century*, p. 146.

100 Cecil Holness quoted in Phillips and Phillips, *Windrush*, p. 90.

101 White, *London in the Twentieth Century*, p. 147.

102 Patterson, *Dark Strangers*, p. 199.

103 Wybrow, *Britain Speaks Out*, p. 55; Marwick, *The Sixties*, p. 237.

104 Marwick, *The Sixties*, pp. 237–8.

105 Holmes, *John Bull's Island*, p. 313.

106 Faith, *Poor Me*, p. 77.

107 Paul Stephenson quoted in Phillips and Phillips, *Windrush*, p. 126.

108 Rudy Braithwaite quoted in Phillips and Phillips, *Windrush*, p. 164.

109 On racist violence between 1948 and 1958, see Holmes, *John Bull's Island*, p. 256; White, *London in the Twentieth Century*, p. 145.

110 Quoted in Mike Phillips and Charlie Phillips, *Notting Hill in the Sixties* (London, 1997), p. 26. On North Kensington and its history, see also Phillips and Phillips, *Windrush*, pp. 105–9; White, *London in the Twentieth Century*, pp. 118–19, 147–8.

111 *Kensington News and West London Times*, 21 November 1958, quoted in Phillips and Phillips, *Windrush*, p. 109.

112 Pearl Jephcott, *A Troubled Area: Notes on Notting Hill* (London, 1964), pp. 33–4.

113 White, *London in the Twentieth Century*, p. 148.

114 *Sunday Times*, 7 July 1963; *Observer*, 21 July 1963; Timmins, *The Five Giants*, pp. 189–90.

115 *The Times*, 29 August 1963, quoted in Timmins, *The Five Giants*, p. 190.

116 George Rhoden quoted in Akhtar and Humphries, *The Fifties and Sixties*, pp. 67–8.

117 Terri Quaye, 'Taking It on the Road', in Sara Maitland, ed., *Very Heaven: Looking Back at the 1960s* (London, 1988), p. 34.

118 Phillips and Phillips, *Windrush*, p. 112.

119 See Phillips and Phillips, *Notting Hill in the Sixties*, pp. 52–5.

120 White, *London in the Twentieth Century*, p. 148.

121 See Paul Rock and Stanley Cohen, 'The Teddy Boy', in Bogdanor and Skidelsky, eds, *The Age of Affluence*, pp. 288–318; Stanley Cohen, *Folk Devils and Moral Panics: The Creation of the Mods and Rockers* (London, 1972).

122 Rudy Braithwaite quoted in Phillips and Phillips, *Windrush*, p. 162.

123 *Tribune*, 5 September 1958.

124 See Dilip Hero, *Black British White British: A History of Race Relations in Britain* (London, 1991), p. 40; Phillips and Phillips, *Windrush*, pp. 166–70; Holmes, *John Bull's Island*, p. 259.

125 Phillips and Phillips, *Windrush*, p. 171.

126 As argued in Phillips and Phillips, *Windrush*, pp. 173–4.

127 White, *London in the Twentieth Century*, pp. 148–9.

128 The following narrative of the Notting Hill riots is based on Phillips and Phillips, *Windrush*, pp. 170–80; Hero, *Black British White British*, pp. 39–40; White, *London in the Twentieth Century*, pp. 148–50.

129 *The Times*, 2 September 1958.

130 *Kensington News and West London Times*, 5 September 1958, quoted in Phillips and Phillips, *Windrush*, pp. 176–7.

131 *Manchester Guardian*, 2 September 1958.

132 White, *London in the Twentieth Century*, p. 149.

133 *Kensington News and West London Times*, 5 September 1958.

134 Quoted in Davis, *Youth and the Condition of Britain*, p. 147.

135 *Daily Mirror*, 1 September 1958 and 3 September 1958.

136 See Hero, *Black British White British*, p. 41; Harry Golbourne, *Race Relations in Britain since 1945* (London, 1998), pp. 70–2.

137 James Wickenden, *Colour in Britain* (Oxford, 1958), pp. 38–9.

138 Wickenden, *Colour in Britain*, pp. 39–40.

139 Marwick, *The Sixties*, p. 238.

140 *Daily Telegraph*, 25 September 1997.

141 Horne, *Macmillan 1957–1986*, pp. 421–3; Saggar, *Race and Politics in Britain*, p. 73; Robert Miles and Annie Phizacklea, *White Man's Country* (London, 1984), p. 44.

142 There is some controversy over the carnival's origins. Jerry White cites three different sources for the rival dates of 1959, 1961–2 and 1966, and concludes that the dilemma is irresolvable: see White, *London in the Twentieth Century*, p. 167.

143 Weight, *Patriots*, p. 295.

144 Phillips and Phillips, *Windrush*, p. 179; Weight, *Patriots*, p. 295.

145 *The Times*, 2 September 1958.

146 Robert Skidelsky, *Oswald Mosley* (London, 1975), pp. 513–14; see also Richard Thurlow, *Fascism in Britain* (second edition: London, 1998).

147 See Phillips and Phillips, *Windrush*, pp. 182–8.

148 Hill, *Sex, Class and Realism*, p. 89.

149 See Durgnat, *A Mirror for England*, pp. 64–5; Hill, *Sex, Class and Realism*, pp. 83–6.

150 On this scene, see Hill, *Sex, Class and Realism*, p. 86.

151 Jonathon Green, *Days in the Life: Voices from the English Underground 1961–1971* (London, 1998), pp. 50–1; White, *London in the Twentieth Century*, p. 339.

152 Barry Miles quoted in Green, *Days in the Life*, p. 10.

153 Monica Dickens, *The Heart of London* (London, 1961), p. 48.

154 Courtney Tulloch quoted in Green, *Days in the Life*, pp. 10–11; the phrase comes from Norman Mailer.

155 Barry Miles quoted in Green, *Days in the Life*, p. 10.

156 See Tony Gould, *Inside Outsider: The Life and Times of Colin MacInnes* (London, 1983), p. 138.

157 Colin MacInnes, *England, Half English* (London, 1961), p. 30.

158 Colin MacInnes, *City of Spades* (A&B edition: London, 1980), pp. 12, 66, 177. For a wider discussion of this novel, see Sinfield, *Literature, Politics and Culture in Post-war Britain*, pp. 127–8.

159 Sinfield, *Literature, Politics and Culture in Post-war Britain*, p. 170.

160 On *Absolute Beginners*, see Bergonzi, *Wartime and Aftermath*, p. 176; Steven Connor, *The English Novel in History, 1950–1995* (London, 1996), p. 90.

161 Colin MacInnes, *Absolute Beginners* (A&B edition: London, 1980), pp. 172–3.

162 MacInnes, *Absolute Beginners*, pp. 179–80.

163 MacInnes, *Absolute Beginners*, p. 203.

CHAPTER 10: I'M ALL RIGHT, JACK

1 Aldgate and Richards, *Best of British*, p. 180; Ed Sikov, *Mr Strangelove: A Biography of Peter Sellers* (London, 2002), p. 129.

2 Aldgate and Richards, *Best of British*, p. 182.

3 Alexander Walker, *Peter Sellers* (London, 1982), pp. 55–7.

4 Walker, *Peter Sellers*, pp. 100–1; Sikov, *Mr Strangelove*, p. 115.

5 *The Times*, 7 January 1959.

6 *The Times*, 26 July 1974. See also the introduction to Burton, O'Sullivan and Wells, eds, *The Family Way*, pp. 6–11.

7 Julian Petley, 'The Pilgrim's Regress: The Politics of the Boultings' Films', pp. 15–34, and Marcia Landy, 'Nation and Imagination in *Private's Progress*', pp. 175–88, both in Burton, O'Sullivan and Wells, eds, *The Family Way*.

8 Raymond Durgnat, 'St Smallwood: Or, Left of *Heaven's Above!*', in Burton, O'Sullivan and Wells, eds, *The Family Way*, p. 218.

9 Walker, *Peter Sellers*, pp. 106–7.

10 See Walker, *Peter Sellers*, pp. 107–8; Roger Lewis, *The Life and Death of Peter Sellers* (London, 1994), pp. 408–10.

11 Lewis, *The Life and Death of Peter Sellers*, p. 409.

12 Walker, *Peter Sellers*, p. 109.

13 Sikov, *Mr Strangelove*, p. 352; see also Walker, *Peter Sellers*, pp. 109–12.

14 On the theme song, see Aldgate and Richards, *Best of British*, p. 175; Petley, 'The Pilgrim's Regress', p. 28.

15 See Lewis, *The Life and Death of Peter Sellers*, p, 421; Aldgate and Richards, *Best of British*, pp. 177–8; Wells, 'Comments, Custard Pies and Comic Cuts: the Boulting Brothers at Play, 1955–65', p. 61; Sikov, *Mr Strangelove*, pp. 125–6.

16 *Daily Express*, 14 August 1959. See also Hill, *Sex, Class and Realism*, p. 197, which discusses the politics of the film.

17 Hill, *Sex, Class and Realism*, pp. 147–9; Aldgate and Richards, *Best of British*, p. 176; Petley, 'The Pilgrim's Regress', p. 28.

18 See Hill, *Sex, Class and Realism*, p. 149.

19 *The Times*, 17 August 1959; Walker, *Peter Sellers*, p. 113.

20 Durgnat, *A Mirror for England*, p. 72.

21 Shaw, *British Cinema and the Cold War*, pp. 160–1.

22 Quoted in Murphy, *Sixties British Cinema*, p. 44; see also Durgnat, *A Mirror for England*, p. 72; Shaw, *British Cinema and the Cold War*, pp. 160–6.

23 *The Times*, 14 March 1960.

24 Quoted in Shaw, *British Cinema and the Cold War*, p. 165.

25 *The Times*, 16 May 1960.

26 *The Times*, 18 May and 20 May 1960.

27 Willmott and Young, *Family and Class in a London Suburb*, p. 103.

28 For a good, brief summary, see Robert Taylor, 'Industrial Relations', in Marquand and Seldon, eds, *The Ideas That Shaped Post-War Britain*, pp. 88–121; or Owen, *From Empire to Europe*, pp. 433–4.

29 Quoted in Marwick, *British Society since 1945*, p. 47.

30 Sampson, *Anatomy of Britain*, p. 554.

31 Marwick, *British Society since 1945*, pp. 164–5; Jefferys, *Retreat from New Jerusalem*, pp. 112–13; Gilmour and Garnett, *Whatever Happened to the Tories*, pp. 147–8.

32 Childs, *Britain since 1945*, p. 103.

33 Sampson, *Anatomy of Britain*, p. 568.

34 *The Campaign Guide 1964* (London, 1964), p. 153, quoted in Childs, *Britain since 1945*, p. 103.

35 Sampson, *Anatomy of Britain*, p. 562.

36 Sampson, *Anatomy of Britain*, p. 562; Childs, *Britain since 1945*, p. 102; Jefferys, *Retreat from New Jerusalem*, p. 112; Aldgate and Richards, *Best of British*, p. 174.

37 Michael Shanks, *The Stagnant Society* (Harmondsworth, 1961), p. 85; Owen, *From Empire to Europe*, pp. 434–5.

38 Sampson, *Anatomy of Britain*, p. 95; Owen, *From Empire to Europe*, p. 434.

39 Jefferys, *Retreat from New Jerusalem*, p. 113.

40 *The Times*, 4 November 1959.

41 Unidentified trade unionist, 1950, quoted in Taylor, 'Industrial Relations', p. 97.

42 Shanks, *The Stagnant Society*, p. 93.

43 Shanks, *The Stagnant Society*, pp. 78, 73–4.

44 Shanks, *The Stagnant Society*, p. 102.

45 Shanks, *The Stagnant Society*, p. 236.

46 Macmillan diary, 26 May 1959, quoted in Horne, *Macmillan 1957–1986*, p. 143.

47 Brittan, *The Treasury under the Tories*, p. 205; Dell, *The Chancellors*, p. 254.

48 Lamb, *The Macmillan Years*, pp. 64–5.

49 Horne, *Macmillan 1957–1986*, p. 237.

50 Macmillan diary, 16 February 1960, quoted in *Macmillan 1957–1986*, p. 236.

51 Macmillan diary, 26 February 1960, quoted in *Macmillan 1957–1986*, p. 238.

52 PREM 11/2962, Macmillan to Amory, 27 February 1960.

53 Lamb, *The Macmillan Years*, pp. 66–7.

54 Lamb, *The Macmillan Years*, p. 68.

55 Horne, *Macmillan 1957–1986*, p. 239.

56 Quoted in Horne, *Macmillan 1957–1986*, p. 240.

57 Dell, *The Chancellors*, p. 258.

58 Gilmour and Garnett, *Whatever Happened to the Tories*, p. 165.

59 *The Times*, 23 July 1960; Dell, *The Chancellors*, p. 259.

60 *The Times*, 23 July 1960; Horne, *Macmillan 1957–1986*, pp. 241–2; Thorpe, *Alec Douglas-Home*, pp. 207–9.

61 On Home at the Foreign Office, see Thorpe, *Alec Douglas-Home*, pp. 205–69, an extremely sympathetic but perfectly reliable account.

62 Macmillan diary, 15 September 1960, quoted in Horne, *Macmillan 1957–1986*, p. 245.

63 Cairncross quoted in Lamb, *The Macmillan Years*, p. 69; see also Brittan, *The Treasury under the Tories*, p. 210; Dell, *The Chancellors*, pp. 258–9.

64 Horne, *Macmillan 1957–1986*, p. 246; Lamb, *The Macmillan Years*, p. 69. The strike in the car industry was provoked in part by a dispute over the length of the mid-morning tea break afforded to Ford workers.

65 Macmillan diary, 30 November 1960, quoted in Horne, *Macmillan 1957–1986*, p. 247.

66 Horne, *Macmillan 1957–1986*, p. 247.

67 Lamb, *The Macmillan Years*, p. 72.

68 See Lamb, *The Macmillan Years*, pp. 69–72; Dell, *The Chancellors*, pp. 260–3.

69 Lamb, *The Macmillan Years*, p. 74.

70 On the 'little budget', see Lamb, *The Macmillan Years*, pp. 74–5; Dell, *The Chancellors*, pp. 264–5.

71 *The Economist*, 29 July 1961.

72 Morgan, *The People's Peace*, p. 211.

73 Jefferys, *Retreat from New Jerusalem*, p. 92; Brittan, *The Treasury under the Tories*, p. 236.

74 *The Times*, 13 July and 26 July 1961.

75 Lamb, *The Macmillan Years*, p. 76; Holt, *Second Amongst Equals*, pp. 39–40. For a slightly more generous verdict, see Brittan, *The Treasury under the Tories*, p. 238.

76 Macmillan diary, 24 March 1962, quoted in Harold Macmillan, *At the End of the Day, 1959–1961* (London, 1973), p. 59.

77 Shanks, *The Stagnant Society*, pp. 139–74.

78 Nigel Harris, *Competition and the Corporate State: British Conservatives, the State and Industry, 1945–1964* (London, 1972), p. 157; Jefferys, *Retreat from New Jerusalem*, p. 125; Dell, *A Strange Eventful History*, pp. 82–96.

79 Hansard, 25 and 26 July 1962.

80 Lamb, *The Macmillan Years*, p. 77; Gilmour and Garnett, *Whatever Happened to the Tories*, p. 167.

81 Sampson, *Anatomy of Britain*, p. 281; Childs, *Britain since 1945*, pp. 138–9; Gilmour and Garnett, *Whatever Happened to the Tories*, p. 167.

82 Lamb, *The Macmillan Years*, pp. 78–9.

83 Dell, *The Chancellors*, pp. 267, 272–3; Owen, *From Empire to Europe*, p. 451.

84 Gilmour and Garnett, *Whatever Happened to the Tories*, p. 170.

85 See Horne, *Macmillan 1957–1986*, pp. 253–5, 332–4; Shepherd, *Iain Macleod*, pp. 259–62; Jefferys, *Retreat from New Jerusalem*, pp. 92–3.

86 *The Times*, 15 March 1962; see also Lamb, *The Macmillan Years*, p. 443; Shepherd, *Iain Macleod*, p. 273; Jefferys, *Retreat from New Jerusalem*, p. 94.

87 Shepherd, *Iain Macleod*, p. 274.

88 Macmillan diary, 24 March and 16 April 1962, quoted in Horne, *Macmillan 1957–1986*, pp. 336–7.

89 Lamb, *The Macmillan Years*, p. 445; Sked and Cook, *Post-war Britain*, p. 181.

90 *The Times*, 15 and 16 March 1962. Schedule A was an unpopular tax on owner-occupied houses, which hit lower-middle-class homeowners particularly badly.

91 See Jefferys, *Retreat from New Jerusalem*, pp. 172–4.

92 Thorpe, *Selwyn Lloyd*, p. 334.

93 On the 1962 budget, see Lamb, *The Macmillan Years*, pp. 81–3; Dell, *The Chancellors*, pp. 274–6; Jefferys, *Retreat from New Jerusalem*, pp. 170–1.

94 CAB 128/35, Macmillan to Lloyd, 22 June 1962; Horne, *Macmillan 1957–1986*, p. 340; Dell, *The Chancellors*, pp. 276–8.

95 Shepherd, *Iain Macleod*, pp. 278–9.

96 Macmillan diary, 21 June 1962, quoted in Horne, *Macmillan 1957–1986*, p. 341.

97 Macmillan diary, 8 July 1962, quoted in Horne, *Macmillan 1957–1986*, pp. 341–2.

98 *Daily Mail*, 12 July 1962; Howard, *RAB*, pp. 291–2; Shepherd, *Iain Macleod*, p. 279.

99 Thorpe, *Selwyn Lloyd*, pp. 342–4.

100 Macmillan diary, 14 June 1962, quoted in Horne, *Macmillan 1957–1986*, p. 343.

101 See Thorpe, *Selwyn Lloyd*, pp. 342–54; Horne, *Macmillan 1957–1986*, pp. 343–4; Lamb, *The Macmillan Years*, pp. 447–8.

102 *The Times*, 14 July 1962.

103 Horne, *Macmillan 1957–1986*, p. 344.

104 Anthony Royle quoted in Horne, *Macmillan 1957–1986*, p. 345.

105 Hennessy, *The Prime Minister*, pp. 70, 75–6.

106 Harold Watkinson, *Turning Points* (Salisbury, 1986), p. 161.

107 Kilmuir, *Political Adventure*, p. 324; Lamb, *The Macmillan Years*, p. 449.

108 Horne, *Macmillan 1957–1986*, p. 346.

109 Horne, *Macmillan 1957–1986*, p. 346.

110 Horne, *Macmillan 1957–1986*, p. 346.

111 Horne, *Macmillan 1957–1986*, p. 348.

112 Thorpe, *Selwyn Lloyd*, p. 354; Dell, *The Chancellors*, p. 280.

113 Thorpe, *Selwyn Lloyd*, p. 353.

114 Lamb, *The Macmillan Years*, p. 451; Jefferys, *Retreat from New Jerusalem*, p. 97.

115 Quoted in Horne, *Macmillan 1957–1986*, p. 350.

116 *Daily Telegraph*, 21 July 1962; see also Horne, *Macmillan 1957–1986*, pp. 348–9; Jefferys, *Retreat from New Jerusalem*, pp. 96–7.

CHAPTER 11: TV WITH AUNTIE

1 *Ariel*, January 1960, quoted in Briggs, *The History of Broadcasting in the United Kingdom: Volume V*, p. 311.

2 *Daily Star*, 17 December 1959. On Greene, see Hewison, *Too Much*, pp. 24–7; Briggs, *The History of Broadcasting in the United Kingdom: Volume V*, pp. 311–25.

3 Quoted in Hewison, *Too Much*, p. 26; see also Hugh Carleton Greene, *The Third Floor*

Front: A View of Broadcasting in the 1960s (London, 1969).

4 Marwick, *Class*, p. 157.

5 Anthony Smith, *British Broadcasting* (Newton Abbott, 1974), p. 62.

6 Colls, *Identity of England*, p. 61.

7 McKibbin, *Classes and Cultures*, pp. 459–60.

8 Marwick, *Class*, p. 157; Asa Briggs, *The History of Broadcasting in the United Kingdom: Volume I: The Birth of Broadcasting* (Oxford, 1995), p. 222.

9 Sampson, *Anatomy of Britain*, p. 601.

10 Lewis, *The Fifties*, p. 210.

11 Robert Giddings, 'Radio in Peace and War', in Bloom and Day, eds, *Literature and Culture in Modern Britain: Volume Two*, p. 133; Stuart Laing, 'The Production of Literature', in Sinfield, ed., *Society and Literature 1945–1970*, p. 154.

12 Chris Williams, quoted in Akhtar and Humphries, *The Fifties and Sixties*, p. 128.

13 Krishan Kumar, 'The Social and Cultural Setting', in Ford, ed., *From Orwell to Naipaul*, pp. 26–7; Weight, *Patriots*, p. 169.

14 McKibbin, *Classes and Cultures*, p. 471.

15 See Kumar, 'The Social and Cultural Setting', p. 27; Akhtar and Humphries, *The Fifties and Sixties*, pp. 128–30.

16 The pilot for the series was first transmitted in 1950, but the first official episode was not broadcast until 1 January 1951.

17 Quoted in Weight, *Patriots*, p. 159; see also McKibbin, *Classes and Cultures*, p. 471; Akhtar and Humphries, *The Fifties and Sixties*, p. 129; and a plethora of websites devoted to the programme.

18 Sinfield, *Literature, Politics and Culture in Post-war Britain*, p. 51.

19 Briggs, *The History of Broadcasting in the United Kingdom: Volume V*, pp. 53–7.

20 *Punch*, 3 April 1957; see Briggs, *The History of Broadcasting in the United Kingdom: Volume V*, p. 55.

21 Briggs, *The History of Broadcasting in the United Kingdom: Volume V*, p. 579. On the Third Programme, see Kate Whitehead, *The Third Programme: A Literary History* (Oxford, 1989).

22 Lez Cooke, 'Television', in Bloom and Day, eds, *Literature and Culture in Modern Britain: Volume Three*, p. 177.

23 Morris, 'Technology 1956–99', in Bloom and Day, eds, *Literature and Culture in Modern Britain: Volume Three*, p. 243.

24 Quoted in Clarke, *Shadow of a Nation*, p. 21.

25 Peter Forster, 'J. Arthur Rank and the Shrinking Screen: The Struggles of the Film Industry and the Rise of Television', in Sissons and French, eds, *The Age of Austerity*, p. 279.

26 Hopkins, *The New Look*, p. 403.

27 Pimlott, *The Queen*, p. 207, gives the figure of twenty-seven million; Akhtar and Humphries, *The Fifties and Sixties*, p. 134, give conflicting figures of twenty million and twenty-five million.

28 Weight, *Patriots*, p. 234. Weight gives a surprisingly precise viewing figure of 20.4 million, but he does not cite his source.

29 Hill, *Sex, Class and Realism*, p. 35.

30 The most authoritative source for television licence statistics is Briggs, *The History of Broadcasting in the United Kingdom: Volume V*, Appendix A, p. 1005. The figures for radio licences, rather than combined licences, showed a corresponding decline, and the radio licence was finally abolished in 1971.

31 Cooke, 'Television', p. 178; on the licence fee, see Briggs, *The History of Broadcasting in the United Kingdom: Volume V*, pp. 305–8.

32 See Laing, 'The Production of Literature', p. 155.

33 Hewison, *In Anger*, p. 149.

34 There is an interesting contemporary discussion of this in Hopkins, *The New Look*, pp. 331–2.

35 Hopkins, *The New Look*, pp. 403–4; Lewis, *The Fifties*, p. 219.

36 See the advertisements reprinted in Akhtar and Humphries, *The Fifties and Sixties*, p. 104.

37 Lewis, *The Fifties*, p. 208.

38 Lewis, *The Fifties*, pp. 208–9.

39 On the controversy surrounding the creation of ITV, see Weight, *Patriots*, pp. 244–9.

40 Hopkins, *The New Look*, pp. 399–400; Briggs, *The History of Broadcasting in the United Kingdom: Volume V*, p. 6; Weight, *Patriots*, p. 249.

41 *Manchester Guardian*, 23 September 1955.

42 *Daily Mirror*, 23 September 1955; *News Chronicle*, 23 September 1955; both quoted in Briggs, *The History of Broadcasting in the United Kingdom: Volume V*, pp. 28–9.

43 Lewis, *The Fifties*, p. 215.

44 Briggs, *The History of Broadcasting in the United Kingdom: Volume V*, p. 185.

45 Hewison, *Too Much*, p. 10.

46 Lewis, *The Fifties*, p. 229.

47 Lewis, *The Fifties*, p. 216.

48 Briggs, *The History of Broadcasting in the United Kingdom: Volume V*, p. 12.

49 Lewis, *The Fifties*, p. 216; Cooke, 'Television', p. 179.

50 Briggs, *The History of Broadcasting in the United Kingdom: Volume V*, p. 143.

51 Lewis, *The Fifties*, p. 216.

52 Hughie Green also presented *Double Your Money*: see Weight, *Patriots*, p. 251.

53 Weight, *Patriots*, p. 251.

54 Quoted in Lewis, *The Fifties*, p. 217.

55 Quoted in Weight, *Patriots*, p. 251.

56 Susan Howe quoted in Akhtar and Humphries, *The Fifties and Sixties*, p. 142.

57 Unknown interviewee quoted in Tim O'Sullivan, 'Television Memories and Cultures of Viewing, 1950–1965', in John Corner, ed., *Popular Television in Britain* (London, 1991), p. 174.

58 Hopkins, *The New Look*, p. 411.

59 Lewis, *The Fifties*, p. 211.

60 *Spectator*, 20 January 1956; *Daily Express*, 21 January 1956.

61 *Manchester Guardian*, 7 April 1956, quoted in Briggs, *The History of Broadcasting in the United Kingdom: Volume V*, p. 14.

62 Briggs, *The History of Broadcasting in the United Kingdom: Volume V*, p. 23.

63 *New Statesman*, 5 June 1956.

64 Hopkins, *The New Look*, p. 403.

65 Briggs, *The History of Broadcasting in the United Kingdom: Volume V*, p. 147.

66 Richard Crossman. *Labour in the Affluent Society* (Fabian Tract No. 325: London, 1960), quoted in Hewison, *Too Much*, pp. 10–11. These attitudes were not entirely dead in the early twenty-first century: when I was teaching in the history department at Sheffield, I was amused to discover that one of my colleagues had no television on the grounds that it would corrupt his children. Another thought that Radio 4's *Today* programme was unsuitable for a family audience, but that is another story.

67 *New Statesman*, 26 January 1957.

68 Raymond Williams, *Communications* (London, 1962), p. 79.

69 Doris Lessing, *Walking in the Shade: Volume Two of My Autobiography* (London, 1997), p. 16.

70 Anthony Hartley, *A State of England* (London, 1963), quoted in Hewison, *Too Much*, p. 14.

71 *News of the World*, 1 July 1962.

72 See Briggs, *The History of Broadcasting in the United Kingdom: Volume V*, pp. 259–71.

73 Briggs, *The History of Broadcasting in the United Kingdom: Volume V*, p. 272.

74 The analogy itself is typical Hoggart: see *Encounter*, January 1960. See also Briggs, *The History of Broadcasting in the United Kingdom: Volume V*, p. 273.

75 *Sunday Times*, 1 July 1962; *Observer*, 1 July 1962.

76 *Report of the Committee on Broadcasting 1960* (London, 1962), pp. 16ff.

77 *Report of the Committee on Broadcasting 1960*, pp. 286–8.

78 *The Economist*, 30 June 1962; for similar responses in the *Sunday Telegraph* and elsewhere, see Briggs, *The History of Broadcasting in the United Kingdom: Volume V*, p. 298.

79 Quoted in John Corner, 'General Introduction: Television and British Society in the 1950s', in Corner, ed., *Popular Television in Britain*, p. 10.

80 Briggs, *The History of Broadcasting in the United Kingdom: Volume V*, pp. 297–9.

81 My italics. Briggs, *The History of Broadcasting in the United Kingdom: Volume V*, pp. 403–4.

82 Briggs, *The History of Broadcasting in the United Kingdom: Volume V*, pp. 411–12.

83 Briggs, *The History of Broadcasting in the United Kingdom: Volume V*, pp. 414–15.

84 Briggs, *The History of Broadcasting in the United Kingdom: Volume V*, pp. 30, 1005.

85 Briggs, *The History of Broadcasting in the United Kingdom: Volume V*, p. 222.

86 See Andy Medhurst, 'Every Wart and Pustule: Gilbert Harding and Television Stardom', in Corner, ed., *Popular Television in Britain*, pp. 60–74.

87 On these five programmes, see Lewis, *The Fifties*, pp. 217–18; Briggs, *The History of Broadcasting in the United Kingdom: Volume V*, pp. 161–75.

88 Briggs, *The History of Broadcasting in the United Kingdom: Volume V*, pp. 190–1; Shellard, *British Theatre since the War*, p. 135.

89 Briggs, *The History of Broadcasting in the United Kingdom: Volume V*, p. 143.

90 Quoted in Hewison, *Too Much*, p. 26.

91 Briggs, *The History of Broadcasting in the United Kingdom: Volume V*, p. 323.

92 Briggs, *The History of Broadcasting in the United Kingdom: Volume V*, pp. 344–6.

93 John Reith, *The Reith Diaries* (London, 1975): see diary entries for 12 September 1963, 20 January 1964.

94 Briggs, *The History of Broadcasting in the United Kingdom: Volume V*, p. 395; see also the excellent essay by Jason Jacobs for the online encyclopaedia of television history at <http://www.museum.tv/archives/etv/N/htmlN/newmansydne/newman-sydne.htm>.

95 *Daily Express*, 5 January 1963.

96 George Brandt, *British Television Drama* (Cambridge 1981), p. 16.

97 Hewison, *In Anger*, p. 149; Laing, *Representations of Working-Class Life*, pp. 148–52; Shellard, *British Theatre since the War*, p. 135.

98 See Laing, *Representations of Working-Class Life*, pp. 150–1.

99 For instance, Taylor, *Anger and After*, pp. 197–9.

100 *Daily Telegraph*, 30 May 1960. See also Laing, 'The Production of Literature', p. 160; Shellard, *British Theatre since the War*, p. 138; Cooke, 'Television', p. 180.

101 *Daily Mail*, 19 April 1962.

102 Laing, 'The Production of Literature', p. 160; Briggs, *The History of Broadcasting in the United Kingdom: Volume V*, p. 396.

103 Irene Shubik, *Play for Today* (London, 1975), p. 38.

104 Lacey, *British Realist Theatre*, p. 116.

105 Briggs, *The History of Broadcasting in the United Kingdom: Volume V*, p. 520.

106 Hewison, *Too Much*, pp. 31–2; Laing, 'The Production of Literature', p. 160; Briggs, *The History of Broadcasting in the United Kingdom: Volume V*, p. 519.

107 Cooke, 'Television', pp. 184–5.

108 Michael Tracey and David Morrison, *Whitehouse* (London, 1979), p. 96.

109 Lacey, *British Realist Theatre*, pp. 71, 116.

110 Briggs, *The History of Broadcasting in the United Kingdom: Volume V*, p. 210.

111 Briggs, *The History of Broadcasting in the United Kingdom: Volume V*, p. 211, n. 6.

112 Peter Goddard, '*Hancock's Half-Hour*: A Watershed in British Television Comedy', in Corner, ed., *Popular Television in Britain*, pp. 75–89; Briggs, *The History of Broadcasting in the United Kingdom: Volume V*, pp. 211–15.

113 See Roger Wilmut, *Tony Hancock: 'Artiste'* (London, 1978).

114 *Independent*, 4 June 2004.

115 *Daily Mirror*, 10 December 1960.

116 See Laing, *Representations of Working-Class Life*, pp. 188–9; BBC feature, 8 December 2000, online at <http://news.bbc.co.uk/1/hi/entertainment/1061044.stm>; Daran Little, *The Coronation Street Story* (London, 2001).

117 *Spectator*, 24 March 1961.

118 Dyer et al., *Coronation Street*, p. 4; Laing, *Representations of Working-Class Life*, pp. 184–5.

119 *New Statesman*, 12 January 1962; see also Laing, *Representations of Working-Class Life*, pp. 189–90; Lacey, *British Realist Theatre*, p. 119.

120 Lacey, *British Realist Theatre*, p. 118.

121 On Barlow and Hoggart, see Lawton, *1963*, pp. 36–7; Hill, *Sport, Leisure and Culture in Twentieth-Century Britain*, p. 107.

122 One article on the history of the show in 2001, for example, called it 'extraordinarily

poorly made': see BBC feature, 5 March 2001, online at <http://news.bbc.co.uk/ 1/hi/entertainment/1203144.stm>; Hylton, *Magical History Tour*, p. 65.

123 Those viewers who preferred ITV to the BBC had their own alternative to *Dixon of Dock Green*, a series called *No Hiding Place* which was almost as successful, running for 236 episodes between 1959 and 1967 with Raymond Francis as the snuff-taking Chief Superintendent Lockhart, a rather more lofty individual than the bluff George Dixon. See Aldgate and Richards, *Best of British*, pp. 133, 142.

124 Ted Willis, *Evening All: Fifty Years over a Hot Typewriter* (London, 1991), p. 70.

125 Aldgate and Richards, *Best of British*, p. 127.

126 Aldgate and Richards, *Best of British*, p. 131.

127 McKibbin, *Classes and Cultures*, p. 452.

128 Aldgate and Richards, *Best of British*, p. 126.

129 Briggs, *The History of Broadcasting in the United Kingdom: Volume V*, p. 431.

130 Willis, *Evening All*, p. 190; Briggs, *The History of Broadcasting in the United Kingdom: Volume V*, p. 431.

131 Geoffrey Gorer, *Exploring English Character* (London, 1955), p. 213.

132 McKibbin, *Classes and Cultures*, p. 329.

133 Clive Emsley, 'The English Bobby', in Roy Porter, ed., *Myths of the English* (Cambridge 1992), p. 118.

134 Durgnat, *A Mirror for England*, pp. 136, 54–5.

135 Durgnat, *A Mirror for England*, p. 57; Pimlott, *Harold Wilson*, p. 267.

136 White, *London in the Twentieth Century*, p. 303.

137 *Observer*, 19 March 1971.

138 Murphy, *Sixties British Cinema*, p. 202.

139 Quoted in Stuart Laing, 'Banging in Some Reality: The Original Z-Cars', in Corner, ed., *Popular Television in Britain*, p. 127; on the evolution of *Z Cars* see also Laing, *Representations of Working-Class Life*, pp. 169–81.

140 *Radio Times*, 28 December 1961; Laing, 'Banging in Some Reality', p. 129.

141 Laing, 'Banging in Some Reality', pp. 128–9; Aldgate and Richards, *Best of British*, pp. 141–2.

142 Briggs, *The History of Broadcasting in the United Kingdom: Volume V*, p. 428.

143 Aldgate and Richards, *Best of British*, pp. 142–3.

144 *Guardian*, 5 January 1962.

145 *Bolton Evening News*, 5 January 1962, quoted in Briggs, *The History of Broadcasting in the United Kingdom: Volume V*, p. 428.

146 Laing, 'Banging in Some Reality', pp. 129, 135; Briggs, *The History of Broadcasting in the United Kingdom: Volume V*, pp. 433–4.

147 *New Statesman*, 5 July 1963.

148 Briggs, *The History of Broadcasting in the United Kingdom: Volume V*, p. 430.

149 Laing, 'Banging in Some Reality', p. 139; Briggs, *The History of Broadcasting in the United Kingdom: Volume V*, pp. 433–4, 526. The title music of *Z Cars* lived on, however, being played every fortnight to greet the dashing heroes of Everton Football Club as they stepped on to the turf of Goodison Park.

150 Laing, 'Banging in Some Reality', pp. 127–9, 133–4.

151 Hylton, *Magical History Tour*, p. 73.

152 See the discussions in Laing, 'Banging in Some Reality', pp. 125–44; Briggs, *The History of Broadcasting in the United Kingdom: Volume V*, p. 341.

153 Sillitoe, *Saturday Night and Sunday Morning*, p. 184.

CHAPTER 12: THE TEENAGE CONSUMER

1 Roger Sabin, *Adult Comics: An Introduction* (London, 1993), pp. 25–6; McKibbin, *Classes and Cultures*, p. 498.

2 Martin Barker, *A Haunt of Fears: The Strange History of the British Horror Comics Campaign* (London, 1984), p. 182.

3 Marcus Morris, foreword to *Best of Eagle* (London, 1977). Morris was an unconventional character. As vicar of St James', Birkdale, Lancashire, he had converted the parish magazine into a national Christian periodical, the *Anvil*, attracting articles from eminent contributors like C. S. Lewis and Harold Macmillan. He was often at odds with the Church hierarchy and eventually worked in publishing full-time, although he remained a priest. Perhaps unusually for a modern man of God, he was also an enthusiastic bon viveur, drinker and womaniser. See Sally Morris and Jan Hallwood, *Living with Eagles: Marcus Morris, Priest and Publisher* (London, 1998).

4 For the genesis of the Dan Dare character, see Morris, foreword to *Best of Eagle*.

5 Weight, *Patriots*, p. 342.

6 Quoted in Webster, *Looka Yonder!*, p. 193.

7 *Picture Post*, 17 May 1952.

8 See Barker, *A Haunt of Fears*, esp. pp. 1–27, 159–69.

9 Linda Shanovitch quoted in Akhtar and Humphries, *The Fifties and Sixties*, p. 22.

10 Unknown interviewee quoted in Pressley, *The Best of Times*, p. 95.

11 Akhtar and Humphries, *The Fifties and Sixties*, p. 22.

12 See Sheila Rowbotham, *A Century of Women: The History of Women in Britain and the United States* (London, 1999), pp. 282–3; Akhtar and Humphries, *The Fifties and Sixties*, pp. 21–2.

13 Davis, *Youth and the Condition of Britain*, p. 168; Mary Ingham, *Now We Are Thirty: Women of the Breakthrough Generation* (London, 1981), p. 65.

14 *Valentine*, 19 January 1957, quoted in Penny Tinkler, 'Girlhood and Growing Up', in Zweiniger-Bargielowska, ed., *Women in Twentieth-Century Britain*, p. 47.

15 *Daily Mirror*, 15 November 1963. There is a nice analysis of these magazines, from which these examples are taken, in Marwick, *The Sixties*, pp. 72–3; see also Tinkler, 'Girlhood and Growing Up', p. 47.

16 Peter Laurie, *The Teenage Revolution* (London, 1965), p. 65.

17 Fogg, *Boutique*, pp. 92–5; Marwick, *The Sixties*, p. 73.

18 Stevenson, *British Society 1914–45*, p. 148.

19 Stevenson, *British Society 1914–45*, p. 163; Marwick, *British Society since 1945*, pp. 35–6, 64; Jackson, *The Middle Classes*, p. 16.

20 Marwick, *British Society since 1945*, p. 74.

21 See Stevenson, *British Society 1914–1945*, pp. 150–6.

22 Jeffrey Weeks, *Sex, Politics and Society: The Regulation of Sexuality since 1800* (second edition: London, 1989), p. 203.

23 See Benjamin Spock, *The Common Sense Book of Baby and Child Care* (New York: 1946). It remained a bestseller for the rest of the century: see Sutherland, *Reading the Decades*, p. 98.

24 *Housewife*, April 1952, quoted in Akhtar and Humphries, *The Fifties and Sixties*, p. 15.

25 On names, see Marwick, *British Society since 1945*, p. 76.

26 Sinfield, *Literature, Politics and Culture in Post-war Britain*, p. 206.

27 Martin Pugh, *Women and the Women's Movement in Britain, 1914–1959* (London, 1992), p. 296; Mary Abbott, *Family Affairs: A History of the Family in Twentieth-Century England* (London, 2003), pp. 99–100; John Bowlby, *Child Care and the Growth of Love* (Harmondsworth, 1953), p. 105.

28 Quoted in Pugh, *Women and the Women's Movement in Britain*, p. 297.

29 John Gardner quoted in Akhtar and Humphries, *The Fifties and Sixties*, p. 18.

30 *Guardian*, 13 September 1965.

31 See Akhtar and Humphries, *The Fifties and Sixties*, pp. 18–21, from which much of this section draws.

32 Akhtar and Humphries, *The Fifties and Sixties*, p. 19.

33 *Independent*, 16 October 2003.

34 Paul Parker quoted in Akhtar and Humphries, *The Fifties and Sixties*, pp. 19–20.

35 Pressley, *The Best of Times*, p. 59.

36 See Ingham, *Now We Are Thirty*, p. 49.

37 Unknown interviewee quoted in Pressley, *The Best of Times*, p. 58.

38 Akhtar and Humphries, *The Fifties and Sixties*, p. 28.

39 Briggs, *The History of Broadcasting in the United Kingdom: Volume V*, p. 176.

40 Briggs, *The History of Broadcasting in the United Kingdom: Volume V*, pp. 178–80; Akhtar and Humphries, *The Fifties and Sixties*, p. 136.

41 See Akhtar and Humphries, *The Fifties and Sixties*, pp. 27–8. Much of my information comes from the website of the British Association of Toy Retailers at <http://www.batr.co.uk>.

42 See Gary Gillatt, *Doctor Who from A to Z* (London, 1998), pp. 16–21.

43 Unknown interviewee quoted in Pressley, *The Best of Times*, p. 68.

44 Unknown interviewee quoted in Pressley, *The Best of Times*, p. 53.

45 Akhtar and Humphries, *The Fifties and Sixties*, p. 22.

46 Akhtar and Humphries, *The Fifties and Sixties*, p. 24.

47 Lamb, *The Macmillan Years*, pp. 431–42; Lawton, *1963*, pp. 284–5.

48 For the Girl Adventurers, see Pressley, *The Best of Times*, p. 71.

49 See Judd, *Empire*, pp. 201–13; Jackson, *The Middle Classes*, pp. 212–19.

50 Weight, *Patriots*, p. 287. His implication is that children were somehow forced to choose between being Scouts and listening to pop music, when of course they could quite happily do both.

51 These figures are provided by the Scout Association website at <http://www.scoutbase.org.uk/library/history/census.htm>. Scouting numbers reached their

peak during the late 1980s; by the end of the century they had suffered a slight dip but still remained above 500,000. In 1995 there were over twenty-five million Scouts of various kinds worldwide.

52 See Marcus Crouch, *Treasure Seekers and Borrowers: Children's Books in Britain 1900–1960* (London, 1962); Elaine Moss, *Part of the Pattern: A Personal Journey Through the World of Children's Books, 1960–1985* (London, 1986).

53 Frank Richards was actually the pen name of Charles Hamilton, who wrote a staggering 100,000 words of children's fiction a week. See Mary Cadogan, *Frank Richards: The Chap behind the Chums* (London, 2000). For the other popular children's authors, see Peter Berresford Ellis and Piers Williams, *By Jove, Biggles! The Life of Captain W. E. Johns* (London, 1981); Mary Cadogan, *Richmal Crompton: The Woman behind William* (London, 1984); Barbara Stoney, *The Enid Blyton Story* (London, 1992); Mark O'Hanlon, *Beyond the Lone Pine: A Biography of Malcolm Saville* (Worcester, 2001). On Arthur Ransome, see Christina Hardyment, *Arthur Ransome and Captain Flint's Trunk* (London, 1984); Hugh Brogan, *The Life of Arthur Ransome* (London, 1985).

54 Bernard T. Harrison, 'Books for Younger Readers', in Ford, ed., *From Orwell to Naipaul*, pp. 357–71.

55 See Timmins, *The Five Giants*, pp. 65–100.

56 Hennessy, *Never Again*, p. 158.

57 Davis, *Youth and the Condition of Britain*, p. 94.

58 Timmins, *The Five Giants*, p. 92.

59 McKibbin, *Classes and Cultures*, p. 226.

60 'Laura', in Landau, ed., *Growing Up in the Sixties*, p. 1.

61 Linda Shanovitch quoted in Akhtar and Humphries, *The Fifties and Sixties*, p. 26.

62 Gunn and Bell, *Middle Classes*, p. 167.

63 Butler, *The Art of the Possible*, pp. 124–5.

64 Laurie, *The Teenage Revolution*, p. 141.

65 Sampson, *Anatomy of Britain*, p. 184.

66 Barnett, *The Audit of War*, p. 302.

67 McKibbin, *Classes and Cultures*, p. 227.

68 Coates and Silburn, *Poverty*, pp. 122–4.

69 Jackson, *Working-Class Community*, pp. 150–1.

70 McKibbin, *Classes and Cultures*, pp. 264–5.

71 Jackson, *Working-Class Community*, pp. 152–3.

72 Gunn and Bell, *Middle Classes*, p. 167.

73 Timmins, *The Five Giants*, pp. 74–5.

74 Timmins, *The Five Giants*, pp. 95–6.

75 See Sampson, *Anatomy of Britain*, p. 175; Addison, *Now the War Is Over*, p. 169.

76 McKibbin, *Classes and Cultures*, pp. 35, 235.

77 Hopkins, *The New Look*, p. 172; McKibbin, *Classes and Cultures*, p. 238.

78 McKibbin, *Classes and Cultures*, p. 246.

79 McKibbin, *Classes and Cultures*, p. 246. On homosexuality in public schools, see Weeks, *Sex, Politics and Society*, p. 109.

80 Oldham, *Stoned*, p. 31.

81 Unknown interviewee quoted in Pressley, *Changing Times*, p. 57.

82 Sampson, *Anatomy of Britain*, p. 184.

83 McKibbin, *Classes and Cultures*, pp. 248–52.

84 Timmins, *The Five Giants*, p. 156.

85 Timmins, *The Five Giants*, pp. 156–7; McKibbin, *Classes and Cultures*, p. 258.

86 Timmins, *The Five Giants*, p. 157.

87 Hewison, *In Anger*, pp. 169–70.

88 Arthur Koestler, 'Introduction', in Koestler, ed., *Suicide of a Nation? An Enquiry Into the State of Britain Today* (London, 1963), p. 14.

89 *Daily Mirror*, 13 November 1963.

90 Jim Tomlinson, *The Politics of Decline: Understanding Post-war Britain* (Harlow, 2000), pp. 23–4.

91 Annan, *Our Age*, p. 501.

92 Ministry of Education, *Higher Education: Report*, 1963, p. 268, quoted in Davis, *Youth and the Condition of Britain*, p. 108.

93 Timmins, *The Five Giants*, pp. 200–3. The most conspicuous critic of the expansion drive, however, was the novelist Kingsley Amis, as will be discussed in the forthcoming sequel to this book.

94 Annan, *Our Age*, p. 501.

95 Annan, *Our Age*, p. 507.

96 Morgan, *The People's Peace*, pp. 233–5; Clarke, *Hope and Glory*, p. 288.

97 See Simon Frith and Howard Horne, *Art into Pop* (London, 1987), p. 29.

98 George Melly, *Revolt into Style* (reissued edition: Oxford, 1989), p. 146.

99 Pearce Marchbank quoted in Green, *Days in the Life*, pp. 32–3.

100 Quoted in Frith and Horne, *Art into Pop*, pp. 74–5.

101 Hewison, *Too Much*, p. 63; Frith and Horne, *Art into Pop*, pp. 74–5, 81; Marwick, *The Sixties*, p. 57. Pop musicians of the sixties who studied at art schools included John Lennon, Paul McCartney, Ray Davies, Keith Richards and Pete Townshend.

102 Mel Calman quoted in Abbott, *Family Affairs*, p. 106.

103 James, *Warrior Race*, p. 730.

104 See Trevor Royle, *The Best Years of their Lives: The National Service Experience 1945–63* (London, 1986): see also Weight, *Patriots*, pp. 307–11, a nice summary.

105 Quoted in Nicholas Crowson, 'Citizen Defence: The Conservative Party and its Attitude to National Service', in Richard Weight and Abigail Beach, eds, *The Right to Belong: Citizenship and National Identity in Britain* (London, 1998), p. 214.

106 T. B. Beveridge, *A Guide for the National Service Man* (London, 1953), pp. 10–11, quoted in Weight, *Patriots*, p. 309.

107 James, *Warrior Race*, p. 730.

108 Carpenter, *That Was Satire That Was*, pp. 32–3.

109 Adrian Walker, *Six Campaigns: National Servicemen on Active Service 1948–1960* (London, 1993), pp. 4, 26.

110 Royle, *The Best Years of their Lives*, p. 250.

111 Quoted in B. S. Johnson, *All Bull: The National Servicemen* (London, 1973), p. 257.

112 Royle, *The Best Years of their Lives*, p. 308.

113 Royle, *The Best Years of their Lives*, p. 307.

114 Walker, *Six Campaigns*, p. 47.

115 Royle, *The Best Years of their Lives*, p. 306.

116 CAB 129/86, 26 March 1957; Lamb, *The Macmillan Years*, pp. 282–3.

117 Carpenter, *That Was Satire That Was*, pp. 9, 33, 43.

118 David Lodge, *Ginger, You're Barmy* (London, 1962); Taylor, *After the War*, pp. 85–8.

119 See Petley, 'The Pilgrim's Regress', pp. 15–34, and Landy, 'Nation and Imagination in *Private's Progress*', pp. 175–88.

120 Murphy, *Sixties British Cinema*, p. 250.

121 Weight, *Patriots*, p. 311.

122 MacInnes, *Absolute Beginners*, p. 12.

123 Green, *All Dressed Up*, p. xi.

124 Marwick, *The Sixties*, p. 17.

125 Hobsbawm, *Interesting Times*, p. 224.

126 Green, *All Dressed Up*, p. xiii.

127 See the excellent discussion in Thomas Hine, *The Rise and Fall of the American Teenager* (New York, 2000).

128 See David Fowler, *The First Teenagers: The Lifestyle of Young Wage-Earners in Interwar Britain* (London, 1995), a very important work.

129 Marwick, *The Sixties*, pp. 41–2.

130 Akhtar and Humphries, *The Fifties and Sixties*, p. 44.

131 Laurie, *The Teenage Revolution*, p. 9.

132 Davis, *Youth and the Condition of Britain*, p. 170.

133 Marwick, *The Sixties*, pp. 43–4.

134 Mark Abrams, *The Teenage Consumer* (London, 1959), pp. 13–14.

135 Mark Abrams, *Teenage Consumer Spending in 1959* (London, 1961), pp. 4–5; Laurie, *The Teenage Revolution*, pp. 9–10.

136 Ministry of Education, *The Youth Service in England and Wales* (London, 1960), p. 24.

137 Abrams, *Teenage Consumer Spending in 1959*, pp. 4–5.

138 Abrams, *The Teenage Consumer*, p. 18.

139 Abrams, *Teenage Consumer Spending in 1959*, p. 5.

140 *Everybody's Weekly*, 3 July 1957.

141 Laurie, *The Teenage Revolution*, pp. 20–1.

142 Dave Gregory quoted in Akhtar and Humphries, *The Fifties and Sixties*, p. 44.

143 Faith, *Poor Me*, pp. 8–11. Adam Faith was, of course, born as Terry Nelhams.

144 Lawson, *Twiggy in Black and White*, pp. 37–8, 41. Twiggy Lawson, meanwhile, was born as Lesley Hornby.

145 Faith, *Poor Me*, p. 11.

146 Faith, *Poor Me*, p. 22.

147 Lawson, *Twiggy in Black and White*, p. 35.

148 Laurie, *The Teenage Revolution*, p. 151.

149 Unknown interviewee quoted in Pressley, *Changing Times*, p. 18.

150 Unknown interviewee quoted in Pressley, *Changing Times*, p. 43.

151 Lawson, *Twiggy in Black and White*, pp. 35–6.

152 Lawson, *Twiggy in Black and White*, p. 22.

153 Faith, *Poor Me*, p. 10.

154 *Daily Mail*, 1 April 1957.

155 MacInnes, *Absolute Beginners*, p. 38.

156 Davis, *Youth and the Condition of Britain*, p. 121.

157 Benson, *The Rise of Consumer Society*, ch. 7; Blake, 'Popular Music since the 1950s', pp. 232–3.

158 Quoted in Laurie, *The Teenage Revolution*, p. 18.

159 Weight, *Patriots*, p. 301.

160 Davis, *Youth and the Condition of Britain*, pp. 47–9.

161 Davis, *Youth and the Condition of Britain*, p. 44.

162 David Hughes, 'The Spivs', in Sissons and French, eds, *Age of Austerity*, pp. 84–5.

163 Wain, *Hurry On Down*, p. 179.

164 Nik Cohn, *Today There Are No Gentlemen* (London, 1971), pp. 29–30.

165 Hopkins, *The New Look*, p. 427.

166 Rock and Cohen, 'The Teddy Boy', pp. 289–90.

167 Rock and Cohen, 'The Teddy Boy', pp. 294–5.

168 Hopkins, *The New Look*, p. 428; Cohn, *Today There Are No Gentlemen*, p. 30.

169 *Daily Express*, 12 May 1954.

170 *Daily Mirror*, 28 October 1953; see also Rock and Cohen, 'The Teddy Boy', pp. 290–1.

171 See Rock and Cohen, 'The Teddy Boy', pp. 288–318; Cohen, *Folk Devils and Moral Panics*.

172 *Daily Mail*, 26 April 1954, quoted in Rock and Cohen, 'The Teddy Boy', p. 296.

173 Mick Johns quoted in Akhtar and Humphries, *The Fifties and Sixties*, p. 41.

174 Ray Pratt quoted in Akhtar and Humphries, *The Fifties and Sixties*, p. 41.

175 *Evening News*, 12 May 1954, quoted in Rock and Cohen, 'The Teddy Boy', p. 301.

176 Cohn, *Today There Are No Gentlemen*, p. 28.

177 Green, *All Dressed Up*, p. 5.

178 See Green, *All Dressed Up*, pp. 5–12.

179 The names mean, respectively, 'Half-Strong', 'Leather Jackets', 'Blackshirts' and 'Style Boys': Lewis, *The Fifties*, p. 118.

180 Davis, *Youth and the Condition of Britain*, p. 143.

181 Robert Roberts, *The Classic Slum: Salford Life in the First Quarter of the Century* (Harmondsworth, 1973), pp. 155–6; Davis, *Youth and the Condition of Britain*, p. 44.

182 Geoffrey Pearson, *Hooligan: A History of Respectable Fears* (London, 1983), p. 202.

183 Rock and Cohen, 'The Teddy Boy', pp. 308–9.

184 Green, *All Dressed Up*, p. 11.

185 Davis, *Youth and the Condition of Britain*, pp. 147, 164.

186 Davis, *Youth and the Condition of Britain*, p. 151.

187 Lewis, *The Fifties*, p. 118.

188 Montgomery, *The Fifties*, p. 173.

189 Marwick, *British Society since 1945*, p. 148.

190 Marwick, *British Society since 1945*, p. 149.

191 *The Times*, 13 September 1956.

192 Lewis, *The Fifties*, p. 129.

193 Davis, *Youth and the Condition of Britain*, pp. 147, 152–4.

194 *Daily Mirror*, 13 September 1958.

195 *Daily Mirror*, 6 March 1959. See Davis, *Youth and the Condition of Britain*, pp. 152–4.

196 Durgnat, *A Mirror for England*, pp. 58–60.

197 Hill, *Sex, Class and Realism*, pp. 108–9; Murphy, *Sixties British Cinema*, pp. 131–3.

198 Hill, *Sex, Class and Realism*, pp. 80–1.

199 Hill, *Sex, Class and Realism*, p. 82.

200 Howard, *RAB*, pp. 261–2.

201 Howard, *RAB*, p. 264.

202 Home Office, *Penal Practice in a Changing Society* (London, 1959); Andrew Gamble, *The Conservative Nation* (London, 1974), p. 82.

203 Weight, *Patriots*, pp. 313–14.

204 *Daily Express*, 16 November 1960, quoted in Marwick, *The Sixties*, p. 62.

205 Durgnat, *A Mirror for England*, p. 137.

206 Ministry of Education, *The Youth Service in England and Wales* (London, 1960). See also Mark K. Smith, 'The Albemarle Report and the Development of Youth Work in England and Wales', *The Encyclopedia of Informal Education*, July 2002, online at <http://www.infed.org/youthwork/albemarle_report.htm>.

207 Ministry of Education, *The Youth Service in England and Wales*, pp. 15, 53.

208 Ministry of Education, *The Youth Service in England and Wales*, p. 17.

209 Ministry of Education, *The Youth Service in England and Wales*, p. 61.

210 *Daily Mirror*, 4 February 1960, quoted in Davis, *Youth and the Condition of Britain*, p. 110.

211 See Smith, 'The Albemarle Report and the Development of Youth Work in England and Wales'.

212 Laurie, *The Teenage Revolution*, pp. 43–4.

213 Ministry of Education, *The Youth Service in England and Wales*, p. 33.

214 Davis, *Youth and the Condition of Britain*, p. 129; Steven Fielding, *The Labour Governments 1964–1970: Volume 1: Labour and Cultural Change* (Manchester, 2003), pp. 182–5.

215 Marwick, *The Sixties*, p. 55. John Davis argues that young people have, since 1945, always been presented by the contemporary media and even by many historians as much more iconoclastic than they actually are: see Davis, *Youth and the Condition of Britain*.

216 *Daily Herald*, 5 October 1954.

217 *The Times*, 26 May 1956.

218 Abrams, *Must Labour Lose?*, p. 58.

219 Ministry of Education, *The Youth Service in England and Wales*, pp. 32–3.

220 Laurie, *The Teenage Revolution*, p. 110.

221 *Observer*, 22 September 1963.

222 Frank Musgrove, *Youth and the Social Order* (London, 1964), pp. 21–2.

223 Zweig, *The Student in an Age of Anxiety*, pp. 200–1.

224 Jackson, *Working-Class Community*, pp. 22, 34–35.

225 Quoted in Davis, *Youth and the Condition of Britain*, p. 157.

226 *Daily Mirror*, 15 September 1958.

227 Ministry of Education, *The Youth Service in England and Wales*, p. 15.
228 See Gorer, *Exploring English Character*; Michael Schofield, *The Sexual Behaviour of Young People* (London, 1965); and Geoffrey Gorer, *Sex and Marriage in England Today* (London, 1971). There will be more on this in the sequel to this book.
229 Laurie, *The Teenage Revolution*, p. 114.
230 See Cohen, *Folk Devils and Moral Panics*.
231 Blake, 'Popular Music since the 1950s', p. 232.
232 Quoted in Hill, *Sex, Class and Realism*, p. 11.
233 Laurie, *The Teenage Revolution*, p. 20.
234 Home Office, *Report of the Committee on Children and Young Persons* (London, 1960), pp. 7–8.
235 Iain Chambers, *Popular Culture: The Metropolitan Experience* (London, 1986), pp. 41–2.

CHAPTER 13: ROCK AND ROLL BABIES

1 *Independent on Sunday*, 6 August 2000.
2 The foxtrot is a good example. See Iain Chambers, *Popular Culture: The Metropolitan Experience* (London, 1986), p. 124.
3 Not everybody was impressed by the contributions of the new American composers. During the war it became apparent that Winston Churchill had never heard of Irving Berlin and indeed believed him to be the philosopher Isaiah Berlin, despite having met the latter on a previous occasion. See Colls, *Identity of England*, p. 188.
4 McKibbin, *Classes and Cultures*, p. 390.
5 Bergonzi, *Wartime and Aftermath*, p. 168; Bleil, Driver and Sarnaker, 'Popular Music in Britain, 1930–1955', p. 220.
6 Blake, 'Popular Music since the 1950s', pp. 225–6.
7 Addison, *Now the War Is Over*, pp. 128–9; Iain Chambers, *Urban Rhythms: Pop Music and Popular Culture* (Basingstoke, 1985), p. 42.
8 Graham Bell quoted in Akhtar and Humphries, *The Fifties and Sixties*, p. 36. See also the description of a South Wales dance hall poised between British conservatism and American enthusiasm in Amis, *That Uncertain Feeling*, pp. 85–6.
9 Blake, 'Popular Music since the 1950s', p. 224.
10 Hennessy, *Never Again*, p. 447.
11 Davis, *Youth and the Condition of Britain* p. 166.
12 McKibbin, *Classes and Cultures*, pp. 411–12.
13 *Daily Mirror*, 11 May 1954.
14 On the *NME* chart, see the obituaries of Percy Dickins in the *Guardian*, 19 February 2002, and the *Independent*, 5 March 2002. There were of course several competing charts during this period: for example, *Melody Maker*, *Record Retailer*, *Record Mirror* and *Music Week* all ran charts of their own, and there were often slight differences between them. Since different writers use different charts, rarely acknowledging their exact sources, it is a sad fact that consistent and definitive statistics are not really available.

15 Oldham, *Stoned*, p. 17.

16 Alma Cogan had no fewer than twenty-one hits between 1954 and 1961, but only one number one. See Bleil, Driver and Sarnaker, 'Popular Music in Britain, 1930–1955', pp. 228–9; McKibbin, *Classes and Cultures*, p. 416.

17 James Miller, *Flowers in the Dustbin: The Rise of Rock and Roll, 1947–1977* (New York, 1999), pp. 34–9, 72.

18 Charlie Gillett, *The Sound of the City: The Rise of Rock and Roll* (revised edition: London, 1983), pp. 1–15; Miller, *Flowers in the Dustbin*, pp. 83–6.

19 Miller, *Flowers in the Dustbin*, p. 151.

20 Bill Haley overcomes parental fears by playing rock and roll music at a dance, whereupon the teenage audience fails to riot. Alan Freed, incidentally, plays a moralistic disc jockey who explains that the purpose of rock and roll is to prevent children from turning into delinquents. See Miller, *Flowers in the Dustbin*, pp. 87–93.

21 Oldham, *Stoned*, pp. 28–9.

22 Dave Palmer quoted in Akhtar and Humphries, *The Fifties and Sixties*, pp. 42–3. For the Croydon incident, see Ian Whitcomb, *After the Ball* (New York, 1972), pp. 225–8.

23 Davis, *Youth and the Condition of Britain*, p. 161.

24 Oldham, *Stoned*, p. 29.

25 Philip Norman, *Shout! The True Story of the Beatles* (London, 1981), p. 21.

26 *Melody Maker*, 5 May 1956.

27 *Daily Mail*, 4 September 1956.

28 *Daily Mail*, 5 September 1956.

29 *The Times*, 13 September 1956.

30 *Melody Maker*, 10 October 1956.

31 Elsie Murphy quoted in Akhtar and Humphries, *The Fifties and Sixties*, p. 42.

32 Norman, *Shout!*, p. 21.

33 McKibbin, *Classes and Cultures*, p. 412.

34 *Independent*, 5 March 2002.

35 Kinn quoted in Oldham, *Stoned*, p. 21.

36 *New Musical Express*, 24 February 1956.

37 McKibbin, *Classes and Cultures*, p. 412.

38 Davis, *Youth and the Condition of Britain*, p. 166.

39 Paul Griffiths, 'Music', in Boris Ford, ed., *The Cambridge Cultural History of Britain, Volume 9: Modern Britain* (London, 1992), p. 49.

40 Ian MacDonald, *The People's Music* (London, 2003), pp. 71–2, 197–8.

41 McKibbin, *Classes and Cultures*, p. 458; Hopkins, *The New Look*, pp. 431–2.

42 Briggs, *The History of Broadcasting in the United Kingdom: Volume V*, pp. 509–11.

43 See 'Radio Luxembourg,' in Colin Larkin, ed., *The Virgin Encyclopedia of Sixties Music* (London, 1997), p. 364.

44 Unknown interviewee quoted in Pressley, *Changing Times*, p. 39.

45 John Hill, 'Television and Pop: The Case of the 1950s', in Corner, ed., *Popular Television in Britain*, p. 92; Briggs, *The History of Broadcasting in the United Kingdom: Volume V*, pp. 202–3; on the heterogeneity of the acts, see Clayson, *Beat Merchants*, p. 29.

46 *Birmingham Mail*, 18 February 1957, quoted in Hill, 'Television and Pop', p. 92.

47 See Eddi Fiegel, *John Barry: A Sixties Theme* (London, 1998), pp. 53–5.

48 *Cornish Guardian*, 6 February 1958, quoted in Briggs, *The History of Broadcasting in the United Kingdom: Volume V*, p. 509.

49 Briggs, *The History of Broadcasting in the United Kingdom: Volume V*, p. 204.

50 Hill, 'Television and Pop', pp. 96–100.

51 *Reynolds News*, 28 January 1962; Hill, 'Television and Pop', pp. 101–3; Briggs, *The History of Broadcasting in the United Kingdom: Volume V*, pp. 206–9.

52 Amis, *Lucky Jim*, p. 227.

53 Colls, *Identity of England*, pp. 358–71.

54 Tony Bacon, *London Live: From the Yardbirds to Pink Floyd to the Sex Pistols* (London, 1999), p. 40.

55 See Ewan MacColl and Peggy Seeger, eds, *The Singing Island* (New York, 1960).

56 R. Vaughan Williams and A. L. Lloyd, eds, *The Penguin Book of English Folk Songs* (Harmondsworth, 1959), p. 7.

57 *Melody Maker*, 10 June 1961; see also Bacon, *London Live*, p. 41; Colls, *Identity of England*, p. 368.

58 MacDonald, *The People's Music*, p. 194.

59 Weight, *Patriots*, p. 159.

60 Tony Palmer, *All You Need Is Love: The Story of Popular Music* (London, 1976) pp. 212–13; Chas McDevitt, *Skiffle: The Definitive Inside Story* (London, 1997); Mike Dewe, *The Skiffle Craze* (London, 1998).

61 Quoted in Peter Leslie, *Fab: The Anatomy of a Phenomenon* (London, 1965), p. 67.

62 *Jazz Journal*, July 1953, quoted in Bacon, *London Live*, p. 24.

63 Spencer Leigh, *Puttin' On the Style: The Lonnie Donegan Story* (London, 2003); Bruce Eder, 'Skiffle', at <http://www.allmusic.com>; *Independent*, 5 November 2002; Philip Norman, *The Stones* (London, 1993), p. 31.

64 Melly, *Revolt into Style*, p. 26.

65 Gillett, *The Sound of the City*, p. 259; Clayson, *Beat Merchants*, p. 31.

66 *Picturegoer*, 1 September 1956, quoted in Clayson, *Beat Merchants*, p. 30.

67 Palmer, *All You Need Is Love*, p. 213.

68 Leslie, *Fab*, p. 72.

69 Melly, *Revolt into Style*, p. 27.

70 Melly, *Revolt into Style*, p. 26; Hopkins, *The New Look*, p. 434.

71 For the transition from professionals to amateurs, see MacDonald, *The People's Music*, pp. 192–209.

72 Hopkins, *The New Look*, p. 433.

73 Hopkins, *The New Look*, p. 434.

74 Clayson, *Beat Merchants*, pp. 33–5.

75 Bacon, *London Live*, p. 25; Clayson, *Beat Merchants*, p. 35.

76 Clayson, *Beat Merchants*, p. 36.

77 Faith, *Poor Me*, pp. 14–15.

78 Norman, *Shout!*, pp. 21–6.

79 Norman, *The Stones*, pp. 33–4.

80 Clayson, *Beat Merchants*, p. 31; Bacon, *London Live*, p. 26.

81 *Daily Mail*, 1 April 1957.

82 Bacon, *London Live*, pp. 22–5; Faith, *Poor Me*, pp. 16–17.

83 Faith, *Poor Me*, p. 16.

84 Hill, 'Television and Pop', pp. 95–6; Bacon, *London Live*, pp. 8, 29.

85 Norman, *Shout!*, p. 38; Clayson, *Beat Merchants*, p. 42.

86 Pete King quoted in Oldham, *Stoned*, p. 106.

87 Oldham, *Stoned*, p. 25.

88 Melly, *Revolt into Style*, p. 2.

89 Maureen Cleave quoted in Pressley, *Changing Times*, p. 32.

90 *Encounter*, December 1957.

91 *Melody Maker*, 31 May 1958.

92 Melly, *Revolt into Style*, pp. 53–4; Clayson, *Beat Merchants*, p. 40. On Parnes, see Johnny Rogan, *Starmakers and Svengalis: The History of British Pop Management* (London, 1988).

93 'Billy Fury', in Larkin, ed., *The Virgin Encyclopedia of Sixties Music*, p. 207; Clayson, *Beat Merchants*, p. 41.

94 Clayson, *Beat Merchants*, p. 41.

95 Reviews in *New Musical Express* and *Daily Sketch* quoted in 'Cliff Richard', in Larkin, ed., *The Virgin Encyclopedia of Sixties Music*, p. 373; and Oldham, *Stoned*, p. 35.

96 Melly, *Revolt into Style*, pp. 56–7.

97 See Steve Turner, *Cliff Richard: The Biography* (London, 1998).

98 The name Adam Faith was a conflation of the names of two of Good's old friends from Oxford. Faith owed a lot to the Oxford connection: he had been originally discovered by the producer Nick Dewey, another university friend of Good's and a Balliol man. See the *Independent*, 18 March 2003.

99 Leslie, *Fab*, p. 80.

100 Faith, *Poor Me*, pp. 25–47; Fiegel, *John Barry*, pp. 65–9.

101 *Independent*, 10 March 2003. His last words, spoken on his deathbed in 2003, were remarkably similar, and no less accurate: 'Channel Five: it's all shit, isn't it? Christ, the crap they put on there, it's a waste of space.'

102 Faith, *Poor Me*, pp. 59–76; *Independent*, 10 March 2003.

103 *Encounter*, December 1957.

104 Leslie, *Fab*, pp. 77–8; Melly, *Revolt into Style*, p. 50; Bacon, *London Live*, p. 33.

105 *Encounter*, December 1957.

106 *Daily Mirror*, 6 April 1959.

107 Clayson, *Beat Merchants*, p. 25; Davis, *Youth and the Condition of Britain*, p. 166.

108 Melly, *Revolt into Style*, pp. 50, 56–8.

109 Faith, *Poor Me*, pp. 45–6, 79–81.

110 See Blake, 'Popular Music since the 1950s', p. 227; Melly, *Revolt into Style*, pp. 56–7; Clayson, *Beat Merchants*, p. 46; Davis, *Youth and the Condition of Britain*, p. 165.

111 Norman, *Shout!*, pp. 132–6.

112 Matthew, *Trad Mad*, pp. 7–8.

113 Matthew, *Trad Mad*, pp. 5–6.

114 Addison, *Now the War Is Over*, pp. 136–7; Melly, *Revolt into Style*, pp. 22–3; Hewison, *Too Much*, p. 62.

115 Addison, *Now the War is Over*, pp. 136–7.

116 Francis Newton, *The Jazz Scene* (London, 1959), p. 247. Hobsbawm reflects on his jazz interests in his memoir *Interesting Times*, pp. 225–7.

117 Jackson, *Working Class Community*, pp. 127–35.

118 Carpenter, *The Angry Young Men*, p. 8.

119 Addison, *Now the War Is Over*, p. 138.

120 Newton, *The Jazz Scene*, p. 232; see also Gillett, *The Sound of the City*, pp. 258–9; Jim Goldbolt, *A History of Jazz in Britain, 1919–50* (London, 1984), esp. ch. 12. To make matters more complicated, within the anti-modernist camp a further internal split divided 'trad' enthusiasts, who liked the Dixieland jazz of the 1900s, from 'revivalists', who preferred the Chicago music of the 1920s. The distinction between trad and revivalist jazz was a pretty obscure and complicated one, and most casual listeners assumed that trad and revivalism were effectively the same thing. In what follows, I treat trad and revivalist jazz as a single phenomenon. For more on this, see Chambers, *Urban Rhythms*, p. 48.

121 Addison, *Now the War Is Over*, p. 138; Humphrey Lyttelton, *I Play as I Please* (London, 1954), pp. 116–25.

122 Bacon, *London Live*, pp. 13–21.

123 Bacon, *London Live*, p. 20; and see John Fordham, *Jazz Man: The Amazing Story of Ronnie Scott and his Club* (London, 1995).

124 *Melody Maker*, 29 July 1950.

125 Peter Maguire, 'What Did You Do in the Great Trad War, Daddy?', *European Cultural Digest*, October 1998, online at <http://www.europeandigest.com/ecd04/docs/digest06.htm>. On Lyttelton's background, see Peter Alex, *Who's Who in Pop Radio* (London, 1966).

126 Melly, *Revolt into Style*, p. 35.

127 See Bacon, *London Live*, p. 36.

128 Although it is worth noting that Chris Barber's Jazz Band had reached the Top Ten in 1959 with 'Petite Fleur', the first time that a trad band recorded a significant chart hit.

129 Matthew, *Trad Mad*, pp. 30–1.

130 See 'Kenny Ball' and 'The Temperance Seven', in Larkin, ed., *The Virgin Encyclopedia of Sixties Music*, pp. 29, 437.

131 On Bilk's publicity, see Leslie, *Fab*, pp. 105–12, written by the mastermind behind it.

132 Melly, *Revolt into Style*, p. 61; and see Newton, *The Jazz Scene*, p. 223.

133 Hylton, *Magical History Tour*, p. 48; see also 'Acker Bilk', in Larkin, ed., *The Virgin Encyclopedia of Sixties Music*, p. 56.

134 Lewis, *The Fifties*, p. 140.

135 Melly, *Revolt into Style*, pp. 67–8.

136 Ian Campbell, 'Music against the Bomb', in Minnion and Bolsover, eds, *The CND Story*, p. 115; Hewison, *In Anger*, p. 165; Bacon, *London Live*, p. 16.

137 Quoted in Leslie, *Fab*, p. 124.

138 Matthew, *Trad Mad*, pp. 113–16; Murphy, *Sixties British Cinema*, p. 135.

139 Matthew, *Trad Mad*, p. 76.

140 Matthew, *Trad Mad*, p. 82.

141 Matthew, *Trad Mad*, pp. 122–3, 128.

142 Norman, *Shout!*, pp. 71–7. There are hundreds, if not thousands of books on the Beatles, and dozens of erroneous anecdotes and myths have accumulated over the years. The most reliable authorities seem to be Norman, *Shout!*; Mark Lewisohn, *The Complete Beatles Chronicle* (London, 1992); and Ian MacDonald, *Revolution in the Head* (revised edition: London, 1997). The best and most informative of the individual biographies, meanwhile, is Barry Miles, *Paul McCartney: Many Years from Now* (London, 1997), which benefits from Miles' extensive interviews with his subject.

143 Norman, *Shout!*, p. 5.

144 Norman, *Shout!*, p. 6.

145 Quoted in Miles, *Paul McCartney*, p. 44.

146 Norman, *Shout!*, pp. 40–3.

147 McCartney quoted in Miles, *Paul McCartney*, p. 15.

148 McCartney quoted in Miles, *Paul McCartney*, pp. 12–14; Norman, *Shout!*, pp. 15–16.

149 Norman, *Shout!*, pp. 11–12, 20–3, 27–8.

150 Norman, *Shout!*, p. 24; Gillett, *The Sound of the City*, p. 263.

151 Norman, *Shout!*, pp. 30–2; Miles, *Paul McCartney*, pp. 25–9.

152 Norman, *Shout!*, pp. 32–3.

153 Norman, *Shout!*, p. 49.

154 See Norman, *Shout!*, pp. 39–54.

155 Norman, *Shout!*, pp. 57–64; MacDonald, *Revolution in the Head*, pp. 344–6.

156 Clayson, *Beat Merchants*, pp. 74, 82.

157 Clayson, *Beat Merchants*, pp. 73–5.

158 Norman, *Shout!*, pp. 78–80.

159 Norman, *Shout!*, pp. 78–93; Miles, *Paul McCartney*, pp. 58–73.

160 Norman, *Shout!*, p. 81.

161 MacDonald, *Revolution in the Head*, p. 43.

162 Miles, *Paul McCartney*, pp. 63–5, 76–8; Norman, *Shout!*, p. 90.

163 Quoted in Clayson, *Beat Merchants*, p. 99.

164 Norman, *Shout!*, p. 108; Clayson, *Beat Merchants*, p. 101; Miller, *Flowers in the Dustbin*, pp. 180–1; and see also Spencer Leigh and Pete Frame, *Let's Go Down the Cavern* (London, 1984).

165 See 'The Cavern', in Larkin, ed., *The Virgin Encyclopedia of Sixties Music*, p. 101.

166 Norman, *Shout!*, pp. 110–12.

167 As argued by almost every writer who discusses the Beatles, with the notable exceptions of Alan Clayson and Ian MacDonald.

168 Chambers, *Urban Rhythms*, p. 61.

169 See Clayson, *Beat Merchants*, pp. 60–1.

170 Clayson, *Beat Merchants*, pp. 58–9, 88.

171 Clayson, *Beat Merchants*, p. 101.

172 Lawton, *1963*, p. 96; Norman, *Shout!*, pp. 99–102; Miles, *Paul McCartney*, p. 80.

173 *Mersey Beat*, 31 August 1961, quoted in Norman, *Shout!*, p. 111.

174 Peter Brown and Steven Gaines, *The Love You Make: An Insider's Story of the Beatles* (London, 1983), pp. 55ff.

175 See Ray Coleman, *The Man Who Made the Beatles: An Intimate Biography of Brian Epstein* (London, 1989).

176 Brian Epstein and Derek Taylor, *A Cellarful of Noise* (London, 1964), pp. 46–7; Norman, *Shout!*, p. 125.

177 Miles, *Paul McCartney*, p. 85.

178 Epstein interviewed on BBC Radio, 1964, transcribed in Lewisohn, *The Complete Beatles Chronicle*.

179 Miller, *Flowers in the Dustbin*, p. 183.

180 Norman, *Shout!*, pp. 130–1; Miles, *Paul McCartney*, p. 88.

181 Miles, *Paul McCartney*, p. 84; Miller, *Flowers in the Dustbin*, pp. 182–3.

182 Norman, *Shout!*, p. 137; Levy, *Ready, Steady, Go*, pp. 86–7.

183 Reprinted in Lewisohn, *The Complete Beatles Chronicle*, p. 54.

184 *Mersey Beat*, 4 January 1962, quoted in Norman, *Shout!*, p. 134.

185 *Mersey Beat*, 15 February 1962, quoted in Clayson, *Beat Merchants*, p. 104.

186 Levy, *Ready, Steady, Go*, p. 75.

187 MacDonald, *Revolution in the Head*, p. 47.

188 Norman, *Shout!*, pp. 134–6.

189 Clayson, *Beat Merchants*, pp. 95–6.

190 See Clayson, *Beat Merchants*, p. 98.

191 Norman, *Shout!*, p. 112.

192 Lewisohn, *The Complete Beatles Chronicle*, p. 53.

193 Quoted in Norman, *Shout!*, p. 143.

194 Norman, *Shout!*, p. 145.

195 See George Martin with Jeremy Hornsby, *All You Need Is Ears* (London, 1979).

196 Martin with Hornsby, *All You Need Is Ears*, pp. 120–32; Norman, *Shout!*, p. 144.

197 MacDonald, *Revolution in the Head*, pp. 49–50.

198 Martin with Hornsby, *All You Need Is Ears*, pp. 120ff; Norman, *Shout!*, p. 147.

199 Norman, *Shout!*, pp. 98, 148.

200 Norman, *Shout!*, pp. 150–1.

201 Norman, *Shout!*, p. 154.

202 For a sympathetic biography, see Alan Clayson, *Ringo Starr: Straight Man or Joker?* (London, 1991).

203 *New Musical Express*, 15 February 1963.

204 Al Aronowitz, 'The Beatles: Music's Gold Bugs', *Saturday Evening Post*, March 1964, online at <www.rocksbackpages.com>.

205 See MacDonald, *Revolution in the Head*, p. 84; MacDonald, *The People's Music*, pp. 43–6. For Martin's plan to make McCartney 'leader', see Norman, *Shout!*, p. 148.

206 Miles, *Paul McCartney*, p. 67.

207 McCartney quoted in Miles, *Paul McCartney*, p. 31.

208 McCartney quoted in Miles, *Paul McCartney*, p. 36.

209 Lewisohn, *The Complete Beatles Chronicle*, pp. 361–5.

210 McCartney quoted in Miles, *Paul McCartney*, p. 37.

211 MacDonald, *Revolution in the Head*, pp. 68–9.

212 *New Musical Express*, 4 January 1963.

213 See George Thomson Geddes, *The Shadows: A History and Discography* (Glasgow, 1981). For a good example of a writer dismissing the Shadows, see Lawton, *1963*, p. 90.

214 Although, as Charlie Gillett points out, historians often overlook the impact of Johnny Kidd and the Pirates, whose breakthrough single 'Shakin' All Over' (1960) was one of the first British releases in which a driving guitar rhythm effectively carried the song. See Gillett, *The Sound of the City*, p. 256.

215 Clayson, *Beat Merchants*, p. 55; Fiegel, *John Barry*, p. 59.

216 MacDonald, *Revolution in the Head*, pp. 51–3.

217 Norman, *Shout!*, p. 157.

218 Norman, *Shout!*, pp 159–60; MacDonald, *Revolution in the Head*, p. 53.

219 Norman, *Shout!*, p. 161; MacDonald, *Revolution in the Head*, p. 56.

220 MacDonald, *Revolution in the Head*, pp. 47, 56.

221 Norman, *Shout!*, p. 168.

222 MacDonald, *The People's Music*, p. 44.

223 MacDonald, *Revolution in the Head*, pp. xii, 94–5.

224 McCartney later recalled: 'I arrived at the meeting to find that Brian [Epstein] and John had already independently decided that the billing would be "songs by John Lennon and Paul McCartney". I said, "What about McCartney–Lennon?" They said, "We'll do this for now and we can change it around to be fair at any point in the future."' See 'Sir Paul defends Credit Switch', online at <http://news.bbc.co.uk/1/hi/entertainment/music/2588347.stm>, 19 December 2002; MacDonald, *The People's Music*, pp. 43–6.

225 See Lewisohn, *The Complete Beatles Chronicle*, pp. 88–135.

226 *Evening Standard*, 26 January 1963.

227 Norman, *Shout!*, pp. 184–5.

228 *Daily Mirror*, 21 June 1963; Norman, *Shout!*, p. 176; Lawton, *1963*, p. 106.

229 See Gillett, *The Sound of the City*, pp. 264–5; Jeffrey Richards, *Films and British National Identity* (Manchester, 1997), pp. 255–8.

230 *Daily Mirror*, 10 September 1963.

231 *Evening Standard*, 17 October 1963.

232 Melly, *Revolt into Style*, p. 73.

233 *Sunday Express*, 20 October 1963.

234 Quoted in Norman, *Shout!*, p. 185.

235 *Evening Standard*, 26 January 1963.

236 'Frank Ifield', in Larkin, ed., *The Virgin Encyclopedia of Sixties Music*, p. 244.

237 *Daily Mirror*, 2 October 1963.

238 Davis, *Youth and the Condition of Britain*, p. 166; Norman, *Shout!*, p. 182.

239 Booker, *The Neophiliacs*, p. 233.

240 See Leslie, *Fab*, p. 92.

241 *New Musical Express*, 15 February 1963.

242 MacDonald, *The People's Music*, p. 192.

243 *New Musical Express*, 4 January 1963.

244 *New Musical Express*, 5 April 1963.

245 *Daily Mirror*, 7 February 1964.

246 *Daily Mirror*, 2 November 1963.

247 *Melody Maker*, 7 May 1963.

248 *Disc*, 24 November 1962, quoted in Clayson, *Beat Merchants*, p. 106.

249 Clayson, *Beat Merchants*, pp. 119–22.

250 Clayson, *Beat Merchants*, p. 125.

251 Norman, *Shout!*, p. 177.

252 Norman, *Shout!*, p. 176.

253 Hewison, *Too Much*, pp. 67–9.

254 McCartney quoted in Miles, *Paul McCartney*, p. 161.

255 McCartney quoted in Miles, *Paul McCartney*, p. 150.

256 MacDonald, *Revolution in the Head*, pp. 73–6.

CHAPTER 14: LIVE NOW, PAY LATER

1 Horne, *Macmillan 1957–1986*, pp. 351–2.

2 Butler, *The Art of the Possible*, p. 232.

3 PREM 5/374, Bligh to Macmillan, 19 April 1962.

4 Douglas Jay, *Change and Fortune: A Political Record* (London, 1980), p. 324; Dell, *The Chancellors*, p. 283.

5 Holt, *Second Amongst Equals*, p. 103.

6 Watkins, *A Short Walk down Fleet Street*, pp. 136–7.

7 Maudling, *Memoirs*, pp. 21, 24, 27.

8 Maudling, *Memoirs*, p. 31.

9 Anthony Howard and Richard West, *The Making of the Prime Minister* (London, 1965), p. 55.

10 Maudling, *Memoirs*, p. 103.

11 Brittan, *The Treasury under the Tories*, pp. 254–9; Maudling, *Memoirs*, pp. 102–5; Dell, *The Chancellors*, pp. 290–1.

12 Quoted in Lamb, *The Macmillan Years*, p. 92.

13 PREM 11/4202, Macmillan to Maudling, 26 February 1963.

14 Maudling, *Memoirs*, pp. 105–22; Lamb, *The Macmillan Years*, pp. 94–5.

15 Maudling, *Memoirs*, p. 112.

16 Dell, *The Chancellors*, p. 292.

17 Hansard, 3 April 1963.

18 Maudling, *Memoirs*, p. 113.

19 Hansard, 4 April and 8 April 1963, quoted in Dell, *The Chancellors*, p. 294.

20 Pinto-Duschinsky, 'Bread and Circuses?', p. 55; Brittan, *The Treasury under the Tories*, pp. 273–5, 280–2.

21 Pinto-Duschinsky, 'From Macmillan to Home, 1959–1964', p. 156; Eric Hobsbawm cited in Lacey, *British Realist Theatre*, p. 10.

22 *New Statesman*, 2 January 1960.

23 *Guardian*, 19 December 1962.

24 Shanks, *The Stagnant Society*, p. 174.

25 Williams, *Hugh Gaitskell*, p. 384.

26 Jefferys, *Retreat from New Jerusalem*, pp. 198–9.

27 Quoted in Gamble, *The Conservative Nation*, p. 78.

28 See Walker, *Hollywood, England*, pp. 168–9.

29 Lamb, *The Macmillan Years*, pp. 100–1; Dell, *The Chancellors*, pp. 297–9.

30 Hansard, 14 April 1964.

31 Dell, *The Chancellors*, pp. 300–2; Kenneth O. Morgan, *Callaghan: A Life* (Oxford, 1997), pp. 203–5.

32 Maudling, *Memoirs*, p. 116.

33 Maudling, *Memoirs*, pp. 111–18; Holt, *Second Amongst Equals*, pp. 154, 206–7.

34 Cairncross quoted in Dell, *The Chancellors*, p. 302.

35 Dell, *The Chancellors*, p. 303.

36 Dell, *The Chancellors*, p. 292.

37 Pinto-Duschinsky, 'From Macmillan to Home, 1959–1964', pp. 154–5.

38 Pinto-Duschinsky, 'Bread and Circuses?', p. 57; Oppenheimer, 'Muddling Through: The Economy, 1959–1964', p. 139.

39 Oppenheimer, 'Muddling Through: The Economy, 1959–1964', p. 147; see also Wright, *Britain in the Age of Economic Management*, p. 21; Jefferys, *Retreat from New Jerusalem*, p. 111.

40 Pinto-Duschinsky, 'Bread and Circuses?', p. 57.

41 PREM 11/3287, Harrod to Macmillan, 11 October 1961.

42 See Wright, *Britain in the Age of Economic Management*, pp. 62–3; Hennessy, *Never Again*, p. 99.

43 Pinto-Duschinsky, 'Bread and Circuses?', p. 57; Alan S. Milward, *The European Rescue of the Nation State* (London, 1992), p. 128.

44 Childs, *Britain since 1945*, p. 100. By 1976 the British share would have shrunk still further to a paltry 9 per cent.

45 On the 'ideology of declinism' that became fashionable in the late fifties, see Jim Tomlinson, *The Politics of Decline: Understanding Post-war Britain* (Harlow, 2000), pp. 1–29.

46 Sampson, *Anatomy of Britain*, p. 568; Oppenheimer, 'Muddling Through: The Economy, 1959–1964', p. 144; Childs, *Britain since 1945*, p. 103.

47 Oppenheimer, 'Muddling Through: The Economy, 1959–1964', p. 144.

48 Dell, *A Strange Eventful History*, pp. 152–3; see also Dell, *Political Responsibility and Industry* (London, 1973), passim; Marwick, *British Society since 1945*, p. 28.

49 Gamble, *Britain in Decline*, pp. 115, 118.

50 Gamble, *Britain in Decline*, p. 112; Wright, *Britain in the Age of Economic Management*, p. 148.

51 Quoted in Peter Clarke, 'The Keynesian Consensus and its Enemies', in Marquand and Seldon, eds, *The Ideas That Shaped Post-War Britain*, p. 84.

52 Skidelsky, 'The Fall of Keynesianism', p. 51.

53 Pinto-Duschinsky, 'Bread and Circuses?', p. 59.

54 Wright, *Britain in the Age of Economic Management*, p. 21. Many scholars now think that this competitive decline was greatly exaggerated: see, for instance, Tomlinson, *The Politics of Decline*, pp. 4–5.

55 Young, *This Blessed Plot*, p. 166; Owen, *From Empire to Europe*, p. 450.

56 Brown, *In My Way*, p. 205.

57 Brown, *In My Way*, p. 204.

58 Young, *This Blessed Plot*, pp. 170–1.

59 Rosen, *The Transformation of British Life*, p. 157.

60 Annan, *Our Age*, p. 480.

61 Lamb, *The Macmillan Years*, pp. 102–25.

62 Quoted in Lamb, *The Macmillan Years*, p. 129.

63 On EFTA, see Lamb, *The Macmillan Years*, pp. 126–57.

64 Young, *This Blessed Plot*, p. 119; Lamb, *The Macmillan Years*, pp. 132–3.

65 Macmillan diary, 9 July 1960, quoted in Horne, *Macmillan 1957–1986*, p. 256.

66 Quoted in Young, *This Blessed Plot*, p. 119.

67 The figures are from Clarke, *Hope and Glory*, p. 279.

68 CAB 134/1820. See also Lamb, *The Macmillan Years*, pp. 136–8; Young, *This Blessed Plot*, pp. 120–1.

69 See Lamb, *The Macmillan Years*, pp. 125–55.

70 See Sked and Cook, *Post-War Britain*, pp. 168–9; Horne, *Macmillan 1957–1986*, pp. 256–7; Young, *This Blessed Plot*, p. 128; Gilmour and Garnett, *Whatever Happened to the Tories*, pp. 158–61.

71 Horne, *Macmillan 1957–1986*, pp. 257–8; Young, *This Blessed Plot*, p. 128.

72 Hansard, 2 August 1961.

73 Horne, *Macmillan 1957–1986*, p. 260.

74 Lamb, *The Macmillan Years*, p. 158.

75 Harold Macmillan, *Britain, the Commonwealth and Europe* (London, 1961), pp. 5–10.

76 Young, *This Blessed Plot*, pp. 128–9.

77 See Young, *This Blessed Plot*, pp. 129–30; Weight, *Patriots*, p. 334; Lamb, *The Macmillan Years*, pp. 158–9.

78 PREM 11/4415, 'Public Opinion and the Common Market', 18 September 1962, quoted in Weight, *Patriots*, pp. 338–9.

79 *Daily Mirror*, 4 June 1962.

80 Young, *This Blessed Plot*, p. 146.

81 Radice, *Friends and Rivals*, pp. 118–21.

82 Hansard, 2 August 1961.

83 Quoted in Philip Ziegler, *Wilson: The Authorised Life* (London, 1993), p. 131.

84 Michael Postan, 'Political and Intellectual Progress', in W. T. Rodgers, ed., *Hugh Gaitskell 1906–1963* (London, 1964), p. 98.

85 Williams, *Hugh Gaitskell*, p. 390.

86 Jenkins, *A Life at the Centre*, p. 145.

87 Jay, *Change and Fortune*, p. 282.

88 Williams, *Hugh Gaitskell*, p. 391.

89 Williams, *Hugh Gaitskell*, pp. 403–4.

90 Williams, *Hugh Gaitskell*, pp. 404–8; Young, *This Blessed Plot*, pp. 162–3.

91 Radice, *Friends and Rivals*, p. 121.

92 Edward Heath, *Travels: Peoples and Places in my Life* (London, 1977), p. 115.

93 John Campbell, *Edward Heath: A Biography* (London, 1993), p. 121.

94 See Miriam Camps, *Britain and the European Community, 1955–1963* (Oxford, 1964).

95 Sir Patrick Reilly quoted in Lamb, *The Macmillan Years*, p. 199.

96 Sir Eric Roll quoted in Campbell, *Edward Heath*, p. 120.

97 Quoted in Horne, *Macmillan 1957–1986*, p. 111.

98 Macmillan diary entries for 28 May, 18 June and 27 June 1959, quoted in Horne, *Macmillan 1957–1986*, pp. 133–4.

99 Macmillan diary, 1 December 1962, quoted in Horne, *Macmillan 1957–1986*, p. 428.

100 John Newhouse, *De Gaulle and the Anglo-Saxons* (London, 1970), pp. 210–11; Lamb, *The Macmillan Years*, pp. 191–2.

101 Jean Lacouture, *De Gaulle: The Ruler 1945–1970* (London, 1991), p. 358; Horne, *Macmillan 1957–1986*, pp. 445–6.

102 Horne, *Macmillan 1957–1986*, pp. 358–450; Lamb, *The Macmillan Years*, p. 202.

103 See Ashton, *Kennedy, Macmillan and the Cold War*, passim; Young, *This Blessed Plot*, p. 143.

104 See Lamb, *The Macmillan Years*, p. 192; Young, *This Blessed Plot*, pp. 133, 143.

105 Horne, *Macmillan 1957–1986*, p. 451.

106 *Daily Express*, 30 January 1963.

107 Quoted in Weight, *Patriots*, p. 357.

108 *The Times*, 30 January 1963; Camps, *Britain and the European Community*, p. 492.

109 Camps, *Britain and the European Community*, p. 493; Nora Beloff, *The General Says No* (Harmondsworth, 1963), pp. 162–4; Campbell, *Edward Heath*, pp. 130–1.

110 Horne, *Macmillan 1957–1986*, p. 448.

111 Macmillan diary, 30 January 1963 and 4 February 1963, quoted in Horne, *Macmillan 1957–1986*, pp. 447–8.

112 Howard, *RAB*, p. 297; Benn diary, 20 February 1963.

113 Cosgrave, *The Strange Death of Socialist Britain*, p. 84.

114 David Butler and Anthony King, *The British General Election of 1964* (London, 1965), p. 79.

115 See Howard, *RAB*, pp. 249–92.

116 Levin, *The Pendulum Years*, p. 173; see also Horne, *Macmillan 1957–1986*, pp. 423–5.

117 *Guardian*, 9 April 1962.

118 See Gamble, *Britain in Decline*, pp. 20–1; Morgan, *The People's Peace*, pp. 197–201; Jefferys, *Retreat from New Jerusalem*, pp. 110–30; Tomlinson, *The Politics of Decline*, pp. 21–6.

119 *Newsweek*, September 1963, quoted in Booker, *The Neophiliacs*, p. 212.

120 Tomlinson, *The Politics of Decline*, p. 22.

121 Examples included Eric Wigham, *What's Wrong with the Unions?* (Harmondsworth, 1961); and Rex Malik, *What's Wrong with British Industry?* (Harmondsworth, 1964). See also Barnes, 'From Eden to Macmillan, 1955–1959', p. 104; Morgan, *The People's Peace*, p. 197.

122 Shonfield, *British Economic Policy since the War* (Harmondsworth, 1958); Sampson, *Anatomy of Britain*; Anthony Hartley, *A State of England* (London, 1963); Nicholas Davenport, *The Split Society* (London, 1964).

123 *The Economist*, 14 September 1963.

124 Sampson, *Anatomy of Britain*, p. 633.

125 On 'modernisation' in the early sixties, see Pimlott, *Harold Wilson*, pp. 299–301; Jefferys, *Retreat from New Jerusalem*, pp. 122–8; Tomlinson, *The Politics of Decline*, pp. 21–3; Rodney Lowe and Neil Rollings, 'Modernising Britain, 1957–64: A Classic Case of Centralisation and Fragmentation?', in R. A. W. Rhodes, ed., *Transforming British Government, Volume 1: Changing Institutions* (London, 2000).

126 Levin, *The Pendulum Years*, p. 243.

127 Arthur Koestler, ed., *Suicide of a Nation? An Enquiry into the State of Britain Today* (London, 1963), pp. 13–14, 239.

128 Malcolm Muggeridge in Koestler, ed., *Suicide of a Nation?*, p. 29.

129 Horne, *Macmillan 1957–1986*, p. 529.

130 Jefferys, *Retreat from New Jerusalem*, p. 99; Horne, *Macmillan 1957–1986*, p. 351.

131 *Private Eye*, 15 June 1962; Carpenter, *That Was Satire That Was*, pp. 173–4.

132 PREM 11/4250, 'Cabinet, October 25th, Modernising Britain'; Jim Tomlinson, 'Conservative Modernisation 1960–1964: Too Little, Too Late?', *Contemporary British History* 3, 1997, pp. 18–38; Hennessy, *The Prime Minister*, p. 261.

133 CAB 129/111, C62 (201), 'Modernisation of Britain', 30 November 1962; Horne, *Macmillan 1957–1986*, p. 469.

134 *Sunday Times*, 7 October 1962.

135 *Guardian*, 11 January 1963.

136 Earl of Longford, *Five Lives* (London, 1964), pp. 242–3; Williams, *Hugh Gaitskell*, p. 424.

137 Williams, *Hugh Gaitskell*, pp. 425–8.

138 Jenkins, *A Life at the Centre*, p. 147.

139 Howard and West, *The Making of the Prime Minister*, p. 13.

140 *Evening News*, 19 January 1963, quoted in Williams, *Hugh Gaitskell*, p. 425.

141 Williams, *Hugh Gaitskell*, pp. 447–2, 455.

142 Marquand, *The Progressive Dilemma*, pp. 123–36; Morgan, *Labour People*, pp. 220–30. Denis Healey thought that Gaitskell would not have been 'an ideal Prime Minister' because 'he really didn't recognise the possibility of honest dissent and he was also hopelessly intellectual in his approach': see Austin Mitchell and David Wienir, eds, *Last Time: Labour's Lessons from the Sixties* (London, 1997), pp. 21–2.

143 Pimlott, *Harold Wilson*, pp. 252–60; Ziegler, *Wilson*, pp. 134–7; Horne, *Macmillan 1957–1986*, pp. 455–6.

CHAPTER 15: A GANG OF LOW SCHOOLBOYS

1 Colley, *Britons*, p. 236.

2 Quoted in Pimlott, *The Queen*, p. 216.

3 Charles Petrie, *The Modern British Monarchy* (London, 1961), p. 26.

4 Hoggart, *The Uses of Literacy*, p. 110.

5 Pimlott, *The Queen*, pp. 240–2.

6 Ben Pimlott presents this argument especially strongly: see Pimlott, *The Queen*, p. 215.

7 Hopkins, *The New Look*, p. 303.

8 Pimlott, *The Queen*, p. 267.

9 Weight, *Patriots*, p. 236.

10 *Picture Post*, 2 June 1952.

11 *Sunday Dispatch*, 25 August 1955. See Weight, *Patriots*, pp. 236–7, for more on this theme.

12 Pimlott, *The Queen*, pp. 266–8.

13 Sampson, *Anatomy of Britain*, p. 37.

14 Weight, *Patriots*, p. 320.

15 *National and English Review*, August 1957.

16 On the reaction, see Masters, *The Swinging Sixties*, p. 180; Pimlott, *The Queen*, pp. 280–1.

17 *National and English Review*, September 1957.

18 Pimlott, *The Queen*, p. 283; Brendon and Whitehead, *The Windsors*, p. 154.

19 *Daily Mirror*, 7 August 1957

20 Pimlott, *The Queen*, pp. 281–2.

21 Quoted in Lewis, *The Fifties*, p. 182.

22 Gregory Wolfe, *Malcolm Muggeridge: A Biography* (London, 1995), p. 289.

23 Wolfe, *Malcolm Muggeridge*, p. 303.

24 *New Statesman*, 22 October 1955.

25 *Saturday Evening Post*, 19 October 1957.

26 Some modern historians have also repeated this error, no doubt unwittingly: for example, Weight, *Patriots*, p. 319.

27 Wolfe, *Malcolm Muggeridge*, p. 295.

28 Wolfe, *Malcolm Muggeridge*, pp. 295–6; on the schoolboys at Sandringham, see Lewis, *The Fifties*, p. 183.

29 Wolfe, *Malcolm Muggeridge*, p. 296; Briggs, *The History of Broadcasting in the United Kingdom: Volume V*, p. 145.

30 Wolfe, *Malcolm Muggeridge*, p. 296.

31 Pimlott, *The Queen*, p. 283.

32 Brendon and Whitehead, *The Windsors*, p. 155; Briggs, *The History of Broadcasting in the United Kingdom: Volume V*, p. 144; Pimlott, *The Queen*, pp. 291–2.

33 See Pimlott, *The Queen*, p. 315.

34 Pimlott, *The Queen*, p. 292.

35 *New Statesman*, 30 January 1960.

36 Pimlott, *The Queen*, p. 314.

37 *Observer*, 4 February 1962.

38 Tom Maschler, 'Introduction', in Maschler, ed., *Declaration* (London, 1957), pp. 7–8.

39 Maschler, 'Introduction', pp. 8–9.

40 Jacobs, *Kingsley Amis*, p. 194.

41 Hewison, *In Anger*, p. 136.

42 Colin Wilson, 'Beyond the Outsider', p. 56; Bill Hopkins, 'Ways without a Precedent', p. 138; Stuart Holroyd, 'A Sense of Crisis', p. 185 – all in Maschler, ed., *Declaration*.

43 Kenneth Tynan, 'Theatre and Living', in Maschler, ed., *Declaration*, p. 116.

44 Ritchie, *Success Stories*, pp. 170–3; Carpenter, *The Angry Young Men*, pp. 171–84, 198.

45 Doris Lessing, 'The Small Personal Voice', in Maschler, ed., *Declaration*, pp. 22–5.

46 See Tynan, 'Theatre and Living', pp. 112ff; Hewison, *In Anger*, p. 137.

47 Anderson, 'Get Out and Push!', pp. 157–9.

48 Marwick, *British Society since 1945*, p. 132.

49 Bergonzi, *The Situation of the Novel*, p. 144.

50 Osborne, 'They Call It Cricket', p. 76.

51 Osborne, 'They Call It Cricket', p. 74.

52 Carpenter, *The Angry Young Men*, p. 181.

53 Lewis, *The Fifties*, p. 182.

54 Ritchie, *Success Stories*, p. 44.

55 For the reviews, see Ritchie, *Success Stories*, pp. 44–5; Carpenter, *The Angry Young Men*, pp. 182–3.

56 *Observer*, 13 October 1957.

57 Ritchie, *Success Stories*, p. 130.

58 Reprinted in John Osborne, *Damn You, England: Collected Prose* (London, 1994), pp. 193–4.

59 Carpenter, *The Angry Young Men*, p. 206.

60 Wain, *Hurry On Down*, p. 84.

61 *New Statesman*, 29 August 1953.

62 Sisman, *A. J. P. Taylor*, p. 214, and see p. 427, n. 16; *Spectator*, 23 September 1955.

63 See Hewison, *In Anger*, p. 166; Weight, *Patriots*, p. 268.

64 *Listener*, 1 November 1956, quoted in Hewison, *In Anger*, p. 167.

65 Quoted in Hewison, *In Anger*, p. 167.

66 Hewison, *In Anger*, p. 167.

67 Annan, *Our Age*, p. 9.

68 See Valentine Cunningham, *British Writers of the Thirties* (Oxford, 1988).

69 Annan, *Our Age*, pp. 11–12.

70 Sampson, *Anatomy of Britain*, p. 225.

71 Sampson, *Anatomy of Britain*, pp. 225–6.

72 Annan, *Our Age*, pp. 14–15.

73 Annan, *Our Age*, p. 15.

74 Lewis, *The Fifties*, p. 159.

75 On the old-boy network in *A Dance to the Music of Time*, see Bergonzi, *The Situation of the Novel*, p. 123.

76 See Taylor, *After the War*, pp. 155–6.

77 *Listener*, 18 April 1957.

78 Bergonzi, *Wartime and Aftermath*, p. 134.

79 See Bergonzi, *The Situation of the Novel*, p. 134; Stevenson, *The British Novel since the Thirties*, pp. 136–7.

80 See Pimlott, *Harold Wilson*, p. 328.

81 Bergonzi, *The Situation of the Novel*, p. 144.

82 *Queen*, August 1959.

83 *Queen*, August 1959.

84 Ranelagh, *Thatcher's People*, pp. 59–70; see also Hewison, *In Anger*, p. 128.

85 Quoted in Marwick, *British Society since 1945*, p. 134.

86 Thomas, 'The Establishment and Society', p. 18.

87 See Hewison, *In Anger*, pp. 167–8.

88 See Porter, '"Never-Never Land"', p. 130; Cannadine, *Class in Britain*, p. 147.

89 Tomlinson, *The Politics of Decline*, p. 25.

90 Sampson, *Anatomy of Britain*, p. xi.

91 Sampson, *Anatomy of Britain*, pp. xix–xiii.

92 Sampson, *Anatomy of Britain*, p. 624.

93 Sampson, *Anatomy of Britain*, foldout chart between pp. 34 and 35.

94 Sampson, *Anatomy of Britain*, pp. 621–31.

95 Sampson, *Anatomy of Britain*, p. 633.

96 Sampson, *Anatomy of Britain*, pp. 634–5.

97 Sampson, *Anatomy of Britain*, p. 638.

98 See Hewison, *Too Much*, pp. 3–5.

99 Carpenter, *That Was Satire That Was*, pp. 1–15.

100 McKibbin, *Classes and Cultures*, p. 515.

101 Both examples are quoted in Weight, *Patriots*, pp. 67–8.

102 Marwick, *The Sixties*, p. 3. Carpenter, *That Was Satire That Was*, pp. 5–6, also makes great play of the drab formality of the fifties.

103 Sikov, *Mr Strangelove*, pp. 50–1, 65.

104 The definitive work on the Goons is Roger Wilmut and Jimmy Grafton, *The Goon Show Companion: A History and Goonography* (London, 1976). On their influences, see Walker, *Peter Sellers*, p. 82; Lewis, *The Life and Death of Peter Sellers*, p. 147; McKibbin, *Classes and Cultures*, p. 472.

105 Sikov, *Mr Strangelove*, pp. 64–5.

106 Lewis, *The Life and Death of Peter Sellers*, pp. 151–3, 166; Stuart Ward, 'No Nation Could Be Broker: The Satire Boom and the Demise of Britain's World Role', in Ward, ed., *British Culture and the End of Empire*, p. 95.

107 Quoted in Carpenter, *That Was Satire That Was*, p. 54.

108 Ronald Bergan, *Beyond the Fringe . . . and Beyond* (London, 1989), pp. 3–13; Carpenter, *That Was Satire That Was*, pp. 93–4.

109 See Carpenter, *That Was Satire That Was*, pp. 18–26, 60–87.

110 Carpenter, *That Was Satire That Was*, p. 85.

111 Carpenter, *That Was Satire That Was*, pp. 106–7.

112 *Daily Mail*, 24 August 1960.

113 Carpenter, *That Was Satire That Was*, pp. 96–9.

114 Carpenter, *That Was Satire That Was*, p. 107; *Daily Mail*, 24 August 1960.

115 Bergan, *Beyond the Fringe*, p. 36; Carpenter, *That Was Satire That Was*, p. 104.

116 Bergan, *Beyond the Fringe*, pp. 32–3; Carpenter, *That Was Satire That Was*, pp. 100–3.

117 Bergan, *Beyond the Fringe*, p. 33.

118 Carpenter, *That Was Satire That Was*, pp. 103, 109.

119 Carpenter, *That Was Satire That Was*, p. 112.

120 Bergan, *Beyond the Fringe*, pp. 37–8.

121 Carpenter, *That Was Satire That Was*, p. 113.

122 Alan Bennett, *Writing Home* (revised edition: London, 1997), p. 321.

123 Carpenter, *That Was Satire That Was*, p. 114.

124 *Daily Mail*, 11 May 1961.

125 *Observer*, 14 May 1961.

126 Bergan, *Beyond the Fringe*, p. 23.

127 Bergan, *Beyond the Fringe*, pp. 44–51

128 Bergan, *Beyond the Fringe*, pp. 33–4.

129 *Daily Mail*, 11 July 1961; Carpenter, *That Was Satire That Was*, pp. 128–36.

130 Carpenter, *That Was Satire That Was*, pp. 130–2.

131 Carpenter, *That Was Satire That Was*, pp. 132–47.

132 Quoted in Carpenter, *That Was Satire That Was*, p. 140.

133 See Bergan, *Beyond the Fringe*, pp. 246–8; Carpenter, *That Was Satire That Was*, pp. 264–7.

134 Malcolm Muggeridge had edited *Punch* between 1953 and 1957: see Wolfe, *Malcolm Muggeridge*, pp. 266–92.

135 See introduction to Ingrams, ed., *The Life and Times of Private Eye*, pp. 7–9; Patrick Marnham, *The Private Eye Story: The First 21 Years* (London, 1983), pp. 13–34; Carpenter, *That Was Satire That Was*, pp. 32–59.

136 Carpenter, *That Was Satire That Was*, p. 179.

137 Marnham, *The Private Eye Story*, p, 42; Carpenter, *That Was Satire That Was*, pp. 180–1.

138 Marnham, *The Private Eye Story*, pp. 85–6; Carpenter, *That Was Satire That Was*, pp. 172, 268.

139 Introduction to Ingrams, ed., *The Life and Times of Private Eye*, p. 8.

140 On the early issues of *Private Eye*, see Marnham, *The Private Eye Story*, pp. 28–37; Carpenter, *That Was Satire That Was*, pp. 159–68.

141 *Observer*, 18 February 1962.

142 *Sunday Times*, 21 October 1962.

143 *Observer*, 8 July 1962.

144 On the fate of these projects, see Carpenter, *That Was Satire That Was*, pp. 178–9.

145 Carpenter, *That Was Satire That Was*, pp. 206–7.

146 Carpenter, *That Was Satire That Was*, pp. 211–15.

147 Melly, *Revolt into Style*, p. 183.

148 Carpenter, *That Was Satire That Was*, p. 217.

149 There is a detailed description of the first edition in Carpenter, *That Was Satire That Was*, pp. 216–23.

150 Ned Sherrin, *A Small Thing – Like An Earthquake* (London, 1983), p. 67.

151 Briggs, *The History of Broadcasting in the United Kingdom: Volume V*, pp. 350–1.

152 *Sunday Telegraph*, 25 November 1962.

153 Quoted in Carpenter, *That Was Satire That Was*, p. 224.

154 Carpenter, *That Was Satire That Was*, p. 213.

155 This no doubt helps to explain the greater coherence and wit of British comedies by comparison with, say, their American counterparts. For the *TW3* writers, see Frischauer, *David Frost*, p. 49; Hewison, *Too Much*, p. 29; Carpenter, *That Was Satire That Was*, p. 243.

156 Carpenter, *That Was Satire That Was*, p. 225; Frischauer, *David Frost*, p. 47.

157 See Briggs, *The History of Broadcasting in the United Kingdom: Volume V*, p. 357.

158 Frischauer, *David Frost*, pp. 20–35; Carpenter, *That Was Satire That Was*, p. 207

159 In fact, although he edited *Granta*, he was only the secretary of the Footlights, never the president. See David Frost, *An Autobiography: Part One* (London, 1993), p. 19.

160   Booker, *The Seventies*, p. 200.

161 Ingrams, ed., *The Life and Times of Private Eye*, p. 11; Frischauer, *David Frost*, p. 60. The drowning incident is described in Frischauer, *David Frost*, p. 64.

162 Booker, *The Neophiliacs*, p. 187.

163 *Evening Standard*, 28 January 1963.

164 Carpenter, *That Was Satire That Was*, pp. 234–5.

165 Carpenter, *That Was Satire That Was*, pp. 240, 253.

166 *Daily Mail*, 10 December 1962.

167 Carpenter, *That Was Satire That Was*, p. 239.

168 Carpenter, *That Was Satire That Was*, p. 244.

169 Carpenter, *That Was Satire That Was*, pp. 245–6.

170 Carpenter, *That Was Satire That Was*, p. 256.

171 Levin, *The Pendulum Years*, p. 319; Carpenter, *That Was Satire That Was*, p. 256.

172 Tracey and Morrison, *Whitehouse*, p. 46.

173 Briggs, *The History of Broadcasting in the United Kingdom: Volume V*, pp. 353, 360.

174 Carpenter, *That Was Satire That Was*, p. 269.

175 *Daily Herald*, 30 September 1963.

176 Sherrin, *A Small Thing*, p. 89.

177 Carpenter, *That Was Satire That Was*, pp. 275–6.

178 Sherrin, *A Small Thing*, p. 78.

179 Carpenter, *That Was Satire That Was*, p. 276.

180 Briggs, *The History of Broadcasting in the United Kingdom: Volume V*, p. 372.

181 Briggs, *The History of Broadcasting in the United Kingdom: Volume V*, p. 372; Carpenter, *That Was Satire That Was*, pp. 277–8.

182 PREM 11/3668, Macmillan to Bevins, 10 December 1962.

183 PREM 11/3668, Bevins to Macmillan, 12 December 1962.

184 For example, Green, *All Dressed Up*, p. 66.

185 *Guardian*, 14 November 1963; see also Carpenter, *That Was Satire That Was*, p. 280.

186 Carpenter, *That Was Satire That Was*, p. 281.

187 Frischauer, *David Frost*, pp. 69–76; Carpenter, *That Was Satire That Was*, p. 297.

188 Frischauer, *David Frost*, pp. 81–3; Masters, *The Swinging Sixties*, p. 25; Clarke, *Shadow of a Nation*, p. 225.

189 Booker, *The Neophiliacs*, p. 286.

190 Frischauer, *David Frost*, p. 9.

191 Clarke, *Shadow of a Nation*, p. 203.

192 Introduction to Ingrams, ed., *The Life and Times of Private Eye*, p. 17; Bergan, *Beyond the Fringe*, p. 251.

193 Bergan, *Beyond the Fringe*, pp. 91–8, 149, 198–9, 253–4.

194 Carpenter, *That Was Satire That Was*, p. 298.

195 *Guardian*, 14 November 1963.

196 Pimlott, *Harold Wilson*, p. 304.

197 Carpenter, *That Was Satire That Was*, p. 273.

198 Hewison, *Too Much*, p. 27.

199 Bergan, *Beyond the Fringe*, p. 23.

200 Carpenter, *That Was Satire That Was*, p. 249.

201 See Green, *All Dressed Up*, pp. 65–6.

202 *New Statesman*, 24 August 1962.

203 Carpenter, *That Was Satire That Was*, p. 148.

204 Briggs, *The History of Broadcasting in the United Kingdom: Volume V*, p. 363.

205 Carpenter, *That Was Satire That Was*, p. 311.

206 *Observer*, 8 July 1962.

207 *Private Eye*, 9 March 1962.

208 Carpenter, *That Was Satire That Was*, p. 182.

209 Carpenter, *That Was Satire That Was*, p. 183.

210 Hitchens, *The Abolition of Britain*, p. 173.

211 Frost, *An Autobiography: Part One*, p. 47.

212 Marnham, *The Private Eye Story*, pp. 74–5; Carpenter, *That Was Satire That Was*, p. 291.

CHAPTER 16: THE SECRET AGENT

1 Walker, *Hollywood, England*, p. 189.

2 *Spectator*, 12 October 1962.

3 *New Statesman*, 9 October 1962; *Monthly Film Bulletin*, October 1962, quoted in James Chapman, *Licence to Thrill: A Cultural History of the James Bond Films* (London, 1999), p. 86.

4 See Chapman, *Licence to Thrill*, p. 88.

5 John Cork and Bruce Scivally, *James Bond: The Legacy* (London, 2002), pp. 48–9.

6 Chapman, *Licence to Thrill*, p. 70.

7 Michael Denning, *Cover Stories: Narrative and Ideology in the British Spy Thriller* (London, 1987), p. 40.

8 Hennessy, *The Secret State*, pp. 1, 3.

9 Aldrich, *The Hidden Hand*, pp. 378–81.

10 Andrew Boyle, *The Climate of Treason* (second edition: London, 1980), pp. 401–8; Aldrich, *The Hidden Hand*, p. 421.

11 Boyle, *The Climate of Treason*, pp. 1–124. On the Apostles, see Annan, *Our Age*, pp. 304–7; Hobsbawm, *Interesting Times*, pp. 187–90.

12 Boyle, *The Climate of Treason*, p. 437.

13 Hewison, *In Anger*, p. 166.

14 *Daily Mirror*, 24 September 1955.

15 Colls, *Identity of England*, p. 90.

16 Annan, *Our Age*, pp. 160–1; on the 'cult of homosexuality', see pp. 134–69.

17 Sinfield, *Literature, Politics and Culture in Post-war Britain*, p. 77.

18 *Sunday Pictorial*, 25 September 1955.

19 CAB 21/4530, 'Civil Servants as Security Risks', 26 April 1957.

20 Lord Hailsham, 'Homosexuality and Society', in J. Tudor Rees and Harley V. Usill, eds, *They Stand Apart: A Critical Survey of the Problems of Homosexuality* (London, 1955), pp. 22, 24, 27.

21 Quoted in Stephen Jeffery-Poulter, *Peers, Queers and Commons: The Struggle for Gay Law Reform from 1950 to the Present* (London, 1991), pp. 48–9.

22 Annan, *Our Age*, p. 160.

23 Cooper, 'Looking Back on Anger', pp. 257–8; Sinfield, *Literature, Politics and Culture in Post-war Britain*, pp. 79–81; Rebellato, *1956 and All That*, pp. 156–223.

24 John Vassall, *Vassall: The Autobiography of a Spy* (London, 1975), p. 66.

25 Edward Gibbon, *The History of the Decline and Fall of the Roman Empire: Volume III* (London, 1995), pp. 510–11; Weeks, *Sex, Politics and Society*, pp. 100, 107.

26 Quoted in Masters, *The Swinging Sixties*, p. 109.

27 McKibbin, *Classes and Cultures*, p. 321.

28 Weeks, *Sex, Politics and Society*, pp. 240–1.

29 Masters, *The Swinging Sixties*, p. 108.

30 Newburn, *Permission and Regulation*, p. 48; Hansard, 3 December 1953.

31 Rebellato, *1956 and All That*, p. 157.

32 Masters, *The Swinging Sixties*, pp. 110–14; *Report of the Committee on Homosexual Offences and Prostitution* (London, 1957), p. 130.

33 Patrick Higgins, *Heterosexual Dictatorship: Male Homosexuality in Postwar Britain* (London, 1996), pp. 282–3; Dudley Edwards, *Newspapermen*, pp. 247–51.

34 *Sunday Pictorial*, 25 May 1952, 1 June 1952; see also the discussion in Sinfield, *Literature, Politics and Culture in Post-war Britain*, pp. 77–8; Weeks, *Sex, Politics and Society*, p. 241; Dudley Edwards, *Newspapermen*, pp. 247–50.

35 *Sunday Mirror*, 28 April 1963.

36 Nigel West, *Friends: Britain's Secret Post-War Intelligence Operations* (London, 1988), pp. 82–5; Dorril, *MI6*, pp. 617–18.

37 Rhodes James, *Anthony Eden*, p. 436; see also Thorpe, *Eden*, p. 472.

38 Dorril, *MI6*, pp. 619–20.

39 See J. Bernard Hutton, *Frogman Extraordinary* (London, 1960); and for an additional selection of Crabb conspiracy theories, see 'How Buster Crabb Died', in *Diver*, June 1996, online at <http://www.divernet.com/history/crabb696.htm>.

40 Quoted in Dorril, *MI6*, p. 619.

41 Nicholas Elliott, *With my Little Eye: Observations along the Way* (Norwich, 1992), pp. 24–6.

42 Boyle, *The Conduct of Treason*, p. 449; Thurlow, *The Secret State*, p. 321.

43 See Christopher Andrew, *Secret Service: The Making of the British Intelligence Community* (London, 1988); and especially Dorril, *MI6*, pp. 3–6.

44 Christopher Felix, *A Short Course in the Secret War* (revised edition: Lanham, New York, 1992), pp. 55–6.

45 George Blake, *No Other Choice: An Autobiography* (London, 1990), pp. 166–8.

46 See Jerrold L. Schecter and Peter S. Deriabin, *The Spy Who Saved the World: How a Soviet Colonel Changed the Course of the Cold War* (New York, 1992); Aldrich, *The Hidden Hand*, pp. 619–20.

47 Peter Wright, *Spycatcher* (New York, 1987), p. 162; Aldrich, *The Hidden Hand*, pp. 142–79, 392–420; Dorril, *MI6*, pp. 161–449, 662–5.

48 Dorril, *MI6*, pp. 660–1.

49 Thurlow, *The Secret State*, pp. 317–18.

50 Dorril, *MI6*, pp. 722–3.

51 See Greville Wynne, *The Man from Moscow* (London, 1967); Schecter and Deriabin, *The Spy Who Saved the World*, pp. 294–5, 334–47; Dorril, *MI6*, pp. 704–8.

52 See David Cannadine, 'Fantasy: Ian Fleming and the Realities of Escapism', in Cannadine, *In Churchill's Shadow*, p. 284.

53 Lycett, *Ian Fleming*, p. 220.

54 See Lycett, *Ian Fleming*, passim; John Pearson, *The Life of Ian Fleming* (London, 1966) and Cannadine, 'Ian Fleming and the Realities of Escapism', pp. 279–311.

55 Lycett, *Ian Fleming*, pp. 245–6.

56 Lycett, *Ian Fleming*, pp. 187ff; Cork and Scivally, *James Bond: The Legacy*, pp. 12–13; Cannadine, 'Ian Fleming and the Realities of Escapism', p. 285.

57 Pearson, *The Life of Ian Fleming*, p. 206; Lycett, *Ian Fleming*, p. 226.

58 *Books and Bookmen*, May 1963, quoted in Chapman, *Licence to Thrill*, p. 1.

59 Lycett, *Ian Fleming*, p. 243.

60 Walker, *Hollywood, England*, pp. 182–3; Raymond Benson, *The James Bond Bedside Companion* (London, 1984), pp. 7–8.

61 Denning, *Cover Stories*, p. 92; Stuart Laing, 'The Production of Literature', in Sinfield, ed., *Society and Literature 1945–1970*, pp. 127–8.

62 Tony Bennett and Janet Woollacott, *Bond and Beyond: The Political Career of a Popular Hero* (London, 1987), pp. 26–7.

63 Cannadine, 'Ian Fleming and the Realities of Escapism', p. 280; Denning, *Cover Stories*, p. 21.

64 *New Statesman*, 5 April 1958.

65 Kingsley Amis, *The James Bond Dossier* (London, 1966) pp. 9, 144.

66 Leroy L. Panek, *The Special Branch: The British Spy Novel 1890–1980* (Bowling Green, Ohio, 1981), pp. 212–14.

67 Umberto Eco, 'The Narrative Structure in Fleming', in Oreste del Buono and Umberto Eco, eds, *The Bond Affair* (trans. R. A. Downie: London, 1966), p. 58; see also Denning, *Cover Stories*, p. 97.

68 See Joseph S. Meisel, 'The Germans are Coming! British Fiction of a German Invasion, 1871–1913', in *War, Literature and the Arts* 2:2, Fall 1990, pp. 41–77; Denning, *Cover Stories*, pp. 11–12, 27–58; Colin Watson, *Snobbery with Violence: Crime Stories and their Audience* (London 1971), pp. 242–50.

69 See Richard Usborne, *Clubland Heroes* (London, 1953).

70 Gertrude Himmelfarb, *Victorian Minds* (New York, 1970), pp. 271–2.

71 Cannadine, 'Ian Fleming and the Realities of Escapism', pp. 288–90.

72 Richard Usborne, introduction to 'Sapper', *Bulldog Drummond*, (London, 1983); Chapman, *Licence to Thrill*, pp. 27–8.

73 Cannadine, 'Ian Fleming and the Realities of Escapism', p. 287.

74 *Times Literary Supplement*, 17 April 1953.

75 Benson, *The James Bond Bedside Companion*, p. 3; Lycett, *Ian Fleming*, p. 223.

76 See Benson, *The James Bond Bedside Companion*, pp. 59–61.

77 Ian Fleming, *Moonraker* (London, 1955), ch. 4. There are so many different editions of the James Bond novels that it seems sensible, following David Cannadine's example, to give chapter rather than page references. In the present case, I am using a Marks and Spencer omnibus edition from the mid-1980s which few readers will have immediately to hand, although I thoroughly recommend it.

78 Nick Foulkes, 'The Style Secrets of James Bond', in Jay McInerney et al., *Dressed to Kill: James Bond: The Suited Hero* (Paris, 1996), p. 65.

79 Panek, *The Special Branch*, pp. 207–8.

80 Denning, *Cover Stories*, pp. 1–2, 93.

81 See Cannadine, 'Ian Fleming and the Realities of Escapism', p. 281.

82 Amis, *The James Bond Dossier*, pp. 88–92.

83 Ian Fleming, *From Russia with Love* (London, 1957), ch. 5.

84 Amis, *The James Bond Dossier*, pp. 86–7.

85 Fleming, *From Russia with Love*, ch. 4.

86 On SMERSH and SPECTRE, see Cannadine, 'Ian Fleming and the Realities of Escapism', p. 306; Chapman, *Licence to Kill*, pp. 30–1.

87 *Spectator*, 9 October 1959.

88 Ian Fleming, *Thrilling Cities* (London, 1963), pp. 85, 90, quoted in Cannadine, 'Ian Fleming and the Realities of Escapism', p. 293.

89 *Spectator*, 9 October 1959.

90 Fleming, *Moonraker*, ch. 3.

91 Fleming, *Moonraker*, ch. 16.

92 Ian Fleming, *Dr No* (London, 1958), ch. 20.

93 Ian Fleming, *You Only Live Twice* (London, 1964), ch. 8.

94 Denning, *Cover Stories*, pp. 109–10.

95 Durgnat, *A Mirror for England*, p. 151.

96 Fleming, *Dr No*, ch. 8.

97 See Cannadine, 'Ian Fleming and the Realities of Escapism', p. 301, a nice passage.

98 Fleming, *Casino Royale*, ch. 4.

99 Fleming, *Casino Royale*, ch. 15.

100 Denning, *Cover Stories*, p. 108.

101 Ian Fleming, *Goldfinger* (London, 1959), ch. 19.

102 Cannadine, 'Ian Fleming and the Realities of Escapism', p. 298.

103 Fleming, *Casino Royale*, ch. 1; *From Russia with Love*, ch. 9.

104 John Lanchester, 'Bond in Torment', *London Review of Books*, 5 September 2002; Lycett, *Ian Fleming*, pp. 179–82.

105 Fleming, *Casino Royale*, ch. 17.

106 Fleming, *Dr No*, ch. 13.

107 Fleming, *From Russia with Love*, ch. 25.

108 Ian Fleming, *The Spy Who Loved Me* (London, 1962), ch. 14.

109 Fleming, *Casino Royale*, ch. 23.

110 Ian Fleming, *On Her Majesty's Secret Service* (London, 1963), ch. 4.

111 Ian Fleming, *Thunderball* (London, 1961), ch. 2.

112 See Denning, *Cover Stories*, pp. 35, 102; Nick Foulkes, 'The World of 007', in McInerney et al., *Dressed to Kill*, p. 62.

113 Denning, *Cover Stories*, pp. 103–5.

114 Fleming, *Moonraker*, ch. 5.

115 Fleming, *From Russia with Love*, ch. 11.

116 Fleming, *Casino Royale*, ch. 7.

117 This, according to John Lanchester, comes to sixteen units: see 'Bond in Torment', *London Review of Books*, 5 September 2002.

118 Fleming, *Thunderball*, ch. 1.

119 Stevenson, *The British Novel since the Thirties*, p. 145; Chapman, *Licence to Thrill*, p. 68.

120 Quoted in Foulkes, 'The Style Secrets of James Bond', p. 80.

121 Reprinted in McInerney et al., *Dressed to Kill*, p. 14.

122 Denning, *Cover Stories*, p. 100.

123 *Sunday Times*, 4 February 1962; on Bond and *Playboy*, see Chapman, *Licence to Thrill*, p. 36.

124 *Twentieth Century*, March 1958.

125 Quoted in Pearson, *The Life of Ian Fleming*, p. 304.

126 Bennett and Woollacott, *Bond and Beyond*, pp. 238–9.

127 Walker, *Hollywood, England*, p. 184; Lycett, *Ian Fleming*, p. 393.

128 Cork and Scivally, *James Bond: The Legacy*, p. 31.

129 Walker, *Hollywood, England*, p. 197.

130 Pearson, *The Life of Ian Fleming*, pp. 333–4.

131 Quoted in Denning, *Cover Stories*, p. 94.

132 See Lycett, *Ian Fleming*, p. 221.

133 Denning, *Cover Stories*, p. 34.

134 Fleming, *Casino Royale*, ch. 20.

135 The film *Ring of Spies* (1963) is a good example: see Murphy, *Sixties British Cinema*, pp. 220–1; Shaw, *British Cinema and the Cold War*, pp. 58–60.

136 On the place of Deighton and le Carré in the tradition of British spy fiction, see Panek, *The Special Branch*, pp. 220–57.

137 Denning, *Cover Stories*, p. 121.

138 Len Deighton, *The Ipcress File* (London, 1962), p. 62.

139 Deighton, *The Ipcress File*, pp. 14–15.

140 Deighton, *The Ipcress File*, p. 80.

141 Deighton, *The Ipcress File*, p. 17.

142 Walker, *Hollywood, England*, pp. 304–5.

143 Deighton, *The Ipcress File*, p. 22.

144 Deighton, *The Ipcress File*, p. 97.

145 *Daily Telegraph*, 14 February 2002.

146 *Independent*, 17 February 2002. Le Carré's background and relationship with his father are most intimately explored in *A Perfect Spy* (London, 1986), regarded by many reviewers as among the best British novels since the war.

147 John le Carré, *Call for the Dead* (Penguin edition: Harmondsworth, 1964), p. 13.

148 Panek, *The Special Branch*, p. 241.

149 *Encounter*, May 1966.

150 Le Carré, *Call for the Dead*, p. 7.

151 John le Carré, *A Murder of Quality* (Penguin edition: Harmondsworth, 1964), p. 24.

152 Le Carré, *Call for the Dead*, p. 10.

153 Denning, *Cover Stories*, pp. 35, 110; Panek, *The Special Branch*, p. 240.

154 *Washington Post*, 9 October 1977.

155 See Panek, *The Special Branch*, pp. 248–51.

156 *Encounter*, May 1966.

157 John le Carré, *The Looking-Glass War* (London, 1965), p. 231.

158 Denning, *Cover Stories*, p. 122.

159 John le Carré, *The Spy Who Came In from the Cold* (London, 1963), p. 134.

160 Le Carré, *The Spy Who Came In from the Cold*, p. 20.

161 Le Carré, *The Spy Who Came In from the Cold*, pp. 231–2.

162 Murphy, *Sixties British Cinema*, p. 224.

163 Paul Dehn quoted in Murphy, *Sixties British Cinema*, pp. 224–5.

164 Bradbury, *The Modern British Novel*, p. 384.

165 Quoted on the Pan edition of 1964.

166 See Panek, *The Special Branch*, pp. 256–7; Stevenson, *The British Novel since the Thirties*, p. 145; Bradbury, *The Modern British Novel*, p. 288.

167 Cork and Scivally, *James Bond: The Legacy*, pp. 58–9.

168 Clive Irving, Ron Hall and Jeremy Wallington, *Scandal '63: A Study of the Profumo Affair* (London, 1963) p. 45; Horne, *Macmillan 1957–1986*, p. 457; Hylton, *Magical History Tour*, pp. 28–9.

169 Blake, *No Other Choice*, pp. 194–205; Hylton, *Magical History Tour*, pp. 29–30; Dorril, *MI6*, pp. 704–5.

170 On Macmillan and the trial, see Horne, *Macmillan 1957–1986*, pp. 457–9; Tom Bower, *The Perfect English Spy: Sir Dick White and the Secret War 1935–90* (London, 1995), pp. 266–71; Hylton, *Magical History Tour*, p. 30.

171 Hylton, *Magical History Tour*, p. 31.

172 Macmillan diary, 28 September 1962, quoted in Horne, *Macmillan 1957–1986*, p. 460.

173 Horne, *Macmillan 1957–1986*, p. 461.

174 Matthew Parris, *Great Parliamentary Scandals* (London, 1995), p. 129.

175 Vassall, *Vassall*, pp. 66–7.

176 *Daily Mail*, 23 October 1962; Lawton, *1963*, pp. 4–5.

177 Parris, *Great Parliamentary Scandals*, p. 134.

178 *Sunday Pictorial*, 28 October 1962, 4 November 1962.

179 Undated newspaper reports quoted in Parris, *Great Parliamentary Scandals*, p. 132.

180 *News of the World*, 11 November 1962.

181 *Daily Mail*, 29 October 1962.

182 Horne, *Macmillan 1957–1962*, pp. 462–3.

183 Lawton, *1963*, pp. 11–12.

184 Quoted in Lawton, *1963*, pp. 7–8.

185 See Horne, *Macmillan 1957–1962*, pp. 463–4; Lawton, *1963*, pp. 7–11; Parris, *Great Parliamentary Scandals*, pp. 136–8.

186 Lawton, *1963*, p. 10; *The Times*, 23 November 1962.

187 Horne, *Macmillan 1957–1962*, p. 464.

CHAPTER 17: SCANDAL

1 Norman, *Shout!*, p. 165.

2 Horne, *Macmillan 1957–1986*, p. 468.

3 Macmillan diary, 9 March 1963, quoted in Horne, *Macmillan 1957–1986*, p. 436; Pimlott, *Harold Wilson*, p. 266; Jefferys, *Retreat from New Jerusalem*, p. 103.

4 Horne, *Macmillan 1957–1986*, p. 470.

5 Jefferys, *Retreat from New Jerusalem*, pp. 102–3.

6 See, for example, the poll published in the *Daily Mail*, 7 May 1963.

7 On Ward, see Irving, Hall and Wallington, *Scandal '63*, pp. 25–39; Summers and Dorril, *Honeytrap*, pp. 29–78.

8 Summers and Dorril, *Honeytrap*, p. 41.

9 Summers and Dorril, *Honeytrap*, pp. 55–7.

10 Summers and Dorril, *Honeytrap*, p. 55.

11 Lawton, *1963*, pp. 133–4. For some wild stories, see Summers and Dorril, *Honeytrap*, pp. 50–3.

12 Quoted in Summers and Dorril, *Honeytrap*, p. 86.

13 *Tit-Bits*, 22 March 1958, quoted in Irving, Hall and Wallington, *Scandal '63*, p. 7.

14 On Keeler's background, see Irving, Hall and Wallington, *Scandal '63*, pp. 6–13. Summers and Dorril, *Honeytrap*, pp. 85–90, is informative but a little sensationalist, while Christine Keeler, *Christine Keeler: The Truth At Last* (London, 2001) is extremely unreliable.

15 Summers and Dorril, *Honeytrap*, pp. 108–12.

16 *Lord Denning's Report* (Cmnd 2152: London, 1963), reprinted as *John Profumo and Christine Keeler, 1963* (London, 1999), pp. 18–24; Irving, Hall and Wallington, *Scandal '63*, pp. 56–66; Thorpe, *Alec Douglas-Home*, p. 238.

17 See *Lord Denning's Report*, pp. 151–8; Summers and Dorril, *Honeytrap*, pp. 106–30, 147–56.

18 The most judicious discussion is in Aldrich, *The Hidden Hand*, pp. 628–9.

19 *Lord Denning's Report*, pp. 9–10; Irving, Hall and Wallington, *Scandal '63*, pp. 47–50; Summers and Dorril, *Honeytrap*, pp. 132–4. The quotation from Lady Astor is in *Honeytrap*, p. 134.

20 Quoted in Summers and Dorril, *Honeytrap*, pp. 50–1.

21 Summers and Dorril, *Honeytrap*, p. 135.

22 Quoted in Hylton, *Magical History Tour*, p. 94.

23 Irving, Hall and Wallington, *Scandal '63*, pp. 50–1.

24 Irving, Hall and Wallington, *Scandal '63*, pp. 14–24; Horne, *Macmillan 1957–1986*, pp. 471–2; Summers and Dorril, *Honeytrap*, pp. 67–8.

25 Summers and Dorril, *Honeytrap*, pp. 137–9.

26· On the officer class, see Shepherd, *Iain Macleod*, p. 292.

27 *Lord Denning's Report*, p. 11; Summers and Dorril, *Honeytrap*, p. 136.

28 *Lord Denning's Report*, pp. 13–15; Irving, Hall and Wallington, *Scandal '63*, pp. 52–3; Lamb, *The Macmillan Years*, p. 455.

29 *Lord Denning's Report*, p. 15.

30 In her most recent autobiography – one of several – Keeler claims that Profumo later made her pregnant and paid for her to have an abortion. There is no evidence for this and since the accusation first surfaced in 2001, it can almost certainly be dismissed.

31 White, *London in the Twentieth Century*, pp. 338–9.

32 *Lord Denning's Report*, pp. 25–6; Summers and Dorril, *Honeytrap*, pp. 168–9.

33 *Lord Denning's Report*, pp. 25–6; Summers and Dorril, *Honeytrap*, pp. 168–9.

34 HO 300/8, 'West End Jazz and Dance Clubs', 15 September 1964, quoted in Weight, *Patriots*, pp. 304–5.

35 *Lord Denning's Report*, pp. 25–6; Summers and Dorril, *Honeytrap*, pp. 168–169.

36 Edgecombe's story is well told in Phillips and Phillips, *Windrush*, pp. 193–196; see also *Lord Denning's Report*, pp. 27–9; Summers and Dorril, *Honeytrap*, pp. 193–5.

37 *Daily Mirror*, 15 December 1962.

38 On Keeler's indiscretion, see Summers and Dorril, *Honeytrap*, pp. 172–3.

39 *Queen*, August 1962.

40 Irving, Hall and Wallington, *Scandal '63*, p. 76.

41 *Lord Denning's Report*, pp. 30–6; Irving, Hall and Wallington, *Scandal '63*, pp. 76–8.

42 *Lord Denning's Report*, pp. 64–76.

43 *Lord Denning's Report*, p. 76; Horne, *Macmillan 1957–1986*, p. 495.

44 Quoted without citation in Lamb, *The Macmillan Years*, p. 457.

45 *Westminster Confidential*, 8 March 1963, quoted in Lawton, *1963*, pp. 137–8; Lamb, *The Macmillan Years*, pp. 458–9.

46 PREM 11/4368, Sir John Hobson to Timothy Bligh, 13 March 1963; see Lamb, *The Macmillan Years*, p. 459.

47 *Lord Denning's Report*, pp. 79–87; Summers and Dorril, *Honeytrap*, p. 231.

48 *Daily Express*, 15 March 1963.

49 *Daily Sketch*, 16 March 1963; *Daily Mail*, 20 March 1963; see also Irving, Hall and Wallington, *Scandal '63*, pp. 90–6.

50 *Private Eye*, 22 March 1963. Montesi was an Italian politician of the time who became famously embroiled in scandal. Note that the story repeats the fiction that Profumo was a Cabinet minister.

51 Irving, Hall and Wallington, *Scandal '63*, pp. 87–8.

52 On Wigg, see Irving, Hall and Wallington, *Scandal '63*, pp. 67–8; Horne, *Macmillan 1957–1986*, p. 473; Pimlott, *Harold Wilson*, p. 286.

53 Irving, Hall and Wallington, *Scandal '63*, pp. 68–71.

54 *Lord Denning's Report*, pp. 30–6; Irving, Hall and Wallington, *Scandal '63*, pp. 76–8.

55 Hansard, 21 March 1963; George Wigg, *George Wigg* (London, 1972), pp. 262–6.

56 See Irving, Hall and Wallington, *Scandal '63*, pp. 100–2.

57 Irving, Hall and Wallington, *Scandal '63*, p. 104.

58 *Sunday Telegraph*, 2 January 1994.

59 *Lord Denning's Report*, p. 106; Denning interview quoted in Lamb, *The Macmillan Years*, pp. 461–2.

60 Shepherd, *Iain Macleod*, pp. 104–5, 294–5.

61 Lamb, in *The Macmillan Years*, p. 463, suggests that Profumo could have recovered from an early resignation; but, given the moral climate of the day and the inevitable publicity that would result, this is not necessarily likely.

62 Lamb, *The Macmillan Years*, pp. 460–1.

63 *Lord Denning's Report*, pp. 113–15.

64 Horne, *Macmillan 1957–1986*, p. 474.

65 Macmillan diary, 22 March 1963, quoted in Horne, *Macmillan 1957–1986*, p. 476.

66 Carpenter, *That Was Satire That Was*, p. 255.

67 See Lawton, *1963*, pp. 323–4.

68 Lamb, *The Macmillan Years*, pp. 464–5.

69 Pimlott, *Harold Wilson*, p. 289; Gilmour and Garnett, *Whatever Happened to the Tories*, p. 182.

70 Pimlott, *Harold Wilson*, pp. 289–91; Horne, *Macmillan 1957–1986*, pp. 476–7; Lamb, *The Macmillan Years*, pp. 465–6.

71 Lamb, *The Macmillan Years*, pp. 466–7.

72 Macmillan diary, 30 May 1963, quoted in Horne, *Macmillan 1957–1986*, p. 477.

73 One example, predictably enough, is the ever-sensational Summers and Dorril, *Honeytrap*, pp. 139–46.

74 Lamb, *The Macmillan Years*, p. 467.

75 Horne, *Macmillan 1957–1986*, p. 477.

76 *Lord Denning's Report*, pp. 132–3.

77 Butler, *The Art of the Possible*, p. 235; Howard, *RAB*, p. 298.

78 Irving, Hall and Wallington, *Scandal '63*, pp. 146–8.

79 Summers and Dorril, *Honeytrap*, pp. 244–5.

80 *Sunday Telegraph*, *Sunday Mirror* and *News of the World*, all 9 June 1963.

81 Macmillan diary, 7 July 1963, quoted in Horne, *Macmillan 1957–1986*, p. 478.

82 Quoted in Masters, *The Swinging Sixties*, p. 92.

83 Redmayne quoted in Horne, *Macmillan 1957–1986*, p. 479.

84 Quoted in Horne, *Macmillan 1957–1986*, p. 492.

85 Horne, *Macmillan 1957–1986*, p. 494.

86 Horne, *Macmillan 1957–1986*, pp. 494–5; see also Howard and West, *The Making of the Prime Minister*, p. 51.

87 Lamb, *The Macmillan Years*, pp. 470–1.

88 Pimlott, *Harold Wilson*, p. 292.

89 Levin, *The Pendulum Years*, p. 63.

90 Cockerell, *Live from Number Ten*, pp. 90–1; Lawton, *1963*, pp. 149–50.

91 Levin, *The Pendulum Years*, pp. 63–4.

92 *The Times*, 17 June 1963.

93 Masters, *The Swinging Sixties*, p. 93; *Private Eye* quoted in Lawton, *1963*, p. 151.

94 Heffer, *Like the Roman*, pp. 310–16.

95 Irving, Hall and Wallington, *Scandal '63*, p. 120; Hansard, 17 June 1963.

96 Hansard, 17 June 1963.

97 Hansard, 17 June 1963.

98 Crossman diary, 22 June 1963, quoted in Pimlott, *Harold Wilson*, p. 296.

99 Hansard, 17 June 1963.

100 Lawton, *1963*, p. 154.

101 Heffer, *Like the Roman*, p. 315.

102 Hansard, 17 June 1963.

103 On Birch, the speech and its effect, see Horne, *Macmillan 1957–1986*, pp. 482–3; Heffer, *Like the Roman*, pp. 315–16.

104 Sampson, *Macmillan: A Study in Ambiguity*, p. 226.

105 Butler, *The Art of the Possible*, p. 235.

106 *Daily Telegraph*, *The Times*, *Daily Mail*, all 18 June 1963.

107 David Bruce to Dean Rusk, 18 June 1963, quoted in Horne, *Macmillan 1957–1986*, p. 483.

108 Gilmour and Garnett, *Whatever Happened to the Tories*, p. 183. Horne, *Macmillan 1957–1986*, p. 484.

109 Macmillan diary, 7 July 1963, quoted in Horne, *Macmillan 1957–1986*, p. 479.

110 *The Times*, 11 June 1963.

111 Lamb, *The Macmillan Years*, p. 473.

112 *Sunday Times*, 9 June 1963.

113 *Sunday Times*, 7 July 1963; *Observer*, 21 July 1963; Timmins, *The Five Giants*, pp. 189–91; Robert Rowland, '*Panorama* in the Sixties', in Aldgate, Chapman and Marwick, eds, *Windows on the Sixties*, pp. 158–9.

114 The cartoon is reprinted in Martin Walker, *Daily Sketches: A Cartoon History of British Twentieth-Century Politics* (London, 1978), p. 171.

115 *Private Eye*, 14 July 1963.

116 Walker, *Daily Sketches*, p. 168; 'Macmillan Confesses' reprinted in Carpenter, *That Was Satire That Was*, p. 257.

117 *Private Eye*, 5 April 1963.

118 Jefferys, *Retreat from New Jerusalem*, p. 105.

119 Horne, *Macmillan 1957–1986*, pp. 484–6.

120 Benn diary, 13 June 1963.

121 Benn diary, 18 June 1963.

122 Quoted in Ziegler, *Wilson*, p. 145.

123 See Boyle, *The Climate of Treason*, pp. 191–335.

124 Thurlow, *The Secret State*, p. 297.

125 Boyle, *The Climate of Treason*, pp. 441–6; Aldrich, *The Hidden Hand*, pp. 436–7.

126 Boyle, *The Climate of Treason*, pp. 448–69.

127 Ziegler, *Wilson*, pp. 146–7.

128 Macmillan diary, 12 July 1963, quoted in Horne, *Macmillan 1957–1986*, pp. 465–6.

129 Boyle, *The Climate of Treason*, p. 495.

130 Boyle, *The Climate of Treason*, pp. 475–9; Brendon and Whitehead, *The Windsors*, pp. 164–5.

131 Boyle, *The Climate of Treason*, p. 502.

132 *Esquire*, September 1967; Wolfe, *Malcolm Muggeridge*, pp. 187–92, 327.

133 John le Carré, introduction to Bruce Page et al., *Philby: The Spy Who Betrayed a Generation* (London, 1977), pp. 31, 27.

134 Quoted in Dorril, *MI6*, pp. 211–12.

135 Boyle, *The Climate of Treason*, p. 471.

136 Horne, *Macmillan 1957–1986*, p. 466; Thurlow, *The Secret State*, pp. 302–5. The Fifth Man was in fact not Hollis at all, who was completely blameless, but a relatively minor figure, John Cairncross.

137 On sex as a symbol of wider social trends, see Weeks, *Sex, Politics and Society*, p. 11.

138 Irving, Hall and Wallington, *Scandal '63*, p. 208.

139 Irving, Hall and Wallington, *Scandal '63*, p. 208.

140 Macmillan diary, 7 July 1963, quoted in Horne, *Macmillan 1957–1986*, pp. 484–5.

141 Horne, *Macmillan 1957–1986*, p. 485.

142 Levin, *The Pendulum Years*, p. 49.

143 *Lord Denning's Report*, pp. 194–213.

144 Brendon and Whitehead, *The Windsors*, pp. 159–60.

145 *Daily Mirror*, 24 June 1963.

146 *Lord Denning's Report*, pp. 202–6. For Ward's own accounts of such occasions, see Summers and Dorril, *Honeytrap*, pp. 50–3.

147 Irving, Hall and Wallington, *Scandal '63*, p. 124.

148 Lamb, *The Macmillan Years*, p. 472. Sandys was only one of a number of candidates; others included Sigismund von Braun, the brother of the inventor of the V2 rocket, and the Hollywood actor Douglas Fairbanks Junior. According to some accounts, Fairbanks *was* in the photograph, but only in the capacity of a masturbating onlooker rather than as an active participant. See the *Independent*, 6 February 2004.

149 Horne, *Macmillan 1957–1986*, p. 486; Lamb, *The Macmillan Years*, p. 473.

150 *Lord Denning's Report*, p. 211.

151 Denning's notes quoted in Lamb, *The Macmillan Years*, p. 482.

152 Denning to Macmillan, undated, quoted in Lamb, *The Macmillan Years*, pp. 479–80: this is from Denning's private archive, which remains closed.

153 *Lord Denning's Report*, p. 209; Levin, *The Pendulum Years*, p. 48.

154 Quoted in Lawton, *1963*, p. 156.

155 Reprinted in Gardiner, *From the Bomb to the Beatles*, p. 125.

156 Benn diary, 3 July 1963.

157 Lawton, *1963*, p. 165.

158 Anthony Howard and Richard West, *The Making of the Prime Minister* (London, 1965), p. 51.

159 Irving, Hall and Wallington, *Scandal '63*, p. 148.

160 Lawton, *1963*, p. 146.

161 Irving, Hall and Wallington, *Scandal '63*, p. 201. The best account of the trial is still Ludovic Kennedy, *The Trial of Stephen Ward* (Harmondsworth, 1965).

162 Summers and Dorril, *Honeytrap*, pp. 301–4.

163 Summers and Dorril, *Honeytrap*, pp. 304–5.

164 *News of the World*, 4 August 1963.

165 See the analysis of poll data in Irving, Hall and Wallington, *Scandal '63*, pp. 222–3.

166 *Daily Mail*, 2 August 1963; Macmillan diary, 2 August 1963, quoted in Horne, *Macmillan 1957–1986*, p. 488.

167 Quoted in Jefferys, *Retreat from New Jerusalem*, p. 106.

168 Macmillan diary, 19 September 1963, quoted in Horne, *Macmillan 1957–1986*, p. 490.

169 Masters, *The Swinging Sixties*, p. 101; Horne, *Macmillan 1957–1986*, p. 490.

170 Macmillan diary, 27 September 1963, quoted in Horne, *Macmillan 1957–1986*, p. 490.

171 Summers and Dorril, *Honeytrap*, p. 310.

172 Gilmour and Garnett, *Whatever Happened to the Tories*, p. 181; Pimlott, *Harold Wilson*, p. 285.

173 Weight, *Patriots*, p. 368.

174 For changes in sexual morality and behaviour during the sixties, see the forthcoming sequel to this book.

175 'Annus Mirabilis', in Larkin, *Collected Poems*, p. 167.

176 *The Times*, 4 July 1963.

177 Pimlott, *Harold Wilson*, p. 286.

178 Quoted in Jefferys, *Retreat from New Jerusalem*, p. 106.

179 See Horne, *Macmillan 1957–1986*, p. 496.

180 Quoted in Horne, *Macmillan 1957–1986*, p. 527.

181 Macmillan diary, 16 August 1963, quoted in Horne, *Macmillan 1957–1986*, p. 530.

182 Macmillan diary, 5 September 1963, quoted in Horne, *Macmillan 1957–1986*, p. 531.

183 Horne, *Macmillan 1957–1986*, p. 534.

184 Macmillan diary, 6 October 1963, quoted in Horne, *Macmillan 1957–1986*, p. 536.

185 Macmillan diary, 7 October 1963, quoted in Horne, *Macmillan 1957–1986*, pp. 538–9.

CHAPTER 18: THE MAGIC CIRCLE

1 Macmillan diary, 8 October 1993, quoted in Horne, *Macmillan 1957–1986*, p. 540.

2 Howard, *RAB*, p. 308.

3 Horne, *Macmillan 1957–1986*, pp. 540–1.

4 Horne, *Macmillan 1957–1986*, p. 541; Howard, *RAB*, p. 309; Heffer, *Like the Roman*, p. 320.

5 Randolph S. Churchill, *The Fight for the Tory Leadership* (London, 1964), pp. 97–8; *Spectator*, 17 January 1964; Thorpe, *Alec Douglas-Home*, pp. 276–7.

6 Macmillan diary, 8 October 1993, quoted in Horne, *Macmillan 1957–1986*, p. 541.

7 Horne, *Macmillan 1957–1986*, p. 542.

8 Horne, *Macmillan 1957–1986*, p. 543.

9 *The Times*, 12 January 1994.

10 Horne, *Macmillan 1957–1986*, p. 544.

11 Sir Harold Evans, *Downing Street Diary: The Macmillan Years 1957–1963* (London, 1981), pp. 296–7.

12 *Daily Mail*, 9 October 1963; *Evening Standard*, 9 October 1963; Horne, *Macmillan 1956–1987*, pp. 543–5; Thorpe, *Alec Douglas-Home*, pp. 279–80.

13 Quoted in Thorpe, *Alec Douglas-Home*, p. 281.

14 Howard, *RAB*, p. 310; Thorpe, *Alec Douglas-Home*, pp. 280–4.

15 Howard, *RAB*, pp. 310–11; Heffer, *Like the Roman*, pp. 320–1.

16 Churchill, *The Fight for the Tory Leadership*, pp. 101–102.

17 Horne, *Macmillan 1957–1986*, pp. 545–6.

18 Churchill, *The Fight for the Tory Leadership*, p. 107.

19 Thorpe, *Alec Douglas-Home*, p. 285.

20 *Sunday Times*, 13 October 1963.

21 *The Times*, 10 October 1963.

22 *Daily Telegraph*, 10 October 1963.

23 Quoted in Lawton, *1963*, p. 298.

24 Horne, *Macmillan 1957–1986*, pp. 552–3; Hailsham, *A Sparrow's Flight*, p. 349; Thorpe, *Alec Douglas-Home*, pp. 260–1.

25 Macmillan diary, 5 September 1963, quoted in Horne, *Macmillan 1957–1986*, p. 531.

26 Hailsham, *A Sparrow's Flight*, p. 350.

27 Amery quoted in Shepherd, *Iain Macleod*, p. 309; see also Nigel Fisher, *Harold Macmillan: A Biography* (London, 1982), p. 235.

28 Pearce, *The Lost Leaders*, pp. 121–2.

29 Hailsham, *A Sparrow's Flight*, pp. 320–2, 327.

30 See, for instance, the section in which he describes the death of his wife Mary, killed in a riding accident, and discusses the relationship between grief and faith: Hailsham, *A Sparrow's Flight*, pp. 397–404.

31 Horne, *Macmillan 1957–1986*, p. 554.

32 Macmillan diary, 14 October 1963, quoted in Horne, *Macmillan 1957–1986*, p. 554.

33 Hailsham, *A Sparrow's Flight*, p. 352.

34 Churchill, *The Fight for the Tory Leadership*, pp. 108–9; Hailsham, *A Sparrow's Flight*, pp. 352–3.

35 Before he succeeded to the Hailsham title he was known as Quintin Hogg.

36 Dennis Walters, *Not Always with the Pack* (London, 1989), p. 125.

37 Butler, *The Art of the Possible*, p. 242; Gilmour and Garnett, *Whatever Happened to the Tories*, p. 193. Churchill also took it upon himself to ring Lord Home's suite and ask him to back Hailsham. When Home himself answered the telephone, the horrified Churchill put his hand over the instrument and exclaimed: 'Goodness, how sad. They live like bloody coolies these days.' See Pearce, *The Lost Leaders*, p. 377.

38 Hailsham, *A Sparrow's Flight*, p. 354.

39 Gilmour and Garnett, *Whatever Happened to the Tories*, p. 192.

40 Unknown interviewee quoted in Thorpe, *Alec Douglas-Home*, p. 286.

41 *Sunday Pictorial*, 6 January 1963; on Maudling's long run as the heir apparent, see Lamb, *The Macmillan Years*, pp. 476ff.

42 Thorpe, *Alec Douglas Home*, p. 273.

43 Maudling, *Memoirs*, pp. 124–5.

44 Maudling, *Memoirs*, p. 127; Shepherd, *Iain Macleod*, p. 316.

45 *Sunday Express*, 4 October 1973.

46 Maudling, *Memoirs*, pp. 126-8.

47 *The Times*, 12 October 1963.

48 Shepherd, *Iain Macleod*, p. 316.

49 Thorpe, *Alec Douglas-Home*, pp. 294-5.

50 Cyril Connolly, *Enemies of Promise* (Harmondsworth, 1961), p. 245.

51 See Thorpe, *Alec Douglas-Home*, pp. 9-18, 36-8.

52 Thorpe, *Alec Douglas-Home*, p. 28.

53 Thorpe, *Alec Douglas-Home*, p. 61.

54 Quoted in Hennessy, *The Prime Minister*, p. 278.

55 An obvious parallel is the American President Franklin D. Roosevelt, for whom the traumatic experience of poliomyelitis was a similarly defining moment.

56 Thorpe, *Alec Douglas-Home*, pp. 108-10, 115.

57 Thorpe, *Alec Douglas-Home*, p. 208.

58 *News of the World*, 25 September 1960; Andrei Gromyko, *Memoirs* (London, 1989), p. 158.

59 *Observer*, 16 September 1962.

60 Horne, *Macmillan 1957-1986*, pp. 544-5; Thorpe, *Alec Douglas-Home*, pp. 282-283.

61 On Home as Macmillan's confidant, see Thorpe, *Alec Douglas-Home*, p. 255.

62 Walters, *Not Always with the Pack*, p. 111; Thorpe, *Alex Douglas-Home*, p. 293.

63 Gilmour and Garnett, *Whatever Happened to the Tories*, p. 187

64 Thorpe, *Selwyn Lloyd*, p. 375; Thorpe, *Alec Douglas-Home*, pp. 293-4.

65 Walters, *Not Always with the Pack*, p. 127; Gilmour and Garnett, *Whatever Happened to the Tories*, p. 192.

66 *Daily Mail*, 12 October 1963; Thorpe, *Alec Douglas-Home*, p. 295.

67 Roy Jenkins, *Portraits and Miniatures* (London, 1993), p. 46.

68 Horne, *Macmillan 1957-1986*, p. 551; Howard, *RAB*, p. 313.

69 Thorpe, *Alec Douglas-Home*, p. 296.

70 Howard, *RAB*, pp. 313-14; Thorpe, *Alec Douglas-Home*, pp. 296-7; Shepherd, *Iain Macleod*, p. 318.

71 *Sunday Mirror*, 13 October 1963.

72 *News of the World*, 13 October 1963; Churchill, *The Fight for the Tory Leadership*, pp. 121-3.

73 *Daily Telegraph*, 12 October 1963.

74 *Observer*, 13 October 1963; *Sunday Telegraph*, 13 October 1963.

75 Churchill, *The Fight for the Tory Leadership*, p. 124; *Daily Express*, 14 October 1963.

76 *Daily Express*, 16 October 1963.

77 Macmillan diary, 14 October 1963, quoted in Horne, *Macmillan 1957-1986*, pp. 553-4.

78 Macmillan diary, 14 October 1963, quoted in Horne, *Macmillan 1957-1986*, p. 555.

79 Pimlott, *The Queen*, pp. 326, 328.

80 Horne, *Macmillan 1957-1986*, p. 555.

81 Howard, *RAB*, p. 316.

82 Tim Bligh, 'Top Secret Note for the Record', 15 October 1963, quoted in Horne, *Macmillan 1957-1986*, p. 556; Thorpe, *Alec Douglas-Home*, pp. 298-301.

83 PREM 11/5008, 15 October 1963.

84 Ramsden, *The Winds of Change*, p. 203.

85 Redmayne to Macmillan, 16 October 1963, quoted in Thorpe, *Alec Douglas-Home*, pp. 302–3.

86 Gilmour and Garnett, *Whatever Happened to the Tories*, pp. 194, 198; Jefferys, *Retreat from New Jerusalem*, p. 181.

87 Jim Prior, *A Balance of Power* (London, 1986), p. 33.

88 William Whitelaw, *The Whitelaw Memoirs* (London, 1989), p. 58; Shepherd, *Iain Macleod*, pp. 323–4.

89 Horne, *Macmillan 1957–1986*, pp. 559–61.

90 Heffer, *Like the Roman*, p. 326.

91 Thorpe, *Alec Douglas-Home*, p. 307; Shepherd, *Iain Macleod*, pp. 324–7.

92 Gilmour and Garnett, *Whatever Happened to the Tories*, p. 199.

93 Gilmour and Garnett, *Whatever Happened to the Tories*, p. 198.

94 Thorpe, *Alec Douglas-Home*, p. 311.

95 Howard, *RAB*, pp. 316–17.

96 Shepherd, *Iain Macleod*, p. 327.

97 *Spectator*, 17 January 1964.

98 Shepherd, *Iain Macleod*, p. 328.

99 Robert Shepherd, *Enoch Powell* (London, 1996), p. 259.

100 Heffer, *Like the Roman*, pp. 326–7.

101 Quoted in Horne, *Macmillan 1957–1986*, pp. 562–3.

102 Pimlott, *The Queen*, p. 328.

103 Shepherd, *Iain Macleod*, pp. 329–31; Heffer, *Like the Roman*, pp. 325–6.

104 *Spectator*, 17 January 1964.

105 Walters, *Not Always with the Pack*, p. 132.

106 Recollections of Sir Ian Gilmour in Gilmour and Garnett, *Whatever Happened to the Tories*, p. 200.

107 Howard, *RAB*, p. 318; Shepherd, *Iain Macleod*, pp. 331–2; Heffer, *Like the Roman*, pp. 326–8.

108 Thorpe, *Alec Douglas-Home*, p. 312.

109 Pimlott, *The Queen*, p. 329.

110 Quoted in Horne, *Macmillan 1957–1986*, p. 565.

111 Macmillan, *At the End of the Day*, p. 515.

112 Macmillan diary, 18 October 1963, quoted in Horne, *Macmillan 1957–1986*, p. 566.

113 Pimlott, *The Queen*, p. 332.

114 Horne, *Macmillan 1957–1986*, p. 566.

115 Thorpe, *Alec Douglas-Home*, pp. 313–14.

116 Howard, *RAB*, pp. 320–1, 399.

117 Thorpe, *Alec Douglas-Home*, pp. 314–15.

118 Maudling, *Memoirs*, p. 130.

119 Hennessy, *Muddling Through*, p. 237.

120 Howard and West, *The Making of the Prime Minister*, pp. 93–4; Thorpe, *Alec Douglas-Home*, pp. 287, 318; Jefferys, *Retreat from New Jerusalem*, pp. 182–3; Gilmour and Garnett, *Whatever Happened to the Tories*, p. 192.

121 Thorpe, *Alec Douglas-Home*, p. 318.

122 Howard, *RAB*, pp. 316–18.

123 Hailsham, *A Sparrow's Flight*, p. 356.

124 As argued in Lamb, *The Macmillan Years*, p. 498.

125 Pimlott, *The Queen*, p. 333; Gilmour and Garnett, *Whatever Happened to the Tories*, p. 200.

126 Howard, *RAB*, pp. 304, 318.

127 Walters, *Not Always with the Pack*, pp. 132–3.

128 Heffer, *Like the Roman*, p. 331.

129 Reginald Bevins, *The Greasy Pole* (London, 1965), p. 145; see also Howard, *RAB*, p. 320.

130 Butler, *The Art of the Possible*, p. 250.

131 Howard, *RAB*, p. 322: this is usually seen as an oblique dig at Macmillan.

132 Home to Butler, 22 October 1963, reprinted in Howard, *RAB*, pp. 322–3.

133 *Spectator*, 17 January 1964.

134 Macmillan diary, 19 October 1963, quoted in Horne, *Macmillan 1957–1986*, p. 569.

135 Quoted in Hennessy, *The Prime Minister*, p. 252.

136 Walters, *Not Always with the Pack*, p. 111.

137 Pimlott, *The Queen*, p. 332.

138 *Spectator*, 17 January 1964. The phrase 'personal moral integrity' had originally been coined by Edward Boyle, who eventually caved in and remained in the government despite his initial protestations. By quoting Boyle, Macleod was mocking his colleague's treachery.

139 Reginald Bennett quoted in Shepherd, *Iain Macleod*, p. 336.

140 Heffer, *Like the Roman*, p. 331.

141 *Spectator*, 17 January 1964.

142 Shepherd, *Iain Macleod*, pp. 358–9.

143 Shepherd, *Iain Macleod*, p. 362.

144 *Spectator*, 24 January 1964.

145 Berkeley quoted in Shepherd, *Iain Macleod*, p. 365.

146 *Spectator*, 14 February 1964.

147 Turner, *Macmillan*, pp. 274–5.

148 Lamb, *The Macmillan Years*, pp. 14–15.

149 Horne, *Macmillan 1957–1986*, p. 214.

150 *Sunday Times*, 20 October 1963; *Observer*, 20 October 1963.

151 Pearce, *The Lost Leaders*, p. 126.

152 *Sunday Express*, 20 October 1963.

153 Benn diary, 14 October and 18 October 1963.

154 Macmillan diary, 18 January 1964, quoted in Thorpe, *Alec Douglas-Home*, pp. 344–5.

155 Thorpe, *Alec Douglas-Home*, p. 344.

156 *Sunday Express*, 20 October 1963.

157 Quoted in Levin, *The Pendulum Years*, p. 246.

158 *Sunday Express*, 20 October 1963.

159 Cockerell, *Live from Number Ten*, p. 98; Carpenter, *That Was Satire That Was*, pp. 275–6.

CHAPTER 19: ON TO 1964

1 Thorpe, *Alec Douglas-Home*, p. 335.
2 Thorpe, *Alec Douglas-Home*, p. 324; Gilmour and Garnett, *Whatever Happened to the Tories*, p. 204.
3 *Evening Standard*, 31 October 1963.
4 *Daily Express*, 11 November 1963.
5 *New Musical Express*, 6 December 1963.
6 *Daily Mirror*, 15 October 1963
7 *Daily Express*, 15 October 1963.
8 Norman, *Shout!*, p. 181.
9 *New Musical Express*, 8 November 1963.
10 *New Musical Express*, 8 November 1963; Norman, *Shout!*, p. 191.
11 Lawton, *1963*, p. 109.
12 *Daily Mail*, 6 November 1963.
13 *Daily Mirror*, 6 November 1963.
14 Norman, *Shout!*, p. 192; Lawton, *1963*, p. 116.
15 *New Musical Express*, 15 November 1963.
16 Norman, *Shout!*, p. 183.
17 Lizzie Bawden quoted in Lawton, *1963*, pp. 112–13.
18 Norman, *Shout!*, p. 183.
19 Quoted in Leslie, *Fab*, p. 149.
20 Quoted in Norman, *Shout!*, p. 193.
21 *News of the World*, 17 November 1963.
22 Payne and Morley, eds, *The Noël Coward Diaries*, p. 501.
23 *Daily Telegraph*, 2 November 1963.
24 Watkins, *A Short Walk down Fleet Street*, p. 95.
25 *New Statesman*, 28 February 1964.
26 Dell, *The Chancellors*, pp. 298–9.
27 Norman, *Shout!*, p. 201; Lawton, *1963*, p. 115.
28 Advertisements reprinted in *NME Originals: The Beatles*, 3 April 2002, pp. 29–31.
29 *Daily Mirror*, 9 December 1963.
30 Norman, *Shout!*, p. 201.
31 Lawton, *1963*, p. 116.
32 *Daily Mail*, 24 December 1963.
33 See Norman, *Shout!*, pp. 203–4.
34 *New Musical Express*, 20 December 1963.
35 *New Musical Express*, 3 January 1964.
36 Lawton, *1963*, p. 116.
37 Norman, *Shout!*, p. 204.
38 *The Times*, 27 December 1963.
39 Quoted in Miller, *Flowers in the Street*, p. 212.
40 *Sunday Times*, 29 December 1963.
41 *New Musical Express*, 31 May 1963.

42 Norman, *Shout!*, p. 195.

43 *New Musical Express*, 3 January 1963.

44 Coates and Silburn, *Poverty*, p. 18; Dorothy Cole, 'Poverty in Britain Today – The Evidence', *Sociological Review*, 1962, pp. 257–82; Brian Abel-Smith and Peter Townsend, 'The Poor and the Poorest', *Occasional Papers on Social Administration* 6, December 1965.

45 CAB 21/4965, 'Recreational Trends in Britain', May 1963.

46 Sampson, *Anatomy of Britain*, p. 579.

47 Weight, *Patriots*, p. 324; McKibbin, *Classes and Cultures*, p. 84.

48 Willmott and Young, *Family and Class in a London Suburb*, pp. 31–3.

49 Akhtar and Humphries, *The Fifties and Sixties*, p. 121.

50 On fishing, see McKibbin, *Classes and Cultures*, pp. 356–7.

51 Briggs, *The History of Broadcasting in the United Kingdom: Volume V*, Appendix A, p. 1005.

52 See James Chapman, '*The Avengers*: Television and Popular Culture during the "High Sixties"', in Aldgate, Chapman and Marwick, eds, *Windows on the Sixties*, pp. 37–8; and James Chapman, *Saints and Avengers: British Adventure Series of the 1960s* (London, 2002), pp. 62–74.

53 *TV Times*, 20 September 1963.

54 Akhtar and Humphries, *The Fifties and Sixties*, p. 28.

55 Chapman, *Saints and Avengers*, pp. 63–6.

56 Briggs, *The History of Broadcasting in the United Kingdom: Volume V*, p. 416.

57 John Tulloch and Manuel Alvarado, *Doctor Who: The Unfolding Text* (London, 1983), p. 32. On the origins of *Doctor Who*, see David J. Howe and Stephen James Walker, *Doctor Who: The Television Companion* (London, 1998), pp. 1–3.

58 Briggs, *The History of Broadcasting in the United Kingdom: Volume V*, p. 420.

59 Quoted in Tulloch and Alvarado, *Doctor Who: The Unfolding Text*, p. 17.

60 See Gillatt, *Doctor Who from A to Z*, p. 14.

61 Gillatt, *Doctor Who from A to Z*, pp. 53–4.

62 See Howe and Walker, *Doctor Who: The Television Companion*, p. 10.

63 On the creation of the Daleks, see Briggs, *The History of Broadcasting in the United Kingdom: Volume V*, p. 422; Howe and Walker, *Doctor Who: The Television Companion*, pp. 15–16.

64 Quoted in Howe and Walker, *Doctor Who: The Television Companion*, p. 15; see also Gillatt, *Doctor Who from A to Z*, p. 17.

65 Gillatt, *Doctor Who from A to Z*, p. 18.

66 Howe and Walker, *Doctor Who: The Television Companion*, p. 40.

67 Tulloch and Alvarado, *Doctor Who: The Unfolding Text*, pp. 56, 44.

68 Tulloch and Alvarado, *Doctor Who: The Unfolding Text*, p. 44.

69 Laing, 'The Production of Literature', pp. 123–7.

70 Levin, *The Pendulum Years*, p. 104; Lawton, *1963*, p. 177; Sutherland, *Reading the Decades*, pp. 55–6.

71 Sutherland, *Reading the Decades*, pp. 65–6.

72 Lycett, *Ian Fleming*, p. 419.

73 Fleming, *On Her Majesty's Secret Service*, ch. 27.

74 Quoted in Lycett, *Ian Fleming*, p. 416.

75 Chapman, *Licence to Thrill*, pp. 89–90; Cork and Scivally, *James Bond: The Legacy*, p. 49.

76 Chapman, *Licence to Thrill*, p. 97; Cork and Scivally, *James Bond: The Legacy*, pp. 52–9.

77 *Kinematograph Weekly*, 24 October 1963.

78 Sadly, he had to cancel it to attend a crisis meeting with Home, Butler and Hailsham: see Thorpe, *Alec Douglas-Home*, p. 314.

79 Lycett, *Ian Fleming*, p. 430; Cork and Scivally, *James Bond: The Legacy*, pp. 59, 51.

80 *Guardian*, 13 August 1963.

81 Walker, *Hollywood, England*, pp. 138–45; Laing, *Representations of Working-Class Life*, pp. 135–8; Aldgate and Richards, *Best of British*, pp. 216–17.

82 Quoted in Chapman, *Licence to Thrill*, p. 68.

83 Walker, *Hollywood, England*, p. 167.

84 Benn diary, 31 December 1963.

85 *Sunday Times Magazine*, 4 February 1962: on its cultural significance, see the discussion in Booker, *The Neophiliacs*, pp. 47–8.

86 *The Times*, 2 October 1963; Pimlott, *Harold Wilson*, pp. 302–4.

87 Ziegler, *Wilson*, pp. 143–4.

88 King and Wybrow, eds, *British Political Opinion*, p. 8.

89 Speech at Birmingham, 19 January 1964, reprinted in Harold Wilson, *The New Britain: Labour's Plan* (Harmondsworth, 1964), p. 10; see also the verbatim extracts in Howard and West, *The Making of the Prime Minister*, pp. 115–16; and Ziegler, *Wilson*, p. 144.

SELECT BIBLIOGRAPHY

What follows is a list of the books cited in the Notes. The full details of academic articles, newspapers and other materials can be found in the notes themselves.

Mary Abbott, *Family Affairs: A History of the Family in Twentieth-Century England* (London, 2003)

Mark Abrams, *The Teenage Consumer* (London, 1959)

Mark Abrams, *Teenage Consumer Spending in 1959* (London, 1961)

Mark Abrams and Richard Rose, *Must Labour Lose?* (Harmondsworth, 1960)

Paul Addison, *Now the War Is Over: A Social History of Britain 1945–1951* (London, 1985)

Miriam Akhtar and Steve Humphries, *Some Liked It Hot: The British on Holiday at Home and Abroad* (London, 2000)

Miriam Akhtar and Steve Humphries, *The Fifties and Sixties: A Lifestyle Revolution* (London, 2001)

Anthony Aldgate, *Censorship and the Permissive Society: British Cinema and Theatre 1955–1965* (Oxford, 1995)

Anthony Aldgate, James Chapman and Arthur Marwick, eds, *Windows on the Sixties: Exploring Key Texts of Media and Culture* (London, 2000)

Anthony Aldgate and Jeffrey Richards, *Best of British: Cinema and Society from 1930 to the Present* (London, 1999)

Brian Aldiss and David Wingrove, *Trillion Year Spree: The History of Science Fiction* (London, 1986)

Richard J. Aldrich, *Espionage, Security and Intelligence in Britain, 1945–1970* (Manchester, 1998)

Richard J. Aldrich, *The Hidden Hand: Britain, America and Cold War Secret Intelligence* (London, 2001)

Peter Alex, *Who's Who in Pop Radio* (London, 1966)

Kenneth Allsop, *The Angry Decade* (London, 1958)

Al Alvarez, *Where Did It All Go Right?* (London, 1999)

Leopold S. Amery, *The Framework of the Future* (Oxford, 1944)

Kingsley Amis, *Lucky Jim* (London, 1954)

Kingsley Amis, *That Uncertain Feeling* (London, 1955)

Kingsley Amis, *I Like It Here* (London, 1958)

Kingsley Amis, *Take a Girl Like You* (London, 1960)

Kingsley Amis, *The James Bond Dossier* (London, 1966)

Kingsley Amis, *Girl, 20* (London, 1971)

Kingsley Amis, *Memoirs* (London, 1991)

Kingsley Amis, *The King's English* (London, 1997)

Christopher Andrew, *Secret Service: The Making of the British Intelligence Community* (London, 1988)

Noël Annan, *Our Age: The Generation That Made Post-War Britain* (London, 1990)

Lorna Arnold and Katherine Pyne, *Britain and the H-Bomb* (London, 2001)

Nigel Ashton, *Kennedy, Macmillan and the Cold War: The Irony of Interdependence* (London, 2002)

Clement Attlee, *Empire into Commonwealth* (Oxford, 1961)

A. J. Ayer, *Language, Truth and Logic* (second edition: London, 1946)

Tony Bacon, *London Live: From the Yardbirds to Pink Floyd to the Sex Pistols* (London, 1999)

George Ball, *The Discipline of Power* (London, 1968)

Simon Ball, *The Guardsmen: Harold Macmillan, Three Friends, and the World They Made* (London, 2004)

Martin Barker, *A Haunt of Fears: The Strange History of the British Horror Comics Campaign* (London, 1984)

Correlli Barnett, *The Collapse of British Power* (London, 1972)

Correlli Barnett, *The Audit of War: The Illusion and Reality of Britain as a Great Nation* (London, 1986)

Correlli Barnett, *The Lost Victory: British Dreams, British Realities, 1945–1950* (London, 1995)

Correlli Barnett, *The Verdict of Peace: Britain Between her Yesterday and the Future* (London, 2001)

Stan Barstow, *A Kind of Loving* (Harmondsworth, 1962)

C. J. Bartlett, *The Special Relationship: A Political History of Anglo-American Relations since 1945* (London, 1992)

Frank Bealey and Henry Pelling, *Labour and Politics, 1900–1906* (London, 1958)

Francis Beckett, *Enemy Within: The Rise and Fall of the British Communist Party* (London, 1995)

Michael Bell, *F. R. Leavis* (London, 1988)

Nora Beloff, *The General Says No* (Harmondsworth, 1963)

Tony Benn, *Years of Hope: Diaries, Papers and Letters, 1940–62* (London, 1994)

Tony Benn, *Out of the Wilderness: Diaries, 1963–67* (London, 1987)

Alan Bennett, *Writing Home* (revised edition: London, 1997)

Tony Bennett and Janet Woollacott, *Bond and Beyond: The Political Career of a Popular Hero* (London, 1987)

John Benson, *The Rise of Consumer Society in Britain 1880–1980* (London, 1994)

Raymond Benson, *The James Bond Bedside Companion* (London, 1984)

Ronald Bergan, *Beyond the Fringe . . . and Beyond* (London, 1989)

Bernard Bergonzi, *The Early H. G. Wells: The Scientific Romances* (Manchester, 1961)

Bernard Bergonzi, *The Situation of the Novel* (London, 1970)

Bernard Bergonzi, *Wartime and Aftermath: English Literature and its Background, 1939–1960* (Oxford, 1993)

John Betjeman, *Collected Poems* (London, 2001)

T. B. Beveridge, *A Guide for the National Service Man* (London, 1953)

Reginald Bevins, *The Greasy Pole* (London, 1965)

A. H. Birch, *Small Town Politics* (Oxford, 1959)

George Blake, *No Other Choice: An Autobiography* (London, 1990)

Clive Bloom and Gary Day, eds, *Literature and Culture in Modern Britain: Volume Three: 1956–1999* (London, 2000)

Vernon Bogdanor and Robert Skidelsky, eds, *The Age of Affluence* (London, 1970)

Christopher Booker, *The Neophiliacs: The Revolution in English Life in the Fifties and Sixties* (revised edition: London, 1992)

Christopher Booker, *The Seventies: Portrait of a Decade* (Harmondsworth, 1980)

Tom Bower, *The Perfect English Spy: Sir Dick White and the Secret War 1935–90* (London, 1995)

John Bowlby, *Child Care and the Growth of Love* (Harmondsworth, 1953)

D. George Boyce, *Decolonisation and the British Empire, 1775–1997* (London, 1999)

Andrew Boyle, *The Climate of Treason* (London, 1980)

John Boyd-Carpenter, *Way of Life* (London, 1980)

Duncan Brack and Iain Dale, eds, *Prime Minister Portillo, and Other Things That Never Happened* (London, 2003)

Malcolm Bradbury, *The Modern British Novel* (London, 1993)

Richard Bradford, *Lucky Him: The Life of Kingsley Amis* (London, 1991)

John Braine, *Room at the Top* (London, 1991)

George Brandt, ed., *British Television Drama* (Cambridge, 1981)

Piers Brendon and Phillip Whitehead, *The Windsors: A Dynasty Revealed, 1917–2000* (London, 2000)

John Brewer, *The Pleasures of the Imagination: English Culture in the Eighteenth Century* (London, 1997)

Paul Brians, *Nuclear Holocausts: Atomic War in Fiction, 1895–1984* (Kent, Ohio, 1987)

Asa Briggs, *The History of Broadcasting in the United Kingdom: Volume I: The Birth of Broadcasting* (Oxford, 1995)

Asa Briggs, *The History of Broadcasting in the United Kingdom: Volume V: Competition* (Oxford, 1995)

Samuel Brittan, *The Treasury under the Tories 1951–1964* (Harmondsworth, 1964)

Stephen Brooke, *Reform and Reconstruction* (Manchester, 1985)

George Brown, *In My Way* (Harmondsworth, 1972)

Peter Brown and Steven Gaines, *The Love You Make: An Insider's Story of the Beatles* (London, 1983)

Alan Bullock, *Ernest Bevin: Foreign Secretary 1945–1951* (London, 1983)

Oreste del Buono and Umberto Eco, eds, *The Bond Affair* (trans. R. A. Downie: London, 1966)

John Burnett, *Liquid Pleasures: A Social History of Drinks in Modern Britain* (London, 1999)

Alan Burton, Tim O'Sullivan and Paul Wells, eds, *The Family Way: The Boulting Brothers and Postwar British Film Culture* (Trowbridge, 2000)

David Butler and Anthony King, *The British General Election of 1964* (London, 1965)

David Butler and Richard Rose, *The British General Election of 1959* (London, 1960)

Lord Butler, *The Art of the Possible: The Memoirs of Lord Butler* (Harmondsworth, 1973)

Alec Cairncross, *The British Economy since 1945* (Oxford, 1992)

Angus Calder, *The Myth of the Blitz* (London, 1991)

Peter Calvocoressi, *The British Experience 1945–75* (Harmondsworth, 1979)

John Campbell, *Nye Bevan and the Mirage of British Socialism* (London, 1987)

John Campbell, *Edward Heath: A Biography* (London, 1993)

John Campbell, *Margaret Thatcher: Volume One: The Grocer's Daughter* (London, 2000)

Miriam Camps, *Britain and the European Community, 1955–1963* (Oxford, 1964)

Edward du Cann, *Two Lives* (London, 1995)

David Cannadine, *The Decline and Fall of the British Aristocracy* (New Haven, 1990)

David Cannadine, *G. M. Trevelyan: A Life in History* (London, 1992)

David Cannadine, *Class in Britain* (London, 2000)

David Cannadine, *Ornamentalism: How the British Saw their Empire* (London, 2001)

David Cannadine, *In Churchill's Shadow: Confronting the Past in Modern Britain* (London, 2002)

David Carlton, *Anthony Eden: A Biography* (London, 1981)

Humphrey Carpenter, *That Was Satire That Was: The Satire Boom of the 1960s* (London, 2000)

Humphrey Carpenter, *The Angry Young Men: A Literary Comedy of the 1950s* (London, 2002)

John le Carré, *The Spy Who Came In from the Cold* (London, 1963)

John le Carré, *Call for the Dead* (Harmondsworth, 1964)

John le Carré, *A Murder of Quality* (Harmondsworth, 1964)

John le Carré, *The Looking-Glass War* (London, 1965)

C. C. Carter and H. C. Brentnall, *Man the World Over* (Oxford, 1952)

Brian Catchpole, *The Korean War, 1950–1953* (London, 2000)

Curtis Cate, *The Ides of August* (London, 1978)

Malcolm Chalmers and William Walker, *Uncharted Waters: The UK, Nuclear Weapons and the Scottish Question* (Edinburgh, 2001)

Iain Chambers, *Urban Rhythms: Pop Music and Popular Culture* (Basingstoke, 1985)

Iain Chambers, *Popular Culture: The Metropolitan Experience* (London, 1986)

Lisa Chaney, *Elizabeth David: A Mediterranean Passion* (London, 1998)

James Chapman, *Licence to Thrill: A Cultural History of the James Bond Films* (London, 1999)

James Chapman, *Saints and Avengers: British Adventure Series of the 1960s* (London, 2002)

David Childs, *Britain since 1945: A Political History* (London, 1979)

Randolph S. Churchill, *The Fight for the Tory Leadership* (London, 1964)

Mark Clapson, *Invincible Green Suburbs, Brave New Towns* (Manchester, 1998)

Nick Clarke, *The Shadow of a Nation: The Changing Face of Britain* (London, 2003)

Peter Clarke, *A Question of Leadership: From Gladstone to Thatcher* (London, 1992)

Peter Clarke, *Hope and Glory: Britain 1900–1990* (London, 1996)

Peter Clarke and Clive Trebilcock, eds, *Understanding Decline: Perceptions and Realities of British Economic Performance* (Cambridge, 1997)

Alan Clayson, *Ringo Starr: Straight Man or Joker?* (London, 1991)

Alan Clayson, *Beat Merchants: The Origins, History, Impact and Rock Legacy of the 1960s British Pop Groups* (London, 1995)

H. A. Clegg et al., *A History of British Trade Unions since 1889* (Oxford, 1964)

Ken Coates and Richard Silburn, *Poverty: The Forgotten Englishmen* (Harmondsworth, 1970)

Michael Cockerell, *Live from Number Ten: The Inside Story of Prime Ministers and Television* (London, 1988)

Stanley Cohen, *Folk Devils and Moral Panics: The Creation of the Mods and Rockers* (London, 1972)

Nik Cohn, *Today There Are No Gentlemen* (London, 1971)

Ray Coleman, *The Man Who Made the Beatles: An Intimate Biography of Brian Epstein* (London, 1989)

Linda Colley, *Britons: Forging the Nation 1707–1837* (New Haven, 1992)

Robert Colls, *Identity of England* (Oxford, 2002)

Cyril Connolly, *Enemies of Promise* (Harmondsworth, 1961)

Steven Connor, *The English Novel in History, 1950–1995* (London, 1996)

Robert Conquest, ed., *New Lines* (London, 1956)

Don Cook, *Forging the Alliance: NATO, 1945–1950* (London, 1989)

William Cooper, *Scenes from Provincial Life* (Harmondsworth, 1961)

Richard Coopey, Steven Fielding and Nick Tiratsoo, eds, *The Wilson Governments 1964–1970* (London, 1993)

John Cork and Bruce Scivally, *James Bond: The Legacy* (London, 2002)

John Corner, ed., *Popular Television in Britain* (London, 1991)

Patrick Cosgrave, *The Strange Death of Socialist Britain* (London, 1993)

Noël Coward, *Pomp and Circumstance* (London, 1960)

Noël Coward, *The Lyrics of Noël Coward* (London, 1965)

Nicholas Crafts and Nicholas Woodward, eds, *The British Economy since 1945* (Oxford, 1991)

Anthony Crosland, *The Future of Socialism* (London, 1956)

Richard Crossman, ed., *New Fabian Essays* (London, 1952)

Richard Crossman, *Labour in the Affluent Society* (London, 1960)

Richard Crossman, *The Backbench Diaries* (ed. Janet Morgan: London, 1981)

Marcus Crouch, *Treasure Seekers and Borrowers: Children's Books in Britain 1900–1960* (London, 1962)

Valentine Cunningham, *British Writers of the Thirties* (Oxford, 1988)

John Darwin, *Britain and Decolonisation: The Retreat from Empire in the Post-War World* (London, 1988)

John Darwin, *The End of the British Empire: The Historical Debate* (Oxford, 1991)

Nicholas Davenport, *The Split Society* (London, 1964)

Elizabeth David, *A Book of Mediterranean Food* (London, 1991)

Grace Davie, *Religion in Britain since 1945: Believing without Belonging* (Oxford, 1994)

Christie Davies, *Permissive Britain: Social Change in the Sixties and Seventies* (London, 1975)

Norman Davies, *The Isles: A History* (London, 1999)

John Davis, *Youth and the Condition of Britain: Images of Adolescent Conflict* (London, 1990)

Gary Day, ed., *Literature and Culture in Modern Britain: Volume Two: 1930–1955* (London, 1997)

Len Deighton, *The Ipcress File* (London, 1962)

Edmund Dell, *Political Responsibility and Industry* (London, 1973)

Edmund Dell, *The Chancellors: A History of the Chancellors of the Exchequer, 1945–90* (London, 1996)

Edmund Dell, *A Strange Eventful History: Democratic Socialism in Britain* (London, 2000)

Roy Denman, *Missed Chances: Britain and Europe in the Twentieth Century* (London, 1996)

Michael Denning, *Cover Stories: Narrative and Ideology in the British Spy Thriller* (London, 1987)

Mike Dewe, *The Skiffle Craze* (London, 1998)

Monica Dickens, *The Heart of London* (London, 1961)

Stephen Dorril, *MI6: Fifty Years of Special Operations* (London, 2000)

J. C. R. Dow, *The Management of the British Economy, 1945–60* (Cambridge, 1964)

David Dowling, *Fictions of Nuclear Disaster* (London, 1987)

Christopher Driver, *The Disarmers: A Study in Protest* (London, 1964)

Ruth Dudley Edwards, *Newspapermen: Hugh Cudlipp, Cecil Harmsworth King and the Glory Days of Fleet Street* (London, 2003)

Charles Duff, *The Lost Summer: The Heyday of the West End Theatre* (London, 1995)

Peggy Duff, *Left, Left, Left* (London, 1971)

Elizabeth Durbin, *New Jerusalems: The Labour Party and the Economics of Democratic Socialism* (London, 1985)

Raymond Durgnat, *A Mirror for England: British Movies from Austerity to Affluence* (London, 1970)

Richard Dyer et al., *Coronation Street* (London, 1981)

Nicholas Elliott, *With my Little Eye: Observations along the Way* (Norwich, 1992)

D. J. Enright, ed., *Poets of the 1950s* (Tokyo, 1955)

Brian Epstein and Derek Taylor, *A Cellarful of Noise* (London, 1964)

Sir Harold Evans, *Downing Street Diary: The Macmillan Years 1957–1963* (London, 1981)

Adam Faith, *Poor Me* (London, 1961)

Gene Feldman and Max Gartenberg, eds, *Protest: The Beat Generation and the Angry Young Men* (London, 1959)

Christopher Felix, *A Short Course in the Secret War* (Lanham, New York, 1992)

Rachel Ferguson, *Passionate Kensington* (London, 1939)

Paul Ferris, *Sir Huge: The Life of Huw Wheldon* (London, 1990)

Paul Ferris, *Sex and the British: A Twentieth-Century History* (London, 1993)

Eddi Fiegel, *John Barry: A Sixties Theme, from James Bond to Midnight Cowboy* (London, 1998)

Steven Fielding, *The Labour Governments 1964–1970: Volume 1: Labour and Cultural Change* (Manchester, 2003)

Nigel Fisher, *Harold Macmillan: A Biography* (London, 1982)

Ian Fleming, *Casino Royale* (London, 1953)

Ian Fleming, *Moonraker* (London, 1955)

Ian Fleming, *From Russia with Love* (London, 1957)

Ian Fleming, *Dr No* (London, 1958)

Ian Fleming, *Goldfinger* (London, 1959)

Ian Fleming, *Thunderball* (London, 1961)

Ian Fleming, *The Spy Who Loved Me* (London, 1962)

Ian Fleming, *On Her Majesty's Secret Service* (London, 1963)

Ian Fleming, *Thrilling Cities* (London, 1963)

Ian Fleming, *You Only Live Twice* (London, 1964)

Ian Fleming, *Octopussy* (London, 1966)

Tom Fleming, ed., *Voices out of the Air: The Royal Christmas Broadcasts, 1932–1981* (London, 1981)

Marnie Fogg, *Boutique: A Sixties Cultural Phenomenon* (London, 2003)

Boris Ford, ed., *The Cambridge Cultural History of Britain, Volume 9: Modern Britain* (London, 1992)

Boris Ford, ed., *The New Pelican Guide to English Literature: Volume 8: From Orwell to Naipaul* (revised edition: London, 1998)

John Fordham, *Jazz Man: The Amazing Story of Ronnie Scott and his Club* (London, 1995)

David Fowler, *The First Teenagers: The Lifestyle of Young Wage-Earners in Interwar Britain* (London, 1995)

Noble Frankland, ed., *Documents on International Relations 1956* (Oxford, 1959)

Lester Friedman, ed., *British Cinema and Thatcherism: Fires Were Started* (London, 1993)

Willi Frischauer, *David Frost: A Biography* (London, 1971)

Simon Frith and Howard Horne, *Art into Pop* (London, 1987)

David Frost, *An Autobiography: Part One* (London, 1993)

David Frost and Ned Sherrin, eds, *That Was The Week That Was* (London, 1963)

Peter Fryer, *Staying Power: The History of Black People in Britain* (London, 1985)

Aleksandr Fursenko and Timothy Naftali, *One Hell of a Gamble: The Secret History of the Cuban Missile Crisis* (New York, 1997)

Paul Fussell, *The Anti-Egotist: Kingsley Amis, Man of Letters* (Oxford, 1994)

John Gallagher, *The Decline, Revival and Fall of the British Empire* (Cambridge, 1982)

George H. Gallup, ed., *The Gallup International Public Opinion Polls: Great Britain 1937–1975, Volume I* (New York, 1976)

Andrew Gamble, *The Conservative Nation* (London, 1974)

Andrew Gamble, *Britain in Decline: Economic Policy, Political Strategy and the British State* (fourth edition: London, 1994)

Juliet Gardiner, *From the Bomb to the Beatles: The Changing Face of Post-War Britain* (London, 1999)

George Thomson Geddes, *The Shadows: A History and Discography* (Glasgow, 1981)

Gary Gillatt, *Doctor Who from A to Z* (London, 1998)

Charlie Gillett, *The Sound of the City: The Rise of Rock and Roll* (London, 1983)

Philip Gillett, *The British Working Class in Postwar Film* (Manchester, 2003)

Ian Gilmour and Mark Garnett, *Whatever Happened to the Tories: The Conservatives since 1945* (London, 1997)

Ralph Glasser, *Gorbals Boy at Oxford* (London, 1988)

Harry Golbourne, *Race Relations in Britain since 1945* (London, 1998)

Jim Goldbolt, *A History of Jazz in Britain, 1919–50* (London, 1984)

David Goldsworthy, *Colonial Issues in British Politics, 1945–61* (Oxford, 1971)

J. H. Goldthorpe, D. Lockwood, F. Bechhofer and J. Platt, *The Affluent Worker: Political Attitudes and Behaviour* (Cambridge, 1968)

Joseph A. Gomez, *Peter Watkins* (Boston, 1979)

Howard Goorney, *The Theatre Workshop Story* (London, 1981)

Geoffrey Gorer, *Exploring English Character* (London, 1955)

Geoffrey Gorer, *Sex and Marriage in England Today* (London, 1971)

Anthony Gorst and Lewis Johnman, *The Suez Crisis* (London, 1997)

Anthony Gorst, Lewis Johnman and Wm Scott Lucas, eds, *Contemporary British History, 1931–61: Politics and the Limits of Policy* (London, 1991)

Tony Gould, *Inside Outsider: The Life and Times of Colin MacInnes* (London, 1983)

Margaret Gowing, *Independence and Deterrence: Britain and Atomic Energy, 1945–1952* (London, 1979)

Jonathon Green, *Them: Voices from the Immigrant Community in Contemporary Britain* (London, 1990)

Jonathon Green, *Days in the Life: Voices from the English Underground, 1961–1971* (Pimlico edition: London, 1998)

Jonathon Green, *All Dressed Up: The Sixties and the Counter-Culture* (London, 1998)

Hugh Carleton Greene, *The Third Floor Front: A View of Broadcasting in the 1960s* (London, 1969)

John Griffiths, *The Survivors* (London, 1965)

Henri Grimal, *Decolonization: The British, French, Dutch, and Belgian Empires, 1919–1963* (London, 1978)

Andrei Gromyko, *Memoirs* (London, 1989)

Simon Gunn and Rachel Bell, *Middle Classes: Their Rise and Sprawl* (London, 2003)

Lord Hailsham, *A Sparrow's Flight: Memoirs* (London, 1990)

John D. Hargreaves, *Decolonization in Africa* (London, 1988)

Jennifer Harris, Sarah Hyde and Greg Smith, *1966 and All That* (London, 1986)

José Harris, *William Beveridge: A Biography* (Oxford, 1977)

Nigel Harris, *Competition and the Corporate State: British Conservatives, the State and Industry, 1945–1964* (London, 1972)

Anthony Hartley, *A State of England* (London, 1963)

Cate Haste, *Rules of Desire: Sex in Britain: World War I to the Present* (London, 1994)

Roy Hattersley, *Who Goes Home? Scenes from a Political Life* (London, 1995)

Denis Healey, *The Time of My Life* (London, 1989)

Edward Heath, *Travels: Peoples and Places in my Life* (London, 1977)

Edward Heath, *The Course of My Life: My Autobiography* (London, 1998)

Simon Heffer, *Like the Roman: A Life of Enoch Powell* (London, 1998)

Mohammed Heikal, *Cutting the Lion's Tail: Suez through Egyptian Eyes* (London, 1986)

Peter Hennessy, *Cabinet* (Oxford, 1986)

Peter Hennessy, *Never Again: Britain 1945–1951* (London, 1992)

Peter Hennessy, *Muddling Through: Power, Politics and the Quality of Government in Postwar Britain* (London, 1996)

Peter Hennessy, *The Prime Minister: The Office and its Holders since 1945* (London, 2000)

Peter Hennessy, *The Secret State: Whitehall and the Cold War* (London, 2002)

Peter Hennessy and Anthony Seldon, eds, *Ruling Performance: British Governments from Attlee to Thatcher* (Oxford, 1989)

Dilip Hero, *Black British White British: A History of Race Relations in Britain* (London, 1991)

Liz Heron, ed., *Truth, Dare or Promise? Girls Growing Up in the Fifties* (London, 1985)

Robert Hewison, *In Anger: Culture in the Cold War 1945–60* (London, 1981)

Robert Hewison, *Too Much: Art and Society in the Sixties 1960–1975* (London, 1986)

Michael Hickey, *The Korean War: The West Confronts Communism, 1950–1953* (London, 2000)

Patrick Higgins, *Heterosexual Dictatorship: Male Homosexuality in Postwar Britain* (London, 1996)

Jeffrey Hill, *Sport, Leisure and Culture in Twentieth-Century Britain* (London, 2002)

John Hill, *Sex, Class and Realism: British Cinema 1956–1963* (London, 1986)

Gertrude Himmelfarb, *Victorian Minds* (New York, 1970)

Donald Hinds, *Journey to an Illusion: The West Indian in Britain* (London, 1966)

Thomas Hine, *The Rise and Fall of the American Teenager* (New York, 2000)

Peter Hitchens, *The Abolition of Britain: The British Cultural Revolution from Lady Chatterley to Tony Blair* (revised edition: London, 2000)

Eric Hobsbawm, *Industry and Empire* (Harmondsworth, 1969)

Eric Hobsbawm, *Age of Extremes: The Short Twentieth Century 1914–1991* (London, 1994)

Eric Hobsbawm, *The New Century: In Conversation with Antonio Polito* (London, 2000)

Eric Hobsbawm, *Interesting Times: A Twentieth-Century Life* (London, 2002)

J. A. Hobson, *Imperialism* (reprinted edition: London, 1961)

Richard Hoggart, *The Uses of Literacy* (Harmondsworth, 1958)

R. F. Holland, *European Decolonization 1918–1981* (Basingstoke, 1985)

Colin Holmes, *John Bull's Island: Immigration and British Society, 1871–1971* (London, 1988)

Stuart Holroyd, *Contraries: A Personal Progression* (London, 1975)

Richard Holt, *Sport and the British: A Modern History* (Oxford, 1990)

Richard Holt, *Second Amongst Equals: Chancellors of the Exchequer since the Second World War* (London, 2001)

Harry Hopkins, *The New Look: A Social History of the Forties and Fifties in Britain* (London, 1964)

Derek Hopwood, *Egypt: Politics and Society 1945–1990* (third edition: London, 1993)

Alistair Horne, *Macmillan 1894–1956: Volume I of the Official Biography* (London, 1988)

Alistair Horne, *Macmillan 1957–1986: Volume II of the Official Biography* (London, 1989)

Anthony Howard, *RAB: The Life of R. A. Butler* (London, 1987)

Anthony Howard, *Crossman: The Pursuit of Power* (London, 1990)

Anthony Howard and Richard West, *The Making of the Prime Minister* (London, 1965)

David J. Howe and Stephen James Walker, *Doctor Who: The Television Companion* (London, 1998)

Emmet John Hughes, *The Ordeal of Power: A Political Memoir of the Eisenhower Years* (London, 1963)

J. H. Huizinga, *Confessions of a European in England* (London, 1958)

J. Bernard Hutton, *Frogman Extraordinary* (London, 1960)

Stuart Hylton, *Magical History Tour: The 1960s Revisited* (Stroud, 2000)

Mary Ingham, *Now We Are Thirty: Women of the Breakthrough Generation* (London, 1981)

Richard Ingrams, ed., *The Life and Times of Private Eye* (London, 1971)

Clive Irving, Ron Hall and Jeremy Wallington, *Scandal '63: A Study of the Profumo Affair* (London, 1963)

Alan A. Jackson, *The Middle Classes 1900–1950* (Nairn, 1991)

Brian Jackson, *Working Class Community* (Harmondsworth, 1968)

Lesley Jackson, *The Sixties: Decade of Design Revolution* (London, 1998)

Eric Jacobs, *Kingsley Amis: A Biography* (London, 1995)

Lawrence James, *The Rise and Fall of the British Empire* (London, 1994)

Lawrence James, *Warrior Race: A History of the British at War* (London, 2001)

Douglas Jay, *Change and Fortune: A Political Record* (London, 1980)

Stephen Jeffery-Poulter, *Peers, Queers and Commons: The Struggle for Gay Law Reform from 1950 to the Present* (London, 1991)

Kevin Jefferys, *Retreat from New Jerusalem: British Politics, 1951–64* (London, 1997)

Kevin Jefferys, *Anthony Crosland* (London, 1999)

Roy Jenkins, *A Life at the Centre* (London, 1991)

Roy Jenkins, *Portraits and Miniatures* (London, 1993)

Roy Jenkins, *Churchill* (London, 2001)

Pearl Jephcott, *Rising Twenty* (London, 1953)

Pearl Jephcott, *A Troubled Area: Notes on Notting Hill* (London, 1964)

B. S. Johnson, *All Bull: The National Servicemen* (London, 1973)

Matthew Jones, *Conflict and Confrontation in South East Asia, 1961–1965: Britain, the United States, Indonesia and the Creation of Malaysia* (Cambridge, 2001)

Mervyn Jones, *Michael Foot* (London, 1994)

Peter Jones, *America and the Labour Party: The Special Relationship at Work* (London, 1997)

Denis Judd, *Empire: The British Imperial Experience from 1765 to the Present* (London, 1996)

Miles Kahler, *Decolonization in Britain and France* (Princeton, 1984)

Dennis Kavanagh, *Thatcherism and British Politics: The End of Consensus?* (Oxford, 1987)

Christine Keeler, *Christine Keeler: The Truth At Last* (London, 2001)

Ludovic Kennedy, *The Trial of Stephen Ward* (Harmondsworth, 1965)

Lord Kilmuir, *Political Adventure: The Memoirs of the Earl of Kilmuir* (London, 1964)

Anthony King and Robert J. Wybrow, eds, *British Political Opinion 1937–2000: The Gallup Polls* (London, 2001)

Arthur Koestler, *The Yogi and the Commissar* (London, 1945)

Arthur Koestler, ed., *Suicide of a Nation? An Enquiry into the State of Britain Today* (London, 1963)

Keith Kyle, *Suez* (London, 1991)

Robert Lacey, *Majesty* (London, 1977)

Stephen Lacey, *British Realist Theatre: The New Wave in Context, 1956–1965* (London, 1995)

Jean Lacouture, *Nasser* (London, 1973)

Jean Lacouture, *De Gaulle: The Ruler 1945–1970* (London, 1991)

Stuart Laing, *Representations of Working-Class Life 1957–1964* (Basingstoke, 1986)

Richard Lamb, *The Macmillan Years 1957–1963: The Unfolding Truth* (London, 1995)

George Lamming, *The Emigrants* (London, 1954)

Cecile Landau, ed., *Growing Up in the Sixties* (London, 1991)

Marcia Landy, *British Genres: Cinema and Society, 1930–1960* (Princeton, 1991)

Paul Langford, *A Polite and Commercial People; England 1727–1783* (Oxford, 1989)

Colin Larkin, ed., *The Virgin Encyclopedia of Sixties Music* (London, 1997)

Philip Larkin, *All What Jazz* (London, 1964)

Philip Larkin, *Jill* (London, 1964)

Philip Larkin, *Collected Poems* (London, 1990)

Peter Laurie, *The Teenage Revolution* (London, 1965)

Twiggy Lawson, *Twiggy in Black and White* (London, 1997)

John Lawton, *1963: Five Hundred Days* (London, 1992)

Zachary Leader, ed., *The Letters of Kingsley Amis* (London, 2000)

Spencer Leigh, *Puttin' On the Style: The Lonnie Donegan Story* (London, 2003)

Spencer Leigh and Pete Frame, *Let's Go Down the Cavern* (London, 1984)

Peter Leslie, *Fab: The Anatomy of a Phenomenon* (London, 1965)

Doris Lessing, *Walking in the Shade: Volume Two of My Autobiography* (London, 1997)

Bernard Levin, *The Pendulum Years: Britain and the Sixties* (revised edition: London, 1977)

Shawn Levy, *Ready, Steady, Go! Swinging London and the Invention of Cool* (London, 2002)

Peter Lewis, *The Fifties* (London, 1978)

Roger Lewis, *The Life and Death of Peter Sellers* (London, 1994)

Mark Lewisohn, *The Complete Beatles Chronicle* (London, 1992)

Alison Light, *Forever England: Femininity, Literature and Conservatism between the Wars* (London, 1991)

Daran Little, *The Coronation Street Story* (London, 2001)

Selwyn Lloyd, *Suez 1956: A Personal Account* (London, 1978)

David Lodge, *Ginger, You're Barmy* (London, 1962)

Lord Longford, *Five Lives* (London, 1964)

Wm Roger Louis and Robin W. Winks, eds, *The Oxford History of the British Empire: Volume V: Historiography* (Oxford, 1999)

Andrew Lycett, *Ian Fleming* (London, 1995)

Humphrey Lyttelton, *I Play As I Please* (London, 1954)

Ewan MacColl and Peggy Seeger, eds, *The Singing Island* (New York, 1960)

Callum MacDonald, *Britain and the Korean War* (Oxford, 1990)

Ian MacDonald, *Revolution in the Head* (revised edition: London, 1997)

Ian MacDonald, *The People's Music* (London, 2003)

Colin MacInnes, *England, Half English* (London, 1961)

Colin MacInnes, *Absolute Beginners* (London, 1980)

Colin MacInnes, *City of Spades* (London, 1980)

Norman and Jeanne Mackenzie, *The Life of H. G. Wells: The Time Traveller* (revised edition: London, 1987)

Harold Macmillan, *Britain, the Commonwealth and Europe* (London, 1961)

Harold Macmillan, *Riding the Storm, 1956–59* (London, 1971)

Harold Macmillan, *At the End of the Day, 1959–1961* (London, 1973)

Harold Macmillan, *The Middle Way: A Study of the Problem of Economic and Social Progress in a Free and Democratic Society* (Wakefield, 1978)

Sara Maitland, ed., *Very Heaven: Looking Back at the 1960s* (London, 1988)

Rex Malik, *What's Wrong with British Industry?* (Harmondsworth, 1964)

Peter Mandler, *The Fall and Rise of the Stately Home* (New Haven, 1997)

Sir Arthur de la Mare, *Perverse and Foolish: A Jersey Farmer's Son in the British Diplomatic Service* (Jersey, 1994)

James Margach, *The Abuse of Power* (London, 1978)

Patrick Marnham, *The Private Eye Story: The First 21 Years* (London, 1983)

David Marquand, *The Progressive Dilemma: From Lloyd George to Blair* (second edition: London, 1999)

David Marquand and Anthony Seldon, eds, *The Ideas That Shaped Post-War Britain* (London, 1996)

George Martin with Jeremy Hornsby, *All You Need Is Ears* (London, 1979)

Arthur Marwick, *Class: Image and Reality in Britain, France and the USA since 1930* (London, 1980)

Arthur Marwick, *British Society since 1945* (Harmondsworth, 1982)

Arthur Marwick, *The Sixties: Cultural Revolution in Britain, France, Italy, and the United States, c.1958–c.1974* (Oxford, 1998)

Tom Maschler, ed., *Declaration* (London, 1957)

Mass-Observation, *Puzzled People: A Study of Popular Attitudes to Religion, Ethics, Progress and Politics in a London Borough* (London, 1948)

Brian Masters, *The Swinging Sixties* (London, 1986)

Brian Matthew, *Trad Mad* (London, 1962)

Reginald Maudling, *Memoirs* (London, 1978)

Ernest R. May and Philip D. Zelikow, eds, *The Kennedy Tapes: Inside the White House during the Cuban Missile Crisis* (London, 1997)

Chas McDevitt, *Skiffle: The Definitive Inside Story* (London, 1997)

Jay McInerney et al., *Dressed to Kill: James Bond: The Suited Hero* (Paris, 1996)

Robert McKenzie and Allan Silver, *Angels in Marble: Working-Class Conservatives in Urban England* (London, 1968)

Ross McKibbin, *Classes and Cultures: England 1918–1951* (Oxford, 1998)

David Alan Mellor and Laurent Gervereau, eds, *The Sixties: Britain and France, 1962–1973: The Utopian Years* (London, 1997)

George Melly, *Revolt into Style* (Oxford, 1989)

Keith Middlemas, *Power, Competition and the State: Volume One: Britain in Search of a Balance, 1940–61* (Basingstoke, 1986)

Drew Middleton, *The British* (London, 1957)

Barry Miles, *Paul McCartney: Many Years from Now* (London, 1997)

Robert Miles and Annie Phizacklea, *White Man's Country* (London, 1984)

James Miller, *Flowers in the Dustbin: The Rise of Rock and Roll, 1947–1977* (New York, 1999)

R. S. Milne and H. C. Mackenzie, *Marginal Seat: A Study of Voting Behaviour in the Constituency of Bristol North East at the General Election of 1955* (London, 1958)

Alan S. Milward, *The European Rescue of the Nation State* (London, 1992)

Alan S. Milward, *The Rise and Fall of a National Strategy 1945–1963* (London, 2002)

John Minnion and Philip Bolsover, eds, *The CND Story* (London, 1983)

Austin Mitchell and David Wienir, eds, *Last Time: Labour's Lessons from the Sixties* (London, 1997)

Nancy Mitford, ed., *Noblesse Oblige: An Enquiry into the Identifiable Characteristics of the English Aristocracy* (London, 1956)

J. M. Mogey, *Family and Neighbourhood: Two Studies of Oxford* (Oxford, 1956)

John Montgomery, *The Fifties* (London, 1965)

Bart Moore-Gilbert and John Seed, eds, *Cultural Revolution? The Challenge of the Arts in the 1960s* (London, 1992)

Kenneth O. Morgan, *Labour People: Hardie to Kinnock* (second edition: Oxford, 1992)

Kenneth O. Morgan, *Callaghan: A Life* (Oxford, 1997)

Kenneth O. Morgan, *The People's Peace: British History since 1945* (second edition: Oxford, 1999)

James (Jan) Morris, *Farewell the Trumpets: An Imperial Retreat* (London, 1978)

Sally Morris and Jan Hallwood, *Living with Eagles: Marcus Morris, Priest and Publisher* (London, 1998)

Blake Morrison, *The Movement: English Poetry and Fiction of the 1950s* (Oxford, 1980)

Elaine Moss, *Part of the Pattern: A Personal Journey through the World of Children's Books, 1960–1985* (London, 1986)

Andrew Motion, *Philip Larkin: A Writer's Life* (London, 1993)

Philip Murphy, *Party Politics and Decolonization: The Conservative Party and British Colonial Policy in Tropical Africa, 1951–1964* (Oxford, 1995)

Robert Murphy, *Sixties British Cinema* (London, 1992)

Robert Murphy, ed., *The British Cinema Book* (second edition: London, 2001)

Frank Musgrove, *Youth and the Social Order* (London, 1964)

Iain Nairn, *Outrage* (London, 1955)

Robin Neillands, *A Fighting Retreat: The British Empire 1947–1997* (London: 1996)

Tim Newburn, *Permission and Regulation: Law and Morals in Post-War Britain* (London, 1992)

John Newhouse, *De Gaulle and the Anglo-Saxons* (London, 1970)

John Newsom, *The Education of Girls* (London, 1948)

Francis Newton, *The Jazz Scene* (London, 1959)

Harold Nicolson, *Letters and Diaries: Volume III: 1945–1962* (London, 1968)

Philip Norman, *Shout! The True Story of the Beatles* (London, 1981)

Philip Norman, *The Stones* (London, 1993)

June Norris, *Human Aspects of Redevelopment* (Birmingham, 1962)

Anthony Nutting, *No End of a Lesson: The Story of Suez* (London, 1967)

Anthony Nutting, *Nasser* (London, 1972)

Andrew Loog Oldham, *Stoned* (London, 2000)

George Orwell, *Coming Up for Air* (Harmondsworth, 1962)

George Orwell, *The Road to Wigan Pier* (Harmondsworth, 1962)

George Orwell, *The Collected Essays, Journalism and Letters of George Orwell: Volume II* (Harmondsworth, 1970)

George Orwell, *The Collected Essays, Journalism and Letters of George Orwell: Volume IV* (Harmondsworth, 1980)

John Osborne, *Look Back in Anger* (London, 1957)

John Osborne, *The Entertainer* (London, 1957)

John Osborne, *Almost a Gentleman: An Autobiography, Volume II: 1955–1966* (London, 1991)

John Osborne, *Damn You, England: Collected Prose* (London, 1994)

David Owen, *Time to Declare* (London, 1992)

Geoffrey Owen, *From Empire to Europe: The Decline and Revival of British Industry since the Second World War* (London, 1999)

Bruce Page et al., *Philby: The Spy Who Betrayed a Generation* (London, 1977)

Tony Palmer, *All You Need Is Love: The Story of Popular Music* (London, 1976)

Leroy L. Panek, *The Special Branch: The British Spy Novel 1890–1980* (Bowling Green, Ohio, 1981)

Frank Parkin, *Middle-Class Radicalism: The Social Bases of the Campaign for Nuclear Disarmament* (Manchester, 1968)

Matthew Parris, *Great Parliamentary Scandals* (London, 1995)

Sheila Patterson, *Dark Strangers: A Sociological Study of the Absorption of a Recent West Indian Migrant Group in Brixton, South London* (Harmondsworth, 1963)

Kathleen Paul, *Whitewashing Britain: Race and Citizenship in the Postwar Era* (Ithaca, New York, 1997)

Graham Payn and Sheridan Morley, eds, *The Noël Coward Diaries* (London, 1982)

Edward Pearce, *The Lost Leaders: The Best Prime Ministers We Never Had* (London, 1997)

Edward Pearce, *Denis Healey: A Life in our Times* (London, 2002)

Geoffrey Pearson, *Hooligan: A History of Respectable Fears* (London, 1983)

John Pearson, *The Life of Ian Fleming* (London, 1966)

Henry Pelling, *The Origins of the Labour Party 1880–1900* (London, 1954)

Charles Petrie, *The Modern British Monarchy* (London, 1961)

Henry Phelps-Brown, *The Growth of British Industrial Relations* (London, 1959)

Henry Phelps-Brown, *The Origins of Trade Union Power* (Oxford, 1985)

Mike Phillips and Charlie Phillips, *Notting Hill in the Sixties,* (London, 1997)

Mike Phillips and Trevor Phillips, *Windrush: The Irresistible Rise of Multi-Racial Britain* (London, 1999)

Andrew Pierre, *Nuclear Politics: Anglo-American Defence Relations 1939–1980* (London, 1981)

Ben Pimlott, *Hugh Dalton* (London, 1985)

Ben Pimlott, ed., *The Political Diary of Hugh Dalton, 1918–40, 1945–60* (London, 1986)

Ben Pimlott, *Harold Wilson* (London, 1992)

Ben Pimlott, *Frustrate Their Knavish Tricks: Writings on Biography, History and Politics* (London, 1994)

Ben Pimlott, *The Queen: A Biography of Elizabeth II* (London, 1996)

Edward Platt, *Leadville: A Biography of the A40* (London, 2000)

Martin Polley, *Moving the Goalposts: A History of Sport and Society since 1945* (London, 1998)

Clive Ponting, *1940: Myth and Reality* (London, 1990)

Roy Porter, ed., *Myths of the English* (Cambridge, 1992)

Raymond Postgate, ed., *The Good Food Guide 1951–1952* (London, 1951)

Anthony Powell, *Books Do Furnish a Room* (London, 1971)

Alison Pressley, *The Best of Times: Growing Up in Britain in the 1950s* (London, 1999)

Alison Pressley, *Changing Times: Being Young in Britain in the '60s* (London, 2000)

J. B. Priestley, *Angel Pavement* (London, 1930)

J. B. Priestley, *Journey down a Rainbow* (London, 1955)

J. B. Priestley, *Thoughts in the Wilderness* (London, 1957)

J. B. Priestley, *English Journey* (London, 1997)

Jim Prior, *A Balance of Power* (London, 1986)

Martin Pugh, *Women and the Women's Movement in Britain, 1914–1959* (London, 1992)

Giles Radice, *Friends and Rivals: Crosland, Healey and Jenkins* (London, 2002)

Ron Ramdin, *The Making of the Black Working Class in Britain* (Aldershot, 1987)

John Ramsden, *The Winds of Change: Macmillan to Heath, 1957–1975* (London, 1996)

John Ranelagh, *Thatcher's People: An Insider's Account of the Politics, the Power and the Personalities* (London, 1992)

Arthur Ransome, *Bohemia in London* (London, 1907)

Terence Rattigan, *Collected Plays: Volume II* (London, 1953)

Simon Raven, *Alms for Oblivion: Volume II* (London, 1998)

Dan Rebellato, *1956 and All That: The Making of Modern British Drama* (London, 1999)

J. Tudor Rees and Harley V. Usill, eds, *They Stand Apart: A Critical Survey of the Problems of Homosexuality* (London, 1955)

John Reith, *The Reith Diaries* (London, 1975)

David Reynolds, *Rich Relations: The American Occupation of Britain 1942–1945* (London, 1995)

R. A. W. Rhodes, ed., *Transforming British Government, Volume 1: Changing Institutions* (London, 2000)

Robert Rhodes James, *Anthony Eden* (London: 1986)

Robert Rhodes James, *A Spirit Undaunted: The Political Role of George VI* (London, 1998)

Jeffrey Richards, *Films and British National Identity* (Manchester, 1997)

Harry Ritchie, *Success Stories: Literature and the Media in England, 1950–1959* (London, 1989)

Robert Roberts, *The Classic Slum: Salford Life in the First Quarter of the Century* (Harmondsworth, 1973)

W. T. Rodgers, ed., *Hugh Gaitskell 1906–1963* (London, 1964)

Johnny Rogan, *Starmakers and Svengalis: The History of British Pop Management* (London, 1988)

C. H. Rolph, ed., *The Trial of Lady Chatterley* (Harmondsworth, 1961)

Andrew Rosen, *The Transformation of British Life 1950–2000* (Manchester, 2003)

Sheila Rowbotham, *A Century of Women: The History of Women in Britain and the United States* (London, 1999)

Sheila Rowbotham, *Promise of a Dream: Remembering the Sixties* (London, 2000)

Seebohm Rowntree and G. R. Lavers, *Poverty and the Welfare State* (London, 1951)

Trevor Royle, *The Best Years of their Lives: The National Service Experience 1945–63* (London, 1986)

Deborah S. Ryan, *The Ideal Home through the Twentieth Century* (London, 1997)

Roger Sabin, *Adult Comics: An Introduction* (London, 1993)

Shamit Saggar, *Race and Politics in Britain* (London, 1992)

Edward Said, *Orientalism: Western Concepts of the Orient* (New York, 1978)

Edward Said, *Culture and Imperialism* (London, 1993)

Anthony Sampson, *Anatomy of Britain* (London, 1962)

Anthony Sampson, *Macmillan: A Study in Ambiguity* (London, 1967)

Raphael Samuel, *Island Stories: Unravelling Britain* (London, 1998)

George Santayana, *Soliloquies in England* (London, 1922)

'Sapper', *Bulldog Drummond* (London, 1983)

Simon Schama, *A History of Britain: The British Wars 1603–1776* (London, 2001)

Jerrold L. Schecter and Peter S. Deriabin, *The Spy Who Saved the World: How a Soviet Colonel Changed the Course of the Cold War* (New York, 1992)

Arthur M. Schlesinger, Jr, *A Thousand Days* (Boston, 1965)

Michael Schofield, *The Sexual Behaviour of Young People* (London, 1965)

L. V. Scott, *Macmillan, Kennedy and the Cuban Missile Crisis* (London, 1999)

Anthony Seldon, *Churchill's Indian Summer: The Conservative Government, 1951–55* (London, 1981)

Michael Shanks, *The Stagnant Society* (Harmondsworth, 1961)

Tony Shaw, *British Cinema and the Cold War: The State, Propaganda and Consensus* (London, 2001)

Dominic Shellard, *British Theatre since the War* (London, 1999)

Dominic Shellard, ed., *British Theatre in the 1950s* (Sheffield, 2000)

Dominic Shellard, *Kenneth Tynan: A Life* (New Haven, 2003)

Robert Shepherd, *Iain Macleod: A Biography* (London, 1994)

Robert Shepherd, *Enoch Powell* (London, 1996)

Ned Sherrin, *A Small Thing – Like an Earthquake* (London, 1983)

Tom Shippey, *J. R. R. Tolkien: Author of the Century* (London, 2000)

Andrew Shonfield, *British Economic Policy since the War* (Harmondsworth, 1958)

Anthony Short, *The Communist Insurrection in Malaya, 1948–1960* (London, 1975)

Irene Shubik, *Play for Today* (London, 1975)

Evelyn Shuckburgh, *Descent to Suez* (London, 1986)

Folarin Shyllon, *Black People in Britain, 1555–1833* (London, 1977)

Ed Sikov, *Mr Strangelove: A Biography of Peter Sellers* (London, 2002)

Alan Sillitoe, *The Loneliness of the Long-Distance Runner* (London, 1961)

Alan Sillitoe, *Saturday Night and Sunday Morning* (London, 1990)

Andrew Sinclair, *The Breaking of Bumbo* (London, 1959)

Alan Sinfield, ed., *Society and Literature 1945–1970* (London, 1983)

Alan Sinfield, *Literature, Politics and Culture in Post-war Britain* (London, 1989)

Adam Sisman, *A. J. P. Taylor: A Biography* (London, 1994)

Michael Sissons and Philip French, eds, *Age of Austerity* (Oxford, 1989)

Alan Sked and Chris Cook, *Post-War Britain: A Political History* (second edition: London, 1984)

Robert Skidelsky, *Oswald Mosley* (London, 1975)

Robert Skidelsky, *John Maynard Keynes: The Economist as Saviour 1920–1937* (London, 1992)

Robert Skidelsky, *John Maynard Keynes: Fighting for Britain 1937–1946* (London, 2000)

Anthony Smith, *British Broadcasting* (Newton Abbott, 1974)

C. P. Snow, *The Masters* (Harmondsworth, 1956)

C. P. Snow, *Corridors of Power* (Harmondsworth, 1966)

Muriel Spark, *The Comforters* (London, 1957)

Benjamin Spock, *The Common Sense Book of Baby and Child Care* (New York, 1946)

Donald Spoto, *Laurence Olivier* (London, 1991)

Margaret Stacey, *Tradition and Change: A Study of Banbury* (Oxford, 1960)

Jo-Mary Stafford, *Light in the Dust: An Autobiography 1930–1960* (Stourbridge, 1995)

Carolyn Steedman, *Landscape for a Good Woman* (London, 1986)

Robert Stephens, *Knight Errant* (London, 1995)

John Stevenson, *British Society 1914–45* (Harmondsworth, 1984)

John Stevenson and Chris Cook, *Britain in the Depression: Society and Politics 1929–39* (London, 1994)

Randall Stevenson, *The British Novel since the Thirties: An Introduction* (London, 1986)

Graham Stewart, *Burying Caesar: Churchill, Chamberlain and the Battle for the Tory Party* (London, 1999)

Frances Stonor Saunders, *Who Paid the Piper? The CIA and the Cultural Cold War* (London, 2000)

Anthony Summers and Stephen Dorril, *Honeytrap: The Secret World of Stephen Ward* (London, 1987)

John Sutherland, *Bestsellers: Popular Fiction of the 1970s* (London, 1981)

John Sutherland, *Reading the Decades: Fifty Years of the Nation's Bestselling Books* (London, 2002)

Matthew Sweet, *Inventing the Victorians* (London, 2001)

A. J. P. Taylor, *English History 1914–1945* (Oxford, 1965)

A. J. P. Taylor, *A Personal History* (London, 1983)

D. J. Taylor, *After the War: The Novel and England since 1945* (London, 1994)

John Russell Taylor, *Anger and After: A Guide to the New British Drama* (Harmondsworth, 1963)

John Russell Taylor, *The Second Wave: British Drama of the Sixties* (London, 1978)

D. R. Thorpe, *Selwyn Lloyd* (London, 1989)

D. R. Thorpe, *Alec Douglas-Home* (London, 1996)

D. R. Thorpe, *Eden: The Life and Times of Sir Anthony Eden, First Earl of Avon 1897–1977* (London, 2003)

Richard Thurlow, *The Secret State: British Internal Security in the Twentieth Century* (Oxford, 1994)

Richard Thurlow, *Fascism in Britain* (second edition: London, 1998)

Nicholas Timmins, *The Five Giants: A Biography of the Welfare State* (London, 1995)

Nick Tiratsoo, ed., *From Blitz to Blair: A New History of Britain since 1939* (London, 1997)

Richard Titmuss, *Essays on 'The Welfare State'* (London, 1958)

Richard Titmuss, *Income Distribution and Social Change: A Study in Criticism* (London, 1962)

J. R. R. Tolkien, *The Hobbit, or There and Back Again* (London, 1981)

Jim Tomlinson, *The Politics of Decline: Understanding Post-war Britain* (Harlow, 2000)

Michael Tracey and David Morrison, *Whitehouse* (London, 1979)

John Tulloch and Manuel Alvarado, *Doctor Who: The Unfolding Text* (London, 1983)

John Turner, *Macmillan* (London, 1994)

Steve Turner, *Cliff Richard: The Biography* (London, 1998)

Twiggy, *Twiggy: An Autobiography* (London, 1976)

Richard Usborne, *Clubland Heroes* (London, 1953)

Fred Vanderschmidt, *What the English Think of Us* (New York, 1948)

Peter Vansittart, *In the Fifties* (London, 1995)

John Vassall, *Vassall: The Autobiography of a Spy* (London, 1975)

Ralph Vaughan Williams and A. L. Lloyd, eds, *The Penguin Book of English Folk Songs* (Harmondsworth, 1959)

Meredith Veldman, *Fantasy, the Bomb, and the Greening of Britain: Romantic Protest, 1945–1980* (Cambridge, 1994)

John Wain, *Living in the Present* (London, 1955)

John Wain, *Strike the Father Dead* (London, 1962)

John Wain, *Hurry On Down* (Harmondsworth, 1979)

George Walden, *Lucky George: Memoirs of an Anti-Politician* (London, 1999)

Adrian Walker, *Six Campaigns: National Servicemen on Active Service 1948–1960* (London, 1993)

Alexander Walker, *Hollywood, England* (London, 1974)

Alexander Walker, *Peter Sellers* (London, 1982)

Martin Walker, *Daily Sketches: A Cartoon History of British Twentieth-Century Politics* (London, 1978)

Dennis Walters, *Not Always with the Pack* (London, 1989)

Stuart Ward, ed., *British Culture and the End of Empire* (Manchester, 2001)

Keith Waterhouse, *Billy Liar* (Harmondsworth, 1962)

Alan Watkins, *A Short Walk down Fleet Street* (London, 2000)

Harold Watkinson, *Turning Points* (Salisbury, 1986)

Colin Watson, *Snobbery with Violence: Crime Stories and their Audience* (London, 1971)

Patricia Waugh, *The Harvest of the Sixties: English Literature and its Background, 1960–1990* (Oxford, 1995)

Duncan Webster, *Looka Yonder! The Imaginary America of Populist Culture* (London, 1988)

Jeffrey Weeks, *Sex, Politics and Society: The Regulation of Sexuality since 1800* (second edition: London, 1989)

Richard Weight, *Patriots: National Identity in Britain 1940–2000* (London, 2002)

Richard Weight and Abigail Beach, eds, *The Right to Belong: Citizenship and National Identity in Britain* (London, 1998)

Jann Wenner, ed., *Lennon Remembers: The Rolling Stone Interviews* (Harmondsworth, 1972)

Nigel West, *Friends: Britain's Secret Post-War Intelligence Operations* (London, 1988)

John Westergaard and Henrietta Resler, *Class in a Capitalist Society* (Harmondsworth, 1977)

Ian Whitcomb, *After the Ball* (New York, 1972)

Eric W. White, *The Arts Council of Great Britain* (London, 1975)

Jerry White, *London in the Twentieth Century* (London, 2001)

Kate Whitehead, *The Third Programme: A Literary History* (London, 1989)

Mary Whitehouse, *Whatever Happened to Sex?* (Hove, 1977)

William Whitelaw, *The Whitelaw Memoirs* (London, 1989)

James Wickenden, *Colour in Britain* (Oxford, 1958)

George Wigg, *George Wigg* (London, 1972)

Eric Wigham, *What's Wrong with the Unions?* (Harmondsworth, 1961)

Francis Williams, *The American Invasion* (London, 1962)

Philip M. Williams, *Hugh Gaitskell* (Oxford, 1982)

Philip M. Williams, ed., *The Diary of Hugh Gaitskell 1945–1956* (London, 1983)

Raymond Williams, *Culture and Society 1780–1950* (London, 1958)

Raymond Williams, *Communications* (London, 1962)

Raymond Williams, *Culture Is Ordinary* (London, 1990)

Ted Willis, *Evening All: Fifty Years over a Hot Typewriter* (London, 1991)

Peter Willmott and Michael Young, *Family and Class in a London Suburb* (London, 1960)

Roger Wilmut, *Tony Hancock: 'Artiste'* (London, 1978)

Roger Wilmut and Jimmy Grafton, *The Goon Show Companion: A History and Goonography* (London, 1976)

A. N. Wilson, *The Victorians* (London, 2002)

Angus Wilson, *Anglo-Saxon Attitudes* (Harmondsworth, 1958)

Angus Wilson, *The Middle Age of Mrs Elliot* (Harmondsworth, 1961)

Angus Wilson, *A Bit off the Map* (Harmondsworth, 1968)

Angus Wilson, *The Old Men at the Zoo* (London, 1979)

Angus Wilson, *Late Call* (London, 1982)

Colin Wilson, *The Outsider* (London, 1956)

Colin Wilson, *Religion and the Rebel* (London, 1957)

Elizabeth Wilson, *Only Halfway to Paradise: Women in Postwar Britain: 1945–1968* (London, 1980)

Elizabeth Wilson, *Adorned in Dreams: Fashion and Modernity* (London, 1988)

Harold Wilson, *The New Britain: Labour's Plan* (Harmondsworth, 1964)

P. G. Wodehouse, *Plum Pie* (London, 1966)

Gregory Wolfe, *Malcolm Muggeridge: A Biography* (London, 1995)

John Wood, ed., *A Nation Not Afraid: The Thinking of Enoch Powell* (London, 1965)

Giles Worsley, *England's Lost Houses: From the Archives of* Country Life (London, 2002)

J. F. Wright, *Britain in the Age of Economic Management: An Economic History since 1939* (Oxford, 1979)

Peter Wright, *Spycatcher* (New York, 1987)

Robert J. Wybrow, *Britain Speaks Out, 1937–87: A Social History as Seen through the Gallup Data* (London, 1989)

Greville Wynne, *The Man from Moscow* (London, 1967)

Hugo Young, *This Blessed Plot: Britain and Europe from Churchill to Blair* (London, 1998)

Michael Young and Peter Willmott, *Family and Kinship in East London* (London, 1957)

Philip Ziegler, *Wilson: The Authorised Life* (London, 1993)

Ferdynand Zweig, *The Student in an Age of Anxiety: A Survey of Oxford and Manchester Students* (London, 1963)

Ina Zweiniger-Bargielowska, ed., *Women in Twentieth-Century Britain* (Harlow, 2001)

INDEX